HISTORIOGRAPHY

CLIO BIBLIOGRAPHY SERIES

Africa Since 1914

American Popular Culture

The American Presidency

The American South, Volume I

The American South, Volume II

Communism in the World Since 1945

European Immigration and Ethnicity in the
  United States and Canada

Historiography, Volume I

Historiography, Volume II

The History of Canada

Indians of the United States and Canada

Indians of the United States and Canada, Volume II

Labor in America

Latin American Politics

The Middle East in Conflict

Military History of the United States

Religion and Society in North America

Social Reform and Reaction in America

Urban America

Women in American History

Women in American History, Volume II

HISTORIOGRAPHY

An Annotated Bibliography of Journal Articles, Books, and Dissertations

Volume I

Susan K. Kinnell
Editor

Foreword by
Georg G. Iggers

ABC-CLIO
Santa Barbara, California
Oxford, England

Library of Congress Cataloging-in-Publication Data

Historiography: an annotated bibliography of journal
    articles, books, and dissertations.

    (Clio bibliography series)
    Includes indexes.
    1. Historiography—Bibliography.   2. Kinnell,
Susan K.   II. Series.
Z6208.H5H57   1987   016.907′2   87-14427
[D13]
ISBN 0-87436-490-6 (v. 1)
ISBN 0-87436-168-0 (set)

© 1987 by ABC-Clio, Inc.

ABC-Clio, Inc.
2040 Alameda Padre Serra, Box 4397
Santa Barbara, California

Clio Press Ltd.
55 St. Thomas Street
Oxford, England

Printed and bound in the United States of America.

TABLE OF CONTENTS
Volume I

FOREWORD

Historiography, depending upon our definition, is either a very old or a relatively recent art. Etymologically the word means "the writing in history." In this sense, the beginnings of historiography date back to the ancient Near and Far East. It is questionable whether there was any community that did not keep its collective memory alive through either an oral or written tradition, whether in Vedic India, Homeric Greece, or Sub-Saharan Africa. Since at least the time of Thucydides in the fifth century B.C., Greece, and Ssu-ma Chien in the second century B.C., China, a continuous tradition of historical writing has existed that distinguishes history from mythology and poetry and seeks to reconstruct the past. Yet in modern usage the term has had two additional meanings: (1) to refer to the study of the history of historical writing as distinct from the writing of history; and (2) to refer to the concern with theoretical and methodological questions that relate to historical writing. These two meanings are intertwined since it is impossible to write a critical history of historical writing without considering the presuppositions upon which such history rests. It is in the latter two senses that the term is generally used today and that the titles abstracted in this volume have been chosen.

In order for historiography to develop these last two meanings, it was necessary for historians first to become aware of what they were doing as historians. In the Western world history came into its own as a profession in the nineteenth century, centered at the universities. Long before this time, however, there existed an awareness of the critical sense with which the historian must approach evidence in order to truthfully recapture the past. But the historian was generally a person of letters or an antiquarian who viewed history as an art rather than as a science. The conception of history as a science—not in the sense of the natural sciences seeking laws and generalizations, but nevertheless as a professional discipline requiring intensive training in the systematic application of research methods—was a development of the nineteenth century. Only then did a lively concern with the history of historical writing emerge.

One of the first important historiographical works was Leopold von Ranke's famous essay "In Criticism of Modern Historians," published in 1824 as an appendix to his first major work on the rise of the modern European political system. The importance of the essay did not lie in its survey of the previous literature on the topic but in its methodological attempt to examine this literature in terms of scientific standards of scholarly research. This critical note became important for the numerous attempts thereafter to write history in a manner that would meet the scholarly requirements of the profession. The most common form for the discussion of historical literature was the review essay or even the book review in the newly established scholarly journals.

At the same time, there was a new interest in a more general history of historical writing. The first important history of historiography, by Ludwig Wachler, appeared in the 1810's and dealt with the German tradition of historical writing essentially as a form of literature. Later histories of historiography, prime among them Eduard Fueter's *Geschichte der neueren Historiographie* (*History of Modern Historical Writing*; Munchen and Berlin: R. Oldenbourg, 1911), on historical writing in Europe since the Renaissance, dealt more broadly with methodological aspects of historical studies. At the same time Fueter and George P. Gooch, the latter in *History and Historians in the Nineteenth Century* (London and New York: Longman's, Green, and Co., 1913), sought to locate historical writing in the broader currents of intellectual history as did James Westfall Thompson in *A History of Historical Writing* (New York: Macmillan Co., 1943), a two-volume study of history since antiquity. In 1937, sociologist Harry Elmer Barnes attempted to do this and at the same time relate the history of historical writing to social conditions in his work of the same title, as did Ernst Breisach in *Historiography: Ancient, Medieval, Modern* (Chicago: University of Chicago Press, 1983), the only recent attempt at a comprehensive history of historical writing and historical thought in the West since antiquity.

Closely related and parallel to these histories of historical writings were careful examinations of the basic theoretical and methodological presuppositions on which historical scholarship rests. There were occasional works dealing with these concerns before the nineteenth century; we need only refer to Lucian's essay on the writing of history in Greco-Roman antiquity or Jean Bodin's "Method for Easily Understanding History" of 1566. Perhaps the most serious attempt in the eighteenth century in this regard was Johann Martin Chladenius' little-known work on historical science. But systematic treatises had to wait until the nineteenth century when history as a professional discipline emerged.

It is therefore no accident that serious discussions of the theory and method of historical writing began then and were particularly prevalent in Germany. An early succinct statement of the "Task of the Historian" was Wilhelm von Humboldt's essay by this name written in 1821. Leopold von Ranke preceded his great lecture courses with introductory remarks on the nature of historical studies. In 1858 J. G. Droysen began to give his influential lectures on history as a humanistic science dealing with unique contexts of meaning, which he distinguished sharply from Thomas Buckle's attempt in England to find laws of historical development. In a less systematic fashion Jakob Burckhardt in Basel expounded his thoughts on the nature of history as an intellectual discipline, and later in the century Wilhelm Dilthey sought to explore the logic of inquiry of *Geisteswissenschaften* (the cultural sciences).

These attempts at formulating a theory of historical writing and of historical knowledge in a systematic fashion must be distinguished from philosophies of history in the traditional sense as found in the writings of Georg Friedrich Hegel, Auguste Comte, Oswald Spengler, or even Karl Marx, who sought to find a pattern of world history. But they should also be distinguished from the practical manuals of historical methodology, such as those of Ernst Bernheim (1888) and Charles Langlois and Charles Seignobos (1899), which were popular in the early twentieth century. It must be added, however, that Bernheim at least was very much aware of the theoretical problems that underlay methodological practice. Almost all of these attempts to deal with the theory of historical writing, i.e., the theory of historiography, proceeded from an idealistic position often labeled historicism—the view that history is the key to understanding things human, that it is made up of the ideas, intentions, and value notions of human beings, and that these must be reexperienced in their concrete uniqueness and cannot be recaptured in abstract concepts.

This idea—which proceeded from nineteenth-century, German idealist philosophy—was widely shared elsewhere during the first half of the twentieth century by theorists of historiography such as R. G. Collingwood, Jose Ortega y Gasset, and Henri Marrou. Yet at the same time important theorists of historical knowledge such as Max Weber, Karl Mannheim and Raymond Aron recognized that this intuitive approach to the sources which the former had demanded did not suffice to grasp historical relationships. The historian, like any other scientist, must work with clear concepts that recognize the uniqueness and integrity of the historical world.

Historical writing in the nineteenth and much of the twentieth century essentially reflected the idealistic notions regarding the character of the human or cultural sciences previously described. The focus of history was on individuals, ideas, and institutions. An elitist bias permeated historical writing and historical thought with a primary emphasis on politics and political leaders and a virtual neglect of the broad masses of the population. In its claim to be scientific, the new professional history stressed the importance of documentary evidence but concentrated on the papers of state that had recently been made available in the public archives rather than on sources illuminating social and economic conditions.

By the end of the nineteenth century, the assumptions upon which this history rested became increasingly problematic. It was considered too narrow and insufficiently concerned with the broad aspects of culture and society. At the same time its claim to be scientific was questioned because of its onesided stress on narrative to the neglect of theory and analysis, considered to be essential aspects of any science. One early challenge to the dominant style of professional history came from outside the profession from Marxism, which developed its own theory of historiography. According to Marxism, political history could only be understood in the context of social conflict. In the place of a history that concentrated on the great political leaders, Marxist historiography emphasized the development of social forces. However, it also shared with the more traditional belief that historical writing must deal with continuous processes in time that could and should be narrated but wished to embed its narrative of events into an explanatory, analytic framework. Much of professional historical writing in the twentieth century accepted the notion that the scope of historical writing must be extended to include economic, social, and cultural factors without accepting the Marxist notion of the primacy of economic forces or the centrality of the class struggle.

But in a sense even Marxist historiography was very traditional. It continued to assign a central role to events and ideas even if it viewed them in the context of economic and social conflict. A much more radical challenge to the conception of a history which progressed in time and in which human beings played a decisive part was formulated by the social historians assembled around the journal *Annales d'histoire économique et sociale* (later *Annales: Économies, Sociétés, Civilisations*) founded in France in 1929. Its first editors, Marc Bloch and Lucien Febvre, and their later disciples, were more interested in writing a history that described the great impersonal, geographical, biological, and economic factors as well as the social and cultural structures within which history took place than in narrating a course of events as the traditional professional historical scholars and Marxists had done. Several conceptions were challenged that had previously been fundamental to historians. One was the notion of historical continuity. Among the *Annales* historians, Fernand Braudel questioned whether the historian could work with a linear concept of time. Instead he preferred to apply different conceptions of time to the various aspects of human life, the almost immobile environment of human geography, the slowly changing economic, social, and cultural institutions and patterns, and the rapidly changing political sphere, each requiring different methods. A second notion emphasized the centrality of human agency in historical change. Braudel stressed the limits of human liberty—the role of the silent forces that operated independently of human consciousness and shaped it. Other historians in the *Annales* tradition were more concerned with cultural factors; but they saw culture in the patterns of everyday life and outlook (*mentalité*) of the population at large rather than in terms of the work of individuals.

This new view of history lent itself to two very different, but not mutually exclusive, methodological approaches. The one was quantitative: Particularly in the area of demographic, economic, and social life, statistical series could be established. Yet *mentalités* and ways of life often required a semiotic approach that sought to understand the symbolic meaning of collective human behavior.

Both the Marxist and the *Annales* schools have deeply influenced the way in which historians write history. But most historians have arrived at their approaches to history independently of both these orientations, though often in ways that resemble them. New concerns have marked historical writing in the years since World War II, and particularly within the past two decades. These reflect the changed political climate both domestically and internationally. There is a much greater interest in aspects of everyday life. Working-class history has turned from the study of the organized working-class movement to that of life patterns and outlook. The same is true of women's history, which has not only gained increasing attention but has also gone beyond the history of the movement to the conditions under which women worked and lived. Questions that seldom before had interested professional historians are now becoming important topics of research including sexuality, gender roles, childhood, death, leisure time, and many others bearing on human existence. The need to understand these in depth led to the application of psychological and psychoanalytical explanations in history, which in their Freudian form did not escape serious challenge. Methodologically, while particularly economic and demographic history relied heavily on quantifiable empirical evidence, many cultural and social historians questioned the applicability of mathematical models to complex, meaning-filled human relations and continued to emphasize the central role of qualitative methods of comprehending these relations.

Not only new topics but also new geographical regions became objects of historical study. Professional historians in the nineteenth century had been primarily interested in the history of the Western world. The non-Western world, if it was studied at all, was approached from the perspective of Western imperial expansion. While the national history of the Western states was not neglected after World War II, it was now approached with greater emphasis on the social and economic context in which political decisions were made. At the same time greater emphasis was given to the in-depth studies of regional and local history. The history of the non-Western world was now viewed very differently. Not only did Western scholars turn increasingly to the history of other areas of the world once dominated by Europe—Africa, the Middle East, Latin America, the Far East and Southern Asia—but they and the new indigenous generation of professional historians in these regions increasingly discovered the extent to which these areas and peoples had an autonomous history of their own. Traditional methods of political history no longer sufficed to study these societies. The old documentary approach was replaced or at least supplemented by the utilization of concepts and methods derived from a variety of social sciences, including cultural anthropology.

In the late 1980's, conceptions of the ways in which historiography is a scientific enterprise thus differ remarkably from those that dominated historical research in the nineteenth century. The Rankean faith that the historian can reconstruct the past through mere immersion into the sources has been largely abandoned. The conception of what constitutes a source has been vastly expanded to include not only written documents but also oral testimony and, more importantly, many less directly personal forms of evidence including birth records, price lists, works of art and literature, folk traditions, and forms of speech and language, all of which reveal elements of social and attitudinal structures. Historians have increasingly emphasized that no meaningful historical writing is possible that is not guided by the explicit questions of the historian. The concept that historical studies can be a scientific enterprise—scientific not in the sense of the natural sciences but of a systematic inquiry which seeks to honestly reconstruct the past—has been questioned but not abandoned.

Skepticism regarding the scientific character of history has taken several forms. One argument, popular in the United States in the 1930's (e.g., Carl Becker and Charles Beard), held that since every history reflected the subjective interests of the historian, it told us more about the historian than about the past. A similar note was raised by Theodor Lessing in Germany and others who suggested that history has no meaning; therefore the historian did not reconstruct the past but constructed it. Under the influence of French structuralist and poststructuralist literary criticism, in very recent years a number of American theorists of historiography have argued that the historian deals with texts that are to be interpreted in terms of their inherent literary and linguistic structure without any direct relation to a historical reality. Hayden White has thus argued that scholarly historical interpretation is no less speculative than grand style philosophy of history, having its roots not in the historian's truthful understanding of the past but in the literary strategies with which the historian consciously or subconsciously chooses to write.

At the other extreme is the effort of the cliometricians in the United States, such as Robert Fogel, who wish to turn history into a rigorous, theoretical social science. Most historians, however, occupy a middle ground. They continue to believe that the historian can obtain a degree of understanding of past societies, cultures, and individuals, and that this understanding requires both a reliance on empirical, at times quantitative, evidence and an appreciation of the qualitative aspects of historical existence. They maintain a profound commitment to historical honesty. They are aware that they approach their subject matter with explicit questions that reflect the perspectivity of their standpoint but their goal is to be guided by their findings and to avoid imposing their biases on their subject matter. There is undoubtedly a much greater awareness of the complexities of the historian's enterprise today than in the days of Ranke, and hopefully more humility, but by no means despair, about the possibility of obtaining knowledge about things human.

In a period of intense discussion on the tasks of the historian, an immense widening of the subject matter of history, and a growing diversity of methodological and conceptual approaches, this volume of abstracts of recent historiographical essays is particularly needed.

Georg G. Iggers
University at Buffalo
State University of New York

EDITOR'S PREFACE

. . . any written history involves the selection of a topic and an arbitrary delimitation of its borders—cutting off connections with the universal. Within the borders arbitrarily established, there is a selection and organization of facts by the processes of thought. This selection and organization—a single act—will be controlled by the historian's frame of reference composed of things deemed necessary and things deemed desirable.

Charles A. Beard
Presidential Address delivered before the
American Historical Association in Urbana,
Illinois, December 28, 1933.

Historians of all disciplines recognize the need for a current comprehensive reference guide to the art and theory of historiography, and the compilation of this bibliography from ABC-CLIO's databases is the first step toward filling that need. With the continued collaboration of historians, both on the staff of ABC-CLIO and in the academic world, the editor created the framework for this bibliography and examined, selected, and classified the over 8,000 citations. The arrangement of the material facilitated division into two volumes that, because each has its own index, can stand alone and be used separately. Together they offer a complete picture of the state of history writing over the last fifteen years.

Volume I covers bibliographies, conferences, books, dissertations, and individual historians. All of these chapters include a wide range of topics, or describe many topics. Also included in Volume I are chapters on methodologies and specific topics in historiography. The full range of revisionist and Marxist historiography is here, as well as the newer quantitative methodologies. Volume II has a geographic classification and covers virtually every region of the world. Included is the art and theory of history writing in different times, by different people, about different places.

The classification scheme adopted allows for general, all-inclusive articles; articles on specific geographic places, specific topics, and historians; and theoretical or methodological articles. Defining the borders of some of these topics frequently proved difficult, and editorial decisions had to be made as to the placement of certain items. No attempt was made to create categories or to force importance on existing categories by such decisions, but rather to allow the weight of the existing scholarship to determine the size and importance of the chapters.

The rotated string index, ABC-SPIndex, allows the researcher several points of access to the topics covered in the bibliography. At the end of each index string is a chronological descriptor, often with two sets of dates—one reflecting the periods covered by the historiographer, the other reflecting the time of authorship. This unique subject profile index allows immediate screening for material of interest. The informative abstracts of the journal articles provide additional information on the scope and relevance of the article for the user.

ABC-CLIO's history databases cover over 2,000 major scholarly journals published in over 40 languages. From this source abstracts of articles published from 1970 to 1985 were selected, along with book and dissertation citations. The books were selected by ABC-CLIO editors for their importance to historians in all fields, and were reviewed in at least one major scholarly journal. Along with the 158 dissertations from Dissertations Abstracts International, these writings cover the art and theory of writing history from the earliest times to the present. They are not limited to those published in the English language, nor to journals of North America and western Europe.

ABC-CLIO is committed to the dissemination of information and knowledge throughout the world—for scholars, researchers, and students—and invites all user comments, questions, and suggestions. Without the help of historians and librarians the world over, these publications would not be possible. With the reactions and input of readers, they will continue to reflect the highest standards of academic research.

LIST OF ABBREVIATIONS

A.	Author-prepared Abstract
Acad.	Academy, Academie, Academia
Agric.	Agriculture, Agricultural
AIA	Abstracts in Anthropology
Akad.	Akademie
Am.	America, American
Ann.	Annals, Annales, Annual, Annali
Anthrop.	Anthropology, Anthropological
Arch.	Archives
Archaeol.	Archaeology, Archaeological
Art.	Article
Assoc.	Association, Associate
Biblio.	Bibliography, Bibliographical
Biog.	Biography, Biographical
Bol.	Boletim, Boletin
Bull.	Bulletin
c.	century (in index)
ca.	circa
Can.	Canada, Canadian, Canadien
Cent.	Century
Coll.	College
Com.	Committee
Comm.	Commission
Comp.	Compiler
DAI	Dissertation Abstracts International
Dept.	Department
Dir.	Director, Direktor
Econ.	Economy, Econom-.
Ed.	Editor, Edition
Educ.	Education, Educational
Geneal.	Genealogy, Genealogical, Genealogique
Grad.	Graduate
Hist.	History, Hist-.
IHE	Indice Historico Espanol

Illus.	Illustrated, Illustration
Inst.	Institute, Institut-.
Int.	International, Internacional, Internationaal, Internationaux, Internazionale
J.	Journal, Journal-prepared Abstract
Lib.	Library, Libraries
Mag.	Magazine
Mus.	Museum, Musee, Museo
Nac.	Nacional
Natl.	National, Nationale
Naz.	Nazionale
Phil.	Philosophy, Philosophical
Photo.	Photograph
Pol.	Politics, Political, Politique, Politico
Pr.	Press
Pres.	President
Pro.	Proceedings
Publ.	Publishing, Publication
Q.	Quarterly
Rev.	Review, Revue, Revista, Revised
Riv.	Rivista
Res.	Research
RSA	Romanian Scientific Abstracts
S.	Staff-prepared Abstract
Sci.	Science, Scientific
Secy.	Secretary
Soc.	Society, Societe, Sociedad, Societa
Sociol.	Sociology, Sociological
Tr.	Transactions
Transl.	Translator, Translation
U.	University, Universi-.
US	United States
Vol.	Volume
Y.	Yearbook

Abbreviations also apply to feminine and plural forms.
Abbreviations not noted above are based on *Webster's Third New International Dictionary*
and the *United States Government Printing Office Style Manual*.

1. BIBLIOGRAPHIES, ARCHIVES, CONFERENCES, AND JOURNAL REVIEWS

1. Adomoniene, Ona. LIETUVOS TSR MA ISTORIJOS INSTI-TUTO LEIDINIŲ 1979 M. BIBLIOGRAFIJA [Bibliography of the publications of the Historical Institute of the Lithuanian Academy of Sciences, 1979]. *Lietuvos Istorijos Metraštis [USSR] 1979: 140-142.* A list with complete bibliographical details of planned publications of the institute for the year.   A. E. Senn

2. Amalvi, Christian. CATALOGUES HISTORIQUES ET CON-CEPTIONS DE L'HISTOIRE [Historical catalogs and conceptions of history]. *Storia della Storiografia [Italy] 1982 (2): 77-101.* The bibliographical classification in the French National Library's historical catalog illustrates what such catalogs reveal about the historical and social concepts prevailing at the time of their compilation. Published by Napoleon III's order between 1855 and 1895, the catalog of French history is hierarchically divided, revealing its monarchist orientation and the favoring of political and administrative structures over social movements and individuals. Newer sections indicate French historiography's evolution in modern times. Based on the National Library's historical catalog; 8 notes. Italian and English summaries.   G. Herritt

3. Anania, Francesca, ed. LA GERARCHIA DEI FINANZIA-MENTI CNR PER LE DISCIPLINE STORICHE [The hierarchy of National Research Council backing for the historical disciplines]. *Quaderni Storici [Italy] 1984 19(2): 669-677.* Supplements a previous article, Francesca Anania's "I Temi della Ricerca Storica in Italia: Le Erogazioni del CNR dal 1967" [Subjects of historical research in Italy: Output of the National Research Council from 1967], *Quaderni Storici 1984 19(1): 271-292.* Lists grants to the first 20 directors of research, 1967-80, as well as subjects and costs of their individual projects. Lists donations by the National Research Council to research in history, 1971-82. 6 notes.
                                        R. Grove

4. Arnesen, Elbjørg. HOVEDFAGS-, MAGISTERGRADS- OG SPESIALOPPGAVER OM LOKALHISTORISKE EMNER 1978-80 [Main subject, master's degree, and special assignments on local history topics, 1978-80]. *Heimen [Norway] 1981 18(12): 805-818.* This Norwegian Institute of Local History list based on information from Oslo, Bergen, Trondheim, and Tromsø universities and subdivided according to area covered by the assignment. It includes history, toponomy, archaeology, ethnology, and folkore.
                                        D. F. Spade

5. Batho, Gordon R. HISTORY BOOKS FOR SCHOOLS: 33. *History [Great Britain] 1974 59(195): 60-68.* A bibliographic essay surveying current British publishing in the main areas of secondary education history. The titles mentioned illustrate two trends: 1) an increasing though still limited interest in world history; 2) a new emphasis, in the teaching of British history, on economic and social themes as against the traditional politico-militaristic-dynastic history.
                                        R. V. Ritter

6. Becker, Gerhard. HISTORIE IN DER KRISE: DER WEST-DEUTSCHE HISTORIKERTAG 1967 IN FREIBURG I. BR [History in crisis: the West German historians' conference, 1967, in Freiburg im Breisgau]. *Zeitschrift für Geschichtswissenschaft [East Germany] 1968 16(2): 206-215.* Reports on the participants, themes, and shortcomings of the 27th Conference of West German Historians, denouncing the claims of the conference to represent all German historians. Most papers and speeches reflected the imperialist political content of West German historiography and education. Trends in American social sciences have thrown West German historiography into disarray. Based on conference presentations, and secondary works; 17 notes.   J. B. Street

7. Behrendt, Lutz-Dieter. INTERNATIONALE KONFERENZ ZUR ENTWICKLUNG DER GESCHICHTE DER GESCH-ICHTSWISSENSCHAFT IN DEN SOZIALISTISCHEN LÄNDERN [International conference on the development of the historical science's history in socialist lands]. *Beiträge zur Geschichte der Arbeiterbewegung [East Germany] 1979 21(4): 608-610.* The December 1978 conference in Moscow of leading historians from socialist lands.   G. E. Pergl

8. Beinart, Haim. KITVEI YITSHAK BAER, RESHIMA BIBLIO-GRAFIT [The writings of Professor Isaac Baer: a bibliographical list]. *Zion [Israel] 1979 44: 321-339.* This is the concluding article in a volume of *Zion* dedicated to Professor Isaac Baer. The first part is a chronological list of all of Baer's writings on Jewish history. The second part arranges the writings according to subject, Hebrew articles preceding articles in other languages within each section, and with cross references to the chronological list, which spans the period 1913-79.   N. Eilan

9. Benson, Susan Porter; Brier, Steve; Entenmann, Robert; Goldstein, Warren; and Rosenzweig, Roy. EDITORS' INTRODUCTION. *Radical Hist. Rev. 1981 (25): 3-8.* Outlines the editorial policy of the *Radical History Review,* an alternative forum for leftist historians, in contrast to "mainstream" historical journals and the forces of the "New Right."

10. Bernadskaia, E. V. PO STRANITSAM SBORNIKA "SRED-NIE VEKA" [Perusal of the collection of papers *Srednie Veka*]. *Voprosy Istorii [USSR] 1983 (3): 114-121.* Reviews 13 issues (nos. 31-43) of the journal *Srednie Veka,* 1968-1982. The bulk of the 60 topical papers deal with socioeconomic conditions, the genesis of feudalism and capitalism, ideological, cultural, and political developments in Western Europe in the 11th-17th centuries. The remainder comprise methodological and historiographic studies and book reviews. 6 notes.   N. Frenkley

11. Boiadzhieva, Elena. PROBLEMI NA SUVREMENNATA NAUCHNOINFORMATSIONNA DEINOST V ISTORI-CHESKATA NAUKA [Problems of contemporary scientific informational activity in historical scholarship]. *Istoricheski Pregled [Bulgaria] 1976 32(2): 82-95.* Surveys various means of distributing historical and historiographical information in Europe and North America particularly emphasizing historical institutes in the USSR and Eastern Europe. The means employed include computerized retrieval systems, bibliographical journals and collections, abstracts, and libraries. Based on periodical literature and other secondary works; table, graph, 57 notes.   F. B. Chary

12. Bojović, Jovan R. PEDESET GODINA *ISTORIJSKIH ZAPISA* 1927-77 [Fifty years of *Istorijski Zapisi,* 1927-77]. *Istorijski Zapisi [Yugoslavia] 1977 30(1): 5-11.* Reviews the 50-year history of the journal *Istorijski Zapisi* and assesses its contribution to Montenegrin and Yugoslav historiography.

13. Borruso, Edoardo. LO STORICO FRA CULTURA E OR-GANIZZAZIONE [The historian between culture and organization]. *Italia Contemporanea [Italy] 1982 146-147: 161-164.* Reviews Ilaria Porciani, *L' "Archivio Storico Italiano": Organizzazione della Ricerca ed Egemonia Moderata nel Risorgimento* (1979), and Manuela Doglio, *La "Nuova Rivista Storica" e la Storiografia del '900 (1917-45)* [Nuova Rivista Storica 1980 (3-4)].   E. E. Ryan

14. Boudot, François. LES OBSTACLES A LA DIFFUSION DE L'INFORMATION ET DU SAVOIR [Obstacles to the dissemination of information and knowledge]. *Bull. d'Hist. Moderne et Contemporaine [France] 1980 (12): 205-216.* Describes the obstacles

that exist for historians and social scientists in obtaining and disseminating information, which include censorship of sources, destruction of documents, technical difficulties, and financial concerns.

15. Bowers, Fredson. SCHOLARSHIP AND EDITING. *Papers of the Biblio. Soc. of Am. 1976 70(2): 161-188.* Emphasizes the necessity of adhering to original texts and remaining true to original style in editing of 17th- and 18th-century literature.

16. Brather, Hans-Stephan and Wick, Peter. GRUNDSÄTZE EINER KLASSIFIZIERUNG DER GESCHICHTSWISSENSCHAFT. EINE INFORMATIONSWISSENSCHAFTLICHE UNTERSUCHUNG [Bases of a classification of historiography: an investigation from the standpoint of the science of information systems]. *Jahrbuch für Geschichte [East Germany] 1975 13: 351-397.* Historiography today includes a vast number of publications which grow at an enormous rate every year. To organize this material into forms more easily accessible to researchers is the essential task of information sciences. Computers can be useful in this work, but the manifold areas of historical knowledge must first be organized into coherent classes and sub-classes. The author proposes the outlines of such a system of organization, including classification by period, geographical area, and subject ("structural-genetic division"). 75 notes, 3 appendixes. J. C. Billigmeier

17. Broadus, John R. SOVIET HISTORIANS AND THE EASTERN QUESTION OF THE EIGHTEENTH CENTURY. *East European Q. 1981 15(3): 357-375.* A complete review of the work of Soviet historians on the relations between Russia and the Ottoman Empire in the 18th century. Each work is identified, its thesis described, and its sources analyzed. All the Soviet historians treat imperial Russian policy favorably and discern progressive results from Russian actions. Based on the cited works; 41 notes.

C. R. Lovin

18. Bucchi, Sergio. NOTE SULLA FORMAZIONE DELL'ARCHIVIO SALVEMINI [Notes on the formation of the Salvemini archive]. *Ponte [Italy] 1980 36(1): 45-61.* Gaetano Salvemini, noted historian and political writer, died in 1957 leaving a large body of work which was subsequently edited by friends and disciples; traces the efforts to assemble and organize the Salvemini legacy.

19. Bugai, N. F. MEZHDUNARODNYE NAUCHNYE SVIAZI INSTITUTA ISTORII SSSR AN SSSR (1976-1980 GG.) [International links of the USSR Academy of Sciences Historical Institute, 1976-80]. *Istoriia SSSR [USSR] 1982 (3): 214-219.* Lists all the contacts with countries abroad made by the USSR's Academy of Sciences Institute of History between 1976 and 1980. The links were with socialist countries of Eastern Europe and the Far East and with nonsocialist countries in Europe and America. The joint symposiums and conferences resulted in several publications, such as one on Russo-Swiss economic links in the 18th century, and a publication of Byzantine legislative documents in West Germany is said to be imminent. 3 notes. D. N. Collins

20. Buonajuto, Mario. STORIOGRAFIA, STRUTTURA E FONTI ARCHIVISTICHE [Historiography, structure and archival sources]. *Rassegna degli Archivi di Stato [Italy] 1974 34(2-3): 494-503.* Discusses the relationship between historiographical methodology and archives.

21. Carbonell, Charles-Olivier. LA NAISSANCE DE LA *REVUE HISTORIQUE*. UNE REVUE DE COMBAT (1876-1885) [The birth of the *Revue historique*: a disputatious journal, 1876-85]. *Rev. Hist. [France] 1976 255(2): 331-351.* During the first 10 years of its existence, the *Revue historique* strove to represent the objective methodology of scientific history. In struggling against the monarchical clericalism of its rival journal, the *Revue des questions historiques*, however, the *Revue historique* proved to be rather firmly Protestant and republican in tone. Each of the leading contributors, led by its founder, Gabriel Monod, were Protestant and most of the articles on religion in the modern era tended toward anti-Catholicism. Based on Vols. 1-10 of *Revue historique*; 35 notes.
G. H. Davis

22. Chavarría, Jesús. A PRECIS AND A TENTATIVE BIBLIOGRAPHY ON CHICANO HISTORY. *Aztlán 1970 1(1): 133-141.* Presents a schematic outline and bibliography on Chicano history.
S

23. Cherepnin, L. V. DISPUTED QUESTIONS IN STUDY OF *THE PRIMARY CHRONICLE* FROM THE 1950'S TO THE 1970'S. *Soviet Studies in Hist. 1974-75 13(3): 57-91.* Discusses in detail questions of dating, reconstruction, interpretation, and evaluation of this chronicle, the basic source for Kievan and Suzdalian history, and reviews the approaches of various Soviet historians (A. A. Shakhmatov, M. D. Priselkov, D. S. Likhachev, V. M. Istrin, N. K. Nikol'skii, S. A. Bugoslavskii, I. P. Eremin, L. V. Cherepnin, et al.) who are active in the field. From *Istoriia SSSR* 1972 (4).

24. Cherepnin, L. V. VO VSEORUZHIE VESTI BOR'BU S BURZHUAZNOI ISTORIOGRAFIEI (IZ OPYTA RABOTY SEKTORA FEODALIZMA INSTITUTA ISTORII AN SSSR) [All-out fight against bourgeois historiography: a study project of the Department of Feudalism of the Institute of History, Academy of Sciences, USSR]. *Istoriia SSSR [USSR] 1962 6(1): 200-208.* Reviews anti-Soviet propaganda in Western literature during the 1950's, and discusses ways to counter it. One of the most effective research tools was a project, begun in 1959, which would compile an exhaustive card file on foreign publications with biographical, political and professional profiles of their authors, and all available information on major historical research centers, institutes, universities and publishing houses in Western Europe and the United States. 8 notes. N. Frenkley

25. Cherkasov, N. S. REGIONAL'NAIA KONFERENTSIIA PO METODOLOGII ISTORII, ISTORIOGRAFII I ISTOCHNIKOVEDENIIU [The regional conference on the methodology of history, historiography and sourcekeeping]. *Voprosy Istorii [USSR] 1979 (5): 134-136.* Presents abstracts of papers delivered at the west Siberian conference held 30 January-1 February 1979 at Tomsk.
V. Sobeslavsky

26. Cole, C. Robert. A BIBLIOGRAPHY OF THE WORKS OF A. J. P. TAYLOR, 1934-1975. *Bull. of Biblio. and Mag. Notes 1976 33(4): 170-177, 181, (5): 212-216.* Parts I and II. Provides a bibliography of the writings of A. J. P. Taylor; divides his work into four categories: major volumes, scholarly and popular articles, book reviews, and polemical works.

27. Connell-Smith, Gordon. THE HISTORIAN AND CONTEMPORARY SOCIETY. *Contemporary Rev. [Great Britain] 1978 232 (1346): 124-128.* Examines the role and responsibilities of professional historians in contemporary society and argues that they should take "a good, hard look at what they are about" and not leave the field of history in society to surveyors of popular entertainment and nostalgia.

28. Conzemius, Victor. LA SAINT-SIEGE ET LA DEUXIEME GUERRE MONDIALE, DEUX EDITIONS DE SOURCES [The Holy See and World War II: two editions of source materials]. *Rev. d'Hist. de la Deuxième Guerre Mondiale et des Conflits Contemporains [France] 1982 32(128): 71-94.* Two collections of documents published between 1965 and 1980 are crucial to the study of the papacy during World War II. They are Piere Blet, et al. ed., *Actes et Documents du Saint-Siège Relatifs à la Seconde Guerre Mondiale*, 10 vol., and Dieter Albrecht, ed., *Der Notenwechsel zwischen dem Heiligen Stuhl und der Deutschen Reichsregierung*, 3 vol. The contents of these 13 volumes are described, evaluated, and related to other sources. 51 notes. G. H. Davis

29. Coupal, Jean-Paul. LES DIX DERNIERES ANNEES DE LA *REVUE D'HISTOIRE DE L'AMERIQUE FRANCAISE*, 1972-1981 [The last 10 years of the *Revue d'Histoire de l'Amérique*

Française, 1972-81]. Rev. d'Hist. de l'Amérique Française [Canada] 1983 36(4): 553-567. Quantitative review of articles published in the journal and of its contributors since 1972. 4 tables, 3 notes.

R. Aldrich

30. Cox, Richard J. AMERICAN ARCHIVAL HISTORY: ITS DEVELOPMENT, NEEDS, AND OPPORTUNITIES. *Am. Arch. 1983 46(1): 31-41.* Although there is a considerable body of literature on American archival history written by both archivists and historians, many areas of the subject have yet to be covered. These include: European influences on American archival practices, local government records, college and university archives, and archival theory and practice. There are specific needs for studies of the interrelationships of the various types of archival institutions on the state level, studies of regional variations among archival repositories, and a one-volume history of American archives. 38 notes.

G.-A. Patzwald

31. Curato, Federico. STORIOGRAFIA ROMENA D'OGGI [Romanian historiography today]. *Risorgimento [Italy] 1973 25(1): 42-51.* Presents a checklist with detailed bibliographical information of recent Romanian historical and historiographical writings of interest to Italian scholars. Cites in particular articles pertaining to European history in the late 19th century. Secondary sources; 4 notes, biblio. Article to be continued.

C. Bates

32. Czeike, Felix. ZEITSCHRIFTENÜBERSCHAU [Journal survey]. *Wiener Geschichtsblätter [Austria] 1980 35(4): 191-198.* Provides an annotated bibliography of 1979 and 1980 issues of Austrian and German periodicals on geography, literature, music, genealogy, labor movements, museums, and urban planning pertaining to Austrian history.

33. Dašić, Miomir. ISTORIJSKI ZAPISI—TEMELJ CRNOGOR-SKE ISTORIOGRAFIJE [Historical Notes—the basis of Montenegrin historiography]. *Jugoslovenski Istorijski Časopis [Yugoslavia] 1977 16(3-4): 155-184.* Reviews the subjects covered by the Montenegrin journal *Historical Notes*, 1927-77, and assesses the journal's cultural influence and its social and academic value. Secondary sources; 48 notes.

J. Bamber

34. Delannoi, Gil. *ARGUMENTS*, 1956-1962, OU LA PAREN-THESE DE L'OUVERTURE [*Arguments*, 1956-62, or the parenthetical opening]. *Revue Française de Science Politique [France] 1984 34(1): 127-145.* Analyzes the historical work accomplished by the review *Arguments*, 1956-62, which opened a digression in the French intellectual world during a period of questioning brought about by de-Stalinization.

35. Deutsch, Robert; Joyeux, Frank; and Sznapka, Marian. DIE ENTWICKLUNG DER KOOPERATION DURCH DIE IN-TERNATIONALEN KONGRESSE FÜR HISTORISCHE WISSENSCHAFTEN [The development of cooperation through the international congresses for historical sciences]. *Rev. Roumaine D'Hist. [Rumania] 1976 15(1): 93-117.* Describes the five congresses for historical sciences held since 1950, noting their organization, functional changes, participants, important themes, discussions, and general impact on the historical sciences.

36. Deutsch, Robert. PERIODICE DE ISTORIE DIN ROMÂNIA ÎN ULTIMII TREIZECI DE ANI [Romanian historical periodicals in the last 30 years]. *Anale de Istorie [Rumania] 1974 20(1): 165-172.* Evaluates the main emphases, tone, and themes of Romanian historiography as reflected in the major periodicals, grouped in four periods: from 23 August 1944 to the end of 1947; 1948-55; 1956-65; and 1965-present. Discusses the conflict between traditional Romanian history of the prewar era and scientific dialectical materialism of the late 1940's and early 1950's, as reflected in *Revista istorică* of the Iorga school and *Revista istorică română* of the modern concept. Most attention is paid to the evolution of *Studii, Analele Institutului de studii istorice şi social-politice de pe lîngă C.C. al P.C.R.*, and the recent (1967) popular monthly, *Magazin istoric*. A feature common to all Romanian publications is the

weeding out of erroneous theses and scientifically unfounded conclusions not conforming to modern reality. Primary sources; 26 notes.

G. J. Bobango

37. Dixon, Diana and Sutcliffe, Anthony. CURRENT BIBLIOG-RAPHY OF URBAN HISTORY. *Urban Hist. Y. [Great Britain] 1982: 79-134.* Provides a bibliography of books relating to urban history listed in the *British National Bibliography* between 1 July 1980 and 30 June 1981, supplemented by the scanning of a large number of periodicals, and by the selections sent by the foreign correspondents of the *Urban History Yearbook*. The entries are classified under these headings: general, population, physical structure, social structure, economic activity, communications, politics and administration, shaping the urban environment, urban culture, and attitudes to cities. An index of towns is also included.

G. L. Neville

38. Djurdjev, Branislav. TACHE FONDAMENTALE DE LA SCIENCE HISTORIQUE [The basic task of historical science]. *Godišnjak Društva Istoričara Bosne i Hercegovine [Yugoslavia] 1976 21-27: 269-271.* Discusses the report by P. Brezzi and E. Sestan "L'historiographie comme science historique" presented at the 14th International Congress of Historical Sciences in San Francisco in 1975, which reviews the development of historiography, ca. 1800-1975.

39. Dmitriev, S. S. ISTORIIA ISTORICHESKOI NAUKI V SSSR. SOVETSKII PERIOD. OKTIABR' 1917-1967 G. BIBLIOGRA-FIIA. M. NAUKA. 1980. 155 ST. [History of historical scholarship in the USSR: Soviet period, October 1917-1967. Bibliography (1980), 155 pp.]. *Voprosy Istorii [USSR] 1982 (1): 119-125.* Reviews a bibliography of Soviet historiography; containing 11,053 entries and covering 50 years of Soviet power, 1917-67.

40. Doglio, Manuela. LA "NUOVA RIVISTA STORICA" E LA STORIOGRAFIA DEL '900 (1917-1945) [The *Nuovo Rivista Storica* and 20th-century historiography, 1917-45]. *Nuova Riv. Storica [Italy] 1980 64(3-4): 334-377.* Reviews the development of historical studies in Italy through the perspective offered by the history of one journal. The chief figure in this period is Benedetto Croce in his fight against positivism on the one hand and with the Fascist ideology on the other. The *Nuova Rivista* played a significant role in the struggle against Fascism. During the Fascist period the journal kept the horizons of the discipline open, especially through a careful review of work done abroad. 200 notes.

J. V. Coutinho

41. Dossick, Jesse J., comp. DOCTORAL DISSERTATIONS, 1976-1977. *Slavic Rev. 1977 36(4): 734-947.* The list of doctoral dissertations separates the American and Canadian titles (including one from Australia), from the British list. Due to nonuniformity in reporting, the list includes 41 titles from 1973 to 1975; the 1977 listings are also far from complete. This is the output from 80 universities in the first list, and from eight in the British section.

R. V. Ritter

42. Drozdowski, Marian. LES ACTIVITÉS DES HISTORIENS DE POZNAŃ [The activities of Poznań historians]. *Acta Poloniae Hist. [Poland] 1977 35: 217-232.* Presents a bibliography of the studies of Poznań historians, 1970-75, centering around Poznań University, its institutes, and the numerous periodicals published in Poznań. Many of these publications deal with Poland's western frontier, Polish-German relations, and the German occupation during World War II. There are also notable publications on the history of Lithuania, and monographs on the history of Greater Poland and of small towns.

H. Heitzman-Wojcicka

43. Eckhardt, Thorvi. BALKANZEITSCHRIFTEN, IV [Balkan journals, part IV]. *Österreichische Osthefte [Austria] 1968 10(1): 44-49.* Continued from a previous article. Reviews the 1963-67 issues of the Romanian historical journal *Revue des Etudes Sud-Est Eu-ropéennes.*

44. Eley, Geoff. MEMORIES OF UNDER-DEVELOPMENT: SOCIAL HISTORY IN GERMANY. *Social Hist. [Great Britain] 1977 (6): 785-791.* Reviews the first volume of the new journal *Geschichte und Gesellschaft. Zeitschrift für Historische Sozialwissenschaft,* (Göttingen; Vandonhoeck und Rupprecht, 1975), welcoming its contribution to the study of social history, which has been unduly neglected by West German historians since World War II. Secondary sources; 17 notes. N. Dejevsky

45. Ellsworth, S. George. TEN YEARS: AN EDITOR'S REPORT. *Western Hist. Q. 1979 10(4): 420-436.* The author has resigned after having served as editor of *The Western Historical Quarterly* for its first ten years. He reports on his "stewardship" of the *Quarterly* by relating its establishment at Utah State University, the story of its operations, and its general underlying guidelines. He considers the *Quarterly* as "the chief visual representative of the field of western American history" and of the sponsoring Western History Association. Ellsworth is optimistic for western American history; the prospects "have never been better." Illus., 3 notes.

D. L. Smith

46. Enriquez del Arbol, Eduardo. REFLEXIONES SOBRE METODOLOGIA PARA UN ESTUDIO DE LA PRENSA [Reflections on methodology for the study of the press]. *Anuario de Hist. Contemporánea [Spain] 1981 8: 249-262.* Discusses problems and advantages involved in using newspapers as historical sources.

47. Epshtein, A. D. METODOLOGICHESKIE I ISTORIOGRAFICHESKIE VOPROSY ISTORICHESKOI NAUKI V "TRUDAKH TOMSKOGO UNIVERSITETA" (1963-1969 GG) [Methodological and historiographical problems of historical research in the *Works of Tomsk University,* 1963-69]. *Novaia i Noveishaia Istoriia [USSR] 1971 (5): 144-152.* In the 1960's Tomsk University developed into one of the centers of historiographical research in the USSR; it published six collections, 1961-69, containing 63 articles which have become a bibliographical rarity. Most articles dealt with the methods and philosophies of foreign historians, either singly or in groups, but some discussed problems such as the gnosiological bases of historical research, objectivity and political loyalty, and the interaction of history with the present. C. I. P. Ferdinand

48. Erdmann, Karl Dietrich. FRAGEN AN DIE SOWJETISCHE GESCHICHTSWISSENSCHAFT [A few questions put before Soviet historiography]. *Geschichte in Wissenschaft und Unterricht [West Germany] 1978 29(7): 451-456.* Reports the proceedings of the third Soviet-German Historians' Conference at Munich. Topics were "Europe between Revolution and Restoration, 1797-1815," where agreement could be reached, and "Historicism and Modern History," where controversial opinions about the processes of historical development and methods of historical inquiry were voiced. Secondary works; note. H. W. Wurster

49. Feenstra, R. COMPLEMENT A LA BIBLIOGRAPHIE DES TRAVAUX HISTORIQUES DE E. M. MEIJERS (1880-1954) [Addenda to the bibliography of the historical works of E. M. Meijers (1880-1954)]. *Tijdschrift voor Rechtsgeschiedenis [Netherlands] 1980 48(4): 373-376.* Provides addenda and errata to R. Feenstra's bibliography of the historical works of Eduard Maurits Meijers (1880-1954) in *Tijdschrift voor Rechtsgeschiedenis* 1955 23: 426-451. Notes publications relating to Meijers and his works that have appeared since 1957. 13 notes. R. O. Khan

50. Felice Cardot, Carlos. EN LOS XXV AÑOS DEL DEPARTAMENTO DE PUBLICACIONES [On the 25th anniversary of the publications department]. *Bol. de la Acad. Nac. de la Hist. [Venezuela] 1983 66(264): 1077-1082.* Describes the activities of the department of publications of the National Academy of History during the 25 years of its existence. Its publications, especially in the field of colonial history, have earned the academy an international reputation. J. V. Coutinho

51. Foerg, Irmgard and Pringle, Annette, comp. POST-WAR PUBLICATIONS ON GERMAN JEWRY: A SELECTED BIBLIOGRAPHY OF BOOKS AND ARTICLES 1979. *Leo Baeck Inst. Year Book 1980 25: 363-441.* Contains 1,080 entries, classified and annotated. F. Rosenthal

52. Fomin, V. PROBLEMY VTOROI MIROVOI VOINY NA STRANITSAKH VENGERSKOGO VOENNO-ISTORICHESKOGO VESTNIKA [The problems of World War II in the pages of Hungary's *Military and Historical Bulletin*]. *Voenno-Istoricheskii Zhurnal [USSR] 1972 (12): 92-97.* Covers articles and reviews published during 1969-72.

53. Frolova, I. I. LITERATURA PO ISTORII SREDNIKH VEKOV, VYSHEDSHAIA V SSSR V 1978 G. [Medieval history studies published in the USSR in 1978]. *Srednie Veka [USSR] 1981 44: 372-390.* Continued from previous articles (see *Srednie Veka* 1978 [42]; 1980 [43]). Lists 296 books and articles arranged alphabetically under name of country and four periods of feudalism, as well as under general headings: handbooks, bibliographies, historiography, etc. Cites 16 titles published in 1976 and 1977 supplementing previous listings. Note. N. Frenkley

54. Gabel, Christopher R. BOOKS ON OVERLORD: A SELECT BIBLIOGRAPHY AND RESEARCH AGENDA ON THE NORMANDY CAMPAIGN, 1944. *Military Affairs 1984 48(3): 144-148.* Presents a select bibliography and research topics on Operation Overlord, the 1944 cross-channel invasion of France by the Western Allies. Overlord is one of the most significant military actions in history, a rare occasion when mighty nations commend their fates to the outcome of a single battle. The schools of historical interpretation concerning the commanders stem directly from the rivalries and controversies that arose among these individuals during the campaign itself. Overlord merits continued historical inquiry.

A. M. Osur

55. Galos, Adam. HISTORIA POLSKI LUDOWEJ NA ŁAMACH SOBÓTKI [The history of Poland in the journal *Sobótka*]. *Śląski Kwartalnik Hist. Sobótka [Poland] 1980 35(1): 97-103.* Surveys the historiographic achievements and shortcomings of the *Śląski Kwartalnik Historyczny Sobótka* over the 34 years of its existence.

56. Georgian, Lucia. COLECȚIA *BIBLIOTHECA HISTORICA ROMANIAE:* O CONTRIBUȚIE IMPORTANTĂ LA AFIRMAREA ȘTIINȚEI ISTORICE ROMÂNEȘTI PE PLAN INTERNAȚIONAL [The *Bibliotheca Historica Romaniae:* an important contribution to the assertion of Romanian historical studies on an international level]. *Studii și Articole de Istorie [Romania] 1973 (24): 162-165.* Surveys the contribution of this series of publications to international historiography, 1963-73.

57. Gerardi, Donald F. BOOKS IN THE FIELD: HISTORIOGRAPHY. *Wilson Lib. Bull. 1968 42(5): 485-496.*

58. Gersman, Elinor Mondale. HISTORIOGRAPHY AND BIBLIOGRAPHY. *Hist. of Educ. Q. 1975 15(2): 227-249.* Bibliography of materials printed 1973-74 pertaining to education, 17th-20th centuries, with special sections for historiography and bibliography, women, family and youth, and professionalism, as well as geographic delineations: Africa, Asia, Australia, Canada, Europe, Great Britain, Latin America, and the United States.

59. Goetz, Helmut. DIE NUNTIATURBERICHTE DES 16. JAHRHUNDERTS ALS KOMPLEMENTÄRQUELLE ZUR GESCHICHTSSCHREIBUNG [The reports of the nuncios of the 16th century as a complementary source for the writing of history]. *Quellen und Forschungen aus Italienischen Archiven und Bibliotheken [Italy] 1973 53: 214-226.* Describes the organization and functioning of the office of the papal nuncios, and comments on the many uses that can be made of their reports in historical research, especially for biography, means of communication, military and social history, and church history and architecture. The reports are less helpful for economic history. Based on various editions of the reports and secondary works; 61 notes. J. B. Street

60. Grabmüller, Hans-Jürgen. DIE RUSSISCHEN CHRONIKEN DES 11.-18. JAHRHUNDERTS IM SPIEGEL DER SOWJETFORSCHUNG (1917-1975) [The Russian chronicles during the 11th-18th centuries in Soviet research]. *Jahrbücher für Geschichte Osteuropas [West Germany] 1976 24(3): 394-416.* Russian scholars like D. S. Lichachev and Soviet ones like M. N. Tikhomirov have catalogued, arranged, and analyzed leading 11th-18th-century annals and chronicles. Serious historiographical surveys of these sources first began in the 19th century under D. V. Polenov and A. I. Markevich. 187 notes. J. R. Goldman

61. Grigulevich, I. R.; Udal'tsova, Z. V.; and Chubar'ian, A. O.. PROBLEMY NOVOI I NOVEISHEI ISTORII NA XV MEZHDUNARODNOM KONGRESSE ISTORICHESKIKH NAUK [Problems of modern and contemporary history at the 15th International Congress of Historical Sciences]. *Novaia i Noveishaia Istoriia [USSR] 1981 (4): 23-40.* The congress in Bucharest, August 1980, discussed problems of modern and contemporary history at plenary sessions, panels, and meetings of various international commissions and organizations of the International Congress of Historical Sciences. J

62. Grishin, V. M. OB OSVESHCHENII VOPROSOV ISTORII PARTII V ZHURNALE *KOMMUNIST MOLDAVII* [Questions of Party history in the journal *Moldavian Communist*]. *Voprosy Istorii KPSS [USSR] 1966 (2): 121-124.* Discusses the periodical's material published during 1965, dealing with the history of local Party organizations.

63. Grönroos, Gun. FINLÄNDSK HISTORISK LITTERATUR 1981: BIBLIOGRAFISKT URVAL [Finnish historical literature 1981: a bibliographical selection]. *Hist. Tidskrift för Finland [Finland] 1983 68(2): 206-228.*

64. Hának, Peter. GESCHICHTSSCHREIBUNG UND ZEITGEMÄSSHEIT. REFLEXION ÜBER DEN WIENER HISTORIKERKONGRESS [Historiography and actuality: reflections on the Viennese congress of historians]. *Österreichische Osthefte [Austria] 1966 8(1): 42-44.* In the field of methodology, historiography is one of the most conservative sciences. Some contributions at the 12th International Congress of Historical Sciences in Vienna showed that the research of sociological structures and comparative methods are a great enrichment for the historian.

65. Haun, Horst and Heinz, Helmut. ZUR GRÜNDUNG DER *ZEITSCHRIFT FÜR GESCHICHTSWISSENSCHAFT*: DER ERSTE JAHRGANG DER ZEITSCHRIFT [Foundation of the *Zeitschrift für Geschichtswissenschaft*: the first volume of the journal]. *Zeits. für Geschichtswissenschaft [East Germany] 1981 29(3): 226-238.* Recounts the history of the founding by East German historians of *Zeitschrift für Geschichtswissenschaft* in 1953 and explains the journal's role in East German historiography, the publication of textbooks, and the refutation of imperialist interpretations of history. Based on the first volume of the journal; 91 notes. G. E. Pergl/S

66. Hecht, David. THE HISTORY OF RUSSIA AND EASTERN EUROPE: A SURVEY OF SCHOLARLY AND RELATED WRITINGS (1966-1970). *Ann. of the Am. Acad. of Pol. and Social Sci. 1975 (417): 120-141.* A survey of studies on the history of Russia and Eastern Europe published between 1966 and 1970, organized chronologically. "Great interest has been manifested in evaluating the Bolshevik Revolution a half-century after 1917. Perhaps as a consequence of détente in Soviet-American political relations, earlier American-Russian historical relations have been studied with renewed interest." Writings covering the different nationalities, regions, and religions are also noted. 63 notes. D. D. Cameron

67. Hegemann, Margot. BIBLIOTHECA HISTORICA ROMANIAE [Bibliotheca Historica Romaniae]. *Jahrbuch für Geschichte der Sozialistischen Länder Europas [East Germany] 1972 16(1): 199-206.* Review article on the *Bibliotheca Historica Romaniae* series, published by the history section of the Romanian Academy of Arts and Sciences (1963-70), which includes studies, monographs, and documents in Russian, French, English, German, and Romanian.

68. Heinz, Helmut and Sumpf, Fredi. ZUR ENTWICKLUNG DER PARTEIGESCHICHTSSCHREIBUNG IN DER DDR: 1976 bis 1980 [Development of the historiography of the Party in East Germany: 1976-80]. *Beiträge zur Geschichte der Arbeiterbewegung [East Germany] 1981 23(2): 208-217.* A bibliography of monographs and document collections on the history of East Germany's ruling Socialist Unity Party and its antecedents, 1848-1961. 4 notes. A. Schuetz

69. Heller, Ilse. DER JAHRGANG 1982 DER ZEITSCHRIFT *VOPROSY ISTORII* [The 1982 volume of the journal *Voprosy Istorii*]. *Zeitschrift für Geschichtswissenschaft [East Germany] 1984 32(3): 246-249.* The 1982 edition of *Voprosy Istorii*, true to its tradition, is concerned mostly with Russian history. The 10 historical articles about capitalist countries are mainly focused on the United States, but England, France, Israel, Brazil, and South Africa are also mentioned. Russian history from the 14th to the 20th centuries is the subject of 15 articles. The remainder of the articles cover current historical events. Note. T. Kuner

70. Heller, Ilse. DER JAHRGANG 1978 DER ZEITSCHRIFT *VOPROSY ISTORII* [The 1978 volume of the journal *Voprosy Istorii*]. *Zeitschrift für Geschichtswissenschaft [East Germany] 1980 28(5): 476-481.* In 1977 *Voprosy Istorii* was awarded the Red Banner of Labor medal as the foremost history journal in the USSR. The 1978 volume of the journal is devoted mainly to the history of Russia and also contains information about important meetings and conferences of historians at home and abroad. Articles dealing with modern world history and peoples' movements are also presented. G. E. Pergl

71. Heller, Ilse. DIE SOWJETISCHE GESCHICHTSWISSENSCHAFT ANFANG DER ZWANZIGER JAHRE: DIE ZEITSCHRIFTEN *PROLETARSKAJA REVOLJUCIJA* UND *KRASNAJA LETOPIS* [Soviet historical science at the beginning of the 1920's: the periodicals *Proletarskaia Revoliutsiia* and *Krasnaia Letopis'*]. *Zeitschrift für Geschichtswissenschaft [East Germany] 1984 32(1): 27-35.* After the revolution there was an urgent need for the creation of a Soviet historical scientific institution. Teaching young historians new principles, research, and standards based on Marxist concepts were all new and demanding undertakings. *Proletarskaia Revoliutsiia* and *Krasnaia Letopis'* were two new journals established to represent the new institution. Both periodicals were catalysts for new scientific and social developments. Between 1931 and 1941 *Proletarskaia Revoliutsiia* published 132 issues. Between 1922 and 1937 *Krasnaia Letopis'* published 64 issues. 53 notes. T. Kuner

72. Hellwig, David J. AFRO-AMERICAN VIEWS OF IMMIGRANTS, 1830-1930: A HISTORIOGRAPHICAL-BIBLIOGRAPHICAL ESSAY. *Immigration Hist. Newsletter 1981 13(2): 1-5.*

73. Henderson, Kathleen. PICTURES IN HISTORY. *Hist. Workshop J. [Great Britain] 1976 1: 208-210.* Describes a number of recent books which indicate the value of illustrations in published historical works. The books include Hilary and Mary Evans's and Andra Nelki's *The Picture Researcher's Handbook, An International Guide To Picture Sources and How to Use Them* (Newton Abbot: David and Charles, 1975) and Gordon Winter's *The Country Camera* (Harmondsworth: Penguin, 1965) and *Cockney Camera* (Harmondsworth: Penguin, 1975). N. Dejevsky

74. Henning, Eckart. DAS GEHEIME STAATSARCHIV BERLIN-DAHLEM: RÜCKBLICK ANLÄSSLICH SEINES DOPPELJUBILÄUMS 1874-1924-1974 [Secret state archives in Berlin-Dahlem: a retrospective on its double jubilee 1874-1924-1974]. *Archivar [West Germany] 1975 28(2): 143-150.* An overview of the history and academic importance of the Dahlem archives for German historical research.

75. Hildebrand, Karl-Gustaf. EMIL HILDEBRAND OCH HISTORISK TIDSKRIFT [Emil Hildebrand and *Historisk Tidskrift*]. *Hist. Tidskrift [Sweden] 1980 (1-2): 62-91.* Reviews the early history of the periodical *Historisk Tidskrift*, founded in 1881 in Sweden, and analyzes its content. One of the most influential persons in shaping the journal during its first 20 years was its editor, Emil Hildebrand, historian and archivist. This study evaluates his performance and some of his personal contributions to the journal, a large part of which were reviews. During his editorship the journal became a representative for standards and ideas of advanced historians, mainly through his furthering of critical research. Private letters, Hildebrand's diary, and the journal. T. Parker

76. Holmgaard, Jens. ADMINISTRATIONSHISTORIE SOM ARKIVNØGLE [Administration history as archive key]. *Arkiv [Denmark] 1980 8(1): 44-50.* One aspect of administration history is the "key aspect": knowledge of historical administrative contexts as the precondition for interpreting the material. In the debate on archives as research institutions, some have gone too far in seeing the archivist as central to the interpretation of provenance. This must remain the function of the historian. The material is arranged on principles of provenance and the duty of the archivist is to provide the historian with the key, in the service of research. Archives could facilitate research by improving registration in some subject areas and generally observe and record any potentially interesting information. K. S. Williams

77. Horn, Maurycy. DIAŁALNOŚĆ ŻYDOWSKIEGO INSTYTUTU HISTORYCZNEGO W POLSCE W LATACH 1967-1979 [The activity of the Jewish Historical Institute in Poland, 1967-79]. *Biuletyn Żydowskiego Instytutu Hist. w Polsce [Poland] 1979 (3): 7-20.* Continued from a previous article.

78. Hudson, Kenneth. MONUMENTS TO WHOM? THE STATE OF INDUSTRIAL ARCHEOLOGY. *Encounter [Great Britain] 1974 42(5): 72-77.* A review article discussing the range of periodical literature and other publications devoted to industrial archeology, commenting that "the movement to academise industrial archeology is more than usually sad," particularly in view of the tendency to exclude the human and social aspects of the subject. "It is surely meaningless to talk of 'technological change' and 'industrial monuments.' People, not steam engines, have monuments... the workers... are an essential element in what we are accustomed to label, far too glibly, 'technology' and 'technological change.' " notes, 7 biblio. D. H. Murdoch

79. Hudzenko, P. P. and Shatalina, F. P. PO STORINKAKH BIULETENNIA "ARKHIVY UKRAINY" [From the pages of the bulletin *Archives of the Ukraine*]. *Ukraïns'kyi Istorychnyi Zhurnal [USSR] 1980 (7): 65-77.* Describes the present format of the bulletin—an organ of the Main Archive Administration of the Council of Ministers of the Ukrainian SSR and defines its task since its founding in 1917, the coverage of specialized historical disciplines studied in the Ukraine, the other Soviet republics, socialist countries, and other foreign nations.

80. Hundert, Gershon. RECENT STUDIES RELATED TO THE HISTORY OF THE JEWS IN POLAND FROM EARLIEST TIMES TO THE PARTITION PERIOD. *Polish R. 1973 18(4): 84-99.* A bibliography of works published 1960-72, with an introduction.

81. Iunitskaia, R. Z. and Tsyrul'nikov, Ia. S. BIOGRAFICHESKAIA KHRONIKA V. I. LENINA: ISTOCHNIKOVAIA BAZA, NEKOTORYE PRIEMY RABOTY S ISTOCHNIKAMI [Bibliographical chronicle of V. I. Lenin: sources and some methods to work with the sources]. *Voprosy Istorii KPSS [USSR] 1983 (4): 119-127.* Describes the sources on which the new fundamental collection of 12 volumes on the life and work of Lenin was compiled. The sources included his manuscripts; drafts of speeches; letters to his friends, editors, and officials; resolutions of the Party Congresses and minutes of other meetings; cables, memos, and calendars with his notes; newspapers and magazines of the time; interviews with foreign correspondents; and memoirs of contemporaries. Based on archival material; 36 notes. R. Kirillov

82. Kalembka, Sławomir. STRUKTURA TREŚCI I FORM PUBLIKACJI "ZAPISEK HISTORYCZNYCH": ZMIANY W LATACH 1908-1979 [Structure of the form and content of the publication of *Zapiski Historyczne*, 1908-79]. *Zapiski Hist. [Poland] 1982 47(3): 7-22.* Analyzes the changes in the layout and thematic preference in the Polish historical journal *Zapiski Historyczne,* 1908-79, stressing the shift from the ecclesiastical to the economic and social history of the Pomeranian region.

83. Kalenychenko, P. M. and Pavlenko, V. V. UKRAINSKATA ISTORICHESKA NAUKA ZA ISTORIIATA NA BULGARIIA I UKRAINSKO-BULGARSKITE OTNOSHENIIA [Ukrainian historiography on the history of Bulgaria and Ukrainian-Bulgarian relations]. *Izvestiia na Inst. po Istoriia na BKP [Bulgaria] 1980 43: 87-107.* Survey of historiography from World War II to the present, analyzing books, pamphlets, and articles dealing with Bulgaria's history, socialist development, and development of USSR-Bulgarian ties during that period.

84. Kamenetski, B. A. SOVETSKAIA BIBLIOGRAFIIA ISTORIOGRAFICHESKOI LITERATURY PO VSEOBSHCHEI ISTORII [Soviet bibliography of historiographical literature on world history]. *Novaia i Noveishaia Istoriia [USSR] 1973 (5): 158-164.* Describes existing bibliographical aids for world history generally and on specific problems, and mentions specialist bibliographies in preparation. Refers principally to the use of a bibliography of historical bibliographies, Soviet bibliographies of foreign bibliographies, and the significance of retrospective bibliographies. Considers recent Soviet bibliographies of Ancient History, the 20th century, and specific countries, and discusses principles behind the science. Examines the two-volume *History of Historical Science in the USSR* and stresses the need for more Soviet bibliographies of foreign history. Secondary sources; 3 notes. C. R. Pike

85. Kampuš, Ivan and Šercar, Tvrtko. STANJE ČASOPISA NA PODRUČJU POVIJESNIH ZNANOSTI U SR HRVATSKOJ KOJE FINANCIRAJU SAMOUPRAVNE INTERESNE ZAJEDNICE ZA ZNANOST [The state of historical journals published in the Croatian SR and financed by the Self-Managed Interest Society for Scientific Endeavors]. *Radovi: Inst. za Hrvatsku Povijest [Yugoslavia] 1981 14(1): 359-374.* Studies the state of the 24 historical periodicals published in Croatia and financed by the Self-Managed Interest Society for Scientific Endeavors. Using data supplied by the journals' editorial staffs, analyzes the periodicity of publication (either regularly or irregularly), the types of articles published, the average number of articles per issue, their average length, and the influence of the editorial staffs on the methodology of the articles. Based on questionnaires and other primary and secondary sources; 6 tables, 2 appendixes, map, 18 notes. German summary. S. L. Kaufman

86. Kandus, Nataša. BIBLIOGRAFIJA SODELAVCEV INŠTITUTA ZA ZGODOVINO DELAVSKEGA GIBANJA ZA LETO 1982 [Bibliography of collaborators of the Institute for the History of the Workers' Movement for 1982]. *Prispevki za Zgodovino Delavskega Gibanja [Yugoslavia] 1983 23(1-2): 221-229.*

87. Kenyon, J. P. VICTORIAN HISTORY MEN: ARCHIVES AND SOURCES. *Hist. Today [Great Britain] 1983 33(Apr): 11-16.* Discusses the haphazard research methods employed by 19th-century British historians and the progress made during that period to open and catalog public records and archives.

88. Keresztesi, Michael. PROLEGOMENA TO THE HISTORY OF INTERNATIONAL LIBRARIANSHIP. *J. of Lib. Hist. 1981 16(2): 435-448.* Discusses several aspects of the history of international librarianship, including the lack of research on the subject,

evidence of interest, the scope of the subject, major hypotheses underlying historical research in the field, and sources and uses of the history of international librarianship. Secondary sources; 23 notes.

J. Powell

89. Kerkkonen, Martti. ARKIVMATERIAL OCH HISTORIESYN: KRONORÄKENSKAPER FRÅN SVENSKA TIDEN SOME BASMATERIAL FÖR HISTORIEFORSKNING [Public record material and the historical view: crown accounts from the Swedish period as a basis for historical research]. *Hist. Arkisto [Finland] 1975 (70): 98-127.* The availability of unusually complete public fiscal archives for Finland, 1500-1800, greatly influenced the evolution of Finnish historiography after 1859, when these archives were opened to scholars. Historians shifted away from political and nationalist questions and examined economic, social, and cultural developments. Finnish historiography became increasingly empirical. Primary sources; 37 notes.

R. G. Selleck

90. Khadzhinikolov, Veselin. DVADESET GODINI SPISANIE *ISTORICHESKI PREGLED* [Twenty years of publication of *Istoricheski Pregled*]. *Istoricheski Pregled [Bulgaria] 1964 20(2-3): 3.* The 20th anniversary of the publication of the journal coincided with the celebrations to mark the 1944 socialist revolution in Bulgaria. The journal was founded by a group of progressive historians in Sofia, and initially its readers were teachers and students, although by 1953 it had a mass readership. Its aims are: 1) to explain the basic history of Bulgaria, particularly the growth of the workers' movement and the role of the Party; 2) to inspire socialist patriotism, proletarian internationalism, and Bulgarian-Soviet friendship; 3) to counter the falsifications of middle-class and reactionary historians; 4) to present international views of Bulgaria; and 5) to report the most important internal and external political developments. 2 notes.

A. J. Evans

91. Khadzhinikolov, Veselin. SPISANIE "ISTORICHESKI PREGLED" I NASHATA ISTORICHESKA NAUKA [The journal *Istoricheski Pregled* and our historiography]. *Istoricheski Pregled [Bulgaria] 1969 25(2-3): 18-29.* Discusses the development and achievements of *Istoricheski Pregled* which began publication after 9 September 1944, as a scholarly journal emphasizing the Marxist-Leninist interpretation of history. In that time the development of the review has paralleled the development of Bulgarian historical studies—both growing in complexity. Since 1944, 141 issues have appeared, including over 1,500 articles and other items. Note.

F. B. Chary

92. Khaidler, Vol'fgang. ZHURNAL *PREPODAVANIE ISTORII I GRAZHDANOVEDENIIA* (GDR) [*Teaching History and Civic Affairs*, East Germany]. *Prepodavanie Istorii v Shkole [USSR] 1980 (2): 69-71.* Survey by the chief editor of this East German journal of some recent articles, covering both theoretical and practical matters in ancient and modern history, mainly, but not exclusively, in the Socialist countries.

93. Kittross, John M., comp. A BIBLIOGRAPHY OF HISTORICAL ARTICLES PUBLISHED IN THE *JOURNAL OF BROADCASTING*, 1956-1982. *Hist. J. of Film, Radio and Television [Great Britain] 1984 4(1): 90-98.* The *Journal of Broadcasting* is a scholarly quarterly magazine published by the Broadcast Education Association (formerly the Association for Professional Broadcasting Education) in Washington, D.C. In selecting items from the *Journal* for inclusion in the bibliography, the compiler has omitted theses and dissertations, articles which presented data more than eight years old at the time of publication, and articles on law, foreign and international broadcasting, and programming in which the historical component was only minor.

94. Kolosova, E. V. LICHNYE ARKHIVY ISTORIKOV I ISTORIOGRAFIIA [Historiography and the personal archives of historians]. *Sovetskie Arkhivy [USSR] 1971 (4): 20-27.* Outlines the contribution of the private collections of D. I. Ilovaiski (1832-1920), N. P. Barsukov (1838-1906), S. D. Sheremet'ev (1844-1918), and other Russian historians to modern historiography, citing their locations in Soviet archives.

95. Kosul'nikov, A. P. RAZRABOTVANETO NA PROBLEMITE NA ISTORIKO-PARTIINATA NAUKA V SPISANIE "VOPROSY ISTORII KPSS" [Solution to problems of historical party science in *Voprosy Istorii KPSS*]. *Izvestiia na Inst. po Istoriia na BKP [Bulgaria] 1974 30: 7-26.* Describes the progress made by the Soviet publication *Voprosy Istorii KPSS*, 1970-72, in realizing the ideological tasks set by the 24th Party Congress. Since its founding in 1957 it has creatively developed and deepened its Marxist-Leninist analysis of history. It has dealt successfully with problems such as the Paris Commune, Trotskyism, proletarian hegemony, and Lenin's novel proletarian party. But it has not published enough specialized articles on the methodology of writing Marxist-Leninist history. Only recently has attention been given to Party historiography. Some articles are not critical enough. Nearly half of each issue is on contemporary themes. Reviews need to be more detailed, scientific, and critical. 24 notes.

C. S. Masloff

96. Kozlitin, I. P. PUBLIKATSII PO ISTORII PROMYSHLENNOSTI I RAZVITIE METODOV KHOZIAISTVOVANIIA V SSSR [Publications on the history of industry and the development of economical methods in the USSR]. *Voprosy Istorii [USSR] 1972 (9): 155-165.* During the 1950's and 1960's more than 150 special collections containing some 1,000 documents on the development of Soviet industry, 1917-72, were published. Major sources of information include the publications of the Communist Party, historical archives, and the works and documents of Lenin. 47 notes.

S. J. Talalay

97. Król, Edmund. LITERATURA O PZPR W ZBIORACH BIBLIOTEKI WSNS [Literature on the Polish United Workers' Party in the collections of the library of the Higher School of Social Studies]. *Z Pola Walki [Poland] 1978 21(4): 241-257.* A bibliography on the Polish United Workers' Party, including archival sources, published scholarly works, and doctoral theses covering a wide range of subjects relating to the Party.

98. Kukushkin, Iu. S. XV MEZHDUNARODNYI KONGRESS ISTORICHESKIKH NAUK [The 15th International Historical Congress]. *Prepodavanie Istorii v Shkole [USSR] 1981 (2): 16-17.* The 15th International Historical Congress, held in Bucharest in August 1980, demonstrated the increasing authority of Soviet historical science and the continuing weakness of bourgeois scholarship.

99. Kul'chitski, S. V. and Shatalina, Ie. P. OSNOVNI ZDOBUTKY RADIANS'KOI ISTORYCHNOI NAUKY V 1975-1979 RR. [The essential achievements of Soviet historical studies, 1975-79]. *Ukrains'kyi Istorychnyi Zhurnal [USSR] 1981 (3): 71-82.* Reviews the work of Soviet historians in all fields of historiography as they were presented at the 15th International Congress of Historians, Bucharest, August 1980.

100. Lalaj, Ana. "GJURMIME ALBANOLOGJIKE," (SERIA E SHKENCAVE HISTORIKE), NR. XII-1982, PRISHTINË, 1983 [*Gjurmime Albanologjike* (Historical Sciences Series) 1982 12, Prishtinë, 1983]. *Studime Historike [Albania] 1984 38(3): 155-160.* Surveys 1982 articles in *Gjurmime Albanologjike* on the history of Kosovo.

G.-D. L. Naçi

101. Leczyk, Marian. STOSUNKI POLSKI-RADZIECKIE W LATACH 1918-45 W HISTORIOGRAFII POLSKI LUDOWEJ [Polish-Soviet relations, 1918-45, in the historiography of Poland]. *Kwartalnik Hist. [Poland] 1979 86(2): 429-449.* A survey of Polish historians' books and articles published in Poland and the USSR on various aspects of Polish-Soviet foreign relations. Research is scarce on the period, and knowledge of unofficial aspects of Polish-Soviet relations, such as the Polish Communist movements, is insufficient. 128 notes.

H. Heitzman Wojcicka

102. Legnani, Massimo. NUOVE RIVISTE, NUOVA STORIA? [New reviews, new history?]. *Italia Contemporanea [Italy] 1982 (149): 120-124.* Examines three new Italian scholarly journals devoted to history: *Passato e Presente*, *Cheiron*, and *Storia della Storiografia*. The first two have the possibility of bringing fresh perspectives to Italian publications in history.

E. E. Ryan

103. LeGoff, Jacques. PAST AND PRESENT: LATER HISTO-
RY. *Past and Present [Great Britain] 1983 (100): 14-28.* Past and
Present has chosen to print examples and case studies rather than
detailed, exhaustive articles. The large majority have concerned the
16th to 19th centuries with a British bias geographically and in the
choice of authors. Five principal characteristics can be discerned in
the scope of the articles: the wish to exemplify a historical problem,
an interest in debate, the primacy of social history, an investigation
of history from below, and an interest in culture and education. 3
notes.   J. G. Packer

104. Lehotská, D. HISTORIOGRAPHIE DE L'ARCHIVISTIQUE
SLOVAQUE EN 1960-1977 [Historiography of Slovak archival science, 1960-77]. *Studia Hist. Slovaca [Czechoslovakia] 1980 (11):
275-300.* A comprehensive study of the organization and the scientific production of Slovak archives; notes the progress, especially
important since 1975, of the organization and techniques of the Slovak archives which, thanks to their high standards reached in the
practice of archival science, have received the support of the Communist Party's organs.   G. P. Cleyet

105. Levykin, K. G. O NEKOTORYKH PROBLEMAKH IS-
TOCHNIKOVEDENIIA [Several problems of source study].
Voprosy Istorii [USSR] 1972 (1): 152-158. Reviews S. O. Shmidt's,
ed., *Istochnikovedenie. Teoreticheskie i metodicheskie problemy*
(Moscow, 1969). The book contains articles by Soviet historians on
problems of historical research, including the definition of its basic
categories, the classification of historical resources, methodology,
and the relationship of archive work to other fields. The scholars
who have contributed to the book link their conclusions to the most
recent achievements of the historical sciences while maintaining a
Marxist-Leninist viewpoint. 6 notes.   R. Permar

106. Lindgrén, Susanne. FINLÄNDSK HISTORISK LITTERA-
TUR 1974, BIBLIOGRAFISKT URVAL [Finnish historical literature 1974; a bibliographical selection]. *Historisk Tidskrift för
Finland [Finland] 1975 60(2): 154-160.* A selective and briefly annotated bibliography of books and articles concerning Finnish history, published during 1974, written mainly in Finnish and Swedish.
                                                    R. G. Selleck

107. Lindgrén, Susanne. FINLÄNDSK HISTORISK LITTERA-
TUR 1979: BIBLIOGRAFISKT URVAL [Historical literature from
Finland, 1979: a bibliographical selection]. *Hist. Tidskrift för Finland [Finland] 1980 65(2): 210-223.* A selective bibliography of historical research published in Finland, both books and articles,
chiefly in the Finnish and Swedish languages, during 1979.
                                                    R. G. Selleck

108. Lindgrén, Susanne. FINLÄNDSK HISTORISK LITTERA-
TUR 1980: BIBLIOGRAFISKT URVAL [Finnish historical literature 1980: a bibliographical selection]. *Hist. Tidskrift för Finland
[Finland] 1981 66(2): 217-232.* A selective list of monographs and
articles about Finnish and general history, mostly by Finns and
published in Finland. The works cited are in major European languages, Scandinavian languages, and Finnish.   R. G. Selleck

109. Lindgrén, Susanne. FINLÄNDSK HISTORISK LITTERA-
TUR 1975: BIBLIOGRAFISKT URVAL [Finnish historical literature 1975: a bibliographical selection]. *Hist. Tidskrift för Finland
[Finland] 1976 61(2): 190-200.* A briefly annotated bibliography of
books and articles on Finnish historiography, published chiefly in
the Finnish and Swedish languages.   R. G. Selleck

110. Lipski, Stephan. ZEITSCHRIFTENBERICHT [Report on
journals]. *Geschichte in Wissenschaft und Unterricht [West
Germany] 1971 22(7): 439-448.* Reviews the 1970 volumes of the
*American Historical Review, Zeitschrift für Geschichtswissenschaft,
Saeculum, Vierteljahreshefte für Zeitgeschichte,* and *Europa-Archiv
und Aussenpolitik.*

111. Lukan, Walter. GESCHICHTSWISSENSCHAFT IN JUGOS-
LAWIEN (1965-1975) [Historiography in Yugoslavia, 1965-75].
Österreichische Osthefte [Austria] 1976 18(2): 193-194. Reviews
new publications of Yugoslavian historians between 1965-75. 4
notes.

112. Łysiak, Ludwik et al. O WYDAWANIU ŹRÓDEŁ
HISTORYCZNYCH—ANKIETA [A questionnaire on the publications of historical sources]. *Kwartalnik Hist. [Poland] 1983 90(1):
141-163.* Answers to a questionnaire concerning publication of historical source material in contemporary Poland by a number of
Polish historians. The questions include a general assessment of editions of historical source material, continuing or discontinuing current series of historical publications, typographical format, and
bilingual editions.   M. Hernas

113. Malina, Peter. NIEDERÖSTERREICHISCHE ZEITUNGEN
UND ZEITSCHRIFTEN SEIT 1918: EINIGE BIBLIOGRAPHIS-
CHE UND QUELLENKRITISCHE BEMERKUNGEN [Lower
Austrian newspapers and periodicals since 1918: some remarks on
bibliography and source criticism]. *Unsere Heimat [Austria] 1982
53(1): 27-40.* The regional press of Lower Austria is an indispens-
able source for the history of the Austrian province, especially for
daily life and social customs.

114. Mangoni, Luisa. *SOCIETA:* STORIA E STORIOGRAFIA
NEL SECONDO DOPOGUERRA *[Società:* history and historiography in the period after World War II]. *Italia Contemporanea [Italy]
1981 33(145): 39-58.* The Italian journal, *Società,* began publication in 1947 following the policy suggested by Delio Cantimori in
1944. The policy aimed to abolish the gap between culture and the
interests and aspirations of the people. It also aimed to reestablish
contact between Italian culture and modern historical, political, social, and economic thought. Historical materialism was to be its
principal method. Though concerned primarily with history during
its first two years of publication, the journal paid little attention to
Italian history and the development of Fascism. After 1949, it was
mainly concerned with Italian literature, particularly of the contemporary era. Even so, an important debate appeared in 1949-50 concerning popular culture and the lower classes. Based on primary
sources, including a press proof of a volume never published.
                                                    E. E. Ryan

115. Martin, Michel. HISTOIRE ET ACTUALITÉ: LA *REVUE
HISTORIQUE* PENDANT LA PREMIÈRE GUERRE MONDI-
ALE [History and current events: the *Revue Historique* during
World War I]. *Rev. Historique [France] 1976 255(2): [518]: 433-
468.* During World War I the *Revue Historique* was not technically
mobilized for war service and pretended to remain objective. However, it made frequent use of the past to support the French policies of the present. Its articles focused on the background of
Alsace-Lorraine, criticized German historians for historical propaganda, and characterized German history as bad. Past examples of
cooperation with France's allies were stressed and Anglo-French
struggles deemphasized. French historians stressed national unity
and the theme of sacrifice for the nation. Ancient history was applied in the analogy of Germans to Huns and references to Tacitus
and the Punic Wars. 80 notes, biographical annotations.
                                                    G. H. David

116. Martínez Carreras, José U. NOTA SOBRE LA REVISTA
"CUADERNOS DE HISTORIA MODERNA Y CONTEMPO-
RANEA" [Note on the journal *Cuadernos de Historia Moderna y
Contemporanea*]. *Rev. de Estudios Int. [Spain] 1981 2(3): 695-697.*
Provides a summary of recent articles in the journal, which was
first published in 1980 at the University of Madrid. The journal
emphasizes modern history and historiography.   D. Ardia

117. Meikle, Jeffrey L. AMERICAN DESIGN HISTORY: A BIB-
LIOGRAPHY OF SOURCES AND INTERPRETATIONS.
American Studies International 1985 23(1): 3-40. Traces the development of design history from its origins in the 1930's. Includes
works on industrial design and designers of the 1920's-30's, the
post-World War II "good design" movement, the heightened social
consciousness in design in the 1960's-70's, and the recent reempha-

sis on style. Includes surveys, critical studies, biographical and autobiographical works, museum catalogs, periodicals, and reference works. 2 photos, biblio.   R. E. Noble

118. Miller, Stuart T. THE VALUE OF PHOTOGRAPHS AS HISTORICAL EVIDENCE. *Local Historian [Great Britain] 1983 15(8): 468-473.* Victorian photographs provide a valuable historical source for research on 19th-century British social customs, material culture, and daily life. Nonetheless, such photos are not always representative and can be misleading to students of the past.

119. Milošević, Miloš. NEKI OBLICI EFEKTIVNOG ARHIVISTIČKOG DOPRINOSA RAZVOJU ISTORIJSKE NAUKE [The contribution of archives to the development of historiography]. *Arhivist [Yugoslavia] 1965 15(1-2): 13-17.* Based on an analysis of the problems of archives in Yugoslavia, concludes that a publication should be created which describes how to catalog archives. The publication would include information about basic principles of decimal classification and alphabetical order.
                                              J. Hunjic/S

120. Minoski, Mikhailo. ISTORISKATA NAUKA VO MAKEDONSKATA TEKOVNA BIBLIOGRAFIIA (1951-1971) [Historical science and the Macedonian Heritage Bibliography, 1951-71]. *Istorija [Yugoslavia] 1980 16(2): 213-217.* Reviews the first 20 years of publication of *Makedonskata Tekovna Bibliografiia* [The Macedonian Heritage Bibliography], analyzing statistically its coverage of books and journals year by year; discusses its declared aims and its contribution to Macedonian historiography.

121. Monod, Gabriel. IL Y A CENT ANS... DU PROGRÈS DES ÉTUDES HISTORIQUES EN FRANCE DEPUIS LE XVIᵉ SIÈCLE [100 years ago: on the progress of historical studies in France since the 16th century]. *Rev. Hist. [France] 1976 255(2): 297-324.* This is the first article printed in the *Revue historique* in 1876 which explains the program of the new journal while describing changes in historical studies in France since the 16th century. Citing a number of significant writings, it shows the influences of French historiography before it attained the scientific status of the mid-19th century. One of seven items in a special edition on the centennial anniversary of *Revue historique*. 91 notes.
                                              G. H. Davis

122. Monticone, Alberto. ARCHIVI SONORI E STORIOGRAFIA [Sound archives and historiography]. *Storia e Pol. [Italy] 1983 22(1): 167-173.* Tape recorders make possible a greater utilization of sound sources in the study of history.   A. Canavero

123. Moritz, Erhard. DER JAHRGANG 1973 DER POLNISCHEN ZEITSCHRIFT "WOJSKOWY PRZEGLĄD HISTORYCZNY" [The 1973 volume of the Polish journal *Wojskowy Przegląd Historyczny*]. *Militärgeschichte [East Germany] 1975 14(2): 214-221.* Reviews the 1973 volume of the Polish historical journal *Wojskowy Przegląd Historyczny*, which analyzes the formation of the Polish People's Army, its role in World War II, the Polish resistance movement against fascism, and the cooperation of the Polish People's Army with the Red Army.   R. Wagnleitner

124. Motte, Olivier. LES ORIGINES DES *MELANGES D'ARCHEOLOGIE ET D'HISTOIRE* [The origins of *Mélanges d'Archéologie et d'Histoire*]. *Mélanges de l'École Française de Rome. Moyen Age-Temps Moderne [Italy] 1982 94(1): 393-483.* Recounts the growth of *Mélanges d'Archéologie et d'Histoire*, 1880-82, and the early years of the French Academy at Rome under Auguste Geffroy.

125. Natan, Zhak. PETNADESET GODINI "ISTORICHESKI PREGLED" [Fifteen years of *Istoricheski Pregled*]. *Istoricheski Pregled [Bulgaria] 1960 16(1): 3-11.* Distinguishes three periods in the history of this periodical, corresponding to the three main periods of Communist rule in Bulgaria: 1945-48, when the periodical's outlook, though antifascist, was not fully Marxist-Leninist; 1948-56, characterized by rapid development, guided and aided by the Communist Party; and 1956-60, when progress was freed from the bur-

densome cult of personality. Evaluates some major historical and historiographical problems tackled by *Istoricheski Pregled* during this time, noting continuing weaknesses.   F. A. K. Yasamee

126. Naumov, V. P. RAZRABOTKA PROBLEM ISTORII ISTORICHESKOI NAUKI [An inquiry into the history of historical science]. *Istoriia SSSR [USSR] 1977 (1): 228-231.* Reports on the work of the Sector for the History of Historical Science, Institute of History, Academy of Sciences of the USSR, during the 1970's, listing the various monographs and collective works on historiography and methodology produced by the members of the sector. These studies have dealt mostly with the history of the USSR, but a number of publications have been concerned with prerevolutionary Russian history as well.   N. Dejevsky

127. Negoiu, I. and Manolescu, R. CERCETAREA ÎN DOMENIUL ISTORIEI MEDIEVALE A ROMÂNIEI ŞI UNIVERSALE [Research in Romanian and world medieval history]. *Analele U. Bucureşti: Istorie [Romania] 1973 22(1): 17-35.* Surveys historiographical research on medieval Romania undertaken by the teaching staff at the departments of Romanian and world medieval history, 1948-73, comprising the publication of document collections, original scientific works, studies and articles. Outstanding scientific contributions were made in world medieval history, Byzantine studies, and Southeast European history.
                                              RSA 11:998

128. Neumann, Victor A. FRAGEN DER ALLGEMEINEN UND RUMÄNISCHEN GESCHICHTSSCHREIBUNG IN EINER FORTSCHRITTLICH GESINNTEN SIEBENBÜRGISCH-DEUTSCHEN ZEITSCHRIFT [Questions regarding world and Romanian historiography in a progressive Transylvanian-German journal]. *Rev. Roumaine d'Hist. [Romania] 1978 17(3): 519-527.* Founded during the 1840's, *Magazin für Geschichte, Literatur und alle Denk-und Merkwürdigkeiten Siebenbürgens* (Journal for history, literature and all noteworthy and remarkable matters regarding Transylvania) was inspired by Wilhelm von Humboldt and Leopold von Ranke. Discusses the contributors to and contents of issues published during 1844-46, and considers romantic historiography. The editor, historian Anton Kurz, a German democrat, introduced new ideas about historical research.   T. Parker/S

129. Nielsen, Sabine. AUFGABENSTELLUNG UND THEMATISCHE BEREICHE DES "JAHRBUCHS FÜR DIE GESCHICHTE MITTEL- UND OSTDEUTSCHLANDS." BIBLIOGRAPHISCH-SYSTEMMATISCHER WEGWEISER DURCH DEN AUFSATZTEIL DER BÄNDE 1-32 [Tasks and areas of thematic concern of the *Jahrbuch für Geschichte Mittel- und Ostdeutschlands:* a systematized bibliographic guide to the articles in volumes 1-32]. *Jahrbuch für die Geschichte Mittel- und Ostdeutschlands [West Germany] 1984 33: 1-34.* The 25th year of the founding of the Historic Commission of Berlin seems an appropriate time to take stock of its developments and achievements, one of which is the publication of the *Jahrbuch für die Geschichte Mittel- und Ostdeutschlands*. While the *Jahrbuch* appeared as early as 1952, it was not until its takeover by the Historical Commission that continuity as well as the completion of its projected tasks could be assured. The *Jahrbuch's* central focus is the former state of Prussia as well as its successor territories from earliest times to the present. In the absence of appropriate scholarly journals from East Germany, it has extended its scope to include these regions also. Particular emphasis is placed on the historic roots of the centuries'-old conflict between Germans and Poles with the need to achieve a better understanding between these two peoples a paramount objective of the Historic Commission. Based on articles in the *Jahrbuch;* 4 illus., 14 notes.   S. A. Welisch

130. Orekhov, V. A. LENINSKAIA "ISKRA" V OSVESHCHENII SOVREMENNOI ANGLO-AMERIKANSKOI BURZHUAZNOI ISTORIOGRAFII [V. I. Lenin's *Iskra* in the interpretation of modern US and British bourgeois historians]. *Istoriia SSSR [USSR] 1972 (1): 202-213.* Describes false conceptions of V. I. Lenin's *Iskra* newspaper. Western historians have examined only

the activity of Lenin's *Iskra* (Nos. 1-52) and ignore the period of the Menshevik *Iskra* (53-112), and have misinterpreted *Iskra's* history. 49 notes.

131. Otruba, Gustav. ZEITSCHRIFTENSCHAU 1966 [Survey of journals, 1966]. *Österreich in Geschichte und Literatur [Austria] 1968 12(2): 99-109*. Bibliography of Austrian historical journals published in 1966.

132. Papa, Antonio. CAMERA OSCURA E NUOVA STORIO-GRAFIA [Camera obscura and new historiography]. *Belfagor [Italy] 1983 38(2): 195-206*. The use of photography in historical publications and research has been delayed in Italy by prejudices among historians and by the fascist monopoly of the medium for its propaganda purposes, obstacles which have only recently been removed.

133. Papadrianos, Iōannēs A. GIOUGKOSLAVIKES MELETES KATA TA ETĒ 1978-1980 GIA TĒN ANATOLIKĒ KRISĒ (1875-1878). PRŌTĒ KATAGRAFĒ [Yugoslavian studies, 1978-80, on the Eastern Crisis, 1875-78: first inventory]. *Valkanika Symmeikta [Greece] 1981 1: 93-113*. Prints a bibliography of Yugoslavian historiography on the Eastern Question.

134. Paskaleva, Virginia. PODGOTOVKATA ZA XIV MEZHDU-NARODEN KONGRES NA ISTORICHESKITE NAUKI V SAN FRANTSISKO (22-29 AVGUST 1975 G.) [Preparation for the 14th International Congress on the Historical Sciences in San Francisco (22-29 August 1975)]. *Istoricheski Pregled [Bulgaria] 1974 30(2): 136-140*. Surveys previous meetings, the present leadership of the committee, and the plans for the 1975 meeting in San Francisco including the program.   F. B. Chary

135. Paterson, Thomas G. THE PRESENT DANGER OF THOUGHT CONTROL: ARE WE TO LEAVE TO A GOVERNMENT CENSOR THE DEFINITION OF WHAT IS "MEANINGFUL"? *Society for Historians of American Foreign Relations. Newsletter 1984 15(3): 32-41*. Unfair restrictions on access to government documents amount to censorship of research sources for historiography. Reprinted from *AHA Perspectives* 1984 22(4).

136. Pazdur, Jan. STORIA ED ETNOGRAFIA NELL'ESPERIENZA DELLA RIVISTA K.H.K.M., 1953-1974 [History and ethnography: the experience of the *Quarterly of History of Material Culture*, 1953-74]. *Quaderni Storici [Italy] 1976 11(1): 38-53*. The quarterly is an official publication of the Institute of History of Material Culture of the Polish Academy of Science and is intended to unite ethnographers and historians in a program to promote the understanding of the history of civilization and of industrial archaeology in European terms. The history of material culture follows an original approach in Poland where the methods and interpretation are based on Marxism. Research is intended to demonstrate that an objectivized way of thinking is a stable value and that it can be preserved in the usefulness of man-made objects. *The Quarterly of History of Material Culture* supports the protection of monuments and illustrates methods of historical research which give full consideration to the laboratory and field investigations of archaeologists and ethnographers.   J

137. Pentti, Raili. FINLÄNDSK HISTORISK LITTERATUR 1983: BIBLIOGRAFISKT URVAL [Finnish historical literature, 1983: a bibliographical selection]. *Historisk Tidskrift för Finland [Finland] 1984 69(2): 178-200*. A selective list of monographs and articles about Finnish and general history, mostly by Finns and published in Finland. The works listed are in major European languages, Scandinavian languages, and Finnish.   R. G. Selleck

138. Petriakov, G. V. and Sazonov, I. S. BOL'SHEVISTSKAIA *PRAVDA* V 1912-1917 GODAKH: OBZOR ISTORIKO-PARTIINOI LITERATURY [The Bolshevik newspaper *Pravda*, 1912-17: a survey of Party-historical literature]. *Voprosy Istorii KPSS [USSR] 1962 (2): 162-174*. Analyzes existing literature on *Pravda*, 1912-17, and suggests the need for a general study.

139. Petrisov, Vasile. REVISTA "MAGAZIN ISTORIC" LA 15 ANI DE LA APARIȚIE [The *Magazin Istoric* during 15 years of publication]. *Anale de Istorie [Romania] 1982 28(2): 96-104*. The *Magazin Istoric* originated in 1967 in the innovative atmosphere of the 9th Conference of the Romanian Communist Party. It was the first journal of its kind in Romania, aiming to provide historical culture for a mass readership which, through the readers' letters, was given a chance to participate. It aimed to make the best use of the continuity of Romanian history as a unifying factor, involving all the centers of historical research. But it also looked further afield to world history, research in foreign archives, and participation in conferences.   J. P. H. Myers

140. Plakhova, R. E. and Tokareva, E. S. VSESOIUZNAIA NAUCHNAIA KONFERENTSIIA "MARKSIZM-LENINIZM I RAZVITIE ISTORICHESKOI NAUKI V STRANAKH ZAPAD-NOI EVROPY I AMERIKI" [The all-union scientific conference on "Marxism-Leninism and the development of historical science in Western Europe and America"]. *Novaia i Noveishaia Istoriia [USSR] 1983 (6): 202-204*. The conference on Marxism and history in Western Europe and America was held in Moscow, 31 January-2 February 1983. It was organized jointly by the Soviet Academy of Science's Scientific Council on the History of Historical Science and the Institute of World History. Over 250 historians from 45 institutions of higher education in 29 Soviet cities took part. Prints summaries of the main papers, which emphasized the growing influence of Marxism-Leninism on Western historical science. Secondary sources.   G. Dombrovski

141. Poulsen, Henning. SPECIELLE KILDEPROBLEMER I DEN NYESTE TIDS HISTORIE [Special source problems in current history]. *Historie [Denmark] 1966 7(1): 25-38*. Discusses the sources used in writing modern history. When the psychological makeup and the ideological perspectives of eyewitnesses and reporters are examined, the validity of contemporary reports can be more thoroughly evaluated.

142. Pronshtein, A. P. PRO ROL' SPETSIAL'NYKH (DO-POMIZHNYKH) ISTORYCHNYKH DYSTSYPLIN U ROZ-KRYTTI INFORMATSIINOHO ZNACHENNIA ISTORYCHNYKH DZHEREL [The role of specialized auxiliary historical disciplines for disclosing the informational significance of historical sources]. *Ukrains'kyi Istorychnyi Zhurnal [USSR] 1970 (8): 21-28*. Discusses the role of such disciplines as chronology, metrology, numismatics, and diplomatics in solving a number of general problems of history.

143. Riska, Celia. FINLÄNDSK HISTORISK LITTERATUR 1982: BIBLIOGRAFISKT URVAL [Finnish historical literature, 1982: a bibliographical selection]. *Hist. Tidskrift för Finland [Finland] 1983 68(4): 464-481*. A selective list of monographs and articles about Finnish and general history, mostly by Finns and published in Finland. The works listed are in major European languages, Scandinavian languages, and Finnish.   R. G. Selleck

144. Róziewicz, Jerzy. THE 25TH ANNIVERSARY OF THE "QUARTERLY JOURNAL OF THE HISTORY OF SCIENCE AND TECHNOLOGY" (1956-1980). *Kwartalnik Hist. Nauki i Techniki [Poland] 1980 25(4): 769-774*. Discusses the history of the *Kwartalnik Historii Nauki i Techniki*, established in Poland in 1956, initially as the organ of the Committee for the History of Science at the Polish Academy of Sciences, and from 1963 of the Institute of the History of Science and Technology, and finally of the Institute of the History of Science, Education, and Technology at the Polish Academy of Sciences. The journal features articles on the history of science, especially Polish science. The article lists the members of the editorial committees, provides circulation data, and describes subject matter. Primary sources; 2 tables, 4 notes.
                                                    J. Powell

145. Ruge, Wolfgang. NEUE BEITRÄGE ZUR GESCHICHTE DER NEUEN UND NEUESTEN ZEIT [New contributions on recent history]. *Zeitschrift für Geschichtswissenschaft [East Germany] 1973 21(7): 844-852*. Reviews the annual issues of the Russian historical journal *Novaia i Noveishaia Istoriia* of 1971 and 1972.

146. Rybář, Miloš. ZGODOVINSKE PUBLIKACIJE V LETU 1979 [Historical publications in 1979]. *Zgodovinski Časopis [Yugoslavia] 1980 34(3): 371-384.* Complete bibliography of Slovene historical monographs for 1979.   T. Hočevar

147. Rybář, Miloš. ZGODOVINSKE PUBLIKACIJE V LETU 1978 [Historical publications in 1978]. *Zgodovinski Časopis [Yugoslavia] 1979 33(3): 511-524.* Bibliography of books on history published in Slovenia during 1978.   T. Hočevar

148. Sakharov, A. M. O NEKOTORYKH METODOLOGI-CHESKIKH VOPROSAKH NA XIV MEZHDUNARODNOM KONGRESSE ISTORIKOV (ZAMETKI DELEGATA) [A few methodological problems at the 14th International Congress of Historians: notes of a delegate]. *Vestnik Moskovskogo U. Seriia 9: Istoriia [USSR] 1976 (3): 3-22.* Discusses ideological struggles occurring between Marxist and non-Marxist historians at this 1975 conference. Bourgeois historians presented their pluralist and anti-Marxist views, showing the fall of interest in history. The historical idealist view was expressed by Italian historians who defended the position of the Frankfurt School. Marxist historians strongly defended their views against pluralism. 6 notes.   D. Balmuth

149. Sautter, Udo. AMERIKANISCHE GESCHICHTSDISSERTATIONEN [American historical Ph.D. theses]. *Geschichte in Wissenschaft und Unterricht [West Germany] 1973 24(9): 564-567.* In the 1960's American historical doctoral dissertations showed a trend toward 20th-century topics, especially the New Deal, the Cold War, national socialism, the Russian revolution, and biographical studies of Franklin D. Roosevelt, Woodrow Wilson and Adolf Hitler.   R. Wagnleitner

150. Schäfer, Karl Heinz. 1813 DIE FREIHEITSKRIEGE IN DER SICHT DER MARXISTISCHEN GESCHICHTSSCHREIBUNG DER DDR [The wars of liberation in 1813 East German Marxist historiography]. *Geschichte in Wissenschaft und Unterricht [West Germany] 1970 21(1): 2-21.* A bibliography of reference books, monographs, dissertations, and articles published in East Germany. East German historians have propagated a specific interpretation of history, especially through their one-sided use of quotations from Marx and Lenin. East German historiography has become an educational instrument in the hands of the government. As in 1813, the German people have their "best friend" in the Russian people; as in 1813, the German people have to fight for national unity and independence. 124 notes, biblio.

151. Schück, Herman. "CENTRALORGAN FOR DEN SVENSKA HISTORISKA FORSKNINGEN": HISTORISK TIDSKRIFT FRÅN SEKELSKIFTET TILL 1960-TALETS BÖRJAN [Central organ for Swedish historical research: Historisk Tidskrift from the turn of the century to the early 1960's]. *Hist. Tidskrift [Sweden] 1980 (1-2): 92-139.* A preliminary charting of the history of the Swedish journal *Historisk Tidskrift* from the turn of the century to the early 1960's, this study uses as source material the journal itself and the minutes from the board and annual meetings. During this period there were five editors: Emil Hildebrand (1881-1905); Torvald Höjer (1906-20); Sven Tunberg (1921-33); Nils Ahnlund (1934-49); and Torvald Höjer (1949-61). *Historisk Tidskrift,* minutes from its board and annual meetings.   T. Parker

152. Șerban, Constantin and Șerban, Victoria. BIBLIOGRAFIE ISTORICĂ SELECTIVĂ COMENTATĂ (1972) [A select historical bibliography with comments, 1972]. *Studii și Articole de Istorie [Romania] 1973 (21): 125-136.* Lists Romanian books and articles on historical subjects.

153. Serczyk, Jerzy. PROBLEMATYKA POMORSKA W CZASOPIŚMIENNICTWIE POLSKIM DO ROKU 1908 (PRZYCZYNEK BIBLIOGRAFICZNY) [The Pomeranian issues in the Polish periodicals up to 1908: a bibliographic contribution]. *Zapiski Hist. [Poland] 1982 47(4): 267-277.* Analyzes the historical perspectives and the preferred topics in the history of Pomerania in Polish periodicals.

154. Sestan, Ernesto. L*"ARCHIVIO STORICO ITALIANO" NELL'ETÀ DEL RISORGIMENTO [The *Archivio Storico Italiano* during the Risorgimento]. *Riv. Storica Italiana [Italy] 1981 93(1): 49-54.* Reviews Ilaria Poriani's *L*"Archivio Storico Italiano": Organizazione delle Ricerca ad Egemonia Moderata* (1979), which describes the background of Italy's oldest historical journal during the first three quarters of the 19th century and examines the relations of the *Archivio* with other historical schools in Italy and abroad.   J. V. Coutinho/S

155. Sherman, I. L. "UKRAINSKYI ISTORYCHNYI ZHURNAL" K LENINSKOMU IUBILEIU [The *Ukrainian Historical Journal* on the anniversary of Lenin's birth]. *Voprosy Istorii [USSR] 1971 (7): 164-167.* Provides a survey of the *Ukrainian Historical Journal,* 1968-70. As part of the preparations for the centenary of V. I. Lenin's birth, the contents became more topical, wide-ranging and interesting. Articles on Lenin's historical approach took a central place. Other authors dealt with Lenin's treatment of particular Soviet or world events and attention was paid to his treatment of the Ukrainian question. Foremost among these was a study of the Leninist attitude to international labor migration in the contemporary period. The periodical continued its attacks on the views of Western historians and discusses aspects of Marxist-Leninist historiography and methodology. There were also articles on German occupation of the Ukraine in World War I.   E. R. Sicher

156. Sirotkin, V. G. and Prokopenko, S. A. NOVYI MEXHDUNARODNYI ZHURNAL *ISTORIIA ISTORIOGRAFII* [New international journal, *History of Historiography*]. *Voprosy Istorii [USSR] 1984 (2): 163-167.* In August 1980 during the 15th International Congress of Historical Sciences in Bucharest, an International Commission on Historiography was created, including 106 historians from 26 countries. In conjunction with this commission a new journal, the *History of Historiography,* has begun publication. The authors detail two issues, including the reaction of historians and information on new publications. 7 notes.   S. J. Talalay

157. Siupiur, Elena. PUBLICATIONS PERIODIQUES PARUES A L'OCCASION DU XVe CONGRES INTERNATIONAL DES SCIENCES HISTORIQUES [Periodicals published on the occasion of the 15th Historical Sciences International Conference]. *Rev. des Études Sud-Est Européennes [Romania] 1981 19(1): 170-172.* Gives an annotated list of Romanian reviews on the historiography of Romania and related disciplines.   G. P. Cleyet/S

158. Spira, Thomas. NEUERE HISTORISCHE ZEITSCHRIFTEN IN UNGARN, VIII [Recent historical periodicals in Hungary, 8]. *Österreichische Osthefte [Austria] 1977 19(4): 295-304.* Reviews the 1970 and 1972 issues of the Hungarian historical journals *Levéltári Közlemények* and the 1971-74 issues of *Történelmi Szemle.*

159. Spirin, L. M. SUSTOIANIE I PERSPEKTIVI NA RAZVITIE NA ISTORIKO-PARTIINATA NAUKA V SSSR [Composition and development perspectives in Party scholarship in the USSR]. *Izvestiia na Inst. po Istoriia na BKP [Bulgaria] 1972 28: 7-36.* Analyzes the ideological and thematic content of Soviet Communist Party historiography, 1967-71, when ca. 3,000 books and brochures were published.

160. Steensgaard, Niels. ADMINISTRATIONSHISTORIE MELLEM HJAELPEVIDENSKAB OG HISTORIEFORSKNING [Administration history between auxiliary science and historical research]. *Arkiv [Denmark] 1980 8(1): 51-53.* The most important contribution of archivists lies in their unbiased, positive approach to source material. The drawing of conclusions, however, belongs to another sphere. The two functions are often called "administration history," but one is an auxiliary science, subject to its own discipline; the other is research, subject only to the discipline of the historian.   K. S. Williams

161. Stella, Vittorio. LA STORIOGRAFIA E L'ARCHIVISTICA, IL LAVORO D'ARCHIVIO E L'ARCHIVISTA [Historiography and archivistics, the work of the archive and the archivist]. *Rassegna degli Archivi di Stato [Italy] 1972 32(2): 269-284.* A study of the historiographical implications of the work of archivists.

162. Šťovíček, Ivan. K VYDÁVÁNÍ NOVODOBÝCH HISTORICKÝCH PRAMENŮ: OTÁZKY TEORIE A METODIKY V EVROPSKÝCH SOCIALISTICKÝCH ZEMÍCH V SEDMDESÁTÝCH LETECH [On the publication of modern historical sources: questions of theory and methodology in the European socialist states in the 1970's]. *Arch. Časopis [Czechoslovakia] 1981 31(3): 152-161.* The recent upsurge in interest in the publishing of historical sources has led to the elaboration of systems of editorial rules in the socialist countries, some states having progressed further than others. 65 notes.

163. Šťovíček, Ivan. VÝBĚROVÁ BIBLIOGRAFIE K TEORII A PRAXI VYDÁVÁNÍ PRAMENŮ K NOVÝM A NEJNOVĚJŠÍM DĚJINÁM [A selected bibliography for the theory and practice in publishing of the resources of modern and contemporary history]. *Sborník Archivních Prací [Czechoslovakia] 1976 26(1): 203-218.* Bibliography of publications in theory and practice in modern historiography, listing over 300 works, mostly European and Soviet but including some American.   G. E. Pergl

164. Stow, George B. BODLEIAN LIBRARY MS BODLEY 316 AND THE DATING OF THOMAS WALSINGHAM'S LITERARY CAREER. *Manuscripta 1981 25(2): 67-76.* Reviews arguments about the histories written by Thomas Walsingham, a St. Albans monk. Internal evidence in Walsingham manuscripts, particularly MS Bodley 316, suggests that the chronology of Walsingham's literary activities should be revised. 42 notes.
M. D. Dibert

165. Strugar, Vlado. APERÇU BIBLIOGRAPHIQUE [Bibliographical survey]. *Rev. d'Hist. de la Deuxième Guerre Mondiale [France] 1972 22(87): 53-62.* Presents a comprehensive survey of Yugoslavian literature on the role of Yugoslavia during World War II. This historiography covers all aspects of the problem—military, political, social, economic, and especially the experience of the country and its inhabitants under the fascist terror. Studies on the political collaborators are especially passionate. 78 notes.   J. P. Fox

166. Székely, György. BESZÁMOLÓ A XV. NEMZETKÖZI TÖRTÉNETTUDOMÁNYI KONGRESSZUSRÓL (BUKAREST, 1980. AUGUSZTUS 10-17.) [Report on the 15th International Conference of Historical Sciences, Bucharest, 10-17 August 1980]. *Magyar Tudományos Akad. Filozófiai és Történettudományok Osztályának Közleményei [Hungary] 1980 29(3): 271-279.* Summarizes the major themes, historians, and countries participating in the conference. Sixty-six countries were represented by 2,700 historians. The four major themes of the conference were: Western Europe as the forum for the convergence of civilizations; peace in a historical context; federated states and the idea of federation in history; and women in society.   A. M. Pogany

167. Tabachnikov, B. Ia. PROBLEMY NOVEISHEI ISTORII I METODOLOGII V ZHURNALE *KWARTALNIK HISTORYCZNY* ZA 1970-1976 GODY [Problems of recent history and methodology in the journal *Kwartalnik Historyczny*, 1970-76]. *Voprosy Istorii [USSR] 1977 (6): 181-187.* Analyzes the seven-year output of this quarterly, published by the Institute of History of the Polish Academy of Sciences, Warsaw. Articles on Polish history of the 19th and 20th centuries predominate, though there are occasional papers on other socialist countries as well as England and France, and rarely on Italy and the United States. Almost none are on Germany, probably because Germany is covered primarily in *Przegląd Zachodni.* 8 notes.   N. Frenkley

168. Teodor, Pompiliu. LA *REVUE HISTORIQUE DU SUD-EST EUROPEEN* ET LE MODELE DES *ANNALES* [The *Revue Historique du Sud-Est Européen* and the model of *Annales*]. *Rev. Roumaine d'Hist. [Romania] 1981 20(4): 773-782.* The *Revue Historique du Sud-Est Européen,* founded by Nicolae Iorga in 1924, was a continuation of the earlier *Bulletin* of the Institute for Southeast Europe. Its importance, during the 17 years of its publication under Iorga's guidance, was to demonstrate the interdependence between the development and historic transformations of all the nations in Southeast Europe, and to place these, as a distinct entity,

in the context of European and universal history. After 1940, under the editorship of Gheorghe Brătianu and M. Berza, the *Revue* remained faithful to Iorga's principles, while displaying strongly the influence of the historical innovations of the French traditions of Marc Bloch and Lucien Febvre in *Annales.* 33 notes.
G. J. Bobango

169. Tikhvinski, S. L. GENERAL'NAIA ASSAMBLEIA MKIN [General Assembly of ICHS]. *Voprosy Istorii [USSR] 1977 (12): 203-208.* Proceedings of the General Assembly of the International Commission of Historical Sciences attended by representatives of 25 national committees and held at Puerto de la Cruz, Canary Islands, 28-29 July 1977. The topics of major papers were assigned to the respective delegations to be presented at the forthcoming 15th International Congress of Historical Sciences, whose four sections will be entitled: Major Themes of Study, Problems of Methodology, History by Chronological Periods, and International Committees and Commissions.   N. Frenkley

170. Troitskaia, L. M. "PASIFIK KHISTORIKEL REV'IU' (1974-1981) [Pacific Historical Review, 1974-1981]. *Novaia i Noveishaia Istoriia [USSR] 1984 (1): 209-216.* Analyzes articles on early to middle 19th-century American history published in this quarterly journal, including studies on the Monroe Doctrine, political and commercial relations with Britain, Russia, Central America, and East Asia, missionary activity in China and the opium trade. American bourgeois historians include economic, religious and social factors in political analyses thereby creating an illusion of objectivity. Yet, by criticizing only minor points in US foreign policy, they try to obscure American capitalist aggression and expansionism. 35 notes.   N. Frenkley

171. Valeva, Elena L. and Drosneva, Elka D. ISTORIOGRAFSKI CHETENIA V INSTITUTA PO SLAVIANOVEDENIE I BALKANISTIKA PRI AKADEMIATA NA NAUKITE V SSSR [History readings at the Institute of Slavic and Balkan studies at the Academy of Sciences in SSSR]. *Istoricheski Pregled [Bulgaria] 1980 36(4): 93-96.* Report on the bimonthly readings in history at the Institute for Slavic and Balkan Studies, Moscow University, which have taken place since 1978 under the auspices of the Soviet Academy of Sciences.   B. R. Pach

172. VanHelleputte, Michel. A PROPOS D'UNE HISTOIRE FRANÇAISE DE LA LITTERATURE ALLEMANDE [A French history of German literature]. *Rev. Belge de Philologie et d'Hist. [Belgium] 1961 39(3): 816-839.* Reviews *Histoire de la Littérature Allemande* (1959). The work features the most complete bibliography and chronological table yet to appear with accurate dates provided throughout. A new hierarchy of values is also evident in the attention accorded to different writers and epochs. Compares the work with contemporary German histories, noting a tendency in the French history to organize its materials according to genres and schools of thought. 68 notes.   A. W. Howell/S

173. Vasić, Ankica. BIBLIOGRAFIJA ISTORIJSKIH ČLANAKA U GODIŠNJAKU FILOZOFSKOG FAKULTETA U NOVOM SADU (1956-1975) [Bibliography of historical archives published in the Almanac of the Faculty of Philosophy, Novi Sad, 1956-75]. *Zbornik za Istoriju [Yugoslavia] 1977 16: 195-201.* A bibliography of the historical articles published in the Almanac of the Faculty of Philosophy, Novi Sad (Godisnjak Filozofskog Fakulteta u Novom Sadu), 1956-75. The bibliography is classified by year of publication and volume and number of journal, and has an author index.
J. Bamber

174. Veen, Theo. EEN *FUNDGRUBE* VOOR DE HISTORISCHE WETENSCHAP: DE ALTHUSIUS-BIBLIOGRAFIE [A source of information for historical science: the Althusius bibliography]. *Bijdragen en Mededelingen Betreffende de Geschiedenis der Nederlanden [Netherlands] 1979 94(1): 89-96.* Review article of Hans U. Scupin and Ulrich Scheuner, eds., *Althusius-Bibliographie. Bibliographie zur politische Ideengeschichte und Staatslehre, zum Staatsrecht und zur Verfassungsgeschichte des 16. bis 18 Jahrhundert* [Althusius-Bilbiography: bibliography of the history of political thought, political science, concerning constitution-

al law and constitutional history, 16th-18th centuries] 2 vol. (Berlin, 1973). The bibliography includes letters and works by the German political thinker Johannes Althusius (1557-1638) and cites literature on political theory and constitutional law and history. Although the editors did not attempt to make this an all inclusive bibliography many important works were omitted. 14 notes.

G. D. Homan

175. Vidnians'kyi, S. V. and Moroz, V. K. ISTORIIA ZARU-BIZHNYKH SLOV'IANS'KYKH NARODIV NA STORINKAKH "PROBLEM SLOV'IANOZNAVSTVA" [The history of other Slavic nations in *Problemy Slavianoznavstva*]. *Ukrains'kyi Istorychnyi Zhurnal [USSR] 1982 (3): 38-48.* The journal *Problemy Slavianoznavstva* [Problems in Slavic studies] has been published in Lvov, Ukraine, since 1970. The author reviews the five issues published between the 25th and 26th congresses of the Communist Party of the Soviet Union, which have discussed the history of the Slavic peoples and have included special studies on the links between Eastern European states. 4 notes. N. M. Diuk

176. Vol'ski, S. A. et al. TRIBUNA UKRAINSKIKH ISTORIKOV [Platform of Ukrainian historians]. *Istoriia SSSR [USSR] 1962 6(1): 166-174.* Review of the first five years of publication of *Ukrains'kyi Istorychnyi Zhurnal* (1957-61).

177. Voskresenskaia, N. O. ZHURNAL *SOVETSKIE ARKHIVY* I VOPROSY KOMPLEKTOVANIIA GOSUDARSTVENNOGO ARKHIVNOGO FONDA SSSR I ISPOL'ZOVANIIA EGO MATERIALOV V SOVETSKOI ISTORIOGRAFII [The journal *Sovetskie Arkhivy* and the problems of stocking the Soviet state archives and using their material in Soviet historiography]. *Istoriia SSSR [USSR] 1983 (4): 82-90.* The journal *Sovetskie Arkhivy* [Soviet archives] was founded in 1922 following a decree by Lenin that the Russian Federation's archives should be reorganized and centralized. It is now the organ of the Main Archives Administration of the Council of Ministers of the USSR and is published in conjunction with the Marxism-Leninism Institute of the Communist Party of the Soviet Union's Central Committee and the Institute for the History of the USSR at the Soviet Academy of Sciences. The journal has always served as a focal point of reference for archival institutions throughout the country in their constant efforts to increase Soviet archival holdings. It has laid down specific guidelines on stocking procedures. Through regular and careful analysis of the experiences of those using reference rooms at the state archives, the journal has given constant advice on how services can be improved. 60 notes. J. Bamber

178. Voss, Jürgen. LITERATURWISSENSCHAFTLICHE HILFSMITTEL FÜR DEN HISTORIKER: DIE BIBLIOGRAPHIEN CIORANESCU [Materials for the historian from the study of literature: the bibliographies of Cioranescu]. *Francia [France] 1974 2: 692-700.* Alexandre Cioranescu, with his three-volume *Bibliographie de la litterature française du dix-septième siècle* (Paris: CNRS, 1965-66), and similar works on the 16th and 18th centuries in French literature, has classified the literature far more thoroughly and precisely than have previous works of a similar nature. For the history of research and historiography, and in all areas of intellectual history, these bibliographies will become standard research tools. 51 notes. J. C. Billigmeier

179. Vozár, Jozef. L'HISTORIOGRAPHIE SLOVAQUE À L'ÉPOQUE DU FÉODALISME TARDIF: LA MOISSON DE 1960-1977 [Slovak historiography on the period of late feudalism: the harvest of 1960-77]. *Studia Hist. Slovaca [Czechoslovakia] 1980 (11): 101-139.* Focuses on the outlines of activity, the tendencies, the evolution, and the importance of the number of authors and periodicals, monographs, and collections of historical research. 152 notes. G. P. Cleyet

180. Vujačić, Slobodan. *ZAPISI* I POKRET SOCIJALNE LITER-ATURE U CRNOJ GORI [*Zapisi* and the social sciences in Montenegro]. *Istorijski Zapisi [Yugoslavia] 1977 30(1): 207-214.* Examines the role and influence of the periodical *Zapisi* in promoting the study of social sciences and historiography in Montenegro, 1927-33.

181. Vulchev, Veselin. OSVOBODITELNITE BORBI V MAKE-DONIIA I ODRINSKO (1878-1912). BULGARSKA ISTORI-CHESKA KNIZHNINA 1945-1979 [The liberation struggles in Macedonia and the district of Adrianople, 1878-1912: Bulgarian historical literature, 1945-79]. *Izvestiia na Inst. za Istoriia [Bulgaria] 1981 (25): 327-368.* A list of 536 historical writings published in Bulgaria between 1945 and 1 October 1979 about the struggles of the Bulgarian population in Macedonia and the district of Adrianople for liberation from the Turkish yoke from the liberation of Bulgaria to the Balkan War in 1912. Based on Bulgarian documents. B. R. Pach

182. Vynar, Lubomyr. DVADTSIATYLITTIA *UKRAINS'KOHO ISTORYKA* (1963-1983) I ZAVDANNIA UKRAINS'KYKH ISTORYKIV [The 20th anniversary of the *Ukrainian Historian* (1963-83) and the tasks of Ukrainian historians]. *Ukrains'kyi Istoryk 1983 20(2-4): 5-24.* On the occasion, in 1983, of the 20th anniversary of the *Ukrainian Historian,* a scholarly journal of the Ukrainian Historical Association, the editor-in-chief summarizes its genesis, growth, and accomplishments; analyses perspectives for its development in the future; and outlines very ambitious aims for Ukrainian historians, stressing the need for the publication of monographs, especially in the field of Ukrainian historiography. Based on the author's private papers, as well as on published primary and secondary sources; 28 notes. A. B. Pernal

183. Vynar, Lubomyr. Z PERSPEKTYVY DESIAT'OCH ROKIV: "UKRAINS'KYI ISTORYK," 1963-1973 [Ten years of the *Ukrainian Historian,* 1963-73]. *Ukrains'kyi Istoryk 1973 10(3/4): 5-28.* Reviews the genesis and achievements of the *Ukrainian Historian* during its first ten years. It was founded in November 1963 to coordinate the work of Ukrainians and foreign historians specializing in the Ukraine and Ukrainians all over the world.

A. Mina

184. Waite, Stephen V. F., ed. ANNUAL BIBLIOGRAPHY FOR 1975 AND SUPPLEMENT TO PRECEDING YEARS: HISTORY. *Computers and the Humanities 1976 10(2): 106-113.* A bibliography of journal articles pertaining to historiography and methodology in European and American history.

185. Watkins, T. H. THE PURLOINED PAST. *Manuscripts 1978 30(4): 260-262.* The past is being stolen by criminals who have been looting historical documents and photographs from American archives. Reviews the current situation and the attempts to protect our documentary heritage. Illus. Reprinted from *American Heritage 1978 29(5): 48-49.* D. A. Yanchisin

186. Watkins, T. H. THE PURLOINED PAST. *Am. Heritage 1978 29(5): 48-49.* Theft of historical documents and photographs from archives is widespread, sometimes unreported and even unnoticed, extremely difficult to prevent, and harmful to the field of history. Illus. D. J. Engler

187. Winslow, Donald J. CURRENT BIBLIOGRAPHY ON LIFE-WRITING. *Biography 1978 1(4): 76-81.* Annotated list of books and articles about biography, autobiography, and related aspects of life writing in British and American publications, restricted mainly to publications in 1977, but occasionally some significant works in 1976 or 1978. The most active area of current interest is autobiography, with psychohistory and psychobiography also favored topics. Based on journals and publishers' lists. J

188. Zalewski, Wojciech. REFERENCE MATERIALS IN RUSSIAN-SOVIET AREA STUDIES, 1974-1975. *Russian Rev. 1976 35(3): 322-335.* Covers 1974 imprints and as many 1975 titles as possible. The majority are Russian but some attention is paid to Western language sources as well. Titles discussed are bibliographies under the headings: current, regional, institutional, subject, economy, population, foreign policy, geography, philosophy, literary; periodicals: lists, indexes and new titles; guides to institutions and institutional collections; student aids; linguistic aids; historiographies and historical bibliographies; reference aids; encyclopedias and guides. R. B. Valliant

189. Zeitzer, Glen. A PLACE FOR ALL: RECENT TRENDS IN AMERICAN PEACE HISTORY WRITING. *Am. Studies Int. 1981 19(3-4): 49-57.* Analyzes trends in the writing of peace history and lists aids and surveys, source collections, monographs, biographies of leading pacifists, unpublished dissertations, and anthologies of both source material and essays. Many of the authors were activists in the peace movement. The ferment of the 1960's and 1970's, including the Vietnam issue, stimulated the writing of peace history, now established as a legitimate, scholarly pursuit. 4 notes.

R. E. Noble

190. Žekulin, N. G. CANADIAN PUBLICATIONS ON THE SOVIET UNION AND EASTERN EUROPE. *Can. Slavonic Papers [Canada] 1980 22(4): 519-538.* This fourth annual bibliography cites over 300 works, including 12 dissertations, by Canadian scholars.

J. F. Harrington

191. Zhidkov, G. P. V NAUCHNOM SOVETE PO ISTORII ISTORICHESKOI NAUKI [Scientific Council on the History of Historical Science]. *Voprosy Istorii [USSR] 1979 (12): 118-120.* Summarizes 24 papers presented at the first session of the Northwest regional chapter of the Scientific Council on the "History of Historical Science," held in Kaliningrad on 28-30 May 1979 under the auspices of the department of history of the Academy of Sciences (USSR) and Kaliningrad University. Main topics included structuring of curricula and textbooks, research methodology, and development of criteria for so-called periodization of Soviet, pre-Soviet, and foreign history, and comparative analyses of Soviet and foreign studies.

N. Frenkley

192. Zimmermann, Fritz. 25 JAHRE BZG [25 years of *Beiträge zur Geschichte*]. *Beiträge zur Geschichte der Arbeiterbewegung [East Germany] 1984 26(1): 3-12.* Commemorates the first quarter of *Beiträge zur Geschichte der Arbeiterbewegung* [Contributions to the history of the labor movement]. Sets it in the context of East German historiography of Communist parties and movements and of the working class. 9 notes.

R. Grove

193. Zlateva, Ani and Toninska, Boianka. PERIODICHNI IZDANIIA V BULGARIIA, SUDERZHASHTI ISTORICHESKI MATERIALI (1878-1944 G.) [Periodicals in Bulgaria containing historical material (1878-1944)]. *Istoricheski Pregled [Bulgaria] 1974 30(3): 112-119.* Surveys Bulgarian scholarly and popular journals containing historical articles from the liberation from Turkey to the advent of popular democratic rule (1878-1944). Although there were many such journals, there was no good scholarly Bulgarian journal dealing exclusively with this era of history. Based on the periodical literature surveyed; 27 notes.

F. B. Chary

194. Zuber, Frederick R. AMERICAN PUBLICATIONS ON AUSTRIAN HISTORY. *Austrian Hist. Y. 1976-77 12-13(pt. 2): 361-373.* Provides a list of books and articles published in the United States in 1975 and 1976. The bibliography is divided into Middle Ages, 1500-1789, 1789-1918, and since 1918, and into special sections on Austria, Hungary, the Northern Slavs, and the Southern Slavs.

J. W. Thacker, Jr.

195. —. BIBLIOGRAFIJA JUGOSLOVENSKE ISTORIOGRAFIJE (1966-1974) [Bibliography of Yugoslav historiography, 1966-74]. *Vojnoistorijski Glasnik [Yugoslavia] 1978 29(1): 224-234, (2): 171-182, (3): 163-177.* A bibliography of historical books published in Yugoslavia between 1966 and 1974, covering those authors with initials R-Z.

J. Bamber

196. —. BIBLIOGRAFIJA JUGOSLOVENSKE ISTORIOGRAFIJE 1966-1974 (KNJIGE) [A bibliography of Yugoslav historiography, 1966-74: Books]. *Vojnoistorijski Glasnik [Yugoslavia] 1975 26(1): 293-306.* Gives a bibliography of books on historiography published in Yugoslavia, 1966-74, covering the letters I, J, and K.

197. —. BIBLIOGRAFIJA JUGOSLOVENSKE ISTORIOGRAFIJE 1975-1978 [Bibliography of Yugoslav historiography, 1975-78]. *Vojnoistorijski Glasnik [Yugoslavia] 1980 31(1): 307-321.* Bibliography of history books and historical novels published in Yugoslavia, 1975-78, covering the letters N through R.

J. Bamber

198. —. BIBLIOGRAFIJA STRANE ISTORIOGRAFIJE O DRUGOM SVETSKOM RATU (1971-1974) [Bibliography of foreign historiography on World War II, 1971-74]. *Vojnoistorijski Glasnik [Yugoslavia] 1980 31(1): 322-330.* Lists foreign books on the history of World War II published 1971-74, by author, letters L-N.

J. Bamber

199. —. BIBLIOGRAPHIE CHOISIE D'OUVRAGES D'HISTOIRE PUBLIÉS EN HONGRIE EN 1978 [A selected bibliography of historical works published in Hungary in 1978]. *Acta Hist. [Hungary] 1980 26(3-4): 497-515.* A selected bibliography of monographs and periodical articles primarily on Hungarian history from 1526 to the present published in Hungary in 1978.

A. M. Pogany

200. —. BIBLIOGRAPHIE D'OEUVRES CHOISIES DE LA SCIENCE HISTORIQUE HONGROISE 1969-1973 [Bibliography of select works of Hungarian historical writing, 1969-73]. *Études Hist. Hongroises [Hungary] 1975 (2): 505-603.* Reviews 1,058 recently published historical works, divided into two sections: 1) Hungarian history to the present, and 2) general, covering antiquity, the Middle Ages, and the modern period, with a section on Russia and the international workers' movement.

201. —. COMPARATIVE BIBLIOGRAPHY—1981. *Hist. in Africa 1981 8: 365-374.* A bibliography of recent works on the study of history.

A. C. Drysdale

202. —. IL CENTRO PER LA STORIA DELL'UNIVERSITÀ DI PADOVA: STRUTTURA E RECENTE ATTIVITÀ [The Center for the History of the University of Padua: structure and recent activities]. *Quaderni per la Storia dell'Università di Padova [Italy] 1983 16: 189-192.* Presents a brief history of the Centro per la Storia dell'Università di Padova, together with a list of its current officers and a report on its current legal standing and publications.

203. —. KNIGY O SOVREMENNOM POLOZHENII, ISTORII, KUL'TURE I IAZYKAKH ZARUBEZHNYKH SLAVIANSKIKH NARODOV VYSHEDSHIE V SOVETSKOM SOIUZE V 1977 G [Books on the contemporary situation, history, culture, and languages of foreign Slav nations published in the USSR in 1977]. *Sovetskoe Slavianovedenie [USSR] 1978 (3): 117-124.* The list includes publications on the following themes: 1) general problems of the European socialist countries: general, international relations, economics and economic cooperation, Party life, state and law, reference works and bibliographies; and 2) foreign socialist countries: history, culture and science, and linguistics.

V. Sobeslavsky

204. —. LITERATURBERICHT [Review of the literature on Reformation history]. *Arch. für Reformationsgeschichte [West Germany] 1980 (Beiheft 9): 1-182.* An annual annotated bibliography, consisting of citations from monographs, journal articles, and festschriften on Reformation history. Topics covered include: 1) pre-Reformation history, 2) Luther, Zwingli, and Calvin, 3) Protestantism, 4) humanism, 5) Catholic reform, 6) literature, art, and music, 7) the European countries, 8) the state: constitution, administration, law, and 9) society and economy.

205. —. NATIONAL REGISTRY FOR THE BIBLIOGRAPHY OF HISTORY: LISTING OF BIBLIOGRAPHIC WORK IN PROGRESS, MARCH 1981-FEBRUARY 1983. *Bull. of Biblio. 1983 40(2): 117-123.*

206. —. NY LOKALHISTORISK LITTERATUR 1981: BIBLIOGRAFISK FORTEGNELSE UTARBEIDET VED NORSK LOKALHISTORISK INSTITUTT (NLI) [New local history literature, 1981: bibliographical inventory prepared at the Norwegian Institute of Local History (NLI)]. *Heimen [Norway] 1982 19(2): 105-122.* A

list of local history material published in 1981, including town, district, and community histories, local history periodicals, source editions, and bibliographies, arranged by area.   D. F. Spade

207.   —. PUBLICHNO OBSUZHDANE NA SP. *ISTORICHESKI PREGLED* [Public debate on *Istoricheski Pregled*]. *Istoricheski Pregled [Bulgaria] 1960 16(5): 114-127.* The debate, marking the 15th anniversary of the founding of the periodical, was held at the Bulgarian Academy of Sciences on 28 April 1960 and was attended by staff and contributors as well as by teachers of history and museum employees. D. Kosev, the Director of the Historical Institute at the Academy of Sciences, opened the proceedings with a speech summarizing the periodical's achievements. Following other speeches there was a general discussion of questions of historiography, education, and the form and content as well as the political perspective of *Istoricheski Pregled*.   F. A. K. Yasamee

208.   —. SEN-KYHYAKU-SHICHIJYONEN NO REKISHI GAKKAI: KAIKO TO TEMBŌ [Historical study in Japan, 1975: prospect and retrospect]. *Shigaku Zasshi [Japan] 1976 85(5): 1-382.* A special issue which provides a bibliography of historical works published in Japan in 1975 dealing with: general history; historical theory; Japan; Asia; Africa; Europe; America; recent publications; and Western history.

209.   —. SEN-KYHYAKU-SHICHIJROKUNEN NO REKISHI GAKKAI-KAIKO TO TEMBŌ [Historical study in Japan, 1976: reviews and prospects]. *Shigaku Zasshi [Japan] 1977 86(5): 1-376; 1978 87(5): 1-410.* Lists and reviews articles and books published in Japan in 1976 dealing with: historical theory; Japan; Asia; Africa; Europe; and the United States. Includes information about the authors and provides a separate bibliography of recent publications on Western history.

210.   —. TRUDY PREPODAVATELEI ISTORICHESKOGO FAKUL'TETA, OPUBLIKOVANNYE V ZARUBEZHNOI PECHATI I RETSENZII NA IKH RABOTY [The works of the historical faculty professors published abroad and commentary]. *Vestnik Moskovskogo U., Seriia 9: Istoriia [USSR] 1972 27(4): 91-94.* Lists 64 entries of works by professors of history, generally followed by reviews, that had been published abroad from 1968 through the first half of 1971. This list has been compiled on the basis of materials at the Institute of Scientific Information and the Fundamental Social Science Library at the Academy of Science of the USSR by A. S. Strelkova, editor-in-chief of the Scientific Library, named after A. M. Gor'kii, at the Moscow State University.   L. Kalinowski

211.   —. VAZHNEISHIE STAT'I I MATERIALY PO SOVREMENNOMU POLOZHENIIU, ISTORII, KUL'TURE, IAZYKAM ZARUBEZHNYKH SLAVIANSKIKH NARODOV OPUBLIKOVANNYKH V SOVETSKIKH PERIODICHESKIKH IZDANIIAKH V 1977 G [The most important articles and material on the contemporary situation, history, culture, and languages of foreign Slav nations published in Soviet periodicals in 1977]. *Sovetskoe Slavianovedenie [USSR] 1978 (2): 121-125.* Includes publications on the following themes: 1) the general problems of the development of the European socialist countries; 2) international relations and mutual socialist economic assistance; and 3) economics and economic cooperation within Comecon.   V. Sobeslavsky

2. BOOKS

212. *Annual Studies of America, 1973.* Moscow: Nauka, 1973. 352 pp.

213. Ackroyd, Joyce, transl. and commentary. *Lessons from History: Arai Hakuseki's Tokushi yoron.* New York: U. of Queensland Pr., 1982. 417 pp.

214. Adamček, Josip; Gross, Mirjana; and Pavličević, Dragutin, ed. *Odjel za Hrvatsku Povijest: Deset Godina Rada, 1971-1981* [Croatian history department: 10 years of work, 1971-81]. Zagreb: Sveučilište u Zagrebu—Institut za Hrvatsku Povijest, 1981. 68 pp.

215. Adams, Ramon F. *More Burs under the Saddle: Books and Histories of the West.* Norman: U. of Oklahoma Pr., 1979. 182 pp.

216. Ado, A. V. and Meier, M. S., ed. *Novaia Istoriia: Ukazatel' Literatury Izdannoi v SSSR na Russkom Iazyke 1917-1940. Vol. 1, Obshchii Otdel: Pervyi Period Novoi Istorii 1640-1870 GG.* [Modern history: index of literature published in Russian in the USSR, 1917-40. Vol. 1, general section: early modern period, 1640-1870]. Moskovski Gosudarstvennyi Universitet. Nauchnaia Biblioteka Imeni A. M. Gor'kogo. Moscow: Izdatel'stvo Moskovskogo U., 1980. 357 pp.

217. Ajello, Raffaele, ed. *Pietro Giannone e il Suo Tempo: Atti del Convegno di Studi nel Tricentenario della Nascita* [Pietro Giannone and his times: acts of the scholarly congress held on the tricentennial of his birth]. Storia e Diritto series. 2 vol. Naples, Italy: Jovene, 1980. 942 pp.

218. Akademiia Nauk SSSR. *Istoriia i Istoriki: Istoriograficheskii Ezhegodnik, 1978* [History and historians: historiographical yearbook for 1978]. Moscow: Nauka, 1981. 352 pp.

219. Akademiia Nauk SSSR. *Osnovnye problemy istorii SShA v amerikanskoi istoriografii ot kolonial'nogo perioda do grazhdanskoi voiny 1861-1865* [Basic problems of the history of the USA in American historiography from the colonial period to the Civil War, 1861-1865]. Moscow: "Nauka," 1971. 371 pp.

220. Altschuler, Glenn C. *Race, Ethnicity, and Class in American Social Thought, 1865-1919.* (American History Series.) Arlington Heights, Ill.: Harlan Davidson, 1982. 160 pp.

221. Anderson, M. *Approaches to the History of the Western Family, 1500-1914.* (Studies in Economic and Social History.) New York: Macmillan, 1982. 96 pp.

222. Anderson, M. *Historians and Eighteenth-Century Europe, 1715-1789.* New York: Oxford U. Pr., 1979. 251 pp.

223. Angle, Paul M. *On a Variety of Subjects.* Chicago: Chicago Hist. Soc. and Caxton Club, 1974. 192 pp.

224. Ankersmit, F. R. *Narrative Logic: A Semantic Analysis of the Historian's Language.* Boston: Martinus Nijhoff, 1983. 265 pp.

225. Aoki, Michiko and Dardess, Margaret B. *As the Japanese See It: Past and Present.* Honolulu: U. Pr. of Hawaii, 1981. 315 pp.

226. Arai Hakuseki. *Lessons from History: The Tokushi Yoron.* Ackroyd, Joyce, transl. St. Lucia, Australia: U. of Queensland Pr., 1982. 417 pp.

227. Ash, James L., Jr. *Protestantism and the American University: An Intellectual Biography of William Warren Sweet.* Dallas: Southern Methodist U. Pr., 1982. 163 pp.

228. Aydelotte, William O. *Quantification in History.* Reading, Mass.: Addison-Wesley, 1971. 181 pp.

229. Bailey, Thomas A. *Probing America's Past: A Critical Examination of Major Myths and Misconceptions.* 2 vols. Lexington, Mass.: Heath, 1973. 442; 430 pp.

230. Baker, Donald N. and Harrigan, Patrick J., ed. *The Making of Frenchmen: Current Directions in the History of Education in France, 1679-1979.* Waterloo, Ont.: Hist. Reflections Pr., 1980. 646 pp.

231. Bannon, John Francis. *Herbert Eugene Bolton: The Historian and the Man, 1870-1953.* Tucson: U. of Arizona Pr., 1978. 296 pp.

232. Barber, John. *Soviet Historians in Crisis, 1928-1932.* New York: Holmes & Meier, 1981. 194 pp.

233. Basarab, John. *Pereiaslav 1654: A Historiographical Study.* (Canadian Library in Ukrainian Studies series.) Edmonton: U. of Alberta, Canadian Inst. of Ukrainian Studies, 1982. 322 pp.

234. Bebbington, D. W. *Patterns in History: A Christian View.* Downers Grove, Ill.: InterVarsity Pr., 1980. 211 pp.

235. Berger, Carl. *The Writing of Canadian History: Aspects of English-Canadian Historical Writing, 1900-1970.* New York: Oxford U. Pr., 1976. 300 pp.

236. Bernard, Jean-Paul. *Les Rébellions de 1837-38: Les Patriotes du Bas-Canada dans la Mémoire Collective et Chez les Historiens* [The rebellions of 1837-38: the patriots of Lower Canada in the collective memory and in history's ivory tower]. Montreal: Boréal Express, 1983. 349 pp.

237. Biale, David. *Gershom Scholem: Kabbalah and Counter-History.* Cambridge: Harvard U. Pr., 1979. 279 pp.

238. Billington, Ray Allen. *Frederick Jackson Turner: Historian, Scholar, Teacher.* New York: Oxford U. Pr., 1973. 599 pp.

239. Bishop, Ferman. *Henry Adams.* Twayne's United States Authors Series, no. 293. Boston: Twayne, 1979. 157 pp.

240. Blackbourn, David and Eley, Geoff. *Mythen Deutscher Geschichtsschreibung: Die Gescheiterte Bürgerliche Revolution von 1848* [Myths of German historiography: the failed bourgeois revolution of 1848]. Frankfurt: Ullstein Materialien, 1980. 139 pp.

241. Blackwell, Richard J., comp. *A Bibliography of the Philosophy of Science, 1945-1981.* Westport, Conn.: Greenwood, 1983. 585 pp.

242. Blumenberg, Hans. *The Legitimacy of the Modern Age.* Wallace, Robert M., transl. Cambridge, Mass.: MIT Pr., 1983. 677 pp.

243. Breisach, Ernst. *Historiography: Ancient, Medieval, & Modern.* Chicago: U. of Chicago Pr., 1983. 475 pp.

244. Brock, William R. *The United States: 1789-1890.* Ithaca, N.Y.: Cornell U. Pr., 1975.

245. Brook, Michael and Rubenstein, Sarah P., comp. *A Supplement to Reference Guide to Minnesota History, 1970-80.* St. Paul: Minnesota Hist. Soc., 1983. 68 pp.

246. Brown, Kenneth and Roberts, Michael, ed. *Using Oral Sources. Vansina and Beyond.* Adelaide, Australia: U. of Adelaide, Dept. of Anthrop., 1980. 130 pp.

247. Brown, Richard Maxwell. *Strain of Violence: Historical Studies of American Violence and Vigilantism.* New York: Oxford, 1975. 397 pp.

248. Brownlee, John S. *History in the Service of the Japanese Nation.* Toronto: University of Toronto-York University Joint Centre on Modern East Asia, 1983. 188 pp.

249. Brožek, Josef and Pongratz, Ludwig J., ed. *Historiography of Modern Psychology: Aims, Resources and Approaches.* Toronto: Hogrefe, 1980. 336 pp.

250. Bugliarello, George and Doner, Dean B., ed. *Symposium on the History and Philosophy of Technology, Chicago, 1973.* Urbana: U. of Illinois Pr., 1979. 384 pp.

251. Buijtenhuijs, Rob. *Essays on Mau Mau: Contributions to Mau Mau Historiography.* Leiden: African Studies Centre, 1982. 224 pp.

252. Burke, Peter. *Sociology and History.* Controversies in Sociology, no. 10. Winchester, Mass.: Allen & Unwin, 1980. 116 pp.

253. Burrow, J. W. *A Liberal Descent: Victorian Historians and the English Past.* New York: Cambridge U. Pr., 1981. 308 pp.

254. Burton, J. K. *Napoleon and Clio: Historical Writing, Teaching and Thinking During the First Empire.* Durham, N.C.: Duke U. Pr., 1979. 219 pp.

255. Büsch, Otto. *Industrialisierung un Geschichtswissenschaft: Ein Beitrag zur Thematik ind Methodologie der Historischen Industrialisierforschung* [Industrialization and historiography: a contribution to the theme and methodology of historical research in industrialization]. Barclay, David E., transl. (Historische und Pädagogische Studien, no. 10.) 2d revised ed. West Berlin: Colloquium, 1979. 168 pp. English translation of entire text.

256. Butterfield, Herbert. *The Origins of History.* New York: Basic Books, 1981. 252 pp.

257. Canary, Robert H. and Kozicki, Henry, ed. *The Writing of History: Literary Form and Historical Understanding.* Madison: U. of Wisconsin Pr., 1978. 165 pp.

258. Cannon, John, ed. *The Historian at Work.* Winchester, Mass.: Allen & Unwin, 1980. 210 pp.

259. Carpenter, Ronald H. *The Eloquence of Frederick Jackson Turner.* San Marino, Calif.: Huntington Lib., 1983. 230 pp.

260. Carroll, Berenice A., ed. *Liberating Women's History: Theoretical and Critical Essays.* Urbana: U. of Illinois Pr., 1976. 434 pp.

261. Cartwright, William H. and Watson, Richard L., Jr., eds. *The Reinterpretation of American History and Culture.* Washington: Natl. Council for the Social Studies, 1973. 554 pp.

262. *Cesare Barbieri Courier. Mussolini and Italian Fascism.* Painter, Borden W., ed. Hartford, Conn.: Cesare Barbieri Center of Italian Studies, Trinity Coll., 1980. 63 pp.

263. Chalfont, Lord, ed. *Waterloo: Battle of Three Armies.* New York: Knopf, 1980. 240 pp.

264. Chan, Ming K. *Historiography of the Chinese Labor Movement 1895-1949.* Stanford: Hoover Inst. Pr., 1981. 232 pp.

265. Chandra, Pramod. *On the Study of Indian Art.* Cambridge, Mass.: Harvard U. Pr., 1983. 134 pp.

266. Chaudhuri, Sashi Bhusan. *English Historical Writings on the Indian Mutiny, 1857-1859.* Calcutta: World Press Private, 1979. 368 pp.

267. Cheney, Roberta Carkeek. *The Big Missouri Winter Count.* Happy Camp, Calif.: Naturegraph, 1979. 63 pp.

268. Cherepnin, L. V. *Voprosy Metodologii Istoricheskogo Issledovaniia: Teoreticheskie Problemy Istorii Feodalizma* [Questions of the methodology of historical investigation: theoretical problems in the history of feudalism]. Moscow: Nauka, 1981. 278 pp.

269. Christie, Jean and Dinnerstein, Leonard, eds. *Decisions and Revisions: Interpretations of Twentieth-Century American History.* New York: Praeger, 1975. 371 pp.

270. Clark, Peter. *Henry Hallam.* (Twayne European Authors Series, no. 330.) Boston: Twayne, 1982. 146 pp.

271. Cochran, Thomas C. *Social Change in America: The Twentieth Century.* New York: Harper and Row, 1972. 178 pp.

272. Cochrane, Eric. *Historians and Historiography in the Italian Renaissance.* Chicago: U. of Chicago Pr., 1981. 640 pp.

273. Codignola, Luca, ed. *Canadiana 2: Storia e Storiografia Canadese* [Canadian history and historiography]. Venice, Italy: Marsilio Editori, 1979. 124 pp.

275. Cohen, Paul A. *Discovering History in China: American Historical Writing on the Recent Chinese Past.* (Studies of the East Asian Institute, Columbia University.) New York: Columbia U. Pr., 1984. 243 pp.

276. Cohen, Warren I., ed. *New Frontiers in American-East Asian Relations: Essays Presented to Dorothy Borg.* New York: Columbia U. Pr., 1983. 294 pp.

277. Combs, Jerald A. *American Diplomatic History: Two Centuries of Changing Interpretations.* Berkeley: U. of California Pr., 1983. 413 pp.

278. Connell, W. F. *A History of Education in the Twentieth Century World.* New York: Teachers College Pr., Columbia U., 1981. 478 pp.

279. Cooper, John Milton, Jr. *Causes and Consequences of World War I.* New York: Quadrangle Books, 1972. 360 pp.

280. Copleston, Frederick. *On the History of Philosophy and Other Essays.* Totowa, N.J.: Barnes & Noble, 1980. 160 pp.

281. Craton, Michael, ed. *Roots and Branches: Current Directions in Slave Studies.* New York: Pergamon, 1979.

282. Craven, William G. *Giovanni Pico della Mirandola: Symbol of His Age, Modern Interpretations of a Renaissance Philosopher.* (Travaux d'Humanisme et Renaissance, no. 185.) Geneva: Droz, 1981. 173 pp.

283. Crow, Jeffrey J. and Tise, Larry E., ed. *Writing North Carolina History.* Chapel Hill: U. of North Carolina Pr., 1979. 247 pp.

284. Dahlhaus, Carl. *Foundations of Music History.* Robinson, J. B., transl. New York: Cambridge U. Pr., 1983. 177 pp.

285. Dawidowicz, Lucy S. *The Holocaust and the Historians.* Cambridge, Mass.: Harvard U. Pr., 1981. 187 pp.

286. Delzell, Charles F., ed. *The Future of History: Essays in the Vanderbilt University Centennial Symposium*. Nashville, Tenn.: Vanderbilt U. Pr., 1977. 263 pp.

287. DeMause, Lloyd. *Foundations of Psychohistory*. New York: Creative Roots, 1982. 336 pp.

288. Dennis, Frank Allen, ed. *Southern Miscellany: Essays in History in Honor of Glover Moore*. Jackson: U. Pr. of Mississippi, 1981. 202 pp.

289. DeVoto, Bernard. *The Letters of Bernard De Voto*. Wallace Stegner, ed. Garden City, N.Y.: Doubleday, 1975. 393 pp.

290. Dickens, A. G. *Reformation Studies*. London: Hambledon, 1982.

291. Diener, Edward. *Reinterpreting American History: A Critical Look at Our Past*. New York: Philosophical Lib., 1975. 217 pp.

292. Dobie, J. Frank. *Prefaces*. Boston: Little, Brown, 1975. 204 pp.

293. Dougherty, James J. et al, comps., eds. *Writings on American History, 1973-74: A Subject Bibliography of Articles*. Washington: Am. Hist. Assoc. and Millwood, N.Y.: Kraus-Thomson, 1974. 266 pp.

294. Douglas, Roy. *From War to Cold War, 1942-48*. New York: St. Martin's, 1981. 224 pp.

295. Duminy, Andrew and Ballard, Charles, ed. *The Anglo-Zulu War: New Perspectives*. Natal, South Africa: U. of Natal Pr., 1981. 179 pp.

296. Dunn, John. *Political Obligation in Its Historical Context: Essays in Political Theory*. New York: Cambridge U. Pr., 1980. 355 pp.

297. Dusinberre, William. *Henry Adams: The Myth of Failure*. Charlottesville: U. Pr. of Virginia, 1980. 250 pp.

298. Dyos, H. J. *Exploring the Urban Past: Essays in Urban History by H. J. Dyos*. Reeder, David and Cannadine, David, ed. New York: Cambridge U. Pr., 1982.

299. Elkins, Stanley M. *Slavery: A Problem in American Institutional and Intellectual Life*. 3rd ed. rev. Chicago: U. of Chicago Pr., 1976. 320 pp.

300. Elton, G. R. *F. W. Maitland*. New Haven: Yale U. Pr., 1985. 128 pp.

301. Emmer, P. C. and Wesseling, H. L., ed. *Reappraisals in Overseas History: Essays on Post-War Historiography about European Expansion*. Comparative Studies in Overseas History, vol. II. Leiden: Leiden U. Pr.; The Hague: Martinus Nijhof, 1979. 248 pp.

302. Enteen, George M.; Gorn, Tatiana; and Kern, Cheryl. *Soviet Historians and the Study of Russian Imperialism*. Pennsylvania State University Studies, no. 45. University Park: Pennsylvania State U. Pr., 1979. 60 pp.

303. Erbe, Michael. *Zur Neueren Französischen Sozialgeschichtsforschung: Die Gruppe um die* Annales [The new French social history research: the *Annales* group]. Erträge der Forschung, no. 110. Darmstadt: Wissenschaftliche Buchgesellschaft, 1979. 159 pp.

304. Faulenbach, Bernd. *Ideologie des Deutschen Weges: Die Deutsche Geschichte in der Historiographie zwischen Kaiserreich und Nationalsozialismus* [Ideology of the German path: German history in the historiography between the empire and National Socialism]. Munich: Beck, 1980. 516 pp.

305. Faulk, Odie B. and Stout, Joseph A., Jr., eds. *The Mexican War: Changing Interpretations*. Chicago: Swallow, 1973. 244 pp.

306. Fell, John L. *A History of Films*. New York: Holt, Rinehart and Winston, 1979. 588 pp.

307. Felt, Thomas E. *Researching, Writing and Publishing Local History*. Nashville: Am. Assoc. for State and Local Hist., 1976. 165 pp.

308. Ferguson, Arthur B. *Clio Unbound: Perception of the Social and Cultural Past in Renaissance England*. Duke Monographs in Medieval and Renaissance Studies, no. 2. Durham, N.C.: Duke U. Pr., 1979. 443 pp.

309. Feuerwerker, Albert, ed. *Chinese Social and Economic History from the Song to 1900: Report of the American Delegation to a Sino-American Symposium, Beijing, 26 October-1 November, 1980*. (Michigan Monographs in Chinese Studies, no. 45.) Ann Arbor: U. of Michigan Pr., 1982. 182 pp.

310. Filion, Maurice, ed. *Hommage à Lionel Groulx* [Homage to Lionel Groulx]. Montreal: Leméac, 1978. 224 pp.

311. Fischer-Galati, Stephen et al., ed. *Romania between East and West: Historical Essays in Memory of Constantin C. Giurescu*. (East European Monographs, no. 103.) Boulder, Colo.: East European Monographs, 1982. 414 pp.

312. Fitzsimons, M. A. *The Past Recaptured: Great Historians and the History of History*. Notre Dame, Ind.: U. of Notre Dame Pr., 1983. 230 pp.

313. Floud, Roderick. *An Introduction to Quantitative Methods for Historians*. Princeton: Princeton U. Pr., 1973. 220 pp.

314. Fogel, Robert William and Elton, G. R. *Which Road to the Past?: Two Views of History*. New Haven: Yale U. Pr., 1983. 136 pp.

315. Foner, Eric. *Politics and Ideology in the Age of the Civil War*. New York: Oxford U. Pr., 1980. 250 pp.

316. Frantz, Joe B.; Jackson, W. Turrentine; Hollon, W. Eugene; Wolfskill, George; and Rundell, Walter, Jr. *Essays on Walter Prescott Webb*. Kenneth R. Philp and Elliott West, ed., Walter Prescott Webb Memorial Lectures, 10. Austin: U. of Texas Pr., 1976. 123 pp.

317. Frazer, Derek and Sutcliffe, Anthony, ed. *The Pursuit of Urban History*. Baltimore: Arnold, 1983. 482 pp.

318. Fulton, Richard M., ed. *The Revolution That Wasn't: A Contemporary Assessment of 1776*. Port Washington, N.Y.: Kennikat, 1981. 247 pp.

319. Furman, Necah Stewart. *Walter Prescott Webb: His Life and Impact*. Albuquerque: U. of New Mexico Pr., 1976. 222 pp.

320. Gagnon, Nicole and Hamelin, Jean. *L'Homme Historien* [The historian]. St. Hyacinthe, Que.: Edisem, 1979. 127 pp.

321. Gagnon, Serge. *Le Québec et ses Historiens de 1840 à 1920: La Nouvelle-France de Garneau à Groulx* [Quebec and its historians from 1840 to 1920: New France from Garneau to Groulx]. Cahiers d'Histoire de l'Université Laval, no. 23. Quebec: Pr. de l'U. Laval, 1978. 474 pp.

322. Ganz, Peter, ed. *Jacob Burckhardt: Über das Studium der Geschichte. Der Text der "Weltgeschichtlichen Betrachtungen"* [Jacob Burckhardt: on the study of history. The text of "Views on World History"]. Munich: C. H. Beck, 1982.

323. Garcia de la Huerta I., Marcos. *Chile 1891: La Gran Crisis y su Historiografía: Los Lugares Comunes de Nuestra Conciencia Historica* [Chile 1891: the great crisis and its historiography: the common places of our historical consciousness]. Santiago: U. of Chile, Centro de Estudios Humanisticos, 1981. 214 pp.

324. Gearhart, Suzanne. *The Open Boundary of History and Fiction: A Critical Approach to the French Enlightenment.* Princeton: Princeton University Press, 1984. 300 pp.

325. Gerster, Patrick and Cords, Nicholas, eds. *Myth and Southern History.* 2 vols., Chicago: Rand McNally, 1974. 351 pp.

326. Gilmore, Al-Tony, ed. *Revisiting Blassingame's* The Slave Community: *The Scholars Respond.* Contributions in Afro-American and African Studies, no. 37. Westport, Conn.: Greenwood, 1978. 206 pp.

327. Godechot, Jacques. *Regards sur l'Epoque Révolutionnaire* [Views of the era of the French Revolution]. Toulouse, France: Privat, 1980. 441 pp.

328. Goodwyn, Lawrence. *Democratic Promise: The Populist Movement in America.* New York: Oxford U. Pr., 1976. 718 pp.

329. Gossman, Lionel. *The Empire Unpossess'd: An Essay on Gibbon's* Decline and Fall. New York: Cambridge U. Pr., 1981. 160 pp.

330. Goudoever, A. P. van. *Romanian History, 1848-1918: Essay from the First Dutch-Romanian Colloquium of Historians, Utrecht 1977.* Historische Studies, 36. Groningen, Netherlands: Wolters-Noordhoff in cooperation with the Instituut voor Geschiedenis der Rijksuniversiteit te Utrecht, 1979. 159 pp.

331. Goveia, Elsa V. *A Study on the Historiography of the British West Indies to the End of the Nineteenth Century.* Washington, D.C.: Howard U. Pr., 1980. 181 pp.

332. Granatstein, J. L. and Stevens, Paul, ed. *A Reader's Guide to Canadian History. Vol. 2: Confederation to the Present.* Toronto: U. of Toronto Pr., 1982. 321 pp.

333. Gransden, Antonia. *Historical Writing in England. Vol. 2: 1307 to the Early Sixteenth Century.* London: Routledge & Kegan Paul, 1982.

334. Grele, Ronald J., ed. *Envelopes of Sound: Six Practitioners Discuss the Method, Theory and Practice of Oral History and Oral Testimony.* Chicago: Precedent, 1975. 154 pp.

335. Guggisberg, Hans Rudolf. *Alte und Neue Welt in Historischer Perspektive: Sieben Studien zum Amerikanischen Geschichts- und Selbstverständnis* [Old and new world in historical perspective: Seven studies on American history and self-definition]. Bern, Switzerland: Lang, 1973. 154 pp.

336. Guntau, Martin, ed. *Biographien Bedeutender Geowissenschaften der Sowjetunion: 19 Biographische Darstellungen zu Bedeutenden Gelehrten der Russischen und Sowjetischen Geologiegeschichte* [History of geological sciences in the USSR: 19 biographical sketches of significant Russian and Soviet scholars in the history of geology]. Schriftenreihe für Geologische Wissenschaften, no. 14. Berlin, East Germany: Akademie-Verlag, 1979. 199 pp.

337. Gutman, Herbert G. *Slavery and the Numbers Game: A Critique of* Time on the Cross. Blacks in the New World. Urbana: U. of Illinois Pr., 1975. 183 pp.

338. Haddad, Yvonne Yazbeck. *Contemporary Islam and the Challenge of History.* Albany: State U. of New York Pr., 1982. 257 pp.

339. Haines, Gerald K. and Walker, J. Samuel, ed. *American Foreign Relations: A Historiographical Review.* Contributions in American History, no. 90. Westport, Conn.: Greenwood, 1981. 369 pp.

340. Halsted, Caroline Amelia. *The Crown and Tower: The Legend of Richard III: A Condensation of Caroline Amelia Halsted's Important Biography of 1844,* Richard III as Duke of Gloucester and King of England *with the Views of Other Authors and Additional Commentary.* Snyder, William H., ed. Sea Cliff, N.Y.: Richard III Soc., 1981. 295 pp.

341. Handlin, Oscar. *Truth in History.* Cambridge, Mass.: Harvard U. Pr., 1979. 437 pp.

342. Hareven, Tamara K., ed. *Transitions: The Family and the Life Course in Historical Perspectives.* New York: Academic, 1978. 304 pp.

343. Harvey, Fernand. *Le Mouvement Ouvrier au Québec* [The labor movement in Quebec]. 2d ed., Montreal: Boréal Express, 1980. 330 pp.

344. Hatch, Nathan O. and Noll, Mark A., ed. *The Bible in America: Essays in Cultural History.* New York: Oxford U. Pr., 1982. 191 pp.

345. Hays, Samuel P. *American Political History as Social Analysis: Essays.* Knoxville: U. of Tennessee Pr., 1980. 459 pp.

346. Heller, L. G. *Communicational Analysis and Methodology for Historians.* New York: New York U. Pr., 1972. 179 pp.

347. Henige, David P. *Oral Historiography.* New York: Longman, 1982. 150 pp.

348. Hepburn, A. C. *Minorities in History.* New York: St. Martin's, 1979. 251 pp.

349. Hexter, J. H. *On Historians.* Cambridge: Harvard U. Pr., 1979. 310 pp.

350. Hiden, John and Farquharson, John. *Explaining Hitler's Germany: Historians and the Third Reich.* New York: Barnes & Noble, 1983. 237 pp.

351. Hildebrand, K. *The Third Reich.* Falla, P. S., transl. Winchester, Mass.: Allen & Unwin, 1984. 184 pp.

352. Hindle, Brooke, ed. *Early American Science.* New York: Sci. Hist. Publ., 1976. 213 pp.

353. Hoerder, Dirk, ed. *American Labor and Immigrant History, 1877-1920's: Recent European Research.* (Working Class in American History series.) Urbana: U. of Illinois Pr., 1983. 286 pp.

354. Holt, Stephen. *Manning Clark and Australian History, 1915-1963.* New York: U. of Queensland Pr., 1982. 207 pp.

355. Hoopes, James. *Oral History: An Introduction for Students.* Chapel Hill: U. of North Carolina Pr., 1979. 155 pp.

356. Horst, Ulrich. *Unfehlbarkeit und Geschichte: Studien zur Unfehlbarkeitsdiskussion von Melchior Cano bis zum I. Vatikanischen Konzil* [Infallibility and history: studies on infallibility from Melchior Cano to Vatican Council I]. (Wallerberger Studien der Albertus-Magnus-Akademie, Theologische Reihe, no. 12.) Mainz, West Germany: Matthias-Grünewald, 1982. 262 pp.

357. Hoskin, Michael. *Stellar Astronomy: Historical Studies.* Chalfont St. Giles, England: Sci. Hist. Publ., 1982. 197 pp.

358. Hourani, Albert Habib. *Europe and the Middle East.* Berkeley: U. of California Pr., 1980. 226 pp.

359. Hromnik, Cyril A. *Indo-Africa. Towards a New Understanding of the History of Sub-Saharan Africa.* Cape Town and Johannesburg: Juta, 1981. 168 pp.

360. Hulliung, Mark. *Citizen Machiavelli.* Princeton: Princeton U. Pr., 1984. 299 pp.

361. Illeritski, V. E. *Sergei Mikhailovich Soloviër* [Sergei Soloviëv]. (Nauchnye Biografii series.) Moscow: Nauka, 1980. 190 pp.

362. Jaffa, Harry V. *How to Think about the American Revolution: A Bicentennial Celebration.* Durham, N.C.: Carolina Academic Pr., 1978. 183 pp.

363. Jeffrey, Ian. *Photography: A Concise History.* (World of Art Library.) New York: Oxford U. Pr., 1982. 248 pp.

364. Jenkins, John H. *Basic Texas Books: An Annotated Bibliography of Selected Works for a Research Library.* Austin, Tex.: Jenkins, 1983. 648 pp.

365. Jennings, Francis. *The Invasion of America: Indians, Colonialism, and the Cant of Conquest.* Chapel Hill: U. of North Carolina Pr. for Inst. for Early Am. Hist. and Culture, 1975. 369 pp.

366. Johnson, Richard, ed. *Making Histories: Studies in History-Writing and Politics.* Minneapolis: U. of Minnesota Pr., 1983. 379 pp.

367. Jones, Gareth Stedman and Samuel, Raphael, ed. *Culture, Ideology and Politics.* London: Routledge & Kegan Paul, 1982.

368. Jorland, Gérard. *La Science dans la Philosophie: Les Recherches Epistémologiques d'Alexandre Koyré* [Science in philosophy: the epistemological research of Alexandre Koyré]. (Bibliothèque des Idées.) Paris: Gallimard, 1981. 372 pp.

369. Kammen, Michael, ed. *The Past Before Us: Contemporary Historical Writing in the United States.* Ithaca, N.Y.: Cornell U. Pr., 1980. 524 pp.

370. Kao, George, ed. *The Translation of Things Past: Chinese History and Historiography.* Hong Kong: Chinese U. Pr., 1982. 200 pp.

371. Katz, Michael B. *Poverty and Policy in American History.* New York: Academic, 1983. 289 pp.

372. Kennedy, Thomas C. *Charles A. Beard and American Foreign Policy.* Gainesville: U. of Florida Pr., 1975. 199 pp.

373. Kenyon, John. *The History Men: The Historical Profession in England since the Renaissance.* Pittsburgh: U. of Pittsburgh Pr., 1984. 322 pp.

374. Keylor, William R. *Jacques Bainville and the Renaissance of Royalist History in Twentieth-Century France.* Baton Rouge: Louisiana State U. Pr., 1979. 349 pp.

375. Kinner, Klaus. *Marxistische deutsche Geschichtswissenschaft, 1917 bis 1933: Geschichte und Politik im Kampf der KPD* [German Marxist historiography, 1917-33: history and politics in the struggle of the German Communist Party]. (Akademie der Wissenschaften der DDR, Schriften des Zentralinstituts für Geschichte, no. 58.) Berlin: Akademie, 1982. 526 pp.

376. Kippur, Stephen A. *Jules Michelet: A Study of Mind and Sensibility.* Albany: State U. of New York Pr., 1981. 269 pp.

377. Kirkendall, Richard S., ed. *The Truman Period as a Research Field: A Reappraisal, 1972.* Columbia: U. of Missouri Pr., 1974. 246 pp.

378. Kliuchevski, V. O. *Neopublikovannye Proizvedeniia* [Unpublished works]. Moscow: Nauka, 1983. 416 pp.

379. Kloss, B. M. *Nikonovskii Svod i Russkie Letopisi XVI-XVII Vekov* [The Nikon codex and Russian chronicles, 16th-17th centuries]. Moscow: Nauka, 1980. 312 pp.

380. Köhler, Henning. *Das Ende Preussens in Französischer Sicht* [The end of Prussia in French view]. (Veröffentlichungen der Historischen Kommission zu Berlin, 53.) New York: Walter de Gruyter, 1982. 122 pp.

381. Kolko, Gabriel. *Main Currents in Modern American History.* New York: Harper and Row, 1976. 433 pp.

382. Koselleck, Reinhart, ed. *Historische Semantik und Begriffsgeschichte* [The semantics of history and the history of concepts]. (Sprache und Geschichte, no. 1.) Stuttgart: Klett-Cotta, 1979. 400 pp.

383. Kremer, Ulrich Michael. *Die Reformation als Problem der Amerikanischen Historiographie* [The reformation as a problem of American historiography]. Wiesbaden, W. Germany: Franz Steiner, 1978. 265 pp.

384. Krishna, Gopal, ed. *Contributions to South Asian Studies,* no. 1. New York: Oxford U. Pr., 1979. 197 pp.

385. LaCapra, Dominick. *Rethinking Intellectual History: Texts, Context, Language.* Ithaca, N.Y.: Cornell U. Pr., 1983. 350 pp.

386. Lamonde, Yvan. *Historiographie de la Philosophie au Québec, 1853-1970* [Historiography of Philosophy in Quebec, 1853-1870]. Collection "Philosophie," Les Cahiers du Quebec. Montreal: HMH, Ltée, 1972. 241 pp.

387. Lane, Ann J., ed. *Mary Ritter Beard: A Sourcebook.* New York: Schocken, 1977. 252 pp.

388. Latham, Edward Connery, ed. *United Statesiana: Seventy-Six Works of American Scholarship Relating to America as Published During Two Centuries from the Revolutionary Era of the United States Through the Nation's Bicentennial Year.* Washington: Assoc. of Res. Lib., 1976. 165 pp.

390. Lauren, Paul Gordon, ed. *Diplomacy: New Approaches in History, Theory, and Policy.* New York: Free Pr., 1979. 286 pp.

391. Leder, Lawrence H., ed. *The Colonial Legacy. Vol. 4, Early Nationalist Historians.* New York: Harper and Row, 1974. 344 pp.

392. Lee, Susan Previant and Passell, Peter. *A New Economic View of American History.* New York: Norton, 1979. 410 pp.

393. Lenin, Vladimir Il'ich and Trotsky, Leon. *Kronstadt.* Mutnick, Barbara, ed. New York: Pathfinder, 1979. 159 pp.

394. León-Portilla, Miguel; Gurría Lacroix, Jorge; and Frost, Elsa Cecilia et al. *Fray Juan de Torquemada, Monarquía Indiana, Vol. VII: Estudios sobre la Vida de Fray Juan de Torquemada, el Plan y la Estructura de su Obra, las Fuentes de Que se Valió para Escribir la Misma, su Idea de la Historia, su Pensamiento Teológico, las Imágenes Que se Formó del Mundo Indígena y del Mundo Hispánico, el Aprovechamiento Que se ha Hecho en Tiempos Posteriores de su Obra, Bibliografía acerca de Esta, Glosario de Vocablos Indígenas y de Arcaísmos e Indices analíticos de las Veintiún Libros Rituales y* Monarquía Indiana [Friar Juan de Torquemada, *Indian Monarchy,* Vol. 7: studies on the life of Friar Juan de Torquemada, the plan and structure of his work, the sources he used to write the same, his concept of history, his theological thought, the images he shaped of the indigenous world and of the Hispanic world, the use made of his work in later times, bibliography of that use, glossary of indigenous words and of archaisms and analytic indexes of the

21 ritual books and *Indian Monarchy].* Mexico City: Inst. de Investigaciones Históricas, U. Nacional Autónoma de México, 1983. 756 pp.

395. Lepenies, Wolf, ed. *Geschichte der Soziologie: Studien zur Kognitiven, Sozialen, und Historischen Identität einer Disziplin* [History of sociology: studies on the cognitive, social and historical identity of a discipline]. (Suhrkamp Taschenbuch Wissenschaft, no. 367.) 4 vol. Frankfurt: Suhrkamp, 1981. 1811 pp.

396. LeRoy Ladurie, Emmanuel. *The Territory of the Historian.* Reynolds, Ben and Reynolds, Siân, transl. Chicago: U. of Chicago Pr., 1979. 345 pp.

397. Levandovski, A. A. *Iz Istorii Krizisa Russkoi Burzhuazno-Liberal'noi Istoriografii: A. A. Kornilov* [From the history of the crisis of Russian bourgeois-liberal historiography: Aleksandr A. Kornilov]. Moscow: Moscow U. Pr., 1982. 178 pp.

398. Lichtman, Allan J. and French, Valerie. *Historians and the Living Past: Theory and Practice of Historical Study.* Arlington Heights, Ill.: AHM Publ., 1978. 267 pp.

399. Litman, Jacob. *The Economic Role of Jews in Medieval Poland: The Contribution of Yitzhak Schipper.* Lanham, Md.: University Press of America, 1985. 306 pp.

400. Lloyd-Jones, Hugh; Pearl, Valerie; and Worden, Blair, ed. *History and Imagination: Essays in Honour of H. R. Trevor-Roper.* London: Duckworth, 1981.

401. Locher, Gottfried W. *Die Zwinglische Reformation im Rahmen der Europäischen Kirchengeschichte* [The Zwinglian Reformation in the framework of European church history]. Göttingen: Vandenhoeck & Ruprecht, 1979. 714 pp.

402. Loewenberg, Bert James. *American History in American Thought: Christopher Columbus to Henry Adams.* New York: Simon and Schuster, 1972. 731 pp.

403. Lord, Donald C. *John F. Kennedy: The Politics of Confrontation and Conciliation.* Barron's Educational Series. Woodbury, N.Y.: Barron, 1977. 458 pp.

404. Lorwin, Val R. and Price, Jacob M., eds. *The Dimensions of the Past: Materials, Problems, and Opportunities for Quantitative Work in History.* New Haven, Conn. and London: Yale U. Pr., 1972.

405. Lottinville, Savoie. *The Rhetoric of History.* Norman: U. of Oklahoma Pr., 1976. 258 pp.

406. Lynn, Kenneth S. *The Air-Line to Seattle: Studies in Literary and Historical Writing about America.* Chicago: U. of Chicago Pr., 1983. 227 pp.

407. Maddox, Robert James. *The New Left and the Origins of the Cold War.* Princeton: Princeton U. Pr., 1973. 169 pp.

408. Magdol, Edward and Wakelyn, Jon L., ed. *The Southern Common People: Studies in Nineteenth-Century Social History.* Contributions in American History, no. 86. Westport, Conn.: Greenwood, 1980. 386 pp.

409. Malone, Michael P., ed. *Historians and the American West.* Lincoln: U. of Nebraska Pr., 1983. 449 pp.

410. Manniche, Jens C. *Den Radikale Historikertradition: Studier i Dansk Historievidenskabs Forudsaetninger og Normer* [Radical historical tradition: studies in Danish historiography—its assumptions and norms]. (Jysk Selskab for Historie, no. 38.) Aarhus, Denmark: Universitetsforlaget, 1981. 439 pp.

411. Marica, George Em. *Studii de Istoria şi Sociologia Culturii Române Ardelene din Secolul al XIX-lea: Vol. 3, George Bariţiu—Istoric* [Studies in the history and sociology of Transylvanian Romanian culture in the 19th century, vol. 3, Goerge Bariţiu, historian]. Cluj-Napoca, Romania: Dacia, 1980. 253 pp.

412. Maud, Ralph. *A Guide to B.C. Indian Myth and Legend: A Short History of Myth Collecting and a Survey of Published Texts.* Vancouver: Talonbooks, 1982. 218 pp.

413. May, Ernest R. and Thomas, James C., Jr., eds. *American-East Asian Relations: A Survey.* Harvard Studies in American-East Asian Relations, 1. Cambridge, Mass.: Harvard U. Pr., 1972. 425 pp.

414. McLennan, Gregor. *Marxism and the Methodologies of History.* London: NLB, 1982.

415. McNaught, Kenneth J. and Bercuson, David J. *The Winnipeg Strike: 1919.* Don Mills, Ont.: Longman, 1974. 126 pp.

416. Medvedev, Roy A. *The October Revolution.* New York: Columbia U. Pr., 1979. 232 pp.

417. Meilink-Roelofsz, M. A. P., ed. *Dutch Authors on West Indian History: A Historiographical Selection.* Yperen, Maria J. L. van, transl. (Koninklijk Instituut voor Taal-, Land- en Volkenkunde, Translation Series, no. 21.) The Hague: Nijhoff, 1982. 384 pp.

418. Melanson, Richard A. *Writing History and Making Policy: The Cold War, Vietnam, and Revisionism.* Lanham, Md.: U. Pr. of Am., 1983. 254 pp.

419. Metz, Karl Heinz. *Grundformen Historiographischen Denkens: Wissenschaftsgeschichte als Methodologie; Dargestellt an Ranke, Treitschke und Lamprecht; Mit einem Anhang über zeitgenössische Geschichts theorie* [Original historiographic thought: the science of history as methodology; represented by Ranke, Treitschke, and Lamprecht; with a supplement on contemporary history theory]. Münchener Universitäts-Schriften, Reihe der Philosophischen Fakultät, no. 21. Munich: Wilhelm Fink, 1979. 737 pp.

420. Mikio Sumiya and Koji Taira. *An Outline of Japanese Economic History, 1603-1940: Major Works and Research Findings.* Tokyo: U. of Tokyo Pr., 1979. 372 pp.

421. Miller, Joseph C., ed. *The African Past Speaks: Essays on Oral Tradition and History.* Hamden, Conn.: Shoe String, 1980. 284 pp.

422. More, Henry. *The Elizabethan Jesuits: Historia Missionis Anglicanae Societatis Jesu (1660) of Henry More.* Edwards, Francis, ed. & transl. London: Phillimore, 1981. 400 pp.

423. Moreno Bonett, Margarita. *Nacionalismo Novohispano: Mariano Veytia; Historia Antigua, Fundación de Puebla, Guadalupanismo* [Mexican nationalism: Mariano Veytia: ancient history, the foundation of the town, and *Guadalupanismo*]. Mexico City: U. Nac. Autonóma, 1983. 347 pp.

424. Morison, Samuel Eliot. *Sailor Historian: The Best of Samuel Eliot Morison.* Emily Morison Beck, ed. Boston: Houghton Mifflin, 1977. 431 pp.

425. Mosca, Liliana. *Il Madagascar nella Vita di Raombana Primo Storico Malgascio (1809-1855)* [Madagascar in the life of Raombana (1809-55), the first Malagasy historian]. Naples: Giannini, 1980. 309 pp.

426. Moscow Institute of the International Working Class Movement. *The International Working-Class Movement: Problems of History and Theory. Vol. 1, The Origins of the Proletariat and its Evolution as a Revolutionary Class.* Chicago: Progress, 1981. 674 pp.

427. Mozzarelli, Cesare and Olmi, Giuseppe, ed. *La Corte nella Cultura e nella Storiografia: Immagini e Posizioni tra Otto e Novecento* [The court in culture and historiography: image and position in the 18th and 19th centuries]. (Europa delle Corti, Centro Studi sulle Società di Antico Regime, Biblioteca del Cinquecento, no. 21.) Rome: Bulzoni, 1983. 284 pp.

428. Mudroch, Vaclav. *The Wyclyf Tradition.* Athens: Ohio U. Pr., 1979. 91 pp.

429. Muise, D. A., ed. *A Reader's Guide to Canadian History. Vol. 1: Beginnings to Confederation.* Toronto: U. of Toronto Pr., 1982. 248 pp.

430. Muller, C. F. J.; VanJaarsveld, F. A.; VanWijk, Theo; and Boucher, Maurice. *South African History and Historians: A Bibliography.* Pretoria: U. of South Africa, 1979. 411 pp.

431. Nash, Gary B., ed. *Class and Society in Early America.* Vol. 1, Interdisciplinary Approaches to History Series; Gerald E. Stearn, ed. Englewood Cliffs, N.J.: Prentice-Hall, 1970. 205 pp.

432. Neatby, Hilda. *The Quebec Act: Protest and Policy.* Canadian Historical Controversies. Toronto: Prentice-Hall, 1972. 142 pp.

433. Newmyer, Kent, ed. *Historical Essays in Honor of Kenneth R. Rossman.* Crete, Nebr.: Doane Coll., 1980. 208 pp.

434. Novack, George, ed. *America's Revolutionary Heritage.* New York: Pathfinder, 1976. 414 pp.

435. Oakley, Francis. *Omnipotence, Covenant, and Order: An Excursion in the History of Ideas from Abelard to Leibniz.* Ithaca, N.Y.: Cornell University Press, 1984. 165 pp.

436. O'Brien, Michael. *The Idea of the American South, 1920-1941.* Baltimore: Johns Hopkins U. Pr., 1979. 273 pp.

437. O'Connor, John E. and Jackson, Martin A., ed. *American History/American Film: Interpreting the Hollywood Image.* New York: Ungar, 1979. 290 pp.

438. Okinshevich, Leo, comp. *U.S. History and Historiography in Post-War Soviet Writings, 1945-1970: A Bibliography.* Santa Barbara, Calif.: ABC-CLIO, 1976. 431 pp.

439. Olson, James S. *Slave Life: A Historiography and Selected Bibliography.* Lanham, Md.: U. Pr. of Am., 1983. 119 pp.

440. O'Neill, James E. and Krauskopf, Robert W., eds. *Research on the Second World War.* National Archives Conferences, Vol. 8. Washington: Howard U. Pr., 1976. 302 pp.

441. Owens, W. R. *Seventeenth-Century England: A Changing Culture. Vol. 2, Modern Studies.* Totowa, N.J.: Barnes & Noble, 1981.

442. Palmer, Bryan D. *The Making of E. P. Thompson: Marxism, Humanism and History.* Toronto: New Hogtown, 1981. 145 pp.

443. Pascoe, Rob. *The Manufacture of Australian History.* New York: Oxford U. Pr., 1979. 207 pp.

444. Pecchioli, Renzo. *Dal "Mito" di Venezia all' "Ideologia Americana"* [The "myth" of Venice in American ideology]. Venice: Marsilio, 1983. 283 pp.

445. Pereyra, Carlos et al. *Historia ¿Para Que?* [History, for what?]. Mexico City: Siglo Veintiuno, 1980. 245 pp.

446. Pérez, Louis A., Jr. *Historiography in the Revolution: A Bibliography of Cuban Scholarship, 1959-1979.* (Reference Library of Social Science, Vol. 90.) New York: Garland, 1982. 318 pp.

447. Pfisterer, Karl Dieterich. *The Prism of Scripture: Studies on History and Historicity in the Work of Jonathan Edwards.* Bern, Switzerland: Lang, 1975. 381 pp.

448. Philipp, Werner. *Ausgewählte Schriften* [Selected writings]. Torke, Hans-Joachim, ed. (Forschungen zur Osteuropäischen Geschichte, vol. 33.) Wiesbaden, West Germany: Otto Harrasowitz for Osteuropa-Institut an der Freien Universität Berlin, 1983. 304 pp.

449. Philp, Kenneth R. and West, Elliott, ed. *Essays on Walter Prescott Webb.* Walter Prescott Webb Memorial Lectures, vol. 10. Austin: U. of Texas Pr., 1976. 124 pp.

450. Pigaffeta, Antonio. *The Philippines: Pigafetta's Story of Their Discovery by Magellan.* Lévesque, Rodrigue, transl. Quebec: Lévesque, 1980. 133 pp.

451. Pole, J. R. *Paths to the American Past.* New York: Oxford U. Pr., 1979. 348 pp.

452. Porciani, Ilaria. *L'Archivio Storico Italiano: Organizzazione della Ricerca ed Egemonia Moderata nel Risorgimento* [The Archivio Storico Italiano: organization of research and moderated hegemony in the Risorgimento]. Biblioteca di Storia Toscana Moderna e Contemporanea, Studi e Documenti, no. 20. Florence: Leo S. Olschki, 1979. 302 pp.

453. Porter, Dale H. *The Emergence of the Past: A Theory of Historical Explanation.* Chicago: U. of Chicago Pr., 1981. 205 pp.

454. Potter, David M. *History and American Society: Essays of David M. Potter.* Don E. Fehrenbacher, ed. New York: Oxford U. Pr., 1973. 422 pp.

455. Prečan, Vilém, ed. *Acta Creationis. Unabhängige Geschichtsschreibung in der Tschechoslowakei, 1969-1980* [Acta creationis. Independent historiography in Czechoslovakia, 1969-80]. Hanover, West Germany: Vilém Prečan, 1980. 252 pp.

456. Prittie, Terence Cornelius Farmer. *The Velvet Chancellors: A History of Post-War Germany.* New York: Holmes & Meier, 1979. 286 pp.

457. Quinn, D. B., ed. *The Hakluyt Handbook.* Second Series, Vols. 144-145. 2 vols., London: Hakluyt Soc., 1974. 707 pp.

458. Ranke, Leopold von. *The Secret of World History: Selected Writings on the Art and Science of History.* Wines, Roger, ed. and transl. Bronx, N.Y.: Fordham U. Pr., 1981. 276 pp.

459. Ranum, Orest. *Artisans of Glory: Writers and Historical Thought in Seventeenth-Century France.* Chapel Hill: U. of North Carolina Pr., 1980. 351 pp.

460. Reid, Anthony and Marr, David. *Perceptions of the Past in Southeast Asia.* Singapore: Heinemann Educ. Books (Asia) for the Asian Studies Assoc. of Australia, 1979. 436 pp.

461. Reikhberg, G. E. and Shurygin, A. P. *Burzhuaznaia Istoriografiia Oktiabria i Grazhdanskoi Voiny v Sibiri* [Bourgeois historiography of the October Russian Revolution and the civil war in Siberia]. Novosibirsk, USSR: Nauka, 1981. 60 pp.

462. Reinitz, Richard. *Irony and Consciousness: American Historiography and Reinhold Niebuhr's Vision.* Lewisburg, Pa.: Bucknell U. Pr., 1980. 230 pp.

463. Repgen, Konrad, ed. *Forschungen und Quellen zur Geschichte des Dreissigjährigen Krieges* [Research and sources on the history of the Thirty Years War]. (Schriftenreihe der Vereinigung zur Erforschung der Neueren Geschichte, vol. XII.) Münster, West Germany: Aschendorff, 1981.

464. Riasanovsky, Nicholas V. *The Image of Peter the Great in Russian History and Thought.* New York: Oxford University Press, 1985. 352 pp.

465. Robinson, Chandler A., ed., comp. *J. Evetts Haley and the Passing of the Old West.* Austin, Tex.: Jenkins, 1978. 239 pp.

466. Robinson, John L. *Bartolomé Mitre: Historian of the Americas.* Washington: U. Pr. of Am., 1982. 117 pp.

467. Rodrigues, José Honório. *História da História do Brazil.* Volume 1, *Historiografia Colonial* [Historiography of colonial Brazil]. Braziliana, no. 21. São Paulo: Edítora Nacional, 1979. 534 pp.

468. Roebuck, Graham. *Clarendon and Cultural Continuity.* New York: Garland, 1981.

469. Rosenberg, Charles, ed. *Healing and History: Essays for George Rosen.* New York: Sci. Hist. Publ.; Neale Watson Academic Publ., 1979. 262 pp.

470. Rosenberg, Rosalind. *Beyond Separate Spheres: Intellectual Roots of Modern Feminism.* New Haven: Yale U. Pr., 1982. 288 pp.

471. Rosenfeldt, Niels Erik, ed. *Sovjetunionens Historie 1917-1970: En Forskningsoversigt* [Soviet history, 1917-70: a survey of research]. Problemer i Ruslands og Sovjetunionens historie, no. 1. Århus: Jysk Selskab for Historie and Universitetsforlaget, 1979. 282 pp.

472. Ross, Stanley R. et al, ed. *Guide to the Hispanic American Historical Review, 1956-1975.* Durham, N.C.: Duke U. Pr., 1980. 432 pp.

473. Rotberg, Robert I. and Rabb, Theodore K., ed. *Climate and History: Studies in Interdisciplinary History.* Princeton, N.J.: Princeton U. Pr., 1981. 280 pp.

474. Rousseau, G. S. and Porter, Roy, ed. *The Ferment of Knowledge.* Studies in the Historiography of Eighteenth-Century Science. New York: Cambridge U. Pr., 1980. 500 pp.

475. Roy, Michel. *L'Acadie Perdue* [Lost Acadia]. Montreal: Québec-Amérique, 1978. 204 pp.

476. Rozman, Gilbert, ed. *Soviet Studies of Premodern China: Assessments of Recent Scholarship.* (Michigan Monographs in Chinese Studies, no. 50.) Ann Arbor: University of Michigan Press, 1984. 247 pp.

477. Russo, David J. *Families and Communities: A New View of American History.* Nashville, Tenn.: Am. Assoc. for State and Local Hist., 1974. 322 pp.

478. Samuel, Raphael, ed. *People's History and Socialist Theory.* History Workshop Series. Boston: Routledge & Kegan Paul, 1981. 417 pp.

479. Schlatter, Richard, ed. *Recent Views on British History: Essays on Historical Writing since 1966.* New Brunswick, N.J.: Rutgers University Press, 1984. 525 pp.

480. Schlobach, Jochen. *Zyklentheorie und Epochenmetaphorik: Studien zur Bildlichen Sprache der Geschichtsreflexion in Frankreich von der Renaissance bis zur Frühaufklärung* [Cyclical theory and the metaphor of epochs: studies of figurative language in historical thought in France from the Renaissance to early Enlightenment]. (Humanistische Bibliothek: Reihe I: Abhandlungen, no. 7.) Munich: Fink, 1980. 387 pp.

481. Schware, Robert. *Quantification in the History of Political Thought: Toward a Qualitative Approach.* Contributions in Political Science, no. 55. Westport, Conn.: Greenwood, 1981. 168 pp.

482. Scott, Anne Firor. *Making the Invisible Woman Visible.* Urbana: U. of Illinois Pr., 1984. 387 pp.

483. Sevost'ianov, G. N., ed. *Osnovnye Problemy Istorii SShA v Amerikanskoi Istoriografii: Ot Kolonial'nogo Perioda do Grazhdanskoi Voiny, 1861-1865* [Basic problems in the history of the U.S.A. in American historiography: From the colonial period to the Civil War, 1861-1865]. Akademiia Nauk SSSR, Institut Vseobshchei Istorii. Moscow: Izdatel'stovo "Nauka," 1971. 373 pp.

484. Seyssel, Claude de. *The Monarchy of France.* Kelley, Donald R., ed.; Hexter, J. H. and Sherman, Michael, transl. New Haven: Yale U. Pr., 1981. 211 pp.

485. Shaffer, Arthur H., ed. *The Politics of History: Writing the History of the American Revolution, 1783-1815.* Chicago: Precedent, 1975. 228 pp.

486. Sharpe, Lesley. *Schiller and the Historical Character: Presentation and Interpretation in the Historiographical Works and in the Historical Dramas.* (Oxford Modern Languages and Literature Monographs.) New York: Oxford U. Pr., 1982. 211 pp.

487. Short, K. R. M., ed. *Feature Films as History: Selected Papers from a Conference Sponsored by Zentrum für Interdisziplinare Forschung, University of Bielefeld Held in 1979.* Knoxville: U. of Tennessee Pr., 1981. 192 pp.

488. Siegel, James. *Shadow and Sound: The Historical Thought of a Sumatran People.* Chicago: U. of Chicago Pr., 1979. 282 pp.

489. Silva Herzog, Jesús. *Collección Cuadernos Americanos: Comprensión y Crítica de la Historia* [The *Cuadernos Americanos* collection: understanding and critique of history]. Mexico City: Nueva Imagen, 1982. 533 pp.

490. Silva Herzog, Jesús. *De la Historia de Mexico, 1810-1938: Documentos Fundamentales, Ensayos y Opiniones* [The History of Mexico, 1810-1938: fundamental documents, essays, and opinions]. Mexico City: Siglo Veinte, 1980. 300 pp.

491. Silver, Thomas B. *Coolidge and the Historians.* Durham, N.C.: Carolina Acad. for Claremont Inst. 159 pp.

492. Simon, Günther. *Kleine Geschichte der Chemie* [Short history of chemistry]. Praxis Schriftenreihe. Abteilung Chemie, 35. Cologne, West Germany: Aulis Verlag Deubner, 1980. 148 pp.

493. Siracusa, Joseph M. *New Left Diplomatic History and Historians: The American Revisionists.* Port Washington, N.Y.: Kennikat Pr., 1973. 138 pp.

494. Skinner, A. E. *Texas Library History: A Bibliography.* Phoenix, Ariz.: Oryx, 1983. 88 pp.

495. Smith, Donald B. *Le "Sauvage" Pendant la Période Héroique de la Nouvelle-France (1534-1663) d'après les Historiens Canadiens-Français des 19ᵉ et 20eRET Siècle* [The "savage" during the heroic period of New France, 1534-1663, according to the French Canadian historians of the 19th and 20th centuries]. 1974. Reprint ed., Montreal: Hurtubise HMH, 1979. 137 pp.

496. Smith, Henry, ed. *Learning from Shōgun: Japanese History and Western Fantasy.* Santa Barbara, Calif.: U. of California, Program in Asian Studies, 1980. 160 pp.

497. Sobolev, G. L. *Oktiabr'skaia Revoliutsiia v amerikanskoi istoriografii 1917-1970-e gody* [The October Revolution in American historiography, 1917-70]. Leningrad: Nauka, 1979. 247 pp.

498. Sonnichsen, C. L. *The Ambidextrous Historian: Historical Writers and Writing in the American West.* Norman: U. of Oklahoma Pr., 1981. 120 pp.

499. Soviet Union, Academy of Science, Institute of World History. *Materials of the First Symposium of Soviet Americanists (November 30-December 3, 1971).* 2 vols., Moscow: Inst. of World Hist. of Acad. of Sci., 1973. 502 pp.

500. Spear, Thomas. *Kenya's Past: An Introduction to Historical Method in Africa.* New York: Longman, 1981. 155 pp.

501. Stave, Bruce M. *The Making of Urban History: Historiography Through Oral History.* Beverly Hills, Calif.: Sage Publ., 1977. 336 pp.

502. Stedman Jones, Gareth and Samuel, Raphael, ed. *Culture, Ideology and Politics.* London: Routledge & Kegan Paul, 1982.

503. Steffen, Jerome O., ed. *The American West: New Perspectives, New Dimensions.* Norman: U. of Oklahoma Pr., 1979. 238 pp.

504. Sternsher, Bernard. *Consensus, Conflict, and American Historians.* Bloomington: Indiana U. Pr., 1975. 432 pp.

505. Stevens, John D. and Garcia, Hazel Dicken. *Communication History.* Sage Commtext, no. 2. Beverly Hills, Calif.: Sage, 1980. 159 pp.

508. Stoddard, Ellwyn R.; Nostrand, Richard L., and West, Jonathan P., ed. *Borderlands Sourcebook: A Guide to the Literature on Northern Mexico and the American Southwest.* Norman: U. of Oklahoma Pr., 1983. 445 pp.

509. Strout, Cushing. *The Veracious Imagination: Essays on American History, Literature, and Biography.* Middletown, Conn.: Wesleyan U. Pr., 1981. 301 pp.

510. Sumiya, Mikio and Taira, Koji. *An Outline of Japanese Economic History, 1603-1940: Major Works and Research Findings.* Tokyo: U. of Tokyo Pr., 1979. 372 pp.

511. Swagerty, W. R. *Scholars and the Indian Experience: Critical Reviews of Recent Writing in the Social Sciences.* (History of the American Indian Bibliographical Series.) Bloomington: Indiana U. Pr., 1984. 268 pp.

512. Swierenga, Robert P., ed. *Beyond the Civil War Synthesis: Political Essays of the Civil War Era.* Contributions in American History. Westport, Conn.: Greenwood, 1975. 348 pp.

513. Swierenga, Robert P., ed. *Quantification in American History: Theory and Research.* New York: Atheneum, 1970. 417 pp.

514. Swigger, Boyd Keith, comp. *A Guide to Resources for the Study of the Recent History of the United States in the Libraries of the University of Iowa, the State Historical Society of Iowa, and in the Herbert Hoover Presidential Library.* Iowa City: U: of Iowa Lib., 1977. 283 pp.

515. Tafuri, Manfredo. *Theories and History of Architecture.* New York: Icon/Harper & Row, 1980. 324 pp.

516. Temu, Arnold and Swai, Bonaventure. *Historians and Africanist History: A Critique: Postcolonial Historiography Examined.* London: Zed, 1982. 187 pp.

517. Thomas, Jack Ray. *Biographical Dictionary of Latin American Historians and Historiography.* Westport, Conn.: Greenwood, 1984. 420 pp.

518. Thompson, Kenneth W. *Cold War Theories. Vol 1: World Polarization, 1944-1953.* Baton Rouge: Louisiana State U. Pr., 1981. 223 pp.

519. Tishkov, V. A., ed. *Problemy Istoriografii Kanady* [Problems of Canadian historiography]. Moscow: Nauka, 1981. 310 pp.

520. Tobin, Gregory M. *The Making of a History: Walter Prescott Webb and the Great Plains.* Austin: U. of Texas Pr., 1976. 184 pp.

521. Torke, Hans-Joachim, ed. *Forschungen zur Osteuropäischen Geschichte* [Research in Eastern European history]. (Osteuropa-Institut an der Freien Universität Berlin. Historische Veröffentlichungen, vol. 28.) West Berlin: Otto Harrassowitz, 1981. 381 pp.

522. Tosh, John. *The Pursuit of History: Aims, Methods and New Directions in the Study of Modern History.* New York: Longman, 1984. 205 pp.

523. Tripathi, Dwijendra and Tiwari, S. C., ed. *Themes and Perspectives in American History.* Hyderabad, India: Am. Studies Res. Centre, 1978. 275 pp.

524. Tropfke, Johannes. *Geschichte der Elementarmathematik.* Vol. 1: *Arithmetik und Algebra* [The history of elementary mathematics. *Vol. I:* arithmetic and algebra]. Vogel, Kurt; Reich, Karin; and Gericke, Helmuth, ed. Revised ed. Berlin: Walter de Gruyter, 1980. 742 pp.

525. Trottier, Louise. *Les Forges: Historiographie des Forges du Saint-Maurice* [The forges: historiography of the steel mills of St. Maurice]. Montreal: Boréal Express, 1980. 172 pp.

526. Tuchman, Barbara. *Practicing History: Selected Essays.* New York: Knopf, 1981. 306 pp.

527. Tucker, Robert W. and Hendrickson, David C. *The Fall of the First British Empire: Origins of the War of American Independence.* Baltimore: Johns Hopkins U. Pr., 1982. 450 pp.

528. Turner, Frederick Jackson. *Frederick Jackson Turner's Legacy: Unpublished Writings in American History.* 1965. Wilbur R. Jacobs, ed. Reprint ed., Lincoln: U. of Nebraska Pr., 1977. 217 pp.

529. Turoff, Barbara K. *Mary Beard as Force in History.* Dayton, Ohio: Wright State U., 1979. 85 pp.

530. Tuska, Jon. *Billy the Kid: A Bio-Bibliography.* Westport, Conn.: Greenwood, 1983. 235 pp.

531. Valle, James E. *Rocks and Shoals: Order and Discipline in the Old Navy, 1800-1861.* Annapolis, Md.: Naval Inst., 1980. 341 pp.

532. Vaughan, Alden T. and Billias, George Athan, eds. *Perspectives on Early American History: Essays in Honor of Richard B. Morris.* New York: Harper and Row, 1973. 405 pp.

533. Veyne, Paul. *Writing History: Essay on Epistemology.* Moore-Rinvolucri, Mina, transl. New York: Wesleyan University Press, 1984. 336 pp.

534. Viatkin, R. V. and Svistunova, N. P., ed. *Istoricheskaia Nauka v KNR* [Historiography in the People's Republic of China]. Rev. ed. Moscow: Nauka, 1981. 357 pp.

535. Vilar, Pierre. *Une Histoire en Construction: Approche Marxiste et Problématiques Conjoncturelles* [A history in construction: Marxist approach and situational problems]. Paris: Gallimard, 1982.

536. Walker, Don D. *Clio's Cowboys: Studies in the Historiography of the Cattle Trade.* Lincoln: U. of Nebraska Pr., 1981. 210 pp.

537. Walsh, Margaret. *The American Frontier Revisited.* (Studies in Economic and Social History.) London: Macmillan, 1981. 88 pp.

538. Watson, Charles A. *The Writing of History in Britain: A Bibliography of Post-1945 Writings about British Historians and Biographers.* (Garland Reference Library of Social Science, no. 91.) New York: Garland, 1982. 726 pp.

539. Watts, Jim and Davis, Allen F. *Generations: Your Family in Modern American History.* New York: Knopf, 1974. 210 pp.

540. Wehler, Hans-Ulrich. *Historische Sozialwissenschaft und Geschictsschreibung: Studien zu Aufgaben und Traditionen Deutscher Geschichtswissenschaft* [Historical social sciences and the writing of history: studies in purposes and traditions of German historical studies]. Göttingen: Vandenhoeck & Ruprecht, 1980. 409 pp.

541. Wehler, Hans-Ulrich, ed. *200 Jahre Amerikanische Revolution und Moderne Revolutionsforschung* [200 year anniversary of the American Revolution and research on modern revolutions]. Göttingen: Vandenhoeck and Ruprecht, 1976. 287 pp.

542. Weitzman, David. *Underfoot: An Everyday Guide to Exploring the American Past.* New York: Scribner's, 1976. 191 pp.

543. Williams, Gwyn A. *The Welsh in their History.* Totowa, NJ: Croom Helm, 1982. 206 pp.

544. Williams, Karel. *From Pauperism to Poverty.* Boston: Routledge & Kegan Paul, 1981. 383 pp.

545. Wilson, Joan Hoff. *Ideology and Economics: U.S. Relations with the Soviet Union, 1918-1933.* Columbia: U. of Missouri Pr., 1974. 192 pp.

546. Woll, Allen. *A Functional Past: The Uses of History in Nineteenth-Century Chile.* Baton Rouge: Louisiana State U. Pr., 1982. 211 pp.

547. Wrigley, Chris. *A. J. P. Taylor: A Complete Annotated Bibliography and Guide to His Historical and Other Writings.* Hassocks, Great Britain: Harvester, 1982. 607 pp.

548. Yeager, Gertrude Matyoka. *Barros Arana's* Historia Jeneral de Chile: *Politics, History, and National Identity.* (Monograph Series in History and Culture.) Fort Worth: Texas Christian U. Pr., 1981. 187 pp.

549. Yerushalmi, Yosef Hayim. *Zakhor, Jewish History and Jewish Memory.* (The Samuel and Althea Stroum Lectures in Jewish Studies series.) Seattle: U. of Washington Pr., 1983. 144 pp.

550. Young, Marilyn Blatt, ed. *American Expansionism: The Critical Issues.* Boston: Little, Brown, 1973. 184 pp.

551. Zitomersky, Joseph, ed. *On Making Use of History: Research and Reflections from Lund.* (Lund Studies in Int. Hist., no. 5.) Lund, Sweden: Esselte Studium, 1982. 206 pp.

552. ——. *Annali dell'Istituto Storico Italo-Germanico in Trento: Jahrbuch des Italienisch-Deutschen Historischen Instituts in Trient. Vol. 6* [Yearbook of the Italo-German Historical Institute in Trent]. Bologna: Il Mulino, 1982. 545 pp.

553. ——. *Cartografía y Relaciones Históricas de Ultramar. Tomo V: Colombia, Panamá y Venezuela* [Cartography and overseas historical accounts. Vol. 5: Colombia, Panama, and Venezuela]. Madrid: Servicio Histórico Military; Servicio Geográfico del Ejército, 1981. 642 pp.

554. ——. *Cartografía y Relaciones Históricas de Ultramar. Tomo I: América en General* [Cartography and overseas historical accounts. Vol. 1: America in general]. Reprint ed. (original publ. 1950). Madrid: Servicio Histórico Militar; Servicio Geográfico del Ejército, 1983. 551 pp.

3. DISSERTATIONS

555. Aay, Henry. "Conceptual Change and the Growth of Geographic Knowledge: A Critical Appraisal of the Historiography of Geography." Clark U. 1978. 393 pp. *DAI 1979 39(10): 6331-6332-A.*

556. Abram, Leonard Gerald. "The American Eye: The Influence of Pragmatism and Impressionism on Henry Adams' Portrayal of Character in *The History of the United States.*" U. of Maryland 1978. 237 pp. *DAI 1979 39(8): 4944-A.*

557. Ahmad, Anis. "Two Approaches to Islamic History: A Critique of Shibli Nu 'Mani's and Syed Ameer Ali's Interpretations of History." Temple U. 1980. 242 pp. *DAI 1981 42(2): 742-A.* DA8115848

558. Alteahrt, M. "Studien zur Geschichte des Historischen Zeitschriftenwesens in Österreich im Vormärz" [Studies in the history of Austrian periodical literature in history in the early 19th century]. U. of Vienna [Austria] 1979. 354 pp. *DAI-C 1983 44(1): 61; 8/317c.*

559. Amariglio, Jack Leon. "Economic History and the Theory of Primitive Socio-Economic Development." U. of Massachusetts 1984. 434 pp. *DAI 1984 45(1): 260-A.* DA8410254

560. Andisheh, Lida. "'Abbas Iqbal Ashtiyani (1897-1956) (A Study in Modern Iranian Intellectual History)." U. of Utah 1982. 289 pp. *DAI 1982 43(4): 1255-A.* DA8220771

561. Angelo, Richard Michael. "Unassigned Frequencies: Four Essays on the Historiography of American Education." Temple U. 1979. 164 pp. *DAI 1979 39(11): 6583-6584-A.*

562. Arx, Jeffrey Paul von. "Preventive Progress: A Study of the Relationship of Religion, Politics and the Historiography of Progress in the Work of Some Nineteenth Century British Historians." Yale U. 1980. 419 pp. *DAI 1981 42(1): 339-A.* DA8109822

563. Barolsky, Ruth Lassow. "A Study of Henry Adams' *History of the United States.*" U. of Virginia 1980. 429 pp. *DAI 1980 41(4): 1728-A.* DA8022676

564. Belonzi, Arthur A. "Roger Burlingame, 1889-1967: Historian." St. John's U. 1975. 234 pp. *DAI 1976 36(8): 5489-5490-A.*

565. Benander, Donald Henry. "Revisionist Criticism of John Dewey's Theory of Schooling." U. of Massachusetts 1980 143 pp. *DAI 1981 41(7): 2991-A.* 8101303

566. Bernard, Claude Eliane. "Le Problème Romanesque du Chouan: Mythe, Histoire, Roman, d'Après *Les Chouans* de Balzac, *Le Chevalier des Touches* et *L'Ensorcelée* de Barbey d'Aurevilly et *Quatrevingt-Treize* de Hugo" [The problem of the romantic royalist: myth, history, and novel in Balzac's *Les Chouans*, Barbey d'Aurevilly's *Le Chevalier des Touches* and *L'Ensorcelée*, and Hugo's *Quatrevingt-Treize*]. Princeton U. 1983. 699 pp. *DAI 1984 45(1): 198-A.* DA8409121

567. Björk, R. K. "Den Historiska Argumenteringen. Konstruktion, Narration och Kolligation—Förklaringsresonemang hos Nils Ahnlund och Erik Lönnroth" [The historical argumentation. Construction, narration, and colligation—explanatory reasoning in works by Nils Ahnlund and Erik Lönnroth]. Uppsala U. [Sweden] 1983. 340 pp. *DAI-C 1984 45(1): 34; 9/132c.* Almqvist & Wiksell, publ.

568. Blair, Carole. "An Archaeological Critique of the History of Rhetorical Theory: Beyond Historical-Critical Dualism in the Analysis of Theoretical Discourse." Pennsylvania State U. 1983. 257 pp. *DAI 1984 45(1): 16-A.* DA8409018

569. Blaser, Lowell Kent. "Between Science and Art: Henry Adams, Carl Becker, and History in America." U. of North Carolina, Chapel Hill 1977. 376 pp. *DAI 1977 38(6): 3676-A.*

570. Boles, Joseph David. "Clio in Crisis: The Historiographic Impulse in the Writings of H. D." Rutgers U., New Brunswick 1983. 399 pp. *DAI 1983 43(11): 3592-A.* DA8308421

571. Boling, Becky Jo. *"Terra Nostra:* Historia del Deseo" [*Terra Nostra:* the history of a desire]. Northwestern U. 1982. 230 pp. *DAI 1983 43(10): 3329-3330-A.* DA8305463

572. Boos, F. "Über das Wertfreiheitspostulat der Sozialwissenschaften: Eine Geschichtliche Betrachtung" [The neutrality postulate of the social sciences: a historical view]. Vienna U. of Commerce [Austria] 1981. 234 pp. *DAI-C 1984 45(3): 683; 9/2790c.*

573. Bost, David Herbert. "History and Fiction: The Presence of Imaginative Discourse in Some Historical Narratives of Colonial Spanish America." Vanderbilt U. 1982. 224 pp. *DAI 1982 43(4): 1159-A.* DA8221365

574. Bourne, Michael Lee. "Vision and Bunk: A Consideration of Historical Drama." Indiana U. 1977. 255 pp. *DAI 1978 38(11): 6403-A.*

575. Boyle, Susan C. "Social Mobility in the United States: Historiography and Methods." U. of Missouri, Columbia 1981. 266 pp. *DAI 1982 42(9): 4116-4117-A.* DA8205367

576. Bravo-Gozalo, J. M. "Problematica e Historia de la Historiografia Literaria Inglesa" [A history of English literary historiography]. Valladolid U. [Spain] 1980. 442 pp. *DAI-C 1981 42(4): 699; 6/4563c.*

577. Brewster, Philip James. "Wilhelm Raabes Historische Fiktion im Kontext. Beitrag zur Rekonstruktion der Gattungsproblematik Zwischen Geschichtsschreibung und Poesie im 19. Jahrhundert" [Wilhelm Raabe's historical fiction in context: a study of the reconstruction of the generic problem between 19th-century historiography and poetry]. Cornell U. 1983. 436 pp. *DAI 1984 44(9): 2778-A.* DA8328699

578. Butts, Francis T. "Perry Miller and the Ordeal of American Freedom." Queen's U. [Canada] 1981. *DAI 1981 42(4): 1759-A.*

579. Byerman, Keith Eldon. "Two Warring Ideals: The Dialectical Thought of W. E. B. Du Bois." Purdue U. 1978. 385 pp. *DAI 1979 40(1): 246-A.*

580. Cantu, Roberto. "La Invencion de America: Historia y Filosofia de la Historia en la Obra de Edmundo O'Gorman" [Spanish text]. U. of California, Los Angeles 1982. 403 pp. *DAI 1982 43(4): 1159-A.* DA8219655

581. Chan, Virginia Mayer. "Historical Consciousness in Eighteenth-Century China; a Case Study of Zhao Yi and the 'Zhexi' Historians." Harvard U. 1982. 379 pp. *DAI 1982 43(6): 2057-2058-A.* DA8222604

582. Chung, Young Hong. "An Analysis of the Historical Purposes and Mechanisms of American Education in the Revisionist Paradigm." U. of Pittsburgh 1981. 138 pp. *DAI 1982 43(1): 93-A.* DA8213135

583. Cohen, Lester H. "The Course of Human Events: American Historical Writing in the Revolutionary Era." Yale U. 1974. 421 pp. *DAI 1975 36(1): 458-A.*

584. Conte, Robert Sal. "The Attribution of Motives in Recent American Historical Writing: An Analysis of Form and Explanation." Case Western Reserve U. 1975. 257 pp. *DAI 1976 37(1): 506-A.*

585. Cook, Lowell Anthony. "Luther, Herder, and Ranke: The Reformation's Impact on German Idealist Historiography." North Texas State U. 1983. 197 pp. *DAI 1984 44(8): 2550-A.* DA8327018

586. Cornell, John Fenlon. "Purpose in Nature: A Study of the History of Teleology." U. of Chicago 1981. *DAI 1982 42(10): 4557-4558-A.*

587. Cragun, LeAnn. "Mormons and History: In Control of the Past." U. of Hawaii 1981. *DAI 1982 42(12): 5219-A.*

588. Crawford, Stephen Cooban. "Quantified Memory: A Study of the WPA and Fisk University Slave Narrative Collections." U. of Chicago 1980. *DAI 1981 41(9): 4140-A.*

589. Culbreth, B. Spencer. "American Foreign Policy in the 1920's: Isolation or Involvement? A Problem in Instruction and Learning." Middle Tennessee State U. 1978. 365 pp. *DAI 1978 39(3): 1757-A.*

590. Desan, Philippe. "Le Développement du Concept de Méthode en France au XVIᵉ Siècle." (French text) University of California, Davis 1984. 250 pp. *DAI 1985 45(11): 3358-A.* DA8501751

591. Devine, Paul Kevin. "Time Stands Fixt: The Theme of History in Milton's *Paradise Lost.*" Vanderbilt U. 1982. 233 pp. *DAI 1982 43(4): 1150-A.* DA8221371

592. Diefenthaler, Jon Thomas. "H. Richard Niebuhr: The Shaping of the American Religious Historian." U. of Iowa 1976. 304 pp. *DAI 1977 37(12): 7902-A.*

593. Dobay, Clara Marie Viator. "Essays in Mormon Historiography." U. of Houston 1980. 347 pp. *DAI 1981 42(1): 345-A.* 8115454

594. Eberan, B. E. "Luther? Friedrich 'der Grosse'? Wagner? Nietzsche?... Wer war an Hitler Schuld? Die Debatte um der Schuldfrage 1945-1949" [Luther? Frederick the Great? Wagner? Nietzsche?... Who was responsible for Hitler? The debate over the question of guilt, 1945-49]. University of Stockholm [Sweden] 1983. 281 pp. *DAI-C 1984 45(4): 931; 9/3880c.*

595. Ekman, B. "The End of a Legend: Ellen Glasgow's History of Southern Women." Uppsala U. [Sweden] 1979. 171 pp. *DAI-C 1981 41(4): 689; 5/4579c.*

596. Emanuel, Gary Lynn. "An Analysis of the Textbook Treatment of the Reconstruction Period: Changes that Occurred between Editions of College Level Survey Textbooks." U. of Northern Colorado 1979. 158 pp. *DAI 1979 40(5): 2837-A.*

597. Evans, Michael Jay. "Machiavelli: Historian, Comic, and Tragic." (Volumes I and II) U. of Michigan 1980. 626 pp. *DAI 1980 41(2): 758-A.* DA8017254

598. Evans, Richard William. "In Quest of a Useable Past: Young Leftist Historians in the 1960's." Case Western Reserve U. 1979. 299 pp. *DAI 1979 39(11): 6840-A.*

599. Fairchild, Sharon Louise. "George Sand, Historian of Her Time in Her *Correspondance* (1812-June 1835)." Wayne State U. 1980. 520 pp. *DAI 1980 41(4): 1627-A.* DA8022751

600. Faragasso, Frank Thomas. "Guglielmo Ferrero: History and Morality." City U. of New York 1981. 307 pp. *DAI 1981 41(12): 5213-A.* DA8112754

601. Farr, James Fulton. "Competing Models of the Method and History of Social Inquiry." U. of Minnesota 1979. 549 pp. *DAI 1980 40(9): 5166-A.* DA8006607

602. Flanary, Barbara Jean Dawson. "The Conflicts of the Second Spanish Republic: An Historiographical Survey." Memphis State U. 1981. 384 pp. *DAI 1982 42(11): 4901-A.* DA8208405

603. Flatt, Donald Franklin. "Historians View Jacksonian Democracy: A Historiographical Study." U. of Kentucky 1974. 219 pp. *DAI 1975 36(3): 1755-A.*

604. Fleischer, Cornell Hugh. "Gelibolulu Mustafa Ali Efendi, 1541-1600: A Study in Ottoman Historical Consciousness." Princeton U. 1982. 601 pp. *DAI 1982 43(4): 1141-A.* DA8221588

605. Freitag, W. D. "Der Entwicklungsbegriff in der Musikgeschichtsschreibung" [The concept of development in the history of music]. University of Hamburg [West Germany] 1976. 292 pp. *DAI-C 1985 46(3): 576; 46/2729.*

606. Furtek, Joanne. "A Social History of Crime and Law Enforcement in the United States and Western Europe, 1630-1980." (Vol. 1-2) Carnegie-Mellon U. 1983. 693 pp. *DAI 1984 44(12): 3780-A.* DA8400061

607. Gamson, Ian Calder. "The American Historian and the Concept of Manifest Destiny, 1845-1849." U. of Minnesota 1973. 275 pp. *DAI 1974 34(11): 7148-A.*

608. Gephart, Ronald Michael. "Revolutionary America, 1763-1789: A Bibliography." Northwestern U. 1980. 120 pp. *DAI 1980 41(6): 2735-A.* 8026807

609. Glasberg, Ronald Peter. "The Contextualization of the *Annales* School, 1949-1968: An Experiment in Historiography." U. of Toronto (Canada) 1980. *DAI 1980 41(6): 2722-A.*

610. Glaubauf, K. "Bismarck und der Aufstieg des Deutschen Reiches in der Darstellung Heinrich Friedjungs" [Bismarck's interpretation of H. Friedjung and his description of the rise of the German empire]. U. of Vienna [Austria] 1979. 250 pp. *DAI-C 1983 44(1): 61; 8/320c.*

611. Goggin, Jacqueline Anne. "Carter G. Woodson and the Movement to Promote Black History." U. of Rochester 1984. 416 pp. *DAI 1984 45(1): 270-A.* DA8409140

612. Goodale, Jesse Robinson. "The Nature and Development of Eighteenth-Century Commonwealthman Political and Historical Thought." Columbia U. 1979. 407 pp. *DAI 1981 42(6): 2802-A.* DA8125291

613. Gool, S. Y. "Mining Capitalism and Black Labour in the Early Industrial Period in South Africa: A Critique of the New Historiography." Lund U. [Sweden] 1983. 244 pp. *DAI-C 1985 46(2): 327. 10/1588c.*

614. Graham, Matt Patrick. "The Utilization of 1 and 2 Chronicles in the Reconstruction of Israelite History in the Nineteenth Century." Emory U. 1983. 517 pp. *DAI 1984 44(8): 2495-A.* DA8328058

615. Haecker, Dorothy A. "The Historical Way of Knowing." U. of Kansas 1981. 222 pp. *DAI 1982 42(7): 3184-A.* DA8128775

616. Hail, Francina Kercheville. "Thomas Paine: An Interpretive Study of the Treatment of Paine by Biographers, Historians and Critics." U. of New Mexico 1977. 384 pp. *DAI 1977 38(6): 3680-A.*

617. Heafer, Dianne Lewis. "A Historiographical Study of the Taney Court and the Dred Scott Decision." U. of Houston 1983. 253 pp. *DAI 1984 44(12): 3781-A.* DA8403909

618. Herold, David Edward. "A Species of Literary Lion: Essays on Morison, Freeman, DeVoto, and Becker and the Writing of History." U. of Minnesota 1973. 247 pp. *DAI 1974 34(11): 7134-A.*

619. Hesse, R. "Geschichtswissenschaft in Praktischer Absicht: Vorschläge und Kritik" [Practical historiography: proposals and critique]. U. of Constance [West Germany] 1979. 175 pp. *DAI-C 1981 42(2): 230; 6/1567c.* Steiner, publ.

620. Hilgendorf, Mark Steven. "Revisionist Interpretations of Slavery in Senior High School American History Textbooks." Duke U. 1982. 164 pp. *DAI 1983 43(8): 2624-A.* DA8301523

621. Hitchcock, Maxine Cacace. "From Anathema to Aggiornamento: The Contest Between Sarpi and Pallavicino over the Council of Trent and the Adjudication by Vatican II." U. of California, Santa Cruz 1980. 347 pp. *DAI 1980 41(5): 2251-A.* DA8025871

622. Hosmer, John Harelson. "The Dunning School and Reconstruction According to Jim Crow." U. of Arizona 1983. 403 pp. *DAI 1983 44(3): 835-A.* DA8315287

623. Hostetter, Philip Alan. "The Interpretation of Fascism by American Social Scientists." Am. U. 1982. 474 pp. *DAI 1982 43(6): 2128-A.* DA8225564

624. Jakfalvi-Leiva, Susana. "Las Ideas Lingüísticas del Inca Garcilaso y el Sujeto-Traductor de la Conquista del Incario" [The linguistic ideas of the Inca Garcilaso and the subject-translator of the conquest of the Incario]. Syracuse U. 1982. 268 pp. *DAI 1983 44(1): 181-A.* DA8310461

625. Johnson, Robert Andrew. "Political Ideology and Political Historiography: Reporting the Populists." U. of California, Berkeley 1981. 200 pp. *DAI 1982 42(12): 5232-A.* DA8211976

626. Kambayashi, Kikuko. "The Expansion of Treatments of Japan in High School Textbooks in American History, 1951-1972." U. of Michigan 1975. 276 pp. *DAI 1975 36(3): 1344-A.*

627. Kirby, Linda Kaye. "Communism, The Discovery of Totalitarianism, and the Cold War: *Partisan Review*, 1934 to 1948." U. of Colorado 1974. 220 pp. *DAI 1975 35(12): 7840-7841-A.*

628. Kruse, Jens. "Poetische Struktur und Geschichte in Goethes *Faust II*" [Poetic structure and history in Goethe's *Faust II*]. U. of California, Los Angeles 1982. 479 pp. *DAI 1982 43(4): 1138-A.* DA8219708

629. Kryder, Elizabeth Anne Giannone. "Humanizing the Industrial Workplace: The Role of the Early Personnel Manager: 1897-1920." Bowling Green State U. 1982. 218 pp. *DAI 1982 43(4): 1265-A.* DA8220238

630. Lack, Paul Dean. "Urban Slavery in the Southwest." Texas Tech U. 1973. 358 pp. *DAI 1974 34(9): 5875-A.*

631. Lagos, Ramona. "El Concepto de la Literatura en la Obra de Jorge Luis Borges: Nivel Teorico y Praxis Literaria" [The concept of literature in the work of Jorge Luis Borges: theoretical level and literary practice]. U. of Arizona 1982. 387 pp. *DAI 1982 43(3): 817-A.* DA8217499

632. Lambert, Paul Frank. "Pioneer Historian: The Life of Joseph B. Thoburn." Oklahoma State U. 1975. 211 pp. *DAI 1977 37(9): 6012-A.*

633. Lecoanet, Regis Marcel. "La Philosophie dans *L'Encyclopédie*" [Philosophy in the *Encyclopédie*]. City U. of New York 1981. 211 pp. *DAI 1981 42(4): 1664-A.* DA8120761

634. Leiby, John Severn. "Report to the King: Colonel Juan Camargo y Cavallero's Historical Account of New Spain, 1815." Northern Arizona U. 1983. 233 pp. *DAI 1983 44(4): 1177-A.* DA8319237

635. Lemons, William Everett, Jr. "The Western Historical Perspectives of DeVoto, Webb, Dobie, and Hyde." U. of Minnesota 1973. 411 pp. *DAI 1974 34(11): 7158-7159-A.*

636. Lenk, I. "Die Wiener *Neuen Zeitungen* 1571-1600. Ihre Mediengeschichtliche Entwicklung und Ihre Bedeutung als Quellen zur Zeitgeschichte" [Newsletters in Vienna, 1571-1600: their evolution and value as historical sources] U. of Vienna [Austria] 1979. 466 pp. *DAI-C 1983 44(3): 442; 8/2024c.*

637. Lewis, Guy Loran. "Daniel Gookin, Superintendent and Historian of the New England Indians: A Historiographical Study." U. of Illinois, Urbana-Champaign 1973. 245 pp. *DAI 1974 34(9): 5876-5877-A.*

638. Lewis, Robert Earl. "The Humanistic Historiography of Francisco Lopez de Gomara (1511-1559)." U. of Texas at Austin 1983. 434 pp. *DAI 1984 44(9): 2784-A.* DA8329845

639. Lopez, Claudio, Jr. "Germán Arciniegas: His Interpretation of the American History and Reality" [Spanish text]. U. of Connecticut 1982. 196 pp. *DAI 1982 43(5): 1561-A.* DA8224540

640. Lystra, Karen Anne. "Perry Miller and American Puritan Studies: A Case Study in Scholarly Community." Case Western Reserve U. 1973. 428 pp. *DAI 1974 34(11): 7135-7136-A.*

641. MacLean, Gerald Martin. "Time's Witness: English Historical Poetry, 1600-1660." U. of Virginia 1981. 296 pp. *DAI 1982 43(5): 1555-A.* DA8219063

642. Mawer, David Ronald. "The Return of the Catholic Past: The Debate between François-Xavier Garneau and His Critics, 1831-1945." McGill U. 1977. *DAI 1978 38(7): 4220-A.*

643. McCaffrey, Raymond Aloysius. "Assassination of American Presidents: An Analysis of the Literature." Fordham U. 1982. 219 pp. *DAI 1982 43(1): 272-A.* DA8213247

644. McKenzie, Lionel Andrew. "The Guicciardinian Prince: A Study in the Meaning of Prudence from Bodin to Richelieu." Johns Hopkins U. 1980. 428 pp. *DAI 1980 41(3): 1172-A.* DA8020267

645. McPartland, Thomas Joseph. "Horizon Analysis and Historiography: The Contribution of Bernard Lonergen toward a Critical Historiography." U. of Washington 1976. 642 pp. *DAI 1976 37(5): 3078-A.*

646. Mealy, Charles Richard. "An Investigation of Historiography, Selected Bibliographic References, and Information Storage and Retrieval Systems Related to Graduate Study and Research in the History of Physical Education." U. of Oregon 1973. 101 pp. *DAI 1974 34(12): 7573-7574-A.*

647. Medland, William James. "The American-Soviet Nuclear Confrontation of 1962: An Historiographical Account of the Cuban Missile Crisis." Ball State U. 1980. 243 pp. *DAI 1981 41(8): 3695-A.* DA8104663

648. Miehls, Don George. "The Self in History: A Contemporary View." Texas Christian U. 1982. 413 pp. *DAI 1983 43(9): 3079-A.* DA8303261

649. Morgan, James Calvin. "Negro Culture in the United States: A Study of Four Models for Interpreting Slavery in the United States." New York U. 1982. 424 pp. *DAI 1982 43(6): 1919-A.* DA8214884

650. Morrison, Katherine Long. "Henry Adams and His Brothers: A Study of American Conservative Thought." U. of Toronto [Canada] 1979. *DAI 1980 40(9): 5057-A.*

651. Naphtali, Zvia Segal. "On the Logic of Inquiry of Historical Sociology: An 'Explication-de-Texte' of Studies on Collective Protest and Revolution." New York U. 1981. 736 pp. *DAI 1982 42(12): 5274-A.* DA8211001

652. Neils, Patricia C. "China in the Writings of Kenneth Scott Latourette and John King Fairbank." U. of Hawaii 1980. *DAI 1980 41(3): 1112-A.*

653. Newell, William Dixon. "The Problem of American Entry into Twentieth Century World War: A Study in Conflicting Historiography." U. of Idaho 1982. 203 pp. *DAI 1982 43(5): 1642-A.* DA8224573

654. Norris, Roy William. "The Rhetoric of Bruce Catton: History as Literature." U. of Kansas 1977. 255 pp. *DAI 1978 38(7): 4170-4171-A.*

655. Nusbaum, Mary Antoine. "The Post-Progressive Historians: Elements of Existentialism in Recent Interpretations of Nineteenth Century America." U. of Toledo 1979. 292 pp. *DAI 1980 40(8): 4718-4719-A.*

656. Okie, Packard Laird, Jr. "Augustan Historical Writing, the Rise of Enlightenment Historiography in England." U. of Kansas 1982. 402 pp. *DAI 1983 43(12): 4008-A.* DA8309342

657. Peachy, William Samuel. "A Year in Selânikî's History: 1593-4." Indiana University 1984. 660 pp. *DAI 1985 45(11): 3357-A.* DA8501471

658. Pfisterer, Karl Dieterich. "The Prism of Scripture: Studies on History and Historicity in the Work of Jonathan Edwards." Columbia U. 1973. 388 pp. *DAI 1974 35(1): 570-A.*

659. Phillips, William Houston, Jr. "The Economic Performance of Late Victorian Britain: Traditional Historians and Growth." Massachusetts Inst. of Tech. 1980. *DAI 1980 41(3): 1162-A.*

660. Prednewa, Ludmila. "Pushkin's *Captain's Daughter:* Pushkin's Historical Outlook." U. of Pennsylvania 1982. 244 pp. *DAI 1982 43(3): 821-A.* DA8217165

661. Preiss, H. "Die Abiponer im Spiegel der Quellen des Zeitraumes von 1527 bis in die Zweite Hälfte des 19. Jahrhunderts" [The Abipon in historical sources, 1527-19th century]. U. of Vienna [Austria] 1979. 301 pp. *DAI-C 1983 44(3): 480; 8/2185c.*

662. Priest, Quinton. "Historiography and Statecraft in Eighteenth Century China: The Life and Times of Chao I (1727-1814)." U. of Arizona 1982. 473 pp. *DAI 1983 43(12): 4006-A.* DA8309038

663. Randolph, Scott Kellogg. "An Analysis of the Committee on the Role of Education in American History and Lawrence Cremin's Revisionist View of the Nature of History of American Education." Rutgers U. 1976. 181 pp. *DAI 1977 37(12): 7578-7579-A.*

664. Rankin, Elizabeth Anne. "Englishmen on the Acropolis: An Historiography of the Architecture of the Parthenon ca. 1750-1850." U. of the Witwatersrand (South Africa) 1979. *DAI 1980 41(3): 834-A.*

665. Ranson, Leonard Buckland. "The Vocational Basis for the Founding of Harvard College: An Alternative to Samuel Morison and Winthrop Hudson." U. of Iowa 1979. 177 pp. *DAI 1979 40(5): 2515-2516-A.*

666. Reilingh, Maarten A. "Paradigm and Style in American Theatre Historiography." Bowling Green State U. 1984. 157 pp. *DAI 1985 45(9): 2697-A.* DA8428396

667. Roper, John Herbert. "Ulrich Bonnell Phillips: His Life and Thought." U. of North Carolina, Chapel Hill 1977. 256 pp. *DAI 1977 38(6): 3685-A.*

668. Rothberg, Morey David. "Servant to History: A Study of John Franklin Jameson, 1859-1937." Brown U. 1983. 356 pp. *DAI 1983 43(11): 3686-A.* DA8228327

669. Ruff, Robert Monroe. "Orthodox, Realist, and Revisionist Interpretations of the Origins of the Cold War, 1962-1972." U. of Georgia 1973. 216 pp. *DAI 1974 34(8): 5076-5077-A.*

670. Sabia, Daniel Robert, Jr. "A Historiography of Histories of Political Theory." U. of Minnesota 1978. 521 pp. *DAI 1979 39(12): 7503-A.*

671. Sanders, Gary Burton. "Freud and Clio: A Historiographical Inquiry into Psychohistory." North Texas State U., 1976. 313 pp. *DAI 1976 37(4): 2364-A.*

672. Saxton, Russell Steele. "Ethnocentrism in the Historical Literature of Territorial New Mexico." U. of New Mexico 1980. 504 pp. *DAI 1980 41(5): 2261-2262-A.* 8025036

673. Scriabine, Christine Brendel. "Upton Sinclair: Witness to History." Brown U. 1973. 207 pp. *DAI 1974 34(10): 6660-A.*

674. Searle, Howard Clair. "Early Mormon Historiography: Writing the History of the Mormons, 1830-1858." U. of California, Los Angeles 1979. 534 pp. *DAI 1980 40(10): 5562-A.*

675. Sexton, Robert Louis. "Regional Choice and Its Effect on Historical Interpretations in the Mid-nineteenth Century." U. of Colorado, Boulder 1980. 137 pp. *DAI 1981 41(8): 3677-A.* 8103135

676. Sharp, Edward Frank. "The Cold War Revisionists and Their Critics: An Appraisal." U. of North Carolina, Chapel Hill 1979. 291 pp. *DAI 1980 41(1): 395-A.* 8013995

677. Shi, David Emory. "Matthew Josephson: The Evolution of a Historian." U. of Virginia, 1976. 373 pp. *DAI 1977 37(10): 6708-A.*

678. Silva, Nelson Lehmann Da. "The 'Civil Religion' of the Modern State: A Historiographical Study." U. of California, Davis 1980. 178 pp. *DAI 1981 41(12): 5205-A.* DA8112020

679. Silver, Thomas Barton. "Prelude to an Interpretation: Coolidge and the Historians." Claremont Grad. School 1980. 195 pp. *DAI 1981 41(8): 3718-A.* 8103832

680. Simmons, Edward Gordon. *"Histoire Generale de Languedoc:* A Study of Maurist Historiography." Vanderbilt U. 1980. 241 pp. *DAI 1981 41(7): 3227-A.* DA8101686

681. Simpler, Steven Houston. "A Critical Analysis of the Church History Writings of Roland H. Bainton." Baylor U. 1981. 287 pp. *DAI 1981 42(4): 1681-A.* DA8120229

682. Sims, Amy R. "Those Who Stayed Behind: German Historians and the Third Reich." Cornell U. 1979. 429 pp. *DAI 1979 39(11): 6900-6901-A.* DA7910835

683. Siskron, Herbert Evans, Jr. "An Examination of Various Critical Models and Methods of Film Analysis with Accompanying Images and Interpretations of the American National Experience as Reflected in the American Film from 1893 to 1977: A Study in Philosophical Historiography with Emphasis on the Process of Validating Films as Primary Source Materials for Historical Research." U. of North Carolina, Chapel Hill 1977. 377 pp. *DAI 1977 38(6): 3686-A.*

684. Smith, John David. "The Formative Period of American Slave Historiography, 1890-1920." U. of Kentucky 1977. 488 pp. *DAI 1977 38(5): 3002-A.*

685. Smith, Larry Douglas. "The Historiography of the Origins of Anti-Missionism Examined in Light of Kentucky Baptist History." Southern Baptist Theological Seminary 1982. 268 pp. *DAI 1982 42(12): 5213-A.* DA8212717

686. Sommerbauer, L. H. "Konzeptanalyse des Geschichtsunterrichtes und der Schulhistoriographie in Österreich und Frankreich im 20. Jh., Untersucht am Beispiel der Darstellung des Barockzeitalters in der Lehrbüchern" [Analysis of concepts in history teaching and historiography in France and Austria in the 20th century: representation of the Baroque era in textbooks]. U. of Vienna [Austria] 261 pp. *DAI-C 1984 45(3): 666; 9/2716c.*

687. Spadafora, David Charles. "Recollection and Foresight: The Idea of Progress in High Eighteenth-Century Britain." Yale U. 1981. 540 pp. *DAI 1981 42(6): 2814-2815-A.* DA8125507

688. Spahn, Theodore Jurgen. "The Treatment of Six Controversial Topics in Selected General Encyclopedias." U. of Michigan 1979. 346 pp. *DAI 1980 40(10): 5233-A.* DA8007841

689. Speck, Beatrice F. "W. E. B. DuBois: A Historiographical Study." Texas Christian U. 1974. 291 pp. *DAI 1974 35(5): 2880-A.*

690. Staggenborg, Robert Gerard. *"New Literary History* and the Postmodern Paradigm: Implications for Theatre History." Louisiana State U. 1983. 176 pp. *DAI 1983 44(4): 913-A.* DA8318027

691. Staudenmaier, John M. "Design and Ambience: Historians and Technology: 1958-1977." U. of Pennsylvania 1980. 401 pp. *DAI 1981 41(10): 4479-A.* DA8107805

692. Stolz, E. "Die Interpretation der Modernen Welt bei Ernst Troeltsch. Zur Neuzeit- und Säkularisierungsproblematik" [Ernst Troeltsch's interpretation of the modern world: the problems of modernity and secularization]. University of Hamburg [West Germany] 1979. 519 pp. *DAI-C 1985 46(1): 52; 10/325c.*

693. Stuart, Bruce Wayne. "American Religious Historiography: William Warren Sweet, Perry Miller and Sidney E. Mead." U. of Minnesota 1984. 409 pp. *DAI 1984 45(5): 1434-A.* DA8418542

694. Sullivan, Jonathan Gray. "Perry Miller's *The New England Mind: From Colony to Province*: An Historiographic Study." Emory U. 1974. 259 pp. *DAI 1975 35(11): 7209-A.*

695. Taxel, Joel Arthur. "The Depiction of the American Revolution in Children's Fiction: A Study in the Sociology of School Knowledge." U. of Wisconsin, Madison 1980. 371 pp. *DAI 1981 41(9): 3868-A.* 8020586

696. Taylor, Antonia Magdalena. "Analisis del 'Discurso Historico' en Bernal Díaz del Castillo" [Analysis of the historical narrative in Bernal Díaz del Castillo]. City U. of New York 1982. 395 pp. *DAI 1982 43(5): 1568-A.* DA8222985

697. Thomas, Jack Douglas, Jr. "Interpretations of American Catholic Church History: A Comparative Analysis of Representative Catholic Historians, 1875-1975." Baylor U. 1976. 270 pp. *DAI 1977 38(1): 419-A.*

698. Tinsley, Barbara Sher. "Faithful and Reformed: The Life and Works of Florimond de Raemond (1540-1601)." Stanford U. 1983. 468 pp. *DAI 1983 44(5): 1546-A.* DA8320788

699. Toher, Martha Dimes. "The Lessons of the Past: Imagination and Narrative in Washington Irving's Histories." Duke U. 1984. 252 pp. *DAI 1985 45(8): 2529-2530-A.* DA8423968

700. Travis, Frederick Francis. "George Kennan and Russia, 1865-1905." Emory U. 1974. 511 pp. *DAI 1975 35(11): 7238-A.*

701. Übelhack, R. "Das Problem der Objektivität in der Geschichtswissenschaft" [The problem of objectivity in the science of history]. University of Erlangen-Nürnberg [West Germany] 1982. 274 pp. *DAI-C 1984 45(4): 954; 9/4003c.*

702. Urza, Carmelo. "Historia, Mito y Metafora en *La Saga/Fuga* de J. B. de Torrente Ballester" [History, myth, and metaphor in J. B. de Torrente Ballester's *Saga/Fuga*]. U. of Iowa 1981. 445 pp. *DAI 1982 42(11): 4824-A.* DA8210054

703. Uyenaka, Shuzo. "A Study of Baishoron: A Source for the Ideology of Imperial Loyalism in Medieval Japan." U. of Toronto [Canada] 1979. *DAI 1980 40(8): 4705-A.*

704. Vittoz, Stanley Herbert. "The American Industrial Economy and the Political Origins of Federal Labor Policy between the World Wars." York U. [Canada]. 1979. *DAI 1980 40(9): 5147-A.*

705. Vogt, Allen Roy. "'An Honest Fanatic': The Images of the Abolitionist in the Antebellum and Historical Minds." U. of Houston 1984. 423 pp. *DAI 1985 45(9): 2974-2975-A.* DA8428104

706. Wagner, Douglas H. "Marxism, Freudianism, and the Historian: A Study of the Methodological and Human Situations Current in Contemporary Historical Study." Fordham U. 1974. 268 pp. *DAI 1974 35(3): 1607-1608-A.*

707. Welliver, Edith Harriet Bean. "Lessing's Image of the Middle Ages." Washington U. 1982. 312 pp. *DAI 1983 43(12): 3926-A.* DA8310944

708. Williams, James Wayne. "The Indianapolis Police, 1820-1883: A Case Study of the Social Control Perspective in Recent Historiography." Indiana U. 1981. 206 pp. *DAI 1982 42(7): 3255-3256-A.* 8128053

709. Winterhager, F. "Der Bauernkrieg von 1525 in der Historischen Literatur: Positionen der Forschung vom Vormärz bis Heute" [The peasant war of 1525 in historical literature: research positions from the period of Vormärz to today]. Free University of Berlin [West Germany] 1979. 234 pp. *DAI-C 1984 45(4): 928; 9/3867c.*

710. Woodward, Michael Vaughan. "Ellis Merton Coulter and the Southern Historiographic Tradition." U. of Georgia 1982. 284 pp. *DAI 1982 43(1): 244-245-A.* DA8214313

711. Zamora, Margarita Montserrat. "Language and History in the *Comentarios Reales.*" Yale U. 1982. 190 pp. *DAI 1982 43(5): 1562-A.* DA8221771

712. Zantop, Susanne M. "'Vorarbeiten zu einer Geschichtsschreibung der Gegenwart': Heinrich Heines *Französische Zustände* und Mariano Jose de Larras *Articulos*" [Preliminary work on a historiography of the present: Heinrich Heine's *Französische Zustände* and Mariano José de Larra's *Articulos*]. Harvard U. 1984. 317 pp. *DAI 1985 45(12): 3633-A.* DA8503590

4. INDIVIDUAL HISTORIANS

713. Adams, Thomas R. STUART CAPEN SHERMAN. *Pro. of the Am. Antiquarian Soc. 1983 93(1): 51-54.* Sherman pursued books and whales during his diverse career. A professional librarian, Sherman also authored books on whaling and developed major collections in that area. His list of whaling logbooks will be published posthumously. He also had an interest in the history of printing, and developed collections and courses on that topic.
J. A. Andrew III

714. Afferica, Joan. ACADEMICIAN LEV VLADIMIROVICH CHEREPNIN, 1905-1977: IN MEMORIAM. *Slavic Rev. 1980 39(4): 633-668.* Traces the career of a major contributor to the advancement of Soviet historiography. Quotes extensively from his works and those of his colleagues. Based on journals, interviews, Soviet government sources; photo, 130 notes.
R. B. Mendel

715. Aktepe, M. Münir. VAK'A-NÜVİS AHMED LÜTFÎ EFENDİ VE TÂİHÎ HAKKINDA BÂZI BİLGİLER [The chronicler Ahmed Lütfî Efendi and some information regarding his *History*]. *Tarih Enstitüsü Dergisi [Turkey] 1979-80 10-11: 121-152.* Recounts the official career of Ahmed Lütfî Efendi (1816-1907), Ottoman court historian from 1865 until his death. Lütfî's official history covers the years 1825-76 and contains 15 volumes, of which seven were published during his lifetime and one after his death. Describes and gives the location of all 15 manuscript volumes and lists Lütfî's other works. 7 photos.
F. A. K. Yasamee

716. Al'bina, L. L. VOL'TER: ISTORIK V SVOEI BIBLIOTEKE [Voltaire: the historian in his library]. *Novaia i Noveishaia Istoriia [USSR] 1979 (2): 145-154.* After Voltaire's death Catherine II bought his personal library and transported it to St. Petersburg in 1779. About 28% of his books are historical. Voltaire's habit of writing marginalia in these books shed light on his scientific and creative method. Voltaire was very thorough in his research and his reactions to the ideas he read were often violent. 65 notes.
V. Sobeslavsky

717. Aldridge, A. Owen. PROBLEMS IN WRITING THE LIFE OF VOLTAIRE: PLURAL METHODS AND CONFLICTING EVIDENCE. *Biography 1978 1(1): 5-22.* Scholars have disagreed over whether emphasis should be placed on Voltaire's (1694-1778) ideas and writings or on his personal relations, particularly his humanitarian activities and unorthodox sex life. They disagree also on the weight which should be given to his statements about himself and to statements made by contemporaries in the form of published criticism, newspaper reports, and anecdotal reminiscences.
J

718. Almaş, Dumitru. CONCEPȚIA DESPRE REVOLUȚIE LA J. MICHELET [J. Michelet's concept of revolution]. *Analele Universității București: Istorie [Rumania] 1969 18(2): 55-64.* States that the French historian Jules Michelet (1798-1874) expressed his ideas on revolution in several of his works, including *Histoire de la Révolution Française.* His ideas were derived from his personal experience of the events of 1830 and 1848 and from polemics with theorists of the Restoration period. Michelet held an idealistic view of revolution, regarding it as a reincarnation of justice and equality, and considered that the French Revolution was inspired by the love of peace and mankind in general. He regarded revolution as a major step in the path towards liberty. The author considers Michelet's views an important influence on contemporary society. Secondary sources; 36 notes.
P. T. Herman

719. Amiantov, Iu. N. IZ ISTORII POISKOV LENINSKIKH TRUDOV [The history of Lenin's research work]. *Voprosy Istorii [USSR] 1970 (3): 101-111.* Discusses Soviet historiography on V. I. Lenin's works. After the October Revolution the Communist Party and Soviet government made Lenin's prerevolutionary and postrevolutionary works widely available. The publication of Lenin's collected works began in 1920. Manuscripts were collected by the Central Party Archive in Moscow and in Leningrad, from abroad as well as from within Russia. Valuable works on the subject include those by M. N. Pokrovski, Baturin, Martov, Gorev, and M. N. Tikhomirov. Based on the complete works of Lenin and secondary sources; 16 notes.
L. Smith

720. Andonov-Poljanski, Hristo. THE HISTORIOGRAPHIC THOUGHT OF BLAZHÉ KONESKI. *Macedonian Review [Yugoslavia] 1984 14(1): 88-95.* Examines the contribution to Macedonian historiography of the eminent scholar and writer Blazhe Koneski through his scholarly, literary, and poetic work.

721. Andonov-Poljanski, Hristo. ISTORIOGRAFSKATA MISLA NA EDVARD KARDELJ [The historiographical thought of Edvard Kardelj]. *Istorija [Yugoslavia] 1979 15(1): 45-52.* Analyzes the contribution made by the prominent Yugoslav political theorist Edvard Kardelj (1910-79) to historiography, particularly his writings on the historical aspects of Yugoslavia's national question.

722. Andonov Poljanski, Hristo. THE HISTORIOGRAPHIC THOUGHT OF BLAZHÉ KONESKI. *Macedonian Review [Yugoslavia] 1984 14(1): 88-95.* Examines the contribution to Macedonian historiography of the eminent scholar and writer Blazhé Koneski through his scholarly, literary, and poetic work.

723. Arab-Ogly, E. A. "ISSLEDOVANIE ISTORII." A. TOYNBEE V OTSENKE ZHURNALA "DIOGÈNE" [A. Toynbee's *A Study of History* as evaluated by the journal *Diogène*]. *Voprosy Filosofii [USSR] 1957 (2): 201-204.* Examines the June 1956 issue of the UNESCO journal *Diogène* which was entirely devoted to a discussion of Arnold Toynbee's *A Study of History* and which included an article by Toynbee himself.

724. Armbruster, Adolf. JOHANN FILSTICH UND SÜDOSTEUROPA [Johann Filstich and Southeast Europe]. *Rev. des Études Sud-Est Européennes [Romania] 1980 18(1): 47-61.* Johann Filstich and his contributions to the development of Romanian and Southeastern European historiography. 51 notes.
G. F. Jewsbury

725. Arnstein, Walter L. GEORGE MACAULAY TREVELYAN AND THE ART OF HISTORY: A CENTENARY REAPPRAISAL. *Midwest Q. 1976 18(1): 78-97.* George Macaulay Trevelyan (1876-1962) is often criticized for being a Whig historian, an English nationalist, a popular author, and a traditional historian in a period of new historical methods. His own historical interests were strongly influenced by his family and personal background. He did not view history as a science, but rather felt that its value lies in the educational processes involved in its study. The historian's primary responsibility is to combine the ability to reconstruct the story of human thoughts and actions with the ability to communicate this story to the widest audience possible. Trevelyan's own works, which are both scholarly and readable, support the ideas he advocated. Note, biblio.
S. J. Quinlan

726. Aston, B. W. RUPERT NORVAL RICHARDSON. *Great Plains J. 1979 18: 114-119.* Born in Texas in 1891, Rupert Norval Richardson's life "has been devoted to two areas of work, Hardin-Simmons University and regional history." He graduated from Hardin-Simmons in 1912 and returned in 1917 "to begin an employment" that spanned 61 years. He taught history and served in various administrative positions, including president (1945-53). His writing and continuous dedication to history has brought him numerous awards both in and outside the field. He has used his frontier traits "not only to become an outstanding historian, but also an outstanding citizen of his church, city, state and nation." From a special section on "Historians of the Southern Plains." 22 notes.
O. H. Zabel

727. Bailey, Thomas A. THE FRIENDLY RIVALS: BEMIS AND BAILEY. *Soc. for Hist. of Am. Foreign Relations. Newsletter 1979 10(1): 12-17.* Author recalls his career rivalry and professional friendship with Samuel Flagg Bemis, comparing their achievements in the field of diplomatic history, 1935-73.

728. Bailyn, Bernard. MORISON: AN APPRECIATION. *Massachusetts Hist. Soc. Pro. 1977 89: 112-123.* A personal memoir of historian Samuel Eliot Morison (1887-1976). A student and professor at Harvard for more than 40 years, Morison was a prolific author of the "old school," known for his narrative flair and his personalized, humanistic books. Based on the author's relationship with Morison, the recollections of Paul Buck, Oscar Handlin, John H. Parry, and the late Frederick Merk, and other material.
G. W. R. Ward

729. Bajcurová, Tamara. DEJINY VEL'LEJ OKTÓBROVEJ SO-CIALISTICKEJ REVOLÚCIE V METODOLOGICKEJ KONCEP-CII DR. J. SLAVÍKA [The history of the October Revolution in the methodological conception of Dr. J. Slavík]. *Slovanský Přehled [Czechoslovakia] 1982 68(6): 476-483.* The neo-Kantian historian of the 1920's and 1930's, J. Slavík, subjected the events of the October Revolution to an idealist analysis in the spirit of Tomáš Garrigue Masaryk (1850-1937), his mentor. He argued that Russia was not developed sufficiently to have any meaningful revolution, bourgeois or socialist. Under his influence a massive anti-Soviet propaganda campaign spread throughout the academic world of Czechoslovakia. An attempt to reedit and revive his work and ideas was made by the reactionary anti-Soviet forces in 1968-69. 40 notes.
B. Reinfeld

730. Ball, Terence. ON RE-READING ROUSSEAU AND HIS CRITICS. *Midwest Q. 1980 21(3): 333-346.* In the 200 years since his death, Jean Jacques Rousseau has been interpreted in various and contradictory ways. In the 18th and 19th centuries there was a tendency to compartmentalize his thought and to use it in support of a variety of sects and creeds. In the first third of the 20th century, Rousseau's thought was dealt with as a coherent whole and in a scholarly manner. After the rise of totalitarian regimes, however, Rousseau was incorrectly indicted as a precursor of totalitarianism, particularly by Jacob Talmon in *The Origins of Totalitarian Democracy* (1952). Critics who rejected Talmon's thesis have mistakenly identified Rousseau as a democrat.
M. E. Quinlivan

731. Barnes, James J. BANCROFT, MOTLEY, PARKMAN AND PRESCOTT: A STUDY OF THEIR SUCCESS AS HISTORIANS. *Literature and Hist. [Great Britain] 1977 (5): 55-72.* George Bancroft, John Lathorp Motley, Francis Parkman and William H. Prescott comprised the first distinct school of American historians to gain European recognition. They all turned to historical studies relatively late in lives after gaining affluence in other professions. They tended to specialize in their studies and were more concerned with archival study than is generally recognized. All of them were driven by an ambition to succeed as historians, and they measured success largely by their reception in Europe. Primary and secondary sources; 50 notes.
N. Dejevsky

732. Baz-Fotiade, Laura. RUMUNSKI IZSLEDVANIIA I OTZ-IVI ZA ZHIVOTA I TVORCHESTVOTO NA HRISTO BOTEV [Romanian research and reflections on the life and work of Khristo Botev]. *Istoricheski Pregled [Bulgaria] 1978 34(6): 84-98.* Surveys historical publications and celebrations in Romania in honor of Khristo Botev on the centenary of his birth in 1848, and reviews numerous books and articles on Botev.

733. Beattie, Margaret and Bogue, Allan G. PAUL W. GATES. *Great Plains J. 1979 18: 22-32.* No other historian has so intensively and extensively studied the American land disposal system and its implications. Paul W. Gates is author of nine books since the 1920's and numerous articles and reviews. Summarizes Gates's major works and presents his key themes. From a special section on "Historians of the Northern Plains." 25 notes, biblio.
O. H. Zabel

734. Bec, Christian. L'HISTORIOGRAPHIE BOURGEOISE À FLORENCE À LA FIN DU XVIᵉ SIECLE: GIULIANO DE RICCI [Urban historiography in Florence at the end of the 16th century: Giuliano de'Ricci]. *Rev. des Etudes Italiennes [France] 1974 20(3/4): 238-266.* Discusses the surviving writings of Giuliano de' Ricci (1543-1606), which reflect not only a courtier's view of Florence under the Medicis, but a somewhat more candid evaluation of other Italian writers. A grandson of Niccolò Machiavelli and independently wealthy, Ricci was able to devote his career to a succession of public offices while publishing a prolific series of works devoted to artistic, political, and religious criticism. Ironically, he failed to complete the one literary work with which he was charged by a Church Commission; the collection, editing, and publishing of the expurgated works of his grandfather Machiavelli. Research based largely upon Ricci's own published works and other published primary and secondary sources. 170 notes.
A. Blumberg

735. Behrendt, Lutz-Dieter; Laskowski, S.; and Ruckick, K. NEUE SOWJETISCHE ARBEITEN ÜBER LENIN ALS HISTO-RIKER [Recent Soviet works on Lenin as a historian]. *Zeitschrift für Geschichtswissenschaft [East Germany] 1970 18(3): 403-412.* Reviews about 70 new Soviet publications on Lenin's works on Russian and European history.

736. Belfiglio, Valentine J. THE CHRISTOPHER COLUMBUS OF AMERICAN STUDIES. *Italian Americana 1979 5(1): 37-46.* In 1924, Giovanni Schiavo wrote a history of Italian Americans in Chicago, which led to further histories of the American Revolution, the colonial period, individual Italians who contributed to American civilization, particular states, and the Mafia, 1924-62.

737. Bell, Whitfield J., Jr. LYMAN HENRY BUTTERFIELD. *Pro. of the Am. Antiquarian Soc. 1983 93(1): 47-51.* Butterfield was a historian, biographer, and the first editor-in-chief of *The Adams Papers.* He began his editorial career in 1944 at Franklin and Marshall College with the discovery of a hitherto unknown letter describing the beginning of that institution. This led him to work on the *Letters of Benjamin Rush, The Papers of Thomas Jefferson,* and finally to the directorship of the Institute of Early American History and Culture. He joined *The Adams Papers* staff in 1954. Twenty volumes later he retired, in 1975.
J. A. Andrew III

738. Berges, Wilhelm. REDEN ZUM 70. UND 80. GE-BURTSTAG VON HANS HERZFELD. AUS DEM NACHLASS HERAUSGEGEBEN VON DIETRICH KURZE [Addresses commemorating the 70th and 80th birthdays of Hans Herzfeld: edited by Dietrich Kurze from the written legacy of Hans Herzfeld]. *Jahrbuch für die Gesch. Mittel- und Ostdeutschlands [West Germany] 1983 32: 93-107.* The phases of Hans Herzfeld's life (1892-1917, 1917-33, 1933-45, and post-1945) coincide with and reflect epochal periods in German history. Finding meaning for the political and social shifts of his times, Hans Herzfeld did not despair but recorded and assessed them. He labored well into the post-World War II period to reevaluate his earlier findings on bourgeois liberalism, on questions relating to World War I, and on issues of militarism and democracy. Tolerant of the opinions of others, beloved teacher, prolific author, researcher, and administrator, Hans Herzfeld continued his numerous pursuits well after retirement, easing the way for many both at home and abroad who found his work exemplary and worthy of emulation. Based on the writings of Hans Herzfeld; 15 notes.
S. A. Welisch

739. Berindei, Dan. EUDOXIU HURMUZAKI ŞI ISTORIOGRA-FIA EPOCII SALE [Eudoxiu Hurmuzaki and contemporary historiography]. *Rev. Arhivelor [Romania] 1974 36(4): 516-520.* Traces the work of the Romanian historian E. Hurmuzaki (1812-74) in collecting and publishing documents and emphasizes the novelty of his approach.

740. Biagianti, Ivo. POLITICI E STORICI DEL CINQUECEN-TO: FILIPPO DE' NERLI (1485-1556) [Sixteenth-century politicians and historians: Filippo de' Nerli (1485-1556)]. *Archivio Storico Italiano [Italy] 1975 133(1-4): 45-100.* A biography and a survey of the historiography concerning the Florentine historian

Filippo de' Nerli (1485-1556), a disciple of Machiavelli and a follower of the Medicis. Filippo de' Nerli wrote his *Commentaries* on the history of Florence from 1215 to 1556. Based on archival and secondary sources; 169 notes. Article to be continued.

A. Canavero

741. Bizzocchi, Roberto. NON TOCCA LA NOSTRA TERRA LEWIS NAMIER D'INGHILTERRA [Lewis Namier of England does not touch our land]. *Belfagor [Italy] 1982 37(2): 220-223.* The British historian of the 18th century, who has analyzed forms of aggregation and consensus in the ruling class, deserves to be better known in Italy.

742. Black, J. L. INTERPRETATIONS OF POLAND IN NINETEENTH CENTURY RUSSIAN NATIONALIST-CONSERVATIVE HISTORIOGRAPHY. *Polish Rev. 1972 17(4): 20-41.* Examines three anti-Polish Russian historians of the 19th century who wrote on the 1772 and 1793 partitions of Poland: Nikolai Karamzin (1766-1826), Mikhail Pogodin (1800-1875), and Sergei Soloviëv (1820-1879).

743. Black, Pamela M. LAURENCE NOWELL'S "DISAPPEARANCE" IN GERMANY AND ITS BEARING ON THE WHEREABOUTS OF HIS COLLECTANEA 1568-1572. *English Hist. Rev. [Great Britain] 1977 92(363): 345-353.* Refutes the assumption that Laurence Nowell's literary and historical writings ceased because of a lack of interest. Rather, his four and one-half year absence on the Continent restrained his output. The author discusses new documentation consisting of a petition to the Court of Requests by Nowell's heirs and an answer by William Lambarde, Nowell's friend and the caretaker of his goods and chattels. Nowell's books and manuscripts were not bequeathed to Lambarde in 1568. Intending to return, Nowell had left the materials in Lambarde's hands for safekeeping. Rather than a lack of "humour to continue," Nowell went to the continent to "broaden his knowledge" and "to augment his collection of historical material." The projected material was destined for Holinshed's *Chronicles.* Based on the documents from the Court of Requests and the Court of Chancery, Robin Flower's 1935 article in the *Proceedings of the British Academy,* and manuscripts in the library at Corpus Christi College, Cambridge; 17 notes.

R. J. Gromen

744. Bogue, Allan G. FREDERICK JACKSON TURNER: HISTORIAN, SCHOLAR, TEACHER; AN ESSAY REVIEW. *Pacific Northwest Q. 1973 64(4): 175-177.* Reviews Ray Allen Billington's *Frederick Jackson Turner: Historian, Scholar, Teacher* (New York: Oxford U. Press, 1973). A well-written and carefully reasoned account of the life of a many-sided academic leader. Outlines the development and professional impact of his ideas, especially his frontier thesis. Turner's ideas challenge historians to develop and test adequate conceptual tools for understanding frontier processes and sectional interaction.

R. V. Ritter

745. Boia, Lucian. ACTIVITATEA ISTORIOGRAFICĂ A LUI EUDOXIU HURMUZAKI [Eudoxiu Hurmuzaki's historical writings]. *Rev. Arhivelor [Romania] 1974 36(4): 521-525.* Summarizes E. Hurmuzaki's posthumous *Fragmente zur Geschichte der Rumänen,* and draws attention to the book's originality.

746. Bolognani, Bonifacio. INCONTRO DELL'EUROPA CON LA CINA NEL SECOLO XVII: MARTINO MARTINI [Meeting of Europe and China in the 17th century: Martino Martini]. *Mondo Cinese [Italy] 1978 6(2): 121-140.* Martino Martini occupies the first place among writers who dedicated themselves to the study of Chinese history and geography in the 17th century. It is to Martini's credit that he laid the foundations for a cultural meeting between Europe and China: with his works on Chinese history and geography, *De Bello Tartarico, Sinicae Historie decas Prima, Novus Atlas Sinensis,* he occupies a very important place in the field of historiography and cartography.

J

747. Bourke, Paul. POLITICS AND IDEAS: THE WORK OF RICHARD HOFSTADTER. *Hist. Studies [Australia] 1976 17(67): 210-218.* A review article which analyzes the work and influence of the late Richard Hofstadter. *The Hofstadter Aegis,* edited by S.

Elkins and E. McKitrick (New York, 1974), is a tribute to Hofstadter in the form of a collection of essays on a variety of historical subjects by 11 of his students. Examines Hofstadter's concern for the historical and contemporary role of intellectuals, his search for a new approach to political analysis, his intellectual role, the consequences of his work, and his appeal outside the United States. Secondary sources; 8 notes.

R. G. Neville

748. Boyer, John W. A. J. P. TAYLOR AND THE ART OF MODERN HISTORY. *J. of Modern Hist. 1977 49(1): 40-72.* Examines the influences on British historian A. J. P. Taylor, including his mentors Alfred F. Pribham and Lewis Namier, and the work which Taylor did in both German and British historiography, 1930's-70's. Assesses Taylor's particular style in terms of his personal prejudices and his tendency to accept history not only as interpretation but also as a subjective cultural experience.

G. A. Hewlett

749. Briceño Perozo, Mario. HOMENAJE AL HERMANO NECTARIO MARÍA. EL MAESTRO NECTARIO MARÍA [Homage to Brother Nectario María: the teacher Nectario María]. *Bol. de la Acad. Nac. de la Hist. [Venezuela] 1976 59(236): 655-662.* Testimonial to Christian Brother Nectario María (b. 1896), who is a prelate, educator, and teacher of history, geography, geology, and mineralogy. He also enjoys baseball and has been a major figure in popularizing the sport. As a scholar he has worked with North American archaeologists on pre-Columbian and prehistoric ruins, written a major Venezuelan historical work used in primary schools, produced over seven local and regional histories, and copied thousands of documents relating to Venezuela housed in the Archivo General de las Indias in Spain. The Brother's words of thanks follow. 2 notes.

J. R. Grusin

750. Briggs, Asa. REVIEW ESSAY: GEORGE MACAULEY TREVELYAN. *Hist. and Theory 1981 20(3): 344-352.* Reviews Mary Moorman's *George Macauley Trevelyan* (1980). Moorman, Trevelyan's daughter, is more concerned with the historian's life before 1918 than with a developmental assessment of his work. Trevelyan is the prime 20th-century exponent of what Herbert Butterfield has termed the Whig interpretation of history. The emphasis is on his observations on 20th-century events rather than on historiography. The most interesting sections deal with Trevelyan's initiation into the profession. Attention is also directed toward his idea that historiography—Whiggish or otherwise—should appeal and instruct a large public. He had an interest in social as well as parliamentary history. 20 notes.

W. J. Reedy

751. Brown, Elizabeth A. R. HENRI PIRENNE: A BIOGRAPHICAL AND INTELLECTUAL STUDY. *Hist. & Theory 1976 15(1): 66-76.* Review essay on Bryce Lyon, *Henri Pirenne: A Biographical and Intellectual Study* (Ghent: E. Story-Scientia, 1974). Ironically at a time when the New History, which envisions individuals as powerless, is flourishing, so is biography. And it is even more ironic that the first massive biography should be written about Henri Pirenne (1862-1935), "a man who decried history which was too constricted, too much like biography." Yet there is justification for the appearance of this first extensive study of Pirenne, "because of the wealth of material he left behind," which was carefully cataloged by his son Jacques, and "because of the influence his particular kind of history" had during and after his lifetime. But Lyon's work is deficient in criticism and simplifies the immense complexity of his subject. 55 notes.

D. A. Yanchisin

752. Brown, Ronald C. A DEDICATION TO THE MEMORY OF FRED A. SHANNON, 1892-1963. *Arizona and the West 1978 20(1): 1-4.* Fred Albert Shannon (1892-1963) was educated at state universities in Indiana and Iowa. His published doctoral dissertation on the Civil War won the Pulitzer and Winsor prizes. He taught in public schools in Indiana, at colleges in Iowa and Kansas, and for two decades at the University of Illinois. His principal contribution to Western history was to force reconsideration of conventional theories and illusions such as the "safety valve" thesis. He believed that industrial and urban forces were more important than the frontier in molding American history. His standards of research and in-

terpretation were high, and his uncompromising assaults on the scholarship of others kept him in the center of controversy. Illus., biblio.

D. L. Smith

753. Bruhat, Jean. ALBERT SOBOUL (1914-1982) [Albert Soboul (1914-82)]. *Rev. d'Hist. Moderne et Contemporaine [France] 1982 29(Oct-Dec): 673-679.* A tribute to Albert Soboul (1914-82), assessing his importance in the historiography of the French Revolution. While interested in all aspects of the Revolution, his enthusiasm and scientific approach came together best when discussing the *sansculottes* of Paris and the events of the Year II. Although characterized by both a concrete explanation of events and a desire for theorization, his approach was not schematic. Many of the criticisms of his work have been based on a superficial reading of it. In addition, his membership in the French Communist Party prevented full justice being done to his scholarship in some quarters. 22 notes.

D. J. Nicholls

754. Bucher, Henry H. CANONIZATION BY REPETITION: PAUL DU CHAILLU IN HISTORIOGRAPHY. *Rev. Française d'Hist. d'Outre-mer [France] 1979 66(1-2): 15-32.* An examination of the career of French explorer Paul Du Chaillu (1831-1903), which challenges many of the generally accepted beliefs about him and examines the contemporary controversies surrounding his discoveries. Based on contemporary periodicals; illus., 95 notes.

D. G. Law

755. Buganov, V. I. SOVETSKAIA LITERATURA O PRIE-MAKH RABOTY V. I. LENINA S ISTOCHNIKAMI [Soviet literature on V. I. Lenin's approach to his sources]. *Voprosy Istorii [USSR] 1970 (9): 129-136.* Lenin's writings are distinguished by the wealth of sources he used and his experience in using documentary evidence is of considerable significance. The author reviews the literature on Lenin's treatment of statistical sources and finds that some works appeared during Lenin's lifetime. Interest in this aspect of scholarship grew in the 1930's but a voluminous literature did not appear until the 1960's. 43 notes.

V. Sobeslavsky

756. Butts, Francis T. THE MYTH OF PERRY MILLER. *Am. Hist. Rev. 1982 87(3): 665-694.* Seeks to rehabilitate the reputation of Perry Miller as a historian of American Puritanism. Revisionist discussion of his work is based on a "misleading caricature," and as a result his critics have failed to appreciate his philosophical assumptions, "contesting figments of their own imaginations and not the reality of Miller's history." The unacknowledged consequence of this revisionism has been to reinforce Miller's scholarship. "Without grasping his philosophical premises, the revisionists have accepted and amplified many of his particular themes," but they mistakenly stress his themes of stasis, resistance to change, and decline, while ignoring his equally prominent themes of transformation, growth, and advance. 88 notes.

R. Schlesinger

757. Cacciatore, Giuseppe. DILTHEY E LA STORIOGRAFIA TEDESCA DEL OTTOCENTO [Dilthey and 19th-century German historiography]. *Studi Storici [Italy] 1983 24(1-2): 55-89.* Wilhelm Dilthey (1833-1911) believed that German scholarship in the 19th century founded and shaped universal historiography. Dilthey's main views on historiography and the main representatives of the German movement, who, in his opinion, had emancipated historical science and consciousness, are examined. 100 notes.

J. V. Coutinho

758. Cadoni, Giorgio. NOTE MACHIAVELLIANE [Notes on Machiavelli]. *Storia e Pol. [Italy] 1983 22(1): 138-152.* Continued from an earlier article. In 1979 Mario Martelli supposed that the 26 chapters of Machiavelli's *Principe* were written in two different periods, in 1513 and 1518. This theory was renewed by Martelli in 1981 ("La Struttura Deformata," *Studi di Filologia Italiana,* 1981 39: 77-116) but refuted by Gennaro Sasso and more recently by Giorgio Inglese ("De Principatibus Mixtis," *Cultura,* 1982 20: 276-301). Cadoni accepts nearly all the remarks of the latter, underlining Martelli's incongruities. Secondary sources; 21 notes.

A. Canavero

759. Carpenter, Ronald H. CARL BECKER AND THE EPI-GRAMMATIC FORCE OF STYLE IN HISTORY. *Communication Monographs 1981 48(4): 318-339.* Discusses the academic career of Carl Becker in the early 20th century, focusing on his epigrammatic style, which was prominent in his popular history works, especially in his essay, *Kansas* (1910), and in his high school textbook, *Modern History* (1931), and on Becker's influence on later American historiography.

760. Casanuovi, Gian Luca. MATERIALISMO E STORIOGRA-FIA IN CROCE NEGLI ANNI 1896-1897 [Historical materialism and historiography in Croce, 1896-97]. *Archivio Storico Italiano [Italy] 1977 135(1-2): 3-100.* Benedetto Croce (1866-1952) was not a philosopher by profession, but a historian. His philosophical research arose from the necessity of clearing up some actual problems met in his historiographical work. In this period of his life, Croce was not an orthodox Marxist; he only accepted some Marxist premises for his historiographical writings. Based on Croce's works; 107 notes.

A. Canavero

761. Cedronio, Marina. CROCE, GENTILE, LA STORIA E LE SCIENZE SOCIALI [Croce, Gentile, history, and the social sciences]. *Mélanges de l'École Française de Rome. Moyen Age-Temps Modernes [Italy] 1981 93(1): 361-400.* Benedetto Croce and Giovanni Gentile were opposed to the spirit of the *Annales* school; their attitude was founded on their conception of the social sciences and illustrates the difference between French and Italian historiography.

762. Cherepnin, L. V. AKADEMIK MIKHAIL MIKHAILOVICH BOGOSLOVSKII [Academician Mikhail Mikhailovich Bogoslovskii]. *Istoricheskie Zapiski Akademii Nauk SSR [USSR] 1974 (93): 223-271.* Professor of Russian history at Moscow University since 1911 and member of the Academy of Sciences of the USSR since 1926, Mikhail M. Bogoslovskii (1867-1929) continued the historiographical tradition of Vasilii O. Kliuchevskii (1842-1911) and was one of the best representatives of Russian bourgeois historiography. Although not a Marxist he contributed to the development of historical scholarship in the Soviet Union. His most important works include *Oblastnaia reforma Petra Velikogo: Provintsiia 1719-1727 gg.* [The regional reform of Peter the Great: The Province, 1719-27] (Moscow: 1902); *Zemskoe samoupravlenie na russkom severe v XVII v.* [Local self government in the Russian north in the 17th century] (2 vols.; Moscow: 1909-12,); and the unfinished *Petr I: Materialy dlia biografii* [Peter I: Materials for a biography] (5 vols.; Moscow: 1940-48). Based on Bogoslovskii's papers in various Soviet archives and on his published works; 229 notes.

J. C. Mills, Jr.

763. Cochrane, Eric. CAESAR BARONIUS AND THE COUNT-ER-REFORMATION. *Catholic Hist. Rev. 1980 66(1): 53-58.* Report on the findings of a conference on the life and works of Catholic historian Caesar Baronius (1538-1607). The historical perspectives of his contemporaries seem not to have touched him too deeply; his political and historical assumptions were often decidedly dated. Baronius did not place truth at the head of his historical legion, but rather effectiveness. He remains interesting because, despite his faults, his works helped launch a completely new way of viewing, and an end of Renaissance learning as a consequence of the Counter-Reformation.

V. L. Human

764. Cochrane, Eric. CESARE BARONIO E LA CONTRORI-FORMA [Caesar Baronius and the Counter-Reformation]. *Studi Storici [Italy] 1979 20(4): 927-932.* Analyzes the presentations made at the conference on the theme, "Baronio the historian, and the Counterreformation," held at Sora, Italy, 6-10 October 1979. The conference considered all aspects of the life and work of the 16th-century writer who was influential in the Counter-Reformation. Primary sources.

E. E. Ryan

765. Cohen, Mendel F. INCOMPLETENESS AND CONTEXTU-AL IMPLICATION IN HISTORY. *Clio 1983 12(3): 261-274.* Histories are necessarily subjective accounts of the past and do not follow fixed criteria that guide the historian in choosing facts or statements for his work. The historian depends on his own values

to determine the form and content of the history he writes. But the historian cannot control the contextual references or implications a reader may find in his work. 9 notes. T. P. Linkfield

766. Colbert, Thomas B. JAMES C. MALIN. *Great Plains J. 1979 18: 48-54.* Born in 1893 and educated at Baker University and the University of Kansas, James C. Malin taught at the latter from 1921 to 1964. Insisting upon the uniqueness of individuals and events and attacking historical relativism, he authored some 16 books, most of which dealt with state and local history and particularly with Kansas and the northern Great Plains of which he is one of the foremost historians. From a special section on "Historians of the Northern Plains." 18 notes. O. H. Zabel

767. Comanducci, Paolo. MABLY NELLA RECENTE STORIOGRAFIA [Mably in recent historiography]. *Pensiero Pol. [Italy] 1975 8(2): 219-230.* Suggests that Gabriel Bonnet de Mably's (1709-85) fame as a revolutionary is not entirely merited. At the turn of the 19th century, the bourgeoisie sought to polemicize the fragments in Mably's works that can be interpreted as antibourgeois and communist. At the same time, followers of Babeuf sought to glorify those same fragments. Not until the end of World War II was Mably's thought reconsidered in its entirety. Although elements of communist utopian thought are present in his writings, there are many other references to moderation and gradualism and defenses of monarchy. Based on Mably's writings and other secondary sources; 42 notes. M. T. Wilson

768. Comte, Bernard. FRANÇOIS DELPECH (1935-1982) [François Delpech (1935-82)]. *Cahiers d'Hist. [France] 1982 27(1): 5-7.* François Delpech (1935-82), assistant professor at the University of Lyons and director of the U.E.R. des Sciences Historiques et Géographiques, Art et Environnement. Highlights the career of this noted French historian of religions, emphasizing his contribution to Jewish history and humanistic historical research. Note.

G. P. Cleyet

769. Congdon, Lee. HISTORY AND POLITICS IN HUNGARY: THE REHABILITATION OF OSZKÁR JÁSZI. *East European Q. 1975 9(3): 315-329.* Discusses how the changing political regimes after 1919 in Hungary affected the reputation of the historian and political activist, Oszkár Jászi. Jászi's radical ideas in the period just before and during World War I and his active participation in political life until Bela Kun's takeover in 1919 have made him a significant figure in Hungarian history. He was condemned by Horthy and the Stalinists but in the period 1945-48 and since the Hungarian revolution of 1956 his reputation has been rehabilitated. Even though he was not a Marxist, he was the first to face up to Hungary's most difficult problems, according to the most recent historical interpretation. Published sources; 57 notes. C. R. Lovin

770. Cooper, Thomas W. MCLUHAN AND INNIS: THE CANADIAN THEME OF BOUNDLESS EXPLORATION. *J. of Communication 1981 31(3): 153-161.* Discusses Canadian historian Harold Adams Innis's "three gifts" to Marshall McLuhan: "an example of social research which resembled modern art and would easily lend itself to the terms of contemporary art criticism"; a constant jump "from field to field and century to century so as to inspire McLuhan's employment of montage"; and his "foreign academic tongue which would enable McLuhan, through lively translation, to become Innis's best-known commentator," and compares and contrasts their writings on the role of communications in history; 1930's-70's.

771. Cornevin, R. ROBERT DELAVIGNETTE. *Bull. des Séances de l'Acad. Royale des Sci. d'Outre-Mer [Belgium] 1977 (1): 43-47.* This obituary for Robert Delavignette (1897-1976) describes his career in French colonial government, his role as director and governor of the École Nationale de la France d'Outre-Mer, and his contributions to African journalism, colonial historiography and African literature. Photo, biblio. R. O. Khan

772. Cronin, James. CREATING A MARXIST HISTORIOGRAPHY: THE CONTRIBUTION OF HOBSBAWM. *Radical Hist. Rev. 1979 (19): 87-109.* Discusses the work of English Marxist historian Eric J. Hobsbawm in an evaluation of his writings and his contribution to Marxist historiography.

773. Crowell, John C. PERRY MILLER AS HISTORIAN: A BIBLIOGRAPHY OF EVALUATIONS. *Bull. of Biblio. and Mag. Notes 1977 34(2): 77-85.* Includes reviews and evaluations of the historiography of Perry Miller, 1933-77.

774. Cunningham, Raymond J. THE GERMAN HISTORICAL WORLD OF HERBERT BAXTER ADAMS: 1874-1876. *J. of Am. Hist. 1981 68(2): 261-275.* Traces the postgraduate career of Herbert Baxter Adams as he pursued his doctorate at Heidelberg and Berlin Universities. Adams's training in German historical scholarship determined the direction and content of his professional approach in training historians at Johns Hopkins. In Germany Adams acquired a lifelong enthusiasm for *Kulturgeschichte.* 54 notes.

T. P. Linkfield

775. Daalder, H. STEIN ROKKAN: DALLO STUDIO DEL CASO NORVEGESE ALL'ANALISI COMPARATA [Stein Rokkan: from the Norwegian case to comparative analysis]. *Riv. Italiana di Scienza Pol. [Italy] 1980 10(3): 343-368.* Stein Rokkan (1921-79) has been one of the most well-known political scientists of our age, and the value of his contribution to the progress of comparative studies has been widely acknowledged. The author recalls Rokkan's life and work, underlining the salient aspects of his career in five sections: a brief biography, the cultural background, the research that brought him international fame, a characterization of his work and approach, and his remarkable intellectual legacy. J/S

776. Dalitz, R. H. and Stone, G. C. DOCTOR BERNARD CONNOR: PHYSICIAN TO KING JAN III SOBIESKI AND AUTHOR OF *THE HISTORY OF POLAND,* 1698. *Oxford Slavonic Papers [Great Britain] 1981 14: 14-35.* Irish emigrant Bernard Connor (1665?-98) was briefly appointed personal physician to King Jan III Sobieski of Poland in 1674. After his return to England, Connor published in 1698 his *History of Poland.* This work, the first of its kind in England and an important source both for the bibliography of Slavonic studies in Great Britain and for the history of 17th-century Poland, has been neglected. Accounts of and sources for Connor's life are here examined to correct previous errors. 105 notes, appendix. D. H. Murdoch

777. Danilov, A. I. S. D. SKAZKIN I NEKOTORYE VOPROSY ISTORIOGRAFICHESKOGO ANALIZA [S. D. Skazkin and certain aspects of historiographical analysis]. *Voprosy Istorii [USSR] 1974 (8): 3-9.* Examines the approach to historiographical problems manifested by academician S. D. Skazkin—one of the founders of the Soviet school of research in the history of the Middle Ages. Whatever aspect of research we take—the historiography of the West-European peasantry, the feudal state, the transition from the period of antiquity to the Middle Ages, the historiography of the Renaissance or the problem of land ownership in the French countryside of the 18th century—it is invariably characteristic of S. D. Skazkin to display a profound class analysis of historical phenomena, making it possible to trace their essence. At the same time, S. D. Skazkin always emphasized the class limitation of bourgeois historiography which determines its methodological nature and inevitably leads to idealism in interpreting the substance of the historical process. The young generation of Soviet researchers in medieval history must learn from S. D. Skazkin to use all the achievements of historical knowledge to advance in science, to carry on a consistent struggle against every departure from the methodology of Marxism-Leninism and against all varieties and manifestations of bourgeois ideology. J

778. Dascălu, Nicolae and Buşe, C. OPERA SCRISĂ A LUI NICOLAE TITULESCU ŞI LOCUL ACESTUIA ÎN ISTORIOGRAFIA CONTEMPORANĂ [The written works of Nicolae Titulescu and his place in contemporary historiography]. *Revista de Istorie [Romania] 1982 35(4): 483-510.* Examines all written material signed by Nicolae Titulescu including studies of civil law, speeches

and conferences, personal documents, original works in the political and juridical fields, and unpublished manuscripts. The rich historiography dedicated to Titulescu is also examined and shows his important contribution to the development of his country. Based on Nicolae Titulescu's writings and secondary sources; 153 notes, biblio. French summary.   P. D. Herman

779. deKay, Ormonde, Jr. OUR MOST POETIC CIVIL WAR HISTORIAN: A TALK WITH BRUCE CATTON. *Manuscripts 1977 29(3): 155-159.* Catton reflects on his writings about the Civil War, his use of manuscripts, his research assistant, his visits to historical sites, and his decision to write history. Illus.
                                                           D. A. Yanchisin

780. Devleeshouwer, Robert. ALBERT SOBOUL ET LA BELGIQUE [Albert Soboul and Belgium]. *Ann. Hist. de la Révolution Française [France] 1982 54(4): 572-574.* Examines Soboul's influence on Belgian historians.   R. Aldrich

781. Diószegi, István. ARATÓ ENDRE EMLÉKEZETE (1921-1977) [Remembrance of Endre Arató, 1921-77]. *Századok [Hungary] 1981 115(4): 820-825.* Tribute to Endre Arató, historian of Czechoslovakian history.   T. Kuner

782. Donnert, Erich. POKROVSKIJS STELLUNG IN DER SOWJETISCHEN GESCHICHTSWISSENSCHAFT [Pokrovski's position in Soviet historiography]. *Wissenschaftliche Zeitschrift der Friedrich-Schiller-Universität Jena. Gesellschafts- und Sprachwissenschaftliche Reihe [East Germany] 1963 12(1): 11-24.* Before the Russian Revolution, Mikhail N. Pokrovski (1868-1932) supported the theories of Nikolai Bukharin and Leon Trotsky in his historical works. In the 1920's Pikrovski's works on Russian history became the standard works of Russian Marxist-Leninist historiography, and were used as textbooks in schools. 67 notes.   R. Wagnleitner

783. Dorpalen, Andreas. HEINRICH VON TREITSCHKE. *J. of Contemporary Hist. [Great Britain] 1972 7(3/4): 21-35.* Analyzes the close relationship between the historical and political career of Heinrich von Treitschke (1834-96). Devoted to the idea of Prussian-led German unification, he propounded his views as a university lecturer, Reichstag deputy, and historian. Despite extensive research, his writings served as a tool for his political goal; to give historical backing and moral sanction to German nationalism. His anti-democratic, militaristic, anti-Semitic views were widely influential in Germany but illustrate his failure as an objective, scholarly historian. Primary and secondary sources; 25 notes.
                                                           B. A. Block

784. Dukes, Paul. RUSSIA AND MID-SEVENTEENTH CENTURY EUROPE: SOME COMMENTS ON THE WORK OF B. F. PORSHNEV. *European Studies Rev. [Great Britain] 1974 4(1): 81-88.* Considers the contributions of B. F. Porshnev to the comparative political and social history of 17th-century Europe and Russia.

785. Ekirch, Arthur A., Jr. REFLECTIONS ON PROBLEMS OF MILITARISM AND HISTORY IN TOLSTOY'S *WAR AND PEACE. Peace and Change 1982 8(4): 1-5.* Discusses Tolstoy's concern with major philosophical questions in his novel *War and Peace,* and his concern with issues regarding militarism and the recording of history.

786. Ekmečić, Milorad. SERGEJ ALEKSANDROVIČ NIKITIN (1901-1979) [Sergei Aleksandrovich Nikitin (1901-79)]. *Jugoslovenski Istorijski Časopis [Yugoslavia] 1979 18(1-2): 230-231.* Obituary of S. A. Nikitin, a Soviet historian and noted specialist on the history of the South Slavs. Nikitin was the author of two monographs on Russian-South Slav links of the 19th century, and edited works on Bulgarian and Yugoslav history.
                                                           F. A. K. Yasamee

787. Eley, Geoff et al. THE DAVID ABRAHAM CASE: TEN COMMENTS FROM HISTORIANS. *Radical History Review 1985 (32): 75-96.* Prints responses of 10 historians to the criticism aimed at Princeton Marxist historian David Abraham and his book, *The Collapse of the Weimar Republic* (1981). Weimar Germany histori-

an Henry Turner of Yale University is leading an attack against the book, which began with the questioning of the veracity of several documents. The debate has raised serious questions about academic politics and concerns over disagreements in interpretation becoming the basis for bitter feuding. 2 notes.   C. F. Howlett

788. Ellis, Richard N. ROBERT G. ATHEARN. *Great Plains J. 1979 18: 5-9.* Athearn was born in 1914 in Montana and trained as a historian at the University of Minnesota. He has taught at the University of Colorado since 1947. His impact on western history depends especially upon effective training of graduate students, numerous publications (which the article discusses), and his activities in the historical profession. From a section on "Historians of the Northern Plains."   O. H. Zabel

789. Elton, G. R. HERBERT BUTTERFIELD AND THE STUDY OF HISTORY. *Historical Journal [Great Britain] 1984 27(3): 729-743.* An assessment of Herbert Butterfield's contribution to the study of history. His writings were primarily devoted to historiography and to the question of the relationship between history and religion. He opened up several new territories and themes in his writings on the 18th century. Deficiencies in his understanding of history involved the treatment of source materials and historical evidence. He also failed to resolve the problem of reconciling history with Christian faith. In his wish to find in history an aid to influence the present he became a propagandist. 13 notes.
                                                           H.-J. Kaiser

790. Engel-Janosi, Friedrich. VOM ANFANG DER GESCHICHTE: SIGMUND FREUD, MIRCEA ELIADE, ARNOLD J. TOYNBEE [The beginning of history: Sigmund Freud, Mircea Eliade, Arnold J. Toynbee]. *Wiener Beiträge zur Geschichte der Neuzeit [Austria] 1974 1: 13-27.* Examines the writings of Sigmund Freud, 1912-30, Mircea Eliade, ca. 1950's, and Arnold J. Toynbee, ca. 1930-50, which contain their ideas on the origins of history.

791. Erickson, Ann K. E. V. TARLE: THE CAREER OF A HISTORIAN UNDER THE SOVIET REGIME. *Am. Slavic and East European Rev. 1960 19(2): 202-216.* Soviet historian Evgeni Tarle (1875-1952) resolutely followed Communist Party edicts on historiography, reinterpreting events, sometimes as many as three times, in accordance with changing Party attitudes, 1936-52.

792. Erofeev, N. A. LEWIS NAMIER AND HIS PLACE IN BOURGEOIS HISTORIOGRAPHY. *Soviet Studies in Hist. 1976-1977 15(3): 26-50.* Reviews the career and contributions of Polish-born British historian Lewis Namier (1888-1960). Namier was essentially a conservative and an apologist for the British establishment, though he did much to discredit the traditional Whig interpretation of British history.

793. Eyice, Semavi. J. VON HAMMER-PURGSTALL VE SEYAHATNÂMELERİ: HAMMER'İN TARİHİCOĞRAFYA, TOPOĞRAFYA VE SANAT TARİHİNE HİZMETİ [J. von Hammer-Purgstall and his travel accounts: his historiography, topography, and skill in historical work]. *Belleten [Turkey] 1982 46(183): 535-550.* Josef von Hammer-Purgstall (1774-1856), Austrian diplomat, traveller, and historian, published his principal works between 1811 and 1836, covering mainly the Balkans, the Levant, and Constantinople. He wrote his memoirs between 1841 and 1852, a condensation of which was published in Vienna in 1940. His skilled research, linguistic knowledge, and speed of work far outweigh any errors in his contributions to the scientific knowledge of the history, geography, and topography of an area then little-known to Europeans. Based on a paper given in March 1982 at a seminar on Josef von Hammer-Purgstall organized by the Faculty of History, University of İstanbul; 8 plates, 44 notes.   J. P. H. Myers

794. Faulk, Odie B. SEYMOUR V. "IKE" CONNOR. *Great Plains J. 1979 18: 72-78.* Seymour V. Connor (b. 1923) entered the University of Texas in 1940 to study mechanical engineering. After service in World War II he took an M.A. in English (1948) and a Ph.D. in History (1952). He was Texas state archivist for a time, but most of his teaching career has been at Texas Tech University.

He has written and edited numerous books on the Southwest always insisting upon accuracy and readable prose. From a special section on "Historians of the Southern Plains." O. H. Zabel

795. Fearnley-Sander, Mary. WILLIAM ROSCOE, HISTORIAN. *Clio 1981 10(2): 183-198.* Explores the incongruity between the admiration for the Medici family of Renaissance Florence and the devotion to the cause of the French Revolution by the British historian William Roscoe (1753-1831). The lesson he derived from the French Revolution was emancipation of the mind, and Roscoe emphasized a parallel development during the Reformation and the Italian Renaissance in two works, *The Life of Lorenzo de' Medici* (1796) and *The Life and Pontificate of Leo X* (1805). 30 notes. T. P. Linkfield

796. Ferriss, William H. FREDERICK JACKSON TURNER AND HIS PRESENTISM. *Pro. and Papers of the Georgia Assoc. of Hist. 1982: 113-122.* Frederick Jackson Turner is often considered preeminent among American historians, but his obsession with the present often made it impossible to write history books, even in order to fulfill publishers' contracts. He supported US imperialism as manifest destiny. Much of his history is either patriotic myth or outright propaganda. 46 notes. R. Grove

797. Fine, John V. A., Jr. and Kleimola, A. M., ed. STUDIES IN EARLY MODERN RUSSIAN HISTORY AND LITERATURE IN HONOR OF THE SIXTIETH BIRTHDAY OF H. W. DEWEY. *Russian Hist. 1980 7(1-2): 1-10.*
Fine, John V. A., Jr.; Kleimola, A. M.; and Challis, Natalia. AN APPRECIATION, pp. 1-3. Reviews the academic career of Horace William Dewey and his influence on students and Russian historical and literary studies.
Fine, John V. A., Jr. and Kleimola, A. M. H. W. DEWEY: PUBLISHED WORKS, pp. 4-10. Lists year by year the 86 publications by H. W. Dewey from 1956 to 1979. G. E. Munro

798. Fishbone, Jonathan D. JOHANN JAKOB BACHOFEN AS AN HISTORICAL THEORIST. *Continuity 1983 (7): 77-97.* Although Johann Jakob Bachofen (1815-87) is now known mostly for his theory of matriarchy as propounded in *Das Mutterrecht* (1861), he also wrote an essay entitled *Die Grundgesetze der Volkersentwicklung und der Historiographie* (1864) which discussed the value of historical knowledge for understanding culture. In it Bachofen took issue with the methodology of contemporary German classical scholarship and argued instead for investigation into its religious foundations. He especially distrusted positivism and its obsession with facts. W. A. Wiegand

799. Floto, Inga. 60'ERNES DILEMMA: NOGET OM AT SKRIVE HISTORIE [The dilemma of the 60's: something about writing history]. *Fortid og Nutid [Denmark] 1976 26(3): 379-389.* Presents and applies the theories of Gene Wise, Thomas Kuhn, and Kenneth Burke on Danish contemporary historical research. 13 notes. A. Erlandson

800. Fontaine, P. F. M. KASPAR PEUCER: DE VOORTZETTER VAN MELANCHTON'S GESCHIEDWERK [Kaspar Peucer: successor to Melanchthon's historical work]. *Kleio [Netherlands] 1979 20(9): 398-406.* Discusses the life and work of Kaspar Peucer (1525-1602), pupil and son-in-law of Philipp Melanchthon (1497-1560) whose *Chronicon Carionis Philippicum* he continued to the period of Emperor Charles V. Born in Silesia, Peucer studied mathematics and medicine at Wittenberg University, became its rector 1560-68, and court physician to the elector of Saxony. Imprisoned in 1574 for crypto-Calvinist activities, he was released and banished 1586. Peucer's historical outlook is closer than Melanchthon's to modern historiography, with its differentiation between religious and secular history and emphasis on politics. He concentrates narrowly on German history and antipopish polemics. Primary sources; 13 notes. G. Herritt

801. Fox, Edward Whiting. HISTORY AND MR. TOYNBEE. *Virginia Q. Rev. 1960 36(3): 458-468.* Proposes that Arnold J. Toynbee's contributions to historiography were assigning history the task of being a study of human experience, justifying history as a search for meaningful uniformities in the development of human societies, and determining the base of history to be theodicy.

802. Freiberg, Malcolm. STEWART MITCHELL. *Massachusetts Hist. Soc. Pro. 1957-60 72: 361-363.* Memorium dedicated to Stewart Mitchell (1892-1957), American historical editor and Director of the Massachusetts Historical Society.

803. Freidel, Frank. FREDERICK MERK. *Massachusetts Hist. Soc. Pro. 1977 89: 181-183.* A memoir of Frederick Merk (1887-1977), Gurney Professor of History and Political Science emeritus at Harvard University, and a renowned historian of the westward movement. After graduation from the University of Wisconsin in 1911, Frederick Merk studied and taught at Harvard with Frederick Jackson Turner and others. Frederick Merk retired from teaching in 1957 and published six volumes during his last two decades. His *History of the Western Movement,* the culmination of his life's work, appeared posthumously in 1978. Based on the author's personal relationship with Frederick Merk, and on unpublished and published material. G. W. R. Ward

804. Friedman, Lawrence and Shaffer, Arthur H. DAVID RAMSAY AND THE QUEST FOR AN AMERICAN HISTORICAL IDENTITY. *Southern Q. 1976 14(4): 351-371.* Examines the life and literary efforts of American historian David Ramsay. His attitudes and philosophies are accounted for. Concludes that he assisted in the development of the nationalist school of writing. Time and circumstances were responsible for this. 37 notes. R. W. Dubay

805. Friguglietti, James. LES ETATS-UNIS DANS LA PENSEE HISTORIQUE D'ALBERT MATHIEZ [The United States in the historical thought of Albert Mathiez]. *Ann. Hist. de la Révolution Française [France] 1982 54(4): 640-653.* Mathiez enjoyed great influence among American historians for his works on the French Revolution. He was also interested in the history and economy of the United States, although he frequently criticized the American government and its politics. 36 notes. R. Aldrich

806. Fuks-Mansfeld, R. G. DAVID FRANCO MENDES ALS GESCHIEDSCHRIJVER [David Franco Mendes as historian]. *Studia Rosenthaliana [Netherlands] 1980 14(1): 29-43.* Surveys the work of David Franco Mendes (1713-92), Hebrew poet and historian.

807. Gadzhiev, K. S. K KRITIKE ODNOI BURZHUAZNOĬ KONTSEPTSII ISTORII SSHA [Towards a criticism of one bourgeois conception of U. S. history]. *Novaia i Noveishaia Istoriia [USSR] 1975 (4): 164-181.* Attacks the ideology of Arthur M. Schlesinger, Jr. as the author of the doctrine of *Realpolitik* in the 1960's. Describes Schlesinger's life and the development of his ideas. Discusses his interpretation of American history and the American economic system. Surveys Schlesinger's published writings. His political views from the 1950's until after the Watergate Affair reflect the contradictions of the American scene. Primary and secondary sources; 74 notes. E. R. Sicher

808. Gagné, Suzanne. LIONEL GROULX: HISTORIEN D'HIER OU D'AUJOURDHUI [Lionel Groulx: a historian of the present or the past]. *Rev. d'Hist. de l'Amerique Française [Canada] 1978 32(3): 455-462.* The writings of Lionel Groulx (1878-1967), the prominent French Canadian historian, are still relevant. "They call people to freedom. Lionel Groulx was a great historian who understood the thoughts of the nation, an historian not only of yesterday but also of our time." 9 notes. M. R. Yerburgh

809. Galante Garrone, Alessandro. SALVEMINI E L'ILLUMINISMO [Salvemini and the Enlightenment]. *Ponte [Italy] 1981 37(5): 432-445.* Gaetano Salvemini was professor at Harvard and historian of the Enlightenment; traces the vicissitudes of his own rationalist historiography.

810. Garin, Eugenio; Vivarelli, Ann, transl. ERNESTO RAGIONIERI *J. of Modern Hist. 1980 52(1): 85-105.* Review essay of the intellectual development and historiography of Italian historian Ernesto Ragionieri (1926-75), his association with Gaetano Salvemini, Pasquale Villari, Carlo Morandi, and Luigi Einaudi, and the journal *Belfagor.* Translated from *Belfagor* 1978 33(3): 297-320; 24 notes.   S

811. Garlato, Francesco. NIEBUHR E LA STORIA DI ROMA [Niebuhr and the history of Rome]. *Nuova Antologia [Italy] 1969 507(2028): 507-528.* Barthold Niebuhr (1776-1831) was a German historian of Rome whose works were profoundly influenced by the times in which he lived; the themes and problems of his world enabled him to pinpoint Roman sociopolitical achievements.

812. Garrett, Wendell D. WALTER MUIR WHITEHILL. *Massachusetts Hist. Soc. Pro. 1978 90: 131-139.* An informal memoir of Walter Muir Whitehill (1906-78), a well-known figure in New England historical and historic preservation circles, a long-time member of the Massachusetts Historical Society, and Director and Librarian of the Boston Athenaeum for more than 25 years. Walter Whitehill was a prolific writer. Garrett utilizes four of his favorite books as springboards from which to remember Walter Whitehill's education, career, habits, and character. Based on an analysis of Walter Whitehill's writings, and the author's personal relationship with him.   G. W. R. Ward

813. Gavigan, Johannes. DER KLAGENFURTER JOHANNES VIDAL O. S. A. (1705-1795) [Johannes Vidal O. S. A. from Klagenfurt (1705-92)]. *Carinthia I [Austria] 1977 167: 69-83.* The Augustinian hermit-monk Johannes Vidal (1705-92) became librarian and historian of the Carinthian monastery of Völkermarkt, 1767-68, where he became famous as the author of a history of the monastery, 1256-1772.

814. Geldbach, Erich. FRIEDRICH LUDWIG JAHN: JUGENDHEILAND ODER BANAUSE? ZUR JAHN-INTERPRETATION DES 19. JAHRHUNDERTS [Friedrich Ludwig Jahn: savior of youth or philistine?, the Jahn interpretations of the 19th century]. *Stadion [West Germany] 1978 4(1): 168-187.* Discusses whether Friedrich Ludwig Jahn (1778-1852) really was an inspiring revolutionary or a misleading Philistine. Opinions throughout the 19th century differ considerably, but there can be no doubt that the strength of the aura surrounding Jahn provoked such extreme judgments. In the light of all the divergent opinions, preconceptions, and misjudgments, we must agree with the statement that "every generation will have its own Jahn." 61 notes.   M. Geyer

815. Georgescu, Valentin Al. RENOVATION DE VALEURS EUROPEENNES ET INNOVATIONS ROUMAINE CHEZ D. CANTEMIR: STATISTIQUE DESCRIPTIVE, ETHNOPSYCHOLOGIE, HISTOIRE DU DROIT, THEORIE DE L'IDEE IMPERIALE [Renewal of European values and Romanian innovations in D. Cantemir: descriptive statistics, ethnopsychology, history of law, and theory of the imperial idea]. *Rev. des Etudes Sud-Est Européennes [Romania] 1982 20(1): 3-23.* An analytic review of the personality, scholarship, and work of Dimitrie Cantemir (1673-1723), prince of Moldavia (1693; 1710-11). A pioneer in the cultural history of Moldavia, this famous historian left an important body of work dealing with history and various branches of the social and legal sciences. As the innovator behind the theory of "imperial principle," his thought and political actions were marked by a resistance to Ottoman authority. 60 notes.   G. P. Cleyet

816. Gerstein, Linda. IVANOV-RAZUMNIK: THE REMEMBRANCE OF THINGS PAST. *Can.-Am. Slavic Studies 1974 8(4): 532-538.* Razumnik Vasil'evich Ivanov, pen-name "Ivanov-Razumnik," was the great historian of the Russian intelligentsia. In his classic *History of Russian Social Thought* he defined the intelligentsia as an ethical category significant for its rejection of vulgar middle-class values. He saw the struggle for existence of the 20th-century Russian intelligentsia as a reflection and continuation of that of the 19th. In his search for meaning in the past he was the archetypical Russian *intelligent.* 13 notes.   G. E. Munro

817. Gibbs, William E. and Castle, Alfred L. MAURICE GARLAND FULTON: HISTORIAN OF NEW MEXICO AND THE SOUTHWEST. *New Mexico Hist. Rev. 1980 55(2): 121-138.* Relates the life and career of Maurice Garland Fulton (1877-1955) from 1922. In 1968, his work on the Lincoln County War was published. Fulton's historical reputation was enhanced by his editing of works on Theodore Roosevelt, Billy the Kid (William Bonney), and Josiah Gregg. As a regional historian Fulton made significant contributions to historical scholarship through his published works, which any serious history student of New Mexico and the Southwest must consult. Based on the Fulton Papers in the Special Collections Library of the University of Arizona, Tucson, Arizona, and other primary sources; 2 illus., 55 notes.   P. L. McLaughlin

818. Gieysztor, Aleksander. TADEUSZ MANTEUFFEL HISTORYK I OBYWATEL (1902-1970) [Tadeusz Manteuffel (1902-70): historian and citizen]. *Nauka Polska [Poland] 1981 29(3-4): 73-79.* Commemorates Polish historian Tadeusz Manteuffel, organizer of the Institute of History of the Polish Academy and author of influential studies in historiography.

819. Giguère, Georges-Émile. LIONEL GROULX: BILAN D'APPRÉCIATIONS [Lionel Groulx: assessment of appreciations]. *Action Natl. [Canada] 1979 68(6): 466-490.* While Msgr. Lionel Groulx was the foremost historian of French Canada, he envisioned a Quebec expressing a nationalism rooted in ethnic origin, culture, social life, and religion. In this, he differed from the purely political nationalism of Henri Bourassa. There is no evidence to support claims that Msgr. Groulx was a fascist, intransigent and intolerant, who romanticized French Canadian history. He was neither a xenophobe nor a racist, and accusations of anti-Semitism are equally unjust. 25 notes.   A. W. Novitsky

820. Gilbert, Felix. THE NEW EDITION OF JOHANN GUSTAV DROYSEN'S *HISTORIK. J. of the Hist. of Ideas 1983 44(2): 327-336.* Uses a new edition of Johann Gustav Droysen's *Historik* edited by Peter Leyh (1977) as the starting point for a reconsideration of the recent, renewed interest in this German historian's writings. While Droysen wrote on Hellenism and the development of Prussia, he is now remembered for the philosophical and methodological views expressed in those lectures given and revised between the 1850's and the 1880's and collected in *Historik.* The earlier versions of the work were heavily influenced by Hegel, but already took issue with the partisan scholarship of Haller and the narrowly political focus of Ranke. Later, his concern centered on differentiating the historical studies from speculative idealism on the one hand and the nomological natural sciences on the other. This aspect had an impact on Dilthey. Above all, Droysen came to see the course of history as an ethical process and the historian's task as deeply and appropriately committed to liberal values. 30 notes.   W. J. Reedy

821. Gindin, Claude. LA PENSÉE HISTORIQUE DE JEAN MEUVRET. QUELQUES-UNS DE SES ENSEIGNEMENTS [The historical thought of Jean Meuvret: a few of his teachings]. *Pensée [France] 1973 (169): 92-102.* Studies the writings of Jean Meuvret (d. 1971) on the French economy under the ancien regime, as reflected in his last book, *Studies on Economic History (1971).* Notes the profound effect of his philosophy on Marxist historiography.

822. Gindin, I. F. RUSSIA'S INDUSTRIALIZATION UNDER CAPITALISM AS SEEN BY THEODOR VON LAUE. *Soviet Studies in Hist. 1972 11(1): 3-55.* Surveys the scholarship of Sovietologist Theodor Von Laue, 1950's-60's, and characterizes him as a bourgeois historian with basic misconceptions about Soviet life and desire for modernization, capitalism, industrialization in the USSR, and Russian revolutionary movements, 1900-17.

823. Giuzelev, Vasil. PROUCHVANIIATA NA PROFESOR IVAN DUICHEV VURKHU BULGARSKATA ISTORIIA [The research of Professor Ivan Duichev on Bulgarian history]. *Istoricheski Pregled [Bulgaria] 1978 34(1): 85-92.* Discusses the career of the medieval historian Ivan Simeonev Duichev (b. 1907). Duichev has published over 500 books and articles on all eras of medieval Bulgaria. He studied with Vasil N. Zlatarski (1866-1935), Petur S.

Mutafchiev (1883-1943), and Iordan Ivanov (1876-1953) among others. Duichev's contribution to Bulgarian historiography has had a profound and lasting effect. Based on the works of Duichev; 49 notes.   F. B. Chary

824. Glatz, Ferenc. SZAKTUDOMÁNYOS KÉRDÉSFELTEVÉSEK ÉS TÖRTÉNETI-POLITIKAI KONCEPCIÓK. (A FIATAL SZEKFŰ GYULA BÉCSI ÉVEINEK TÖRTÉNETÉBŐL) [Asking questions in specialized fields of scholarship and the historical political concept: on the history of the Viennese years of young G. Szekfű]. *Történelmi Szemle [Hungary] 1974 17(3): 396-420.* Having spent 28 years at one of the richest European archives, Das Kaiserliche and Königliche Haus-, Hof- und Staatsarchiv, Vienna, G. Szekfű, the most prominent bourgeois Hungarian historian, returned home on his appointment as professor of the Budapest University in 1925. Specializing in the Hungarian matters of the monarchy, he viewed his country's past from a less parochial view than his colleagues back home. While loyal to the 1867 compromise, he perceived that continuing Austrian hegemony in joint affairs was based on the excellent machinery of constitutional and administrative efficiency. Highlights Szekfű's understanding of the problems of the nationalities and his amiable contacts with Czech and Croatian colleagues.   E. E. Soos/S

825. Głombik, Czesław. ZADANIA HISTORII FILOZOFII W OCENIE I BADANIACH STEFANA PAWLICKIEGO [The tasks of the history of philosophy in the assessment and studies by Stefan Pawlicki]. *Studia Filozoficzne [Poland] 1972 (11-12): 81-95.* Reviews the historical works of Stefan Pawlicki (1839-1916) and appraises their merits in the analysis of the history of philosophy and the postulates he presents with regard to historical and philosophical research.

826. Gogarten, Hermann. DAVID HUME ALS GESCHICHTSSCHREIBER. EIN BEITRAG ZUR ENGLISCHEN HISTORIOGRAPHIE DES 18. JAHRHUNDERTS [David Hume as historian: a contribution to English historiography of the 18th century]. *Arch. für Kulturgeschichte [West Germany] 1979 61(1): 120-153.* Introduces and criticizes Hume's historical work; deals with Hume's purpose in writing and the three methodological problems of organization, principles of selection, and use of sources; and closes with observations on the relationship of Hume's history and philosophy. 167 notes.   H. D. Andrews

827. Gogoneață, Nicolae. CONCEPȚIA LUI A. D. XENOPOL ASUPRA PREVIZIUNII ÎN ISTORIE [A. D. Xenopol's concept of prediction in history]. *Studii și Articole de Istorie [Romania] 1968 12: 31-38.* Clarifies apparently-conflicting views expressed by Romanian historian Alexandru D. Xenopol about the nature of history. He believed in the possibility of predicting, if not concrete happenings, at least the general direction of historical development. 29 notes.   F. Kellogg

828. Goldberg, A. L. IURII KRIZHANICH V ZARUBEZHNOI ISTORIOGRAFII (1940-1970 GODY) [Juraj Križanić in foreign historiography, 1940-70]. *Istoriia SSSR [USSR] 1976 (1): 201-205.* Reviews recent foreign historiography on the life and thought of the eminent Slavist Juraj Križanić (1618-83). In recent years research on Križanić, the leading exponent of Slavic thought in the 17th century, has significantly increased because of the relevance of much of his work to contemporary problems. Although comparatively little primary material on Križanić has been published, scholars have devoted much attention to his political, cultural, and religious views. At the same time, very little has been done on Križanić's geographical and ethnographical observations or on his philosophical conceptions. 35 notes.   J. W. Long

829. Gómez Martínez, José L. DILTHEY EN LA OBRA DE AMÉRICO CASTRO [Dilthey in the work of Américo Castro]. *Ábside [Mexico] 1973 37(4): 461-471.* Discusses the influence of Wilhelm Dilthey on the 20th-century Spanish historian Américo Castro, showing the philosophical similarities of Dilthey's work to the thought of José Ortega y Gasset and discussing the ways in which Castro's work is a practical application of these philosophical concepts.

830. Goodman, Jennifer Robin. THE CAPTAIN'S SELF-PORTRAIT: JOHN SMITH AS CHIVALRIC BIOGRAPHER. *Virginia Mag. of Hist. and Biog. 1981 89(1): 27-38.* Analyzes romantic elements in the historical writings of European and US adventurer John Smith, including Chaucerian to Elizabethan chivalric themes. Smith depicted himself as the one true knight operating in conditions much colored with romanticism. The last compromises Smith's work as historian. 34 notes.   P. J. Woehrmann

831. Gorskaia, N. A. PAMIATI AKADEMIKA B. D. GREKOVA [B. D. Grekov: in memoriam]. *Voprosy Istorii [USSR] 1982 (4): 109-116.* Review article of the major historical works of Boris D. Grekov (1882-1953). His studies, published 1912-52, deal with Russian feudalism, serfdom, socioeconomic development, and legal status of peasants, mainly 15th-17th centuries. His work shows his gradual endorsement of Marxism. 30 notes.   N. Frenkley

832. Gottfried, Paul. LUKACS' *THE YOUNG HEGEL* REEXAMINED. *Marxist Perspectives 1979-80 2(4): 144-155.* A critical evaluation of George Lukács's *The Young Hegel*, Rodney Livingstone, transl. (London, 1975), which discusses Georg Hegel's early philosophy, 1790's, from a Marxist-Leninist perspective.

833. Goulding, Stuart D. FRANCIS PARKMAN AND THE JESUITS. *Hist. Today [Great Britain] 1974 24(1): 22-31.* Gives biographical data on historian Francis Parkman (1823-93) and discusses his treatment of 17th-century Jesuit missionaries in *The Conspiracy of Pontiac: Pioneers of New France in the New World* (1865) and *Jesuits* (1867).

834. Grabski, Andrzej F. FRANCISZEK BUJAK AND ECONOMIC HISTORY: A DISCUSSION OF HIS METHODOLOGICAL VIEWS. *Studia Historiae Oeconomicae [Poland] 1981 16: 3-27.* After outlining the development of interest in economic history in several European countries during the 19th and early 20th centuries, the ideological and methodological views and work of the distinguished Polish economic historian Franciszek Bujak are analyzed. Special attention is paid to an assessment of H. Madurowicz-Urbańska's multivolume *Wybór Pism* [Selected works] (1976-) on Bujak. Bujak's lecture at the Jagiellonian University on 15 November 1905, which, according to Madrowicz-Urbańska was "the first attempt in Polish scholarship to define the meaning of economic history," is also analyzed. 87 notes.   G. L. Neville

835. Grabski, Andrzej F. KARL LAMPRECHT I HISTORIOGRAFIA POLSKA [Karl Lamprecht and Polish historiography]. *Kwartalnik Hist. Nauki i Techniki [Poland] 1981 26(2): 315-334.* Discusses the varied reception by Polish historians of the historiography of Karl Lamprecht during the 1890's and early 1900's. His history of Germany was labeled by some as overly materialist. His historico-cultural approach in 1900, in contrast to his previous emphasis on economic history, drew more adherents in Poland. The leading advocate of this approach was Wacław Sobieski. 62 notes.
                                                 M. A. Zurowski

836. Gracheva, L. E. VOPROSY REVOLIUTSIONNOGO DVIZHENIIA ROSSII V TRUDAKH GEORGIIA BAKALOVA [Questions of the revolutionary movement in Russia in the works of Georgi Bakalov]. *Sovetskoe Slavianovedenie [USSR] 1984 (2): 37-50.* Georgi Bakalov (1873-1939) was one of the founders of the school of Marxist historical science in Bulgaria and was active in the international socialist movement. He believed the Russian revolutionary movement began to have an impact in Bulgaria from the 1860's onward. He was a friend of G. V. Plekhanov and explored the role of Russian emigrants in Bulgaria. Secondary sources; 34 notes.   S. F. Jones

837. Grafenauer, Bogo. MESTO SIMONA RUTARJA V SLOVENSKOM ZGODOVINOPISJU [Simon Rutar's place in Slovene history]. *Goriški Letnik [Yugoslavia] 1976 3: 9-19.* Discusses the importance and contribution of Simon Rutar's writings to the study of Slovenia's history.

838. Grant, H. Roger. LEWIS ATHERTON. *Great Plains J. 1979 18: 10-14.* Atherton was born in 1905 in Missouri and trained as an historian at the University of Missouri. He taught at his alma mater from 1936 to 1973. In addition to other published works, his *The Cattle Kings* focuses on the Great Plains. Also an outstanding teacher and "idea" man, he directed dissertations of many prominent historians. 17 notes. From a section on "Historians of the Northern Plains."   O. H. Zabel

839. Graubard, Stephen R. EDWARD GIBBON: *CONTRARIA SUNT COMPLEMENTA. Daedalus 1976 105(3): 171-187.* It is possible that the standard intellectual portrait of Edward Gibbon (1737-94) needs to be revised to account for the seemingly contradictory aspects of his life, character, and writings which are not in fact contradictory but rather complementary. Such a portrait would elucidate the unique qualities which appear in his history. For, while Gibbon resembled the respected historians of his time, he emphasized and integrated his materials in a manner which shed new light. It was only in the presentation of his own age that Gibbon failed, and his talents for nuance, irony, qualification, and surprise deserted him. 51 notes.   E. McCarthy

840. Green, Donald E. GILBERT C. FITE. *Great Plains J. 1979 18: 93-98.* Gilbert C. Fite, born in South Dakota in 1918 and educated at the Universities of South Dakota and Missouri, spent 25 years teaching at the University of Oklahoma. From 1971 to 1978 he was president of Eastern Illinois University. Since then he has taught at the University of Georgia. He is a "superb teacher" and active scholar with special interest in the history of American agriculture. His "most significant contribution" to the history of the Great Plains is probably *The Farmer's Frontier, 1865-1900* (1966). From a special section on "Historians of the Southern Plains." Note on sources.   O. H. Zabel

841. Grendi, Edoardo. NORBERT ELIAS: STORIOGRAFIA E TEORIA SOCIALE [Norbert Elias: historiography and social theory]. *Quaderni Storici [Italy] 1982 17(2): 728-739.* Discusses Norbert Elias's historiography, particularly regarding social relationships and processes.   J/S

842. Grigoraş, Nicolae. ORIGINEA, FORMAŢIA ŞI PREOCUPĂRILE ISTORICE ALE MITROPOLITULUI DOSOFTEI [The origins, training, and historical interests of Metropolitan Dosoftei]. *Rev. de Istorie [Romania] 1974 27(10): 1485-1499.* Surveys the life and works of Metropolitan Dosoftei, especially his contributions to Romanian historiography from his study of Romanian language and culture, and discusses the sources he used.

843. Häikiö, Martti. SIR LEWIS NAMIER (1888-1960). *Historiallinen Aikakauskirja [Finland] 1975 73(1): 25-35.* A survey of the intellectual career of the Polish-English historian, Sir Lewis B. Namier (1888-1960). His greatest achievement was a new type of political history focusing on the lives of active politicians. Namier's specialty was the British House of Commons, particularly during the era of the American Revolution. He placed high value on a conservative, dynastic basis for political life. Based on Namier's published writings; 49 notes.   R. G. Selleck

844. Hall, John Whitney. E. H. NORMAN ON TOKUGAWA JAPAN. *J. of Japanese Studies 1977 3(2): 365-374.* Evaluates the historical scholarship of the writings of E. H. Norman in his *Origins of the Modern Japanese State* (1975). This reprint of Norman's *Japan's Emergence as a Modern State* (1940), two previously unpublished manuscripts, and an analytical introduction by editor John Dower strongly endorse the narrative skills and analytical powers of this scholar. Norman's views on feudalism in Tokugawa Japan, although largely drawn from Japanese sources and subsequently challenged by later researchers, were bold, imaginative, and convincing. Based on Western sources; 5 notes.   S. H. Frank

845. Halperin, John. *EMINENT VICTORIANS* AND HISTORY. *Virginia Q. Rev. 1980 56(3): 433-454.* Lytton Strachey's *Eminent Victorians* (1918) shows that Strachey was not a dependable historian. He was uninterested in politics; he and others in the Bloomsbury group were against Victorianism. Much of Strachey's

presentation is "pure fabrication" and the author gives specific examples from *Eminent Victorians* on Cardinal Henry E. Manning (1808-92), Florence Nightingale (1820-1910), Thomas Arnold (1795-1842) and William Ewart Gladstone (1809-98). Strachey was correct only with General Charles George Gordon (1833-85).   O. H. Zabel

846. Hargreaves, Mary W. M. A DEDICATION TO THE MEMORY OF JAMES ORIN OLIPHANT, 1894-1979. *Arizona and the West 1983 25(4): 308-312.* James Orin Oliphant completed his doctoral studies at Harvard University, where he became a recognized authority on the cattle industry in Oregon country. At Bucknell University, where he served for most of his academic career, he also became known for his pioneering studies on the home missionary movement in the westward expansion of the American frontier. Illus., biblio.   D. L. Smith

847. Hauser, Oswald. A. J. P. TAYLOR. *J. of Modern Hist. 1977 49(1): 34-39.* A short review by a German colleague of the works of A. J. P. Taylor, a British historian, focusing on Taylor's allegedly anti-German views, 1938-45.

848. Herkless, John L. EIN UNERKLÄRTES ELEMENT IN DER HISTORIOGRAPHIE VON MAX LENZ [An unexplained element in the historiography of Max Lenz]. *Hist. Zeitschrift [West Germany] 1976 222(1): 81-104.* Previous explanations of Max Lenz's (1850-1932) dependence on Leopold von Ranke in writing on Germany between Luther and Bismarck have overlooked the influence of John Robert Seeley (1834-95) on Lenz's conception of imperialism. 91 notes.   G. H. Davis

849. Herwig, Holger H. ANDREAS HILLGRUBER: HISTORIAN OF "GROSSMACHTPOLITIK" 1871-1945. *Central European Hist. 1982 15(2): 186-198.* Describes the main arguments in the works of Andreas Hillgruber and evaluates his importance to modern German historiography. Refers to the following works: *Deutschlands Rolle in der Vorgeschichte der Beiden Weltkriege* (1967, 1979), *Kontinuität und Diskontinuität in der Deutschen Aussenpolitik von Bismarck bis Hitler* (1969, 1971), *Grossmachtpolitik und Militarismus im 20. Jahrhundert* (1974), *Deutsche Grossmacht- und Weltpolitik im 19. und 20. Jahrhundert* (1977, 1979), *Die Gescheiterte Grossmacht: Eine Skizze des Deutschen Reiches 1871-1945* (1980, 1981).   C. R. Lovin

850. Herzhod, H. I. V. V. VOROVSKYI IAK ISTORYK PARTII [V. V. Vorovski as a Party historian]. *Ukrains'kyi Istorychnyi Zhurnal [USSR] 1981 (10): 129-132.* One of Lenin's closest comrades-in-arms, Vorovski distinguished himself as a prolific writer on political theory and the Communist Party's development.   V. Bender

851. Holden, William Curry. J. EVETTS HALEY. *Great Plains J. 1979 18: 99-106.* J. Evetts Haley has published "more than two hundred articles and books" which have cut a wide swath across the historical landscape of the Southwest. Born in poverty, he graduated from West Texas State Normal College and took a master's degree in history at the University of Texas. After that he worked for the Panhandle-Plains Museum and then as a collector of archival material for the University of Texas. The latter position was sacrificed to his activist conservative leadership against Franklin Roosevelt's reelection in 1936. He then developed a successful career in ranching, but never neglected his historical endeavors. From a special section on "Historians of the Southern Plains."   O. H. Zabel

852. Holmes, Larry E. SOVIET REWRITING OF 1917: THE CASE OF A. G. SHLIAPNIKOV. *Slavic Rev. 1979 38(2): 224-242.* Examines A. G. Shliapnikov's principles, methodology, impartiality, and historical interpretations. Discusses his academic and political courage, his contributions to and impact on Soviet historiography as a historian-memoirist. Sponsored by the Research Committee of the University of South Alabama; from a paper presented at the 16th Southern Conference on Slavic Studies, Birmingham, Alabama, 22 October 1977. 100 notes.   R. B. Mendel

853. Holotík, L'udovít. PODNĚTY Z MARXOVHO HISTORICKÉHO DIELA [Impulses from Marx's historical work]. *Hist. Časopis [Czechoslovakia] 1983 31(2): 153-163.* The validity of Marx's conclusions in his historical works still exists. His *Class Struggles in France* was a monumental achievement which demonstrated his ability to evaluate political, social, and psychological events. Based on Marx's works. G. E. Pergl/S

854. Horn, Maurycy. MEYER BAŁABAN—SHEFER FUN GESHIKHTE-SHUL VEGN YIDN IN POYLN [Meyer Balaban—head of the historical school of Polish Jewry]. *Bleter far Geszichte [Poland] 1983 21: 7-55.* Meyer Balaban (1877-1942) was the preeminent historian of Polish Jewry. In a career that spanned four decades, Balaban published 20 books, over 100 articles in learned journals, and another 100 in popular magazines. Balaban was a follower of Simon Dubnow, who stands in apposition to Heinrich Gratz, the first comprehensive Jewish historian. Balaban specialized in local Jewish histories, Hasidism in Poland, Polish-Jewish history as reflected in legal documents, Jewish sectarians, and the bibliography of Polish Jewish history, particularly in primary source materials. English and Polish summaries. D. Roth

855. Howe, Daniel Walker and Finn, Peter Elliott. RICHARD HOFSTADTER: THE IRONIES OF AN AMERICAN HISTORIAN. *Pacific Hist. R. 1974 43(1): 1-23.* An historiographic study of the work of Richard Hofstadter as an American historian, based on his writings, which attempts to "reconstruct by inference the motivating intelligence behind [them]." Hofstadter was always his own man, peculiarly sensitive to the ironies of history, always the liberal, but not entirely acceptable to conservative, radical, or liberal. Given to stripping away illusions, he was never able to fulfill the healing function of "scholar-as-psychotherapist," and offered "no new sense of corporate identity." 64 notes. R. V. Ritter

856. Hurezeanu, Damian. LUCREŢIU PĂTRĂŞCANU ŞI FENOMENUL ISTORIC ROMANESC (1821-1944) [Lucretiu Patrascanu and the phenomenon of Romanian history, 1821-1944]. *Rev. de Istorie [Romania] 1975 28(10): 1479-1504.* Analyzes the vital contributions of theoretician and Communist activist Lucretiu Patrascanu (1900-54) to the progress of historical thought in Romania, especially in his major works, *Un veac de frămîntări sociale* [A century of social struggles], *Problemele de bază ale României* [Basic problems of Romania], and *Sub trei dictaturi* [Under three dictators]. The historian's central preoccupation was seeking a logical structure for historical phenomena and this, combined with his view of history as a social process, his strong class position, and his emphasis on the role of the masses, laid the essential basis for the writing of modern history in Romania. Secondary sources; 66 notes. G. J. Bobango

857. Hurezeanu, Damian. MIHAI EMINESCU—UN PASIONAT AL ISTORIEI [Mihai Eminescu, a passionate lover of history]. *Revista de Istorie [Romania] 1982 35(1): 115-137, (2): 313-338.* Part 1. Romanian poet Mihai Eminescu possessed an extraordinary love of history. His "historical culture" was impressive in its amplitude and variety. Eminescu studied ancient and medieval Romanian history, examined closely the evolution of national historiography, and had a precise understanding of the characteristics of European historiography. Part 2. Examines the expressions of Eminescu's romanticism in his reflections on history. Eminescu's philosophical poems contain examples of his romantic vision of history and also show Schopenhauer's influence. Explores Eminescu's views on Romanian history. 153 notes. French summary. P. D. Herman/S

858. Illeritski, V. E. SOVETSKIE ISTORIKI O S. M. SOLOV'EVE [Soviet historians on S. M. Soloviëv]. *Voprosy Istorii [USSR] 1981 (11): 124-130.* Sergei Soloviëv is deemed the greatest historian of prerevolutionary Russia. His *History of Russia from Most Ancient Times* was published in volumes, the first of which appeared in 1851 followed by a volume each consecutive year until the end of his life. Soloviëv's historical concepts were criticized by the government and historians of his time. Only after the October Revolution in Russia did his works find genuine appreciation. A review of publications by Soviet historians devoted to Soloviëv and his contribution to historical science indicates that much work has been done in this respect, although more comprehensive research is needed to determine Soloviëv's contribution to Russian historical thought and concepts. S. M. Levy

859. Inchikian, H. G. B. M. KNUNYANTS [B. M. Knunyants]. *Patma-Banasirakan Handes. Istoriko-Filologicheskii Zhurnal [USSR] 1979 (1): 3-14.* Traces the career of Bogdan Knunyants (1879-1911), whose life was a total dedication to the ideas of socialism and democracy. In Soviet historiography he is regarded as one of the first authors who seriously researched the role of the Soviets during the Russian Revolution of 1905-07. He joined the Russian revolutionary movements in St. Petersburg in 1897 when he was a student of 19. Active in the Caucasus and Russia, he was tried and imprisoned many times. In 1905 he went to Geneva, where he met with Lenin. Back in Russia he wrote revolutionary articles and took part in various committee meetings. Condemned to life in exile, he escaped and lived his last years in Baku under a false name, continuing his revolutionary activities to the end. Over 50 works by him still survive. 28 notes. A. Nassibian

860. Irmscher, Johannes. FRIEDRICH AUGUST WOLF ALS VERTRETER AUFKLÄRERISCHEN GESCHICHTSDENKENS [Friedrich August Wolf as a representative of enlightened historical thinking]. *Jahrbuch für Gesch. [East Germany] 1982 25: 7-22.* Esteems classical scholar Friedrich August Wolf (1759-1824) for his modern method of textual criticism. Wolf explained ancient phenomena according to historical conditions instead of by applying current linguistic usage. Wolf also dealt with the history of literature, politics, mythology, and numismatics. 105 notes. I. Malwitz

861. Ivanov, Iu. F. NAUCHNAIA DEIATEL'NOST' N. N. LIUBOVICHA [The scientific activity of N. N. Liubovich]. *Sovetskoe Slavianovedenie [USSR] 1980 (4): 82-93.* Nikolai Liubovich (1855-1935) studied history in Kiev and later took up a teaching post at Warsaw University where he remained until 1915. His research interests were Polish history and the Reformation. In contrast to the majority of historians of his day, Liubovich considered that social and economic factors provided the explanation for historical events. His work on the Reformation showed that religious ideas reflected social reality. A more detailed study of the career of Liubovich needs to be undertaken. Based on Soviet archives and secondary sources; 67 notes. G. Dombrovski

862. Jacobs, Wilbur R. SHERBURNE FRIEND COOK: REBEL-REVISIONIST (1896-1974). *Pacific Historical Review 1985 54(2): 191-199.* Although trained academically as a physiologist, most of Sherburne Friend Cook's work was in the area of historical demography. From the beginning, his research and conclusions sparked controversy. His academic productivity was prodigious, rapidly promoting him through the rank of associate professor. But so unusual were his methodologies and conclusions that it took several years before he could be advanced to the rank of full professor. Among his more controversial contributions were his estimation of the pre-Columbian Indian population at 100 million, his questioning whether there was a tendency among Mexican Americans to seek civil rather than religious weddings, and his interpretation of the size of Indian potsherds—"the size would depend upon how far the oldest woman will walk to dump her garbage." His lifetime work totaled some 160 research publications. Based on the Library Key to the Sherburne F. Cook Papers, Bancroft Library, University of California, Berkeley, and interviews; 31 notes. H. M. Parker, Jr.

863. Jaeck, Hans-Peter. VON DER *HENRIADE* ZUM *SIÈCLE DE LOUIS XIV*: MOTIVE UND VORAUSSETZUNGEN DER GESCHICHTSSCHREIBUNG VOLTAIRES [From the *Henriade* to the *Siècle de Louis XIV*: motives and assumptions in the historical writings of Voltaire]. *Jahrbuch für Geschichte [East Germany] 1979 19: 147-178.* Voltaire's qualities as an historian have not always been justly appreciated. There has been little investigation of his knowledge, methods of research, and manner of formulating and solving historical problems. This essay examines the early stages of Voltaire's historical writing, from the *Henriade* (1723) to the *Siècle de Louis XIV* (1739). In this period Voltaire's motives, assumptions

and intentions developed from an "anti-despotic, anti clerical, critical" approach to history to a new conception of a "bourgeois-civilizing, philosophic" history. Voltaire always brought an open, inquisitive mind to the study of history. He was unencumbered by preconceived theories, had an eye for historical change, and employed an analytic method. Based on Voltaire's published writings and correspondence; 132 notes.   J. B. Street

864. Jamiołkowska, Danuta. JAN LEO—HISTORYK PRUS [Jan Leo: historian of Prussia]. *Komunikaty Mazursko-Warmińskie [Poland] 1976 4(134): 455-468.* Leo (1572-1635) attended the seminary and the Jesuit college in Braunsberg (Polish, Braniewo) and was ordained in 1596. He spent most of his life serving as deacon and canon and devoting himself to the study of the history of Warmia. He completed the *Historia Prussiae* around 1625, which traces the history of East Prussia from the earliest times to Leo's own day. The author discusses Leo's sources and the significance of *Historia Prussiae*'s favorable treatment of the Poles. Based on archival and secondary material; 90 notes, appendix.   R. Seitz

865. Jemnitz, János. LENIN ÉS A TÖRTÉNETTUDOMÁNY [V. I. Lenin and historical science]. *Történelmi Szemle [Hungary] 1970 13(2): 210-222.* V. I. Lenin did not write long historical works, but had a very clear conception of the history of the working-class movement and its periodization. His analysis of the history of the Paris Commune, and his reflections on Russian history, and his biographical articles are important historical sources.   I. Hont

866. Jennings, Francis. FRANCIS PARKMAN: A BRAHMIN AMONG UNTOUCHABLES. *William and Mary Quarterly 1985 42(3): 305-328.* Despite the praise given to Francis Parkman's works over the last century, his writings exhibit errors and distortion in the use of historical sources. Parkman edited quotations in order to improve diction, leaving the quotations conveying a different meaning. Parkman also made unwarranted exaggerations, such as inflating the importance of the Indian chief Pontiac. He consistently depicted Indians as brute beasts, even in instances where this was contrary to the evidence, revealing his racial and class prejudices. Based on Francis Parkman's works and on primary sources; 121 notes.   H. M. Ward

867. Johannsen, Robert W. DAVID POTTER, HISTORIAN AND SOCIAL CRITIC: A REVIEW ESSAY. *Civil War Hist. 1974 20(1): 35-44.* A review of *History and American Society: Essays of David M. Potter* (New York, Oxford U. Press, 1973), published two years after Potter's death. Following a sketch of Potter's life and work, the author analyzes the substance of the essays. Divided into two parts, the theory and practice of history, and studies on the American character, the writings measure the breadth and depth of Potter's mind and the importance of his contributions to our understanding of history.   E. C. Murdock

868. Jones, Billy M. ODIE B. FAULK. *Great Plains J. 1979 18: 85-92.* Odie B. Faulk (b. 1933) spent his early years in East Texas, served in the Marine Corps during the Korean War, and attended Texas Tech University. His career has included teaching at Texas A & M, editing *Arizona and the West*, teaching at Oklahoma State University (1968-77), and since 1978 serving as director of the Memphis State University Press. He has been particularly productive of authored and edited 31 books and 40 articles on topics concerning the Southwest. From a special section on "Historians of the Southern Plains."   O. H. Zabel

869. Jones, Myrddin. A LIVING TREASURY OF KNOWLEDGE AND WISDOM: SOME COMMENTS ON SWIFT'S ATTITUDE TO THE WRITING OF HISTORY. *Durham U. J. [Great Britain] 1975 67(2): 180-188.* Analyzes the knowledge of and preoccupation with history of Jonathan Swift (1667-1745), and how this influenced his writing with special reference to *Gulliver's Travels*. Primary and secondary sources; 36 notes.
                                                        R. G. Neville

870. Jones, Oakah L. A DEDICATION TO THE MEMORY OF MAX L. MOORHEAD, 1914-1981. *Arizona and the West 1984 26(1): 1-4.* Max L. Moorhead was trained in Spanish and Mexican

borderlands history at the University of California, Berkeley. He established a reputation as a meticulous scholar and authority on Spanish documents in Spain, Mexico, and the American Southwest. His monographs on Spanish Indian policies, the presidio as a frontier institution, and the Santa Fe-Chihuahua route are the standard accounts on these subjects. For three decades he was a highly regarded teacher at the University of Oklahoma. Illus., biblio.
                                                        D. L. Smith

871. Jones, Robert H. FRED ALBERT SHANNON. *Great Plains J. 1979 18: 55-59.* Born in Missouri (1893), Fred A. Shannon was educated at Indiana State Teachers College and the Universities of Indiana and Iowa. He taught at numerous colleges, including the University of Illinois (1940-64). Shannon was not "primarily a historian of the Great Plains," but "was vitally interested in American agriculture" so works such as *The Farmer's Last Frontier, An Appraisal of Walter Webb's The Great Plains,* and others dealt with the Great Plains. Not always tactful and hating hypocrisy and pomposity, he often enlivened historical meetings. From a special section on "Historians of the Northern Plains." 7 notes.
                                                        O. H. Zabel

872. Jussim, Marco. MACHIAVELLI NELLO SPECCHIO DELLA CRITICA SOVIETICA DEGLI ANNI '70 [Machiavelli and Soviet critics in the 1970's]. *Storia e Pol. [Italy] 1983 22(2): 339-352.* Studies on Niccolò Machiavelli in the USSR developed mainly after 1970. Marxist historiography attributes primary importance to discovering to what degree Machiavelli's thought advanced social progress and to define his relationship to humanism. Analyzes works by V. I. Rutenburg, R. I. Chlodovski, L. M. Batkin, F. M. Burlatski, and K. M. Dolgov. Secondary sources; 45 notes.
                                                        A. Canavero

873. Jütte, Robert. ZWISCHEN STÄNDESTAAT UND AUSTROFASCHISMUS: DER BEITRAG OTTO BRUNNERS ZUR GESCHICHTSSCHREIBUNG [Between the corporate state and Austrofascism: Otto Brunner's contribution to historiography]. *Jahrbuch des Instituts für Deutsche Geschichte [Israel] 1984 13: 237-262.* Otto Brunner, the historian and archivist, argued that it was not the responsibility of historians to convey antiquated knowledge but to point out tendencies in the past epochs which still influenced the present. To Brunner interpretation of history and understanding the political present went hand in hand. His basic theme was the relationship between Austria's monarchy and individual German lands. The concept of the modern Austrian state was alien to him. Hence, Brunner applauded the annexation of Austria by Germany in 1938. Based on Austria's archival sources, newspapers and secondary sources; 131 notes.   S. P. Forgus

874. Kalenova, L. S. NAUCHNAIA KONFERENTSIIA "ISTORIIA I FILOLOGIIA TURTSII" [A scientific conference on the history and philology of Turkey]. *Narody Azii i Afriki [USSR] 1977 (3): 170-177.* Soviet scholars participated in the 5-8 October 1976 conference dedicated to the scholar on Turkey, academician Vladimir Gordlevsky (1876-1976), which took place in the Oriental Institute at the Academy of Sciences of the USSR. Reports were given on the scientific, pedagogical, and social work of Gordlevsky, especially his contributions to the study of history and philology. The conference was divided into three sections on history and Oriental studies; literature, art, culture, and philosophy; and linguistics.
                                                        L. Kalinowski

875. Karl, Barry D. FREDERICK JACKSON TURNER: THE MORAL DILEMMA OF PROFESSIONALIZATION. *Rev. in Am. Hist. 1975 3(1): 3-7.* Review article prompted by Ray Allen Billington's *Frederick Jackson Turner: Historian, Scholar, Teacher* (New York: Oxford U. Pr., 1973) which discusses Turner's career and his influence on American historiography and the modern historical profession.

876. Kashtanov, S. M. ALEKSANDR ALEKSANDROVICH ZIMIN—ISSLEDOVATAL' I PEDAGOG [Aleksandr Aleksandrovich Zimin, scholar and teacher]. *Istoriia SSSR [USSR] 1980 (6): 152-157.* Aleksandr Zimin (1920-80), professor of history at

the Moscow State Historical Archives Institute, 1950-70, wrote some 300 major studies in Russian history of the feudal era, methodology and historiography, original research, and historical bibliography.

N. Frenkley

877. Kawecka, Krystyna; Żarnowska, Anna; and Piber, Andrzej. 80-LECIE URODZIN PROF. ŻANNY KORMANOWEJ; BIBLIOGRAFIA PRAC PROF. DR. ŻANNY KORMANOWEJ [Tribute to Professor Żanna Kormanowa and her bibliography]. *Z Pola Walki [Poland] 1980 23(4): 196-216.* Professor Żanna Kormanowa celebrated her 80th birthday 11 August 1980. Her bibliography covers over 50 years of steady and fruitful work focused on the history of the working class. Professor Kormanowa was the first to offer in 1948 a university seminar on the topic at the Institute of History, University of Warsaw. In addition to her own scholarly production, Professor Kormanowa is also known as an outstanding pedagogue; she has been the director of 29 doctoral dissertations and many masters' theses. Based on Kormanowa's bibliography, 1925-80.

I. Lukes

878. Kemp, Peter and Marchetti, François. L'HISTOIRE COMME RÉCIT ET COMME PRATIQUE, ENTRETIEN AVEC PAUL RICOEUR [History as story-telling and a practice: a conversation with Paul Ricoeur]. *Esprit [France] 1981 (6): 155-165.* An interview with French philosopher Paul Ricoeur (b. 1913), who discusses the function of historical narrative, Marxist ideology and utopia, and social and cultural creativity.

879. Khadzhinikolov, Veselin. AKADEMIK ZHAK NATAN I BULGARSKATA ISTORICHESKA NAUKA [Academician Zhak Natan and Bulgarian historical science]. *Istoricheski Pregled [Bulgaria] 1972 28(5): 3-21.* Surveys the career of Zhak Natan (b. 1902) and analyzes his influence on Bulgarian historiography on the occasion of his 70th birthday. Natan, the son of a poor Jewish brush maker, became a member of the Communist Party in 1920 and was jailed several times for his activities in the Party. In 1938 he wrote his most famous work, *History of the Bulgarian Economy,* but he influenced Bulgarian historiography in all fields as an author and editor, particularly as chief editor of *Istoricheski Pregled.* Among other things, he publicized the democratic progressive ideology of the Bulgarian national liberation movement of the 19th century, overlooked by other Marxist historians. After World War II he was particularly influential in bringing Marxist-Leninist methodology to Bulgarian historiography. Based on the works of Zhak Natan; 43 notes.

F. B. Chary

880. Kirshner, Julius. RECENSORI E STORICI IN AMERICA: J. H. HEXTER [Reviewers and historians in America: J. H. Hexter]. *Studi Storici [Italy] 1982 23(2): 317-324.* In his reviews of historical works, the American scholar, J. H. Hexter, has used intemperate language as well as questionable tactics and judgment. He has also revealed the low esteem in which he holds post-Renaissance culture in Italy, as compared with cultural developments in France and England. Primary sources; 2 notes.

E. E. Ryan

881. Knei-Paz, Baruch. THE REVOLUTIONARY AS HISTORIAN: LEON TROTSKY'S *HISTORY OF THE RUSSIAN REVOLUTION* REVISITED. *State, Government and Int. Relations [Israel] 1978 12: 97-107.* Leon Trotsky's *History of the Russian Revolution* is notable for its epic presentation and artistic approach: Trotsky the dramatic revolutionary of 1917 is reflected in the work of Trotsky the historical dramatist.

882. Kogălniceanu, Ion M. VASILE M. KOGĂLNICEANU: UN DEMN URMAȘ AL TATĂLUI SĂU [Vasile M. Kogălniceanu: a worthy successor to his father]. *Magazin Istoric [Romania] 1981 15(4): 22-23, 54.* Surveys the life and work of the Romanian historian Vasile Kogălniceanu, 1863-1942, fourth son of the Wallachian statesman Mihail Kogălniceanu, 1817-91, whose official correspondence was published in 1893.

883. Kolakowski, Leszek. STANISLAW BRZOZOWSKI: MARXISM AS HISTORICAL SUBJECTIVISM. *Survey [Great Britain] 1976 22(3-4): 247-266.* Little known outside of Poland, Stanislaw Brzozowski greatly influenced the intellectual history of 20th-century Poland, being one of the first to contrast Karl Marx and Friedrich Engels. He is most closely associated with the philosophy of labor; that is, man's contact with reality is achieved through labor. Brzozowski's socialism is defined solely in terms of the struggle for free labor, a state in which the laborer while at work is not subject to a higher authority. Uninterested in proletarian revolution, Brzozowski was concerned only with the need for the mind and will of the working class to rise to a level where workers were in full control of the processes of society. Secondary sources; 19 notes.

D. R. McDonald

884. Konig, Michael F. HENRY D. BARROWS: CALIFORNIA RENAISSANCE MAN. Dodd, Horace L. and Long, Robert W., ed. *People of the Far West* (Brand Book no. 6; San Diego: Corral of the Westerners, 1979): 131-137. Recounts the career of Henry D. Barrows of Los Angeles, California, historian, US marshal, school superintendent, agriculturalist, and Republican Party leader, 1854-77.

885. Kopčan, Vojtech. MICHAL MATUNÁK A JEHO DIELO [Michal Matunák and his work]. *Hist. Časopis [Czechoslovakia] 1981 29(1): 75-83.* Deals with the life and work of Slovak historian Michal Matunák (1866-1932), who made significant contributions to the study of Ottoman expansion in Slovakia. Analyzes Matunák's main works and refers to the archival material used by him as well as his methodology.

J

886. Křivský, Pavel. PALACKÝ A HORMAYR [Palacký and Hormayr]. *Strahovská Knihovna [Czechoslovakia] 1976 (11): 63-77.* Evaluates the importance of historian Joseph von Hormayr (1781-1848) and of his teaching on Palacký's historiographical work.

887. Król, Marcin. PROFILE: MICHAL BOBRZYŃSKI. *Polish Perspectives [Poland] 1973 16(10): 36-44.* Assesses the humanitarian and scholarly contribution of the popular Polish historian Michal Bobrzyński (1849-1935) in his two-volume *Outline of the History of Poland,* published in 1878.

888. Kučera, Matúš. F. V. SASINEK—FOUNDER OF MODERN SLOVAK HISTORIOGRAPHY. *Studia Historica Slovaca [Czechoslovakia] 1984 13: 201-216.* Assesses the contributions of František Víťazoslav Sasinek (d. 1914) to the development of Slovak historiography. His methodology was deficient due to the oppression of Slovaks and other minority groups in Hungary and his resulting lack of a solid scientific education. Nevertheless, his influence on Slovak nationalism and independence movements was significant. 28 notes.

R. Grove

889. Kučera, Matúš. PROFIL HISTORICKÉHO DIELA FRANTIŠKA VÍŤAZOSLAVA SASINKA [The character of F. V. Sasinek's works in Slovak history]. *Hist. Časopis [Czechoslovakia] 1981 29(2): 195-207.* F. V. Sasinek is the founder of the national Slovak historiography. In his works he dealt mainly with the oldest history of the Slovaks, their role in the Hungarian Kingdom, as well as with the position of the Slovaks among other Slavonic nations. F. V. Sasinek's works were of a great importance even during the author's life.

J

890. Kuczyńska, Alicja. PAMIĘCI UCZONEGO: PRZEMÓWIENIE WYGŁOSZONE NA PLENARNYM POSIEDZENIU KOMITETU NAUK FILOZOFICZNYCH 3 CZERWCA 1980 R. [In memory of a scholar: a speech at the meeting of the Committee of Philosophical Sciences, 3 June 1980]. *Studia Filozoficzne [Poland] 1980 (9): 17-21.* A speech in memory of the Polish historian of philosophy, Władysław Tatarkiewicz, assessing his contributions in the fields of historiography and aesthetics.

891. Kuhn, Helmut. DAS PROBLEM EINER PHILOSOPHISCHEN HISTORIOGAPHIE: ZUM WERK VON ERIC VOEGELIN [The problem of a philosophical historiography: the work of Eric Voegelin]. *Zeits. für Pol. [West Germany] 1981 28(2): 116-129.* Describes the philosophical and historical nature of Voegelin's work in political science, highlighting some of his main theories and phases of development.

892. Kulynych, I. M. and Pavlenko, O. H. ISTORIIHRAFIIA TA DZHERELOZNAVSTVO: F. FISHER PRO ZAHARBNYTSKI PLANY NIMETS'KOHO IMPERIALIZMU V PERSHYI SVITOVYI VIINI [Historiography and research: F. Fisher on the occupation plans of German imperialism during World War I]. *Ukrains'kyi Istorychnyi Zhurnal [USSR] 1980 (8): 135-142.* Provides a general background to Fritz Fisher of Hamburg University, West Germany. Analyzes his works and in particular those dealing with German expansionist plans in World War I.

893. Labrousse, Ernest. GEORGES HAUPT, A NEMZETKÖZI SZOCIALIZMUS FRANCIA TÖRTÉNETÍRÓJA [Georges Haupt, the French historiographer of international socialism]. *Világtörténet [Hungary] 1979 (2): 93-97.* In his youth (1949-58) Haupt published in Romanian. In 1958, he emigrated to France and began to publish in French.   R. Hetzron

894. Lacroix, Benoît. LIONEL GROULX CET INCONNU [The unknown Lionel Groulx]. *Rev. d'Hist. de l'Amérique Française [Canada] 1978 32(3): 325-346.* An intimate portrait of Fr. Lionel Groulx (1878-1967), the eminent French Canadian historian. During an incredibly long and productive career, Fr. Groulx wrote more than 30 books and hundreds of articles. Though his world consisted primarily of books, libraries, and research, he often wrote in a popular style so that history could be enjoyed by a much larger audience. He taught for more than 50 years. 7 notes.
M. R. Yerburgh

895. Lasch, Christopher. WILLIAM APPLEMAN WILLIAMS ON AMERICAN HISTORY. *Marxist Perspectives 1978 1(3): 118-127.* Praises William Appleman Williams's writings on American history, 1950's-70's.

896. Laughlin, Henry A. FERRIS GREENSLET. *Massachusetts Hist. Soc. Pro. 1957-60 72: 379-384.* Ferris Greenslet (1875-1959) was an author, editor, intellectual, historian, and member of the Massachusetts Historical Society from 1916 to 1959.

897. Launius, Roger D. A BIBLIOGRAPHY OF THE WORKS OF T. HARRY WILLIAMS. *Louisiana Hist. 1984 25(1): 5-28.* Covers Williams's work by year and publication. Williams won fame for his studies of the Civil War era and as an interpreter of recent Southern politics. The common thread through his writing is an attempt to understand power and its uses in American history.
R. E. Noble

898. Leal, Ildefonso. CARACCIOLO PARRA LEON Y LA HISTORIOGRAFIA VENEZOLANA [Caracciolo Parra León and Venezuelan historiography]. *Bol. de la Acad. Nac. de la Hist. [Venezuela] 1972 55(218): 186-192.* Speech given in 1972 honoring Caracciolo Parra León, a Latin American historian of the early 20th century, among whose major works were *La Instrucción en Caracas, 1567-1725* and *Filosofía Universitaria Venezolana, 1788-1821.*

899. Leckie, William H. CARL COKE RISTER. *Great Plains J. 1979 18: 120-123.* Carl Coke Rister (1889-1955) was a friendly "Baptist with a Puritan conscience." Describes Rister's teaching techniques and insists that with graduate students he was a particularly fine teacher. Rister taught at Hardin-Simmons (10 years), Oklahoma (22 years), and Texas Tech (3 years). A productive scholar, he wrote 10 books while at Oklahoma and two more were published posthumously. Best known was *Western America*, coauthored with LeRoy Hafen, which was widely used as a textbook. From a special section on "Historians of the Southern Plains." 3 notes.   O. H. Zabel

900. Lefebvre, Georges. LETTRES À ALFRED RUFER (1935-1945) [Letters to Alfred Rufer, 1935-45]. *Ann. Hist. de la Révolution Française [France] 1980 52(4): 615-620.* Eight letters discussing Georges Lefebvre's research on the French Revolution, current events, and his personal life.   R. Aldrich

901. Leith, James A. L'INFLUENCE DE SOBOUL AU CANADA [Soboul's influence in Canada]. *Ann. Hist. de la Révolution Française [France] 1982 54(4): 585-588.* Examines influence of Albert Soboul on Canadian historians and their criticisms of his works on the French Revolution.   R. Aldrich

902. Leonidov, L. VOENNO-ISTORICHESKIE ISSLEDOVANIIA A. M. ZAIONCHKOVSKOGO [The military-historical research of A. M. Zaionchkovski]. *Voenno-Istoricheskii Zhurnal [USSR] 1972 (6): 99-104.* Although he was not a Marxist, the works of A. M. Zaionchkovski (1862-1926) are of great value to the historian of military operations of the Eastern Front during World War I, and his ideas helped in the construction of the Red Army.

903. Levenberg, S. SIMON DUBNOV: HISTORIAN OF RUSSIAN JEWRY. *Soviet Jewish Affairs [Great Britain] 1982 12(1): 3-17.* Discusses Russian-Jewish historian Simon Dubnow and his belief in the cultural and social durability of the Diaspora; examines Dubnow's historiography of Russian and East European Jews.

904. Lewis, Gordon K. MR. CHURCHILL AS HISTORIAN. *Historian 1958 20(4): 387-414.* Winston Churchill's historiography (primarily *World Crisis, History of the Second World War,* and *History of the English Speaking People),* rather than being incisive history, reveals itself to be the product of a particular social class, achieving importance for the insight it provides into the thought processes of a great statesman and for the light that his interpretation of the past sheds on the present.

905. Liu, Nicolae. JULES MICHELET ÎN CONŞTIINŢA ROMÂNEASCĂ [Jules Michelet in the conscience of the Romanians]. *Rev. de Istorie [Romania] 1974 27(3): 363-384.* Occasioned by the centennial of the death of the great French historian, the author recalls Michelet's life and work in the political, scientific, social, and artistic conscience of the Romanian people, in the creation of eminent representatives of Romanian culture and historiography.   RSA 11:1660

906. Ljubšić, Radoš. BIBLIOGRAFIJA RADOVA DRAGOSLAVA STRANJAČKOVIĆA [Bibliography of the works of Dragoslav Stranjačković]. *Istorijski Glasnik [Yugoslavia] 1978 (1-2): 201-212.* A bibliography, by year of publication, of the works of Dragoslav Stranjačković, (1901-66) a Serbian historian of the 19th and early 20th centuries.

907. Lobodovs'kyi, Iuzef. SOLZHENITSYN IAK ISTORYK I POLITYK [Solzhenitsyn as a historian and politician]. *Sučasnist [West Germany] 1975 (11): 90-98.* A translated reprint of an article, first published in the London Polish periodical *Viadomosti,* July 1975, whose author criticizes Solzhenitsyn's historical judgment and political attitudes.

908. Locher, Gottfried W. UNSER WEGWEISER: DIE SWINGLI-BIBLIOGRAPHIE ULRICH GÄBLERS [Our trailblazer: the Zwingli bibliography of Ulrich Gäbler]. *Zwingliana [Switzerland] 1979 15(1): 50-56.* Surveys Gäbler's scholarship and that of other scholars on Ulrich Zwingli, 1897-1972. Biblio.
D. R. Stevenson

909. Lönne, Karl-Egon. ZUR TEXTGESTALTUNG DER WERKE BENEDETTO CROCES [On text structure in the works of Benedetto Croce]. *Quellen und Forschungen aus Italienischen Archiven und Bibliotheken [Italy] 1971 50: 355-381.* Examines the question of whether a new historical edition of Benedetto Croce's (1866-1952) works is needed because of changes in concept and content in earlier editions. Describes in detail the different editions of some of Croce's early works. In most cases substantial changes were so minimal that a complete historical edition would not be worth the effort. Based on Croce's works; 77 notes.
J. B. Street

910. Lovera DeSola, Roberto J. LA OBRA HISTÓRICA DE AUGUSTO MIJARES [Historical work of Augusto Mijares]. *Bol. Hist. [Venezuela] 1974 12(35): 256-283.* Augusto Mijares, a classic essayist of Venezuela's history, is noted for his revision of Venezue-

lan historiography. Beginning with the 18th century, he sought to discover the motivating forces of the independence movements by studying the ideas and prominent figures of the period rather than events. *Lo afirmativo venezolano* (1963) is an important collection of essays in which Mijares reinterpreted Venezuela's social, and political past. 40 notes. G. Pizzimenti

911. Lūsis, K. K. R. VIPERS CEL·LĀ UZ MATERIĀLISTISKO VĒSTURES IZPRATNI [Robert Vipper on the way to a materialist understanding of history]. *Latvijas PSR Zinātņu Akadēmijas Vēstis [USSR] 1976 (3): 102-113*. Critically examines the approach of Russian historian Robert I. Vipper (1859-1954) to dialectical materialism before 1940, and discusses his gradual renunciation of idealistic principles during 1941-54; his philosophical writings reflected this change.

912. Lynn, Kenneth S. ONLY YESTERDAY. *Am. Scholar 1980 49(4): 513-518*. Traces the motivations and prejudices of journalist Frederick Lewis Allen's best-selling book of 1931, *Only Yesterday*. Allen's view of history derived from his Puritan heritage, professional training, and political liberalism. F. F. Harling

913. MacDougall, H. A. NEWMAN—HISTORIAN OR APOLO-GIST? *Can. Hist. Assoc. Hist. Papers 1968: 152-163*. Analyzes Cardinal John Henry Newman's contribution to history. As an Oxford Reformer, John Henry Newman came to history because of a desire to reform the Church of England, moving to an acceptance of Rome after studying the Early Church. Although he introduced evolutionary theory into theological study before Darwin enunciated the biological theory, Newman did regard history as an autonomous enterprise. He used facts and chronology to further a moral cause. Based on manuscripts in the Cambridge University Library and secondary works; 41 notes. G. E. Panting

914. Maciu, Vasile. V. I. LENIN: ISTORIC [V. I. Lenin: historian]. *Studii și Articole de Isorie [Rumania] 1970 (15): 15-21*. Emphasizes the historical basis of Lenin's political theory, and analyzes the historical content of his work.

915. Madaj, M. J. OBITUARIES. *Catholic Hist. Rev. 1978 64(1): 138*. A remembrance of Father Joseph Vincent Swastek (1913-77), who died unexpectedly on 5 September 1977. Fr. Swastek was ordained in 1940, and thereupon began graduate work at the University of Notre Dame, Catholic University, Ottawa University, and the University of Michigan. He specialized in Polish American history, in which discipline he was both a pioneer and a leader. He was a charter member of the Polish American Historical Association and very active in its affairs for a quarter century. He published extensively. V. L. Human

916. Magdolenová, Anna. PETER KELLNER-HOSTINSKÝ AKO HISTORIK [Peter Kellner-Hostinský as a historian]. *Hist. Časopis [Czechoslovakia] 1981 29(1): 103-115*. Characterizes Peter Kellner-Hostinský's historical works on the economic, political, and cultural history of Hungary and quotes some other works in which his interests are presented together with his relations to the history of the Slavs. Kellner-Hostinský supported Slovak political ideology in his works and tried to find its historical role within the struggle of the Slovaks for their equal rights with the Hungarian nation. J

917. Mangoni, Luisa. ALFREDO ORIANI E LA CULTURA POLITICA DEL SUO TEMPO [Alfredo Oriani and the political culture of his time]. *Studi Storici [Italy] 1984 25(1): 169-180*. Revises the view, expressed by Benedetto Croce and widely accepted, that Alfredo Oriani was an isolated thinker. His works, *Il Matrimonio* (1923) and *La Lotta Politica in Italia: Origini della Lotta Attuale (476-1887)* (1925) can be related not only to Italian thinkers of his time but especially to the historical studies of France by Hippolyte Taine and the call for moral and intellectual reform in the work of Ernest Renan. In *La Rivolta Ideale* (1924), Oriani shed light on the *fin-de-siècle* crisis of political authority, nationalism, antidemocratic idealism as well as on problems of the Italian state, race, and political traditions. 45 notes. J. W. Houlihan

918. Mańkowski, Zygmunt. O TWÓRCZOŚCI CZESŁAWA MADAJCZYKA [The writing of Czesław Madajczyk]. *Kwartalnik Hist. [Poland] 1981 88(3): 761-769*. Celebrates the 25th anniversary of Madajczyk's historical writing. A prolific author, Madajczyk's interest is in German policy in occupied Poland. His research concentrates on the period between the two world wars. In the field of general history his studies center on the Third Reich and fascism. H. Heitzman-Wojcicka

919. Manley, Kenneth R. JOHN RIPPON AND BAPTIST HISTORIOGRAPHY. *Baptist Q. [Great Britain] 1979 28(3): 109-125*. Biography of John Rippon (1751-1836), Baptist pastor in Southwark, England, and his contribution to the writing of early Baptist history.

920. Marini, Giuliano. IL METODO DI SAVIGNY IN ALCUNI GIUDIZI DELL'ANNO 1883 [The method of Savigny according to some judgments of the year 1883]. *Pensiero Pol. [Italy] 1982 15(1): 308-316*. In 1883 several German writers explained the contributions of Friedrich Karl von Savigny (1779-1861) to historical science. All underlined his refusal of a Hegelian type of system and unilateral historicism and his insistence on the role of individuals whose unreflected interaction, rather than collective forces, constitutes the web of history. 34 notes. J. V. Coutinho

921. Marino, Adrian. N. IORGA ET LES PREMIERS SIGNES DE LA MODERNISATION ROUMAINE [N. Iorga and the first signs of Romania's modernization]. *Synthesis [Romania] 1979 6: 93-96*. The historian Nicolae Iorga was the first to uncover the influence of the European Enlightenment on Romanian culture and civilization. He systematically documented the depth and development of this progressive, modernist, and antifeudal ideology in his country. Note. J. V. Coutinho

922. Markishka, Darina. VIKTOR IVANOVICH GRIGOROVICH I MINALOTO NA BULGARSKIIA NAROD [Viktor Ivanovich Grigorovich and the past of the Bulgarian people]. *Istoricheski Pregled [Bulgaria] 1978 34(1): 67-84*. Traces the career of the 19th-century Slavicist, Viktor Grigorovich (1815-76) and discusses the contributions he made to the study of Bulgarian history, language, and folklore. During 1844-47 Grigorovich made an extensive journey in European Turkey visiting Bulgarian monasteries and villages. Papers and publications based on the research accomplished during this journey were a major initial contribution to the field of Bulgarian studies. Based on Grigorovich's works and other published memoirs; 145 notes. F. B. Chary

923. Markov, Walter. ALBERT SOBOUL ET L'HISTORIOGRAPHIE D'EXPRESSION ALLEMANDE [Albert Soboul and German-language historiography]. *Ann. Hist. de la Révolution Française [France] 1982 54(4): 567-571*. Through translations of his works, visits to universities, and teaching, Soboul had a great influence on German-speaking historians of the French Revolution. R. Aldrich

924. Marlinski, S. Ia. ALEKSEI ALEKSEEVICH POKROVSKI [Aleksei Alekseevich Pokrovski]. *Istoriia SSSR [USSR] 1974 (5): 140-144*. An appreciative evaluation of the teaching and historical research of Aleksei Pokrovski (1875-1954) by one of his students. All of Pokrovski's work had a bibliographical character. He was the foremost authority on the documents, registers, public prints, etc., of Russia before and after the revolution and greatly extended historical and archaeological investigation. The author suggests the value of an archival organization of Pokrovski's own work. 16 notes. J. Wilkinson

925. Marsina, Richard. SAMUEL TIMON A JEHO PREDSTAVY O NAJSTARŠÍCH DEJINÁCH SLOVÁKOV [Samuel Timon (1675-1736) and his ideas on the earliest history of the Slovaks]. *Hist. Časopis [Czechoslovakia] 1980 28(2): 238-251*. Samuel Timon is considered a pioneer in the critical historiography of Hungary. He taught at Trnava University and Košice University. Timon wrote the first critical synthesis of the history of Hungary, 1000-1578, and the history of Pannonia before the kingdom of Hungary

was established as well as historical biographies of Hungarian cardinals and works on topography. Timon considered the predecessors of the Slovaks as the oldest inhabitants of Pannonia.

J/S

926. Marsina, Richard. SAMUEL TIMON AND HIS VIEWS ON THE EARLY SLOVAK HISTORY. *Studia Historica Slovaca [Czechoslovakia] 1984 13: 91-105.* Adapts and expands an earlier article. Samuel Timon (1675-1737) founded modern Hungarian critical historiography. He studied the history and topography of Pannonia before and during the Hungarian monarchy. He regarded the Slavic ancestors of the Slovaks as the oldest extant population of the region. 83 notes.
R. Grove

927. Martín Gallardo, Francisco. FERMÍN CABALLERO Y MENÉNDEZ PELAYO [Fermín Caballero and Menéndez Pelayo]. *Bol. de la Biblioteca de Menéndez Pelayo [Spain] 1975 52(1-4): 313-327.* Documents the high esteem in which Fermín Caballero (1800-76) was held by Marcelino Menéndez Pelayo (1856-1912). An appendix of five letters from Fermín and his son Félix, 1875-95, suggests that a fifth and still unpublished volume of Caballero's major work, *Conqueses Ilustres,* had been completed before his death. 15 notes.
L. H. Nelson

928. Maslin, M. A. TEORETICHESKOE NASLEDIE N. G. CHERNYSHEVSKOGO V SOVREMENNOI BOR'BE IDEI [The theoretical heritage of Nikolai Chernyshevsky and its role in the contemporary ideological struggle]. *Acta U. Carolinae Phil. et Hist. [Czechoslovakia] 1979 (4): 141-157.* Criticizes the works of F. B. Randall, J. P. Scanlan, N. G. O. Pereira, V. Terras, R. Kindersley, and J. A. Rogers—American writers and historians who deny the originality of Chernyshevsky's philosophical ideas and stress the political nature of his aesthetics. Shows the impact Chernyshevsky had on the transformation of the anthropological principle into the general concept of social and political determinism.
R. Kirillov

929. McCaffery, Larry. STANLEY ELKINS: A BIBLIOGRAPHY 1957-77. *Bull. of Biblio. and Mag. Notes 1977 34(2): 73-76.* Includes works by Elkins and critical evaluations of them.

930. McGill, William J. HERBERT BUTTERFIELD AND THE IDEA OF LIBERTY. *South Atlantic Q. 1971 70(1): 1-12.* Butterfield's criticism of the "Whig interpretation of history" centers on their simplistic perception of history rather than on their interest in liberty. Instead of the gradual triumph of liberty over tyranny, Butterfield sees history as the complex paradox of man's refusal to accept liberty or its responsibilities. Liberty must be understood in terms of its spiritual origin in the freedom of conscience and in the historical struggle to produce tangible freedoms in order to withstand the pressures of society. The historian's role is not to fix blame for injustices, but to increase human understanding necessary for liberty by the pursuit of truth. Based on Butterfield's writings and secondary sources; 34 notes.
W. L. Olbrich

931. McGinnis, A. C. JOHN P. MORROW, JR. *Arkansas Hist. Q. 1978 37(3): 278-279.* Obituary of surveyor, engineer, and Arkansas historian John Patterson Morrow, Jr. (1907-78). Illus.
G. R. Schroeder

932. McIntyre, W. D. PHILIP ROSS MAY (1929-77). *Hist. News [New Zealand] 1977 (35): 13.* Discusses Philip Ross May's career in historical research and his works on gold rushes in New Zealand and California.

933. McKinney, Gordon B. THE WORLD OF WILLIAM LYNWOOD MONTELL. *Appalachian J. 1984 11(3): 255-259.* Surveys the work of oral historian William Lynwood Montell, who in his three books has illuminated the black and white cultures of Appalachia.

934. McNeill, John T. JOHN FOXE: HISTORIOGRAPHER, DISCIPLINARIAN, TOLERATIONIST. *Church Hist. 1974 43(2): 216-229.* Records the salient facts of John Foxe's life (1516-87). Foxe was a man of widely varied interests and talents who served as an irenic spirit amid contending forces and played a minor role in

public life while researching and writing the works that would bring him fame. Foxe was a sometime historiographer, a martyrologist, a humanist, an Erasmian, a Puritan, and an Anglican; he was the Elizabethan Eusebius and an Erastian precursor of Elizabethan nationalism. An independent thinker, Foxe was not unduly influenced by either the continental reformers or the Elizabethan divines. Based on V. Norskov Olsen's *John Foxe and the Elizabethan Church,* editions of Foxe's work, and other secondary sources; 37 notes.
M. D. Dibert

935. Megill, Allan. FOUCAULT, STRUCTURALISM, AND THE ENDS OF HISTORY. *J. of Modern Hist. 1979 51(3): 451-503.* Though he has written many allegedly historical works, Michel Foucault is a myth-maker rather than a historian in any conventional sense. Sometimes labeled a structuralist, he was never a structuralist in the senses usually intended by his commentators. But at least until *The Archaeology of Knowledge* (1969) he was a structuralist in the broader sense of adhering to a quasi-scientific Apollonian formalism, claiming to uncover the structures according to which past thought was organized. Even in his early work, however, there was an arbitrariness that set him apart from conventional historians, and more recently he has acknowledged that, following the line established by Nietzsche in *The Use and Disadvantage of History,* he intends his history to be taken as myth. But the status of such a historiography is questionable, for if it purports to examine the past from the standpoint of the present, its conception of the present is equally a myth.
J

936. Melent'ev, Iu. S. FILOSOFIIA N. G. CHERNYSHEVSKOGO I NEKOTORYE VOPROSY SOVREMENNOI IDEOLOGICHESKOI BOR'BY [N. G. Chernyshevsky's philosophy and some problems of the present-day ideological struggle]. *Voprosy Filosofii [USSR] 1978 (6): 43-56.* Characterizes the main features of the philosophy of Nikolai Chernyshevski, his attitude toward philosophical systems of the past, and his philosophical and social stand on the Russian realities of the 1850's-60's. Concentrates on recent philosophical and sociological conflicts in appraising Chernyshevski's heritage. Russian emigré writers N. Berdyaev, N. Lossky, V. Zenkovsky, and A. Filippov take a reactionary anti-Soviet stand, while American students represent a second trend; M. M. Laserson, J. H. Billington, F. B. Randall, C. A. Moser, G. P. Scanlan, F. P. Woerlin, N. G. Pereira, and R. W. Mathewson are singled out.
J/S

937. Meloni, Vittorio. I SEMINARI INTERNAZIONALI GAETANO MOSCA [The Gaetano Mosca international seminars]. *Risorgimento [Italy] 1984 36(2): 249-255.* Reviews the historiography on the political thought of Gaetano Mosca, including his theory of class politics, his ideas about colonialism, his relationship to the sociology of right and to the party system, and the influence of his ideas on intellectuals and class politics. Gaetano Mosca Archives and secondary sources; 8 notes.
J. W. Houlihan

938. Meshkov, O. V. and Dibrova, S. S. PARTIINYI DIIACH, VCHENYI-ISTORYK (DO 90-RICHCHIA Z DNIA NARODZHENNIA M. M. POPOVA) [A Party worker, scholar, and historian (for the 90th anniversary of the birth of N. N. Popov)]. *Ukrains'kyi Istorychnyi Zhurnal [USSR] 1981 (1): 110-115.* Nikolai Nikolaevich Popov (1890-1940) was born in Kutaisi, Georgia and became a Communist Party worker in Transcaucasia, the Ukraine, and Russia. He is credited with writing the first biography of V. I. Lenin and the outline of the history of the Communist Party. Primary Party sources and Popov's writings; 17 notes.
I. Krushelnyckyj

939. Meyer, Klaus. THEODOR SCHIEMANN UND DIE RUSSISCHE GESCHICHTE [Theodor Schiemann and Russian history]. *Zeitschrift für Ostforschung [West Germany] 1979 28(4): 588-601.* Klaus Meyer's *Theodor Schiemann als politischer Publizist* (1956) considers Theodor Schiemann as a publicist, but the Baltic German historian's role as a scholar has been given little consideration. After 1887, Schiemann made early 19th-century Russian history the center of his work. *Geschichte Russlands unter Nikolaus I,* 4 vol. (1904-19) was a political biography of Tsar Nicholas I and at the same time a study of Russia's political system. His other works are

period studies and an attempt at popularization. Schiemann's norms and values were those of Prussia, and he marks the beginning of German historical interest in Russia.   J/S

940. Mikus, Joseph A. ROBERT WILLIAM SETON-WATSON'S CENTENNIAL. *Jednota Ann. Furdek 1980 19: 135-138.* Examines the Slovak aspects of R. W. Seton-Watson's historiography of the Habsburg Empire on the centennial of the historian's birth.

941. Miliband, S. D. SPISOK OSNOVNYKH TRUDOV DOK-TORA ISTORICHESKIKH NAUK S. A. MKHITARIANA (K 70-LETIIU SO DNIA ROZHDENIIA) [The main works of historian S. A. Mkhitarian, on his 70th birthday]. *Narody Azii i Afriki [USSR] 1981 (3): 245-246.* A list of the main works of S. A. Mkhitarian on Vietnam and Indochina, many of which appeared in the journal *Voprosy Ekonomiki.* The list does not include book reviews, editorial work, or newspaper articles.   S. J. Talalay

942. Milutinović, Kosta. FRANJO RAČKI I ILARION RU-VARAC [Franjo Rački and Ilarion Ruvarac]. *Zbornik za Istoriju [Yugoslavia] 1980 (21): 159-170.* Describes the contributions of the Croatian Rački and the Serbian Ruvarac to the exploration of the Yugoslav past. 63 notes.   P. J. Adler

943. Milutinović, Kosta. SIMA LUKIN LAZIĆ I STANOJE STANOJEVIĆ [Sima Lukin Lazić and Stanoje Stanojević]. *Zbornik za Istoriju [Yugoslavia] 1981 (23): 205-210.* In the late-19th century, a polemic was carried on between adherents of the oldstyle chauvinist historiography, and the modern, rationalist, documentary style among the Serbs of Hungary. An exemplar of the first was Sima Lukin Lazić, a self-taught popularizer who wrote in Serbian almanacs and newspapers of the day. Lazić's views were severely contested by Stanoje Stanojević, one of a rising number of scientifically trained historians who gathered around Ilarion Ruvarac in an attempt to dispel the fictions and mythical preconceptions that had harmed the progress of national historiography for many years. 24 notes.   P. J. Adler

944. Mommsen, Wolfgang J. IN MEMORIAM KARL-GEORG FABER 1925-1982 [In memoriam: Karl-Georg Faber (1925-82)]. *Storia della Storiografia [Italy] 1982 (2): 3-10.* Commemorates Faber's contributions to regional and political historiography and the theory of history. A founding member of the International Commission for the History of Historical Sciences, coeditor of this journal, and faculty member at Münster University, Faber turned from work in German regional and political history to theoretical problems of historiography after 1950. A historian in the tradition of ideologically inspired political history, Faber, in his last, still unpublished, writings, defended a critically reformed historicism against the Annales School's "new history." Based on K.-G. Faber's works; 16 notes.   G. Herritt

945. Monguillot, Manuel Salvat. ALTAMIRA Y LA HISTORIA [Altamira and history]. *R. Chilena de Hist. y Geografía [Chile] 1966 (134): 180-196.* A judgment on the work of the Spanish historiographer Rafael Altamira y Crevea (1866-1951), who criticized "modern" tendencies and established bases for the correct teaching of history. His methods helped spread the idea of "integral history" (political, social, etc.), opened unexplored avenues in the investigation of Indian law, and recognized the importance of critical evaluation of sources. Primary sources; 42 notes.   L. R. Atkins

946. Montpensier, Roy Stone de. MAITLAND AND THE INTERPRETATION OF HISTORY. *Am. J. of Legal Hist. 1966 10(4): 259-281.* Discusses the historiography and methodology of British historian Frederic William Maitland (1850-1906), particularly his *Domesday Book and Beyond,* concluding that he was more an interpreter according to Whig political ideology; also explores Maitland's concept of the law and jurisprudential history reflected in his works.

947. Morato, Josefina and Oñate, Modesta. BIBLIOGRAFIA DEL DOCTOR PEDRO BOHIGAS BALAGUER [Bibliography of Doctor Pedro Bohigas Balaguer]. *Biblioteconomía [Spain] 1971 28(73/*

74): 3-30. Describes the works of Pedro Bohigas Balaguer which include studies on history and literature, principally Catalan. Appendixes.   A. V. (IHE 85350)

948. Moscati, Laura. FEDERICO SCLOPIS STORICO DEI LONGOBARDI [Federico Sclopis, historian of the Lombards]. *Rassegna Storica del Risorgimento [Italy] 1979 66(3): 259-276.* Historian Federico Sclopis (1798-1878) said that the German tribes did not unite Italy because of the interference of the Catholic Church and the invasion of the Franks. Sclopis evaluated the favorable contribution to Italy of the German institutions which affected the juridical, administrative, and social aspects. Based on the Sclopis Papers at the Accademia delle Scienze di Torino, and secondary sources.
A. Sbacchi

949. Mühlpfordt, Günter. KARL HAGEN: EIN PROGRESSIVER HISTORIKER IM VORMÄRZ ÜBER DIE RADIKALE REFORMATION [Karl Hagen: a progressive Vormärz historian on the radical Reformation]. *Jahrbuch für Geschichte [East Germany] 1980 21: 63-101.* A study of the political ideas, activities, and writings of Karl Hagen (1810-68), historian, publicist, and radical social democrat. His libertarian ideology is linked through Hegel to the Reformation. His *History of the Reformation* (1841-44) is important for its inclusion of the reform movement in its dual structure of moderate and radical elements. In cooperation with Johann Wirth, another prominent democrat, Hagen published *Braga* in 1838-39, a platform for a historical democratic view.   T. Parker

950. Mulryan, John. SIR PHILIP AND THE SCHOLARS: A REVIEW ARTICLE. *Cithara 1974 13(2): 76-82.* Reviews recent historiography on Sir Philip Sidney (1554-86), a British Renaissance man.

951. Murrah, David J. WILLIAM CURRY HOLDEN. *Great Plains J. 1979 18: 107-113.* Holden was born in Texas in 1896 and educated at the University of Texas. He received a Ph.D. in history in 1928. His teaching career centered on Texas Technological College and he made an indelible impression there as "historian-archeologist-anthropologist-museum director and author (11 books, 50 articles). He directed the West Texas Museum for 36 years, created Texas Tech University's The Southwest Collection and served in various administrative capacities. Without Holden much of west Texas history would have perished. From a special section on "Historians of the Southern Plains." 21 notes.   O. H. Zabel

952. Myslivchenko, A. G. EVOLIUTSIIA MIROVOZZRENIIA ERIKA GEIERA [Evolution of Erik Geijer's world outlook]. *Voprosy Filosofii [USSR] 1974(9): 123-131.* Analyzes the world outlook of the eminent Swedish historian and philosopher of the first half of the 19th century, Erik Gustav Geijer. In the first period of his activity Geijer stood for romanticism and conservatism. In the second, however, he reverted to bourgeois democracy and liberalism. In the last period, before Marx, Geijer suggested remarkable ideas on the formation of new class contradictions; he also hazarded a conjecture on the material nature of motive forces of history. However, the author argues the groundlessness of the attempts of some scholars to consider Geijer as a supporter of theism and particularly as a "Marxist before Marx." The personality principle was fundamental in Geijer's views and it accompanied the mainstream of Swedish philosophy. The main specific feature of that philosophy was a constant interest for ethical and human problems.   J

953. Naidenov, M. E. M. N. POKROVSKII I EGO MESTO V SOVETSKOI ISTORIOGRAFII [M. N. Pokrovski and his place in Soviet historiography]. *Istoriia SSSR [USSR] 1962 6(3): 48-71.* Discusses the political and historical philosophy of Mikhail N. Pokrovski (1868-1932) and his gradual shift, 1890-1920's from bourgeois idealism to economic materialism and, finally, to Marxism. Though errors in his economic theories and an insufficient knowledge of Marxist dialectics are blameworthy, the posthumous, official rejection of his historical concepts under Stalin's cult of personality is inexcusable. 26 notes.   N. Frenkley

954. Nardin, V. V. OSNOVNYE VOPROSY ISTORICHESKOI KONTSEPTSII M. N. POKROVSKOGO [Basic problems of M. N. Pokrovski's concept of history]. *Vestnik Moskovskogo U. Seriia 9: Istoriia [USSR] 1970 25(5): 19-31.* Deals with the critical evaluation of the socioeconomic, political, and historical philosophy of Mikhail Nikolaevich Pokrovski (1868-1932) in Soviet historiography: idolized in the 1920's, vilified in the 1930's-mid-1950's, Pokrovski is now being objectively reappraised. Four stages are recognized in Pokrovski's evolution from historic idealism, 1896-1907, to economic materialism, 1908-14, Marxist concept of history, 1908-14, and a deviation toward a bourgeois economic conception, 1915-27, repudiated in the final years of his life. 64 notes.

N. Frenkley

955. Nasko, Siegfried. BIBL CONTRA SRIBIK. EIN BEITRAG ZUR HISTORIOGRAPHISCHEN POLEMIK UM METTERNICH [Bibl versus Srbik: a contribution on the historiographical polemic on Metternich]. *Österreich in Geschichte und Literatur [Austria] 1971 (15)9: 497-513.* Analyzes the confrontation in the 1920's between the liberal Austrian historian Viktor Bibl (1870-1947) and the traditional national historian Heinrich von Srbik (1878-1951) on the interpretation of Metternich's role. Based on Bibl's and Srbik's works and secondary literature; 59 notes.

R. Wagnleitner

956. Nazarov, V. D. NAUCHNAIA KONFERENTSIIA PAMIATI AKADEMIKA L'VA VLADIMIROVICHA CHEREPNINA [Seminar in memory of Academician Lev Vladimirovich Cherepnin]. *Istoriia SSSR [USSR] 1981 (6): 208-210.* Discusses the proceedings at a seminar organized by the Academy of Sciences of the USSR and Moscow State University and held 26-28 November 1980 in memory of the Soviet historian Academician Lev Vladimirovich Cherepnin (1905-77). More than 120 historians from 38 academic organizations, universities, archival centers, museums, and journals from all over the USSR described Cherepnin's contribution to the study of the formation and development of the centralized Russian state. In his opening report, Academician V. T. Pashuto hailed Cherepnin's innovative work in the sphere of methodology, especially his comparative historical analysis. A. D. Gorskii reviewed Cherepnin's writing on the Russian state in the 14th to 16th centuries and the land councils from the 16th to 18th centuries. Other speakers included A. A. Preobrazhenski, who examined Cherepnin's study of the class struggle in the 17th to 18th centuries.

J. Bamber

957. Neumann, Wilhelm. DER PARACELSUS-RING DER STADT VILLACH FÜR GOTBERT MORO [The Paracelsus Circle of the town of Villach for Gotbert Moro]. *Carinthia I [Austria] 1979 169: 311-317.* In 1979 in Villach Professor Gotbert Moro was honored by admission to the Paracelsus Circle for his work on the physician and alchemist Paracelsus (1493-1531) since 1950.

958. Nevler, V. E. N. G. CHERNYSHEVSKII V ITAL'IANSKOI ISTORIOGRAFII [N. G. Chernyshevski in Italian historiography]. *Istoriia SSSR [USSR] 1980 (5): 216-221.* Considers the place in modern Italian historiography of the 19th-century Russian revolutionary Nikolai Chernyshevski. Italian historians of various political persuasions recognize Chernyshevski's sympathy with the Risorgimento and regard him with esteem. Chernyshevski's ideas attracted the attention of all the leading Italian thinkers of the second half of the 19th century and continue to influence contemporary Italian historiography. 37 notes.

J. W. Long

959. Nevler, V. E. A. V. LUNACHARSKII-ISTORIK ITALII [Anatoli Lunacharski: historian of Italy]. *Voprosy Istorii [USSR] 1978 (8): 202-206.* Recalls an often-overlooked aspect of Lunacharski's activities, i.e., his interest in Italian affairs, which originated in 1905 when he worked as a journalist under Lenin in Switzerland. During the next 10 years or more he familiarized himself with Italian politics. Apart from contributions to Lenin's papers, *Vpered* and *Proletarii*, Lunacharski's only publications in this field were *Italy and the War* (Petrograd, 1917) and two later articles in 1923 and 1929. Based on Russian printed sources.

J. P. H. Myers

960. Newman, Edgar and Friguglietti, James. ALBERT SOBOUL ET LES HISTORIENS DES ETATS-UNIS [Albert Soboul and the US historians]. *Ann. Hist. de la Révolution Française [France] 1982 54(4): 589-593.* Examines the influence of Soboul's work on American historians and his visits to the United States.

R. Aldrich

961. Niedermayer, Franz. ADIOS A HANS RHEINFELDER, AMIGO DE ESPAÑA [Farewell to Hans Rheinfelder, friend of Spain]. *Arbor [Spain] 1972 81(315): 97-100.* Gives a necrological note on the German Hispanist, Hans Rheinfelder, a professor at the University of Munich.

R. O. (IHE 84011)

962. Norman, Birger. ANTECKNINGAR OM EN BERÄTTELSE [Notes on a report]. *Hist. Tidskrift [Sweden] 1970 (1): 4-15.* Birger Norman was asked by the editors of *Historisk Tidskrift* to write about the knowledge he gained in writing his book on the 1931 strike in Ådalen. He describes his thoughts on the need to read and write history, and on history as literature.

B. L. Jeppesen

963. Nunis, Doyce B., Jr. A DEDICATION TO THE MEMORY OF MAYNARD J. GEIGER, O.F.M., 1901-1977. *Arizona and the West 1978 20(3): 198-202.* Franciscan Fr. Maynard Joseph Geiger (1901-77) completed his philosophical and theological studies in California and was ordained to the priesthood. His M.A. work at St. Bonaventure College, New York, in English and Spanish were preparatory for his doctorate in Hispanic American history in 1937 at The Catholic University of America, Washington, D. C. His professional career was spent as archivist and historian at Mission Santa Barbara, California. His early writings focused on Spanish Florida. Later his scholarship was concerned with the Franciscan missionaries in California, particularly Junípero Serra. Illus., biblio.

D. L. Smith

964. Nunis, Doyce B., Jr. MEMORIAL TO REV. MAYNARD J. GEIGER, O.F.M. *J. of California and Great Basin Anthrop. 1977 4(2): 155-172.* Maynard J. Geiger (1901-77), a Franciscan priest at Mission Santa Barbara, California, wrote on Mission and Indian life; includes an extensive bibliography of his articles, books, and newspaper articles, 1936-76.

965. Oestreich, Gerhard. ESSAYS ON HINTZE. *Hist. and Theory 1978 17(1): 99-112.* Review article on *The Historical Essays of Otto Hintze,* edited by Felix Gilbert with the assistance of Robert M. Berdahl (New York: Oxford U. Pr., 1975). Although Gilbert's translation contains only isolated selections of Hintze's work, it is a welcome introduction to one of the major historical thinkers of the 20th century. Discusses Hintze's life and the development of his thought, which is only now being discussed by historians in Germany. In his preoccupation with Marx, Hintze developed "a theory of history within the literature of sociology," which was his major contribution. 20 notes.

D. A. Yanchisin

966. O'Muiri, Reamonn. LAMHSCRIBHINN STAIRE AN BHIONAIDIGH [Bennett's historical manuscript]. *Seanchas Ard Mhacha [Ireland] 1978 9(1): 123-127.* Discusses Arthur Bennett's (1793-1879) life and literary interests and describes the contents of *Wars of Ireland* or the encounters of Gael and Gall, begun in 1844. Gives information on Bennett's efforts to have his work published. Based on the manuscript in private possession of Brendan McEoin, Downpatrick, Co. Down with a copy in the Public Record Office, Belfast.

967. Ortega y Medina, Juan A. OTRA VEZ HUMBOLDT, ESE CONTROVERTIDO PERSONAJE [Humboldt once more, this controversial personality]. *Hist. Mexicana [Mexico] 1976 25(3): 423-454.* Discusses the continuing historiographical polemic on the role and personality of Alexander von Humboldt (1769-1859), especially in recent works by Jaime Labastida which show Humboldt the nationalist in inner conflict with Humboldt the universal scientist. 44 notes.

S. P. Carr

968. Pach, Zsigmond Pál. [V. I. LENIN'S WORKS AND INTERPRETATIONS OF HISTORY]. *Történelmi Szemle [Hungary] 1970 13(2): 207-209, 256-259.*

—. MEGNYITÓ A MTA TÖRTÉNETTUDOMÁNYI INTÉZETE TUDOMÁNYOS ÜLÉSÉN LENIN SZÜLETÉSÉNK 100 ÉVFORDULÓJA ALKALMÁBÓL [Opening speech of the commemorative scientific session at the Historical Institute of the Hungarian Academy of Sciences to celebrate the 100th birthday of Lenin], *pp. 207-209.* There are three possible approaches to Lenin's work on history: 1) to study Lenin's own historical writings, 2) to consider his theoretical contribution to the understanding of historical phenomena; and 3) to assess his role in the development of historical materialism.

—. ZÁRSZÓ [Afterword], *pp. 256-259.* In pursuing historical research one should utilize Lenin's methodological insights which rest on an acceptance of Karl Marx's and Friedrich Engels's teachings, on the correct periodization of history, on the comparative method, and on the extensive use of historical statistics.   I. Hont

969. Papoulidis, Constantin. SYNODIS D. PAPADIMITRIOU [Synodis D. Papadimitriou]. *Makedoniká [Greece] 1975 16: 174-203.* Synodis D. Papadimitriou (1859-1921) was born in Salonika. He became a famous medievalist teaching at the University of Odessa. 99 notes., biblio.   A. J. Papalas

970. Paquette, Jean-Marcel. FRANÇOIS-XAVIER DE CHARLEVOIX OU LA MÉTAPHORE HISTORIENNE: CONTRIBUTION À UNE SYSTÉMATIQUE DU RECIT HISTORIOGRAPHIQUE [François-Xavier de Charlevoix or the historical metaphor: Contribution to a systematization of a historiographical narrative]. *Recherches Sociographiques [Canada] 1974 15(1): 9-19.* François-Xavier de Charlevoix's (1682-1761) narratives of New France provided modern historians with a sound perspective and an advanced historical methodology in their work. The importance of Charlevoix in this historiographical realm remains unacknowledged.   A. E. LeBlanc

971. Parente, Luigi. GIUSTINO FORTUNATO STORICO DEL RISORGIMENTO [Giustino Fortunati, historian of the Risorgimento]. *Rassegna Storica del Risorgimento [Italy] 1976 63(4): 422-440.* Giustino Fortunato, a historian of the Risorgimento, concentrated his studies primarily on the regions of Southern Italy and the city of Naples. A very thorough and precise analysis of historical data characterizes his work but perhaps even more characteristic is his bias as a member of a pro-Bourbon family of large landholders in Lucania. Fortunato never understood the dynamic of social classes and the consequences of their struggles nor did he comprehend the importance of the emerging human sciences such as demography, sociology, or psychoanalysis. 76 notes.
                                                      M. T. Wilson

972. Parry, G. J. R. WILLIAM HARRISON AND HOLINSHED'S CHRONICLES. *Historical Journal [Great Britain] 1984 27(4): 789-810.* Investigates the influence of William Harrison's works on Raphael Holinshed's *Chronicles of England, Scotlande and Irelande* (1577). Harrison, the author of the *Description of Britain* published in Holinshed's *Chronicles,* also worked on a chronology. The manuscript of Harrison's *Great English Chronology* shows that Holinshed used it for his own work, but he also censored it because of its Puritan view of history. Based on manuscripts of William Harrison and other primary sources; 104 notes.
                                                      H. J. Kaiser

973. Pascoe, Louis B. OBITUARIES. *Catholic Hist. Rev. 1978 64(1): 138-139.* A tribute to Father Harry J. Sievers (1921-77), who died unexpectedly in the Bronx, New York, on 18 October 1977. Fr. Sievers completed his undergraduate work at Loyola University of Chicago. He received his M.A. from Loyola and his Ph.D. from West Baden College, in Indiana. He was ordained in 1953. He taught at several universities, and specialized in research on American presidents. Among his extensive achievements in this field, he was commissioned to write, and completed, the definitive three-volume biography of Indiana's only president, Benjamin Harrison, though his research was not limited to the life of that presi-

dent. Fr. Sievers was a member of the American Catholic Historical Association, and Dean of the Graduate School of Arts and Sciences at Fordham University at the time of his death.
                                                      V. L. Human

974. Perticone, Giacomo. FILOSOFIA E STORIOGRAFIA NEL PENSIERO DI GIORGIO SIMMEL (1858-1918) [Philosophy and historiography in the thought of Georg Simmel (1858-1918)]. *Storia e Politica [Italy] 1969 8(1): 3-13.*

975. Petranović, Branko. JOVAN MARJANOVIĆ [Jovan Marjanović]. *Jugoslovenski Istorijski Časopis [Yugoslavia] 1981 20(1-4): 5-14.* Assesses Jovan Marjanović's contribution to Yugoslav historiography on World War II. His impeccable attention to detail in examining sources has been an example to later generations of scholars, yet his meticulousness did not hamper a lively approach and writing style. Jovan Marjanović will be remembered for particularly useful work on unearthing archival material concerning the Yugoslav Communist Party in Moscow. Also of special interest are his works *Prilozi Istoriji Sukoba Narodnooslobodilačkog Pokreta i Četnika Draže Mihailovića u Srbiji 1941 Godine* [Contributions to the history of the conflict between the national liberation movement and Draža Mihailović's Chetniks in Serbia in 1941] and *Ustanak i Narodnooslobodilački Pokret u Srbiji 1941* [The uprising and the national liberation movement in Serbia in 1941]. He did much to promote the study of Yugoslav history abroad and took part in many international seminars.
                                                      J. Bamber

976. Pier, Arthur S. MARK ANTONY DEWOLFE HOWE. *Massachusetts Hist. Soc. Pro. 1957-60 72: 408-438.* Mark Howe (1864-1960) was an historian, biographer, and poet.

977. Pleterski, Janko. ZGODOVINSKA MISEL SLOVENSKIH MARKSISTOV V ČASU SPERANSOVE KNJIGE [Historical views of the Slovene Marxists at the time of Sperans's book]. *Zgodovinski Časopis [Yugoslavia] 1979 33(4): 533-544.* On the occasion of the 40th anniversary of the publication of *Razvoj slovenskega narodnega vprasanja* [Development of the Slovene national question] by Edvard Kardelj (pseudonym Sperans), the author considers the historiographical activity of the Slovene Marxists, 1932-41, including Ivo Grahor, Dusan Kermavner, Boris Kidric, Vladimir Martelanc, Joze Vilfan, and Boris Ziherl.

978. Podrimavský, Milan. SLOVENSKÉ DEJINY V DIELE Š. M. DAXNERA [Slovak history in the works of Š. M. Daxner]. *Hist. Časopis [Czechoslovakia] 1981 29(4): 506-521.* Discusses the political and historical works of Š. M. Daxner, a leader of the Slovak bourgeois national movement of the 19th century.   J/S

979. Polišenský, Josef and Mikell, Charles. FRANTIŠEK LÜTZOW A PRAHA, 1902-1911 [Francis Lützow and Prague, 1902-11]. *Sborník Národního Muzea v Praze Řada C: Literární Historie [Czechoslovakia] 1973 18(3-5): 71-85.* A Bohemian aristocrat with English family ties, Count Francis Lützow (1849-1916) frequently resided in London. His books on Bohemia, Prague, and John Hus familiarized English readers with Czech history and national aspirations. Lützow was active on behalf of Czech participation in the Exposition of 1906 and in the Olympics of 1908. Based on the Lützow papers in the National Museum in Prague; 64 notes. English summary.   R. E. Weltsch

980. Popescu-Optaşi, Nicolae. ISTORIEI TRANSILVANIEI ÎN PREOCUPĂRILE ŞTIINŢIFICE ALE LUI R. W. SETON-WATSON [Transylvanian history in the scholarly concerns of R. W. Seton-Watson]. *Rev. de Istorie [Romania] 1980 33(1): 169-176.* Surveys the life and works of the British historian Robert W. Seton-Watson (1879-1951), noting his sympathy for Romanian territorial unification. Traces his academic career and political life, relates them to his views on Romania, and stresses the importance of his activities in publicizing the justifications for the Romanian position on Transylvania. 43 notes.   R. O. Khan

981. Popișteanu, Cristian. IN DIALOG CU JOHN SANNESS [Talking with John Sanness]. *Magazin Istoric [Romania] 1982 16(3): 18-19.* A 1980 interview with John Sanness, president of the Nobel Peace Prize Committee, on the relationship of national to international history, Norwegian history, his lectures on World War II, and Romania.

982. Porter, Roger J. GIBBON'S *AUTOBIOGRAPHY*: FILLING UP THE SILENT VOID. *Eighteenth-Cent. Studies 1974 8(1): 1-26.* Throughout his *Autobiography*, Edward Gibbon (1737-94) displayed an obsession with success and fame. In examining the events of his life, Gibbon asserted that every choice and act was undertaken deliberately to further his work as a historian. Despite his attempt to illustrate his control over life, Gibbon admitted that much is subject to chance and circumstance. To defend himself against his consequent fears of deprivation and disorder, Gibbon preoccupied himself with the activity of "filling up" life's emptiness through study. Nonetheless, he discovered that much of what he wrote in the *Decline and Fall* could be applied to individual lives as well. Overall, the events of his own life can be seen to parallel the same natural laws of prosperity, adversity, decay, and impending obscurity displayed by kingdoms and empires. Primary and secondary works; 25 notes.   R. C. Robbins

983. Poster, Mark. ALTHUSSER ON HISTORY WITHOUT MAN. *Pol. Theory 1974 2(4): 393-409.* An exploration of the social theory and historiography of Louis Althusser.

984. Poster, Mark. FOUCAULT E LA STORIA [Foucault and history]. *Comunità [Italy] 1983 37(185): 231-253.* Michel Foucault proposes a new way of interpreting history and linking it with today's political battles. He is an antihistorical historian who, while writing history, calls into question all the canons of the trade.

985. Prawitt, Leo. PHILIPP MATTHÄUS HAHN: EIN VERZEICHNIS DER SEKUNDÄRLITERATUR ZU LEBEN UND WERK [Philipp Matthäus Hahn: an index of the secondary literature on his life and work]. *Blätter für Württembergische Kirchengeschichte [West Germany] 1980-81 80-81: 175-203.* An extensive bibliography in chronological order, which would serve as the basis for a Hahn archive.

986. Price, Jacob M. PARTY, PURPOSE, AND PATTERN: SIR LEWIS NAMIER AND HIS CRITICS. *J. of British Studies 1961 1(1): 71-93.* Examines the historiography of British historian Sir Lewis Namier, 1929-53.

987. Price, Jeffrey Thomas and Baylen, J. O. A POSITIVIST HISTORIAN: H. T. BUCKLE. *Q. Rev. of Hist. Studies [India] 1972/73 12(1): 43-47.* Henry Thomas Buckle (1832-62), author of *The History of Civilization in England*, held that the task of the historian is to discover the laws which determine the conduct of men. Handicapped by this philosophy of history and by the lack of a critical spirit, he nonetheless merits some credit for increasing the scope of historical study to include geographic and sociologic factors, the use of statistics, and comparisons between European and non-European civilizations. 27 notes.   J. M. McCarthy

988. Pronin, P. V. SPISOK NAUCHNYKH TRUDOV S. M. TROITSKOGO [A list of the scholarly works of S. M. Troitski]. *Istoricheski Zapiski Akademii Nauk SSSR [USSR] 1977 98: 360-366.* Bibliography of books, articles, and reviews by the Soviet historian S. M. Troitski (1930-76), mainly concerned with the history of Russia in the 17th and 18th centuries.

989. Prunk, Janko. HISTORIOGRAFSKI ELEMENTI V DELU BORISA KIDRIČA [Historiographic elements in the works of Boris Kidrič]. *Prispevki za Zgodovino Delavskega Gibanja [Yugoslavia] 1978-79 18-19(1-2): 63-68.* Discusses the contributions of historian Boris Kidrič to the historiography of Slovenia.   J/S

990. Qualey, Carlton C. THEODORE C. BLEGEN. *Norwegian-American Studies 1962 21: 3-13.* Theodore C. Blegen served as the editor of the publications of the Norwegian-American Society, 1925-60, but beyond his interest in Norwegians in America,

he also served as the dean of the graduate school at the University of Minnesota. His main interests in terms of historiography included immigrant studies and local history, the latter of which he spent a great deal of his spare time pursuing, and in many cases, defending. While his writings on immigrant history covered a diversity of ethnic groups, his main area of interest was with the Norwegian Americans. Secondary sources; 9 notes, biblio.   G. A. Hewlett

991. Radu, Gil. METODA LUI NICOLAE IORGA ÎN SCRIEREA ISTORIEI [Nicolae Iorga's method in writing history]. *Analele U. București: Filosofie [Romania] 1978 27: 65-72.* Analyzes the methodology of the Romanian historian Nicolae Iorga, noting his emphasis on the correct use of sources and the placing of historical facts in their wider contemporary context.

992. Rae, Thomas I. THE HISTORICAL WRITING OF DRUMMOND OF HAWTHORNDEN. *Scottish Hist. Rev. [Great Britain] 1975 54(1): 22-62.* William Drummond (1585-1649), Scottish poet and man of letters, turned to historical writing in his later years. His *History of the Five Jameses* has not received much attention from modern historians who regard it as derivative because it deals with years which do not include any part of the lifetime of the author. The availability of both rough drafts and the finished manuscripts makes possible this analysis on the evolution of the study, the sources utilized, and the attitudes and ideals which moulded Drummond's interpretation. 97 notes, 2 appendixes.
                    N. W. Moen

993. Raitio, Tuire. PENTTI RENVALLIN BIBLIOGRAFIA [A bibliography of Pentti Renvall]. *Hist. Aikakauskirja [Finland] 1983 81(2): 119-122.* A partial bibliography of publications by the Finnish historian Pentti Renvall (1907-74) from 1929 through 1974.
                    R. G. Selleck

994. Ravetz, Alison. THE TRIVIALISATION OF MARY WOLLSTONECRAFT: A PERSONAL AND PROFESSIONAL CAREER RE-VINDICATED. *Women's Studies Int. Forum 1983 6(5): 491-499.* There has been a sustained and systematic marginalization and devaluation of Mary Wollstonecraft with the result that her work is neutralized. This orignated with her husband, William Godwin, and Godwin's distortions have since been perpetuated by all biographers despite the fact that contrary testimony is available.
                    J/S

995. Renucci, Paul. UNE TRAGÉDIE DE LA "RAISON DE DIEU," LA "IUDIT" DE FEDERICO DELLA VALLE [A tragedy of the *Reason of God*, the *Judith* by Federico della Valle]. *Rev. des Études Italiennes [France] 1978 24(1-3): 174-194.* Examines the historiography of Federico della Valle (1560?-1628), an Italian writer who had remained little known until 1929, when Italian critic Benedetto Croce (1866-1952) discussed his personality and work in *Storia dell'età barocca*. Gives an appraisal and comments on della Valle's *Iudit* [Judith], a tragedy printed in 1627-28.

996. Ricuperati, Giuseppe. PAUL HAZARD E LA STORIOGRAFIA DELL'ILLUMINISMO [Paul Hazard and Enlightenment historiography]. *Riv. Storica Italiana [Italy] 1974 86(2): 372-404.* Examines the origins of and influences upon the historian Paul Hazard, whose primary fame came from his contributions to the intellectual origins of the French Revolution. Considers Hazard's studies of the French Enlightenment and compares and contrasts them with many works written during the 20th century. Careful attention is given to the environment in which these works were written. Primary and secondary sources; 115 notes.
                    M. T. Wilson

997. Robinson, Cecil. A DEDICATION TO THE MEMORY OF HARVEY FERGUSON, 1890-1971. *Arizona and the West 1973 15(4): 310-314.* A biographical sketch and historiographic evaluation of Harvey Ferguson (1890-1971), who achieved stature as a major interpreter of the cultural history of the Southwest. His 15 books and several articles draw heavily upon his boyhood and later experiences in New Mexico. Illus., biblio.   D. L. Smith

998. Rohwer, Jürgen; Ulrich, Christine, transl. ADMIRAL GORSHKOV AND THE INFLUENCE OF HISTORY UPON SEA POWER. *US Naval Inst. Pro. 1981 107(5): 150-173.* Admiral of the Fleet S. G. Gorshkov, the Soviet Navy's commander-in-chief, has studied history for many years and has published a number of books and articles on it and on the future of the Soviet navy. But Admiral Gorshkov is not a student of history for history's sake, but a student of history for political purposes. Therefore, he uses history to convince the Soviet civilian hierarchy of the important role the Soviet navy is playing on today's international stage and the roles that navy should be groomed for in the future. He has succeeded in convincing the Soviet Union's present political leaders of the importance of a large navy, one that they can use as an instrument of policy. Secondary sources; 17 photos. A. N. Garland

999. Roman, Louis. INFLUENȚA MATERIALISMULUI DIALECTIC ȘI ISTORIC ASUPRA OPEREI LUI IOAN BOGDAN [The influence of historical and dialectical materialism on the works of Ioan Bogdan]. *Rev. de Istorie [Romania] 1979 32(12): 2303-2317.* Examines the works of the Romanian scholar Ioan Bogdan (1864-1919) and asserts that he only expressly formulated dialectical and historical materialist ideas after applying them in his analyses of topics such as social structures and the relation between internal and external factors and between phenomena and processes. Also notes dialectical traits in his research techniques, particularly his scrupulous work on poorly documented periods. 60 notes. French summary. R. O. Khan

1000. Roper, John Herbert. C. VANN WOODWARD'S EARLY CAREER: THE HISTORIAN AS DISSIDENT YOUTH. *Georgia Hist. Q. 1980 64(1): 7-21.* Describes the early career of C. Vann Woodward (b. 1908), noted Southern historian, including people who influenced him in his liberal radical stands against racism, concluding with the completion of his dissertation which was published as *Tom Watson: Agrarian Rebel* (1938). Based on interviews with Woodward; 10 notes. G. R. Schroeder

1001. Ross, Stanley R. SAN MARTÍN AS SEEN IN UNITED STATES TEXTBOOKS. *Inter-American Rev. of Biblio. 1979 29(1): 41-52.* Compares the views of José de San Martín through the study of 11 university textbooks in Latin American history published between 1950 and 1977. They differ in his early career in Spain, his motivation in returning to Latin America, and the amount of support he received from Buenos Aires. They all laud his energy, talent, and character, and praise his achievement and that of his army in crossing the Andes. Agreeing that San Martín's meeting with Simón Bolívar at Guayaquil in July 1822 was unsatisfactory, they are sympathetic to San Martín. 39 notes.
B. D. Johnson

1002. Rothberg, Morey D. "TO SET A STANDARD OF WORKMANSHIP AND COMPEL MEN TO CONFORM TO IT": JOHN FRANKLIN JAMESON AS EDITOR OF THE *AMERICAN HISTORICAL REVIEW*. *Am. Hist. Rev. 1984 89(4): 957-975.* Describes the efforts of John Franklin Jameson, first editor of the *American Historical Review*, to establish narrow scholarly standards for the journal during his tenure from 1895 to 1901 and from 1905 to 1928. Jameson was not very successful in meeting this goal. Historical writing could not be restricted to conform to Jameson's rigid commitment to nationalism and institutional history. In addition, other historians rejected his partisan view of what constituted serious scholarship. Based on documents in the Library of Congress and on secondary sources; 2 fig., 26 notes.

1003. Rottler, Ferenc. FRAKNÓI VILMOS TÖRTÉNETÍRÓI PÁLYAKEZDŐSE (1861-1871) [First period of Vilmos Fraknói's historiographical work (1861-71)]. *Századok [Hungary] 1969 103(5/6): 1046-1076.* Reviews Vilmos Fraknói's relationships with several leading Hungarian historians, especially Arnold Ipolyi, Flóris Rómer, and Ferenc Toldy; his work at the Magyar Történelmi Társulat (Hungarian Historical Association); and his biography on Cardinal Péter Pázmány, a pioneering work in church historiography.

Concludes that traces of rationalism and positivism are present in Fraknói's first publications in spite of his conservative Catholic philosophy. Based partly on unpublished documents.
F. S. Wagner

1004. Rubene, M. A. and Rubenis, A. A. KRITICHESKOE ISSLEDOVANIE SOOTNOSHENIIA "VREMIA—CHELOVEK—ISTORIIA" V FENOMENOLOGII E. GUSSERLIA [A critical study of the correlation "time—man—history" in the phenomenology of E. Husserl]. *Latvijas PSR Zinātņu Akad. Vēstis [USSR] 1983 (12): 23-33.* A critical analysis of the views of the German philosopher Edmund Husserl (1859-1938) on history, the human role in history, and sociohistorical problems. Primary sources; 24 notes. R. Vilums

1005. Rüger, Adolf. DIEDRICH WESTERMANNS BEITRAG ZUR GESCHICHTSSCHREIBUNG ÜBER AFRIKA [Diedrich Westermann's contribution to African historiography]. *Wissenschaftliche Zeitschrift der Humboldt-U. [East Germany] 1976 25(2): 197-202.* Discusses the contributions of Diedrich Westermann to the writing of African history.

1006. Rumiantsev, A. M. V. I. LENIN I ISTORICHESKAIA NAUKA [V. I. Lenin and the science of history]. *Novaia i Noveishaia Istoriia [USSR] 1970 (2): 3-6.* Soviet historical science prides itself on having Lenin as its inspiration, on having an ideology based on Marxism-Leninism, thus making it Party- and people-oriented; on being totally objective; and seeking only the truth in order to create a Communist society. Lenin stressed the importance of understanding history for future development; he answered all important questions concerning historical development; realised that history showed mankind 's destined path towards communism; and saw that the Russian October Revolution was the result of the universal development of mankind. Based on collected works of Lenin. 12 notes. L. Smith

1007. Rundell, Walter, Jr. WALTER PRESCOTT WEBB. *Great Plains J. 1979 18: 130-139.* "Had Walter Prescott Webb not become a world-renowned historian, he might well have been an eminent businessman.... " Historians remember him as author of *The Great Plains* (1931), *The Great Frontier* (1952), *The Texas Rangers* (1935), and *Divided We Stand* (1937). Describes Webb's "acquisitive instincts" and their implementation in publication of widely used textbooks, selling of movie rights to *The Texas Rangers*, and real estate dealings in Austin. His income from royalties and profits was often more than his professorial salary. "He died a wealthy man." From a special section on "Historians of the Southern Plains." 39 notes. O. H. Zabel

1008. Rytkönen, Seppo. ZUR DATIERUNG EINES UNVERÖFFENTLICHTEN MANUSKRIPTS VON B. G. NIEBUHR [The dating of an unpublished manuscript by B. G. Niebuhr]. *U. of Turku. Inst. of General Hist. Publ. [Finland] 1967 1: 53-60.* Examines the Danish born historian and statesman Barthold Georg Niebuhr's (1776-1831) unpublished manuscript on Roman history believed to have been written in Copenhagen, 1803-05.

1009. Sakharov, A. M. LOMONOSOV-ISTORIK V OTSENKE RUSSKOI ISTORIOGRAFII [An evaluation of Lomonosov as a historian in Russian historiography]. *Vestnik Moskovskogo U., Seriia 9: Istoriia [USSR] 1961 16(5): 3-18.* Discusses the influence of changing philosophical and political trends during the 18th-20th centuries on the evaluation of the historical views of the first Russian scientist and humanist Mikhail Lomonosov (1711-65). Examines 40 studies on Lomonosov, noting differences in their sociohistorical bias. Full recognition of his importance as a historian came only after the 1940's. 73 notes. N. Frenkley

1010. Salimbeni, Fulvio. FRANCESCO DI MANZANO E LA STORIOGRAFIA DEL SUO TEMPO [Francesco di Manzano and the historiography of his time]. *Archivio Storico Italiano [Italy] 1984 142(2): 283-313.* Describes and evaluates the scholarly contributions of Francesco di Manzano, 19th-century Italian historian, who specialized in the study of Friuli. Di Manzano's research, methodology, and writing emphasized the richness of Friuli's cultural and political past, which has influenced the subsequent work of other historians of the region. Based on di Manzano's writings and secondary sources; 83 notes.

1011. Šamberger, Zdeněk. MLADÝ PALACKÝ A JEHO ZAKLADATELSKÝ VÝZNAM PRO ČESKOU VĚDU [Young Palacký and his importance as a founder of Czech historical science]. *Strahovská Knihovna [Czechoslovakia] 1976 (11): 17-48.*

1012. Sand, Shlomo. PROLEGOMENI AD UNA CRITICA DELLA STORIOGRAFIA SORELIANA: DUE LEGGENDE DA SFATARE [Prolegomena to a critique of Sorel historiography: two legends to undo]. *Ann. della Fondazione Luigi Einaudi [Italy] 1982 16: 329-382.* Despite Croce and Gramsci, who attempted to correct a widespread false impression, the work of Georges Sorel (d. 1922) still suffers from his reputation, created by Mussolini, as the spiritual father of fascism. Of the many misconceptions concerning Sorel, the author examines, first, Sorel's influence on and relations with the trade union movement of his time, and second, the alleged admiration of the later Sorel for fascism. 80 notes, biblio.
                                    J. V. Coutinho

1013. Sanlés Martínez, Ricardo. EL PADRE GUILLERMO A TRAVES DE SU CORRESPONDENCIA [Father Guillermo through his correspondence]. *Estudios [Spain] 1984 40(146-147): 83-114.* Discusses the importance of the 172 letters preserved in the archives of the Mercedarians as research sources for the biography and as background to the historiography of Guillermo Vázquez Núñez, historian and member of that Spanish religious order.

1014. Sarbei, V. H. ISTORYCHNI POHLIADY H. S. SKOVORODY (DO 250-RICHCHIA VID DNIA NARODZHENNIA) [The historical views of H. S. Skovoroda: the 250th anniversary of his birth]. *Ukrains'kyi Istorychnyi Zhurnal [USSR] 1972 (11): 54-62.* Discusses the views of some of the prerevolutionary Ukrainian historians whose work can be incorporated into Soviet historiography in connection with the study of the philosophy of history of H. S. Skovoroda, outstanding 18th-century Ukrainian philosopher.

1015. Saunders, Christopher. GEORGE MCCALL THEAL AND LOVEDALE. *Hist. in Africa 1981 8: 155-164.* Little has been written about South African historian George Theal's career before the late 1870's. His years employed at Lovedale Seminary near Alice were marked by his sympathetic views toward the natives. His *Compendium of South African History and Geography*, published during these years, reflects his attitudes. Once he left Lovedale for a government job, his sympathies shifted to the white frontier farmers, and he denounced his early book as being "defective." Primary sources; 41 notes.
                                    A. C. Drysdale

1016. Schleier, Hans. JOHANNES ZIEKURSCH [Johannes Ziekursch]. *Jahrbuch für Geschichte [East Germany] 1969 3: 137-196.* Johannes Ziekursch (1876-1945) published three volumes entitled *Political History of the New German Empire* (1925-30), interpreting Bismarck's antidemocratic unification of Germany as the start of the 1918 fall of the German Empire. Educated in Bonn, Breslau, and Munich, on the faculty of Breslau University and already known for his work on the influence of the Catholic Church on 17th- and 18th-century German history, the regional histories of Saxony, Prussia, and Silesia, including his *Hundred Years of Silesian Agrarian History* (1915), Ziekursch experienced great academic censure for his leftist views. As an opponent of Nazism his work was no longer published, but he continued to teach at Cologne University. Although unnoticed by West German historians, Ziekursch's work is an important source for East German historians. 168 notes.
                                    M. A. Hoobs

1017. Schleier, Hans. KARL LAMPRECHT ALS INITIATOR EINER INTENSIVIERTEN FORSCHUNG ÜBER DIE GESCHICHTE DER GESCHICHTSSCHREIBUNG [Karl Lamprecht, initiator of intensified research into the history of historiography]. *Storia della Storiografia [Italy] 1982 (2): 38-56.* Discusses the polemics in Germany in the 1890's over the "method controversy" regarding Karl Lamprecht's new historiographical concepts and methods, which were to have lasting effects on German bourgeois historiography. In opposition to Leopold von Ranke's politically oriented historiography, Lamprecht's concept of cultural history and causalgenetic methods aimed at a total view of the history of historical science. Heavily attacked by the majority of his German academic colleagues but honored outside Germany, Lamprecht founded the Royal Saxonian Institute for Cultural and Universal History in 1909 and actively supported the work of his followers. Based on Lamprecht's publications; 54 notes. Italian and English summaries.
                                    G. Herritt

1018. Schmidt, James. JÜRGEN HABERMAS E LE DIFFICOLTA DELL ILLUMINISMO [Jürgen Habermas and the difficulties of the Enlightenment]. *Comunità [Italy] 1983 37(185): 102-125.* For about a quarter of a century Jürgen Habermas has attempted to keep a skeptical eye on theories of progress and his faith in the Enlightenment.

1019. Schnabel, Franz. WERNER NÄF UND DIE DEUTSCHE GESCHICHTE [Werner Näf and German history]. *Schweizer Beiträge zur Allgemeinen Geschichte [Switzerland] 1960-61 18-19: 109-117.* Werner Näf's main contribution in the field of German history was the interpretation of the development of the Holy Roman Empire and the role of the German territories in the spirit of Leopold Ranke.

1020. Schorsch, Ismar. FROM WOLFENBÜTTEL TO WISSENSCHAFT: THE DIVERGENT PATHS OF ISAAK MARKUS JOST AND LEOPOLD ZUNZ. *Leo Baeck Inst. Year Book [Great Britain] 1977 22: 109-128.* The careers of Isaak Markus Jost (1793-1860) and Leopold Zunz (1794-1860) indicate the extremes of Jewish assimilation. Jost, author of the first modern history of the Jews, was a student of Voltaire's rationalism and measured the past in terms of the present; his historiography judged, condemned, applauded, and could not muster much sympathy for the field of religion. Zunz, the father of modern Jewish scholarship, applied Herder's insights and revealed cultural creativity and growth where the philosophe saw only error and degeneration. In uncovering the nature of the past, Zunz believed he could influence the shape of the present. 74 notes.
                                    F. Rosenthal

1021. Schulin, Ernst. FRIEDRICH MEINECKES STELLUNG IN DER DEUTSCHEN GESCHICHTSWISSENSCHAFT [Friedrich Meinecke's place in German historical study]. *Hist. Zeitschrift [West Germany] 1980 230(1): 4-29.* Friedrich Meinecke's (1862-1954) long career as a professional historian can be divided into five periods characterized by his basic approach to history. At first he retained the Prussian-Kleindeutsch traditions of Heinrich von Treitschke and Heinrich von Sybel. After 1906 he developed a social history approach and during the Weimar period, the history of ideas. Under the Nazis he concentrated on nonpolitical intellectual history but afterwards he worked on nonelitist collective intellectual history. Meinecke has less influence now than he did a generation ago, but his work is not outmoded. Based on works of historical theory; 50 ref.
                                    G. H. Davis

1022. Schweinzer, Silvia. UNE CONTRIBUTION A L'HISTORIOGRAPHIE DE L'ANCIEN REGIME: PAULINE DE LEZARDIERE ET SON OEUVRE [A contribution to the historiography of the old régime: Pauline de Lézardière and her work]. *Francia [France] 1980 8: 573-594.* Traces the life and work of the French writer Pauline de Lézardière (1754-1835), who wrote *The Theory of the Political Laws of the French Monarchy* (1792). Examines her contribution to the historiography of the old régime. She was exiled to Holland in 1796, but returned to France in 1801 and continued her historical research and writing until her death in 1835. The author also discusses her personality and political ideology as revealed in her works and her personal letters, as well as describing her position within late 18th- and early 19th-century historiography and her methods of writing. A list of her works both published and unpublished is also included. Based on Pauline de Lézardière's writings and personal letters and secondary sources; 110 notes, appendix.
                                    G. L. Neville

1023. Scott, Franklin D. THE SAGA OF NELS M. HOKANSON: IMMIGRANT AND IMMIGRANT HISTORIAN. *Swedish Pioneer Hist. 1978 29(3): 198-208.* Nels M. Hokanson was born in Copenhagen of Swedish parents in 1885. In 1887 the family came to America and settled in St. Paul, Minnesota. After four or five years the family moved to Aitkin, Minnesota, where Nels lived until he joined a circus band at age 16. Discusses his life and times, based on his published writings and especially on autobiographical notes which he prepared in 1977-78. Hokanson's concern with his Swedish compatriots began in childhood and continued throughout his life. He is best known for his book, *Swedish Immigrants in Lincoln's Time.* It was first published in 1942 and is now being reprinted. He has written many articles for Swedish American journals. Photo, 11 notes.   C. W. Ohrvall

1024. Segovia, Eduardo. LA OBRA HISTORIOGRAFICA DE BOSSUET [Bossuet's historiography]. *Rev. de Hist. Americana y Argentina [Argentina] 1968-69 7(13-14): 231-251.* Examines the influence of Jacques Bénigne Bossuet on 20th-century intellectual history in France.

1025. Senkowska-Gluck, Monika. GEORGES LEFEBVRE—HISTORYK REWOLUCJI FRANCUSKIEJ [Georges Lefebvre, historian of the French Revolution]. *Kwartalnik Hist. [Poland] 1976 83(2): 278-286.* Georges Lefebvre (1874-1959) brought important innovations to the historiography of the French Revolution—he was the first to depart from strictly political to social and economic aspects. The author describes the path which led him to a university career, and underlines the innovative character of his principal works. 22 notes.   H. Heitzman-Wojcicka

1026. Şerban, Constantin. ECOURI ROMÂNEŞTI ÎN OPERA LUI LUIGI FERDINANDO MARSILI (250 ANI DE LA MOARTE) [Romanian echos in the work of Luigi Ferdinando Marsili: 250 years after his death]. *Revista de Istorie [Romania] 1980 33(11): 2169-2187.* Luigi F. Marsili, an Italian scientist of European reknown, conducted intensive political, diplomatic, military, and scientific activity in Romania. Documents illustrate Marsili's interest in the historical, geographical, and linguistic origins of the Romanian people and their Daco-Roman continuity in the regions of the Carpathians and the Danube. Marsili's scientific work encompassed all phases of Romanian life and is considered a precious Medieval historical source. 98 notes. French summary.
                                                   T. Z. Herman

1027. Şerban, Constantin. MEDALION ISTORIC: JULES MICHELET (1798-1874) [Historical portrait: Jules Michelet, 1798-1874]. *Studii şi Articole de Istorie [Romania] 1974 25: 45-50.* Discusses Michelet's origin, studies, and teaching career and his historiography with special reference to the *History of France.* His relations with the Romanian revolutionaries of 1848 are also examined.   RSA 11:1672

1028. Sestan, Ernesto. RINASCIMENTO E CRISI ITALIANA DEL CINQUECENTO NEL PENSIERO DI FEDERICO CHABOD [The Renaissance and the Italian crisis of the 16th century in the thought of Federico Chabod]. *Riv. Storica Italiana [Italy] 1960 72(4): 676-686.* Refers to Chabod's evaluation of the Renaissance as a unique cultural phenomenon, in spite of the earlier rediscovery of antiquity in the 13th century. Discusses also Chabod's interpretation of Machiavelli's writings. Based on Chabod's works.
                                                   F. Pollaczek/S

1029. Shanski, D. N. I. N. BOLTIN I EGO OTSENKA V OTECHESTVENNOI ISTORIOGRAFII [I. N. Boltin and his assessment in national historiography]. *Vestnik Moskovskogo U., Seriia 8: Istoriia [USSR] 1977 (6): 41-55.* Investigates reactions by Russian historians to the publications of Ivan Boltin (1735-92), 1780-1977, suggesting problems which still need to be discussed. Criticisms have stressed his unfamiliarity with sources, and his support for the enlightened autocracy of Catherine II. His supporters have concentrated on his participation in preparing manuscripts for publication and his broad interest in philosophical, philological, and literary questions. Slavophiles liked his attempts to restore pride in Russia; opponents of serfdom approved of his "progressive conservative"

views toward the peasants. He is now regarded as an apologist of unlimited monarchy, yet not totally reactionary, and it is as yet unclear whether he may be regarded as an early historical determinist. Secondary sources; 111 notes.   D. N. Collins

1030. Shapiro, Herbert. LINCOLN STEFFENS: LIGHT AND SHADOW ON HIS HISTORICAL IMAGE. *Am. J. of Econ. and Sociol. 1972 31(3): 319-326.*

1031. Shattuck, Henry L. ELLERY SEDGWICK. *Massachusetts Hist. Soc. Pro. 1957-60 72: 395-396.* Ellery Sedgwick (1872-1959) was an editor and member of the Massachusetts Historical Society from 1914 until 1959.

1032. Shavit, Yaacob. HA-ŠIMUŠ ŠEL MAŚKILIM YEHUDIM BE-MIZRAḤ EYROPAH BE-MIŠNATO ŠEL HENRI TOMAS BAQL [The works of Henry Thomas Buckle and their application by the *Maskilim* of Eastern Europe]. *Zion [Israel] 1984 49(4): 401-412.* The works of the English historian Henry Thomas Buckle (1821-62) enjoyed widespread influence among the "Western" intelligentsia of Russia beginning in the 1860's. This influence spread to the Jewish intelligentsia, who used Buckle's historicophilosophical positions to buttress their claim that intellectuals are the creators of civilization's progress and to support the revival of the Jewish nation in its historic homeland. Judah Leib Levin disputed Buckle's notions on the role of morality in human advancement. Buckle's work provided a basis for describing Jewish history as a "history without geography." 48 notes. English summary.
                                                   J/J. D. Sarna

1033. Shevchenko, F. P. ISTORYCHNE MYNULE U SPRYINIATTI BOHDANA KHMEL'NYTS'KOHO [The historical past in the works of Bogdan Khmelnitsky]. *Ukrains'kyi Istorychnyi Zhurnal [USSR] 1982 (2): 90-100.* Khmelnitsky, leader of the Ukrainian Cossacks in the successful revolution against the Polish state in 1648, had conducted considerable research into previous Ukrainian history. His writings are collected in a modern edition *Dokumenty Bohdana Khmel'nyts'koho* (1960), and bears testimony to his sophisticated approach to history. He took a progressive view of the role of social classes in the Ukraine and based his own activities on his view of history until his death in 1654. 69 notes.
                                                   N. M. Diuk

1034. Shevtsov, V. I. GUSTAV EVERS I RUSSKAIA ISTORIOGRAFIIA [Gustav Evers and Russian historiography]. *Voprosy Istorii [USSR] 1975 (3): 55-70.* Analyzes the historical views expounded by the prominent Russian scientist Gustav Evers during the first three decades of the 19th century and defines his place in Russian historiography. Gustav Evers was the first theoretician of the primitive communal system and the first sociologist in Russian historiography to draw the attention of scientists to the problem of society and social relations. Practical application of the new methods of cognition, the close study of political and legal relationships both in their historical and juridical aspects constituted an important distinctive feature of Evers' investigations which contributed to the development of the history of Russian law. The numerous research works produced by Gustav Evers clearly reflect the close interaction of Russian and German scientific thought. Side by side with carefully studying the achievements of West European science, he imbibed the advanced ideas and valuable conclusions of Russian historians and proved capable of effectively applying them in the process of his research in the history of Russia, which became the principal subject of his investigations.   J

1035. Shibata, Michio; Chizuka, Tadami; and Ninomiya, Hiroyuke. ALBERT SOBOUL ET LES HISTORIENS JAPONAIS [Albert Soboul and Japanese historians]. *Ann. Hist. de la Révolution Française [France] 1982 54(4): 600-603.* Examines influence of Soboul on Japanese historians, particularly H. Kohachiro Takahashi (1912-82), Soboul's friend and the most important Japanese historian of the French Revolution.   R. Aldrich

1036. Shirai, Atsushi. [STUDIES CONCERNING WILLIAM GODWIN IN JAPAN].

—. NIHON NI OKERU GODOUIN KENKY SHI [The history of studies concerning William Godwin in Japan]. *Mita Gakkai Zasshi [Japan] 1966 59(6): 101-113.* Continued from a previous article.

—. ROBĀTO ŌEN TO UIRIAMU GODOUIN [Robert Owen and William Godwin]. *Mita Gakkai Zasshi [Japan] 1966 59(12): 21-44.*

—. NIHON NI OKERU GODOUIN KENKY [The history of studies concerning William Godwin in Japan]. *Mita Gakkai Zasshi [Japan] 1967 60(8): 135-143.*

1037. Šidak, Jaroslav. IVAN KUKULJEVIĆ—OSNIVAČ MODERNE HRVATSKE HISTORIOGRAFIJE [Ivan Kukuljević: the founder of modern historiography]. *Hist. Zbornik [Yugoslavia] 1972-73 (25-26): 5-29.* Even though Kukuljević was not an educated researcher, his historiographical activity made him a renowned collector and editor of historical sources. He was the founder in 1850 of the Society for Yugoslav History and Antiquity, and the publisher of the *Archives for Yugoslav History,* 1851-75. Kukuljević mainly covered biographical material. His many-sided scientific and organizational activities created a solid basis for modern Croatian historiography. 115 notes.   A. C. Niven

1038. Šidak, Jaroslav. LJUDEVIT GAJ KAO HISTORIOGRAFSKI PROBLEM [Ljudevit Gaj as a historiographical problem]. *Radovi: Inst. za Hrvatsku Povijest [Yugoslavia] 1973 3: 7-34.* Explains how the work of the Croatian pan-Slavist and nationalist Ljudevit Gaj (1809-72) was initially regarded as important only for Croatia's language and literature, and that his role in Croatia's national reawakening was treated seriously in historiography only from about 1920.

1039. Silberstein, Laurence J. HISTORICAL SOCIOLOGY AND JEWISH HISTORIOGRAPHY: A REVIEW ESSAY. *J. of the Am. Acad. of Religion 1974 42(4): 692-698.* Discusses two monographs by Jacob Katz describing 18th-century assimilation of European Jews into European culture and society. Katz examined this change in the light of the social, political, cultural, and economic processes which were occurring in Europe. Primary and secondary sources; 18 notes.   E. R. Lester

1040. Šimeček, Zdeněk. K METODOLOGII DÍLA FRANTIŠKA PALACKÉHO [The methodology in the works of František Palacký]. *Slovanský Přehled [Czechoslovakia] 1976 62(3): 211-220.* František Palacký valued the historical research of his immediate predecessors, especially Gelasius Dobner and František Pelcl, who carefully documented their works and included long bibliographies. Palacký's first task was the collection and editing of important sources. He worked with Pelcl in the compilation of a diplomatic history, and even approached the nobility for support in establishing new archives for important material from all regions of Czechoslovakia. Palacký insisted that Czech history should be based on primary sources. 52 notes.   B. Kimmel

1041. Simić, Miodrag. BIBLIOGRAFIJA RADOVA PROFESORA DR JOVANA MARJANOVIĆA [Bibliography of works by Professor Dr. Jovan Marjanović]. *Jugoslovenski Istorijski Časopis [Yugoslavia] 1981 20(1-4): 45-50.* Lists 93 works by Jovan Marjanović, chiefly concerning Yugoslavia in general and Serbia in particular during World War II. Title, publisher, date of publication, and number of pages are given and the bibliography is subdivided as follows: books (14); coauthored books (9); major journal articles and monographs (27); major newspaper articles (17); collaboration in encyclopaedias (3); lectures and book prefaces (6); editorial works (6); translation of Marjanović's works in English (2), Italian (2), Chinese (1), Russian (1), Hungarian (2), and Romanian (1).   J. Bamber

1042. Singal, Daniel Joseph. BEYOND CONSENSUS: RICHARD HOFSTADTER AND AMERICAN HISTORIOGRAPHY. *Am. Hist. Rev. 1984 89(4): 976-1004.* Evaluates the position of Richard Hofstadter in American historiography. Hofstadter's historical scholarship is usually placed within the "consensus school," which emphasizes the absence of ideological politics in US history. Hofstadter's early work pointed out consensus in the American political tradition in order to condemn the system, not praise it. As his career proceeded, however, he came to share the view that American political culture was unique and exemplary because it was non-ideological. This changing viewpoint as well as his broad interests make Hofstadter's work difficult to classify. Secondary sources; 2 fig., 55 notes.   S

1043. Sked, Alan. READING HISTORY: METTERNICH. *Hist. Today [Great Britain] 1983 33(June): 43-47.* Metternich's reputation among historians as a reactionary figure who held back history is strange, given the placidity of his tenure.

1044. Sojková, Zdenka. JAROSLAV VLČEK O SLOVENSKÝCH DĚJINÁCH A DĚJEPISCÍCH (DO ROKU 1900) [Jaroslav Vlček on Slovak history and historical documents up to 1900]. *Hist. Časopis [Czechoslovakia] 1981 29(1): 64-74.* Investigates Vlček's approach to the problems of Slovak history and its development. Deals with Vlček's relations to contemporary Slovak historians, as well as to Czech and Russian Slovakists. Vlček is a chronicler of his own age and that of the Matica period, a historian of Ludevit Štúr's movement, then the historian of the romantic generation and of the Slovak national revival from the point of view of the philosophy of European history.   J/S

1045. Sokolov, O. D. M. N. POKROVSKII: VYDAIUSHCHIISIA ORGANIZATOR NAUCHNO-ISSLEDOVATEL'SKOI RABOTY V SSSR [M. N. Pokrovski: prominent research organizer in the USSR]. *Voprosy Istorii [USSR] 1969 (6): 30-45.* Describes the contributions of Marxist historian Mikhail Nikolaevich Pokrovski (1868-1932) to the advancement of historical research and pedagogy in the Soviet Union in the 1920's, his teaching career and fight against bourgeois Western corruption of history. 41 notes. English summary pp. 221-222.   N. Frenkley

1046. Sokolov, O. D. M. N. POKROVSKII: OUTSTANDING ORGANIZER OF RESEARCH IN THE USSR. *Soviet Studies in Hist. 1970 8(4): 322-352.* Chronicles the life of Soviet historian M. N. Pokrovski (1868-1932) who began his career as a bourgeois historian but eventually, under the influence of V. I. Lenin, founded the Marxist school of Soviet historiography, perfecting the tenets of Leninist historical process, 1917-31.

1047. Stansky, Peter. REVIEW ESSAY: ELIE HALEVY. *Hist. and Theory 1982 21(1): 143-149.* Critically reviews Myrna Chase's *Elie Halévy: An Intellectual Biography* (1980). While Halévy's goal of writing a full interpretation of 19th-century England remained incomplete insofar as he never finished his book on the 1852-95 era, his stress on the intellectual and cultural accounting for England's Victorian liberty and stability remains relevant. He is especially remembered for the "Halévy thesis" concerning the socioeconomic implications of Methodism. His last writings reveal a fear that the growth of state power might endanger the English democratic tradition.   W. J. Reedy

1048. Staur, C. RICHARD HOFSTADTER OG DEN LIBERALE TRADITION [Richard Hofstadter and the liberal tradition]. *Hist. Tidsskrift [Denmark] 1979 79(1): 80-95.* Hofstadter did not write with the specialist in mind and his work often lacks a careful investigation of the primary sources. Originally influenced by C. A. Beard, he later became critical of Beard's approach to history, and particularly his simplistic view of the relationship between economic interest and belief. Hofstadter stressed that a society's economic interests are not always obvious to its members. He also believed that the conflict between a conservative and a liberal tradition in American politics was a myth fabricated by the school of progressive historians. Ironically the so-called "liberal" school of thought was the more conservative.   M. A. Bott

1049. Stave, Bruce M. A CONVERSATION WITH SAM BASS WARNER JR. *J. of Urban Hist. 1974 1(1): 85-110.* Recounts Warner's formal college training, the books and people who influenced him, and how he came to write *Street Car Suburbs* (1969), *The*

Private City (1971), and *The Urban Wilderness* (1972). Warner has moved from city planning to fieldwork and sees a need for more systematic studies.   S. S. Sprague

1050. Stave, Bruce M. A CONVERSATION WITH ANTHONY R. SUTCLIFFE. *J. of Urban Hist. 1981 7(3): 335-379.* This interview with Anthony R. Sutcliffe, urban historian of England and France, covers both his personal background and professional contributions. Discusses the state of urban history in England. 46 notes, biblio.   T. W. Smith

1051. Steinacker, Eppo. ZUM ACHTSIGSTEN GEBURTSTAG EUGEN ROSENSTOCK-HUESSYS [On the 80th birthday of Eugen Rosenstock-Huessy]. *Wort und Wahrheit [West Germany] 1969 24(3): 275-277.* Celebrates the 80th birthday of Eugen Rosenstock-Huessy, Austrian historian and philanthropist, whose creation in the area of voluntary work in the 1920's became a model for the American Peace Corps 20 years later. After 1938 he found refuge in the United States. His *European Revolutions* became a standard work of modern historiography. He now lives in Four Wells, Vermont.   G. E. Pergl

1052. Steinmetz, Max. SCHRIFTEN UND BRIEFE THOMAS MÜNTZER. ZUM ERSCHEINEN EINER WESTDEUTSCHEN MÜNTZERGESAMTAUSGABE [Writings and letters of Thomas Müntzer: publication of a complete edition of the works of Müntzer in West Germany]. *Zeitschrift für Geschichtswissenschaft [East Germany] 1969 17(6): 739-748.* Describes the state of research—especially in socialist countries—on peasant leader Thomas Müntzer (1489?-1525) and his associates. Although Müntzer did not found a religious sect, he was a major theoretician of both Anabaptism and social action. Only about one-third of his works are liturgical; his other writings include important pieces advocating radical social reforms. Based on Müntzer's works and their current interpretations; 33 notes.   G. H. Libbey

1053. Steirer, William F., Jr. EUGENE D. GENOVESE: MARXIST-ROMANTIC HISTORIAN OF THE SOUTH. *Southern R. 1974 10(4): 840-850.*

1054. Štih, Bojan. BLEIWEIS 1982: ALI HERETIČNI KENOTAF NEKEMU IDEJNOZGODOVINSKEMU VREDNOTENJU [Janez Bleiweis, 1982, or, a heretical cenotaph for certain ideohistorical evaluations]. *Zbornik za Zgodovino Naravoslovja in Tehnike [Yugoslavia] 1983 7: 175-180.* In the light of his sceptical attitude toward so-called historical science, the author comments ironically on the opinions so far held concerning Dr. Janez Bleiweis.   J

1055. Strand, Wilson E. DAVID HUME, HISTORIAN. *Social Sci. 1975 50(4): 195-203.* The philosopher David Hume (1711-76) freed English historiography from party politics with his *History of England* (1754).

1056. Summers, Anne. THOMAS HODGKIN (1910-1982). *Hist. Workshop J. [Great Britain] 1982 (14): 180-182.* An obituary of Thomas Lionel Hodgkin, outlining his varied career and assessing his achievement. As a civil servant in Palestine in the 1930's he became an anti-imperialist and Communist. He later joined the Oxford Extra-Mural Delegacy in North Staffs and then in Africa. Resigning his position, he devoted himself to the study of African and Third World history and politics, and later wrote a history of Vietnam, *Vietnam: The Revolutionary Path* (1981). The serious study of African history owes much to his scholarship, which he undertook despite the uncertainty of assuming different positions in order to pursue his interest in the unfashionable and the invisible.   D. J. Nicholls

1057. Suratteau, Jean-René. GEORGES LEFEBVRE, DISCIPLE DE JAURÈS? [Georges Lefebvre, disciple of Jaurès?]. *Ann. Hist. de la Révolution Française [France] 1979 51 (3): 374-398.* Reprinted from *Bulletin de la Société d'Études Jaurésiennes*, 1978 (69-70): 18-27. Although he never met Jean Jaurès, Georges Lefebvre remained deeply influenced by him throughout his career as a historian of the French Revolution. Lefebvre's Marxist analysis of economic and social conditions owes much to Jaurès's interpretation, but he went further in his analysis of biological and psychological factors, including the irrational side of human behavior. Lefebvre's other concerns were the perfecting of historical methodology and the expansion of the scope of historical study. Based on Lefebvre's writings; 34 notes.   J. Friguglietti

1058. Svet, Ia. M. UIL'IAM KHIKLING PRESKOTT I EGO "OTKRYTIE AMERIKI" [William Hickling Prescott and his discovery of America]. *Novaia i Noveishaia Istoriia [USSR] 1977 (1): 134-142.* With the publication in New York in 1843 and London in 1848 of his *History of the Conquest of Mexico*, William Hickling Prescott's name became a household word. Details his life and works and discusses his approach and reputation. His works are now largely outdated but he is still regarded as the corypheus of romantic historiography. Based on Prescott's works and secondary accounts; 16 notes.   D. N. Collins

1059. Szulkin, Michał. SZYMON DUBNOW—WYBITNY HISTORYK ŻYDOWSKI [Simon Dubnow—an outstanding Jewish historian]. *Biuletyn Żydowskiego Instytutu Historycznego w Polsce [Poland] 1975 93(1): 3-26.* Simon Dubnow (born 1860, murdered by the Nazis in 1941) was a self-taught person who, relying entirely on himself, acquired enormous historical knowledge and enriched Jewish historiography. He began his scientific production in the columns of Jewish periodicals printed in Russian ("Woschod"). He carried out his historical researches against an extensive social and economic background—trying to give a synthesis of the history of Jews. He was one of the founders of the Historical-Ethnographical Commission in Petersburg which contributed to the intensification of researches in the history of Jews. In Dubnow's rich and varied scientific production particular place is occupied by the history of Jews in Poland. In his works on Frankists, an 18th century semi-Christian Jewish Sect, he attempted to give a new outlook on the transformations which had taken place among the Polish Jews in the 18th century. His longer sojourn in Vilna contributed to enlivening the life of this former "centre of Jewish culture," and to founding (in 1925) the Jewish Scientific Institute ("Yivo") in the works of which Dubnow actively participated. Of fundamental importance is his 10-volume *Weltgeschichte des jüdischen Volkes*—which appeared translated into many languages. Valuable memoirs of Dubnow entitled *Kniga zhizni* (The Book of Life) composed of 3 volumes show his extraordinary course of life and give an abundance of facts. The last (third) volume of Dubnow's memoirs, printed in Riga in 1940, was found in the collections of Staatsbibliothek in Berlin.   J

1060. Szvák, Gyula. VASZILIJ OSZIPOVICS KLJUCSEVSZKIJ [Vasili Osipovich Kliuchevski]. *Világtörténet [Hungary] 1981 (4): 111-117.* Kliuchevski's work influenced most historical studies of his time in Russia. Although not a follower of Marxist historical theories, his works, especially *The boyar duma in old Russia* which describes 10th-18th century Russia, are written in a unique and exceptionally brilliant manner. His ability to place individuals within the framework of their historical environment enabled him to offer a more complex evaluation of the individual than could be done even by the most elaborate biographies. Plate, 5 notes.

T. Kuner

1061. Tanzone, Daniel F. JOHN C. SCIRANKA: OUTSTANDING SLOVAK AMERICAN FRATERNALIST. *Jednota Ann. Furdek 1978 17: 151-160.* Discusses John Coleman Sciranka (b. 1902), a historian and journalist, and his involvement with Slovak American organizations since 1924.

1062. Tarabuzzi, Gianfranco. ECHI ITALIANI SETTECENTESCHI DELLA STORIOGRAFIA INGLESE [English historiography in Italy during the 18th century]. *Archivio Storico Italiano [Italy] 1980 138(3): 390-440.* Analyzes the success of some English writers in Italy. Examines the histories of David Hume, Adam Ferguson, and Edward Gibbon published between 1736 and 1765. Based on research in Italian libraries.   A. Canavero

1063. Tarcov, Nathan. PHILOSOPHY & HISTORY: TRADITION AND INTERPRETATION IN THE WORK OF LEO STRAUSS. *Polity 1983 16(1): 5-29.* That Leo Strauss should continue to be examined and explained, attacked and defended, is surely an indication of how successful a teacher he was. Not long ago, John Gunnell objected to his uses of history and tradition. Strauss regarded tradition as a problem, not as a norm, his thesis about exoteric writing was not intended to place his own interpretations beyond debate, and he thought of history and philosophy as being virtually inseparable.
J

1064. Tikhvinski, S. L. and Peskova, G. N. VYDAIUSHCHIISIA RUSSKII KITAEVED N. IA. BICHURIN (K 200-LETIIU SO DNIA ROZHDENIIA) [The famous Russian sinologist, N. Ia. Bichurin: tribute on the 200th anniversary of his birth]. *Novaia i Noveishaia Istoriia [USSR] 1977 (5): 146-159.* Biography of Nikita Bichurin (1777-1853) and critical analysis of his scientific contributions to sinology. Bichurin's outstanding knowledge of China's language, history, and culture did not prevent him from drawing unfounded parallels between China and Europe and from idealizing aspects of the sociopolitical structure and legal system of the repressive Manchu monarchy. His contemporaries, especially the well-known Russian democrat and literary critic Vissarion Belinski (1811-48), faulted him for this. Based on Bichurin's unpublished studies; 73 notes.
N. Frenkley

1065. Timpanaro, Sebastiano. GIROLAMO VITELLI E FRANCESCO DE SANCTIS (IN UNA LETTERA A LUIGI RUSSO DEL 1924) [Girolamo Vitelli and Francesco De Sanctis (in a letter to Luigi Russo, 1924)]. *Belfagor [Italy] 1979 34(3): 305-314.* Publication of Girolamo Vitelli's letter to Luigi Russo adds to the particularly sparse knowledge of the relationship between Vitelli and Francesco De Sanctis; it serves also to clarify academic reactions to De Sanctis's evolution to neoidealist historiography.

1066. Todd, Janet M. MARY WOLLSTONECRAFT: A REVIEW OF RESEARCH AND COMMENT. *British Studies Monitor 1977 7(3): 3-23.* Reviews recent writing and research on the career and writings of Mary Wollstonecraft under the categories of letters, works, biographical and critical comment, biographies, and historical and critical studies. 57 notes.
R. Howell

1067. Todd, Janet M. THE NEW SCHOLARSHIP: REVIEW ESSAYS: THE BIOGRAPHIES OF MARY WOLLSTONECRAFT. *Signs: J. of Women in Culture and Soc. 1976 1(3 Pt.1): 721-734.* Mary Wollestonecraft's (1759-97) personality has overshadowed her works and an understanding or misunderstanding of her life has colored critical evaluations of her theses and statements regarding feminism. Despite her complexity, biographers present her favorably or disapprovingly, for their own purposes, by suppressing facts in her life or distorting her character. Her unconventional behavior linked immorality and feminism in many minds to the discredit of feminism for several decades; but, conversely, she represented a possibility of freedom which countered a dangerous and constricting coupling of purity and feminism in the 19th century. Primary and secondary sources; 22 notes.
S. E. Kennedy

1068. Todorov, Goran D. ISTORICHESKITE VUZGLEDI NA PAISII KHILENDARSKI [The historical views of Paisi of Hilendar]. *Izvestiia na Inst. za Istoriia [Bulgaria] 1968 (20): 95-165.* Analyzes *Istoriia Slavianobulgarska,* the master work of Paisi of Hilendar (1722-98), praising his analysis of the political structure and cultural life of medieval Bulgaria, his assessment of the regressive influence of Ottoman rule, his objectivity, rationalism, methodology, and use of sources. Attempts to relate the history, finished in 1762, to Paisi's life and era, and contemporary Bulgarian problems.
F. A. K. Yasamee

1069. Todorov, Goran D. and Angelov, D. N. S. DERZHAVIN KATO ISTORIK NA BULGARSKI NAROD [N. S. Derzhavin as an historian of the Bulgarian people]. *Istoricheski Pregled [Bulgaria] 1963 19(6): 74-93.* Nikolai Derzhavin (1877-1953) adopted Marxism after the Russian Revolution. He was sympathetic to Bulgaria over the Macedonian question and castigated the Bulgarian middle class. His *History of Bulgaria* in four volumes, published after World War II, is a monumental work. The first volume deals with the foundation of the Bulgarian State, to the year 681; the second with the first and second Bulgarian kingdoms, social status, religion, and other aspects of the country's history; the third covers the years of Turkish occupation and provides a Marxist interpretation of the decline of the Ottoman Empire in the 18th and 19th centuries, and a full account of the struggles of the Bulgarian independence movement. The final volume considers Bulgaria since 1878, particularly its efforts to achieve independence and social justice. Based on Derzhavin's works; 81 notes.
A. J. Evans/S

1070. Topolski, Jerzy. JANA RUTKOWSKIEGO KONCEPCJA HISTORII KULTURY MATERIALNEJ [Jan Rutkowski's conception of history of material culture]. *Kwartalnik Hist. Kultury Materialnej [Poland] 1980 28(4): 461-467.* Jan Rutkowski (1886-1949) was the first Polish (and, perhaps, European) scholar to concern himself with the history of material culture. His *Economic History of Poland,* (1946), was a methodological achievement which anticipated modern attitudes toward the history of material culture by many years. Rutkowski was a true precursor of the contemporary model of historical research. Secondary sources; 27 notes.
I. Lukes

1071. Trapl, Miroslav. PROF. PH. DR. DIMITR KRANDŽALOV. *Acta Universitatis Palackianae Olomucensis-Historica [Czechoslovakia] 1972 (18): 159-162.* Reviews the life and work of Bulgarian historiographer and professor of Eastern European history at the University of Olomouc (since 1948), Dimitr Krandžalov (1907-71). His own education started before World War II at the University of Prague; in 1945 he became a teacher at the University of Sofia. Krandžalov's scientific research concentrated mainly on fighting the romanticism and false nationalism in the history of this century and on the question of the first Slavic settlements in the Balkans.
G. E. Pergl

1072. Trépanier, Pierre. MARCEL TRUDEL ET DONALD CREIGHTON [Marcel Trudel and Donald Creighton]. *Action Natl. [Canada] 1980 69(9): 707-715.* Although his study of Voltaire is misguided and he is wrong in comparing the Quebec intellectual renaissance of the 1840's and 1850's to the Enlightenment, Marcel Trudel's work on 17th-century Canada is rivaled only by that of Lucien Campeau and André Vachon. Trudel's best work is characterized by breadth, exactitude, and erudition, correcting the errors of Garneau and Lanctôt. Far more passionate is Donald Creighton, who understands that history is more than doctrines and abstractions. As Trudel is prolific and conscientious, Creighton is a historian in the grand tradition. Note.
A. W. Novitsky

1073. Treves, Piero. UN DIMENTICATO CRITICO LOMBARDO DEL MOMMSEN [A forgotten Lombard critic of Mommsen]. *Nuova Riv. Storica [Italy] 1958 42(2): 185-204.* Discusses Giuseppe Brambilla's critical study of Theodor Mommsen, the renowned German historian of the ancient world, in the context of Italian historiography and the events preceding the unification of Italy in 1870. Brambilla's thought was limited neither by contemporary academic conformity nor traditional historiography, and his writing was tempered by native Lombard realism. His attitude was that of a liberal European opposed both to anachronistic ideologies of the past and to the pseudo-scientific exaltation of the concept of materialism. Based on Brambilla's works and secondary sources; 21 notes.
C. E. King

1074. Tropper, Peter G. ABT MAGNUS KLEIN VON GÖTTWEIG UND SEINE "PRIVATURKUNDENLEHRE": EIN BEITRAG ZUR WISSENSCHAFTSGESCHICHTE DES 18. JAHRHUNDERTS [The Abbot Magnus Klein from Göttweig and his "private palaeography": a contribution to the history of 18th-century scholarship]. *Mitteilungen des Inst. für Österreichische Geschichtsforschung [Austria] 1981 89(3-4): 269-286.* Traces the life and academic and theological career of Magnus Klein (1717-83), the abbot of the Benedictine monastery in Göttweig, Lower Austria, and pays particular attention to his contribution to 18th-century historiography through his studies in palaeography. The author provides a detailed examination of a handwritten manuscript by Klein in which he attempted to elaborate his theory concerning the importance of investigating "private documents" in order to gain a deeper appreciation of the legal and administrative history in Austria during the Middle Ages. Based on Klein's manuscript held in the library in the monastery in Göttweig and secondary sources; 113 notes.   G. L. Neville

1075. Troy, Frederick S. EDMUND BURKE AND THE BREAK WITH TRADITION: HISTORY VERSUS PSYCHOHISTORY. *Massachusetts Rev. 1981 22(1): 93-132.* Describes the 10-volume *Correspondence of Edmund Burke,* Thomas W. Copeland, ed. As four-fifths of these letters were heretofore unpublished, their publication is of immense assistance to historians. A recent psychobiography of Burke demonstrates that Burke is too complex for modern biographers. He must be studied in terms of 18th-century Britain, and cannot be analyzed from the viewpoint of modern concepts. Burke was a devout Anglican, a Christian humanist, and believed in broad social reform. Based on Burke's correspondence.
                                                        E. R. Campbell

1076. Turner, J. Munsey. ROBERT FEATHERSTONE WEARMOUTH (1882-1963): METHODIST HISTORIAN. *Pro. of the Wesley Hist. Soc. [Great Britain] 1982 43(5): 111-116.* A miner turned Primitive Methodist minister, Robert Featherstone Wearmouth could comprehend and chronicle in his histories how Methodism, no less than Marxism, shaped the British labor movement.

1077. Ullrich, Horst. F. ENGELS KAMPF GEGEN F. W. J. SCHELLING UND DIE BÜRGERLICHE PHILOSOPHIEGESCHICHTSSCHREIBUNG [F. Engels's struggle against F. W. J. Schelling and the bourgeois historiography of philosophy]. *Wissenschaftliche Zeitschrift der Friedrich-Schiller-Universität Jena. Gesellschafts- und Sprachwissenschaftliche Reihe [East Germany] 1976 25(1): 157-161.* Between 1841-45 Friedrich Engels published anonymous pamphlets against Friedrich von Schelling and his followers who tried to discredit Georg Hegel's philosophy at the University of Berlin.

1078. Uskova, E. I. NAUCHNYE TRUDY F. A. KOGAN-BERNSHTEIN [Scientific works of F. A. Kogan-Bernshtein]. *Srednie Veka [USSR] 1981 44: 394-396.* Lists 36 original studies and translations, published from 1927 to 1979, by Faina Abramovna Kogan-Bernshtein (1899-1976), professor of history at the Moscow University and the Moscow State Historical Archives Institute, who also published under the name of F. Mesin. Note.
                                                        N. Frenkley

1079. Van Orman, Richard A. OSCAR OSBURN WINTHER. *Great Plains J. 1979 18: 60-63.* Oscar Osburn Winther (1903-70), child of Danish immigrants, was educated at the University of Oregon, Harvard, and Stanford. He taught at various places, but primarily at the University of Indiana. His major work and publications were in the field of transportation history (*The Transportation Frontier,* et al.) His most popular work was *The Great Northwest,* but Winther considered *The Old Oregon Country* his best. He also is known for the three editions of his bibliography on the periodical literature of the Trans-Mississippi West. Selected bibliography of Winther. From a special section on "Historians of the Northern Plains."

1080. Várkonyi, Ágnes R. SZEREMLEI SÁMUEL ÉS A MEZŐVÁROSOK TÖRTÉNETÉNEK HISTORIOGRÁFIÁJA [Sámuel Szeremlei and the historiography of agricultural towns]. *Századok [Hungary] 1974 108(4): 915-930.* Szeremlei was the major historian of Hungarian towns in the second half of the 19th century. He used the positivistic approach of contemporary bourgeois historical science. He later abandoned the provincial approach and put it in the wider context, reviewing history as a continuum. In 1908 he was elected a corresponding member of the Hungarian Academy of Sciences. 44 notes.   G. Hetzron

1081. Velkov, Dragan. SPISOK NA OBJAVENI TRUDOVI NA PROFESOROT D-R ALEKSANDAR APOSTOLOV [The published works of Professor Aleksandar Apostolov]. *Istorija*

[Yugoslavia] 1980 16(2): 13-15. Bibliography of published works, mainly on Macedonian history, by Aleksandar Apostolov, Professor of History at the University of Skopje.

1082. Vickers, Brian. FRANCES YATES AND THE WRITING OF HISTORY. *J. of Modern Hist. 1979 51(2): 287-316.* Reviews *The Rosicrucian Enlightenment* by Frances Yates and concludes that Yates's proposed rewriting of Renaissance history is an edifice with no foundations.

1083. Vidnians'kyi, S. V. ODYN Z OSNOVOPOLOZHNYKIV MARKSYSTS'KOI ISTORIOHRAFII V CHSSR (DO 100-RICHCHIA Z DNIA NARODZHENNIA Z. NEIEDLOHO) [One of the founders of Marxist historiography in the Czechoslovakian SSR: the 100th anniversary of the birth of Z. Nejedly]. *Ukrains'kyi Istorychnyi Zhurnal [USSR] 1978 (2): 130-133.* A biographical sketch of the prominent Czech historian, Z. Nejedly, one of the best chroniclers of the decline of capitalism, who welcomed the October Revolution as an event of great world significance. Analyzes works written by Nejedly before and after he joined the Communist Party, in 1929. Describes his work as professor at Moscow University after the Nazis occupied Czechoslovakia, where he was instrumental in founding Marxist-Leninist Slavic studies. On his return to Czechoslovakia after the war, he played an active part in opposing counterrevolutionary forces and in securing the Communist victory in 1948. He was a historian of a new breed, born of the October Revolution and its ideals. 15 notes.
                                                        V. A. Packer

1084. Voth, Grant L. THE ARTIST AND THE PAST: REFLECTIONS ON TWO NEW GIBBON BOOKS. *Eighteenth-Cent. Studies 1974/75 8(2): 213-221.* Reviews two new works on Edward Gibbon and their relationship to Leo Braudy's seminal study *Hume, Fielding and Gibbon: Narrative Form in History and Fiction.* The first, David Jordan's *Gibbon and His Roman Empire* (Chicago: U. of Illinois Pr., 1971), draws on Braudy's work but broadens the discussion of the influences on the *persona* Gibbon created as the narrator of the *Decline and Fall.* Jordan's book is disappointing because it offers no new insights on the second half of the *Decline and Fall.* In offering a new conceptual framework, it has created, along with Braudy's study, the circumstances for a reconsideration of the second half of the *Decline and Fall* in light of Gibbon's changing awareness of his function as artist and historian. The second work, R. N. Parkinson's *Edward Gibbon* (New York: Twayne, 1973), is a biographical criticism of the *Decline and Fall* in terms of various emotional experiences in Gibbon's life. This approach sheds little new light on Gibbon's history. 10 notes.
                                                        R. C. Robbins

1085. Vranoussi, Era. ECHOS DE L'OEUVRE DE CANTEMIR DANS LES MILIEUX GRECS [Echos of Cantemir's work in Greek circles]. *Istanbul à la Jonction des Cultures Balkaniques, Méditerranéennes, Slaves et Orientales aux XVIᵉ-XIXeRET Siècle* (Bucharest: AIESEE, 1973): 461-474. The literary and historical works of Dimitrie Cantemir were widely read in Greek-speaking educated circles throughout the Balkans and outside the Ottoman Empire, in Odessa, Vienna, and other centers of Hellenism in exile. Cantemir was not looked down upon as a Romanian; in those days the elite of all Christian nations in the Balkans considered themselves Greeks, and used the Greek language for all formal purposes. Cantemir's histories were used by Greek historians like Athanasios Komnenos-Hypsilantis, but he was criticized by Dimitrios Katartzis for writing his *History of the Ottoman Empire* in Latin instead of Greek, and for composing Turkish-style music. 28 notes.   J. C. Billigmeier

1086. Waeber, Paul. LECTEURS ET AMIS GENEVOIS D'AUGUSTIN THIERRY: AMIEL, JAMES GALIFFE, SISMONDI, JEAN D'ESPINE [Readers and Genevan friends of Augustin Thierry: Amiel, James Galiffe, Sismondi, Jean d'Espine]. *Mus. de Genève [Switzerland] 1979 (191): 3-9.* Four different interpretations, 1825-60, of Augustin Thierry, historian of the ancient Gaul and Celt societies, by four of his contemporaries: Amiel, James Galiffe, Sismondi, and Jean d'Espine.

1087. Wagner, Henry R. HENRI TERNAUX COMPANS: A BIBLIOGRAPHY. *Inter-American Rev. of Biblio. 1957 (3): 239-254.* Bibliography of the historiographical works of Henri Ternaux-Compans, including his translations and works on Latin America, 1826-57.

1088. Wallot, Jean-Pierre. GROULX HISTORIOGRAPHE [Groulx historiography]. *Rev. d'Hist. de l'Amérique Française [Canada] 1978 32(3): 407-433.* An historiographic analysis of the writings of Fr. Lionel Groulx (1878-1967), distinguished Canadian historian. 95 notes.   M. R. Yerburgh

1089. Weber, Hermann. ERICH MATTHIAS ZUM GEDÄCHTNIS (21.8.1921-23.3.1983) [Erich Matthias in memoriam (21 August 1921-23 March 1983)]. *Jahrbuch für die Gesch. Mittel- und Ostdeutschlands [West Germany] 1983 32: 269-270.* With the death of Erich Matthias, professor of political science and history at the University of Mannheim and from 1977 member of the Historical Commission of Berlin, German historiography has lost one of its leading representatives. Giving new dimension to studies of political parties, Matthias made significant contributions to the interpretation of the November 1918 revolution, while his exemplary work on social democracy has influenced subsequent scholarship. In 1979 he turned his attention to a multivolume edition of source materials on the German trade union movement, 1914-49. Thanks to his foresight, the project is well under way and can successfully be brought to completion.   S. A. Welisch

1090. Weisberger, Bernard A. MAKING HISTORY. *Am. Heritage 1981 32(3): 105-107.* Interview with historian C. Vann Woodward on his career, his books, and his views on historical trends. Illus.
                    J. F. Paul

1091. West, Carroll Van. DEMOCRATIC IDEOLOGY AND THE ANTEBELLUM HISTORIAN: THE CASE OF HENDERSON YOAKUM. *J. of the Early Republic 1983 3(3): 319-339.* Though Henderson Yoakum's *History of Texas from Its First Settlement in 1685 to Its Annexation to the United States in 1846* (1855) is still highly regarded, questions linger as to whether Yoakum was merely a propagandist for Sam Houston or the prototypical 19th-century American historian—an instructor in patriotic values and destiny. A staunch Tennessee Democrat in the Jefferson-Jackson agrarian tradition, Yoakum successfully served in Tennessee politics. An ideologue not given to pragmatic politics, he gradually disengaged himself from party infighting and moved to Texas in 1845. Yoakum noted that Stephen Austin mirrored the revolutionary tradition more than Houston and that this tradition gave impetus to the Texas revolt. Rather than a tribute to Houston, Yoakum's *History* was a commemoration of revolutionary democratic principles and a plea for a strong union based on the agrarian tradition. 46 notes.   G. A. Glovins

1092. White, Hayden V. [THE LATER PHILOSOPHY OF R. G. COLLINGWOOD]. *Hist. and Theory 1965 4(2): 244-252.* Reviews Alan Donagan's *The Later Philosophy of R. G. Collingwood* (1962). Collingwood initiated inquiry into the nature and function of historical knowledge, a subject long dismissed by British historians as unnecessary until the social dislocations of the 20th century brought about the kind of self-doubt long familiar to Continental historians. The reviewer elaborates on the Hobbesian aspect of Collingwood's philosophy as it relates to the ordinary language movements.

1093. Wieseltier, Leon. ETWAS ÜBER DIE JUDISCHE HISTORIK: LEOPOLD ZUNZ AND THE INCEPTION OF MODERN JEWISH HISTORIOGRAPHY. *Hist. and Theory 1981 20(2): 135-149.* Examines the career and scholarship of the early 19th-century German-Jewish savant, Leopold Zunz. Zunz launched the modern historiographical study of Judaism with his *Etwas über die Rabbinische Literatur* (1818). For Zunz, inspired by the philological inquiries of August Wilhelm Boeckh, the Jewish historian "was to be a new source of cultural authority, a rival of the rabbi and the philosopher." He was committed to the belief that Jewish historiography could have far-reaching and beneficial implications for Jewish identity. His goal was nothing less than to research and define all aspects of historical Jewish culture. This entailed approaching religious texts as human-created, temporal objects. Zunz work shows the influence of Herder. 42 notes.   W. J. Reedy

1094. Wintle, Michael J. THREE UNPUBLISHED LETTERS BY T. B. MACAULAY. *Notes and Queries [Great Britain] 1981 28(4): 322-324.* Reprints three previously unpublished letters written in 1847 and 1849 by T. B. Macaulay to Jonkheer Johannes Cornelius de Jonge, state archivist in The Hague, 1831-53, requesting information for his book, *History of England.*

1095. Wolle, Stefan. AUGUST LUDWIG VON SCHLÖZERS NESTOR-EDITION (1802-1809) IM GEISTIGEN UND POLITISCHEN UMFELD DES BEGINNENDEN 19. JH. [August Ludwig von Schlözer's *Nestor* (1802-09) in the intellectual and political arena at the beginning of the 19th century]. *Jahrbuch für Gesch. der Sozialistischen Länder Europas [East Germany] 1982 25(2): 139-152.* The German historian August Ludwig von Schlözer (1735-1809) was a Normanist, a believer in the significant impact of the Normans on Europe, including the Normans' influence on Russia in the establishment of Kiev. Schlözer's *Nestor. Russische Annalen in Ihrer Slavonischen Grundsprache Verglichen, Übersetzt und Erklärt* [Nestor: Russian annals in their original Slavonic compared, translated, and interpreted], 5 vol. (1802-09), offered new and more accurate interpretations of the origins of the Slavs, especially the Russians, based on a critical study of original sources and an enlightened, liberal understanding of history. The work stimulated study of Russian history in Germany and in Russia, where Schlözer became well known and his work often cited.   S

1096. Woodbridge, Hensley C. WILLIAM HICKLING PRESCOTT: A BIBLIOGRAPHY. *Inter-American Rev. of Biblio. 1959 9(1): 48-77.* Bibliography of William Hickling Prescott's historiography on Spain and Latin America includes American first editions (and their subsequent translations), biographical and critical studies, and previous bibliographies on Prescott, 1838-1955.

1097. Woodward, C. Vann. ALLAN NEVINS: DEFENDER OF THE FAITH. *Rev. in Am. Hist. 1976 4(1): 25-26.* Review article prompted by Allan Nevins's *Allan Nevins on History* (New York: Scribner's, 1975).

1098. Woodward, Michael Vaughan. THE PUBLICATIONS OF ELLIS MERTON COULTER TO 1 JULY 1977. *Georgia Hist. Q. 1977 61(3): 268-278.* Provides a bibliography of books and articles authored, coauthored and edited by Ellis Merton Coulter during 1912-77. His writings deal primarily with Southern history and Georgia history in particular. The list excludes book reviews and newspaper articles.   G. R. Schroeder

1099. Wynar, Lubomyr R. DMYTRO DOROSHENKO—VYDATNYI DOSLIDNYK UKRAINS'KOI ISTORIOHRAFII I BIBLIOHRAFII [Dmytro Doroshenko: a renowned researcher in Ukrainian historiography and bibliography]. *Ukrains'kyi Istoryk 1982-83 19-20(3-4, 1): 40-78.* Analyzes the enormous contributions made by Dmytro Ivanovych Doroshenko (1882-1951) in the fields of Ukrainian historiography and historical bibliography. Doroshenko published an outstanding work: *Ohliad Ukrains'koi Istoriohrafii* [A survey of Ukrainian historiography] (Prague, 1923), as well as numerous monographs, studies and reviews devoted to historical labors of leading Ukrainian historians. The foundation for the latter field was *Ukazatel Istochnikov dlia Oznakomleniia s Iuzhnoi Rus'iu* [A guide to sources for knowledge of Southern Rus] (St. Petersburg, 1904). He continued to add to it various publications with the passage of time. Very valuable were his articles and reviews in non-Ukrainian journals, especially those which appeared in the *Zeitschrift für Osteuropäische Geschichte* (1931-34), for they made the history of Ukraine accessible to foreign readers. Appends selected bibliographies: a bibliography relating to bibliographies of works by Doroshenko and a bibliography of works about him. Based chiefly on Doroshenko's publications; 106 notes, appendix.   A. B. Pernal

1100. Zeil, Wilhelm. GESCHICHTE UND KULTUR SLAWIS-CHER VÖLKER IM WISSENSCHAFTLICHEN WIRKEN VON LEOPOLD KARL GOETZ (1868 BIS 1931) [History and culture of the Slavic peoples in the scholarly works of Leopold Karl Goetz (1868-1931)]. *Jahrbuch für Geschichte der Sozialistischen Länder Europas [East Germany] 1984 28: 235-252.* Goetz was interested in Slavs in Germany, in Russia, and in the USSR. He was not a professional philologist, and he preferred to view Slavic cultures and peoples in a broad historical context. He believed in "a world of Slavs" and deplored political and cultural divisiveness among the various Slavic peoples. 101 notes.   D. R. Stevenson

1101. Zhukov, Ie. M. [V. I. LENIN AND THE HISTORICAL METHOD].
—. V. I. LENIN I METODOLOGICHESKIE OSNOVY ISTORI-CHESKOI NAUKI [V. I. Lenin and the methodological base of the science of history]. *Novaia i Noveishaia Istoriia [USSR] 1970 (2): 7-17.* The foundation and development of Soviet historical science is inextricably bound up with Lenin, whose works are the basis for all subsequent Marxist historical studies, especially concerning economics and politics. Anti-Marxist historians have attempted to falsify history in various ways, and Lenin fought against their subjective and idealistic falsifications. Based on the collected works of Lenin; 30 notes.
L. Smith

—. LENIN, ISTORIIA, SOVREMENNOST' [Lenin, history, modernity]. *Novaia i Noveishaia Istoriia [USSR] 1970 (4): 3-11.* Though not a professional historian, Lenin was capable of examining historical data with assiduity, detecting the most important tendencies in any epoch. Based on Lenin's writings; 11 notes.   D. N. Collins

1102. Zub, Alexandru. THE BUCKLEAN IMPACT ON ROMA-NIAN CULTURE. *Anuarul Institutului de Istorie şi Arheologie "A. D. Xenopol" [Romania] 1983 (Supplement 4): 189-199.* Discusses the impact of the work of the English historian Henry Thomas Buckle (1821-62) in Europe during the 1860's, and on Romanian society in particular. Buckle's *History of Civilization in England*, in which he attempted to make history as exact a science as possible, was translated into German, French, and Russian, and all versions were circulated in Romanian. Analyzes Buckle's definition of civilization and shows how his ideas were applied in Romania by the academic Titu Maiorescu and the *Junimea* circle, and considers the views of other contemporary Romanian writers who accepted or refuted Buckle's theories, which, by the end of the century, had become unfashionable. Secondary sources; 84 notes.
G. L. Neville

1103. Zub, Alexandru. CONSTANTIN C. GIURESCU UND DER URSPRUNG SEINER SYNTHESE DER RUMÄNISCHEN GESCHICHTE [Constantin C. Giurescu and the origins of his synthesis of Romanian history]. *Südost-Forschungen [West Germany] 1979 38: 191-205.* Giurescu was the third modern Romanian historian who can be said to have succeeded in presenting a fully matured view of his nation's historical development. Like his predecessors Xenopol and Iorga, his work posits a definite philosophy of history and historical explanations. Giurescu rejected his former patron, Iorga, and went his own way, more concerned with the methodology of research and the exploration of archival material than with wide-ranging explanation or all-encompassing theories.
P. J. Adler

1104. Zub, Alexandru. CONSTANTIN C. GIURESCU: PERSPECTIVĂ ISTORIOGRAFICĂ [Constantin C. Giurescu: an historiographical perspective]. *Anuarul Inst. de Istorie şi Arheologie "A. D. Xenopol" [Romania] 1979 16: 489-500.* Traces the major historiographical influences on the Romanian historian Constantin C. Giurescu (1901-77), particularly his predecessors A. D. Xenopol and Nicolae Iorga, and notes how this is reflected in his works. Describes his education and the development of his career, his relations with his contemporaries, and the influence of his publications. 96 notes.   R. O. Khan

1105. Zub, Alexandru. A. D. XENOPUL AND THE NEW "SE-RIAL HISTORY." *Rev. Roumaine d'Hist. [Romania] 1980 19(2-3): 511-519.* Although he does not mention the name of the Romanian historian anywhere in his vast and impressive works of history and historiography, Pierre Chaunu's 1960 discussions of "serial history," the possibility of explaining things in a causal, genetic manner while retaining the individual uniqueness of the historical fact, find their origins in the work of Alexander D. Xenopol, professor at the University of Iaşi, who devoted an entire chapter to the theory in his *Principes fondamentaux de l'histoire* (1899) and produced what remains basically the definitive text on the theme, *Théorie de l'histoire*, in 1908. It was Xenopol's brilliant synthesis of the *Zeitgeist* of his day which made of the causal relation a methodological principle and allowed narrative history to become explicative history. 84 notes.   G. J. Bobango

1106. Zub, Alexandru. KOGĂLNICEANU ŞI IORGA (NOTE ISTORIOGRAFICE) [Kogălniceanu and Iorga: historiographical notes]. *Anuarul Institutului de Istorie şi Arheologie [Romania] 1973 10: 247-254.* Compares the writings of Mihail Kogălniceanu and Nicolae Iorga, as well as Iorga's comments on Kogălniceanu's thoughts on historiography and cultural directions. Both men were historians, scholars, orators, and statesmen, and they shared the same ideas about the organic development of society. Based on published materials; 47 notes.   F. Kellogg

1107. Zub, Alexandru. L'ESPRIT CRITIQUE DANS L'OEUVRE DE M. KOGALNICEANU [The critical spirit in the work of M. Kogălniceanu]. *Rev. Roumaine d'Hist. [Romania] 1972 11(2): 281-302.* Mihail Kogălniceanu stands as the founder of modern Romanian historiography, as the author of many works on Romanian history, as the initiator of the first Moldavian historical journal, but also as the formulator of a more critical spirit in Romanian historical methodology. He wrote numerous works on the history of Wallachia, Moldavia and of the Romanians living outside the principalities, as well as of the gypsies, but his greatest contribution, perhaps, was his dictum, stated in 1840, "the first duty which I have imposed on myself is that of telling the truth." 125 notes.
J. C. Billigmeier

1108. —. APPUNTI PER UNA BIBLIOGRAFIA MAZZINIANA [Notes for a bibliography of Mazzini]. *Bollettino della Domus Mazziniana [Italy] 1983 29(2): 109-219.* Provides an annotated bibliography of recent historical scholarship on Giuseppe Mazzini (1805-72), Italian patriot and revolutionary, and the Risorgimento.

1109. —. BIBLIOGRAFIA DEGLI SCRITTI DI ERNESTO RAGIONIERI [A bibliography of the writings of Ernesto Ragionieri]. *Italia Contemporanea [Italy] 1975 26(120): 37-63.* Lists all the works of the modern Italian historian Ernesto Ragionieri from 1946 to 1975. The first part includes all of Ragionieri's contributions that appeared as monographs and in specialized periodicals. The second part is a compilation of all the titles of articles written by Ragionieri for *Nuovo Corriere* in Florence, and *L'Unità* (both the Rome and Milan editions).   M. T. Wilson

1110. —. DR. R. COKE WOOD MEMORIAL SERVICE. *California Historian 1980 26(3): 27-30.*
Shebl, James M. COMMENT, *p. 27.*
Lamson, Berenice. THE MAN, *pp. 27-28.*
Limbaugh, Ronald. THE TEACHER, *p. 28.*
Covello, Leonard. THE WRITER, *p. 28.*
Payne, Walter. THE HISTORIAN, *p. 29.*
Hand, Clifford. R. COKE WOOD AT PACIFIC, *p. 29.*
Lambert, Rick. MY GRANDFATHER, *p. 29.*
Chrystal, William. BENEDICTION, *p. 30.*
Eulogies given at the memorial service of Dr. R. Coke Wood (1905-79), American historian and writer, at Morris Chapel, University of the Pacific.

1111. —. [FOR ERWIN WALTER PALM'S 70TH BIRTHDAY]. *Jahrbuch für Geschichte von Staat, Wirtschaft und Gesellschaft Lateinamerikas [West Germany] 1983 20: xxvii-lvi.*
Palm, Erwin Walter. VITA [Vita], *pp. xxvii-xxxiv.* Autobiographical, chronological resume of Erwin Palm's life.

Kügelgen Kropfinger, Helga von. BIBLIOGRAFIA DE LAS PUBLICACIONES DE ERWIN WALTER PALM [Bibliography of Erwin Walter Palm's publications], *pp. xxxv-1*. A list of 128 items written, edited, or translated by Erwin Palm.

Treue, Wolfgang. ERWIN WALTER PALM Y EL PROYECTO MEXICO DE LA FUNDACION ALEMANA PARA LA INVESTIGACION CIENTIFICA [Erwin Walter Palm and the Mexico Project of the German Foundation for Scientific Investigation], *pp. li-lvi*. Palm made significant contributions to the German Foundation for Scientific Investigation after 1957. Palm played a fundamental role in the Mexico Project of the German Foundation.   T. Schoonover

1112. —. THE HISTORICAL WRITINGS OF JOEL HURSTFIELD, 1944 TO 1978. Clark, Peter; Smith, Alan G. R.; and Tyacke, Nicholas, ed. *The English Commonwealth, 1547-1640: Essays in Politics and Society* (New York: Barnes & Noble, 1979): 205-214. A chronological bibliography of 1) the books, articles, and lectures and 2) reviews by historian Joel Hurstfield, who wrote primarily about Tudor England.

1113. —. HVORDAN BLIR MAN HISTORIKER: INTERVJU MED SVERRE STEEN [How one becomes a historian: interview with Sverre Steen]. *Samtiden [Norway] 1980 89(6): 27-32*. Reminiscences of Steen's early life and his opinions on the nature of history-writing and the role of the historian.

1114. —. IN MEMORIAM: MAYNARD J. GEIGER, O.F.M. *Pacific Hist. Rev. 1977 46(4): 684-685*. Maynard J. Geiger, archivist at Mission Santa Barbara 1937-77 and historian of Franciscan missionary activities in the Spanish Borderlands, died 13 May 1977. He was born in Lancaster, Pennsylvania, in 1901 and earned his Ph.D. in 1937 from Catholic University.   W. K. Hobson

1115. —. IN MEMORIAM: T. HARRY WILLIAMS, 1909-1979. *Louisiana Hist. 1979 20(3): 245-246*. T. Harry Williams was an outstanding historian of the Civil War, the American military, and the political history of the modern South. In addition to being an award-winning author, he was for 38 years one of the most widely known, popular, and respected professors at Louisiana State University.   D. B. Touchstone

1116. —. AN INTERVIEW WITH WILLIAM APPLEMAN WILLIAMS. *Radical Hist. Rev. 1979-80 (22): 65-91*. Interviews leftist activist and historian William Appleman Williams.

1117. —. LI ZHI (1527-1602) IN CONTEMPORARY CHINESE HISTORIOGRAPHY: NEW LIGHT ON HIS LIFE AND WORKS. *Chinese Studies in Hist. 1979-80 13(1-2): ix-xviii, 3-207*. Entire issue devoted to the life and thought of Li Zhi (Li Chih) anti-Confucian philosopher and 20th-century historiography surrounding him.

1118. —. LIUDMILA ZHIVKOVA I BULGARSKATA ISTORICHESKA NAUKA [Liudmila Zhivkova and Bulgarian historical science]. *Istoricheski Pregled [Bulgaria] 1982 38(5): 3-9*. Liudmila Zhivkova's death in 1981 at the age of 39 was a great loss to Bulgarian historiography. She worked at the Institute of Balkanistics at the Bulgarian Institute of Sciences. An expert in Anglo-German antagonisms in the Balkans prior to World War II, she well understood Great Power interest in the Balkans. She promoted Bulgarian culture, especially understanding of Bulgaria's 1,300 years of statehood. An outstanding and original Marxist-Leninist thinker, she was able to analyze Bulgaria's transition from imperialist oppression to today's socialist independence. She inculcated respect for Bulgaria's religious past and rich history of the Church and its iconography. Based on Liudmila Zhivkova's works, press reports, and Party documents; 15 notes.   A. J. Evans

1119. —. [THE METHOD OF HISTORICAL WRITING] (Danish text). *Historie [Denmark] 1982 14(2): 272-304*.

Tandrup, Leo. OMKRING "RAVN" [Concerning "Ravn"], *pp. 272-284*. The author's biography, *Ravn I-II* (1980), of the Danish historian, Kristian Erslev (1852-1930), has touched off much debate in Denmark.

Manniche, Jens C. OM HISTORIESKRIVNINGENS METODIK: ET SVAR FRA EN "TROLD" TIL EN BONDE [The method of historical writing: a reply from a "troll" to a peasant], *pp. 285-304*. Tandrup has asserted that Erslev was not a cold, objective scholar but was torn between positivism and neoidealism, objective historical research and subjective historical writing, yet Tandrup's own methods are too subjective. Based on *Ravn I-II* and reviews of it; 60 notes.
                                          J. R. Christianson

1120. —. PAMIATI AL'BERA SOBULIA [In memory of Albert Soboul]. *Novaia i Noveishaia Istoriia [USSR] 1983 (1): 199-202*. An obituary of the French Marxist historian Albert Soboul (1914-82), who was an honorary Doctor of Moscow State University. His works, which concentrate on the French Revolution are listed. Several of them were translated into Russian and published in the USSR. In 1982, he spoke at a meeting of the Learned Council of the USSR Academy of Sciences (Institute of General History) on the subject of "Philosophers and Revolution." 31 notes, biblio.
                                          D. N. Collins

1121. —. PAUL RICOEUR: ENTREVUE [Paul Ricoeur: an interview]. *Hist. Reflections [Canada] 1974 1(2): 213-229*. Records an interview with Professor Paul Ricoeur, outlining his views on various questions of historiography and methodology.

1122. —. PROF. DR. VÁCLAV KRÁL, DR.SC. 9.2.1926-12.12. 1983 [Václav Král, 1926-83]. *Slovanský Přehled [Czechoslovakia] 1984 90[i.e., 70](1): 1*. Prints an obituary of the editor-in-chief of *Slovanský Přehled*, Václav Král. He was a beloved teacher of sociology and history and a highly respected scholar. He wrote extensively on a number of subjects, but is best known for his interest in Czechoslovak-Soviet relations, and most recently in Marxist historiography. In all his writing, Král furthered the progress of socialism under the leadership of the Czechoslovak Communist Party.
                                          B. Reinfeld

1123. —. THE PUBLISHED WORKS OF J. H. HEXTER: A BIBLIOGRAPHY. Malament, Barbara C., ed. *After the Reformation: Essays in Honor of J. H. Hexter* (Philadelphia: U. of Pennsylvania Pr., 1980): 355-360. Bibliography of historian J. H. Hexter's books, edited editions, articles, review articles and reviews, and correspondence.

1124. —. SPISOK OSNOVNYKH RABOT DOKTORA ISTORICHESKIKH NAUK VADIMA ALEKSANDROVICHA ALEKSANDROVA [A list of major works of Dr. V. A. Aleksandrov on his 60th birthday]. *Sovetskaia Etnografiia [USSR] 1982 (3): 143-146*. Lists major works of Vadim A. Aleksandrov, a Russian historian.

1125. —. VASZIL ZLATARSZKI (1866-1935) [Vasil Zlatarski (1866-1935)]. *Világtörténet [Hungary] 1980 (1): 68-86*. One of the most important representatives of bourgeois historiography in Bulgarian is presented here, with excerpts of his writings. Primary sources; portrait, biblio.   R. Hetzron

1126. —. VERÖFFENTLICHUNGEN VON WERNER NÄF [Publications by Werner Näf]. *Schweizer Beiträge zur Allgemeinen Geschichte [Switzerland] 1960-61 18-19: 34-42*. Bibliography of 100 publications on Swiss, German, and European history by the Swiss historian Werner Näf (1894-1959).

5. METHODOLOGY AND SCHOOLS OF HISTORIOGRAPHY - GENERAL

1128. Afanas'ev, O. A. O ZADACHAKH I PREDMETE ISTORIOGRAFII [The aims and subject of historiography]. *Novaia i Noveishaia Istoriia [USSR] 1978 (4): 212-214.* Reports the proceedings of the current session of Historiographic Wednesdays held at the Department of History of the Academy of Sciences of the USSR, 30 November 1977, that debated N. A. Eroteev's report "On the aims and subject of historiography," which discussed such topics as the dangers of overspecialization, the need to differentiate between historiography and bibliographic studies, as well as between philosophy and factual historical research, and the importance of critical analysis of Russian prerevolutionary and Western bourgeois studies. N. Frenkley

1129. Affeldt, Werner. ASPEKTE DER KÖNIGSERHEBUNG PIPPINS IN DER HISTORIOGRAPHIE DES 19. JAHRHUNDERTS [Aspects of Pépin III's elevation to the throne in the historiography of the 19th century]. *Arch. für Kulturgeschichte [West Germany] 1977 59(1): 144-189.* On the basis of an admittedly selective overview of 22 primarily German historians writing about Pépin III (714?-768), asserts there is no single interpretation, no schools, no clear types, nor even a line of development based on methodology. What is clear is that methods and use of sources in 19th-century German historiography were affected by political and philosophical attitudes, which in some cases led to manipulation of facts and sources. 92 notes. H. D. Andrews

1130. Alatoseva, A. I. and Kirieva, R. A. VIEC NGHIEN CUU LICH SU KHOA HOC LICH SU O LIEN XO TRONG GIAI DOAN HIEN NAY [Current studies in historiography in the USSR]. *Nghien Cuu Lich Su [Vietnam] 1981 (6): 49-57, 64.* Surveys recent Soviet work on research, methodology, expansion of historical sources and topics, increased interest in contemporary history, cooperative projects with foreign scholars, and continued criticism and refutation of bourgeois ideology and sociology. J/S

1131. Anchor, Robert. REVIEW ESSAY. *Hist. and Theory 1975 14(3): 326-335.* A review article on Alice Kohli-Kunz's *Erinnern und Vergessen. Das Gegenwärtigsein des Vergangenen als Grundproblem historischer Wissenschaft* (Berlin: Duncker & Humblot, 1973) and Joachim and Orlinde Radkau's *Praxis der Geschichtswissenschaft. Die Desorientiertheit des historischen Interesses* (Düsseldorf: Bertelsmann U., 1972). The argument of both critiques of modern, especially German, historical thought is that "the study of history has lapsed into insignificance and irrelevance" because historians have failed to appreciate the implications of historical theory. They have not taken into account the effect of psychological forces in the making and the study of history nor the retention of outmoded, distorting concepts. The author seriously questions some of the psychological (or metapsychological) assumptions of the authors as to motivations implicit in historical research. 11 notes. R. V. Ritter

1132. Ankersmit, F. R. EEN MODERNE VERDEDIGING VAN HET HISTORISME: GESCHIEDENIS EN IDENTITEIT [A modern defense of historicism: history and identity]. *Bijdragen en Mededelingen betreffende de Geschiedenis der Nederlanden [Netherlands] 1981 96(3): 453-474.* Historicism has been discredited because it was often associated with objectionable political concepts or was not considered scientific enough. At least four definitions of historicism can be identified. The one considered the most workable contends that only a historical approach enables one to trace the identity or individuality of objects; the essence of identity is in their history. We only know history in terms of historical interpretation, therefore, history must be associated with the identity of historical interpretations. Thus, history is a theory of historical writing and not a theory of historical phenomena. Secondary materials; 25 notes. G. D. Homan

1133. Arac, Jonathan. NARRATIVE FORM AND SOCIAL SENSE IN *BLEAK HOUSE* AND *THE FRENCH REVOLUTION*. *Nineteenth-Century Fiction 1977 32(1): 54-72.* Compares Thomas Carlyle's *The French Revolution* (1837) and Charles Dickens' *Bleak House* (1852-53) in terms of narrative form and social sense to show that the writing of history and literature share a similar literary mode in Victorian writing.

1134. Aron, Raymond. RÉCIT, ANALYSE, INTERPRÉTATION, EXPLICATION: CRITIQUE DE QUELQUES PROBLÈMES DE LA CONNAISSANCE HISTORIQUE [Narrative, analysis, interpretation, explication: criticism of some problems of historical understanding]. *Arch. européennes de sociologie [Great Britain] 1974 15(2): 206-242.* A methodological postscript to *Republique imperiale, les Etats-Unis dans le monde 1945-1972.* Shows that the route to impartiality in contemporary history lies in incorporating the four literary skills of the title. 8 notes. M. L. Lifka

1135. Aydelotte, William O. THE SEARCH FOR IDEAS IN HISTORICAL INVESTIGATION. *Social Sci. Hist. 1981 5(4): 371-392.* Examines basic methods for improving creativity and imagination in scientific and social scientific work. Basic theories of creativity are reviewed and evaluated. Major factors considered include the advantages of hard steady work versus relaxation and leisure time, and solitude versus social and intellectual interaction. Based on a presidential address to the Social Science History Association, November 1980; 4 notes, biblio. L. K. Blaser

1136. Bagge, Povl. DR. LEO TANDRUP OG KR. ERSLEVS AFHANDLING "HISTORIESKRIVNING" [Dr. Leo Tandrup and Kristian Erslev's treatise on historiography]. *Historisk Tidsskrift [Denmark] 1980 80(2): 452-457.* In Charles Victor Langlois and Charles Seignobos's *Introduction aux Études Historique*, Seignobos maintained that historical syntheses like Theodor Mommsen's *Römische Geschichte* were chiefly works of art. Seignobos found true historical scholarship in monographs and books of reference such as Pauly-Wissowa's *Realencyclopädie*. In 1911 this prompted the leading Danish historian, Kristian Erslev, to write his treatise on the writing of history (i.e. historiography in the sense *Geschichtsschreibung* as distinct from historical research or *Geschichtsforschung*). Despite the kinship between the two categories of historical writing, which Erslev calls obvious, he makes a great point of their differences. He emphasizes that the *Geschichtsforscher* has to restrict his subject matter because the prime duty of a scientist is to prove everything he says. This the *Geschichtsschreiber* (e.g., Mommsen) does not and cannot do. At the same time Erslev defends the freedom entailed in *Geschichtsschreibung*. He says it gives the reader less, though in some respects more, than *Geschichtsforschung*. Among the merits of *Geschichtsschreibung* he underlines its ability to paint a vivid picture of the past and to move the reader in a way that scholarly historical research does not. In a paper published in 1940 in *Historisk Tidsskrift* (and reprinted together with Erslev's treatise in a separate publication in 1978), Povl Bagge argues against several of Erslev's views. In 1979 the historian Leo Tandrup published two volumes dealing with Erslev's life and work and criticizing Povl Bagge's views, alleging that Erslev in reality believed in only a very slight difference between *Geschichtsschreibung* and *Geschichtsforschung*. In his subsequent rejoinder, Povl Bagge argues that Leo Tandrup's criticism is based on a series of misreadings and erroneous interpretations of Erslev's treatise and Povl Bagge's paper. J

1137. Bailyn, Bernard. THE CHALLENGE OF MODERN HISTORIOGRAPHY. *Am. Hist. Rev. 1982 87(1): 1-24.* Advocates the creation of new, more comprehensive narrative structures that will appeal to a wider reading public. Three recent trends that will shape, enrich, and complicate these works are 1) the discovery of "latent" events (those unknown to, or not clearly understood by, contemporaries), and their relation to "manifest" events; 2) a rescaling of perspective, through "transnational communication," to identify "large-scale spheres and systems organized as peripheries and cores"; and 3) the description of "interior" or subjective experience (based on nonverbal or behavioral expressions), and its relation to external events. Comprehensive narration is "the ultimate purpose of all historical scholarship." Presidential address at the 96th meeting of the American Historical Association; 48 notes.

R. Schlesinger

1138. Bann, Stephen. REVIEW ESSAY: THE EMPIRE UNPOSSESS'D. *Hist. and Theory 1983 22(2): 199-207.* Reviews Lionel Gossman's *The Empire Unpossess'd: An Essay on Gibbon's Decline and Fall* (1981). Rather than examining Edward Gibbon's classic work in terms of its methodology, Gossman, asking the questions "Why and how do we read Gibbon?," analyzes the text as a piece of imaginative literature. To do this, Gossman resorts to the critical techniques of such French theorists as Roland Barthes. A major objective is to expose the "masks" that occlude textual transparency in Gibbon. Moreover, abandoning a merely rhetorical or formal exegesis, Gossman also employs a psychoanalytic approach and interprets parts of the book as "the text of the life" of a writer with relationships and physical peculiarities that affected the figurations and metaphors in his historiography. 12 notes.

W. J. Reedy

1139. Barany, George. ON TRUTH IN MYTHS. *East European Q. 1981 15(3): 347-355.* A commentary on myth in history as exemplified in three articles in the same issue of *East European Quarterly.* The author accepts the debunking of historical myths as the legitimate duty of historians and emphasizes that the accuracy of a myth may not be as important as what the myth aims to do and how the myth is understood by those who accept it. Secondary sources; 17 notes.

C. R. Lovin

1140. Barbagallo, Francesco. LA STORIA TRA PASSATO E FUTURO [History between the past and the future]. *Studi Storici [Italy] 1984 25(1): 105-117.* Places contemporary historiography in the context of the general crisis resulting from the pluralization of values, showing how the past and future are historically determined terms: the future has traditionally been linked to the myth of progress and the past has been investigated only in order to explain the present. Yet historians have made sense out of history by assuming a rectilinear model of progress—be it positivistic or Marxist—and now that recent studies especially of the history of science have shattered the rectilinear model, historians need to face once again the problem of making sense not only of history but of life. 29 notes.

J. W. Houlihan

1141. Bardach, Juliusz et al.; Szwarc, Andrzej, ed. JAK UPRAWIAĆ HISTORIĘ NAJNOWSZĄ? [How to pursue recent history?]. *Przegląd Hist. [Poland] 1981 72(3): 515-525.* A record of the discussion among historians on how to take advantage of the current relaxation of censorship to improve the quality and veracity of historical research, writing, and education, especially of the postwar era. Censorship has vastly distorted the truth in the past, and attempts must be made to do as much work as soon as possible in case the opportunity passes. Based on a discussion organized by *Przegląd Historyczny* on 10 January 1981.

L. A. Krzyzak

1142. Barg, M. A. ISTORICHESKOE SOZNANIE KAK PROBLEMA ISTORIOGRAFII [Historical awareness as a historiographic problem]. *Voprosy Istorii [USSR] 1982 (12): 49-66.* Presents two understandings of the concept "historical awareness": a broad one, i.e., as a characterization of the culture of the given epoch and a narrow, specialized one, i.e., as a sphere of transformation of the dominating world-view into an axiological system of the historian. In the first case the type of historicism is analyzed within a cultural context, while in the second the historian discloses the degree to which the worldview situation influences the formation of the type of historical thinking.

J

1143. Barg, M. A. VOPROSY METODA V SOVREMENNOI BURZHUAZNOI ISTORIOGRAFII [Problems of method in contemporary bourgeois historiography]. *Voprosy Istorii [USSR] 1972 (9): 63-81.* The article observes the influence of such phenomena as social and political changes taking place in the postwar world, and success of Marxist historical science, as well as progress outlined in the postwar period in linguistics, economy, psychology—contiguous "sciences about man"—on bourgeois historiography. After a universally recognized bankruptcy of the neo-Kantian methodology in history, bourgeois historiography resorted to empiric sociology in search of a new methodological orientation. The latter, in its turn, being in need of an integral historiosophic theory, turned to historiography looking for a way to overcome a static character which prevails in this science—that of a structural-functional picture of the world. However, while following this path, bourgeois historiography will meet only with new disappointments. The analysis of attempts of bourgeois historians to overcome methodological crisis in bourgeois historical science makes it possible to reveal the trend and essence of the tendencies characteristic of modern development in historical science in Western countries.

J

1144. Barnard, F. M. ACCOUNTING FOR ACTIONS: CAUSALITY AND TELEOLOGY. *Hist. and Theory 1981 20(3): 291-312.* Argues that intentionality and teleological causation are prerequisites for the understanding of history as the record of identifiable agencies—actors, reasons, and purposes. Without these, the study of human history becomes an absurdity and indeed incomprehensible. The "done" cannot be separated from the "doers" unless we find it acceptable to collapse all directional explanations into conditional explanations. As R. G. Collingwood maintained, intentional actions are the "essential stuff" of historiography. 32 notes.

W. J. Reedy

1145. Bender, Thomas. THE NEW HISTORY—THEN AND NOW. *Reviews in American History 1984 12(4): 612-622.* Charles and Mary Beard's *The Rise of American Civilization* (1927) was a work of historical synthesis going beyond the narrow political histories of the day to include economic and social factors in its explanation of the development of American culture, and its broad scope reveals the specialization and insularity of present-day historical research.

1146. Bérard, Robert N. APPROACHES TO NINETEENTH-CENTURY HISTORIOGRAPHY. *New Scholar 1978 5(2): 369-375.* Review article prompted by Maurice Maldelbaum's *History, Man and Reason: A Study In Nineteenth-Century Thought* (Baltimore: Johns Hopkins U. Pr., 1974) and Hayden White's *Metahistory: The Historical Imagination in Nineteenth-Century Europe* (Baltimore: Johns Hopkins U. Pr., 1974). However, Charles Rearich's *Beyond the Enlightenment: Historians and Folklore in Nineteenth-Century France* (Bloomington: Indiana U. Pr., 1974) and John Clive's *Macaulay: The Shaping of the Historian* (New York: Alfred A. Knopf, 1974) make fresh approaches.

D. K. Pickens

1147. Berkhofer, Robert F., Jr. THE TWO NEW HISTORIES: COMPETING PARADIGMS FOR INTERPRETING THE AMERICAN PAST. *OAH Newsletter 1983 11(2): 9-12.* Compares two differing approaches in American history: the social science historians, who apply the quantifying approach of the social sciences to historical topics, and the Marxian radical historians, who reject quantifying as a way of understanding social processes.

1148. Bishop, Morris. ESSAY: WHAT IS IMPORTANT IN HISTORY? *Am. Heritage 1967 19(1): 2-3.* Suggests historians tend to exalt the unimportant and fail to emphasize what is important for the nonprofessional reader. Illus.

J. F. Paul

1149. Blaas, P. HET ENGAGEMENT EN DE HISTOIRE ÉVÉNEMENTIELLE [Engagement and incidental history]. *Tijdschrift voor Geschiedenis [Netherlands] 1974 87(3): 397-409.* Discusses French "incidental history" and English "record history" between 1880 and 1920 through such representative writers as Numa Denis Fustel de Coulanges (1830-89) and Frederic William

Maitland (1850-1906). Their views on past and present anachronisms brought about fundamental changes in history's social function and the relation between historical study and engagement, the historian's engagement being his concern for a present endangered by anachronisms, which made for greater objectivity toward the past in the specialized study of institutional history and its unpredictable processes. 31 notes.   G. Herritt

1150. Blanke, Horst Walter; Fleischer, Dirk; and Rusen, Jorn. THEORY OF HISTORY IN HISTORICAL LECTURES: THE GERMAN TRADITION OF *HISTORIK*, 1750-1900. *History and Theory 1984 23(3): 331-356.* Examines the development and diversity of the German tradition of *Historik* from the 18th to the 20th centuries. *Historik* encompasses the nature and practice of historical writing, research, and thinking. The word is most familiar from J. G. Droysen's book of that name, which was compiled from his lectures after his death. There have been four major traditions of reflection on history: the humanistic-rhetorical, the auxiliary-encyclopedic, the historico-philosophical, and the epistemological. The oldest is the first, which received its original formulation in the thought of S. J. Baumgarten, G. A. Will, and K. W. von Rotteck. Essentially, the "theory" of history evolved hand-in-hand with the professionalization of historical studies in the late 18th and early 19th centuries. 121 notes.   W. J. Reedy

1151. Blight, James G. THE STRUCTURE OF HISTORIANS' REVOLUTIONS? *Rev. in Am. Hist. 1981 9(3): 313-318.* Review essay of Gene Wise's *American Historical Explanations: A Strategy for Grounded Inquiry*, 2d ed. (1980), which analyzes the sources, contexts, and methodologies of eminent American historians.

1152. Bobinska, Celina. KRYTYKA WEWNETRZNA ZRODLA A ANALIZA KLASOWA [Internal criticism of historical sources and social analysis]. *Kwartalnik Hist. [Poland] 1963 70(3): 551-559.* In traditional historiography, social analysis of historical sources has been often misunderstood. The author sees a value in examining a historian's outlook, his opinion about history, his attitude toward the various social classes and various political events. All these circumstances are reflected in his general outlook, his choice of historical sources, and the manner in which he represents the material. All these factors are important especially as they relate to the formation of a national history.   J. Wilczek

1153. Bogue, Allan G. EMERGING THEORETICAL MODELS IN SOCIAL AND POLITICAL HISTORY. *Am. Behavioral Scientist 1973 16(5): 625-629.* The editor's introduction to six essays in historiography and methodology.

1154. Borelli, Giorgio. SU ALCUNE TENDENZE DELLA STORIOGRAFIA ITALIANA [Some trends in Italian historiography]. *Econ. e Storia [Italy] 1981 2(2): 242-251.* Beginning with the heritage of the philosophical and historical work of Benedetto Croce, examines some recent trends, including: the Marxist influence of Antonio Gramsci; the effort toward a total historiography, beyond events of political history, seizing the texture of socioeconomic institutions; the school of Bologna, the Lombardo-Venetian school; and the impact of French developments, especially the work of Fernand Braudel and the *Annales* school.
                          J. V. Coutinho

1155. Bouwsma, William J. THE RENAISSANCE AND THE DRAMA OF WESTERN HISTORY. *Am. Hist. Rev. 1979 84(1): 1-15.* This essay calls attention to the virtual collapse in recent historiography of the venerable conception of the Renaissance as a decisive turning point in the drama of Western history and to the substitution for it of the vague notion of the Renaissance as an "age of transition" to the modern world. This shift is attributed to a general tendency in recent historiography to minimize process in favor of structure. However valuable in some respects, structuralist history is not well adapted to explain change. As a result, it has undermined the dramatic organization of Western history and—since historiography cannot finally dispense with dramatic patterns of some kind—opened the way for a "myth of apocalyptic modernization" that rejects the relevance of all but the most recent past to the present. The traditional idea of the Renaissance, since it saw

the modern world as the goal of linear history, was itself vitiated by apocalypticism. Detached from this metahistorical assumption, however, it is still useful to explain much (if not all) in contemporary culture, in the meaning of that term now common among anthropologists.   A

1156. Bouwsma, William J. *THE WANING OF THE MIDDLE AGES* BY JOHAN HUIZINGA. *Daedalus 1974 103(1): 35-43.* The *Waning of the Middle Ages* (Haarlem, 1919) was old-fashioned history. Huizinga's real contribution was his exhortation to the historian to use his inevitable subjectivity and his dependence on his own culture. The historian had to penetrate beneath the evidence to ask questions relative to his own time. Primary and secondary sources; 17 notes.   E. McCarthy

1157. Bowie, Andrew. NEW HISTORIES: ASPECTS OF THE PROSE OF ALEXANDER KLUGE. *J. of European Studies [Great Britain] 1982 12(3): 180-208.* Suggests why Alexander Kluge's writings are of interest as a contribution to the debate on the possibilities of literary form as a response to modern history and to a reassessment of the role of traditional historiography.

1158. Brezzi, Paolo. LA STORIA E LA PROMOZIONE UMANA [History and human advancement]. *Studium [Italy] 1976 72(6): 771-785.* Argues that modern historiographical methods such as group and multi-disciplinary research, computer aid, etc., may produce such a complete picture of the past that it could contribute to human advancement in a way that previous histories could not do.

1159. Brichford, Maynard. HISTORIANS AND MIRRORS: A REVIEW ESSAY. *Am. Archivist 1973 36(3): 397-402.* Reviews six books: Geoffrey R. Elton's *The Practice of History* (London: Sydney U. Press, 1967), Robin W. Winks', ed., *The Historian as Detective: Essays on Evidence* (New York: Harper & Row, 1969), Robert F. Berkhofer's *A Behavioral Approach to Historical Analysis* (New York: Free Press, 1969), David H. Fischer's *Historians' Fallacies: Toward a Logic of Historical Thought* (New York: Harper & Row, 1970), John Higham's *Writing American History: Essays on Modern Scholarship* (Bloomington: Indiana U. Press, 1970), and Jack H. Hexter's *Doing History* (Bloomington: Indiana U. Press, 1971). The books were written by historians in response to the effects on history by new methods of social scientists, philosophers, and natural scientists. States the theme of each work. The ideas are useful to archivists, whose role differs from that of historians. Archivists must consider some questions about records, and must write about archivists and what they do.   D. E. Horn

1160. Bromley, Yu. and Shkaratan, O. THE GENERAL AND THE PARTICULAR IN HISTORICAL, ETHNOGRAPHICAL, AND SOCIOLOGICAL RESEARCH. *Current Anthrop. 1972 13(5): 569-574.* Stresses the connectedness of the three disciplines in exploring historical cultural structures, treating each as a scientific (as opposed to humanistic) pursuit.

1161. Brown, Theodore M. PUTTING PARADIGMS INTO HISTORY. *Marxist Perspectives 1980 3(1): 34-63.* Thomas S. Kuhn's *The Structure of Scientific Revolutions* (Chicago, 1962) has been instrumental in initiating a widespread movement in historiography toward applying the concept of the paradigm to the interpretation of history.

1162. Bruneau, William A. LOGIC AND PRAGMATISM: THE FOUNDATIONS OF FRENCH HISTORICAL TRAINING AND RESEARCH, 1880-1914. *Pro. of the Ann. Meeting of the Western Soc. for French Hist. 1978 6: 307-316.* Investigates a series of books, mostly manuals of logic and the theory of knowledge, that included a chapter or two on applied philosophy in history and the social sciences. Without clarification of the notions of reason, cause, effect, moral duty, and law that underlay changing theories and practices of historical research, it is difficult to know to what extent French historians saw their work as a contribution to the newly emerging social sciences and to what extent history teachers believed their work was merely a branch of moral and civic education. There is evidence that French historians, confronted with writings that showed how history differed from science, knew and respected the difference, and that they wrote moralistic history fully understanding the logical and intellectual consequences of doing so. 27 notes.   A/J

1163. Burton, David H. HISTORY, HUBRIS AND THE HEISENBERG PRINCIPLE. *Thought* 1975 50(196): 84-93. Historians tend to emphasize either a fixed past or the process of historical change. Whichever emphasis historians choose, they bring to their work logical and scientific subjectivity. In order to test this proposition, the career of Theodore Roosevelt between 1909 and 1919 is examined.   J. C. English

1164. Butterfield, Herbert; Poo, Mu-chou, transl. JEN-LEI HUA WANG-SHIH (2) HSI-YANG SHIH-HSÜEH-SHIH CHIH YEN-CHIU (SHANG) [Man on his past: the study of the history of historical scholarship]. *Ssu yü Yen (Thought and Word) [Taiwan]* 1976 13(6): 389-394. Translates the first two sections of chapter two of Herbert Butterfield's *Man On His Past: The Study of the History of Historical Scholarship* (Cambridge: Cambridge U. Pr., 1955). Discusses the rise of the German historical school. Eighteenth-century German historians at the University of Göttingen laid the foundation for later German innovations in the study of history. 36 notes.   T. P. Massey

1165. Butterfield, Herbert; Poo Mu-chou, transl. JEN-LEI HUA-WANG-SHIH (2) HSI-YANG HSÜEH-SHIH CHIH YEN-CHIU (B) [Man on his past: the study of the history of historical scholarship (Chapter II-2)]. *Ssu yü Yen (Thought and Word) [Taiwan]* 1976 14(1): 48-56. A translation of the last two sections of Herbert Butterfield's second chapter from *Man On His Past: The Study of the History of Historical Scholarship* (Cambridge U. Pr., 1955). Butterfield continues his discussion of the works of 18th-century German historians at the University of Göttingen. He points out the important contributions these historians made in developing the concept of universal history and in developing critical methods of inquiry.   T. P. Massey

1166. Capobianco, Laura and D'Agostino, Guido. DALLA STORIA SCIENZA ALLA STORIA MATERIA [From history as science to the matter of history]. *Italia Contemporanea [Italy]* 1984 (156): 114-119. Reviews Scipione Guarracino's *Guida alla Storiografia e Didattica della Storia* [Guide to historiography and the teaching of history] (1983). The first section of the book surveys the development of historiography from the 15th century to the present and discusses the crucial issues at various times; the second half investigates modern methodologies and contributions. Guarracino establishes a theoretical plane with six levels: knowledge of facts, conceptualization, elaboration, analysis, explication, and valuation, and applies this scheme to selected modern historians.   J. W. Houlihan

1167. Caracciolo, Alberto. FRA "STORICO" E "BIOLOGICO": APPUNTI SU CRISI DEL REALE E CRISI DEL SAPERE [Between "historical" and "biological": notes on crises of reality and crises of knowing]. *Quaderni Storici [Italy]* 1977 12(2): 551-555. Discusses, with a number of biologists, approaches which can be adopted today when studying certain historical aspects of the relationship between historical man and nature.   J

1168. Carbonell, Charles-Olivier. POUR UNE HISTOIRE DE L'HISTORIOGRAPHIE [For a history of historiography]. *Storia della Storiografia [Italy]* 1982 (1): 7-25. Various and conflicting theories and methodologies of historiography have served to underline the essential relativity of historical knowledge and have opened the way to a new history of historiography, one in which the essential point is not the document itself but its relationship with the culture and society in which it had its genesis. This does not preclude other approaches—bibliographic, elitist, or progressionist—but it means that they must be supplemented by new ones. 37 notes.   J. V. Coutinho

1169. Carroll, David. HISTORY AS WRITING. *Clio* 1978 7(3): 443-461. The scholarly debate over Jacques Derrida's *De La Grammatologie* [Of Grammatology], first published in 1967 and translated into English in 1976, has been unproductive because scholars have distorted Derrida's conception of literature. Derrida views history as the principal support of metaphysics; they have similar assumptions and implications. In the Western tradition, historical writing has been too narrow in scope. Because writing is the framework in which history is conceived, Derrida prefers as broad a definition of writing as possible, one that includes trace, supplement, difference, and spacing. 20 notes.   T. P. Linkfield

1170. Chartier, Roger. COMMENT ON ECRIVAIT L'HISTOIRE AU TEMPS DES GUERRES DE RELIGION [How history was written at the time of the Wars of Religion]. *Ann.: Économies, Sociétés, Civilisations [France]* 1974 29(4): 883-887. Analyzes the work of George Huppert, especially his book *The Idea of Perfect History* (Evanston: U. of Illinois Pr., 1970), examining his thesis that a new historical methodology arising from a new philosophical outlook appeared in 1560-1600. Huppert's view that 17th-century historical writing represented a regression is debatable, but his general thesis is stimulating. 15 notes.   R. Howell

1171. Chastenet, Jacques. À QUOI SERT L'HISTOIRE? [What is history good for?]. *Nouvelle Rev. des Deux Mondes [France]* 1977 (6): 513-518. Reflects on the nature and purpose of historical research today, and some problems in distinguishing legend from history, attempting to protect historical study from becoming a popular fad.

1172. Chaunu, Pierre. L'HISTOIRE SERIELLE. BILAN ET PERSPECTIVES [Serial history: balance-sheet and perspectives]. *Rev. Roumaine d'Hist. [Romania]* 1970 9(3): 459-484. Distinguishes between quantitative and serial history and charts the development of the latter since the 1930's. It was then the need for a serial historical method was first felt. Taking the form of a scientific history of prices, as did the first French serial historian, François Simiand, it attempted to respond to the needs of economists. In the 40's and 50's, serial history was extended to include a greater range of subjects, such as industrial production, population, and rates of exchange. Its growth was so rapid, in fact, that by the late 50's and 60's, it could claim a position of preeminence among historical methods. At present, serial history can be applied to virtually any subject, though three fields in particular stand out: geographical history, natural history, and, most important, demographic history. Secondary sources; 61 notes.   A. W. Howell

1173. Clark, Stuart. BACON'S HENRY VII: A CASE-STUDY IN THE SCIENCE OF MAN. *Hist. and Theory* 1974 13(2): 97-118. Although historians since the 19th century have treated prescientific history with a disdain equal to natural science before Galileo, they have searched for foundations of scientific history in earlier works. "What happens when a 'pre-scientific' historian is caught in this deadly cross fire is admirably illustrated by Francis Bacon's *History of the Reign of King Henry the Seventh*" (1622), which was long accepted as the final word on Henry VII until Bacon's abuse of evidence was exposed in the 1890's. A judgement of Bacon's methodology according to the standards of contemporary scholars or those of 19th century historians is immaterial, because "the important and paradoxical point is that a work condemned as 'unscientific' from the modern historiographical point of view should turn out to be saturated with the scientific assumptions of the Baconian *doctrine de homine*." 54 notes.

         D. A. Yanchisin

1174. Clifford, Geraldine Jonçich. HISTORY AS EXPERIENCE: THE USES OF PERSONAL-HISTORY DOCUMENTS IN THE HISTORY OF EDUCATION. *Hist. of Educ. [Great Britain]* 1978 7(3): 183-196. Describes the contribution by American historians of education to the methodology of historical inquiry. Considers the concept of grass-roots history, the potential evidence of documents of personal history, and the methodological problems associated with them. Outlines the uses of this approach for studying 19th-century American education and its effect on personal relations and attitudes at the time. 52 notes.

1175. Cline, Howard F. MISSING AND VARIANT PROLOGUES AND DEDICATIONS IN SAHAGÚN'S *HISTORIA GENERAL*: TEXTS AND ENGLISH TRANSLATIONS. *Estudios de Cultura Náhuatl [Mexico] 1971 9: 237-251.* Transcribes and translates into English several unpublished sections of Bernardino de Sahagún's *Historia General,* particularly the various prologues. Table, biblio. I. M. (IHE 90083)

1176. Clive, John. HISTORIOGRAPHY II: THE MOST DISGUSTING OF THE PRONOUNS. *Am. Scholar 1976-77 46(1): 104-108.* Twentieth-century historians have written as if the most disgusting pronoun that they can insert into their work is "I." The insertion of self or autobiographical feelings can strengthen and objectify histories. F. F. Harling

1177. Cochrane, Eric. THE TRANSITION FROM RENAISSANCE TO BAROQUE: THE CASE OF ITALIAN HISTORIOGRAPHY. *Hist. and Theory 1980 19(1): 21-38.* Explores the cultural meaning of the stylistic term "baroque." Although specialists in a number of fields have reached tentative conclusions about what the term connotes, the nature of Italian baroque historiography remains unclear. Renaissance histories were characterized by four attributes: the concept of change through time and human effort, the rhetoric and language of the ancients, the use of psychological causal explanations, and the desire not only to inform but to morally or politically educate the reader. By the beginning of the 16th century, however, historiography in Italy started to suffer from a "crisis of content." Humanist insight gave way under the impact of the Counter-Reformation to precepts that were platitudinous, ahistorical, and politically inconsequential. The ancients were no longer paradigmatic. 70 notes. W. J. Reedy

1178. Colish, Marcia L.; Woodman, Harold D.; and Alpern, Mildred. THREE NOTES ON THE RELATIONSHIP BETWEEN WRITING AND TEACHING HISTORY. *Hist. Teacher 1980 13(4): 543-550.* Presents three views of the relationships between the writing and teaching of history. Marcia L. Colish of Oberlin College urges history writers to bring the enthusiasm of research and publication to their students. Harold D. Woodman of Purdue University agrees with that idea and recommends that history teachers make special efforts to keep up to date and present the latest views from the most recent books and journals. Mildred Alpern of Spring Valley Senior High School in New York discusses the problems of teaching effectively and keeping abreast of current scholarly interpretations. Based on papers read at the annual meeting of the American Historical Association in December 1979. S. H. Frank

1179. Commager, Henry Steele. SHOULD THE HISTORIAN MAKE MORAL JUDGMENTS? *Am. Heritage 1966 17(2): 27, 87-93.* Cites the views of William Hickling Prescott (1796-1859), Theodore Parker (1810-66), Mandell Creighton (1843-1901), Lord Acton (John Emerich Edward Dalberg-Acton, 1834-1902), James Anthony Froude (1818-94), and John Lothrop Motley (1814-77). "We should not confuse moral with professional judgment. In the field of his professional competence the scholar has the same obligation as the judge, the teacher, the physician, the architect . . . . We want professional judgments from a doctor or a lawyer or an engineer; and we have a right to professional judgments from a scholar as well." Illus. D. D. Cameron and S

1180. Conkin, Paul K. [REVIEW ESSAY: TRUTH IN HISTORY]. *Hist. and Theory 1980 19(2): 224-237.* Critically reviews Oscar Handlin's *Truth In History* (Cambridge: Harvard U. Pr., 1979). Handlin's work is an "inept, often naive commentary on the historical profession." He reveals a deep disillusionment about recent developments and questions the integrity and truthfulness of many contemporary historians. While he attempts to explain what truth in the research and writing of history really means, his own understanding of such truth is both simplistic and confused. Moreover, in warning historians about the grave pitfalls of faddishness and ideological commitment he tends to vitiate the "external" purpose of historiography: human self-understanding. History must in some sense be morally useful if historians want public support for undertakings. As long as strict methodological canons are followed, Handlin's fears are exaggerated. W. J. Reedy

1181. Coover, Edwin R. SOCIOECONOMIC STATUS AND STRUCTURED CHANGE. *Social Sci. Hist. 1977 1(4): 437-459.* Assesses context, critical background, and ascription of socioeconomic studies applied to historical evaluation, 1925-53, and proposes the use of socioeconomic status evaluation as a tool to evaluate development of socioeconomic structural change.

1182. Cruz, Paulo Werneck da. A HISTORIA E AS NOVAS CONDIÇÕES DO PENSAMENTO CIENTIFICO [History and the new conditions of scientific thought]. *Revista do Instituto Histórico e Geográfico Brasileiro [Brazil] 1983 (339): 83-90.* Describes the developments in historical research since the 18th century when historians began to evaluate the evolution of society and employ new research methods. Discusses the interaction among philosophical, sociological, scientific, and historical methods of analysis. J. V. Coutinho

1183. Čumpelíková, Barbora. PŘÍSPĚVEK K DISKUSI O POJMU TRADICE [A contribution to the discussion about tradition]. *Hist. a Vojenství [Czechoslovakia] 1981 30(1): 177-185.* Discusses the significance of tradition in historiography. Secondary sources; 7 notes. G. E. Pergl/S

1184. Cunningham, Raymond J. IS HISTORY PAST POLITICS? HERBERT BAXTER ADAMS AS PRECURSOR OF THE "NEW HISTORY." *Hist. Teacher 1976 9(2): 244-257.* A discussion of Herbert Baxter Adams as a precursor of the New History. The author holds that, upon close examination, Adams' approach to the study of history presaged the social and cultural emphasis of the New History. Adams also advanced the presentism which was a hallmark of the New History. Primary and secondary sources; 54 notes. P. W. Kennedy

1185. Danilov, A. I. PROBLEMA KONTINUITETA V ISTORIOGRAFII FRG [The continuity problem in West German historiography]. *Voprosy Istorii [USSR] 1981 (3): 67-81.* The continuity problem is a key to an understanding of the character and essence of West German historical research. The author shows that there is no unity on this problem, discusses diverse views and concepts, and correlates them to concrete historical problems of Germany's recent past and contemporary developments. The treatment of the continuity problem by bourgeois historians is closely linked with present-day reality. J

1186. Davidson, James West. THE NEW NARRATIVE HISTORY: HOW NEW? HOW NARRATIVE? *Reviews in American History 1984 12(3): 322-334.* Discusses the resurgence of narrative history, which is descriptive rather than analytical and uses literary techniques to convey truths about human nature as well as historical fact.

1187. Dawidoff, Robert. JUST BECAUSE THINGS CHANGE, THAT DOESN'T MEAN THEY STAY THE SAME. *Rev. in Am. Hist. 1980 8(2): 145-154.* Review essay of Oscar Handlin's *Truth in History* (Cambridge, Mass.: Belknap Pr. of Harvard U. Pr., 1979); covers 1970's.

1188. DeGiorgi, Fulvio. RETORICA E STORICITA: HENRI PIRENNE [Rhetoric and historicity: Henri Pirenne]. *Critica Storica [Italy] 1983 20(1): 121-129.* Historians of historiography have concentrated on the ideas of history entertained by great historians and their links with the general currents of thought, and sometimes on their methodology. This note concentrates on the narrative structure of a historical work, that is, the organization of researched facts by means of general ideas in the *History of Europe* of the Belgian historian Henri Pirenne. 34 notes. J. V. Coutinho

1189. DeMichelis, Fiorella Pintacuda. ALLE ORIGINI DELLA "HISTOIRE TOTALE": JULES MICHELET [The origins of "total history": Jules Michelet]. *Studi Storici [Italy] 1980 21(4): 835-854.* Examines the basis for regarding Jules Michelet as the founder of a tradition of historical studies that came to include such later historians as Lucien Febvre, Fernand Braudel, and Jacques Le Goff. Michelet synthesized his view of history in his work, *Introduction a l'Histoire Universelle* (1831). Michelet has affirmed the positive and autonomous character of historical research and its openness to all the rich and multiple aspects of human life. Primary sources; 62 notes.

E. E. Ryan

1190. DeVries, Jan; with commentary by Namias, Jerome and Herlihy, David. MEASURING THE IMPACT OF CLIMATE ON HISTORY: THE SEARCH FOR APPROPRIATE METHODOLO-GIES. *J. of Interdisciplinary Hist. 1980 10(4): 599-630.* Examines methodologies for the measurement of the impact of climate on economic conditions in preindustrial Europe. Uses as case studies several provinces of the Netherlands to show how detailed meteorological data provide correlations between climate and dairy production, arable crop yields, canal transportation, and fuel prices, 17th-18th centuries. Secondary sources; 3 tables, 4 fig., 45 notes.

J. Powell/S

1191. Diephouse, David J. CLIO'S MIRROR AND MODERN CONSCIOUSNESS. *Fides et Hist. 1980 13(1): 65-71.* Reviews the following recent works: Eric J. Leed's *No Man's Land: Combat and Identity in World War I* (1979), Carl E. Schorske's *Fin-de-Siècle Vienna: Politics and Culture* (1980), and Robert Wohl's *The Generation of 1914.* Although these books differ considerably in tone and theme, taken together they provide evidence that history has continuing vitality and still reflects important insights into the human condition.

M. E. Quinlivan

1192. Djirković, Sima. METODOLOŠKI PROBLEMI PROUČAVANJA SREDNJOVEKOVNIE SRPSKE ISTORIJE [Methodological problems in the researching of medieval Serbian history]. *Istorijski Glasnik [Yugoslavia] 1978 (1-2): 63-68.* The postwar historiography of the Serbian Middle Ages underwent a considerable change in approach to that of a social rather than a philological nature. Certain hangovers from prewar methodology are currently evident in the arrangement and usage of the available source material. The two main fields of endeavor by medievalists are the correction of distortions, in part induced by a faulty methodology and in part by excessive dependence on philological tools, and the better organization and accessibility of medieval sources and their wider utilization.

P. J. Adler

1193. Dmitriev, S. S. MEMUARISTIKA KAK FENOMEN KUL'TURY [Memoirs as a cultural phenomenon]. *Istoriia SSSR [USSR] 1981 (6): 125-131.* Discusses how memoirs are used as historical sources and how the various types of memoir writing can be categorized. Basically, there are two genres. The first serves to give historians a factual reconstruction of historical events; such an approach is not necessarily outmoded and has its uses. The second is more reflective and seeks to examine the natural laws of history and to analyze socioideological and class trends. This latter type is exemplified in A. G. Tartakovski's *1812 God i Russkaia Memuaristika* [1812 and Russian memoir writing] (1980). Note.

J. Bamber

1194. Donat, Ion. L'ANALYSE GÉOGRAPHIQUE DANS L'HISTOIRE [Geographic analysis in history]. *Rev. Roumaine d'Hist. [Romania] 1975 14(2): 211-239.* Urges greater interdisciplinary cooperation among all researchers through the use of better methodology brought about by contemporary techniques and the growth of knowledge. The work of gathering material is only the first step of the historian's task; the second, that of interpreting and communicating it, is the result of art and talent and depends on the depth of understanding and the criteria of evaluation chosen. The author discusses better usage of maps for assessment of the territorial distribution of mass phenomena, and reviews the development of statistical, demographic, and the cartographic studies and sources throughout the 19th and early 20th centuries in Romania. Primary and secondary sources; 16 maps showing density, peasant land distribution, administrative districting, etc., 1831-1912; 23 notes.

G. J. Bobango

1195. Dray, William H. REVIEW ESSAY: THE DIALECTIC OF ACTION. *Hist. and Theory 1981 20(1): 83-91.* Reviews Frederick A. Olafson's *The Dialectic of Action: A Philosophical Interpretation of History and the Humanities* (1979). Olafson argues that a humanistic, value-laden image of man should guide the inquiries of

historians. He sharply distinguishes man from nature. Drawing on Heidegger, Olafson posits historicity as a major constituent of human nature. This in turn implies that teleological explanations rather than logical "covering-law" models are not appropriate to historiography. In considering interpretive teleology on the social level, cyclical and linear processes may be distinguished. Olafson's emphasis on the centrality of actions in history led him to put forward some unwarranted assertions about the sorts of causal judgments that historians are entitled to make.

W. J. Reedy

1196. Droysen, Johann Gustav; Hu Ch'ang-chih, transl. TZU JAN YÜ LI SHIH [Nature and history]. *Ssu yü Yen (Thought and Word) [Taiwan] 1982 20(4): 74-83.* A translation of Johann Gustav Droysen's (1818-1884) "Natur und Geschichte" (1868), reprinted in P. Leyh's *Historik* (1977). The objective of this translation is to familiarize Taiwan historians with the principles of German historical scholarship, one of the preeminent models for historical study that should be applied to Chinese history. 14 notes.

J. A. Krompart

1197. Duckworth, Mark. NEW PLOTS FOR OLD: WAS THERE HISTORY BEFORE RANKE? *Melbourne Hist. J. [Australia] 1982 14: 73-91.* Discusses the development of thought regarding the methodologies of history, the objectivity and subjectivity of history and the techniques of historiography in Western culture over three centuries.

1198. Dufeil, Michel-Marie. HISTOIRE CLASSIQUE, HISTOIRE CRITIQUE: REFLEXIONS SUR LE TEXTE ET L'OBJET [Classical history, critical history: reflections on the text and the subject]. *Hist. and Theory 1982 21(2): 223-233.* Contends that there is a clear distinction between the "classical historiography" of the past and the "critical historiography" of the last several decades. The basic difference hinges on contemporary realization that written texts are not the sole foundation of retrospective knowledge and that writing is a datum that needs to be historically explained in civilization. Modern historians are beginning to make fuller use of material artifacts and their contexts by borrowing techniques and working assumptions from anthropology and linguistics. There is increased skepticism not only about the veracity of written records but about their source priority.

W. J. Reedy

1199. Durocher, René. PERSECTIVES D'AVENIR EN HISTOIRE [Perspectives of the future in history]. *Transactions of the Royal Society of Canada [Canada] 1982 20: 213-216.* Recently, traditional history and the new history have coexisted. Traditional history is based on the positivist beliefs that facts are self-evident and that their recitation renders them intelligible. The new history uses untraditional methods and sources to construct its interpretations. With the ascendency of the new history, historians will be more likely to specialize and identify with the social sciences. They will be less nationalistic with the decline in interest in politics in favor of economic and social forces. 3 notes.

A. W. Novitsky

1200. Egan, Kieran. PROGRESS IN HISTORIOGRAPHY. *Clio 1979 8(2): 195-228.* Reviews some of the significant changes in historiography from Herodotus to Jacob Burckhardt and defines a general criterion by which historiographical progress can be measured. The five categories or stages of progress used are mythic, romantic, philosophic, alienating ironic, and sophisticated ironic. Models drawn from other disciplines cannot be applied to the progress of historiography. Progress in historiography means reducing the mental constraints on inquiry by overcoming any presuppositions the historian might have about the past.

T. P. Linkfield

1201. Elbrønd-Bek, Bo. OM DEN HISTORISKE ROMAN [Historical novels]. *Historie [Denmark] 1983 14(4): 651-667.* The imaginative process of the historian and the writer of historical fiction is often quite similar. R. G. Collingwood in 1946 asserted that the historian tries to recapture the thoughts of people in the past but does so from the point of view of his own situation, so the process is always critical and the results are relevant to the historian's own times. Some writers of historical fiction merely use the past as the background for adventure stories or idealize it in escapist terms. The best ones, however, show the relevance of past to present as historians do. J. R. Christianson

1202. Elekes, Lajos. HISTORISME, A-HISTORISME ET ANTI-HISTORISME DANS LA SCIENCE BOURGEOISE DE NOTRE TEMPS [Historicism, ahistoricism, and anti-historicism among contemporary bourgeois scholars]. *Études Hist. Hongroises [Hungary] 1975 1: 59-88.* Examines the bourgeois approach to historiography over the last three quinquennial World Congresses. Argues that it is essentially 19th-century and misguided, and it is too European-oriented. Examines the work of the Committee on Historiography, established by the Social Science Research Council in New York, 1923. Assesses the statements of various western historians such as Geoffrey Barraclough on the need to reevaluate the role of the historian and history writing. 15 notes. A. Alcock

1203. Elekes, Lajos. LE PROBLÈME DE L'HISTOIRE ET DE LA MÉTHODE DANS LA SCIENCE BOURGEOISE MODERNE [The problem of history and method in modern bourgeois science]. *Études Hist. Hongroises [Hungary] 1980 (2): 515-550.* Bourgeois scholars engaged in methodological research in history since World War II can be divided into two groups. The first group has produced formalized research approaches useful for some kinds of studies but not applicable universally. These approaches are not suitable for discovering the objective distinctiveness of any concrete area of research or the optimal methods of investigating it. The other group has focused on the unique features of historiography. Besides the Oxford school, the trends of R. G. Collingwood, Ludwig Wittgenstein, movements influenced by Benedetto Croce at US universities and research institutes, and other German and Western European schools exist, but they all attempt to disassociate themselves from their spiritual forebears. They study arbitrarily selected discrete phenomena of historiography and therefore also fail to achieve their stated goal of discovering a universally applicable method. Bibliographical note. Russian summary.

1204. Engelberg, Ernst. ÜBER THEORIE UND METHODE IN DER GESCHICHTSWISSENSCHAFT [On theory and methodology in historical science]. *Zeitschrift für Geschichtswissenschaft [East Germany] 1971 19(11): 1347-1366.* Both German historicism and Western European positivism lack the Marxist-Leninist understanding of dialectics and laws of historical development; even bourgeois historians, however, recognize that empiricism without theory is meaningless.

1205. Engel-Janosi, Friedrich. DIE WAHRHEIT DER GESCHICHTE [The truth of history]. *Wort und Wahrheit [West Germany] 1967 22(12): 765-775.* Discusses the significance of truth in modern historiography; the conception of historical truth has changed. Cites past historians, explaining their approach to the problem of truth in history. Sees the necessity of embracing myths as an indivisible part of modern historical research. G. E. Pergl

1206. Enteen, George M. VARIETIES OF HISTORIOGRAPHY. *Hist. of European Ideas [Great Britain] 1981 2(3): 247-254.* Review of *The Past Before Us,* a collection of essays on the current state of historical studies, edited by Michael Kammen. The essays show a weakening of traditional narrative history and the growing attention being given to social history. Kammen's introduction calls for a balance between the study of events and the analysis of structures. S. R. Smith

1207. Erdélyi, Ilona T. A VORMÄRZ PERIODIZÁCIÓS FOGALOMRÓL [Conceptual recognition of time period of Vormärz]. *Helikon Világirodalmi Figyelő [Hungary] 1982 28(1): 4-9.* Introduces the contents of an issue of *Helikon Világirodalmi Figyelő.* The expression *Vormärz* was used originally to describe historical happenings before March 1848 and it was closely associated with the Metternich era. In current historical research *Vormärz* covers the period between 1815 and 1848. *Restaurationsepoche, Junges Deutschland,* or the more frequently appearing

Biedermeierzeit was also used by historians to cover this period, which was seething with immense changes in the political and literary world. T. Kuner

1208. Ernst, Joseph E. and Merrens, H. Roy. PRAXIS AND THEORY IN THE WRITING OF AMERICAN HISTORICAL GEOGRAPHY. *J. of Hist. Geography 1978 4(3): 277-290.* Primary sources are used increasingly by historical geographers, especially travel accounts, topographies, and geographies. However, the contemporary observers and recorders had their biases and prejudices. Additionally, present-day scholars using those same sources also have similar problems with subjectivity. The idea of the geographer as impersonal and completely objective observer is no longer acceptable. Examples of both problems are cited, including Thomas Jefferson's *Notes on the State of Virginia* and those who have since studied Jefferson and his work. Scholars today must be aware of their subjectivity as they create their own version of the past. A dialogue between those studying similar topics should derive a more balanced and objective understanding. Secondary sources; 68 notes. A. J. Larson

1209. Ferrari, Liliana. SOCIALNA, LOKALNA IN NACIONALNA ZGODOVINA: RAZPRAVA V TEKU [Social, local, and national history: the discussion continues]. *Kronika [Yugoslavia] 1980 28(3): 153-157.* Italian historiography in the postwar period has drifted noticeably toward an emphasis on local history in imitation of the interest of Anglo-Saxon historians in oral history in recent years. Younger historians must be cautioned that rigorous application of tried and tested methodology is necessary in all historical studies, whatever fashion may bring. J/S

1210. Finley, M. I. "PROGRESS" IN HISTORIOGRAPHY. *Daedalus 1977 106(3): 125-142.* If it is correct to speak of history as an ideological activity, it is clear that the measurement of progress is a problem since ideologies change. An increase in the number of known facts, improved techniques, accumulating historical experiences, and changes in stresses or models do not necessarily indicate progress. Secondary sources; 50 notes. E. McCarthy

1211. Flaherty, David H. PRIVACY AND CONFIDENTIALITY: THE RESPONSIBILITIES OF HISTORIANS. *Rev. in Am. Hist. 1980 8(3): 419-429.* Discusses the problems historians face in protecting the privacy of individuals about whom they write, focusing on social scientists, economists, and epidemiologists who use "personal data for contemporary research"; questions whether historians should be included in this group of researchers, who work under a code of ethics regarding their subjects' privacy.

1212. Flaig, Herbert. THE HISTORIAN AS PEDAGOGUE OF THE NATION. *History [Great Britain] 1974 59(195): 18-32.* Studies the roles of three German historians of the last half of the 19th century who were pivotal in linking history to the present: Gustav Droysen (1808-84), Heinrich von Sybel (1817-95), and Henrich von Treitschke (1834-96). Discusses and evaluates them as educators of the nation, thereby illustrating the growing importance of the intellectual. They believed that the professional historian was not responsible to his discipline alone. Historical scholarship should also enrich and in turn be enriched by the wider world of public life. History, in their hands, became politicized, while political life was given greater historic awareness. They saw the importance of instilling a knowledge and awareness of a common past in the nation's youth in order to develop a sense of patriotism and shared destiny. 80 notes. R. V. Ritter

1213. Flint, John T. CONCEPTUAL TRANSLATIONS IN COMPARATIVE STUDY: A REVIEW ARTICLE. *Comparative Studies in Soc. and Hist. 1976 18(4): 502-516.* A review essay discussing the relationship between comparative studies and the monographic resources upon which they depend, emphasizing the importance of the process of conceptual translation in comparative studies.

1214. Florea, Ion. CRITICA DENATURĂRII RAPORTULUI DINTRE ISTORIE SI LOGIC ÎN FILOZOFIA BURGHEZĂ A ISTORIEI [Criticism of the misrepresentation of the relation between history and logic in the middle-class philosophy of history]. *Anale de Istorie [Romania] 1971 17(4): 79-91.* Criticizes 20th-century bourgeois historiography as denying the social implications of developments in the natural sciences, causing contradictions between the laws of history, divorcing causal from logical explanation in history, history from sociology, and historical from structural analysis. Considers the denial of social law and objective logic as an expression of the middle-class ideological crisis in captialism's imperialist stage, presenting social and historical science as weapons of progressive proletarian ideology. Pays particular attention to the works of Wilhelm Dilthey, Georges Gurvitch, Régis Jolivet, H. I. Marrou, Oswald Spengler, Karl Popper, Emile Callot, V. I. Lenin, Karl Marx, and Friedrich Engels; 52 notes. R. O. Khan

1215. Floto, Inga. DE SENASTE ÅRS DANSKE HISTORIOGRAFISKE DEBAT [Danish historiographical debate in the 1970's]. *Scandia [Sweden] 1981 47(2): 245-254.* Prior to the 1970's Danish historiography was dominated by the empirical school founded by Kristian Erslev a century ago. During the last decade, however, historians influenced by Thomas Kuhn have rebelled against this historical approach. Jens Chr. Manniche's recent book *Den Radikale Historikertradition* [The radical historical tradition] (1981) summarizes the controversy through its discussion of Erslev's historical and political ideology. Nevertheless, Manniche failed to consider the sociological implications of Erslev's work. Based on a lecture presented at the Nordic History Conference, Jyväskylä, Finland, August, 1981. 13 notes. English summary.
L. B. Sather

1216. Floto, Inga. TRADITIONSKRITIK [The critique of tradition]. *Hist. Tidsskrift [Denmark] 1979 79(2): 358-371.* Current debates among Danish historians over methodology and ideology reflect a basic paradigm shift in Danish historiography. During 1880-1920 a model of scientific history was established in Denmark, emphasizing critical use of sources and an implicitly progressive ideology. From 1920 to 1960 the ideology became dominantly relativist, but methodology remained positivist. Since 1960 a Marxist-oriented movement has sought to replace scientific by "socialized" history. This effort, though still incomplete, is an understandable response to contemporary conditions. Based on recent Danish historiographic articles and monographs; 30 notes.
R. G. Selleck

1217. Foa, Anna; Calvi, Giulia; and Schulte van Kessel, Elisja. CORPI SENZA STORIA. SULL'ULTIMO LIBRO DI CAMPORESI [Bodies without history: on Piero Camporesi's latest book]. *Quaderni Storici [Italy] 1984 19(2): 627-640.* Reviews Piero Camporesi's *La Carne Impassibile,* underlining the limits of the scientific paradigm the author employs as it opposes present time order and plain legibility to the disorder and fundamental unintelligibility of the past.
J

1218. França, José Agosto. HISTORIA E IMAGEN [History and image]. *Anais da Acad. Portuguesa da Hist. [Portugal] 1977 24(2): 179-190.* The historian not only writes but rewrites history. History is always in flux in all its forms: poetic, symbolic, and statistical. History includes all branches of human knowledge. It is both scientific and artistic, and is a symbol of the total human reality.
J. D. Barnard

1219. Franzina, Emilio. GLI SMARRIMENTI DI CLIO [Clio bewildered]. *Belfagor [Italy] 1980 35(3): 346-352.* The crisis in modern historical studies, both as regards methodology and subject matter, as seen in the report of a seminar sponsored by the National Institute for the Study of the History of the Liberation Movement in Italy: the problems of change and the social function of the past are all presented in new terms.

1220. Frederickson, George M. COMPARATIVE HISTORY. Kammen, Michael, ed. *The Past Before Us: Contemporary Historical Writing in the United States* (Ithaca, N.Y.: Cornell U. Pr., 1980): 457-473. US historiography on comparative history since the 1960's "has been concerned less with the dynamics of entire societies than with the role and character of particular ideas, institutions, modes of social and political action, or environmental challenges in a small number of national settings, most often only two." Interest largely concerns what can be learned that is new about US history from analogous situations elsewhere: slavery and race relations, geographic expansion and settlement, and women's rights. Comparative history, however, represents only a fraction of the total US historical output, and most work being done in it is accomplished by nonhistorians or historians on vacation from single-subject historiography. 53 notes.
S

1221. Fumaroli, Max. AUX ORIGINES DE LA CONNAISSANCE HISTORIQUE DU MOYEN AGE: HUMANISME, RÉFORME ET GALLICANISME AU XVIᵉ SIÈCLE [The origins of historical knowledge in the Middle Ages: humanism, Reformation, and Gallicanism in the 16th century]. *Dix-Septième Siècle [France] 1977 29(1-2): 5-29.* Analyzes the part played in the birth of medieval critical scholarship by Protestant ecclesiology, German humanism and its rehabilitation of the "barbarians" and French humanism and its gallican apologetics of Christian monarchy. The author dwells in particular on the works and theories of Flaccus Illyricus, the real founder of medieval Church critical history; Germanists Jean Carion, Jean Sleidan, and François Hotman, who advocated a new allegiance to Northern Europe; and representatives of medieval Gallicanism, Pierre Pithou, Étienne Pasquier and Jacques de Thou. Secondary sources; 10 notes.
G. P. Cleyet

1222. Fure, Odd-Bjørn. PROBLEMER, METODE OG TEORI I HISTORIEFORSKNINGEN: HISTORIE—OG VITENSKAPSOPPFATNING I JENS ARUP SEIPS TEORETISKE PRODUKSJON [Problems, method, and theory in historical research: concepts of history and knowledge in the theoretical work of Jens Arup Seip]. *Hist. Tidsskrift [Norway] 1983 62(4): 373-403.* A historiographical discussion of Norwegian historian Jens Arup Seip's work. Distinct changes can be seen in three of the four major categories of his thought since 1940: his general view of society, the relationship between determinism and voluntary action, and concepts of historical time. Seip's emphasis upon norm-regulated behavior has not changed, however. His theories of knowledge have dealt mainly with the relationship between empirical knowledge and the construction of models. Seip in this regard has continued to adhere to the former and his debates with Norwegian social scientists have led to a greater skepticism of the latter. Secondary sources; 96 notes. English summary.
L. B. Sather

1223. Furet, François. FROM NARRATIVE HISTORY TO HISTORY AS A PROBLEM. *Diogenes [Italy] 1975 (89): 106-123.* Discusses methodological aspects of the narrative style in French historiography in the 1970's.

1224. Gadzhiev, K. S. "DEDALUS" O KRIZISE SOVREMENNOI AMERIKANSKOI ISTORIOGRAFII [Daedalus on the crisis of contemporary American historiography]. *Voprosy Istorii [USSR] 1972 (7): 182-189.* Examines many discussions, some published in the American journal *Daedalus,* on the role of history in a system of social sciences. American historiography seems to be suffering from a lack of cohesion among its many branches. History must be seen within the context of a complex social sphere, not divided up into social, political, and intellectual categories. 10 notes.
S. J. Talalay

1225. Gagnon, Serge. LA NATURE ET LE RÔLE DE L'HISTORIOGRAPHIE—POSTULATS POUR UNE SOCIOLOGIE DE LA CONNAISSANCE HISTORIQUE [The nature and role of historiography: postulates for a sociology of historical knowledge]. *Rev. d'Hist. de l'Amérique Française [Canada] 1973 26(4): 479-531.* Defines the role of the modern historians and the use that can be made of historiography in modern historical research, relying on methods used in sociology and psychology. Thus the personality of the historian is taken into account, for the historian belongs to a class, an ethnic group, and a period which are to be reflected in his work. Secondary sources; 94 notes.
C. Collon

1226. Gallerano, Nicola. CERCATORI DI TARTUFI CONTRO PARACADUTISTI: TENDENZE RECENTI DELLA STORIOGRAFIA SOCIALE AMERICANA [Truffle grubbers versus parachutists: recent trends in American social historiography]. *Passato e*

Presente [Italy] 1983 (4): 181-196. Using Thomas Kuhn's model for the understanding of scientific revolutions, surveys recent trends in American historiography to analyze the epistemological bases of recent research, the role of traditional and professional outlooks, and the sociopolitical context. The field is divided not between fact (truffle) finders and model builders (parachutists), but between seekers of truth and seekers of meaning, those who look for explanations and those who look for interpretations. 42 notes.

J. V. Coutinho

1227. Gardiner, Patrick. LOUIS GOTTSCHALK, ED., *GENERALIZATION IN THE WRITING OF HISTORY. Hist. and Theory 1965 4(3): 349-352.* Reviews the articles, written primarily by historians, in Louis Gottschalk's, ed., *Generalization in the Writing of History: A Report of the Committee on Historical Analysis of the Social Science Research Council.* The work investigates "how practicing historians envisage the problem of generalization within the context of their own specific aims and enquiries."

1228. Gaus, Helmut. HISTORIOGRAFIE, ENGAGEMENT EN WETENSCHAP [Historiography, engagement, and science]. *Tijdschrift voor Geschiedenis [Netherlands] 1974 87(3): 339-352.* Changing views of historiography in the 20th century have led to a mistaken polarization of the concepts objectivity and engagement. When this polarization is eliminated, history as a science has meaning. Historiography, when viewed as the study of recurrent human behavior and its laws, engages in the synthesis of a recreated past leading to nonpartisan participation in current events. 20 notes.

G. Herritt

1229. Gay, Peter. STYLE IN HISTORY. *Am. Scholar 1974 43(2): 225-236.* The Count de Buffon's epigram, "the style is the man," serves as the basis for the introduction to the author's *Style in History* (New York: Basic Books, 1974). "The cultivated manner of the writer instructively expresses his personal past as well as the culture's ways of thinking, feeling, believing and working." That style must have ambiguity, give pleasure, inform, lend to truth, and point to beauty. Historical styles best illustrated are from the works of Edward Gibbon, Jacob Burckhardt, Thomas B. Macaulay, and Leopold von Ranke.

C. W. Olson

1230. Génicot, Léopold. NOVA ET VETERA: SUR LE PROGRÈS DES MÉTHODES HISTORIQUES [Nova et vetera: the progress of historical methods]. *Rev. de l'Inst. de Sociologie [Belgium] 1980 (2): 175-185.* Discusses the means of adapting scientific methods to history for improving and modernizing historic methodology.

1231. George, C. H. HILL'S CENTURY: FRAGMENTS OF A LOST REVOLUTION. *Sci. and Soc. 1976-77 40(4): 479-486.* J. H. Hexter's attacks on the writings of Christopher Hill indicate that the former lacks an even elementary understanding of Marxist conceptualization and analysis. An examination of recent publications by Hill and those influenced by his work stress Hill's genuine contribution to historical understanding of the early modern period in Great Britain in such areas as the relationship of science to society, the association between Protestantism and the rise of capitalism, the place of the professions in 17th-century England, and the basic social attitudes of propertied classes. Among the problems that Hill has not as yet formulated or resolved are the specific results of the shift in society from oral to printed communication and concomitant changes in language usage, the perplexing problem of development of religious thought in the highly secularized society of the 17th century, and Hill's analytical employment of the concept of Puritanism.

N. Lederer

1232. Giard, Luce. LE MOMENT POLITIQUE DE LA PENSÉE [The political moment of thought]. *Esprit [France] 1978 (5): 44-57.* The history of the Frankfurt School from its beginnings in 1922 to the present, emphasizing its analytical methods and approaches.

1233. Gilliam, Harriet. THE DIALECTICS OF REALISM AND IDEALISM IN MODERN HISTORIOGRAPHIC THEORY. *Hist. and Theory 1976 15(3): 231-256.* Modern historiographic theory is divided into the camps of realism and idealism. Internal dialogue

has often been aimed at accommodating an opposite view, using the dialectic as a means of increasing knowledge. The author reviews crucial terms and methods including the idea of fact, the idea of causality, the idea of historical truth, and history as a story exhibiting change. 80 notes.

D. A. Yanchisin

1234. Glatz, Ferenc. A TÖRTÉNETTUDOMÁNY ÉS A KÖZGONDOLKODÁS TÖRTÉNETI ELEMEI [The historical elements of the study of history and of common thinking]. *Társadalmi Szemle [Hungary] 1980 35(1): 47-57.* There is a correlation between common thinking and historical ideology: applied history can be used as positive propaganda.

1235. Glénisson, Jean and Day, John, transl. FRANCE. Iggers, Georg G. and Parker, Harold T., ed. *International Handbook of Historical Studies: Contemporary Research and Theory* (Westport, Conn.: Greenwood Pr., 1979): 175-192. Historiography in France since World War II has been influenced by the *Annales* school, Marxism, and the increasing use of quantitative methods, particularly by the medievalists. Fernand Braudel, the heir to the *Annales* tradition established by Marc Bloch and Lucien Febvre, dominated historiography until the 1970's. The intellectual climate then changed with methodological inquiry in vogue and the development of the New History. Part of this was the concept of *mentalité*, the mental images individuals and groups have of their situations and the conduct resulting from these images. 20 notes.

1236. Glénisson, Jean. UMA HISTÓRIA ENTRE DUAS ERUDIÇÕES (NOTAS SOBRE ALGUMAS PRÁCTICAS E ALGUNS DOGMAS DA ATUAL HISTORIOGRAFIA FRANCESA) [A history between two disciplines: notes on some practices and dogmas of current French historiography]. *Rev. de Hist. [Brazil] 1977 55(110): 433-462.* Inquires whether there is a specifically French historiography, by surveying current trends. Characterizes it as a plethora of methodologies in contrast with the 19th century, with a rapid development of the instruments of the historian particularly for the manipulation of extensive statistical data by computer. Developments in the human sciences and computerization have also produced a revolution in documentation, considerably increasing the range and type of documentation available. Examines the historian's elaboration of problems for himself to solve rather than being led to conclusions by undirected study of limited data. Expansion of sources has also effected a transformation of critical methods of reading data, here presented as a preoccupation with quantification. 56 notes.

R. O. Khan

1237. Goetzmann, William H. TIME'S AMERICAN ADVENTURES: AMERICAN HISTORIANS AND THEIR WRITING SINCE 1776. *Am. Studies Int. 1981 19(2): 5-47.* Explores the development of American historical writing, its interrelations with the changing intellectual and cultural climate, and the various schools of history that have emerged. Reprinted from *Social Science Quarterly* 1976. 3 portraits, 7 notes, biblio.

R. E. Noble

1238. Goldie, Mark. OBLIGATIONS, UTOPIAS, AND THEIR HISTORICAL CONTEXT. *Hist. J. [Great Britain] 1983 26(3): 727-746.* Reviews the methodological considerations of three modern historians and two new studies of utopianism: Frank Manuel and Fritzie Manuel's *Utopian Thought in the Western World* (1979) and J. C. Davis's *Utopia and the Ideal Society: A Study of English Utopian Writing 1516-1700* (1981). Current studies of John Locke reveal many methodological contrasts, especially between historical contextualism and linguistic contextualism; the considerations that lead to these contrasts are apparent as well in the two new utopian histories, both of which adhere to linguistic contextualism. 59 notes.

R. M. Twisdale

1239. Golob, Eugene O. THE IRONY OF NIHILISM. *Hist. and Theory 1980 19(4): 55-65.* Attacks Hayden White's *Metahistory* (Baltimore: Johns Hopkins U. Pr., 1973) for failing to understand the historiographical process as analyzed by such philosophers as R. G. Collingwood and Louis Mink. White begins by trying to measure historical thinking and knowledge against his image of positivism. When he finds it wanting and ignores idealist accounts of history as an autonomous mode of knowing, he leaps to the conclusion that history is nothing but "a matter of moral or aesthetic predisposal." White assumes that fictional narrative and historiographical narrative are identical and that in each the choice of linguistic devices preforms the content. This however omits the fact that mode of employment does not necessarily negate truth-value. His libertarian desire to release us from the "burden" of historical false consciousness hides a deeply Cartesian rationalism and innatism. 16 notes. W. J. Reedy

1240. Gorman, J. L. OBJECTIVITY AND TRUTH IN HISTORY. *Inquiry [Norway] 1974 17(4): 373-397.* Examples of historical writing are analyzed in detail, and it is demonstrated that, with respect to the statements which appear in historical accounts, their truth and value-freedom are neither necessary nor sufficient for the relative acceptability of historical accounts. What is both necessary and sufficient is the acceptability of the selection of statements involved, and it is shown that history can be objective only if the acceptability of selection can be made on the basis of a rational criterion of relevance. "Relevance" and "significance" are distinguished. The conditions of rationality of a criterion of acceptability are examined with special reference to Popper's criterion of "falsifiability," which is shown to fail to apply to historical writing. General conclusions are drawn about the implications of the argument for the possibility of the "unity of science," and about the conditions which need to be met if history is to be objective. J

1241. Gorodetski, E. N. HISTORIOGRAPHY AS A SPECIAL BRANCH OF HISTORICAL SCIENCE. *Soviet Studies in Hist. 1976 14(4): 3-39.* Follows the development of historiography in Russia from the 1820's to 1974. While remaining within the complex of historical disciplines, historiography has identified the area of investigation that distinguishes it from other branches of historical scholarship, and at the same time seeks to integrate within its boundaries the principal branches of historical knowledge.

1242. Gorodetski, E. N. ISTORIOGRAFIIA KAK SPETSIAL'NAIA OTRASL' ISTORICHESKOI NAUKI [Historiography as a special branch of historical science]. *Istoriia SSSR [USSR] 1974 (4): 96-116.* The first works on historiography appeared in Russia in the 1820's and 1830's, written mainly by M. T. Kachenovskii and M. P. Pogodin. The author traces the formation of historiography as a special branch of historical science from its inception to the present day. Historiography attempts to unite into its framework the history of all the branches of historical science. Primary and secondary sources; 2 tables, 34 notes. L. Kalinowski

1243. Gorodetski, E. N. LENINSKAIA LABORATORIIA ISTORICHESKOGO ISSLEDOVANIIA [Lenin's method of historical research]. *Voprosy Istorii [USSR] 1982 (4): 3-25.* Lenin's works are used by the author to illustrate his approach to historical facts, their analysis and the establishment of their interdependence, which is of great methodological importance for the historian in mastering the methods of objective scientific research. In this context, the author discusses Lenin's method of analyzing statistical and other sources, and the role of artistic images in Lenin's works. Lenin skilfully used statistical data which were for him a scientific instrument in studying the past and present, while an artistic image was an organic part of his argumentation, an element of the historical and sociological synthesis. J

1244. Grafton, Anthony T. JOSEPH SCALIGER AND HISTORICAL CHRONOLOGY: THE RISE AND FALL OF A DISCIPLINE. *Hist. and Theory 1975 14(2): 156-185.* By reviewing the work of Joseph Justus Scaliger (1540-1609), the author examines Renaissance chronological literature with the idea of attempting to establish "what chronologers were trying to do and how their discipline changed in the course of the period 1500 to 1700." Scaliger was a meticulous scholar, who placed chronology on a scientific basis in validating earlier forgeries and repudiated the sole dependence on Biblical chronology. Yet after Scaliger, chronology declined as a valid historical methodology. Appendixes provide an explanation of Scaliger's corrections to calendrical antiquities. 110 notes. D. A. Yanchisin

1245. Graus, František. DIE EINHEIT DER GESCHICHTE [The unity of history]. *Hist. Zeitschrift [West Germany] 1980 231(3): 632-649.* Reflections on the harmful effects of specialization in historical research, division of history into national units and periods or epochs, especially the concept of *Zeitgeschichte* (contemporary history). The recurring aspect of anti-Semitism is an example of a topic which has been misperceived because of almost exclusive attention to the contemporary period and on one country, Nazi Germany. Other distortions come from questionable conceptions adapted from social science disciplines into historical practice. G. H. Davis

1246. Grew, Raymond. THE CASE FOR COMPARING HISTORIES. *Am. Hist. Rev. 1980 85(4): 763-778.* Historians react ambivalently to comparative history and have reason for their distrust, whether the term is taken to mean the comparison of civilizations, of major topics, of historical processes, or of institutions. Conventional understanding implies that comparison requires extensive research in more than one society and uses taxonomies that are insensitive to particularities. All of these objections can be met. For historians, comparison is unavoidable and invaluable when they pose questions, define problems, design research, and test hypotheses. Generally, historical comparison seems most effective at a kind of middle range in which problems are significant but clearly defined and the analysis is attentive to context. A study of the last 500 manuscripts submitted to the journal, *Comparative Studies in Society and History: An International Journal,* suggests seven kinds of topics that especially invite this treatment, for comparative history is not a particular kind of history and there is no comparative method. Based on literature on comparative history and on the manuscripts submitted; 37 notes. A

1247. Groppi, Angela. I SENTIMENTI E I LORO STORICI [Feelings and their historians]. *Memoria: Riv. di Storia delle Donne [Italy] 1981 (1): 53-64.* In a 1941 article Lucien Febvre suggested opening a vast inquiry into the fundamental emotions of mankind and their modalities. Comments on nearly 50 years of attempts to read feelings not only as psychological and physiological but as social phenomena and on the methods and concepts used to identify their historical dimension. Biblio. J. V. Coutinho

1248. Gross, David L. THE "NEW HISTORY" AND BEYOND: THE VIEW FROM THE SEVENTIES. *Social Sci. J. 1978 15(2): 23-38.* Analyzes James Harvey Robinson's *The New History: Essays Illustrating the New Historical Outlook* (1912) in terms of perspective on critical history and compares turn-of-the-century "new historians" with American historians in the 1970's to determine similarities in methodologies and presuppositions.

1249. Haenens, Albert d'. DE L'HISTORIOGRAPHIE COMME MANIFESTATION DE L'IMAGINAIRE [Historiography as a manifestation of the scope of imagination]. *Rev. de l'U. de Bruxelles [Belgium] 1981 (1-2): 207-215.* Analyzes the social and psychological significance of historiography as a manifestation of the practice of history in a given group and examines the influence of the historians' research on their productions and practices.

1250. Hall, A. Rupert. ON WHIGGISM. *Hist. of Sci. [Great Britain] 1983 21(1): 45-59.* Herbert Butterfield (1900-79) critically characterized the Whig interpretation of history as an "abridgement" in which the historian already knows the moral of his tale. He failed to recognize the extent to which the account of the past is inevitably influenced by the changing present. Butterfield believed history should be simply a statement of what occurred and he distrusted patterns, but history is not simply a compilation of facts and inductive generalizations. The study of the history of science was founded on a Whig view of history. It has been told as a record of successes, inevitably seeking for precursors and precedents. "Rightness" or "wrongness" is of the essence of the contemporary context of science. The science historian cannot avoid the burden of superior knowledge. The Whiggish idea of progress is inevitably built in. 23 notes. J. G. Packer

1251. Hall, John R. THE TIME OF HISTORY AND THE HISTORY OF TIMES. *Hist. and Theory 1980 19(2): 113-131.* Examines the nature of social time utilized in historiography. The "objective" temporal framework and chronology assumed by historians since Leopold von Ranke has been increasingly challenged in recent years by the relativity of multiple scales of time (as in the work of Braudel and the *Annales* school) and by subjective appreciations of time (as in the phenomenology of Alfred Schutz). The phenomenologists have isolated four types of subjective temporal orientation; synchronic, diachronic, strategic and eternal. If this phenomenological typology can augment the sociological approach of Max Weber and the structuralist, Marxian perspective of Louis Althusser, then the traditional ideology of objectivist time may "be replaced with a 'history' of times." Primary sources; 41 notes.

W. J. Reedy

1252. Hancock, Sir Keith. THE HISTORIAN AND HIS EVIDENCE. *J. of the Soc. of Archivists [Great Britain] 1976 5(6): 337-345.* Examines the process of historical investigation in three areas: the conduct of war, biography, and land use. In the first area, war, the author discusses the problems of coping physically and intellectually with the millions of files of documents available, and comments on the Civil Series of the British History of World War II. Under biography he discusses the inventory, preservation, and management of the Smuts archive. Land use comprises a summary of the author's research in the history of land tenure and use in Italy.

L. A. Knafla

1253. Handke, Horst. GESCHICHTSDENKEN IN DER ANPASSUNG ÖKONOMISCHE UND SOZIALE FRAGESTELLUNGEN IN DER HISTORIOGRAPHIE DER BRD [Historical thinking in perspective: economic and social questions posed by West German historians]. *Jahrbuch für Wirtschaftsgeschichte [East Germany] 1980 (2): 209-228.* The spate of West German historiographical works produced in the 1970's are rooted in conservative capitalist theory despite new perspectives represented such as the "new left," the Fischer school, and the structuralism of the *Annales* school. Reviews three collections of representative theoretical essays. 60 notes.

E. L. Turk

1254. Hanisch, Ernst. KRITISCHE GESCHICHTSWISSENSCHAFT [Critical history]. *Zeitgeschichte [Austria] 1974 1(5): 126-132.* The new critical West German historiography links up with the work of critical liberal scholars in the pre-Fascist era. Intense contacts with scholars in Anglo-Saxon countries helped to overcome the fixation on "German historiography." Social history has reached a position of priority only comparable to the role of political history in the past. The theoretical discussion of the relevance of the analyzed subject for society helps to avoid false objectivism. 36 notes.

R. Wagnleitner

1255. Harris, Carl V. THE UNDERDEVELOPED HISTORICAL DIMENSION OF THE STUDY OF COMMUNITY POWER STRUCTURE. *Hist. Methods Newsletter 1976 9(4): 195-200.* Discusses the recent historiography of community studies. Divides it into a power-elite school which finds economic and social power resting in the hands of elites and a pluralist school which argues that no group really dominates local government. Pluralists denounce the power elitist's reputationalist method and the conspiracy theory of interest politics. The major difference between the two schools is the problem of the meaning of history and the meaning to be found in history. Neither school has a satisfactory solution. 16 notes.

D. K. Pickens

1256. Harrison, Joseph H., Jr. THE HYBRID MUSE: HER PEDIGREE AND HER PREDICAMENT. *Clio 1982 11(3): 283-290.* Reviews the ancient tradition of duality in the writing of history—history as art and history as science—and laments the modern tendency toward narrow specialization with the accompanying de-emphasis on prose style. Historians and students of history should give serious consideration to history as literature. 13 notes.

T. P. Linkfield

1257. Hartman, Geoffrey H. HISTORY-WRITING AS ANSWERABLE STYLE. *New Literary Hist. 1970 2(1): 73-84.* An interdisciplinary examination of art, literature, and historiography.   S

1258. Hausmann, Frank-Rutger. ZUM VERHÄLTNIS VON DICHTUNG UND GESCHICHTSSCHREIBUNG IN DER FRANZÖSISCHEN KLASSIK [The relationship between literature and history in the French classical period]. *Saeculum [West Germany] 1976 27(1): 36-49.* A long period of stagnation in the development of historiography occurred between the end of the 16th century, when historians such as Etienne Pasquier (1529-1615) broke radically from traditions established during the Middle Ages and the Renaissance, and the founding of the Ecole des Chartres in 1821 under the patronage of the Académie des Inscriptions et Belles Lettres, when history achieved recognition as a separate discipline. The author offers several reasons for the nondevelopment of historical methodology in the French classical period, a time when literary interest in history was at its peak. The rise of absolute monarchy, the influence of the Counter-Reformation, the popularity of Cartesian and Pyrrhonian philosophies, which deemphasized the importance of historical fact, the pervasiveness of Aristotle's theories of poetics, which ranked history as less important than literature, and the theoretical formulations of the *doctrine classiques* contributed to the stagnation. 45 notes.

M. A. Butler

1259. Hayden, J. Michael. "NEW" HISTORY: NEW BOTTLES AND OLD WINE. *Can. J. of Hist. [Canada] 1980 15(3): 409-411.* Reviews Peter Burke's *Popular Culture in Early Modern Europe* (1978), Peter Burke's, ed., *New Cambridge Modern History, XIII. Companion Volume* (1979), Emmanuel LeRoy Ladurie's *The Territory of the Historian* (1979), and William H. McNeill's *The Human Condition, An Ecological and Historical View* (1980), with special emphasis on the theories from other disciplines affecting the study of history.

J. Powell

1260. Haywood, Ian. THE MAKING OF HISTORY: HISTORIOGRAPHY AND LITERARY FORGERY IN THE EIGHTEENTH CENTURY. *Lit. and Hist. [Great Britain] 1983 9(2): 139-151.* Discusses the role literature played in 18th-century historiography and how reliance on it as a primary source made forgeries easier. In their drive to establish valid foundational sources for their authentic histories, 18th-century historians often overlooked the fact that many of their sources were of purely literary value (e.g., ballads, verse chronicles, etc.). Since historical fiction was not yet an accepted prose form, some historians seeking to humanize the past used forgeries to achieve their aim. A detailed inspection of James Macpherson's *Fragments of Ancient Poetry* examines the use of oral history, while Thomas Chatterton's manuscripts illustrate the use of gradation in forgeries. Based on the writings of John Toland, David Hume, John Locke, and Thomas Innes and the forgeries of James Macpherson, Thomas Chatterton, and Jeffrey Keating; 32 notes.

M. M. A. Lynch

1261. Heckenast, Gusztáv. MI A TÖRTÉNETI TÉNY? [What is a historical fact?]. *Történelmi Szemle [Hungary] 1980 23(4): 677-680.* The historian's job is to reconstruct facts of bygone days from documents that are still available. Since most of this work consists of writing, there is a strong tendency to accept only written documentation and reject all other sources. However, modern practice shows that, even in the absence of material facts, by using analogy and hypothesis, historical facts can be recreated to a great degree, or at least history can be rewritten and reevaluated by the historian.

T. Kuner

1262. Hegel, Georg; Harris, H. S., ed. FRAGMENTS OF HISTORICAL STUDIES. *Clio 1977 7(1): 113-134.* Georg Hegel's student and biographer Karl Rosenkranz first published these documents in 1843. The original manuscripts have been lost, and precise dating for these fragments is impossible. They are translated here for the first time. The fragments cover the Oriental spirit, Greece, Rome, the medieval world, the modern world, and modern historians. 30 notes.

T. P. Linkfield

1263. Heidorn, Günter. ZUM WECHSELVERHÄLTNIS VON WELT- UND NATIONALGESCHICHTE. EIN BEITRAG ZU EINEM METHODOLOGISCHEN PROBLEM [On the relationship of universal to national history: a problem of methodology]. *Wissenschaftliche Zeitschrift der U. Rostock. Gesellschafts- und Sprachwissenschaftliche Reihe [East Germany] 1972 21(2): 173-182.* The relationship of universal to national history in Marxist-Leninist historiography corresponds to the dialectics relating the general and the particular. National traditions and special historical developments are all based on general laws of history.

1264. Heikkilä, Hannu. ELÄMÄHISTORIALLISEN TUTKIMUK-SEN LÄHTÖKOHDISTA [Points of departure for the study of life history]. *Hist. Arkisto [Finland] 1984 (82): 51-59.* Examines problems encountered by sociologists in the United States and England in the use of life history data for empirical research and considers the relevance of this methodology for current historical studies. Based on English-language monographs; 22 notes.
R. G. Selleck

1265. Hennig, John. DAS WESEN DES GEWESENEN [The reality of things past]. *Geschichte in Wissenschaft und Unterricht [West Germany] 1967 18(11): 673-681.* Examines whether the truth which history must have if it is properly to be called a science exists simply by virtue of the insight or understanding of individuals or whether it possesses an existence apart from its being perceived. 17 notes.
J. M. McCarthy

1266. Hennig, John. KRITISCHES BEWUSSTSEIN UND GESCHICHTE [Critical consciousness and history]. *Geschichte in Wissenschaft und Unterricht [West Germany] 1974 25(4): 227-237.* Discusses the topic in three parts: the history of critical consciousness, and critical consciousness and history in the objective and subjective senses. Secondary sources; 18 notes.
R. Wagnleitner

1267. Hermerén, Göran. HISTORISKA FÖRKLARINGAR [Historical explanations]. *Historisk Tidskrift [Sweden] 1973 93(2): 212-238.* A discussion of the nature of explanation in historical studies, and arguments for and against various theories such as the dualism of Wilhelm Dilthey (1833-1911), the monism of Carl Gustav Hempel, and the rationalism of William H. Dray. Based on published sources; 3 notes, biblio.
R. G. Selleck

1268. Hernadi, Paul. CLEO'S COUSINS: HISTORIOGRAPHY AS TRANSLATION, FICTION, AND CRITICISM. *New Literary Hist. 1976 7(2): 247-257.* The problems inherent in the writing of history are analogous to those confronting translators, novelists, and critics.

1269. Hernadi, Paul. THE EROTICS OF RETROSPECTION: HISTORYTELLING, AUDIENCE RESPONSE, AND THE STRATEGIES OF DESIRE. *New Literary Hist. 1981 12(2): 243-252.* The analogous genres of historytelling and storytelling have a human significance whose aesthetic and epistemological aspects cannot be analyzed apart.

1270. Heuss, Alfred. DAS PROBLEM DES "FORTSCHRITTS" IN DEN HISTORISCHEN WISSENSCHAFTEN [The problem of "progress" in the discipline of history]. *Zeitschrift für Religions- und Geistesgeschichte [West Germany] 1979 31(2): 132-146.* Whether there is progress in the discipline of history is a moot question. The discovery of new sources produces a kind of progress, and there have been great historical works. Although historical writings are cumulative, history gets rewritten periodically. Consequently, there is the possibility of decline as well as progress in the writing of history. Secondary sources; 8 notes.
J. D. Hunley

1271. Heydemann, Günther. RELATIVIERUNG DES DOGMAS? [Will the dogma become more flexible?]. *Geschichte in Wissenschaft und Unterricht [West Germany] 1980 31(3): 159-171.* Theory and methodology of historical research have developed greatly in

East Germany since the Seventh Party conference of the Communist Party in 1967, which stressed the importance of historical knowledge for a socialist consciousness. Confrontation with West Germany required qualified historical research in order to stop Western influence. The basis for this development is the model of the economic formations of society, which best fits Marxist theory of social development. 33 notes.
H. W. Wurster

1272. Heyl, John D. KUHN, ROSTOW, AND PALMER: THE PROBLEM OF PURPOSEFUL CHANGE IN THE SIXTIES. *Historian 1982 44(3): 299-313.* Clarifies the historiographical context into which Thomas Kuhn's *The Structure of Scientific Revolutions* (1962) appeared. Together with Walt W. Rostow's *The Stages of Economic Growth: A Non-Communist Manifesto* (1960) and Robert R. Palmer's *The Age of Democratic Revolution: A Political History of Europe and America, 1760-1800*, 2 vol. (1959, 1964), Kuhn's works contributed significantly to the "interpretation of discontinuous, purposeful change" that played an important role in the historiography of the 60's. The academic world was never the same after their works had their day. The strength of each work lay in its conceptual design—the process of change forced by a purposeful constituent. The historiographical achievement of these works lies in the questions they left behind. 53 notes.
R. S. Sliwoski

1273. Holdheim, W. Wolfgang. AUERBACH'S *MIMESIS*: AESTHETICS AS HISTORICAL UNDERSTANDING. *Clio 1981 10(2): 143-154.* Although Erich Auerbach claimed that aesthetic considerations were secondary when he wrote history, the way he wrote history was very aesthetic. Auerbach wanted to illustrate how history should be written, and with that goal in mind he used the *figura* concept in *Mimesis*, his best known work. 20 notes.
T. P. Linkfield

1274. Holmberg, Åke. VÄRLDSHISTORIA: KONSTRUKTION, REALITET? [World history: an artificial construction or a reality?]. *Historielärarnas Förenings Årsskrift [Sweden] 1983-84: 6-8.* No written history is congruent with the course it tries to relate. The writer constructs actively through discrimination, passively through lack of knowledge. The history of the world can be regarded as one history or several separate ones. The most suitable geographical frame must be found for each theme considered. Other units of measurement of time may be more appropriate than solar movement; a measurement of time that is related to people or generations would be preferred. The periodization of history is too narrow; we need time periods that reflect global processes. There is a need for more relative, more pertinent synchronisms to replace the strictly chronological approach. The system of dividing world history into time periods has to be elastic enough to combine comparable units for thematic treatment, even if the years do not match. Paper given at a lecture at Historiska Institutionen in Lund, Sweden, 1983.
B. Darshana-Reed

1275. Holth, Gunnar. Å SKRIVE SITT LIV: NOTATER OM SELVBIOGRAFIEN [To write one's life: notes on autobiography]. *Samtiden [Norway] 1983 92(6): 20-29.* Discusses the tradition of autobiographical writing in Europe from St. Augustine (354-430) to 1983. Published sources; 7 illus., 11 notes, biblio.
R. G. Selleck

1276. Hong, Thai. MOT VAI SUY NGHT VE VIEC VAN DUNG PHUONG PHAP LUAN SU HOC NOI CHUNG VAO VIEC NGHIEN CUU GIAI CAP CONG NHAN VA PHONG TRAO CONG NHAN [Some reflections on the methodology of the study of the history of the working class and of the labor movement]. *Nghien Cuu Lich Su [Vietnam] 1981 (1): 65-68.*

1278. Horlick, Allan S. GOOD HISTORY AND HISTORICAL QUESTIONS. *Hist. of Educ. Q. 1973 13(2): 173-183.* Review essay of David Hackett Fischer's *Historians' Fallacies* (Harper and Row,

1970) and J. H. Hexter's *The History Primer* (Basic Books, 1971). Both search for history's uniqueness and "whether special rules of logic characterize historical thinking and discourse." Secondary sources; 28 notes.   L. C. Smith

1279. Horowitz, Mark R. WHICH ROAD TO THE PAST? *Hist. Today [Great Britain] 1984 34(Jan): 5-10.* Uses G. R. Elton's *Tudor Revolution in Government* (1953) and R. W. Fogel's *Time on the Cross* (1974) as examples of the two historians' different approaches, which they themselves had compared in *Which Road to the Past? Two Views of History* (1983).

1280. Huang Chun-chieh, trans. K'O HSÜEH FANG FA YU SHIH HSÜEH CHIA TI KUNG TSO [Scientific method and the work of historians]. *Thought and Word [Taiwan] 1972 9(6): 359-364.* Translation from English into Chinese of Geoffrey Barraclough's article "Scientific Method and the Work of Historian" which originally appeared in *Logic, Methodology and Philosophy of Science*, edited by Ernest Jagel, Patrick Suppes and Alfred Tarski (Stanford: Stanford U. Pr., 1962).   C. C. Brown

1281. Huang Chun-chieh. LI-SHIH CHIAO-YÜ TI JEN-WEN I-I [The humanist significance of historical education]. *Ssu yü Yen (Thought and Word) [Taiwan] 1981 18(6): 85-91.* Quotes major Chinese and Western historians to demonstrate that historical studies are not just concerned with miscellaneous facts relating to individual persons. Historical education can be of intense importance in influencing the choices and destiny of mankind. To strengthen the humanist significance of historical education, three areas should be addressed: any focus on individual history must be converted to a concern for the history of civilization; local and parochial interest must be balanced with a focus on all mankind; historians must make their work useful to their own time. 13 notes.   J. A. Krompart

1282. Hughes, Peter. [THE WRITING OF HISTORY]. *Hist. and Theory 1978 17(3): 367-374.* Review essay of Michel de Certeau's *L'Écriture de l'Histoire* (Paris: Gallimard, 1975). Certeau poses the quandary of modern historiography between the shortcomings of rhetorical analysis and the tendency for quantitative approaches to remystify history. His studies of cultural and religious history illustrate the direction modern history should take in going beyond rhetoric to the impulses that create rhetoric. 15 notes.   D. A. Yanchisin

1283. Hull, David L. CENTRAL SUBJECTS AND HISTORICAL NARRATIVES. *Hist. and Theory 1975 14(3): 253-274.* A study of the relation between historiography and the philosophy of science to show that the conflict between them which is sometimes claimed is more apparent than real. "If historical narratives are viewed as descriptions of historical entities as they persist through time, then the currently accepted analysis of science need not be modified in order to account for the unity evident in historical narratives." Such unity is provided not so much by the connections between the events related as by the unity and continuity of the historical entities. The author illustrates and develops this notion with examples from various sciences, where it can be seen most clearly in those disciplines which possess highly developed theories. The general applicability of the analysis presented is the strongest possible argument in its favor. 35 notes.   R. V. Ritter

1284. Hux, Samuel. "SO THE KING SAYS—SAYS HE...": HISTORICAL NOVEL/FICTIONAL HISTORY. *Western Humanities Rev. 1979 33(3): 189-201.* Contrasts the historical novel with fictional history, comparing both to traditional history, from Herodotus to Doctorow, and argues that the former inspire the reader to believe and remember later as fact what is obviously not.

1285. Ianziti, Gary. FROM FLAVIO BIONDO TO LODRISIO CRIVELLI: THE BEGINNINGS OF HUMANISTIC HISTORIOGRAPHY IN SFORZA MILAN. *Rinascimento [Italy] 1980 20: 3-39.* Research on humanistic historiography of the 15th century has emphasized the role of Leonardo Bruni (1369-1444) in constructing a history based on human rather than divine energies that conveys an understanding of the complexity of politics. Flavio Biondo (1392-

1463) emulated Bruni and created a new vocabulary to describe the novel realities of war and politics. Biondo in turn served as a model for Lodrisio Crivelli in his biography of Francesco Sforza written soon after 1460. Crivelli employed the new historiography with its capacity of comprehending the complexity of political reality as a means of legitimizing the Sforza seizure of power in Milan in 1450. Printed primary sources; 50 notes.   J. R. Banker

1286. Iggers, Georg G. FEDERAL REPUBLIC OF GERMANY. Iggers, Georg G. and Parker, Harold T., ed. *International Handbook of Historical Studies: Contemporary Research and Theory* (Westport, Conn.: Greenwood Pr., 1979): 217-232. West German historians have been conventional in their approach to history until recently, following Leopold von Ranke's model of narrative, event-oriented history, which is concerned with politics conceived as the pursuit of national interest. They have been relatively uninterested in social and economic considerations. Fritz Fischer's *Der Griff nach der Weltmacht: die Kriegsziel Politik des Kaiserlischen Deutschlands, 1914-1918* (1960) gave impetus to historiograhical change with its emphasis on the interrelationship of economic interest, social class relations, and politics. Despite growing interest in social processes, events and personalities still receive great attention. Historians reject as speculative comprehensive theories of historical development. In the tradition of Marx and Weber, they emphasize the qualitative aspects that go into the understanding of history as the product of human actions. Secondary sources; 63 notes, biblio.

1287. Iggers, Georg G. INTRODUCTION: THE TRANSFORMATION OF HISTORICAL STUDIES IN HISTORICAL PERSPECTIVE. Iggers, Georg G. and Parker, Harold T., ed. *International Handbook of Historical Studies: Contemporary Research and Theory* (Westport, Conn.: Greenwood Pr., 1979): 1-14. The secular narrative of political and military events and human motivations that constituted historiography from the time of Thucydides to recent years has declined in popularity and has been supplemented by an extended scope of historical study which uses new methodologies and technologies to study non-Western and nonelite aspects of life. Discusses new approaches, especially the *Annales* and Marxist. 14 notes.   S

1288. Iggers, Georg G. THE NEW HISTORIOGRAPHY IN HISTORICAL PERSPECTIVE. *Australian J. of Pol. and Hist. [Australia] 1971 17(1): 44-55.* Discusses the 20th-century confrontation between the idealist and social science traditions in historical scholarship. Concentrates on four major influences: the traditional idealist school (much alive in diplomatic history); Marxism; Weber; and the *Annales* school. Recent developments are microhistory (where objective factual knowledge may be possible) and the study of society at the subconscious level with aid from psychology and anthropology.   W. D. McIntyre

1289. Iggers, Georg G. THE UNIVERSITY OF GÖTTINGEN 1760-1800 AND THE TRANSFORMATION OF HISTORICAL SCHOLARSHIP. *Storia della Storiografia [Italy] 1982 (2): 11-37.* Observes the growth in historiographical professionalism at Göttingen University as the school made the transition from the old type of institution dedicated to teaching to the modern one emphasizing research. The university's most representative historians showed great diversity in their perspectives. Based on Göttingen University historiographical works; 73 notes. French and German summaries.   G. Herritt

1290. Ihnatowicz, Ireneusz. DIE HILFSWISSENSCHAFTEN ZUR GESCHICHTE DES 19. UND 20. JAHRHUNDERTS NACH DEM ZWEITEN WELTKRIEG [The auxiliary sciences for the history of the 19th and 20th centuries: contributions after World War II]. *Jahrbuch für Gesch. [East Germany] 1981 23: 491-502.* Discusses the need for historians to deal with new source material, such as photographs or tape recordings, as well as master new disciplines, such as sociology or psychology, and acquire quantitative skills for the study of mass processes in history. Lists the relevant new contributions from Poland. Biblio.   A. Schuetz

1291. Jablonski, Henryk. O RZETELNA OCENE STANU NAUK HISTORYCZNYCH [A fair appraisal of the present state of historical research]. *Kwartalnik Hist. [Poland] 1965 72(1): 3-7.* The unification of scientific research and the mutual corroboration of sciences are among the most typical contemporary trends. While technical knowledge does not yet allow combined research, it is obligatory for a historian to have a considerable knowledge of psychology, sociology, economy, and the law. Knowledge on the formation of social conscience is of great importance. The inaugural address at the Committee for Historic Sciences of the Polish Academy of Sciences, Warsaw, 3-4 June, 1964. J. Wilczek

1292. Jann, Rosemary. FROM AMATEUR TO PROFESSIONAL: THE CASE OF THE OXBRIDGE HISTORIANS. *J. of British Studies 1983 22(2): 122-147.* The "Oxbridge" historians of the late 19th century were out of step with important changes in continental and American historiography, and in other professional disciplines. Their acceptance of critical standards and methods of scholarship was imitative and incomplete, lagging well behind that of less prestigious British universities. The "Oxbridge" historians, unlike other professionals, did not seek to monopolize expertise, but to guarantee their discipline's repute among an intellectual and social elite. Hence in determining professional status at Oxford and Cambridge, accomplishment in research was depreciated, teaching was emphasized, published "literary history" retained much prestige, and a degree of amateurism prevailed. Based on the published writings of late 19th-century Oxford and Cambridge historians; 98 notes. D. M. Cregier

1293. Jensen, Bernard Eric. ET BIDRAG TIL REVISIONEN AF METODELAERENS GRUNDLAG [An appendix to the revision of methodological foundations]. *Hist. Tidsskrift [Denmark] 1976 76: 113-148.* The time has come for a critical approach to historical analysis using the methods and structural techniques borrowed from the social sciences. The synthesis must be a balance of subjectivity-objectivity which requires a structural methodology to solve the dilemma in all circumstances. The historian must treat materials as an element of perception and must play an active role. Instruction in this method (derived in part from the *Annales* school) is necessary for the utilization of a structuralism where creativity is possible but must be acquired. Based on a consideration of Henning Poulsen's *Studier i historisk methode* (Copenhagen, 1972). R. E. Lindgren

1294. Jovičić, Stevan. FILM KAO ISTORIJSKI IZVOR [Film as historical source material]. *Istorijski Glasnik [Yugoslavia] 1977 (1-2): 39-70.* The film has unique advantages to the historical researcher as a source material. It is a sort of "everyman's literature," available as a means of informing and influencing vast masses of people who would not otherwise be reachable by another art form. It is ideally suitable for propaganda usage, and has been so used by many groups for many purposes. The documentary form ranks with autobiography and newspapers as a source of information on historical events and personages, and the art film provides as forceful and valid a projection of the subjective reality of a given epoch as any other medium. P. J. Adler

1295. Jutikkala, Eino. KATSAUS SUOMEN HISTORIANTUTKI-MUKSEEN JA -KIRJOITUKSEEN 1900-LUVUN ENSI PUOLISKOLLA [A survey of Finland's historical research and writing in the first half of the 1900's]. *Hist. Aikakauskirja [Finland] 1983 81(2): 83-88.* The dominant trends in Finnish historiography from 1900 to 1950 derived from the influence of Leopold von Ranke (1795-1886), emphasizing source criticism and objectivity, along with strong nationalism focused on state politics and individual leaders. The minority trend followed the collectivist approach of Karl Lamprecht (1856-1915). R. G. Selleck

1296. Kaczyńska, Elżbieta. ŻYCIE ZAWODOWEGO RE-WOLUCJONISTY-PRZYCZYNEK DO DYSKUSJI O BIOGRA-FIACH POSTACI HISTORYCZNYCH (NAD KSIĄŻKĄ ANDRZEJA NOTKOWSKIEGO: LUDWIK WARYŃSKI OSSO-LINEUM WROCŁAW 1978) [The life of a professional revolutionary: towards a discussion of biographies of historical personages. On Andrzej Notkowski's *Ludwik Waryński* (1978)]. *Z Pola Walki [Poland] 1981 23[i.e., 24](2): 197-202.* Comments on the conventions of the genre of historical biography, focusing on A. Notkowski's work on Ludwik Waryński. Though aimed at the reading public, accurate presentation of the historical background is vital. The genre is rarely represented in historiography, given as it is to fanciful psychological interpretations, although the work reviewed is exempt from this criticism. M. Hernas

1297. Kalashnikova, N. Iu. KRITIKA ISTORICHESKOGO LI-BERALIZMA G. BATTERFILDOM [H. Butterfield's critique of historical liberalism]. *Vestnik Leningradskogo Universiteta: Seriia Istorii, Iazyka i Literatury [USSR] 1984 (1): 34-38.* British historiography is in a state of deep crisis because of the bankruptcy of non-Marxist conceptions of history, and H. Butterfield (b. 1900) is a case in point. His critique of the Whig interpretation of history has destroyed much of the groundwork upon which bourgeois historiography rests. His neoconservatism cannot resurrect bourgeois history—it is dying. Secondary works; 15 notes. English summary. D. N. Collins

1298. Kalberg, Stephen. MAX WEBER'S TYPES OF RATIO-NALITY: CORNERSTONES FOR THE ANALYSIS OF RATIO-NALIZATION PROCESSES IN HISTORY. *Am. J. of Sociol. 1980 85(5): 1145-1179.* Max Weber's four types of rationality, as identified by the scholastic Stephen Kalberg, "can serve as the logical prerequisite for an exploration of the vicissitudes of rationalization process in history at all levels of sociocultural process."

1299. Kammen, Michael. INTRODUCTION: THE HISTORIAN'S VOCATION AND THE STATE OF THE DISCIPLINE IN THE UNITED STATES. Kammen, Michael, ed. *The Past Before Us: Contemporary Historical Writing in the United States* (Ithaca, N.Y.: Cornell U. Pr., 1980): 19-46. Surveys the interest which American historians have taken in the writing of history and in judging each other's interpretations of events. Examines trends in historiography such as chauvinism, national self-criticism, liberalism, conservatism, radicalism, objectivity, subjectivity, pluralism, and cosmopolitanism. Notes the cross-fertilization between history and the other social sciences. Decries the lack of pedagogical training for professional historians. Comments on the increased interest in methodology and observes that all the phenomena mentioned above are reflected in the contents of the present volume. 64 notes. S

1300. Kan, A. S. SHVEDSKAIA ISTORIOGRAFIIA V XX VEKE (OSOBENNOSTI I ETAPY) [Swedish historiography in the 20th century: special features and stages]. *Voprosy Istorii [USSR] 1971 (11): 81-96.* In the opening part of this century philosophical idealism, political conservatism, and nationalism (the Uppsala school) predominated in Swedish historiography. In the first decade of the century there emerged liberal historiography in the sphere of Sweden's modern history and the critical-positivist Lund school in the sphere of medieval history. In the period between the two World Wars the Lund school was particularly instrumental in destroying several patriotically-romantic versions of traditional historiography and thereby contributing to the general qualitative growth and extension of the range of problems dealt with in historical research works. The same period witnessed the appearance of the first Marxist historians. J

1301. Kann, Robert A. BETRACHTUNGEN ZUM RELEVANZ-PROBLEM IN DER GESCHICHTSSCHREIBUNG DER NEUZEIT [Notes on the problem of relevance in the historiography of the modern period]. *Anzeiger der Österreichischen Akad. der Wissenschaften. Philosophisch-Historische Klasse [Austria] 1979 116(1): 28-44.* Historical research can only be relevant when it is applied to problems of human activities without adopting ideas of any laws dominating historical developments, a historian only being able to suggest hypotheses of the past.

1302. Kaplanoff, Mark D. THE EMPEROR'S NEW CLOTHES. *Rev. in Am. Hist. 1981 9(1): 1-6.* Review essay of *The Past Before Us: Contemporary Historical Writing in the United States*, edited by Michael Kammen (1980).

1303. Kedourie, Elie. HISTORY, THE PAST AND THE FUTURE. *American Scholar 1983-84 53(1): 109-115.* Examines the origins of the writing of history, the purpose of the examination of the past, the philosophy of history, and other aspects of historiography. F. F. Harling

1304. Kelley, Donald R. FACES IN CLIO'S MIRROR: MISTRESS, MUSE, MISSIONARY. *J. of Modern Hist. 1975 47(4): 679-690.* Review article on recent books that study the development of European historical thought and writing, with special reference to the 14th to 17th centuries. 8 notes. P. J. Beck

1305. Kellner, Hans. TIME OUT: THE DISCONTINUITY OF HISTORICAL CONSCIOUSNESS. *Hist. and Theory 1975 14(3): 275-296.* Studies possible responses which a historian may make to missing, nonexistent, or unavailable information. The problem is aggravated by the fact that historians "do not know exactly what they do not know." From among four possible responses to this problem the author emphasizes the fourth: "a study of the types of non-available information and the structure of its effective loss or destruction." The whole problem is a reflection of the fundamentally flawed character of historical knowledge qua knowledge. However, these informational gaps can be subjected to analytic categorization. 50 notes. R. V. Ritter

1306. Kennan, George F. THE EXPERIENCE OF WRITING HISTORY. *Virginia Q. Rev. 1960 36(2): 205-214.* Continuing complexity in world affairs, vast differences in individual perspective, and the seemingly endless march of events make historiography an infinitely difficult and continual pursuit.

1307. Kerr, Thomas J., IV. THE SOCIAL SCIENCES, HUMANITIES AND HISTORY: THE EYE OF THE BEHOLDER. *Liberal Educ. 1974 60(4): 489-499.* Discusses the problem of fragmented perception in social science and historical analysis, offering guidelines toward a holistic perception of events.

1308. Kersten, Krystyna. HISTORYK—TWÓRCĄ ŹRÓDEL [The historian: a creator of sources]. *Kwartalnik Hist. [Poland] 1971 78(2): 313-330.* Discusses modern research methods which are available to historians, listing questionnaires, meetings with veterans, memoirs, and interviews as possible sources. The intellectual development and social relation of witnesses to an historic event influence the nature of their testimony. Witnesses may be influenced by the social environment, language, and the intellectual and cultural level of the interviewer. Russian summary. 34 notes. B. Lubelski

1309. Khodakovski, N. I. "TEORIIA I METODIKA SOVETSKO-GO ISTOCHNIKOVEDENIIA" [Study and methods of Soviet source criticism]. *Sovetskie Arkhivy 1976 (1): 109-111.* Reviews A. T. Nikolaeva's *Teoriia i metodika sovetskogo istochnikovedeniia. Uchebnoe posobie dlia studentov zaochnogo fakul'teta* [Theory and method of Soviet source criticism. A textbook for students of the extramural faculty] (Moscow, 1975) and compares it to 15 other Soviet publications on the subject; concludes it is a progressive contribution to the literature on the subject.

1310. Kibel, Alvin C. REVIEW ESSAY: THE VERACIOUS IMAGINATION. *Hist. and Theory 1982 21(2): 315-320.* Critically reviews Cushing Strout's *The Veracious Imagination: Essays on American History, Literature, and Biography* (1980). The book posits a link between history and fiction by viewing narrative as a mode of explanation independent of scientific forms of argumentation. For the historian, judgments of causality are always retrospective evaluations of reconstructed stories. Strout opposes his view to that of both the structuralists and the deconstructionists, but never adequately explores or justifies the meaning of his own tenets. He avoids the totalizing and Hegelian-Marxist perspective of the realist historical narrative of Frederic Jameson, or Hayden White, but fails to plausibly account for the ground and effects of narrative realism. Secondary sources; 5 notes. W. J. Reedy

1311. Kieniewicz, Stefan et al. O SYNTEZACH HISTORYCZNY-CH [Concerning historical syntheses]. *Kwartalnik Hist. [Poland] 1982 89(4): 627-639.* Discusses the purpose and method of writing historical syntheses. Unfortunately there is disagreement among historians on the definition of synthesis, partly because its intended audience often influences its character. Article to be continued. J. J. Kulczycki

1312. Kieniewicz, Stefan. PRZESZŁOŚĆ NARODOWA W OCZACH SPOŁECZEŃSTWA I W OCHACH HISTORYKA [The national past in the eyes of society and in the eyes of a historian]. *Kwartalnik Hist. [Poland] 1980 87(2): 435-445.* Polish historians today tend to be relatively free in their choice of method and subject when studying the distant past. There are considerably more restrictions in the study of the recent past because of a dearth of sources, lack of access to information because of reasons of state, and interference by the authorities. Originally presented as a paper at the 10 January 1980 meeting of the Committee of Historical Sciences of the Polish Academy of Sciences. H. Heitzman-Wojcicka/S

1313. Kilunov, A. F. PARTIINIST' ISTORYCHNOHO DOS-LIDZHENNIA I KRYTYKA BURZHUAZNOHO OB'IEKTYVIZMU [Party spirit in historical research and criticism of bourgeois objectivity]. *Ukrains'kyi Istorychnyi Zhurnal [USSR] 1970 (1): 31-43.* Criticizes the approach of bourgeois historians who claim to be objective in their analyses of historical events, suggesting that objectivity is impossible.

1314. Kirkendall, Richard S. A PROFESSION OF MANY PARTS. *Public Hist. 1981 3(4): 65-74.* Review essay of *The Past Before Us: Contemporary Historical Writing in the United States,* edited by Michael Kammen (1980), which focuses on "the expansion of old specialties and the proliferation of new specialties and of new methods" but neglects the area of public history.

1315. Kjaergaard, Thorkild. FAGMAEND OG AMATØRER [Professionals and amateurs]. *Fortid og Nutid [Denmark] 1976 26(4): 507-515.* Discusses the attitude of professional historians to amateurs, arguing that the work of the latter is often valuable.

1316. Kjelland, Arnfinn. HVORDAN DEFINERE LOKALHIS-TORIE: ET FORSLAG VED VICTOR SKIPP, ENGELSK LO-KALHISTORIKER [Defining local history: a suggestion from the English local historian Victor Skipp]. *Heimen [Norway] 1982 19(3): 165-170.* Skipp's definition is a "descriptive" one: local history is what is found on bookshelves. His four categories become three in a Norwegian context: country settlement and town and district histories. Histories limited by area can also be treated thematically (economic history, social history, and so on). Three methodological possibilities exist: data collection, narrative and descriptive history, and detail analysis. All three are important and should support each other. Based on "Local History: A New Definition," *The Local Historian* 1981 14(6): 325-331 and (7): 392-399, by Victor Skipp. See also the "local history debate" in *Heimen* 1979 16(3) and 1980 17(1), (3). D. F. Spade

1317. Klein, Milton M. THE HISTORIAN'S BUSINESS. *New York Hist. 1983 64(1): 51-63.* The historian's raw materials in reconstructing past events are written records and each reconstruction is an invention, because the historian brings to historical writing a set of biases and predilections which color his work. There are historians today who employ the social sciences to comprehend past behavior. Knowledge of history is valuable; the chief virtue of history is its ability to ask questions of the human race. 11 notes. R. N. Lokken

1318. Kocka, Jürgen. THEORIEORIENTIERUNG UND THEO-RIESKEPSIS IN DER GESCHICHTSWISSENSCHAFT. ALTE UND NEUE ARGUMENTE [Theory orientation and theory skepticism in historiography: old and new arguments]. *Hist. Social Res. [West Germany] 1982 (23): 4-19.* Examines the use of theory in history, particularly its application in West German historiography during the past two decades.

1319. Köhler, Oskar. DIE VIELEN "GESCHICHTEN" UND DIE EINE "FUNDAMENTALGESCHICHTE" [The many "histories" and the one "fundamental history"]. *Saeculum [West Germany]* 1978 29(2): 107-146. Discusses modern scientific theories of history, suggesting that they discourage historians of narrative history. Secondary material; 113 notes. R. Wagnleitner

1320. Konstan, David. THE FUNCTION OF NARRATIVE IN HAYDEN WHITE'S *METAHISTORY*. *Clio* 1981 11(1): 65-78. Reviews and analyzes Hayden White's *Metahistory: The Historical Imagination in Nineteenth-Century Europe* (1973). White examines eight historians and philosophers of history and the conflict between the narrative impulse for each writer and the mode of argument he chose for his narrative style. 11 notes. T. P. Linkfield

1321. Kosolapov, V. V. SOTSIAL'NI FUNKTSII ISTORYCHNOI NAUKY V ROZVYNUTOMU SOTSIALISTYCHNOMU SUSPIL'STVI [The social functions of historical science in an advanced socialist society]. *Ukraïns'kyi Istorychnyi Zhurnal [USSR]* 1976 (4): 53-64. Deals with the important role of historical science as one of the most important branches of social knowledge and as one of the factors influencing the management of social processes in a socialist society.

1322. Kossmann, E. H. KANTELEND GESCHIEDBEELD [Changing historical image]. *Bijdragen den Mededelingen betreffende de Geschiedenis der Nederlanden [Netherlands]* 1984 99(1): 55-62. Reviews W. W. Mijnhardt's *Kantelend Geschiedbeeld. Nederlandse Historiographie sinds 1945* [Changing historical image: Dutch historiography since 1945] (1983). The 19th and 20th centuries receive relatively little attention in this volume, although these periods are of considerable importance. Comparisons with other historical writings reveal that Dutch historiography tends to lag behind and is less interested in non-Dutch subjects. The reviewer concludes that it is difficult for Dutch historians to compete with those from the United States, France, Germany, and England. G. D. Homan

1323. Kouri, Erkki. ENGLANNIN HISTORIANTUTKIMUKSEN KEHITYS HARRASTELUSTA TIETEEKSI [The development of historical research in England from a hobby to a science]. *Hist. Aikakauskirja [Finland]* 1978 76(4): 307-330. Describes developments in historiography in Great Britain from 1724 to the present. History as a research discipline began in 1867, with the appointment of William Stubbs (1825-1901) at Oxford University. While Oxford has focused on English history, Cambridge has focused on general history, building on the work of J. E. E. D. Acton (1834-1902). Debate on the nature and goals of historical studies has always flourished, but since 1945 history has become more specialized and professional, as reflected in the current work of G. R. Elton at Cambridge. 121 notes. R. G. Selleck

1324. Kovács, Endre. ISMERETELMÉLETI PROBLÉMÁK A MAI POLGÁRI TÖRTÉNETIRÁSBAN [Epistemological problems in contemporary bourgeois historiography]. *Történelmi Szemle [Hungary]* 1968 11(4): 349-372. Questions about the meaning of history have proved barren for bourgeois thinkers. Therefore they have turned increasingly toward the problems of historical epistemology. In this respect they represent a relativistic view. However, they have realized the dangers of extremism and continuously try to find a compromise between objectivism and subjectivism. Reviews the work of R. Aron, H.-I. Marrou, G. Barraclough, Th. Litt, R. Wittram, O. F. Anderle, Arnold J. Toynbee and the Annales circle. I. Hont

1325. Koval'chenko, I. D. THE HISTORICAL SOURCE IN LIGHT OF THE THEORY OF INFORMATION. *Social Sci. [USSR]* 1983 14(4): 100-114. Discusses the study of historical sources from the information theory viewpoint, using examples from historic social and economic data.

1326. Kudrna, Jaroslav. K VÝVOJOVÝM TENDENCÍM POZITIVISTICKÉ HISTORIOGRAFIE [Development tendencies of positivist historiography]. *Československý Časopis Hist.*

[Czechoslovakia] 1976 24(1): 1-21. Attempts to ascertain the depth of the influence of philosophical and sociological positivism on historical science. Positivism may create a larger rationality, but that cannot solve all real problems of historical science. G. E. Pergl

1327. Kudrna, Jaroslav. ZU EINIGEN FRAGEN DES METHODENSTREITS IN DER FRANZÖSISCHEN HISTORIGRAPHIE UM 1900 [On certain issues of the methodological conflict in French historiography around 1900]. *Sborník Prací Filosofické Fakulty Brněnské University: Řada Historická [Czechoslovakia]* 1983 32(30): 69-83. Between the sociologizing and idiographic trends in the debate conducted in *Revue de Synthèse Historique* stood Henri Berr, whose views were a compromise which went further methodologically than the bourgeois Rankean historiography of the day.

1328. Kudrna, Jaroslav. ZU EINIGEN FRAGEN DES METHODENSTREITS IN DER FRANZÖSISCHEN HISTORIOGRAPHIE UM 1900 [Some questions on the methodological struggle in French historiography around 1900]. *Storia della Storiografia [Italy]* 1983 (3): 62-78. Shows the influence of Karl Lamprecht on the debates over historical methodology in France surrounding the founding of the journal *Revue de Synthèse Historique* [Review of historical synthesis]. Lamprecht influenced Henri Berr, whose philosophy underlay that of French sociologist Emile Durkheim, who felt that history should be subsumed by sociology. Historians resisted Durkheim's approach and came to see sociology as ancillary to history. 43 notes. English and French summaries. R. Grove

1329. Kunina, A. E. O NEKOTORYKH METODOLOGICHESKIKH PROBLEMAKH AMERIKANSKOI BURZHUAZNOI ISTORIOGRAFII (1945-1955) [Some methodological problems of American bourgeois historiography, 1945-55]. *Amerikanskii Ezhegodnik [USSR]* 1983: 200-218. After World War II, a new stage began in the history of bourgeois historical thought. The Social Science Research Council was created in 1923 for the planning and coordination of scientific work. Represented in the council were the American Association of Political Science, the American Economic Association, the American Sociological Society, the American Anthropological Association, the American Statistical Association, the American Psychological Association, and from 1925, the American Historical Association. In 1942, at a New York conference, the decision was made to accept the Commission on Historiography, which undertook to examine methodological problems of American historiography. The question of methods and directions after World War II is highlighted. 106 notes. S. J. Talalay

1330. Kylunov, A. F. PRO PRYRODU ISTORYCHNOHO FAKTU [The nature of historical facts]. *Ukraïns'kyi Istorychnyi Zhurnal [USSR]* 1965 (8): 52-58. Discusses Western and Soviet definitions of "historical fact" and its function in the process of writing history.

1331. Lamontagne, Roland. OPINIONS EN HISTOIRE [Viewpoints in history]. *Rev. d'Hist. de l'Amérique Française [Canada]* 1967 21(2): 181-184. Defines the structuralist approach to historical study and outlines the techniques and interpretations employed in an interdisciplinary framework with international collaboration: this is exemplified by the historian Fernand Braudel, the *Annales* school, and the Centre International de Synthèse. Pierre Chaunu contributes a definition of serial history, and Frédéric Mauro writes on history and structure. P. Herman

1332. Langholm, Sivert. VERDI-ELEMENTER I HISTORISKE TEORIER [Value elements in historical theories]. *Historie [Denmark]* 1966 7(1): 61-76. Discusses how historians make evaluations in their research with particular reference to Norwegian historiography.

1333. Laroui, Abdallah. FOR A METHODOLOGY OF ISLAMIC STUDIES: ISLAM SEEN BY G. VON GRÜNEBAUM. *Diogenes [Italy]* 1973 (83): 12-39. Discusses 20th-century philologist, historian, and culturalist Gustave von Grünebaum's methodology in 11th-century Islamic studies and culture.

1334. Leffler, Phyllis K. THE *HISTOIRE RAISONNÉE*, 1660-1720: A PRE-ENLIGHTENMENT GENRE. *J. of the Hist. of Ideas 1976 37(2): 219-240.* Describes *l'histoire raisonnée*, an historical genre which introduced "many of the characteristics of Enlightenment historiography." The genre developed, becoming less moralistic and less concerned with literary form than its humanistic predecessors had been. It eventually advanced ideas, notably the theory of progress and historical relativism which would be characteristic of Enlightenment historiography. Published primary and secondary sources; 98 notes.　　　　　　　　　 D. B. Marti

1335. Lehikoinen, Anja. HISTORIANTUTKIMUS SAKSAN LIITTOTASAVALLASSA TOISEN MAAILMANSODAN JÄLKEEN [Historical research in West Germany after World War II]. *Hist. Aikakauskirja [Finland] 1976 74(4): 337-346.* Since 1945, historians in West Germany have been working out the consequences of the 1945 collapse for German historical scholarship. Most have agreed on the need to revise traditional historical views focused on the nation state, but they disagree on how radical a revision is necessary. Interest in recent history and in social history has led to use of new methodologies, with major foreign influences coming from France and the United States. Presently historians are generally more explicitly engaged in social and political issues than before World War II. 41 notes.　　　　 R. G. Selleck

1336. Lehikoinen, Anja. OBJEKTIIVISUUDESTA JA ARVOSTUKSISTA HISTORIANTUTKIMUKSESSA [Objectivity and valuation in historical research]. *Hist. Aikakauskirja [Finland] 1983 81(4): 275-280.* Examines current debates among European historians on the nature and possibility of objectivity in historical research, with particular attention to discussion in West Germany and to ideas of the Swedish historian Göran Hermerén in *Värdering och Objektivitet* [Valuation and objectivity] (1972). Based on published books and articles; 39 notes.　　　　　　 R. G. Selleck

1337. Leicester, H. M., Jr. THE DIALECTIC OF ROMANTIC HISTORIOGRAPHY: PROSPECT AND RETROSPECT IN *THE FRENCH REVOLUTION. Victorian Studies 1971 15(1): 7-17.* A study of the relations of theory and practice in Thomas Carlyle's (1795-1881) historical writing, "the ways theory and practice affect and alter one another in the concrete act of the writing of history." Carlyle's historiography included what he called "narrative" and "action," two modes of historical interpretation, the prospective and retrospective; the former is linear, the latter is solid, that is, often simultaneous. In *The French Revolution* this theory was put into play concretely to produce a "Carlylean interpretation" dynamically, out of the process of working with the materials of history—a respeaking of theory in the context of a concrete interpretive experience. But beyond this act of retrospective interpretation there arises immediately in the present a new prospective experience in which the writer and his work can only be "fulfilled in the completion of dialogue with other consciousness." 14 notes.　　　　　　　　　　　　 R. V. Ritter

1338. Lepkowski, Tadeusz. KILKA UWAG O HISTORYCZNEJ BIOGRAFISTYCE [Comments on historical biography]. *Kwartalnik Hist. [Poland] 1964 71(3): 711-726.* A paper resulting from the discussion of the aims of historical biography organized by *Kwartalnik Historyczny*. Considers biography the oldest form of historical writing, and stresses the lasting appeal of the genre. Isolates two main kinds of biography: erudite, "pure" biography, exemplified by the *Polish Biographical Dictionary*, Kazimierz Lepszy, ed,; and the official, sociological, propaganda-type biography, exemplified by Krystyna Zienkowska's *Jacek Jezierski*. Explains that the political biographies of revolutionary leaders are fragmentary because the political beliefs are the most important factor in them.
　　　　　　　　　　　　　　　　　 J. Wilczek/S

1339. Lepore, Ettore. STORIOGRAFIA CONTEMPORANEA E DIBATTITO TEORICO [Contemporary historiography and theoretical debate]. *Studi Storici [Italy] 1984 25(1): 131-138.* Reviews Paolo Rossi's edition *La Teoria della Storiografia Oggi*, which collects essays arising out of a conference held at Turin in 1982. The volume faces the split between historiographical theories based on philosophy and epistemology and those based on concrete historic

research. Arthur C. Danto traces the development of a philosophy of mind, which agrees with the essay of Hayden White. Wolfgang J. Mommsen notes the problems of historical social science and, along with Francois Furet, discusses the rapport between history and science. The essays of Reinhart Koselleck and Jerzy Topolsky deal with historic definitions of temporal awareness, especially in the modern age, and the structure of events. 6 notes.
　　　　　　　　　　　　　　　　　 J. W. Houlihan

1340. Levin, David. [AMERICAN HISTORICAL EXPLANATIONS]. *Clio 1974 3(3): 341-346.* Reviews Gene Wise's *American Historical Explanations: A Strategy for Grounded Inquiry* (Homewood, Ill.: Dorsey Press, 1973), the first part of which is addressed to students in a first course in historiography. Studies relationships between the assumptions of Progressive historians and a group Wise calls Counter-Progressive historians.　　 S

1341. Levin, David. FORMS OF UNCERTAINTY: REPRESENTATION OF DOUBT IN AMERICAN HISTORIES. *New Literary Hist. 1976 8(1): 59-74.* Discusses the historiography in terms of the way in which historians deal with the issues of uncertainty in historical fact, both their own and that of their subjects.

1342. Li Hung-ch'i. CHIN-TAI HSI-YANG SHIH-HSÜEH CHIH FA-CHAN [The rise of modern Western historiography: a brief survey]. *Ssu yü Yen (Thought and Word) [Taiwan] 1977 15(4): 238-256, (5): 343-360.* Part I. Surveys Western historiography from the Renaissance to the rise of the German schools in the late 18th century. 53 notes. Part II. Focuses on Georg Hegel, August Comte, and Wilhelm Dilthey. Comte's positivist theories on the comparative and scientific study of mankind undermined Hegel's idealist philosophy of history. Dilthey, in turn, while accepting Comte's comparative theories, rejected the equation of historical methods with the methods of the natural sciences, arguing that history must have its own epistemology. Includes a brief appreciation of the cultural historian Jakob Burckhardt and the social historian Numa Denis Fustel de Coulanges. 48 notes.　　　　 T. P. Massey

1343. Liebel, Helen. RANKE'S FRAGMENTS ON UNIVERSAL HISTORY. *Clio 1973 2(2): 145-159.* Allowing that only God "knew" universal history, Ranke focused on factual, critical historiography of nations, viewed as more than the sum of their parts but yet as a product of creative human history. 65 notes, appendix.
　　　　　　　　　　　　　　　　　 A. H. Auten

1344. Logan, George M. SUBSTANCE AND FORM IN RENAISSANCE HUMANISM. *J. of Medieval and Renaissance Studies 1977 7(1): 1-34.* Analyzes the various interpretations of Renaissance humanism, reinterpreting the coherence of Renaissance humanism as an intellectual tradition of late medieval and early modern Europe. Discusses Paul Kristeller's approach to the definitional problem of the Renaissance, eschewing its substance for its medium, the cycle of *studia humanitatis* which all humanists shared (rhetoric, poetry, history, and moral philosophy). Questioning this approach, the author takes a dialectical one, asserting that what binds Renaissance humanists together is their substantive study of classical rhetoric and history, and the practical use they made of these studies for understanding the current problems confronting their society. Endowing them with a perception of the complexities of human life, this double vision led to the evolution of a series of subtraditions which gave substance to the relativism, detachment, and skepticism that came to mark modern man. 81 notes.
　　　　　　　　　　　　　　　　　 L. A. Knafla

1345. Löwe, Bernd P. METHODOLOGIE DER GESELLSCHAFTSWISSENSCHAFTEN UND IDEOLOGISCHER KLASSENKAMPF [Methodology of the social sciences and ideological class struggle]. *Zeitschrift für Geschichtswissenschaft [East Germany] 1973 21(9): 1074-1087.* The methodological discussion of bourgeois historiography is only one manifestation of the crisis of bourgeois ideology. The bases of this conflict are socioeconomic and sociopolitical changes within bourgeois society.

1346. Lower, Arthur R. M. SHAPING THE PAST. *Dalhousie R.* *[Canada] 1975 55(1): 103-113.* A philosophical statement on the need to organize knowledge into understandable patterns. The process of writing history calls for much collecting, throwing out, rearranging, and looking for similarities. Historians try to classify their own past; this takes the form of myth, legend, tradition, belief, dogma, concept, or thesis. The article relates this to famous historians such as Spengler, Toynbee, Meinecke, Hobbes, Gibbon, Lord Clarendon, and Ranke. Note.   C. Held

1347. Lozek, Gerhard. ZUR THEORIEDISKUSSION IN DER NICHTMARXISTISCHEN GESCHICHTSWISSENSCHAFT EN-DE DES 19./ANFANG DES 20. JAHRHUNDERTS [Theoretical discussion in non-Marxist historiography from the end of the 19th to the beginning of the 20th centuries]. *Zeitschrift für Geschichtswissenschaft [East Germany] 1984 32(5): 395-404.* Theory and methodology were the two main concerns of non-Marxist historians at the end of the 19th century. New developments in biology, anthropology, and zoology, changes in society and the social sciences, and increasing revolutionary political awareness of the working class in capitalist countries helped to a great extent to overcome this narrow approach to historical science. Today, Marxist and non-Marxist historians still employ different approaches and procedures. 51 notes.   T. Kuner

1348. Lucas, Stephen E. THE SCHISM IN RHETORICAL SCHOLARSHIP. *Q. J. of Speech 1981 67(1): 1-20.* Reassesses the relationship between history and criticism with respect to intrinsic and extrinsic analysis of public address, the role of evaluation in rhetorical scholarship, and the nature of critical and historical method.   J/S

1349. Lupu, N. Z. PARTINITATE ŞI OBIECTIVITATE ÎN ŞTIINŢA ISTORIEI [Partisanism and objectivity in historical science]. *Anale de Istorie [Rumania] 1973 19(1): 79-92.* Analyzes the study of history as both a subjective and an objective process, and the vital role of the historian as a militant partisan in bringing about social progress, of contributing to the transformation of society, and advancing the creation of socialism and communism. History cannot be divorced from the historian who writes it, nor can the historian really view historical events other than with his own class outlook. As Charles Beard noted, history as such can never be reproduced, but remains always incomplete and subjective, due to the nature of its sources. By bringing to his task a knowledge of the laws of social development, the Marxist historian raises history to a science, insofar as it can be a true mirror of the real historic process. Marxism allows us to reveal the existence of "objective historic realities" which exist independently of the conceptions of men, individuals, classes, or social groups. Thus Marxist historiography gears its interpretations not "according to the political needs of the moment," but to the truth of life and the social processes. Secondary sources; 26 notes.   G. J. Bobango

1350. Lutz, Heinrich. HISTORISCHES VERSTEHEN UND MORALISCHES URTEILEN ANGESICHTS DER ERFAHRUNGEN DES 20. JAHRHUNDERTS [Historical understanding and moral judgment given the experiences of the 20th century]. *Veröffentlichungen des Verbandes Österreichischer Geschichtsvereine [Austria] 1967 17: 16-30.* The developments of the 20th century do not only motivate the historian to analyze and judge the immediate past, but also initiate a reinterpretation of earlier history in the light of these developments. Not the accumulation of new knowledge alone, but a deep and critical reflection of historical methods can lead to a satisfactory historical understanding and moral judgment. Based on secondary literature; 17 notes.   R. Wagnleitner

1351. Lynch, Katherine A. LOCAL AND REGIONAL STUDIES IN HISTORICAL DEMOGRAPHY. *Hist. Methods 1982 15(1): 23-29.* Identifies several trends in methodology. First, larger databases have become available and are being used in an increasingly successful manner. Secondly, interdisciplinary studies are now realities rather than just academic desires. Lastly, in the historical period between the late Middle Ages and the development of modern statistical records, it is now possible to measure the impact of epidemic diseases on past demographic crises. Family reconstitution technique and regional studies are contributing to the larger historiographic synthesis that should be forthcoming in the future. 28 notes.   D. K. Pickens

1352. Lynn, Kenneth S. THE REGRESSIVE HISTORIANS. *Am. Scholar 1978 47(4): 471-500.* Believes that Bernard Bailyn and Eugene D. Genovese are regressive historians. Criticizes them for viewing history too simplistically. Finds the reductionism and nihilism of Leo Marx far more reprehensible than the notions of Bailyn and Genovese. Identifies Bailyn with "the Age of Rubbish" and Genovese's ideas as a black power update of the Uncle Remus stories. Pleads for a return to the rediscovery of complexity in history and the notions of multiplicity of forces.   F. F. Harling

1353. MacPherson, Mary. HISTORIOGRAPHY, ITS IMPLICATIONS FOR BUILDING LIBRARY COLLECTIONS. *Can. Lib. J.* *[Canada] 1976 33(1): 39-45.* Libraries must change their antiquated and arbitrary acquisition and classification policies to reflect the increasingly interdisciplinary tone of publishing and research. The methodology of historiography provides a model for these changes. 22 notes, biblio.   L. Johnson

1354. Mägdefrau, Werner. ZUM KAMPF UM EINE NEUE GESCHICHTSWISSENSCHAFT AN DER FRIEDRICH-SCHILLER-UNIVERSITÄT JENA [The struggle for a new historical science at the Friedrich-Schiller University, Jena]. *Wissenschaftliche Zeitschrift der Friedrich-Schiller U. Jena. [East Germany] 1966 15(1): 63-77.* Discusses the introduction of history with a Marxist interpretation at the Friedrich-Schiller University at Jena and the opposition of bourgeois historians, 1945-65.

1355. Malaurie, Guillaume. CRISE DE L'HISTOIRE: DEPLACER LES QUESTIONS [A crisis of history: a shift in issues]. *Esprit [France] 1981 (2): 48-65.* Discusses new perspectives on history as to interpretation, methodology, and notions of civilization, based on the reviews of recent historical works.

1356. Mandelbaum, Maurice. THE PRESUPPOSITIONS OF *METAHISTORY*. *Hist. and Theory 1980 19(4): 39-54.* Examines and challenges fundamental assumptions of Hayden White's *Metahistory* (1973). One of White's most important presuppositions is his lumping together of historians and philosophers of history for his paradigmatic, tropal analysis of historiographical discourse. He ignores the major differences in the methods and goals of these two groups. His second primary assumption is presupposing that "the order bestowed by the historian on his materials represents a poetic act." He thus leaves out of account what is usually seen as the purposes of historical writings, "to discover, depict, and explain what has occurred in the past." The basic difficulty is that White's tropological approach is fundamentally ahistorical. Moreover, this approach has constrained him to adopt relativism. 9 notes.   W. J. Reedy

1357. Mann, Golo. THE OLD HISTORY AND THE NEW: THOUGHTS ON THE CRISIS OF THEORY AND PRACTICE. *Encounter [Great Britain] 1978 51(2): 11-17.* Discusses the causes of the crisis in the study of history, and the benefits of historical narrative, including biography, as an important method of studying history as opposed to structural analysis or the history of events.

1358. Manniche, Jens C. TYSK-KRITISK SKOLE OG FRANSK-KRITISK SKOLE. ET BIDGAG TIL STUDIET AF HISTORIE-TEORETISKE SYNSPUNKTER I DANMARK [German and French critical schools: a contribution to the study of theoretical historical viewpoints in Denmark]. *Hist. Tidsskrift [Denmark] 1975 75(1): 39-59.* Recent growth of interest in historical theory and method causes this examination of Erik Arup, Kristian Erslev, Aage Friis, and Vilhelm la Cour. Arup supports the interpretive, conceptual French school. Arup has been criticized by the older historians for his "fantasy" but defends himself on the grounds that historians are responsible for creation of order and reasonable judgments when sources are inadequate. He reasons that individuals act in the same fashion regardless of time. Erslev opposed Arup, although he was close to Arup at times. Arup's methodology represents an interest in the purposes and objectives of historical writing.

R. E. Lindgren

1359. Maqrahī, Mīlād al-. MULĀHAZĀT HAWL KITĀBAT AL-TĀRĪKH WA-AL-BAHTH AL-TĀRĪKHĪ [Observations on historiography and the study of history]. *Majallat al-Buhūth al-Tārīkhīya [Libya] 1984 6(2): 477-488.* Argues that the importance of history and its principal objective must be the true explanation of past events, the study of which gives wisdom and understanding. Documents and all other possible sources are most important, and a properly critical use must be made of them, together with an appreciation of their economic, social, and political setting, in order to arrive at historical truth. The historian's role is that of commentator and interpreter. 14 notes.

C. H. Bleaney

1360. Marcus, John T. THE CHANGING CONSCIOUSNESS OF HISTORY. *South Atlantic Q. 1961 60(2): 217-225.* Examines the evolution of historiography, 1920's-60's, and indicates new conceptions of history manifest in a changed sense of time, increasing awareness of the interdependence of social organization, and the abandonment of the absolute.

1361. Martin, Warren B. HISTORY, EDUCATION, AND CHANGE. *Pacific Historian 1965 9(2): 59, 102-104.* Argues that historiography is biased by personal and provisional value judgements.
S

1362. Mason, Paul T. THE HISTORIAN'S CRAFT. *Clio 1972 1(3): 66-72.* Reviews David Hackett Fischer's *Historians' Fallacies: Toward a Logic of Historical Thought* (New York: Harper and Row, 1970); Robert F. Berkhofer's, Jr. *A Behavioral Approach to Historical Analysis* (New York: Free Press, 1969); J. H. Hexter's *The History Primer* (New York: Basic Books, 1971); and Arthur Marwick's *The Nature of History* (New York: Alfred A. Knopf, 1971). Historians scrutinizing their discipline are borrowing from logic and social science while retaining an interest in prose narration. History per se (*contra* Marwick) is not anathema to limited research frameworks or to technical language. But the role of dialogue among historians in history writing is often overlooked. 7 notes.
A. H. Auten

1363. Mata Gavidia, José. HISTORIOGRAFÍA [Historiography]. *Rev. de Filosofía de la U. de Costa Rica [Costa Rica] 1977 15(41): 165-174.* Historiography essentially is a search into that which is authentic, and the circumstances surrounding the historical event. The authentic consists of man as a social being, his culture and his freedom to take action, but never neglecting the historical circumstances in which the action takes place. Secondary sources; 4 notes.
H. J. Miller

1364. Maternicki, Jerzy. FORSCHUNGEN ZUR GESCHICHTSSCHREIBUNG UND -METHODOLOGIE IN POLEN [Research on historiography and historical methodology in Poland]. *Jahrbuch für Gesch. [East Germany] 1981 23: 437-469.* The history of historiography and historical methodology have become quite fashionable in recent years. This trend has helped produce biographies and new editions of Poland's classical historians. While non-Polish histories have generally received little attention, non-Polish methodological work, including quantitative history and psychohistory, has been received with interest. Most Polish authors treat methodology only as a marginal topic of their own research. Biographical article. 111 notes.
A. Schuetz

1365. Maternicki, Jerzy. HISTORYCY O HISTORII [Historians on history]. *Kwartalnik Hist. [Poland] 1968 75(2): 405-409.* M. H. Serejski's *Historians on History: From Adam Naruszewicz to Stanisław Kętrzyński, Vol. 1, 1775-1918* and *Vol. 2, 1918-1939* is a collection of important materials which were unavailable or known only to a few historiographers. Now a new "historians on

history" is needed to focus on theory and methodology and to include the perspectives of philosophers, sociologists, lawyers, economists, and journalists. Secondary sources; 30 notes.
I. Lukes

1366. Matthews, Fred. "HOBBESIAN POPULISM": INTERPRETIVE PARADIGMS AND MORAL VISION IN AMERICAN HISTORIOGRAPHY. *Journal of American History 1985 72(1): 92-115.* Stresses the need for historians to shift their emphasis from fragmented studies to consideration of broader models of social behavior and to look for elements of agreement and disagreement among these models. Historians should place more emphasis on intellectual studies, especially critical studies of major interpretive works that have themselves projected models for analyzing American history. Secondary sources; 39 notes.
T. P. Linkfield

1367. Mauro, Frédéric. STRATÉGIE ET HISTOIRE [Strategy and history]. *R. d'Hist. Moderne et Contemporaine [France] 1969 16(3): 480-482.* Comments on the article by Jean Baptiste Duroselle calling for a history of strategy. Strategy applies not only to war and peace among nations but to domestic politics, elections, political parties, economic development, and labor-management relations. The work of historians in defining the forms and explaining the mechanism and dynamics of strategy will complement that of the new French historical school.
J. D. Falk

1368. Maza, Manuel. LAS HISTORIAS DE LOS HISTORIADORES TAMBIEN SON HISTORIAS: ANALISIS HISTORICO [The stories of the historians are also stories: historical analysis]. *Estudios Sociales [Dominican Republic] 1984 17(56): 5-22.* Analyzes the nature, goals, techniques, methodology, and inherent tensions of scientific historiography with a short annotated bibliography.

1369. Mazza, Mario. RITORNO ALLE SCIENZE UMANE. PROBLEMI E TENDENZE DELLA RECENTE STORIOGRAFIA SUL MONDO ANTICO [Return to the humane sciences: problems and trends in recent historiography on the ancient world]. *Studi Storici [Italy] 1978 19(3): 469-507.* During the 19th century, the historiography of ancient civilization developed rapidly. Though political history predominated, there were numerous works which applied the insights of the social sciences to ancient history, works such as those of Jane Ellen Harrison on ancient Greek religion. In the early 20th century, under the influence of Leopold von Ranke and Benedetto Croce, the historiography of antiquity turned toward historicism, a doctrine which, consistent with German and Italian idealism, sought to free history from "material" causation. Beginning much earlier, but gaining force after World War II, an opposite trend has emphasized study of the social, economic, environmental, and intellectual milieux of Greek and Roman society, bringing in the methodology and the body of knowledge of sociology, anthropology, psychology, economics, and other social sciences. 128 notes.
J. C. Billigmeier

1370. McAuley, James J. IMAGINED FACTS—HISTORY-MAKING AND THE IMAGINATIVE PROCESS. *Organon 1971 2(2): 39-41.* History is a matter of interpretation for the facts simply are not known. The imagination should be used to seek out historical truth. This can be done through reading contemporary fiction or by crystallizing history in verse. 2 notes, illustrative poem.
P. W. Kennedy

1371. McCormick, Richard P. THE COMPARATIVE METHOD: ITS APPLICATION TO AMERICAN HISTORY. *Mid-America 1974 56(4): 231-247.* Advocates the comparative method—"to identify and measure relationships between specified variables and some particular phenomenon within two or more historical environments"—rather than the less systematic comparative approach for analytical studies of certain problems in the past. Among the problems involved in the comparative method, one aspect often overlooked is the prospect of conducting comparative research on an intranational basis. In fact this may be the true area for the comparative method as compared to the grand scale of the comparative approach. Based on printed materials; 44 notes.
T. D. Schoonover

1372. McCullagh, C. Behan. INTERPRETATION IN HISTORY. *Australian J. of Pol. and Hist. [Australia] 1971 17(2): 215-229.* Three kinds of interpretation are discussed: descriptive, implicative and causal. Descriptive interpretations may be cultural, classificatory or functional. Implicative interpretation involves three operations: rough classification of evidence; a close look at the related period, and elaboration of one theory about its origin. Causal interpretation may also involve a simply explanatory interpretation. Interpretations cannot be definitive, since they are not exhaustive but always selective; being tentative, they are always open to revision.

W. D. McIntyre

1373. McCullagh, C. Behan. REVIEW ESSAY: NARRATIVE LOGIC. *History and Theory 1984 23(3): 394-403.* Reviews F. R. Ankersmit's *Narrative Logic: A Semantic Analysis of the Historian's Language* (1983). Ankersmit develops a theory about the nature of the interpretations that historians engage in whenever they write about the past. His perspective is influenced by the work of Georg Simmel and Johan Huizinga. The main focus is what he terms "narrative substances"—the view of the past supplied and imposed by the mode known as *narratio*. Yet Ankersmit fails to give a clear and systematic account of what these "substances" really consist of and how they operate. To say that they are ineluctable "points of view" is not to offer a thorough analysis. However, he discusses several other topics in a stimulating way. 10 notes.

W. J. Reedy

1374. McNeill, William H. A DEFENCE OF WORLD HISTORY. *Tr. of the Royal Hist. Soc. [Great Britain] 1982 32: 75-89.* Contrasts the relatively modern preoccupation with history seen within the context of nations and states with the older tradition of world history to stress the value of the latter. Emphasizes the importance of the study of interactions between civilizations, particularly the "threats and promises arising from contacts with strangers," in order that historians might acquire "a vision of the ecumenical setting within which each separate national state and more local community lived and moved and had its being." Concludes with an appeal "to reflect anew about how the world's history can be adequately conceived."

D. H. Murdoch

1375. Mérei, Gyula. KORSZERŰ TÖRTÉNETÍRÁS [Up-to-date historiography]. *Magyar Tudomány [Hungary] 176 21(10): 599-606.* Non-Marxist historians are urging a methodological and ideological reform of the science of history. Those Marxist historians who have overcome the pitfalls of dogmatism, while maintaining the same basic principles, are putting emphasis on the application of modern research tools and procedures. The two trends are compared with the presentation of various views.

R. Hetzron

1376. Mérei, Gyula. STRUKTURATÖRTÉNET-KUTATÁS AZ NSZK TÖRTÉNETÍRÁSÁBAN [Structural history research in West German historiography]. *Párttörténeti Közlemények [Hungary] 1974 20(3): 88-117.* Up to the mid-1950's, the historicism of Leopold von Ranke, Friedrich Meinecke, and Gerhard Ritter dominated West German historiography. In 1951 Theodor Schieder began to advocate closer relationship between history and sociology. During the 1960's a new school of historians, the structuralists, took the lead at various congresses. They emphasized the importance of the inner structure of society and employed models for historical analysis. The author gives a Marxist critique of German structuralist methodology. 90 notes.

P. I. Hidas

1377. Miller, David Harry and Steffen, Jerome O. [TRENDS IN HISTORIOGRAPHY]. Miller, David Harry and Steffen, Jerome O., ed. *The Frontier: Comparative Studies,* Vol. 1 (Norman: U. of Oklahoma Pr., 1977): 3-10. American historians in the 19th century rejected comparative analysis as a valid historical approach, believing that historical phenomena were unique. They refused to generalize. In response, some historians attempted to make history relevant. If truth could not ultimately be known and generalizations about human experiences could not be drawn, then history should be used for social utility, with the historian molding his analysis to

fit contemporary needs. The fear that this approach damaged the credibility of the profession motivated some historians to develop the field of comparative history. 9 notes. S

1378. Minei, Nicolae. SHERLOCK HOLMES ÎN ARHIVE [Sherlock Holmes in the archive]. *Magazin Istoric [Romania] 1982 16(6): 49-52.* Robin W. Winks edited a series of essays, *Historian as Detective* (1970), which illustrates the resemblances between the work of the historian and that of the detective.

1379. Mink, Louis O. THE THEORY OF PRACTICE: HEXTER'S HISTORIOGRAPHY. Malament, Barbara C., ed. *After the Reformation: Essays in Honor of J. H. Hexter* (Philadelphia: U. of Pennsylvania Pr., 1980): 3-21. J. H. Hexter is concerned with four characteristics of the theory of historiography: 1) professionalism, or the practice of professional historiography as a discipline; 2) the avoidance of arguments on methodology, reflecting Hexter's distaste for "relativism, economic interpretation, tunnel history and factor analysis"; 3) his criticism of analytical philosophy of history as distinguished from the speculative; and 4) the rhetorical function of historiography as an expression of the historian's thought. S

1380. Mironets, N. I. KHUDOZHESTVENNAIA LITERATURA KAK ISTORICHESKII ISTOCHNIK (K ISTORIOGRAFII VOPROSA) [Fiction as a historical source: on the historiography of the problem]. *Istoriia SSSR [USSR] 1976 (1): 125-141.* A historiographical review on the use of literature as a historical source. The problem of the employment of literature in the study of history has long attracted the attention of philosophers, literary critics, historians, and other specialists. From their studies it is clear that literary works often reflect the essence of historical events, the characteristic features of a period, real social relationships, and the dialectics of social processes. Thus the use of literature in the study of history can assist the development of the historical conceptions of the masses. 89 notes.

J. W. Long

1381. Mironets, N. I. LITERATURE AS A HISTORICAL SOURCE (TOWARD THE HISTORIOGRAPHY OF THE PROBLEM). *Soviet Studies in Hist. 1978 17(2): 57-84.* Examines attempts to study a number of boundary problems of literary research, art studies, and other disciplines, including history.

1382. Momigliano, Arnaldo. HISTORY IN AN AGE OF IDEOLOGIES. *Am. Scholar 1982 51(4): 495-507.* Critical history began with Hecataeus of Miletus, Herodotus, and Thucydides. Their ethos was individualism and free speech. Their professional training was minimal, and truth was their motto. The basis of all history is evidence alone. Rhetoric has no place in historical investigation. A final warning, "Beware of the historian-prophet!"

F. F. Harling

1383. Momigliano, Arnaldo. LINEE PER UNA VALUTAZIONE DELLA STORIOGRAFIA NEL QUINDICENNIO 1961-1976 [Lines for evaluating historiography, 1961-76]. *Riv. Storica Italiana [Italy] 1977 89(3-4): 596-609.* The characteristics of the work done during this period are twofold: 1) the consolidation of tendencies which emerged during the preceding period, e.g. the appearance of a Third World historiography, the decline of Soviet-type Marxism and increasing spread of reformed Marxist interpretations in Western Europe and North America; achronic structuralist interpretations side by side with traditional diachronic ones; the blurring of frontiers between history and sociology or anthropology, and history and academic theology; and 2) attention to oppressed and minority groups, to intellectual forms associated with subordinate classes, to the symbolic aspects of social life, to problems of communication, of the family, of development, of the increasing role of science and technology in the texture of social life. 22 notes, biblio.

J. V. Coutinho

1384. Mommsen, Wolfgang J. DIE GESCHICHTSWISSENSCHAFT IN DER MODERNEN INDUSTRIEGESELLSCHAFT [The discipline of history in modern industrial society]. *Vierteljahrshefte für Zeitgeschichte [West Germany] 1974 22(1): 1-17.* Following the destruction of historicism as a unified basis of historical scholarship, history has turned toward structural analysis, more relevant to modern man's conception of society. Similarly social science is moving away from an anti-historical approach of detailed empirical studies, demonstrating its need for historical perspective and comparison. "Historical thinking" is still crucial because of its comparative perspective as an "anti-ideological weapon" against determinism, opening the way toward communication across ideological barriers. Based on historical and sociological theory; 17 notes.   D. Prowe

1385. Montgomery, David. HISTORY AS HUMAN AGENCY. *Monthly Rev. 1981 33(5): 42-48*. Reviews E. P. Thompson's *Poverty of Theory and Other Essays* (1978), a collection of four essays attacking structuralism in its Marxist and anti-Marxist guises.

1386. Morel, Bernard. CONJUGUER L'HISTOIRE. CONJONCTURE ET PROSPECTIVE [To read history: conjuncture and prospective]. *Actualité Econ. [Canada] 1975 51(2): 194-208*. The purpose of prospective, as a new way of understanding history, is to define the prospects which make the future. The future is the result and expression of different projects of economic groups and classes, which clash within a complex economic and social formation.   J/S

1387. Morgenthau, Hans. REMARKS ON THE VALIDITY OF HISTORICAL ANALOGIES. *Social Res. 1972 39(2): 360-364*. Warns that all similarities and dissimilarities of historical social movements must be examined carefully and responsibly before analogies are drawn; makes specific reference to analogies drawn between the Weimar Republic in Germany, 1919-32, and the United States in the 1960's.

1388. Morris, Richard B. HISTORY OVER TIME. *William and Mary Q. 1984 41(3): 455-463*. The author notes early influences on his career in history and law. Historians should recognize the value of narrative history and avoid the "nonlanguage" prevalent among many quantitative social historians. Historians must write for each other. They should also reevaluate their earlier works; self-criticism is essential. Contribution to "Early American Emeriti: A Symposium of Experience and Evaluation."   H. M. Ward

1389. Moutsopoulos, E. MODELES HISTORIQUES ET MODELES CULTURELS [Historical models and cultural models]. *Humanitas [Mexico] 1981 22: 19-23*. There are four models upon which history may be interpreted: poetic models, religious models, scientific models, and synthetic models.

1390. Müller, Joachim. SCHILLERS WALLENSTEIN ALS BEISPIEL EINES HISTORISCH-LITERARISCHEN PORTRÄTS [Schiller's *Wallenstein* as example for a historical literary portrait]. *Wissenschaftliche Zeitschrift der Friedrich-Schiller-Universität Jena. Gesellschafts- und Sprachwissenschaftliche Reihe [East Germany] 1969 18(1): 165-168*. Before Friedrich von Schiller published his drama, *Wallenstein*, he published his *History of the Thirty Years War* (1791-93), using history in a dialectical process to develop the dramatic personality.

1391. Munz, Peter. FROM HISTORICISM TO HISTORY. *Landfall [New Zealand] 1958 12(2): 144-147*. Discusses the confusion between the truly scientific approach to history and the notion that historical laws exist from which future history can be predicted.

1392. Murav'ev, V. A. and Sakharov, A. M. ON THE TEACHING OF HISTORIOGRAPHY ON HIGHER EDUCATIONAL INSTITUTIONS OF THE USSR. *Soviet Studies in Hist. 1976 14(4): 40-55*. Questionnaires about the teaching of historiography which were circulated to Soviet universities and teachers colleges in 1970 and 1972 brought responses indicating that there are great differences among institutions of higher learning in the teaching of this important subject, and efforts to standardize and improve the teaching of historiography must be made to eliminate such discrepancies.

1393. Murphy, George G. S. THE "NEW" HISTORY. *Explorations in Entrepreneurial Hist. 1965 2(2): 132-146*. Examines the idea that current history is "new" in some cases because it is

coming closer to what a modern empiricist might demand of it, and for the first time has a really defensible set of techniques. This is not so much due to a growing philosophic awareness on the part of historians, but to other reasons which seem to indicate that the move to a "new" history will continue. 20 notes.

                                                    D. D. Cameron

1394. Murphy, James J. THE HISTORIOGRAPHY OF RHETORIC: CHALLENGES AND OPPORTUNITIES. *Rhetorica 1983 1(1): 1-8*. The historiography of rhetoric "faces a number of challenges, including challenges of definition, of comprehensives, of interculturality, and of method," and particular rhetorics must be understood as episodes in a common human endeavor.

1395. Nagl-Docekal, Herta. ZUM PROBLEM DES RELATIVISMUS IN DER MEUREN AMERIKANISCHEN GESCHICHTSTHEORIE [The problem of relativism in recent American theories of history]. *Wiener Beiträge zur Geschichte der Neuzeit [Austria] 1974 1: 128-141*. Analyzes the relativist theory of history, 1942-74, and asks if the relativist concept of rational explanation can counter neopositive historiography.

1396. Nedoncelle, Maurice. COMPRÉHENSION ET INCOMPRÉHENSION DU GÉNIE DANS L'ÉTUDE DU PASSÉ [The comprehension and incomprehension of genius in the study of the past]. *Rev. d'Hist. et de Philosophie Religieuses [France] 1975 55(1): 27-36*. The historical recreation and analysis of men of genius requires of the historian a kind of poetic intuition, verified by the examination of the subject's actions and works. 13 notes.

1397. Nelson, John S. TROPAL HISTORY AND THE SOCIAL SCIENCES: REFLECTIONS ON STRUEVER'S REMARKS. *Hist. and Theory 1980 19(4): 80-101*. Reassesses Hayden White's *Metahistory* (1973) and Nancy S. Struever's critique of it. Both White and Struever see rhetoric as central to historiography but both restrict and contort the meanings and historiographical role of tropes. Struever sees them as modalities of argument within a purely linear, positivist conception of history. She prefers Renaissance tropes to "poetic" tropes. She fails to realize that White's tropes are more than literary devices; they embody styles of thought. Struever wants to defend an "ideal Rationalism" no longer convincing or efficacious. On the other hand, White has not pushed his "rhetoric of inquiry" far enough. He has backed away from fully exploring the nature of tropes, of their "elective affinity," of the relevance of tropal history to modern social science and, most importantly, of the implications of an ironic philosophy of history. 27 notes.   W. J. Reedy

1398. Nikiforov, E. A. TEORETICHESKIE PROBLEMY ISTORIOGRAFII. V. NAUCHNOM SOVETE PO PROBLEME "ISTORIIA ISTORICHESKOI NAUKI" [Theoretical problems of historiography: the Scientific Council on the problem of "The History of Historical Science"]. *Istoriia SSSR [USSR] 1978 (4): 208-211*. A summary of the discussion held in December 1977 at the Scientific Council in Moscow. Historians from Moscow and other cities discussed problems of methodology in historical research. Contemporary science demands an historiographical approach to every historical subject. The chief function of historiography is to raise the quality and efficacy of historical research.

                                                    J. W. Long

1399. Nissen, Henrik S. TRAEK AF DEN HISTORISK-METODISKE DEBAT I NORDEN I 1960ERNE OG -70ERNE [Features of the Scandinavian debate on history and its methodology in the 1960's and 1970's]. *Historisk Tidsskrift [Denmark] 1980 80(2): 405-417*. Four interconnected problems concerning the study of history and its methodology have been hotly debated in Scandinavia during the past 20 years. The problems debated have partly been inspired by the Anglo-Saxon discussion on historical explanation and partly based on the study of the so-called "critical breakthrough" in historiography around the turn of the century in Scandinavia. The four problems are: 1) what is a historical fact?, 2) what are the consequences when distinctions lie in the historian's use of the material and not in the material itself?, 3) what is the role of the master theory seen in the light of point number 2?, and

4) (closely linked with 3) what are the conditions for the use of the hypothetic-deductive method in historical research? Using as a starting point Arthur Danto's *Analytical Philosophy of History,* the author demonstrates that a greater emphasis placed on the narratological element in the science of history solves some of the problems under debate, or at least helps to illuminate the problems from another and particularly relevant point of view.   J

1400. Noble, David W. PARADIGMS, PROGRESS AND THE INTERPRETATION OF HISTORY. *Can. Rev. of Am. Studies [Canada] 1982 13(3): 321-332.* Revolution against theories and interpretations of Progressive historians has created turmoil for professional historians since the 1940's. Books reviewed here discuss those matters: June Goodfield's *An Imagined World: A Study of Scientific Discovery* (1981); Michael Kammen, ed., *The Past before Us: Contemporary Historical Writing in the United States* (1980); Richard Reinitz's *Irony and Conscience: American Historiography and Reinhold Niebuhr's Vision* (1980); Cushing Strout's *The Veracious Imagination: Essays on American History, Literature, and Biography* (1981); and Daniel J. Wilson's *Arthur O. Lovejoy and the Quest for Intelligibility* (1980).   H. T. Lovin

1401. Nore, Ellen. CHARLES A. BEARD'S ACT OF FAITH: CONTEXT AND CONTENT. *J. of Am. Hist. 1980 66(4): 850-866.* Charles A. Beard's defense in the early 1930's of the relativistic or subjective approach to the writing of history did not constitute a sharp or sudden break with his earlier career. During the 1920's and 1930's, Beard was merely following the theoretical science of his time into new and uncertain areas. For Beard the act of writing history was similar to the quantum jumps taken by physicists such as Niels Bohr and Albert Einstein in their efforts to escape the determinism of Newtonian physics. Beard's flight from historical determinism led him toward relativism, but he never became an absolute relativist. Several factors influenced Beard's relativism regarding historical knowledge, including the New History, the writings of Benedetto Croce, and the social theory of Karl Mannheim. 48 notes.   T. P. Linkfield

1402. Nybom, Thorsten. EMANCIPATORISK HISTORIEFOR-SKNING I FÖRBUNDSREPUBLIKEN TYSKLAND [Emancipatory historical research in the Federal Republic of Germany]. *Hist. Tidskrift [Sweden] 1982 (2): 202-216.* Conservative historians emphasizing politics and diplomacy ruled the German historical world until the 1960's. Fritz Fischer's work and Theodor Adorno and Jürgen Habermas's critical theory encouraged the development of new theoretical and methodological approaches to historical study. American and British influences have helped to shape a new school of "emancipated historians" who agree that an explicit use of theory and close cooperation with other social sciences is both desirable and unavoidable. They also recognize that theoretical models and conceptual frameworks should not be regarded as historical laws but as convenient means for the generation of new knowledge. Based on published secondary works; 50 notes.   L. B. Sather

1403. Oldfield, Adrian. MORAL JUDGMENTS IN HISTORY. *Hist. and Theory 1981 20(3): 260-277.* Considers the nature of moral judgments, the criteria on which they are based, and their function in historical writing. Discusses the objections to such historiographical judgments advanced by Herbert Butterfield, George Kitson Clark, and E. H. Carr. These objections are either based on a misunderstanding of moral judgments or simply cannot be sustained. Because he knows the consequences of past events and actions, the historian *qua* historian makes coherent sense out of the "incoherence of lived experience." If he is to transcend chronicle and assess the meaning and significance of his subject he is required to make moralistic "synoptic judgments." The historian's descriptive language concerning historical individuals or societies is unavoidably and, at least connotatively, moral. Secondary sources; 29 notes.   W. J. Reedy

1404. Olegina, I. N. METODOLOGICHESKIE VOPROSY ISTORICHESKOI NAUKI (K DISKUSSII S A. GERSHENKRO-NOM.) [The methodological problems of history: comments on a discussion with Alexander Gerschenkron]. *Vestnik Leningradskogo*

U.: Seriia Istorii, Iazyka, i Literatury [USSR] 1976 (20): 37-46. A discussion of several of the methodological problems Gerschenkron considered in his article "Criticism From Afar; A Reply." The author refutes Gerschenkron and other critics by pointing out their misunderstanding of the scientific bases of Soviet historiography. The author discusses the basic principles of historical materialism and the methods of historical science in general by discussing the roles of social and economic frameworks. Article to be continued. 44 notes.   G. F. Jewsbury

1405. Olegina, I. N. O PRICHINNOSTI, NEOBKHODIMOSTI I ZAKONOMERNOSTI V ISTORII (K DISKUSSII S. A. GERS-HENKRONOM) [Causality, necessity, and regularity in history: comments on a discussion with A. Gerschenkron]. *Vestnik Leningradskogo U.: Seriia Istorii, Iazyka, i Literatury [USSR] 1977 (2): 37-45.* Continued from a previous article (see preceding abstract). A polemical response to Alexander Gerschenkron's article "Criticism From Afar; A Reply" which criticised Soviet historiography. The author refutes Gerschenkron's arguments, clarifies his incorrect presentations, and asserts that Marxism as a scientific theory has proved effective and that it is not mere dogma but a developing system. 33 notes.   G. F. Jewsbury/S

1406. Oliver, Ivan. THE "OLD" AND THE "NEW" HERME-NEUTICS IN SOCIOLOGICAL THEORY. *British J. of Sociol. [Great Britain] 1983 34(4): 519-553.* Examines some recent developments in hermeneutics, with particular reference to the relationships between 20th-century hermeneutic philosophy and the foundations of 19th-century German historical and social studies.

1407. Osinovskii, I. N. TOMAS MOR I EGO BURZHUAZNYE KRITIKI [Thomas More and his bourgeois critics]. *Novaia i Noveishaia Istoriia [USSR] 1978 (3): 55-69.* Criticizes the biased bourgeois interpretation of Thomas More's *Utopia.* Modern Western writers have ignored the very essence and originality of More's enlightened philosophy and emasculated his innovative ideas by tracing them back to medieval concepts. More, a father of utopian communism, looked to the future, not the past. Though his criticism of absolutism and feudalism was tempered by 16th-century political traditions, he overcame the bourgeois blindfolds of humanism by castigating the class divisions and social inequality of his time and denounced private ownership as the root of poverty and exploitation. 78 notes.   N. Frenkley

1408. Özbaran, Salih. TARİHÇİLİK ÜZERİNE BAZI ÇAĞDAŞ GÖRÜNÜŞLER [Some contemporary views on historiography]. *Tarih Dergisi [Turkey] 1979 (32): 587-606.* Considers the views expressed on the writing of history by a series of contemporary historians from Britain, the United States, France, and Turkey under three headings: what is history? What is its purpose? Is it a science? These views are evaluated with regard to the need to counter the prejudices against history prevalent in modern Turkish society and the highly individual, even random, nature of the views expressed is questioned. 55 notes.   T. C. Stanley

1409. Pamlényi, Ervin. A HISTORIOGRÁFIA TÁRGYÁRÓL ÉS MÓDSZERÉRŐL [The subject and method of historiography]. *Történelmi Szemle [Hungary] 1974 17(4): 552-557.* The subject of historiography is still an important, much-debated issue of both Marxist and bourgeois historians. Uncertainty exists with regard to the term historiography itself. Sometimes it is understood to mean history writing, but in ever-widening circles it means the history of history writing. The author outlines the differing bourgeois and Marxist concepts of historiography, arguing that the most logical and clearest definition of the subject of historiography has come from L. V. Tcherepnin.   J

1410. Parker, Christopher J. W. ACADEMIC HISTORY: PARA-DIGMS AND DIALECTIC. *Literature and Hist. [Great Britain] 1979 5(2): 165-182.* Discusses "history's own history," its developing educational role in the universities and its fundamental characteristics as a discipline. The author accepts that T. Stoianovich's identification of exemplar and developmental paradigms in *French Historical Method: The "Annales" Paradigm* (1975), can be applied to history's development as a discipline in 19th-century England, but that the functional-structural paradigm for the 20th century would be either inappropriate or premature. Primary sources; 76 notes.   R. D. Black

1411. Parker, Harold T. THE ANNALES CIRCLE AND THE MARXIST INTERPRETATION. *Consortium on Revolutionary Europe 1750-1850: Pro. 1974: 45-51.* Both the Marxist interpretation of the French Revolution and the *Annales* school can be seen as reactions against the narrowness and simplicities of the post-Rankean school of professional historians. The Marxists are prisoners of the concept of the bourgeois revolution and the *Annales* circle tends to make man too passive a part of history, but from the contradiction between the older narrative history and these two schools there is emerging a higher synthesis of method. 6 notes.
                                                      R. Howell

1412. Parker, Harold T. SOME CONCLUDING OBSERVATIONS. Iggers, Georg G. and Parker, Harold T., ed. *International Handbook of Historical Studies: Contemporary Research and Theory* (Westport, Conn.: Greenwood Pr., 1979): 419-431. Historiography in the 20th century and especially since World War II has moved toward not only plural forms of investigation but also "reintegration at a more complex level." Describes modes of historical understanding, the trend toward synthesis, and the integration of methods and approaches. 10 notes.

1413. Parkerson, Donald. INTERNAL MIGRATION: RESEARCH THEMES AND NEW DIRECTIONS. *OAH Newsletter 1983 11(3): 17-19.* Internal migration during the 19th and 20th centuries is a newly popular topic with interdisciplinary historians; several new methodologies to determine causes are being developed.

1414. Parlato, Giuseppe. IPOTESI SULLA STORIA, DI ANNA LISA CARLOTTI [Hypothesis on history, by Anna Lisa Carlotti]. *Storia Contemporanea [Italy] 1979 10(1): 167-170.* Reviews Anna Lisa Carlotti's *Ipotesi sulla storia* (Milano: Giuffré, 1977). The value of this book is in its stressing the need for a cooperation between all sciences and disciplines in comprehending the planet Earth and its history—to put into practice the famous "total history" and to present a hypothesis which will be evaluated and discussed as a working thesis. 2 notes.   J. C. Billigmeier

1415. Partington, Gordon Geoffrey. HISTORICAL GENERALIZATION. *Hist. Teacher 1980 13(3): 385-400.* Examines the problems of historical generalization. Although care must be exercised in attaching labels to nations, eras, events, personalities, and undocumented stereotyping must be avoided, it is necessary to assign categories of interpretation to the ingredients of history. Explores the works of many historians on this subject. Secondary sources; 38 notes.   S. H. Frank

1416. Passos, Maria Lúcia Perrone de Faro. UMA HISTÓRICA ENTRE DUAS ERUDIÇÕES (REFLEXÕES SOBRE A METODOLOGIA HISTÓRICA ATUAL EM FRANÇA) [History between two types of scholarship: reflections on the present historical methodology in France]. *Rev. de Hist. [Brazil] 1976 54(107): 277-279.* Surveys historical methodology in France during the last decade. The hegemony established by the *Annales* school has been challenged, particularly through the advance of Marxist orthodoxy. Significant developments have occurred through the use of computers; documentation has been revolutionized with technological innovations; there has been a shift away from history as narrative, with the subsequent emergence of the history of ideas and mentalities replacing economic history. Read by Jean Glénisson in May 1976 at the Faculty of Humanities, University of São Paulo. Secondary sources; 2 notes.   P. J. Taylorson

1417. Patrushev, A. I. TRADITSII "NEMETSKOGO ISTORIZMA" V BURZHUAZNOI ISTORIOGRAFII FRG [The traditions of German historicism in the bourgeois historiography of West Germany]. *Voprosy Istorii [USSR] 1975 (10): 90-103.* Analyzes the legacy of the traditional theoretical-methodological basis of German bourgeois historiography, German historicism, in contemporary West German historiography. Notwithstanding the extensive use of

the most up-to-date socioscientific methods by West German historians, there did not occur any radical methodological reorientation in West German bourgeois historiography and the majority of historians in the Federal Republic of Germany continue to cling, though in a slightly modified form, it is true, to the cornerstone of German historicism, the principle of individualization of historical phenomena. As a result of this approach, West German bourgeois historiography is unable to overcome the general crisis in the methodology of bourgeois historical science.   J

1418. Peltier, Michel. L'HISTOIRE SANS PARTI-PRIS? UNE LÉGENDE.... [History without taking sides? A legend....]. *Écrits de Paris [France] 1975 (349): 59-63.* Discusses various attempts since the 19th century to write objective history and concludes that the role of the historian compels him to judge events as well as record them.

1419. Perceval-Maxwell, Michael. LES HUMANITÉS FACE AUX ANNÉES 1980: LA PLACE DE L'HISTOIRE [The humanities in the 1980's: the place of history]. *Tr. of the Royal Soc. of Can. [Canada] 1980 18: 113-125.* The discipline of history is not exclusively the domain of professionals. Popular history retains much of its traditional narrative character, even as the didacticism of earlier generations has been discredited. Although economic and political forces have reduced the significance of national frontiers, much history continues to be written from a national perspective. Marxist historians, influential on both the popular and academic levels, are among the few remaining adherents of a progressive determinism. The major force for the expansion of the discipline's frontiers remains the French *Annales* school, but quantitative history has made significant advances. Contemporary historians complement and supplement, but do not displace, the work of previous generations. 23 notes.   A. W. Novitsky

1420. Perlak, Bernard. SOZIALGESCHICHTE JAK PROGRAM REORIENTACJI ZACHODNIONIEMIECKIEGO HISTORYZMU [Sozialgeschichte as a program of reorientation of West German historiography]. *Przegląd Zachodni [Poland] 1981 37(5-6): 163-183.* After the collapse of the German Reich at the end of World War II, West German historians began to reorient their science of history, which up to that time was conservative, describing state roles and great leading political personalities. A similar effort occurred in France as the *Annales* school, but West German historians opposed this development because it showed some convergence with Marxist positions. *Annales* historians recognized the personal element in history and noted fluctuations and diversions in long-run trends. To West German historians history has to be based on sociological types and has to recognize the role of great personalities whose influence may be for good or evil. Primary sources.
                                                      M. Krzyzaniak

1421. Pessen, Edward. A HISTORIAN'S PERSPECTIVE. *Prologue 1975 7(4): 243-248.* American historical scholarship is in a state of crisis. The "impenetrable writing style" of some "new historians," who are evidently convinced that history is a social science, is ineffably dull. History's central subject matter is the individual and the unique. Impersonal statistics can inform the scholar, but as V. O. Key reminded us, correlations are not causes. Some "radical" historians defeat their purpose by narrowly examining the past only for evidence that bears on current issues. Whatever their persuasion, the purpose of historians in studying history is to understand it; admonitions to uniformity must be resisted to the end. 15 notes.   W. R. Hively

1422. Pessen, Edward. SOME CRITICAL REFLECTIONS ON THE NEW HISTORIES. *South Atlantic Q. 1979 78(4): 478-488.* Focuses on problems inherent in the New Histories. These are static if not ahistorical; they rely on quantitative evidence, which breeds imprecision; they give short shrift to individuals; they are not a joy to read, lacking in literary beauty; much of this historiography is not accessible to the general readers or to nonspecialist scholars; some writers give the mistaken impression that their work is more scientific, clinically detached, more capable of achieving disinterested truths than traditional history; and the New Historians are guilty of making excessive claims. If there is one historical truth more timeless than others, it is that the quality of a historical work depends not on the modishness either of its themes or methodology but on its originality of thought and on the quality of its research, analysis and literary style. H. M. Parker, Jr.

1423. Petrick, Fritz. BEMERKUNGEN ZUR "HISTORISCHEN METHODE" [Notes on the "Historical Method"]. *Wissenschaftliche Zeitschrift der Ernst-Moritz-Arndt-Universität Greifswald [East Germany] 1977 26(Sonderheft 1): 43-46.* In his book of 1905, *Historical Method*, Ernst Bernheim stresses the necessity of the interpretation of historical sources in a materialist way, thus turning a subjective into an objective view.

1424. Petrovich, Michael B. STRUCTURAL HISTORY AND YUGOSLAV MARXISM. *Slavic Rev. 1980 39(2): 292-296.* Review essay of Mirjana Gross's *Historijska Znanost: Razvoj, Oblik, Smjerovi* supplement 3 (Zagreb: Sveuciliste u Zagrebu, Institut za Hrvatsku Povijest, 1976), a controversial manual dealing with the development, structure, procedures, and directions of historical science. Primary sources. R. B. Mendel

1425. Pflanze, Otto. BISMARCKS HERRSCHAFTSTECHNIK ALS PROBLEM DER GEGENWÄRTIGEN HISTORIOGRAPHIE [Bismark's leadership technique as a problem of contemporary historiography]. *Hist. Zeits. [West Germany] 1982 234(3): 561-600.* Organization of historical data in models is useful for comparative history. Several biographical models based on Otto von Bismarck's leadership techniques reveal faults as well as advantages in model methodology. The most frequently used models in Bismarck historiography are "negative integration," amalgamation policy, "Bonapartism," and "social imperialism." Historians must recognize that in comparisons differences may be as important as similarities. Two faults in the models examined are: 1) the assumption that motivations are known for behaviors covered by the models and 2) the exclusion of data not applied to the model. Historians in general have not made good use of social science methodology. Based on the works of important Bismarck scholars and Bismarck's collected works; 52 notes. G. H. Davis

1426. Philipp, June. TRADITIONAL HISTORICAL NARRATIVE AND ACTION-ORIENTED (OR ETHNOGRAPHIC) HISTORY. *Hist. Studies [Australia] 1983 20(80): 339-352.* Criticizes the view of L. Stone and P. Abrams on the relationship of traditional historical narrative and "new" history. Considers the views of W. H. Walsh, E. H. Carr, J. H. Hexter, T. Judt, and E. P. Thompson. Suggests that historians differentiate between two orders of discourse, their own and that of historical actors. Traditional narrative history is event oriented, while ethnographic history is action-oriented. Getting inside actions means reconstructing the experience and meanings expressed by the participants. 59 notes.
W. D. McIntyre

1427. Phillips, Mark. THE REVIVAL OF NARRATIVE: THOUGHTS ON A CURRENT HISTORIOGRAPHICAL DEBATE. *U. of Toronto Q. [Canada] 1983-84 53(2): 149-165.* History is both an art and a science. Historians, however, have not always given both equal critical attention. They have recently lost faith in scientific history, and there has been renewed interest in narrative. Narrative, however, has a different meaning now. The new "narrative" means the organization of material in a chronologically sequential order with content aligned into a single coherent story. It deals with the specific rather than the statistical. Discusses this definition with reference to recent works. Historical narrative presupposes events in chronology, but the underlying story can be reversed, cut across, or frozen. A renewed interest in the text's literary qualities is part of the revival of narrative, but historians generally reject the formulations of literary critics or philosophers. 26 notes. E. R. Campbell

1428. Pietrzak-Pawlowska, Irena. O NIEKTÓRYCH TENDENCJACH WSPÓŁCZESNEJ HISTORIOGRAFII W SWIETLE MIĘDZYNARODOWYCH KONGRESÓW [Certain trends in contemporary historiography in the light of international congresses]. *Kwartalnik Hist. [Poland] 1966 73(2): 492-495.* Describes controversial trends at the last three International Congresses of Historical

Sciences in Rome, 1955, in Stockholm, 1960, and in Vienna, in 1965. The program of these congresses aimed at the integral interpretation of historical processes, which is a broader approach than a mere chronology. One of the innovations was the comparative, synthetic interpretation of the history of Europe and other continents in the light of the economic theory of growth.

J. M. Wilczek

1429. Pillorget, René. DIE BIOGRAPHIE ALS HISTORIOGRAPHISCHE GATTUNG: IHRE HEUTIGE LAGE IN FRANKREICH [Biography as a historiographic genre: its present status in France]. *Hist. Jahrbuch [West Germany] 1979 99: 327-354.* Discusses new trends in the use of biographies in French historiography. Biographies of individual personalities are replaced with short biographical notes about average persons representing whole social or political groups. The role of personalities or heroes in history is restricted in favor of quantitative biographies of various social groups. New psychoanalytic methods are also used in the explanation of historical events. In spite of these new trends the role of individual personalities in decisionmaking and in shaping history cannot be denied and therefore individual biographies will remain an important historiographic source. Original article in French; 66 notes. R. Vilums

1430. Pitz, Ernst. GESCHICHTSSCHREIBUNG IM WANDEL DER INTERESSEN UND METHODEN. PLÄDOYER FÜR MEHR VERGLEICHENDE GESCHICHTSBETRACHTUNG [The transformation of attitudes and methods in historiography: a plea for a more comparative consideration of history]. *Archivar [West Germany] 1975 28(3): 237-255.* Explains that historical science is forced to adapt to changes of attitude toward history from generation to generation.

1431. Polreichová, Helena. KRISE HISTORICKÉHO VĚDOMÍ? [A crisis of historical consciousness?]. *Československý Časopis Historický [Czechoslovakia] 1969 17(3): 396-406.* A reply to an article by the Czech historian František Graus, "Contemporary crisis of our historical knowledge," *Czechoslovakian historical review,* 1968 16(4): 485-504. Based on author's stay in the United States and study of changing historiographical tendencies in that country. Seeks to bring to the attention of her Czechoslovak colleagues the more recent findings of quantitative and multidisciplinary approaches to the study of history. 34 notes. L. D. Orton

1432. Porciani, Ilaria. NUOVI CONTRIBUTI ALLA STORIA DELLA STORIOGRAFIA [New contributions to the history of historiography]. *Studi Storici [Italy] 1977 18(2): 217-229.* Reviews recent works dealing with historiography and with the history of historiography, including the works of authors such as Muratori, Giannone, Niebuhr, Ranke, Sybel, Haym, Treitschke, Hartmann, Tocqueville, Taine, Renan, Piganiol, Dehio, Jorga, Volpe, Droysen, Hintze, Croce, and Levi della Vida, covering such subjects as the historiography of the Moslem world, the Moslems in Sicily, the Norman conquest of England, and French historiography. 20 notes.
J. C. Billigmeier

1433. Presle, Micheline and Marechal, Jean. HISTOIRE ET GÉOGRAPHIE, D'HIER À AUJOURD'HUI, DÉVELOPPEMENT ET TRANSFORMATION [History and geography from yesterday till today: development and transformation]. *Cahiers de Clio [Belgium] 1980 (61): 26-47.* Analyzes history since the Renaissance; examines its evolution, new documentary sources and methods, its relation with sociology and economics, structuralism, and Marxism. Article originally published in *Activités d'éveil (Sciences sociales), Bulletin de liaison du cycle élémentaire. Institut de recherche pédagogique* 1978 (17): 9-47.

1434. Preston, Joseph H. WAS THERE AN HISTORICAL REVOLUTION? *J. of the Hist. of Ideas 1977 38(2): 353-364.* Reviews scholarly writing about the development of historiography in early modern Europe. Some historians have argued that a revolution in historiography occurred between the 14th and 17th centuries, but they have focused on different points within that long period and on different countries. Historiographical change went on over too long a period and with too much continuity to be called revolutionary. 63 notes.   D. B. Marti

1435. Pronshtein, A. P. O PREDMETE ISTOCHNIKOVEDENIIA KAK NAUCHNOI ISTORICHESKOI DITSIPLINY [Source study as a scientific historical discipline]. *Istoriia SSSR [USSR] 1977 (5): 161-173.* One of the most important criteria for the definition of a science as an independent branch of knowledge is the definition of its subject matter. The subject matter of source study is the historical source with all the information it contains considered as a product of social development. In this sense the historian must evaluate the source as a phenomenon of social life as well as the bearer of the information which it embodies. This circumstance defines the subject matter of source study and entitles it to consideration as an independent branch of historical science. 80 notes.

J. W. Long

1436. Prosperi, Adriano. PREMESSA [Foreword]. *Quaderni Storici [Italy] 1982 17(2): 391-410.* Historiography has traditionally been considered the science of the dead. The recent fortune of historical thanatology has attracted attention to this specific aspect of historiography. Some of the problems and questions connected with historical relations between living and dead that an anthropologically oriented historiography should reflect upon are examined here.

J

1437. Pundeff, Marin. B. A. GRUSHIN, *OCHERKI LOGIKI ISTORICHESKOGO ISSLEDOVANIIA. Hist. and Theory 1964 4(1): 72-78.* Reviews B. A. Grushin's *Ocherki Logiki Istoricheskogo Issledovaniia* [Essays on the logic of historical study: the evolutionary process and the problems of its scientific reconstruction] (1961). The work, based on lectures in a course on "Problems of the Logic of Historical Study," 1958-59, examines the dialectical methodology in the social sciences.

1438. Rabb, Theodore K. TOWARD THE FUTURE: COHERENCE, SYNTHESIS, AND QUALITY IN HISTORY. *J. of Interdisciplinary Hist. 1981 12(2): 315-332.* To show how historians are divided in their aims and preoccupations, the quest for meaning, the flight from materialism, and the epistemological implications of qualifications are explored. The idea that works of synthesis as a means of establishing coherence of historical research is feasible must be abandoned, because they cannot cover all fields anymore. Nevertheless, common interests and aims among historians as well as the standards of judging quality create a sense of professional cohesion. To define quality as the central unifying trait several elements that establish the standards of quality are developed. Secondary sources; 19 notes.   H. J. Kaiser

1439. Racevskis, Karlis. A RETURN TO THE HEAVENLY CITY: CARL BECKER'S PARADOX IN THE STRUCTURALIST PERSPECTIVE. *Clio 1979 8(2): 165-174.* Reexamines Carl Becker's *The Heavenly City of the Eighteenth-Century Philosophers* (1932) and the controversy surrounding his thesis in relation to current French structuralist theories. Because the basic ideas of Becker's critics concerning the Enlightenment were formed on a different epistemological level than were Becker's, their criticisms of Becker's work were frequently ill-founded. Having detached himself from a cause-effect analysis of the Enlightenment as the origin of certain modern ideas, Becker demonstrated that the 18th century had retained all the principal attitudes essential to the Christian religion of the 13th century. Becker never claimed the two periods

were related in a cause-effect sequence, but he did posit that philosophy fulfilled the same needs for the 18th century that Christianity did for the 13th.   T. P. Linkfield

1440. Rapport, Leonard. FORGING THE PAST. *OAH Newsletter 1983 11(3): 11-15.* Discovery and publication of important historical documents later found to be forgeries have caused great concern for researchers who rely on written documentation.

1441. Redlich, Fritz. WORK LEFT UNDONE. *Harvard Lib. Bull. 1973 21(1): 5-19.* Discusses contemporary issues and problems of historical scholarship, 1890-1950's, based on a speech by the author on his 80th birthday.   S

1442. Reinalter, Helmut. ZUR GRUNDLAGENDISKUSSION DER GESCHICHTE [The basic discussion of history]. *Österreich in Geschichte und Literatur [Austria] 1977 21(4): 234-240.* The reformation of traditional historiography has to be based on improved means of interpretation, comparisons, structural analysis, and systematical theoretical reflections. Secondary literature; 19 notes.

R. Wagnleitner

1443. Reinitz, Richard. THE USE OF IRONY BY HISTORIANS AND VICE-VERSA TOWARD A METHODOLOGY OF LIBERATION. *Clio 1977 6(3): 275-288.* As writers of history, American historians must give more attention to irony as a literary device in their interpretations of the past. Used rhetorically, irony can be a conservative device showing the divisiveness of a people. Used on a dramatic level, irony can have a humanizing and therapeutic effect. As a literary device, irony helps clarify the meaning the historian gives to the past. The context of the particular work he writes about determines the historian's use of irony. American historians should use irony for its therapeutic value in interpreting the past. Secondary sources; 27 notes.   T. P. Linkfield

1444. Remond, René. ORIENTATIONS DE LA RECHERCHE HISTORIQUE EN FRANCE [Trends in historical research in France]. *Storia e Pol. [Italy] 1973 12(4): 556-560.* French historians are concerned with the most recent periods of contemporary history, since they no longer attach extreme importance to public archives nor believe that it is possible to study historical periods only after a long lapse of time. The leading trend is now to study the structures of reality, extending research to the so-called deep forces, and looking for the help of other social sciences. The fields where these trends are most dominant are: economic and social history, political history, and history of culture and beliefs.   A. Canavero

1445. Renvall, Pentti. DE HISTORISKA SLUTLEDNINGARNAS HELHETSKARAKTER [The characteristics of historical analysis]. *Historie [Denmark] 1966 7(1): 50-60.*

1447. Repgen, Konrad. METHODEN-ODER RICHTUNGSKÄMPFE IN DER DEUTSCHEN GESCHICHTSWISSENSCHAFT SEIT 1945? [Methods-or-factions disputes in German historiography since 1945]. *Geschichte in Wissenschaft und Unterricht [West Germany] 1979 30(10): 591-610.* Despite an intense discussion about theory in German historical research, there is no modern handbook on the history of the subject. History is often understood as the history of the 19th and 20th centuries, and an often-voiced slogan says that history belongs to the social sciences. Although the adherents of this slogan claim to have a new method, they are but a new faction with specific and different opinions about present-day Germany and do not really have new methods. This is proven by a synopsis of the major struggles among German historians from 1859 to the Fischer controversy. Real struggles, not merely academic debates, were always struggles of factions, not of methods. Different political opinions or basic convictions about life were at stake, but both parties used the same methodology. The same is true for the struggle between the Wehler-Kocka group and their opponents. Biblio.

H. W. Wurster

1448. Richardson, R. C. METHODOLOGIES OF HISTORY. *Literature and Hist. [Great Britain] 1979 5(2): 220-224.* Reviews recent works on historiography and historical method by A. Momigliano, Leonard Krieger, Charles Diehl, Emmanuel Le Roy Ladurie and J. Topolski. Discussed Momigliano's debunking of Vico and praise of Croce, Krieger's demonstration that Ranke was not an objective historian, Diehl's view that Americans were highly selective in their assimilation of German scholarship in the 19th century, Le Roy Ladurie's preoccupation with quantification and computers, and Topolski's obsession with methodology for its own sake. Concludes that methodology and historiography can never be independent disciplines, separate from the study of history.

R. D. Black.

1449. Richter, Karel. TEORETICKÉ OTÁZKY TRADIC VE VZTAHU K VOJENSKOHISTORICKÝM VÝZKUMÚM [Theoretical questions of tradition in the context of military historical research]. *Hist. a Vojenství [Czechoslovakia] 1982 31(6): 84-104.* Tradition is, basically, defined as "historically created customs, ways and norms of behavior, transferred by man from generation to generation." Because traditions are just fragments of the past, a relatively compact picture of history could be brought forward only by perfect historic knowledge. There is no way to equal education based on history with an education based on traditions only. The Czechoslovak Institute of Military History published a series of studies that bring the problem of tradition into an accurate connection with historic sciences used in military education. 35 notes.

G. E. Pergl

1450. Ricuperati, Giuseppe. STORIOGRAFIA E INSEGNAMENTO DELLA STORIA [Historiography and history teaching]. *Passato e Presente [Italy] 1982 (2): 183-200.* Discusses the changes which have been introduced in the teaching of history from the elementary to the higher secondary level in recent years, and especially the problems raised by the method of teaching history as research. 18 notes.

J. V. Coutinho

1451. Ringdal, Nils Johan. PERSPEKTIV PA HISTORIGRAFIEN [Perspective on historiography]. *Hist. Tidsskrift [Norway] 1981 60(1): 84-88.* Discusses Georg G. Iggers's attempts to view postwar European historiography in *New Directions in European Historiography* through Thomas S. Kuhn's ideas regarding scientific development. Iggers fails to carry out Kuhn's approach because historical research rarely acts as a normal science as understood by Kuhn.

L. B. Sather

1452. Ringe, Donald A. THE FUNCTION OF LANDSCAPE IN PRESCOTT'S *THE CONQUEST OF MEXICO. New England Q. 1983 56(4): 569-577.* When William H. Prescott's *The Conquest of Mexico* first appeared it was praised for its elements of style, and its use of landscapes in particular. Prescott wrote for a generation of readers who expected meaning to be embodied in the landscape. He used nature thematically, as a moral standard against which the actions of men could be judged. His landscapes were carefully designed to communicate the evils brought about by human passions, the despoliation of nature accompanying the advent of the white man, and the impermanence of all things, including mighty empires. 13 notes.

R. S. Sliwoski

1453. Robin, Régine. VERS UNE HISTOIRE DES IDÉOLOGIES [Toward a history of ideologies]. *Ann. Hist. de la Révolution Française [France] 1971 43(2): 285-308.* Seeks models for the historiography of ideologies. Criticizes the dominant school in historiography, which enshrines objectivity as its goal. Criticizes Claude Lévi-Strauss both for his assertion that there is no objective history,

and for his advocacy of linguistic models for the study of society and history. The study of linguistics does not provide any procedure for new discovery. 41 notes.

J. C. Billigmeier

1454. Rodríguez Casado, Vicente. EL VALOR HISTÓRICO DE "LO DADO" [The historical value of "the given"]. *Archivo Hispalense [Spain] 1973 55(171-173): 213-217.* Man cannot isolate himself from the influence of "the given," i.e., the historical and socioeconomic circumstances in which he lives. This influence, however, should not be understood in a deterministic sense.

A. D. (IHE 86588)

1455. Rodríguez Sánchez, Angel. ¿QUE ES SER HISTORIADOR? [What does it mean to be a historian?]. *Cuadernos Hispanoamericanos [Spain] 1983 (394): 171-180.* The historian is a scientist in search of truth. The process requires choosing instruments and organizing the search. Since to write history is to interpret the past from the present, every historian must make clear his own reality, thought, commitments, and intellectual evolution so as to elucidate the actual present from which he is trying to interpret that past. The researcher must be subject to research, too, for the historian cannot claim to be a neutral narrator of events. Impartiality for the historian must mean above all clear understanding of the fact that no final interpretation of any historical event can be expected. This will also be the source of the liberty and freedom from which he must work uncompromisingly. 51 notes.

C. Pasadas-Ureña

1456. Romano, Ruggiero. HISTORY TODAY. *Int. Social Sci. J. [France] 1981 33(4): 641-649.* Describes the historian as "the memory of mankind" and identifies the new element in historiography in the last 50 years as the penetration of economics by history and a renewed awareness of communal problems ranging from social organization to beliefs, showing how history has turned to economics, sociology, and psychology, assimilating many of their techniques but only a few of their concepts.

1457. Romano, Sergio. BIOGRAPHIE ET HISTORIOGRAPHIE [Biography and historiography]. *Rev. d'Hist. Diplomatique [France] 1982 96(1-2): 43-56.* Of all the historical genres, biography is the most futile, the most arrogant, the most reactionary, and the most irrational. Yet, as the lives of Giuseppe Volpi, Ludovico Toeplitz, and Philippe Ariès indicate, the cultural and semantic study of the destinies of certain individuals can further understanding of certain contradictions of one's national history. French translation of an Italian article which originally appeared in *Risorgimento*, 1981 1: 93-100; 2 notes.

W. J. Roosen

1458. Roorda, D. J. and Emmer, P. C. GESCHIEDBEOEFENING IN SOORTEN [Kinds of history studies]. *Kleio [Netherlands] 1975 16(9): 407-422.* Discusses historical trends which have evolved since the 8th century. Until recent times, historians tended to be generalists who used an intuitive approach which emphasized events precipitated by human motivation. Some historians rejected this approach and relied instead on demographic and other archival data suitable for computers. They became technocrats who stressed the impersonal forces of history by concentrating on social and economic structures. These differences threatened to polarize historians. But there are indications that historians, seeking to overcome limitations within their craft, have begun to borrow techniques from each other, and this new development will strengthen the field of history. Biblio.

R. C. Alltmont

1459. Rosenmayr, Leopold. LEBENSALTER, LEBENSVERLAUF UND BIOGRAPHIE [The times, passage of life, and biography]. *Wiener Beiträge zur Geschichte der Neuzeit [Austria] 1979 6: 47-67.*

1460. Rundell, Walter, Jr. PHOTOGRAPHS AS HISTORICAL EVIDENCE: EARLY TEXAS OIL. *Am. Archivist. 1978 41(4): 373-398.* While historians generally employ photographs in the same manner as written documents, there are special concerns related to the preparation of photographic histories, including: historical quality of the photograph, pictorial quality of both original and reproduction, optical distortion and bias on the part of the photographer, repositories' unsystematic collection practices, and accurate identification of subjects. Based on author's experience preparing book *Early Texas Oil: A Photographic History, 1866-1936;* 14 photos, 15 notes.   G.-A. Patzwald

1461. Rüsen, Jörn. ZUM PROBLEM DER HISTORISCHEN OBJEKTIVITÄT [The problem of objectivity in history]. *Geschichte in Wissenschaft und Unterricht [West Germany] 1980 31(3): 188-198.* Whereas the bourgeois version of the theory of historical epistemology denies the validity of value judgments in historical research and establishes its scientific character on method, the Marxist version establishes objectivity on the identity of the values of the historian and those of the progressive classes and developments he analyzes. By considering historical writing as narrative texts it is possible to take something from both, because convincing narrative texts must be truthful and make sense. This combines method and values, because truth in history must be examined by method, but values only give sense to a text. 17 notes.
                                                H. W. Wurster

1462. Rutman, Darrett B. NOTES TO THE UNDERGROUND: HISTORIOGRAPHY. *J. of Interdisciplinary Hist. 1972 3(2): 373-383.* Reviews: Callcott, George H., *History in the United States, 1800-1860: Its Practice and Purpose* (Baltimore, The Johns Hopkins Press, 1970); Clark, G. Kitson, *The Critical Historian* (Basic Books, 1967); Postan, M. M., *Fact and Relevance: Essays on Historical Method* (Cambridge University Press, 1971); Richter, Melvin, ed., *Essays in Theory and History: An Approach to the Social Sciences* (Harvard, 1970). Callcott presents a brisk dissertation on America's romantic historians, their intellectual origins and their rise and fall. Clark elaborates the "established position of today." Postan's essays span his own career from the 1930's to the 1960's, are largely methodological, and discuss the "philosophic quandaries of the discipline." Richter edits a volume of essays by scholars now or formerly associated with a Harvard interdisciplinary social science general education course, all of them behavioralists, critical of traditional history and intent on change. 8 notes.   R. V. Ritter

1463. Ryszka, Franciszek. POLITISCHE WISSENSCHAFT UND GESCHICHTSGEWISSENSCHAFT: EINIGE METHODOLOGISCHE BEMERKUNGEN [Political science and historical consciousness: some methodological remarks]. *Acta Poloniae Hist. [Poland] 1973 27: 139-157.* Examines some of the methods available to researchers in fields of political science and history. Begins by defining politics and the three tasks of political science: analysis and description, creation of a theory of politics, and practical and prognostic conclusions. History provides background and materials for political science, and consideration should be given to applying comparative and qualitative semantics and opinion polls to historical study. Also asserts that mathematical methods are equally valuable to historians and political scientists both of whom often need to classify and quantify information before studying it further.
                                                A. Armstrong

1464. Rytkönen, Seppo. HISTORIANKIRJOITUKSEN PERINNE JA KESKEISET SUUNNAT [The tradition and central directions of writing of history]. *Turun Hist. Arkisto [Finland] 1976-31: 16-32.* The tradition of historical writing may be divided into three branches. The first is the Western tradition which had its origins in the Greek example. The second tradition is represented by the Chinese who developed it in relation to Confucianism. The third is the Mohammedan tradition which originated in Islam. Each of the three developed independently. Not until the 19th century did they interact. When Western Civilization spread, its tradition of historical writing followed and decreased the influence of the other traditions. They did not disappear, but fell subject to "modernization." The unification of the traditions due to the influence of the Western world is the direction of present-day development.   J

1465. Sakharov, A. M. O NEKOTORYKH VOPROSAKH ISTORIOGRAFICHESKIKH ISSLEDOVANII [Some problems of historiographic research]. *Vestnik Moskovskogo U. Seriia 9: Istoriia [USSR] 1973 28(6): 19-34.* Discusses the methodology of historical research used from the early 19th century to the present. Ideological changes in the study of historical processes, principles applied

to the dating of stages in historical and sociopolitical development, and conceptual differences between various historiographic trends are discussed. 39 notes.   N. Frenkley

1466. Sakharov, A. M. O PREDMETE ISTORIOGRAFICHESKIKH ISSLEDOVANII [Historiographical studies]. *Istoriia SSSR [USSR] 1974 (3): 90-112.* Russia's first students of historiography were unclear in the 1820's and 1830's regarding the precise perameters of the discipline, a task of definition which has been left to Soviet scholars. A recent Russian textbook on historiography edited by V. E. Illeritskii and I. A. Kudriavtsev (1971) is imprecise in defining the subject. The author reviews the ideas on historiography set forth by L. V. Cherepnin, A. I. Danilov, S. L. Peshlich, M. V. Nechkina, S. A. Tokarev, A. L. Shapiro, S. O. Shmidt and others, concluding that Cherepnin's and Nechkina's concepts were correct. Historiography is the study and analysis of historical sources. The history of the historical sciences should not be termed historiography. Primary and secondary sources; 86 notes.
                                                L. Kalinowski

1467. Sakharov, A. M. ON THE SUBJECT OF HISTORIOGRAPHIC RESEARCH. *Soviet Studies in Hist. 1975 13(4): 3-43.* Reviews the literature on historiography, 1820's-1973, and defines historiography as the analysis of the literature on particular historical problems, asserting that the history of historical scholarship is a different field.

1468. Salov, V. I. ISTORICHESKII FAKT I SOVREMENNAIA BURZHUAZNAIA ISTORIOGRAFIIA [Historical fact and contemporary bourgeois historiography]. *Novaia i Noveishaia Istoriia [USSR] 1973 (6): 43-56.* Analyzes the conflict between Marxist-Leninist and bourgeois historiography. Surveys Lenin's views on the study of history, and describes the bourgeois approach, based on C. L. Becker's *What are Historical Facts?* Contrasts bourgeois attempts to find meaning in historical facts with the Marxist-Leninist concept of fact in the overall historical process, and considers bourgeois debates over the independence of historical facts, the Leninist class-based evaluation of social phenomena, and the bourgeois use of facts in anti-Communism. Reproduces positive bourgeois assessments of the achievements of Soviet historians. Secondary sources, 73 notes.   C. R. Pike

1469. Samuel, Raphael. ART, POLITICS AND IDEOLOGY. *Hist. Workshop J. [Great Britain] 1978 (6): 101-106.* Appeals to historians to consider artistic works as historical sources. The bias of most historiography is literary or statistical and not visual, and hence iconography is neglected as a means of acquiring a perception of the politics or ideology of the past. Works of art are often a metaphorical rather than a realistic reflection of their times. Historians should verse themselves in the symbolic language peculiar to each artist and the aesthetic ideology characteristic of the latter's era.
                                                G. M. Alexander

1470. Savelle, Max. HISTORIAN'S PROGRESS OR THE QUEST FOR SANCTA SOPHIA. *Pacific Hist. Rev. 1958 27(1): 1-26.* Assesses historiography, 1910-58.

1471. Scanlan, James P. REVIEW ESSAY: *SOVREMENNAIA FILOSOFIIA ISTORII. Hist. and Theory 1983 22(3): 311-317.* Reviews *Sovremennaia Filosofiia Istorii* (1980) by the Soviet Estonian philosopher Eeero N. Loone, of Tartu State University. Loone's work marks a dramatic shift from the usual approach of Soviet thinkers to the philosophy of history. Loone shows great respect for Western contributions in this area, especially the writings of Collingwood, Mandelbaum, and Hempel. Loone distinguishes three types of historiography: reconstructive, empirical, and theoretical. His work departs from strict Marxist ideas and suggests that historical developments may be interpreted within new paradigms in the future.   W. J. Reedy

1472. Schaff, Adam. THE HISTORIAN'S ENGAGEMENT AND THE OBJECTIVE NATURE OF HISTORICAL TRUTH. *Tijdschrift voor Geschiedenis [Netherlands] 1974 87(3): 310-320.* The absolute objectivity demanded of the historian through the 19th century is as impossible to achieve as is the absolute engagement advocated by Marxists, Presentists, and K. Mannheim. The historian should be partisan to a specified theoretical standpoint only and engaged by taking its side; objectivity should lie in recognizing the subjective factor in cognition and eliminating its impact in the handling of source materials.　　　　　　　　　　G. Herritt

1473. Schlebecker, John T. THE USE OF OBJECTS IN HISTORICAL RESEARCH. *Agric. Hist. 1977 51(1): 200-208.* Historical objects are a useful but neglected aid to research. By examining objects historians can get a better idea of the environment in which events happened. In agricultural history objects may be used for such diverse functions as seeing how machines worked, determining horsepower, discovering which farm tasks were the most difficult, and in comparing European and American technology. 16 notes.
　　　　　　　　　　D. E. Bowers

1474. Schleier, Hans. EXPLIZITE THEORIE, IMPERIALISMUS, BISMARCK UND HERR WEHLER [Explicit theories, imperialism, Bismarck, and Mr. Wehler]. *Jahrbuch für Geschichte [East Germany] 1972 6: 477-500.* Hans-Ulrich Wehler's *Bismarck und der Imperialismus* (1969) is a thorough consideration of the colonial policy of Otto von Bismarck, and of the economic, social, and political forces behind it. Wehler has brought new sources and new techniques into play, rendering his work valuable for Marxist-Leninist historians. The author reflects constantly on his own methodology, and one can thus measure what bourgeois, structural historiography has to offer and what it cannot. 58 notes.
　　　　　　　　　　J. C. Billigmeier

1475. Schmidt, Helmut D., ed. SCHLÖZER ON HISTORIOGRAPHY. *Hist. and Theory 1979 18(1): 37-51.* Introduces and reproduces August Ludwig Schlözer's (1735-1809) "On History," an English translation of *Schlözer uber die Geschichtsverfassung (Schreiben über Mably an seinen deutschen Herausgeber)* in *Litterarische Chronik,* vol. 1 (Bern, 1785). Originally it was an open letter to the German publisher of Gabriel Bonnet de Mably's essay on historiography, *De la manière d'écrire l'histoire* (Strasbourg, 1784). Schlözer rejected Mably's belief in the superiority of the classical historians and considered history to be an autonomous, critical science. 11 notes.　　　　　　R. V. Ritter

1476. Schnelle, Kurt. METODOLOGÍA E HISTORIA: ALGUNAS REFLEXIONES SOBRE LA OBRA DE R. MENÉNDEZ PIDAL [Methodology and history: thoughts on the work of Ramón Menéndez Pidal]. *Islas [Cuba] 1979 (64): 3-13.* Literary tradition documents past history; minstrel poetry and epics did recount contemporary history as spectators rather than as intellectual efforts, part of the German influence on Spain's intelligentsia in the Middle Ages; Ramón Menéndez Pidal tries to bridge history and philology methodologically, an approach much discussed by historians W. Kienast, E. R. Curtius, and Leo Spitzer, who saw in the *Poem of Mio Cid* more fiction than history, in contrast to Menéndez Pidal.

1477. Schoubye, Jørgen. HISTORIE, VIDENSKAB OG HISTORIOGRAFI [History, science, and historiography]. *Historisk Tidsskrift [Denmark] 1980 80(2): 355-404.* At the same time as the interest in history as subject for research and education has increased, the need for a description of the many types of activities which enter into historical research and the teaching of history has increased enormously. Two main trends within the fields of the theory and history of science seem to be able to meet this demand. This applies to the school which has sprung up around the conservative American physicist and historian, Thomas S. Kuhn, and the neo-Marxist theory of science. Taking as his starting-point Jean Piaget's book on structuralism, and with reference to Adam Schaff's *History and Truth* and Eric J. Hobsbawm's treatise on Karl Marx's contribution to historical research, the author demonstrates that the Kuhnian paradigm theory has significant points of similarity with the form of genetic or generative structuralism that the above-mentioned authors represent. The goal of generative structuralism is to develop a method for the study of structures under development. It has abandoned the standpoint that there is an irreconcilable incompatibility between structure and process. Referring to Erling Ladewig Petersen's epochmaking structural analysis of Erik Arup's

works, the author stresses the importance of generative structuralism for historiographical research, including the significance of the Kuhnian concepts of paradigm.　　　　　　　　　J/S

1478. Schüle, Klaus. KRITIK DER HISTORIOGRAPHIE [Critique on historiography]. *Geschichte in Wissenschaft und Unterricht [West Germany] 1969 20(3): 151-159.* Tries to classify historians' work on the basis of modern French historiography. Subdivides historiography into five major sections: 1) bibliographies, reviews, conferences; 2) history, contemporary history, related humanities and sciences; 3) theory of history and methodology; 4) current tendencies in historiography, history of historiography; and 5) special problems of historiography. Suggests using the term recording of history only when examining the results of the historian's work, and using the word historiography for examining the development of the recording of history. 63 notes.
　　　　　　　　　　S. Boehnke

1479. Schulin, Ernst. ZWEI BÜCHER ZUR FRANZÖSISCHEN GESCHICHTSWISSENSCHAFT DES SPÄTEN 19. JAHRHUNDERTS [Two books on French historiography of the late 19th century]. *Francia [France] 1978 6: 592-598.* Review article about Charles-Olivier Carbonell's, *Histoire et Historiens, une mutation idéologique des historiens français,* (Toulouse, 1976) and William R. Keylor's, *Academy and Community: the Foundation of the French Historical Profession,* (Cambridge, Massachusetts, 1975) which analyze the development of new methods, and the theoretial gaps, in French historiography, 1866-1914.　　　　　R. Wagnleitner

1480. Schumann, Hans-Gerd. THE PROBLEM OF CONSERVATISM: SOME NOTES ON METHODOLOGY. *J. of Contemporary Hist. [Great Britain] 1978 13(4): 803-817.* The problem with the historical study of conservatism lies in the methodology of history itself. History deals with the particular in a determinant past, whereas the term "conservatism" is a generalization applied to a sociological category. The historian tends to consider one layer of conservatism, or any other abstraction, after the other and thus have a mental stack of areas of conservation. The true method should be multidisciplinary. The entire social, economic, and political configuration should be considered as a unit. Pitfalls, such as seeing conservatism as only the counterpart of the rationalism of the Enlightenment, or looking for underlying human patterns of conservatism could be avoided. The meaning of conservatism would then clearly be a function of the entire situation.
　　　　　　　　　　M. P. Trauth

1481. Seifert, Arno. DROYSEN UND DIE OBJEKTIVITÄT [Droysen and objectivity]. *Hist. Jahrbuch [West Germany] 1979 99: 414-424.* A critical review of a new edition of Johann Gustav Droysen's *Historik,* vol. 1, Peter Leyh, ed. (Stuttgart: Fromann-Holzboog, 1977). Droysen was a prominent German historian and philosopher whose lecture series on encyclopedias and methodology of history was first published under the title *Historik* in 1857 and several times revised. The new edition is based on Droysen's preserved manuscripts and includes Broysen's outline *(Grundriss)* not included in earlier editions. Therefore the new edition is an important contribution to the historiography of the 19th century. 17 notes.　　　　　　　　　　R. Vilums

1482. Serejski, Marian H. HISTORIA HISTORIOGRAFII A NAUKI HISTORYCZNE [History of historiography and historical sciences]. *Kwartalnik Hist. [Poland] 1963 70(3): 535-547.* Discusses the scope, the goals, the methods, and the role of the history of historiography and postulates that the essence of historical research be concerned with history of the human mind in the constantly changing world. Until the present all historians of historiography concentrated mainly on historical thought, and a new science has emerged recently: the history of the historical sciences. There is a close relationship between the history of civilization, the history of history, and history of sciences. All three define the progress of man.　　　　　　　　　　J. Wilczek

1483. Serejski, Marian H. and Dutkiewicz, Józef. HISTORIA—NAUKA—IDEOLOGIA [History—science—ideology]. *Kwartalnik Hist. [Poland] 1965 72(3):*

611-618. A joint review article on Celina Bobinska's *Historyk, fakt, metoda* [Historian, fact, and the method] (Warsaw: Książka i Wiedza, 1964). The reviewers praise the book for its comprehensive discussion of problems neglected by Marxist methodology. They criticize the author's imprecision in her definition of the uniqueness and nonrepetition of historical fact. They agree with her postulates concerning inadequacy of the source material, source-supplies, and historical criticism in many recent publications. J. Wilczek

1484. Sheehan, Bernard W. THE PROBLEM OF MORAL JUDGMENTS IN HISTORY. *South Atlantic Quarterly 1985 84(1): 37-50.* The greatest risk of the historian involves imposing his moral values on previous ages. Even if a natural moral law could be discovered, no common moral code has ever been accepted throughout the world's population. At the same time, to stress the diversity of moral views neither undermines the concept of natural law nor supports a thoroughgoing cultural relativism. Secondary sources; 34 notes. H. M. Parker, Jr.

1485. Šimeček, Zdeněk. JIŽNÍ MORAVA A VLASTIVĚDNÉ ZÁJMY JOSEFA DOBROVSKÉHO [Southern Moravia and Josef Dobrovský's interest in local history]. *Časopis Matice Moravské [Czechoslovakia] 1983 102(1-2): 98-119.* As vice-rector and then rector of the General Seminar at Hradisko near Olmütz, Josef Dobrovský was able to study the Old Czech monuments in Moravian archives and libraries. He was also interested in dialects and archaeology. Historiography of the day was underdeveloped and conspicuously weak on dating. Through Alexej Habrich, prior of the Rajhrad monastery, Dobrovský came into contact with a number of cases of misdating through serious misinterpretation of the evidence (misreading of medieval numerals, a too-ready willingness to see a 12th-century abbot's monogram in a 16th-century stonemason's mark, and other such errors). Dobrovský is credited with the serious revision of history in the light of archaeological evidence. Based on archival sources, correspondence, and some secondary literature; 69 notes. L. Short

1486. Simionescu, Paul. CONSEMNAREA ISTORIOGRAFICĂ ȘI SENSUL INVESTIGAȚIILOR ETNOLOGICE [Historiographical record and the significance of ethnological investigations]. *Rev. de Istorie [Rumania] 1978 31(10): 1813-1824.* Examines the increasing interrelationship between historiography and ethnology as they become more objective sciences, with historiography broadening its sources beyond the written word and seeking to explain the internal mechanisms of social development. A vast body of data requires more coherent and rigorous analysis, civilization being comprehended by interpreting the entire body of monuments it leaves behind. 40 notes. R. O. Khan

1487. Sjödell, Ulf. HISTORIKERN I TIDEN: SYNSPUNKTER PA BEVISPROBLEM I HISTORIOGRAFISK FORSKNING [The historian as a function of his time: viewpoints of problems of proof in historiographical research]. *Scandia [Sweden] 1975 41(1): 87-12.* Analyzes the influence of trends and contemporary tendencies on historiographical research, and asserts the need for objectivity. Emphasizes the importance of research traditions. Secondary sources; 202 notes. U. G. Jeyes

1488. Skyum Nielsen, N. BILLEDER OG HISTORIE [Pictures and History]. *Hist. Tidsskrift [Denmark] 1978 78: 454-460.* Reviews Axel Bolvig's *Billeder-sadan set* (Copenhagen: Gyldendal, 1974) and Paul Eller's *Historisk Ikonografi* (Copenhagen, 1964). Bolvig's book is a study in the use of pictures as source material, and he draws on the most advanced theories in sociology and linguistics in treating pictures as symbols. Eller's book is poorly illustrated, but the text is scholarly and lucid. M. A. Bott

1489. Smirnov, V. F. and Tabachnikov, B. Ia. O RAZVITII ISTORII ISTORICHESKOI NAUKI V STRANAKH SOTSIALISTICHESKOGO SODRUZHESTVA [The development of a history of historical science in the countries of the socialist community]. *Novaia i Noveishaia Istoriia [USSR] 1979 (3): 207-209.* A conference entitled "Basic Directions in Contemporary Study of the History of Historical Science in Socialist Countries" was held in Moscow 11-13 December 1978. There was an emphasis on the important role of historiographical research, especially in the struggle with bourgeois and reformist ideologies. Most of the lectures were devoted to an analysis of the fundamental stages in the development of, and the contemporary position of, historiography in Communist countries. L. J. Seymour

1490. Smith, Daniel Scott. EARLY AMERICAN HISTORIOGRAPHY AND SOCIAL SCIENCE HISTORY. *Social Sci. Hist. 1982 6(3): 267-292.* Examines the impact of the recent social science history trend on the study of early American history, an area that has been especially congenial to social science history practitioners. Social science methodology has played a major role in many key issues of colonial history: the declining emphasis on American uniqueness and continuity, Anglicization of colonial America, modernization, economic growth theories, personality types, and the local hierarchy dichotomy. Secondary sources; biblio. L. K. Blaser

1491. Smith, Daniel Scott. SOCIOBIOLOGY AND HISTORY. *Journal of Interdisciplinary History 1982 13(2): 301-310.* Reviews Charles J. Lumsden and Edward O. Wilson's *Genes, Mind, and Culture: The Coevolutionary Process* (1981); Alexander Rosenberg's *Sociobiology and the Preemption of Social Sciences* (1980); *Sociobiology Examined* (1980), edited by Ashley Montagu; *Sociobiology and Human Politics* (1981), edited by Elliott White; and Peter J. Wilson's *Man, the Promising Primate* (1980). Sociobiology, with its application of Darwinian evolutionary theory to social behavior, has had less impact on history than it has had on other social sciences. Sociobiology could amplify historical research by illuminating the limitations that genetics had placed on cultural development. 11 notes. R. deV. Brunkow

1492. Smith, M. Brewster. DAVID C. MCCLELLAND, *THE ACHIEVING SOCIETY.* *Hist. and Theory 1964 3(3): 371-380.* Reviews David C. McClelland's work (1961) which proposes achievement as a psychological motivation for historical development. Despite its shortcomings, the work is valuable for its bold approach to history from an outside discipline; it deserves the close attention of specialists in many disciplines.

1493. Smitten, Jeffrey. ROBERTSON'S *HISTORY OF SCOTLAND:* NARRATIVE STRUCTURE AND THE SENSE OF REALITY. *Clio 1981 11(1): 29-47.* Few modern historians have appreciated William Robertson's *History of Scotland during the Reigns of Queen Mary and of King James VI* (1759) because they have misunderstood the structure of his work. Instead of achieving unity through a patterned sequence of events, Robertson achieved it by arranging events and characters around a network of contrasts. The most striking example of this method is Robertson's presentation of historical characters as contrasting pairs. 29 notes. T. P. Linkfield

1494. Smolenski, N. I. SOTSIAL'NO-EKONOMICHESKIE TERMINY I PONIATIIA V NATSIONAL'NO-POLITICHESKOI ISTORIOGRAFII GERMANII XIX V. [Social and economic terms and concepts in 19th-century German national and political historiography]. *Srednie Veka [USSR] 1982 45: 225-242.* The historians of the 19th-century German national-political school, such as H. Sybel, J. G. Droysen, and L. Ranke, used social and political categories inconsistently. Their theories of history did not admit the importance of economic factors, but a close reading of their writings indicates that they could not dispense with an examination of economic phenomena. However, the narrowness of their political ideology and the one-sided nature of the concepts employed weakened both their social and economic analysis. Secondary sources; 82 notes. G. Dombrovski

1495. Sprandel, Rolf. WIE SIEHT DIE GESCHICHTSWISSENSCHAFT SICH SELBST? [How do the historical sciences view themselves?]. *Saeculum [West Germany] 1979 30(2-3): 187-196.* Reviews the retrospective self-image of the historical sciences over the centuries and postulates a merging of cumulative and functional approaches to modern historical writing. 57 notes. S. Beer

1496. Stone, Lawrence. IL RITORNO ALLA NARRAZIONE: RIFLESSIONI SU UNA VECCHIA NUOVA STORIA [Reflections on history: return to narration]. *Comunità [Italy] 1981 35(183): 1-25.* Historians have always told stories but recently in France such history has been decried as *événementielle;* now however there are signs of a subterranean current which seems to involve various eminent new historians in some form of narration.

1497. Stone, Lawrence. THE REVIVAL OF NARRATIVE: REFLECTIONS ON A NEW OLD HISTORY. *Past & Present [Great Britain] 1979 (85): 3-24.* Charts some recent changes in historical writings and the revived use of narrative by "new historians," principally in France, Great Britain and the United States. This has been based on disillusionment with various modes of "scientific history," whether Marxist economic determinism, demographic determinism, or cliometrics. The end of monocausal explanation and disappointing results of quantification have led a small but significant group of historians to a form of writing using a particular event to illuminate many aspects of a particular society, often drawing upon anthropological approaches and using the problematic concept of *mentalité.* 43 notes.   D. J. Nicholls

1498. Strel's'kyi, V. I. KOMPLEKSNE VYVCHENNIA DZHEREL—VAZHLYVA UMOVA IKH NAUKOVOHO VYKORYSTANNIA [Comprehensive study of sources: an important condition for their scientific use]. *Ukrains'kyi Istorychnyi Zhurnal [USSR] 1981 (1): 51-57.* Stresses the methodological importance of a comprehensive study of source materials in historical research, indicates the necessity of establishing genealogical and other links in the documents, and concludes that only a synthesis between documents and facts opens the way to broad historical generalizations. Works by Lenin and others; 12 notes.   I. Krushelnyckyj

1499. Struever, Nancy S. TOPICS IN HISTORY. *Hist. and Theory 1980 19(4): 66-79.* Criticizes tropological philosophy of history as it appears in Hayden White's *Metahistory* (1973). White has reduced rhetoric to considerations of style, a reduction that obscures and distorts the historian's argumentative deployment of language. What he has neglected is the centrality of *topoi* to the disciplines of rhetoric, law, and history. Topics are the realm of our common humanity and our shared issues. They are not the rather vacuous formalities of White's linguistic approach to historiography. History's political role, which White himself recognizes, requires that historiography not become "rhetorical technocracy." Historical writings must not be relegated to private and isolated literary tests. 36 notes.   W. J. Reedy

1500. Sturges, R. P. FROM COLLECTED BIOGRAPHY TO PROSOPOGRAPHY. *Lib. Rev. [Great Britain] 1976 25(5/6): 210-213.* Suggests that 19th-century attitudes contained elements favorable to biographical compilations and compares these to modern attitudes which stress prosopography.

1501. Sundell, Jan-Olof. LAURITZ WEIBULL OCH DEN HISTORISKA FORSKNINGEN [Lauritz Weibull and historical research]. *Svensk Tidskrift [Sweden] 1977 64(9): 396-400.* Professor Lauritz Weibull of Lund initiated the school of scientific historiography known as historical criticism. A successor of his, Professor Birgitt Odén, has published a book on the opposition that he encountered. The author confirms that Professor Odén's account of the sensational disputes between conservative and radical historians is a true one, but emphasizes that there were conservative professors like Arthur Stille who entirely accepted the results of Weibull's medieval research. Weibull won such acceptance that he was appointed a professor at the University of Lund.
       L. G. G. Twyman

1502. Suolahti, Jaakko. HISTORIANTUTKIMUKSEN MURROS [The change in historical research]. *Hist. Aikakauskirja [Finland] 1981 79(1): 45-51.* A critical discussion of Geoffrey Barraclough's survey of current historiography in the UNESCO volume, *Main Trends of Research in the Social and Human Sciences,* Part II (The Hague: Mouton, 1978). Expansion of historical research to include

new conceptual frameworks, methodologies, topics, and geographical areas not only enriches the body of historical knowledge but also makes synthesis more difficult and more necessary.
       R. G. Selleck

1503. Suvanto, Pekka. HISTORIANTUTKIMUKSEN UUSIA LÄHESTYMISTAPOJA [New methods of approach in historical research]. *Hist. Arkisto [Finland] 1982 (77): 12-23.* Surveys trends in European and North American historical research since 1945, including interest in economic and social history, methodological discussion of Thomas Kuhn's concept of paradigms, cultural radicalism, neo-Marxism, the *Annales* school, and the structuralist approach. Based on historical monographs; 38 notes.
       R. G. Selleck

1504. Tandrup, Leo. EN VEJ UD AF NUTIDENS OG HISTORIKERNES KRISE [A way out of the current crisis in history and society]. *Historie [Denmark] 1984 15(2): 234-255.* History is not simply entertaining a handful of colleagues with obscure details nor following academic fads. The historian must have a unified view, based on a strong but dynamic sense of personal identity. Love of others, for example, can inspire a historian to see things from the viewpoint of another and thus understand that person's historical situation. Thus the historian's development as a human being has a decisive influence upon his historical writing. Based on writings by current and past historians and social philosophers; 53 notes.
       J. R. Christianson

1505. Tannenbaum, Edward R. JERZY TOPOLSKI, *METHODOLOGY OF HISTORY. Hist. and Theory 1979 18(2): 243-250.* A review of Jerzy Topolski's *Methodology of History,* Olgierd Woitasiewicz, transl. (Dordrecht: D. Reidel, 1976), which reviews the major problems of methodological research on historiography and assesses the major results. There are major self-contradictions both in the handling of methodology and in the handling of historical data. Topolski reflects the growing sophistication with which Marxist theory is used by historians, yet he fails to subject his own and others' presuppositions and tacit assumptions to critical scrutiny. 8 notes.   R. V. Ritter

1506. Taylor, A. J. P. THE HISTORIAN AS BIOGRAPHER. *Wiener Beiträge zur Geschichte der Neuzeit [Austria] 1979 6: 254-261.* An essay on the rivalry between biography and historiography with an explanation of technical problems of both disciplines.

1507. Tellenbach, Gerd. GEDANKEN ÜBER HISTORISCHE FORSCHUNG IN "TRIVIALBEREICHEN" [Thoughts on historical research in trivial areas]. *Saeculum [West Germany] 1979 30(2-3): 210-225.* Addresses itself to the perennial problem of progress in the historical sciences generally and examines the contributory potential of trivia to the study of universal history and the expansion of historical knowledge. 25 notes.   S. Beer

1508. Tessitore, Fulvio. LA STORIOGRAFIA COME SCIENZA [Historiography as science]. *Storia della Storiografia [Italy] 1982 (1): 48-88.* Examines the problem of historiography understood as a science, beginning with Comte and the French positivist historians. Surveys the debate provoked by their ideas in Italian intellectual circles, where some writers contended that there was no such thing as a positivist historiography because such historiography betrayed every theoretical and methodological principle of positivism. Argues that there is a positivist historiography just as there is an idealist one, although a true historian would refuse to package the past in any preestablished system. 201 notes.   J. V. Coutinho

1509. Tessitore, Fulvio. LA STORIOGRAFIA COME SCIENZA [Historiography as science]. *Pensiero Pol. [Italy] 1982 15(1): 127-172.* Discusses the philosophical and methodological debates regarding the nature of historical research in the late 19th century. The debates concerned the search for general laws in historical study and the understanding of unique and non-repeatable situations, the relation of the particular to the universal, the nature of historical knowledge, and the significance of various philosophical schools to the problems of historical research. 201 notes.

J. V. Coutinho

1510. Teute, Fredrika J. VIEWS IN REVIEW: A HISTORIOGRAPHICAL PERSPECTIVE ON HISTORICAL EDITING. *Am. Archivist 1980 43(1): 43-56.* Following standards set in the early 1950's, the editors of letterpress editions of the papers of noted Americans provide copious annotations which, while purporting to be objective, often reveal the editors' biases. These annotations also cause collections to become voluminous and result in extensive publication delays. Editorial projects should "devote more energy to publishing the documents and less to the writing of history in the form of annotation" thereby freeing funds to support other worthwhile endeavors. 63 notes.

G.-A. Patzwald

1511. Thelander, Jan. HISTORIA, TEORI OCH KUNSKAPSUTVECKLING: OM FRÅGANDETS KONST I FORSKNINGSPROCESSEN [History, theory, and knowledge development: the art of questioning in the research process]. *Scandia [Sweden] 1982 48(2): 303-348.* History as well as other aspects of the Western scientific tradition has become a part of the "problem culture" that primarily stresses answers. In order, however, to maintain its own identity as a discipline and retain a holistic approach to it, history must stress the role of the question in the research process. 2 fig., 140 notes. English summary.

L. B. Sather

1512. Thorsen, Niels. NYERE TENDENSER I AMERIKANSK HISTORIOGRAFI: DEBATTEN OM "CONFLICT" OG "CONSENSUS" [New trends in American historiography: The debate on "conflict" and "consensus"]. *Historisk Tidsskrift [Denmark] 1974 74(1): 342-363.* The new trend is the activist, New Left history, with its critique of "progressive" history. Within this historical writing is the development of a pluralistic social interpretation that conflicts with older historical writings in their emphasis on conflict and a more diffuse character of the American society. Primarily analyzes Daniel Boorstin and Richard Hofstadter, but uses William Williams and other American historians for comment and contrast. The concept of radicals as participants in history is ebbing out.

R. E. Lindgren

1513. Thuillier, Guy. RÉFLEXIONS SUR L'HISTOIRE [Reflections on history]. *Hist. Reflections [Canada] 1981 8(2): 191-204.* Thinking about death influences the professional and personal attitudes of the historian. The desire to produce work that will live on after one's death leads the historian to adopt certain strategies and to seek to dominate time. In order to conquer boredom—one's own and the reader's—the historian must write necessary, well-researched, and clear works. 6 notes.

M. Schumacher

1514. Todorova, Antoaneta. NIAKOI METODOLOGICHESKI PROBLEMI NA ISTORIIATA [Some methodological problems of history]. *Istoricheski Pregled [Bulgaria] 1977 33(1): 82-91.* Criticizes the coverage of methodology in Bulgarian historiography after 1944 by comparing it with the achievements of Soviet scholars. Surveys Bulgarian and Soviet studies in the field of methodology and also covers their controversies with Western historians. Investigates the state of methodology in various sections of Bulgarian historical science, for example in military and Party history, and ethnography. Based on Marxist classics and Soviet scientific literature; 42 notes.

S. Troebst

1515. Tokody, Gyula. AZ ELSŐ VILÁGHÁBORÚ UTÁNI FORRADALMI VÁLTOZÁSOK HATÁSA A NAGYNÉMET TÖRTÉNETÍRÁSRA [The effect of revolutionary changes following World War I on Pan-German historiography]. *Századok [Hungary] 1969 103(5/6): 990-1023.* Discusses postwar historiographical trends in Germany and Austria. German and Austrian historians took no cognizance of the October Revolution of 1917 but were influenced only by the revolutionary effects of the German revolution of 1918-19. The philosophy and methodology of the *gesamtdeutsch* historical school is scrutinized, particularly the historical writings of Heinrich Srbik and Raimund Friedrich Kaindl.

F. S. Wagner

1516. Topolski, Jerzy. GŁÓWNE TENDENCJE ROZWOJOWE HISTORIOGRAFII XIX I XX W. [The main developmental tendencies of historiography in the 19th and 20th centuries]. *Kwartalnik Historyczny [Poland] 1983 90(4): 839-858.* Developments in the study of history have led to the acceptance of certain "standard principles" as requisites for professional historians, and have gradually led to modern historiography. The "factographic" model (initiated by the German L. von Ranke, 1795-1886) was attacked by Positivist historiography (such as that of the Briton H. T. Buckle, 1820-62), which attacked the episodic character of the "factographic" model in the name of scientific discovery of general laws. Twentieth-century historiography involves attempts at an understanding of global history and includes interdisciplinary studies, with Marxist analysis providing only one of the important inspirations. Table. French summary.

L. A. Krzyzak

1517. Torstendahl, Rolf. HISTORISKA SKOLOR OCH PARADIGM [Historical schools and paradigms]. *Scandia [Sweden] 1979 45(2): 151-170.* The attempt by Birgitta Odén to interpret the work of the Swedish historian Lauritz Weibull (1873-1961) around 1900 as the introduction of a new paradigm in Swedish historiography suffers from weaknesses in both the logical structuring of evidence and the conceptualization of a "paradigm" in the social sciences and humanities. The concept of paradigm, if freed from Thomas S. Kuhn's specific usage, can be useful in analyzing changes in historiography, but other concepts such as minimal demands and optimum norms can also be useful in recognizing significant differencs between schools of historical thought. Based on Swedish- and English-language discussions of the nature of scholarly research; 47 notes. English summary.

R. G. Selleck

1518. Trask, David. A NOTE ON RELEVANCE AND HISTORY. *Clio 1972 1(3): 34-39.* To refute the charge of irrelevancy, historians must realize their professional identity. History is the study of past processes in a space-time continuum, offering psychic solace in the face of mortality as well as utilitarian and recreational values.

A. H. Auten

1519. Trépanier, Pierre. PLAIDOYER POUR L'HISTOIRE COMME GENRE LITTÉRAIRE [Plea for history as a literary genre]. *Action Natl. [Canada] 1981 70(10): 811-821.* In the 20th century, the perception of history as a social science, the development of historical materialism, and quantification have minimized concern with style. In addition, both academic history and the use of history as propaganda have restricted the historian's audience. The proper role of the historian is to bridge the gap between generations and to make the experience of the past intelligible. The historian must write well not only to communicate knowledge, but also to transport the reader to other cultures and times. Despite recent emphasis on abstraction and theory, history remains the science of the concrete and the art of narrative and description. The art of writing is not a superfluous refinement but an absolute essential for history.

A. W. Novitsky

1520. Troitskaia, L. M. SOVREMENNYE ISTORIKI-"PROGRESSISTY" M. DZHENSEN I DZH. T. MEIN I PROBLEMY RANNEI AMERIKANSKOI ISTORII [The modern "progressive" historians M. Jensen and J. T. Main and early American history]. *Amerikanskii Ezhegodnik [USSR] 1981: 143-159.* Twentieth-century historiography of early American history has been characterized by a battle between conservative and democratic trends. In the 1960's-70's there was a move from "neoconservatism" to "progressive" concepts in a modernized form. Merrill Jensen began this progressive approach, which has been continued in recent years by other historians, including Jackson T. Main. The progressives are strict adherents to bourgeois objectivism, focusing attention on social and economic problems and conflicts. However, historiographical relativism has left its mark; Jensen and Main concede that subjectivism and conflicting facts can lead to diverse interpretations. 56 notes.   J. Bamber

1521. Trukan, G. A.; Protopopov, A. A.; and Volk, S. S. LENINSKII IUBILEI I SOVETSKAIA ISTORIOGRAFIIA [V. I. Lenin's Jubilee and Soviet historiography]. *Istoriia SSSR [USSR] 1971 (3): 159-168.* Reviews Jubilee literature on history, published 1968-70, which has several characteristic features: important themes, complex analyses of problems, hitherto uninvestigated topics, and the use of genuine historical methods.

1522. Tu Wei-yun. PI-CHIAO LI-SHIH YÜ SHIH-CHIEH SHIH [Comparative history and universal history]. *Ssu yü Yen (Thought and Word) [Taiwan] 1978 15(6): 402-406.* The comparative approach is an important tool in the writing of world and universal history. It can be universally applied, leading to a deeper understanding of historical problems and helping avoid cultural biases. Based on Western historiographical sources; 30 notes.
                                                              T. P. Massey.

1523. Ultee, Maarten. MICHEL FELIBIEN AND THE *HISTOIRE DE LA VILLE DE PARIS:* THE MAKING OF AN HISTORIAN. *Pro. of the Ann. Meeting of the Western Soc. for French Hist. 1982 10: 236.* Discusses the methodology used in Michel Félibien's *Histoire de la Ville de Paris* [History of Paris] (1725), which was commissioned by the local government. Abstract only.   S

1524. Valota, Bianca. STORIA E BIOGRAFIA [History and biography]. *Storia della Storiografia [Italy] 1982 (1): 89-100.* Reports on a seminar on the study of biography sponsored by the Brodolini Foundation in Milan, October 1981. The seminar was attended by psychologists, psychiatrists, and historians of various persuasions. There was apparent a renewed scholarly interest in biography in contrast with the quantitative and serial tendencies of several schools. Of special interest was the question of the influence of biographical studies on the problem of the periodization of history.   J. V. Coutinho

1525. VanJaarsveld, F. A. NUWE RIGTINGS IN DIE EUROPESE GESKIEDSKRYWING [New directions in European historiography]. *Historia [South Africa] 1981 26(1): 2-23.* Reports on work being done at the Ecole des Hautes Etudes en Sciences Sociales, Paris and the universities of Berlin, Bielefeld, Göttingen, and Munich. Describes meetings there with representatives of the various new approaches to historiography linking history and the social sciences. Based on interviews.   G. Herritt/S

1526. VanJaarsveld, F. A. OBJEK EN METODE IN DIE WETENSKAP VAN DIE GESKIEDENIS, 1825-1980 [Object and method in the science of history, 1825-1980]. *Historia [South Africa] 1982 27(1): 14-46.* Surveys the developments and constant changes of objects and methods in historiography from Leopold von Ranke (1795-1831) and the beginning of history as a science to its present form. Ranke's interpretive method and the emphasis on political science predominated throughout the 19th century and are still influential today. The developing social sciences with their different objectives and methods have challenged his views and demonstrated the complex nature of historical research. 132 notes.   G. Herritt

1527. Vasiliev, V. At. OBSUZHDANE NA POROZHENIIATA, NANESENI OT KULTA KUM LICHNOSTTA V ISTORI-CHESKATA NAUKA [A consideration of the difficulties caused by the cult of personality in the historical sciences]. *Istoricheski Pregled [Bulgaria] 1963 19(2): 142-149.* In early 1963 the Bulgarian Academy of Sciences Institute of History held two conferences on the effects of the cult of personality on Bulgarian historical science. The main speakers included Zhan Noton, D. Kosev, and Vl. Topencharov. It was agreed that the cult had done much harm to historical studies, and that ideological vigilance and loyalty to true Leninism was necessary to overcome the damage.
                                                              A. J. Evans

1528. Verhaegen, Benoît. HISTOIRE IMMÉDIATE ET ENGAGEMENT POLITIQUE; ESSAI SUR LES RELATIONS ENTRE LA CONNAISSANCE, LA PRATIQUE POLITIQUE ET LA CONSCIENCE [Immediate history and political engagement: an essay on the relations between cognition, practical politics, and conscience]. *Tijdschrift voor Geschiedenis [Netherlands] 1974 87(3): 330-338.* Defines the terms, methods, objectives, and engagement of "immediate" history, a discipline which is based on historical materialism and places man and his environment into a dialectical relationship. Using history's documentary techniques as well as the oral methods of anthropology and sociology, the "immediate" historian is engaged in the critical, theoretical, and practical analysis of contemporary revolutions, and therefore in the collective transformation of society. 12 notes.   G. Herritt

1529. Vierhaus, Rudolf. HANDLUNGSSPIELRÄUME: ZUR REKONSTRUKTION HISTORISCHER PROZESSE [Freedom of action: reconstruction of historical processes]. *Hist. Zeits. [West Germany] 1983 237(2): 290-309.* Julius Caesar's crossing of the Rubicon in 49 BC and Frederick the Great's invasion of Silesia in 1740 are examples of historical actions based on decisions that required evaluation of the immediate situation. Without careful analysis of the context of decisions and resulting actions, biographical, social, structural, or narrowly conceived explanations of such events are prone to error. Based on works of historical theorists; 15 citations.   G. H. Davis

1530. Viikari, Matti. SAKSALAISEN HISTORISTISEN HISTORI-ANKIRJOITUKSEN TRADITIOSTA JA SEN KRIISISTÄ VUOSI-SADAN VAIHTEESSA [The tradition of historicist historiography in Germany and its crisis at the turn of the century]. *Hist. Arkisto [Finland] 1978 71: 101-120.* Examines the limitations of the historicist tradition in German historiography from its founder, Leopold von Ranke (1795-1886), to 1914. Though ostensibly objective, rejecting theory and relying on factual sources, the historicists were implicitly conservative supporters of the Prussian state and the German Empire, and thus not capable of meeting the new challenges of social and economic history associated with advancing capitalism. Biblio.   R. G. Selleck

1531. Ward, Paul L. [NEW DIRECTIONS IN EUROPEAN HISTORIOGRAPHY]. *Hist. and Theory 1976 15(2): 202-212.* Reviews Georg G. Iggers' *New Directions in European Historiography* (Middletown, Conn.: Wesleyan U. Pr., 1975). His "book deserves attention as an illuminating survey of the international dimension of current work in history." His sampling of current trends in European historiography is instructive and well-defined, its thesis being Rankean historical scholarship and its antithesis the revolt of the *Annales* historians in France, the revisionists in West Germany, and Marxist historians throughout Europe. 14 notes.   D. A. Yanchisin

1532. Warden, G. B. INEQUALITY AND INSTABILITY IN EIGHTEENTH-CENTURY BOSTON: A REAPPRAISAL. *J. of Interdisciplinary Hist. 1976 6(4): 585-620.* Critiques the hypothesis that increasing inequality was characteristic of pre-Revolutionary America and that it explains the growth and acceptance of revolutionary ideology. The inequality argument is not persuasive because it is based on incomplete and inaccurate records, fails to take other quantitative information into account, and ignores other more familiar library sources. Quantitative methods do not make literary evidence and interpretation obsolete. It was the instability, rather than the inequality, of society which accelerated the process of mistrust, extremism, and ultimately rebellion. 3 tables, 55 notes.
                                                              R. Howell

1533. Watelet, Hubert and Dubé, Jean-Claude. RENCONTRES DE L'HISTORIOGRAPHIE FRANÇAISE AVEC L'HISTOIRE SOCIALE (XVIᵉ SIÈCLE-1830) [Encounters of French historiography with social history, 16th century-1830]. *Social Hist. [Canada] 1977 10(20): 205-209.* The six articles published in this issue were first presented at conferences at the universities of Saint-Paul and Ottawa. They have no rigorously geographical or chronological links, though most are studies of France during the Old Regime. One has a largely European setting and another discusses the impact of the Revolution of 1830 on historians. The articles suggest that French historians are finally showing serious interest in historiography and sociology. 16 notes. — D. F. Chard

1534. Watts, Lee. READING AND WRITING IN HISTORY: A BRIEF SUMMARY OF MICHEL FOUCAULT AND JACQUES DERRIDA. *Melbourne Hist. J. [Australia]* 1981 13: 37-39. Discusses the theoretical constructs of history, as form and process, of French structuralists Michel Foucault and Jacques Derrida, and considers the implications of structuralist methodology for literary history.

1535. Weinryb, Elazar. THE JUSTIFICATION OF A CAUSAL THESIS: AN ANALYSIS OF THE CONTROVERSIES OVER THE THESES OF PIRENNE, TURNER, AND WEBER. *Hist. & Theory* 1975 14(1): 32-56. Uses Morton White's criticism of the "simple-minded regularists" to defend the methodological bases of the great causal historical theories of Henri Pirenne, Frederick Jackson Turner, and Max Weber. The aim of the justification is to develop a theory regarding the formulation of causal theories as a proper historical method. 96 notes. — D. A. Yanchisin

1536. Wengraf, A. E. CAN HISTORY BE OBJECTIVE? *Lock Haven Rev.* 1967 9: 42-47. Discusses problems of ethnocentrism and sociological influences in the writing of history in the 1960's, emphasizing methodology and semantical ambiguities.

1537. Werneck da Cruz, Paulo. A HISTORIA E AS NOVAS CONDIÇÕES DO PENSAMENTO CIENTIFICO [History and the new conditions of scientific thought]. *Rev. do Inst. Hist. e Geog. Brasileiro [Brazil]* 1981 (332): 213-220. Discusses the change and evolution of ideas, science, and of the spirit of a given age, and how they affect the study of history, the view of the past, and the nature of society at any given moment. Social sciences and methodologies and the physical sciences have greatly affected the nature and use of history. — R. Garfield

1538. Westbrook, Robert. GOOD-BYE TO ALL THAT: AILEEN KRADITOR AND RADICAL HISTORY. *Radical History Review* 1984 (28-30): 69-89. Reviews Aileen Kraditor's *The Radical Persuasion, 1880-1917: Aspects of the Intellectual History and Historiography of Three American Radical Organizations* (1981), a critique of American radical organizations, the historians of these groups, and radical history in general. Kraditor, a radical historian turned conservative, has written a polemical work that is too often guilty of the very mistakes she attributes to radical historians. 3 illus.

1539. Weymar, Ernst. DIMENSIONEN DER GESCHICHTSWISSENSCHAFT: GESCHICHTSFORSCHUNG—THEORIE DER GESCHICHTSWISSENSCHAFT—DIDAKTIK DER GESCHICHTE. TEIL I [Dimensions of historiography: historical research, theory, and teaching. (Part 1)]. *Gesch. in Wiss. und Unterricht [West Germany]* 1982 33(1): 1-11. This essay, dedicated to the author's former teacher, Karl Dietrich Erdmann, begins a four-part discussion of the new consciousness among West German historians ("a republic of historians") since 1945. Postulates an emerging consensus within West German historiography with reference to problems, functions, and teaching of history. This first part attempts to sketch briefly the postwar development of historical research in Germany as a background for subsequent analysis of historical interpretations and their integration into the current teaching of history. German historiography since World War II has moved beyond narrow political concerns to encompass broader areas of society. 19 notes. — L. D. Wilcox

1540. White, Hayden. INTERPRETATION IN HISTORY. *New Literary Hist.* 1973 4(2): 281-314. Presents 19th-century theories of historiography and attempts to separate ideology from methodology.

1541. White, Hayden. THE VALUE OF NARRATIVITY IN THE REPRESENTATION OF REALITY. *Critical Inquiry* 1980 7(1): 5-27. Discusses the relationship between historiography and literary narrative in the context of the recording of what is real, imaginary, and desired, with reference to the *Annals of St. Gall,* Richerus of Rheims's *History of France,* and Dino Compagni's *Chronica,* 1310-12; considers the fortunes of the narrative form in the writings of more modern historians, and Hegel's philosophy of history in terms of "historicity" and "narrativity."

1542. Wieder, D. Lawrence. SOME HISTORIANS' METHODS IN THE ANALYSIS OF THOUGHT. *West Georgia Coll. Studies in the Social Sci.* 1981 20: 16-25. Using ethnomethodology as developed by Harold Garfinkel, describes some methods used by historians to grasp and reason with the thoughts of historical figures, particularly the "reasoning with" the historical subject, "reasoning on behalf of" the historical subject, and "reasoning through" an idea.

1543. Wiley, Roland John. CHAIKOVSKII'S VISIT TO PRAGUE IN 1888. *Slavic Rev.* 1981 40(3): 433-443. Using Pëtr Ilich Tchaikovsky's own works, speeches, and correspondence, shows how documents are used or misused to write history and explores the Russian composer's reasons for considering his Prague sojourn an important element in furthering his career in musical composition. An earlier version of this article was presented to the 10th World Congress of the Czechoslovak Arts and Sciences in Washington, D.C. on 18 October 1980; 39 notes. — R. B. Mendel

1544. Willcox, W. B. AN HISTORIAN LOOKS AT SOCIAL CHANGE. *J. of Social Issues* 1983 39(4): 9-23. Historians have been subject to diverse intellectual currents since the 18th century, many of which have suggested new explanations of historic events and behavior. Reflection shows, however, that history is too complex to conform to theoretical laws of causality, and the problem is compounded by the fact that historical sources are at best no more than someone's impression of what happened. Reprint of an article orginally published in *Journal of Social Issues* 1961 17(1): 50-65. — D. Powell

1545. Williams, William Appleman. A HISTORIAN'S PERSPECTIVE. *Prologue* 1974 6(3): 200-203. A historian's analysis of the reasons for his personal methodology. Claims that all facts, myths, beliefs, actions, and reactions are related. Great movements, ideas, and events of history can usually be presented in a single paragraph, for a given comment or action serves as their distillation. Photo, biblio. — V. L. Human

1546. Williams, William Appleman. THOUGHTS ON READING HENRY ADAMS. *J. of Am. Hist.* 1981 68(1): 7-15. Discovers in Henry Brooks Adams the inspiration for defining the historian's social responsibility. This responsibility goes beyond uncovering facts; it involves warnings, prophecy, and outlining alternatives for society. For Adams, historians had to participate in creating a new social outlook; they had to raise questions and inspire thought, as well as provide answers to such questions as who, what, and where. The presidential address delivered before the Organization of American Historians at Detroit, 2 April 1981. — T. P. Linkfield

1547. Woolf, Daniel R. RECENT WRITINGS ON HISTORIOGRAPHY. *Queens's Quarterly [Canada]* 1984 91(3): 524-539. Reviews the following historiographical works: Herbert Butterfield's *The Origins of History* (1981), Eric Cochrane's *Historians and Historiography in the Italian Renaissance* (1981), J. W. Burrow's *A Liberal Descent* (1981), Deborah Wormell's *Sir John Seeley and the Uses of History* (1980), and John Kenyon's *The History Men* (1983). Historiography can indeed be an esoteric discipline, and in some ways it is a step further from reality than history itself, but it can also serve the same reflective role that critical theory plays in the study of literature. 26 notes. — L. V. Eid

1548. Zhukov, E. M. K VOPROSU O KRITERIIAKH PERIODIZATSII ISTORII [Concerning criteria for the periodization of history]. *Novaia i Noveishaia Istoriia [USSR]* 1979 (1): 3-12. The theory of successive socioeconomic formations is the basis for a general understanding of the historical process. The problem of periodization is complicated because it is difficult to find a single criterion for a substantiated division of the world historical process and of regional or local histories. That is why, even for the periodization of the world historical process, the formation principle should be supplemented somewhat. The concept of historical epoch, the Marxist-Leninist content of which is revealed in the article, is most convenient in this respect.　　　　　　　　　　　　　　　J

1549. Zietsman, P. H. "THE DEATH OF THE PAST" OF DIE LEWENDE VERLEDE? [*The Death of the Past* or the living past?]. *Kleio [South Africa] 1971 3(2): 34-38.* A review article on J. H. Plumb's *The Death of the Past* (1969).

1550. Zub, Alexandru. N. IORGA ET LA METHODE REGRESSIVE DANS L'HISTORIOGRAPHIE [Nicolae Iorga and the regressive method in historiography]. *Rev. Roumaine d'Hist. [Romania] 1981 20(4): 765-772.* Although Iorga himself was responsible for some of the criticisms aimed at his methodology, since he seldom dwelt other than casually on the problem of the historian's attitude toward facts and the relation between content and expression, analysis of the prolific dean's philosophical origins and major historiographic influences reveals much of his thought in this regard. Based on Iorga's *Généralités* and secondary analyses; 39 notes.　　　　　　　　　　　　　　G. J. Bobango/S

1551. Zuluaga, Rosa M. LA LLAMADA "NUEVA HISTORIA" [The so-called "new history"]. *Rev. de Hist. Americana y Argentina [Argentina] 1978-80 10(19-20): 87-101.* The conception of history as a social science was formulated in the early 19th century, reinforced by Marx's historical materialism, and best represented in the work of the group of the French journal *Annales*. Examines the concepts, traces the development, and assesses the work produced by the *Annales school* and concludes that, however valuable its contribution, history must remain an autonomous research, independent of the methods and concepts of the "human sciences" and of social history. 19 notes.　　　　　　　　J. V. Coutinho

1552. —. [HISTORICAL NARRATIVE]. *Geschichtsdidaktik [West Germany] 1980 5(4): 383-397.*
Jung, Michael. GESCHICHTSERZÄHLUNG HEUTE: DIE WIEDERGEBURT EINER UNTAUGLICHEN EN METHODE [History narrative today: the rebirth of an unsuitable method], *pp. 383-391.* Discusses problems and drawbacks connected with the use of historical narrative.
Tocha, Michael. AUF DIE INHALTE KOMMT ES AN [It depends on the content], *pp. 393-397.* Response to Michael Jung.

1553. —. [HISTORY TEACHING AND DIDACTICISM] (Italian text).
Pitocco, Francesco. DIDATTICA DELLA STORIA E STORIOGRAFIA [History teaching and historiography]. *Quaderni Storici [Italy] 1981 16(1): 313-337.* Joining a discussion opened by an article by Edoardo Grendi in an earlier issue of *Quaderni*, the author argues that the problem of the teaching of history in schools cannot be dissociated from the problem of teacher-formation and the pedagogical model which it perpetuates. There is no difference between the old and new approaches to the teaching of history and the old and new approaches to pedagogy. Grendi's article in *Quaderni* 1979 14(2): 698-707. 2 notes.
Grendi, Edoardo. LO STORICO E LA DIDATTICA INCOSCIENTE (REPLICA A UNA DISCUSSIONE) [The historian and unconscious didacticism: reply to a discussion]. *Quaderni Storici [Italy] 1981 16(1): 338-346.* Replying to the discussion occasioned by his earlier article, argues that the discourse on historical research and its teaching and communication is no other than a reflection on the role of the historian. Attention must therefore be paid to the personal qualifications of the historian, who cannot do away with his own subjectivity; autobiography is the first necessary exercise in history.
　　　　　　　　　　　　　　J. V. Coutinho

1554. —. AN INTERVIEW WITH JOHN WILKINSON: RETROSPECTIVE FUTUROLOGY. *Center Mag. 1972 5(6): 59-62.* Presents *Center Magazine* Senior Fellow John Wilkinson's current Futurology concept as a method for viewing history.

1555. —. [MORE ON HISTORIOGRAPHICAL COMMON SENSE]. *Quaderni Storici [Italy] 1979 14(3): 1135-1151.*
Caracciolo, Alberto. L' *HOMO FABER* EL IL SUO ROVESCIO [*Homo faber* and his reverse], *pp. 1133-1144.* Response to Edoardo Grendi's earlier article [*Quaderni Storici* 1979 14(2)]. Observes that while the microanalytical method proposed by the latter to bring history closer to the student's immediate experience is effective for certain levels of knowledge it is not equally useful for others or for particular periods: it is of little help, for example, in cases involving vast "categories" such as the centralized states, the world market, the universal presence of mass media, or the international diffusion of technologies. If historical knowledge is to correspond to the experience of contemporary man, it must above all emphasize the contradictions between the supposed "dominion of nature" and the actual effect of contaminating, altering and destroying nature produced by such accelerated progress.
Villani, P. SENSO COMUNE E SENSO DELLA STORIA [Common sense and a sense of history], *pp. 1144-1151.* A more critical view of the historical process and a closer link between history teaching and the real, everyday experience of the young must not however reduce the attention paid to the great, fundamental, phenomena that accompany the development of civilization.　　　　　　　　　　　　　　J

1556. —. "THE PEASANT WAR IN GERMANY" BY FRIEDRICH ENGELS: 125 YEARS LATER. *J. of Peasant Studies [Great Britain] 1975 3(1): 89-135.*
Bak, Janos. *pp. 89-98.* Discusses the history, main points, and the enduring significance of the work.
Wohlfeil, Rainer. *pp. 98-103.* Discusses the historiographical context of the work.
Engelberg, Ernst. *pp. 103-107.* Discusses Wohlfeil's essay and additional historiographical concerns.
Vogler, Günter. *pp. 108-116.* Discusses Wohlfeil's essay and argues that the notion of an early bourgeois revolution requires further study.
Friedman, Edward. *pp. 117-123.* Analyzes the aspect of religion and revolution in the work.
Greussing, Kurt and Kippenberg, Hans G. *pp. 123-131.* Relates the arguments of the work to situations in the Middle East.

1557. —. QU'EST-CE QUE L'HISTOIRE DE L'HISTORIOGRAPHIE? [What is history of historiography?]. *Storia della Storiografia [Italy] 1982 (2): 102-111.*
Walker, Lawrence D. THE HISTORY OF HISTORICAL RESEARCH AND WRITING VIEWED AS A BRANCH OF THE HISTORY OF SCIENCE, *pp. 102-107.* Historiography is a branch of intellectual history and its study is best modelled after the history of science, in which the subject is scientific, but the discipline of history is not; their synthesis serves scientific, objective truth.
Netchkina, M. V. L'HISTOIRE DE L'HISTORIOGRAPHIE: PROBLEMES METHODOLOGIQUES DE L'HISTOIRE DE LA SCIENCE HISTORIQUE [The history of historiography: methodological problems of the history of historical science], *pp. 108-111.* Discusses the attention given to methodological questions in Marxist-Leninist history of historical science and the integral part played by the history of science in its problems.　　　　　　　　　　　　　　G. Herritt

1558. —. [RUSSIA AND THE WEST]. *Slavic Rev. 1964 23(1): 1-30.*
Roberts, Henry L. RUSSIA AND THE WEST: A COMPARISON AND CONTRAST, *pp. 1-12.* Chronicles political, social, and philosophical links between the USSR and Western Europe, 1870's-1945, highlighting changing attitudes in the methodology and historiography of comparative analysis.
Raeff, Marc. RUSSIA'S PERCEPTION OF HER RELATIONSHIP WITH THE WEST, *pp. 13-19.* Discusses contrast analysis as a method of historiography, highlighting the basic entity of national identity as a basis for comparative studies and tracing the concept through Russian history, 1630's-1880's.

Szeftel, Marc. THE HISTORICAL LIMITS OF THE QUESTION OF RUSSIA AND THE WEST, *pp. 20-27.* Examines the relationship between Russia and the West, 1840's-1917, highlighting geographical, historical, and cultural limitations to Russia's inclusion in Western European social and cultural history.

Roberts, Henry L. REPLY, *pp. 28-30.* Comments on criticisms of his paper.

1559. —. [SOURCE CRITICISM]. *Historie [Denmark] 1974 11(1): 105-141.*

Pasternak, Jakob. DEN HALVRUSTNE KILDEKRITIK [Tarnished source criticism], *pp. 105-136.* Studies the source criticism proposed by Henrik Nissen. Discusses the central problem that Henrik Nissen and his critics have tackled but not resolved systematically. The author develops his own approach and adds some concluding remarks regarding the state of source criticism in Denmark today.

Sjøqvist, Viggo. SVAR TIL DEN RUSTFRIE KILDEKRITIK [Answer to stainless source criticism], *pp. 137-141.* Discusses the validity and source of Jakob Pasternak's source criticism for other historians.
B. L. Jeppesen

1560. —. [THE TEACHING OF HISTORY: PROBLEMS AND METHODS]. *Cahiers Pédagogiques 1967 (65): 5-83, (66): 7-152.*
L'ENSEIGNEMENT DE L'HISTOIRE - PROBLÈMES GÉNÉRAUX [The teaching of history - general problems], *pp. 5-83.* The first section, "Research and Teaching," deals with selected concepts and approaches: social class and social stratification, the mobility and wealth of French society during the last hundred years, the quantitative approach to history, the pre-historic period, and a review of books describing fundamental changes and trends in modern Europe since the 16th century. The second section, "General Problems," includes the organization of material, the social, intellectual and cultural objectives of teaching history, student attitudes toward the discipline, the selection of subject matter, the relation of history and science, and the reformation of teaching methods. Based on secondary sources and personal observations; biblios.

L'ENSEIGNMENT DE L'HISTOIRE - MÉTHODES [The teaching of history - methods], *pp. 7-152.* Combined with extracts of responses received from a questionnaire sent to history professors by the editors of *Cahiers Pédagogiques*, are sections dealing with the use of primary source materials and audio-visual aids, the use of the textbook and the notebook, classroom techniques, interdisciplinary courses, the measurement of students' achievement, and the professional preparation of history teachers. Based on secondary works and the personal observations and experiences of the contributors. J. S. Gassner

1561. —. [THE TRUTH ABOUT THE RENAISSANCE]. *Bibliothèque d'Humanisme et Renaissance [Switzerland] 1982 44(3): 645-648, 657-660.*

Kuntz, Marion L. and Kuntz, Paul G. TRUTH IN HISTORY: WASWO'S IDEOLOGICAL RELATIVISM *VS.* KRISTELLER'S EMPIRICAL OBJECTIVISM, *pp. 645-648.* Richard Waswo's review of Paul O. Kristeller's *Renaissance Thought and Its Sources* (1981) misunderstands Kristeller's objectivism and seeks to impose ideology on the study of history.

Waswo, R. LEARNING TO LOVE RELATIVE TRUTHS, *pp. 657-660.* Interpretation, and even ideology, must inform all understanding of truth. M. Schumacher/S

1562. —. UNA QUESTIONE DI CONFINE [A question of limits]. *Memoria: Rivista di Storia delle Donne [Italy] 1983 (9): 50-65.*

DiCori, Paola. *pp. 50-55.* Begins the discussion on the essay of Gianna Pomata, "La Storia delle Donne: una Questione di confine in N. Tranfaglia, ed., *Il Mondo Contemporaneo*, vol. 10 part 2, pp. 1435-1469."

Calvi, Giulia. *pp. 55-58.* Discusses integrative history and the new women's history.

Stella, Simonetta Piccone. *pp. 58-61.* Notes Pomata's attempt both to pluralize historical disciplines and to interrelate them.

Arioti, Maria. *pp. 62-65.* Notes the necessity of combining anthropology and history, of refusing general methodologies and relativizing the problem of feminine subordination.
J. W. Houlihan

Marxist Methodology and Historiography

1563. Ballvora, Shyqri. LIGJËSIA E PËRGJITHSHME DHE FAKTI HISTORIK NË ZHVILLIMIN SHOQËROR [Historical fact in social development]. *Studime Hist. [Albania] 1978 32(1): 59-84.* Criticizes bourgeois and revisionist historiography, which, confining itself to historical fact, ignores Marxist-Leninist rules and methodology. This results in the negation of the philosophical and practical approach. Whilst non-Marxist historians are defeated by the absence of certain historical facts, Marxist-Leninist historians can discover these facts and complete the historical picture.
G.-D. L. Naci

1564. Barg, M. A. THE HISTORICAL FACT: STRUCTURE, FORM, CONTENT. *Soviet Studies in Hist. 1977 16(1): 3-47.* A Marxist definition of historical fact as well as an exploration of its nature.

1565. Barg, M. A. KATEGORII "VSEMIRNO-ISTORICHESKII" I "LOKAL'NO-ISTORICHESKII" V MARKSISTSKO-LENINSKOM ISTORIZME [The categories world-historic and local-historic in Marxist-Leninist historiography]. *Voprosy Istorii [USSR] 1980 (1): 61-78.* The Marxist conception of "world-historic" embraces the cognitive principle of history as a science. From this point of view the correlation of world-historic and local-historic is disclosed in the concept "limitation" or, which is the same thing, "classical forms." This concept is analyzed in the article both in ontological and cognitive aspects. Its application in historiographical practice is illustrated on three levels: 1) world-historic as the interaction of a number of coexisting socioeconomic formations; 2) world-historic within the framework of one formation taken singly; 3) world-historic within the framework of the local-historic process. The author brings out the dialectical interdependence of the categories he examines. 60 notes. J

1566. Bartel, Horst and Schmid, Walter. GESCHICHTSWISSENSCHAFT UND GESCHICHTSBEWUSSTSEIN BEI DER GESTALTUNG DES ENTWICKLETEN SOZIALISMUS [Historiography and historical consciousness in the formation of developed socialism]. *Einheit [East Germany] 1978 33(3): 254-260.* In the ideological struggle with bourgeois theories of history during the period of the formation of an advanced socialist society, the consciousness-forming function of Marxist-Leninist historiography has been to strengthen proletarian internationalism and socialist patriotism.

1567. Bensing, M. and Druzhinin, N. M. OBMEN MNENIIAMI MEZHDU PROFESSOROM M. BENZINGOM (GDR) I AKADEMIKOM N. M. DRUZHININYM [An exchange of opinions between Professor M. Bensing (East Germany) and Academician N. M. Druzhinin]. *Novaia i Noveishaia Istoriia [USSR] 1971 (1): 129-139.* Letters between the Soviet historian Nikolai M. Druzhinin and Professor Manfred Bensing of Leipzig University in 1969 discuss historiography, the history of culture, the problem of bringing together historians in different fields, attitudes toward collective research, and other methodological problems of the contemporary Marxist historian. E. R. Sicher

1568. Bernstein, Howard R. MARXIST HISTORIOGRAPHY AND THE METHODOLOGY OF RESEARCH PROGRAMS. *Hist. and Theory 1981 20(4): 424-449.* Selectively reviews and appropriates the views of Imre Lakatos and Larry Laudan on the concept of a "research program" with which to measure the fruitfulness and vitality of the Marxist trend in historiography. 58 notes.
W. J. Reedy

1569. Berthold, Werner. ZUR ENTWICKLUNG DER MARXIS-TISCH-LENINISTISCHEN GESCHICHTSWISSENSCHAFT ZU EINER VOLL ENTFALTETEN WISSENSCHAFTLICHEN SPEZIALDISZIPLIN [The development of Marxist-Leninist historical science into a fully evolved special scholarly discipline]. *Beiträge zur Geschichte der Arbeiterbewegung [East Germany] 1984 26(1): 13-24.* Traces the evolution of Marxist historiography. Explores the relationship between the Communist Party and the study of history in Communist countries. Focuses on the development of methodology compatible with ideology in the USSR and East Germany. Revision of a presentation to the third Rostock symposium on historical science, 2 December 1982; 29 notes.　　　　　　R. Grove

1570. Boiadzhiev, Georgi. KOMPLEKSNYI PODKHOD PRI ANALIZE ISTORICHESKOGO PROTSESSA [The complex approach to the analysis of historical processes]. *Bulgarian Hist. Rev. [Bulgaria] 1976 4(4): 78-84.* Discusses the Marxist concept of a "complex" approach to historical research and proposes a working definition of this approach. Examines the typology of this methodology, which is not synonymous with the "integral" and "systematic" methods, and gives examples of historical events which have to be studied in supranational frames of reference. On the other hand, argues that regional circumstances must also be taken into account, although strictly speaking there is no historical problem that is not complex. Suggests that computer analysis can be of assistance in the processing of complicated data in the application of this methodology. 22 notes.　　　　　　E. R. Sicher

1571. Bordzhiev, Georgi. O KOMPLEKSNOM RASKRYTII AKTIVNOSTI CHELOVEKA MARKSISTSKOI ISTORIOGRAFIEI [Marxist historiography and its all-embracing revelation of the activity of man]. *Bulgarian Hist. Rev. [Bulgaria] 1979 7(2): 78-87.* An examination of the Marxist approach to the role of man in history, a problem on which in 1973 the author produced a comprehensive study: man is central to any understanding of events. Reviews the relations between Bulgaria and the USSR, 1944-65, indicating the path for future historians. Based mainly on Russian but also some Bulgarian and Polish secondary sources, 55 notes.
　　　　　　J. P. H. Myers

1572. Bychko, I. V. ISTORIKO-FILOSOFSKOE ISSLEDOVANIE: OPYT METODOLOGICHESKOGO ANALIZA [Historical and philosophic research: essay in methodological analysis]. *Voprosy Filosofii [USSR] 1984 (9): 104-112.* Describes the leading principles of Marxist historiography and philosophy as the adherence to the Party spirit and historicism.

1573. Cambel, Samuel. OTÁZKY VÝVOJA SOCIALISTICKEJ SPOLOČNOSTI V NAŠEJ MARXISTICKEJ HISTORIOGRAFII [Problems of socialist social development in Marxist historiography]. *Hist. Časopis [Czechoslovakia] 1982 30(1): 66-72.* Explains some problems of Marxist historiography of contemporary history; many caused by the short time-span that divides the researcher from the event. Those participating in events described could be viewed as co-creators of the history, and their personal reminiscences may be valuable. The time factor must not be an obstacle to full historical knowledge. Marx himself in his description of events in France of 1848 and of the case of Napoleon III provided an outstanding example of the writing of the history of events at which he was present. 10 notes.　　　　　　G. E. Pergl

1574. Chernov, A. B. LENIN, ISTORIA I SOVREMENNOST': XV NAUCHNAIA KONFERENTSIA KOMISSII ISTORIKOV SSSR I GDR [Lenin, history, and contemporary times: the 15th Joint Conference of Historians of the USSR and the GDR]. *Voprosy Istorii KPSS [USSR] 1970 (6):139-141.* Summarizes the speeches of Soviet and East German historians at their 15th congress at which the influence of Leninist ideas on the world revolutionary process was stressed.

1575. Čistozvonov, A. N. ÜBER DIE STADIAL-REGIONALE METHODE BEI DER VERGLEICHENDEN HISTORISCHEN ERFORSCHUNG DER BÜRGERLICHEN REVOLUTIONEN DES 16. BIS 18. JAHRHUNDERTS IN EUROPA [About the phased-regional method in the comparative historical research of the bourgeois revolutions of the 16th to the 18th century in Europe]. *Zeitschrift für Geschichtswissenschaft [East Germany] 1973 21(1): 31-48.* The Marxist historical school considers bourgeois revolutions to be objective necessities for the transformation of feudalism to capitalism. As the bourgeois revolutions were an organic part of a global, complex process of the development of capitalism, the phased-regional method should be applied instead of the national-regional. A phased region is a group of countries, not necessarily a geographic unity, which show the same type of basic laws of development within a historical process. Therefore, bourgeois revolutions should not be categorized as "early" or "late," but as revolutions of the phase of manufacture, industries, and the imperialistic phase of capitalism. Secondary sources; 32 notes.
　　　　　　R. Wagnleitner

1576. Danilov, A. I. ISTORICHESKOE SOBYTIE I ISTORICHESKAIA NAUKA [A historical event and historiography]. *Srednie Veka [USSR] 1980 43: 13-31.* Explores the role of a historical event as a fundamental unit of human activity. The cause-and-effect occurrences of such events form a historical process. Criticizes the quantitative method and structural concept of bourgeois historical methodology and historiography. Based on works of Engels, Lenin, and Marx; 40 notes.　　　　　　R. Kirillov

1577. Dement'ev, I. P. OSNOVNYE NAPRAVLENIIA I SHKOLY V AMERIKANSKOI ISTORIOGRAFII POSLEVOENNOGO VREMENI [The principal trends and schools in American historiography of the post-war period]. *Voprosy Istorii [USSR] 1976 (11): 67-90.* The author gives a generalizing characteristic of the development of American historiography during the postwar period, shedding light on the evolution of its principal trends and schools. The attention in the article is focussed on the politico-ideological significance of one or another historical conception, methodology, analysis of the new techniques of research and critical tendencies in the historiography of the last decade. In conclusion the author examines a number of works produced by Marxist historians in the U.S.A.
　　　　　　J

1578. Doernberg, Stefan. PROLETARISCHER INTERNATIONALISMUS UND GESCHICHTSWISSENSCHAFT [Proletarian internationalism and historiography]. *Zeitschrift für Geschichtswissenschaft [East Germany] 1969 17(1-2): 87-91.* As national states do not exist as isolated historical realities, Marxist-Leninist historiography has to promote world historical research, exploding nationalist, individualist thinking on the basis of the theory of proletarian internationalism.

1579. Döhring, Rolf, et al. GESCHICHTSWISSENSCHAFT UND GESCHICHTSBEWUSSTSEIN [Historical science and historical consciousness]. *Zeitschrift für Geschichtswissenschaft [East Germany] 1968 16(8): 1049-1056.* Theoretical discussion of the role of socialist historical consciousness and how it is an expression of Marxism-Leninism in East German society.

1580. Döhring, Rolf and Meier, Helmut. SOZIALISTISCHES GESCHICHTSBEWUSSTSEIN—WESENTLICHES ELEMENT SOZIALISTISCHER BEWUSSTHEIT [Socialist historical consciousness: decisive element of socialist consciousness]. *Einheit [East Germany] 1976 31(5-6): 542-555.* Of all scientific contributions to the strengthening of a socialist consciousness, Marxist historiography probably is the most important for the development of a fundamental socialist personality.

1581. Dorpalen, Andreas. HISTORY AND POLITICS: AN EAST GERMAN ASSESSMENT. *Central European Hist. 1979 12(1): 83-90.* Reviews *Unbewältigte Vergangenheit* (1977), by East German historians, which points out that West German historians are "willing helpmates of monopoly capitalism." The work is useful because it does serve as a corrective to Western historiography, and it does show how Marxist-Leninist ideology affects historical writing. 9 notes.　　　　　　C. R. Lovin

1582. Dowd, Douglas F. MAKING HISTORY FROM THE LEFT. *Maryland Hist. 1981 12(2): 9-22.* Compares the work of the Marxist historians Immanuel Wallerstein and Perry Anderson within the context of a summary of radical historiography. Anderson introduced the global historical context for a revision of Marxist theory and Wallerstein's studies provide a Third World perspective for the analysis of capitalism. 11 notes. G. O. Gagnon

1583. Engelberg, Ernst. ÜBER GEGENSTAND UND ZIEL DER MARXISTISCH-LENINISTISCHEN GESCHICHTSWISSENSCHAFT [The subject and goal of Marxist-Leninist historiography]. *Zeitschrift für Geschichtswissenschaft [East Germany] 1968 16(9): 1117-1145.* The subject of Marxist-Leninist historiography cannot be rigid and unchanging as the bases of superstructures of various formations of society: economy, culture, ideology, and politics, show structural differences, the analysis of which has to be the humanistic sense of history which is finally achieved only after the introduction of communism.

1584. Faber, Karl-Georg. DIE GESCHICHTLICHE WELT UND DIE MARX'SCHE BASIS-ÜBERBAU-THEORIE [The historical world and the Marxian basis-superstructure theory]. *Hist. Zeitschrift [West Germany] 1974 Bieheft 3(Neue Folge): 47-73.* The methodological distinction between historical "basis" and "superstructure" lies at the heart of Marxist social theory. It creates problems in theory, however, especially the difficulty of classifying any group of historical phenomenon as "basic" or "superstructural." A close analysis of the concepts "relics" and "traditions" as sources of historical knowledge reveals that they reflect the theoretical intentions of "basis" and "superstructure." This analysis also shows that there can be no clear distinction between "basis" and "superstructure," which grew out of Marx's polemical tactics. 72 notes.
G. H. Davis

1585. Fricke, Dieter. GESCHICHTSWISSENSCHAFT UND GESCHICHTSBEWUSSTSEIN [Historical science and historical consciousness]. *Zeitschrift für Geschichtswissenschaft [East Germany] 1968 16(5): 624-630.* Theoretical discussion of the Marxist view of history, social historical consciousness, and the development of a socialist society.

1586. Galkin, I. S. VELIKAIA OKTIABR'SKAIA SOTSIALISTICHESKAIA REVOLIUTSIIA I BOR'BA IDEI V ISTORICHESKOI NAUKE NA SOVREMENNOM ETAPE [The Great October Socialist Revolution and the struggle of ideas in historical science at the present time]. *Vestnik Moskovskogo U., Seriia 8: Istoriia [USSR] 1977 (5): 14-25.* Discusses ways in which Soviet historians have fulfilled V. I. Lenin's command to carry on the ideological battle through historical science, with particular reference to Moscow State University's historians. The anti-Communism of US historians in the 1950's was channeled into attempts to construct non-Marxist visions of the future, such as W. Rostow's *Stages of Economic Growth* and Bell's conception of post-industrial society. These concepts, as well as those of historians who see historical development as dictated by anthropological and psychological factors, are attacked by Marxist-Leninists. Non-Marxist historians from nonsocialist countries, like Ernst Nolte from West Germany often adopt Marxist attitudes but are attacked for eclecticism and even sophisticated studies based on quantitative methods, such as Fogel and Engerman's study of American slavery, are criticized for the use of doubtful data. The author suggests that despite the quantitative growth of western historical research, many historians sell themselves as a marketable product. 26 notes. D. N. Collins

1587. Gawrecki, Dan. HISTORIOGRAFIE ČELEM K BUDOUCNOSTI [Historiography faces the future]. *Československý Časopis Hist. [Czechoslovakia] 1983 31(5): 744-747.* Reviews the festschrift by this title, dedicated to Jaroslav Purš, edited by Ondřej Felcman, Leoš Jeleček, Tomáš Vojtěch, and Josef Žemlička, and published in Prague by the Czechoslovak Academy of Sciences in 1982. More than 30 historians contributed discussions of Marxist historiography or its applications to specific problems in Czechoslovak and world history. R. E. Weltsch

1588. Glatz, Ferenc. MARXI ELMÉLET ÉS TÖRTÉNETI SZAKTUDOMÁNY [Marxist theory and the science of history]. *Történelmi Szemle [Hungary] 1983 26(3-4): 353-366.* Points out that Marx's ideas, including his thoughts on history, became known mainly through the interpretative, popularizing works of Mehring, Plekhanov, Bukharin, and above all Stalin, leading to a simplified and stereotyped version. The leaders and participants of the working-class movement had direct contact with his writings, but only with those that were concerned with the revolutionary events and periods. Western non-Marxist historians started to read Marx only following the 1960's. The future of Marxist history lies in the combination of the theoretical grounds of Marxism with the proper scholarly handling of evidence, and that can not only enhance historical insight but can also lead to changes in the historical methodology inherited from the 19th century. Based on a paper read at a conference held in Budapest on 20 May 1983 commemorating the centenary of the death of Marx. Russian and English summaries.
G. Jeszenszky

1589. Gottschling, Ernst. METHODOLOGISCHE FRAGEN DER MARXISTISCH-LENINISTISCHEN KRITIK BÜRGERLICHER IDEOLOGIE [Methodological questions of the Marxist-Leninist criticism of bourgeois ideology]. *Wissenschaftliche Zeitschrift der Ernst-Moritiz-Arndt-Universität Greifswald [East Germany] 1977 26(Sonderheft 1): 23-31.*

1590. Hall, Stuart. MARXISM AND CULTURE. *Radical Hist. Rev. 1978 (18): 5-14.* Presents several reasons for the recent interest in several areas of radical historical study, discussing in particular the role of Marxist historiography in the study of cultural and social history.

1591. Hartmann, Günter; Schneider, Kurt; and Berthold, Walter. GESCHICHTSWISSENSCHAFT UND GESCHICHTSBEWUSSTSEIN [Historical science and historical consciousness]. *Zeitschrift für Geschichtswissenschaft [East Germany] 1968 16(6): 769-773.* Discusses the relationship of the Marxist-Leninist concept of history and socialist historical consciousness.

1592. Hobsbawm, Eric J. MARX E LA CONOSCENZA STORICA [Karl Marx and historical knowledge]. *Studi Storici [Italy] 1983 24(3-4): 335-346.* Discusses Marx's materialist conception of history and its influence on past and present historical studies. Marx's work remains the essential basis of any historical analysis; his influence in nonsocialist countries is greater than ever. But in most countries Marx's work is the starting point, not the point of arrival of research. Today Marxist history is pluralistic and cannot be isolated from other historical reflection and research. 7 notes.
J. V. Coutinho

1593. Hroch, Miroslav. KOMPARATIVNÍ METODA V MARXISTICKÉ HISTORIOGRAFII. MOŽNOSTI A MEZE JEJÍHO VYUŽITÍ [Comparative method in Marxist historiography and its use]. *Československý Časopis Historický [Czechoslovakia] 1972 20(5): 631-647.* The use of comparative method in Marxist historiography could open further research for analogical historical situations, social development, and the relationship of the common and the extraordinary in history. However, this method cannot produce a universal change in modern historical research. Printed sources; 29 notes. G. E. Pergl

1594. Ivanov, V. V. PROBLEMA SOOTNOSHENIIA ISTORII I SOVREMENNOSTI V BURZHUAZNOI LITERATURE 60-KH GODOV [The relationship between history and the present in bourgeois literature of the 1960's]. *Voprosy Istorii [USSR] 1971 (11): 184-191.* A Marxist analysis of material published during the 1960's by Anglo-American, French, and West German historians, including publications from the 13th International Congress of Historical Sciences, which examine the relationship between history and the present day. Various methodological approaches are used to analyze the relationship between history and the social role of historical study, and politics. Primary sources; 38 notes. R. Permar

1595. Jaeck, Hans-Peter. PROBLEMS OF HISTORICAL EXPLANATION AND MARXIST THEORY OF SOCIETY AND HISTORICAL PROCESS. *Studia Hist. Oeconomicae [Poland] 1980 15: 21-27.* Examines the ways in which Karl Marx's early historical studies contributed to the origin of his theory of historical materialism and examines questions concerning the general methodology of history including historical explanation. The dialectical and materialist theory of history and society can be successful historical explanations.   G. L. Neville/S

1596. Kakhk, Iu. O NEKOTORYKH NOVYKH IAVLENIIAKH VO VZAIMOOTNOSHENIIAKH MARKSISTSKOI TEORII I BURZHUAZNOI ISTORICHESKOI NAUKI [Some new phenomena in relations between Marxist theory and bourgeois historical science]. *Eesti NSV Teaduste Akadeemia. Toimetised [USSR] 1977 26(4): 338-343.* Recent Western historiography is pessimistic, sees a "crisis of history," and is dissatisfied with the absence of a fundamental theory of historical science. Some historians express the necessity of using methods from sciences other than history or of fusing history and sociology. Marxism, to the contrary, is said to be the best theory for use in historical search. American historians, in using econometric methods and models of alternative development, were in essence repeating some of the principles applied by V. I. Lenin at the beginning of the 20th century. Marxist influence on bourgeois historiography increases each year.   J/S

1597. Kondratieva, T. S. O MATERIALISTICHESKOI TENDENTSII V ISTORIKO-SOTSIOLOGICHESKOI MYSLI FRANTSUZSKOGO PROSVESHCHENIIA [Materialistic trends in historical-sociological thoughts of the French Enlightenment]. *Vestnik Moskovskogo U., Seriia 9: Istoriia [USSR] 1972 27(4): 36-49.* Many bourgeois historians see in the philosophes of the Enlightenment not Karl Marx's forerunners but his "anticipators". They try to belittle the historical significance of Marx's discoveries. Marxist historians, while carrying on polemics with Western historians, are trying to determine objectively the place of the ideological inheritance of the Enlightenment in the development of sociohistorical thought. The author investigates some aspects of this unsolved problem by examining the ideas of Rousseau, Montesquiou, Diderot, Mornet, Voltaire, Turgo, Mellier, Mably, Morelli and Barnave. The link between the Enlightenment and dialectical materialism is that in the 18th century human thought already worked in the direction of Marx's discovery, i.e., there was already a tendency for the materialistic understanding of history. 50 notes.
    L. Kalinowski

1598. Kosarev, A. I. ISTORICHESKII FAKT, EGO PONIATIE I OPISANIE [Historical fact, its comprehension and description]. *Sovetskoe Gosudarstvo i Pravo [USSR] 1970 (7): 75-82.* Discusses the problems involved in determining what constitutes historical fact and in describing its essence: as opposed to the bourgeois approach, the Marxist one correctly emphasizes the complexity and proper context of each historical fact.

1599. Křížek, Jurij. NĚKTERÉ PROBLÉMY HISTORICKÉHO VÝZKUMU [Some problems of historical research]. *Československý Časopis Hist. [Czechoslovakia] 1982 30(6): 862-891.* Marxists recognize both the material preconditions of long-term social development and the significance of concrete processes, particular events, or even accidents. Only by giving careful attention to both aspects can historians contribute scientifically to a knowledge of society. A clear theoretical understanding and definition of the historical phenomenon under investigation will help the historian to avoid eclecticism or accumulations of undigested facts. Based on writings of Marx, Engels, Lenin, and Soviet theoreticians; 88 notes. Russian and German summaries.   R. E. Weltsch

1600. Küttler, Wolfgang. BEGRIFFSBILDUNG UND GESETZESPROBLEMATIK IN GESCHICHTE UND GESCHICHTSERKENNTNIS [Shaping of terms and problems of laws in history and historical perception]. *Zeits. für Geschichtswissenschaft [East Germany] 1981 29(9): 779-797.* A contribution to the contemporary discussion in East Germany of problems and requirements pertaining to research in socialist history, this lecture's theme encompasses the relations of concepts, theory, and the perception of laws in multiple connections. The comments focus on a few selected problem areas, introduced by a short summarization of previous Marxist research in the social sciences. The requirements for the creation of concepts and the assertion of laws in the historical process and research are examined and the system of generalized statements and ideas and their function in the Marxist-Leninist science

of history are discussed. Lecture given at the 3d Convention of the Departmental Commission on the Theory, Methodology and History of the Science of History of the Historical Society of East Germany in November 1980 in Berlin.   T. Parker

1601. Law, Robin. THE MARXIST APPROACH TO HISTORICAL EXPLANATION. *Tarikh [Nigeria] 1978 6(1): 40-50.* Outlines the basic Marxist model of historical interpretation as described by Karl Marx and discusses it as a theoretical method used in the writing of history.

1602. McLennan, Gregor. RICHARD JOHNSON AND HIS CRITICS, TOWARDS A CONSTRUCTIVE DEBATE. *Hist. Workshop Journal [Great Britain] 1979 8: 157-166.* The Louis Althusser standpoint in Richard Johnson's "Thompson, Genovese, and Socialist-Humanist History" (*Hist. Workshop* 1978 6: 79-100), is heavily qualified, and the arguments of his critics are undermined by their assumption of an "authentic Marxism" from which to theorize on the forces and relations of production. These inconsistencies are rooted in Marx's work itself. 3 notes.   C. B. Bailey

1603. Mogil'nitski, B. G. KARL MARKS I FRIDRIKH ENGEL'S—ISTORIKI ISTORICHESKOI NAUKI [Karl Marx and Friedrich Engels, historians of historical science]. *Novaia i Noveishaia Istoriia [USSR] 1984 (1): 3-18.* Discusses the materialistic interpretation of history by Marx and Engels. They introduced the class element as motive force in historical development and rejected the idealistic positivist philosophy of contemporaneous historians. The Marxist materialistic perception of history (expanded by Lenin) succeeded in debunking the tendentious falsifications of history in bourgeois historiography, particularly that of German historians of the late 19th century. 70 notes.   N. Frenkley

1604. Mogil'nitski, B. G. O SOTSIAL'NYKH FUNKTSIIAKH SOVREMENNOI BURZHUAZNOI ISTORICHESKOI NAUKI [The social functions of contemporary bourgeois historical science]. *Istoriia SSSR [USSR] 1978 (5): 189-206.* Reviews recent Western literature on the social functions of historical science. Marxist historiography seeks to deepen and enrich the knowledge of the past and to reveal fully all the cognitive possibilities of history. Bourgeois historiography falsifies the past in an effort to impede social progress and preserve capitalism. Contemporary bourgeois historiography finds itself in a condition of crisis for which there is no solution. As a result, contemporary bourgeois historians are emphasizing the limited possibilities for the social influence of historical science. 75 notes.   J. W. Long

1605. Nichițelea, Pamfil. PRESENTEISMUL ÎN GÎNDIREA ISTORICĂ CONTEMPORANĂ [Presentism in contemporary historical thought]. *Rev. de Istorie [Rumania] 1976 29(3): 413-429.* A Marxist analysis of the most widespread subjectivist-relativist theory of history, presentism. The main figures are Benedetto Croce, Charles Beard, Carl Becker, and Conyers Read. Croce's influence was in the direction of introducing subjective idealist views into contemporary historiography. The others introduced relativism via the "New History," negating the laws of history and rejecting historical materialism for presentism. Historical truth becomes a "noble dream," an illusion, necessitating the constant rewriting of history. Though it deals with real problems, presentism's relativism makes it overall a reactionary theory. Secondary sources; 52 notes.
    P. E. Michelson

1606. Nolte, Ernst; Kimber, Robert and Kimber, Rita, trans. THE RELATIONSHIP BETWEEN "BOURGEOIS" AND "MARXIST" HISTORIOGRAPHY. *Hist. & Theory 1975 14(1): 57-73.* There is a polarity between bourgeois and Marxist historiography to which every historian responds. But there are few differences between the two historiographies; their methodologies are not unalike nor are they direct opposites—each shares the common heritage of Western thought. They differ only on the question of skepticism addressed to the concept of a classless society, "an idea that is at the heart of Marxism . . . the one real dividing line between bourgeois and Marxist historiography." 44 notes.   D. A. Yanchisin

1607. Rüdiger, B. ÜBER PLATZ UND AUFGABEN DER QUELLENKUNDE IN DER MARXISTISCH-LENINISTISCHEN GESCHICHTSWISSENSCHAFT [The position and task of source studies in Marxist-Leninist historiography]. *Zeitschrift für Geschichtswissenschaft [East Germany] 1973 21(6): 679-683.*

1608. Santsevych, A. V. ZNACHENNIA I PRYNTSYPY SKLADANNIA KHRONIK Z ISTORII [The meaning and principles of compiling chronicles from history]. *Ukrains'kyi Istorychnyi Zhurnal [USSR] 1977 (5): 80-88.* Stresses the importance of following correct principles in compiling chronicles, quoting examples of post-1917 works, where the chronological approach of Marxism-Leninism has been used.

1609. Schleier, Hans. KOLLOQUIUM ZU PROBLEMEN DER METHODOLOGIE DER MARXISTISCH-LENINISTISCHEN GESCHICHTSWISSENSCHAFT [Colloquium on problems of methodology in Marxist-Leninist historiography]. *Zeitschrift für Geschichtswissenschaft [East Germany] 1970 18(9): 1192-1196.* Lists the contributors and summarizes the papers and discussions at the colloquium on problems of methodology of Marxist-Leninist historiography held in Berlin in June 1970. Some 100 scholars, including guests from many socialists countries, took part.

J. B. Street

1610. Shevchenko, V. METODOLOHIA I METODYKA ISTORYCHNYKH DOSLIDZHEN'. METODOLOHICHNI ASPEKTY VZAIEMOZV'IAZKU ISTORIYI TA SUCHASNOYI PARTIYNOHO BUDIVNYTSTVA [The methodology and method of historical research: the methodological aspects of studying historical roots and the present practice of Party work]. *Ukrains'kyi Istorychnyi Zhurnal [USSR] 1979 215(2): 51-60.* The Communist Party must constantly update its scientific forms and methods of work and, while keeping sight of its Marxist-Leninist origins, incorporate the achievements of the natural and social sciences into its methodology so it may have the advantage of the best methods for fulfilling policies of the Communist Party of the Soviet Union and building communism.

L. Djakowska

1611. Shishkin, A. F. ISTORIIA I NRAVSTVENNOSTY [History and morality]. *Voprosy Filosofii [USSR] 1978 (4): 130-142.* The most common accusation against Marxist theory since its inception is that it fatalistically views history and human actions. We cannot make concessions in understanding determinism, moderate it, or limit the field of its application contrary to Lenin's requirement. We can rightly estimate the services of historical figures only if we correctly understand social progress. Marxism requires, above all, that estimates of the historical activity of statesmen, religious reformers, and leaders of social movements should be based on the links of their activity with the position and interests of social classes and their role in the development of society in the historical epoch under review. Efforts to ensure peace and the security of nations require common standards of ethics.

J/S

1612. Smolenski, N. I. ISTORICHESKAIA DEISTVITEL'NOST' I ISTORICHESKOE PONIATIE [Historical reality and historical conception]. *Voprosy Istorii [USSR] 1979 (2): 3-15.* The basic content of this work consists in the attempt to prove that scientific historical conception emerges first of all as a reflection of the historical process in its developed form, of its maturest variant. Marx, Engels, and Lenin proceeded from the premise that the substance of historical categories depends on the degree of maturity of the historical process or of the thing reflected. A mature form of the historical process constitutes the basis of the concept in the sense that it opens the possibility of cognizing other phenomena of one and the same class both within the limits of one and the same epoch and in relation to the progressive development of history as a whole, every new stage in which serves as the starting point of cognizing the past. Primary sources; 61 notes.

J

1613. Stoianov, Zheliazko. KARL MARKS I NEKOTORYE METODOLOGICHESKIE PROBLEMY ISTORICHESKOI NAUKI [Karl Marx and some methodological problems of historiography]. *Bulgarian Hist. Rev. [Bulgaria] 1983 11(1): 3-21.* For Karl Marx historical science aimed to discover all forms of antagonism and ex-

ploitation in society. Political action could then be based on objective truth. Marx recognized that the Communist Party was devoted to objective truth, and therefore commitment to the Communist Party was logically a commitment to objective truth. He thus answered the objections of those theoreticians who argued that commitment to the Communist Party was incompatible with loyalty to objectivity. Marx specifically denounced subjectivism and relativism. Thus Marxist theory enjoins Party commitment as a prerequisite of profound socialist change. Based on Marx's works and secondary material; 53 notes.

A. J. Evans

1614. Stoianov, Zheliazko. KARL MARKS I NIAKOI TEORETICHESKI PROBLEMI NA ISTORICHESKATA NAUKA [Karl Marx and some theoretical problems of history]. *Istoricheski Pregled [Bulgaria] 1978 34(2): 4-23.* Discusses some problems of historiography in the light of Marxism, analyzing the role of sources in historical understanding, the nature and place of facts in historical investigation, and the mutual relationship between objectivity and subjectivity in historical understanding. Marxism-Leninism is a powerful historical tool in the service of the proletarian class. Based on the works of Marx, Friedrich Engels, V. I. Lenin, and other authors; 88 notes.

F. B. Chary

1615. Stojanov, Željazko. ON THE NATURE OF DESCRIPTION IN HISTORICAL COGNITION. *Bulgarian Hist. Rev. [Bulgaria] 1977 5(2): 93-99.* Analyzes historical description from a Marxist viewpoint, relating it to historical events, facts, and explanation. Historical facts are socially-important historical events established by the historian and whose authenticity is demonstrated by their reflection in concrete historical sources. These facts form the starting point in every historical description, whose main functions are the systematization of historical facts followed by the designation of the results. Description and explanation are interdependent. Cites modern theoretical works in English and Russian. 23 notes.

E. M. Sirriyeh

1616. Streisand, Joachim. DIE MARXISTISCH-LENINISTISCHE GESCHICHTSWISSENSCHAFT ALS GESELLSCHAFTSWISSENSCHAFT UND IHRE BEZIEHUNGEN ZU DEN NATURWISSENSCHAFTEN [Marxist-Leninist historiography as part of the social sciences and its relation to the natural sciences]. *Zeitschrift für Geschichtswissenschaft [East Germany] 1973 21(3): 289-300.*

1617. Streisand, Joachim. GESCHICHTSBILD UND GESCHICHTSBEWUSSTSEIN BEI DER GESTALTUNG DER ENTWICKELTEN SOZIALISTISCHEN GESELLSCHAFT [Historical image and historical consciousness in the formation of a developed socialist society]. *Zeitschrift für Geschichtswissenschaft [East Germany] 1969 17(1-2): 33-51.* Marxist-Leninist historiography and the creation of socialist consciousness are interrelated in the task of working out a historical image showing that the progressive trends of German history have reached their culmination in the creation of the East German state.

1618. Streisand, Joachim. GESCHICHTSBILD—GESCHICHTSBEWUSSTSEIN — GESCHICHTSWISSENSCHAFT [Historical image—historical consciousness—historical science]. *Zeitschrift für Geschichtswissenschaft [East Germany] 1967 15(5): 822-834.* Analyzes East German historiography as one of the means to strengthen historical knowledge of the confrontation between the classes and class interests for the establishment of an internationalist socialist historical consciousness.

1619. Strel's'kyi, V. I. VIDBIR FAKTIV PRY ISTORYCHNOMU DOSLIDZHENNI V SVITLI LENINS'KOI TEORII PIZNANNIA [The selection of facts in historical research in the light of Lenin's theory of knowledge]. *Ukrains'kyi Istorychnyi Zhurnal [USSR] 1975 (6): 37-44.* Explains dialectical materialism and its use as a starting point for all research in history and the social sciences, with reference to V. I. Lenin's writings and Soviet historiography, 1917-75.

1620. Thai, Nghiem Van. MAY NET VE SU HOC TRONG THOI DAI NGAY NAY [Some traits of current historiography at the present time]. *Nghien Cuu Lich Su [Vietnam] 1981 (6): 58-64.*

Rejects the faulty and reactionary views of bourgeois and colonialist theoreticians and historians toward historical science and presents a summary of the struggle of historical Marxist views, especially of Soviet historians, in recent decades.   J/S

1621. Topolski, Jerzy. INSPIRACJE LENINOWSKIE W BADANIACH HISTORYCZNYCH [Leninist inspiration in historical research]. *Nowe Drogi [Poland]* 1975 (4): 23-33. Surveys Lenin's historical writings and the method by which he linked theory and practice, indicating their importance as a source of inspiration for all Marxist historians.

1622. Topolski, Jerzy. LENINE ET LES SCIENCES HISTORIQUES [Lenin and the historical sciences]. *Acta Poloniae Hist. [Poland]* 1970 22: 5-17. Lenin elaborated the revolutionary theory of historical materialism whose two principal theories were the theory of the revolution and the theory of unequal development of capitalism. The author analyzes Lenin's theory of the historical process in the field of general historical sciences and explains the necessity of the historical method for the construction of the mentioned theory. Based on Lenin's works; 18 notes.
                    H. Heitzman-Wojcicki

1623. Topolski, Jerzy. METHODOLOGICAL PROBLEMS OF APPLICATIONS OF THE MARXIST THEORY TO HISTORICAL RESEARCH. *Social Res.* 1980 47(3): 458-478. Karl Marx's historical materialistic theories of the process of history, of transformations of that process, and of socioeconomic formations provide the historian with certain methodological directives; G. Bois's *Crise du Feodalisme* (1976), an analysis of the feudal formation, while it successfully follows most of the directives derived from Marx's theories, fails to take into account conclusions that follow from the directive of combining the objective and the subjective factors (in this case the relation between feudal incomes and feudal needs) when formulating a historical synthesis.

1624. Topolski, Jerzy. WSPOŁCZESNE PROBLEMY METODOLOGICZNE NAUK HISTORYCZNYCH [Contemporary methodological problems of historical sciences]. *Kwartalnik Historyczny [Poland]* 1974 81(3): 528-545. A review of major philosophical-methodological trends in contemporary historiography stresses Marxism and the conceptions which try to combine Marxism and non-Marxism. Among the new concepts are noteworthy theories based on Christian philosophy. Also deals with three methodological tendencies of contemporary historiography: 1) the tendency toward interdisciplinary approaches, notably in social history, 2) models in the new economic history, and 3) quantification. Biblio.
                    H. Heitzman-Wojcicki

1625. Vasilev, Kiril. LENIN I NYAKOI METODOLOGICHESKI PROBLEMI NA ISTORICHESKATA NAUKA [Lenin and some methodological problems of historical science]. *Izvestiia na Inst. po Istoriia na BKP [Bulgaria]* 1970 23: 5-79. Analyzes several contemporary problems of methodology within Russian and Bulgarian Marxist historical theory and practice. Leninism serves as the key to solving problems of integrating history with philosophy, mathematics, sociology, and psychology, through unifying traditional methods of research with the most recent trends. Bulgarian historians have not fully absorbed V. I. Lenin's example of applying statistics and mathematics in historical study, nor his early form of systems theory. 162 notes.   C. S. Masloff

1626. Voskanian, A. M. and Navasardian, R. G. V. I. LENINE EV PATMAGITUTYAN METODOLOGIAKAN MI KANI HARTSER [V. I. Lenin and certain methodological problems in historiography]. *Patma-Banasirakan Handes. Istoriko-Filologicheskii Zhurnal [USSR]* 1969 (2): 15-28. After 1893 Lenin opposed the subjective-idealistic approach of the pre-Marxian historiographers and based his theory of class struggle on a scientific interpretation of history. He discovered that the study of history and social relations were inseparable from the practical problems of class struggle.

1627. Wiener, Jonathan M. [*SOCIAL ORIGINS OF DICTATORSHIP AND DEMOCRACY*]. *Hist. and Theory* 1976 15(2): 146-175. The radical loner, Barrington Moore, Jr., offered a neo-

Marxian alternative to the prevailing modernization theories in his *Social Origins of Dictatorship and Democracy* (Boston: Beacon Pr., 1966). His three divergent routes to the modern world—bourgeois revolution, revolution from above, and peasant revolution—have become progressively more popular since his work's original publication in 1966. "Moore's theory focuses on social classes as the crucial units of analysis. It rests on the implicit Marxian thesis that particular classes favor political structures which protect or further their socio-economic interests." Discussions of Moore's thesis in the last 10 years have been of five kinds: 1) debate over method, 2) consideration of conceptual issues, 3) efforts to situate Moore as a theorist, 4) examinations of case studies, and 5) new applications. 158 notes.   D. A. Yanchisin

1628. Zhukov, E. M. [V. I. LENIN AND THE HISTORICAL METHOD].
—. V. I. LENIN I METODOLOGICHESKIE OSNOVY ISTORICHESKOI NAUKI [V. I. Lenin and the methodological base of the science of history]. *Novaia i Noveishaia Istoriia [USSR]* 1970 (2): 7-17. The foundation and development of Soviet historical science is inextricably bound up with Lenin, whose works are the basis for all subsequent Marxist historical studies, especially concerning economics and politics. Anti-Marxist historians have attempted to falsify history in various ways, and Lenin fought against their subjective and idealistic falsifications. Based on the collected works of Lenin; 30 notes.
                    L. Smith
—. LENIN, ISTORIIA, SOVREMENNOST' [Lenin, history, modernity]. *Novaia i Noveishaia Istoriia [USSR]* 1970 (4): 3-11. Though not a professional historian, Lenin was capable of examining historical data with assiduity, detecting the most important tendencies in any epoch. Based on Lenin's writings; 11 notes.
                    D. N. Collins

1629. —. [J. H. HEXTER'S CRITIQUE OF CHRISTOPHER HILL'S HISTORICAL METHODS]. *J. of British Studies* 1979 19(1): 122-136.
Palmer, William G. THE BURDEN OF PROOF: J. H. HEXTER AND CHRISTOPHER HILL, *pp. 122-129*. Denies J. H. Hexter's charge that Christopher Hill, in his studies of 17th-century England, has tailored evidence to fit a Marxist model. Hill no longer treats history in bald Marxist terms, but concedes that it is an interfusion of materialism, idealism, and many other variables. Hexter overlooks weaknesses in his own work similar to those of which he accuses Hill. 26 notes.
Hexter, J. H. REPLY TO MR. PALMER: A VISION OF FILES, *pp. 130-136*. Hill is a prisoner of his filing system. He continues to use categories of evidence established 40 years ago. Although Hill may, as Palmer claims, have renounced his early monocular view of history, he ignored contradictory data because they were not in his files. 7 notes.   D. M. Cregier

1630. —. O NEKOTORYKH VOPROSAKH METODOLOGII ISTORII KPSS [Problems in the methodology of the history of the CPSU]. *Voprosy Istorii KPSS [USSR]* 1977 (5): 97-104.
Duchenko, N. V., *pp. 97-100*. Discusses the methodology of Marxist scholarship on the history of the Communist Party of the Soviet Union. The principle of Party loyalty requires of the historian a conscious defense of the interests of the proletariat.
Zlobin, V. I., *pp. 100-104*. The author supports the principle of Party loyalty; however, no distinct historical methodology exists for the study of Party history. Based on the published works of Marx, Engels, Lenin, and Leonid Brezhnev; 20 notes.
                    L. E. Holmes

The Annales School

1631. Abosch, Heinz. ZWEIFEL AM ENGAGEMENT: ENTTÄUSCHTE FRANZÖSISCHE INTELLEKTUELLE [Doubts about commitment: disillusioned French intellectuals]. *Schweizer Monatshefte [Switzerland]* 1982 62(5): 387-391. The works of French historians like Fernand Braudel, Georges Duby, and Emmanuel Le Roy Ladurie all represent a giving up of empty doctrines and the belief in "historical laws" for concentration on regional details, history being interpreted in a multi-dimensional structural way.

1632. Afanas'ev, Iu. N. EVOLIUTSIIA TEORETICHESKIKH OS- NOV SHKOLY "ANNALOV" [Evolution of the theoretical basis of the *Annales* school]. *Voprosy Istorii [USSR] 1981 (9): 77-92.* Analyzes the methodological principles of the French historians associated with the *Annales* journal from its inception in 1929 to our day in the context of contemporary historiography. Discussing their theoretical and concrete historical studies, he singles out three main stages in the development of this school.   J

1633. Afanas'ev, Iu. N. VCHERA I SEGODNIA FRANT- SUZSKOI *NOVOI ISTORICHESKOI NAUKI* [The past and present of France's *Nouvelle Histoire*]. *Voprosy Istorii [USSR] 1984 (8): 32-50.* The traditions of the *Annales* school and its founders, Marc Bloch and Lucien Febvre, are being consistently developed within the *Nouvelle Histoire* framework. Its essentially broader range of problems and more precise methods of analysis greatly contributed to enlarging the body of historical knowledge. F. Braudel, C. Mazoric, G. Duby, J. Le Goff, and other historians of the *Nouvelle Histoire* school widely draw on the best traditions of the *Annales* school. However, the last 15 years have seen some negative developments as well: revision of some traditional propositions and conceptions, increased doubts about the possibility of objective historical knowledge, excessive interest in a form, and subjective idealism. Some scholars (F. Furent, E. Le Roy Ladurie, and P. Veyne, among others) even resorted to anti-Marxist pronouncements.   J

1634. Aymard, Maurice. LES *ANNALES* ET L'ITALIE *[Annales* and Italy]. *Mélanges de l'Ecole Française de Rome. Moyen Age- Temps Modernes [Italy] 1981 93(1): 401-417.* Analyzes the success of the journal *Annales: Economies, Sociétés, Civilisations* in Italy from the beginning. Describes the creation of an *Annales* network and the place occupied by Italy and Italians in the periodical and school, as well as the resistance of academic circles in terms of Franco-Italian scientific and cultural relations.

1635. Bartolommei, Sergio and Spini, Andrea. "DISCORSI" E "RIVOLUZIONI": LA STORIA DEI "NOUVEAUX HISTO- RIENS" ["Discourses" and "revolutions": the history of France's "new historians"]. *Riv. Critica di Storia della Filosofia [Italy] 1979 34(1): 26-34.* Reviews *Discours, histoire et révolutions* (1975) by Jean-Marie Goulemot and discusses the attempts by contemporary French historians to redefine their aims, methods, and problems and to unify the discourse of and on history by a practice which understands the writing of. history as a theoretico-ideological construction.

1636. Battini, Michele. VIS A TERGO. CIVILTA, SOCIETA E STORIA SECONDO E. DURKHEIM E M. MAUSS [Look behind: civilization, society, and history according to E. Durkheim and M. Mauss]. *Storia della Storiografia [Italy] 1983 (4): 30-70.* Traces the influence of Emile Durkheim and his nephew Marcel Mauss on 20th-century French historiography, particularly the *Annales* school. However, Fernand Braudel and the other *Annales* historians developed only one of many possible implications of the sociologists' work. Another was the opposed structuralism of Claude Lévi-Strauss. 91 notes. French and German summaries.
                                    R. Grove

1637. Blumenau, S. F. "ANNALY" I PROBLEMY FRANT- SUZSKOI BURZHUAZNOI REVOLIUTSII KONTSA XVIII VEKA *[Les annales* and problems of the French bourgeois revolution of the late 18th century]. *Vestnik Moskovskogo U., Seriia 8: Istoriia [USSR] 1978 (3): 68-87.* A critique of the French historical journal *Annales, économies, sociétés, civilisations* from the Soviet standpoint, and of the school of historians connected with it, who in the 1960's reassessed the French Revolution. In attempting to pull bourgeois history out of the rut of narrowly political history, the *Annales* school placed more attention on economic and social matters. The author follows editorial policy from 1946 onwards and

considers changes in the traditional interpretations of the French Revolution. Based on articles in *Annales* and secondary works; 104 notes.   D. N. Collins

1638. Bogucka, Maria. NOWA HISTORIA ["New history"]. *Kwartalnik Hist. [Poland] 1976 63(4): 896-902.* A review of a French collection of 33 essays entitled *Faire de l'histoire* (Paris: Gallimard, 1974). The essays postulate a radical renovation of history and seem to present a self-analysis of the work of French historians from the circle of *Annales*, influenced by Bloch, Febvre and Braudel. The "new history" breaks with traditional problems and approaches and with old objects of historical studies. It is linked with quantitative methods and wants to analyze mass events rather than single ones. The second volume discusses new methods of study in archaeology, economy, demography, history of art while Vol. 3 presents new objects of study, such as climate, the subconsciousness, language, health, and public opinion. 44 notes.
                                    H. Heitzman-Wojcicka

1639. Boia, Lucian. L'HISTORIOGRAPHIE ROUMAINE: ET L'ECOLE DES "ANNALES": QUELQUES INTERFERENCES [Romanian historiography and the *Annales* school: some interferences]. *Analele U. București: Istorie [Romania] 1979 28: 31- 40.* The "new history," of which the French journal *Annales: Economies, Sociétés, Civilisations* is the most outstanding and representative example, is not an exclusively French product. Much has been written about its influence outside France but nothing on its relations with Romanian historiography, with which it had very close contact especially between the two wars. Romanian historians made a substantial contribution to the new study. 21 notes.
                                    J. V. Coutinho

1640. Bruneau, William A. AN APOLOGIA FOR BIOGRAPHY IN FRENCH HISTORY. *Pro. of the Ann. Meeting of the Western Soc. for French Hist. 1980 8: 568-576.* Argues that *Annales* historians have concentrated too exclusively on such topics as social structures, quantification, and anthropology. They have nearly killed the art of biography among professional French historians. A middle ground is possible, one that would combine an awareness of broad social and economic structures with the role of individuals. 23 notes.   T. J. Schaeper

1641. Bulhof, Ilse N. THE COSMOPOLITAN ORIENTATION TO HISTORY AND FERNAND BRAUDEL. *Clio 1981 11(1): 49- 63.* Uses Fernand Braudel's *Capitalism and Material Life 1400-1800* (1967) to demonstrate the potential and advantages of the cosmopolitan approach to writing history. By widening his investigative scope to include non-Western peoples and cultures, the cosmopolitan historian can escape the self-centered confines of his own civilization, as Braudel does in his work. Braudel uses the entire world as a stage, not just Western civilization. 27 notes.
                                    T. P. Linkfield

1642. Burguière, André. HISTÓRIA DE UNA HISTÓRIA: EL NACIMIENTO DE *ANNALES* [Story of a history: the birth of *Annales*]. *Rev. Española de Investigaciones Sociológicas [Spain] 1980 (12): 21-36.* *Annales: Économies, Sociétés, Civilisations,* born *Annales d'Histoire Économique et Sociale,* is unusual in many ways; it is history that combines the social sciences, its direct and polemic style invites discussion, so that even its enemies have become part of the group surrounding *Annales,* it approaches history from the present and then goes into the past, and it is an economic and psychological (rather than the conventional political and diplomatic) approach to history.

1643. Cantù, Francesca. ASPETTI DI METODOLOGIA DELLA RICERCA NELLA STORIOGRAFIA DELLE *ANNALES* [Aspects of research methodology in the historiography of the *Annales* school]. *Mélanges de l'École Française de Rome. Moyen Age- Temps Modernes [Italy] 1981 93(1): 433-455.* The research methodology of the *Annales* school is characterized by interdisciplinarity, attention to new frontiers of study and interpretation, and a focus on epistemological problems; within this context, examines two methodological and epistemological models: that of quantitative and serial history and that of conceptualizing history.

1644. Civolani, Eva. SOLLECITAZIONI METODOLOGICHE DELLE *ANNALES* NELLA STORIOGRAFIA DEL MOVIMENTO OPERAIO IN ITALIA [Methodological impulses from *Annales* in the historiography of the workers' movement in Italy]. *Mélanges de l'Ecole Française de Rome. Moyen Age-Temps Modernes [Italy] 1981 93(1): 419-432.* Many obstacles have delayed the meeting of the historiography of the Italian workers' movement and the methodology of the journal *Annales: Economies, Sociétés, Civilisations,* including different intellectual and philosophical traditions and different understandings of relevant concepts like social class, causality in history, and model.

1645. Dubuc, Alfred. L'INFLUENCE DE L'ÉCOLE DES ANNALES AU QUÉBEC [The influence of the *Annales* school in Quebec]. *Rev. d'Hist. de l'Amérique Française [Canada] 1979 33(3): 357-386.* The *Annales* school began to influence Quebec historians and sociologists in the 1950's, reaching a peak with the work of Jean Hamelin and Fernand Ouellet on social and economic history and the history of attitudes. That influence has waned since the late 1960's, due to competition from other schools of historiography, notably the Marxist one. 98 notes. R. Aldrich

1646. Elmore, Richard. VIEW FROM THE RIVE GAUCHE: A COMMENT ON *ANNALES* HISTORIOGRAPHY. *Psychohistory Rev. 1978 7(2): 30-35.* Assesses the contributions of the group of French historians known as the *Annales* school, such as Marc Bloch, Lucien Febvre and their successors. Argues that psychoanalytic theory has not been utilized by *Annales* historians because they minimize the importance of individual historical actors in favor of explanation based on economic, sociological, and group psychological theories. Reviews recent writings of the *Annales* school and asserts that their emphasis on such "contextual factors" as location, class, production, and mentality in determining human behavior continue in the *Annales* tradition. Argues that the *Annales* might profit by inclusion of historians who blend contemporary social and behavioral sciences in creating new history. J. M. Herrick

1647. Esteva, Juan. LA HISTORIA Y EL ACTUAL DEBATE EPISTEMOLÓGICO [History and the current epistemological debate]. *Bol. de la Soc. Española de Hist. de la Farmacia [Spain] 1980-81 31-32(124-125): 287-297.* History, the Cinderella of epistemology, did not abandon the determinist-positivist approach—as other sciences had already done—until Lucien Febvre and Marc Bloch, with their *Annales* school, introduced a new methodology.

1648. Faber, Karl-Georg. COGITO ERGO SUM HISTORICUS NOVUS: BEMERKUNGEN ZU "DIE GESCHICHTE DER ANNALES, ERZÄHLT VON FRANÇOIS FURET" [I think, therefore I am a new historian: remarks on the history of the *Annales,* told by François Furet]. *Hist. Zeits. [West Germany] 1983 236(3): 529-537.* From the introduction to François Furet's *L'Atelier de l'Histoire* (1982) it is not clear whether the methodology of the *Annales* school led or just accompanied the transformation of historical investigation to a more scientific, total view. Distinctions between "events history" and "structural history" are not as clear as *Annales* theoreticians once proclaimed. G. H. Davis

1649. Fontana i Làzaro, Josep. ASCENS I DECADÈNCIA DE L'ESCOLA DELS "ANNALES" [Rise and decline of the *Annales* school]. *Orígens del capitalisme* (Esplugues de Llobregat: Editorial Ariel, 1974): 283-298. Following Henri Pirenne (1862-1935), who claimed that historiographical theorizing could be based on erudition, Lucien Fèbvre (1878-1956) and Marc Bloch (1886-1944) founded the journal, *Annales,* in which history is defined as the science of man's diverse activities and creations, for which the tools would be supplied by other disciplines. Fernand Braudel's *La Méditerranée* (1949) was an important attempt to utilize the *Annales* definition and formula, which states that history has various temporal rhythms. But the relations among these parallel rhythms are not noticed by Braudel. The indiscriminate use of new tools (computers, etc.), that dismiss *a priori* theories, is bringing about the decline of the *Annales* school. J. M. (IHE 94175)

1650. Furet, François. BEYOND THE *ANNALES*. *J. of Modern Hist. 1983 55(3): 389-410.* The intellectual legacy of *Annales* ("more than a journal—and less than a doctrine") "was a simple and powerful idea: history was to be freed to wander in every field." Beyond that, *Annales* historians have "offered an almost boundless range of topics and methods..." Unifying that diversity, however, is their common belief that "history absorbs the social sciences instead of simply representing the temporal dimension of those sciences." Concomitant with the spread of *Annales* ideas, all but traditional historians have tended to abandon the study of given periods in favor of particular issues or problems, including those previously considered outside the purview of history: the ones exhibiting immobility over time. This, again, has partly been the legacy of the social sciences. J. D. Hunley

1651. Horsgor, Michael. TOTAL HISTORY: THE *ANNALES* SCHOOL. *J. of Contemporary Hist. [Great Britain] 1978 13(1): 1-13.* Traian Stoianovich's *French Historical Method, The Annales Paradigm* (Ithaca: Cornell U. Pr., 1976) surveys the techniques of the current French *Annales* school of history led by Fernand Braudel. France now ranks with Greece and Germany in masterful innovation in historiography. The *Annales* method is shaped around a trinity: serialism, the critical examination of very long trends in demographic or economic processes; structuralism, the analysis of the impact of conjunctures, that is factors of cyclical or oscillatory movement; and functionalism, the study of the interaction of the three traditional fields of interest—economies, societies, and civilizations—the dynamics of their triple relationship, and their hierarchical and dialectical interdependence. Braudel himself now recognizes the weakness of the *Annales* school, its neglect of political history. Political-historical studies are being produced. The motif of the *Annales* is "History is the science of the sciences of man." 25 notes. M. P. Trauth

1652. Kudrna, Jaroslav. IDEOLOGISCHE ASPEKTE UND METHODOLOGISCHE GRUNDLAGEN DER FRANZÖSISCHEN "ANNALES" SCHULE [Ideological aspects and methodological foundations of the French *Annales* school]. *Zeits. für Geschichtswissenschaft [East Germany] 1981 29(3): 195-204.* Describes the founding of the *Annales* school of historiography in France in the 1920's and its influence on methodological discussions among historians elsewhere. *Annales'* supporters attacked the style of political historiography which, transferred by Gabriel Monod, was a direct descendant of the methodology of Leopold von Ranke. Examines the birth of the *Annales* as a reaction to the economic and social crisis of the capitalist system of the 1930's. Some look at the historiography reflected in the *Annales* as writing of the crisis and recession of the colonial empires. But its orientation on stable epochs marks the school as basically conservative. 53 notes. G. E. Pergl

1653. Kudrna, Jaroslav. K NĚKTERÝM ASPEKTŮM GENEZE METOD ŠKOLY ANNALES [Some aspects of the genesis of the methods of the Annales school]. *Sborník Prací Filosofické Fakulty Brněnské U.: Řada Hist. [Czecholsovakia] 1980 29(27): 131-142.* The modern French Annales School of historiography owes much to certain 19th-century historians and to sociology, the integration of sociological methods and models coming much later in France than in Russia.

1654. LeRoy Ladurie, Emmanuel. DIX ANNÉES DE RECHERCHES HISTORIQUES [Ten years of historical research]. *Histoire [France] 1978 (2): 60-65.* Examines a decade of work on medieval and modern history. Some recent studies have increased our understanding of social groups, attitudes, and mores. History is a strict but literary discipline which must call on the imagination and offer reading pleasure as well. J

1655. LeRoy Ladurie, Emmanuel. RECENT HISTORICAL "DISCOVERIES." *Daedalus 1977 106(4): 141-155.* Since history rests at the center of an interdisciplinary approach, the term discoveries may be inaccurate. There have been several finds in the recent decade. Historical sociology of specific groups has been an active area and focused on such groups as the Breton nobility or the French army. Social history has moved to the study of minorities (Basques,

Occitans, and Jurassians) and of majorities (peasants). Historians have begun investigations of sex practices, eating patterns, or beliefs on death—areas formerly covered by ethnologists. Quantitative history also has become a major field. Secondary sources; 5 notes.

E. MacCarthy

1656. Mauro, Frederic. OS ESTUDOS HISTÓRICOS EM FRANÇA: DECLÍNIO OU EVOLUÇÃO? [French historical studies: decline or evolution?]. *Rev. de Hist.* [Brazil] 1974 49(99): 5-14. Speculates on the future of French historiography in the wake of the success of the *Annales* school of French historical studies. The increasing popularity of the discipline may cause a deterioration in the quality of French historical work, and a vulgarization evidenced by popularization of history in nonprofessional journals and audiovisual presentations. Balancing this pessimism is an optimistic climate for future French historical studies. In addition to being the vanguard for the "new" social history, French historians are continuing to make important contributions to interpretation of French history.

C. A. Preece

1657. Moote, A. Lloyd. THE ANNALES HISTORIANS. *Queen's Q.* [Canada] 1978 85(3): 496-504. Review article prompted by Traian Stoianovich, *French Historical Method: The Annales Paradigm* (Ithaca: Cornell U. Pr., 1976) and Robert Forster and Orest Ranum, eds., *Family and Society: Selections from the Annales: Économies, Sociétés, Civilizations*, translated by Elborg Forster and Patricia M. Ranum (Baltimore: Johns Hopkins U. Pr., 1976). Comments on the impact of the school of historiography which grew up around the journal *Annales*, founded 1929, and on Stoianovich's treatment of the subject. In the last decade this highly influential school has perhaps become more flexible, while continuing its healthy opposition to a narrative history which uncritically attempts to derive one year's "big stories" from those of the preceding year.

L. W. Van Wyk

1658. Motoike, Ritsu. "ANARU" ENO MICHI: FURANSU NO DENTÔTEKI REKISHIGAKU HIHAN [The road to the *Annales* school: a criticism of traditional historiography in France]. *Shisō (Iwanami Shoten)* [Japan] 1982 (702): 14-30. The *Annales* school was generated from critical reviews of traditional historiography in *Année Sociologique* and *Revue de Synthèse Historique*, which attacked not positivism but the history of ordinary events. The *Annales* school was established through the efforts to overcome old schools by eagerly absorbing methods and findings of the humanities. 30 notes.

S. Hayashida

1659. Pillorget, René. FROM A CLASSICAL TO A SERIAL AND QUANTITATIVE STUDY OF HISTORY: SOME NEW DIRECTIONS IN FRENCH HISTORICAL RESEARCH. *Durham U. J.* [Great Britain] 1977 69(2): 207-216. The 1929 founding of the journal *Annales d'histoire economique et sociale* (now *Annales: Economies, Sociétés, Civilisations*) by Marc Bloch and Lucien Febvre signaled the formation of a new school of French historians who emphasize economic and social history.

1660. Ratcliffe, Barrie M. THE DECLINE OF BIOGRAPHY IN FRENCH HISTORIOGRAPHY: THE AMBIVALENT LEGACY OF THE *ANNALES* TRADITION. *Pro. of the Ann. Meeting of the Western Soc. for French Hist.* 1980 8: 556-567. Even though the trend had started earlier, the *Annales* school of history that arose in the late 1920's turned French historiography even further away from the writing of biographies. With a few exceptions, *Annales* writers have avoided discussing individuals and have concentrated instead on such things as climate, geography, and long-term developments. In recent years some scholars have noted various deficiencies in the *Annales* approach, and today there are signs of an increasing interest in narrative and biography among professional historians. 72 notes.

T. J. Schaeper

1661. Renzi, Paolo. DEGLI INCONTRI MARGINALI DI UN NUOVOTIPO, OVVERO: LE "ANNALES" E LA STORIOGRAFIA ITALIANA [Marginalia of a new type, or, *Annales* and Italian historiography]. *Nuova Riv. Storica* [Italy] 1979 63(5-6): 635-667. Discusses a conference dealing with the impact of the *Annales*

School of French historiography on Italian historical thought and practice. The conference was sponsored by the École Français de Rome in 1979.

J. J. Renaldo

1662. Revel, Jacques. HISTOIRE ET SCIENCES SOCIALES: LES PARADIGMES DES *ANNALES* [History and the social sciences: the *Annales* paradigms]. *Ann.: Écon., Soc., Civilisations* [France] 1979 34(6): 1360-1376. Examines the nature of the *Annales* paradigm. At present, we lack the sociological studies needed to understand more clearly the nature, over the last 50 years, of the movement which has coalesced around the journal founded by Marc Bloch and Lucien Febvre. The identity of *Annales* is undoubtedly bound up with a scientific project, a network, institutions, a form of sensibility; still, it has undergone some marked changes. This article seeks to understand the logic behind these changes by analyzing the shifting relations between history and the social sciences over the last half century. These relations are explicitly at the heart of the *Annales* enterprise, and they help us to understand the shifts and adjustments of an intellectual policy. 25 notes.

J

1663. Romano, Sergio. LE *ANNALES* E L'ITALIA, STORIA DI METODI E STORIA DI "ATTORI" [The *Annales* school and Italy: history of methods and history of actors]. *Mélanges de l'École Française de Rome. Moyen Age-Temps Modernes* [Italy] 1981 93(1): 457-463. Italian historians tend to write history as the life of an actor's—the people of God, the nation, the proletariat; whereas the French historians of the *Annales* school see history as the development of human techniques.

1664. Roos, Marjoke de. DE ONTKETENDE GESCHIEDENIS [Unleashed history]. *Spiegel Hist.* [Netherlands] 1981 16(10): 556-560. A discussion of the work of the French School for Advanced Studies and Social Sciences during the 1970's. The school has gone beyond the economic and demographic orientation of Fernand Braudel and Marc Bloch to develop an integral history that employs psychology, anthropology, and social theory. Discusses the works of Jacques Le Goff and Emmanuel Le Roy Ladurie. 7 illus.

C. W. Wood, Jr.

1665. Ruiz Martín, Felipe. EL CINCUENTENARIO DE *ANNALES: ÉCONOMIES, SOCIÉTÉS, CIVILISATIONS* [The semicentennial of *Annales: Économies, Sociétés, Civilisations*]. *Rev. Española de Investigaciones Sociológicas* [Spain] 1980 (12): 9-14. Under Lucien Febvre and Marc Bloch, the *Annales* achieved international standing early, bringing the French school of historiography to the rest of the world; their purpose was an integration of the social sciences.

1666. Schueler, Klaus. DIE TENDENZEN DER NEUEREN FRANZOESISCHEN HISTORIOGRAPHIE UND IHRE BEWERTUNG: EIN UEBERBLICK [Tendencies in recent French historiography and its evaluation: an overview]. *Geschichte in Wissenschaft und Unterricht* [West Germany] 1968 19(4): 229-233. In this century French historiography has developed into a social science from a positive science. The main impulse came in the 1920's from the journal *Annales*, which integrated economic and social history, demography, geography, and psychology. Despite some criticism, the approach of the *Annales* school prevails strongly in French historiography. Critics such as Jacques Droz fear an overemphasis on economic facts, but admit the great methodological advantages of the *Annales* approach. The criticism of some German historians such as Theodor Schieder and Gerhard Ritter results from a difference of approach: French historians turn their interest to the social aspects of history while German historians tend to stress the personal and state-political aspects. 21 notes.

L. H. Schmidt

1667. Takeoka, Yuriharu. *ANNALES* SCHOOL AND SERIAL HISTORY. *Shakai-Keizai-Shigaku* [Japan] 1978 44(4): 28-39. Offers a background of the development of serial history, outlining its basic tenets, and compares it with quantitative methods of economic history focusing on how each method deals with conflict and historical analysis, 1950's-70's.

1668. Wallerstein, Immanuel. BRAUDEL, LE "ANNALES" E LA STORIOGRAFIA CONTEMPORANEA [Braudel, the *Annales*, and contemporary historiography]. *Studi Storici [Italy] 1980 21(1): 5-17.* Investigates the reasons why the *Annales: Économies, Sociétés, Civilisations* and Fernand Braudel exercised so great an influence on the intellectual world between 1945 and 1973. Both the *Annales* school and Braudel emphasized global explanations and economic and social factors in the study of history. While there were some areas of agreement between members of the school and Marxists, their differences were radical. Primary sources; 28 notes.
E. E. Ryan

1669. Wallerstein, Immanuel. FERNAND BRAUDEL, HISTORIAN, "*HOMME DE LA CONJONCTURE.*" *Radical Hist. Rev. 1982 (26): 104-119.* An appreciation of Fernand Braudel and the historiography of the *Annales* school, 1945-68, using Braudel's own notion of *conjoncture* to examine the relationships among *Annales*, Marxism, and those that opposed him.

1670. Wilson, Stephen. "THEY ORDER... THIS MATTER BETTER IN FRANCE": SOME RECENT BOOKS ON MODERN FRENCH HISTORIOGRAPHY. *Hist. J. [Great Britain] 1978 21(3): 721-735.* Examines four monographs on modern French historiography of the *Annales* school that recently have become familiar to English-speaking audiences in translation. The approaches popularized by such historians as Aries, Braudel, Brémond, Chevalier, Foucault, Goubert, Labrousse, Le Bras, Lefebvre, Le Roy Ladurie, and Mandrou have tended to extend the scope and interest of historical study to include aspects of societies of the past that were previously ignored or studied in isolation; ignore political, diplomatic, and narrative history; and combine history with such disciplines as geography, psychology, sociology, and social anthropology. The close ties existing between French sociology and the humanities, and the centralized institutional framework within which French academic history developed are instrumental in accounting for its notable influence, scope, and coherence; 37 notes.
L. J. Reith

1671. Winock, Michel; Ilbert, Robert; and Agulhon, Maurice. LA NOUVELLE HISTOIRE [The new history]. *Histoire [France] 1979 (9): 114-117.* Review article of *Annales* school historiography in Jacques Le Goff's *La Nouvelle Histoire* (Paris: Encyclopédies du Savoir Moderne, 1978) and Pierre Chaunu's *Histoire quantitative, histoire sérielle* (Paris: Cahiers des Annales, 1978) in addition to François Furet's *Penser la Révolution française* (Paris: Gallimard, 1978).

1672. Worobec, Christine. CONTEMPORARY HISTORIANS ON THE MUSCOVITE PEASANTRY. *Can. Slavonic Papers [Canada] 1981 23(3): 315-327.* Discusses the French *Annales* school of historiography and its impact on Soviet historical research, revealing much about the study of the Muscovite peasantry in the late 16th and early 17th centuries. Works by V. I. Koretskii, S. O. Shmidt, V. A. Aleksandrov, and others suggest a growing realization among Soviet historians that such elements as geographical features, psychology, sociology, cultural developments, biological, and demographic factors may not necessarily belong to either of the long-stressed substructure or superstructure phenomenon in historical development. While far from achieving the total view of reality urged by Fernand Braudel and his colleagues, the Soviets have indeed been affected by bourgeois historiographic thought. Secondary sources; 43 notes.
G. J. Bobango

1673. —. [THE ANNALES SCHOOL]. *J. of Econ. Hist. 1978 38(1): 58-80.*
Forster, Robert. ACHIEVEMENTS OF THE ANNALES SCHOOL, *pp. 58-76.*
North, Douglass C. DISCUSSION, *pp. 77-80.*
Describes the various kinds of history pursued by the *Annales* School in France, assesses the school's accomplishments and shortcomings, and indicates what special relevance it has for economic historians. The strengths of the *Annales* School lie in an openness to the various approaches of neighboring disciplines, chiefly sociology and anthropology, an imaginative use of sources, especially those that can be treated "in series," and

a sensitivity to new historical problems, particularly those relating to preindustrial societies. For the American-trained economic historian, the principal deficiency of the school is its failure to employ theory or develop a unified, explicit methodology.
J

1674. —. LES *ANNALES*, 1929-1979 [*Annales*, 1929-79]. *Ann.: Écon., Soc., Civilisations [France] 1979 34(6): 1344-1346.* Discusses the role the *Annales* school has played in modern historiography since the founding of the journal, *Annales: Économies, Sociétés, Civilisations*.

1675. —. LOS *ANNALES*: 1929-1979 [*Annales*: 1929-79]. *Rev. Española de Investigaciones Sociológicas [Spain] 1980 (12): 15-19.* Describes the functions of history and historiography as the posing of questions, of seeking many answers rather than one, not in order to divide but to integrate; Marc Bloch and Lucien Febvre of *Annales: Économies, Sociétés, Civilisations* have been very successful in these respects.

Language and Terminology in Historiography

1676. Barg, M. A. PRINTSIP SISTEMNOSTI V MARKSISTSKOM ISTORICHESKOM ISSLEDOVANII [The principle of taxonomy in Marxist historical research]. *Istoriia SSSR [USSR] 1981 (2): 78-98.* The treatment of society as a complex and constantly developing system was clearly formulated by Marx in his teachings on socioeconomic formations. Lenin also stressed the systematic character of the study of society. But development of society is not exclusively due to changes and improvements of the means of material production; it is also due to improvements in the means of communication—language and human thought. Thus, the specifics of every historical period must be defined through systematic study of its mentality as well as its material development. A paradigmatic approach to historical studies is essential in historiographical studies.
S. M. Levy

1677. Bontinck, F. REMARQUES MARGINALES A VANSINA, "THE DICTIONARY AND THE HISTORIAN" [Marginal remarks to Vansina: "The Dictionary and the Historian"]. *Hist. in Africa 1976 3: 155-156.* Criticizes Zaïrean historian Jan Vansina's occasional neglect of appropriate old dictionaries; insufficient lexicographical research may lead to erroneous conclusions.

1678. Dan, Ilie. IMPLICATIONS HISTORIQUES DANS L'ETUDE DE LA TOPONYMIE ROUMAINE [Historical implications in the study of Romanian toponomy]. *Rev. Roumaine d'Hist. [Romania] 1983 22(1): 33-46.* Along with history and archaeology, the study of toponomy can contribute to a knowledge of the historic past by clarifying geographic, social, and linquistic problems. Place-names to a historian can have the value of historic documents, and can furnish clues to the appearance or disappearance of peoples and their ethnic symbiosis such as that between the Romanians and other populations. The economic and sociocultural development of a region may also be traced by studying its place-names, which furnish clues to population displacements, names of people, conquests, and migrations. 60 notes.
G. J. Bobango

1679. Farsobin, V. V. K ISTORII SKLADYVANIIA PONIATIIA "ISTOCHNIKOVEDENIE" [The history of the definition of *istochnikovedenie*]. *Istoriia SSSR [USSR] 1981 (6): 108-116.* Discusses the polemics conducted over the years by Soviet historians on how to define the concept of *istochnikovedenie* [the study of sources]. It has been the subject of numerous articles, monographs, books, and seminars. Basically, there are two schools of thought: one holds that *istochnikovedenie* is the classification of different kinds of sources; the other, that it is the problem of source study, not source form, that is important. S. O. Shmidt, for example, subdivides *istochnikovedenie* into groupings such as statistical sources, legal documents, memoirs, letters, and other classifications. V. V. Farsobin, on the other hand, defines as branches of the study the search for sources, paleography, textology, proof of the validity of sources, archaeography, and other investigative processes. Secondary sources; 54 notes. J. Bamber

1680. Girard, Louis. HISTOIRE ET LEXICOGRAPHIE [History and lexicography]. *Ann.: Econ., Soc., Civilisations [France] 1963 18(6): 1128-1132.* Reviews Jean Dubois's *Le Vocabulaire Politique et Social en France de 1869 à 1872, à travers les Oeuvres des Ecrivains, les Revues et les Journaux* [Political and social vocabulary in France, 1869-72, through author's works, reviews, and journals] (1962), which analyzes lexical items of interest to historians in terms of the structure of lexicology. Historians need to take such studies seriously in order to avoid illusory and arbitrary arguments. Note.

1681. Hernadi, Paul. RE-PRESENTING THE PAST: A NOTE ON NARRATIVE HISTORIOGRAPHY AND HISTORICAL DRAMA. *Hist. & Theory 1976 15(1): 45-51.* Examines the use of language by historians in contrast to that employed by dramatists in picturing the past and their methods of staging. In representing the past the historian translates events but does not provide a simple mirror to the past by quoting verbatim as does the dramatist. Moreover, the history tellers of the theater always leave their presentations open with the promises of more to come. 9 notes.
D. A. Yanchisin

1682. Kamerbeek, J., Jr. HET BEGRIP "HISTORISCHE OVER-GANGSPERIODE" KRITISCH BEKEKEN [The concept "historical transition period" regarded critically]. *Forum der Letteren [Netherlands] 1968 9(4): 203-224.* Illustrates how the concept "transitional period," originally used by John Stuart Mill with reference to his own times, became a catchword in the later 19th- and early 20th centuries. "Transition period" was applied indiscriminately, with derogatory meanings, to any historical period and the persons living in it, thereby subjectively degrading both. Primary and secondary materials; 80 notes. G. Herritt

1683. Küttler, Wolfgang. WISSENSCHAFTSSPRACHE, BEGRIFFS- UND THEORIEBILDUNG IN DER HISTORISCHEN FORSCHUNG UND DARSTELLUNG. ZUM PROBLEM DER SPRACHE DES HISTORIKERS [Learned language and the formation of concept and theory in historical research and representation: the historian's language]. *Zeitschrift für Geschichtswissenschaft [East Germany] 1980 28(6): 532-543.* Masters of strict scientific analysis and the descriptive narrative formulation of historical materials are the giants of historiography. The author shows the steps of the historian's creative work from the language of the primary sources to modern speech and terminology, explaining the rules of scientific Marxist methodology. 49 notes. G. E. Pergl

1684. Levitt, Joseph. RACE ·AND NATION IN CANADIAN ANGLOPHONE HISTORIOGRAPHY. *Can. Rev. of Studies in Nationalism [Canada] 1981 8(1): 1-16.* Analyzes Canadian-Anglophone historians' use of the terms "race" and "nation." By "nation," they have meant one Canadian community or a sovereign state, and this meaning has remained unchanged. Early uses of "race" suggested that mental traits were transmitted through the blood, but this implication is totally absent in present-day works. 35 notes. R. Aldrich

1685. Milis, L. TAALKONFLIKT EN TAALGRENS ALS ONDERWERP VAN HISTORISCH ONDERZOEK [Language conflict and language boundary as subject for historical research]. *Tijdschrift voor Geschiedenis [Netherlands] 1975 88(3): 301-312.* Language is one of the most important expressions of social and cultural identity. A historian must be concerned with the linguistic situation in a given area and era and study language conflicts with great objectivity. The author cites examples from 19th-century French and Belgian history and shows how national bias led to gross distortions. Based on secondary materials; 29 notes.
G. D. Homan

1686. Mommsen, Wolfgang J. DIE SPRACHE DES HISTO-RIKERS [The language of the historian]. *Historische Zeitschrift [West Germany] 1984 238(1): 57-58.* The rhetorical traditions which bound 19th-century historians to their cultural heritages weakened as historians adopted more scientific modes of expression. In the late 20th century, a worldwide revival of narrative changed historical style. Historiography was regarded as a literary endeavor rather than as mere communication of research results. The relationship between theory, research, and narration was discussed in the writings of Jack Hexter, Golo Mann, Haydon White, and others. 39 notes. G. H. Davis

1687. Murru, Furio. NOTE PER UN MODELLO STORIOGRA-FICO DELLA LINGUISTICA [Notes toward a historiographical model of linguistics]. *Critica Storica [Italy] 1982 19(3): 373-391.* Until recently linguistic research has systematically avoided any reference to its predecessors. After examining certain methods and models of a new historiographical approach to the science, the author proposes a tentative alternative and more comprehensive model for futher discussion, clarification, and elucidation. 24 notes.
J. V. Coutinho

1688. Palmieri, Stefano. GLI STORICI A PRATO [The historians at Prato]. *Nuova Riv. Storica [Italy] 1982 66(3-4): 399-404.* The Society of Italian Historians held its annual congress at Prato in April 1982 on the theme "The Historian and His Language." Among the topics discussed were: the experience of the European intellectual lexicon and historical research; Italian vernacular sources and their lexicon; borrowings by the scientific language from the historiographical; analysis of the language of the Enlightenment historians; the contribution of the Marxist lexicon to Italian historiography, and the historical language of Benedetto Croce. Based on the work of the congress. J. V. Coutinho

1689. Pitschmann, Benedikt. P. MATTHIAS HÖFER VON KREMSMÜNSTER UND SEIN ETYMOLOGISCHES WÖRTERBUCH (1815) [P. Matthias Höfer of Kremsmünster and his etymological dictionary (1815)]. *Jahrbuch des Oberösterreichischen Musealvereins [Austria] 1970 115(1): 199-210.* Analyzes the importance of the etymological dictionary of Matthias Höfer for Austrian historiography. 117 notes, biblio.

1690. Ricuperati, Giuseppe. LINGUAGGIO E MESTIERE DEL-LO STORICO NEL PRIMO SETTECENTO [Language and the historian's craft in the early 18th century]. *Studi Storici [Italy] 1983 24(1-2): 7-36.* During the counter-Reformation, historiography had somewhat lost its proper identity with other scientific disciplines under the influence and predominance of sacred and ecclesiastical history. By the early 18th century, changes had occurred in the historian's craft that were manifested in the language employed by historians. 111 notes. J. V. Coutinho

1691. Sillars, Malcolm O. DEFINING MOVEMENTS RHETORI-CALLY: CASTING THE WIDEST NET. *Southern Speech Communication J. 1980 46(1): 17-32.* Since Leland Griffin published "The Rhetoric of Historical Movements" in 1952, movement theory's emphasis on linearity, cause, intent, and definition has become too restrictive; theorists should apply the criteria of usefulness and carefully when identifying and studying movements.

1692. Struever, Nancy S. HISTORIOGRAPHY AND LINGUIS-TICS. Iggers, Georg G. and Parker, Harold T., ed. *International Handbook of Historical Studies: Contemporary Research and Theory* (Westport, Conn.: Greenwood Pr., 1979): 127-150. Historians and linguists must develop a strong inclusive theory on the structures and processes of communication as well as language, performance as well as competence, and speech as well as language. Pressures for the formalization of such a theory have been exerted by various schools of philosophy. For the historian, the "theory is pragmatic in two senses: it demands the consideration of texts in the context of use, and it has practical applications to specific problems of historical inquiry." 16 notes, biblio. S

1693. Tortarolo, Edoardo. SUL LINGUAGGIO DELLA STORIO-GRAFIA ILLUMINISTICA [On the language of the historiography of the Enlightenment]. *Studi Storici [Italy] 1983 24(1-2): 37-53.* By employing the methods of the history of concepts developed in Germany, attempts to identify the problems that interested the historians of the Enlightenment, particularly Voltaire, the Encyclopedists, and the writers of the Göttingen school. This provisional attempt inquires into the perspective in which these scholars looked at the past and the language they predominantly used. 80 notes.

J. V. Coutinho

1694. Veit-Brause, Irmline. A NOTE ON *BEGRIFFSGESCHICHTE*. *Hist. and Theory 1981 20(1): 61-68.* Identifies and summarizes the trends in contemporary European, particularly German, historiography that can be grouped under the term *Begriffsgeschichte*. Like the *histoire non-événementielle* popularized by the *Annales* school, this tendency studies the "participant" conceptualizations that accompanied changes in the past. The central claim is that keywords for describing philosophical, political, social, and economic experience must be related to specific lexical contexts. Words and their meaning change over time. *Begriffsgeschichte* concentrates on delimiting "whole clusters of semantic fields." This effort imperceptibly merges with the objectives of cultural anthropology. Secondary sources; 20 notes.

W. J. Reedy

1695. Zilch, Reinhold. "JUNKER" ALS HISTORISCHE KATE-GORIE BEI KARL MARX UND FRIEDRICH ENGELS [Junker as a historical category in the views of Karl Marx and Friedrich Engels]. *Zeits. für Geschichtswissenschaft [East Germany] 1981 29(12): 1140-1147.* The lack of a complete definition of the term *Junker* by Marx and Engels has resulted in problems of communication among historians in East Germany. Based on works by Marx and Engels.

T. Parker/S

1696. —. [INSIDERS AND OUTSIDERS IN AMERICAN HISTORICAL NARRATIVE AND AMERICAN HISTORY]. *Am. Hist. Rev. 1982 87(2): 390-423.*
Moore, R. Lawrence. INSIDERS AND OUTSIDERS IN AMERICAN HISTORICAL NARRATIVE AND AMERICAN HISTORY, *pp. 390-412.* Suggests reasons why disagreements about the value of terms like "insider" and "outsider" have no ultimate solution, and some ways in which historians can make better sense of "insider-outsider" conflict within the context of American pluralism.
Gaustad, Edwin S. COMMENT, *pp. 413-415.* Accepts author's "clarifying directions" but claims he debases the value of insider-outsider terminology "so that it can no longer circulate among historians."
Wise, Gene. COMMENT, *pp. 416-419.* Author is "on target" but has not put together the "dramatistic language" needed to gain leverage on his materials.
Moore, R. Lawrence. REPLY, *pp. 420-423.* Insider-outsider disputes form a central theme in American history. 54 notes.

R. Schlesinger

Quantitative Methods and the Statistical Approach

1697. Alexander, Manfred. ZUR VERWENDUNG VON LOCH-KARTEN, ELEKTRONISCHER DATENVERARBEITUNG UND STATISTISCHEN METHODEN IN DER SOWJETISCHEN HISTORIOGRAPHIE. [On the use of punch-cards, electronic data processing and statistical methods in Soviet historiography]. *Jahrbücher für Geschichte Osteuropas [West Germany] 1974 22(1): 88-124.* Reviews recent Soviet literature on historical use of electronic data processing and the use of statistical methods in the USSR since the 1960's. These methods are still contested by many Soviet historians, but the special status of economic and social history in the Soviet Union has caused an increasing number of researchers to experiment with the new techniques. 155 notes.

R. G. Young

1698. Alter, George. HISTORY AND QUANTITATIVE DATA: A REVIEW. *Hist. Methods 1981 14(3): 145-148.* In the essays in Jerome M. Clubb and Erwin K. Scheuch, ed., *Historical Social Research: The Use of Historical Research: The Use of Historical and*

Process-Produced Data (1980), the main concern is with the methodological challenge that statistical data is for historians trained in the conventional techniques. Apparently historians still seek to recreate the past "as it really happened" rather than develop general principles of human behavior, the major objective of social science. 24 notes.

D. K. Pickens

1699. Arcila Farías, Eduardo. LA HISTORIA CUANTITATIVA Y SUS PROBLEMAS [Quantitative history and its problems]. *Histórica [Peru] 1981 5(2): 141-147.* Introduces a research project of the Central University of Venezuela on the historical development of the colonial Public Treasury of the old province of Caracas, involving the use of statistical and other econometric methods. Criticizes tendencies of the quantitative school of historiography which denature history and negate historical narrative. 3 notes, biblio.

J. V. Coutinho

1700. Beliavskaia, I. A. and Popova, E. I. SOVETSKO-AMERIKANSKII KOLLOKVIUM PO PRIMENENI-IU KOLICHESTVENNYKH METODOV V ISTORII [Soviet-American colloquium on the use of quantitative methods in history]. *Amerikanskii Ezhegodnik [USSR] 1981: 276-288.* Describes a conference held in the Estonian capital of Tallinn, 26-30 May 1981, at which Soviet and American historians discussed the use of quantitative methods in historiography. The meeting followed one held in Baltimore in 1978 at which the reports were submitted by the Soviet side. The Tallinn seminar heard 10 reports by the Americans, most of which concentrated on the growth of quantitative methodology in the United States. In the main report, Allan G. Bogue stressed that in the past 15 years hundreds of articles and dozens of books had been published in the United States on the subject, special cliometrical journals had come out, and historical data banks had been set up. Quantitative methods such as the use of functions, models, correlation, regression, and factor analysis are in everyday use. 3 notes.

J. Bamber

1701. Blumin, Stuart M. "THE NEW URBAN HISTORY" UP-DATED. *Rev. in Am. Hist. 1975 3(3): 293-299.* Asking what is new about the new urban history and "where is the study of the urban past heading," reviews *The New Urban History: Quantitative Explorations by American Historians* (Princeton, N.J.: Princeton U. Pr., 1975) edited by Leo F. Schnore; outlines the book's content, analyzes the book within the context of urban historiography, and discusses the various methodologies used by contributors to the book.

1702. Bode, Frederick; Grogono, Peter; and Ginter, Donald E. A REVIEW OF OPTIMAL INPUT METHODS: FIXED FIELD, AND THE EDITED TEXT. *Hist. Methods Newsletter 1977 10(4): 166-176.* A general consideration of fixed and free-field formatting to indicate economical methods for developing small and large historical data bases. Discusses the problems of editing sources for input into a raw data file and producing an analytical file encoded and formatted to suit the desired analysis. 14 notes.

D. K. Pickens

1703. Bolkhovitinov, N. N. VSTRECHA SOVETSKIKH I AMERIKANSKIKH ISTORIKOV [A meeting of Soviet and American historians]. *Novaia i Noveishaia Istoriia [USSR] 1976(1): 208-210.* Reports on the proceedings of a colloquium of Soviet and US historians following the 14th International Congress of Historical Sciences in San Francisco, California, 30-31 August 1975. A comparison of American blacks and Russian serfs revealed the importance of comparing sources and statistics. Note.

V. A. Packer

1704. Borodkin, L. I. and Sokolov, A. K. ISTORIK I IZUCHE-NIE SOTSIALNYKH PROTSESSOV (OB ISPOL'ZOVANII MAS-SOVYKH ISTOCHNIKOV I KOLICHESTVENNYKH METODOV IKH ANALIZA V NOVEISHEI ZARUBEZHNOI ISTORIOGRA-FII) [The historian and the study of social processes: the use of mass sources and quantitative methods of their analysis in recent foreign historiography]. *Istoriia SSSR [USSR] 1983 (1): 178-194.* Reviews recent western historiography on the application of quantitative methods to the study of mass sources, focusing on J. M.

Clubb and E. K. Scheuch, eds., *Historical Social Research* (1980). This collection reflects the technical progress made in the West in the 1970's with respect to quantitative methods but suffers from incorrect bourgeois interpretations of findings. Soviet historians should utilize the techniques of recent quantitative study of mass sources while bringing to their analysis Marxist theoretical and methodological principles. 40 notes.   J. W. Long

1705. Brachmann, Bothe. DIE AUSWIRKUNGEN DER MODERNEN INFORMATIONSÜBERLIEFERUNG AUF DIE WECHSELBEZIEHUNG ZWISCHEN GESCHICHTSBILD UND INFORMATIONSBASIS [The effect of modern means of information on the interrelation between historical image and information basis]. *Zeitschrift für Geschichtswissenschaft [East Germany] 1969 17(1-2): 62-68.* The scientific-technological revolution with its rapid quantitative growth of information makes it necessary for historians to organize a qualitative limitation of information, that is a maximum of information has to be achieved with a relative minimum of documents.

1706. Brandstötter, Elisabeth. WISSENSCHAFTLICHE DOKUMENTATION UND INFORMATION IN DER GESCHICHTSWISSENSCHAFT [Documentation and information in historical sciences]. *Zeitgeschichte [Austria] 1981 9(1): 27-32.* The Institut für Maschinelle Dokumentation of the University of Graz has developed a unique database for Austrian historical literature since 1945. Biblio.   M. Geyer

1707. Bullough, Vern and Bullough, Bonnie. THE COMPUTER, THE HISTORIAN, AND SOME VARIABLES OF ACHIEVEMENT: A METHODOLOGY. *Computer Studies in the Humanities and Verbal Behavior 1973 4(3): 117-123.* Discusses the uses of computer analysis in historical research in the 1970's, using social conditions in 18th-century Scotland as a methodological example.

1708. Clubb, Jerome M. and Allen, Howard W. COLLECTIVE BIOGRAPHY AND THE PROGRESSIVE MOVEMENT: THE "STATUS REVOLUTION" REVISITED. *Social Sci. Hist. 1977 1(4): 518-534.* Assesses the possibilities for the use of collective biography or prosopography in the quantitative assessment of history, especially as displayed by George E. Mowry in his 1963 study, *The California Progressives* and Alfred C. Chandler, Jr.'s "The Origins of Progressive Leadership" in Elting E. Morison's (ed.) *The Letters of Theodore Roosevelt* (Cambridge, 1954).

1709. Clubb, Jerome M. QUANTIFICATION AND THE "NEW" HISTORY: A REVIEW ESSAY. *Am. Arch. 1974 37(1): 15-25.* Reviews of recent literature on quantitative approaches to the study of the past. Controversy about the new method has decreased as use has increased in many graduate history programs. *The Dimensions of the Past*, edited by Val R. Lorwin and Jacob M. Price (New Haven: Yale University, 1972), is a major addition to the literature. Its essays by many experts cover international research. Discusses appropriate areas for the application of such methods and lists the kinds of materials future historians will want. Based on secondary sources; 14 notes.   D. E. Horn

1710. Coover, Edwin R. SOCIAL INDICATORS FROM SURVEY DATA. *Hist. Methods Newsletter 1977 10(2): 49-65.* Discusses research difficulties in using the derivation of social indicators. The time span is limited to the last 40 years of US and European history and the survey data poses conceptual problems of moving from isomorphic indicators to abstraction. The other two problem areas are statistics and data processing. The original observer and the historian must have the same perception of the public opinion data. 11 fig., 38 notes.   D. K. Pickens

1711. Dyba, Marian. METODY I WYNIKI. Z WARSZTATU HISTORYKA DZIEJÓW SPOŁECZEŃSTWA POLSKIEGO. POD REDAKCJĄ ST. KALABIŃSKIEGO WARSZAWA 1980 [Methods and Results: from the workshop of the historian of Polish society, ed. S. Kalabiński, Warsaw 1980]. *Z Pola Walki [Poland] 1981 23[i.e., 24](2): 202-207.* Reviews the lierature on quantitative meth-

ods in the social sciences, pointing out trends highlighted in the publication of papers on the subject edited by S. Kalabiński, *Methods and Results* (1980).   M. Hernas

1712. Fitch, Nancy E. STATISTICAL AND MATHEMATICAL METHODS FOR HISTORIANS: AN ANNOTATED BIBLIOGRAPHY OF SELECTED BOOKS AND ARTICLES. *Hist. Methods 1980 13(4): 222-231.* Based on the 1980 Newberry Library Summer Institute in Quantitative Methods.   D. K. Pickens

1713. Fure, Eli. SKIPPERSKJØNN OG STOKASTIKK [Educated guesswork and stochastic modeling]. *Hist. Tidsskrift [Norway] 1983 62(4): 404-418.* Historical works often qualify statistical analyses in ways which suggest an implicit but unreported method of separating the relevant and systematic from the unimportant and mundane. It is possible to formulate a probability or stochastic model to evaluate such conclusions openly. Examples included are taken from recent works on legal proceedings in Norway on sorcery in the 16th century, and changes in the fertility rates in a Norwegian parish from 1870 to 1910. Table, chart, 17 notes. English summary.   L. B. Sather

1714. Gavrila, Irina. CUANTIFICAREA ÎN ISTORIE: VALOARE ŞI LIMITE [Quantifying in historiography: advantages and limits]. *Rev. de Istorie [Romania] 1979 32(5): 895-903.* Examines the application of mathematical methods and the use of computers in historical research, briefly surveying the most important work carried out in economic, political, and demographic history with new methods devised in the United States, USSR, Great Britain, and France. Analyzes the basic problems confronting the researcher seeking to apply mathematical methods in historical research and concludes that these methods together with the rapid working of computers offer a major contribution to increasing the scientific rigor of historical research. 17 notes. French summary.   R. O. Khan

1715. Goldman, Lawrence. THE ORIGINS OF BRITISH "SOCIAL SCIENCE": POLITICAL ECONOMY, NATURAL SCIENCE AND STATISTICS, 1830-1835. *Hist. J. [Great Britain] 1983 26(3): 587-616.* Maintains the impossibility of a history of British social sciences in the 19th century because no coherent discipline as such existed in Great Britain at the time. This is illustrated by a consideration of the origins of the Statistical Society of London (now the Royal Statistical Society); its founders and subsequent members had conflicting, often contradictory views of its purposes and methodology. This reflected similar confusion throughout Great Britain at the time regarding the socioeconomic applications of the science of statistics—or social science. 189 notes.   R. M. Twisdale

1716. Granasztói, György. A SZÁMÍTÓGÉPEK A TÖRTÉNETTUDOMÁNYBAN [Computers in historiography]. *Történelmi Szemle [Hungary] 1972 15(1-2): 29-47.* Computer study has not displaced traditional historical methodology, but it has made the analysis and classification of source material simpler. It is particularly useful for Marxist historians who use scientific methods in their study of society. The FORCOD system of computers has helped them greatly in the study of such subjects as 15th- and 16th-century Hungarian social history. Secondary sources; 5 tables, diagram, 4 fig., 17 notes.   H. Szamuely

1717. Griswold del Castillo, Richard. QUANTITATIVE HISTORY IN THE AMERICAN SOUTHWEST: A SURVEY AND CRITIQUE. *Western Hist. Q. 1984 15(4): 407-426.* Reviews published materials that have used quantitative methods and data as a principal source for investigation of American Southwest subjects. Surveys the main research directions and themes developed by scholars and predicts a steadily increasing output of published scholarship, especially on the social history of pueblos, haciendas, missions, presidios, and ranchos of the far northern frontiers of New Spain and Mexico. Mexican immigration, the development of border cities, and Mexican-American trade and investment relations are prime contemporary subject prospects for quantitative studies. 63 notes.   D. L. Smith

1718. Gutman, Myron P. GOLD FROM DROSS? POPULATION RECONSTRUCTION FOR THE PRE-CENSUS ERA. *Hist. Methods 1984 17(1): 5-19.* Reviews E. A. Wrigley and R. S. Schofield's *The Population History of England, 1541-1871* (1981), which examines methodological issues. The "English technique" is based on data of poor quality and uses models and technical assumptions that attempt to answer larger questions; the French method uses better data and is more conservative and accurate. Wrigley and Schofield worked back in time from 1871, the date of the first modern census. 7 tables, 15 notes, biblio.　　　D. K. Pickens

1719. Herzog, Bodo and Horstmann, Werner. DER COMPUTER ALS HILFSMITTEL DES HISTORIKERS? [The computer as an aid to the historian?] *Tradition [West Germany] 1972 17(2): 84-100.* Using computers one can test the results of an 18th-century assessment to determine which of three locations would have been best for the erection of an iron foundry. With very exact mathematical means, from exact data, the authors answer their own question. 21 notes.　　　J. C. Billigmeier

1720. Holmes, Jack D. L. A NEW LOOK AT SPANISH LOUISIANA CENSUS ACCOUNTS: THE RECENT HISTORIOGRAPHY OF ANTONIO ACOSTA. *Louisiana Hist. 1980 21(1): 77-86.* Briefly describes the research of a young Spanish demographer-historian, Antonio Acosta Rodríquez, whose careful studies of the censuses of Spanish colonial Louisiana will cause some reassessment of this period in Louisiana history. Cites in full the 74 census reports analyzed in Acosta's PhD dissertation (U. of Seville, 1976). Based on census reports in the Archivo General de Indias, Seville; 80 notes.　　　D. B. Touchstone

1721. Jensen, Richard; *Public Historian* Editors, interviewers. THE ACCOMPLISHMENTS OF THE NEWBERRY LIBRARY FAMILY AND COMMUNITY HISTORY PROGRAMS. *Public Hist. 1983 5(4): 49-61.* Interviews Richard Jensen about his tenure as head of the Newberry Library's Family and Community History Center and his role in training scholars in quantitative history.

1722. Kahk, J. RECENT RESULTS OF SOVIET HISTORIANS IN USE OF MATHEMATICAL METHODS AND COMPUTERS IN AGRARIAN HISTORY. *Hist. Tidskrift [Sweden] 1974 (3): 414-421.* A description of some of the recent findings (since 1965) of Soviet historians using quantitative methods in the field of agrarian history. Soviet historians have concentrated their attention primarily on the agrarian history of Russia particularly during the first half of the 19th century, and have concluded that feudal exploitation of the peasantry was the most significant factor determining the economic well-being of the peasant holding. Secondary sources; 8 notes.　　　O. Hoidal

1723. Kahk, Juhan. QUANTITATIVE HISTORICAL RESEARCH IN ESTONIA: A CASE STUDY IN SOVIET HISTORIOGRAPHY. *Social Sci. Hist. 1984 8(2): 193-200.* Soviet historians began to explore quantitative computer techniques in the late 1950's. Estonian historians have recently made rapid progress in this area. Many individuals and research teams have quantitative history projects underway at the present. Historiographical essay based on published sources; 4 notes, biblio.　　　L. K. Blaser

1724. Katz, Michael B. QUANTIFICATION AND THE SCIENTIFIC STUDY OF HISTORY. *Hist. Methods Newsletter 1973 6(2): 63-68.* Reviews William Aydelotte's *Quantification in History* (Reading, Mass.: Addison-Wesley, 1971) and Lee Benson's *Toward the Scientific Study of History—Selected Papers* (Philadelphia: Lippincott, 1972). Quantification and the scientific study of history are desirable, but the historian's ability to discover general laws and the application of 20th-century concepts to the past are questionable. Stresses "the intellectual content of technical concerns" in defense of "new historical procedures." The success of these books will be marked by the extent to which they "become part of a conventional wisdom."　　　D. K. Pickens and S

1725. Kousser, J. Morgan. HISTORY QUASSHED: QUANTITATIVE SOCIAL SCIENTIFIC HISTORY IN PERSPECTIVE. *Am. Behavioral Scientist 1980 23(6): 885-904.* Identifies nine qualities

that have produced a striking variation between the course of development of quantitative methods in history and that in the rest of the social sciences, reviews the rise of Quantitative Social Scientific History (QUASSH), and suggests that the future of history as a discipline will be best served by combining conventional historical skills with sophisticated cliometric analysis.

1726. Kousser, J. Morgan. QUANTITATIVE SOCIAL-SCIENTIFIC HISTORY. Kammen, Michael, ed. *The Past Before Us: Contemporary Historical Writing in the United States* (Ithaca, N.Y.: Cornell U. Pr., 1980): 433-455. The introduction of quantitative social science into American history, 1957-61, offered new ways of interpreting the past. The addition of quantifiable data as a primary source allowed material considered unusable before the advent of data processing to now supplement old evidence. Comparison of statistics gathered over a period of time enabled historians to consider not only events but also systems, structures, and patterns. 5 tables, 51 notes.　　　S

1727. Koval'chenko, I. D. and Selunskaja, N. V. SOWJETISCHE ERFAHRUNGEN BEI DER ANWENDUNG MATHEMATISCH-STATISTISCHER METHODEN IN HISTORISCHEN UNTERSUCHUNGEN [Soviet experiences in the use of mathematical-statistical methods in historical investigations]. *Jahrbuch für Wirtschaftsgeschichte [East Germany] 1972 (4): 11-22.* Describes the application of mathematical methods and electronic calculation by Soviet historians to the discovery of the inner mechanisms of historical processes. Cites cases of the application of correlative analysis, regression analysis, and factor analysis to problems of the peasantry in the 19th century, the aristocracy in northern France in the 12th to 14th century, the economic structure and peasant duties in Estonia in the 17th to 19th century, taxation and property in Byzantium in the 14th century, and other Russian agrarian problems. Discusses problems arising from incomplete sources and techniques for successfully applying mathematical methods. Secondary works; table, 19 notes.　　　J. B. Street

1728. Lebrun, Pierre. HISTOIRE QUANTITATIVE ET DÉVELOPPEMENT DE LA BELGIQUE AU XIXᵉ SIÈCLE: ÉTAT DES RECHERCHES, RÈGLES MÉTHODOLOGIQUES, CHOIX ÉPISTÉMOLOGIQUES [Quantitative history and development in Belgium in the 19th century: the state of research, methodology, epistemological choices]. *Cahiers de Clio [Belgium] 1980 (64): 35-58.* Reviews 10 volumes, edited by the Royal Academy of Belgium, which comprise the first part of an extensive historical study-in-progress; seven volumes focus on 19th-century Belgium under the collective title *Histoire quantitative et développement de la Belgique, 1830-1913.*

1729. Liveanu, V. ON THE UTILIZATION OF MATHEMATICAL METHODS IN HISTORY IN ROMANIA: SOME METHODOLOGICAL REMARKS. *Rev. Roumaine d'Hist. [Romania] 1974 13(2): 323-334.* Discusses experiments conducted by Romanian researchers, and their preference for mathematical models and the machine in the statistical analysis of correlations. Mathematics and the computer may help improve the current theory of history. A paper presented at the international conference on "History and the Computer," Uppsala, 1973.　　　RSA 11:1661

1730. Lückerath, Carl August. ELEKTRONISCHE DATENVERARBEITUNG IN DER GESCHICHTSWISSENSCHAFT? [Data processing in historical studies?]. *Geschichte in Wissenschaft und Unterricht [West Germany] 1969 29(6): 321-329.* Explains the functioning of computers and provides examples of their application to history. However, in the process of standardization historians must be aware that qualitative precision cannot be reached. Fig., 16 notes.　　　S. Boehnke/S

1731. McCaa, Robert. MICROCOMPUTER SOFTWARE DESIGNS FOR HISTORIANS: WORD PROCESSING, FILING, AND DATA ENTRY PROGRAMS. *Historical Methods 1984 17(2): 68-74.* Provides some concepts for a software design that edits, stores, and retrieves narrative text and quantitative data. Word processing is critical. Data Star is the best of an imperfect group of instruments. Table; 12 notes. D. K. Pickens

1732. Miskimin, Harry. THE QUALITY OF QUANTITATIVE WORK: A REVIEW ARTICLE. *Comparative Studies in Soc. and Hist. [Great Britain] 1975 17(2): 253-258.* Reviews V. Lorwin and J. M. Price, eds., *The Dimensions of the Past: Materials Problems, and Opportunities for Quantitative Work in History* (New Haven: Yale U. Press, 1972); E. A. Wrigley, ed., *Nineteenth-Century Society: Essays in the Use of Quantitative Methods for the Study of Social Data* (Cambridge: Cambridge U. Press, 1972); and W. O. Aydelotte, A. G. Bogue, and R. W. Fogel, eds., *The Dimensions of Quantitative Research in History* (Princeton: Princeton U. Press, 1972).

1733. Neveux, Hugues. À PROPOS DE L'HOMMAGE À ERNEST LABROUSSE: LA POSTÉRITÉ D'UNE OEUVRE MAGISTRALE [Homage to Ernest Labrousse: the posterity of a teacher's work]. *Rev. d'Hist. Écon. et Sociale [France] 1976 54(2): 252-257.* Reviews the collection *Conjoncture économique, structures sociales: Hommage à Ernest Labrousse* (Paris-The Hague: Publications et L'École Pratique des Hautes Études, 1974) and considers Labrousse's contribution to French quantitative historiography. The dominance of themes of cyclical economics and its relation to social structures demonstrates Labrousse's influence on modern French historians. 21 notes. R. O. Khan

1734. Pool, D. I. THE HISTORIOGRAPHER IN COMPUTERLAND: A REVIEW ARTICLE. *Social Hist. [Canada] 1975 8(15): 165-174.* Quantitative historical data provides information at the structural level rather than at the sociopsychological level; it reports on behavior rather than attitudes. Record linkage is an important quantitative technique. It can be conducted at the micro-level (person, family, household, or work unit) or at the macro-level (society, community, parish, county, industry, etc.). Secondary sources; 20 notes. W. K. Hobson

1735. Popova, E. I. and Stankevich, S. B. MATEMATICHESKIE METODY V AMERIKANSKOI ISTORIOGRAFII POLITICHESKOI BOR'BY V KONGRESSE S.SH.A. [Mathematical methods in American historiography on the political struggle in Congress]. *Amerikanskii Ezhegodnik [USSR] 1981: 118-142.* Mathematical studies of voting patterns in Congress were proposed at the turn of the century by F. G. Turner and were improved in the 1920's-30's by political scientists H. Roach and S. Rice. Interest in the quantitative approach rose in the 1970's, when the tension between the executive branch and Congress intensified. One out of every 10 articles in the *American Political Science Review* in the 1970's, for instance, was a statistical analysis of voting trends. Journals such as *Computers and Humanities* and *Historical Methods Newsletter,* as well as countless books and articles, have provided a quantitative breakdown for a wide range of variables thought to affect voting and voting behavior in Congress. 79 notes. J. Bamber

1736. Rico, Luisa F. ¿UNA HISTORIA CUANTITATIVA? [A quantitative history?]. *Anuario de Hist. [Mexico] 1978-79 10: 325-332.* Discusses a number of attempts to use quantitative methods in historical research, concludes that more explicit attention to mathematical methods is needed. Based on Aydelotte, W. O; Bogue, A. G.; and Fogel, R. W. *The Dimensions of Quantitative Research in History,* (1972). C. G. P. Gillespie

1737. Roy, Ian and Porter, Stephen. THE POPULATION OF WORCESTER IN 1646. *Local Population Studies [Great Britain] 1982 (28): 32-43.* Examines population trends of Worcester, England in 1646, explaining problems in interpretation of statistics and historiography.

1738. Saveth, Edward N. CLIOMETRICS AND TRUTH IN AMERICAN HISTORY. *San José Studies 1979 5(2): 75-84.* Overview of arguments between historiographers who retain traditional interpretive methods and, more recently, those who have begun to use quantifiable data.

1739. Sedelow, Walter A., Jr. and Sedelow, Sally Yates. FORMALIZED HISTORIOGRAPHY, THE STRUCTURE OF SCIENTIFIC AND LITERARY TEXTS. *J. of the Hist. of the Behavioral Sci. 1978 14(3): 247-263.* Part I. SOME ISSUES POSED BY COMPUTATIONAL METHODOLOGY. The examination of theorizing and techniques for scientific language analysis applied to history clearly generalizes to imply a domain of applicability potentially coextensive for behavioral scientists with the scope of cultural behavior. The computer and related science and technology are moving toward a relationship vis-à-vis symbolic acts analogous to microscopy for the subvisual in scale and telescopes for astronomic phenomena. Content analysis is one of the points of departure from which present ideas and algorithms have moved on. How far, both at present and in the future, is the authors' subject. Article to be continued. J

1740. Selunskaya, N. B. PROBLEMY IZUCHENIIA MASSOVYKH ISTORICHESKIKH ISTOCHNIKOV V SOVREMENNOI AMERIKANSKOI ISTORIOGRAFII [Problems of study of mass historical sources in modern American historiography]. *Istoriia SSSR [USSR] 1975 (4): 201-207.* Describes and criticizes the quantitative method in analyzing history as used by such American historians as A. Bogue, Lee Benson, R. Swierenga, R. Fogel, L. Davis, V. Lorwin, J. Price, D. Landes, W. Aydelotte and others. Dissatisfaction with the descriptive method led these historians to quantitative analysis; however, according to one of them, (L. Davis), only certain small problems may be solved by quantitative history. General, complex problems that unite social, economic and political aspects are "outside of the methodology of the 'new history' ", and their solution depends on a general theory which, up till now, has not been worked out. The author agrees with L. Davis and goes on to say that the positivist views of the US historians bring them to the rejection of the possibility of learning the natural laws of historical development, determine their programmatic approach to the methods of investigation, and lead to nihilism in the evaluation of historical sources and of the empirical approach in analysis. Based on primary sources; 15 notes. L. Kalinowski

1741. Sharpless, John. POPULATION REDISTRIBUTION IN THE AMERICAN PAST: EMPIRICAL GENERALIZATIONS AND THEORETICAL PERSPECTIVES. *Social Sci. Q. 1980 61(3-4): 401-417.* Considers urban demographic shifts from a historical perspective, using Frederick Jackson Turner's *The Frontier in American History* (1920), George W. Pierson's "The M-Factor in American History" (1962), and Rowland T. Berthoff's *An Unsettled People: Social Order and Disorder in American History* (1971). The study of population and demography in the United States certainly engaged historians in the past. Social scientists have not monopolized the data. 54 notes. M. Mtewa

1742. Smith, Daniel Scott. THE ESTIMATES OF EARLY AMERICAN HISTORICAL DEMOGRAPHERS: TWO STEPS FORWARD, ONE STEP BACK, WHAT STEPS IN THE FUTURE? *Hist. Methods 1979 12(1): 24-38.* Comments on the lack of a consensus among historical demographers and their often tragic failure to correctly present their numbers. They also need to relate their data to social and economic structure. Except for death, each man experiences the other statistical events in the context of family life. 3 tables, 61 notes. D. K. Pickens

1743. Sprague, D. N. A QUANTITATIVE ASSESSMENT OF THE QUANTIFICATION REVOLUTION. *Can. J. of Hist. [Canada] 1978 13(2): 177-192.* Historical analyses have become increasingly quantitative, but it is not clear whether this development has resulted in theoretically sophisticated forms of historical analysis. The author examines the content of 349 examples of quantitative history published between 1967 and 1976 and classifies the articles by levels of theoretical sophistication. While the majority of the quantitative analyses have been no more sophisticated than conventional interpretive history, there is a trend toward increases in both quantitative elegance and theoretical sophistication. 27 notes. J. Moore

1744. Velichkov, Aleksandur. METODOLOGICHESKI OSO-BENOSTI V RAZVITIETO I PRILOZHENIETO NA KOLI-CHESTVENITE METODI V OBLASTTA NA ISTORICHESKITE NAUKI V SSSR I SASHT [Methodological peculiarities in the development and the application of quantitative methods in the field of historical sciences in the USSR and the United States]. *Istoricheski Pregled [Bulgaria] 1980 35(2): 72-79*. Examines recent American and Soviet historical literature using quantitative methods. Describes the techniques and applications. Despite objections from traditional historians, quantitative methods will prove a useful tool in the future. 44 notes.　　　　　　　　　　F. B. Chary

1745. Velichkov, Aleksandur. ZA PRILOZHENIETO NA KOLI-CHESTVENITE METODI V ISTORICHESKOTO IZSLEDVANE [The application of quantitative methods in historical research]. *Istoricheski Pregled [Bulgaria] 1975 31(4): 85-98*. Explains the use of statistics and quantitative methods in historiography. Discusses the types of areas these methods can be applied and various statistical tools used. Also describes the use of quantitative methods in the United States and the USSR. These methods are a powerful new historical tool that should be used in Bulgaria. Secondary materials; 84 notes.　　　　　　　　　F. B. Chary

1746. Velichkov, Aleksandur G. METODOLOGICHESKI OSO-BENOSTI V RAZVITIETO I PRILOZHENIETO NA KOLI-CHESTVENITE METODI V OBLASTTA NA ISTORICHESKITE NAUKI V SSSR I SASHT [Methodological peculiarities in the development and the application of quantitative methods in the field of historical sciences in the USSR and the United States]. *Istoricheski Pregled [Bulgaria] 1980 36(2): 72-79*. Examines recent American and Soviet historical literature using quantitative methods, describing techniques and applications. Despite objections from traditional historians, quantitative methods will prove a useful tool. 44 notes.　　　　　　　　　　F. B. Chary

1747. Vorontsov, G. A. NEKOTORYE NOVEISHIE NAPRAV-LENIYA V BURZHUAZNOI ISTORIOGRAFII FRG [Some of the latest trends in West German bourgeois historiography]. *Voprosy Istorii [USSR] 1974 (9): 64-86*. The author critically analyzes the contemporary methods and forms of historically substantiating the policy followed by the bourgeois government in West Germany. The growing politicization of bourgeois historiography is based on the application of quantitative methods, machine processing and modelling, with the aid of which bourgeois scientists are endeavoring to find a way out of the methodological crisis. The article examines the methods of quantitative analysis and machine processing of historical material, the possibilities and limits of applying computers in this sphere. Considerable attention is devoted by the author to the methodological problems of historical modelling, to the concrete methods of constructing models.　　　J

1748. Weibull, Jørgen. KVANTITATIV METOD I HISTORISK FORSKNING [The quantitative method in historical research]. *Historie [Denmark] 1966 7(1): 39-49*. Characterizes the quantitative method in historiography as a means of utilizing source material. This is not a new concept, but the growing interest in social and economic factors together with the modern technical possibilities for handling mass data have strengthened the interest in the quantitative method. Points to a few interpretational problems that statistical handling of mass data can produce, and suggests that the interpretative and critical skills of history must be weakened by correlative efficients, tables, and diagrams.　　B. L. Jeppesen/S

1749. —. THE FRANCHISE IN SEVENTEENTH-CENTURY MASSACHUSETTS. *William and Mary Q. 1977 34(3): 446-458*.
Ginsberg, Arlin J. IPSWICH, *pp. 446-452*. Compares the arguments and interpretations of sources by Thomas Franklin Waters and B. Katherine Brown in their treatment of the franchise in 17th-century Ipswich. Evaluates the several town lists used by these authors and notes the problems of duplication, nonresidency, and other discrepancies. Waters held that 28.4 percent adult males could vote, and Brown posited that 77.6 percent could. Ginsberg's analysis finds Waters' estimate nearly correct. Offers advice on quantitative investigation. 20 notes.

Wall, Robert E. DEDHAM AND CAMBRIDGE, *pp. 453-458*. Takes issue with B. Katherine Brown's criticism of his use of sources in his work on suffrage in Dedham and Cambridge. Objects to the accusation that he relied too heavily on vital statistics and not enough upon tax records. Lists 15 residents of Dedham who were not on tax lists and prints the names of 72 Cambridge residents who did not sign a petition of 1664. Defends his thesis that the franchise declined during 1647-66.
　　　　　　　　　　　　　　　　　　　　　H. M. Ward

Oral History and Folk History

1750. Abbasov, A. M. ROZVYTOK ISTORYCHNOHO KRAIEZ-NAVSTVA NA POLTAVSHCHYNI V KHODI PIDHOTOVKY VYDANNIA [The development of historical study of local folklore in the Poltava region during prepublication preparation]. *Ukrains'kyi Istorychnyi Zhurnal [USSR] 1976 (8): 59-65*. Describes amateur researchers' contribution to the volume of *Istoriia mist i sil Ukrains'koi RSR* [History of towns and villages of the Ukraine] (1974) devoted to Poltava Oblast.

1751. Amirian, Lemyel. KARABAGH: HISTORY AND LEGEND. *Armenian Rev. 1982 35(4): 390-398*. Fact and legend intertwine in the history of Karabagh and the rest of Armenia; records of culture and craftsmanship exist from 521 BC to the present.

1752. Blomstedt, Yrjö. MYYTIT JA MYYTINSÄRKİJÄT [Myths and myth-breakers]. *Hist. Arkisto [Finland] 1982 (77): 7-11*. Myths are created and shattered in historical studies because the assumptions and goals of historical research itself change over time.
　　　　　　　　　　　　　　　　　　　　　R. G. Selleck

1753. Bunkse, Edmund V. LATVIAN FOLKLORISTICS. *J. of Am. Folklore 1979 92(364): 196-214*. The collection and study of folklore has been the most important endeavor of Latvian cultural nationalism. Latvian folklore centers on the *dainas*, short quatrain folksongs, as analyzed by three succeeding schools: the mythological, historical-geographical, and Marxist-Leninist. Based in part on *daina* texts; 52 notes.　　　　　　　　W. D. Piersen

1754. Clayton, Lawrence. FACTUALITY VERSUS ARTISTIC LICENSE IN WESTERN FOLK SONGS. *West Texas Historical Association Year Book 1982 58: 176-180*. Although historians cannot rely on Western folk songs for complete accuracy, they will be surprised to discover how many accurate details are contained in the lyrics.　　　　　　　　　　　　　　　M. L. Tate

1755. Cohn, Norman. WAS THERE EVER A SOCIETY OF WITCHES? MYTHS AND HOAXES OF EUROPEAN DEMON-OLOGY. *Encounter [Great Britain] 1974 43(6): 26-41*. Discusses superstitions, hoaxes, and historiography regarding witchcraft and demonology in Europe from the 11th to 20th centuries. Article to be continued.

1756. Crawford, Charles W. THE DEVELOPMENT OF ORAL HISTORY RESEARCH IN TENNESSEE. *West Tennessee Hist. Soc. Papers 1975 29: 100-108*. Defines oral history as "a new discipline involving cooperative effort by a participant in history, a historian, and a machine." After succinctly describing seven programs active in Tennessee in oral history interviewing, the author then suggests some of the needs for oral history research in Tennessee: the country music industry; the culture and folklore of the Cumberland Plateau; notable events in recent Tennessee history; the post–World War II "war" at Athens; the experience of minorities who have been separated from the majority of the state's population; and the amount and kind of change occurring in selected Tennessee communities. Based on primary and secondary sources; 22 notes.
　　　　　　　　　　　　　　　　　　　　　H. M. Parker, Jr.

1757. DeCaro, F. A. ORAL HISTORY AND FOLKLORE IN SEVENTEENTH CENTURY ENGLAND. *Kentucky Folklore Record 1982 28(3-4): 33-39*. Discusses the overlap of oral history and folklore and the work of two early English scholars: John Aubrey, whose *Brief Lives,* written with Oxford scholar Anthony Woods, was an early monument to oral history and dealt chiefly with authors and bishops educated at Oxford after 1500; and Sir Nicholas L'Estrange (d. 1655), who compiled one of the most extensive collections of historical traditions associated with the courts of Elizabeth I and James I.

1758. D'Haenens, Albert. ORALITE, HISTOIRE ET MEMOIRE COLLECTIVE: DE LA RELATION OCCIDENTALE A LA TRADITION ET A L'HISTOIRE ORALES [Orality, history, and collective memory: Western relations to oral tradition and history]. *Cahiers de Clio [Belgium] 1983 (75-76): 14-23.* Describes the precedence of written over oral history in the West since the Middle Ages as "true" history and the reawakened interest during the 20th century in oral history due to the proliferation of audiovisual materials to record and reproduce such history.

1759. Dixon, Elizabeth I. ARROWHEAD IN RETROSPECT. *J. of Lib. Hist. 1967 2(2): 126-128.* A discussion of the success of the First National Colloquium on Oral History. Primary sources.
                                                                A. C. Dewees

1760. Egan, Kieran. MYTHICAL AND HISTORICAL REFERENCE TO THE PAST. *Clio 1973 2(3): 291-307.* Examines how myths deal with historical events in an effort to clarify the distinction between myth and history, using examples from ancient Egypt and medieval Europe.

1761. Eliade, Mircea. SOME OBSERVATIONS ON EUROPEAN WITCHCRAFT. *Hist. of Religions 1975 14(3): 149-172.* Briefly examines the major stages in the historiography of witchcraft, especially the work of Margaret Murray's *The Witch-Cult in Modern Europe* (1921). Shows the continuity of some important pagan rituals and beliefs relating to fertility and health in the development of European witchcraft. Discusses the Italian *benandanti* of the 16th and 17th centuries and the Romanian *stigoi* and *călusari* as examples of this trend. Shows the universality of charges of witches' orgies and cannibalism made against all heretics and even early Christians. Asserts that witches' orgies reflected a radical rebellion against contemporary religious and social standards and a desire to return to "beginning times." Secondary sources; 65 notes.
                                                                T. L. Auffenberg

1762. Estes, Leland L. INCARNATIONS OF EVIL: CHANGING PERSPECTIVES ON THE EUROPEAN WITCH CRAZE. *Clio 1984 13(2): 133-147.* Modern scholars continue to show interest in the European witch craze of the 16th and 17th centuries, searching for a new explanation for the evil behind the idea itself and for the focus of its often violent activities. Over the decades, scholars have shifted their emphasis from investigating the origin of the evil behind the craze to analyzing the objects and victims of witch-hunting. Secondary sources; 35 notes.   T. P. Linkfield

1763. Goodman, R. S. and Pryluck, Calvin. THE TAPE RECORDED INTERVIEW AS DATA FOR FILM HISTORY. *Speech Monographs 1972 39(4): 306-311.* "This study considered the nature of interview data as a significant problem in film historiography. Two extant interviews with a single individual were compared and were evaluated in the light of additional evidence. The investigation focused upon the quality of interview data. Interview data were noted to suffer from the problems of (1) failure of memory, (2) archetypal memory, and (3) the inability to accurately transcribe expression of mood. Interviews were found to have value as primary sources, as a means for determining the mood and intent of the oral rendition, and as a means for the researcher to get a better feeling for men and historical periods."   J

1764. Hodara, Joseph. HISTORIA, HEROES Y ANTIHEROES [History, heroes, and antiheroes]. *Estudios de Asia y Africa [Mexico] 1984 19(3): 335-341.* Man's ubiquitous subjectivity seems to demand the existence of heroes as exemplary models. This does not mean that history could be reduced to juxtaposition of their biographies. The hero's quality does not derive from his identity nor from the tasks he is assigned in history, for he always needs an audience which also seeks to enter in history acting as his accomplice.

19th-century romanticism and nationalism, 20th-century totalitarianism and spread of secular religions cannot be fully explained without the human appetite for heroism, which keeps alive our trust in historicity. 6 notes.   C. Pasadas-Ureña

1765. Houston, Joan. THE WITCHCRAFT CRAZE OF THE SIXTEENTH AND SEVENTEENTH CENTURIES. *Flinders J. of Hist. and Pol. [Australia] 1973 3: 54-60.* Criticizes existing interpretations as, for example, by Hugh Trevor-Roper for failing to fully understand the real nature of society during the 16th-17th centuries. Analyzes the source and nature of the European witchcraft craze during these centuries. Secondary sources; 40 notes.
                                                                P. J. Beck

1766. Johansen, Jens Christian V. TAVSHED ER GULD... [Silence is golden...]. *Hist. Tidsskrift [Denmark] 1982 81(2): 401-423.* This survey concentrates on three main areas of research into European and American witch-hunts: their origin, function, and termination. Micro studies of the history of witch-hunts in specific regions, published in the last 15 years, show great local variation preventing a general synthesis. Based on documents in the Danish Record Office and secondary sources; 76 notes.
                                                                H. C. Andersen

1767. Joyner, Charles W. ORAL HISTORY AS COMMUNICATIVE EVENT: A FOLKLORIST PERSPECTIVE. *Oral Hist. Rev. 1979: 47-52.* To develop a viable study of folk history, the historian must utilize the modes of analyses developed by folklorists. Oral memoirs hide the truth from the perceptive historian no more than other documents. 13 notes.   D. A. Yanchisin

1768. Kuschel, Rolf and Monberg, Torben. HISTORY AND ORAL TRADITIONS: A CASE STUDY. *J. of the Polynesian Soc. [New Zealand] 1977 86(1): 85-95.* Independent accounts of the late 19th century adventures of a Bellona islander known as Tom by William T. Wawn in *The South Sea Islanders and the Queensland Labour Trade* (1893), and by Daniel Tuhanuku, a Bellonese oral historian in the 1970's, show that properly understood oral histories have considerable value as history in the Western sense.

1769. Lindahl, Carl. "IT'S ONLY FOLKLORE...": FOLKLORE AND THE HISTORIAN. *Louisiana History 1985 26(2): 141-154.* Explains how folklore aids the historian. Much folk history is fact, and even when inaccurate it reveals "cultural fact"—the everyday lives and concerns of a people—and "emotional fact"—how a people views itself today and uses folk history to substantiate that view and pass it on to the next generation. Based on field work, folklore collections, newspapers, and secondary sources; 24 notes.
                                                                R. E. Noble

1770. Linder, Robert D. WANTED: SERIOUS HISTORIANS OF THE OCCULT. *Fides et Hist. 1973 6(1): 60-70.* Review-essay on nine books (1972-73) dealing with satanism, witchcraft, spiritualism, and other aspects of the occult sciences. Argues that these books should be taken seriously as source material on the occult, even if they are inadequate as histories. Although uneven and riddled with methodological and definitional problems, the volumes point up the need for serious scholarship in the occult. 38 notes.
                                                                R. Butchart

1771. Mohrmann, Ute. VOLKSKUNDE UND KULTURGESCHICHTE [Scientific folklore and cultural history]. *Zeitschrift für Geschichtswissenschaft [East Germany] 1974 22(7): 799-800.* Marxist-Leninist historiography needs scientific folklore studies for the analysis of the material culture and the living conditions of the working classes, as traditional historical sources usually lead toward a culture of the upper classes only.

1772. Murphy, Lawrence R. LUCIEN B. MAXWELL: THE MAKING OF A WESTERN LEGEND. *Arizona and the West 1980 22(2): 109-124.* Frontier mythmaking is a complicated process, especially when it concerns the American West. As a case study, the development of the legend of New Mexico rancher Lucien B. Maxwell (1818-75) is traced through the writings of novelists, popular writers, and historians. The paucity of solid historical evidence has encouraged authors to exercise their imaginations to concoct tales about his life. Understanding the mythmaking process will help historians to separate truth from legend. 9 illus., 20 notes.

D. L. Smith

1773. Oliver, Peter. ORAL HISTORY: ONE HISTORIAN'S VIEW. *Can. Oral Hist. Assoc. J. [Canada] 1975/76 1: 13-19.* Affirms the importance of oral history as a tool for the historian to assess daily life and popular thought during the modern age.

1774. Opie, John. FREDERICK JACKSON TURNER, THE OLD WEST, AND THE FORMATION OF A NATIONAL MYTHOLOGY. *Environmental Rev. 1981 5(2): 79-91.* Discusses the historiography of Frederick Jackson Turner, and its contribution to US folk history and popular mythology.

1775. Portelli, Alessandro. THE PECULIARITIES OF ORAL HISTORY. *Hist. Workshop J. [Great Britain] 1981 (12): 96-107.* Discusses the attitude of historians to oral history, asserting that written and oral sources demand different methods of interpretation. Considers the importance of listening to tapes as oral sources, rather than reading transcripts, which lose the class connotations and tonal nuances of speech. Oral history tells less about the factual aspects of events than about their meaning and effect on contemporaries in psychological terms. Factual credibility is usually seen as the prerogative of written sources, but oral sources have a psychological credibility that makes them as valuable to the historian. 21 notes.

1776. Rundell, Walter, Jr. MAIN TRENDS IN U.S. HISTORIOGRAPHY SINCE THE NEW DEAL: RESEARCH PROSPECTS IN ORAL HISTORY. *Oral Hist. Rev. 1976: 35-47.* Reviews the major trends in US historiography since 1933 with particular attention to those works making use of oral history. Oral historians should begin to investigate and gather information while events are still fresh, but they must remember that "Problems inherent in using oral history differ only in degree from those faced in research with literary evidence." The historian must make use of new methodologies and all the analytical advances to be gained from the behavioral and social sciences, but he "must be alert to biases and errors whenever he encounters them." 10 notes.

D. A. Yanchisin

1777. Salimbeni, Fulvio. LA STREGONERIA NEL TARDO RINASCIMENTO [Witchcraft in the later Renaissance]. *Nuova Riv. Storica [Italy] 1976 60(3-4): 269-334.* Examines witchcraft historiography noting that older works on the subject are chiefly descriptive, polemical, or apologetic. Their one-dimensional approach left important questions unanswered. After World War II, the widespread interest in sorcery and demonology attracted much interest. The author surveys the topic, the new research methods employed, the questions raised, and some of the conclusions. New psychoanalytic and social pathologic approaches reveal depths of the subject that had not been previously explored. Of the many students of the subject H. R. Trevor-Roper above all has made a valuable contribution.

H. W. L. Freudenthal

1778. Schafer, William J. FURTHER THOUGHTS ON JAZZ HISTORIOGRAPHY: THAT ROBERT CHARLES SONG. *J. of Jazz Studies 1978 5(1): 19-27.* Reviews jazz history by studying discrepancies between facts and legends, especially those of Jelly Roll Morton, about Robert Charles, a black man in New Orleans who in July 1900, after an attempt to arrest him, killed seven whites (including four policemen) and wounded 20 others with a rifle before being killed himself.

D. J. Engler

1779. Šindelář, B. HON NA ČARODĚJICE V ZÁPADNÍ HISTORIOGRAFII PO DRUHÉ SVĚTOVÉ VÁLCE [The witch hunt in Western historiography since World War II]. *Sborník prací Filosofické Fakulty Brněnské U. Rada Hist. [Czechoslovakia] 1973 22(20): 168-187.* A selective bibliography of the literature relating to the persecution of witches produced by Western scholars since World War II. Despite the existence of a considerable body of research on the persecution of witches, the subject has been largely ignored by the leading historical journals in the West. This neglect

may be due to embarrassment on the part of some bourgeois historians that while the persecution of witches reached epidemic proportions in Western and Central Europe in the 16th and 17th centuries, it was rare in the allegedly backward East European countries where Orthodox Christianity prevailed. 42 notes.

F. H. Eidlin

1780. Sitton, Thad. ORAL LIFE HISTORY: FROM TAPE RECORDER TO TYPEWRITER. *Social Studies 1981 72(3): 121-126.* Oral history offers a unique source for understanding the community, the culture, and the genealogy of a given group of people. 12 notes.

L. R. Raife

1781. Stănculescu, Florea. ISTORIA ORALĂ SI VALOAREA EI CA IZVOR ISTORIC [Oral history and its value as a historic source]. *Analele U. Bucureşti: Istorie [Romania] 1980 29: 36-45.* Oral history dating from the 16th century offers students a glimpse of the spirit and tradition of the Romanian people as it has been transmitted from generation to generation. Oral history also provides a valuable source of information on society, politics, and culture. In addition, changes in the Romanian language and the development of proverbs have been interesting results of oral history projects. Based on secondary sources; 28 notes.

M. A. Preda

1782. Stenberg, Henry G. SELECTED BIBLIOGRAPHY, 1977-1981. *Oral Hist. Rev. 1982 10: 119-132.* This checklist of oral history research contains 237 items divided into four classes: manuals; catalogs and guides; books; periodical articles. Updates John Fox's "Bibliography Up-Date".

D. A. Yanchisin

1783. Strobach, H. EINIGE VOLKSKUNDLICHE PROBLEME DES HISTORISCHEN ERBES [Folklore problems in historical heritage]. *Zeits. für Geschichtswissenschaft [East Germany] 1981 29(7): 611-617.* Discusses the relationship between heritage and tradition and problems concerning customs and ethnic traditions.

T. Parker/S

1784. Strobach, H. METODOLOGICHESKIE PROBLEMY ISTORICHESKOGO IZUCHENIIA FOL'KLORA [Methodological problems of the historical study of folklore]. *Sovetskaia Etnografiia [USSR] 1983 (5): 48-58.* Examines questions currently facing German scholars of folklore, paying particular attention to the problems of sources.

1785. Thompson, E. P. FOLKLORE, ANTHROPOLOGY, AND SOCIAL HISTORY. *Indian Hist. Rev. [India] 1977 3(2): 247-266.* The writing of social history will benefit from the reexamination of old, long-collected folklore material by subjecting it to new questions with a view to recovering lost customs and beliefs. It is equally necessary for a historian in the Marxist tradition to accept that neither the congruities nor the contradictions of the deeper historical process could be handled without attending to the problems raised by anthropologists in their work. 40 notes.

V. Samaraweera

1786. Thompson, Roger. REVIEW ARTICLE: SALEM REVISITED. *J. of Am. Studies [Great Britain] 1972 6(3): 317-336.* Discusses the historiography of witchcraft (alleged) suppression in Salem, Massachusetts, in 1692 and in England. The psychological aspects and social dynamics of the behavior of many principals in the incidents have proven difficult to explain. Although "temporary and insecure [public] authorities" in each case allowed the "mania" to develop, major differences do exist between the Salem and English experiences. Reexamination of the "connexion between witchcraft and Puritanism" is in order. Based on secondary sources; 22 notes.

H. T. Lovin and S

1787. Titon, Jeff Todd. THE LIFE STORY. *J. of Am. Folklore 1980 93(369): 276-292.* Defines "life story" as a "self-contained fiction" of personal narrative ordering the past by present personality. Biography, oral history, and personal history, its historical kin, differ in focusing on events, processes, causes, and effects rather than on the individual. These forms are usually shaped by the stance of the historian and the questions asked of the informant. 50 notes.   W. D. Piersen

1788. Weber, Devra. ORAL SOURCES AND THE HISTORY OF MEXICAN WORKERS IN THE UNITED STATES. *Int. Labor and Working Class Hist. 1983 (23): 47-50.* The paucity of written records on Mexican-American laborers and labor relations during the 1920's-30's requires that scholars use oral history approaches to the subject.

1789. Whitt, Dana Gabbart. THE JUICE OF HISTORY: THE WRITINGS OF A. C. GREENE. *West Texas Hist. Assoc. Year Book 1978 54: 76-81.* Summarizes a 1977 interview of A. C. Greene, conducted by the author, in which Greene discusses his native West Texas, his work, his stress on local history, and belief that the folk element of history—the "juice" of history—should receive greater emphasis in all historical writing.

1790. Wilder, Amos N. BETWEEN REMINISCENCE AND HISTORY: A MISCELLANY. *Massachusetts Hist. Soc. Pro. 1975 87: 105-117.* Informal reminiscence, impromptu recollection, and other forms of oral recital are at the roots of history. In both oral reminiscence and formal history there are omissions, distortions, abstractions, and superficialities; each operates under the same laws and in light of the same hazard. Based on numerous anecdotes and reminiscences from European and American published sources, diaries and autobiographies; note, index.   G. W. R. Ward

1791. Wilson, William A. FOLKLORE AND HISTORY: FACT AMID THE LEGENDS. *Utah Hist. Q. 1973 41(1): 40-58.* A defense of "the validity of folklore as evidence of history." A number of illustrations from Indian, black, and early Utah folklore indicate the accuracy of the historical fact enshrined in such traditions. Equally important is what can be learned of cultural history from the same kind of sources. Perhaps the most important value in folklore study is its indication of what a group of people believe about their past which helps the historian understand the motivations which govern people's lives in the present. 4 photos, 32 notes.
                                              R. V. Ritter

1792. Zguta, Russell. FOLKLORE AS HISTORY: RUSSIAN *BYLINY* AND *ISTORICHESKIE PESNI. Southern Folklore Q. 1971 35(2): 97-120.* Discusses genres of folklore in Russian historical writings from the 1863 to the 20th century, emphasizing the thought of historians L. N. Maikov and V. F. Miller.

The Use of Psychology in History

1793. Ardelt, Rudolf G. PSYCHOANALYSE UND HISTORISCHE BIOGRAPHIK [Psychoanalysis and historical biography]. *Zeitgeschichte [Austria] 1976 3(7): 234-243.* Critically evaluates the relevance of psychoanalytical biographies in modern historiography. 36 notes, biblio.   R. Wagnleitner

1794. Beaver, Harold. PARKMAN'S CRACK-UP: A BOSTONIAN ON THE OREGON TRAIL. *New England Q. 1975 48(1): 84-103.* A psychological and sociological study of Francis Parkman as revealed in his *Journal* and his *The Oregon Trail.* The study centers on his handling of the Indians, whose observation he claims to be the main purpose of his trip. Scholars have strongly disagreed on the merits of his work, but have often failed to properly understand his purposes. His physical and mental breakdown for about two years after his return is a major clue revealing a very unbalanced and neurotic personality unable to cope with the radical contrasts between the values his own upbringing had inculcated and the reality he faced on the trip. Moreover, this same upbringing greatly warped his powers of observation and interpretation. 60 notes.   R. V. Ritter

1795. Brown, Richard D. MODERNIZATION AND THE MODERN PERSONALITY IN EARLY AMERICA, 1600-1865: A SKETCH OF A SYNTHESIS. *J. of Interdisciplinary Hist. 1972 2(3): 201-228.* Explores the concept of modernization as a meaningful synthesis of American development, and questions whether the specific character of the American experience confirms or challenges the conventional model of modernization. The attempt at such an analysis reveals the variants that a particular situation may introduce into modernization models. In this case, America's underpopulation is largely responsible for its unusual path of development. Although existing conceptualizations of modernization have flaws, their emphasis on historical process and their potential for cross-cultural and cross-chronological comparisons give them unusual advantages for such analysis. 161 notes.   R. V. Ritter

1796. Byrnes, Joseph F. SUGGESTIONS ON WRITING THE HISTORY OF PSYCHOLOGICAL DATA. *Hist. and Theory 1977 16(3): 297-305.* Historians must be flexible in their use of psychological analysis. Historians must follow the data and not be limited by a particular psychological theory or methodology. Moreover, historians are not compelled to establish rigid categories to solve problems as therapists and psychometricians. Finally, the historian needs only to defend the terminology he employs for its rationality. 11 notes.   D. A. Yanchisin

1797. Caruso, Igor A. PSYCHOANALYSE UND ENTFREMDUNG [Psychoanalysis and alienation]. *Zeitgeschichte [Austria] 1975 3(1): 1-7.* Economic alienation penetrates every aspect of human life. Psychoanalysis can analyze the subjective manifestations of history in the alienation of an individual. Illus.
                                              R. Wagnleitner

1798. Crunden, Robert M. FREUD, ERIKSON, AND THE HISTORIAN: A BIBLIOGRAPHICAL SURVEY. *Can. R. of Am. Studies 1973 4(1): 48-64.* In American historical writing since 1945 psychoanalytic theories have enjoyed a growing vogue. Professional historians depend heavily on Sigmund Freud (1856-1939) and Erik Erikson for their psychiatric knowledge. The results are not completely satisfactory; sometimes, the writings proved highly controversial. Applying psychoanalysis produced "sexual reductionism" in some writings, notably in histories of King Henry VIII of England. Writings using psychoanalytic theories about Martin Luther, Mohandas Karamchand (Mahatma) Gandhi, and Woodrow Wilson provoked allegations that reformers had been unfairly denigrated. The works of David Donald on Charles Sumner produced the same complaint, especially from "radicals" who refused to accept downgrading of their Abolitionist heroes. Discusses several technical problems that have emerged when historians have tried to use psychoanalytic theory. 30 notes.   H. T. Lovin

1799. Curry, Richard O. A REVIEW ESSAY: CONSCIOUS OR SUBCONSCIOUS CAESARISM? A CRITIQUE OF RECENT SCHOLARLY ATTEMPTS TO PUT ABRAHAM LINCOLN ON THE ANALYST'S COUCH. *J. of the Illinois State Hist. Soc. 1984 77(1): 67-71.* While many historians have emphasized the radicalism of Abraham Lincoln on the issue of slavery, only Harold Hyman, La Wanda Cox, and David Lightner have noted Lincoln's egalitarianism. Recent psychohistorical studies by George B. Forgie, Dwight G. Anderson, and Charles B. Stozier present erroneous interpretations of Lincoln's political motivations. These works are grounded in conjecture, faulty logic, and an inadequate understanding of Lincoln's era. 13 notes.   A. W. Novitsky

1800. Deutsch, Robert. DIE PSYCHOHISTORIE UND DIE SOWJETISCHE GESCHICHTSSCHREIBUNG. ZUR GESCHICHTE EINER GRENZÜBERSCHREITUNG [Psychohistory and Soviet historiography: the history of crossing a boundary]. *Schweizerische Zeits. für Gesch. [Switzerland] 1983 33(2): 168-191.* Psychohistory, dealing with emotionally subconscious and supratemporal aspects of history, is in direct contrast to Soviet historiography, which emphasizes the temporal and lawfully ordered nature of history. Soviet historiography, in its function as an openly repressive tool of the ruling elite, presents a succession of revisionist and self-contradictory interpretations of the history of the Soviet Union and other Communist countries. As a science, it is forced into dependence on a political system and reflects in its contradictions the cyclical changes in that system. Even though some Russian historians, such as M. N. Pokrovsky and N. A. Rojkov, did pioneer work in psychohistory before World War II, the dominant attitude in Communist countries toward psychohistory is one of critical rejection. 44 notes.   H. K. Meier

1801. Himmelfarb, Gertrude. THE "NEW HISTORY." *Commentary 1975 59(1): 72-78.* Reviews Jacques Barzun's *Clio and the Doctors: Psycho-History, Quanto-History, and History* (Chicago: U. of Chicago Press, 1975).

1802. Hugenholtz, F. W. N. LE DECLIN DU MOYEN AGE (1919-1969) [The Waning of the Middle Ages, 1919-69]. *Acta Historiae Neerlandica [Netherlands] 1971 (5): 40-51.* Johan Huizinga's *The Waning of the Middle Ages* appeared in 1919. Although the author was influenced by Burckhardt, his work did not produce the prolonged polemics and intense debates as did that of the Swiss historian. While it was initially received with some skepticism by Dutch colleagues, the book sold some 50,000 copies in the Netherlands and was translated into many foreign languages. It is read especially by non-historians and has become a classic especially because it inaugurated, at least in the Netherlands, the idea of psychological inquiry. 10 notes.   G. D. Homan

1803. King, Richard H. FROM CREEDS TO THERAPIES: PHILIP RIEFF'S WORK IN PERSPECTIVE. *Rev. in Am. Hist. 1976 4(2): 291-296.* Discusses the historiography and theory of Philip Rieff pertaining to psychohistory, interpretation of Freud, and application of psychoanalytic theory to history, 1959-73, in relation to the formation of the modern American mind, popular culture, and cultural and intellectual history.

1804. Kren, George M. PSYCHOHISTORICAL INTERPRETATIONS OF NATIONAL SOCIALISM. *German Studies Rev. 1978 1(2): 150-172.* Surveys the major psychohistorical interpretations of Nazism, including those concentrating on the national leadership and those seeking to understand "followership" and the passivity of the concentration camp victims. This approach proves to be particularly appropriate due to the "large irrational component of National Socialism which traditional historiography has not been able to handle adequately." 55 notes.   R. V. Ritter

1805. LaPenna, Linda. LA PSYCHOHISTORY: PROPOSTE E STUDI NELLA STORIOGRAFIA AMERICANA [Psychohistory: proposals and research in American historiography]. *Quaderni Storici [Italy] 1981 16(2): 574-605.* Psychohistory has been debated in the United States for the past 60 years, but so far there has been more talk than research. In the past decade, however, studies inspired not only by psychoanalysis but also by academic psychology have appeared. Surveys recent essays that have produced new historical insights but expresses skepticism about the future of psychohistory as an autonomous field of research.   J

1806. Lennon, J. Michael and Strozier, Charles B. EMPATHY AND DETACHMENT IN THE NARRATIVES OF ERIKSON AND MAILER. *Psychohistory Rev. 1981 10(1): 18-32.* Erik Erikson's *Gandhi's Truth* (1969) and Norman Mailer's *The Armies of the Night* (1968) demonstrate history and literature can be merged through the sensitive use of empathy by the writer. Psychohistorical studies and the new nonfiction, represented by Erikson and Mailer, are moving into common ground. Both Erikson and Mailer discuss their involvement with and empathy for their subjects. Both blend objective historical fact with their own subjectivities. Both works are landmarks in the convergence of history and narrative literature. 43 notes.   J. M. Herrick

1807. Lewis, Thomas T. ALTERNATIVE PSYCHOLOGICAL INTERPRETATIONS OF WOODROW WILSON. *Mid-America 1983 65(2): 71-85.* Woodrow Wilson has been the subject of widely divergent psychological and psychohistorical interpretations. 80 notes.   P. J. Woehmann

1808. Loewenberg, Peter. PSYCHOHISTORY. Kammen, Michael, ed. *The Past Before Us: Contemporary Historical Writing in the United States* (Ithaca, NY: Cornell U. Pr., 1980): 408-432. Since William L. Langer's 1957 address to the American Historical Association, US historians have increasingly realized that "not only social and political contexts but also personal life and family settings predispose historians to given kinds of materials, values, research problems, and interpretations" despite a wariness to using psychoanalysis. Biography best lends itself to the blending of history and psychoanalysis: Erik H. Erikson's study of Martin Luther related "psychosocial identity crises" to a historical movement. The psychological aspect of ideology and racism—Nazism and anti-Semitism, US attitudes toward Indians and Negroes—has received a great deal of attention. Psychoanalysis also provides insight into intellectual and cultural history, e.g. Carl E. Schorske's studies of 19th-century Vienna and Peter Gay's work on Sigmund Freud. American historians have applied psychohistory "both crudely and well, both daringly and conservatively." 93 notes.   S

1809. Luck, David. A PSYCHOLINGUISTIC APPROACH TO LEADER PERSONALITY: HITLER, STALIN, MAO, AND LIU SHAO-CH'I. *Studies in Comparative Communism 1974 7(4): 426-453.* The Freudian oral-anal pattern is conducive to objective and comparable information about political leaders. Orality involves high self-esteem, impulsiveness, tendency to pull objects towards oneself and alternation of behaviors as well as relative freedom from anxiety while anality represents lower self-esteem, obsessive and compulsive behavior, and relatively high anxiety. An index of the first 1000 images in *Mein Kampf* and in Stalin's *Sochineniia* showed violent oral imagery in Adolf Hitler and violent anal imagery in Joseph Stalin. Hitler's imagery was 59% oral, Mao Tse-tung's 35%, Liu Shao-Ch'i 23%, and Stalin's 14%. 3 tables, 2 figs., 48 notes, appendix.   D. Balmuth

1810. Neuman, R. P. CLIO, EROS, AND PSYCHE: SEPARATION, DIVORCE OR MARRIAGE. *Psychohistory Rev. 1978 7(1): 6-12.* Summarizes the theories of recent historians of sex. Most are anti-Freudian and optimistic about the possibilities for sexual happiness in contemporary Western culture. Havelock Ellis, Alfred Kinsey, and Vern Bullogh were proponents of the view that sexuality is simply biological fact as opposed to the Freudian theory of continual struggle between sexual drives and cultural mores. Psychoanalytic theory can explain such phenomena as the rise of illegitimacy after 1750 as well as the concern over masturbation expressed in the 18th and 19th centuries. The author reviews the writings of Michel Foucault, J. Barker-Benfield, and Edmund Shorter. Contemporary culture has sacrificed the notion of love for the preoccupation with sexual technique. 25 notes.   J. M. Herrick

1811. Raffel, Burton. EMOTIONAL HISTORY: AN EXPLORATORY ESSAY. *Biography 1984 7(4): 352-362.* Presents an overview of "emotional history," a new historical subdiscipline pioneered by the author; emotional history is the study of the "inner lives" of individuals in order to determine "what it was like to be alive then, how it felt being alive, in contrast to being alive today."

1812. Salimbeni, Fulvio. PSICANALISI E STORIOGRAFIA: UN PROBLEMA PLURIDISCIPLINARE [Psychoanalysis and historiography: a multidisciplinary problem]. *Studium [Italy] 1981 77(5): 565-580.* Psychoanalysis joined to historical research can be an effective cognitive tool for the study of religion as well as of the new secularized faith which is psychoanalysis itself.

1813. Salov, V. I. VTORZHENIE PSIKHOANALIZA V BURZHUAZNUIU ISTORIOGRAFIIU [The intrusion of psychoanalysis into bourgeois historiography]. *Novaia i Noveishaia Istoriia [USSR] 1972 (4): 89-105.* Describes the differences between Marxist-Leninist and bourgeois historiography, pointing out that psychoanalysis has entered much of the bourgeois intellectual sphere. For example, much use is made of the theories of Sigmund Freud whose analyses of Leonardo da Vinci and Dostoevski show a disbelief in man's creative abilities, preferring to consider man driven by the baser passions and instincts. Bourgeois psychoanalysis attempts to show that aggression is inevitable and even praiseworthy. It tries to focus attention away from class conflict and Marxism-Leninism to an examination of the dark passions which, it claims, govern the world. Based on American, British, German, and Soviet sources; 84 notes. A. J. Evans

1814. Schmidt, Casper. ALCHEMISTS, CRITICS AND PSYCHO-HISTORIANS. *J. of Psychohistory 1981 8(3): 337-367.* Defines alchemy as a study without the appropriate conceptual tools and believes that the four following books are in an alchemical, rather than a psychohistorical, phase: *Continuities and Discontinuities: Essays in Psychohistory,* edited by Shirley Sugerman (1978); *Quantification and Psychology: Toward A 'New' History,* edited by Harvey J. Graff and Paul Monaco (1980); *New Directions in Psychohistory: The Adelphi Papers in Honor of Erik H. Erikson,* edited by Mel Albin (1980); and *Shrinking History: On Freud and the Failure of Psychohistory,* by David E. Stannard (1980). 10 notes. L. F. Velicer

1815. Strout, Cushing. PSYCHE, CLIO, AND THE ARTIST. Albin, Mel, ed. *New Directions in Psychohistory: The Adelphi Papers in Honor of Erik H. Erikson* (Lexington, Mass.: Heath, 1980): 97-115. The common ground between literary critics, historians, and psychoanalysts is their imaginative participation in other people's experience. Because of this, elements of psychoanalysis, particularly ego psychology and Erik H. Erikson's concepts of identity and the life-cycle, may help preserve the human concreteness of history, biography, and fiction while freeing us from the strictures of conceptual language. This theme is applied in an evaluation of psychobiographies of literary and political figures, addressing the complex movement, back and forth, between the author's life and his text, the essential task of the critic and the biographer. Secondary sources; 56 notes. J. Powell

1816. Talmon, J. L. PSYCHOSOCIAL HISTORY. *Hist. and Theory 1975 14(1): 121-137.* Review-essay prompted by Fred Weinstein and Gerald M. Platt's *The Wish To Be Free. Society, Psyche and Value Change* (Berkeley and Los Angeles: U. of California Pr., 1969) and *Psychoanalytic Sociology. An Essay on the Interpretation of Historical Data and the Phenomena of Collective Behavior* (Baltimore and London: Johns Hopkins U. Pr., 1973). S

1817. Wallace, Edwin, R., IV. HISTORIOGRAPHY IN HISTORY AND PSYCHOANALYSIS. *Bull. of the Hist. of Medicine 1983 57(2): 247-266.* The subject matter, methodology, and problems and possibilities of historians and psychoanalysts are comparable in many ways. The historian and the psychoanalyst both seek to understand past events and their meaning. Both require discrimination and analysis of sources. 30 notes. M. Kaufman

1818. Wehler, Hans-Ulrich. PSYCHOANALYSIS AND HISTORY. *Social Res. 1980 47(3): 519-536.* In the late 1960's German social scientists began to make use of psychoanalytic theory though German historians remained dubious of its value; a costs-benefits analysis of psychoanalytic theory as an aid to historians suggests that, despite undeniable parallels between the two disciplines and the ability of psychoanalysis to offer an occasional historical insight, social psychology will probably prove of more enduring value to the historian because of its applicability to groups as well as individuals.

1819. Zeldin, Theodore. PERSONAL HISTORY AND THE HISTORY OF THE EMOTIONS. *J. of Social Hist. 1982 15(3): 339-347.* More historians should attempt to escape the restraining uniformity of professional conformity. A historical style of topic and presentation that mingles personal understanding and some aspect of the history of human emotions is a sign of a discipline seeking a more pluralistic and accurate reflection of life. Love or loneliness, in a narrow place and time with all the mundane interactions, or as a more psychological and literary analysis, or the reassessing of an existing subject in the light of these human preoccupations would be valuable contributions to historiography. 18 notes. C. M. Hough

1820. —. DISCURSO DE RECEPCION DE DON MAURO TORRES AGREDO [Installation address of Don Mauro Torres Agredo]. *Bol. de Hist. y Antigüedades [Colombia] 1982 69(739): 936-955.*
Torres Agredo, Mauro. PSICOLOGIA DE LAS MASAS [Psychology of the masses], *pp. 936-950.* A review of the phenomenon of mass psychology and its treatment in historical and other literature.
Rodríguez Plata, Horacio. RESPUESTA AL DISCURSO DE DON MAURO TORRES [Reply to the address of Don Mauro Torres], *pp. 951-955.* Pays tribute to Torres as a leading Colombian psychiatrist who has combined his professional training with an interest in history to become an exponent of the psychological dimension in historiography and author of various psychological biographies. D. Bushnell

1821. —. THE PSYCHOHISTORY OF HISTORY: A SYMPOSIUM. *J. of Psychohistory 1981 8(3): 259-279.*
Ebel, Henry. [THE PSYCHOHISTORY OF HISTORY], *pp. 259-261.* History is a dying science.
Ball, Richard A. COMMENT, *pp. 261-263.* Ebel may be correct in predicting the end of history.
DeMause, Lloyd. COMMENT, *pp. 263-264.* Sees a perversion of reading and writing history and believes psychohistory can overcome this.
Orban, Peter. COMMENT, *pp. 264-265.* Writing history is a way to lower one's anxiety.
Beisel, David R. COMMENT, *pp. 265-268.* Since the past is necessary to study the present, history can be turned to better uses.
Binion, Rudolph. COMMENT, *pp. 268-269.* Fears of the past, and therefore of history, cannot be escaped.
Ende, Aurel. COMMENT, *pp. 269-271.* Psychohistory will help the human race survive.
Stein, Howard F. COMMENT, *pp. 271-272.* Discusses paradoxes inherent in studies of history.
Gonen, Jay Y. COMMENT, *pp. 273-275.* The terrors and anxieties of history can be tolerated by psychohistorians.
Raeithel, Gert. COMMENT, *pp. 275-276.* Reflects on the changeability in interpretations of the past.
Ryan, Stephen. COMMENT, *pp. 277-278.* Sees continued human need for history as a psychic buffer.
Ebel, Henry. REPLY, *pp. 278-279.* There is much work available in the field of psychohistory. 2 notes. L. F. Velicer

The Philosophy of History

1822. Assiter, Alison. THE THEORY OF POVERTY OR GOOD OLD ENGLISH WORKING-CLASS HISTORY. *Literature and Hist. [Great Britain] 1979 5(2): 145-152.* Part of a symposium discussing E. P. Thompson's *The Poverty of Theory* (Merlin Pr., 1978). Criticizes Thompson's philosophical techniques, his critique of the French Marxist Louis Althusser, his interpretation of Marx, and his own political conduct.

1823. Bullock, Alan. THE HISTORIAN'S PURPOSE: HISTORY AND METAHISTORY. *Hist. Today [Great Britain] 1979 29(11): 710-714.* Discusses the history of the philosophy of history, from Friedrich Engels to Oswald Spengler to Marc Bloch.

1824. Canfora, Luciano. ANALOGIE ET HISTOIRE [Analogy and history]. *Hist. and Theory 1983 22(1): 22-42.* Examines the roles of analogical thinking in the development of historiography and the philosophy of history. Even the first historian whom the profession recognizes as "scientifically" factual, Thucydides, approached his own account of the Peloponnesian War by reviewing the origins and travails of not only the past itself but earlier attempts to recount that past. In the work of 19th-century theorists such as J. G. Droysen and Wilhelm Dilthey, a preoccupation with historical conceptualizing and writing as efforts at comprehension that required the search for resemblances through analogies became explicitly and elaborately articulated. Reflection on the place of analogy in historiography has recently gained a new acuteness and should never be neglected by self-conscious historians. 47 notes.

W. J. Reedy

1825. Carr, David. REVIEW ESSAY: TEMPS ET RECIT. *History and Theory 1984 23(3): 357-370.* Reviews Paul Ricoeur's *Temps et Récit* (1983). In this work of philosophy of history, Ricoeur examines the relationship between historiography and narration. He considers historical works as literary texts. Like metaphor, narrative seeks to achieve a "synthesis of the heterogeneous." Narration is an "operation of configuration." Ricoeur's book consolidates much of the recent thinking about the functions of narration. But perhaps he does not emphasize enough the configured "poetic" continuity that exists between "life" and "art." 20 notes.   W. J. Reedy

1826. Cherno, Melvin. DILTHEY'S "ALLGEMEINE LAN-DRECHT" AND THE HISTORIOGRAPHY OF ORGANIC CONNECTIONS. *Clio 1977 6(3): 307-326.* Examines an unpublished manuscript by Wilhelm Dilthey (1883-1911) and his philosophy of history. The historian must first discover "organic connections" or some "regular structure" in the relationship between the parts and the whole of his subject. He must then transmit to the reader an understanding of the structure he has discovered by making his work reflect that structure. The historian's art of presenting connections is very similar to that of any creative artist. Dilthey applied this theory to his study of the Prussian Law Code of 1794 by showing the social, political, and intellectual connections underlying the code. 64 notes.   T. P. Linkfield

1827. Chickering, Roger. HISTORY AND MORALITY IN HISTORICAL DRAMA: A HISTORIAN'S PERSPECTIVE ON HOCHHUTH'S SOLDATEN. *German Studies Rev. 1979 2(3): 351-361.* Discusses Rolf Hochhuth's play *Soldaten: Nekrolog auf Genf* (Reinbek, 1967) and its author's moralistic philosophy of history which disregards the complexity of historical events and persons and unconsciously distorts and manipulates them to fit its tenets. The modern historian also distrusts the view that great historical figures like Winston Churchill shape history. Hochhuth's plays and the writings of some historians have given a greatly distorted view of World War II, a war which remains to be reevaluated with scrupulous regard for evidence. Based mostly on Hochhuth's *Soldaten* and other plays; 26 notes.   G. Herritt

1828. Cole, C. Robert. HISTORIANS AND OTHERS: THEORETICAL PERSPECTIVES IN HISTORIOGRAPHY TODAY. *Rocky Mountain Social Sci. J. 1973 10(2): 115-121.* Review essay examining six books on the theory of history.   S

1829. DeVries, Willem A. MEANING AND INTERPRETATION IN HISTORY. *Hist. and Theory 1983 22(3): 253-263.* Philosophers of history who do not believe that historiography can attain nomological generalizations insist that historians' methodology is inherently interpretative. However, too little attention has been paid to the theory of meaning that must be found to ground interpretation. There are four main notions of meaning advanced by linguists: the referential, the behavioral, the ideational, and the translational. Reenactment interpretationists such as R. G. Collingwood have unfortunately flirted with the ideational definition and this preference has led critics to see interpretationist thinking as mystically intuitional. Yet Peter Winch, Charles Taylor, and other hermeneutically inclined interpretationists embrace a translational theory of meaning that allows their approach to interpreting society and history to rest on wide contextual understanding rather than intuition. The ability to succeed at historical interpretation is indeterminate but not mysterious. 14 notes.   W. J. Reedy

1830. Diggins, John P. THE PERILS OF NATURALISM: SOME REFLECTIONS ON DANIEL J. BOORSTIN'S APPROACH TO AMERICAN HISTORY. *Am. Q. 1971 23(2): 153-180.* To Daniel J. Boorstin, American history is essentially "the triumph of matter over mind," the graveyard of abstract theory: "America was the resurrection of practical life." Questions whether the concept of "givenness," values implicit in the acts themselves, sufficiently explains three major episodes in American history: New England Puritanism,

the Revolution and the Constitution, and the Civil War. By an analysis of these three episodes 1) shows how his assumptions force him to exaggerate, if not distort, some central aspects of American intellectual history, 2) demonstrates that certain thinkers whom Boorstin believes to have been antitheoretical were profoundly theoretical in their political and social thought, 3) suggests that the deterministic implications in the idea of "givenness" preclude historical causation and thereby render Boorstin ill-equipped to explain major crises like the Civil War, and 4) points up the latent moral ironies in Boorstin's naturalistic philosophy of history. There needs to be a restoration of theory, ideas, and moral judgment in the study of the American past. 71 notes.   R. V. Ritter

1831. Dray, W. H. R. G. COLLINGWOOD ON THE A PRIORI OF HISTORY. *Clio 1983 12(2): 169-181.* Although critical of positivist historians who sought general patterns or laws in the historical process, Collingwood did insist that historians construct detailed "pictures" of the past, not only by selecting and criticizing their sources but also by using their own prior historical knowledge about the subjects they research. Using his "disciplined imagination" to fill in the gaps left by inadequate sources, the historian can construct a picture of the past that is coherent and continuous. Based mainly on the essays in Collingwood's *The Idea of History* (1946); 9 notes.   T. P. Linkfield

1832. Ginsburg, Jerry. THE IMPLICATIONS OF ANALYTIC PHILOSOPHY OF HISTORY FOR THE PRACTICING HISTORIAN. *Hist. Methods Newsletter 1975 8(3): 121-133.* Reviews Murray Murphey's *Our Knowledge of the Historical Past* (New York: Bobbs-Merrill, 1973), criticizing Murphey's comments on the writings of Carl G. Hempel. Hempel's concept clarification and testing of general laws is productive for historical understanding. The author considers analytic philosophy useful to historians.

D. K. Pickens

1833. Goetz, Hans-Werner. "VORSTELLUNGSGESCHICHTE": MENSCHLICHE VORSTELLUNGEN UND MEINUNGEN ALS DIMENSION DER VERGANGENHEIT. BERMERKUNGEN ZU EINEM JÜNGEREN ARBEITSFELD DER GESCHICHTSWISSENSCHAFT ALS BEITRAG ZU EINER METHODIK DER QUELLENAUSWERTUNG ["Concept History": human concepts and views as a dimension of the past—remarks on a new field of history as a contribution to a method of source evaluation]. *Arch. für Kulturgeschichte [West Germany] 1979 61(2): 253-271.* As here defined, concept history does not reconstruct the past in its actuality, but rather the past as the processed reality of contemporaries. Thus it is the history of past times. Because it deduces neither facts nor structures, it represents, along with event history and structural history, a third way of looking at the past with its own methods and results. It puts the reflections and expressions of the contemporary at the center. It asks not how a certain fact came to exist (event history) or what that fact as a type had in common with other facts (structural history), but how contemporaries saw that certain fact. And like the other two ways of looking at the past, it has both limits and possibilities. 61 notes.

H. D. Andrews

1834. Gottfried, Paul. MYTH, IDEOLOGY, AND AN UNFINISHED TASK FOR CONSERVATIVE HISTORIANS. *Continuity 1982 (4-5): 31-49.* Many theorists have outlined deterministic patterns in history. These deterministic theories are myths, and while the conservative historian should not use them as sufficient cause for explaining historical events, he should consider them as crucial conditioning factors.   W. A. Wiegand

1835. Levine, Joseph M. COLLINGWOOD, VICO AND THE *AUTOBIOGRAPHY*. *Clio 1980 9(3): 379-392.* Suggests a solution to the problem of why R. G. Collingwood failed to acknowledge the influence of Giambattista Vico and other Italian writers when he wrote his *Autobiography* in 1939. Collingwood intended the *Autobiography* as a philosophical argument, a condensed version of the books he had been working on for twenty years. He was trying to demonstrate the social value of the union of philosophy and history, not the origins of the ideas he was preaching. 45 notes.

T. P. Linkfield

1836. Mader, Johann. POLITIK IM "OFFENEN HORIZONT" [Politics in the "open horizon"]. *Wissenschaft und Weltbild* [Austria] 1963 16(2): 81-91. Discusses the philosophy of history of Karl Jaspers and its impact on historiography.

1837. Muret, Philippe. CHASTELAIN PARMI NOUS. A PROPOS D'UN LIVRE RECENT [Chastellain among us: notes on a recent book]. *Rev. Belge de Philologie et d'Hist.* [Belgium] 1983 61(2): 367-372. Reviews of J.-C. Delclos, *Le Témoignage de Georges Chastellain, Historiographe de Philippe le Bon et de Charles le Téméraire* [The testimony of George Chastellain, historiographer of Philip the Good and Charles the Bold]. Declos analyzes Chastellain's *Chronicle,* commenting on his philosophy of history. Based on secondary sources; 12 notes.

B. S. Fetter

1838. Palonen, Kari. AJOPUUTEORIAN AATEKRITIIKIÄ, ELI ERÄITÄ SELITYKSIÄ SUOMALAISEN HISTORIANTUTKI-MUKSEN KONSERVATISMILLE [A conceptual critique of the driftwood theory, or some explanations for the conservatism of Finnish historical research]. *Politiikka* [Finland] 1975 17(2): 110-120. A critique of the driftwood theory of history, as illustrated in modern Finnish historiography, and in particular by Arvi Korhonen's *Barbarossa-suunitelma ja Suomi* [The Barbarossa Plan and Finland] (Porvoo, 1961). Korhonen argues that Finland's entry into the war against the USSR in 1941 was inevitable. His arguments are flawed by naive empiricism, uncritical use of documents, a narrow positivism which ignores options present to decision-makers, a misplaced insistence on the neutrality of historical judgment, and an unexamined political philosophy of mechanistic historical forces. Such a theory only distorts historical analysis and constitutes the promotion of an unacknowledged ideology. 5 notes.

R. G. Selleck

1839. Seifert, Arno. GESCHICHTE ODER GESCHICHTEN: HISTORIE ZWISCHEN METAPHYSIK UND POETIK [History or stories; history between metaphysics and poetics]. *Hist. Jahrbuch* [West Germany] 1978 96(2): 390-410. A review article of several German studies on the philosophy of history. Discusses the role of the historian as distinguished from the chronicler or narrator of historical stories. The task of the historian is to explain the connections of historical events and their meanings.

R. Vilums

1840. Stone, George C. TIME IN DEWEY'S CONCEPT OF HISTORICAL INQUIRY. *Social Sci.* 1975 50(3): 131-135. Proposals concerning a proper principle of time have been offered by historians and philosophers for centuries. One American philosopher, John Dewey, perhaps the most important philosopher America has produced, was no exception. Yet, little has been written about his principle of time as it relates to his concept of historical inquiry. Elucidates John Dewey's principle of time, particularly as it relates to history.

J

1841. Trenard, Louis. LA PLACE DE VOLTAIRE DANS L'HISTORIOGRAPHIE FRANÇAISE [The place of Voltaire in French historiography]. *Kwartalnik Hist. Nauki i Techniki* [Poland] 1979 24(3): 509-522. Discusses Voltaire's concept of historiography as explained in his *Essays on Morals.* Describes pre-Voltairian historians of the classical school, including Jacques Bossuet, who viewed history as a servant of the study of morals and of theology. Bossuet's view of history was to serve the ideas of the 18th-century Enlightenment, to stress that great men were those who were either practically useful or were wise in the style of the philosophes, that history ought to be written to uplift morals. He regarded historical facts such as battle and deeds of monarchs as useless. 4 photos, 29 notes.

M. A. Zurowski

1842. White, Morton. WHY ANNALISTS OF IDEAS SHOULD BE ANALYSTS OF IDEAS. *Georgia R.* 1975 29(4): 930-947. It is impossible to produce a history of ideas without presenting at the same time an analysis and evaluation of those ideas. Thus, the historian, psychologist, or sociologist must be adequately trained in philosophy if he is to give a logical analysis of the ideas he is discussing. This is the only way to present what the author meant as opposed to the ever-present cursory accounts which have virtually no appreciation of the author's intent. Secondary sources; 2 notes.

M. B. Lucas

1843. Zub, Alexandru. DESCRIPTIVISM ŞI "ISTORIE FILOSOFICĂ" (1848-1866) [Descriptivism and philosophical history, 1848-66]. *Anuarul Inst. de Istorie si Arheologie "A. D. Xenopol"* [Romania] 1980 17: 229-241. Discusses the philosophical outlook of Romanian historians, 1848-66, which was marked by important political changes, notably the union of Moldavia and Wallachia in 1859. Many documents were still unknown or unpublished. Romanian nationalism encouraged the Romantic historical writings of Mihail Kogălniceanu (1817-91) and others. The most promising figure was Nicolae Bălcescu (1819-52) in whose writings the narrative and the philosophical approach were united. Based on contemporary historical writings; 90 notes.

A. K. Dalby/S

1844. Zub, Alexandru. LA CONCEPTION HISTORIQUE D'A. D. XENOPOL [The philosophy of history of A. D. Xenopol]. *Rev. Roumaine d'Hist.* [Romania] 1970 9(4): 727-744. Discusses efforts by the late 19th-century Romanian historian, A. D. Xenopol, to discover and define unifying principles between events. Xenopol's belief in the unique development of each culture as opposed to the idea of a common civilization for all people received further treatment in "National Culture," an article published in 1868. Subsequently, Xenopol focused increasingly on Romanian history in which he sought to comprehend the direction rather than merely reproduce the events. His *Itoria romanilor din Dacia Taiana* (1888) attests to this intention. Later works such as *The Fundamental Principles of History* (1899) and *The Reign of Prince Cuza* (1903) show a continuing interest in the problems of causality and historical processes. 91 notes.

A. W. Howell

6. ECONOMIC HISTORY

1845. Archibugi, Daniele. DI UNA DIFFERENZA TRA L'EPOCA DI KEYNES E L'ERA KEYNESIANA [On a difference between the epoch of Keynes and the Keynesian era]. *Studi Storici [Italy] 1984 25(3): 679-696.* Notes that historians have subdivided the history of modern capitalism into two phases: the troubled era of 1913-46 when Keynes was alive and the golden age of 1946-73 when his ideas were most influential. In his lifetime, Keynes argued against the Versailles Treaty and Winston Churchill's plan to return to the gold standard and predicted the ruinous consequences of both. The American New Deal came the closest to putting his ideas into effect, and up until his death in 1946 he worked on international economic problems. His idea has always been pragmatic: to resolve social conflicts that arise from unemployment and inflation and thus to preserve the liberal state. 52 notes.

J. W. Houlihan

1846. Ashworth, William. THE NEWEST AND TRUEST ECONOMIC HISTORY? *Econ. Hist. Rev. [Great Britain] 1982 35(3): 434-442.* Review of Roderick Floud and Donald McCloskey, ed. *The Economic History of Britain since 1700* (2 vol. 1981). Although billed as a new explanation, based on the best quantitative methods and a rigorous application of economic theory, it represents little that is new in economic historiography.

B. L. Crapster

1847. Badía Cabrera, Miguel A. UN EJERCICIO DE DESMITIFICACION HISTORICA: *EL TRIUNFO DEL CONSERVADURISMO* DE GABRIEL KOLKO [Comment on the demythification of history: Gabriel Kolko's *Triumph of Conservatism*]. *Rev. de Ciencias Sociales [Puerto Rico] 1980 22(3-4): 361-377.* Kolko's *Triumph of Conservatism* attacked the traditional interpretation of the Progressive era. Kolko held that the intervention of the state in the economy had neither liberal intentions nor liberal consequences. Federal regulation was not aimed at the protection of small business and the public from the ruinous consequences of monopoly; it was rather the instrument by which big business sought to establish by public decree and administrative initiative what it could not bring about spontaneously: the definitive control of the markets in a few hands. Kolko also analyzed the theoretical presuppositions that prevented the orthodox historians from apprehending the peculiar nature of the relation between the state and the economy. His critique of Karl Marx and Max Weber is not conclusive, and it is precisely a comprehensive philosophy of history, which owes much of its inspiration to Marx and Weber, that notably sets apart *Triumph of Conservatism* from earlier works.

J/S

1848. Bairati, Piero. PER IL BENE DELL'UMANITÀ: BENJAMIN FRANKLIN E IL PROBLEMA DELLA MANIFATTURE [For the good of humanity: Benjamin Franklin and the problem of manufactures]. *Riv. Storica Italiana [Italy] 1978 90(2): 262-293.* Hagiographers portray Benjamin Franklin as a universal genius; detractors see him as a symbol of American "banality." A sound historical view must avoid such extremes. Benjamin Franklin, with his roots in New England Puritanism, adopted as his first journalist pseudonym that of Silence Dogood, an echo of Cotton Mather's *Essays to Do Good.* Raising the material conditions of the people was an important way of doing good in society, and Franklin saw that goal as achievable through economic growth, through an increase in trade and manufacturing. He was, in a very real sense, the Father of the Industrial Revolution in the United States. 100 notes.

J. C. Billigmeier

1849. Balle-Petersen, Poul. CENTER FOR ARBEJDERKULTURSTUDIER [A center for studies in labor culture]. *Arbejderhistorie [Denmark] 1983 (21): 98-100.* Describes activities and plans at the interdisciplinary center established at the University of Copenhagen, Denmark, in 1982.

1850. Banke, Niels. GAMLE OG NYE VURDERINGEN AF ADAM SMITH'S *WEALTH OF NATIONS* (1776) [Old and new interpretations of Adam Smith's *Wealth of Nations* (1776)]. *Nationaløkonomisk Tidsskrift [Denmark] 1976 114(1): 5-25.* In writing the *Wealth of Nations*, Adam Smith prepared well, using notes from his lectures at Glasgow, physiocratic theory, James Steuart's *Inquiry into the Principles of Political Economy*, Étienne Bonnot de Condillac (1715-80), and other writers. He presented such ideas as self-interest, the amorality of economics, the division of labor, the critical analysis of society, price structure, and other subjects. Smith opposed mercantilism, and his theory of capital arose from this opposition. He defended free trade and laissez-faire best. Karl Marx in *Das Kapital* used Smith extensively though criticized him as well. Modern writers find Smith's *Wealth of Nations* well-thought out, logical, and consistently organized. Biblio.

R. E. Lindgren

1851. Barber, Clarence L. ON THE ORIGINS OF THE GREAT DEPRESSION. *Southern Econ. J. 1978 44(3): 432-456.* Examines varying views on the causes of the Great Depression of 1929, examining the economy and social structure as they were affected 1900-31; proposes an alternative hypothesis based on a spending rather than money origin.

1852. Barceló, Alfons. HISTÒRIA I TEORIA ECONÒMICA [History and economic theory]. *Orígens del capitalisme* (Esplugues de Llobregat: Editorial Ariel, 1974): 93-113. Analyzes the use of economic theory in historiography, reviewing systems without a surplus (simple gathering, hunting and fishing, and simple subsistence-level agricultural and livestock economies) and systems with a surplus (slave, capitalist, and socialist economies). The author has used John Hicks's (b. 1904) work as a contrast to his own arguments.

J. Mr. (IHE 94190)

1853. Barg, M. A. OB ODNOI NESOSTOIATEL'NOI KONTSEPTSII ZAPADNOI ISTORIOGRAFII [One defective conception of Western historiography]. *Novaia i Noveishaia Istoriia [USSR] 1973 5: 55-69.* Compares Western and Soviet historiography on the "crisis of the 17th century" and criticizes Western historians' views on transitional eras particularly that between feudalism and capitalism. A study of the contemporary bourgeois conception of economic development and the change in the historical treatment of the "crisis of the 17th century," 1950's-70's, demonstrates the impossibility of understanding the crisis separately from the problem of the transitional era. Secondary sources; 34 notes.

C. R. Pike

1854. Barns, William D. REVISIONIST HISTORIOGRAPHY AND THE PATRONS OF HUSBANDRY. *J. of the West Virginia Hist. Assoc. 1979 3(1): 55-66.* Review article on the Patrons of Husbandry (Grange) in the United States, prompted by books on the movement and other farmers' organizations; covers 1860's-1970's.

1855. Bartley, Numan V. ANOTHER NEW SOUTH? *Georgia Hist. Q. 1981 65(2): 119-137.* Discusses various historians' interpretations of the development of the New South after the Civil War, determining that plantation-oriented leadership continued to control the region until the breakdown of the agricultural economy due to various disasters in the 1920's. 52 notes.

G. R. Schroeder

1856. Basmann, R. L. THE ROLE OF THE ECONOMIC HISTORIAN IN PREDICTIVE TESTING OF PROFFERED "ECONOMIC LAWS." *Explorations in Entrepreneurial Hist. 1965 2(3): 159-186.* Significance in the interpretation of economic history is determined by a combination of econometricians (who formulate and test prediction-statements and statistical computations) and historians (who use facts for formulating historical inferences and explanations).

1857. Bazylow, Ludwik. WIELKI PROLETARIAT—PIERWSZA PARTIA W HISTORII WIELKIEGO RUCHU [The Great Proletariat: the first party in the history of a great movement]. *Kwartalnik Hist. [Poland] 1982 89(2-3): 235-249.* Historians of the workers' movement have often dealt more in mythology, even hagiography, than in history. Ludwik Krzywicki's memoirs contain much material about early Polish socialists, not all of it reliable. Other memoirs are also valuable. Historical studies of the Great Proletariat have contributed to our understanding and there is cause for optimism for growing objectivity. Based on published memoirs; 29 notes. Russian summary. J. J. Kulczycki

1858. Becker, William H. CONTRIBUTIONS DURING THE 1960S TO THE HISTORY OF AMERICAN BUSINESS. *Rev. Int. d'Hist. de la Banque [Switzerland] 1974 8: 216-224.* Business history in the 1960's differed from earlier decades in the sheer volume produced and in the variety of methodology used. Writers were also more interested in developing abstract or theoretical explanations of the growth of business enterprise, the study of strategy and structure by Alfred D. Chandler being one of the best examples of this tendency. Finally the relationship between business and the federal government became a focal point of study. On the whole, the 1960's affirmed the conclusions of the earlier decades regarding the close interrelationship between government and business enterprise. Secondary sources; 19 notes. D. McGinnis

1859. Belgorodskaia, L. V. OSVESHCHENIE RAZVITIIA PARTIINO-SOVETSKOI PECHATI PERVYKH LET NEPA V ISTORICHESKOI LITERATURE [Historical literature on the development of the Soviet Party press during the New Economic Policy]. *Vestnik Leningradskogo U.: Seriia Istorii, Iazyka i Literatury [USSR] 1983 (2): 24-28.* The 1920's saw a crisis of the Soviet Communist Party press. The pressures created by the New Economic Policy were economic, since the papers were no longer subsidized, and ideological, since non-Communist press was allowed to create competition. Since the late 50's, new approaches to the issue have been proposed, such as that the Party press did badly because of poor journalism. Secondary sources; 22 notes. English summary. M. Hernas

1860. Bel'son, Ia. M. ANTINAUCHNOST' KONTSEPTSII SOVREMENNOGO BURZHUAZNOGO GOSUDARSTVOVEDENIIA [Unscholarly concepts of contemporary bourgeois studies on the state]. *Sovetskoe Gosudarstvo i Pravo [USSR] 1981 (10): 120-126.* Criticizes the content and methodology of recent bourgeois historiography on the development and nature of capitalism, in light of materials presented at the 26th Congress of the Communist Party of the Soviet Union.

1861. Bickerton, Ian J. JOHN HAY'S OPEN DOOR POLICY: A RE-EXAMINATION. *Australian J. of Pol. and Hist. [Australia] 1977 23(1): 54-66.* Details the background to Secretary of State John Hay's China policy of 1899-1901 and suggests that recent revisionist interpretations are incorrect. Marilyn Young (1969) and Raymond Esthus (1959) deemed that the Open Door policy concerned commerce, finance, and politics, and suggested that, while the rhetoric stressed Open Door, in reality US policy soon became a pragmatic one of securing only equal access for US trade. An examination of the Philander C. Knox, Francis M. Huntington Wilson, Willard Straight, William Rockhill, and Hay Papers indicates that the Open Door and opposition to foreign spheres were consistently pursued. W. D. McIntyre

1862. Bordo, Michael D. and Schwartz, Anna J. ISSUES IN MONETARY ECONOMICS AND THEIR IMPACT ON RESEARCH IN ECONOMIC HISTORY. *Res. in Econ. Hist. 1977 (supplement 1): 81-129.* Reviews recent analytic developments in monetary economics and surveys the consequent literature in economic history. Covers the changing theories of the nature, origin, and function of money, the role of interest rates and financial intermediaries, effects of monetary disturbances and related issues. Examines the efforts of investigators who have probed into these broad and general areas. The literature is considerable, but too much emphasis has been placed on monetary disturbances to the detriment of other fruitful areas of research. 23 notes, ref. V. L. Human

1863. Braudel, Fernand. PARA UNA ECONOMÍA HISTÓRICA [Toward historical economics]. *Rev. de Occidente [Spain] 1969 (72): 261-272.* Reproduces a chapter from *La historia y las ciencias sociales* (History and the social sciences, IHE 72380), which comments on the importance of the study of the rise and fall of societies, civilizations, economies, and political institutions for the historian. R. O. (IHE 90557)

1864. Braudel, Fernand. A TÉR ÉS AZ IDŐ FELOSZTÁSA EURÓPÁBAN *(CIVILISATION MATERIELLE, ECONOMIE ET CAPITALISME XVᵉ-XVIIeRET SIECLE.* TOME 3. *LE TEMPS DU MONDE.* PARIS, 1979. CÍMŰ KÖNYV I.FEJEZETE PP.11-70) [Division between space and time in Europe: first chapter of *Civilisation Materielle, Economie et Capitalisme XVᵉ-XVIIeRET Siecle.* Vol. 3. *Le Temp du Monde.* Pari, 1979, pp. 11-70]. *Világtörténet [Hungary] 1980 (4): 3-69.* Regardless of political or geographical boundaries, the world always consists of one completely interacting economic unit, regulated by powerful economic centers (Venice, Antwerp, Amsterdam, London, New York). Events are always influenced by the distance of events from these central cities. Historians traditionally concentrate on short cycles in which changes can be easily isolated and studied, but detailed studies of Kondratieff cycles (50-100 years or longer) will provide many unexpected new insights into historical and economic developments. 2 plates, 143 notes. T. Kuner

1865. Breen, T. H. BACK TO SWEAT AND TOIL: SUGGESTIONS FOR THE STUDY OF AGRICULTURAL WORK IN EARLY AMERICA. *Pennsylvania Hist. 1982 49(4): 241-258.* A variety of interpretations of early American agriculture are reviewed. Those of James Henretta and James T. Lemon are discussed in some detail. Breen suggests that a focus upon agricultural production would best enable the historian to understand the cultural values of early American families. 46 notes. D. C. Swift

1866. Brera, Paolo. TEORIA E STORIA DELLO SVILUPPO ECONOMICO: IL CONTRIBUTO DI J. D. GOULD [Theory and history of economic development: the contribution of J. D. Gould]. *Riv. Storica Italiana [Italy] 1977 89(1): 153-159.* Review article of a book by J. D. Gould (Italian translation: *Storia e sviluppo economico* [Bari: Laterza, 1976]). Gould distinguishes between growth, meaning expansion of real per capita wealth, and development, which denotes a change in the structure of society along with economic expansion. Gould does not accept the doctrine of *Einmaligkeit*, the uniqueness and irrepeatability of historical events. While stressing the close similarity of the stages nations pass through on their way to development, Gould concedes that difference may occur, for example, between a country which began industrialization in 1825, before railroads and the mass production of steel, and one that began in 1875, after both had come into existence. 12 notes. J. C. Billigmeier

1867. Brody, David. LABOR AND THE GREAT DEPRESSION: THE INTERPRETATIVE PROSPECTS. *Labor Hist. 1972 13(2): 231-244.* Reviews recent historiography of labor during the Great Depression, and attacks the New Left interpretation of labor as an integral part of the corporate state. The main outline of labor history focuses on its continuance of business unionism, but there are many areas which need interpretive studies. Based on secondary sources. L. L. Athey

1868. Brody, David. THE OLD LABOR HISTORY AND THE NEW: IN SEARCH OF AN AMERICAN WORKING CLASS. *Labor Hist. 1979 20(1): 111-126.* Reviews labor historiography, the stimuli for the "new" labor history, and current methodological and conceptual questions. A "useable framework for our particular labor history" is called for. Secondary sources; 22 notes. L. L. Athey

1869. Buhle, Paul. ANARCHISM AND AMERICAN LABOR. *Int. Labor and Working Class Hist. 1983 (23): 21-34.* Reviews recent historiography of American anarchism of the 1880's-1920's, focusing on the ethnic foundations of anarchist movements and the co-option of anarchism by international Communism after the Russian Revolution of 1917.

1870. Buts'ko, M. O. and Evselevs'kyi, L. I. VYSVITLENNIA PODII PERIODU VELYKOI VITCHYŻNIANOI VIINY U PRAT-SIAKH Z ISTORII FABRYK I ZAVODIV [The elucidation of events from World War II in the history of factories and plants]. *Ukraïns'kyi Istorychnyi Zhurnal [USSR] 1980 (2): 134-140.* Reviews some of the more notable publications on the history of industrial plants in the Ukraine, stressing their propaganda value for inspiring Soviet patriotism and proletarian internationalism. 42 notes.   I. Krushelnyckyj

1871. Buza, János. HISTORIOGRÁFIAI VÁZLAT 1867-1945. KÖZÖTTI ÁR-ÉS BÉRTÖRTÉNETIRÁSUNKRÓL [A sketch of Hungarian historiography dealing with prices and wages, 1867-1945]. *Magyar Tudományos Akad. Filozófiai és Történettudományi Osztályának Közleményei [Hungary] 1977 26(1-2): 187-203.* The branch of historiography dealing with prices and wages was neglected in Hungary after 1945. The author asserts that the ample research, 1867-1900, in some specific fields was not enriched significantly either after World War I or World War II. Based on contemporary books and articles; 104 notes.   CK-AU

1872. Byres, T. J. HISTORICAL PERSPECTIVES ON SHA-RECROPPING. *J. of Peasant Studies [Great Britain] 1983 10(2-3): 7-40.* Sets the sharecropping relationship in its historical context in order to compensate for the ahistorical view evident in much of contemporary scholarship and to illuminate sharecropping's modern situation. Sharecropping is both ancient and widespread; its lineage extends to the ancient civilizations in Greece, China, and India. A review of the pertinent literature is the occasion for a discussion of sharecropping's persistence, spread, and eventual demise in all of Europe except for the north, and in China, India, and Persia. Secondary sources; 47 notes, 72 ref., 2 tables.   B. Stenslie

1873. Carson, Robert B. RAILROADS AND REGULATION RE-VISITED: A NOTE ON THE PROBLEMS OF HISTORIOGRA-PHY AND IDEOLOGY. *Historian 1972 34(3): 437-446.* In his 1965 *Railroads and Regulation, 1877-1916* (New York: W. W. Norton, 1970) Gabriel Kolko asserted that railroad leaders shaped the regulation of their own industry, to their own advantage. Although he does not support Kolko fully, Carson defends the railroad study from some criticism. The controversy is broader than this particular issue, which is an example of a struggle among historians about differing ideological interpretations of business-government relations in the United States. 15 notes.

N. W. Moen

1874. Casanova, Pablo Gonzalez. HISTORICAL SYSTEMS AND SOCIAL SYSTEMS. *Studies in Comparative Internat. Development 1973 8(3): 227-246.* Reviews the history and theory of social change from the 16th century to the present, explaining causal factors and seeking the best means to direct change through revolution and reorganization.

1875. Cesarano, Filippo. ON THE ROLE OF THE HISTORY OF ECONOMIC ANALYSIS. *Hist. of Pol. Econ. 1983 15(1): 63-82.* While economists have sought to find a role for the history of the discipline, most scholars have advanced arguments meant to enlarge the sphere of the subject as opposed to arguments that ascribe a new importance to traditional forms of the history of economic analysis. Signs of dissatisfaction with the present state of economics may be attributed to the decreasing marginal benefit of applying a refined methodological weaponry. Secondary sources; 28 notes, biblio.   T. P. Richardson

1876. Chaunu, Pierre. LES DEPASSEMENTS DE L'HISTOIRE QUANTITATIVE: RETROSPECTIVE ET PERSPECTIVE [Beyond quantitative history: retrospective and perspective]. *Mélanges de la Casa de Velázquez [France] 1972 7: 646-685.* Discusses the prob-

lems and trends of economic history. The new economic history (quantitative history, cliometry), developed in the United States, has surpassed that which developed in connection with the great historical changes of the 1930's. The author proposes a further refinement: the "third quantitative level," centered on the study of systems of civilization and fundamental attitudes toward life and death, and based on the systematic utilization of massive data by computers. The text of the authors's lecture.

P. M. (IHE 86586)

1877. Cheyette, Fredric. FERNAND BRAUDEL: A BIOGRA-PHY OF CAPITALISM. *Wilson Q. 1980 4(2): 102-107.* Discusses Fernand Braudel's *Civilisation Matérielle, Economie, et Capitalisme* (1979); Braudel is continuing the tradition of French historical writing begun by Marc Bloch and Lucien Febvre; and comments on the methods which Braudel employed to interpret the relation of economic factors and social structures.

1878. Chistozvonov, A. N. VII MEZHDUNARODNYI KON-GRESS EKONOMICHESKOI ISTORII [The Seventh International Congress of Economic History]. *Novaia i Noveishaia Istoriia [USSR] 1979 (3): 3-21.* The seventh International Congress of Economic History met in Edinburgh, 13-18 August 1978. Topics discussed included urbanization and social change, the struggle to preserve resources in Europe between 1400 and 1800, and the difference in development between European countries and those on other continents. Keen interest focused on methodological discussions on the New Economic History. This favors a multifaceted approach to research and no reliance on narrow, nondescriptive, factual material. 23 notes.   L. J. Seymour

1879. Chornomaz, I. Sh. RADIANS'KA ISTORIOHRAFIIA RO-BITNYCHOHO KONTROLIU NA UKRAINI: 1917-1918 [Soviet historiography on workers' control in the Ukraine, 1917-18]. *Ukraïns'kyi Istorychnyi Zhurnal [USSR] 1977 (5): 132-139.* Reviews and classifies works written 1920's-70's, on labor control of production.

1880. Clarke, Simon. SOCIALIST HUMANISM AND THE CRI-TIQUE OF ECONOMISM. *Hist. Workshop Journal [Great Britain] 1979 8: 137-156.* Reply to Richard Johnson's "Thomson, Genovese, and Socialist-Humanist Hist.," (*History Workshop* 1978 6: 79-100). Examines the work of Maurice Dobb to assess the theoretical stance of contemporary socialist historians. Dobb's view of production relations is reductive, concentrating on the context of enterprise rather than class. Instead, social relations should be conceived in political and cultural as well as economic terms. A return to Dobb's economism denies the achievement of socialist humanism, the prevailing direction of current Marxist historiography. 13 notes.

C. B. Bailey

1881. Cohen, Jon S. THE ACHIEVEMENTS OF ECONOMIC HISTORY: THE MARXIST SCHOOL. *J. of Econ. Hist. 1978 38(1): 29-57.* Presents a selective survey of the contributions of Marxist scholars to the literature of European economic history. Topics include feudalism and the decline of serfdom, the transition to capitalism, the absolutist state, the crisis of the 17th century, the English Civil War, and the rise of factories. Emphasizes works available in English and stresses the historical development of England. Focuses on works that deal in detail with historical problems and that have had an impact on the work of other historians.

J

1882. Cole, Arthur H. CONSPECTUS FOR A HISTORY OF ECONOMIC AND BUSINESS LITERATURE. *J. of Econ. Hist. 1957 17(3): 333-388.* Surveys British economic and business literature, 17th century-1880, assesses the changing scholarly and popular attitudes toward economics, and discusses the social and cultural impact which economic theory had during the period.

1883. Coleman, D. C. PROTO-INDUSTRIALIZATION: A CONCEPT TOO MANY. *Econ. Hist. Rev. [Great Britain] 1983 36(3): 435-448.* Traces economic historians' origination and development of the concept of protoindustrialization and some difficulties which arise when trying to apply it to England. B. L. Crapster

1884. Comeau, Robert. L'HISTOIRE OUVRIÈRE AU QUÉBEC: QUELQUES NOUVELLES AVENUES [The working class history of Quebec: some new avenues]. *R. d'hist. de l'Amérique française [Canada] 1975 28(4): 579-583.* Recent histories of Quebec's working class emphasize the exploitation of workers. New approaches are needed in retracing and interpreting the evolution of political consciousness among members of that class. Geographic precision, specific job descriptions, accurate wage and salary scales, and full knowledge about living conditions are necessary. A good history of Quebec's working class should be integrated with the general social and economic history of Quebec. Based on secondary works; 7 notes. L. B. Chan

1885. Conlin, Joseph R. INTRODUCTION. Conlin, Joseph R., ed. *At the Point of Production: The Local History of the I.W.W.* (Westport, Conn.: Greenwood Pr., 1981): 3-24. Surveys the histories and the historians of the Industrial Workers of the World (IWW), especially Paul F. Brissenden's *The I.W.W.: A Study of American Syndicalism* (1919), which succeeded as a comprehensive, definitive history of the IWW. Also discusses the works of Fred Thompson, Joyce Kornbluh, Philip S. Foner, Patrick Renshaw, and Melvyn Dubofsky. These illustrate various perspectives whhich supplement Brissenden's classic. The articles in this collection are introduced as examples of what needs to be done in the field of IWW history. Secondary sources. J. Powell

1886. Conlin, Joseph R. L'ORGANIZZAZIONE DEGLI I.W.W. E I SUOI STORICI: RASSEGNA BIBLIOGRAFICA [The organization of the I.W.W. and its historians: a bibliographical summary]. *Movimento Operaio e Socialista [Italy] 1976 22(1-2): 111-131.* The common bind between historians studying the American Labor Movement is that they have centered their attention on the successes: the ever-triumphant order, the adaptability of corporate liberalism, and the all-powerful and unparalleled American Federation of Labor. Radical movements have been described by sympathetic historians as passive victims, powerless in front of an insidious and impregnable culture or destroyed by repression. In light of these assertions, reviews the major works concerning the Industrial Workers of the World. Primary and secondary sources; 39 notes. M. T. Wilson

1887. Conte, Domenico. MONDO AGRARIO E CAPITALISMO ORGANIZZATO: RECENTI LIBRI TEDESCHI [The agrarian world and organized capitalism: recent German books]. *Quaderni Storici [Italy] 1978 13(3): 1122-1130.* Examines the results of West German research into contemporary agrarian history, a discipline with a long tradition in Germany. Pays particular attention to the work of H.-J. Puhle and J. Kocka published in 1974 and 1975. J/S

1888. Cruise, H. F. THE ECONOMIC HISTORIAN AND THE GROWTH DEBATE. *Australian Econ. Hist. Rev. [Australia] 1975 15(2): 83-106.* Discusses the relevance of the ideas of Thorstein Veblen to the perspective of the economic historian on the economic growth debate in Australia. Explores the problems raised for economic analysis by the concern of governments with evaluating the long-term path of the total economy in terms of alternative paths, and what help economic history might provide for this sort of evaluation. Secondary sources; 48 notes. R. B. Orr

1889. Czihak, Hans. GEDANKEN ZUR KOMBINATSGESCHICHTSSCHREIBUNG [Thoughts on the writing of the history of collectives]. *Jahrbuch für Wirtschaftsgeschichte [East Germany] 1972 (3): 251-256.* Reviews the difficulties involved in the writing of the history of collectives, and suggests some principles applicable to different types of collectives. Territorially unified and dispersed collectives require different approaches and emphases. Recommends

collective authorship, balanced attention to the separate parts of a collective, and scrutiny of the workers' role and the communal setting. Secondary works; 3 notes. J. B. Street

1890. Czollek, Roswitha and Šteimanis, Josef. DER FASCHISMUS IM BALTIKUM IN DER SOWJETISCHEN HISTORIOGRAPHIE [Fascism in the Baltic area in Soviet historiography]. *Jahrbuch für Geschichte der Sozialistischen Länder Europas [East Germany] 1980 24(1): 85-102.* Baltic fascism has its roots in the counterrevolutionary movements of 1917-19, in which landless and land-poor people were recruited into the bourgeois-led armed forces. Bourgeois nationalism, rooted in the concern for their own private property and economic enterprises, led to fascism in the 1920's and 1930's. These movements were defeated overwhelmingly in the elections of 14 and 15 July 1940. 48 notes. D. R. Stevenson

1891. Dalchow, Irmtraud. FORSCHUNGSOBJEKT BETRIEBSGESCHICHTE [Research-object business history]. *Wissenschaftliche Zeitschrift der Martin-Luther-Universität Halle-Wittenberg. Gesellschafts- und Sprachwissenschaftliche Reihe [East Germany] 1978 27(1): 105-114.* In contrast to the descriptive aspect of business history in capitalist countries, East German historians who specialize in business history attempt to work out the lawful development of capitalism and the means of exploitation through concrete examples. Secondary literature; 14 notes. R. Wagnleitner

1892. Danilova, L. V. A DISCUSSION OF AN IMPORTANT PROBLEM. *Soviet Studies in Hist. 1966 4(4): 3-12.* Originally published in *Voprosy Filosofii* [USSR] 1965 12. Discusses recent interpretations among Soviet scholars of Marx's concept of the Asiatic Mode of Production, showing that it applies to all early class societies.

1893. Debouzy, Marianne. LA CLASSE OUVRIÈRE AMÉRICAINE: RECHERCHES ET PROBLÈMES [The American working class: Research and problems]. *Mouvement Social [France] 1978 (102): 3-8.* The American working class has always struck European observers, particularly leftists, as distinguished chiefly by negatives: lack of cohesion, lack of class consciousness, lack of revolutionary ideology, and absence of a workers' party. But it exists, nonetheless, and its discontent seems to be growing. The history of the working class in the United States defies schematization; its historians must create new theories to explain its course. 4 notes. J. C. Billingmeier

1894. DelTreppo, Mario. FEDERIGO MELIS AND THE RENAISSANCE ECONOMY. *J. of European Econ. Hist. [Italy] 1981 10(3): 709-742.* Federigo Melis, 20th-century Italian historian, looked at the function of the Renaissance business firms from within and determined that these firms, led by "pure" managers, had decisive and determining effects on the development of society. Melis showed that the impetus given to economic development by the great merchants made the Renaissance a period of economic growth, not one of stagnation as some historians had believed. Business flourished in the Renaissance alongside of the arts and humanities, making the period a true passage from the ancient to the modern world. 93 notes. D. S. Rockwood

1895. DeSantis, Vincent P. THE AMERICAN GILDED AGE REVISITED. *Australian J. of Pol. and Hist. [Australia] 1983 29(2): 354-367.* Presents a historiographical interpretation of US history, 1865-1900, stressing the rise of industrial capitalism and the big corporations; the passing of the frontier; the growth of the cities; and the new immigrant inrush; the spread of railways; and the emergence of the United States as a world power. While writers in the 1930's like V. L. Parrington, C. A. Beard, and M. Josephson condemned the business leaders of the Gilded Age, writers in the 1940's and 1950's like A. Nevins, T. C. Cochran, and E. S. Kirkland stressed their creative contributions. After reviewing the writings of such contemporary critics and reformers as Jacob Riis, Henry George, and Edward Bellamy, the author accepts H. M. Jones's view that the Gilded Age "lived in its own right." W. D. McIntyre

1896. DeVries, Jan. IS THERE AN ECONOMICS OF DECLINE? *J. of Econ. Hist. 1978 38(1): 256-258.* A summary of papers and discussion on the title question presented at a workshop chaired by the author held at the 37th annual meeting of the Economic History Association, 1977. The three papers on the historiography of economic decline were delivered by Gerald Gunderson on the late Roman Empire, Richard T. Rapp on the relationship of foreign trade to economic decline—including 17th-century Italy and Spain, and Donald McCloskey on Great Britain, 19th-20th centuries.

C. W. Olson

1897. Deyon, Pierre. L'ENJEU DES DISCUSSIONS AUTOUR DU CONCEPT DE "PROTO-INDUSTRIALISATION" [The historiographical meaning of protoindustrialization]. *Rev. du Nord [France] 1979 61(240): 9-17.* Summarizes the discussion on the concept of protoindustrialization. The author emphasizes the importance of F. Franklin Mendels's work and distinguishes between points on which there is general agreement and those which require further research.

J/S

1898. Dick, Wolfgang and Golub, Arno. AUFGABEN AUF DEM GEBIET DER GESCHICHTE DER ÖRTLICHEN ARBEITERBEWEGUNG UND BETRIEBSGESCHICHTE IN VORBEREITUNG DES X. PARTEITAGES DER SED [Studies in the field of the history of the local working-class movement and industrial history in preparation for the 10th SED Party conference]. *Beiträge zur Gesch. der Arbeiterbewegung [East Germany] 1980 22(5): 746-750.* Examines the 10th SED Party conference, held in February 1980 in Berlin, whose theme was the history of the local working-class movement and industrial history. The following points were considered: the political and ideological function of this field of history since 1945; the study of regional history, German history, the world revolutionary process, and the worldwide class struggle; the link between research and propaganda; the use of this field of history to unmask the reactionary and aggressive existence of imperialism; the history of the Leuna works before 1945 and an examination of class struggle; the relationship between economic and social policies in industrial history; and the management and leadership of industry. 3 notes.

G. L. Neville

1899. Dick, Wolfgang and Goldmann, Sonja. BETRIEBSGESCHICHTE—DIE GESCHICHTE DES WIRKENS VON MENSCHEN [Trade history: the history of human jobs]. *Beiträge zur Gesch. der Arbeiterbewegung [East Germany] 1984 26(1): 112-121.* Surveys the beginnings of the historiography of trades and of the working class in Germany. 35 notes.

R. Grove

1900. Dimitrov, Dimitür. MONOGRAFIIA, POSVETENA NA SÜVETSKATA ISTORIOGRAFIIA ZA SÜVREMENNOTO RABOTNICHESKO DVIZHENIE [A monograph dedicated to Soviet historiography of the contemporary labor movement]. *Izvestiia na Inst. po Istoriia na BKP [Bulgaria] 1981 45: 516-518.* Review of the second volume of B. I. Rasputnis's *Sovietskaiia Istoriografiia Sovremennogo Rabochego Dvizheniia* [Soviet historiography on the contemporary workers' movement] (1980) as an analytical study of Soviet scholarship on the subject of the socialist and trade union movements in the capitalist world.

1901. Djurović, Borislav. NEKA GLEDIŠTA O AGRARNIM ODNOSIMA U SOCIJALISTIČKIM ZEMLJAMA [Some views on agrarian relations in socialist countries]. *Zbornik za Društvene Nauke [Yugoslavia] 1977 1(62): 165-175.* Discusses characteristic views in Western, Yugoslav, and Soviet literature concerning the socialization of agriculture, collective farms, collectivization in general, and social relations on kolkhoz-type farms during the period 1918-77. Western authors stress the antipeasant nature of collectivization. Yugoslav theories consider the nature of social transformation and make a case for gradual development of social ownership without violent infringements on individual ownership. Soviet writers insist that the only correct socialist transformation is that of the Soviet type; anything else is regarded as a deviation from the Party line. 40 notes.

A. C. Niven

1902. Donno, Antonio. LABOR HISTORY: DALLA STORIA DEL SINDACATO ALLA STORIA OPERAIA [Labor history: from the history of labor unions to the history of labor]. *Nuova Riv. Storica [Italy] 1982 66(3-4): 319-341.* Since the mid 1960's British and American social historians have brought new perspectives and methods to the study of working class history. In contrast to earlier schools, especially the Wisconsin school which denied the existence of a working class in America due to ethnic heterogeneity and constant immigration, and concentrated on the history of labor unions, the new historians focus on the contribution each ethnic group made to the labor movement and class consciousness. Inspired by Marxist concepts they argue that labor history is the history of a social movement and not merely of the struggles of market unionism. 82 notes.

J. V. Coutinho

1903. Dubofsky, Melvyn. GIVE US THAT OLD TIME LABOR HISTORY: PHILIP S. FONER AND THE AMERICAN WORKER. *Labor History 1985 26(1): 118-137.* Analyzes the strengths and weaknesses of two multivolume surveys of American labor: John R. Commons et al., *History of Labor in the United States,* 4 vols. (1918-35) and Philip S. Foner's *History of the Labor Movement in the United States,* 6 vols. (1947-82). 18 notes.

L. F. Velicer

1904. Dziewulsky, Jan. WSPÓŁCZESNE SPORY WOKÓŁ EKONOMICZNYCH I POLITYCZNYCH POGLĄDÓW RÓŻY LUKSEMBURG [Recent controversies on the economic and political views of Rosa Luxemburg]. *Ekonomista [Poland] 1979 (3): 577-615.* Appraisal of Rosa Luxemburg's economic theory has been determined by a political appraisal of her activity, 1950's-70's.

1905. Eichholtz, Dietrich. ALTE UND "NEUE" KONZEPTIONEN. BÜRGERLICHE LITERATUR ZUR WIRTSCHAFTSGESCHICHTE DES FASCHISMUS IN DEUTSCHLAND [Old and "new" conceptions: bourgeois literature on the economic history of fascism in Germany]. *Jahrbuch für Wirtschaftsgeschichte [East Germany] 1971 (3): 231-255.* Reviews many examples of bourgeois historiography since 1945 on the social and economic history of Nazism in Germany, in particular, Arthur Schweitzer's *Big Business in the Third Reich* (Bloomington, 1964); Wolfgang Birkenfeld's *Der synthetische Treibstoff 1933-1945: Ein Beitrag zur nationalsozialistischen Wirtschafts- und Rüstungspolitik* (Göttingen, 1964); and Dieter Petzina's *Autarkiepolitik im Dritten Reich: Der nationalsozialistischen Vierjahresplan* (Stuttgart, 1968). Analyzes the scientific and political conceptions of these works, their discussion of armament and war economy, the role of monopolies and their relationship to government, and war preparations and aims. Birkenfeld's study is a conservative apology for big business in the Nazi era. Petzina and Schweitzer's works are more liberal but serve the same end—supporting Western imperialism. Secondary works; 31 notes.

J. B. Street

1906. Eichholz, Dietrich. ZU EINIGEN FRAGEN DER GESCHICHTE DES DEUTSCHEN IMPERIALISMUS [Some questions on the history of German imperialism]. *Zeitschrift für Geschichtswissenschaft [East Germany] 1976 24(1): 65-74.* Discusses methodological, formal, ideological, and political problems of the writing of an economic history of German imperialism. 10 notes.

R. Wagnleitner

1907. Eley, Geoff. CAPITALISM AND THE WILHELMINE STATE: INDUSTRIAL GROWTH AND POLITICAL BACKWARDNESS IN RECENT GERMAN HISTORIOGRAPHY, 1890-1918. *Hist. J. [Great Britain] 1978 21(3): 737-750.* Examines 15 monographs on recent historiography of Wilhelmine Germany. Takes issue with the thesis that Imperial Germany lacked a modern political system because a preindustrial power elite maintained its antidemocratic power bases by containing the bourgeoisie within the industrial and ideological structures of the traditional society. The economic power of big business facilitated a close control of labor and introduced a company paternalism that restricted political reform. Despite admitted methodological strengths, the historical approach in the works examined appears to ignore the existing ideological continuity that runs from Max Weber through the more recent critical history of the Frankfurt school by way of Eckart Kehr. 20 notes. L. J. Reith

1908. Endo, Teruaki. RECENT STUDIES ON BUSINESS HISTORY OF FRANCE—SERIES ON THE BUSINESS HISTORY OF BANKING AND STEEL-MAKING IN THE NINETEENTH CENTURY. *Keieishigaku [Japan] 1968 3(2): 60-82.* US scholars who pioneered in French business history discovered that most of the business enterprises in France were family-owned, small in scale, and managed conservatively. By contrast, French business historians emphasized the success of national economic planning since the end of World War II and tried to make it clear that the economic development in this period stemmed from various phenomena of the late 19th century: the corporation system, the joint-stock deposit and investment banks, and the technological innovations in the steel industry. To clarify the contributions of 19th-century entrepreneurs to the economic development in France, French scholars have published two journals, *Histoire des Enterprises* and *Revue d'Histoire de la Siderurgie.* Reviews the papers appearing in the two journals, and outlines the development of the banking and the steel-making businesses in France. Article in Japanese. J

1909. Engerman, Stanley L. CONTRACT LABOR, SUGAR, AND TECHNOLOGY IN THE NINETEENTH CENTURY. *J. of Econ. Hist. 1983 43(3): 635-659.* Throughout the world during most of the 19th century, cane sugar was produced on plantations, most frequently with either slave labor or, after slavery was ended, with contract laborers brought in from low-income countries. The diverse sources and recipients of 19th-century contract labor movements were related to political and economic factors, and there were changes in the ethnic composition of the plantation labor force. Transitions in the nature of sugar production raise questions about the study of the relations between institutional and technological changes. J/S

1910. Engerman, Stanley L. DOUGLASS C. NORTH'S *THE ECONOMIC GROWTH OF THE UNITED STATES, 1790-1860* REVISITED. *Social Sci. Hist. 1977 1(2): 248-257.* The first work of "new economic historians" in the early 1960's still stands the test of time. North dealt with one central issue—why the United States economy developed—with little discussion of the impact of that economic growth on social and political issues. Though the book was not a radical departure from "traditional" history, it did attack important new questions. Though new data amplified or modified some of North's arguments, the book still focuses on the important issues in American economic history "with generally useful results." Based on a close reading of North and on secondary works of US economic history since 1961; 32 notes.
T. L. Savitt

1911. Engerman, Stanley L. RECENT DEVELOPMENTS IN AMERICAN ECONOMIC HISTORY. *Social Sci. Hist. 1977 2(1): 72-89.* Discusses recent works in economic history, 1969-70's.

1912. Erofeev, N. A. ANGLIISKAIA BURZHUAZNAIA ISTORIOGRAFIIA O SOTSIAL'NYKH POSLEDSTVIIAKH PROMYSHLENNOGO PEREVOROTA [Bourgeois English historiography on the social consequences of the Industrial Revolution]. *Novaia i Noveishaia Istoriia [USSR] 1983 (2): 59-71.* The question of the social consequences of the Industrial Revolution has long been debated in bourgeois historiography. Most bourgeois historians are trying to conceal the truth about the poverty and sufferings which the Industrial Revolution brought to the toiling masses. Bourgeois historians were not able to refute this obvious truth in the course of the discussion reviewed in the article which took place in the late 1950's-early 1970's. J

1913. Erofeev, N. A. PROMYSHLENNYI PEREVOROT: SODERZHANIE I GRANITSY PONIATIIA [The Industrial Revolution: content and limits of the concept]. *Novaia i Noveishaia Istoriia [USSR] 1984 (6): 78-87.* Discusses specific features, chrono-

logical limits, and consequences of the Industrial Revolution, reviews the historiography of the Industrial Revolution, and expresses his own ideas on the matter. J

1914. Etherington, Norman. THE CAPITALIST THEORY OF CAPITALIST IMPERIALISM. *Hist. of Pol. Econ. 1983 15(1): 38-62.* A focus on forgotten international capitalist literature on the economic imperatives of imperialism. There is reason for investigation of the impact of the idea of economic imperialism on the behavior of the great powers after 1900. Secondary materials; 96 notes.
T. P. Richardson

1915. Falk, Waltraud. ALLGEMEINES UND BESONDERES BEIM ÜBERGANG VON KAPITALISMUS ZUM SOZIALISMUS ALS AUSGANGSPUNKT EINER VERGLEICHENDEN WIRTSCHAFTSGESCHICHTE DES SOZIALISMUS [Generalizations and specifics on the transition from capitalism to socialism as the starting point of a comparative economic history of socialism]. *Jahrbuch für Wirtschaftsgeschichte [East Germany] 1980 (2): 9-30.* A universal history is needed to compare the transition from capitalism to socialism. The historiography, not just the methodology, must be comparative. Although specific details and national developments will vary, basic economic laws exist determining the stages of transition. These stages include the preparatory class struggle, seizure of commanding heights of industry, nationalization, technological modernization, and state economic planning. Based on official statistics and monographs from socialist historians; 42 notes.
E. L. Turk

1916. Farina, Francesco and Marani, Ugo. STRUTTURE MONETARIE E FINANZIARIE DELL'ECONOMIA FASCISTA [The monetary and financial structure of the Fascist economy]. *Quaderni Storici [Italy] 1978 13(3): 1036-1062.* Criticizes a number of recent studies concerning Fascist economic policy in Italy. Emphasizes the importance of both the fiscal and monetary policy measures which the government took to intervene in the economy, especially after 1926, and after the 1929 Wall Street Crash. 44 notes.

1917. Faucher, Daniel. L'ASSOLEMENT TRIENNAL EN FRANCE. [Triennal rotation in France]. *Études Rurales [France] 1961 1: 7-17.* Reviews the historiography of agricultural techniques in France, discussing the development of both biennial and triennial patterns of rotation, and the particular significance of the latter in the economy of Northern France. Secondary works; photo, 21 notes.
T. B. Davies

1918. Feliu, Gaspar. BOSQUEJO PARA UN ESTUDIO DE LA HISTORIA ECONOMICA COMO CIENCIA [Sketch for a study of economic history as science]. *Cuadernos de Hist. Econ. de Cataluña [Spain] 1980 (21): 197-225.* Continued from a previous article (see *Cuadernos de Historia Económica de Cataluña 1979 [20]).* Studies the major developments in economic history, 1900-1945, concentrating on the influence of Schumpeter, Weber, the London School of Economics, American institutionalism and *Business History,* the history of prices, and the influence of Marxism. 148 notes. Article to be continued.
L. H. Nelson

1919. Fink, Gary M. THE FOURTH SOUTHERN LABOR CONFERENCE. *Int. Labor and Working Class Hist. 1983 (23): 62-64.* Discusses recent trends in Southern labor relations historiography as revealed at the 1982 "Southern Labor Studies" conference in Atlanta, Georgia; institutional and social history covering the late 19th-20th centuries have achieved a recent synthesis and reconciliation.

1920. Fischer, Wolfram. SOME RECENT DEVELOPMENTS IN THE STUDY OF ECONOMIC AND BUSINESS HISTORY IN WESTERN GERMANY. *Res. in Econ. Hist. 1977 (supplement 1): 247-285.* Reviews the growth of the study of economic history by universities in West Germany since the 1950's. Individual research into economic history has been in vogue, but the trends of the last decade suggest that cooperative efforts are coming to the fore. No genuinely new textbook has recently been published, but the use of economic history to explain political history is in vogue. Investigations of the business world have not been popular with German economic historians. 130 notes.   V. L. Human

1921. Flynn, Dennis O. EL DESARROLLO DEL PRIMER CAPITALISMO A PESAR DE LOS METALES PRECIOSOS DEL NUEVO MUNDO: UNA INTERPRETACION ANTI-WALLERSTEIN DE LA ESPAÑA IMPERIAL [The development of early capitalism despite precious metals from the New World: an anti-Wallerstein interpretation of imperial Spain]. *Revista de Historia Económica [Spain] 1984 2(2): 29-57.* Immanuel Wallerstein and others have recently claimed that modern capitalism originated in the commercial hegemony of the "center" (Western Europe) over the "periphery" (primarily Latin America and Eastern Europe). The surplus produced by the forced labor of the latter was transferred to the former, but Wallerstein does not explain how the surplus was transferred. In the case of precious metals from America, explains how that transfer was made and also that this surplus did not give rise to capitalism, because it was spent by the Austrian dynasty in imperial military adventures. Biblio., 93 notes.
                                                J. V. Coutinho

1922. Fremdling, Rainer. DIE DREI WICHTIGSTEN WIRTSCHAFTSHISTORISCHEN ZEITSCHRIFTEN DER VEREINIGTEN STAATEN [The three most important journals of economic history in the United States]. *Geschichte und Gesellschaft [West Germany] 1984 10(2): 283-390.* The three high-quality journals, *Research in Economic History, Explorations in Economic History,* and *Journal of Economic History,* show an overwhelming predominance of North American authors. This may be a claim for an elitist, closed society of historians or else a sign of provincial isolation. Tables show diversification of authors, breakdown of articles by applicable centuries, and themes pertaining to inside or outside of North America. Quantifies kilometric and non-kilometric figures in methodology and the frequency of predominantly verbally argumentative articles. 3 tables, 13 notes.   T. Kuner

1923. Gestrin, Ferdo. NEKAJ POGLEDOV NA GOSPODARSKO ZGODOVINO V SLOVENSKEM ZGODOVINOPISJU [Some views of economic history in Slovene historiography]. *Zgodovinski Časopis [Yugoslavia] 1982 36(3): 205-211.* Discusses Slovene historiography on economic history, and its weaknesses, including insufficient attention to economic theory.   J/S

1924. Gibelli, Antonio. GAETANO PERILLO: IL CONTRIBUTO ALLA STORIA DEL MOVIMENTO OPERAIO [Gaetano Perillo: the contribution to the history of the struggle of the labor movement]. *Movimento Operaio e Socialista [Italy] 1976 22(1-2): 8-17.* Documents the contributions of Gaetano Perillo to the history of the working-class struggle, particularly in Liguria. Perillo's contributions were twofold: 1) the creation of centers for historical research, the publication of a bulletin of history and bibliography, and the foundation of the journal *Movimento Operaio e Socialista*; and 2) personal research and extensive writing on working-class struggles. Although he studied the local history of the working class in Liguria his work was not constrained by too narrow a scope but described an autonomous history of the class and the workers' movement. 16 notes.   M. T. Wilson

1925. Gibelli, Antonio. PROLETARIATO DI FABBRICA E CAPITALISMO INDUSTRIALE [Factory proletariat and industrial capitalism]. *Italia Contemporanea [Italy] 1974 26(115): 73-76.* Stefano Merli's *Proletariato di fabbrica e capitalismo industriale, Il caso italiano: 1880-1900* (Florence, 1972) shows the extent of the progress already made, and above all of the profound change of perspective which has overtaken Marxist historiography of the labor movement. Merli's work is a novel and fresh approach which will add much to both political debate and historical scholarship.
                                                J. C. Billigmeier

1926. Giddens, Paul H. WRITING A CORPORATE HISTORY: A PERSONAL MEMOIR. *J. of the Illinois State Hist. Soc. 1981 74(1): 17-30.* In 1946, Giddens, a prominent historian of the petroleum industry, was invited by Chairman of the Board Robert E. Wilson and Conger Reynolds, director of public relations of Stan-

dard Oil Company (Indiana) to prepare a history of that company. Since 1919, the secrecy that had characterized the Standard Oil Trust in previous decades had yielded to a major public relations campaign under Robert W. Stewart and, later, Wilson. The company accepted the conditions stipulated by Giddens, including financial support for both the author and research assistants as well as free access to all relevant materials and assurances of total academic freedom. Although the project was originally scheduled to be completed in two years, *Standard Oil Company (Indiana): Oil Pioneer of the Middle West* was not published by Appleton-Century-Crofts until 3 January 1956. 7 illus., 11 notes.
                                                A. W. Novitsky

1927. Gillet, Marcel. AU XIXe SIÈCLE: INDUSTRIALISATION LINÉAIRE OU INDUSTRIALISATION PAR BONDS? [The 19th century: gradual or spasmodic industrialization?]. *Rev. Econ. [France] 1972 23(5): 723-752.* Since 1945, numerous French economic historians, under the impulse of Ernest Labrousse, have probed deeper into the analysis of social structures and cyclical movements. But Walt W. Rostow presented a growth analysis according to which industrialization would have been insured by short take-off periods. On the other hand, J. Marczewsci and T. J. Markovitch present French industrialization in the 19th century as a slow and quite regular process; the specialists of the New Economic History have made similar revisions as regards the United States. Maurice Levy-Leboyer thinks therefore that it is high time to cross out some results which are still accepted in France. The index of industrial production in France from 1815 to 1914, established by François Crouzet, shows the importance of the leap performed between 1830 and 1860. Jean Bouvier, François Furet, and Marcel Gillet in *Le mouvement du profit en France au XIXe siècle* (1965), have emphasized the great pendulum swings. These authors hope that economists and historians will unite their efforts in order to test the following hypothesis, formulated in the line of their study in *Le bassin houiller du Nord et du Pas-de-Calais de 1815 à 1914* (1971): the 19th century would have witnessed the genesis of a growth and the abortion of a development.   J

1928. Givsan, Hassan. A CRITIQUE OF BAHRO'S ALTERNATIVE WRITING OF HISTORY. *Int. J. of Pol. 1980 10(2-3): 79-98.* Rudolf Bahro's *The Alternative: A Contribution to the Critique of Actually Existing Socialism* (1977) criticizes Marx for overestimating the role of capitalist private property and underestimating the importance of the Asiatic mode of production. Communist revolutions actually developed in countries with the Asiatic mode. Givsan rejects this view, contending that imperial Russia was more capitalistic than Bahro indicates and that Communist revolutions, though occurring in less developed economies, were closely linked with imperialist (capitalist) wars or imperialist-induced crises. 42 ref.   R. E. Noble

1929. Goldberg, Barry. A NEW LOOK AT LABOR HISTORY. *Social Policy 1982 12(3): 54-62.* Review essay focusing on the approach of the new labor historians such as Christopher Hill, Eric Hobsbawm, Albert Soboul, George Rudé, and Edward Thompson, who are " . . . shifting attention from the fate of formal organizations and ideologies to the cultures, work, and communities of the workers in whose name unionists and radicals claim to speak."

1930. Gołębiowski, W. Janusz. A MUNKÁSMOZGALOM MINT A KUTATÁS TÁRGYA: ÁLTALÁNOS PROBLÉMÁK ÉS ÚJ IRÁNYZATOK [The labor movement as research subject: general problems and new directions]. *Párttörténeti Közlemények [Hungary] 1980 26(4): 132-148.* There is a tendency in historiography to seek reciprocal connections between the labor movement and the chronological development of the working class. Modern research must consider development of class consciousness, degrees of participation in social and political activities, the historical development and origin of the working class and its structure, horizontal and vertical mobility in society, and political rights. Current Polish historiography reflects consideration of all these factors. Research on the labor movement will be greatly enriched by using methods of modern sociology.   T. Kuner

1931. Gonçalves Melo, Jayro. BREVES CONSIDERAÇÕES SO-BRE O MERCANTILISMO EM HECKSCHER E DOBB [Thoughts on mercantilism in Heckscher and Dobb]. *Anais de Hist.* [Brazil] *1977 9: 57-62.* Compares and comments on Eli F. Heckscher's *La Epoca Mercantilista* (1943) and Maurice Dobb's *A Evolução do Capitalismo* (1965).

1932. Groth, Margit; Knudsen, Herman; and Leihardt, Kurt. OM STUDIET AF ARBEJDSKAMPE: EN DISKUSSION [The study of labor disputes: a discussion]. *Árbog for Arbejderbevaegelsens Hist.* [Denmark] *1979 9: 184-206.* Edited transcript of a panel discussion among three Danish historians of the labor movement. Based on a meeting held in May 1979; 25 notes.

1933. Gunnarson, Gisli. A STUDY IN THE HISTORIOGRAPHY OF PRICES. *Econ. and Hist.* [Sweden] *1976 19(2): 124-141.* The founders of modern price studies integrated their data collections into general economic theory and economic history, an endeavor neglected by the International Scientific Committee on Price History during the 1920's-30's. Only recently has there been a reunification of data collection and economic-historical interpretations. While historians became more scientific, economists became more history- and society-conscious. Secondary sources; 70 notes.   M. Geyer

1934. Gutnova, E. V. O DVIZHUSHCHIKH SILAKH PER-EKHODA OT FEODALIZMA K KAPITALIZMU [The forces motivating the transition from feudalism to capitalism]. *Voprosy Istorii* [USSR] *1983 (9): 160-165.* Analyzes for the benefit of Soviet historians part of a debate about the structure of preindustrial agrarian society in Europe and its influence on the development of capitalism. The debate has been waged in the pages of *Past and Present* (1976-78), and is continued in an article by Professor Robert Brenner. Brenner's arguments, which are against neo-Malthusianism, echo the attitudes of many Marxist historians, although he seems unaware of this. He also underestimates the importance of peasant uprisings and of the early urban bourgeoisie. 6 notes.

D. N. Collins

1935. Haapala,   Pertti.   MITA   ON TYÖVÄENLUOKKA—ESIMERKKINÄ   TAMPEREEN TYÖVÄESTÖN LUOKKALUONNE VUOSINA 1830-1920 [What is the working class—the example of the class nature of workers in Tampere 1830-1920]. *Hist. Aikakauskirja* [Finland] *1983 81(3): 175-182.* Tests the analytical utility of the concept of a "working class" by examining differentiation and homogeneity among factory workers in Tampere, Finland, 1830-1920. At no time were they a homogeneous group. The concept, but not the reality, of a homogeneous working class emerged as the old patriarchal society declined. Historians should use the concept of "working class" to reflect the ways in which members of a given historical society perceived the division of labor in their environment. Based on published Finnish research; 2 tables, 8 notes.   R. G. Selleck

1936. Hartwell, R. M. GOOD OLD ECONOMIC HISTORY. *J. of Econ. Hist.* 1973 33(1): 28-40. Economic historians prior to World War I were British professors of economics, politically involved and preoccupied with explaining long-term economic evolution. The historians of the first generation saw the importance of other disciplines—law, government, religion, customs, politics—and the need for comparative analysis between different economies and different stages of development. They were concerned with the influence of economic action on freedom, such as the development of the corporation with rights and duties different from its members. These economic historians "determined many of the major historical interests" of the 20th century. 42 notes.   C. W. Olson

1937. Haupt, Georges. HVORFOR EN ARBEJDERBEVAEGEL-SENS HISTORIE? [Why a history of the labor movement?]. *Árbog for Arbejderbevaegelsens Hist.* [Denmark] *1979 9: 7-27.* Discusses problems in the historiography of the European labor movement from 1870 to 1970. Originally published in *New German Critique* 1978 (14).

1938. Haupt, Georges. POURQUOI L'HISTOIRE DU MOUVE-MENT OUVRIER? [Why a history of the workers' movement?]. *Europa* [Canada] *1978 1(2): 103-123.* A genuine scientific but militant history of the labor movement remains to be written, because previous histories have been appropriated by institutional organizations or written by professional historians who have taken a non-militant approach.

1939. Haupt, Heinz-Gerhard and Steinberg, Hans-Josef. TENDANCES DE L'HISTOIRE OUVRIÈRE EN RÉPUBLIQUE FÉDÉRALE ALLEMANDE [Tendencies in labor history in West Germany]. *Mouvement Social* [France] *1977 (100): 133-141.* Outlines West German labor historiography since 1945. The historicist tendency developed mainly by Gerhard Ritter stressed the great influence of political evolution in the labor movement. The structural history tendency, modeled after Dutch theory by such historians as Werner Conze and Otto Brunner in 1951 stressed the effect of social structures, processes, and movements, and the influence of collective socioeconomic forces on labor history. After 1960, a marked change in historiography took place as historians such as Dieter Groh and Hans-Ulrich Wehler stressed integration of the working class into society. 42 notes.   S. Sevilla

1940. Hawley, Ellis W. THE DISCOVERY AND STUDY OF A "CORPORATE LIBERALISM." *Business Hist. Rev. 1978 52(3): 309-320.* Argues that the classic liberal and conservative interpretations of American history do not accurately reflect the ways in which the modern nation has been organized. Rather than a continual business-government conflict, there has been the development of an "organizational sector" between the private enterprise and the public sectors. Introduces a special issue devoted to the study of "corporate liberalism," the attempt to find a "liberal but not-statist alternative to laissez-faire prescriptions" to recurring economic crises. Secondary works; 11 notes.   C. J. Pusateri

1941. Heitz, Gerhard. REGIONALE QUELLEN UND MARXIS-TISCH-LENINISTISCHE   AGRARGESCHICHTE   [Regional sources and Marxist-Leninist agrarian history]. *Archivmitteilungen* [East Germany] *1975 25(4): 138-144.* Stresses the importance of regional sources on agrarian problems and developments for Marxist-Leninist historiography from the Middle Ages to the 19th century.

1942. Heitz, Gerhard. ZUR AGRARGESCHICHTLICHEN KOM-PONENTE DER INDUSTRIEGESELLSCHAFTSTHEORIE [The agricultural-historical component of the theory of industrial societies]. *Wiss. Zeits. der Wilhelm-Pieck-Universität Rostock. Gesellschafts- und Sprachwissenschaftliche Reihe* [East Germany] *1979 28(7-8): 427-431.* Criticizes historians in capitalist countries for simplistic views regarding the agricultural sector of society in their research on the forms of society before and after capitalism and industrialization.

1943. Held, Wieland. LÄNDLICHE LOHNARBEIT IM 15. UND 16. JAHRHUNDERT UNTER BESONDERER BEACHTUNG THÜRINGENS. THEORETISCHE ÜBERLEGUNGEN UND LITERATURBERICHT [Rural paid labor in the 15th and 16th centuries with special consideration for Thuringia: theoretical considerations and report on the literature]. *Jahrbuch für Wirtschaftsgeschichte* [East Germany] *1978 (1): 171-189.* Cites and summarizes the findings of numerous Marxist and bourgeois studies of the question of landless agricultural laborers in the period of transition from feudalism to capitalism in the 15th and 16th centuries in Germany. All the studies address either certain aspects of the question or are based on local geographic areas. A thorough study of the degree of development of capitalist productive relations in Thuringia before the German Peasant War of 1525 would be a specially significant scholarly contribution. Secondary works; 124 notes.   J. B. Street

1944. Henderson, W. O. THE LABOUR FORCE IN THE TEX-TILE INDUSTRIES. *Archiv für Sozialgeschichte* [West Germany] *1976 16: 283-324.* During the Industrial Revolution the textile industries in Great Britain, France, and Germany were the greatest employers. Many of the workers were women and children. At first, work at home dominated over work in the factory. Early factories often employed inexperienced workers with low wages. Living and working conditions were harsh. Violence was the workers' means for securing their position until the middle of the 19th century, followed by unionization and strikes until 1900. The author discusses the controversies over the standard of living in the Industrial Revolution and the cotton factory family. 164 notes.

H. W. Wurster

1945. Hendricks, Rickey L. THE CONSERVATION MOVEMENT: A CRITIQUE OF HISTORICAL SOURCES. *Hist. Teacher 1982 16(1): 77-104.* Historiographical essay on the conservation movement. Major eras in the history of the conservation movement in America are: the turn of the century Progressive era, the New Deal programs of the 1930's, and the ecological movement of the 1960's and 70's. The tension between wilderness preservation and utilitarian perspectives is the chief analytical framework for conservation movement history. 101 notes.

L. K. Blaser

1946. Herden, Rose-Elisabeth. JAHRBUCH—FORUM: "ZU GRUNDTENDENZEN DER BEVÖLKERUNG IN DER GESCHICHTE" [Journal forum: "The Basic Tendencies of Population Movement in History"]. *Jahrbuch für Wirtschaftsgeschichte [East Germany] 1981 (3): 129-136.* Reports on a conference held 16 October 1980 in Berlin, which discussed the basic trends of population movement in history based on the work of Parviz Khalatbari, who has asserted that population movement is a concrete process that always occurs within the framework of specific historical means of production and encompasses both quantitative and qualitative aspects. Other contributions examined the problem of biological and social attitudes in the process of human reproduction, the problem of formulating general trends of population increase and the nature of these trends in different historical eras, and the relationship between productivity, the means of production, and population movement.

G. L. Neville

1947. Hill, Lewis E. INSTITUTIONALISM AS HISTORICAL INTERPRETATION. *Social Sci. J. 1978 15(1): 39-46.* Examines the institutionalist economic theory of Thorstein Veblen and Clarence E. Ayres as historiography.

1948. Hobsbawm, E. J. LABOR HISTORY AND IDEOLOGY. *J. of Social Hist. 1974 7(4): 371-381.* Studies the changes which have taken place in the historiography of labor and labor ideologies. There has been a growing academicism and "radicalization has produced a substantial crop of new labor historians." There needs to be a fresh realization that labor history is concerned with changing as well as with interpreting the world, but also to know what is meant by changing people. "For many of us the final object of our work is to create a world in which working people can make their own life and their own history, rather than to have it made for them by others, including academics." 8 notes.

R. V. Ritter

1949. Hornby, Ove and Mogensen, Gunnar Viby. THE STUDY OF ECONOMIC HISTORY IN DENMARK. RECENT TRENDS AND PROBLEMS. *Scandinavian Econ. Hist. R. [Denmark] 1974 22(1): 61-87.* Since World War II the study of economic history has expanded through publication of specialized studies of which those in agricultural history are the most numerous. Prior to 1945 the field was neglected, and the best work was a general history of Denmark published in German in 1933. Subjects for study cover industries, international commerce, and studies of communication and transport. Research in money and banking has been one of the Danish specialties, especially in institutional histories. Expanding studies, however, call for a general debate on priorities and some form of cooperative work with both state and institutional financial support. Conflict between Marxists and non-Marxists hinder theoretical and ideological frameworks for studies. The need for more training at the universities and support are predominant.

R. E. Lindgren

1950. Horowitz, Daniel. GENTEEL OBSERVERS: NEW ENGLAND ECONOMIC WRITERS AND INDUSTRIALIZATION. *New England Q. 1975 48(1): 65-83.* The 1890's economic writings and statistical studies of Edward Atkinson, David A. Wells, Carroll

D. Wright, and Francis A. Walker reveal their understanding of industrialization, in their attempts to explain US economic growth. In the light of their contributions to an understanding of the period's industrial growth, it is obvious that at least some genteel New Englanders (regardless of the nostalgia characterizing others) really comprehended the forces at work. They were willing and able "to make some sense of the sweep and breadth of industrialization." 44 notes.

R. V. Ritter

1951. Hummel, Jeffrey Rogers. THE MONETARY HISTORY OF AMERICA TO 1789: A HISTORIOGRAPHICAL ESSAY. *J. of Libertarian Studies 1978 2(4): 373-389.* Historical research on money in America before 1789 is dominated by two schools, the hard-money school, represented as early as 1740 by Dr. William Douglass and culminating in the work of Andrew McFarland Davis in 1900, and the managed-money school, represented as early as 1729 by Benjamin Franklin and culminating in the work of Leslie Van Horn Brock in 1941; though the later managed-money treatments are sounder historically, the older hard-money treatments are sounder theoretically in their view that paper money did not generate prosperity in the American colonies but instead generated the boom-bust trade cycle.

1952. Iakovlev, A. AGAINST CONCEPTS THAT VIOLATE THE HISTORICAL APPROACH. *Soviet Studies in Hist. 1973-74 12(3): 3-36.* Reviews recent Soviet and non-Soviet writings, 1966-71, and attacks for their views: I. Zabelin that professionals and paraprofessionals will replace workers in the historical arena; R. Darendorf's ideas that classes are shifting forms reacting to temporary conditions; theorists of convergence and their precursor, Werner Sombart; Herbert Marcuse on the cultural integration of workers into capitalist society; Ortega y Gasset that workers are the dregs of society; Arnold Toynbee's workers are an impediment to progress; I. Shevtsov's nihilism; I. Drozdov's snobbish denial of the historical role of the working class; M. Lobanov's moral superiority of the peasantry; and Alexander Solzhenitsyn as a supporter of the aristocracy.

1953. Ievselevs'ky, L. I. DIAL'NIST' VSEUKRAINS'KOI REDAKTSII *ISTORII FABRYK I ZAVODIV* [The activities of the Ukrainian editorial board of the *History of Factories and Plants*]. *Ukrains'kyi Istorychnyi Zhurnal [USSR] 1976 (6): 84-87.* Portrays the difficulties of the editorial board and its prime mover, writer Maxim Gorky, in starting to write the first history of factories and plants in the Ukraine, 1931-35.

1954. Ignatenko, T. A. ISTPROFY I IKH ROL' V SOVETSKOI ISTORIOGRAFII PROFESSIONAL'NOGO RABOCHEGO DVIZHENIIA [Istprofs (special commissions for the study of the history of the trade union movement) and their role in Soviet historiography of the labor movement]. *Istoricheskie Zapiski Akademii Nauk SSSR [USSR] 1979 104: 240-267.* Clarifies contributions of local *istprof* commissions during the 1920's and 1930's. Concentrates on proletarian trade unions, excluding teachers, postal workers, and other nonproductive cadres. Archival and other primary sources; 88 notes.

V. A. Packer

1955. Ingham, John N. RAGS TO RICHES REVISITED: THE EFFECT OF CITY SIZE AND RELATED FACTORS ON THE RECRUITMENT OF BUSINESS LEADERS. *J. of Am. Hist. 1976 63(3): 615-637.* Analyzes the backgrounds of 696 iron and steel manufacturers in six US cities, ca. 1874-1900. The pattern of social continuity presented by Frances W. Gregory and Irene D. Neu seems more applicable to this data than the "new elite" thesis of Matthew Josephson or Herbert G. Gutman. The typical manufactuer does not conform to the rags and riches stereotype. In the larger, established cities, industrialists belonged to antebellum upper social classes that had controlled the preindustrial economy. In smaller, more recently established cities, however, origins and social status were more complex. Primary and secondary sources; 9 tables, 12 notes.

W. R. Hively

1956. Isen, Chr. ORGANISERET AKTIVITET PÅ FORENINGSBASIS OMKRING ARBEJDERHISTORIEN I RINGKØBING AMT [Organized activity of an association concerning labor history in Ringkøbing Province]. *Arbejderhistorie [Denmark] 1983 (21): 95-98.* Describes activities of the new association for labor history organized in 1983 in Ringkøbing Province on the west coast of Denmark.

1957. Iskenderov, A. A. OSNOVNYE CHERTY I ETAPY KRIZISA BURZHUAZNOI ISTORICHESKOI NAUKI [The basic characteristics and stages of the crisis of bourgeois historiography]. *Novaia i Noveishaia Istoriia [USSR] 1980 (5): 41-59.* The general crisis of capitalism is expressed in the bankruptcy of its ideas. The science of history has been denied an objective scientific base by such men as Arnold J. Toynbee. French and American writers assert that the foundations of bourgeois science are trembling and that the whole basis of the discipline is unstable. They have begun to question the idea of inevitable progress. Three stages of the crisis are distinguishable: the second half of the 19th century to the Bolshevik Revolution, from then to the late 1950's, and the last 20 years. Attempts to bypass the crisis by using specialized methodologies such as quantitative research do not overcome the decline; socialism is on the march, capitalism in retreat. Based on secondary sources in English, French, German, and Russian; 52 notes.

D. N. Collins

1958. Jaanvjark, E. E. and Kala, K. K. OSVESHCHENIE VOPROSOV RAZVITIIA RABOCHEGO KLASSA ESTONSKOI SSR V PERIOD SOTSIALIZMA SOVETSKOI ISTORIOGRAFIEI (1960-1980 GG.) [Interpretation of problems of the development of the working class of Estonia in the socialist period of Soviet historiography, 1960-80]. *Istoriia SSSR [USSR] 1981 (6): 141-149.* Lists and discusses works by Soviet historians published 1960-80 and describing the development of the working class in Estonia. The main book on the subject is *Istoriia Estonskoi SSR* [A History of the Estonian SSR], by V. Maamjagi et al., which gives a comprehensive account of the political, economic, and social development of the Estonian working class. It is particularly useful for a review of the leading role of the Communist Party of Estonia in the republic's industrial development and in the training of workers' cadres. Secondary sources; 49 notes.

J. Bamber

1959. Jabłoński, Henryk. TERAŹNIEJSZOŚĆ I PRZESZŁOŚĆ [Past and present]. *Nowe Drogi [Poland] 1973 (5): 79-80.* Discusses the theoretical problems involved in writing the history of the working-class movement.

1960. Jaeger, Hans. BUSINESS HISTORY IN GERMANY: A SURVEY OF RECENT DEVELOPMENTS. *Business Hist. R. 1974 48(1): 28-48.* This historiograhical essay on German business history, 1918-74, emphasizes the lack of broad views on the subject. Instead there have been company histories and entrepreneurial biographies. The development of the broader view is handicapped by the lack of business schools and chairs of business history in the universities. Company archives, company histories, entrepreneurial biographies, economic history, and social history comprise the available resources. Notes some developments and a developing methodology toward a broader based business history. 90 notes.

R. V. Ritter

1961. Jones, Andrew. THE RISE AND FALL OF THE MANORIAL SYSTEM: A CRITICAL COMMENT. *J. of Econ. Hist. 1972 32(4): 938-944.* Criticizes the model outlined by Douglass C. North and Robert Paul Thomas in *The Journal of Economic History* 1971 31(4) concerning the rise and fall of the manorial system in Western Europe and particularly in England. They failed to distinguish properly between the economic organization of manorialism and the political institution of feudalism; they incorporated part of the Marxian theory of historical evolution which they intended to break away from. Manorialism did not die out ca. 1500. Long after serfdom disappeared a manorial relationship existed in the countryside. North and Thomas have ignored the peasants and sacrificed "factual accuracy to the appeal of the model." 35 notes.

C. W. Olson

1962. Jones, Archer. SOCIAL DARWINISM AND CLASSICAL ECONOMICS: AN UNTESTED HYPOTHESIS. *North Dakota Q. 1978 46(1): 19-31.* US historiography has equated classical economics and social Darwinism, which actually differ on issues such as competition, laissez-faire, and taxation.

1963. Jones, Merfyn. APPROACHES TO MINERS' HISTORY. *Bull. of the Soc. for the Study of Labour Hist. 1981 (43): 71-73.* Reviews John Gaventa's *Power and Powerlessness, Rebellion and Quiescence in an Appalachian Valley* (1980); Alan Campbell's *The Lanarkshire Miners: A Social History of Their Trade Unions* (1979); and Hywel Francis and David Smith's *The Fed: A History of the South Wales Miners in the Twentieth Century* (1980), concentrating on an examination of the authors' different historiographic approaches.

1964. Kalakura, Ia. S. BOR'BA PARTII ZA USKORENIE NAUCHNO-TEKHNICHESKOGO PROGRESSA V PROMYSHLENNOSTI V USLOVIIAKH RAZVITOGO SOTSIALIZMA [The Party's struggle to speed up scientific-technical progress in industry under developed socialism]. *Voprosy Istorii KPSS [USSR] 1976 (4): 123-130.* Reviews Ukrainian publications, 1959-75, dealing with industrialization and improving productivity.

1965. Kalakura, Ia. S. and Petrenko, V. S. KOLKHOZNOE KRESTIANSTVO I SEL'SKOE KHOZIAISTVO UKSSR V UKRAINSKOI SOVETSKOI ISTORIOGRAFII (1945-1975 GG) [Kolkhoz peasantry and agriculture in the Ukrainian SSR, Ukrainian-Soviet historiography, 1945-75]. *Voprosy Istorii [USSR] 1975 (7): 133-138.* Reviews literature published, 1965-75 on the postrevolutionary history of agriculture in the Ukraine. Includes economically-oriented works, as well as those documenting the Communist Party's agricultural policy and improved living conditions. 16 notes.

V. Sobeslavsky

1966. Kanev, D. KONFERENTSIIA NA ISTORITSI NA RABOTNICHESKOTO DVIZHENIE-LINTS, AVSTRIIA [A conference of historians of the labor movement in Linz, Austria]. *Izvestiia na Inst. po Istoriia na BKP [Bulgaria] 1978 (39): 619-623.* Discusses the historians' conference held 20-24 September 1977 in Linz, Austria, in which 20 countries took part in discussions of the problems of the proletarian movement.

1967. Kaye, Harvey J. TOTALITY: ITS APPLICATION TO HISTORICAL AND SOCIAL ANALYSIS BY WALLERSTEIN AND GENOVESE. *Hist. Reflections [Canada] 1979 6(2): 405-419.* Examines the concept of totality of Marxian historical social scientists Immanuel Wallerstein and Eugene Genovese. While they represent the continuation among Marxists of the debate on the transition from feudalism to capitalism, they also extend the debate into new areas. Wallerstein's capitalist world economy is a reconceptualization of transition built on Paul Sweezy's argument of the development and expansion of a market economy. Genovese is more limited but pushes the transition question beyond the economic into "the complex relationships among the political economy, political sociology and psychological and cultural dimensions of class relations." 94 notes.

1968. Khvostova, K. V. METODOLOGICHESKIE PROBLEMY PRIMENENIIA MATEMATICHESKIKH METODOV V ISTORICHESKIKH ISSLEDOVANIIAKH [Methodological problems in the use of mathematical methods in historical research]. *Voprosy Istorii [USSR] 1975 (11): 97-112.* The significance of applying mathematical methods in history consists, from the viewpoint of Marxist historians, in detailing and concretizing historical hypotheses. The employment of these methods heightens the authentic value of the given sources and extends the possibility of verifying the conclusions formulated by historians. The keen interest shown by bourgeois scientists in the mathematical processing of historical information is explained by the essential requirement of bourgeois historiography to manifest a theoretical, problems approach to the study of history. But the attempts of bourgeois historians to employ theories and mathematical models applied in economic science and sociology are insufficiently effective. Research in the historical past calls for the evolvement of special mathematical models. For example, research in the medieval period, owing to the specific character of its phenomena, as well as to the incompleteness of individual sources of mass information, calls, as a rule, for micromodelling intended for the study of microstructures and small social groups.

J

1969. Kiszlov, G. A NEMZETKÖZI MUNKÁSMOZGALOM TÖRTÉNETÉNEK KUTATÁSA A SZOVJETUNIÓBAN [Soviet research on the history of the international labor movement]. *Párttörténeti Közlemények [Hungary] 1977 23(2): 122-158.* Reviews monographs and articles dealing with the history of the international labor movement, published 1971-76, in the USSR. 106 notes.

CK-AU

1970. Klein, Maury. THE ROBBER BARONS. *Am. Hist. Illus. 1971 6(6): 12-22.* One of the early historiographical conflicts concerning the US Industrial Revolution of the late 19th century has been the nature of the men who dominated it, and whether they were "industrial statesmen" or "Robber Barons." Critics saw two types of tycoons; builders, such as John D. Rockefeller and Andrew Carnegie, and wreckers, typified by Jay Gould. Recent studies have focused on themes such as organizational and institutional development, outliving the Robber Barons theory. As for the men, both pirates and pioneers, they did exactly what the prevailing system encouraged them to do, becoming reflections as well as products of their culture. Primary and secondary sources; 9 illus.

D. Dodd

1971. Klemm, Volker. ZUR BEDEUTUNG ALBRECHT DANIEL THAERS FÜR DIE AGRARHISTORIOGRAPHIE [On the significance of Albrecht Daniel Thaer for agrarian historiography]. *Jahrbuch für Wirtschaftsgeschichte [East Germany] 1975 (1): 121-136.* Albrecht Daniel Thaer (1752-1828) laid the foundations of German superiority in the study of agricultural economics which was universally recognized by the end of the 19th century. Thaer's hitherto neglected research in agrarian history, particularly his seminal work, *Grundriss einer Geschichte des Ackerbaus* (1807), was "agrarian history in the broadest sense." Thaer repeatedly criticized feudal restrictions on agricultural productivity and advocated modernization as a practical necessity. Primary and secondary sources; 66 notes.

R. J. Bazillion

1972. Koberdowa, Irena. METODOLOGICZNE ASPEKTY HISTORIOGRAFII MIĘDZYNARODOWEGO RUCHU ROBOTNICZEGO (TEZY) [Methodological aspects of historiography of the international worker's movement]. *Z Pola Walki [Poland] 1978 21(1): 131-137.* Presents 13 theses from the international methodological conference of historians of the labor movement on basic theoretical problems facing the authors and editors of the two-volume *International Workers' Movement* (Warsaw, 1976). Includes as well works by historians from nations other than Poland. The theses stressed the necessity of keeping alive the scientific character of this historiography based on the principles of Marxist methodology.

J/S

1973. Kochanowicz, Jacek. *HOMO OECONOMICUS* I HISTORIA GOSPODARCZA [Homo oeconomicus and economic history]. *Przegląd Historyczny [Poland] 1983 74(3): 517-526.* Reviews Douglas C. North's *Structure and Change in Economic History* (1981), which describes and analyzes the differences between the traditional and new economic histories. The latter, originating in the United States in the 1950's, is also known as econometric history or cliometrics. 33 notes.

A. B. Pernal

1974. Kreder, A. A. EKONOMICHESKII KRIZIS 1929-1933 GG I VNUTRENNIAIA POLITIKA PRAVITEL'STVA G. GUVERA V AMERIKANSKOI BURZHUAZNOI ISTORIOGRAFII [The Great Depression from 1929 to 1933 and the domestic policy of Herbert Hoover's administration in American historiography]. *Amerikanskii Ezhegodnik [USSR] 1982: 163-184.* Analyzes the gradual transformation from the 1930's to the 1970's of the perception of Herbert Hoover's policy during the Great Depression. His policy of noninterference in the economy was initially considered

inefficient. Now, due to Hoover's strong accent on American individualism, it is found more appropriate for the economy. Secondary sources; 65 notes.

R. Kirillov

1975. Kriwoguz, Igor M. W. I. LENIN I RADZIECKA HISTORIOGRAFIA MIĘDZYNARODOWEGO RUCHU ROBOTNICZEGO CZASÓW NOWOŻYTNYCH [V. I. Lenin and Soviet historiography of the modern international labor movement]. *Z Pola Walki [Poland] 1973 19(1): 3-36.* Reviews chronologically the achievements of Soviet historiography covering the international labor movement in the 19th and 20th centuries. The foundation of Soviet historiography is the works of Marx, Engels, and Lenin. Soviet historiography on the international workers' movement has been developing since the first years of the Soviet state and has gone through several stages. The author gives characteristics of these stages, considered in conjunction with each particular resolution of the Central Committee of the CPSU and the directive scientific bodies of the USSR. Each new stage in development indicated a new stage in the struggle against departures from Marxist-Leninist methodology and alien ideological influences. The development of research and the popularization of the history of the international labor movement was accompanied by a fierce ideological struggle against opportunism and bourgeois ideology. The author concentrates on works dealing with activities of Marx, Engels, and Lenin, the development of the workers' movement in Western Europe, the activities of the First and Second Internationals, the history of the Paris Commune, the international influences exerted by Lenin, the Bolshevik current on revolutionary movement in the world, and research on workers' movements in America and Asia.

J

1976. Kucherenko, G. S. SENSIMONIZM V "POLITICHESKOI EKONOMII I POLITIKE" PROSPERA ANFANTENA [Saint-Simonian in Prosper Enfantin's *Political Economy and Politics*]. *Novaia i Noveishaia Istoriia [USSR] 1974 (5): 55-70.* A brief discussion of Barthélemy Prosper Enfantin's writings and an attack on two aspects of bourgeois historiography, which has underestimated Comte de Saint-Simon's role in the movement which acquired his name, and has exaggerated the role of Enfantin in the movement. The latter's influence is deduced from the frequency of his publications in the journal *Le Producteur,* but many of these contributions are incidental and of no substance. Enfantin contributed to only three out of 30 public lectures given by the collaborators of the journal. Bourgeois historians have underestimated Enfantin's economic theory, concentrating instead on his works on the women's question and religion. Marx and Engels, however, stated that Enfantin's contributions to economic thought were profound. Concentrates on Enfantin's writings about capitalism and the position of the working masses, stressing his belief in the class struggle. Based on published documentary sources; 91 notes.

D. N. Collins

1977. Kula, Witold. SPORY DOKOLA PROBLEMU GENEZY KAPITALIZMU AGRARNEGO W DZISIEJSZEJ HISTORIOGRAFII RADZIECKIEJ [The controversy surrounding the genesis of agrarian capitalism in contemporary Soviet historiography]. *Kwartalnik Hist. [Poland] 1964 71(1): 137-142.* Soviet historiography concerning the evolution of capitalism is extensive but uneven. The agrarian structure has been examined thoroughly while other sides of the problem are almost neglected. New research should go beyond the cross-sectional method and be based on long series of occurrences showing general trends.

J. Wilczek

1978. Kuma, Krishna. MULTINATIONAL CORPORATIONS AND TRANSNATIONAL RELATIONS. *J. of Pol. & Military Sociol. 1979 7(2): 291-304.* Review article illustrating different intellectual contexts of eight social science works on multinational corporations. The liberal-diffusionist school believes that multinational corporations facilitate the development of the maximum use of scarce human and material resources. A second school treats the multinationals as imperialistic and undesirable while a third neomercantilist school argues that multinational corporations are best "understood with reference to the complex interplay of national interests on the world scene." The decline of US leadership has fostered economic nationalism and regionalism which will in turn affect the growth of the multinationals.

1979. Lampe, John R. and Jackson, Marvin R. AN APPRAISAL OF RECENT BALKAN ECONOMIC HISTORIOGRAPHY. *East European Q. 1975 9(2): 197-240.* A comprehensive bibliographic essay on works published in the last 10 years on the economic history of the Balkans. After noting the gaps which needed to be filled and the problems with sources and methods, the authors review the literature country by country, including Bulgaria, Yugoslavia, Romania, and Greece. 71 notes. C. R. Lovin

1980. Larsen, Keld D. JEG—EN HÅNDVAERKER ELLER MØDET MED VIRKELIGHEDEN [I: a craftsman or the meeting with reality]. *Arbejder Hist. [Denmark] 1982 18: 17-32.* Discusses some of the problems that face the historian of the working classes in his relations to employer, audience, and material.

1981. Laverychev, V. Ia. and Pushkareva, I. M. NEKOTORYE PROBLEMY IZUCHENIIA ISTORII RABOCHEGO KLASSA ROSSII PERIODA IMPERIALIZMA [Problems involved in the study of Russian working-class history in the period of imperialism]. *Voprosy Istorii [USSR] 1981 (1): 18-34.* In examining the main directions of continued research in the problems of the history of the Russian working class of the period of imperialism, the authors stress the need for a comprehensive approach and discuss some concrete methods of solving the more general problems. In this context, they urge further investigation of the hegemony of the proletariat in the bourgeois-democratic revolution, and of some aspects of Communist Party history, such as the tactic of Left blocs, the struggle against manifestations of opportunism, and development of the strike movement at different stages. Also emphasizes the need for a more precise definition of the working class and a more accurate estimate of its numerical strength, more effective methods of studying the conditions of proletariat, and more stress on the international significance of the Russian labor movement. J

1982. Leab, Daniel J. WRITING HISTORY WITH FILM: TWO VIEWS OF THE 1937 STRIKE AGAINST GENERAL MOTORS BY THE UAW. *Labor Hist. 1980 21(1): 102-112.* Reviews two films: *The Great Sitdown* (1976) by British filmmaker Stephen Peet and *With Babies and Banners* (1978) by Lorraine Gray and Lynn Goldfarb. The films rewrite history from the United Automobile Workers of America (UAW) strikers' and women's perspectives. 20 notes. L. L. Athey

1983. Loone, E. N. BOR'BA TECHENII V SOVREMENNOI ANGLO-AMERIKANSKOI ISTORIOGRAFII ANGLIISKOGO RABOCHEGO DVIZHENIIA NA PERVOM ETAPE OBSHCHEGO KRIZISA KAPITALIZMA [Conflicting trends in contemporary Anglo-American historiography on the British labor movement during the first stage of the general crisis of capitalism]. *Vestnik Moskovskogo Universiteta, Seriia 9: Istoriia [USSR] 1962 17(5): 40-56.* Analyzes Anglo-American literature on the British labor movement of 1919-39 on the basis of some 30 (mainly British) studies published primarily in the 1950's. Differences in appraisal depend on the political philosophy of the individual author and reflect the ideological bias of his socioeconomic class: Marxists and leftist Labourites defend the workers' conduct, while rightist Labourites support collaboration with the middle classes, thus accepting capitalism. 92 notes. N. Frenkley

1984. Lötsch, Manfred. EINIGE BERMERKUNGEN ZUR DISKUSSION ÜBER DEN CHARAKTER DER ARBEITERKLASSE [Some observations on the debate concerning the character of the working class]. *Jahrbuch für Wirtschaftsgeschichte [East Germany] 1973 (2): 209-216.* Jürgen Kuczynski has defined the proletariat as workers operating machines in large plants. This definition is based upon a misuse of Lenin's writings and ignores the views of Marx and Engels who identified the proletariat with wage labor. Moreover, it equates a specific form of capitalism with the system as a whole and, in view of the declining ratio of factory to non-factory workers, it amounts to a theory of the progressive diminution of the proletariat. Secondary works; 16 notes. J. A. Perkins

1985. Macchioro, Aurelio. LA STORIA DEL PENSIERO ECONOMICO FRA STORIA E SCIENZA [The history of economic thought between history and science]. *Nuova Riv. Storica [Italy]* *1974 58(1-2): 1-28.* The distinction between economic thought and economic doctrines is a useful one in the history of economics. The author surveys briefly the history of both, then discusses the confusion between technology and historiography. The so-called laws of diminishing return, of marginal utility, and of the division of labor are part of the operating technique; they do not constitute the subject matter of history. 7 notes. J. C. Billigmeier

1986. Macintyre, Stuart. THE MAKING OF THE AUSTRALIAN WORKING CLASS: AN HISTORIOGRAPHICAL SURVEY. *Hist. Studies [Australia] 1978 18(71): 233-253.* Contrasts E. P. Thompson's definition of class as "something which in fact happens... in human relationships" with Marx's distinction between class "in itself" and "for itself" and compares six Australian writers' use of the concept of class. Ian Turner (1965) uses class as an "objective category: the class of men and women who work for wages." Humphrey McQueen (1970) says the criterion is not ownership but "consciousness," and in the 19th century Australian laboring classes were petit bourgeois. Terry Irving (1967) suggested a working class must have a common relationship to the means of production and a specific class consciousness. Bob Connell (1977) suggests there needs to be a body of wage laborers committed to the destruction of capitalism. John Rickard (1976) sees working- and middle-class traditions which, in the 1890's, led to institutions which enabled them to coexist. Ronald Lawson (1973) sees in Brisbane not class so much as "a ladder, a hierarchy of closely adjacent status positions." The author suggests new avenues of inquiry. W. D. McIntyre

1987. Makkai, Làszlò. ARS HISTORICA: ON BRAUDEL. *Rev. (Fernand Braudel Center) 1983 6(4): 435-454.* Like Leopold von Ranke, Fernand Braudel is an unequalled master of *ars historica* in all three classical senses of the term—as art, craft, and science. Braudel's economic-historical account avoids a simple dogmatic view by presenting the developmental phases of world economics in three dimensions—vertically, horizontally, and chronologically. L. V. Eid

1988. Martin, Albro. UNEASY PARTNERS: GOVERNMENT-BUSINESS RELATIONS IN TWENTIETH-CENTURY AMERICAN HISTORY. *Prologue 1979 11(2): 91-105.* Surveys 20th-century literature on relations between government and business as influenced by the 19th century. Before 1825 the idea of the congruence of business and public interests dominated. After 1825, those with private interests were seen as greedy profiteers seeking to manipulate political power to their own advantage. By 1900 indignant literature was attacking the business community with increasing vehemence. From 1900 to 1930 public opinion held that individuals had the power to limit the unrestrained power of corporations. However, Charles A. Beard and Mary R. Beard's four-volume *Rise of American Civilization* (1927-40) made clear that the "business of America is business." Since 1945, revisionists have shown that Progressive intervention in economic decisionmaking was a mistake. More recently, works have appeared which demonstrate the failure of government regulatory programs. Secondary sources; 25 notes. J. Powell

1989. Masuda, Etsusuke and Newman, Peter. GRAY AND GIFFEN GOODS. *Econ. J. [Great Britain] 1981 91(364): 1011-1014.* Discusses the historiographical treatment of Simon Gray and his economic theories from the 1890's until the 1960's. Relates the basic descriptions on the corn trade as initially provided by Gray and provides the various interpretions that later economic historians and theorists have provided. Both Gray and his academic interpreters could handle distinct exceptions to their economic theories. Secondary sources. W. D. Wrigley

1990. Mathias, Peter. ADAM'S BURDEN: DIAGNOSES OF POVERTY IN POST-MEDIEVAL EUROPE AND THE THIRD WORLD NOW. *Tijdschrift voor Geschiedenis [Netherlands] 1976 89(2): 149-160.* Discusses the debate on poverty in modern Europe and the developing nations. Social thinkers, theologians, and others have searched for universal interpretaions to explain the problem of poverty. Thus, the Calvinists contended that poverty was necessary for a prosperous economy and as an inducement for the poor to exert themselves. Third World nations are poor, according to many, because of their idleness, high leisure preference, and overpopulation. This search for universal causes will smother reality, however, since social theory is not autonomous and absolute but is given significance and relevance in relation to a specific context of time and society. Secondary sources; 19 notes. G. D. Homan

1991. Mauro, Frédéric. CONCEPTUALISATION ET QUANTIFICATION EN HISTOIRE ÉCONOMIQUE [Conceptualization and quantification in economic history]. *R. de la U. Complutense de Madrid [Spain] 1971 20(79): 65-78.* Discusses in general terms the rise of economic history, particularly the development of statistics and quantitative methods in history. Quantification has progressed at the expense of conceptualization; positivism and the scientific method have created a distrust of ideas, aggravated by the confusion between doctrine and theory. Quantification and conceptualization must be used to stimulate each other and economic historians must not only study mathematics and statistics but also appreciate the value of inherited concepts so they can adapt them to present needs. 13 notes.

1992. McClelland, Peter D. MODEL-BUILDING IN THE NEW ECONOMIC HISTORY. *Am. Behavioral Scientist 1973 16(5): 631-652.* One of six essays in this issue dealing with emerging theoretical models in social and political history.

1993. McCloskey, Donald. NEW PERSPECTIVES ON THE OLD POOR LAW. *Explorations in Econ. Hist. 1973 10(4): 419-436.* Summarizes the historiography of the Old Poor Law from 1795 to 1834. Shows that economic analysis of the operation of the system is usually unclear and sometimes self-contradictory. Suggests that in practice the law operated to subsidize income rather than wages. This reduced the supply of effort from agricultural laborers but increased the value of the effort that remained. Based on published documents and secondary accounts. P. J. Coleman

1994. McDonnell, Lawrence T. "YOU ARE TOO SENTIMENTAL": PROBLEMS AND SUGGESTIONS FOR A NEW LABOR HISTORY. *Journal of Social History 1984 17(4): 629-654.* The celebrated new labor history of the 1970's exhibits two tendencies: one conservative, one leftist, and both sentimental to the extent that they ignore many vital and lingering questions about the past and present of the working-class struggle. Herbert Gutman and David Montgomery are the two leading advocates of the pathbreaking work that has given so much new enthusiasm and insight to the field. Though supposedly on two sides of the historiography of American labor, both Gutman and Montgomery cheer the survival of the American working class, ignoring its ongoing struggle with and subservience to capital. 79 notes. C. M. Hough/S

1995. McFarlane, Bruce. THE USE OF ECONOMIC THEORY IN HISTORY: SNOOKS SNOOKERED. *Labor Hist. [Australia] 1976 (31): 83-85.* The author defends his views on the economic theory of Graeme Snooks and its use in historiography, 1957-74.

1996. McGuirl, Barbara and Olson, Gordon L. BUSINESS HISTORY HAS A FUTURE. *Public Hist. 1981 3(3): 153-159.* Account of the day-long seminar conducted by the Grand Rapids Area Council for the Humanities (GRACH) and the Grand Rapids Public Library "to show business leaders the many uses and fundamental features of a corporate history program."

1997. McKenzie, Robert H. RECONSTRUCTION HISTORIOGRAPHY: THE VIEW FROM SHELBY. *Historian 1974 36(2): 207-223.* Evaluates the historiography of Reconstruction from the point of view of the Shelby Iron Company of Shelby, Alabama, from source materials held in the University of Alabama Library covering 1862-1923. This economic environment needs to be understood if one is to understand why decisions made in Washington produced the results they did. 29 notes. R. V. Ritter

1998. McNaught, Kenneth. E. P. THOMPSON VS HAROLD LOGAN: WRITING ABOUT LABOUR AND THE LEFT IN THE 1970S. *Can. Hist. Rev. [Canada] 1981 62(2): 141-168.* Discusses inadequacies of Canadian labor historiography, typified by Harold

Logan's *Trade Unions in Canada* (1948). Labor organization and the reactions of government and business were emphasized, while the real experiences of the working class were neglected. Social change in the 1960's increased Canadian scholars' receptivity to US and European influences, such as the work of E. P. Thompson and of the *Annales* school in France. A marked stress on social history and less biased Marxist interpretations have resulted. However, comprehensive theses explaining the Canadian labor structure, government's labor policy or the political left and labor, have yet to appear. 62 notes. N. A. Newhouse

1999. McQuaid, Kim. THE FRUSTRATION OF CORPORATE REVIVAL DURING THE EARLY NEW DEAL. *Historian 1979 41(4): 682-704.* Recent years have witnessed a shift in New Deal historiography, emphasizing continuities between the 1920's and 1930's. The concept of "corporate liberalism" has emerged from studies investigating the relationship between big business and the state. Examines two quasigovernmental agencies that enjoyed impressive measures of advisory influence during the early years of the New Deal—the Business Advisory Council of the Department of Commerce and the Industrial Advisory Board of the National Recovery Administration. Details the creation, early history, and membership of these agencies, and concludes that, while continuity between the New Era and the New Deal is overdrawn, corporate liberalism did weather the storm. Primary sources; 42 notes. R. S. Sliwoski

2000. Michalski, Stanisław. GENEZA I TEORETYCZNE PRZESŁANKI KULTURY ROBOTNICZEJ [Origins and theoretical premises of working-class culture]. *Z Pola Walki [Poland] 1981 23[i.e., 24](2): 3-22.* Discusses the problem of the formation and function of working-class culture in the works of contemporary Polish historians. All agree that socialism determines changes in the value systems of the workers' culture, enabling them to reorient themselves in the changing world. Working-class culture is not only conditioned by the community, but also it is itself an active conditioning agent. 39 notes. English and Russian summaries. M. Hernas

2001. Mikkelsen, Flemming. STREJKEN SOM KOLLEKTIV AKTION: NYE STREJKEANALYSER INDEN FOR SAMFUNDSVIDENSKABERNE OG HISTORIEVIDENSKABEN [The strike as collective action: new strike analyses in the social and historical sciences]. *Økonomi og Politik [Denmark] 1982 56(4): 98-121.* Examines the current historiography on strikes as social and historical phenomena. Describes the development of the strike from the 18th century to the present, providing an evaluation of causal theory, "interest" theory, and Charles Tilly's conflict theory. The author also compares strikes in Europe and North America, 1900-80, specifically noting Scandinavian activities during this period. 2 illus., 92 notes. D. F. Spade

2002. Mintz, Sidney. A NOTE ON THE DEFINITION OF PEASANTRIES. *J. of Peasant Studies [Great Britain] 1973 1(1): 91-106.* More important than an abstract definition of "the peasantry" is the development of typologies of rural socio-economic groupings. Such typologies should facilitate comparisons between societies whose rural socioloqy reveals broadly similar structures. They might include the following features: the internal composition of the so-called peasant sector; the relationships of different parts of that sector to other, non-peasant rural groups; the social-relational uses made of traditional cultural forms in rural community life, for linking different parts of the peasantry and distinguishing between peasants and non-peasants; and the historical development of the peasant sector. J

2003. Molesti, Romano. MOMENTI DELLO SVOLGIMENTO DELLA STORIA DELLE DOCTRINE ECONOMICHE [Highlights in the development of the history of economic theory]. *Economia e Storia [Italy] 1970 (4): 504-520.* Primarily reviews the works of three modern authors on economic development: R. Gill, D. R. Fusfeld, H. Denis. All three agree on the need to understand economic theory as a product of its time, subject to change in the wake of new economic or social developments. Secondary sources; 39 notes.   F. Pollaczek

2004. Montgomery, David. TO STUDY THE PEOPLE: THE AMERICAN WORKING CLASS. *Labor Hist. 1980 21(4): 485-512.* A historiographical review of the literature on the American working class, concentrating on the studies produced in the last 30 years. 68 notes.   L. F. Velicer

2005. Morales Lezcano, Víctor. NUEVA HISTORIA ECONÓMICA, MODERNIZACIÓN, INTERNACIONALISMO: PARENTESCO DE LOS TRES CAMPOS DE ESTUDIO [New economic history, modernization, and internationalism: the relationship of the three fields of study]. *Anales de Econ. [Spain] 1973 (17): 129-139.* Considers the ideological foundations of the new economic history, a school closely linked to sociology. The school, predominately active in the United States, considers modernization and the incorporation of Western characteristics and values, a lever for the economic growth of developing nations, a thesis convincingly discredited by Andre Gunder Frank (1929-) some years ago. Nonetheless, the new economic history has yielded some noteworthy results within its ideological limitations.
C. M. S. (IHE 88076)

2006. Moramarco, Fred. HAMILTON AND THE HISTORIANS: THE ECONOMIC PROGRAM IN RETROSPECT. *Midcontinent Am. Studies J. 1967 8(1): 34-43.* Alexander Hamilton (1757-1809) was the first Secretary of the Treasury (1789-95). Historical interpretations of his economic policies have taken three courses: the aristocratic view, the mercantile view, and the American or nationalist view. The nationalist view seems to be the most realistic interpretation in terms of the results of Hamilton's programs. 32 notes.
S

2007. Morineau, Michel. JUGLAR, KITCHIN, KONDRATIEFF, ET COMPAGNIE [Juglar, Kitchin, Kondratieff and company]. *Review (Fernand Braudel Center) 1984 7(4): 577-598.* A critical study of the Juglar, Kitchin and Kondratieff economic cycles in history. Explains that such "cycles," mainly because of their sophisticated formulation, are too rigid for offering any validity. Suggests, instead, the study of the more flexible concept of "sequences," which centers on comparing the movements within cycles. 5 fig., 14 notes, ref.   G. P. Cleyet

2008. Morton, Desmond. E. P. THOMPSON DANS DES ARPENTS DE NEIGE: LES HISTORIENS CANADIENS-ANGLAIS ET LA CLASSE OUVRIERE [E. P. Thompson in acres of snow: English-Canadian historians and the working class]. *Rev. d'Hist. de l'Amérique Française [Canada] 1983 37(2): 165-182.* Historiographical essay on Canadian working-class and labor history, particularly the development of a Marxist school of analysis and the influence of the English social historian E. P. Thompson on English-language Canadian historians. 64 notes.   R. Aldrich

2009. Murphy, P. J. THE ORIGINS OF THE 1852 LOCK-OUT IN THE BRITISH ENGINEERING INDUSTRY RECONSIDERED. *Int. Rev. of Social Hist. [Netherlands] 1978 23(2): 242-266.* The accounts of the 1852 lockout and trade union organization by Henry Pelling, J. B. Jeffreys, and Keith Burgess follow too much "an idealised notion of how trade unions should develop." These historians show political or ideological preferences which distort an understanding of factors contributing to this celebrated incident. Offers a new look at the origins and at neglected aspects of the lockout. Based on contemporary newspaper accounts and secondary sources.   G. P. Blum

2010. Nakamura, Hiroji and Aramaki, Masanori. KAHEI SHINYŌGAKUSETSU-SHI KENKYU [Historical studies of money and credit theories]. *Ann. Bull. of the Soc. for the Hist. of Econ. Thought [Japan] 1982 20: 4-17.* Examines Japanese publications concerning books written by classic thinkers on economic theory and traces Japanese historiography of monetary systems, credit, and banking.   M. Kawaguchi

2011. Neuschäffer, Hubertus. CARL FRIEDRICH FRHR. VON SCHOULTZ-ASCHERADEN: EIN BEITRAG ZUM FORSCHUNGSPROBLEM DER AGRARREFORMEN IM OSTSEERAUM DES 18. JAHRHUNDERTS [Carl Friedrich Baron von Schoultz-Ascheraden: a contribution to research problems on land reform in the Baltic region in the 18th century]. *J. of Baltic Studies 1981 12(4): 318-332.* Baron von Schoultz-Ascheraden (1720-82) was a land reformer. Owner of several estates in Livonia, he decreed in 1764 a new law improving the legal status of the peasantry. He was motivated not only by humanitarian ideas, but also by political and economical calculations. Historiographical criticism of his reforms is controversial. His peers condemned him, adherents of the Enlightenment praised him, Marxist historians claim he did not intend to improve the lot of the peasants. Land reforms in the Baltic region were influenced by several political theories. Based on a paper presented at the 6th Conference on Baltic Studies, 5-8 June 1981, at the University of Stockholm; 36 notes.   R. Vilums

2012. Nilsson, Carl-Axel. 1930-TALSKRIS OCH SAMHÄLLSUTVECKLING [The Depression of the thirties and subsequent social developments]. *Hist. Tidskrift [Sweden] 1976 (1): 59-75.* To what extent should the Depression of the early 1930's be viewed as a discontinuity in modern history? The author compares the Marxist view, in which the Depression is placed in the context of the transition from a competitive capitalism to a monopoly variant, with a second view closely related to specific political and economic changes in a short-term perspective. Chart, table, 16 notes. English summary.   A. Erlandsson

2013. Norris, James D. HISTORY AND THE POLITICAL ECONOMY. *J. of Interdisciplinary Hist. 1972 3(2): 363-372.* A review article prompted by Peter Temin's *The Jacksonian Economy* (New York: W. W. Norton, 1969), James Roger Sharp's *The Jacksonians versus The Banks: Politics in the States After the Panic of 1837* (New York: Columbia U. Pr., 1970), and William L. Taylor's *A Productive Monopoly: The Effect of Railroad Control on New England Coastal Steamship Lines, 1870-1916* (Providence: Brown U. Pr., 1970). Each book illustrates that causal relationships between the fluctuations in the economy and government activity, including political fortunes, are being probed by modern techniques of quantification and empirical tests.   R. V. Ritter

2014. O'Brien, P. K. ESSAYS IN BIBLIOGRAPHY AND CRITICISM, LXXVII. AGRICULTURE AND THE INDUSTRIAL REVOLUTION. *Econ. Hist. Rev. [Great Britain] 1977 30(1): 166-181.* Discusses E. L. Jones's *Agriculture and the Industrial Revolution* (Blackwell: Oxford, 1974), which raises important questions about agrarian history, 1650-1815. The author assesses the key factors explaining the parallel growth of agricultural output and industrialization in Great Britain. Traditionally, agriculture has been viewed as a stumbling block to industrial progress; modern agrarian history has demonstrated agriculture's positive contribution to industrialization. Nevertheless, generalizations about an "agricultural revolution" are inappropriate within the context of the British tenurial system. 18 notes.   B. L. Crapster/S

2015. Orlik, I. I. SOTSIALISTICHESKOE SODRUZHESTVO I PROVAL "STRATEGICHESKOGO KONTROLIA" [Socialist cooperation and the collapse of strategic control]. *Istoriia SSSR [USSR] 1976 (5): 3-19.* Examines the rise of Comecon, giving special attention to the efforts of the Western nations to impede the development of economic cooperation between socialist countries, and to the distortion of Comecon history common in Western scholarship. The foreign policy of the United States was in many cases formulated in response to or anticipation of the growing influence of the socialist countries in the world economy. Secondary sources; table, 43 notes.   N. Dejevsky

2016. Ostrander, Gilman M. THE MAKING OF THE TRIANGULAR TRADE MYTH. *William and Mary Q. 1973 30(4): 635-644.* No such pattern as the triangular trade existed as a major factor in colonial commerce, as popularly believed to have been the case with New England, Africa, and the West Indies. Only one author wrote of the so-called triangular trade (before it was "discovered" in the late 19th century): Jeremy Belknap, who stated in

1795 that the trade was negligible in reference to Massachusetts. Discusses those historians who made the myth and why the myth persisted. A major reason for the myth lies in the New England conscience—a willingness to believe the worst of other New Englanders and the animosity between residents of Massachusetts and Rhode Island. Cites historiography on the triangular trade. 28 notes.   H. M. Ward

2017. Pallot, Judith. *KHUTORA* AND *OTRUBA* IN STOLYPIN'S PROGRAM OF FARM INDIVIDUALIZATION. *Slavic Rev. 1984 42[i.e., 43](2): 242-256.* *Khutora* and *otruba* are farm classifications. The peasantry favored *otruba* (a single parcel of farmland separate from house and garden); the government favored *khutora* (a single parcel of farmland which incorporated house and garden). The author analyzes and supports George L. Yaney's revisionist theories regarding the Stolypin land reforms. The government was sensitive to peasant demands, and moderately flexible in implementing land reform and farm settlement. Soviet historians do not agree with Yaney revisionism; they insist that reform was an attempt to impose a predetermined farm plan on the peasantry regardless of the peasants' wishes. Based on Russian archival sources; 59 notes.   R. B. Mendel

2018. Palmer, Bryan D. WORKING-CLASS CANADA: RECENT HISTORICAL WRITING. *Queen's Q. [Canada] 1979-80 86(4): 594-616.* Provides a survey of working-class historiography in Canada, contrasting Canada's first generation of labor historians—who continue to probe working-class radicalism, politics and institutions, largely in the context of the 20th century—with second generation historians who are less firmly entrenched in the profession, more likely to have been trained in the United States and thus more comfortable with the broad range of questions the international literature in working-class literature confronts. Internationalism and Marxism exert a forceful influence on their works. 67 notes.
                                                          J. Powell

2019. Pashkov, Anatolii Ignat'evich. IZUCHENIE ISTORII POLITICHESKOI EKONOMIKI SOTSIALIZMA [Historical study of the political economy of socialism]. *Voprosy Ekonomiki [USSR] 1980 (11): 3-14.* Describes how Soviet economists analyze and elucidate Soviet economic theory and practice and counteract the anti-Soviet, class-biased economic theories of Western countries.

2020. Pepe, Adolfo. L'ORGANIZZAZIONE OPERAIA IN ITALIA NELLA PRIMA FASE DI SVILUPPO INDUSTRIALE [Labor organization in Italy during the first phase of industrial development]. *Storia e Politica [Italy] 1973 12(2): 154-168.* The problem of reconstruction of Italian history in the period of capitalist economic development and of the delineation of class divisions cannot now be said to have found a valid solution. Neither liberal nor Marxist historiography has approached the problem from a fresh and objective perspective. The author discusses his own views, including the question of reformism and that of the anticapitalist role of the Italian working class. Note.   J. C. Billigmeier

2021. Perinbaum, B. Marie. *HOMO AFRICANUS: ANTIQUUS OR OECONOMICUS?* SOME INTERPRETATIONS OF AFRICAN ECONOMIC HISTORY. *Comparative Studies in Soc. and Hist. [Great Britain] 1977 19(2): 156-178.* Examines varying interpretations of African economic history, 19th-20th centuries, focusing on the *antiquus* argument (economic process in a so-called promotive society) and the *oeconomicus* argument (the extent to which traditional economic studies can be applied to African economic history) offered in the 1950's-60's.

2022. Pessen, Edward. SHOULD LABOR HAVE SUPPORTED JACKSON?: OR QUESTIONS THE QUANTITATIVE STUDIES DO NOT ANSWER. *Labor Hist. 1972 13(3): 427-437.* Presents an historiographical essay on approaches to the Age of Jackson. Quantitative studies do not relieve the historian of telling what happened, why it happened, and the consequences. An innovative use of quantitative and qualitative studies is needed to suggest answers to the question posed in the article's title. Based on secondary interpretations; 22 notes.   L. L. Athey

2023. Peterson, Larry. FROM SOCIAL DEMOCRACY TO COMMUNISM: RECENT CONTRIBUTIONS TO THE HISTORY OF THE GERMAN WORKERS' MOVEMENT 1914-1945. *Labour [Canada] 1980 5(Spr): 161-181.* Reviews recent works on the German labor movement and stresses their departure from traditional labor historiography, particularly in their use of new historical approaches and revisionist interpretations.   G. P. Cleyet

2024. Porras Nadales, Antonio. SOCIALISMO Y SOCIEDAD INDUSTRIAL: SAINT-SIMON [Socialism and industrial society: Saint-Simon]. *Rev. de Estudios Pol. [Spain] 1978 (4): 129-148.* Claims that the Comte de Saint-Simon was the first to analyze the historical processes of Western societies from the viewpoint of industrial production and technocracy, even though France was not industrialized by the time of his death in 1825.

2025. Porter, Glenn. RECENT TRENDS IN CANADIAN BUSINESS AND ECONOMIC HISTORY. *Business Hist. R. 1973 47(2): 141-157.* Reviews recent historical writing in Canadian business and economic history. Notes that the economic interpretation of Canada's history, referred to as the Laurentian thesis, has begun to lose its force of late. However, the need for other instructive generalizations supported by sound evidence continues. Secondary sources; 66 notes.   C. J. Pusateri

2026. Price, Jacob M. A NOTE ON THE VALUE OF COLONIAL EXPORTS IN SHIPPING. *J. of Econ. Hist. 1976 36(3): 704-725.* Surveys the history and historiography of the American shipbuilding industry, 1763-75, and its importance as an export of capital-starved colonies. Data from contemporary merchants, clerks of the British Board of Trade, and Lloyds of London insurance records indicate that "shipbuilding in the Thirteen Colonies totalled about 40,000 measured tons annually and was worth about 300,000 pounds sterling, of which at least 18,600 tons worth 140,000 pounds sterling were sold abroad." These figures are considerably higher than those reported by historians 1913-72, and represent an important factor in the colonial balance of trade with Great Britain. 4 tables, 40 notes, appendix.   T. Simmerman

2027. Price, Richard. THEORIES OF LABOUR PROCESS FORMATION. *Journal of Social History 1984 18(1): 91-110.* Discusses recent historiography, mostly on the United States and Great Britain, of labor process formation, a field that was revived in 1974 by Harry Braverman's *Labor and Monopoly Capital: The Degradation of Work in the 20th Century.* Since 1974, the understanding of how the labor process has formed and developed has progressed rapidly, though no consensus exists on the matter. 59 notes.   S

2028. Puissant, Jean. L'HISTORIOGRAPHIE DU MOUVEMENT OUVRIER [Historiography of the labor movement]. *Rev. de l'U. de Bruxelles [Belgium] 1981 (1-2): 175-192.* A historiography of the Belgian labor movement since 1860.

2029. Rapone, Leonardo. IL SINDACALISMO FASCISTA: TEMI E PROBLEMI DELLA RICERCA STORICA [Fascist labor unions: themes and problems of historical research]. *Storia Contemporanea [Italy] 1982 13(4-5): 635-696.* Reviews the political debates among antifascist forces on the character of fascist labor organizations and the relations between the regime and the working class. Surveys the state of historical studies on the subject and identifies the lines of research available to historians. 173 notes.   J. V. Coutinho

2030. Ratcliffe, Barrie M. THE ECONOMIC INFLUENCE OF THE SAINT-SIMONIANS: MYTH OR REALITY? *Pro. of the Ann. Meeting of the Western Soc. for French Hist. 1977 5: 252-262.* The claim that the Saint-Simonians played a significant role in the economy of 19th-century France was forged by contemporary writers to attack aspects of French economy, society, and politics. The myth has been perpetuated in modern historiography, particularly in American writing on 19th-century economic growth and industrialization. The author examines three aspects of the myth: the relationship between membership of the sect and later business or public careers; the originality and importance of Saint-Simonian economic theories, especially their practical proposals; and the power of Saint-Simonian ideology in individual careers or economic growth. Only at the ideological level can the question of Saint Simonianism's influence be considered still open. Based on correspondence in the Bibliothèque de l'Arsenal and works by and about Saint-Simonians. A/J

2031. Romeo, Rosario. LUIGI EINAUDI E LA STORIA DELLE DOTTRINE E DEI FATTI ECONOMICI [Luigi Einaudi and the history of economic doctrines and events]. *Ann. della Fondazione Luigi Einaudi [Italy] 1974 8: 121-141.* Luigi Einaudi (1874-1961) was a historian. Humanist and liberal, he thought that in the moral life of men is the origin and the explanation of historical events. Einaudi wrote historical works of great importance on finances in Savoy at the beginning of the 18th century and on economic policy in World War I. One of 13 articles in a special issue on the centennial of Einaudi's birth. 3 notes. M. de Leonardis

2032. Rose, Günther. ZUR GENESIS UND FUNKTION DER THEORIE DER "INDUSTRIEGESELLSCHAFT" [The origin and function of the theory of the industrial society]. *Zeitschrift für Geschichtswissenschaft [East Germany] 1967 15(1): 20-45.* Discusses the development of the bourgeois theory of the industrial society by American, French, and German historians since the 1940's.

2033. Sabsovich, R. L. ISTORIIA PROFSOIUZOV V TRUDAKH FRANTSUZKIKH ISTORIKOV I SOTSIOLOGOV [The history of trade unions in the works of French historians and sociologists]. *Voprosy Istorii [USSR] 1979 (1): 149-155.* Study of French bourgeois historiography of the trade union question since World War II reveals the existence of a reactionary trend openly hostile to the trade unions and a more objective trend which refrains from open anti-Communism but occupies some false positions. The history of the trade union movement in fact bears out the conclusions of French Marxist historians about the increasing role of unions in France. C. J. Read

2034. Samsonov, A. M. and Korzun, L. I. KNIGI O LIUDIAKH VELIKOGO TRUDOVOGO PODVIGA [Books about labor heroes]. *Voprosy Istorii [USSR] 1983 (6): 116-120.* Discusses the educational, moral, and patriotic significance of a series with the cumulative title *Ocherki o geroiakh truda* [Essays on labor heroes]. The first three volumes published in Moscow (1979-83) contain 85 biographical sketches. 7 notes. N. Frenkley

2035. Sanzhieva, T. E. PROBLEMY ELEKTRIFIKATSII BURIATII V SOVETSKOI ISTORICHESKOI LITERATURE [Problems of the electrification of Buryatia in Soviet historiography]. *Izvestiia Sibirskogo Otdeleniia Akad. Nauk SSSR. Seriia Obshchestvennykh Nauk [USSR] 1980 (3): 3-7.* Since the 1950's the problems of the development of the energy system in the Buryat ASSR have been studied by historians, economists, Party workers, and energy specialists. The effectiveness of energy policies and the social and economic consequences of electrification have been examined. Work has been carried out on the forms and methods of Party activity employed to expand the republic's energy basis. Apart from the works of K. M. Prodaivoda and A. A. Parshkov, research on the electrification of agriculture and of the domestic sector has yet to be undertaken. Secondary sources; 27 notes. G. Dombrovski

2036. Sapelli, Giulio. PER LA STORIA COMPARATA DELLE IMPRESE INDUSTRIALI E BANCARIE: IPOTESI DI LAVORO [A comparative history of industrial and banking enterprises: working hypotheses]. *Ann. dell'Istituto Giangiacomo Feltrinelli [Italy] 1982 22: 329-354.* Discusses whether historical analysis of financial institutions, particularly banking in Italy, can achieve the same successes that have resulted from historical analysis of industrialization, and whether key concepts obtained from the latter are applicable to the former. 86 notes. J. V. Coutinho

2037. Sawer, Marian. THE POLITICS OF HISTORIOGRAPHY: RUSSIAN SOCIALISM AND THE QUESTION OF THE ASIATIC MODE OF PRODUCTION. *Critique [Great Britain] 1978-79 (10-11): 15-35.* Debate on the concept of the Asiatic mode of production was introduced by Lenin in 1925-26, and the debate characterized divergent interpretations of Russian history, reaching back

to dissension between the Bolsheviks and the Mensheviks at the Fourth (Unity) Congress of the Russian Social Democratic Worker's Party in 1906.

2038. Sawer, Marian. THE SOVIET DISCUSSION OF THE ASIATIC MODE OF PRODUCTION. *Survey [Great Britain] 1979 24(3): 108-127.* The concept of the Asiatic mode of production, which was legitimized by newly discovered references to the works of Marx and Engels, provided the *Aziatchiki* a format for the expression of a variety of opinions about Oriental and, in particular, Chinese society which had previously been regarded as incompatible with the Marxist schema of historical progress. However, in the debate that resulted between 1925 and 1931 orthodoxy proved more powerful. Based on original and secondary sources; 69 notes. V. Samaraweera

2039. Scheiber, Harry N. FEDERALISM AND THE AMERICAN ECONOMIC ORDER, 1789-1910. *Law and Soc. Rev. 1975 10(1): 57-118.* Discusses the historiography of political and legal aspects of the relationship between federalism and the economic order in the 19th century, emphasizing the role of the Supreme Court and issues in constitutional law.

2040. Schultz, Helga. "PROTOINDUSTRIALISIERUNG" UND ÜBERGANGSEPOCHE VOM FEUDALISMUS ZUM KAPITALISMUS [Protoindustrialization and the transitional period from feudalism to capitalism]. *Zeitschrift für Geschichtswissenschaft [East Germany] 1983 31(12): 1079-1091.* Discusses the concept of protoindustrialization in Europe, 16th-19th centuries, a concept that was first formulated by F. F. Mendels in the 1970's. Mendels defines protoindustrialization as "the first stage of industrialization characterized by: the increasing seasonal production of the rural population for a market lying outside the region; the symbiosis of rural export and regional development of market orientated development; and the increase in population due to the new demographic conditions of the 'protoindustrial' population." Protoindustrialization is a universally necessary (if inadequate) preliminary stage before industrialization. Examines the work of three Marxist historians who maintain that this concept is, on the one hand, an antirevolutionary theory of bourgeois social and economic historiography that denies the relationships between economic change in agriculture and industry and the bourgeois revolutionary cycle, but on the other, formulates new ideas which are important for Marxist investigation. Secondary sources; 58 notes. G. L. Neville

2041. Schulze, Hans. DER MISSBRAUCH DER PROGNOSE IN DER WESTDEUTSCHEN HISTORIOGRAPHIE [The misuse of prognostication in West German historiography]. *Zeitschrift für Geschichtswissenschaft [East Germany] 1968 16(2): 151-164.* Describes recent attempts of West German and American historians and sociologists to formulate theories of modern development, such as "industrial society," "formed society," and "convergence theory," which purport to show that capitalism is a viable and efficient path to development and is compatible with basic historical trends. These theories provide a pseudoreligious mantle to an expansionist ideology, inculcating subordination of the masses and war-readiness under conditions of state-monopoly capitalism. The theories are unhistorical and thus provide false prognoses of future development. Secondary works; 55 notes. J. B. Street

2042. Schwartz, Harvey. HARRY BRIDGES AND THE SCHOLARS: LOOKING AT HISTORY'S VERDICT. *California Hist. 1980 59(1): 66-79.* Appraises Harry Bridges and his controversial career as leader of the International Longshoreman's and Warehouseman's Union. Retired since 1977, Bridges first gained national attention with his leadership of the international longshoremen's strike and the San Francisco general strike of 1934. For 19 years afterward, the federal government tried to deport Bridges, a native of Australia, but failed to prove his Communist connections. The charge of Communist sympathizer-member has long been attached to Bridges, whose outspoken views have included consistent pro-Soviet statements, approval of Communist unionists, cooperation with Communists, endorsement of the general strike, opposition to American entry in the Korean War, and support of Henry Wallace in 1948. Scholars have varied widely in their assessment of Bridges, from supporting his union activities to condemning his pro-Communist views. Recent scholarly efforts have shown more moderation, and recognize that his view of labor unity was practical, traditional in method, and international in outlook. Calls the question of his relationship to the Communist Party beside the point. Photos, 43 notes.   A. Hoffman

2043. Seltzer, Alan L. WOODROW WILSON AS "CORPORATE LIBERAL": TOWARD A RECONSIDERATION OF LEFT REVISIONIST HISTORIOGRAPHY. *Western Pol. Q. 1977 30(2): 183-212.* Examination of Woodrow Wilson's opposition to artificial combination, the Justice Department's antitrust prosecutions, Wilson's foreign trade policies, and his speeches on foreign trade reveals that Wilson supported vigorous antitrust policy, contrary to left revisionist interpretations.

2044. Shaw, Ronald E. CANALS IN THE EARLY REPUBLIC: A REVIEW OF RECENT LITERATURE. *J. of the Early Republic 1984 4(2): 117-142.* Analyzes the emergence, contribution, and impact of canal studies, particularly during the scholarly writing explosion of the 1950's-60's. Building on the conceptual framework established in George R. Taylor's *Transportation Revolution, 1815-1860* (1951), the writings of Carter Goodrich and his students at Columbia were the first comprehensive investigations of eastern and mideastern canal building. Subsequent interpretations have applied newer quantitative methodologies, focused on the relationship of canal systems to agricultural, regional, and economic development, and probed canal administration and cost-effectiveness. Recently specialized canal analyses have decreased in number, since the latest efforts have attempted to remove canal studies from a phase of transportation development and integrate them into a larger analysis of growth, urbanization, technology, business enterprise, and republicanism. Secondary sources; map, 43 notes.
                                          G. A. Glovins

2045. Shirai, Atsushi and Taka, Tetsuo. AMERIKA KEIZAI SHISÕSHI [History of American economic thought]. *Ann. Bull. of the Soc. for the Hist. of Econ. Thought [Japan] 1981 19: 2-17.* Japanese economic studies have been greatly influenced by American economic studies; however, American economic history has been little studied in Japan. Examines in two parts Japanese publications that have discussed American economic thinkers. The first part, written by Atsushi Shirai, covers up to the Civil War and studies Benjamin Franklin, Thomas Paine, Thomas Jefferson, Alexander Hamilton, and some others; part two, written by Tetsuo Taka, covers from the Civil War to World War I, discussing John Bates Clark, Thorstein Veblen, John Roger Commons, and William C. Mitchell.   M. Kawaguchi

2046. Sipos, Péter. ÜZEMTÖRTÉNET ÉS MUNKÁSMOZGALOM-TÖRTÉNET [Industrial plant history and labor movement history]. *Párttörténeti Közlemények [Hungary] 1972 18(4): 110-125.* Analyzes the relationship between the current state of industrial plant history and Communist Party history. The author suggests an interdisciplinary approach for the industrial studies. Most factory histories provide good research material but authors' analyses of the past, especially of the post-World War II period, are deficient. 29 notes.   P. I. Hidas

2047. Sivachev, N. V. and Savel'eva, I. M. MEZHDUNARODNOE RABOCHEE DVIZHENIE: VOPROSY ISTORII I TEORII [American labor in recent Soviet historiography]. *Labor Hist. 1977 18(3): 407-432.* Surveys recent developments in the history of American labor by Soviet scholars. Based on publications in the USSR; 43 notes.   L. L. Athey

2048. Sivachev, N. V. "NOVYI KURS" F. RUZVEL'TA [The Roosevelt New Deal]. *Voprosy Istorii [USSR] 1981 (9): 45-63.* A survey of the main trends of American historiography on the New Deal that analyzes the economic, social, and political aspects of the New Deal policy as a process of the development of US monopoly capitalism into state-monopoly capitalism. The reforms in industry, agriculture, finance, labor relations, unemployment relief, and the introduction of the social security system are discussed. Reveals the

role of the working class and democratic forces in winning social legislation, analyzes political struggle and the substantial changes in the two party system in the second half of the 1930's.   J

2049. Šneerson, L. M. DIE SOWJETISCHE HISTORIOGRAPHIE UND EINIGE AKTUELLE PROBLEME BEI DER ERFORSCHUNG DER GESCHICHTE DER ARBEITERBEWEGUNG IN DEN ENTWICKELTEN KAPITALISTISCHEN LÄNDERN [Soviet historiography and some recent problems in the research of the history of the workers' movement in the developed capitalist countries]. *Wissenschaftliche Zeitschrift der Friedrich-Schiller-U. Jena. Gesellschafts- und Sprachwissenschaftliche Reihe [East Germany] 1974 23(6): 737-752.* Soviet historians repudiate the theory of the Western revisionist sociologists that the proletariat in Western nations were integrated into modern capitalist society after World War II.

2050. Sogrin, V. V. AMERIKANSKAIA RADIKAL'NAIA ISTORIOGRAFIIA RABOCHEGO I SOTSIALISTICHESKOGO DVIZHENII SSHA [American radical historiography and labor and socialist movements in the United States]. *Amerikanskii Ezhegodnik [USSR] 1982: 136-162.* Discusses the development of radical historiography in the United States in the 1950's-70's. Originated from New Labor and New Left schools, it dealt with the history of labor, disapproved of the concept of the "exceptionalism" of American labor, and considered such factors as the nonfeudal historical structure of the society, immigration, and specific trade union leadership crucial in the slow development of the class consciousness of workers. Secondary sources; 60 notes.   R. Kirillov

2051. Staněk, Tomáš. HISTORIOGRAFIE PRŮMYSLOVÝCH OBLASTÍ A JEJÍ PŘEDMET [The object of historiography of industrial regions]. *Slezský Sborník [Czechoslovakia] 1980 78(1): 15-37.* The historiography of industrialized countries had always been determined primarily by the particular resource of consequence. The method of extraction and the quantity of coal or iron ore was duly noted, but there was not enough integration of social structures, of the population and shifts that were occasioned by economic instability. All the complexities of social and political organizations and their interrelationships in an industrial region should also be compared to similar tensions, contacts and associations in a nonindustrial region of the country. 47 notes.   B. Reinfeld

2052. Stenson, M. R. THE ECONOMIC INTERPRETATION OF IMPERIALISM: A COMMENT ON SOME RECENT WRITINGS. *New Zealand J. of Hist. [New Zealand] 1976 10(2): 178-188.* Examines the analytical gulf between Marxists and liberals and argues that clarification of the major issues must await interpretations encompassing pre- and post-capitalist imperialism and dealing with "root causes." 49 notes.   P. J. Coleman

2053. Sternsher, Bernard. GREAT DEPRESSION LABOR HISTORIOGRAPHY IN THE 1970S: MIDDLE-RANGE QUESTIONS, ETHNOCULTURES, AND LEVELS OF GENERALIZATION. *Rev. in Am. Hist. 1983 11(2): 300-319.* Trends in Great Depression labor historiography since the 1970's include closer examination of the relationship between labor activism and ethnicity and greater emphasis on the "history from the bottom up" perspective of the new social historians.

2054. Stigel, Lars. FAGBEVAEGELSENS BRUG AF HISTORIEN 1950-1980 [The labor movement's use of history, 1950-80]. *Arbejder Hist. [Denmark] 1982 19: 3-11.* The approach of the Danish trade unions to working-class historiography is slowly changing from the ideological and idealistic toward the more useful and pragmatic. Based on trade union journals and secondary sources; 19 notes.

2055. Stolarik, Mark. AGRARIAN PROBLEMS IN SLOVAKIA, 1848-1918: AN HISTORIOGRAPHIC ESSAY. *Social Hist. [Canada] 1974 7(13): 111-120.* Surveys 20th-century Slovak, Magyar, and British historiography on agrarian issues in Slovakia, 1848-1918. Very little appeared prior to 1948 due to historians' preoccupations with political issues. After 1948, Marxist historians have brought social history to the forefront and gained sophistication.

The intensity of Marxist interpretations has been directly proportional to the intensity of the Marxist ideology of the regime under which they were written. Historians have made good use of county and city archives, but ignored church archives. Secondary sources; 22 notes. W. K. Hobson

2056. Stols, Eddy. L'ARCHÉOLOGIE INDUSTRIELLE, UNE SOURCE POUR L'HISTOIRE DU MODE DE VIE DANS UNE SOCIÉTÉ INDUSTRIELLE: PREMIÈRE PARTIE [Industrial archaeology, a source for the history of the way of life in an industrial society. Part I]. *Cahiers de Clio [Belgium] 1980 (63): 38-53.* Reviews and comments on the various literature, documents, museums and other sources which since the 1960's make up the historiography of industrial archaeology. Article to be continued.

2057. Stuijvenberg, J. H. van. ROSTOW'S GROEIFASEN EN HUN GEBRUIK IN DE PRACTIJK VAN DE ECONOMISCHE GESCHIEDSCHRIJVING [Rowstow's growth stages and their use in economic historiography]. *Econ.- en Sociaal-Hist. Jaarboek [Netherlands] 1970 33: 167-185.* Summarizes W. W. Rostow's *The stages of economic growth* (Cambridge, 1960) and observes the use of his notion of a "takeoff" stage in the writings of several historians who have applied Rostow's unbalanced growth theories. They all leave out one or more of the criteria charcterizing the "takeoff," and each interprets it in his own way. The lack of uniformity in the concept is caused by its being a "real-typical" construction not found in reality. Table, notes. G. Herritt

2058. Supple, Barry. ECONOMIC HISTORY IN THE 1980S: OLD PROBLEMS AND NEW DIRECTIONS. *J. of Interdisciplinary Hist. 1981 12(2): 199-205.* In spite of the change of the discipline during the last two decades and its present methodological as well as topical discussions, there is scope for a revival of economic history. Attention must be focused on the results of specialization and the historical roots of economic history. Further considerations of the influences on economic history can ensure substantial and technical developments. Note. H. J. Kaiser

2059. Swierenga, Robert P. LAND SPECULATION AND ITS IMPACT ON AMERICAN ECONOMIC GROWTH AND WELFARE: A HISTORIOGRAPHICAL REVIEW. *Western Hist. Q. 1977 8(3): 283-302.* The Progressive school of land historiography was inspired by the studies of Richard T. Ely and Frederick Jackson Turner at the turn of the 20th century. Benjamin H. Hibbard was especially interested in the effects of land speculation on agricultural development, and he raised a number of perceptive questions for other researchers. Hibbard's work introduced Paul Wallace Gates to the study of land history and Gates has dominated the field since the late 1920's. From the first, Gates accepted "the Progressive, prescriptive approach" and rejected the statistical approach of agricultural economists. Revisionism produced a substantial bill of particulars against land speculators. The winds of revisionism finally affected Gates, and his complaints against land speculators were considerably softened. Revisionist methodology and interpretation of evidence now recognize the positive role of speculators as middlemen between the government and settlers. 46 notes. D. L. Smith

2060. Szakály, Ferenc. ÖSTÖRTÉNET, KÖZÉPKOR [Ancient history, middle ages]. *Századok [Hungary] 1980 114(3): 331-363.* Before 1948 there were few attempts by Hungarian historians to research agricultural history. However, following the dictates of the traditional Marxist position of historical writing, much recent progress has been made in this field of economic history. 236 notes.

T. Kuner

2061. Tenfelde, Klaus. NEUE FORSCHUNGEN ZUR GESCHICHTE DER ARBEITERSCHAFT [Recent research on the history of the working class]. *Archiv für Sozialgeschichte [West Germany] 1980 20: 593-615.* Recent research into the working class examines the basic facts of life and struggle of the working class instead of

observing its abstract role in the historical process, which was the fashion of the past. Studies of the fates of individual companies and of their workers provide rich insights. 59 notes.

H. W. Wurster

2062. Tetiushev, V. I. BURZHUAZNAIA ISTORIOGRAFIIA O METODAKH I ISTOCHNIKAKH OSUSHCHESTVLENIIA INDUSTRIALIZATSII V SSSR [Bourgeois historiography on the origins and methods of industrialization in the USSR]. *Istoriia SSSR [USSR] 1977 (2): 170-183.* Dismisses the views expressed in books and articles written by economic historians in Western Europe, mostly since the 1960's, about the forced, contrived, and uneconomical features of the process of Soviet industrialization. The economic and political conditions in Russia were perfectly suited to this change. 94 notes. N. Dejevsky

2063. Thal, Peter. ZUM WISSENSCHAFTLICHEN GEHALT UND SOZIALEN STANDPUNKT DER THEORIE DES KLASSISCHEN BÜRGERLICHEN ÖKONOMEN ADAM SMITH [On the scientific content and social standpoint of the theory of the classic bourgeois economist Adam Smith]. *Jahrbuch für Wirtschaftsgeschichte [East Germany] 1971 (4): 83-100.* Reviews the attitudes and criticisms of 20th-century economists and historians on Adam Smith's *Inquiry into the Causes and Nature of the Wealth of Nations* (1776). Bourgeois critics have failed to recognize Smith's labor value theory, which contributed to Marxism. Despite Smith's strong criticism of certain bourgeois practices, his book is itself basically bourgeois in viewpoint. Describes the manner in which recent propagandists for capitalism have used Smith's work for political purposes. Secondary works; 80 notes. J. B. Street

2064. Thompson, Dorothy. RADICALS AND THEIR HISTORIANS. *Literature and Hist. [Great Britain] 1977 (5): 104-108.* Reviews David Jones's *Chartism and Chartists* (Allen Lane, 1975), R. G. Kirby's *The Voice of the People, John Doherty 1798-1854: Trade Unionist, Radical and Factory Reformer* (Manchester U. Pr., 1975), and Henry Weisser's *British Working-Class Movements and Europe 1815-48* (Manchester U. Pr., 1975).

2065. Thorsen, Niels. THE SEARCH FOR POWER, INC.: ROBERT WIEBE AND ALAN TRACHTENBERG ON THE GILDED AGE. *Am. Studies in Scandinavia [Norway] 1983 15(2): 69-78.* Robert Wiebe and Alan Trachtenberg offer different views of the years following the Civil War. Wiebe spoke in terms of modernization; of the breakup of "island communities"; and the formation of large political, social, and economic institutions organized on bureaucratic principles of order and specialization. For him, it was a time of confusion and uncertainty. Trachtenberg, on the other hand, saw the advent of the corporation not simply as part of the technological modernization process but as a cultural phenomenon that taught people to think and act in ways conducive to mass organization. 15 notes. R. E. Goerler

2066. Tijn, Th. van. A CONTRIBUTION TO THE SCIENTIFIC STUDY OF THE HISTORY OF TRADE UNIONS. *Int. Rev. of Social Hist. [Netherlands] 1976 21(2): 212-239.* Uses the Dutch diamond industry before 1895, the printing industry prior to 1914, and the De Twente region textile industry before 1940 as case studies to determine the success of trade unions. Labor unions are successful when they become collective bargaining agents and participate in the determination of wages and conditions of employment within the framework of a national collective labor agreement. The author develops an analytical model which includes a group of economic, sociostructural, sociopsychological, and governmental factors as variables. Though no clearcut generalizations are established, the model will be suggestive for the scientific study of trade unions. Based on newspapers, protocols, and secondary sources; 2 tables, appendix. G. P. Blum

2067. Tilly, Charles. PEASANTS AGAINST CAPITALISM AND THE STATE: A REVIEW ESSAY. *Agric. Hist. 1978 52(3): 407-416.* Explores the relationship of peasants and capitalist society as expounded in Frank E. Huggett's *The Land Question and European Society*, R. E. F. Smith's *Peasant Farming in Muscovy*, John D. Bell's *Peasants in Power: Alexander Stamboliski and the Bulgarian*

Agrarian National Union, 1899-1923, Benedict J. Kerkvliet's *The Huk Rebellion: A Study of Peasant Revolt in the Philippines,* and Merilee S. Grindle's *Bureaucrats, Politicians and Peasants in Mexico: A Case Study in Public Policy.* In varying degrees all ignore the rich returns of recent European historiography and fail to further significantly our understanding of the very subject of peasants and capitalism.   R. T. Fulton

2068. Tilly, Richard. SOLL UND HABEN: RECENT GERMAN ECONOMIC HISTORY AND THE PROBLEM OF ECONOMIC DEVELOPMENT. *J. of Econ. Hist. 1969 29(2): 298-319.* A review article on recent German historiography of 19th-century industrialization in Germany. In addition to several monographs, the author considers textbooks, historical periodicals, books of readings, and publications series. In contrast with US and English scholarship, German historians have underrated the significance of industrialization on political development in Germany. Economists who have written significant histories have much less influence on economic historiography than have historians. A whole generation of German scholarship was arrested "thanks to political events after 1930." 60 notes.   C. W. Olson

2069. Topolski, Jerzy. THE ROLE OF THEORY AND MEASUREMENT IN ECONOMIC HISTORY. Iggers, Georg G. and Parker, Harold T., ed. *International Handbook of Historical Studies: Contemporary Research and Theory* (Westport, Conn.: Greenwood Pr., 1979): 43-54. Economic history has been in transition from a traditional form with no interest in theory to one enveloped with theory and quantitative methods. There are three often unclear divisions: 1) inquiry inspired by general theories of historical process; 2) inquiry inspired by economic theory; and 3) inquiry inspired by social theory. Examines the contributions of economic historians in each. 21 notes, biblio.

2070. Vári, András; Wellmann, Imre, commentary. VITÁK AZ ANGOL GAZDASÁGTÖRTÉNETÍRÁSBAN A "MEZŐGAZDASÁGI FORRADALOM" ÉS A "BEKERÍTÉSEK" [Debates in England regarding the economic history of the Agricultural Revolution and the enclosures]. *Agrártörténeti Szemle [Hungary] 1983 25(3-4): 501-523.* Although Toynbee, Lord Ernle, the Hammonds, Tawney, and Marx believed that the system of forceful enclosures of common land created an agricultural revolution, this point of view is often rejected by modern historians. Agriculture was not revolutionized; enclosures simply enabled the large landowner to put his land to produce crops with the best yield and highest financial reward. In effect many of the poor lost their free pastures, but to believe that this caused their absolute ruin is a misinterpretation of the facts. 2 maps, 69 notes. Commentary, pp. 524-527.   T. Kuner

2071. Voroshilov, S. I. PROBLEMY RABOCHEGO DVIZHENIIA V NOVEISHEI AVSTRIISKOI ISTORIOGRAFII [Problems of the labor movement in contemporary Austrian historiography]. *Vestnik Leningradskogo Universiteta: Seriia Istorii, Iazyka i Literatury [USSR] 1984 (1): 28-34.* The establishment of an institute to study working-class history at the University of Linz in Austria has led to a flowering of writing on proletarian history in the country. The author assesses the new insights gained and provides information about discussions at a theoretical conference on the position of the workers, held in 1973, relating in part to Austrian links with the European Economic Community. Based on secondary works in German; 43 notes. English summary.   D. N. Collins

2072. Voskresenski, Iu. V. et al. AKTUAL'NYE ZADACHI IZUCHENIIA ISTORII SOVETSKOGO RABOCHEGO KLASSA [The urgent tasks of studies in the history of the Soviet working class]. *Istoriia SSSR [USSR] 1973 (4): 3-33.* One of the most important tasks for Soviet history is the investigation of the development and creative activity of the working class, its structure and composition, and its periodization. Secondary sources; 69 notes.
                                                                           L. Kalinowski

2073. Voskresenski, Iu. V.; Mitrofanova, A. V.; Poletaev, V. E.; Rogachevskaia, L. S.; Seniavski, S. L.; and Tverdokhleb, A. A. PRESSING TASKS IN THE STUDY OF THE HISTORY OF

THE SOVIET WORKING CLASS. *Soviet Studies in Hist. 1974 13(1): 3-55.* Discusses the problems of targeting research in the history of the working class, establishing the relationship between theoretical and empirical approaches in analyzing the social makeup of the working class, examining intraclass structure, and periodizing the history of this class, and in addition calls attention to problems which—from 1920 to 1974—have been treated inadequately, e.g., sociopolitical activities of the working class, socialist competition, and the workers' standard of living.

2074. Vučo, Nikola. EKONOMSKA ISTORIJA I NJEN ZNAČAJ ZA MUZEOLOŠKO PRIKAZIVANJE ISTORIJE [Economic history and its importance for a museological approach to history]. *Zbornik Istorijskog Muzeja Srbije [Yugoslavia] 1979 15-16: 5-17.* Economic history started to carry weight after Marx and Engels formulated their theory of dialectical and historical materialism. It became a separate scientific discipline in the early 20th century with the growth of the economic sciences at universities. The Museum of History of Serbia in Belgrade has always been aware of the importance of economic history as a branch of the historical sciences and has included it in its scope since the museum's foundation. Accepting the principle that handicraft, industry, agriculture, and mining are the main factors of economic growth, the museum has paid special attention to exhibitions depicting handicrafts and social relations in the history of Serbia.   J. Bamber

2075. Weible, Robert. THE INDUSTRIAL CITY: LOWELL CONFERENCE ON INDUSTRIAL HISTORY, UNIVERSITY OF LOWELL, APRIL 29-30, 1983. *Technology and Culture 1984 25(1): 103-108.* Summarizes papers presented at the conference in Lowell, Massachusetts.   C. O. Smith, Jr.

2076. Willis, F. Roy. THE CONTRIBUTION OF THE *ANNALES* SCHOOL TO AGRARIAN HISTORY: A REVIEW ESSAY. *Agric. Hist. 1978 52(4): 538-548.* Surveys six decades of writing on agrarian history by the *Annales* school, focusing on the problems of agriculture and the life of agrarian societies. Through an evolutionary process the journal provided practical examples for dealing with the French geographical environment in its history. Several writers were important to the direction the school was to take, including Emmanuel Le Roy Ladurie, and Fernand Braudel. Secondary sources; 33 notes.   R. T. Fulton

2077. Winters, Donald L. AGRICULTURAL TENANCY IN THE NINETEENTH-CENTURY MIDDLE WEST: THE HISTORIOGRAPHICAL DEBATE. *Indiana Mag. of Hist. 1982 78(2): 128-153.* During the last 50 years agricultural historians have debated the causes of farm tenancy in the Midwest. Early scholars tended to blame federal land policies for increases in tenancy. Since the 1950's historians have suggested that tenancy had been present almost from the start and was due to a lack of capital and the sharply increasing price of land which prevented or delayed purchase. Only gradually did tenants move to purchase their farms. Historians have also argued as to whether cash renting or sharecropping was the more efficient form of tenancy. 73 notes, map, cartoon.   A. Erlebacher

2078. Woodman, Harold D. ECONOMIC HISTORY AND ECONOMIC THEORY: THE NEW ECONOMIC HISTORY IN AMERICA. *J. of Interdisciplinary Hist. 1972 3(2): 323-350.* A review article prompted by Robert William Fogel and Stanley L. Engerman, eds., *The Reinterpretation of American Economic History* (New York: Harper and Row, 1971), William N. Parker, ed., *The Structure of the Cotton Economy of the Antebellum South* (Washington, D.C.: The Agricultural History Society, 1970), and Lance E. Davis and Douglass C. North's *Institutional Change and American Economic Growth* (Cambridge: Cambridge U. Pr., 1971). These books illustrate the strengths and weaknesses of the new econometric history as practiced in America. "Modern economic theory (like theories from other disciplines) can aid the historian, but it cannot replace the historical imagination, nor can it lead the true believers to the nirvana of scientific history. To think that it can, is to deny history itself."   R. V. Ritter

2079. Wright, Gavin. THE STRANGE CAREER OF THE NEW SOUTHERN ECONOMIC HISTORY. *Rev. in Am. Hist. 1982 10(4): 164-180.* Surveys major themes in the history of Southern economy, emphasizing regional economic development and the role of blacks.

2080. Yellowitz, Irwin. AMERICAN JEWISH LABOR: HISTORIOGRAPHICAL PROBLEMS AND PROSPECTS. *Am. Jewish Hist. Q. 1976 65(3): 203-213.* Although the history of American Jewish labor has been a subject of inquiry for over half a century, the major problems in concept and method have not been resolved. The boundaries of American Jewish labor as distinguished from that of the American Jewish labor *movement* should be defined by the influence of Jewish identity and concerns upon leaders and institutions, and the impact of these major figures and their organizations upon the Jewish community. The complex interaction of Jewish, American, trade union, and socialist concerns deserves further study (e.g., Samuel Gompers or Meyer London as Jewish rather than American Labor leaders) as well as considerations of events and persons outside New York City. 34 notes.   F. Rosenthal

2081. Zaborov, M. A. ISTORIOGRAFICHESKIE ISSLEDOVANIIA O MEZHDUNARODNOM RABOCHEM DVIZHENII NOVOGO VREMENI [Historiographic research works devoted to the contemporary international working-class movement]. *Voprosy Istorii [USSR] 1976 (7): 70-85.* Most of the available research works, with rare exceptions, do not give an integral idea of the impact made by the evolution of historical views and conceptions on the destinies and role of the working class, of the succession of research schools, methods, etc. The efforts to create a generalizing work devoted to the historiography of the entire labor movement encounter serious difficulties connected with the choice of an equitable historiographic criterion for appraising many works devoted to most diverse aspects of research on the working-class movement. The most promising criterion for such appraisals is the stand taken by one or another researcher on the question which is of paramount importance for a clear understanding of the historiographical process—that of the rise of the proletariat as a truly revolutionary class at the different stages of its history.   J

2082. Zaborov, M. A. PROBLEMY ISTORII RABOCHEGO KLASSA ZARUBEZHNYKH STRAN I EGO OSVOBODITEL'NOI BOR'BY V ISSLEDOVANIIAKH SOVETSKIKH UCHENYKH [Problems of the history of the working class of foreign countries and of its liberation struggle in the works of Soviet scholars]. *Novaia i Noveishaia Istoriia [USSR] 1981 (5): 3-24.* Surveys Soviet historiography of the non-Soviet working class published in the second half of the 1970's and early 1980's. Their research is supported by the Communist Party and the state because it analyzes the laws of the world revolutionary movement. 143 notes.   V. Sobell

2083. Zaborov, M. A. RABOCHEE DVIZHENIE NOVOGO VREMINI: K KRITIKE SOVREMENNOI BURZHUAZNOI I SOTSIAL-REFORMISTSKOI ISTORIOGRAFII [The workers' movement of modern times: a critique of the present bourgeois and social reformist historiography]. *Novaia i Noveishaia Istoriia [USSR] 1982 (4): 42-58.*

2084. Zaborov, M. A. VOZNIKNOVENIEMEZHDUNARODNOGO RABOCHEGO DVIZHENIIA I VEKHI EGO RAZVITIIA (V NOVOE VREMIA) [The international working-class movement: origin and principal stages of development in the contemporary period]. *Voprosy Istorii [USSR] 1974 (2): 63-80.* "Examines the main principles and criteria applied to the periodization of the history of the international working-class movement in the contemporary period. Analyzing the various periodization schemes accepted in bourgeois and social-reformist historiography, the author shows that they are essentially based on the negation of general historical laws. That explains why researchers studiously avoid singling out any common boundaries dividing different states in the history of the class struggle of the proletariat as a whole. The author makes an attempt to formulate the distinctions between the 'working-class movement' and 'international working-class movement' concepts, defining the former as a

movement embracing major events of the struggle waged by the factory proletariat, and the latter as a movement dating back to the period of the rise and development of the modern working class. The author draws the conclusion that the working-class movement became international in character already in the period from the latter half of the 18th to the beginning of the 19th centuries, although its development during that period was confined to the national boundaries. The working-class movement is international in its social essence. In conclusion the article analyzes the question concerning the correlation of the general landmarks of the international working-class movement and its boundaries in individual countries, as well as the connection of these landmarks with different stages of civil history."   J

2085. Zalin, Giovanni. ATTIVITA REALI E STRUTTURE FINANZIARIE NELLA GENOVA PRE-INDUSTRIALE. RASSEGNA DI CONTRIBUTI RECENTI [Occupational activities and financial structure in pre-industrial Genoa: a review of recent research]. *Economia e Storia [Italy] 1973 20(4): 492-528.* Provides an economic history of Genoa from the 11th century to the end of the Napoleonic period. Examines shipping, foreign trade, the development and decline of local industries, and Genoa's importance as a financial center of international standing. Secondary sources; 290 notes.   F. Pollaczek

2086. Żarnowska, Anna. LA CLASSE OUVRIÈRE À LA FIN DU XIXᵉ SIÈCLE ET AU DÉBUT DUE XXeRET SIÈCLE (AVANT/1939) DANS LES RECHERCHES HISTORIQUES EN POLOGNE [The working class at the end of the 19th century and at the beginning of the 20th century (before 1939) from historical research in Poland]. *Mouvement Social [France] 1981 (115): 89-102.* Reviews historiography since 1960 of the Polish working class from 1870 to 1939, focusing on the labor movement, the structure of the working class, and its position in capitalist structures. Recent research emphasizes working-class evolution and its dependence on structural transformations in Polish society. 37 notes.

G. P. Cleyet

2087. Zhukov, E. M. AZ ÁLTALÁNOS SZOCIOLÓGIAI ÉS A TÖRTÉNELMI TÖRVÉNYSZERŰSÉGEK KÖLCSÖNÖS VISZONYA [Mutual interrelations of general sociological and historical regularities]. *Századok [Hungary] 1978 112(6): 1165-1178.* Since economic developments are more predictable than political events a law applicable to future expansion can be formulated. This is based on the observation that societies have always been committed to constant progression. The establishment of Communism indicates the great possibilities for development. 33 notes.   T. Kuner

2088. Zieger, Robert H. WORKERS AND SCHOLARS: RECENT TRENDS IN LABOR HISTORIOGRAPHY. *Labor Hist. 1972 13(2): 245-266.* Surveys developments in labor history. Although much of the early work tended to sustain the conservative proclivities of the labor movement, more recent work has been sharply critical. Surveys moderate and radical New Left historial critics. There is a trend toward more localized study and an attempt to penetrate the history of the inarticulate. Based on secondary sources; 62 notes.   L. L. Athey

2089. Zorgbibe, Charles. ENTREPRISES MULTINATIONALES ET SYSTÈME INTERNATIONAL [Multinational enterprises and the international system]. *Défense Natl. [France] 1974 30(8-9): 39-52.* Discusses theses interpreting the worldwide growth of powerful multinational corporations and examines the provisions needed in international law to control them.

2090. Zvada, Ján. PŘEDMĚT DĚJINY MEZINÁRODNÍHO DĚLNICKÉHO HNUTÍ A METODY VÝZKUMU [History of the international labor movement: the field and its research methods]. *Československý Časopis Hist. [Czechoslovakia] 1978 26(1): 97-120.* Calls Marxist-Leninist theory and methodology to the attention of historians by establishing a series of definitions and categorizations. The international workers' movement from 1789 to the present serves as a useful example, for it shows at every turn the interdependence of Marxist theory and historical research. Czechoslovak scholars have not interested themselves sufficiently in methodological problems and guidelines, and thus expose themselves to ideological deviation. 16 notes.   R. E. Weltsch

2091. —. BIBLIOGRAPHIC ESSAY. Cantor, Milton, ed. *American Workingclass Culture: Explorations in American Labor and Social History* (Westport, Conn.: Greenwood, 1979): 423-427. Traces the rise of American labor historiography since the 1960's, emphasizing the influence of E. P. Thompson and Eric Hobsbawn on the more recent scholarship.

2092. —. CONTROVERSY. *New Left Rev. [Great Britain] 1976 (97): 81-104.*
Monds, Jean. WORKERS' CONTROL AND THE HISTORIANS: A NEW ECONOMISM, *pp. 81-100.* Takes issue with James Hinton in Great Britain and David Montgomery in the United States, who have mistaken instances of job control by skilled workers in the late 19th and early 20th centuries for examples of real workers' control.
Hinton, James. REJOINDER, *pp. 100-104.*

2093. —. KEIEI SHIZAKU NO KADAI [Tasks of business history]. *Keieishigaku [Japan] 1966 1(1): 3-107.*
Nakagawa, Keiichiro. TASKS OF BUSINESS HISTORY, *pp. 3-12.* Emphasizes the need for an interdisciplinary approach between business, entrepreneurial, and economic historians. Compares English, US, and Japanese development.
Hazama, Hiroshi. "CULTURAL STRUCTURE" AND BUSINESS HISTORY: ON THE STUDY OF ENTREPRENEURSHIP FROM THE THEORY OF ACTION, *pp. 13-24.* Discusses the Parsons-Smelser model in analyzing the objectives and motivations of business and the personalities of business men. Explains why the two eminent Heiji entrepreneurs, Shibusawa Eiichi and Yasuda Zenjiro, were awarded different social sanctions.
Yui, Tsunehiko. COMMENT, *pp. 25-27.*
—. DISCUSSION, *pp. 28-31.*
Takada, Kaoru. ORGANIZATION AND BUSINESS HISTORY, *pp. 32-40.* Discusses the objectives and ideology of management, the organization of production and distribution, and the businessmen themselves.
Nakagawa, Keiichiro. COMMENT, *pp. 41-44.*
—. DISCUSSION, *pp. 45-50.*
Otsuka, Hisao. ECONOMIC HISTORY AND BUSINESS HISTORY, *pp. 51-62.* Western European capitalism developed through organizational activities. The author urges the cooperation of economic and business historians in economic and business studies.
Kurita, Shinzo. COMMENT, *pp. 63-66.*
—. DISCUSSION, *pp. 67-70.*
Katsura, Yoshio. CONCEPTS OF BUSINESS LEADER, *pp. 71-88.* Explains the meaning of "executive," "administrator," "entrepreneur," and "manager," based on the works of Fritz Redlich.
Yonekawa, Shinichi. COMMENT, *pp. 89-90.*
—. DISCUSSION, *pp. 91-95.*
Inoue, Tadakatsu. APPROACHES TO THE HISTORY OF INDIVIDUAL BUSINESS UNITS, *pp. 96-103.* Distinguishes between five types of business history studies: 1) administrative history developed by N. S. B. Gras and H. M. Larson; 2) business history in East Germany; 3) innovation history based on Schumpeter's concept; 4) Redlich's emphasis on routine in economic growth and developmental innovations; and 5) entrepreneurial history developed by A. H. Cole.
Fuzitsu, Seiji. COMMENT, *p. 104.*
—. DISCUSSION, *pp. 105-107.*
Papers and discussion on business history are from the first annual meeting of the Business History Society in Japan held at the University of Tokyo, November 1965.   S

2094. —. A MUNKÁSMOZGALOM TÖRTÉNETE KUTATÁSÁNAK NEGYEDSZÁZADA [Twenty-five years of research on the history of the labor movement]. *Parttörténeti Közlemények [Hungary] 1973 19(3): 3-18.* In 1946 the Hungarian Communist Party formed a Party History Commission which by

1948 developed the Party History Institute, later called the Labor History Institute. During World War II many labor unions, Social Democratic Party, and illegal Communist documents were destroyed, but most of the relevant police records survived. Until 1957 the absence of trained and experienced staff and the negative features of Party policy lowered the quality of the Institute's output. Since then trained Party historians have emerged, and a synthesis and several popular histories have been published.

P. I. Hidas

2095. —. [REGULATION, PROPERTY RIGHTS, AND DEFINITION OF "THE MARKET"]. *J. of Econ. Hist. 1981 41(1): 103-111.*
Scheiber, Harry N. REGULATION, PROPERTY RIGHTS, AND DEFINITION OF "THE MARKET": "LAW" AND THE AMERICAN ECONOMY, *pp. 103-109.* Identifies four problems in the recent interdisciplinary studies of property rights, law, and economic development in the 19th-century United States. First, recent studies stress too exclusively the positive functions of law in either the "release of entrepreneurial energy" or the exploitative allocation of advantages (by courts and legislatures) to the business interests leading industrialization. Second, the dichotomy between alleged "instrumentalism" as the prevailing judicial style before 1860 and "formalism" after 1865 has been exaggerated. Third, generalizations have been based too much on the eastern states and Wisconsin. Fourth, there has been a failure to identify accurately the winners and losers in the struggle over regulation and the definition of property rights. Thus, although rediscovery of the importance of institutions by economists and the renaissance of legal history among historians and legal scholars constitute welcome (converging) developments in recent scholarship, much more research is needed on these main themes in the literature.
Higgs, Robert. DISCUSSION, *pp. 110-111.*   J

2096. —. RUCH ROBOTNICZY JAKO PRZEDMIOT BADAŃ HISTORII, SOCJOLOGII I POLITOLOGII [Workers' movement studied by historians, sociologists, and political scientists]. *Z Pola Walki [Poland] 1980 23(4): 47-85.*
Kozik, Zenobiuz, *pp. 47-48, 82-84.*
Markiewicz, Władyslaw, *pp. 48-54, 84-85.*
Kłoskowska, Antonina, *pp. 54-57.*
Żarnowski, Janusz, *pp. 57-59.*
Dyoniziak, Ryszard, *pp. 59-62.*
Waldenberg, Marek, *pp. 62-64.*
Kancewicz, Jan, *pp. 64-69.*
Gołębiowski, Bronisław, *pp. 69-71.*
Koberdowa, Irena, *pp. 71-72.*
Dziewulski, Jan, *pp. 73-76.*
Topolski, Jerzy, *pp. 76-78.*
Gołębiowski, Janusz W., *pp. 78-82.* The labor movement is a historico-social phenomenon of enormous complexity which calls for an interdisciplinary approach. The discussion touched on topics from history, sociology, political science, philosophy, literature, and natural sciences.   I. Lukes

Slavery

2097. Boney, F. N. ASSESSMENT OF SOME RECENT WORKS IN BLACK HISTORY: THE CONTINUING SLAVERY DEBATE, AN ESSAY REVIEW. *Georgia Hist. Q. 1974 58(4): 409-413.* The work of Robert William Fogel and Stanley L. Engerman is compared with other standard works in the field. Fogel and Engerman have presented a statistical treatment considering the conditions and the nature of slavery in the antebellum South. While statistically precise, they lack breadth and depth. Their data is based on far too limited data sources. They concluded that slavery was not as bad as previously indicated because the treatment was not excessively harsh, husbands were family leaders, and families were generally kept intact.   M. R. Gillam

2098. Bossy, John. DEMOGRAPHY AND DEMOGOGY: ON THE HISTORY OF RURAL PEOPLE. *Encounter [Great Britain] 1976 46(1): 62-66.* Discusses political attitudes in the current historiography of slavery and rural problems of peasants in Africa and developing nations from the 17th to 20th centuries.

2099. Brandfon, Robert. SPECIFIC PURPOSES AND THE GENERAL PAST: SLAVES AND SLAVERY. *J. of Interdisciplinary Hist. 1972 3(2): 351-362.* Review article prompted by David Brion Davis' *The Slave Power Conspiracy and the Paranoid Style* (Baton Rouge: Louisiana State U. Press, 1970), Eugene D. Genovese's *The World the Slaveholders Made: Two Essays in Interpretation* (New York: Pantheon, 1969), and Robert S. Starobin's *Industrial Slavery in the Old South* (New York: Oxford U. Press, 1970). Sees these books as illustrations of the ambiguities that can develop as historians seek to relate fact and the interpretation of fact, especially when, in the search for new interpretations, they attempt the application of other disciplines, such as sociology and psychology, to history. It is sometimes difficult to recognize their limits, to not substitute means for ends, and to avoid the unconscious substitution of the values of the other disciplines for those of their own. R. V. Ritter

2100. Buganov, V. I. VTOROI KOLLOKVIUM AMERIKAN-SKIKH I SOVETSKIKH ISTORIKOV V SSHA [The 2d Colloquium of American and Soviet Historians in the United States]. *Istoriia SSSR [USSR] 1976 (3): 207-209.* The colloquium was held in August 1975. The Soviet delegation corrected some misconceptions of American historians concerning not only Russian and Soviet but also American history, including slavery. The history of Russian peasants figured prominently in the colloquium. N. Dejevsky

2101. Campbell, Randolph. LOCAL ARCHIVES AS A SOURCE OF SLAVE PRICES: HARRISON COUNTY, TEXAS AS A TEST CASE. *Historian 1974 36(4): 660-669.* An inquiry into the best sources for estimates of the economics of slavery, especially the individual cost of slaves. Most studies have relied on the work of Ulrich B. Phillips (works published during 1905-29), based largely on auction records, which were often unanalyzed group figures. Shows how such figures can be double-checked through the use of local archival records, concentrating the study on slave labor in Harrison County, Texas, having the largest slave population of any Texas county. Bases the study largely on estate inventories of 40 slaveholders from the probate records of 1849-60, which listed slaves individually and with considerable detail. These prices are consistently lower than Phillips' prices, though on the whole not to a marked degree. 20 notes. R. V. Ritter

2102. Cassidy, Frederic G. THE PLACE OF GULLAH. *Am. Speech 1980 55(1): 3-16.* Reexamines Ian Hancock's "A Provisional Comparison of the English-Derived Atlantic Creoles" (1969). New information on the Atlantic slave trade requires a review of Hancock's conclusions that Gullah descended from Sierra Leone Krio and his doubt about the existence of Barbados Creole. The evidence proves the existence of a common pidgin English language source for slaves taken from the West Indies to South Carolina during 1651-70. 6 fig., 17 notes, ref. G. Smith

2103. Conway, Alan. SLAVERY IN THE UNITED STATES. *Hist. News [New Zealand] 1977 (35): 1-6.* The historiography of slavery reveals changing attitudes among 20th-century historians.

2104. Cooper, Frederick. THE PROBLEM OF SLAVERY IN AFRICAN STUDIES. *J. of African Hist. [Great Britain] 1979 20(1): 103-125.* The volume and quality of recent empirical studies of slavery require the development of new conceptual approaches. The most influential approach starts with a functionalist concept of social structure and emphasizes enslavement as an absorption of people into kinship groups, but is inadequate in the dissection of the internal cleavages and dynamics of African societies. A. G. Hopkins emphasizes the purely economic function of slavery while Marxists (especially Claude Meillassoux) have focused on the use of slaves by owners in the struggle for wealth and power. There has been recognition of differences in slave systems between regions and over

time, and also the effects of the slaves' acceptance or resistance. The class basis of slavery was shaped by capitalism as a developing system as well as by market forces. 90 notes.
A. W. Novitsky

2105. Craton, Michael. A CRESTING WAVE? RECENT TRENDS IN THE HISTORIOGRAPHY OF SLAVERY, WITH SPECIAL REFERENCE TO THE BRITISH CARIBBEAN. *Hist. Reflections [Canada] 1982 9(3): 403-419.* The scholarship on slavery, and British Caribbean slavery in particular, has been extensive in the last 25 years. Slave studies have become more sophisticated and interdisciplinary. The social, cultural, and family life of slaves are being examined more closely, as is slave medicine. Key writers include Genovese, Degler, Tannenbaum, Savitt, Beckwith, Mintz, and Price. Slave historiography has become Braudellian in its interest in long-term movements rather than single events. It seeks a balance between micro- and macroscopic studies, particularly in the area of comparative slave studies. 41 notes. M. Schumacher

2106. Craton, Michael. SEARCHING FOR THE INVISIBLE MAN: SOME OF THE PROBLEMS OF WRITING ON SLAVE SOCIETY IN THE BRITISH WEST INDIES. *Hist. Reflections [Canada] 1974 1(1): 37-57.* Discusses divergent historical interpretations and research problems in the study of West Indian plantation societies and slavery. Using computer data, analogous historical trends, and recorded oral traditions, historians must answer five important questions: 1) what were the actual slave society conditions; 2) did slaves accept or reject the plantation system; 3) what alternatives were open to the slave; 4) what social changes occurred during the slavery period; and 5) what happened to West Indian society when slavery formally ended? Contemporary West Indian society is much the same as it was during the slavery period, due to socioeconomic influences. Views of slavery are conditioned by present events and are not based on the slavery period itself. Secondary sources; 23 notes. S

2107. Crocker, Ruth Hutchinson. ULRICH PHILLIPS: A SOUTHERN HISTORIAN RECONSIDERED. *Louisiana Studies 1976 15(2): 113-130.* Ulrich Bonnell Phillips (1877-1934), long considered the foremost American historian of the antebellum South, has been severely criticized by revisionist historians for his sympathetic treatment of slavery and the plantation, especially in his two most famous works, *American Negro Slavery* (1918) and *Life and Labor in the Old South* (1929). His work is typical of the Progressive era in which it was written; he was racist and his view of blacks never changed. However, his use of primary sources and analysis of the social and economic institutions of the South are still significant. Important insights still stand, such as the unique combination of blacks and whites in plantation society and the special role of the plantation aristocracy as the chief power in the antebellum South. Primary and secondary sources; 81 notes. J. Buschen

2108. Curtin, Philip D. THE AFRICAN DIASPORA. *Hist. Reflections [Canada] 1979 6(1): 1-17.* Reviews recent historiography of the slave trade and calls for comparative research on its three major phases, the repopulation of tropical America, the provision of labor for mines and plantations in America and elsewhere, and the supply of specialized servant groups to the Islamic world, all of which share characteristics with other migrations. Relates the African experience to the basic questions examined by migration studies in general, identity and intentions of the migrants and impact of their moving on sending and receiving areas. Both impacts, at least as regards general synthesis, have been less researched than asserted in recent years. The slave trade has been likened economically to the fishing industry, but it may be more aptly compared, in terms of cost distribution, to burglary. 39 notes. S

2109. Davis, David Brion. SLAVERY AND THE POST-WORLD WAR II HISTORIANS. *Daedalus 1974 103(2): 1-16.* Since 1956, five major turning points have occurred in the historiography of slavery: Kenneth Stampp's *Peculiar Institution* (New York: Alfred A. Knopf, 1956) demonstrated the topic's "peculiar urgency", Stanley Elkins' *Slavery* (Chicago: University of Chicago Press, 1959) questioned the cruelty or humaneness of American slavery, Conrad and Meyer's "The Economics of Slavery in the Ante-Bellum

South" in Alfred Conrad and John Meyer, *The Economics of Slavery and Other Econometric Studies* (Chicago: Aldine, 1964) opened the "Cliometric Revolution", Philip D. Curtin's *The Atlantic Slave Trade: A Census* (Madison: University of Wisconsin Press, 1969) expanded the demography of slave trade hemispherically. Direct evidence from slaves has recently become available. The conflict and convergence of this historiography show in Eugene Genovese's *Roll Jordan Roll* (1974) and Robert W. Fogel and Stanley L. Engerman's *Time on the Cross* (Boston: Little Brown, 1974). Secondary sources; 21 notes.   E. McCarthy

2110. Davis, Thomas J. SLAVE TESTIMONY: A REVIEW ESSAY AND A BIBLIOGRAPHY. *Afro-Americans in New York Life and Hist. 1979 3(1): 73-86.* Discusses books of slave testimony which describe personal experiences of antebellum plantation slaves; includes a bibliography.

2111. Degler, Carl. PLANTATION SOCIETY: OLD AND NEW PERSPECTIVES ON HEMISPHERIC HISTORY. *Plantation Soc. in the Americas 1979 1(1): 9-14.* Discusses the historiography of slavery, 1950's-70's. By focusing on the social system, the plantation, instead of the legal system, slavery, the new journal, *Plantation Society in the Americas,* may further historical understanding of: whether slavery was a unique system of labor or part of a free-unfree labor continuum, comparative studies of slavery in and among countries, the effect of slavery on the evolution of black culture, whether slavery was a traditional or capitalistic labor system, and new questions of the relations among values and economic activities. Secondary sources.   R. G. Sherer

2112. Degler, Carl. WHY HISTORIANS CHANGE THEIR MINDS. *Pacific Hist. Rev. 1976 45(2): 167-184.* Reprints the presidential address to the Pacific Coast Branch of the American Historical Association at its 68th annual meeting in August 1975. Investigates the reasons for changes in historical interpretation and uses as an example the reinterpretation of slavery during the last quarter of a century. Three themes have undergone revision: 1) the impact of slavery upon blacks; 2) the profitability of slavery as an economic institution; 3) the comparative history of slavery in the new world. Reveals the importance of historical evidence which, coupled with the value judgments of the investigator, brings past and present together. 20 notes.   R. V. Ritter

2113. Dew, Charles B. THE SAMBO AND NAT TURNER IN EVERYSLAVE: A REVIEW OF "ROLL, JORDAN, ROLL." *Civil War Hist. 1975 21(3): 261-268.* Review article prompted by Eugene D. Genovese's *Roll, Jordan, Roll: The World The Slaves Made* (1974). The main thesis of the book, that a practical "accommodation-resistance" relationship developed between owner and slave, is well-supported by the author's elaborate research and perceptive analysis of that relationship based on his deep understanding of the complexities of the human experience.
                                    E. C. Murdock

2114. Drimmer, Melvin. THOUGHTS ON THE STUDY OF SLAVERY IN THE AMERICAS AND THE WRITING OF BLACK HISTORY. *Phylon 1975 36(2): 125-139.* Despite the large number of comparative works investigating slavery in the Americas which were published during the 1960's and early 1970's, the study of Negroes and their relationship to the system of slavery has been neglected. The existing investigations have thoroughly depicted the world of the slaveholders, but the lives of blacks have been denigrated and/or relegated to a secondary status. Of the many historians mentioned in this article, Stanley Elkins, Eugene Genovese, Orlando Patterson, Ulrich B. Phillips, and Winthrop Jordan are most thoroughly analyzed. Concludes that the history of blacks in the Americas is still to be written. Based on secondary sources; 37 notes.   B. A. Glasrud

2115. Dunn, Richard S. QUANTIFYING SLAVERY AND THE SLAVE TRADE. *J. of Interdisciplinary Hist. 1978 9(1): 147-150.* Review of some recent writings on slavery. To overcome the problem of the incomplete nature of recorded data even for the 19th century, some have resorted to counterfactual analysis and mathematical model building. The result has produced an atmosphere "of scholarly mudslinging rather than mathematical elegance." The abstract mode of computation also tends to hide individual personality and local variety. All these features are abundantly illustrated in the works reviewed. 2 notes.   R. Howell

2116. Finley, M. I. SLAVERY AND THE HISTORIANS. *Social Hist. [Canada] 1979 12(24): 247-261.* The historiography of slavery is a manifestation of contemporary social and political views, such as Marxism. The interest of many historians today in the economics of American Negro slavery reflects in part concern with modern racial tensions. The new historiography of slavery is distinguished from the old by the serious investigation of the complex ideology of the slaves, which, with the psychology of slavery, are most urgently in need of continued inquiry. Secondary sources; 12 notes.
                                    D. F. Chard

2117. Fogel, Robert William. CLIOMETRICS AND CULTURE: SOME RECENT DEVELOPMENTS IN THE HISTORIOGRAPHY OF SLAVERY. *J. of Social Hist. 1977 11(1): 34-51.* Recent statistical examinations of work and sexual practices of American slaves indicate that young slave women were "not overwhelmingly promiscuous" but "prudish." These studies indicate that statistical methodology can be a "useful instrument in the study of culture." 49 notes.   L. E. Ziewacz

2118. Fohlen, Claude. L'ESCLAVAGE AUX ETATS-UNIS: DIVERGENCES ET CONVERGENCES [Slavery in the United States: Divergences and Convergences]. *Rev. Hist. [France] 1977 257(2): 345-360.* American historians neglected the subject of slavery before 1918 when Ulrich B. Phillips published *American Negro Slavery* and in 1929, when he published *Life and Labor in the Old South.* Since then regional studies by Ralph B. Flanders, Charles S. Sydnor, G. G. Johnson, James B. Sellers, and Joe G. Taylor and general interpretations by Kenneth M. Stampp and Stanley Elkins have been published. In 1974 Robert William Fogel and Stanley L. Engerman published *Time on the Cross: The Economics of American Negro Slavery,* which applies the statistical approach referred to as Cliometrics. This book stirred up debate on slavery and the value of quantification in all fields of history. 16 notes.
                                    G. H. Davis

2119. Fohlen, Claude. UN DÉBAT HISTORIOGRAPHIQUE: L'ESCLAVAGE AUX ÉTATS-UNIS [A historiographical debate: Slavery in the United States]. *Bull. de la Soc. d'Hist. Moderne [France] 1977 76(18): 8-16.* Studies the 1974 controversy about slavery as an economically sound and efficient institution which brought prosperity to the South and good working and living conditions for slaves as opposed to free laborers.

2120. Foner, Eric. REDEFINING THE PAST. *Labor Hist. 1975 16(1): 127-138.* A review article prompted by Robert William Fogel and Stanley L. Engerman's *Time on the Cross: The Economies of American Negro Slavery,* 2 volumes (Boston: Little, Brown & Co., 1974). Consensus-oriented, avowedly political, and appearing to be scientific and objective, the work is fundamentally ahistorical, abstracted from actual history, based on flimsy, questionable data, and full of unwarranted inferences. The work is, to use Fogel and Engerman's words about another book, an "exceptional demonstration of the power of ideology to obliterate reality." 2 notes.
                                    L. L. Athey

2121. Fox-Genovese, Elizabeth. POOR RICHARD AT WORK IN THE COTTON FIELDS: A CRITIQUE OF THE PSYCHOLOGICAL AND IDEOLOGICAL PRESUPPOSITIONS OF *TIME ON THE CROSS. Rev. of Radical Pol. Econ. 1975 7(3): 67-83.* Compares the findings in Robert William Fogel's and Stanley L. Engerman's *Time on the Cross* (New York, 1974) with other historians' conclusions on 19th-century slavery in the South.

2122. Friedman, Lawrence J. "HISTORICAL TOPICS SOMETIMES RUN DRY": THE STATE OF ABOLITIONIST STUDIES. *Historian 1981 43(2): 177-194.* Before and after the Civil War those who had worked for emancipation tried to provide a history of the movement. A paradigm of "the growth of a dissenting minority," which secured the eradication of Southern slav-

ery, emerged. Alternate explanations, such as the role of civil liberties, moral issues (pressure of Garrisonians), and the appeal of the Liberty Free Soil-Republican Party, all undermine the "growth" paradigm. Rather than speak of the growth of a dissenting minority, it is better to refer to its constant, articulate presence. Primary sources; 41 notes.
R. S. Sliwoski

2123. Gallerano, Nicola. SCHIAVITÙ E FAMIGLIA NERA IN AMERICA: UN DIBATTITO SULLA "RADICAL HISTORY REVIEW" [Slavery and the black family in America: a debate in the *Radical History Review*]. *Movimento Operaio e Socialista [Italy] 1978 1(4): 426-437.* The *Radical History Review,* founded in the United States in 1973, is attempting to present a more leftist, partly Marxist, interpretation of American history and society than that found in conventional historical periodicals. In 1974, a debate began in the pages of this journal on slavery and the black family, a debate inspired by three books: Stanley L. Engerman's and Robert W. Fogel's *Time on the Cross: The Economics of American Negro Slavery* (Boston, 1974); Eugene Genovese's *Roll Jordan Roll* (New York, 1974); and Herbert Gutmans *The Black Family in Slavery and Freedom, 1750-1925* (New York, 1976). The first was torn apart by the RHR's reviewers; the second two were criticized for certain features and praised for others; 19 notes.
J. C. Billigmeier

2124. Green, Barbara L. SLAVE LABOR AT THE MARAMEC IRON WORKS, 1828-1850. *Missouri Hist. Rev. 1979 73(2): 150-164.* Recent historians have been interested in the political and economic ramifications of industrial slavery. Samuel Massey and Thomas James, the founders of the company, used little slave labor, preferring to recruit skilled white ironworkers from Ohio. Their limited experience with black workers and the knowledge gleaned from their contact with industrialists, who extensively used black labor, show that the slave workers were not the lazy, shiftless, childish, and dishonest workers portrayed by Ulrich B. Phillips and Stanley Elkins. Illus., 56 notes.
W. F. Zornow

2125. Hay, Robert P. "AND TEN DOLLARS EXTRA, FOR EVERY HUNDRED LASHES ANY PERSON WILL GIVE HIM, TO THE AMOUNT OF THREE HUNDRED": A NOTE ON ANDREW JACKSON'S RUNAWAY SLAVE AD OF 1804 AND ON THE HISTORIAN'S USE OF EVIDENCE. *Tennessee Hist. Q. 1977 36(4): 468-478.* In 1804 Andrew Jackson ran an ad for a runaway slave in the Nashville *Tennessee Gazette.* In the 173 years since, biographers of Jackson and students of southern slavery have often failed to find this unusual ad or have misued it when they did. The fact that the ad is being placed in the definitive edition of the Andrew Jackson papers for all researchers to see will help historians make a more balanced assessment of Jackson's attitude toward slaves. Primary and secondary sources; 26 notes.
M. B. Lucas

2126. Hellie, Richard. RECENT SOVIET HISTORIOGRAPHY ON MEDIEVAL AND EARLY MODERN RUSSIAN SLAVERY. *Russian Rev. 1976 35(1): 1-32.* Although slaves made up the second largest segment of the Muscovite population, Soviet historiography had ignored them until very recently. The official canon, laid down in 1932, was that the basic antagonism was between landowners and dependent peasants, not between slaves and slaveowners. Now that the ideological strictures have been somewhat relaxed, a whole series of new books has come out since 1970. The major problem has become "how to reconcile the presence of slavery with the reigning dogma that the period under review is formally a 'feudal' one." Secondary sources; 148 notes.
R. B. Valliant

2127. Higman, Barry W. THE SLAVE POPULATIONS OF THE BRITISH CARIBBEAN: SOME NINETEENTH-CENTURY VARIATIONS. *Eighteenth-Cent. Florida and the Caribbean 1976: 60-70.* The variety of slave populations in the British West Indies "is not explicable by reference to any single demographic cycle, but was a genuine diversity"; historians who compare slavery across nations or empires are using questionable assumptions. Three major groups are defined: slave populations that were naturally increasing, heavily decreasing, and lightly decreasing. It may be worth attempting a typology of the British Caribbean slave populations, but this will require a model more complex than Philip D. Curtin's. Sugar colonies must be separated from nonsugar colonies and considered chronologically, according to stages of settlement. 14 notes, appendix.
W. R. Hively

2128. Issel, William. HISTORY, SOCIAL SCIENCE, AND IDEOLOGY: ELKINS AND BLASSINGAME ON ANTE-BELLUM AMERICAN SLAVERY. *Hist. Teacher 1975 9(1): 56-72.* Discusses and compares Stanley M. Elkins' *Slavery: A Problem in American Institutional and Intellectual Life* (2nd ed.; Chicago: U. of Chicago Press, 1968) and John Blassingame's *The Slave Community: Plantation Life in the Ante-Bellum South* (New York: Oxford U. Press, 1972). States that Elkins' approach to the problem of slavery is conservative and reflects social science attitudes of the 1950's. Blassingame's work, though not above criticism, discusses slavery from a more recent perspective, treating the slaves more as individuals and from their own viewpoint. Primary and secondary sources; 56 notes.
P. W. Kennedy

2129. Johnson, Marion. BULFINCH LAMBE AND THE EMPEROR OF PAWPAW: A FOOTNOTE TO AGAJA AND THE SLAVE TRADE. *Hist. in Africa 1978 5: 345-350.* Examines the history of Bulfinch Lambe, an 18th-century British slave trader, and suggests that Lambe was not a reliable source of information on Dahomey. I. A. Akinjogbin's contention that King Agaja ("the Emperor of Pawpaw") sought to terminate Dahomey's involvement in the slave trade is based on this inaccurate source. 11 notes.

2130. Kilian, Martin A. and Tatom, E. Lynn. MARX, HEGEL, AND THE MARXIAN OF THE MASTER CLASS: EUGENE D. GENOVESE ON SLAVERY. *J. of Negro Hist. 1981 66(3): 189-208.* Eugene D. Genovese represents himself as providing a humanistic-Marxian interpretation of the slave South, but his definitions and categories are inadequate. He uses some psychological interpretations that falsely minimize the terror, tragedy, racism, and economic exploitation of slavery, thus losing the real life process of the master-class relationship.
A. G. Belles

2131. King, Richard H. MARXISM AND THE SLAVE SOUTH: A REVIEW ESSAY. *Am. Q. 1977 29(1): 117-131.* In his works on slavery and the American South, Eugene Genovese incorporates the theoretical concepts of certain 20th-century revisionist Marxists, especially the ideas of Antonio Gramsci and his construct of hegemony. Genovese's analysis of slavery, the black, and the American South elicits criticisms of various portions of his exceedingly important historical contributions. Areas of criticism include Genovese's placing of the master-slave relationship at the center of his interpretation of the American South, his views on southern white guilt over slavery, his employment of Gramsci's construct of hegemony, and his interpretations of southern white class interests, slave religion, the strength of the slave family, the existence of slave culture, and the generation in antebellum times of black nationalism.
N. Lederer

2132. Kiple, Kenneth F. and Kiple, Virginia H. SLAVE CHILD MORTALITY: SOME NUTRITIONAL ANSWERS TO A PERENNIAL PUZZLE. *J. of Social Hist. 1977 10(3): 284-309.* Investigates the nutritional difficulties which must be considered in order to explain the high death rates among slave children because the rates seem inconsistent with the high caloric intake recent cliometric studies report. Certain mechanisms suited for survival in West Africa tended to produce nutritional difficulties in the United States where there was less sunshine. Further nutritional deficits in the slave diet frequently dovetailed with the chemical barriers inherited from Africa. As a result, the black child suffered a high rate of death from convulsions, teething, tetanus, rickets, smothering, protein-calorie malnutrition, pica, and worms. Both those who have depicted the southern planters as paternalists and as capitalists have lacked the understanding that there were elements in the situation largely beyond the planters control. Table, 111 notes.
M. Hough

2133. Klein, Martin A. THE STUDY OF SLAVERY IN AFRICA. *J. of African Hist.* *[Great Britain]* 1978 19(4): 599-609. Review of Suzanne Miers and Igor Kopytoff, eds., *Slavery in Africa. Historical and Anthropological Perspectives* (Madison, 1977) and Claude Meillassoux, *L'esclavage en Afrique précoloniale* (Paris, 1975). The horrors of African slavery were used in the 18th century as justification for the Atlantic trade and in the 19th to encourage intervention and colonial occupation. Since that time, colonial administrators, allied with slaveholding chiefs, sought to convince Europeans that African slavery was benign. Serious study has developed only in the last decade with the publication of A. G. Hopkins's *Economic History of West Africa* (London, 1973). Hopkins, Meillassoux, and Miers and Kopytoff provide contrasting topical interpretations including the absence of freedom, the hereditary nature of slavery, and the introduction of slaves into new environments. Much work remains to be done on the duties and organization of slaves. 38 notes. A. W. Novitsky

2134. Kleinman, Max L. THE DENMARK VESEY CONSPIRACY: AN HISTORIOGRAPHICAL STUDY. *Negro Hist. Bull.* 1974 37(2): 225-228. Studies the slave revolt conspiracy of Denmark Vesey in Charleston, South Carolina, 1821-22, and the 1964 revisionist account of it by historian Richard Wade.

2135. Knudson, Jerry. JEFFERSON THE FATHER OF SLAVE CHILDREN? ONE VIEW OF THE BOOK REVIEWERS. *Journalism Hist.* 1976 3(2): 56-58. Examines Fawn M. Brodie's thesis in *Thomas Jefferson, An Intimate History* (New York, 1974) that Jefferson fathered five children by his slave Sally Hemings, and its reception by the critics.

2136. LeRiverend, Julio. EL ESCLAVISMO EN CUBA (PERSPECTIVAS DEL TEMA) [Slavery in Cuba: reflections on the topic]. *Rev. de la Biblioteca Nac. José Martí [Cuba]* 1980 22(3): 33-51. The historiography of Cuban slavery has many new areas for future scholars to study. New work must be firmly based on exhaustive use of primary sources and a solid knowledge of Marxist theory. Secondary sources; 40 notes. J. A. Lewis

2137. Liedel, Donald E. SLAVERY AND ABOLITION: STANLEY ELKINS AND HIS CRITICS. *J. of Popular Culture* 1971 5(3): 616-619. Examines the debate over slavery and abolitionism between Stanley Elkins and his critics through reviews of Elkins' *Slavery: A Problem in American Institutional and Intellectual Life*, 2nd ed. (Chicago: U. of Chicago Press, 1968); *The Debate Over Slavery: Stanley Elkins and His Critics*, edited by Ann. J. Lane (Urbana: U. of Illinois Press, [1971]); and Aileen S. Kraditor's *Means and Ends in American Abolitionism: Garrison and His Critics on Strategy and Tactics, 1834-1850* (New York: Pantheon Books, [ca 1969]).

2138. Mandić, Oleg. IZ PROBLEM ROBOVLASNIČKE DRUŠTVENO-EKONOMSKE FORMACIJE [The problem of slave-owning socioeconomic formation]. *Historijski Zbornik [Yugoslavia]* 1976-77 29-30: 21-35. Studies the economies of ancient Egypt, Mesopotamia, China, India, and most of the early Mediterranean civilizations to refute the Marxist view of early history as being dominated by slave-owning economies. This notion was suggested by Engels, superficially adopted by Lenin, and finally enshrined as a Marxist dogma by Stalin. Primary sources; 61 notes. S. Košak

2139. McDonald, Roderick A. THE WILLIAMS THESIS: A COMMENT ON THE STATE OF SCHOLARSHIP. *Caribbean Q. [Jamaica]* 1979 25(3): 63-68. Reviews the historiography of slavery and attacks recent challenges to Eric Williams's *Capitalism and Slavery* (1964) by Robert Thomas, Stanley Engerman, and Roger Anstey. Defends Williams' thesis that slavery was essential to the development of the colonies of Western Europe. Secondary sources; 21 notes. R. L. Woodward, Jr.

2140. Mettas, Jean. POUR UNE HISTOIRE DE LA TRAITE DES NOIRS FRANÇAISE: SOURCES ET PROBLÈMES [Towards a history of the French slave trade: sources and problems]. *Rev. Française d'Hist. d'Outre-Mer [France]* 1975 62(1/2): 19-46. A definitive historiographical account of the French slave trade remains to be written, yet it can be written, given the variety and amount of archival material in France and the former colonies. The author poses questions about the methods and geography of the trade, as well as its social, economic, and political consequences for France, the New World colonies, and various West African societies. Based on documents in the Archives Nationales de France, Archives Départementales de Charente-Maritime et Loire-Atlantique, Arquivo Histórico Ultramarino in Lisbon, and secondary sources; 64 notes. L. B. Chan

2142. Milani, Piero A. A PROPOSITO DI UNA NUOVA RIVISTA SULLA SCHIAVITÙ [A new journal about slavery]. *Politico [Italy]* 1980 45(4): 671-684. Singles out special problems relating to slavery on the occasion of the publication of a new journal, *Slavery and Abolition: A Journal of Comparative Studies*. The author is opposed to the widespread propensity to consider modern or colonial slavery separately from ancient and medieval slavery; there is in fact a perfect continuity. Europeans were well accustomed to black slavery before colonialism. Also, explicative and justicative theories of slavery on the part of the Church, jurists, and philosophers were relatively unchanged since the Hellenistic period. J/S

2143. Miller, Randall M. WHEN LIONS WRITE HISTORY: SLAVE TESTIMONY AND THE HISTORY OF AMERICAN SLAVERY. *Res. Studies* 1976 44(1): 13-23. Discusses the necessity of obtaining testimony from Negro slaves in writing the history of plantation slavery in the South from the 1830's to 1860, including the accounts of Frederick Douglass.

2144. Mörner, Magnus. THE IMPACT OF REGIONAL VARIETY ON THE HISTORY OF THE AFRO-LATIN AMERICANS. *Secolas Ann.* 1978 9: 1-13. Comparative slavery in the New World is such a complex subject that wholesale generalizations cannot be safely made about it. The present level of research allows us only to point out the many variations that existed. Secondary sources; 25 notes. J. A. Lewis

2145. Moses, Wilson J. RESTORING THE HARD LINE ON SLAVERY: A. LEON [HIGGINBOTHAM'S] *IN THE MATTER OF COLOR* AND SOME OTHER VIEWS. *UMOJA: A Scholarly J. of Black Studies* 1978 2(3): 189-197. Review essay of A. Leon Higginbotham's *In the Matter of Color, Race and the American Legal Process: The Colonial Period* (New York: Oxford U. Pr., 1978) begins with a survey of historiography on slavery during the 1960's, assessing Higginbotham in that light, and concludes that his identification of present economic, social, and political problems within the black community as the result of 300 years of interaction with a repressive legal system is a correct hypothesis.

2146. Nichols, William W. SLAVE NARRATIVES: DISMISSED EVIDENCE IN THE WRITING OF SOUTHERN HISTORY. *Phylon* 1971 32(4): 403-409. American historians have generally ignored slave narratives because they have not seemed to be reliable evidence. Use of the narratives could provide important information on the slaves' view of slavery. Secondary sources; 15 notes. C. K. Piehl

2147. Olson, James S. SLAVES, PSYCHES AND HISTORY: REVIEW ESSAY. *J. of Ethnic Studies* 1983 11(3): 95-110. Although historians have engaged in considerable scholarly debate during the last 15 years over slavery, a new consensus seems to have emerged concerning the personalities, families, and values of American slaves. The older argument of such writers as Albert Hart, Ulrich B. Phillips, and Charles Sydnor that slaves were inferior, rootless but happy people, has been countered, as have the descriptions of black pathologies central to the work of Kenneth Stampp, E. Franklin Frazier, and Stanley B. Elkins. Although some slaves responded to bondage with docile acquiescence or outright violence, most worked out a tenuous reciprocity with whites as each particular occasion required. At the same time they created a unique blend of African and American customs and values and nurtured a rich family life that provided love and emotional security. 34 notes.

G. J. Bobango

2148. Piras, Giorgio. STUDI RECENTI SUL PROBLEMS STORICO DELLA SCHIAVITÙ [Recent studies concerning the historical problem of slavery]. *Storia Contemporanea [Italy] 1973 4(2): 345-359.* Reviews recent works on the historical problem of slavery in Brazil, Mozambique, and the rest of the New World. Discusses the nature of the encounter between Portuguese feudalism and the system of Negro *regulos* in Mozambique. Examines the peculiar socioeconomic structure of slavery in the Indies and on mainland America. Secondary works; 53 notes.

L. R. Atkins

2149. Pybus, Cassandra. EUGENE D. GENOVESE: THE NEO-MARXIST INTERPRETATION OF THE SLAVE SOUTH. *Flinders J. of Hist. and Pol. [Australia] 1973 3: 32-44.* After discussing the Marxist contribution to history in general and to the study of the Slave South in particular, analyzes the neo-Marxist interpretation of Genovese, with its stress on the totality of slave society and on the internal contradictions of the system which led to war and the system's destruction. Based on the writings of Genovese, Marx, and Gramsci; 47 notes.

P. J. Beck

2150. Russell-Wood, A. J. R. THE BLACK FAMILY IN THE AMERICAS. *Jahrbuch für Geschichte von Staat, Wirtschaft und Gesellschaft Lateinamerikas [West Germany] 1979 16: 267-309.* Recently there has been a great deal of interest in the slave family, much of it general in nature. These studies have revealed blacks who ran away to form separate black settlements and who selected surnames reflecting their past or present culture. Significantly, despite the quantity of new work, no definitive history has been written for any region or republic in Spanish or Portuguese America. Secondary sources; 50 notes.

T. D. Schoonover

2151. Sandin, Bengt. SLAVEN SOM MEDELKLASSAMERI-KAN. FOGEL OCH ENGERMAN OCH DEBATTEN OM SLAVERIET I USA [The slave as a middle-class American: Fogel and Engerman and the discussion of slavery in the USA]. *Hist. Tidskrift [Sweden] 1977 (1): 39-70.* Analyzes Robert William Fogel and Stanley L. Engerman's, *Time on the Cross* (Boston: Little, Brown, 1974), which describes slavery as benfiting slaves materially and socially. Fogel and Engerman use quantitative methods in attempting to be objective and to produce a study unrelated to a particular school of thought. They have failed in both, as their work implies approval of the social structure and continues the consensus tradition in American historiography. Moreover, the book has implications for present American society in suggesting a sound social structure in which the individual can advance through hard work, as the slave could in the institution of slavery as they depict it. 70 notes, ref.

P. A. Hegstad

2152. Shapiro, Herbert. EUGENE GENOVESE, MARXISM, AND THE STUDY OF SLAVERY. *J. of Ethnic Studies 1982 9(4): 87-100.* The work of Eugene Genovese is widely perceived within and beyond the historical profession as a product of creative Marxist scholarship, especially now that his *Roll, Jordan, Roll* has become for many reviewers "a definitive benchmark in the historiography of slavery." A full assessment of his scholarship is in order, due to the crucial questions Genovese raises, and close analysis of works such as *The Political Economy of Slavery* shows his greatest lacunae: the minimizing of the significance of black struggle and the magnifying of whatever elements of passivity can be found among blacks insofar as they actively participated in the

Civil War. Accommodation and the plantation as community are overdone themes. Summarizes critiques of Genovese by King, Gutman, Woodward, and others. 67 notes.

G. J. Bobango

2153. Shapiro, Herbert. THE IMPACT OF THE APTHEKER THESIS: A RETROSPECTIVE VIEW OF *AMERICAN NEGRO SLAVE REVOLTS. Sci. & Soc. 1984 48(1): 52-73.* Herbert Aptheker's thesis expressed in his 1943 book *American Negro Slave Revolts*—that American slavery spawned resistance, including conspiracies and revolts—changed the basic assumptions and interpretations of slave studies. It fell out of favor in the 1950's-60's, though its critics seldom provided evidence to support their dismissals. In the last decade historians have returned to Aptheker's book with renewed respect, and have added much supporting evidence. Secondary sources; 70 notes.

R. E. Butchart

2154. Smith, John David. ALFRED HOLT STONE: MISSISSIPPI PLANTER AND ARCHIVIST/HISTORIAN OF SLAVERY. *J. of Mississippi Hist. 1983 45(4): 262-270.* Considered one of the nation's leading white experts on the "Negro problem" in the early 20th century, Alfred Holt Stone played an even more pivotal, but unrecognized, role as an archivist and historian of slavery. While Stone's writings by modern standards appear racist and outmoded in methodology, his contributions to the historiography of slavery should be better recognized. While seeking materials on antebellum Southern blacks, Stone would raise significant questions pertaining to the slave experience. His investigations revealed that the institution was not a static monolith, but rather a misunderstood, fluid system of racial and economic control. Stone's primary interest in slavery was to use this institution as a comparative model for race and labor relations in his own Jim Crow South. Based on Stone's publications and secondary sources; 17 notes.

M. S. Legan

2155. Smith, John David. DUBOIS AND PHILLIPS: SYMBOLIC ANTAGONISTS OF THE PROGRESSIVE ERA. *Centennial Rev. 1980 24(1): 88-102.* Compares the thought and writings of W. E. B. Du Bois and Ulrich B. Phillips, the Progressive Era's foremost historians on slavery. Both men wrote numerous books and articles on slavery and southern topics. Du Bois stressed the injustice of slavery, the contributions of African culture to black life, and racial equality; Phillips wrote from the perspective of the white middle class, viewed blacks as inferior, and defended southern institutions. Both men could be harshly critical of other scholars, and their opposing viewpoints inevitably brought them into contention. Du Bois reviewed Phillips's work negatively and charged him with racism. In contrast, Phillips all but ignored Du Bois, probably because his southern outlook prevented him from taking black intellectuals seriously. Had Phillips held a broader social perspective, he might have benefited from Du Bois's viewpoints on slavery. 33 notes.

A. Hoffman

2156. Smith, John David. THE HISTORIOGRAPHIC RISE, FALL, AND RESURRECTION OF ULRICH BONNELL PHILLIPS. *Georgia Hist. Q. 1981 65(2): 138-153.* Describes the pioneering historiographical views on slavery of Ulrich B. Phillips in the early 1900's, the criticisms, leveled against his work, particularly in the 1950's and 1960's, and the current reacceptance and acknowledgement of his influence despite criticism of his racism and some of his uses of sources. Based on Phillips's writings and secondary historiographical works; 47 notes.

G. R. Schroeder

2157. Smith, John David. JAMES FORD RHODES, WOODROW WILSON, AND THE PASSING OF THE AMATEUR HISTORIAN OF SLAVERY. *Mid-America 1982 64(3): 17-24.* Contrasts the attitudes and methods of James Ford Rhodes and Woodrow Wilson as historians and more narrowly as interpreters of slavery and the South, largely through analysis of Wilson's anonymous review of Rhodes's *History of the United States from the Compromise of 1850.* Rhodes was the amateur, narrative historian, a neoabolitionist, heavily dependent on travel accounts amassed for his private library; Wilson was the professional, an apologist for the Old South and advocate of synthesizing multiarchival sources. Based on the Wilson Papers and Rhodes's letters from several manuscript collections; 23 notes.

P. J. Woehrmann

2158. Smith, John David. AN OLD CREED FOR THE NEW SOUTH: SOUTHERN HISTORIANS AND THE REVIVAL OF THE PROSLAVERY ARGUMENT, 1890-1920. *Southern Studies 1979 18(1): 75-87.* Scientific historians of the Progressive Era attempted a reevaluation of slavery. Claiming objectivity, they found that slavery had been basically good for blacks, bringing them abundant food, clothing, housing, and care; developing warm, close relationships between blacks and whites; teaching blacks skilled crafts; and introducing them slowly to Christianity, the English language, and civilized manners through education. These views were promoted by white historians such as Ulrich B. Phillips (1877-1934) and black spokesmen such as Booker T. Washington (1856-1915). Secondary sources; 34 notes.   J. J. Buschen

2159. Starr, Raymond. HISTORIANS AND THE ORIGINS OF BRITISH NORTH AMERICAN SLAVERY. *Historian 1973 36(1): 1-18.* A study of the historiography of the rise of American slavery in the colonies, examining the motives of historians writing on the subject. Understanding the relationship of early historians to the question of slavery helps explain the long acceptance of the economic interpretation, and shows how, in the last decade, the argument that race prejudice preceded and may have caused slavery has now become the dominant theme in the historiography of the origins of slavery. Future research using newer analytical tools may be able to come up with more empirically grounded conclusions. 45 notes.   R. V. Ritter

2160. Steirer, William F., Jr. SLAVE OR SUPER-SLAVE: WHO REALLY DID LABOR IN THE SOUTHERN COTTON FIELDS? *Pro. of the South Carolina Hist. Assoc. 1979: 14-27.* Examines the historical literature on slavery since Kenneth Stampp's *The Peculiar Insitution* in 1956, characterizing most of the more recent writers as studying the "super-slaves," those who escaped slavery relatively unscathed. Suggests that a better treatment would discard both the old "Sambo" and the more recent "super-slave" images and treat slaves as human beings. 32 notes.   J. W. Thacker, Jr.

2161. Stewart, James Brewer. POLITICS AND BELIEF IN ABOLITIONISM: STANLEY ELKINS' CONCEPT OF ANTIINSTITUTIONALISM AND RECENT INTERPRETATIONS OF AMERICAN ANTISLAVERY. *South Atlantic Q. 1976 75(1): 74-97.* Stanley M. Elkins located the essence of the American abolitionists in their extremely emotional rejection of all social structures which attempted to deal with slavery. This "anti-institutionalism" destroyed any chance of a peaceful, negotiated solution to slavery. Historians in the 1960's usually rejected out of hand or ignored Elkins' theory. Current historians such as Bertram Wyatt-Brown, Lewis Perry, and the author accept it with modifications. Based on primary and secondary sources; 62 notes.   W. L. Olbrich

2162. Tipton, Frank B., Jr. and Walker, Clarence E. *TIME ON THE CROSS. Hist. & Theory 1975 14(1): 91-121.* Review article prompted by Robert William Fogel and Stanley L. Engerman, *Time on the Cross: The Economics of American Negro Slavery* (Boston: Little, Brown and Co., 1974). Fogel and Engerman used quantitative methods to question the "traditional interpretation" (first propagated by the abolitionists) of slavery as an unworkable economic system. The reviewers examine Fogel and Engerman's alternative, finding it incomplete and their authority questionable, which problems illustrate "some of the difficulties of an attempt to apply systematic quantitative methods to historical data." But traditional methods of research are also unsatisfactory. The reviewers offer some suggestions for future research when the crucial questions "will be the impact of slavery on the economy and social structure of the south." 61 notes.   D. A. Yanchisin

2163. Van Deburg, William L. SLAVE DRIVERS AND SLAVE NARRATIVES: A NEW LOOK AT THE "DEHUMANIZED ELITE." *Historian 1977 39(4): 717-732.* Robert William Fogel and Stanley L. Engerman's *Time on the Cross* and Eugene D. Genovese's *Roll, Jordan, Roll* are historiographical landmarks in research on the leadership roles of slaves in the antebellum period. Using these volumes as points of departure, discusses black leadership qualities in terms of slave drivers, using as evidence the Slave Narrative Collection compiled by the Federal Writers' Project dur-

ing the 1930's. Urges acceptance of these documents as a viable research tool for scholars, particularly for analyzing the existence of slave leadership elites.   M. S. Legan

2164. —. AFRO-AMERICAN SLAVE CULTURE. *Hist. Reflections [Canada] 1979 6(1): 122-155.*

Schuler, Monica. AFRO-AMERICAN SLAVE CULTURE, *pp. 121-137.* Examines the goals and values of African culture in Jamaica, particularly the transformation of various African ethnic groups into a Pan-African society and the role of religion in that process. The survival of 19th-century Central African indentured laborers' social and religious customs (Kumina) demonstrates the uses of ethnicity in institution building and adaptation to a Pan-African context. The pervasive African religion provided a sorcery to counter that of the masters, as in the case of the Myal religion of the 18th- and 19th-century Jamaica.

Karasch, Mary. COMMENTARY ONE, *pp. 138-141.* Compares the Jamaican experience with 19th-century Rio de Janeiro, particularly the development of ethnic-based lay brotherhoods, an elite institution appropriated and manipulated by Africans for their own social protection. 30 notes.

Price, Richard. COMMENTARY TWO, *pp. 141-149.* In Surinam, creolization, African-African syncretism, replaced African ethnic identities with a new Afro-American one much more rapidly than Schuler attests for Jamaica. Her qualitative data on slave life and religion is an important historiographic contribution. 23 notes.

Brathwaite, Edward Kamau. COMMENTARY THREE, *pp. 150-155.* Schuler's isolation of Myalism from other slave religions limits our conception of their complex resources of resistance and deprives Afro-Caribbean religion of its simultaneous secular-political dimension. 11 notes.

2165. —. INDIGENOUS AFRICAN SLAVERY. *Hist. Reflections [Canada] 1979 6(1): 19-83.*

Lovejoy, Paul E. INDIGENOUS AFRICAN SLAVERY, *pp. 19-61.* Analyzes the development of slavery in savanna, coastal, and southern and eastern Bantu regions of Africa in the medieval Islamic era, 11th-16th centuries; the period of the transatlantic slave trade, 16th-19th centuries; the 19th-century switch to legitimate trade goods in West Africa; and the period of abolition and transition, 1890-1940. 92 notes.

Kopytoff, Igor. COMMENTARY ONE, *pp. 62-77.* Lovejoy falls into the essentialist trap that requires systems and processes to be "essentially" one thing or another, and attributes too great influence to the Atlantic, external influences on African slaveries. 23 notes.

Cooper, Frederick. COMMENTARY TWO, *pp. 77-83.* Neither Lovejoy's market-centered analysis nor Kopytoff's kinship-centers pay sufficient attention to the social and economic structures that fostered slavery in particular places and times. 16 notes.

2166. —. SLAVE FAMILY AND ITS LEGACIES. *Hist. Reflections [Canada] 1979 6(1): 183-211.*

Gutman, Herbert G. SLAVE FAMILY AND ITS LEGACIES, *pp. 183-199.* Traces US historiography of the slave family and analyzes various kinds of data to show that slaves' and ex-slaves' real choices on the record suggest the nature of their marriage and family customs. Freedman's Bureau reformers, the retrogressionist theses of scholars like Ulrich B. Phillips, and the subsequent work of sociologist E. Franklin Frazier and his followers all concentrated on the social deprivation and subjection of slave life. Historians began in the 1960's to seek evidence of slaves' own history-making, including the development of family mores internal to slave culture. Freedmen's marriage registers in postbellum North Carolina, intensive study of particular plantations, and examination of 18th-century slave naming practices give clues to important regularities in slave family and society.

Higman, Barry W. COMMENTARY ONE, *pp. 200-203.* Adds West Indian comparative data, particularly parallels to the succeeding historiographical generations. We need to look more closely at the influence of postemancipation social change—urbanization and the concentration of Negro women in domestic service—on the black family.

Engerman, Stanley L. COMMENTARY TWO, *pp. 204-211.* The slave family was always a central concern of pro-slavery defense as well as abolitionist critique, and Frazier's own views changed over time. Summarizes recent work on slave family and fertility, primarily in the United States. 6 notes.   S

2167. —. SLAVERY AND RACE IN SOUTH CAROLINA. *Pro. of the South Carolina Hist. Assoc. 1980: 78-117.*

Terry, George D. SOUTH CAROLINA'S FIRST NEGRO SEA-MEN ACTS, 1793-1803, *pp. 78-93.* Examines the actions taken by the South Carolina Assembly to protect the state from the danger of a slave revolt. The laws that were enforced were severe but felt necessary because of the effect of the slave revolt in Santo Domingo. Under these laws, black seamen were either not allowed to land in Charleston or were required to be locked up while in the port. Similar laws were enacted after the Denmark Vesey affair in 1822. Based on public documents, newspapers, and published works, 38 notes.

Smith, John David. NEGLECTED BUT NOT FORGOTTEN: HOWELL M. HENRY AND THE "POLICE CONTROL" OF SLAVES IN SOUTH CAROLINA, *pp. 94-110.* Reexamines the work of Howell M. Henry (1879-1956) who wrote *The Police Control of the Slave in South Carolina* and was professor of history and economics at Emory and Henry College in Virginia. Based on published works; 46 notes.

Shankman, Arnold and Cox, Edward L. COMMENTARIES ON "SLAVERY AND RACE IN SOUTH CAROLINA," *pp. 111-117.*   J. W. Thacker, Jr.

2168. —. SLAVERY AND THE PROTESTANT ETHIC. *Hist. Reflections [Canada] 1979 6(1): 157-181.*

Anstey, Roger. SLAVERY AND THE PROTESTANT ETHIC, *pp. 157-172.* Analyzes the role of religious forces in the formation and expansion of antislavery movements in the United States and Great Britain and examines its influences in the abolition of the British slave trade, the West Indian emancipation, and US antislavery politics. Theological doctrines—Arminianism, redemptionism, sanctification, and postmillenialism—disposed Protestants to include the slaves among the potentially saved, to hate the institution of slavery, and to strive for earthly reform. Additionally, slavery became a denominational issue, as Anglican Evangelicals, Nonconformists, and Quakers combined to provide the political organization and strategy for abolition and emancipation. 66 notes.

DaCosta, Emilia Viotti. COMMENTARY ONE, *pp. 173-177.* Anstey's reasoning is circular and fails to distinguish causation from concomitance and real motives from the religious rhetoric in which they were dressed. 2 notes.

Davis, David Brion. COMMENTARY TWO, *pp. 177-181.* Explains Anstey's own Christian belief and the way it informed his work on the British abolitionists of the 18th and 19th centuries and their religious conception of politics.   S

7. SOCIAL AND INTELLECTUAL HISTORY

2169. Bajoit, G. MODÈLE CULTUREL, IDÉOLOGIE ET THÉORIE DE L'HISTOIRE [Cultural model, ideology and the theory of history]. *Recherches Sociologiques [Belgium] 1980 11(1): 3-30.* Analyzes the historical explanations proposed by about 20 intellectuals (sociologists and politicians) who had a great effect upon intellectual currents in their time; relates concepts of cultural model and ideology to macrosociological theories of history.

2170. Banac, Ivo. NEW STUDIES ON THE SOCIAL HISTORY OF CROATIA. *Slavic Rev. 1983 42(1): 97-100.* Examines Croatian historiography as exemplified by the following works: *Odjel za Hrvatsku Povijest: Deset Godina Rada, 1971-1981* [Department of Croatian History: 10 years of work, 1971-81] (1981), edited by Josip Adamček, Mirjana Gross, and Dragutin Pavličević; *Društveni Razvoj u Hrvatskoj: od 16. Stoljeća do Početka 20. Stoljeća* [Social development in Croatia: 16th to early 20th centuries] (1981), edited by Mirjana Gross. R. B. Mendel

2171. Beach, William W. A SECOND LOOK: THE AGENDA FOR "SOCIAL SCIENCE HISTORY." *Social Sci. Hist. 1980 4(3): 357-364.* Critique of J. Morgan Kousser's proposal of a close alliance between history and quantitative, analytic social science disciplines in *Social Science History* 1977 1(3). Quantitative, hard core social science disciplines are inherently ahistorical and unable to explain change, and therefore of limited use to historians. 2 notes, 2 ref. L. K. Blaser

2172. Bowers, C. A. WRITING CONTEXT-FREE HISTORY. *Hist. of Educ. Q. 1979 19(4): 499-506.* Reviews Peter Carbone, Jr.'s *The Social and Educational Thought of Harold Rugg.* Harold Ordway Rugg was a leading 20th-century American technocratic, progressive, educational philosopher and psychologist who expounded on the value of imagination, school-centered communities, and social engineering. Condemns Carbone's biographical study for its failure to analyze the social context out of which Rugg's ideas arose and those of the modern age. S. H. Frank

2173. Brady, Thomas A., Jr. SOCIAL HISTORY OF THE REFORMATION [AND] SOZIALGESCHICHTE DER REFORMATION: A CONFERENCE AT THE DEUTSCHES HISTORISCHES INSTITUT, LONDON, MAY 25-27, 1978. *Sixteenth Cent. J. 1979 10(1): 89-92.* A recent Anglo-German conference, chiefly concerning cities in the German Reformation, revealed essential differences between modernists and traditionalists. The former, represented notably by A. G. Dickens and a group from Tübingen, would employ social historical methods to rival the Marxists. They view a two-step Reformation: urban reform followed by a princely one. They are opposed by historians of humanism such as Bernd Moeller and by historians of a neo-Rankean, political tendency, who distrust quantification, prosopography, and class analysis. 11 notes. D. O. McNeil

2174. Burin, S. N. AMERIKANSKAIA ISTOROGRAFIA SOTSIALNYKH OTNOSHENII KOLONIALNOGO PERIODA [American historiography of social relations of the Colonial period]. *Novaia i Noveishaia Istoriia [USSR] 1974 (1): 175-187.* American historians view the colonial period from 1607 as the foundation of the future American state in political, economic, and ideological terms. The trend in the 1920's-30's was toward idealization of the period, with analyses by Charles and Mary Beard, C. M. Andrews, C. P. Nettels, H. S. Commager, A. Nevins, and E. Channing. Interest in the subject increased after World War II, focusing on the position of workers, uprisings, and religion with more detailed social analysis, including works by R. B. Morris, A. E. Smith, C. Bridenbaugh, T. J. Wertenbaker, E. S. Morgan, and W. E. Washburn. Studies appearing in the 1950's-60's examined the social organiza-

tion of the colonies and the position of workers more realistically, as seen in the works of M. Jensen, G. Ostrander, G. B. Nash, R. Berthoff, L. H. Leder, and L. Lemisch. Secondary sources; 80 notes. L. Smith

2175. Čas, Bojan. ZGODOVINA—SOCIOLOGIJA [History and sociology]. *Časopis za Zgodovino in Narodopisje [Yugoslavia] 1980 16(1): 190-214.* Describes the relationship between history and sociology, discussing the relation between the individual and the universal and the formation of sociological historiography. J/S

2176. Chaunu, Pierre. LES ÉLÉMENTS DE LONGUE DURÉE DANS LA SOCIÉTÉ ET LA CIVILISATION DU XVIIᵉ SIÈCLE. LA DÉMOGRAPHIE [Persistent elements in the society and the civilization of the 17th century: demography]. *Dix-Septième Siècle [France] 1975 (106-107): 3-22.* Demography provides an explanatory key to a European civilization which began between 1100 and 1350 and lasted into the 1800's. Historiographical demography was begun around 1950 by Pierre Goubert and Louis Henry. Its original model, based on 20th-century patterns, was greatly improved by J. Hajnal's recognition of the altered structure of early modern marriages: very late compared with other centuries. The nuclear family is older and more widespread than has previously been believed. Insignificant nuances to this general pattern are characteristic of the 17th century. 21 notes. W. J. Roosen

2177. Chiang Jo-min. SHIH NIEN SO SSU SO YEN; *SSU YÜ YEN* CHIN SHIH NIEN LUN WEN NEI JUNG YÜ FAN WEI TI FEN HSI [*Thought and Word* over the past 10 years: a content analysis]. *Ssu yü Yen (Thought and Word) [Taiwan] 1980 18(2): 49-60.* Contributors to *Ssu yü Yen (Thought and Word)* are primarily college and university teachers. Most of the articles in this social sciences publication are in sociology, with history and political science next in frequency. These and other findings are the result of an analysis of *Si yu Yen* issues, 1970-80. 11 tables, biblio. J. A. Krompart

2178. Chirot, Daniel. SOCIOLOGY AND HISTORY: A REVIEW ESSAY. *Hist. Methods 1983 16(3): 121-123.* Blending history and sociology is a delicate scholarly enterprise. Quite often Emile Durkheim's, Max Weber's, and Talcott Parsons's theories are used without close attention being paid to complex historical data. The result is a book such as Philip Abrams's *Historical Sociology* (1982). On the other hand, Charles Tilly's *As Sociology Meets History* (1981) and Craig Calhoun's *The Question of Class Struggle. Social Foundations of Popular Radicalism During the Industrial Revolution* (1982) reveal the inadequacy of the modernization and anomie theories and expose the fallacy in Durkheim's thought. D. K. Pickens

2179. Chudacoff, Howard P. SUCCESS AND SECURITY: THE MEANING OF SOCIAL MOBILITY IN AMERICA. *Rev. in Am. Hist. 1982 10(4): 101-112.* Assesses the historiography of social mobility, examining criteria for defining mobility and determining its significance in society.

2180. Civolani, Eva. "LE MOUVEMENT SOCIAL" [Le Mouvement Social]. *Passato e Presente [Italy] 1982 (1): 176-192.* Though *Le Mouvement Social* appeared as a continuation of an earlier bulletin *L'Actualité de l'Histoire* (1951-60) published by the Institut Français de l'Histoire Sociale, it represented a break in the historical traditions of the Institute. It opened a new level of historical inquiry into the meaning of various social practices and promises to provide the study of the working classes with an adequate theoretical and scientific instrument. 106 notes. J. V. Coutinho

2181. Clark, Charles E. HISTORY, LITERATURE, AND BELKNAP'S "SOCIAL HAPPINESS." *Hist. New Hampshire 1980 35(1): 1-22.* Scientism has challenged history as literature three times in modern history, all in times of uncertainty. Gibbon and his contemporaries at the end of the 18th century, Turner and Beard at the turn of the 20th century, and Berkhofer in the 1960's have sought the certainty they thought an empirically based historical science could create. Jeremy Belknap, who started writing history in such a climate, was influenced by both the Enlightenment and Romanticism. His rationalism combined with a new aesthetic consciousness, and he fashioned a vision of social happiness relevant for a century.   D. F. Chard

2182. Conze, Werner. ZUR SOZIALGESCHICHTE DES KAISERREICHS UND DER WEIMARER REPUBLIK [On the social history of the German empire and the Weimar republic]. *Neue Politische Literatur [West Germany] 1976 21(4): 507-515.* Younger German historians of the late 1960's and 1970's working in German history 1870-1933 have concentrated on the organized potential of the state, economy, and society in their growing politicization, polarization, and differentiation instead of describing events and personalities.

2183. Crubellier, Maurice. ÉDUCATION ET CULTURE: UNE DIRECTION DE RECHERCHE [Education and culture: a research direction]. *Hist. de l'Éduc. [France] 1978 (1): 39-48.* Introduces and analyzes the goals and functions of the Center for Study and Research in Education and Culture (CEREC) established at the University of Rheims in 1975 to research education history and culture in the Champagne-Ardennes region.

2184. Cuff, Robert. THE HISTORIAN AS PESSIMIST. *Can. R. of Am. Studies 1976 7(1): 95-101.* Review article prompted by Robert Wiebe's *The Segmented Society: An Historical Preface to the Meaning of America* (New York: Oxford U. Pr., 1975). Wiebe has attempted to present interpretations of America's development which sharply counter the interpretations of both the consensus historians of the 1950's and America's radical critics of the 1960's. 26 notes.   H. T. Lovin

2185. Cuff, Robert D. AMERICAN HISTORIANS AND THE "ORGANIZATION FACTOR." *Can. R. of Am. Studies 1973 4(1): 19-31.* An exploratory probe of the "organization factor" in American historical writing. Since World War II, scholars have produced a substantial literature dealing with the large-scale organizations that have emerged in the United States and other industrial areas. However, research and writing have proceeded with little attention to methodological difficulties and the need for interdisciplinary enterprise to cope successfully with the complexities of studying social organizations. Treats several specific areas that need attention. Scholars particularly need to address their studies toward the relationships between "values and organizational change." 33 notes.
                                                                      H. T. Lovin

2186. Darnton, Robert. INTELLECTUAL AND CULTURAL HISTORY. Kammen, Michael, ed. *The Past Before Us: Contemporary Historical Writing in the United States* (Ithaca, N.Y.: Cornell U. Pr., 1980): 327-349. Evaluates the present state of intellectual history studies in the United States through a review of curricula and recent publications. Social and intellectual history merged in the early 20th century to challenge traditional perspectives on history. Arthur Lovejoy and Perry Miller established a separate identity for intellectual history in the 1940's and 1950's by elevating it out of the social context. For 30 years it occupied a prominent position in American studies but it has recently declined relative to social history and its subfields of anthropology, popular culture, and political thought. 4 tables, fig., 55 notes.

2187. Davidson, Alastair. PEOPLE'S HISTORY AND POPULAR CULTURE. *Labour History [Australia] 1984 (46): 116-127.* The idea of "the people," traceable in social science writings to Roman times, became in Machiavelli a conception of an entity to be shaped, an understanding echoed by Napoleon and Hitler. The 19th-century French historian Jules Michelet understood the people to refer to the agricultural masses who in their quotidian routine acted as a brake on social change, and this view was maintained by the *Annales* school. People's history in the 20th century was concerned with analyzing the structural definitions which delimited the scope of the discipline. 41 notes.   L. J. Howell

2188. Davis, Harold Eugene. EL PENSAMIENTO SOCIAL EN LAS AMERICAS [Social thought in the Americas]. *Humánitas [Mexico] 1978 19: 85-97.* Surveys the various philosophies contained in histories written in the Americas since the early 19th century, and states that Latin American books reveal an optimistic view of humanity and admit the possibility of real changes in society.

2189. Dormon, James H. COLLECTIVE BEHAVIOR IN THE AMERICAN POPULAR RESISTANCE, 1765-1775: A THEORETICAL PROSPECTUS. *Historian 1979 42(1): 1-17.* Any attempt to resolve the historiographical controversy pertaining to popular participation in the American Revolution depends upon greater analytical precision in dealing with episodes of collective behavior. Discovers in Neil Smelser's model of "collective behavior" a tool to reconcile the arguments in revolutionary scholarship of idealists and realists. After applying the model to Boston's *Liberty* Riot of 1768, concludes that Smelser and other social action theorists may have provided historians with a modus operandi for achieving a new consensus. Primary sources; 47 notes.   R. S. Sliwoski

2190. Doyle, Don H. HISTORY FROM THE TOP DOWN. *J. of Urban Hist. 1983 10(1): 103-114.* Recent historiography has tended to observe history from the bottom up, although sometimes as much can be learned by viewing it from the top down. Perhaps even more can be gained from an integrated study focusing not only on individual classes, but also on the relationships between them.
                                                                      T. W. Smith

2191. Dykstra, Robert R. STRATIFICATION AND COMMUNITY POLITICAL SYSTEMS: HISTORIANS' MODELS. *Am. Behavioral Scientist 1973 16(5): 695-714.* One of six essays in this issue dealing with emerging theoretical models in social and political history.

2192. Eade, Susan. SOCIAL HISTORY IN BRITAIN IN 1976: A SURVEY. *Labor Hist. [Australia] 1976 (31): 38-52.* Examines current thought on social history and historiography among British historians, 1976.

2193. Elsner, Lothar and Heitz, Gerhard. ZUR KONZEPTION DER "INDUSTRIEGESELLSCHAFT": KRITIK DER ROSENBERG-FESTSCHRIFT [On the conception of "industrial society": critique of the Rosenberg *Festschrift*]. *Wissenschaftliche Zeitschrift der U. Rostock. Gesellschafts- und Sprachwissenschaftliche Reihe [East Germany] 1972 21(1 pt. 2): 119-122.* Review article of G. Schultz et al., *Entstehung und Wandel der modernen Gesellschaft. Festschrift für Hans Rosenberg zum 65. Geburtstag*, edited by Gerhard A. Ritter (Berlin, 1970). Although the contributors try to find new interpretations of social development in the 19th and 20th centuries, they do not overcome the ideological basis of anti-Communism. This *Festschrift* is part of the West German social democratic interpretation of social history of the 19th and 20th centuries.

2194. Engelberg, Ernst. PARTEILICHKEIT UND OBJEKTIVITÄT IN DER GESCHICHTSWISSENSCHAFT [Bias and objectivity in historiography]. *Zeitschrift für Geschichtswissenschaft [East Germany] 1969 17(1-2): 74-79.* Historiography cannot be impartial because of its political and social relevance in the totality of social formation, a view strongly opposed to the concept of bourgeois objectivity, which is a disguise for bourgeois class consciousness.

2195. Engerman, Stanley L. UP OR OUT: SOCIAL AND GEOGRAPHICAL MOBILITY IN THE UNITED STATES. *J. of Interdisciplinary Hist. 1975 5(3): 469-489.* Analysis of "the new social history" in the United States with particular respect to Stephan Thernstrom, *The Other Bostonians: Poverty and Progress in the American Metropolis* (Cambridge, Mass., 1973). Although there are reservations about both procedures and conclusions, the critical point is that Thernstrom and others "have clearly shown the basic usefulness of their methods and have greatly advanced our knowledge of what happened among the non-elite." 2 tables, 40 notes.

R. Howell

2196. Fernández Vargas, Valentina. VALOR Y SIGNIFICADO DE LA HISTORIA SOCIAL [The value and meaning of social history]. *Rev. Int. de Sociología [Spain] 1972 30(1/2): 35-53.* Discusses problems of modern historiography's conception of history as a global totality comprised of the different regional histories.

F. L. (IHE 88053)

2197. Field, Martha Heineman. SOCIAL CASEWORK PRACTICE DURING THE "PSYCHIATRIC DELUGE." *Social Service Rev. 1980 54(4): 482-507.* Discusses the assumptions that histories of the social work profession are accurate based on the history of trends and ideas, and that a "psychiatric deluge" inundated social casework practice and theory from 1917 to 1949; concludes that histories of social casework practice neglect a systematic examination of historical case records and that a "psychiatric deluge" did not exist, but rather that psychodynamic theory was integrated slowly into the profession.

2198. Filene, Peter G. AN OBITUARY FOR "THE PROGRESSIVE MOVEMENT." *Am. Q. 1970 22(1): 20-34.* Seeks to resolve and settle the debate historians have been conducting with "The Progressive Movement," which never really existed as a "movement." Major attention to the definition of a "movement" and analysis of its necessary components shows the nonexistence of a coherent progressive program, ideology, membership, and electorate. Concludes that history during 1890-1920 was ambiguous, inconsistent, and "moved by agents and forces more complex than a progressive movement." 48 notes.

R. V. Ritter

2199. Fourquin, Guy. L'ÉTAT DES RECHERCHES FRANÇAISES EN HISTOIRE SOCIALE DU MOYEN ÂGE: QUELQUES APERÇUS DES RÉSULTATS ACQUIS ET DES PROBLÈMES EN SUSPENS [The present state of French research in the social history of the Middle Ages: glimpses at the results and pending problems]. *Rev. du Nord [France] 1978 60(236): 43-55.* Considers the changes in French social historiography from one full of prejudices such as the real or supposed opposition between the nobility and the middle classes, to one concerned with the fundamental components of society: the nuclear family and extended family, clans, and socio-professional groups. The history of rebellions and political history proper may benefit from this new emphasis.

J/S

2200. Gadzhiev, K. S. SOVREMENNAIA AMERIKANSKAIA NEOKONSERVATIVNAIA ISTORIOGRAFIIA I NEKOTORYE PROBLEMY PURITANIZMA [Modern American nonconservative historiography and certain problems of Puritanism]. *Vestnik Moskovskogo U. Seriia 9: Istoriia [USSR] 1973 28(3): 18-31.* Criticizes American studies of the 1930's-60's and their interpretation of sociopolitical developments in 17th-century Puritan society. This so-called neoconservative school maintains that New England Puritans gave rise to a purely American culture, differing radically from European traditions, and distinguished by a dominant democratic and religiously tolerant middle class which precluded ideological conflicts typical for European countries. This theory is disputed: Puritan colonization of America, based on bourgeois social concepts, developed similarly to other bourgeois states harboring antagonistic class and sectarian distinctions. 51 notes.

N. Frenkley

2201. Galvão de Andrada Coelho, Ruy. SOCIOLOGIA E HISTÓRIA [Sociology and history]. *Rev. de Hist. [Brazil] 1969 38(77): 11-25.* Traces the development of history and sociology and their interrelationship from the 1830's. Refutes Durkheim's view of a radical separation and refers to the views and writings of Comte, Lévi-Strauss, Radcliffe-Brown, Weber, and Braudel. Suggests that at a time when many sociologists are attempting to lessen the structuralist dominance, collaboration with historians is essential. Secondary sources; biblio.

P. J. Taylorson

2202. Gégot, Jean-Claude. STORIA DELLA CRIMINALITÀ: LE RICERCHE IN FRANCIA [History of criminality: research in France]. *Quaderni Storici [Italy] 1981 16(1): 192-211.* Describes some of the directions of historical research in France in the last two decades. The history of criminality in France is an essential part of social history and the history of mentalities. 76 notes.

J. V. Coutinho

2203. Grob, Gerald N. REFLECTIONS ON THE HISTORY OF SOCIAL POLICY IN AMERICA. *Rev. in Am. Hist. 1979 7(3): 293-306.* Reviews recent scholarship on social policy in the United States, 1850's-1920's, and suggests areas of investigation yet to be studied: nature of dependency, processual aspects, interaction with the political system, economic considerations, and philosophical concepts of social policy.

2204. Gudavicius, E. EUROPOS IKIFEODALINE VISUOMENE (TARYBINES ISTORIOGRAFIJOS DUOMENYS) [European prefeudal society: Soviet historiographic data]. *Lietuvos TSR Mokslų Akad. Darbai. Serija A: Visuomenės Mokslai [USSR] 1983 (4): 82-89.* Using Soviet literature, defines prefeudal society in Europe and identifies the problem of the genesis of feudalism with the problem of the origins of the exploitation of the majority of the population. "The prefeudal period, if one must distinguish such a period, is nothing other than the period of the genesis of European feudalism." 61 notes.

A. E. Senn

2205. Guelzo, Allen C. REVIVALISM AND SOCIAL HISTORY: SOME OBSERVATIONS ON A REPRINT. *Fides et Hist. 1982 14(2): 61-69.* Examines Timothy L. Smith's *Revivalism and Social Reform: American Protestantism on the Eve of the Civil War* (1957, reprint 1980). Smith's pioneering study linking antebellum evangelical revivalism with perfectionist traditions fails as social history. Written in an era of consensus dominance, Smith's volume was supposedly a departure, a rejection of intellectual history, and yet the historian created his own group of elite reformers. The antebellum reformers were noble and honest, but they eventually stopped short of challenging industrial expansion or American pluralism, and Smith cannot explain why. The author's call for social reform is misleading and anachronistic in 20th-century technological society. Secondary sources; 16 notes.

G. A. Glovins

2206. Handke, Horst. DIE "THEORIE VOM SOZIALEN WANDEL": BESTANDTEIL BÜRGERLICHER SOZIAL- UND WIRTSCHAFTSGESCHICHTSSCHREIBUNG [The "theory of social change" in the writing of bourgeois economic and social history]. *Jahrbuch für Wirtschaftsgeschichte [East Germany] 1980 (3): 135-139.* Reviews of *Sozialer Wandel* [Social change] by Günter Wiswede and Thomas Kutsch (1978). 10 notes.

E. L. Turk/S

2207. Handlin, Oscar and Handlin, Mary F. THE NEW HISTORY AND THE ETHNIC FACTOR IN AMERICAN LIFE. *Perspectives in Am. Hist. 1970 4: 5-24.* Defines the "New History" as social history which displaced institutional history. Proponents of the New History seem most concerned with finding history's villains and heroes and, as a result, have closely identified with the subjects of their studies. In analyzing Reconstruction and the immigration problem, the Handlins show how historians are influenced by the social milieu in which they write. Future historians must resist this temptation and strive for a more apt historical description of what makes the American character.

W. A. Wiegand

2208. Hansen, Lars Ivar. HISTORISK MATERIALISME OG NORSK MIDDELALDER [Historical materialism and the Norwegian Middle Ages]. *Historisk Tidsskrift [Norway] 1974 53(3): 288-304.* Debates the application of Marxist interpretations to the history of the Middle Ages, focusing on the use of subjective or materialistic criteria. At issue was the church's entry into landholding and the change from a primitive, family type of economic production to an individual and feudal form, with the large landholders and church demanding returns through payment of dues or taxes. Civil war must be seen as a part of the conversion of society to a new production system, and the emergence of a dominant class with ensuing class conflict as part of the new system. War proletarianized the rural folk and created the nobility, who built the state apparatus.   R. E. Lindgren

2209. Heitz, Gerhard. ÜBERLEGUNGEN UND ASPEKTE ZUM BÄUERLICHEN KLASSENKAMPF IM SPÄTFEUDALISMUS [Consideration and aspects of the peasant class struggle in late feudalism]. *Acta U. Carolinae Philosophica et Hist. [Czechoslovakia] 1974 (1): 65-74.* In order to understand the peasant class struggle in its full historical meaning, one must proceed from the objective processes of late feudalism. Not only rebellions, but also strikes and flight from the land must be considered. The work of Soviet historians is basic to all understanding of the peasant movements of this period, grounded as it is in scientific Marxism-Leninism. 25 notes.
                                        J. C. Billigmeier

2210. Heitz, Gerhard. VOLKSMASSEN UND FORTSCHRITTE IN DER EPOCHE DES ÜBERGANGS VOM FEUDALISMUS ZUM KAPITALISMUS [Popular masses and progress in the epoch of the transition from feudalism to capitalism]. *Zeitschrift für Geschichtswissenschaft [East Germany] 1977 25(10): 1168-1177.* Discusses 18 theses presented to the 6th Historical Congress of the German Democratic Republic in 1977. In the countryside the popular masses comprised both landed and landless peasants, in the city they included the artisans, merchants, and the preproletariat strata. The lower classes, with varying motives and activities, were the driving force of historical progress. Together they undermined the feudal order. 7 notes.   J. T. Walker

2211. Henretta, James A. SOCIAL HISTORY AS LIVED AND WRITTEN. *Am. Hist. Rev. 1979 84(5): 1293-1333.* Develops a philosophy of historical analysis that combines a critical methodology, social theory, and political ideology. The argument has four components: an explication of the scholarship of the French *Annalistes* and English Marxists first demonstrates the feasibility of coherent systems of historical inquiry and, second, defines the prime features of "social" history. The third section elucidates both the epistemological weaknesses of the American tradition of pragmatic analysis and its great strength: a phenomenological perspective that depicts historical experience "as it was actually lived." The fourth presents an "action model"—a rhetorical strategy for combining a chronological narrative with social analysis and a methodological synthesis of the structural approaches of *Annalistes* and Marxists, the quantitative techniques of social-scientific historians, and the phenomenological perspective of American pragmatic historiography. Commentaries by Robert F. Berkhofer, Jr., and Darrett B. Rutman, with a reply by the author.   A

2212. Henretta, James A. THE STUDY OF SOCIAL MOBILITY: IDEOLOGICAL ASSUMPTIONS AND CONCEPTUAL BIAS. *Labor Hist. 1977 18(2): 165-178.* The study of mobility embodies assumptions about the nature of human motivation and social reality. Striving and success are valued and there is the presupposition of social inequality. A cautious use of these ideas is necessary since they may cause historians to overlook subcultural perceptions of reality not in accord with social mobility. 27 notes.
                                        L. L. Athey

2213. Higham, John. CURRENT TRENDS IN THE STUDY OF ETHNICITY IN THE UNITED STATES. *J. of Am. Ethnic Hist. 1982 2(1): 5-15.* Briefly examines the split among pluralist scholars into those who see cultural differences as intrinsic assets and those who see ethnic groups as part of an exploited working class. The former interpretation is conservative and stresses the ethnic community; the latter is radical and emphasizes class over ethnicity. Higham sees in some of the new research on family, urban, and comparative ethnic history, an attempt to examine "class without Marxism and ethnicity without pluralism," an effort he applauds. 21 notes.   N. C. Burckel

2214. Hiner, N. Ray. AFTER THE FALL: TOWARD A HISTORY OF LIFE IN AMERICA. *Fides et Hist. 1973 6(1): 52-59.* Review essay on the *Life in America Series*, (Boston: Houghton Mifflin, 1968-72). States that the series "provides some definite clues concerning the future shape of American historical scholar-

ship," but concludes that major work toward reconstructing a holistic view of American history is yet to be done, and that the holistic view in fact may never be reached. Secondary sources; 6 notes.
                                        R. Butchart

2215. Hobsbawm, Eric J. THE REVIVAL OF NARRATIVE: SOME COMMENTS. *Past & Present [Great Britain] 1980 (86): 3-8.* Comments on Lawrence Stone's "The Revival of Narrative: Reflections on a New Old History" concerning a supposed disillusionment with economically determinist models of historical explanation and development of a new narrative history. Those historians discussed by Stone in fact do link their small-scale studies with larger questions. The success of social history and the "new historians" in the postwar decades has allowed historians to concentrate on other questions, approaching historical change "ecologically rather than as geologists." It is possible to explain much of what Stone surveys as the continuation of past enterprises by other means, not proofs of their bankruptcy. 19 notes.
                                        D. J. Nicholls

2216. Hoffman, Louise E. FROM INSTINCT TO IDENTITY: IMPLICATIONS OF CHANGING PSYCHOANALYTIC CONCEPTS OF SOCIAL LIFE FROM FREUD TO ERIKSON. *J. of the Hist. of the Behavioral Sci. 1982 18(2): 130-146.* Applied to the interpretation of social phenomena, Freud's insights have been at once extraordinarily fruitful yet susceptible to oversimplification and pejorative stereotyping. A number of his fundamental concepts—the existence of an irrational mass mind, the Oedipal family constellation, the pathology of psychic regression—have, when used to understand collective experience, created powerful myths. Only gradually did he and his successors modify and amplify these myths, resulting in the elaboration of ego psychology and the concept of identity. These concepts connected psychoanalysis with contemporary social, political, and historical thought and allowed more nuanced forms of explanations.   J

2217. Hollingsworth, J. Rogers. PERSPECTIVES ON INDUSTRIALIZING SOCIETIES. *Am. Behavioral Scientist 1973 16(5): 715-740.* One of six essays in this issue dealing with emerging theoretical models in social and political history.

2218. Holton, Robert J. THE CROWD IN HISTORY: SOME PROBLEMS OF THEORY AND METHOD. *Social Hist. [Great Britain] 1978 3(2): 219-233.* Discusses a wide range of recent writings by historians and sociologists who have considered the role of crowds in history, centering on G. Rudé's *The Crowd in History, 1730-1848* (1964). The concept of crowd is still insufficiently precise, crowd study too often conceived in terms of social protest, and an unnecessary differentiation drawn between crowds in preindustrial and industrial societies. Secondary works; 63 notes.
                                        N. Dejevsky

2219. Iriye, Akira. AMERICANOLOGY IN JAPAN. *R. in Am. Hist. 1975 3(2): 143-154.* K. Ōhashi, H. Katō, and M. Saitō, eds. *Amerika no bunka* [American civilization] (Tokyo: Nan'undo, 1969-71), 7 volumes, and M. Saitō, N. Homma, and S. Kamei, eds. *Nihon to Amerika* [Japan and America] (Tokyo: Nan'undo, 1973), 3 volumes, contain some of the few examples of Japanese historiography of American culture, social conditions, and national self-image in the 19th and 20th centuries.

2220. Irmschler, Konrad and Lozek, Gerhard. HISTORISMUS UND SOZIALGESCHICHTE IN DER GEGENWÄRTIGEN BÜRGERLICHEN GESCHICHTSSCHREIBUNG [Historicism and social history in contemporary bourgeois historical writing]. *Zeitschrift für Geschichtswissenschaft [East Germany] 1979 27(3): 195-208.* Discusses recent trends in bourgeois historicism and social history, the two main currents of West German historiography. These trends are the search for wide-ranging theories, such as that of the industrial society or modernization theory; borrowing from cultural anthropology; the revival of Dilthey's concept of *Verstehen*; the theoretical justification of objectivity; and the recent emphasis on empirical data. Marxist-Leninist historians must understand the diversity of these concepts and trends in order to combat them. 56 notes.　　　　　　　　　　　　　　　　J. T. Walker

2221. Irmschler, Konrad. ZUM "HISTORISCH-SOZIALWISSENSCHAFTLICHEN" KONZEPT EINER BÜRGERLICHEN GESELLSCHAFTSGESCHICHTE IN DER HISTORIOGRAPHIE DER BRD [The historical and social science concept of bourgeois social history in West German historiography]. *Zeitschrift für Geschichtswissenschaft* [East Germany] 1980 28(12): 1135-1147. Refutes the ideas expressed in West Germany's *Geschichte und Gesellschaft*, which treats a modern social history within the framework of bourgeois historical thinking. The program worked out by some liberal West German social historians is a clear sign of a growing dilemma among bourgeois historians, who are forced to adopt a defensive attitude toward capitalism in their works. In addition, a group of conservative historians in West Germany regards the liberals as crypto-Marxists. Aggravated conservatism will be the result in West German historiography. 78 notes.
　　　　　　　　　　　　　　　　G. E. Pergl

2222. Irmschler, Konrad. ZUR GENESIS DER THEORETISCH-METHODOLOGISCHEN KONZEPTE VON SOZIAL-, STRUKTUR- UND GESELLSCHAFTSGESCHICHTE IN DER BÜRGERLICHEN HISTORIOGRAPHIE DER BRD [The genesis of theoretical-methodological concepts of social history, structural history, and history of society in West German nonsocialistic historiography]. *Jahrbuch für Gesch.* [East Germany] 1982 25: 341-376. Summarizes diverging lines of West German social history. The discussion in the 1960's endeavored to find new concepts toward history as a social science. Sharpening attacks by conservative historians and publicists against such approaches presumably open a period of theoretical stagnancy. Moreover, the advance of competitive political history can be expected. 133 notes.
　　　　　　　　　　　　　　　　I. Malwitz

2223. Jaurès, Jean. PAGES OBLIÉES: LE RÔLE HISTORIQUE DE LA BOURGEOISIE [Forgotten pages: the historical role of the middle classes]. *Annee Pol. et Econ.* [France] 1973 46(235-236): 237-254. Reprints chapter 10 of Jean Jaurès's *L'Armée nouvelle* (1910) which examines the historical role of the middle classes.

2224. Jay, Martin. CRITICAL THEORY CRITICIZED: ZOLTÁN TAR AND THE FRANKFURT SCHOOL. *Central European Hist.* 1979 12(1): 91-98. A scathing indictment of Zoltán Tar's *The Frankfurt School: The Critical Theories of Max Horkheimer and Theodor W. Adorno* (1977), "neither good history nor successful sociology." The work is full of factual and interpretive errors as well as being poorly conceived and developed. 22 notes.
　　　　　　　　　　　　　　　　C. R. Lovin

2225. Jones, Gareth Stedman. CLASS EXPRESSION VERSUS SOCIAL CONTROL?: A CRITIQUE OF RECENT TRENDS IN THE SOCIAL HISTORY OF "LEISURE." *Hist. Workshop J.* [Great Britain] 1977 4: 162-170. Examines recent trends in research into the history of leisure, the ways the subject has been conceived, and the conceptual instruments employed, with special reference to sociological models of social control, Marxism, and class expression.
　　　　　　　　　　　　　　　　R. G. Neville

2226. Jones, Robert Alun. DURKHEIM'S RESPONSE TO SPENCER: AN ESSAY TOWARD HISTORICISM IN THE HISTORIOGRAPHY OF SOCIOLOGY. *Sociol. Q.* 1974 15(3): 341-358. "Merton has made an important distinction between the 'history' and 'systematics' of sociological theory, and outlined the valuable functions of the former. Most histories of sociology, however, have been 'presentist' or 'Whiggish' in perspective; we propose an 'historicist' alternative. Within this perspective, Durkheim's response to Spencer is analyzed in three areas: (1) the relation between 'individual' and 'society;' (2) evolution and social change; and (3) the scope and method of sociology. In these areas, Durkheim's critical style reveals a repetitive theme which is termed 'inversion.' The essay concludes by re-affirming Merton's distinction and urging that the 'historicist' perspective is the most valid and useful approach to the history of sociology."　　　　　　　　　　J

2227. Judt, Tony. A CLOWN IN REGAL PURPLE: SOCIAL HISTORY AND THE HISTORIANS. *Hist. Workshop J.* [Great Britain] 1979 7: 66-94. Social history is suffering a decline, though the number of publications, and the shift in interests in the 1960's-70's from institutions and events to more varied social concerns, give the discipline every outward appearance of health and energy. The discipline has been abused and degraded by the modern tendency toward lack of theoretical content, obsession with method and technique, reaction against political and economic history in favor of abstraction and models, constant striving after scientific status, and indiscriminate borrowing from other disciplines. Considers how these characteristics have been formed and have come to the fore. Secondary sources; 5 illus., 84 notes.　　A. Fenn/S

2228. Kammen, Michael. CLIO AND THE CHANGING FASHIONS: SOME PATTERNS IN CURRENT AMERICAN HISTORIOGRAPHY. *Am. Scholar* 1975 44(3): 484-496. There is a notable awakening of interest in social history, and a legitimizing of the case study. American historians are examining smaller units of society in greater detail than ever before. During the last five years, historians seem to have discovered anthropology as well as ethnohistory. Articles in learned historical journals have gained as much influence as full-scale books. History is regaining a broad reading public and may supplant the novel.　　　　E. P. Stickney

2229. Karier, Clarence. THE QUEST FOR ORDERLY CHANGE: SOME REFLECTIONS. *Hist. of Educ. Q.* 1979 19(2): 159-177. Historiographical reflections about a paper given by the author in 1970, in light of historiography and events since then. The earlier essay critically analyzed the liberalism illustrated best by the writings of John Dewey and the role of that philosophy in the maintenance of a corporate political economy. The issue is still critical because of the reactionary drift of America and new definitions of what areas fall under the study of history of education. These now include the family, the workplace, the foundations, the mass media, advertising, the military, athletics, and the entertainment industry. 47 notes.　　　　　　　　L. C. Smith

2230. Kilunov, A. F. PRIMENENIE KONKRETNO-SOTSIOLOGICHESKIKH ISSLEDOVANII V ISTORICHESKOI NAUKE [The application of concrete sociological research in historical science]. *Voprosy Istorii* [USSR] 1972 (1): 34-48. The author examines the correlation of sociology and history and the possibilities of applying concrete sociological analysis in historical science. The article shows that the interaction between sociology and history is based on the close connection between the past, present, and future. The application of concrete sociological methods extends the source research basis and the range of problems, enriches methodology with new techniques, promotes closer ties between history and contemporaneity, and increases the social significance of historical research works. The author also discusses the possibility of applying individual sociological methods (observation, interviews, surveys by questionnaire, opinion polls, etc.).　　　　J

2231. Kilunov, A. F. THE USE OF CONCRETE SOCIOLOGICAL RESEARCH IN HISTORICAL SCHOLARSHIP. *Soviet Studies in Hist.* 1973 11(4): 291-318. Discusses the differences between sociology and history, refers to literature and conferences devoted to an integration of the two disciplines, and gives examples of interdisciplinary research as it has been used to study history, 1810-1970.

2232. Kraditor, Aileen S. ON THE HISTORY OF AMERICAN REFORM MOVEMENTS AND ITS LEGACY TODAY. *Continuity* 1980 (1): 37-59. Historians should not use a "good-bad" paradigm when analyzing reform movements in American history. That mode of thinking reflects too much subjective judgment. Most reformers shared common opinions of their fellow man. They perceived him as a flawed individual free to choose, but protective of the concepts of limited government and citizen responsibility. These common values stretched across three overlapping stages in US history with varying intensity: stage 1, 1780-1850; stage 2, 1828-1945; and stage 3, 1890 to the present. The underlying values should be used to research American reform movements, and because they can provide a foundation for explaining most of the inconsistencies inherent in the movements' variant branches, they may help historians minimize the possibility of incorporating their own biases into their interpretations. W. A. Wiegand

2233. Kuklick, Bruce. MYTH AND SYMBOL IN AMERICAN STUDIES. *Am. Q. 1972 24(4): 435-450.* Henry Nash Smith's *Virgin Land* (Cambridge: Harvard U. Pr., 1950), inspired a series of books relating consciousness to society, and demonstrating how "collective images" explain behavior. Explicating the premises of this "humanist school" illustrates its overemphasis on fiction as a shortcut around other historical data, and its misleading presentism in tracing archetypal ideas. Clearer thinking is required in developing an American Studies framework. 57 notes.

W. D. Piersen

2234. Kusmer, Kenneth L. AMERICAN SOCIAL HISTORY: THE BOORSTIN EXPERIENCE. *Rev. in Am. Hist. 1976 4(4): 471-482.* Defines Daniel Boorstin's *The Americans: The Colonial Experience* (1958), *The National Experience* (1965), and *The Democratic Experience* (1973) as consensus historiography and explores Boorstin's observations on selected events, 17th-20th centuries.

2235. Lane, Roger. CRIME AND THE INDUSTRIAL REVOLUTION: BRITISH AND AMERICAN VIEWS. *J. of Social Hist. 1974 7(3): 287-303.* Explores the British and American approaches to the relation between crime and the Industrial Revolution in the late 18th and 19th centuries. The British have accepted and explored the implications of such a relationship; American social scientists have not. The fact that the urban and the industrial revolutions have largely coincided in time in the United States has prevented Americans from identifying their separate effects. 73 notes. R. V. Ritter

2236. Launius, Roger D. THE NATURE OF THE POPULISTS: AN HISTORIOGRAPHICAL ESSAY. *Southern Studies 1983 22(4): 366-385.* Discusses various interpretations of Populism. During 1900-40, many historians looked upon Populism as a progressive reform movement and as an expression of the people's sentiments. In the 1950's, revisionists found the movement to be anti-Semitic, fascist, and irrational. Some blamed this on the decline of the family farm. In the 1960's-70's, scholars again saw Populism as a positive force in the shaping of late 19th-century America and as a rational response to grievances felt by farmers of the Plains and the South. Populism was a political response to economic distress. 85 notes. J. J. Buschen

2237. Leffler, Phyllis K. FROM HUMANIST TO ENLIGHTENMENT HISTORIOGRAPHY: A CASE STUDY OF FRANÇOIS EUDES DE MÉZERAY. *French Hist. Studies 1978 10(3): 416-438.* François Eudes de Mézeray's work represents that 17th-century transitional genre of historical writing, called *histoire raisonnée*, between history as art concept of the Renaissance and history as science of the Enlightenment. It emphasized cultural and social history, a more skeptical tone, and a more critical approach to sources. Providentialism gave way gradually to a secular analysis of human motivation, and history was presented objectively, as a verifiable set of facts. This *histoire raisonnée* became a link between the humanist-literary approach of the Renaissance and the secular and empirical history of the Enlightenment. Primary sources; 113 notes. H. T. Blethen

2238. Lehmann, Hermann. VON DER VERANTWORTUNG DES WISSENSCHAFTLERS (JÜRGEN KUCZYNSKI, STUDIEN ZU EINER GESCHICHTE DER GESELLSCHAFTSWISSEN-SCHAFTEN, 10 BDE) [The responsibility of the scientific scholar: Jürgen Kuczynski's *Studies on the History of Social Science*, 10 volumes]. *Jahrbuch für Wirtschaftsgeschichte [East Germany] 1979 (2): 13-38.* Kuczynski began with a discussion of bourgeois historians, continuing with an analysis of the various schools of political and economic theory which preceded historical materialism. There

are numerous biographical studies, and the series concludes with a summary discussion of the impact and problems of scientific social history. Kuczynski shows how previous historical writing served the ruling classes, the historical periods reflecting their rise and fall. Histories of the coming classless society will have a wholly different cultural perspective. Review based on works of Kuczynski, Marx, Engels, and various historians; 14 notes. E. L. Turk

2239. Lévy, René and Robert, Philippe. LE SOCIOLOGUE ET L'HISTOIRE PENALE [The sociologist and the history of the penal system]. *Ann.: Econ., Soc., Civilisations [France] 1984 39(2): 400-422.* The issue of the relationship of sociology to history, a recurrent one since the origins of social sciences, is today particularly relevant to the sociologist of the penal system. Several reasons lead to a reassessment of this sociology: the failure of classic paradigms, the difficulties of replacing them fruitfully, the sudden changes in the basic elements of the penal problem, and the violence of public debate on the issue. Since the sociologists who tried to act as historians have not been successful, we must turn now towards a dialogue of history and sociology, and "interdisciplinary" reanalysis of the results of both in this field. At first, we must tackle some preliminary conceptual and methodological problems. J

2240. Lozek, Gerhard. AKTUELLE FRAGEN DER ENTWICK-LUNG VON THEORIE UND METHODOLOGIE IN DER BÜRGERLICHEN HISTORIOGRAPHIE [Current developmental problems in theory and methodology in bourgeois historiography]. *Zeitschrift für Geschichtswissenschaft [East Germany] 1977 25(9): 1021-1027.* New developments in the international class struggle have caused bourgeois historians to search for new theories and methodologies. Consequently, many historians, especially in West Germany, have become involved in social history, but within a limited framework. Though they are criticized by their colleagues, these historians, such as H. U. Wehler and Jürgen Kocka, have retained their bourgeois and social reformist ideology. Marxist-Leninist historians must refine and deepen their own concepts in order to combat these new theories and methods. 18 notes.

J. T. Walker

2241. Makkai, László. ARS HISTORICA. MEGJEGYZÉSEK FERNAND BRAUDEL: CIVILISATION MATÉRIELLE, ÉCONOMIE ET CAPITALISME, XVᵉ-XVIIIeRET SIÈCLE C. MŰVÉHEZ [Ars Historica: notes on Fernand Braudel's *Civilisation Matérielle, Économie et Capitalisme, XVᵉ-XVIIIeRET Siècle*]. *Századok [Hungary] 1981 115(1): 206-215.* A review article and critique of Braudel's concept of material civilization. Such considerations were for a long time outside the general historical approach. New inventions are essential because communities must generate new ideas or perish. T. Kuner/S

2242. Mariz, George E. VICTORIAN SOCIAL HISTORY: "THE SILENT HISTORICAL REVOLUTION" REVISITED. *Studies in Hist. and Soc. 1973 4(2): 41-52.* A review article of J. A. Banks and O. Banks, *Feminism and Family Planning in Victorian England* (New York: Schocken Books, 1964); G. Best, *Mid-Victorian Britain, 1815-1875* (New York: Schocken Books, 1972); K. Chesney, *The Victorian Underworld*; E. R. Pike, *Golden Times...* (New York: Schocken Books, 1972); E. P. Thompson and E. Yeo, *The Unknown Mayhew* (New York: Schocken Books, 1971); and J. J. Tobias, *Urban Crime in Victorian England* (New York: Schocken Books, 1972). Demonstrates that the "silent historical revolution" in Victorian social history "is still in progress." However, the new "social history" is anti-Victorian and has led historians to ignore the Victorian upper and middle class. J. O. Baylen

2243. McShane, Clay. ESSAYS IN PUBLIC WORKS HISTORY. *Journal of Urban History 1984 10(2): 223-228.* Reviews *Essays in Public Works History*, a series of 12 essays published during 1976-82 by the Public Works Historical Society. The series covers important issues and figures in public works history, but lacks a broad perspective and includes no comprehensive policy history to consolidate the contributions of the individual essays. 8 notes.

L. J. Howell

2244. Mende, Georg. WAS HEISST: HISTORISCH DENKEN? [What is historical thinking?]. *Zeitschrift für Geschichtswissenschaft* [East Germany] 1969 17(1-2): 69-73. Historical thinking has to be based on the study of concrete social formations, their interrelations, and developments.

2245. Mercier, Roger. L'AMÉRIQUE ET LES AMÉRICAINS DANS L'*HISTOIRE DES DEUX INDES* DE L'ABBÉ RAYNAL. [America and the Americans in the *Histoire des deux Indes* of Abbé Raynal]. *Rev. Française d'Hist. d'Outre-Mer* [France] 1978 65(3): 309-324. French historian and philosopher Guillaume Thomas François Raynal (1713-96) found that America offered a rich source for speculation on the nature of civilization and primitive society, the progress or fall of man, and the concept of the noble savage. The three editions of his *Histoire des deux Indes* between 1770 and 1780 show a shifting view of the European colonies in the Americas, their economic and legal ties with the mother countries, and the reasons for the American Revolution. 66 ref.

D. G. Law

2246. Molnar, Miklos and Deutsch, Robert. HISTOIRE ET SCIENCES HISTORIQUES DANS LES PAYS SOCIALISTES D'EUROPE: ESQUISSE D'UNE TYPOLOGIE HISTORIOGRAPHIQUE [The historical sciences in Europe's socialist countries: outline of a historiographic typology]. *Mouvement Social* [France] 1980 (111): 235-254. Changes in the historiography of the European socialist countries cannot be interpreted only in ideological or institutional terms, but must be linked with a social history of the historians themselves. Marxism underwent changes due to historical events; thus there was first an international history of the ruled people, then a national history of the rulers, while the priority first attached to change moved to duration. Socialist historiography became burdened with myths and taboos which have to be deciphered. There are national differences, but common (and constant) features can be defined.

J

2247. Monkkonen, Eric H. FROM COP HISTORY TO SOCIAL HISTORY: THE SIGNIFICANCE OF THE POLICE IN AMERICAN HISTORY. *J. of Social Hist.* 1982 15(4): 575-591. Describes the historiography of urban government and, specifically, of urban police. Finds that by the 1920's major changes in the philosophy and responsibilities of the police had taken place, enlarging their role from just control of crime and law enforcement to the inclusion of social service functions. Statistical sample of 20 cities from 1860 to 1920; 49 notes.

C. M. Hough

2248. Monter, E. William. REFORMATION HISTORY AND SOCIAL HISTORY. *Archiv für Reformationsgeschichte* [West Germany] 1981 72: 5-12. European history between 1500 and 1650 cannot be studied without a firm knowledge of the Reformation. Areas in which Reformation history and social history might collaborate are the quantification of 16th-century tax and legal records and other documents. Family history might also benefit from such a collaboration. Secondary sources; 25 notes.

J. Powell

2249. Muraskin, William A. THE SOCIAL CONTROL THEORY IN AMERICAN HISTORY: A CRITIQUE. *J. of Social Hist.* 1976 9(4): 559-569. Reviews David Rothman's *Discovery of the Asylum* (1971) and Anthony Platt's *The Child Savers: The Invention of Delinquency* (1969), examining the strengths and weaknesses of social control interpretation. Rothman exemplifies the orthodox view of American historians that there was a homogeneous character to the society. The social control theory is discussed in light of Platt's work. Faults Rothman for writing middle class intellectual history without sufficient supporting data on other groups. Complains that Platt is engaged in a reduction of a culture-bound middle class outlook to petty manipulation of others.

M. Hough

2250. Naganuma, Muneaki. "SHAKAISHI" TO "SHAKAITEKI TEIKOKUSHUGI" RON—H-U. VERA NO SHORON NI TSUITE [Social history and *Sozialimperialismus*: H-U. Wehler's view]. *Rekishi Hyōron* [Japan] 1975 (306): 1-16. Explores several issues in German social history through a detailed study of Hans Ulrich Wehler's historiography. Examines the similarities and differences between Wehler's methodology and that of E. Kehr, G. W.

F. Hallgarten, and Fritz Fischer. Freely using the viewpoint of the "predominance of domestic affairs" and sociological categories, Wehler adopted "the opinion of continuity" with regard to the rise of Nazism. Gerhard Ritter insisted that the Nazis were an exceptional, pathological phenomenon in German history. Wehler used the concept of social imperialism as his own methodological premise. The influence of the Frankfurt School is present in this concept of *Sozialimperialismus* and the idea of imperialism is insufficient for the understanding of the colonies and ambiguous for an analysis of imperialistic economic relations. 51 notes.

I. Matsui

2251. Nicholls, David. THE SOCIAL HISTORY OF THE FRENCH REFORMATION: IDEOLOGY, CONFESSION AND CULTURE. *Social Hist.* [Great Britain] 1984 9(1): 25-43. Assesses the historiographical contribution of the Société de l'Histoire du Protestantisme Français (SHPF), and of university-based professional historians—principally Imbart de la Tour, Romier, Hauser, and Febvre. Identifies three recent features of French historiography: regionalism, confessionalism, and "neo-Weberianism" (illustrated with reference to the work of Janine Garrisson-Estèbe). The *Annales* phase of the 1970's, emphasizing historical determinism, reduced events such as the Reformation to the periphery; recent interest in *mentalités* has, however, reversed this. The author concludes that the Reformation was about power: God's power over humankind, the power of cities, and the power of the state in relation to local power. Secondary sources; 81 notes.

R. G. Rodger

2252. O'Brien, Patricia. CRIME AND PUNISHMENT AS HISTORICAL PROBLEM. *J. of Social Hist.* 1978 11(4): 508-520. Attempts to place Michel Foucault's recent works on crime in perspective. In the contemporary liberal view, and that of conventional historians, the developments of penology since the 1750's represent progress. Various Marxist students differ over whether crime is chiefly important as prepolitical acts of individual desperation or as an indication of bourgeois control of the means of production manifesting itself in the institutional oppression. Foucault expounds a new functionalist view, a sort of "post structuralist anarchism" replacing economic determinism with attention to the techniques of power and its various consequences. 36 notes.

M. Hough

2253. Österberg, Eva. "DEN GAMLA GODA TIDEN": BILDER OCH MOTBILDER I ETT FORSKNINGS-LÄGE OM DET ÄLDRE AGRARSAMHÄLLET [The good old days: contrasting models of traditional peasant society in modern historical research]. *Scandia* [Sweden] 1982 48(1): 31-60. Analyzes trends in Swedish historical research on traditional agrarian society in light of recent British literature on the same subject. Historians from both countries have looked back beyond the 18th century, especially to the 17th, and concur on the mechanisms leading to increased social and economic differentiation. Early court records can be used to show the frequency of land transactions and the values implicit in the punishment of sexual crimes. The early 17th century can therefore be seen as a time of conflict between integrative and disintegrative societal forces. Based on published primary sources; table, 67 notes. English summary.

L. B. Sather

2254. Ouellet, Fernand. LA FORMATION D'UNE SOCIETE DANS LA VALLEE DU SAINT-LAURENT: D'UNE SOCIETE SANS CLASSES A UNE SOCIETE DE CLASSES [The formation of a society in the Saint Lawrence Valley: from a classless to a class society]. *Can. Hist. Rev.* [Canada] 1981 62(4): 407-450. Traditional Canadian historiography has painted the early Canadian society of New France as a homogeneous and harmonious community, neglecting the factors which made for stratification and conflict. This picture began to be questioned in the 1950's. Early Canadian society was a more archaic version of the metropolitan society, a military society dominated by the clergy and nobility. The most significant factor that undermined this social structure was the commercialization of agriculture toward the end of the 18th century. The emergence of a bourgeoisie transformed a society of ranks into a class society. 144 notes.

J. V. Coutinho

2255. Patch, William L., Jr. GERMAN SOCIAL HISTORY AND LABOR HISTORY: A TROUBLED PARTNERSHIP. *J. of Modern Hist. 1984 56(3): 483-498.* Reviews three recent studies and surveys relevant literature published since 1963. German social history was molded by the school of Fritz Fischer, which sought to demonstrate that agrarian and industrial elites dominated Germany from 1866 to 1945 and sought hegemony in Europe to defend their domestic power against democracy and social democracy. Thus, German social history has been characterized by an "exaggerated belief in the ability of elites to manipulate the masses that discourages good peasant and labor history." Especially since 1977 this deficiency has been partially corrected. But there remain many gaps in our knowledge, and German social historians' interest in trade unions "remains exceptional." 53 notes. J. D. Hunley

2256. Pessen, Edward. SOCIAL MOBILITY IN AMERICAN HISTORY: SOME BRIEF REFLECTIONS. *J. of Southern Hist. 1979 45(2): 165-184.* Critical analysis of important questions raised by social mobility research is of greater interest than a report of recent research. Some imbalances are obvious. The professions and slavery have been studied, but rural and even political occupations have not been examined for social mobility. Little attention has been paid to downward mobility. Most important, however, the students of social mobility must try to make their writing less boring, less technical, and directed more at the intelligent general reader. Printed secondary sources; 57 notes. T. D. Schoonover

2257. Pietrzak-Pawłowska, Irena. KONFRONTACJE HISTORYCZNE XX WIEKU [Historical confrontations in the 20th century]. *Kwartalnik Hist. [Poland] 1967 74(3): 805-812.* The International Commission on the History of Social Changes and Structures sponsored the publication of *Mouvements Ouvriers et Depression Economique de 1929 à 1939,* Denise Fauvel-Rouif, ed. The book is based on a broad spectrum of sources on social, political, and economic aspects. This enabled the authors to document the underlying relationships between historical events on the largest scale. Based on secondary sources; 15 notes. I. Lukes

2258. Pisciotta, Alexander W. CORRECTIONS, SOCIETY, AND SOCIAL CONTROL IN AMERICA: A METAHISTORICAL REVIEW OF THE LITERATURE. *Criminal Justice Hist. 1981 2: 109-130.* Research in criminal justice traditionally suffers from a preoccupation with the identification of short-term solutions to combat crime. This essay provides a review of the significant historical accounts of corrections in the United States while categorizing them as being consistent with the assumptions and orientation of the march of progress, radical-Marxist, or social context approaches. The critique of these three metahistorical perspectives produces suggestions for developing a methodology to assess the analytical usefulness of the competing approaches. 77 notes. J. L. Ingram

2259. Quaini, Massimo and Marenco, Franco. DUE SGUARDI SUGLI *ANNALI-PAESAGGIO* [Two looks at the *Annali-Paesaggio*]. *Quaderni Storici [Italy] 1983 18(3): 1019-1034.* Comments on the fifth volume of a history of Italy published by Einaudi: *Storia d'Italia—Annali 5—Il Paesaggio, a Cura di Cesare De Seta* [History of Italy. Vol. 5: the landscape, edited by Cesare De Seta] (1982). The volume takes the landscape as the theme or rather the metaphor around which social history is written. Discusses the advantages and weaknesses of this device, the possibilities of which have been discovered and exploited chiefly in the last 20-odd years. J. V. Coutinho

2260. Rabinbach, Anson. GEORGES HAUPT: HISTORY AND THE SOCIALIST TRADITION. *Mouvement Social [France] 1980 (111): 75-83.* The history of the labor movement can be written apart from the doctrinaire view of traditional socialist historiography, which reduced history to an expression of power and served the very interests of power. Georges Haupt placed a great deal of emphasis on the recognition of regional and national differences as a decisive aspect of social history, and also on the reality of a spirit of international cooperation and respect in the labor movement, thus affirming a commitment to a polyphonous Marxism that could tolerate difference. The writing of the history of the labor movement was for him a way to bring a remedy to a working class which had become indifferent to its own past and to restore its relationship to the socialist tradition. J

2261. Ritcheson, Charles R. THE BRITISH ROLE IN AMERICAN LIFE, 1800-1850. *Hist. Teacher 1974 7(4): 574-596.* Discusses British influence in American life, and American historians' interpretations of that influence. In the early national period of the United States British historians such as Macaulay, Buckle, and Green remained popular in spite of critical evaluations of the Anglo-American relationship by American commentators. Later American historians such as Dunning, Mahan, and Roosevelt spoke more favorably of the Anglo-American connection which was based on economic, social, cultural, religious, ideological, political, and diplomatic factors. To interpreters of this persuasion an Anglo-American community existed from the very beginning of American history. Primary and secondary sources; 53 notes. P. W. Kennedy

2262. Rock, Paul. SOME PROBLEMS OF INTERPRETATIVE HISTORIOGRAPHY. *British J. of Sociol. [Great Britain] 1976 27(3): 353-369.* Examines problems of historiography to show its relevance to and usefulness in sociology and its study of the present and past.

2263. Rodgers, Daniel T. IN SEARCH OF PROGRESSIVISM. *Rev. in Am. Hist. 1982 10(4): 113-132.* Examines the failure of historians writing in the 1970's to agree on a definition for Progressivism; looks at themes and events that have been linked with Progressivism.

2264. Rothman, David J. *THE UPROOTED:* THIRTY YEARS LATER. *Rev. in Am. Hist. 1982 10(3): 311-319.* Oscar Handlin's *The Uprooted* (1951), which portrayed the demoralization of immigrants, was a pioneering work in its use of sociological concepts and its commitment to the idea of history as a humanistic discipline.

2265. Sarna, Jonathan D. THE JEWISH WAY OF CRIME. *Commentary 1984 78(2): 53-55.* Examines recent works on Jewish social history that deal with crime and criminals.

2266. Saurer, Edith. DIECI ANNI DI STUDI AUSTRIACI DI STORIA DELLA CRIMINALITA E DEL DIRITTO PENALE [Ten years of Austrian studies of the history of criminality and of penal law]. *Quaderni Storici [Italy] 1982 17(1): 217-225.* Surveys Austrian historiography of crime and criminals and of criminal law. Discusses the development of the concept of *Kriminalität* [criminality] in Austrian law as well as problems encountered in the historical sources. One of six articles in this issue on criminal sources and social history. 37 ref. R. Grove

2267. Segal, Howard P. TOCQUEVILLE AND THE PROBLEM OF SOCIAL CHANGE: A RECONSIDERATION. *South Atlantic Q. 1978 77(4): 492-503.* Treats the portion of Alexis de Tocqueville's work pertaining to social change—that is, significant changes that affect the outlook and lives of its members. Changes considered include democratization, industrialization, and urbanization. Tocqueville pointed out that all change is gradual, not abrupt, hence the failure of the French Revolution. Whereas many historians see breaks between historical eras, Tocqueville saw history as a continuum, the end of which is not in sight. He also envisaged the probability of order or disorder in any society at any time, which in turn could result in further social change, the nature of which would be unpredictible. Based on Tocqueville's works and secondary sources; 22 notes. H. M. Parker, Jr.

2268. Seidman, Steven. BEYOND PRESENTISM AND HISTORICISM: UNDERSTANDING THE HISTORY OF SOCIAL SCIENCE. *Sociol. Inquiry 1983 53(1): 79-94.* Contrasts "presentist" theories of social science history, which view science as a continuous progression of knowledge to the present, with "historicist" theories that focus on the discontinuities and historical context of social science; focuses on historiography of the social sciences since the 1960's.

2269. Shanin, Teodor. PEASANTRY: DELINEATION OF A SO-CIOLOGICAL CONCEPT AND A FIELD OF STUDY. *Peasant Studies Newsletter 1973 2(1): 1-8.* Reprinted from *European Journal of Sociology* 1971 12: 289-300.

2270. Shanley, Mary Lyndon. THE HISTORY OF THE FAMILY IN MODERN ENGLAND. *Signs 1979 4(4): 740-750.* Reviews the new literature on the family in modern England from the perspective of a political scientist, in particular: Lawrence Stone, *The Family, Sex and Marriage in England 1500-1800* (New York: Harper and Row, 1977); Randolph Trumbach, *The Rise of the Egalitarian Family: Aristocratic Relations in Eighteenth Century England* (New York: Academic Pr., 1978); Louise A. Tilly and Joan W. Scott, *Women, Work and Family* (New York: Holt, Rinehart and Winston, 1978). Individualism as it emerged promoted a new *mentalité* among the aristocrats and a more egalitarian family relationship. Political scientists should note the danger of separating the public sphere from the private.   S. P. Conner

2271. Shapiro, Gilbert. PROSPECTS FOR A SCIENTIFIC SOCIAL HISTORY: 1976. *J. of Social Hist. 1976 10(2): 196-204.* A personal credo on historiography, on the "attempts to incorporate history into social science." "The most important problems—of social change and development, the dynamics of institutional and cultural orders—escape the relatively simplistic theoretical models implicit in most quantitative work" and for this reason will remain marginal to the main stream of historical social science. "Unless we find ways of measuring the subjective, and incorporating it in the theories from which our problems derive, both its description and speculation about its influence will be left to the 'humanists,' and scientific work will serve history . . . only as an ancillary discipline comparable to carbon dating, paleography and numismatics." 6 notes.   R. V. Ritter

2272. Šilbajoris, Rimvydas. THE SCHOLAR'S RECORD AND THE BLIND EYES OF TIME. *J. of Baltic Studies 1975 6(2/3): 239-245.* Humanistic values, rather than considerations of size or power, justify study of the Baltic peoples.
     E. W. Jennison, Jr.

2273. Soboul, Albert. DESCRIPTION ET MESURE EN HISTOIRE SOCIALE [Description and measure in social history]. *Information Historique [France] 1966 28(3): 104-109.* Defines the scope and aims of social history and outlines the development of the discipline in French historiography during the past 40 years. At first social history was associated with the history of circumstances and later with the study of social structures. The author refers to major works in both fields, and elucidates the quantitative and qualitative viewpoints. Primary and secondary sources; 39 notes.
     P. T. Herman

2274. Spoehr, Luther. MUCKRAKING AND MUDSLINGING: LOUIS FILLER VERSUS RECENT AMERICAN HISTORY. *Rev. in Am. Hist. 1977 5(3): 391-396.* Review article prompted by Louis Filler's *The Muckrakers,* a new and enlarged edition of *Crusaders for American Liberalism* (University Park: Pennsylvania State U. Pr., 1976) and Filler's *Appointment at Armageddon: Muckraking and Progressivism in the American Tradition,* Contributions in American Studies no. 20 (Westport, Conn.: Greenwood Pr., 1976); compares Filler's traditional historical interpretation of Progressivism and the recent reassessment of muckrakers and Progressivism.

2275. Stearns, Peter N. TOWARD A WIDER VISION: TRENDS IN SOCIAL HISTORY. Kammen, Michael, ed. *The Past Before Us: Contemporary Historical Writing in the United States* (Ithaca, N.Y.: Cornell U. Pr., 1980): 205-230. The interest in social history during the 1960's led to its appearance in general history courses and texts, but its main strength still lies in research. American social history did not develop independently, having its roots in European research, yet it is distinguished by its emphasis on examining history from the viewpoint of the common people. It is further characterized by an interest in novelty which has led to the steady development of topical subfields such as labor history, women's history, black history, and working-class history. 72 notes.   S

2276. Stock, Brian. LITERARY DISCOURSE AND THE SOCIAL HISTORIAN. *New Literary Hist. 1977 8(2): 183-194.* Discusses historical literature since the 19th century, examining two dominant trends; the tendency toward closer examination of the external world, and the concurrent awareness of inner development patterns.

2277. Szacki, Jerzy. REFLECTIONS ON THE HISTORY OF SOCIOLOGY. *Int. Social Sci. J. [France] 1981 33(2): 248-259.* Discusses sociologists' interest in the history of their own discipline, as exhibited in historical studies of sociology from 1959 to 1976; and suggests that such studies are important for generating continuity and tradition among sociologists and for acquiring a better appreciation of the diversity of sociological research.

2278. Taylor, Robert J. ONE HISTORIAN'S EDUCATION. *William and Mary Q. 1984 41(3): 478-486.* The author recounts his education and career. Criticizes the new social history's emphasis on methodology and calls for greater respect for narrative history. Contribution to "Early American Emeriti: A Symposium of Experience and Evaluation."

2279. Tilly, Charles. VECCHIO E NUOVO NELLA STORIA SOCIALE [Old and new in social history]. *Passato e Presente [Italy] 1982 (1): 31-54.* Discusses the changes that have taken place in the practice of historiography, in the field of social history, 1968-80. The new social history, emphasizing individual human experience and the narrative method, has not displaced the older social history that favored quantitative analysis of social trends. In fact, the latter has revealed the historical specificity of social structure and helped to relate individual experience to societal phenomena. 52 notes.
     J. V. Coutinho

2280. Tilly, Louise A. PEOPLE'S HISTORY AND SOCIAL SCIENCE HISTORY. *Social Sci. Hist. 1983 7(4): 457-474.* There are differences and tensions in the fundamental approaches of practitioners of "people's history" and "social science history." There are, however, also mutual, shared interests that should lead historians to overcome their differences and establish a "social science people's history." Based on published sources; 3 notes, biblio.
     L. K. Blaser

2281. Vanlangenhove, Fernand. LES INVARIANTS DE L'HISTOIRE ET DE L'ETHNOLOGIE [The constants of history and ethnology]. *Acad. Royale de Belgique Bull. de la Classe des Lettres et des Sci. Morales et Pol. [Belgium] 1977 63(11-12): 423-440.* Discusses the recent reappearance—in the work of Paul Veyne and others—of the notion that there are constants in history. The idea was originally broached by sociologists Emile Waxweiler (1867-1916) and Georges Smets (b. 1881). It concerns certain natural aspects of human social behavior, thought, and activity which are unmentioned in the historical documents themselves but which historians must unconsciously presume in order to make ancient behavior and thought intelligible to modern man.   A. H. Kittell

2282. Veltmeyer, Henry. TOWARDS AN ASSESSMENT OF THE STRUCTURALIST INTERROGATION OF MARX: CLAUDE LEVI-STRAUSS AND LOUIS ALTHUSSER. *Sci. and Soc. 1974/75 38(4): 385-421.* Compares the ideologies and the use of structuralism to analyze history and social organization by Karl Marx, Claude Levi-Strauss and Louis Althusser, 19th-20th centuries.

2283. Vericat, José. HISTORIOGRAFÍA Y SOCIOLOGÍA [Historigraphy and sociology]. *Rev. Española de la Opinión Pública [Spain] 1973 (34): 83-102.* Discusses the methodology of historiography and sociology, focusing primarily on the development of the methodology of social sciences and giving the historical bases for 20th-century social thought.

2284. Veysey, Laurence. THE "NEW" SOCIAL HISTORY IN THE CONTEXT OF AMERICAN HISTORICAL WRITING. *Rev. in Am. Hist. 1979 7(1): 1-12.* Discusses the different conceptions of American historians concerning political, social, and intellectual history in the United States, specifically the new social history that emerged as a result of the split between leftists and nonleftists in the 1960's.

2285. Vilar, Pierre. MISÈRE ET RÉVOLUTION DU XVIIIᵉ SIÈCLE: RÉFLEXIONS SUR LE MODÈLE LABROUSSIEN [Misery and revolution in the 18th century: reflections on Labrousse's model]. *Europa [Canada] 1978 1(2): 149-171.*

2286. Vovelle, Michel. ENCORE LA MORT: UN PEU PLUS QU'UNE MODE? [Death again: more than just a fashion?]. *Ann.: Econ., Soc., Civilisations [France] 1982 37(2): 276-287.* Reviews 10 English, French, and Italian language works on death and attitudes toward death. Recent publications cover a wider geographical area and a longer stretch of time. They also display a great variety and sophistication of method. J. V. Coutinho/S

2287. Wescott, Roger W. BOUNDARIES BETWEEN CIVILIZATIONS. *Int. Social Sci. Rev. 1984 59(1): 35-41.* Those philosophers, historians, and sociologists who have attempted to distinguish between civilizations have been hampered by the fact that civilizations are "fuzzy sets": the spatial and temporal boundaries between them are usually blurred. To this analytical problem the writer proposes a solution based on the culture-area principle used by museums of ethnology, a solution which, by focusing on centers or cores rather than on margins or peripheries, acknowledges cultural overlap and stylistic fade-out. J

2288. White, G. Edward. THE SOCIAL VALUES OF THE PROGRESSIVES: SOME NEW PERSPECTIVES. *South Atlantic Q. 1971 70(1): 62-76.* Viewing the Progressive movement in its complexities prevented the consensus school of history from creating any real synthesis of the movement. However, in the light of new monographs, different attitudes toward ethnic groups, and contemporary *angst,* the unifying elements of the movement can be isolated from the mainstream of American thought. The characteristic values are Anglo-Saxonism, moral righteousness, popular elitism, and belief in progress. Identifying social values rather than social backgrounds enables the historian to focus on the Progressives' attempts to reconcile social reality with their ideas. Based on secondary sources; 41 notes. W. L. Olbrich

2289. Wilentz, Sean. ON CLASS AND POLITICS IN JACKSONIAN AMERICA. *Rev. in Am. Hist. 1982 10(4): 45-63.* Looks at the failure of historians to deal with issues of class and social history in Jacksonian political historiography.

2290. Wright, James E. THE ETHNOCULTURAL MODEL OF VOTING: A BEHAVIORAL AND HISTORICAL CRITIQUE. *Am. Behavioral Scientist 1973 16(5): 653-674.* One of six essays in this issue dealing with emerging theoretical models in social and political history. S

2291. Yang, Martin C. I SHÊ HUI HSÜEH YEN KUANG LUN LI SHIH TI CH'UANG TSAO CHÊ [A sociological interpretation of who makes history]. *Thought and Word [Taiwan] 1972 10(2): 1-9.* Criticizes the traditional approach to writing the history of a society or people which unduly stresses the importance of a few leading persons and neglects the role of the masses who actively participate in historical events. The criticism is buttressed with examples from Chinese histories and current agricultural progress in Taiwan. Biographers should emphasize the influences their subjects exert on the masses. C. C. Brown

2292. Zeil, Wilhelm. ZUR PROBLEMATIK DER ANWENDUNG SOZIOLOGISCH-STATISTISCHER FORSCHUNGSMETHODEN IN DER GESCHICHTSWISSENSCHAFT [Problems concerning the application of sociological and statistical ways of research in historiography]. *Jahrbuch für Geschichte der Sozialistischen Länder Europas [East Germany] 1973 17(1): 217-226.* Discusses the relationship between sociology and historiography, and ways of integrating them, to commemorate the publication of *Istoriko-sociologičeskie issledovanija (na materialach slavjanskich stran),* (1970).

2293. Zemsky, Robert. AMERICAN LEGISLATIVE BEHAVIOR. *Am. Behavioral Scientist 1973 16(5): 675-694.* One of six essays in this issue dealing with emerging theoretical models in social and political history.

2294. Zhukov, E. M. O SOOTNOSHENII OBSHCHESOTSIOLOGICHESKIKH I ISTORICHESKIKH ZAKONOMERNOSTEI [The correlation of general sociological and historical regularities]. *Voprosy Filosofii [USSR] 1977 4: 50-61.* Compares the specific features of historical laws with sociological ones. Substantiates some aspects of the materialistic understanding of history, such as the correlation between necessity and chance, the objective and the subjective, and freedom and necessity in social development. Criticizes the idealistic and metaphysical concepts of the historical process. Stresses the topicality of investigating the historical and sociological regularities and suggests ways of solving the complicated problem of the interrelationship of various sciences in studying the development of human society. J

2295. Zielyk, Ihor V. DO PYTANNIA VZAIEMOVIDNOSYN MIZH ISTÓRIIEIU TA SOTSIOLOHIIEIU [The question of the relationship between history and sociology]. *Ukrains'kyi Istoryk 1982 19(1-2): 40-53.*

2296. —. COMMENT AND DEBATE. *Am. J. of Sociol. 1979 84(5): 1238-1244.*
Becker, George. COMMENT ON LENSKI'S "HISTORY AND SOCIAL CHANGE," *pp. 1238-1241.* Asserts that Gerhard Lenski's criticism of Robert Nisbet's *Social Change and History* failed to recognize Nisbet's criticism of neoevolutionism, failed to provide adequate evidence for his own characterization of new revolutionists, and asserted a faulty reliance on a distinction between general and specific evolution.
Lenski, Gerhard. PROBABILISM REASSERTED: A REPLY TO BECKER, *pp. 1242-1244.* Replies to individual criticisms and comments on the current disparity of thought on determinism among sociologists.

Intellectual History
(including Education)

2297. Allen, James Smith. HISTORY AND THE NOVEL: *MENTALITE* IN MODERN POPULAR FICTION. *Hist. and Theory 1983 22(3): 233-252.* Examines the difficulties inherent in social historians making use of novels as documents and assesses the potential offered to such historians by newer trends in literary theory, particularly reader-response criticism. Unlike the internalist formalism of the earlier New Critics, the more externalist, code-oriented perspectives of the structuralists, deconstructionists, and the reception critics present historians with a less arbitrary way of weighing the meanings attached to fictional prose and its themes and values by both authors and audiences. Such types of literary criticism help to reconstruct the mental and moral universes of past creators and consumers of fiction. 70 notes. W. J. Reedy

2298. Alter, Jean V. SOCIOLOGIE DU DÉGUISEMENT: LECTURE CRÉATRICE [Sociology of disguise: creative reading]. *Rev. de l'U. de Bruxelles [Belgium] 1979 (3-4): 333-341.* Affirms the importance of teaching literature of the past and discusses inherent problems in relating past events, social conditions, and values to the present; utilizes Charles Sorel's *Histoire Comique de Francion* (1623) to illustrate the relationship between fiction and history, the dichotomy between appearance and actual state of being, and the role of fiction in disguising history.

2299. Bender, Thomas; Hall, Peter D.; Haskell, Thomas L.; and Mattingly, Paul H. INSTITUTIONALIZATION AND EDUCATION IN THE NINETEENTH AND TWENTIETH CENTURIES. *Hist. of Educ. Q. 1980 20(4): 449-472.* Report on the symposium, "Institutionalization and Education in the Nineteenth and Twentieth Centuries," held at the annual American Educational Research Association, Boston, 8 April 1980. The topic was discussed under three sections: problems of the literature, the problems of interpretation, and the theoretical problem. Secondary studies; 26 notes.

H. M. Parker, Jr.

2300. Berkhofer, Robert F., Jr. CLIO AND THE CULTURE CONCEPT: SOME IMPRESSIONS OF A CHANGING RELATIONSHIP IN AMERICAN HISTORIOGRAPHY. *Social Sci. Q. 1972 53(2): 297-320*. "[The author] contends that the impact of the culture concept upon the American historical profession may be discerned in the popularity of intellectual history, American studies, and the consensus interpretation of the United States past after World War II. He notes in connection with this a conjunction of trends toward a new definition of culture by social scientists, its coming into general scholarly usage, and the internal development of history writing at the time. He believes that just as the culture concept is being refined or discarded in the quest by other social scientists today for greater analytical precision, a parallel trend also appears to be starting in the history profession."

J

2301. Bianchi, L. SULLA STORIOGRAFIA DI PIERRE BAYLE [On the historiography of Pierre Bayle]. *Studi Storici [Italy] 1982 23(2): 415-438*. Reviews three works on Pierre Bayle: Gianni Paganini's *Analisi della Fede e Critica della Ragione nella Filosifia di Pierre Bayle* [Analysis of faith and critique of reason in the philosophy of Pierre Bayle] (1980); Anna Foa's *Ateismo e Maggia. Il Declino della Concezione Magica nel "Dictionnaire" di Pierre Bayle* [Atheism and magic. The decline of the conception of magic in the "Dictionnaire" of Pierre Bayle] (1980); and Massimo Firpo's "Pierre Bayle, gli Eretici Italiani del Cinquecento e la Tradizione Sociniana" [Pierre Bayle, the Italian heretics of the 16th century, and the Socinian tradition] in *Rivista Storica Italiana* 1973 85(3): 612-666. Primary sources; 45 notes.

E. E. Ryan

2302. Bien, Horst. VOM WIRKEN DER RUSSISCHEN KRITISCHEN REALISTEN IN NORWEGEN: ANMERKUNGEN ZU MARTIN NAGS REZEPTIONSHISTORISCHEN SCHRIFTEN [The work of Russian critical realists in Norway: Notes on the reception-historical writings of Martin Nag]. *Nordeuropa [East Germany] 1981 14: 53-61*. Norwegian Slavist Martin Nag has published many works on literary relations between Russia and Norway, an expression of a progressing internationalization of the literary process.

2303. Bitterli, Urs. ROUSSEAU IN WECHSELNDER BELEUCHTUNG [Rousseau in changing light]. *Schweizer Monatshefte [Switzerland] 1978 58(10): 797-803*. New German publications on Jean Jacques Rousseau do not develop a critical approach toward Rousseau's philosophy.

2304. Bouwsma, William J. RIBELLI, LIBERTINI E ORTODOSSI NELLA STORIOGRAFIA BAROCCA [Rebels, libertines, and orthodoxies in Baroque historiography]. *Hist. and Theory 1974 13(3): 305-314*. A review article of Sergio Bertelli's *Ribelli, Libertini e Ortodossi nella Storiografia Barocca* (Florence: La Nuova Italia, 1973) which is concerned with the confrontation between the confessional orthodoxies of early modern Europe and the intellectual challenges which prepared for the Enlightenment. Bertelli allows his thesis to unfold in the course of his narrative of the history of historiography in the period. "It seems to emerge first in his identification of what, in Renaissance historiography, was most fruitful for the future and then in his account of its precarious survival through the seventeenth century." The author challenges Bertelli's view of the place of both the Renaissance and the Enlightenment in the history of historiography. 15 notes.

R. V. Ritter

2305. Bouwsma, William J. INTELLECTUAL HISTORY IN THE 1980S: FROM HISTORY OF IDEAS TO HISTORY OF MEANING. *J. of Interdisciplinary Hist. 1981 12(2): 279-291*. Reports on the past and future of intellectual history. Depending heavily on traditional philosophy, intellectual history underwent a transformation in the last decade toward a new historical genre. In its new state, intellectual history as the history of meaning is concerned with the cultivation and transmission of meaning, turning especially to the arts, anthropology, and linguistics as vehicles for the expres-

sion of meaning. These tendencies of scholarship are expected to grow stronger. New connections with philosophy are also a possibility for the development of new intellectual history. 13 notes.

H. J. Kaiser

2306. Bredsdorff, Thomas. LOVEJOY'S IDEA OF "IDEA." *New Literary Hist. 1977 8(2): 195-212*. Through reformulation of the hypotheses of Arthur O. Lovejoy, the author examines Lovejoy's history of ideas in terms of its inherent idealism and its acceptance of the scholarly pursuit of truth as self-evident.

2307. Breinig, Helmbrecht. "THE SOBER PAGE OF HISTORY": IRVINGS KÜRZERE HISTORISCH-BIOGRAPHISCHE SCHRIFTEN ZWISCHEN FAKTOGRAPHIE UND DICHTUNG ["The Sober Page of History": the factual versus the poetical in Irving's shorter historical and biographical writings]. *Amerikastudien/Am. Studies [West Germany] 1975 20(1): 7-28*. Irving's hitherto neglected shorter historical and biographical works gain new interest when seen in connection with the current discussion of genres and of the distinctive qualities of literature and historiography. They also reflect the state of American literature in the early nineteenth century. The application of a conceptual framework provided by modern literary theory reveals a remarkable generic and structural variety, ranging from the personal essay to semi-fictionalized forms of narrative history and to works taking their structural patterns from legendary material. While Irving remained aloof from the progressivism of his contemporary fellow-historians, his desire to reveal the inherent aesthetic appeal of historical events and characters led him to a lifelong series of experiments in combining the poetical and the factual in his historical writings. The present analysis demonstrates that more often than not he was thwarted in these attempts by his lack of a genuine theory of history and by his own conflicting impulses to write imaginatively and, under the influence of contemporary American attitudes, to avoid getting too absorbed in a world of pure imagination. Where he does achieve a balance, it usually is an achievement more pleasing to the literary critic than to the historian.

J

2308. Brickman, William W. NOTES ON THE HISTORIOGRAPHY OF HIGHER EDUCATION DURING THE 16TH-18TH CENTURIES. *Paedagogica Hist. [Belgium] 1980 20(1): 376-380*. Examines historical writings on higher education produced from the 16th to the 18th centuries. Particular reference is made to Christoph August Heumann and to his *Bibliotheca Historica Academica*, appended to the 1739 edition of Hermann Conring's *De Antiquitatibus Academicis Dissertationes Septem*, as well as to Jacob Middendorp's *Academiarum Orbis Christiani Libri Duo* (1572).

G. L. Neville

2309. Brickman, William W. THEORETICAL AND CRITICAL PERSPECTIVES ON EDUCATIONAL HISTORY. *Paedagogica Hist. [Belgium] 1978 18(1): 42-83*. Defines the scope and contents of educational history, its relation to other fields in history, its relation to the social sciences and humanities, its relation to other educational fields, its values and uses, the qualifications of the educational historian, and concludes with considerations on criticism and controversy in educational history. 85 notes.

J. M. McCarthy

2310. Briggs, Asa. THE STUDY OF THE HISTORY OF EDUCATION. *Hist. of Educ. [Great Britain] 1972 1(1): 5-22*. Stresses the need to consider the history of education not as a self-contained subject, but within the mainstream of historical study. Educational historians must give careful consideration to six specific developments in historiography: the more sophisticated study of local history; a more analytical approach to comparative history; increased attention to statistical studies; the increased use of sociological, anthropological, and psychological concepts; the increasingly analytical approach to political history, with attention focused on administrative and decisionmaking processes; and the changed attitude toward intellectual and cultural history, which lays less stress on the ideas of great thinkers, and more emphasis on the communication of ideas, the significance of language, and forms of control. 48 notes.

L. J. Shepherd

2311. Buss, Allan R. IN DEFENSE OF A CRITICAL-PRESENTIST HISTORIOGRAPHY: THE FACT-THEORY RELATIONSHIP AND MARX'S EPISTEMOLOGY. *J. of the Hist. of the Behavioral Sci. 1977 13(3): 252-260.* Social scientists during the 1920's-30's often ignored the social science epistemology developed by Karl Marx, especially his fact-theory relationship. The author's methodology of critical presentism, which involves judging the past in the context of the present, derives from the Neo-Marxian Frankfurt School. 39 notes. S

2312. Caplat, Guy. LE SERVICE D'HISTOIRE DE L'EDUCATION: HISTORIQUE ET MISSIONS [The "Service d'Histoire de l'Education": historical account and missions]. *Hist. de l'Éduc. [France] 1978 (1): 3-11.* Describes the origins, evolution, and mission of the Educational History Office created in 1977 as part of France's National Institute for Pedagogical Research and oriented toward the promotion of research in the history of education.

2313. Caspard, Pierre. LES ACTIVITES DU SERVICE D'HISTOIRE DE L'EDUCATION [Activities of the Educational History Office]. *Hist. de l'Éduc. [France] 1978 (1): 13-16.* Describes the current activities of the Educational History Office of France's National Institute for Pedagogical Research and its contributions to the study of the history of education.

2314. Ciafardone, Raffaele. L'ILLUMINISMO TEDESCO NELLA LETTERATURA FILOSOFICA DEGLI ULTIMI TRENT'ANNI [The German Enlightenment in the philosophical literature of the last 30 years]. *Verifiche [Italy] 1979 8(2-3): 250-264.* Discusses postwar historiography of the German Enlightenment, 1690-1780.

2315. Clemens, Anna Valdine. ZELDA FITZGERALD: AN UNROMANTIC REVISION. *Dalhousie Rev. [Canada] 1982 62(2): 196-211.* Essentially an examination of four biographies of F. Scott Fitzgerald and Zelda Fitzgerald. *The Far Side of Paradise* (1951), by Arthur Mizener, *Scott Fitzgerald* (1962), by Andrew Turnbull, *Zelda* (1970), by Nancy Milford, and *Exiles in Paradise* (1971), by Sara Mayfield. Each biography is widely discussed with an emphasis on its treatment of Zelda. 30 notes. C. H. Held

2316. Clifford, Geraldine Jonçich. SAINTS, SINNERS, AND PEOPLE: A POSITION PAPER ON THE HISTORIOGRAPHY OF AMERICAN EDUCATION. *Hist. of Educ. Q. 1975 15(3): 257-272.* Historiography of American education tends to cover institutional histories and biographies of great educators; it should also cover "the majority of the middle," who have been responsible during the 17th-20th centuries for education of the American public.

2317. Cohen, Howard. KEEPING THE HISTORY OF PHILOSOPHY. *J. of the Hist. of Philosophy 1976 14(4): 383-390.* Discusses the historiography of philosophy through either recovery of the past or reconstruction of the past.

2318. Cohen, Sol. THE HISTORY OF THE HISTORY OF AMERICAN EDUCATION, 1900-1976: THE USES OF THE PAST. *Harvard Educ. R. 1976 46(3): 298-330.* Discusses trends in the historiography of American education 1900-76, emphasizing struggles in the 1930's and 40's between academicians and advocates of teacher training, and attention to social problems.

2319. Cohen, Sol. NEW PERSPECTIVES IN THE HISTORY OF AMERICAN EDUCATION, 1960-1970. *Hist. of Educ. [Great Britain] 1973 2(1): 79-96.* Since an initiative in 1953 from the Ford Foundation's Fund for the Advancement of Education, there has been an important reconsideration of American educational history in an attempt to move away from earlier preoccupation with the public school system. Points to the new concern with the broader societal aspects of the history of education. Some hitherto neglected areas of study are now being tackled. Notes the use of "methods and insights borrowed from the social sciences." Warns of possible pitfalls in the new approach. Based on secondary sources; 65 notes. L. J. Shepherd

2320. Conkin, Paul K. INTELLECTUAL HISTORY: PAST, PRESENT, AND FUTURE. Delzell, Charles F., ed. *The Future of History: Essays in the Vanderbilt University Centennial Symposium* (Nashville: Vanderbilt U. Pr., 1977): 111-133. There is widespread belief among historians that intellectual history has a troubled present and no future, despite its past achievements. American attempts to characterize the mentality of large groups go back to the Puritans, but the work of Vernon Louis Parrington is the usually accepted modern American beginning. Surveys of courses in American intellectual history in 1955 and by the author in 1974 reveal chaos in course titles and content. Intellectual historians are criticized for being elitist in subject and archaic in method. Because great ideas are produced by few minds, however, the intellectual historian has little choice: concern with popular belief is social history. In addition, intellectual historians focus on meaning and language, necessitating a humanistic rather than a quantitative approach. Increased concern for conceptual precision, greater sophistication in research design, and skepticism about theories developed in other disciplines insures that intellectual history will remain very much a part of the search for man's multidimensional past. 15 notes. P. L. Solodkin

2321. Crubellier, Maurice. L'HISTOIRE EN CRISE D'UNE ECOLE EN CRISE [The unsettled history of a school in trouble]. *Hist. de l'Educ. [France] 1983 (18): 29-48.* Describes a number of publications, recent and reissued, dealing with French primary and secondary education during the 19th and early 20th centuries.

2322. Dampierre, E. de. NOTE SUR *CULTURE* ET *CIVILISATION* [Note on *culture* and *civilization*]. *Comparative Studies in Soc. and Hist. [Great Britain] 1960-61 3(3): 328-340.* Discusses whether a distinction exists between the meanings of the words culture and civilization in English, French, and German historical studies.

2323. De Leon, David. THE COMMUNAL NATURE OF OUR CONSCIOUSNESS: THOUGHTS ON AMERICAN INTELLECTUAL HISTORY. *Rendezvous 1975 10(2): 1-14.* Overview of intellectual history, 1870's-1975, is used to delineate evolution in historiographical interpretation and to emphasize the need to establish some form of value judgment for writing and interpreting history.

2324. Desné, Roland; Simonffy, Zsuzsa, transl. SZUBJEKTIVITÁS VAGY OBJEKTIVITÁS: NEHÉZ HELYZETBEN AZ IRODALOMTÖRTÉNÉSZ [Subjectivity or objectivity: the dilemma of the historian of literature]. *Helikon Világirodalmi Figyelő [Hungary] 1983 29(3-4): 299-303.* Since the selection of the authors and works in any history of literature inevitably reflects the historian's taste and judgment, complete objectivity is beyond our reach. The aim of objectivity can be pursued by examining all the causes and circumstances of the literary works and placing them in the context of the entire cultural and historical background. This multidisciplinary and multilateral approach should also be collective, with a large number of authors participating in any ambitious project of literary history. Read at the second colloquy In Memoriam Werner Krauss in Berlin, 4-5 June 1980. G. Jeszenszky

2325. Dethan, Georges. UNE CONCEPTION NOUVELLE DE LA BIOGRAPHIE? [A new understanding of biography?]. *Rev. d'Hist. Diplomatique [France] 1982 96(1-2): 57-67.* Today biographers must be and are more interested in the private person than in the public one. The first models of this new style of biography are in literary history. It is acceptable for a biographer to be sympathetic toward the subject. Biography is justified by the simple proposition that if humans have always made history, so too have they always told it. 18 notes. W. J. Roosen

2326. Emerson, Roger L. CONJECTURAL HISTORY AND SCOTTISH PHILOSOPHERS. *Historical Papers [Canada] 1984: 63-90.* Recently, many historians have focused on the emergence in 18th-century Scotland of a large number of conjectural histories—accounts of the development of institutions, beliefs, or practices not based on documents or contemporary artifacts—and have analyzed them within the framework of a Marxist-oriented social science. Such a perspective is misguided because the writers of the "golden age" (1730-90) based their works on those of previous generations and could not have held doctrines of economic determinism or historical materialism while reconciling their positions with Calvinist beliefs. The conjectural historians David Hume and Adam Smith, for example, were the products of their intellectual milieu. A paper presented at the annual meeting of the Canadian Historical Association, Guelph, 1984; 90 notes.
D. R. Schweitzer

2327. Etulain, Richard W. THE AMERICAN LITERARY WEST AND ITS INTERPRETERS: THE RISE OF A NEW HISTORIOGRAPHY. *Pacific Hist. Rev. 1976 45(3): 311-348.* Discusses the major booklength works that illustrate the major trends of interpretation exerting the most influence on scholars. The new criticism had little influence on the study of western literature. Hence historical and biographical backgrounds continued, and they still remain important in western literary history. Its historiography may be seen at its best in two books published in 1950: Franklin Walker's *A Literary History of Southern California* and Henry Nash Smith's *Virgin Land: The American West as Symbol and Myth.* Walker's historical and Smith's more holistic emphasis have been the guiding lights of the field. 50 notes.
R. V. Ritter

2328. Etulain, Richard W. RESEARCH OPPORTUNITIES IN WESTERN LITERARY HISTORY. *Western Hist. Q. 1973 4(3): 263-272.* Setting aside for the moment the debate between literary historians and literary critics as to which is the better approach, some western American literature is more suited to the techniques of the former. The literary historian, however, must use the findings of the cultural sociologist, the historian of ideas, the cultural anthropologist, and the literary critic. Even with the increased interest in western literature inspired by Henry Nash Smith's *Virgin Land* (Cambridge: Harvard U. Press, 1950), little research has been done. If scholars avoid "provinciality and regional defensiveness" and concern themselves with stylistic and structural matters, they can make substantial contributions. 26 notes.
D. L. Smith

2329. Feather, John. *THE HISTORY OF BOOKS AS A FIELD OF STUDY: A REVIEW ESSAY. J. of Lib. Hist. 1982 17(4): 463-467.* Reviews Thomas Tanselle's *The History of Books as a Field of Study* (1981). Argues for a broadening of the context of bibliographical endeavor; not only the history of the book is of interest, but its influence as well. Influence is not easily ascertained, but the fact that the whole of Western history is shaped by books demands that the effort be made. Considerable groundwork has been done, but there remains the task of creating a conceptual framework by means of which researchers can synthesize existing data and reach out into new areas.
V. L. Human

2330. Feinberg, Walter. REVISIONIST SCHOLARSHIP AND THE PROBLEM OF HISTORICAL CONTEXT. *Teachers Coll. Record 1977 78(3): 311-336.* Revisionist historians of American education, such as Michael B. Matz and Colin Greer, have attacked traditional historians who found widespread support among the lower classes for public schools as a vehicle of social mobility. They argue that public education was imposed upon the poor by the upper class intent upon preserving a capitalist class system. Revisionists evaluate historical events against current standards, not those prevailing at the time. In fact, the accepted goal of most educational development since the mid-19th century has been to "maximize technological development," a goal not necessarily compatible with the revisionists' ideals of equality of opportunity, upward mobility, and local control. Secondary sources; 35 notes.
E. Bailey

2331. Field, Frank. LITERATURE, SOCIETY AND THE TWENTIETH-CENTURY HISTORIAN. *History [Great Britain] 1979 64(210): 54-58.* Modern British historians have yet to contrib-

ute significantly to the study of the relationship between literature and society. To be sure, the limitations of literature as commentary on an era must be recognized, while at the same time literary works should not be seen simply as social documents. Still, as in the current study of the influence of the Surrealist movement in France between the two world wars shows, an examination of writers' involvement in the problems and politics of society can shed light broadly on the history of a period. 5 notes.
R. P. Sindermann, Jr.

2332. Frigo, Gian Franco. LA STORIOGRAFIA FILOSOFICA ITALIANA DEL POSITIVISMO E DEL NEOKANTISMO [Italian philosophical historiography of positivism and neo-Kantianism]. *Verifiche [Italy] 1983 12(2-3): 195-217.* Comments on Luciano Malusa's *La Storiografia Filosofica Italian nella Seconda Metà dell'Ottocento. I: Tra Positivismo e Neokantismo* [Italian philosophical historiography in the late 19th century. Vol. 1: between postivism and neo-Kantianism] (1977) and its critics. Its main lack is in theory, its main strength in thoroughness.

2333. Frigo, Gian Franco. "L'ATEO DI SISTEMA." IL "CASO SPINOZA" NELLA STORIOGRAFIA FILOSOFICA TEDESCA DALL'*AUFKLÄRUNG* ALLA *ROMANTIK* ["The systematic atheist": the "Spinoza Case" in German historiography of philosophy from the Enlightenment to the Romantic period]. *Verifiche [Italy] 1977 6(4): 811-859.* Discusses the reception of Baruch Spinoza's atheistic philosophy by German historians of philosophy during the Enlightenment and Romantic periods.

2334. Gribaudi, Maurizio. A PROPOSITO DI LINGUISTICA E STORIA [Linguistics and history]. *Quaderni Storici [Italy] 1981 16(1): 236-266.* Models adopted in the field of linguistics lead one to ask how far historians face the problem of the formalization of social behavior. The relationship between the phenomenon and its rule, between individual behavior and social codes is discussed in a comparison between linguistic models and the categories used in historiography to interpret social phenomena. In the second part of the article the writer proposes that the social use of language should be taken into consideration in the practice of research into social history. Referring to the more specific field of sociolinguistics he emphasizes how the study of language and its use as a channel of communication in relationships between individuals permits a more precise definition of individual and group behavior.
J

2335. Guadarrama González, Pablo. EL ANÁLISIS MARXISTA-LENINISTA DE LA HISTORIA DE LA FILOSOFÍA FRENTE A LAS TERGIVERSACIONES DE LA HISTORIOGRAFÍA BURGUESA [Marxist-Leninist analysis of the history of philosophy faced with the misrepresentations of bourgeois historiography]. *Islas [Cuba] 1979 (62): 159-176.* Criticizes bourgeois historiography because it is descriptive, it ignores the specific laws that govern the development of philosophical thought, and it regards philosophers as separate entities, with subjective evaluations, without considering the links between philosophy and the material conditions of society and the class struggle.

2336. Gustavson, Carl G. THE HISTORIOGRAPHY OF BLUE BOOKS. *AHA Newsletter 1978 16(1): 7-9.* Examines the study of college students' history course blue books as a method of reflection for academics when contemplating broad analyses of historiography.

2337. Haddock, B. A. VICO: THE PROBLEM OF INTERPRETATION. *Social Res. 1976 43(3): 535-552.* Examines difficulties in interpreting, and various interpretations of, the philosophy of Giovanni Battista Vico (1668-1744). Difficulties in interpretation arise because his philosophy is suggestive rather than of a systematic nature. The true value of Vico's works on the history of ideas lies in his criterion for judgment of ideas which avoided anachronism.

2338. Halperin, John and Platt, Andrew K. GEORGE ELIOT STUDIES 1945-1975: A BIOCRITICAL SURVEY. *British Studies Monitor 1977 7(3): 24-43.* Analysis of the post-World War II revival of interest in the work of George Eliot and of the recent research and writing under the categories of biography, letters, editions, and bibliographies. 13 notes.   R. Howell

2339. Halpern, Jeanne W. BIOGRAPHICAL IMAGES: EFFECTS OF FORMAL FEATURES ON THE WAY WE SEE A LIFE. *Biography* 1978 1(4): 1-15. When biography is examined as a literary genre, then the selection of materials, the structure of the text, and the style of the prose are singularly important components of the image-making process. The author shows how such formal features not only reflect the biographer's vision of a life but also influence the impression the reader receives. Based on contemporary texts from the documentary to the fictionalized.   J

2340. Hamlin, Cyrus. THE DILEMMA OF ROMANTICISM. *U. of Toronto Q. [Canada]* 1974 44(1): 66-76. Discusses historical and literary criticism about Romanticism in European literature, 1774-1835.

2341. Hammerstein, Notker. JUBILÄUMSSCHRIFT UND ALLTAGSARBEIT. TENDENZEN BILDUNGSGESCHICHTLICHER LITERATUR [Celebratory writings and ordinary work: trends in the literature of the history of education]. *Hist. Zeits. [West Germany]* 1983 236(3): 601-633. Celebratory histories of various universities in Western Europe and the United States produce much new knowledge, but involve intellectual dangers. General studies of higher education, especially with a social historical orientation need to be written. At present, there is the tendency to focus on a particular institution without relating the topic to wider historical concerns. 96 notes.   G. H. Davis

2342. Hazlett, J. Stephen. EDUCATION AND REVOLUTION DURING THE NINETEENTH CENTURY. *Consortium on Revolutionary Europe 1750-1850: Pro.* 1977: 162-166. A common framework for approaching the question of the development of state systems of mass schooling in the 19th century has not been attained because: 1) the models used are imprecise, static, and overlapping; and 2) the object of the inquiry is frequently not well delineated. It is necessary to know more about teaching methods and to discover teachers' opinions and their relations to their job and their community. Secondary sources; 3 notes.   R. Howell

2343. Heath, William G. THOREAU AND OTHERS. *Can. Rev. of Am. Studies [Canada]* 1983 14(4): 447-455. Reviews Richard Bridgman's *Dark Thoreau* (1982), Philip Gura's *The Wisdom of Words: Language, Theology, and Literature in the New England Renaissance* (1981), Anne C. Rose's *Transcendentalism as a Social Movement, 1830-1850* (1981), and Henry David Thoreau's *Journal, Vol. 1: 1837-1844* (1981), which reveal the persistence of scholarly fascination with 19th-century Transcendentalists. 10 notes.   H. T. Lovin

2344. Hiner, N. Ray. WARS AND RUMORS OF WARS: THE HISTORIOGRAPHY OF COLONIAL EDUCATION AS A CASE STUDY IN ACADEMIC IMPERIALISM. *Societas* 1978 8(2): 89-114. Until 1959 colonial education was studied almost solely by educators. Since that time the field has become something of a battleground between historians and educators with benefits, however, accruing to both fields. Educational perspectives have even invaded such fields as religious history and political theory, but much remains to be done that will require the work of scholars from many academic fields. 63 notes.   J. D. Hunley

2345. Holzbachová, Ivana. POTENCIALISMUS NEBO HISTORISMUS? NAD JEDNÍM POKUSEM O ZVĚDEČTĚNÍ HISTORIOGRAFIE [Potentialism or historicism? Thoughts concerning one attempt at a more scientific historiography]. *Československý Časopis Hist. [Czechoslovakia]* 1983 31(6): 885-897. Criticizes Walter Falk's *Vom Strukturalismus zum Potentialismus* (1976) as a failed attempt to solve the problem of Western historiography. Falk rejects and neglects the materialist interpretation of social change. Drawing on several contemporary thinkers in biology, psychology, linguistics, and intellectual history, he exaggerates the significance

of collective consciousness and gives undue weight to unidentified factors of change external to existing social systems. 32 notes. Russian and German summaries.   R. E. Weltsch

2346. Hutton, Patrick H. THE HISTORY OF MENTALITIES: THE NEW MAP OF CULTURAL HISTORY. *Hist. and Theory* 1981 20(3): 237-259. Examines that genre of intellectual history known as the history of mentalities—the study of the culture of the common man. The work of Philippe Ariès, Norbert Elias, and Michel Foucault are comparatively analyzed to chart the emphases of this 20th-century historiographical trend. This trend bears the imprint of the *Annales* approach pioneered in the writings of Lucien Febvre and Marc Bloch. Although they evaluate the implications of the West's civilizing process somewhat differently and focus on divergent specific topics, their historiography converges "upon a theory of civilization which emphasizes man's ongoing effort to establish an equilibrium" between new forms of experience and existing forms of conventional wisdom. Their three dominant subjects are: the pressures of conformity, the accelerating sense of time, and the increasing psychological preoccupation with self. 68 notes.   W. J. Reedy

2347. Kaestle, Carl F. CONFLICT AND CONSENSUS REVISITED: NOTES TOWARD A REINTERPRETATION OF AMERICAN EDUCATIONAL HISTORY. *Harvard Educ. R.* 1976 46(3): 390-396. Discusses the historiography of the influence of class struggle in public education 1950's-70's.

2348. Kaestle, Carl F. EDUCATION AND AMERICAN SOCIETY: NEW HISTORICAL INTERPRETATIONS, INTRODUCTION. *Hist. of Educ. [Great Britain]* 1978 7(3): 170-172. Outlines developments in the history of American education during the 1960's-70's with particular reference to "revisionism." Also discusses each of the papers published in this special issue of the *History of Education* which is devoted to the history of education in the United States. 5 notes.   R. G. Neville

2349. Kemiläinen, Aira. AATE-, ASENNE- JA MIELIPIDEHISTORIA [The history of ideas, attitudes, and opinions]. *Historiallinen Arkisto [Finland]* 1984 (82): 109-125. Discusses research after 1920 in Germany, France, the United States, and Finland on the history of ideas. This term covers two separate topics: articulated ideas that are considered as philosophy, and attitudes and opinions among broad social groups that constitute social history. The latter has been relatively neglected in Finland. 35 notes.   R. G. Selleck

2350. Kett, Joseph. ON REVISIONISM. *Hist. of Educ. Q.* 1979 19(2): 229-235. Review article of Diane Ravitch's *The Revisionists: A Critique of the Radical Attack on the Schools* (New York: Basic Books, 1978). That book provides an important balance to the radical view of American education. Many of the radical writers have serious historical fallacies in their writings.   L. C. Smith

2351. Kouřím, Zdenek. ANDRÉ BARON: MÁS SOBRE EL KRAUSISMO Y MENÉNDEZ PELAYO [André Baron: more on Krausism and Menéndez Pelayo]. *Humánitas [Mexico]* 1979 20: 225-228. Reviews the historiography of Krausism (Karl Krause, 1781-1832, German philosopher) in Spain and its relationship to Marcelino Menéndez Pelayo, who condemned it without hesitation, and Julián Sanz del Río, who accepted it as a valid philosophy. Reviews a monograph by André Baron [*Boletín de la Biblioteca de Menéndez Pelayo* 1972 48(1-4)], which clarifies the distinction between ideology and philosophy with respect to the debate on Krausism.

2352. Labbett, B. D. C. LOCAL HISTORY IN THE CLASSROOM. *Social Studies* 1979 70(2): 62-66. History can be made more meaningful when pupils are allowed to write history based on local events that are of interest to them. The instructor guides them in matters of research, the collection of evidence or facts which relate to local cases, but pupils formulate ideas about events and do the actual writing of the histories. This procedure motivates interest and helps develop skills in handling concepts. 2 notes.

L. R. Raife

2353. Leland, Dorothy. ON READING AND WRITING THE WORLD: FOUCAULT'S HISTORY OF THOUGHT. *Clio 1975 4(2): 225-243.* Michel Foucault seeks to free intellectual history from subjection to transcendence. There are no priorities for thinking man or world "order." Human language intersecting with space creates contingent "realities" set in time. The problem has become that of the meaning of language and its delimiting of thought. 8 notes.

A. H. Auten

2354. Levi, Albert William. *DE INTERPRETATIONE:* COGNITION AND CONTEXT IN THE HISTORY OF IDEAS. *Critical Inquiry 1976 3(1): 153-178.* Allan Janik's and Stephen Toulmin's *Wittgenstein's Vienna* (New York, 1973) and Stephen Marcus's *Engels, Manchester, and the Working Class* (London, 1974), both dealing with the history of ideas, mark a turning point in modern critical interpretation.

2355. Levin, David. CLASSIC STATEMENT: DAVID LEVIN ON "THE LITERARY CRITICISM OF HISTORY." *Clio 1971 1(1): 42-45.* A precis of the first four sections and a reprint of the final fifth section of the essay in David Levin's *In Defense of Historical Literature* (New York, 1967). Argues that literary art is not a mere embellishment but is inherent in historiography. The art of perception in selecting the climactic, the typical, the symbolic, and expressing coherence between events are cited as proof. Also cites the arts of ordering, forming, defining, interpreting, selecting, arranging, and generalizing as instances of literary decision-making. States that literary criticism of historical writing performs the valuable service of highlighting relationships between technique and substance for the historian. 2 notes.

A. H. Auten

2356. Lucas, Christopher J. HISTORICAL REVISIONISM AND THE RETREAT FROM SCHOOLING. *Educ. and Urban Soc. 1974 6(3): 355-362.* A review of Joel H. Spring's book *Education and the Rise of the Corporate State* (Boston: Beacon, 1973).

S

2357. Marcolungo, Ferdinando L. CHRISTIAN WOLFF (1679-1754) E LA STORIOGRAFIA FILOSOFICA [Christian Wolff (1679-1754) and the historiography of philosophy]. *Verifiche [Italy] 1979 8(4): 395-401.* Attempts an overview of the German rationalist philosopher's thinking on historical knowledge and the place that the history of philosophy has in his system, in the context of the current debates concerning the historical dimension of philosophical activity.

2358. Marks, Russell. THE REVISIONIST WORLD VIEW. *Hist. of Educ. Q. 1979 19(4): 507-514.* Reviews *American Education, An Introduction to Social and Political Aspects* by Joel Spring. Suggests how world views shaped historical interpretations and, in particular, how contemporary educational revisionist world views shape the writing of history. Explores Spring's analysis of the political purposes of educational institutions and performance in other social roles. Questions Spring's exposition of the education ideas of Thomas Jefferson and Horace Mann. Secondary sources; 8 notes.

S. H. Frank

2359. McAvoy, William C. A REVIEW OF ENGLISH RENAISSANCE TEXTUAL STUDIES: 1981-1983. *Manuscripta 1984 28(3): 157-169.* Surveys textual studies of non-Shakespearean works from 1475 to 1642 which were published during a two-year period from 1981 until 1983. 43 notes.

M. D. Dibert

2360. McComb, David. CLIO AND KELLER: PSI IN THE HISTORY CLASSROOM. *Teaching Hist.: A J. of Methods 1977 2(1): 17-21.* Fred Keller's Personalized System of Instruction was applied to the US history survey with the results that students learned one-

third more than those taught by the traditional lecture course. Students comments favorably on the methods of the self-paced class and revealed a preference for PSI courses.

A

2361. Mitchell, Allan. THE FRENCH WAY OF DEATH: SOME METHODOLOGICAL QUESTIONS AND SUGGESTIONS. *Pro. of the Ann. Meeting of the Western Soc. for French Hist. 1976 4: 155-163.* Outlines three basic characteristics of French historiography of death: its conception as a branch of social history, its pursuit and expression in terms of attitudes toward death, and its concentration on the early modern period. Analyzes the changing thought of Philippe Ariès on the study of death, noting discrepancies and methodological dilemmas. Suggests topics for preliminary investigation before the history of mentalities or a comprehensive theory of French attitudes toward death can be achieved.

J. D. Falk

2362. Mitchell, Allan. PHILIPPE ARIÈS AND THE FRENCH WAY OF DEATH. *French Hist. Studies 1978 10(4): 684-695.* Three characteristics mark the present interest in death in France: death is conceived as a branch of social history, Frenchmen have dealt with attitudes toward death, and the focus has been on the early modern period. Led by Philippe Ariès, French historians seek to relate the drastic change in attitude when death was regarded as a common and celebrated experience to the present attitude of death as a shameful phenomenon. Secondary sources; 30 notes.

H. T. Blethen

2363. Muccillo, Maria. LA VITA E LE OPERE DI ARISTOTELE NELLA "DISCUSSIONES PERIPATETICAE" DI FRANCESCO PATRIZI DA CHERSO [The life and works of Aristotle in the *Discussiones Peripateticae* by Francesco Patrizi da Cherso]. *Rinascimento [Italy] 1981 21: 53-119.* Francesco Patrizi (1529-97), in his 1571 work, utilized the critical historical tools of Renaissance philology to demystify Aristotle in an attempt to destroy his moral and intellectual authority. Patrizi denied to Aristotle a place in the honorable tradition of pious and occult philosophy that culminates in Christ. Rather, he reduced the Greek writer to a student of physics. Patrizi examined the Aristotelian school from its beginnings to his own day, asserting that the Aristotelians, excepting the immediate heirs, misunderstood or misrepresented their master due to their slavish imitation of him. Patrizi attacked Aristotle and his school in order to affirm the freedom of inquiry from any authority. Based on the printed text of *Discussiones* and other primary sources; 157 notes.

J. R. Banker

2364. Mytrovych, Kyrylo. PORTRET SKOVORODY: U 250-RICHCHIA IOHO NARODZHENNIA [A portrait of Skovoroda: on the 250th anniversary of his birth]. *Sučasnist [West Germany] 1972 (11): 44-55.* A discussion of Grigori Skovoroda's philosophy and a historiographical review of its critics, 1800-1971.

2365. Nies, Fritz. ZEIT-ZEICHEN. GATTUNGSBILDUNG IN DER REVOLUTIONSPERIODE, UND IHRE KONSEQUENZEN FÜR LITERATUR- UND GESCHICHTSWISSENSCHAFT [Time signals: the establishment of genres in the revolutionary period and the consequences for literary history and historiography]. *Francia [France] 1980 8: 257-275.* Traces the evolution of literature in France. New types of periodicals appeared, including directories, reviews and literary articles. In the theater, vaudeville and melodrama emerged. Literature was expected to explain political events and to examine the influence of these events on the daily life of all French people whatever their social status. Secondary sources; 87 notes.

G. L. Neville

2366. Peckham, Howard H. RETROSPECTUS. *William and Mary Q. 1984 41(3): 464-477.* Author's reminiscences of his career as a historian, including his role with the American Association of State and Local History in publishing *American Heritage.* Discusses the development of American intellectual history and notes the value of studying 18th-century history. Contribution to "Early American Emeriti: A Symposium of Experience and Evaluation."

H. M. Ward/S

2367. Piaia, Gregorio. INTORNO ALLE ORIGINI DELLA MODERNA STORIOGRAFIA FILOSOFICA [The origins of modern philosophical historiography]. *Verifiche [Italy] 1979 8(2-3): 211-231.* Describes the contribution of Maria Assunta Del Torre's *Le origini moderne della storiografia filosofica* (Florence: La Nuova Italia, 1976) to the emergence of the history of philosophy as an autonomous discipline; discusses the work in relation to previous historiography of philosophy, 17th-20th centuries.

2368. Potts, David B. "COLLEGE ENTHUSIASM!" AS PUBLIC RESPONSE, 1800-1860. *Harvard Educ. Rev. 1977 47(1): 28-42.* Reviews the historiographical interpretations of the accessibility, popularity, curricular flexibility, and enrollment growth of antebellum American colleges and suggests directions for future research in the area of early 19th-century higher education.

2369. Prosperi, Gianluca. VERSO NUOVI MODELLI DI STORIOGRAFIA LETTERARIA [Toward new models of literary historiography]. *Studium [Italy] 1982 78(2): 229-232.* Giuseppe Petronio's *Teorie e Realtà della Storiografia Letteraria* (1980) analyzes various periods in the history of literature and examines the current debate on the relationship between history and literature.

2370. Puppo, Mario. PROBLEMI DELLA STORIOGRAFIA LETTERARIA [Problems of literary historiography]. *Studium [Italy] 1977 73(5): 633-642.* Benedetto Croce denied that romanticism created a model of the history of literature as a history of the national spirit. The author examines numerous proposals of diverse ideological and methodological circles in order to resolve the difficult problem of literary historiography.

2371. Ranum, Orest. A SKELETON COMES OUT OF THE CLOSET: HISTORIANS EXPLORE ATTITUDES TOWARD DEATH. *Bull. of the Hist. of Medicine 1983 57(3): 450-457.* Reviews five books on death and dying that demonstrate the changing views toward death from ancient to modern times. *La Mort, les Morts dans les Sociétés Anciennes* (1982), edited by Gherardo Gnoli and Jean-Pierre Vernant, examines the concept of death in ancient times, and includes data from archaeological studies and the analysis of ancient texts. Its approach is contrasted with that taken in studies of modern history, including John McManners's *Death and the Enlightenment: Changing Attitudes to Death among Christians and Unbelievers in Eighteenth-Century France* (1981), Gordon Geddes's *Welcome Joy: Death in Puritan New England* (1982), Philippe Ariès's *The Hour of Our Death* (1981), and *Mirrors of Mortality: Studies in the Social History of Death* (1982) edited by Joachim Whaley.   M. Kaufman

2372. Richards, Judith. LITERARY CRITICISM AND THE HISTORIAN: TOWARDS RECONSTRUCTING MARVELL'S MEANING IN *AN HORATIAN ODE. Literature and Hist. [Great Britain] 1981 7(1): 25-47.* Demonstrates the value of genuine cooperation between literary critics and historians in the interpretation of political or public poetry by showing how a close examination both of the general religious and philosophical climate and of the specific political history of the 1640's would seem to preclude certain widely-held critical interpretations of Andrew Marvell's *An Horatian Ode Upon Cromwell's Return from Ireland* (1650). The *Ode* reflects the almost universal contemporary belief that the Civil War in England, the execution of Charles I, and Oliver Cromwell's conquest of Ireland all testified to God's providential ordering of world history; and gives no support to the conventional view of Marvell's own political evolution from royalist to Cromwellian sympathizer between 1650 and 1658. Its contemporary political significance can best be appreciated in the context of the Engagement Controversy of 1649-50. Based on Marvell's poetic works and secondary sources; 69 notes.   M. J. Clark

2373. Russ, Anne J. AMERICAN HIGHER LEARNING SINCE WORLD WAR II: PROFESSIONALISM, BUREAUCRACY, AND MANAGERIAL ELITES. *Trends in Hist. 1982 3(2): 15-31.* Prints a bibliographic essay on the historiography of the growing importance of management as an academic discipline in US colleges and universities.

2374. Simon, W. M. COMTE'S ORTHODOX DISCIPLES: THE RISE AND FALL OF A CÉNACLE. *French Hist. Studies 1965 4(1): 42-62.* The history of positivism in 19th-century France, and the history of the disciples of August Comte in particular, is an example of intellectual history as the study of those who receive and select ideas rather than those who create ideas.

2375. Soikkanen, Hannu. SUOMEN UUSINTA HISTORIAA KOSKEVASTA AATEHISTORIALLISESTA TUTKIMUKSESTA [Research on intellectual history in modern Finnish historiography]. *Hist. Arkisto [Finland] 1978 71: 267-271.* Compares the idealist approach, which studies the ideas expressed by intellectual elites, with more recent studies postulating social and economic determinants, as illustrated by research on Finnish topics.   R. G. Selleck

2376. Starobinski, Jean. THE MEANING OF LITERARY HISTORY. *New Literary Hist. 1975 7(1): 83-88.* The study of literary history, like other branches of historical study, is not entirely retrospective, but is very much rooted in the present.

2377. Stigant, Paul. WONDERFULLY INCOMPREHENSIBLE: HISTORY, THEORY AND THE FUTURE OF *LITERATURE AND HISTORY. Lit. and Hist. [Great Britain] 1982 8(2): 138-146.* Assesses the implications of current debates among socialist and feminist historians for the future of *Literature and History*, making a plea for history to become more prominent in the journal, but a history more aware of theory and its own "problematic." The journal should "confront its politics," asking itself who it is addressing, asking about the changes feminism has wrought on the politics of the Left, and considering more the politics of teaching. Historians should take more note of some of the concepts and abstractions now being used by radical literary critics. Secondary works; 21 notes.   D. J. Nicholls

2378. Storr, Richard J. THE ROLE OF EDUCATION IN AMERICAN HISTORY: A MEMORANDUM FOR THE COMMITTEE ADVISING THE FUND FOR THE ADVANCEMENT OF EDUCATION IN REGARD TO THIS SUBJECT. *Harvard Educ. R. 1976 46(3): 331-354.* Presents the author's views regarding the historiography of American education, originally sponsored by the Ford Foundation's Fund for the Advancement of Education in the 1950's, emphasizing the role of American national characteristics, 1954-70's.

2379. Stout, Harry S. MORAL PHILOSOPHY IN COLONIAL NEW ENGLAND: FROM EARLY PURITAN PIETY TO PERRY MILLER'S MISTAKES. *Fides et Hist. 1983 15(2): 97-102.* Reviews two books by Norman Fiering: *Moral Philosophy at Seventeenth Century Harvard: A Discipline in Transition* (1981) and *Jonathan Edwards' Moral Thought and Its British Context* (1981). Fiering's pathbreaking study of philosophy in colonial New England challenges Perry Miller's paradigm on two counts: first, Puritan piety experienced a transformation not a decline, and second, there was never a monolithic New England mind in the first place. Fiering's fresh analysis of Jonathan Edwards portrays the Northampton pastor as a good synthesizer sifting through the philosophical grains for the proper Calvinist defense, rather than Perry Miller's perception of Edwards as a philosopher-innovator in the company of Locke, Shaftesbury, and Hutchinson. Secondary sources; 5 notes.   G. A. Glovins

2380. Svilpis, J. E. JOHNSON, HUMANISM, AND "THE LAST GREAT REVOLUTION OF THE INTELLECTUAL WORLD." *Studies in Eighteenth-Century Culture 1982 11: 299-310.* Although Samuel Johnson (1709-84) devotes only four words to the term "humanist" in his *Dictionary* (1755), and although modern scholars have underestimated Johnson's historical understanding of Renaissance humanism, which flourished from 1454 to 1582, Johnson's preface to *The English Works of Roger Ascham* (1515-68), author of *The Schoolmaster* (1570), demonstrates his sense of both the limitations and achievements of the movement: on the one hand, as the *Dictionary* definition suggests, humanism was excessively concerned with words rather than tenets and facts; on the other, humanistic training equipped one with literacy, the key to the acquisition of those same tenets and facts. Primary sources; 38 notes. E. L. Keyser

2381. Szanto, Gillian. RECENT STUDIES IN MARVELL. *English Literary Renaissance 1975 5: 273-286.* Since 1945 the historical approach to Andrew Marvell's (1621-78) poetry has come into its own. Wallerstein's *Studies in Seventeenth-Century Poetic* (1950), Legouis' *Andrew Marvell: Poet, Puritan, Patriot* (1965), and Leishman's *The Art of Marvell's Poetry* (1966) have stimulated critics to turn to political, poetic, and cultural traditions for an understanding of Marvell's purposes and effects. Recent full-length studies, notably those by Toliver (1965), Wallace (1968), and Colie (1970), combine literary criticism with pertinent intellectual, theological, and aesthetic history. The search for a philosophical key to Marvell has been widespread; so far, Neoplatonism, Calvinism, baroque aesthetics, and European painting have yielded some explanatory hypotheses about the poetry. The canon and texts of the post-Restoration satires in prose and verse are attracting attention, and Marvell's connection with religious and commercial circles is another new area for study. In short, the present critical trend is to understand Marvell in terms of the culture of his period. J

2382. Thayer, H. S. HISTORY AND PHILOSOPHY. *Social Res. 1980 47(4): 672-685.* Discusses historical scholarship in philosophy from the time of Thales and cites W. K. C. Guthrie's *A History of Greek Philosophy* (1962-78), J. H. Randall's *The Career of Philosophy* (1962-65), and some recent works on the history of philosophy in America, including Bruce Kuklick's *The Rise of American Philosophy* (1977).

2383. Todorova, M. N. HISTORICAL PROBLEMS IN THE WORK OF THE 15TH WORLD CONGRESS OF PHILOSOPHY, (SEPTEMBER 1973-VARNA, BULGARIA). *Bulgarian Hist. Rev. [Bulgaria] 1974 2(1): 99-102.* Reviews the program of this congress on man, science, and technology. Lists the topics discussed at plenary sessions, individual colloquiums, problem and research groups, and mentions important reports in each category.

A. Armstrong

2384. Trénard, Louis. L'HISTOIRE DES MENTALITÉS COLLECTIVES: LES PENSÉES ET LES HOMMES, BILAN ET PERSPECTIVES [History of collective mentalities: thoughts and men, balance and perspectives]. *R. d'Hist. Moderne et Contemporaine [France] 1969 16(4): 652-662.* Discusses the problems and methods of the study of collective mentality, public opinion, and the history of ideas, citing significant works in the field and pitfalls to avoid. 58 notes. J. D. Falk

2385. Tucker, Bruce. EARLY AMERICAN INTELLECTUAL HISTORY AFTER PERRY MILLER. *Can. Rev. of Am. Studies [Canada] 1982 13(2): 145-157.* Since the 1960's, intellectual historians of colonial New England have borrowed heavily from the methodologies and theories of social scientists. But these extensive innovations have not fundamentally changed the pathbreaking scholarship of historian Perry Miller or improved on his artistry. Miller and his successors used sociological theories. Secondary sources; 29 notes. H. T. Lovin

2386. Turi, Gabriele. SOCIALISMO E CULTURA [Socialism and culture]. *Movimento Operaio e Socialista [Italy] 1980 3(2-3): 143-154.* Introducing this issue of *Movimento* devoted to "Socialist Culture and Publishing," discusses the shift of interest in socialist circles from the composition and structures of the working class to the circulation of ideas and the formation of class consciousness. Reviews the literature which illustrates this shift and the debate within European Marxism regarding a purely economic and a more comprehensive reading of works by Marx. 47 notes.

J. V. Coutinho

2387. Tyack, David B. POLITICIZING HISTORY. *Rev. in Am. Hist. 1979 7(1): 13-17.* Review article prompted by Diane Ravitch's *The Revisionists Revised: A Critique of the Radical Attack on the Schools* (New York: Basic Books, 1978) which rejects

the radical interpretation of American educational development of the 1970's in favor of the liberal view of educational history of the 1960's.

2388. Tyack, David B. WAYS OF SEEING: AN ESSAY ON THE HISTORY OF COMPULSORY SCHOOLING. *Harvard Educ. R. 1976 46(3): 355-389.* Discusses the role of economics, social classes, and political systems in the development of compulsory education from 1840 to the 20th century, including problems in historiography.

2389. Vasoli, Cesare. CONSIDERATIONS SUR L'HISTOIRE DE LA PHILOSOPHIE DE LA RENAISSANCE [Remarks on the history of Renaissance philosophy]. *Rev. des Etudes Italiennes [France] 1982 28(3-4): 227-254.* Reviewing recent publications on the history of Renaissance philosophy shows how research in this historical period has helped transform historical studies.

2390. Velde, I. van der. SAMENWERKING TUSSEN HISTORICI EN BEOEFENAREN DER HISTORISCHE PEDAGOGIEK [Cooperation between historians and students of historical pedagogy]. *Kleio [Netherlands] 1965 6(5): 141-146.* Argues that because the interest in educational problems and their history is growing, there is a need for a systematic study of historical pedagogy by both historians and history teachers.

2391. Veschioni Bolla, Teresa. LA FILOSOFIA DI SPINOZA NELLA STORIOGRAFIA FRANCESE CONTEMPORANEA (1960-1977) [Spinoza's philosophy in contemporary French historiography (1960-77)]. *Verifiche [Italy] 1977 6(4): 861-892.*

2392. Veysey, Laurence. THE HISTORY OF EDUCATION. *Rev. in Am. Hist. 1982 10(4): 281-291.* Reviews trends, including revisionist writings of the 1960's-76, and major subfields in the historiography of American education.

2393. Vivarelli, Roberto. IL 1870 NELLA STORIA D'EUROPA E NELLA STORIOGRAFIA [The year 1870 in the history of Europe and in historiography]. *Ann. della Facoltà di Sci. Pol.: Materiali di Storia [Italy] 1980-81 17(5 part 2): 9-28.* Examines the ideas by which the year 1870 came to be considered an important turning in the history of Europe by considering recent studies.

2394. Voegelin, Eric; Opitz, Peter J., transl. MENSCHHEIT UND GESCHICHTE [Humankind and history]. *Zeits. für Pol. [West Germany] 1981 28(2): 150-168.* This excerpt from Eric Voegelin's *Order and History*, Vol. 2, *The World of the Polis* (1957), applies principles of order and history to universal questions on existence and being.

2395. Vovelle, Michel. HISTOIRE DES MENTALITES: HISTOIRE DES RESISTANCES OU LES PRISONS DE LA LONGUE DUREE [History of mentalities: history of resistances or prisons of long duration]. *Hist. of European Ideas [Great Britain] 1981 2(1): 1-18.* Describes and criticizes two interpretations of the history of mentalities. Fernand Braudel characterized the approach as the study of "prisons of long duration," while Ernest Labrousse defined it as the history of "resistances." Both emphasize the inertia of collective attitudes, an interpretation which fails to consider the interplay between intellectual and cultural elites and the masses. At certain periods of history, such as the French Revolution, a powerful dialectic seems to have been operating.

S. R. Smith

2396. Vovelle, Michel. THE HISTORY OF MANKIND IN THE MIRROR OF DEATH. *Pro. of the Ann. Meeting of the Western Soc. for French Hist. 1978 6: 91-109.* Reviews the current state of the historiography of death and its place in the new history of mentalities. Presents two methodologies for the study of the history of death. The first is vertical history, which follows death from experienced, biological, or demographic death to the history of ideas

and discourse about death. The second, history over a long time span, traces attitudes and behavior regarding death from the 13th century to the present and notes stages or periods in that history.
J. D. Falk

2397. Vovelle, Michel. IDEOLOGIES ET MENTALITIES: UNE CLARIFICATION NECESSAIRE [Ideologies and mentalities: a necessary clarification]. *Europa [Canada] 1981 4(1): 17-28.* While many historians assert that the concept of ideology is fundamentally at odds with that of mentality, or attitudes of mind, in fact no such contradiction exists. While ideology may be an indicator of political action, the history of mentalities is the history of the relation between concrete material life of people and the mental image they have of it. 21 notes.
J. F. Harrington, Jr./S

2398. Vovelle, Michel. REDISCOVERY OF DEATH SINCE 1960. *Ann. of the Am. Acad. of Pol. and Social Sci. 1980 (447): 89-99.* Man has always been concerned with and has devised strategic attitudes toward death. Since 1960 there has been a burgeoning of interest, as evidenced by the increase in writings about death, and a distinct shift in conceptualization. The literature is surveyed indicating the loci of increased interest, exploring the concerns of different groups—physicians, family members, clergymen, historians—and discussing the effects of modern life such as the impact of advanced medical technology.
J

2399. Walker, Don D. RIDERS AND REALITY: A PHILOSOPHICAL PROBLEM IN THE HISTORIOGRAPHY OF THE CATTLE TRADE. *Western Hist. Q. 1978 9(2): 163-179.* A philosophical examination of *historical reality* and *mythic reality* as it occurs in the historiography of the Western cattle trade, particularly in the writings of Walker Prescott Webb, Joe B. Frantz, Julian E. Choate, Cordia Sloan Duke, J. Frank Dobie, and Robert R. Dykstra. "As men we are given to mythic versions of ourselves and other men." Historians must arrive at rhetorical meaning "inductively from an empirical configuration of facts" rather than fabricating the configuration from within themselves. "Tell us what you know and how you believe that you know it. Tell us what you assume. Tell us why you take this conceptual trail instead of that one. Then, in mutual trust, perhaps we can together find whatever realities the history of cows and men may grant us." 38 notes.
D. L. Smith

2400. Waller, Gary F. AUTHOR, TEXT, READING, IDEOLOGY: TOWARDS A REVISIONIST LITERARY HISTORY OF THE RENAISSANCE. *Dalhousie Rev. [Canada] 1981 61(3): 405-425.* Recent scholarly articles on the Renaissance reveal that a radical revaluing of the literature of this period is taking place. The works of Louis Althusser and Etienne Balibar, Jonathon Goldberg, Jacques Derrida, a group of French feminists as represented by *The Women's Part: Feminist Criticism of Shakespeare,* and a number of lesser critics are the basis for this study. 47 notes.
C. Held

2401. Ward, Paul L. REVIEW ESSAY: HISTORY SCHOOLBOOKS IN THE 20TH CENTURY. *Hist. and Theory 1980 19(3): 362-370.* Reviews and analytically extends Frances FitzGerald's *America Revised: History Schoolbooks in the Twentieth Century* (Boston: Little, Brown and Co., 1979). FitzGerald sees American history textbooks as an index of the public mind. Her concern has been to reveal writers and publishers as "arbiters of American values" and as the "Ministries of Truth for children." Since early in the century these texts have suffered from multifarious defects. The statewide text choices common in the South motivated publishers to produce books depicting Reconstruction according to regional preconceptions. Similarly, few modern texts have emphasized the class divisions and economic processes of our society. In general, the patriotic tasks of these books has blended poorly with the impact of social studies. Secondary sources; 11 notes.
W. J. Reedy

2402. Weeks, Jeffrey. FOUCAULT FOR HISTORIANS. *Hist. Workshop J. [Great Britain] 1982 (14): 106-119.* Michel Foucault's challenge to the practice of historical investigation must be understood before it can be effectively answered. He has located a new area of historical concern in the history of the discursive realm or "archaeology of knowledge," particularly those intellectual disciplines that since the 18th century have defined the boundaries of the economic, sexual, medical, familial, and disciplinary. Criticizing notions of individuality and essential humanity, he has placed the idea of knowledge as power at the center of intellectual concern. His approach, however, can lead to a new form of crude determinism where the relationship between discourse and social relations remains vague, and all forms of power are placed on the same level with no sense of a hierarchy. Based on Foucault's writings and commentaries on them; illus., 35 notes.
D. J. Nicholls

2403. Wengraf, A. E. HISTORY AND LITERATURE. *Lock Haven Rev. 1966 8: 46-53.* Discusses the philosophical relationship between history and literature in the work of W. B. Gallie and W. H. Dray, 1957-64.

2404. White, Hayden V. THE HISTORICAL TEXT AS LITERARY ARTIFACT. *Clio 1974 3(3): 277-303.* Argues that historical narratives should be recognized as verbal fiction which have more in common with literature than with science. Historians impose meaning on events and facts by encoding them with "culturally provided categories, such as metaphysical concepts, religious beliefs, or story forms." They present all the possible meanings of a given sequence of historical events by providing alternative emplotments of them. "History as a discipline is in bad shape today because it has lost sight of its origins in the literary imagination.... By drawing historiography back once more to an intimate connection with its literary basis, we should not only be putting ourselves on guard against *merely* ideological distortions," but we should also arrive at a theory of history without which it cannot exist as a discipline.
J. D. Falk

2405. Zunde, A. Ia. EVOLIUTSIIA PONIMANIIA PRIRODY FILOSOFII: ISTORIKO-METODOLOGICHESKII OBZOR [Evolution in the conception of philosophy: historical and methodological review]. *Latvijas PSR Zinātņu Akad. Vēstis [USSR] 1982 (9): 33-46.* A survey of changes in the comprehension of philosophy, through the ages from the classical Greek period to contemporary Marxism. 55 notes.
R. Vilums

2406. —. GESCHIEDENIS VAN HET (HISTORISCH) KINDERBOEK [History of (historical) books for children]. *Kleio [Netherlands] 1980 21(11): 306-308.* Presents a historical survey of children's books in general, focusing on Dutch history books and their authors, which first appeared in the Netherlands after 1850. The then popular children's historical novel stressed heroism and patriotism, changing in the early 1900's to present the child with a generally optimistic, idealized picture of the world. The intent of children's books remained pedagogical until about 1942. After that books sought to make the child critical of history and to introduce contemporary world problems.
G. Herritt

Cultural History

2407. Adams, John W. ANTHROPOLOGY AND HISTORY IN THE 1980S: CONSENSUS, COMMUNITY, AND EXOTICISM. *J. of Interdisciplinary Hist. 1981 12(2): 253-265.* Misinterpretations and misapplications of ethnographic findings among historians are problems between anthropology and history. It is necessary for historians, who wish to use anthropological insights, also to choose the appropriate anthropological theory. A reassessment of the place of historical consciousness in ethnography is necessary. For the writing of history it is important to turn to the study of folk history in Western society instead of the exotic. 21 notes.
H. J. Kaiser

2408. Alexander, Malcolm. HISTORICAL SOCIAL SCIENCE: CLASS STRUCTURE IN THE MODERN WORLD SYSTEM. *Australian and New Zealand J. of Sociol. [Australia] 1981 17(1): 56-64.* A trend to repudiate the imposition of rigid schemata on historical reality is seen in the social writings of the 1970's and 1980's.

2409. Andersen, Svend Aage. ARBEJDERKLASSENS KUL-
TURHISTORIE: PROBLEMER OG INDFALDSVINKLER I
STUDIET AF "ARBEJDERKULTUR" [The history of working-
class culture: problems and approaches]. *Årbog for Arbejderbevaegelsens Hist.* *[Denmark]* *1981* 11: 7-41. Surveys postwar theories
and practice of research into 19th- and 20th-century European
working-class culture and emphasizes the need to widen the definitions of "history" and "culture."

2410. Ariès, Philippe; Liang Ch'i-tzu, transl. HSIN T'AI LI SHIH
[The history of mentalities]. *Ssu yü Yen (Thought and Word)*
[Taiwan] *1982* 20(4): 57-73. A translation of Philippe Ariès's
"L'Histoire des Mentalités" in *La Nouvelle Histoire,* J. Le Goff,
ed. (1978). Any two cultures in different times or places have disparate mentalities. The study of the history of mentalities is a philosophical discipline which arose in 20th-century France as the West
became disenchanted with its belief in progress. Biblio.
                                                    J. A. Krompart

2411. Ariès, Philippe. THE SENTIMENTAL REVOLUTION.
Wilson Q. 1982 6(4): 46-53. The author reiterates the main outlines
of his thesis on the historical origins and development in Western
culture of the concept of childhood in his *Centuries of Childhood*
(1962). Points out four areas of innovative research that have
emerged since publication of the work.

2412. Balit, Adolphe; Norris, Colin J., transl. GEO-CULTURAL
MODULATIONS AND CULTURAL COLLISION: MIGRATION
OF CONCEPTS AND FIGURES. *Cultures [France] 1980 7(4):
119-131.* Argues for a change of cultural perception of world history, claiming that the Arab and Islamic peoples have made significant contributions to Western culture, yet are undercelebrated in
contemporary perspectives of history.

2413. Barton, Michael. THE STUDY OF AMERICAN EVERY-
DAY LIFE. *Am. Q. 1982 34(3): 218-221.* Reviews the literature on
daily life in America. There is a fairly long tradition of these historical studies, but they are often poorly documented or fail to draw
significant conclusions. 16 notes.   D. K. Lambert

2414. Bergamasco Lenarda, Lucia. INFANZIA E CLASSI SUB-
ALTERNE IN AMERICA TRA OTTO E NOVECENTO
[Childhood and the lower classes in 19th- and 20th-century
America]. *Movimento Operaio e Socialista [Italy] 1983 6(1): 145-
156.* Analyzes recent historiography on lower-class children. Considers works on black families, the history of education, and child law.
20 notes.   S. Rocchitta

2415. Bernardi, Bernardo. LA STORIA NELLA STORIA DE-
LL'ANTROPOLOGIA [The role of history in anthropology].
Quaderni Storici [Italy] 1977 12(2): 325-339. The relationship between anthropology and history has been approached in different
ways during the development of anthropological theory. The first
phase was marked by research into the problem of the historical
origin of culture and society along the lines of the evolutionistic
and diffusionistic schools. Opposition to any historical research and
internal polemics as to the value of history for anthropology
marked the second phase of structural-functionalist anthropology.
The third phase is related to Lévi-Straussian structuralism in which
the value of history in anthropology is not denied but analysis is
mostly synchronic. The fourth phase is connected to the dynamic
approach whereby culture and society are seen as the product of
cultural processes brought about by four fundamental factors: an-
thropos, ethnos, oikos, and chronos. History, the direct effect of
chronos, is intrinsically connected to all cultural phenomena.
                                                            J

2416. Boia, Lucian. THE HISTORY OF MENTALITIES: A WAY
TO AN ALL-COMPRISING HISTORY. *Rev. des Études Sud-Est
Européennes [Romania] 1980 18(4): 581-584.* Traces the origins of
the history of mentalities back to Herodotus, at the same time accepting the rather minor role played by the mental approach to history overall, until the "historiographic revolution" of the 20th
century. Reasons for the new focus were the crisis of values between the two world wars, and the impact of advances in sociology,

ethnology, and psychology. Research of mentalities will hopefully
provide a more complex view of history using literature and the arts, until now neglected, as historical sources.   J. Cushnie

2417. Boia, Lucian. ISTORIA MENTALITĂȚILOR (CU
PRIVIRE SPECIALĂ ASUPRA SCOLII DE LA "ANNALES")
[The history of mentalities: with special reference to the *Annales*
school]. *Rev. de Istorie [Romania] 1980 33(5): 937-952.* Traces the
emergence of the history of mentalities as an autonomous field for
investigation between the first and second world wars and assesses
the contribution of the *Annales* school, in particular its two founders, Lucien Febvre (1878-1936) and Marc Bloch (1886-1944). Surveys numerous recent French historiographical works influenced by
the school and notes characteristic themes including the history of
the imagination, attitudes toward death, demographic behavior, relations between the sexes, and aspects of myths and popular cults.
Stresses the multidisciplinary nature of such studies and the need
for them to be integrated into the ensemble of historiography. 26
notes. French summary.   R. O. Khan

2418. Bromlei, Iu. V. and Pershits, A. I. F. ENGEL'S I SOVRE-
MENNYE PROBLEMY PERVOBYTNOI ISTORII [Friedrich
Engels and contemporary problems in primitive history]. *Voprosy
Filosofii [USSR] 1984 (4): 44-61.* Views Friedrich Engels's ap-
proach to primitive society in *The Origin of the Family, Private
Property, and the State* and his handling of source material taken
from the work of American anthropologist E. Morgan.

2419. Burchell, R. A. THE HISTORIOGRAPHY OF THE
AMERICAN IRISH. *Immigrants & Minorities [Great Britain] 1982
1(3): 281-305.* The history of the Irish immigration has not been
adequately written except for the period between the famine and
1880. American censuses contain valuable data for this work. The
study of successive generations of Irish Americans faces a problem
of definition because of divisions among the immigrants, particularly that between Catholics and Protestants. Protestants were assimi-
lated more easily into the host society than were Catholics. The
history of the Irish Americans has been mostly an urban history
with important issues related to religion, education, and politics. A
new synthesis of that history is needed based on American census
data. 104 notes.   J. V. Coutinho

2420. Calmy, Christophe. LA SEXUALITÉ AU XIXe SIÈCLE:
ENTRETIEN AVEC ALAIN CORBIN [Sexuality in the 19th century: an interview with Alain Corbin]. *Histoire [France] 1979 (12):
80-82.* Corbin analyzes recent French historiography on Western
sexuality.

2421. Carey, James W. THE PROBLEM OF JOURNALISM HIS-
TORY. *Journalism Hist. 1974-75 1(1): 3-5, 27.* Advocates that the
history of journalism should move away from the old "Whig interpretation" and concentrate on cultural history in order to grasp the
realities of the period studied.

2422. Carson, Cary. DOING HISTORY WITH MATERIAL
CULTURE. Quimby, Ian M. G., ed. *Material Culture and the
Study of American Life* (New York: W. W. Norton, 1978): 41-64.
New trends in historiography which focus on people rather than
processes or trends give a new value to the use of material culture
in historiography.

2423. Cassidy, Keith. FAMILIES, COMMUNITIES AND AMER-
ICAN HISTORY. *Can. Rev. of Am. Studies [Canada] 1978 9(1):
90-95.* In *Families and Communities: A New View of American
History* (Nashville: American Association for State and Local History, 1974), David J. Russo attempted, through a loosely defined
concept of "community," to demonstrate how American history
could be rewritten to serve the contemporary interest in social history. Rejecting writing that focused on the national perspective, he
believes that histories should simultaneously treat the "several levels
of community" that Americans have experienced.
                                                        H. T. Lovin

2424. Chaunu, Pierre. QUELLE IMAGE DE LA CONDITION HUMAINE DONNE AUJOURD'HUI L'HISTOIRE? [What image of the human condition does history present today?]. *Rev. des Travaux de l'Acad. des Sci. Morales et Pol. et Comptes Rendus de ses Séances [France] 1979 132(1): 419-441.* History provides many different, sometimes contradictory, images of the human condition. There is history that examines recent events in microscopic detail, cyclical history, and linear history. The latter, which posits a beginning and an end of time, is in accord with both Genesis and most of the theories of astrophysics. Comments by Roland Mousnier, Jean-Baptiste Duroselle, Pierre-Georges Castex, Fernand Gambiez, Olivier Lacombe, Jean Stoetzel, Edmond Giscard d'Estaing, Jacob Kaplan, and Henri Guitton. Response by the author. Secondary sources; 12 notes. J. R. Vignery

2425. Clark, Stuart. FRENCH HISTORIANS AND EARLY MODERN POPULAR CULTURE. *Past & Present [Great Britain] 1983 (100): 62-99.* Historical explanations of French popular culture such as those of Muchembled, Delumeau, Febvre, Mandrou, and Braudel are vitiated by a general theory that ties meaning logically to the supposed representing and misrepresenting qualities of language, invoking a higher authority than discourse itself, and passing negative judgment. The idea that discourse on culture can be verified by appeal to how the world is, regardless of how it is seen in the discourse, must give way to a relativist account of its "truth-value and its rationality." The strength of a historical relativism drawn from the theory of language is that it helps resolve ambiguities in the notion of "histoire structurale" by appealing to two central principles: the overall arbitrariness of the system of meaning in terms of which the world is organized, and the contextual identity of the individual units of signification that make up these systems. Primary sources; 88 notes. J. G. Packer

2426. Coco, Antonio. PROSPETTIVA ASSIOLOGICA E METODO STORIOGRAFICO NELL'EVOLUZIONE DEL CONCETTO DI CIVILTÀ [Axiological perspective and historiographical method in the evolution of the concept of civilization]. *Pensiero Pol. [Italy] 1979 12(2): 372-379.* Investigates the use of the term "civilization" in the 18th century and the various attempts to explain its meaning by French historian François Guizot, who preferred an empirical approach to the study of history. Assesses the attempts of other historians to apply the knowledge imparted by the "new sciences" to the study of civilization. Based on papers delivered at a conference on "The Study of Man and the Study of Society in the 18th Century." A. Alcock

2427. Cohn, Bernard S. ANTHROPOLOGY AND HISTORY IN THE 1980S: TOWARD A RAPPROCHEMENT. *J. of Interdisciplinary Hist. 1981 12(2): 227-252.* While historians have studied the chronological progressive events of the world, the anthropologist's subject became the study of nonprogressive primitive peoples. At first the comparative method dominated. By the 1920's scholars turned to anthropological fieldwork for a reconstruction of the "ethnographic present." Anthropological impulses on history as well as a revived interest in history on the part of anthropologists can establish a new working relationship between the two fields. Matters of joint interest are named. Secondary sources; 42 notes. H. J. Kaiser

2428. Conze, Werner. NEUE LITERATUR ZUR SOZIALGESCHICHTE DER FAMILIE [New publications on family history]. *Vierteljahrschrift für Sozial- und Wirtschaftsgeschichte [West Germany] 1984 71(1): 59-71.* A report on recent publications in family history with an emphasis on German contributions. The British Cambridge Group and the US journal *Family History* still dominate the theoretical conceptions of German family history. But in recent years a number of documentary and article collections have appeared in Germany, which are increasingly reaching out beyond the traditionally related fields of demography, ethnology, and anthropology to family economic and legal history. 32 notes. D. Prowe

2429. Conzen, Kathleen Neils. HISTORICAL APPROACHES TO THE STUDY OF RURAL ETHNIC COMMUNITIES. Luebke, Frederick C., ed. *Ethnicity on the Great Plains* (Lincoln: U. of Ne-

braska Pr. for the Center for Great Plains Studies, 1980): 1-18. Reviews the concepts scholars have used in analyzing immigrant groups in rural environments and outlines a structure for comparative studies based on family and community history. While some scholars have stressed rapid assimilation as the main characteristics of ethnic life in rural environments, others have emphasized that rural conditions offer favorable opportunities for cultural maintenance. The crucial question is whether a given settlement achieved the measure of concentration or density essential for ethnic community formation. For this reason systematic study of rural ethnicity must include subcounty data on location and residence patterns, and account for the role of institutions in promoting immigrant settlements, as well as such variables as land availability, opportunities for agricultural employment, family size, age, and a wide range of cultural variables which influence the adaptive experience of rural ethnic groups. Secondary sources; 31 notes. J. Powell

2430. Cox, Richard J. THE VARIETY AND USES OF HISTORICAL DOCUMENTATION: FIVE NEW BOOKS. *Manuscripts 1983 35(1): 41-51.* Five publications—James West Davidson and Mark Hamilton Lytle's *After the Fact: The Art of Historical Detection* (1982), Fay D. Metcalf and Matthew T. Downey's *Using Local History in the Classroom* (1982), Elizabeth Hampsten's *Read This Only to Yourself: The Private Writings of Midwestern Women, 1880-1910* (1982), Lillian Schlissel's *Women's Diaries of the Westward Journey* (1982), and George W. McDaniel's *Hearth & Home: Preserving the People's Culture* (1982)—have many faults but indicate the healthy, innovative quality of recent historical work. 5 notes. D. A. Yanchisin

2431. Cremin, Lawrence A. THE FAMILY AS EDUCATION: SOME COMMENTS ON RECENT HISTORIOGRAPHY. *Teachers Coll. Record 1974 76(2): 250-265.* Examines the recent literature in the history of the family with a special focus on America. Values the focus on the role of the family as educator in Bernard Bailyn's *Education in the Forming of American Society* (New York: Norton, 1972), a theme rarely studied. W. H. Mulligan, Jr.

2432. Cuaz, Marco. ALMANACCHI E "CULTURA MEDIA" NELL'ITALIA DEL SETTECENTO [Almanacs and the "middle culture" in 18th-century Italy]. *Studi Storici [Italy] 1984 25(2): 353-362.* Discusses the historiography of almanacs and the popular literature of *colportage.* French historians, such as Pierre Brochon, have emphasized the importance of popular literature in the formation of a French national consciousness and raised the question of the manipulation of public opinion by mass media. Italian historians, however, have produced regional studies unlike the work of the French historians or of Christopher Hill and Keith Thomas on British popular culture. In Italy, calendars, guides to city and court, and educational tracts made up a "middle culture," an area of common sense that, as Gramsci says, always exists between folklore and philosophy. 12 notes. J. W. Houlihan

2433. d'Amelia, Marina. I TURBAMENTI DELLO STORICO: SU ALCUNI STUDI SULLA STORIA DELLA SESSUALITA E DELL'AMORE [Muddying the waters of history: some studies on the history of sexuality and love]. *Memoria: Riv. di Storia delle Donne [Italy] 1983 (7): 98-101.* Reviews four journal issues on the topic: Sexualités Occidentales, *Communications* 1982 (35); Sexuality in History, *Journal of Contemporary History* 1982 (2); Sex, Science and Society in Modern France, *Journal of Modern History* 1982 (2); and On the History of Love, *Journal of Social History* 1982 (spring). All are profoundly disappointing in the themes studied, methods used, material collected, and reading proposed. J. V. Coutinho

2434. Davis, Natalie Z. ANTHROPOLOGY AND HISTORY IN THE 1980S: THE POSSIBILITIES OF THE PAST. *J. of Interdisciplinary Hist. 1981 12(2): 267-275.* Anthropology as a sister discipline has close ties to history. Ethnographical interpretations have given historians a new awareness of various problems of their field. New insights in small-scale interactions, mechanisms of exchange, and notions of gender systems can reveal, for example, questions hidden to historians. Of importance is the historian's awareness of the different anthropological schools as well as of the dangers of misapplications of anthropological interpretations to history. 12 notes.   H. J. Kaiser

2435. Dunn, Tony. AREA STUDIES, THEORY AND PRACTICE. CULTURAL STUDIES AND THE POLITICS OF CULTURE IN BRITAIN: FROM IDEOLOGY TO "LOGOPOEIA." *Journal of Area Studies [Great Britain] 1983 (8): 3-8.* Discusses area studies and cultural studies in Great Britain, the continental approaches, a balance sheet for the practice of cultural studies, and the present challenges.

2436. Ermakov, V. T. IZUCHENIE ISTORII KUL'TURY KAK SYSTEMY [Studies of cultural history as a system]. *Voprosy Istorii [USSR] 1984 (4): 110-115.* Summarizes the proceedings of a conference convened at the Novosibirsk Academic City under the auspices of the Soviet Academy of Sciences in May 1983 and devoted to the problems of cultural history as a system. The issues discussed included systematic integrity of cultural history, appropriateness of evaluative approaches, and culture of socialist societies as the object of social management. 2 notes.   M. Hernas

2437. Esler, Anthony. "THE TRUEST COMMUNITY": SOCIAL GENERATIONS AS COLLECTIVE MENTALITIES. *J. of Pol. and Military Sociol. 1984 12(1): 99-112.* Guidelines toward improved models and methodologies for the study of generational consciousness may be found in the work of historians specializing in the study of collective mentalities. These *mentalités collectives* are conceived of as constituting the root-level structures of thought and feeling that undergird the more complex but superficial formulations of elitist intellectual life. From the *mentalité* historian, the generational researcher might borrow broader definitions of generational consciousness, a variety of methodological innovations, and a willingness to cross disciplinary boundaries for further help in probing the workings of generational consciousness.   J/S

2438. Ferguson, Arthur B. THE NONPOLITICAL PAST IN BACON'S THEORY OF HISTORY. *J. of British Studies 1974 14(1): 1-20.* Relies principally upon the Spalding-Ellis-Heath edition of his works to demonstrate how Francis Bacon (1561-1626) broadened the theory and practice of historical study and writing in Renaissance England to include the history of learning and the arts. Although Bacon's prospectus never encompassed the full scope of what today is called cultural history, he established a paradigm toward which such pioneers as Camden, Spelman, and Selden had been progressing. What is more, Bacon's personal ventures into the new field he envisaged for history demonstrated how richly the broader approach contributed to the sense of period as well as of process. 53 notes.   N. W. Moen

2439. Ferrante, Lucia. STRUTTURE O STRATEGIE? DISCUSSIONE SULLA STORIA DELLA FAMIGLIA [Structures or strategies? Discussions on the history of the family]. *Quaderni Storici [Italy] 1984 19(2): 613-626.* An examination of current concepts in the study of family structure in Europe and the usefulness of such concepts in the historiography of the family. Based on papers presented in Trieste in September 1983 at a conference on modern family structure in Italy and Europe.   J/S

2440. Finkelstein, Barbara. TOLERATING AMBIGUITY IN FAMILY HISTORY: A GUIDE TO SOME MATERIALS. *J. of Psychohistory 1983 11(1): 117-128.* Psychohistorical analysis of the family is a difficult and complex task, and historians regularly shy away from it. Such is the case with three recent books on family history: *Family Life in America* (1981), edited by Mel Albin and Dominick Cavallo; *Loving, Parenting and Dying: The Family Cycle in England and America, Past and Present* (1980), edited by Vivian C. Fox and Martin H. Quett; and *America's Family: A Documentary History* (1982), edited by Donald M. Scott and Bernard Wishy. The first is straight narrative history; the second establishes a theoretical framework which ignores the transitory nature of

child-rearing; and the third posits no theory on the family's historical evolution, although the primary sources cited in the articles demonstrate the complexities and search potential of family history.   W. A. Wiegand

2441. Flandrin, Jean-Louis and Wall, Richard. LES CARACTÉRISTIQUES DE LA FAMILLE OCCIDENTALE ET LEUR ANCIENNETÉ [The characteristics and historical development of the Western family]. *Rev. d'Hist. Moderne et Contemporaine [France] 1978 25(July-Sept): 476-480.* On 23-24 July 1976 the SRCC Cambridge Group for the History of Population and Social Structure discussed the origins and unique characteristics of the modern Western family structure. Over a dozen historians from Europe and the United States discussed changing assessments of this institution in light of recent demographic studies. They concluded not enough information is yet available to differentiate Western familial patterns with certainty. Table.   F. C. Bohm

2442. Flores, Marcello. INFANZIA E SOCIETÀ BORGHESE NELLA RECENTE STORIOGRAFIA [Childhood and bourgeois society in recent historiography]. *Movimento Operaio e Socialista [Italy] 1980 3(4): 497-506.* Recent interest in the history of the family has brought to light much material on childhood as a potential focus of historical research. Reviews some Italian, French, and English works on child labor and abandoned children.
                                      J. V. Coutinho

2443. Galasso, Giuseppe. GLI STUDI DI STORIA DELLA FAMIGLIA E IL MEZZOGIORNO D'ITALIA [Studies of the history of the family and southern Italy]. *Mélanges de l'Ecole Française de Rome. Moyen Age-Temps Modernes [Italy] 1983 95(1): 149-159.* Surveys historiography on the organization of families, marriage, and social change in southern Italy.

2444. Girardet, Raoul. DU CONCEPT DE GENERATION A LA NOTION DE CONTEMPORANEITE [From the concept of generation to the notion of contemporaneity]. *Rev. d'Hist. Moderne et Contemporaine [France] 1983 30(Apr-June): 257-270.* A diachronic study of the history of mentalities that discusses the concept of generation and the influence on mentalities of the synchronism of events. Based on a report presented on 31 October 1981 at the Conference of the Association Française de Science Politique; 11 notes.   G. P. Cleyet

2445. Goubert, Pierre. FAMILY AND PROVINCE: A CONTRIBUTION TO THE KNOWLEDGE OF FAMILY STRUCTURES IN EARLY MODERN FRANCE. *J. of Family Hist. 1977 2(3): 179-195.* Reviews the historiography on family structure in 18th-century France. A uniform family structure did not exist in France, but significant regional variation did occur. The Laslett model of the western, nuclear family has been overemphasized. Biblio., 3 appendixes.   T. W. Smith

2446. Haines, Michael A. FERTILITY, MARRIAGE, AND OCCUPATION IN THE PENNSYLVANIA ANTHRACITE REGION, 1850-1880. *J. of Family Hist. 1977 2(1): 28-55.* Historians have been able to distinguish only the crudest outline of fertility in 19th-century America. Most of their early works were aggregate level analysis in which differences between states or counties were used to explain the fertility transition and to uncover correlates of fertility. Using the child-women ratio on the household level is promising but risky. The potential for bias (e.g. mortality differentials) is great, yet the possibility of significant scholarly progress into this veiled subject is sufficient to justify the attempt. The author finds that strong occupational differentials in fertility did exist. Professionals' families had the lowest fertility, farmers' and miners' the highest. 49 notes.   T. W. Smith

2447. Hareven, Tamara K. CYCLES, COURSES AND COHORTS: REFLECTIONS ON THEORETICAL AND METHODOLOGICAL APPROACHES TO THE HISTORICAL STUDY OF FAMILY DEVELOPMENT. *J. of Social Hist. 1978 12(1): 97-109.* The historical study of the family has undergone significant methodological shifts in the past decade, but a basic objective remains the same, to "explore the interactions between individual time, family time, and historical time." Identifies and analyzes approaches in the study of the family, in particular "family cycle" and "life course." Shifts position from an earlier advocacy of the use of family cycle to a support for the life course concept which offers new perspectives, new questions, and new beneficial methodologies, one of which is age cohorts. Secondary sources; 26 notes.

R. S. Sliwoski

2448. Hareven, Tamara K. THE FAMILY PROCESS: THE HISTORICAL STUDY OF THE FAMILY CYCLE. *J. of Social Hist. 1974 7(3): 322-329.* Proposes a new mode of analysis of family patterns in 19th-century society. The family is viewed as a process over time rather than as a static unit within certain time periods. This model "assumes fluidity, change and transition in family structure... that individuals live through a variety of patterns of family structure and household organization during different stages of their life cycle, and that families and households evolve different types of organization, structure and relationships which are generally obscured in cross-sectional analysis." Supports the validity of this approach by data from a study of family structure in 19th-century Boston. 15 notes.

R. V. Ritter

2449. Hareven, Tamara K. MODERNIZATION AND FAMILY HISTORY: PERSPECTIVES ON SOCIAL CHANGE. *Signs: J. of Women in Culture and Soc. 1976 2(1): 190-206.* The concept of modernization can be a valuable framework in which to study society and particularly the history of the family. It is often assumed in modernization theory that traditional values and patterns of behavior are replaced by modern ones in a continuous and consistent way. However, historical reality is always more complex and illustrates the uneven changes in individual and societal patterns of behavior. Family history must acknowledge diverse patterns of change from pre- to post-modern behavior within families as well as taking into account differences in class and ethnicity. An attempt must be made to evaluate the means by which families balance traditional and modern attitudes and it must be remembered that families did not modernize as units, but that men and women modernized at different rates within the family structure. 38 notes.

S. R. Herstein

2450. Harris, Neil. CULTURAL INSTITUTIONS AND AMERICAN MODERNIZATION. *J. of Lib. Hist. 1981 16(1): 28-47.* Discusses the historiography of cultural institutions and the changing attitudes about them. Historians were instrumental in molding attitudes about cultural institutions as they reworked American history, especially during 1960-79. Replacing an older set of satisfactions with the development of major cultural institutions, a sense of victories and successes, was a long list of discontents, suspicions, and criticisms. Finally, institutions had to ask whether they were to provide standards for society, or simply meet the needs of society. Presented at the Library History Seminar VI, "Libraries & Culture," Austin, Texas, 19-22 March 1980; 21 notes. J. Powell

2451. Hiner, N. Ray. THE CHILD IN AMERICAN HISTORIOGRAPHY: ACCOMPLISHMENTS AND PROSPECTS. *Psychohistory Rev. 1978 7(1): 13-23.* Summary of writings of scholars such as Phillippe Aries, Lloyd de Mause, Philip Greven, and Lawrence Stone, who have revised notions of childhood by examining changing perceptions of children over time. Reviews historiography on children and presents a series of questions to be analyzed in order to produce a more complete history of childhood. Suggests the reductionistic psychological orientation of some historians of childhood must be tempered by the functionalism of the social historian. Secondary sources; 50 notes. J. M. Herrick

2452. Houston, Rab and Smith, Richard. A NEW APPROACH TO FAMILY HISTORY? *Hist. Workshop J. [Great Britain] 1982 (14): 120-131.* Comments on Miranda Chaytor's "Household and Kinship: Ryton in the Late 16th and Early 17th Centuries." Chaytor has raised some important questions, especially about women and children, but has criticized other historians on the basis of inadequate evidence, suggesting that her approach is not as new as she states. Chaytor has not taken historical and geographical context into proper account: some of her statements refer to what happened in exceptional demographic and economic circumstances; she

generalizes from northeast England to the country as a whole; and she uses anthropological studies of Mediterranean countries not applicable to England. The result is an unbalanced view, especially in regard to the sexual division of labor. Secondary works; illus., 51 notes. D. J. Nicholls

2453. Howe, K. R. THE FATE OF THE "SAVAGE" IN PACIFIC HISTORIOGRAPHY. *New Zealand J. of Hist. [New Zealand] 1977 11(2): 137-154.* Compares and contrasts two historiographical traditions. The first, lasting until the early 1950's, portrayed the Pacific islanders as noble savages ravaged by Western influences. The second, which began in the 1940's, portrays the islanders as active, ambitious savages whose way of life was not necessarily ravaged by European contact. Based on published documents, travel accounts, and secondary sources; 54 notes. P. J. Coleman

2454. Illick, Joseph E. MORE ON THE CHILD IN AMERICAN HISTORIOGRAPHY. *Psychohistory Rev. 1979 7(4): 24-25.* Reply to N. Ray Hiner (see abstract 17A:5938). Suggests historians of childhood, such as Hiner and Lloyd deMause, have overlooked the rejection of the father in the 18th and 19th centuries as a possible explanation of change and human behavior. The transformation of childhood from the 19th century to the 20th century, when children were seen as harmless and enjoyable, may be due to modernization, although that theory is merely descriptive, not explanatory. Argues the human personality has changed over time. 10 notes.

J. M. Herrick

2455. Johnson, Richard. EDWARD THOMPSON, EUGENE GENOVESE AND SOCIALIST-HUMANIST HISTORY. *Hist. Workshop J. [Great Britain] 1978 (6): 79-100.* Culturalism, the Marxist socialist-humanist historiographical method employed by E. P. Thompson and Eugene Genovese, was formulated as a reaction against economism, the Marxist methodology of 1930-56, which had an overriding emphasis on the use of the economic concepts as means of interpreting historical development. Culturalism views class consciousness as an equally important historical determinant. It differs from Louis Althusser's structuralism in which economism is replaced by theoretical postulation. Karl Marx's *Das Kapital* had originally incorporated a mixture of economism, culturalism, and structuralism. 51 notes. G. M. Alexander

2456. Kern, Stephen. THE HISTORY OF CHILDHOOD: A REVIEW ARTICLE. *J. of the Hist. of the Behavioral Sci. 1973 9(4): 406-412.* Discusses writings about childhood in psychology and history from 1960-71, emphasizing the theories of Erik Erikson and David Hunt.

2457. Kim, M. P. O KUL'TURE KAK PREDMETE ISTORICHESKOGO IZUCHENIIA [The subject matter of the general historiography of culture]. *Voprosy Istorii [USSR] 1974 (11): 32-38.* Emphasizes the urgent need to question the general historiography of culture so as to work out a clear conception of its actual content. Drawing on his assessment of the progress of research in the history of Soviet culture, the author puts forward his considerations with regard to evolving a new scheme of research in the problem, which would proceed from a broader, more comprehensive, synthetic approach to culture as a complex, multifaceted and, at the same time, intrinsically integral system distinguished for its rich content and multiform functions. The author believes that at the present juncture there emerges the possibility of more fully defining the most important problems and tasks of research in the history of Soviet culture on the basis of generalizing the experience in the field of studying culture and analyzing the present-day cultural realities. The author's proposals are graphically reflected in a scheme reproduced in the concluding part of the article. J

2458. Kolendo, Jerzy. PROBLEMATYKA HISTORII KULTURY MATERIALNEJ W BADANIACH NAD "STAROŻYTNOŚCIAMI" NA PRZEŁOMIE XVIII I XIX W.: PRZYKŁAD A. MONGEZA [Problems in the history of material culture in studies of ancient objects at the turn of the 19th century: example of A. Mongez]. *Kwartalnik Hist. Kultury Materialnej [Poland] 1982 30(2): 173-180.* Views the methodological aspects of the works of the French classical art historian Antoine Mongez

(1747-1838) and their impact on the contemporary studies of the ancient material culture. His *Dictionnaire d'Antiquités* and *Recueil d'Antiquités* provided detailed analyses of the development of shapes, motifs, and materials used in Roman tools and decorations, based on both the written and the direct archeological sources. Despite some serious chronological mistakes and occasional falling for falsifications, Mongez's work shows familiarity with methods of production and deep knowledge of sciences. 4 illus., 31 notes. French summary. M. Hernas

2459. Larkin, Jack. THE VIEW FROM NEW ENGLAND: NOTES ON EVERYDAY LIFE IN RURAL AMERICA TO 1850. *Am. Q. 1982 34(3): 244-261.* Reviews "landmark" books on daily life in rural America. The changes in the everyday life of the meetinghouse and school provide useful examples of research topics. 30 notes. D. K. Lambert

2460. Luckmann, Thomas. PERSÖNLICHE IDENTITÄT UND LEBENSLAUF: GESELLSCHAFTLICHE VORAUSSETZUNGEN [Personal identity and curriculum vitae: social assumptions]. *Wiener Beiträge zur Geschichte der Neuzeit [Austria] 1979 6: 29-46.* Examines personal identity as a form of life in different aspects of development of human society and its relation to nature.

2461. Madajczyk, Czesław. LES MÉMOIRES EN TANT QUE DOCUMENTS DE MASSE: LES POSSIBILITÉS DE LEUR EXPLOITATION DANS LES SCIENCES HUMAINES [Memoirs as popular documents: possibilities of their exploitation in the human sciences]. *Acta Poloniae Hist. [Poland] 1976 33: 165-176.* In 19th-century Poland there was an explosion of memoir writing, especially after the two unsuccessful insurrections. In the 20th century this activity became less spontaneous but very common. There is no country where diary writing, sponsored by the press or by sociologists, achieved such proportions. The author concentrates his attention on postwar memoirs, written chiefly by the peasants as a result of various competitions. However, these diaries are seldom used by historians; they do not recognize them as valid sources. The author thinks that they could be used as testimonies to the formation of the mentality of present day society. Such collections of memoirs should be analyzed by teams formed of the historians, sociologists, and programmers. 12 notes. H. Heitzman-Wojcicka

2462. Maddoli, Gianfranco. APPUNTI SULLA FORMAZIONE CULTURALE DI EDUARD MEYER: LA "GESCHICHTE VON TROAS" E GLI ANNI DI SCHLIEMANN [Points on the cultural formation of Eduard Meyer: *The History of Troy* and the years of Schliemann]. *Riv. Storica Italiana [Italy] 1981 93(3): 809-820.* Despite the lack of evidence of a direct connection between Eduard Mayer (1855-1930) and Heinrich Schliemann, probably due to the hostile reaction to Meyer's *Geschichte von Troas* [History of Troy] (1877), Meyer's historical outlook was greatly influenced by Schliemann from the first. Their intellectual relations reveal the profound late-19th-century rupture between German ancient historians. Meyer belonged to the "fundamentalists," who believed in a factual basis for Greek epic. Out of his daring challenge to the authority of George Grote and Ernst Curtius laid down in the *History* came the founding of a new science of anthropology. Read at the Scuola Normale Superiore di Pisa [The Pisa Superior Normal School] in February 1981; 30 notes. T. F. Mayer

2463. Maksakova, L. V. MEZHDUNARODNYI KOLLOKVIUM PO PROBLEME "VOINA I KUL'TURA (1939-1945)" [International colloquium on the problem of war and culture, 1939-45]. *Voprosy Istorii [USSR] 1978 (3): 181-182.* Describes colloquium discussions on 1) culture as the subject of investigation and its significance during World War II; 2) the defense of spiritual values during the war; 3) culture as a spiritual weapon of the people in the struggle against fascism; and 4) the specific development of culture in the various groups of countries during World War II. The colloquium, 6-9 September 1977, in Warsaw was organized by the Commission on the History of World War II, the Committee on Historical Sciences, and by the Institute of History at the Polish Academy of Sciences. Primary sources. L. Kalinowski

2464. Malizia, Pierfranco. MARX, STORIA E CULTURA [Marx, history, and culture]. *Nuova Riv. Storica [Italy] 1977 61(3-4): 388-403.* Presents various interpretations of Karl Marx's relationship to cultural history in the context of cultural anthropology and Marxist determinism. 45 notes. J. J. Renaldo

2465. Mikkeli, Heikki. MENTALITEETTIEN HISTORIAA: OLIKO 1500-LUVUN IHMINEN AHNE ATEISTI? [The history of mentalities: were people in the 1500's avaricious atheists?]. *Historiallinen Arkisto [Finland] 1984 (82): 127-139.* Discusses research on the history of mentalities by French and other European historians in the period after 1920. 17 notes. R. G. Selleck

2466. Millar, David. ORDINARY PEOPLE, EXTRAORDINARY HISTORY. *Can. Oral Hist. Assoc. J. [Canada] 1981-82 5(1): 19-24.* Describes the contributions being made by local, ethnic, and occupational historians to a better understanding of social classes in Canada.

2467. Mintz, Lawrence E. "RECENT TRENDS IN THE STUDY OF POPULAR CULTURE": SINCE 1971. *Am. Studies Int. 1983 21(5): 88-104.* Surveys the literature, demonstrating the growth of activity and resources and the development of sophisticated research procedures. Covers research tools, bibliographies, anthologies, and general books, and studies that approach popular culture from such perspectives as structuralism, phenomenology, psychoanalysis, quantification, communications theory, and Marxism. The new methodologies reject description, appreciation, and superficial analysis and approach popular culture as a complex social and cultural phenomenon, to be seen as a process involving the production, distribution, and use of the text or artifact under study. Photo, biblio. R. E. Noble

2468. Moreno, Diego and Quaini, Massimo. PER UNA STORIA DELLA CULTURA MATERIALE [Toward a history of material culture]. *Quaderni Storici [Italy] 1976 11(1): 5-37.* Approaches the history of European material culture from an interdisciplinary approach as a framework for the study of the material basis of past European societies. Analyzes the references to material culture in the works of W. Kula and demonstrates how the very categories and concepts of Marxist historiography necessarily require the fusion of disciplines such as historical geography, archaeology, and European ethnology. The application of the concept of *genre de vie* [way of life] to ethnology and human geography is also briefly discussed. The last four sections review the problems posed from a historiographical point of view by post-classical archaeology. It is not enough to adopt material culture as an instrument of historical archaeology unless the means for integrating this into the history of preindustrial European societies have been foreseen. J

2469. Mozzarelli, Cesare. DALLA STORIA DEL DIRITTO ALLA STORIA ISTITUZIONALE E SOCIALE. QUALCHE RIFLESSIONE SU STORICI E GIURISTI NELL'ETA BORGHESE [From legal history to institutional and social history: some reflections on historians and lawyers in the era of the middle classes]. *Nuova Riv. Storica [Italy] 1977 61(3-4): 404-416.* Discusses various changes in the interpretations historians have given to middle-class society. Secondary sources; 49 notes. J. J. Renaldo

2470. Olsen, Ib. DE NYESTE HOVEDRETNINGER INDENFOR DEN FAMILIEHISTORISKE FORSKNING OM VESTEUROPA I PERIODEN CA. 1400 TIL CA. 1800 [The newest trends in family history research concerning Western Europe in the period ca. 1400-1800]. *Hist. Tidsskrift [Denmark] 1983 83(1-2): 166-194.* Discusses results of research on the emergence of the nuclear family in preindustrial England, France, and Germany. Three factors have been especially studied: changes in 1) emotions and consciousness, 2) household size and structure, and 3) inheritance laws. With considerable regional variations, the nuclear family was clearly present in preindustrial times, but a full theoretical explanation has yet to be worked out. Based on published books and articles; 9 tables, 47 notes. R. G. Selleck

2471. Ory, Pascal. HYPOTHESES DE TRAVAIL EN HISTOIRE CULTURELLE: L'EXEMPLE DE LA FRANCE CONTEMPORAINE [Working hypotheses in cultural history: the example of contemporary France]. *Bull. de la Soc. d'Hist. Moderne [France] 1982 81(14): 6-13.* Discusses cultural history as the "social history of representations," with particular reference to France since 1870.

2472. Østberg, Berit. BARN I LOKALHISTORIEN [Children in local history]. *Heimen [Norway] 1982 19(4): 227-231.* Children have been neglected in local history writing. Their culture has greater continuity than that of adults, yet changes constantly. Much about games, songs, rhymes, and customs can be learned from modern children. For earlier times, sources are meagre, but interviewing old people, especially in large gatherings, can produce valuable results.   D. F. Spade

2473. Palmer, Bryan. CLASSIFYING CULTURE. *Labour [Canada] 1981-82 8-9(Aut-Spr): 153-183.* Poses a critique of selected recent writing on US and British working-class culture, arguing against the tendency to categorize culture into discrete ideal types. It argues the importance of locating culture materially and historically, developing a notion of periodization that recognizes particular stages of development and levels of conflict and struggle. As such it poses an implicit rejection of recent Canadian polemics directed against the study of the cultural.   J

2474. Peeters, H. F. M. VIJF EEUWEN GEZIN EN KIND IN WEST-EUROPA. EEN HISTORIOGRAFISCH OVERZICHT. ENKELE LIJNEN EN RICHTLIJNEN [Five centuries of family and child in Western Europe: a historiographic survey—some lines and directions]. *Tijdschrift voor Geschiedenis [Netherlands] 1981 94(3): 343-376.* In recent decades many local, regional, national, and other family studies have appeared. They focus on such problems as the development of the nuclear family, the size of the family, marriage, mortality rates, etc. In Western Europe in the early part of the 19th century the husband married at age 28 and the woman at 25. The average size of the family was five while about 50% of the children died before the age of 20. Studies reveal that family life became more humane and "emotionalized" in the latter part of the 18th century. Sources used by family historians are diaries, autobiographies, memoirs, and letters. Secondary materials; 127 notes.   G. D. Homan

2475. Pershits, A. I. [TRADITIONS AND THE HISTORICAL PROCESS] (Russian text). *Narody Azii i Afriki [USSR] 1981 (4): 69-84, (5): 81-92.* Part 1. TRADITSII I KUL'TURNO-ISTORICHESKII PROTSESS [Tradition and the cultural historical process]. A theoretical discussion of the possibilities and pitfalls of using traditions—and the cultural changes reflected in their evoluton—as source materials in historiography. Part 2. DINAMIKA TRADITSII I VOZMOZHNOSTI IKH ISTOCHNIKOVEDCHESKOGO ISTOLKOVANIIA [The dynamics of traditions and the possibilities of their interpretation as sources]. Uses examples drawn from Arabia, Australasia, and Africa to establish the variety and unpredictability of the forms and tempo with which traditions can be modified. This variability renders their use as historical sources complex. Various methods of differentiation and analysis are discussed, and attention is drawn to the parallels between traditions and vestiges. English summary.   F. A. K. Yasamee

2476. Prude, Jonathan. THE FAMILY IN CONTEXT. *Labor Hist. 1976 17(3): 422-436.* In Bernard Farber's *Guardians of Virtue, Salem Families in 1800* and Michael Anderson's *Family Structure in Nineteenth Century Lancashire* conceptual approaches to the family in historical context are ineffectively developed. Secondary sources; 23 notes.   L. L. Athey

2477. Rollyson, Carl E., Jr. *ABSALOM, ABSALOM!*: THE NOVEL AS HISTORIOGRAPHY. *Literature and Hist. [Great Britain] 1977 (5): 42-54.* William Faulkner's *Absalom, Absalom!* (1936) is a historical novel which shows how common people can comprehend and misunderstand the idea of history in relation to their lives. A number of passages in the novel can profitably be com-

pared with the writings of prominent historians and thinkers on the subject of historical awareness. Based on Faulkner's writings and on secondary sources; 37 notes.   N. Dejevsky

2478. Rousseau, G. S. THE PERFECT BLENDSHIP. *Am. Scholar 1981 50(4): 552-555.* In order to understand the evolution of sex and sensibility, these two concepts must be juxtaposed and viewed as parallel developments.   F. F. Harling

2479. Ryan, Mary P. THE EXPLOSION OF FAMILY HISTORY. *Rev. in Am. Hist. 1982 10(4): 181-195.* The wealth of data resulting from a decade of family history studies has made it necessary to reexamine basic suppositions about the American family.

2480. Sabean, David Warren. THE HISTORY OF THE FAMILY IN AFRICA AND EUROPE: SOME COMPARATIVE PERSPECTIVES. *J. of African Hist. [Great Britain] 1983 24(2): 163-171.* In comparing and evaluating the history of the family in Europe and Africa, there are problems concerning the concept of "family." During certain periods in Europe, as in many African societies, no single word was synonymous with the English term "family." Recently, researchers have defined family by the functions and roles it performed. As a result, they have begun to identify concepts of house, household, and homestead, as being more specific. These concepts are directly related to a consideration of how sources of authority have perceived the family as a unit of production, consumption, and reproduction. Further refinement in the analysis of societies including the correlation of reproduction to production and the reevaluation of kinship relationships must occur before comparison and analysis can be more precise. 48 notes.   J. M. Gilbert

2481. Schlereth, Thomas J. MATERIAL CULTURE STUDIES AND SOCIAL HISTORY RESEARCH. *J. of Social Hist. 1983 16(4): 111-143.* Reviews recent literature on the artifacts, objects, and hardware of history—a growing field of study encompassed by material culture studies. 105 notes.   C. M. Hough

2482. Schlumbohm, Jürgen. ZUM STAND DER KINDHEITSFORSCHUNG [On the state of research on the history of childhood]. *Geschichtsdidaktik [West Germany] 1983 8(4): 305-316.*

2483. Schuppan, Peter. BEMERKUNGEN ZUM GEGENSTAND EINER MARXISTISCHEN KULTURGESCHICHTE [Marxist cultural history]. *Zeitschrift für Geschichtswissenschaft [East Germany] 1974 22(12): 1359-1376.* Marxist historiography must analyze the material culture of all classes in all phases of economic social formations; working and living conditions; and emotional, spiritual and intellectual elements, including ethnology and folklore.

2484. Schuppan, Peter. MARX UND ENGELS ÜBER KULTUR UND KULTURENTWICKLUNG. THEORETISCHE GRUNDLAGEN FÜR EINE GEGENSTANDSBESTIMMUNG DER MARXISTISCH-LENINISTISCHEN KULTURGESCHICHTSSCHREIBUNG [Marx and Engels on culture and cultural development: theoretical bases for a determination of objectivity in Marxist-Leninist cultural historiography]. *Jahrbuch für Volkskunde und Kulturgeschichte [East Germany] 1976 19: 9-54.* The views of Karl Marx and Friedrich Engels on culture and cultural history are the bases for Marxist-Leninist concepts of cultural historiography. The basic Marxist view is that political, religious, literary, and cultural developments in general are epiphenomena of economic developments. This clear theoretical understanding provided the correct path in the labyrinth of facts which confronts the historian. 135 notes.   J. C. Billigmeier

2485. Seigel, Rudolf. ZUR GESCHICHTSSCHREIBUNG BEIM SCHWÄBISCHEN ADEL IN DER ZEIT DES HUMANISMUS: AUS DEN VORARBEITEN ZUR TEXTAUSGABE DER HAUSCHRONIK DES GRAFEN VON ZOLLERN [Historiography on the Swabian aristocracy during the period of humanism: preliminary works for the edition of the family chronicle of the counts of Zollern]. *Zeits. für Württembergische Landesgeschichte [West Germany] 1981 40: 93-119.* Family history as a separate undertaking of the Swabian aristocracy only became fashionable in the 16th century. The aristocratic family chronicle is a distinct category in historiography. These sources stress the origins and the world view of several Swabian families. As far as their genealogical aspects are concerned, these chronicles are "modern" in terms of sources and interpretative skills. Based on documents from several German regional archives; 100 notes.　　　　　　M. Geyer

2486. Sengle, Friedrich; Sz. Érdi, Éva, transl. A BIEDERMEIER KOR [The Biedermeier era]. *Helikon Világirodalmi Figyelő [Hungary] 1982 28(1): 10-16.* Translates the preface to *Biedermeierzeit* (1971). Explains the difficulties encountered in writing a book which is to offer a new insight into the period, without being involved in the traditionally sentimental German approach of yearning for the "good old days" or attempting to present a historically bygone age in a modernized and therefore more entertaining context.　　　　　　T. Kuner

2487. Shore, Miles F. THE CHILD AND HISTORIOGRAPHY. *J. of Interdisciplinary Hist. 1976 6(3): 495-505.* Analyzes the collection of essays edited by Lloyd deMause, *The History of Childhood* (New York, 1974). Despite an evangelistic tone, it is an important and provocative work and should be a strong stimulus to further work in the field on the part of both historians and behavioral scientists. 11 notes.　　　　　　R. Howell

2488. Smith, Daniel B. THE STUDY OF THE FAMILY IN EARLY AMERICA: TRENDS, PROBLEMS, AND PROSPECTS. *William and Mary Q. 1982 39(1): 3-28.* Reviews the literature on family history of the 17th and 18th centuries, with emphasis on the publications of the 1960's and 70's. Until mid-1970, studies focused on historical demography and New England. Since then there has been a shift to demographic foundations and the rest of the colonies. Especially there has been recent interest in parent-child relations and sex-role patterns. Cites the significant interpretive trends, and discusses the leading studies. Secondary literature; 76 notes.　　　　　　H. M. Ward

2489. Sogner, Sølvi Bauge. "ETT LAND, TO KULTURER" [One country, two cultures]. *Heimen [Norway] 1979 18(4): 241-249.* Ståle Dyrvik in *Den Lange Fredstiden, 1720-1784* [The Long Peacetime, 1720-84], ed. Knut Mykland, vol. 8, *Norges Historie* [Norway's History], cites the need for study of 18th-century folk culture. History lacks information on the occupations, customs, and lives of common people. A historical ethnology is needed to answer the many questions about the population such as regional, occupational, and class variations.　　　　　　E. E. Krogstad

2490. Spagnoli, Paul G. PHILIPPE ARIES, HISTORIAN OF THE FAMILY. *J. of Family Hist. 1981 6(4): 434-441.* Reflects on Philippe Ariès's recent autobiography, *Un Historien du Dimanche,* and his body of historical works such as *Centuries of Childhood* and *Western Attitudes towards Death.* Much insight into his historical approach and philosophy is gained by knowledge of his political, family, and occupational background. 6 notes, biblio.　　　　　　T. W. Smith

2491. Spiecker, B. and Groenendijk, L. F. FANTASIES IN RECENT HISTORIOGRAPHY OF CHILDHOOD. *British Journal of Educational Studies [Great Britain] 1985 33(1): 5-19.* Critique of the "main-effect" model employed in contemporary psychohistory of the family and childhood by John Demos, Lloyd de Mause, and Lawrence Stone. The use by these authors of the "nomological-deductive" mode of explanation inherent in the main-effect model results in the assigning of causality to changing relationships between children and adults. Secondary sources; 44 notes.　　　　　　D. G. Nielson

2492. Stage, Sarah J. OUT OF THE ATTIC: STUDIES OF VICTORIAN SEXUALITY. *Am. Q. 1975 27(4): 480-485.* A review essay prompted by recent works on Victorian sexual attitudes in America by Carl N. Degler, Robin and Mark Haller, and Ronald G. Walters. Despite the indicated significance of sex as a factor in history in these works, a full determination of the relationship between sexual ideology and behavior cannot be achieved unless sex-

ual advice literature, such as that used as source material in these studies, is balanced against actual sexual behavior and demographic, economic, social and legal factors.　　　　　　N. Lederer

2493. Stone, Albert E. AUTOBIOGRAPHY IN AMERICAN CULTURE: LOOKING BACK AT THE SEVENTIES. *Am. Studies Int. 1981 19(3-4): 3-14.* Recent critical studies of American autobiography have shifted emphasis from the past, which autobiography recreates, to the self-conscious "I" who remembers and to strategies of self-composition. Historians and social scientists explored autobiography less carefully and imaginatively than did literary critics. Black autobiography received particular attention; less so women's autobiography, which lacks a full-length study and adequate bibliography. American Indian autobiography emerged as a discrete literary and historical subject. Autobiography continues to be "a flourishing national pastime and one of the livelier fields of current American studies." Photo, 40 notes.　　　　　　R. E. Noble

2494. Tanase, Al. THE CULTURAL CONDITION OF THE HISTORICAL FACT. *Rev. Roumaine d'Hist. [Rumania] 1975 14(2): 241-250.* The historical fact is characterized by existential, spatial, and temporal determinations and must be appreciated in its totality, its distinct individuality, or its uniqueness. Many historians have attempted to give "an integrating image" to cover datum, such as Wilhelm Dilthey and Nicolae Iorga with their respective systems of civilization and historical permanences. The author surveys the neo-Kantians' ideas as to the cultural and axiological nature of the historical fact, stressing that a fact becomes historical only when it regards a value objectification; thus according to Heinrich Rickert reference to values is a theoretical device necessary for knowing historical fact. Historical sciences are thus at the same time sciences of culture, for "a people achieves its historical personality only by its culture." History must therefore cease its exclusive preoccupation with the political and examine the phenomena of economic, material, and spiritual culture if it wishes to aspire to integrity and totality. Secondary writings; 11 notes.　　　　　　G. J. Bobango

2495. Thorsen, Niels. FRA FAELLESSKAB TIL FAELLESMARKED: *VOR TIDS KULTURHISTORIE'S* KULTUR [From community to Common Market: the culture of *The Cultural History of Our Times*]. *Hist. Tidsskrift [Denmark] 1982 81(2): 425-441.* Erling Bjøl's *Vor Tids Kulturhistorie* [3 vol., 1978-79] is a symptom of and an element in a cultural development in the Western world and the formation of a new mentality. The concept of an organized society, to which history is contributing, has replaced that of the organic society with a collective memory and awareness. The work is an indication of how history will be written and taught in Denmark in the future. Secondary sources; 18 notes, 26 ref.　　　　　　H. C. Andersen

2496. Tilly, Charles and Tilly, Louise A. STALKING THE BOURGEOIS FAMILY. *Social Sci. Hist. 1980 4(2): 251-260.* Reviews and criticizes the work of two major interpreters of the modern bourgeois family, Christopher Lasch and Lawrence Stone. Both are charged with participating in an idealist reaction against recent social science, and are criticized primarily for their failure to make better use of the tools and methods of the new social history. Ref.　　　　　　L. K. Blaser

2497. Tilly, Louise A. and Cohen, Miriam. DOES THE FAMILY HAVE A HISTORY? A REVIEW OF THEORY AND PRACTICE IN FAMILY HISTORY. *Social Sci. Hist. 1982 6(2): 131-180.* Reviews progress of the past decade in European and American family history. Divides family history into three major approaches—demographic, sentiments (or attitudes), and household economics—and evaluates the major works and strengths and weaknesses of each approach. Newer trends include a "hegemonic-institutional" approach and exploration of the ties between family history and women's history. Suggests areas for future study. Review essay of secondary sources; 7 notes, biblio.　　　　　　L. K. Blaser

2498. Tilly, Louise A. and Cohen, Miriam. LA FAMIGLIA HA UNA STORIA? [Does the family have a history?]. *Passato e Presente [Italy] 1982 (2): 105-145.* Surveys the English-language literature on the history of the family since the 16th century published in the United States, Great Britain, and Western Europe in the last decade. Most of the literature falls into three categories: demographic studies, studies of sentiments and attitudes, and household economy. Discusses the methods used and their possible modifications. Also touches on certain applied versions of the history of the family and the light they throw on new aspects of social reality. 6 photos, 94 notes. J. V. Coutinho

2499. Vann, Richard T. THE MAKING OF THE MODERN FAMILY BY EDWARD SHORTER. *J. of Family Hist. 1976 1(1): 106-117.* During the last two decades Edward Shorter has tried to piece together and synthesize the rapidly growing number of scholarly studies in family history and historical demography. Shorter utilizes the available data to speculate on the familial transition spurred by the Industrial Revolution, concentrating on courtship, the mother-child relationship, and family-community interaction. 5 notes, biblio. T. W. Smith

2500. Vann, Richard T. THE YOUTH OF *CENTURIES OF CHILDHOOD. Hist. and Theory 1982 21(2): 279-297.* Considers the impact and continuing validity of Philippe Ariès's *Centuries of Childhood,* first published in 1960. It pioneered contemporary research in the history of the family and the history of mentalities. Its influence grew throughout the 1970's and citations to it became legion in a variety of disciplines. Though the work blazed an intellectual trail, it is not definitive nor has it gone unchallenged in many of its basic claims. Ariès has an obvious nostalgia for the Middle Ages even though his assertion that the period had no real notion of childhood or the "sentimental" nuclear family has been successfully refuted. 50 notes. W. J. Reedy

2501. Veress, Éva. A TÖRTÉNETILEG VÁLTOZÓ CSALÁD PROBLÉMÁJÁRÓL [The problem of the historically changing family]. *Történelmi Szemle [Hungary] 1983 26(1): 172-175.* So far the social sciences have not produced a concept which could be used by historians in the study of the family. Instead of searching for the definition of the family, historians should try to find out how families function. This approach would help to create a model of the dynamic family within a constantly changing historical framework. 4 notes. T. Kuner

2502. Vicinus, Martha. SEXUALITY AND POWER: A REVIEW OF CURRENT WORK IN THE HISTORY OF SEXUALITY. *Feminist Studies 1982 8(1): 133-156.* Review essay, covering seven books on different aspects of, and theoretical models for the study of, sex and sexuality, published 1978-81. 59 notes. S. Hildenbrand

2503. Vogel, Lise. THE CONTESTED DOMAIN: A NOTE ON THE FAMILY IN THE TRANSITION TO CAPITALISM. *Marxist Perspectives 1978 1(1): 50-73.* Examines family history theory of the 1950's-70's as it perceives transition in the 19th and 20th centuries.

2504. Wheaton, Robert. INTRODUCTION: RECENT TRENDS IN THE HISTORICAL STUDY OF THE FRENCH FAMILY. Wheaton, Robert and Hareven, Tamara K., ed. *Family and Sexuality in French History* (Philadelphia: U. of Pennsylvania Pr., 1980): 3-26. Compares Philippe Ariès's *L'enfant et la vie familiale sous l'ancien règime* (Paris, 1960), with Lawrence Stone's *The Family, Sex and Marriage in England 1500-1800* (New York, 1977). Topics considered by both studies and the essays in this collection include kinship terminology, marriage formation, economic basis of marriage, family size, and parent-child relationships. Three main themes emerge: the great variety of patterns in French familial behavior, subordination of the individual to the needs of the larger kin group, and the slow rate at which changes in the relationship of the simple family to the community and kin group have occurred. 13 notes, biblio.

2505. Wilkinson, Rupert. AMERICAN CHARACTER REVISITED. *J. of Am. Studies [Great Britain] 1983 17(2): 165-187.* The focus of generalizing about American culture, an old intellectual preoccupation, has changed significantly since the 1930's, the most

recent studies probing psychological variables in the character, attitudes, and personal values of Americans. Both American and foreign interpreters have variously traced the roots of American character to contemporary social forces, social institutions, economic ideologies, and conditions peculiar to the United States or inherent to international trends. Others stress the importance of American behaviors such as penchants for individualism. 60 notes. H. T. Lovin

2506. Wilson, Adrian. THE INFANCY OF THE HISTORY OF CHILDHOOD: AN APPRAISAL OF PHILIPPE ARIÈS. *Hist. and Theory 1980 19(2): 132-153.* Critically examines the pathbreaking study of the history of childhood in the West written by Philippe Ariès and translated into English as *Centuries of Childhood* (London, 1962). Ariès's amateur work suffers from three main defects: it relies almost entirely on printed and pictorial evidence; it does not relate its subject to a wider historical and social context; and it consistently assumes a "present-minded" point of view. These shortcomings lead Ariès to misread and misuse the evidence he considers, especially iconographic evidence concerning the evolution of attitudes toward the child. Because it was the pioneering work in the field it has guided researchers for the past 20 years. However, its present-centered character makes its methodological faults inevitable. It is a prime example of what Collingwood condemned as "scissors-and-paste" history. 72 notes. W. J. Reedy

2507. Winock, Michel. L'ENFANT À TRAVERS LES SIÈCLES: ENTRETIEN AVEC PHILIPPE ARIÈS [Children through the centuries: an interview with Philippe Ariès]. *Histoire [France] 1980 (19): 85-87.* Considers the state of historiography by a pioneer of mentalities 20 years after the publication of his *L'Enfant et la vie familiale sous l'Ancien Régime.*

2508. Wirtz, Rainer. ASPETTI DELLA STORIOGRAFIA TEDESCA SULLA CRIMINALITÀ [Aspects of German historiography on criminality]. *Quaderni Storici [Italy] 1981 16(1): 212-224.* Criminology and history have found a very limited field for common research in Germany. Social problems related to crime have been studied within very narrow frameworks. However, certain historians, inspired by the work of Dirk Blasius and F. Sack, have begun to investigate crime as a symptom of the pathology of bourgeois society in the course of its development. 29 notes. J. V. Coutinho

2509. Zak, L. M. SOVREMENNAIA SOVETSKAIA ISTORIOGRAFIIA O PROBLEMAKH NATSIONAL'NO-KUL'TURNOGO STROITEL'STVA [Modern Soviet historiography on problems of cultural development in the national Soviet Republics]. *Istoriia SSSR [USSR] 1971 (5): 82-95.* The history of the development of socialist multinational culture is investigated and studied widely by Soviet historians. The author reviews the works on the subject chronologically and analyzes the important problems of national cultural construction in Soviet historiography. All Soviet republics had much in common during the cultural revolution and so in the historical literature of the national republics there are many general works on the process of cultural construction. However, there are also separate important problems that concern some of the republics: the overcoming of cultural backwardness; the formation of the intelligentsia; the development of national education; the emancipation of women; and the cultural impact of the class struggle. Many works have been written by historians of the republics on these particular problems. Secondary sources; 76 notes. L. Kalinowski

2510. Zub, Alexandru. HISTOIRE ET ANTHROPOLOGIE: LA CONTRIBUTION DE MIRCEA ELIADE [History and anthropology: the contribution of Mircea Eliade]. *Rev. des Etudes Sud-Est Européennes [Romania] 1981 19(2): 301-310.* Provides an overview of the contribution of Mircea Eliade to the development of a new historiography based on cultural anthropology and related disciplines. Secondary sources; 39 notes. L. J. Klass

2511. —. [THE HISTORY OF CULTURE AND THE HISTORY OF EDUCATION]. *Történelmi Szemle [Hungary] 1974 17(3): 421-453.*
Niederhauser, Emil. A KULTÚRTÖRTÉNET KÉRDÉSÉHEZ [The question of cultural history], *pp. 421-429.* Discusses material and spiritual cultural history in the context of the Slovaks in Czechoslovakia before 1938.
Makkai, László. MŰVELŐDÉSTÖRTÉNET MINT ÉRTÉKRENDSZEREK TÖRTÉNETE [The history of education as the history of systems of values], *pp. 429-436.* Marxism views education as a coherent system of values.

Kosáry, Domokos. A MŰVELŐDÉSTÖRTÉNET HELYE A TÖRTÉNELMI SZINTÉZISBEN [The place of the history of education in historical synthesis], *pp. 436-446.* The Enlightenment period, 1711-90, was crucial in Hungarian cultural history.
Hanák, Péter. A KULTÚRTÖRTÉNETI SZINTÉZIS PROBLÉMÁI [Problems of synthesis in cultural history], *pp. 447-453.* Historians must fit specific manifestations of culture into the framework of the historical process. E. E. Soos

8. POLITICAL HISTORY

2512. Barret-Kriegel, Blandine. HISTOIRE ET POLITIQUE OU L'HISTOIRE, SCIENCE DES EFFETS [History and politics or history, science of results]. *Ann.: Economies, Sociétés, Civilisations [France] 1973 28(6): 1437-1462.* Philosophical analysis of the approach to the history of politics in view of the concerns of the *Annales* school of historians. The philosophical bases of the *Annales* school are examined and related to a return to political history which is seen as a science of results rather than of causes. Printed sources; 48 notes.   R. Howell

2513. Baumgold, Deborah. POLITICAL COMMENTARY ON THE HISTORY OF POLITICAL THEORY. *Am. Pol. Sci. Rev. 1981 75(4): 928-940.* Presents the study of the history of political theory as a branch of political studies. Prior to the postwar success of empirical political science, the view would have seemed unexceptional. But the need for a defense against the empiricist attack impelled many theorists to turn to theories of interpretation in search of a philosophical and methodological identity. A preoccupation with issues of interpretation now threatens the customary, political study of the tradition. The author, writing in defense of a political understanding of the field, identifies fundamental propositions distinguishing "political commentary," suggests critical standards appropriate to the enterprise, and criticizes two currently fashionable applications of interpretative theory to the study of politics, historicist commentary and hermeneutical political science.   J

2514. Bodnar, Artur. SYSTEM POLITYCZNY A PODŁOŻE HISTORYCZNE [Political system and historical background]. *Studia Nauk Pol. [Poland] 1981 (1): 11-31.* An analysis of the interrelationship between political system and historical background political science. Defines the political system according to F. Ryszka, J. Kowalski, W. Lamentowicz, and B.N. Topornin. Then, five factors are discussed determining the historical continuity of the social environment and its main properties. In the analysis of political problems it is more correct to use the notion of "socio-historical background," viewed by M. Karwat. Considers three research methods applied to the study of relations between the political system and the historical background of a given society or group; these are the comparative method, the historical method, and the systems method.   J/S

2515. Boucher, David. NEW HISTORIES OF POLITICAL THOUGHT FOR OLD? *Pol. Studies [Great Britain] 1983 31(1): 112-121.* Discusses recent writing on the history of political thought professing to have been inspired in their method by Quentin Skinner, establishing their relation to older work and how far there is a consensus on the appropriate methods for studying the history of political thought. The new histories continue and refine older tendencies. There are elements of textualism, indicating a satisfaction with the literal meaning of some works; contextualism, both linguistic and phenomenal; historical purism, a love of the past for the sake of the past; and historical impurism, the tendency to do something more than history. The new histories can be viewed as defenses of the last bastions of the traditional approaches to the study of the history of political thought against the encroachment of social scientific explanations upon the sphere of historical understanding. Based on secondary works; 30 notes.
                                                      D. J. Nicholls

2516. Ceppa, Leonardo. DIALETTICA DELL'ILLUMINISMO E OPINIONE PUBBLICA: I MODELLI DI HABERMAS E KOSELLECK [The dialectic of Enlightenment and public opinion: the models of Habermas and Koselleck]. *Studi Storici [Italy] 1984 25(2): 343-352.* Discusses the interpretation of Jürgen Habermas concerning bourgeois political conceptions. Starting from the etymology of *Öffentlichkeit*, Habermas notes the essential link between the Enlightenment, liberalization, and the *openness* to public scrutiny of the political system. He traces the changes of *Öffentlichkeit* from the feudal period to the age of mass media. In the Enlighten-

ment, the public sphere included a large degree of public opinion which was mobilized against absolutism. Reinhart Koselleck set up a similar dialectic, and the work of both historians points the way to a historical sense motivated by political awareness of actual problems. 13 notes.   J. W. Houlihan

2517. Cervelli, Innocenzo. SUL RAPPORTO FRA STORIOGRAFIA E POLITICA NELL'ETÀ DELL'IMPERIALISMO. A PROPOSITO DI UN RECENTE LIBRO SU F. MEINECKE [On the relationship of historiography to politics in the age of imperialism. A propos a recent book about F. Meinecke]. *Storia Contemporanea [Italy] 1970 1(3): 577-594.* Discusses a recent study, *Federico Meinecke e la Crisi dello stato nazionale tedesco* (Turin, 1969) by Sergio Pistone, devoted to the political thought of Friedrich Meinecke. Emphasizes the various phases in the evolution of Meinecke's political attitudes, which became progressively more elaborate in contrast to *kleindeutsch* attitudes and the more statically conservative ones in the manner of Heinrich von Treitschke. Pistone misses the connection between historiographic thought and a liberal-imperialistic or social-imperialistic political ideology. But, by interpreting the phenomenon of imperialism in Lenin's terms and noting the striking modernity of the young Max Weber's views on capitalistic economy, one arrives at an adequate historical and political understanding of the connection between historiographic orientation, political thought, and imperialism.   J/S

2518. Chadwick, Owen. HISTORIAN OF EMPIRE. *Modern Asian Studies [Great Britain] 1981 15(4): 877-880.* Reviews Deborah Wormell's *Sir John Seeley and the Uses of History* (1980). Seeley, famous for his studies on imperialism and its history, aimed to improve politics by training future politicians in history and political economy. The readability of Seeley's works does not mean that they are superficial.

2519. Chaimowicz, Thomas. MONTESQUIEU AND TACITUS. *Continuity 1983 (7): 41-54.* Charles de Montesquieu, 18th-century French political philosopher, learned much from classical historians, especially Tacitus. Because he was thoroughly versed in Latin literature, Montesquieu understood the subtleties of the abbreviated form of expression Tacitus used to structure his complex thoughts. Montesquieu found much in Roman history to augment his understanding of French history; contemporary historians cannot expect to understand the foundations of Montesquieu's political theories unless they approach them from this angle.   W. A. Wiegand

2520. Condren, Conal. THE DEATH OF POLITICAL THEORY: THE IMPORTANCE OF THE HISTORIOGRAPHICAL MYTH. *Politics [Australia] 1974 9(2): 146-149.* Discusses the decline of political theory and the insecure position of political theorists in the 1950's-60's. Serious difficulties emerge when the history of political theory is viewed as a separate area of intellectual activity. This orthodox view of the discipline leads to inadequate histories of political theory. Political theorists, philosophers, and political scientists did not challenge this orthodox historiographical perception in the 1950's. The flaws in "the enshrined mythology acted in different ways to undermine the viability of contemporary political theory." Secondary sources; 23 notes.   R. G. Neville

2521. Daalder, H. MODERNE POLITIEKE WETENSCHAP EN HET NUT VAN DE GESCHIEDENIS [Modern political science and the use of history]. *Bijdragen en Mededelingen Betreffende de Geschiedenis der Nederlanden [Netherlands] 1975 90(2): 226-243.* Modern research methods as employed by the behaviorist-oriented political scientist can be successfully applied to the study of history. Dutch historians could study the process of centralization of the Netherlands from the Burgundian to the modern era, including an examination of the 19th century in terms of the social origins of the civil service, the composition of parliament, the development of political parties, and the process of politicization of the bureaucracy. Historians must overcome some of their traditional research approaches to make such studies effective. 21 notes.

G. D. Homan

2522. Dachs, Herbert. ÜBER EINIGE TRENDS IN MODERNEN FÖDERALISMUS [Some trends in modern federalism]. *Zeitgeschichte [Austria] 1975 3(2): 56-64.* A historiographical essay on the development of federalism especially in Austria and the United States, from dynastic federalism to constitutional federalism between the 18th and 20th centuries.   R. Wagnleitner

2523. Dawson, Nelson L. UNEQUAL JUSTICE: MCCARTHY AND HISS. *Midstream 1981 27(4): 13-16.* Compares the treatment of Joseph R. McCarthy and Alger Hiss in history textbooks, with special attention to the liberal bias in these books that dangerously makes Communism appear as just another political option in a pluralistic world.

2524. Dejung, Christoph. TYRANNIS. EIN BEITRAG ZUR GESCHICHTE DES BEGRIFFES "TOTALITARISMUS" [Tyranny: a contribution to the history of the term "totalitarianism"]. *Schweizerische Zeitschrift für Geschichte [Switzerland] 1980 30(3-4): 386-389.* Totalitarianism is an unhistorical term. It was a convenient means to understand some of the social and political phenomena of the 20th century, but it has outlived its usefulness. As a term of vague negativism it cannot be applied to older, traditional ideologies. Being blind toward the social content of a political system and the historical factors that led to its rise, totalitarianism helps little to understand systems of state socialism such as Stalinist Russia or the military dictatorships of Third World countries. It should be replaced by "fascism" which offers itself as a much better tool for the description and analysis of the wide range of phenomena that influenced recent history, from the 1920's to the second spring of fascism in today's Third World.   H. K. Meier

2525. DelNoce, Augusto. IL PROBLEMA DELLA DEFINIZIONE STORICA DEL FASCISMO [The problem of the historical definition of fascism]. *Storia e Politica [Italy] 1976 15(1): 121-170.* Discusses the intellectual and spiritual roots of Fascism in the light of Renzo De Felice's *Le interpretazioni del fascismo* (Bari: 1969, 1971). De Felice finds the ultimate roots of Fascist activism in the naturalism and pessimism of the 19th century (Renan and Taine had influenced young Mussolini). De Felice denies a common nature to the various rightist, anti-Communist, and antidemocratic movements usually grouped together as fascist which swept Europe in the 1920's and 1930's, affirming an irreducible qualitative difference between various conservative and reactionary movements on one hand, and Nazism and Fascism on the other. He also distinguishes between Fascism and Nazism and between Fascism as a movement and Fascism in power. Fascism, he maintains, perished in 1945; there are no Fascists left today; the radicals of the right found in various countries have nothing to do with historical Fascism. 41 notes.   J. C. Billigmeier

2526. De Santis, Vincent P. THE POLITICAL LIFE OF THE GILDED AGE: A REVIEW OF THE RECENT LITERATURE. *Hist. Teacher 1975 9(1): 73-106.* An overview and evaluation of recent literature dealing with the political history of the Gilded Age. Older writers, such as James Bryce and Matthew Josephson, interpreted the period in a negative manner. Numerous revisionist works appeared in the 1950's and 1960's, and these depicted the politics of the Gilded Age in a more positive way. Yet textbooks and general histories of this period many times still stress the older, less positive view. Primary and secondary sources; 6 illus., 76 notes.

P. W. Kennedy

2527. Diggins, John P. POWER AND AUTHORITY IN AMERICAN HISTORY: THE CASE OF CHARLES A. BEARD AND HIS CRITICS. *Am. Hist. Rev. 1981 86(4): 701-730.* Offers a theoretical and methodological examination of the criticisms made against Charles A. Beard (1874-1948) by a number of notable post-World War II historians, among them Richard Hofstadter, Bernard Bailyn, Jack P. Greene, Cecelia Kenyon, Robert Brown,

Lee Benson, and Edmund S. Morgan. The author attempts to refute five specific charges made against Beard: 1) that he read back into the Constitution a conflict between the ideas of liberty and property that has no basis in the emancipatory spirit of the 18th century, 2) that he erred in claiming the Constitution departed from the emancipatory spirit of the Declaration of Independence, 3) that he failed to consider contemporary Whig ideas about economic "independence," political "virtue," and social "deference", 4) that he neglected to study 18th-century intellectual history; and 5) that he mistakenly interpreted James Madison's theory of government as an expression of "economic determinism." In addition, the author attempts to show that one of Beard's ultimate concerns involved the question of authority and its legitimacy in America. Hence, his great classic, *An Economic Interpretation of the Constitution,* may be read as an effort to demonstrate the alienation of economic power from political authority by tracing its genesis to the theories of the framers. Based on the complete works of Beard and the secondary literature of the post-World War II historians, as well as *The Federalist* and other 18th-century primary materials; 88 notes.

2528. Duroselle, Jean-Baptiste. PIERRE RENOUVIN ET LA SCIENCE POLITIQUE [Pierre Renouvin and political science]. *Rev. Française de Sci. Politique [France] 1975 25(3): 561-574.* For Pierre Renouvin, historian, what sort of relationship should history have with political science? Certainly one of dependence since in his opinion there could be no political science without history or, to be more precise, without the data with which history provides the political scientist. In fact, through his enlightened scepticism with regard to political science, Pierre Renouvin condemned the now widespread tendency to speculate upon abstractions representing concrete phenomena before these concrete phenomena have been studied in depth. Lastly, to see political science only as present-day history, lacking in scope and neglected, was to reassert the superior and demanding conception of history that Pierre Renouvin professed throughout his work. History is much more than a science; it is the instrument which provides the human sciences with the raw material that they must shape to their own ends. Which is a modest way of saying that nothing is outside the scope of history.

J

2529. Erdmann, Karl Dietrich. NATIONALSOZIALISMUS—FASCHIMUS—TOTALITARISMUS [National socialism—fascism—totalitarianism]. *Geschichte in Wissenschaft und Unterricht [West Germany] 1976 27(8): 457-469.* Soviet-Marxist theories of fascism cannot explain the fact that fascism was not able to develop in the most highly developed bourgeois-capitalist societies in the United States, Great Britain, and France. The Marxist, the bourgeois-liberal, and the phenomenological explanations of fascism correlate with the three main forces of the 20th century. Based on secondary literature; 30 notes.

R. Wagnleitner

2530. Erényi, Tibor. TÖRTÉNELEM ÉS POLITIKA [History and politics]. *Társadalmi Szemle [Hungary] 1981 36(6): 58-71.* Hiding or distorting history is against the interests of a Marxist state. Society will suffer if historians attempt to glorify or idealize any person or group. Mistakes as well as successful undertakings must be shown in an objective manner. Only by adhering to these principles will historians be able to fulfill the most important role in society, the education of students in their formative years. 8 notes.

T. Kuner

2531. Erofeev, N. A. L. NEMIR I EGO MESTO V BURZHUAZNOI ISTORIOGRAFII [Louis Namier and his place in bourgeois historiography]. *Voprosy Istorii [USSR] 1973 (4): 76-89.* The article analyzes the extensive scientific legacy of the prominent British historian Louis Namier, whose close study of the British 18th-century political scene enabled him to refute the widespread legends concerning the character of the major English political parties and Parliament of that period. Another important scientific service rendered by Namier consists in evolving the methodological principles of studying the history of Parliament through the biographies of individual members of Parliament. The article also briefly examines a number of major works written by Namier's pupils and followers.

J

2532. Ezergailis, Andrew. NATIONALISM IN WORLD POLITICS AND HISTORY. *Nationalities Papers 1975 3(2): 60-88.* Assesses the usefulness of the concept of nationalism in historiography in the 1970's and examines historians' misconceptions about the relation of nationalism to other ideologies, such as imperialism, conservatism, racism, and fascism.

2533. Fay, Victor. CONCEZIONI DIVERSE DELLA DITTATURA DEL PROLETARIATO [Various conceptions of the dictatorship of the proletariat]. *Ponte [Italy] 1977 33(11-12): 1325-1330.*

2534. Femia, Joseph. THE GRAMSCI PHENOMENON: SOME REFLECTIONS. *Pol. Studies [Great Britain] 1979 27(3): 472-483.* Antonio Gramsci's mounting popularity in the English-speaking world has led to a flood of books about him. Some very dubious interpretations have emerged, but even more worrying is the fact that there has been no serious attempt to evaluate his ideas from either an ethical or a scientific point of view. It is clear that Gramsci's thought raises issues of contemporary importance, but the recent English language literature on him is limited in scope and often mistaken in conclusions. 27 notes. R. Howell

2535. Fuchs, Peter. DER ABSOLUTISMUS ALS FORSCHUNGSPROBLEM. ZWEI NEUE BESTANDSAUFNAHMEN [Absolutism as a research problem: two new anthologies]. *Hist. Zeitschrift [West Germany] 1975 220(3): 642-648.* Absolutism is one of the continuing topics of historical research and discussion. This article describes and evaluates the contributions to this topic which appear in two new collections: 1) Walther Hubatsch, ed., *Absolutismus* (Darmstadt, 1973) and 2) Karl Otmar von Aretin, ed., *Der aufgeklärte Absolutismus* (Cologne, 1974).

G. H. Davis

2536. Garrard, John. SOCIAL HISTORY, POLITICAL HISTORY AND POLITICAL SCIENCE: THE STUDY OF POWER. *J. of Social Hist. 1983 16(3): 105-121.* Discusses assumptions and definitions and questions of use and measurement surrounding the terms "political" and "power" in the social sciences and in historical inquiry. 38 notes. C. M. Hough

2537. Geras, Norman. SENSIBILITÀ LETTERARIA E CULTURA POLITICA NEL GIOVANE TROCKIJ [Literary sensitivity and political culture in young Trotsky]. *Ponte [Italy] 1980 36(11-12): 1132-1180.* Not generally valued properly even within the international socialist movement, Leon Trotsky's early writings represent the richest and most inventive part of his work: incisive, precise, lucid in political portraits, he is at his best placing political events in their more complex historical context, as best shown in *1905;* he is not just a political theoretician, but has a great aptitude for historical synthesis.

2538. Goodway, David. THE METIVIER COLLECTION AND THE BOOKS OF GEORGE JULIAN HENRY. *Bull. of the Soc. for the Study of Labour Hist. [Great Britain] 1984 (49): 57-60.* Describes and discusses this wide-ranging collection of books held at Vanderbilt University, Nashville, Tennessee, which were deposited between April 1919 and March 1925. The collection is particularly strong on 19th-century politics and historical works, particularly on the United States.

2539. Gunnell, John G. INTERPRETATION AND THE HISTORY OF POLITICAL THEORY: APOLOGY AND EPISTEMOLOGY. *Am. Pol. Sci. Rev. 1982 76(2): 317-327.* Recent challenges to traditional approaches and purposes for studying the history of political theory have raised questions about its constitution as both a subject matter and subfield of political science. Methodological arguments advocating what is characterized as a more truly historical mode of inquiry for understanding political ideas and recovering textual meaning have become increasingly popular. The relationship of these hermeneutical claims about historicity, such as that advanced by Quentin Skinner, to the actual practice of interpretation is problematical. Such claims are more a defense of a certain norm of historical investigation than a method of interpretation, and the implications of this norm for the reconstitution of the history of political theory require careful consideration.

J

2540. Howe, Daniel Walker. EUROPEAN SOURCES OF POLITICAL IDEAS IN JEFFERSONIAN AMERICA. *Rev. in Am. Hist. 1982 10(4): 28-44.* Examines recent historiography suggesting that Jeffersonian America was more receptive to European political theory than was previously believed.

2541. Hrochová, Věra and Hroch, Miroslav MYTUS KŘÍŽOVÝCH VÝPRAV V BURŽOASNÍ HISTORIOGRAFII [The myth of the Crusades in bourgeois historiography]. *Československý Časopis Hist. [Czechoslovakia] 1975 23(4): 533-564.* Views the 18th-century non-Marxist historiography of the Crusades as an expression of bourgeois society's ideology, used in special conditions for political propaganda by the state, party, or ideological group. The "Crusade idea" became a visible instrument of anticommunism during the Cold War era. Printed sources; 157 notes.

G. E. Pergl

2542. Jensen, Richard. HOW DEMOCRACY WORKS: THE LINKAGE BETWEEN MICRO AND MACRO POLITICAL HISTORY. *J. of Social Hist. 1983 16(3): 27-34.* Describes five succeeding frameworks of interpretation that have characterized the work of political scientists and historians: Baconian, Idealist, Turnerian, Pluralist, and Behavioral. The current behavioralist view is the prevailing mold for political science, the new political history, and the new social history. 18 notes. C. M. Hough

2543. Jong, Rudolf de. DE ONTWIKKELING VAN HET ANARCHISME [The development of anarchism]. *Spiegel Hist. [Netherlands] 1979 14(11): 579-588.* Despite the difficulty of writing a general history of anarchism with its emphasis upon individualism and diversity, a comparative history is possible, for several threads run through the movement as a whole: its search for practical responses to immediate circumstances; its ties with socialism; its emphasis upon spontaneity and direct action by the masses. An examination of the socioeconomic environment that produced it reveals that it was never exclusively agrarian and that immigrants have played an important role throughout its history. Primary sources; 19 illus. C. W. Wood

2544. Kaushik, Asha. THE VITAL CENTRE: A. M. SCHLESINGER, JR., AS HISTORIAN. *Indian J. of Am. Studies [India] 1981 11(2): 17-25.* Arthur M. Schlesinger, Jr.'s theory of liberalism as the "vital center" of American political life occupies a significant place in contemporary historiography. Rejecting both ideological conservatism and radicalism, Schlesinger welcomes both flexibility and pragmatism as liberals must meet changing situations. 28 notes. L. V. Eid

2545. Kraynak, Robert P. HOBBES'S *BEHEMOTH* AND THE ARGUMENT FOR ABSOLUTISM. *Am. Pol. Sci. Rev. 1982 76(4): 837-847.* Hobbes's history of the English Civil War, *The Behemoth,* has been neglected by contemporary scholars, yet it provides the clearest statement of the problem that Hobbes's political science is designed to solve. In *Behemoth,* Hobbes shows that societies such as 17th-century England inevitably degenerate into civil war because they are founded on authoritative opinion. The claim that there is a single, authoritative definition of rightness or truth which is not an arbitrary human choice is an illusion of "intellectual vainglory," a feeling of pride in the superiority of one's opinions which causes persecution and civil strife. By presenting Hobbes's historical and psychological analysis of this problem, illuminates his argument for absolutism and shows that Hobbes is not a precursor of totalitarianism but a founder of liberalism. J

2546. Laslett, J. H. M. PLURALISM, LIBERALISM, AND HISTORY: SEYMOUR MARTIN LIPSET AND HIS WORLDVIEW. *Society 1983 20(5): 64-68.* An overview of the work of political sociologist Seymour Martin Lipset; Lipset has examined two major themes in his work: the uniqueness of the United States and the stability of democracy.

2547. Linse, Ulrich. ANARCHISMUS-THEORIEN [Theories on anarchism]. *Archiv für Sozialgeschichte [West Germany] 1979 19: 585-589*. Recent German studies have contributed to the understanding of anarchism, though they are speculative in some parts.
H. W. Wurster

2548. Lozek, Gerhard. BÜRGERLICHE GESCHICHTSSCHREIBUNG IM ZEICHEN IMPERIALISTISCHER POLITIK [Bourgeois historiography under the sign of imperialist policy]. *Einheit [East Germany] 1975 30(12): 1414-1421*. West German concepts of history use bourgeois parliamentarianism as historical legitimacy for an anti-Communist interpretation of history.
R. Wagnleitner

2549. Ludington, Charles Townsend, Jr. THE NOVELIST AS POLITICAL HISTORIAN IN THE UNITED STATES. *Indian J. of Am. Studies [India] 1982 12(1): 57-68*. Modernists, like Norman Mailer in *Armies of the Night* (1968) and E. L. Doctorow in *Ragtime* (1975), hold that no sense can be made of "history" because external events no longer provide structure. If chaos is the rule, the novelist becomes the better historian. Serious novels that are politically engaged can be ignored only at our peril. 21 notes.
L. V. Eid

2550. Matsuzuka, Shunzō. SUPENSU (THOMAS SPENCE, 1750-1814) KAN NO HENKAN: RADIKARIZUMU KARA SEN-NEN ŌKOKU SHYUGIE [Changing views on Thomas Spence (1750-1814): from radicalism to millennialism]. *Shigaku Zasshi [Japan] 1981 90(1): 67-88*. Enumerating Spence's studies in chronological order, the article explains that Thomas Spence was not only a radical or a pioneer of land-nationalization socialism but also a millenarian. Spence's millennialism was examined and accepted by the socialists of the late 18th century. Around the end of the 19th century and the beginning of the 20th century, some sociologists recognized Spence's land-nationalization theory. Until the middle of this century, Spence was considered a radical; however, in the 1960's Thomas Malcom Knox referred to the "radical biblicism" of Spence. C. Garett and John Feltcher Clews Harrison described that Spence was a millenarian, discussing pre- and post-millennialisms. Spence's theory should be studied further to make clear his principle of the French Revolution and millennialism. 79 notes.
M. Kawaguchi

2551. McKinley, Blaine. ANARCHIST JEREMIADS: AMERICAN ANARCHISTS AND AMERICAN HISTORY. *J. of Am. Culture 1983 6(2): 75-84*. Reviews attitudes of prominent anarchists toward American historical events, such as the American Revolution and the Civil War, and toward historical figures, such as John Brown and George Washington.

2552. Mellon, Stanley. NINETEENTH-CENTURY PERCEPTIONS OF REVOLUTION. Parker, Harold T., ed. *Problems in European History*, (Durham, N.C.: Moore Publ., 1979): 59-71. Twentieth-century observers tend to view the French Revolution as having remade Europe in an institutional sense. It destroyed the power of monarch, aristocracy and church for all time. The succeeding period of restoration was doomed from the start. The people of the 19th century did not share this perspective, and yet, paradoxically, they viewed the revolution in far more heroic dimensions and were far more convinced of its crucial importance. The reason for this was their keener appreciation of the cultural changes, the dramatic and irreversible shift in world views that grew out of the period. Much 20th-century scholarship has suppressed the traumatic quality of the revolution; Americanizing and historicizing it.
L. W. Van Wyk

2553. Mühlpfordt, Günter. AUGUST LUDWIG SCHLÖZER UND DIE "WAHRE DEMOKRATIE": GESCHICHTS- UND OBRIGKEITSKRITIK EINES ANWALTS DER UNDERDRÜCKTEN UNTER DEM ABSOLUTISMUS [August Ludwig Schlözer and the "true democracy": A critique of history and authority by a lawyer of the opressed under absolutism]. *Jahrbuch des Instituts für Deutsche Geschichte [Israel] 1983 12: 29-73*. Schlözer emancipated history from its focus on dynasties, war, and foreign policy. The essence of history to Schlözer was cultural and scientific development and the evolution of legal systems and financial practices. Schlözer applauded the ambitions of the French Revolution and fought for human rights, including the rights of women, the poor, and agricultural labor. He concluded that the only natural political system was democracy. Based on memoirs and secondary sources; 105 notes.
S. P. Forgus

2554. Nezhinski, L. N. SOVIETSKA HISTORIOGRAFIA O REVOLÚCIÁCH ŠTYRIDSIATYCH ROKOV V KRAJINÁCH STREDNEJ A JUHOVÝCHODNEJ EURÓPY [Soviet historiography on revolutions of the 1940's in Central and Southeastern Europe]. *Hist. Štúdie [Czechoslovakia] 1982 26: 179-188*. Revolutions of the 1940's in Europe and Asia became the largest political event in world history, second only to the October 1917 Revolution. Soviet historiography pays constant attention to research about these events because of their enormous value for scientific and political evaluation and historical knowledge. Based on published sources; 24 notes.
G. E. Pergl

2555. O'Gorman, Frank. FIFTY YEARS AFTER NAMIER: THE EIGHTEENTH CENTURY IN BRITISH HISTORICAL WRITING. *Eighteenth Cent.: Theory and Interpretation 1979 20(2): 99-120*. Lewis Namier's description of the structure of 18th-century politics has never been seriously challenged, although modern research has begun to question its relevance to any period significantly earlier or later than the mid-18th century. Despite revisions of his views on the powers of the monarchy, the rise of the cabinet, the structure of Parliament, the development of parties, and the function of ideology in politics, historians owe a debt to Namier for creating a rigorous methodology. Secondary sources; 78 notes.
H. T. Blethen

2556. Peterson, Steven A. BIOPOLITICS: LESSONS FROM HISTORY. *J. of the Hist. of the Behavioral Sci. 1976 12(4): 354-366*. Delineates the boundaries and history of biopolitics as a subdiscipline of social science as well as the historical antecedents to current studies (in three categories: metaphor, evolutionary influences, and public policy implications) through a series of historical examples from European and American history, 16c-20c.

2557. Raitière, Martin N. AMPHIALUS' REBELLION: SIDNEY'S USE OF HISTORY IN *NEW ARCADIA*. *J. of Medieval and Renaissance Studies 1982 12(1): 113-131*. Sir Philip Sidney, in his *New Arcadia* (1584), used the "monarchomach" program with which he was familiar not to uphold the lawful rebellion of a low-status magistrate against the defective rule of a monarch, but to condemn it as an act leading to political unrest and the destruction of the state. The author analyzes the texts and the documents on which the *Arcadia* is based and concludes that Sidney was only nominally a member of the "warrior aristocracy," and that he was completely skeptical of the aristocratic cult of "martial courage" which lay behind the monarchomachs of 16th-century France. The historiographical context is expertly drawn, and Anglo-French-Dutch relationships are placed within this framework. Based on a wide range of documents and interpretive literature; 42 notes.
L. A. Knafla

2558. Rutman, Darrett B. POLITICAL HISTORY: THE NEW AND THE PSEUDO-NEW. *J. of Interdisciplinary Hist. 1972 2(3): 305-310*. A review article prompted by Robert Zemsky's *Merchants, Farmers, and River Gods: An Essay on Eighteenth-Century American Politics* (Boston, Gambit, 1971), Jere R. Daniell's *Experiment in Republicanism: New Hampshire and the American Revolution, 1741-1794* (Cambridge, Mass.: Harvard U. Press, 1970) and Donald B. Cole's *Jacksonian Democracy in New Hampshire, 1800-1851* (Cambridge, Mass.: Harvard U. Press, 1970). Differentiates the methodology of political history as practiced in these three historical studies of the political aspects of American history during mid-18th to the mid-19th centuries. After applying the guidelines of the "truly new political history" concludes that Zemsky is new, Daniell is not, and Cole, though superficially new, fails to meet the standards under careful scrutiny. 7 notes.   R. V. Ritter

2559. Sabia, Daniel R., Jr. POLITICAL EDUCATION AND THE HISTORY OF POLITICAL THOUGHT. *American Political Science Review 1984 78(4): 985-999.* Texts designed to introduce political science students to the history of political thought or to past political theories have been commonplace in the discipline, as have disputes about their pedagogical utility or justifiability, and methodological debates concerning their adequacy or legitimacy. In an effort to address these disputes and some of these debates, three models of historiographical inquiry are examined. Each model represents a particular approach and is defined in terms of three common features. The methodological debates are addressed indirectly by identifying clearly the major features and purposes of these approaches, and directly by consideration of such issues as the nature of a historical tradition, the legitimacy of certain interpretive strategies and presuppositions, and the viability of certain conceptions of past political theory. Each approach can make significant contributions to the education of political science students.   J/S

2560. Sivachev, N. V. NOVYE ISSLEDOVANIIA AMERIKAN-SKIKH UCHENYKH PO ISTORII POLITICHESKIKH PARTII SSHA [New research by American academics on the history of political parties in the USA]. *Novaia i Noveishaia Istoriia [USSR] 1970 (4): 162-169.* A critical bibliography of recent work on political history published in the United States. The works mentioned appeared in the 1960's and covered the whole span of American political development up to the 1964 Republican campaign. Criticizes the bourgeois approach to historiography, yet admits that "new and sometimes unusual methods of study" have emerged. Published secondary works; 34 notes.   D. N. Collins

2561. Smolenski, N. I. PROBLEMA "POLITICHESKOI ISTORII" V SOVREMENNOI BURZHUAZNOI ISTORIOGRAFII FRG [The problem of political history in contemporary West German bourgeois historiography]. *Novaia i Noveishaia Istoriia [USSR] 1980 (5): 158-166.* An investigation of the writing of contemporary West German historians who are opposed to the new interdisciplinary methods of social historians and prefer to concentrate on political history. Details of the debate within West Germany about the possibility of fusing the social sciences and history lead to a look at the political approach to reality. German secondary sources; 75 notes.   D. N. Collins

2562. Strauss, Gerald. THE HOLY ROMAN EMPIRE REVISITED. *Central European Hist. 1978 11(3): 290-301.* Discusses the transformation of the historical view of the Holy Roman Empire resulting from the recent publication of several sound works on its history. Once viewed as a monstrosity, the empire is now seen as a viable political structure which worked because its agencies and processes were capable "of sustaining established institutions, hierarchies, values, and conventions."   C. R. Lovin

2563. Tadić, Božidar. NEKA POLAZNA SHVATANJA O DRUSTVENO-ISTORIJSKOM RAZVOJU KOD TEORETIČARA KONVERGENCIJE [Basic concepts about sociohistorical development held by convergence theorists]. *Istorijski Zapisi [Yugoslavia] 1978 31(1-2): 61-117.* Discusses how sociohistorical development has been analyzed in the last 20 or 30 years by the so-called convergence theorists, who hold that there is no fundamental sociohistorical difference between socialist and capitalist systems.

2564. Tonsor, Stephen J. A FRESH START: AMERICAN HISTORY AND POLITICAL ORDER. *Modern Age 1972 16(1): 2-8.* In the American experience, the notion of "a fresh start" has taken the proportions of a national purpose. But because man cannot evade language, he cannot jettison history. Historians and political scientists as rhetoricians should activate the past into consciousness, where its meaning can be comprehended and its consequences dealt with. 12 notes.   M. L. Lifka

2565. Topolski, Jerzy. REWOLUCJE W DZIEJACH NOWOŻYTNYCH I NAJNOWSZYCH (XVII-XX WIEK) [Revolutions in contemporary and modern times, 17th-20th centuries]. *Kwartalnik Hist. [Poland] 1976 83(2): 251-267.* The term "revolution" is used in different meanings, depending on ideological and theoretical perspective. The author gives examples of inadequate interpretations of European revolutions and of the American Revolution and points out that they deform the image of history. Following Marxist theory, revolutions should be treated as an event possessing an objective meaning (i.e., as a historical process) as well as a subjective meaning (i.e., as human endeavors steered by a definite aim). Revolutions are the highest manifestation of the historical activity of society and their influence on everday development is exceptionally strong. The author proposes a classification of revolutionary movements. 37 notes.   H. Heitzman-Wojcicka

2566. Tully, James H. THE PEN IS A MIGHTY SWORD: QUENTIN SKINNER'S ANALYSIS OF POLITICS. *British J. of Pol. Sci. [Great Britain] 1983 13(4): 489-509.* Discusses Quentin Skinner's writings on interpretation and explanation in history and social science and on the development of early modern political thought; the author describes how Skinner's work sheds light on the present day.

2567. VanderMeer, Philip. COLLECTIVE BIOGRAPHY AND THE NEW POLITICAL HISTORY. *Indiana Social Studies Q. 1980-81 33(3): 5-20.* Discusses the limitations of the traditional narrative and chronological way of studying political history and the responses to it over the past two decades, focusing on collective biography in which information about many individuals in a particular group is collected, rather than focusing on a few "unusual characters."

2568. Villari, Rosario. IL POSTO DELLA STORIA [The role of history]. *Studi Storici [Italy] 1982 23(2): 325-328.* The study of history is essential for contemporary politics. Without an understanding of history, one risks obscuring the major values, such as democracy and socialism, that society has created in the course of its development. History has not been supplanted by other social sciences. Although history's methods may have changed, its contribution to an understanding of the past remains unique.   E. E. Ryan

2569. Weisser, Henry. CHARTISM AND THE HISTORIANS. *British Studies Monitor 1978 8(3): 16-26.* Chartism as a political movement in Great Britian deserves more attention than it has received lately. A review of how historians have handled the movement in the past suggests that considerable responsibility for Chartism's obscurity devolves upon them. Historians must get away from technical disputes and narrow scholarly preoccupations in order to present a picture of Chartism for the general reader. 26 notes.   R. Howell

2570. Westfall, William. HISTORY AS PASSPORT: FRANCES FITZGERALD AND HER CRITICS. *Social Studies 1981 72(2): 52-55.* Serious public and professional criticism of the distortions and inaccuracies plaguing historiography can largely be blamed on politics. 36 notes.   L. R. Raife

2571. Wilsher, J. C. "POWER FOLLOWS PROPERTY"—SOCIAL AND ECONOMIC INTERPRETATIONS IN BRITISH HISTORICAL WRITING IN THE EIGHTEENTH AND EARLY NINETEENTH CENTURIES. *J. of Social Hist. 1983 16(3): 7-26.* Cites 17th-century French and English writers, and 18th- and early-19th-century British historians at length to show their persistent attention to socioeconomic explanations of political developments. By mid-century, scholarly professionalism and the detail of the work of Stubbs and Acton channeled history into the documentary political mold. 107 notes.   C. M. Hough

2572. Yasutake, Hidetake. DENTŌ TO SHITENO AMERIKA MINSHU-SHUGI [American democracy as a tradition]. *Rekishigaku Kenkyū [Japan] 1971 18: 1-11.* The estimation of Jacksonian democracy has an important meaning for the establishment of American national history. By rearranging theories on Jacksonian democracy, the author aims to examine the tradition of American national history of the 20th century. After studying the theories of Frederick Jackson Turner, B. Hammond, and Richard Hofstadter, insists that American democracy must be understood in a worldwide context and also related to the problem of why socialism has not been permitted in American society. Mentions new left historians. M. Ito

2573. Zietsman, P. H. DIE UITBEELDING VAN PERSOON-LIKHEDE EN VAN DIE TYDSKLEUR IN DIE GESKIED-SKRYWING [The representation of personality and of period color in historiography]. *Kleio [South Africa] 1973 5(1): 53-59.* Review article on M. Weiner's *The Sovereign Remedy* (1971).

2574. —. [ON LINCOLN'S POLITICAL RELIGION]. *Pol. Theory 1982 10(4): 520-546.*

Corlett, William S., Jr. THE AVAILABILITY OF LINCOLN'S POLITICAL RELIGION, pp. 520-540. A refutation of some concepts presented in Harry Jaffa's *The Crisis Of the House Divided* (1959), including the view that Lincoln viewed himself as a God among men.

Thurow, Glen E. REPLY TO CORLETT, pp. 541-546.

Communism, Fascism, Marxism, and Totalitarianism

2575. Agosti, Aldo. LA STORIOGRAFIA SULLA TERZA INTERNAZIONALE [The historiography of the Third International]. *Studi Storici [Italy] 1977 18(1): 139-169.* Reviews some 200 works on the history of the Comintern, distinguishing three phases in the historiography of international communism, an early journalistic period, Cold War historiography in the 1950's, and the present period, commencing with works by Annie Kriegel (1963) and W. T. Angress (1964).

2576. Aizin, B. A. PROBLEMY RABOCHEGO DVIZHENIIA I SOVREMENNYI ANTIKOMMUNIZM [Problems of the workers' movement and contemporary anti-Communism]. *Novaia i Noveishaia Istoriia [USSR] 1974 (4): 184-195.* In their attempts to rewrite history, anti-Communist bourgeois historians write of the integration of the working class into the capitalist system. They misquote the works of progressive historians to discredit socialism. For example, Peter Nettl, with an idiosyncratic view of Marxism, and showing sympathy for Eduard Bernstein, belittles Rosa Luxemburg, claiming that the Communist movement in 1914 was isolationist. He misrepresents her attitude towards imperialism, rejects as exaggerated her accounts of the exploitation of workers in capitalist countries, and dismisses Luxemburg's warning concerning the danger of a world war. Luxemburg made mistakes, but reactionary authors have denigrated her works to discredit Marxism. Based on the works of J. P. Nettl, K. Meyer, P. Frölich, V. I. Lenin, B. Kautsky; 35 notes. A. J. Evans

2577. Albrecht, Dieter. ZUM BEGRIFF DES TOTALITARISMUS [On the term totalitarianism]. *Geschichte in Wissenschaft und Unterricht [West Germany] 1975 26(3): 135-141.* Reviews the history of the term totalitarianism since the 1920's, and the postwar discussion of its meaning. Many researchers now regard totalitarianism primarily as the construction of a new society with new values imposed by force. Marxist opponents of this theory deny its validity for both National Socialism and Soviet communism. They stress the differences in the social content of the two systems, despite formal congruities. The author concedes this, but sees totalitarianism as a formal technique of power. The decisive criterion for the victims is the totalitarian demands, and not socioeconomic differences. Therefore National Socialism and Soviet communism are archetypes of totalitarianism. Secondary sources; 9 notes. H. W. Wurster

2578. Ambri, Mariano. "FASCISMI" E FASCISMO ["Fascisms" and fascism]. *Affari Esteri [Italy] 1977 9(34): 351-369.* Discusses several historiographical approaches to Fascism in Italy, recognizing its European antecedents and the tendency to call all 20th-century manifestations of similar historical phenomena fascist.

2579. Anderson, M. F. and Petriakov, G. V. OBSUZHDENIE "OCHERKOV ISTORII KP LATVII" [A discussion of *Sketches on the History of the Latvian CP*]. *Voprosy Istorii KPSS [USSR] 1961 (1): 219-222.* Describes and comments on a meeting in Riga in October 1960 between representatives of the Latvian Communist Party and the Institute of Party History to discuss a projected history of the Latvian Communist Party, 1893-1919.

2580. Barg, M. A. O DVUKH UROVNIAKH MARKSISTSKOI TEORII ISTORICHESKOGO POZNANIIA [Two levels of Marxist theory of historical conception]. *Voprosy Filosofii [USSR] 1983 (8): 107-114.* The Marxist doctrine of socioeconomic formation calls for the study of society as a unified, developing organism and views world history as a unified, organic whole.

2581. Bartel, Horst; Gemkow, Heinrich; and Winkler, Gerhard. OBZOR NAUCHNO-ISSLEDOVATEL'SKOI RABOTY V GDR V OBLASTI ISTORII MARKSIZMA [A survey of scientific research work in the GDR in the sphere of the history of Marxism]. *Voprosy Istorii KPSS [USSR] 1963 (5): 106-118.* Looks at some of the work of East German historians published, 1955-62, on subjects including the state and the Paris Commune.

2582. Belkina, G. L. MARKSIZM I BURZHUAZNAIA MARK-SOLOGIIA: ISTORICHESKIE ETAPY BOR'BY [Marxism and bourgeois Marxology: historical periods of struggle]. *Voprosy Filosofii [USSR] 1976 12: 80-92.* Analyzes the historical periods of the struggle of Marxism and the bourgeois ideology in its Marxological version and shows some predominant trends typical of each period. Although the emergence of Marxology in the narrow sense of the word is associated with bourgeois ideologists' attempts to use Marx's early works against Marxism, the use of Marx's works as arguments against Marxism were really first made in the 19th century. From the beginning of the 20th century they have assumed a quite definite character. J/S

2583. Blinkin, Ia. A. IZDANIIA GUVEROVSKOGO INSTITUTA VOINY, REVOLIUTSII I MIRA [Publications of the Hoover Institution on War, Revolution and Peace]. *Voprosy Istorii [USSR] 1978 (10): 189-195.* That the Hoover Institution on War, Revolution and Peace is a leading anti-Communist center is immediately evident from the views of its Director W. G. Campbell, and of leading collaborators. A brief survey of some of the Institution's publications, including books and the *Russian Review,* illustrates the Institution's falsification of the history of Communism, Leninism, V. I. Lenin, and the history of the USSR. 43 notes. A. P. Oxley

2584. Boev, Petko. NAUCHEN TRUD ZA TRETIIA KONGRES NA KOMUNISTICHESKIIA INTERNATSIONAL [Scholarly work on the third congress of the Comintern]. *Izvestiia na Inst. po Istoriia na BKP [Bulgaria] 1976 34: 395-403.* Review of a compilation of articles by various historians published as *Tretii Kongress Kominterna* (Moscow: Politizdat, 1975) on the 1921 Congress.

2585. Brava, Gian Mario. RIFLESSIONI SULLA STORIA DEL MARXISMO [Reflections on the history of Marxism]. *Studi Storici [Italy] 1982 23(3): 517-540.* A review of two volumes of *Storia del Marxismo* [History of Marxism], edited by Eric J. Hobsbawm, Georges Haupt, Franz Marek, Ernesto Ragionieri, Vittorio Strada, and Corrado Vivanti: vol. 2, *Il Marxismo nell'Età della Seconda Internazionale* [Marxism in the age of the Second International] (1979); vol. 3/1, *Il Marxismo nell'età della Terza Internazionale. Dalla Rivoluzione d'Ottobre alla Crisi del '29* [Marxism in the age of the Third International. From the October revolution to the crisis of '29] (1980); and vol. 3/2, *Dalla Crisi del '29 al XX Congresso* [From the crisis of '29 to the 20th congress] (1981). Primary sources; 71 notes. E. E. Ryan

2586. Cambel, Samuel. O PREDMETE A METODOLOGICKÝCH VÝCHODISKÁCH DEJÍN SOCIALIZMU [History of socialism: the subject and its methodological points of departure]. *Československý Časopis Hist. [Czechoslovakia] 1981 29(3): 350-365.* The history of socialist construction, especially in Czechoslovakia, is a natural topic that awaits concentrated team-work during the 7th Five-Year Plan. The transformation of the village after 1948 is one major field that offers vast, unexplored documentation. Marxist historians must tackle it systematically, while avoiding the pitfalls of a mere positivist accumulation of facts. 24 notes. Russian and English summaries.
R. E. Weltsch

2587. Chistiakov, V. V. ROZA LIUKSEMBURG I MEZHDUNA-RODNOE RABOCHEE DVIZHENIE [Rosa Luxemburg and the international working-class movement (in commemoration of the birth centenary)]. *Voprosy Istorii [USSR] 1971 (3): 65-80.* The opening part of the article is devoted to the characteristic given by Marxist and bourgeois historiography of Rosa Luxemburg's activity in the international working-class movement. The author makes a detailed analysis of Rosa Luxemburg's views on the proletariat, highlighting her significant achievements in this sphere and, at the same time, disclosing her mistakes and their causes. The article sheds light on V. I. Lenin's attitude to Rosa Luxemburg's theoretical works and revolutionary activity. In conclusion the author traces the gradual evolution of Rosa Luxemburg's views towards Leninism, especially after the victory of the Great October Socialist Revolution.
J

2588. Chvostov, Vladimir Michailovič. DIE NEUESTE GESCH-ICHTE DES DEUTSCHEN IMPERIALISMUS IN DER WEST-DEUTSCHEN HISTORIOGRAPHIE [The most recent history of German imperialism in West German historiography]. *Zeitschrift für Geschichtswissenschaft [East Germany] 1967 15(4): 581-594.* West German historians try to prove that the monopoly bourgeoisie had no responsibility for the rise of fascism. They define fascism as the integration of various social groups and stress its popular character without working out the genuine class character of Nazism. 41 notes.
R. Wagnleitner

2589. Cocatre-Zilgien, Andre. REGARDS CRITIQUES SUR LE MARXISME [Critical observations on Marxism]. *Écrits de Paris [France] 1974 (337): 25-37.* Historical events since the 17th century cannot be analyzed according to Marxist principles; other factors, enumerated here, are bases for evaluation.

2590. Cunliffe, John. THE COMMUNIST LEAGUE AND THE "DISSOLUTION QUESTION." *J. of Modern Hist. 1981 53(1): 164.* The controversy over Karl Marx's alleged dissolution of the Communist League in 1848 is misplaced because neither Communist nor non-Communist historians have succeeded in demonstrating that Marx's purported decision could effectively have dissolved the League. Abstract only.
J. D. Hunley

2591. Daline, V. M. THE MOST RECENT FOREIGN LITERA-TURE ON BABEUF. *Soviet Studies in Hist. 1973 11(4): 353-370.* Reviews the literature by and about Babouvism and its founder, Gracchus Babeuf, whom Soviet scholar V. P. Volgin and others consider an early Communist, 1789-1971.

2592. Dentoni, Mario Concetta. CONTADINI E COMMUNISMO: ASPETTI DI UN PROBLEMA STORIOGRAFICO [Peasants and communism: aspects of a historiographic problem]. *Italia Contemporanea [Italy] 1982 (149): 105-111.* The problem of the relationship between Marxism and the world of rural workers remains to be resolved and has become the litmus test for policies of the Left everywhere. Based on primary sources; 30 notes.
E. E. Ryan

2593. Diehl, Ernst. ZU EINIGEN PROBLEMEN UND AUFGA-BEN DER GESCHICHTSWISSENSCHAFT DER DDR IN DER GEGENWÄRTIGEN ETAPPE [Some problems and tasks of historical science in the German Democratic Republic at the present stage]. *Zeitschrift für Geschichtswissenschaft [East Germany] 1969 17(11): 1393-1402.* Suggests that East German historians should recognize that their work is a means of furthering the Marxist-

Leninist workers' struggle, and should discover new ways to present clearly the historical background to the class struggle and relate it to contemporary political affairs. Historians must be critical of themselves and must use their journals for discussion of this problem, the correction of imperialist histories, and general historical criticism. By doing this they will broaden and promote the Marxist-Leninist view of history and society. Secondary materials; 6 notes.
G. H. Libbey

2594. Dziamski, Seweryn. HISTORIA MYŚLI MARKSISTOWS-KIEJ W POLSCE [The history of Marxist thought in Poland]. *Studia Filozoficzne [Poland] 1977 6(139): 55-68.* Traces the history of the studies of Marxism in Poland, 1877-1939, as regards both their sociophilosophical and ideological aspects.

2595. Eichler, Helga and Lehmann, Hannelore. DER DEUTSCHE TERRITORIALSTAATLICHE ABSOLUTISMUS [German territorial-state absolutism]. *Zeitschrift für Geschichtswissenschaft [East Germany] 1970 18(12): 1616-1618.* Reports on a colloquium held in Berlin on 2 May 1970 on absolutism in the German states, 16th-18th centuries. Papers and discussions covered the positions of Karl Marx and Friedrich Engels on German absolutism and the development of this theme in subsequent Marxist historiography.
J. B. Street

2596. Eley, Geoff. WHAT PRODUCES FASCISM: PRE-INDUSTRIAL TRADITIONS OR A CRISIS OF THE CAPITAL-IST STATE. *Pol. & Soc. 1983 12(1): 53-82.* Much of the recent literature on the origins and ideology of fascism has taken on a historical perspective that emphasizes preindustrial traditions. These explanations must be modified to include as well the political, social, and economic stresses of the post-World War I European crises. 54 notes.
D. G. Nielson

2597. Falcionelli, Alberto. "LA SAGRADA FAMILIA." A PROPOSITO DEL CENTENARIO DE LENIN [The Holy Family: Lenin's centenary]. *Rev. de Hist. Americana y Argentina [Argentina] 1968-69 7(13-14): 183-230.* Discusses the historiography of Marxism-Leninism and the almost mystical relation of the one to the other on the centenary of Lenin's birth in 1970.

2598. Francovitch, Carlo. FASCISMO E ANTIFASCISMO [Fascism and antifascism]. *Movimento di Liberazione in Italia [Italy] 1962 (69): 70-76.* Reviews a collection of essays edited by Feltrinelli inquiring into the social, economic, and intellectual history of Italian Fascism and the resistance in its European context, from widely differing viewpoints. Discusses the motives for various approaches and summarizes some of the contributions.
R. O. Khan

2599. Gawrecki, Dan. REVIZIONISTICKÉ FALZIFIKACE VÝZNAMU V. SJEZDU KSČ A JEJICH KRITIKA [Revisionist falsification of the Fifth Congress of the Czechoslovak Communist Party and their criticism]. *Slezský Sborník [Czechoslovakia] 1980 78(2): 88-113.* In the 1960's, culminating in 1968, there appeared a number of revisionist interpretations of the Fifth Party Congress (1929), at which the Leninist-Stalinist model of party structure and discipline was adopted. Jan Mlynárík in the *Literární listy* (Literary Gazette) was the foremost proponent of this interpretation and claimed that at the Fifth Congress of the Czechoslovak Party in 1929 a purge of the social democrats took place and a dogmatic leftist leadership assumed control. This is a falsification of the party's history; in fact, strongly influenced by the Sixth Congress of the Comintern in 1928, the Czechoslovak Party became a truly revolutionary organ. In the last 10 years Marxist historiography has severely criticized the revisionist positions which approached the bourgeois West German historical account of the Czechoslovak Communist Party. 78 notes.
B. Reinfeld

2600. Goetz, Helmut. TOTALITARISMUS—EIN HISTORIS-CHER BEGRIFF [Totalitarianism, a historical term]. *Schweizerische Zeits. für Gesch. [Switzerland] 1982 32(1): 163-174.* Refutation of Christoph Dejung's contention that totalitarianism is a polemical term and has outlived its usefulness in historical contexts. The term was not made famous only by Hannah Arendt, but was widely and approvingly circulated in Mussolini's Italy. Giovanni Gentile, Francesco Ercole, and Emilio Betti together gave a precise and well-rounded picture of totalitarianism in its historical reality. Even though Nazi Germany did not adopt the term, it certainly implemented its content, just as Franco's Spain had many of its characteristics. Wherever basic human rights and constitutional guarantees are being set aside, the doors are opened to hubris and brutality, and totalitarianism is at work. 61 notes.   H. K. Meier

2601. Goranov, Stefan. ISTORIKO-PARTIINATA NAUKA I BORBATA PROTIV ANTIKOMUNIZMA NA SUVREMENIIA ETAP [Party-historical scholarship and the contemporary struggle against anti-Communism]. *Izvestiia na Inst. po Istoriia na BKP [Bulgaria] 1975 32: 481-488.* Reports on a conference on the above theme held in Warsaw on 9-11 April 1974, organized by the Polish Institute for the History of the Workers' Movement, and other bodies, and attended by representatives of other socialist countries.

2602. Gorodets'kyi, Iu. N. PYTANNIA ISTORIOHRAFICHNO-HO DOSLIDZHENNIA U PRATSIAKH V. I. LENINA 1917-1923 [Historiographic research in the works of V. I. Lenin, 1917-23]. *Ukrains'kyi Istorychnyi Zhurnal [USSR] 1970 (2): 27-38.* Analyzes Lenin's *The State and Revolution* and other works in which he places Marx, Engels, and other communists and socialists in the international revolutionary movement.

2603. Gottlieb, Roger S. FEUDALISM AND HISTORICAL MATERIALISM: A CRITIQUE AND SYNTHESIS. *Sci. & Soc. 1984 48(1): 1-37.* Marxist scholars have produced three competing theories of feudalism and the transition to capitalism: a class struggle view associated with Maurice Dobb, Rodney Hilton, Robert Brenner, and others; a world-system view promulgated by Immanuel Wallerstein; and a political and economic fusion view held by Perry Anderson. The author argues "that it is a mistake to try to find an economic core within feudal society; or to base an understanding of that society's internal dynamic and transition to capitalism on an analysis of its economy's 'laws of development' or 'contradictions.'" He finds flaws in all three positions, and argues for a synthesis of all three to produce a sounder theory. Based on secondary sources; 82 notes.   R. E. Butchart

2604. Gräfe, Karl-Heinz; Hübner, Peter; and Teller, Hans. 29. KONFERENZ DER KOMMISSION DER HISTORIKER DER DDR UND DER UDSSR [Conference of the Committee of Historians from East Germany and the USSR]. *Zeits. für Geschichtswissenschaft [East Germany] 1981 29(7): 618-620.* The 29th conference of the Committee of Historians took place in Dresden in October 1980. The theme of the conference was "Bourgeois historiography and communist research on the real communism: analysis and critique." Many of the speeches concerned new trends and shortcomings of bourgeois treatment of socialist development. The main areas of interest were the analysis and critique of bourgeois portrayals of the history of the development of socialist society and questions of war and peace in the history of socialist foreign policy.   T. Parker

2605. Gregor, A. James. FASCISM AND COMPARATIVE POLITICS. *Comparative Pol. Studies 1976 9(2): 207-222.* Discusses recent historical writings on Italian and German fascism.

2606. Gruzdeva, V. P. NIAKOI PROBLEMI V SUVETSKATA ISTORIOGRAFIIA NA KOMUNISTICHESKIIA INTERNATSIONAL [Problems in Soviet historiography of the Communist International]. *Izvestiia na Inst. po Istoriia na BKP [Bulgaria] 1980 42: 135-170.* Examines the sources of information available to historiographers in particular about Lenin's works and works about Lenin's contribution to the construction of the Comintern, as well as slanderous writings in bourgeois, reformist, and Maoist publications. Russian, French, and German summaries.

2607. Haberl, Othmar Nikola. JUGOSLAWISCHE ARBEITEN ZUR GESCHICHTE DER INTERNATIONALEN ARBEITER-BEWEGUNG [Yugoslav writings on the history of the international labor movement]. *Int. Wiss. Korrespondenz zur Gesch. der Deutschen Arbeiterbewegung [West Germany] 1979 15(3): 443-470.*

Reviews the phases of Yugoslav historiography on the international labor movement, handbooks and aids, works on the history of the 1st and 2d Internationals, the history of the Comintern, the history of the international labor movement after 1945, the Soviet-Yugoslav conflict, the conferences of the Communist and Labor Parties, the Chinese Revolution and the Soviet-China conflict, reform communism and Eurocommunism and the reevaluation of proletarian internationalism.

2608. Hartwell, R. M. THE ANTICAPITALIST MENTALITY. *Armidale and District Hist. Soc. J. and Pro. [Australia] 1976 (19): 1-10.* Explains the hostility of historians to capitalism and their support of socialism. Intellectuals are socialists in order to solve social problems erroneously believed to stem from capitalism. Socialism has the attraction of planned development and resembles millenarianism. Socialism also coincides with the spirit of the age, which encourages greater government control. Historians have spread the myth of capitalist exploitation of the working classes. Instead, they should destroy the myths which have discredited capitalism. Secondary sources; 29 notes.   J. L. White

2609. Haun, Horst. DAS KARL-MARX-JAHR 1953 UND DIE ENTWICKLUNG DER MARXISTISCH-LENINISTISCHEN GESCHICHTSWISSENSCHAFT IN DER DDR [The Karl-Marx-Year 1953 and the development of Marxist-Leninist science of history in East Germany]. *Jahrbuch für Geschichte [East Germany] 1979 20: 165-201.* The main task of the Karl Marx Year, celebrated in 1953, was to convey the importance of Karl Marx and to educate the working masses about the irreconcilable battle for the socialist order. During this year there was increased analysis and biographical research on Marx and Engels. Numerous publications on German history and on important events in the international workers' movement were published and new source material explored. An exhibition covering all aspects of communism was held at the Museum for German History in Berlin. Based on material in the Central Party Archives and documents of the Socialist Unity Party.   T. Parker

2610. Hermann, Istvan. V. I. LENIN OB ISTORICHESKOI AL'TERNATIVE [V. I. Lenin on historical alternatives]. *Voprosy Filosofii [USSR] 1980 (12): 97-106.* Considers the problem of historical and social alternatives in the history of class struggle and revolutionary movements. Analyzes Lenin's works and revolutionary activity and the meaning of the concept of historical and social alternatives. Explains the difference between the principal, decisive, and collateral, nondecisive alternatives, illustrated in the alternatives engendered through the revolutionary situation and events in 1917 in Russia and Lenin's theoretical and practical activity in this period. The author analyzes the Leninist solution of decisive alternatives of that time.   J/S

2611. Herzfeldt, Renate and Zimmermann, Fritz. O FAL'SIFIKATSII LENINIZMA V ZAPADNOI GERMANII [The falsification of Leninism in West Germany]. *Voprosy Istorii KPSS [USSR] 1970 (8): 44-56.* Summarizes the works of West German authors who provide a false picture of Lenin and emphasizes the unity of socialist countries in resisting the spread of such unorthodox viewpoints.

2612. Hess, U. and Kinner, K. DIE PARISER KOMMUNE IM GESCHICHTSBILD UND GESCHICHTSDENKEN DER KPD IN DEN JAHREN DER WEIMARER REPUBLIK [The image of the Paris Commune in history and in the historical thinking of the Communist Party of Germany in the years of the Weimar Republic]. *Wissenschaftliche Zeitschrift der Karl-Marx U. Leipzig [East Germany] 1971 20(1): 69-85.* The basic idea in the historical discussion of the Paris Commune by the Communist Party of Germany was the proof that the workers of Paris had in 1871 for the first time tried to establish the dictatorship of the proletariat. The example of the Paris Commune demonstrated how the bourgeoisie allied itself with its arch-enemy in its struggle against the revolutionary proletariat. The historical analysis of the Communist Party of Germany was reached by using the comparative historical meth-

od which made it possible to establish continuity from the revolution of 1848-49 and the Paris Commune to the October revolution. Based on published documents and secondary literature; 80 notes.
R. Wagnleitner

2613. Hill, Christopher; Hilton, R. H.; and Hobsbawm, Eric J. PAST AND PRESENT: ORIGINS AND EARLY YEARS. *Past and Present [Great Britain] 1983 (100): 3-14.* *Past and Present* was initiated by John Morris and a group of other Marxists in 1952. It was planned as a journal in which Marxist and non-Marxist historians who had a common approach to history would collaborate. The journal began in confused finances, but had no trouble maintaining itself. The founding group left or was expelled from the Communist Party in 1956-57, but the journal continued to be regarded as Marxist until the editorial board was enlarged in 1958. Then *Past and Present* gained greater public respectability, larger size, more frequent publication, and increased circulation. J. G. Packer

2614. Hobsbawm, Eric J. MARX AND HISTORY. *New Left Review [Great Britain] 1984 (143): 39-50.* Text of the author's lecture given at the Marx Centenary Conference organized by the Republic of San Marino in 1983.

2615. Hundt, Martin. DAS KOMMUNISTISCHE MANIFEST UND DIE TÄTIGKEIT DES BUNDES DER KOMMUNISTEN NACH DER REVOLUTION VON 1848-1849 [The *Communist Manifesto* and the activities of the Communist League after the Revolution of 1848-49]. *Zeitschrift für Geschichtswissenschaft [East Germany] 1974 22(3): 325-330.* Refutes the contentions of bourgeois historians that the *Communist Manifesto* cannot be considered the party program of the Communist League. The Manifesto was used as a theoretical work to educate the masses as well as the League cadres. It was also a guide for party organization. Therefore, the Manifesto was reprinted by 1851 and widely circulated. Primary and secondary sources; 30 notes. J. T. Walker

2616. Iida, Kanae. DAIICHI INTĀNASHONARY KENKY NI KANSURU SAIKIN NO DŌKŌ [A brief comment on recent studies about the First International]. *Mita Gakkai Zasshi [Japan] 1966 59(12): 103-115.*

2617. Jong, Rudolf de. IETS OVER DE GESCHIEDSCHRIJVING VAN HET ANARCHISME [The historiography of anarchism]. *Spiegel Hist. [Netherlands] 1979 14(11): 628-630.* Review of major works dealing with the history of anarchism written in the late 19th and 20th centuries. Attention is also given to major archival collections and important memoirs.
C. W. Wood

2618. Kandel', E. P. K KRITIKE BURZHUAZNYKH I REVIZIONISTSKIKH KONTSEPTSII O TEORETICHESKOI I REVOLIUTSIONNO-PRAKTICHESKOI DEIATELNOSTI F. ENGELSA [Middle-class revisionist views of the theoretical and practical revolutionary activity of F. Engels]. *Voprosy Istorii KPSS [USSR] 1970 (11): 87-100.* Attacks middle-class revisionist historians' attempts to expose contradictions between the philosophy of Marx and Engels by citing extracts from the works of Engels, 1844-91.

2619. Kanishcheva, N. I. SOVREMENNAIA ZAPADNOGERMANSKAIA BURZHUAZNAIA ISTORIOGRAFIIA O PREDPOSYLKAKH OKTIABR'SKOI REVOLIUTSII [Current West German bourgeois historiography on the preconditions of the October Revolution]. *Istoriia SSSR [USSR] 1983 (4): 160-175.* West German scholars, like all historians in Western Europe, have long understood the global significance of the Bolshevik Revolution of 1917. Their analyses have, however, in the past been consistently tendentious. Nevertheless, the growing influence of the socialist countries and the crisis in the capitalist West led to a realization in Western Europe of the need for better relations with the USSR. This also affected the way in which West German historians approached their study of Soviet history. In the past decade a number of West German scholars, including H. Berding and D. Geyer, have

been more willing than before to realize that the October Revolution was not a chance occurrence and to evaluate objectively the circumstances surrounding it. 98 notes. J. Bamber

2620. Kantor, K. M. MIROVOI REVOLIUTSIONNYI PROTSESS I MEZHDUNARODNOE RABOCHEE DVIZHENIE [The world revolutionary process and the international working class movement]. *Voprosy Filosofii [USSR] 1972 (12): 77-88, 1973 (1): 96-111.* Part I. The relation between the international workers' movement and the world revolutionary process has become a focus of worldwide ideological struggle. The bourgeois and revisionist philosophy of today, trying to disprove the Marxist-Leninist understanding of the historical process as a world revolutionary process directed by the conscious will of the working class and its parties, seeks to counterpose its historiography to this understanding. Anticommunist and revisionist doctrines now posit the breakaway of the international workers' movement from the world revolutionary process, or even oppose the two. These doctrines are based on the most general problems of world history, and the ideology of present-day anticommunism cannot be exposed fully unless its historiosophic foundations are brought to light and the problems of interaction of different civilizations and the evolution of cultures are considered from Marxist positions as important problems of the world revolutionary process. Part II. The sixties saw a reorientation in the diverse trends of modern Right and Left-wing opportunism, reformism, and radicalism, in its historiosophic essentials similar to the one experienced by the avowedly anticommunist, bourgeois antiproletarian ideology. They recognize that the world revolutionary process is advancing toward socialism, but assert that the working class has either no relation whatsoever to this development or only a remote one. The author criticizes these anti-Marxist concepts, and points out that the world revolutionary process and the international working-class movement are inseparable. The world revolutionary process also includes the national liberation movements, the anti-imperialist activities of the developing countries of the Third World and the nonproletarian sections (close to the working class) in the developed capitalist states. The international workers' movement has always been the leading and decisive force in the world revolutionary process, a force that imparts sense to the latter.
J/S

2621. Kaszjanyenko, V. I. A SZOCIALIZMUS FEJLŐDÉSÉNEK SZAKASZAI. A FEJLETT SZOCIALIZMUS KONCEPCIÓJÁNAK HISTORIOGRÁFIÁJA [The phases of the development of socialism: the historiography of the concept of developed socialism]. *Párttörténeti Közlemények [Hungary] 1984 30(3): 191-215.* Gives a survey of the various national and international discussions, published writings, and speeches that deal with the theoretical and practical features characteristic of life and society in general in the countries that follow the pattern of Soviet-type socialism. Based on Soviet and Hungarian publications; 76 notes. G. Jeszenszky

2622. Khalevin, V. M. PROTIV FAL'SIFIKATSII APREL'SKIKH TEZISOV V. I. LENINA V ZAPADNOGERMANSKOI BURZHUAZNOI ISTORIOGRAFII [Against falsification of V. I. Lenin's April Theses in bourgeois West German historiography]. *Vestnik Leningradskogo U.: Seriia Istorii, Iazyka i Literatury [USSR] 1964 19(8): 29-38.* Takes issue with the anti-Leninist bias of Oskar Anweiler, especially his *Rätebewegung in Russland, 1905-1921* (Leiden: Brill, 1958), which insists on a contradiction between Lenin's April Theses and his purported stand against workers' councils (soviets) in 1905-06. Anweiler as well as Georg von Rauch, *Geschichte des bolschewistischen Russland* (Wiesbaden: Rheinische Verlagsanstalt, 1955) and Franz Borkenau, *Der europäische Kommunismus, seine Geschichte von 1917 bis zur Gegenwart* (Bern: Francke, 1952) and other West German studies falsify the true meaning of the April Theses and dispute the consistency of Lenin's ideological dicta by giving credence to distortions and fabrications concocted by Leon Trotsky and others. 53 notes.
N. Frenkley

2623. Khrakovs'ki, I. N. Z ISTORII DOSLIDZHENNIA TEORETYCHNOI SPADSHCHYNY K. MARKSA V URSR [The history of research into Karl Marx's theoretical heritage in the Ukraine].

Ukrains'kyi Istorychnyi Zhurnal [USSR] 1968 (5): 11-16. Reviews specialist and popular studies on Marxism in the Ukrainian SSR, 1921-28.

2624. Khrisanfov, V. I. BOR'BA V. I. LENINA, BOL'SHEVIKOV ZA SPLOCHENIE INTERNATSIONALISTOV V 1914-1917 GG. (KRITICHESKII ANALIZ NEMARKSISTSKOI LITERATURY 60-70-KH GODOV) [The struggle of V. I. Lenin and the Bolsheviks for the consolidation of the Internationalists, 1914-17: a critical analysis of non-Marxist literature, 1960-70's]. *Vestnik Leningradskogo U.: Seriia Istorii, Iazyka i Literatury [USSR] 1982 (2): 5-11.* The majority of works by anti-Communist historians such as B. Lazitch, M. Drachkovitch, and S. Page give only a superficial analysis of the struggle of Lenin and the Bolsheviks for the unification of left forces, 1914-17. Their main concern is to justify the leaders of Social Democracy and, by falsifying facts, to allege the isolation of the Bolsheviks within the international socialist movement. The lack of reference to the work of modern Soviet historians in western literature illustrates the narrow range of source material employed by the researchers. Secondary sources; 24 notes.   G. Dombrovski

2625. Kolpinskii, N. Iu. and Mosolov, V. G. SOVREMENNYE BURZHUAZNYE REFORMISTKIE FAL'SIFIKATORY ISTORII I INTERNATSIONALA [Contemporary bourgeois reformist falsifiers of the history of the First International]. *Voprosy Istorii KPSS [USSR] 1964 (9): 55-66.* Bourgeois and reformist socialist historians of the First International, such as Julius Braunthal, Richard Hostetter, and G. D. H. Cole, underestimate the influence of Marx on socialist movements of that period and overestimate anarchist and reformist influences.

2626. Kuneva, Zhivka. ZA "NISHTETATA" NA MARKSISKATA ISTORIOGRAFIIA (ORGANIZATSIONITE PROBLEMI NA VTORIIA INTERNATSIONAL V MARKSISKATA I NEMARKSISKA LITERATURA) [The "destitute" of Marxist historiography: organizational problems of the Second International discussed in Marxist and non-Marxist literature]. *Izvestiia na Inst. po Istoriia na BKP [Bulgaria] 1977 37: 197-234.* Surveys the literature on the history of the Second International, 1889-1914.

2627. Küttler, Wolfgang and Remer, Claus. FORSCHUNGSAUFGABEN ZUR GESCHICHTE DER SOZIALISTISCHEN LÄNDER [Research problems in the history of the socialist countries]. *Jahrbuch für Geschichte der Sozialistischen Länder Europas [East Germany] 1971 15(1): 9-24.* Underlines the political and ideological importance of historiographic research and studies in East Germany in the last 10 years and outlines the main fields for future research with the central aim of historiography providing a contribution to the formation of a developed social system of socialism by reinforcing the unity between historic and political thinking and, thus, becoming an active force in society.

2628. Kuznetsov, V. N. and Chepurenko, A. Iu. NESOSTOIATEL'NOST' BURZHUAZNYKH INTERPRETATSII MARKSIZMA [The shallow nature of bourgeois interpretations of Marxism]. *Voprosy Istorii KPSS [USSR] 1983 (10): 68-80.* In the struggle against progressive revolutionary ideas, bourgeois Marxologists such as A. Kunzli, J. K. Galbraith, M. Rubel, and P. Vranicki falsify the theories and the history of Marxism in a variety of ways. Some attempt to counterpose the "young" and the "mature" Marx; others try to find contradictions between Marx and Lenin. All the modern interpretations offered by the Marxologists, however, seek to prove the unscientific basis of Marxist theory and its irrelevance to an analysis of the present stage of social development. But praxis is the criterion of truth and has judged in favor of Marxism. Secondary sources; 48 notes.   G. Dombrovski

2629. Laboor, Ernst and Lewin, Erwin. EIN WÜRDIGER BEITRAG MARXISTISCH-LENINISTISCHER HISTORIKER [Contribution of Marxist-Leninist historians]. *Einheit [East Germany] 1977 32(12): 1424-1426.* Reviews the lectures and discussions of the 27th Conference of the Commission of East German

and Soviet Historians in Berlin in September 1977, dealing with the laws of transformation from capitalism to socialism, and critical interpretation of Western historians' views of the Russian Revolution.   R. Wagnleitner

2630. Laschitza, Annelies. FRANZ MEHRING—EIN LEHRMEISTER DER MARXISTISCHEN BIOGRAPHIE [Franz Mehring: a master of Marxist biography]. *Beiträge zur Geschichte der Arbeiterbewegung [East Germany] 1976 18(1): 58-69.* The German left wing welcomed the publication of Franz Mehring's *Karl Marx* (Berlin, 1918) as the first biography of Karl Marx (1818-83) based on materialistic historiography. Mehring was the first author able to characterize all dimensions of Marx's work, and his biography became the basis for historical materialist biographies of Marx. Based on Mehring's book and secondary literature; 45 notes.   R. Wagnleitner

2631. Lavau, Georges. L'HISTORIOGRAPHIE COMMUNISTE [Communist historiography]. *Esprit [France] 1978 (3): 3-19.* Explains the intellectual working process of the French Communist Party through a critical analysis of the *Manuel d'histoire du Parti communiste français* (1964) and the two volumes of *L'Histoire du réformisme en France* (1976).

2632. Ledeen, Michael A. RENZO DE FELICE AND THE CONTROVERSY OVER ITALIAN FASCISM. *J. of Contemporary Hist. [Great Britain] 1976 11(4): 269-283.* Renzo De Felice's book *Intervista sul Fascismo* [Interview on Fascism] (Bari, 1975) is the most provocative scholarly work since A. J. P. Taylor's study of the origins of World War II and the provocation is deliberate. The author sees two elements in Italian fascism: the "fascist movement" and the "fascist regime." The movement represented the demand for the replacement of the ruling class in the tradition of the French Revolution. The actual regime killed the dream of the movement. The success of fascism was based on genuine support for Benito Mussolini. Both movement and regime were destroyed in World War II and cannot be revived. De Felice's thesis challenges traditional Marxist historiography which regards fascism as a reactionary support of capitalism. The debate continues.
     M. P. Trauth

2633. Lewin, Erwin. NEUE SOVJETISCHE ARBEITEN ZUR GESCHICHTE DER KOMINTERN [Recent Soviet works on the history of the Comintern]. *Beiträge zur Gesch. der Arbeiterbewegung [East Germany] 1980 22(5): 770-777.* Discusses recently published works by Soviet writers on the general development of the Comintern, its specific activities, the role of the Comintern within class divisions, its role in the struggle for peace and democracy, and for the national and social liberation of nations, Lenin's influence and leading role in the Comintern, the role of the Bolshevik Party in the formation and development of the Comintern, and various Comintern congresses. In addition the author discusses the collaboration between Soviet historians and historians from other socialist countries on this subject. 58 notes.   G. L. Neville

2634. Longinotti, Liana. FRIEDRICH ENGELS E LA "RIVOLUZIONE DI MAGGIORANZA" [Friedrich Engels and the revolution by the majority]. *Studi Storici [Italy] 1974 15(4): 769-828.* Surveys various evaluations of Engels as theoretician, the nature of his departures from Marx, and his relationship with the German Social Democratic Party. Admits the ambiguities in Engels's views, but draws a sharp distinction between his view of the social democratic path and that of the German Social Democrats. Topics covered include Engels's views on the peasant question, the relationship between peace and socialist revolution, and revolution by the majority. 142 notes.   E. J. Craver

2635. Lozek, Gerhard and Mader, Ursula. DER KAMPF GEGEN DIE IDEOLOGIE DES ANTIKOMMUNISMUS [The struggle against the ideology of anticommunism]. *Zeitschrift für Geschichtswissenschaft [East Germany] 1967 15(4): 686-692.* Reviews the lectures and discussions of a conference of the Institute of the Humanities at Berlin in March 1967, which analyzed theoretical and methodological problems of historiography on the struggle of the socialist movements against anticommunist imperialism since 1917.

2636. Mader, Ursula. THEORETISCHE UND PRAKTISCHE PROBLEME DER GESCHICHTSPROPAGANDA [Theoretical and practical problems of historical propaganda]. *Zeitschrift für Geschichtswissenschaft [East Germany] 1970 18(2): 209-213.* The German Society of Historians which met in Berlin, November 1969, stressed the importance of the Marxist-Leninist historiography for the formation of a socialist consciousness of historical processes.

2637. Magomedov, M. A. PROTIV BURZHUAZNOI IDEOLOGII I REVIZIONIZMA [Against bourgeois ideology and revisionism]. *Voprosy Istorii KPSS [USSR] 1976 (8): 74-86.* Criticizes the attempts by bourgeois writers to discredit Karl Marx and Friedrich Engels as well as those internationalists untrue to V. I. Lenin and Communist Party policy.

2638. Malysh, A. I. KARL MARKS I EGO SOVREMENNYE BURZHUAZNYE KRITIKI [Karl Marx and his contemporary bourgeois critics]. *Voprosy Istorii KPSS [USSR] 1963 (4): 34-47.* Notes the different approaches of Western authors to Karl Marx: some are crudely anti-Communist while others attempt to take a more objective view and characterize Marxism as a mistaken theory, or as no longer having any relevance.

2639. Malysh, A. I. SOVREMENNAIA BURZHUAZNO-REFORMISTSKAIA KRITIKA *KAPITALA* MARKSA [Contemporary bourgeois-reformist criticism of Marx's *Capital*]. *Voprosy Istorii KPSS [USSR] 1961 (2): 157-167.* Attacks contemporary attempts by Western bourgeois historians and theoreticians to discredit Karl Marx's *Das Kapital.*

2640. Mangoni, Luisa. PER UN DEFINIZIONE DEL FASCISMO: I CONCETTI DI BONAPARTISMO E CESARISMO [For a definition of fascism: the concepts of Bonapartism and Caesarism]. *Italia Contemporanea [Italy] 1979 31(135): 17-52.* Refers to historiographical interpretations of the phenomena of totalitarianism, dictatorship, and absolute rule and discusses the political application of the concepts of Bonapartism and Caesarism in the 19th and 20th centuries. Examines the similarities and differences between Fascism and Nazism and focuses on the crisis of the Weimar Republic, 1929-32, discussing the views of H. Arendt, H. A. Winkler, A. Thalheimer, C. Schmitt, and L. Trotsky. Based on the works of C. Schmitt and other sources; 121 notes.   P. J. Durell

2641. Marushkin, B. I. ANTIKOMMUNISTICHESKAIA ISTORIOGRAFIA: IDEOLOGICHESKOE ORUZHIE IMPERIALIZMA [Anti-Communist historiography: the ideological weapon of imperialism]. *Voprosy Istorii KPSS [USSR] 1970 (7): 92-102.* Attacks the falsification and ·distortion of Marxism-Leninism in historical literature.

2642. Masłow, Nikolaj N. O METODOLOGICZNYCH PROBLEMACH BADAŃ HISTORII RUCHU ROBOTNICZEGO I MARKSISTOWSKO-LENINOWSKICH PARTII KOMUNISTYCZNYCH I ROBOTNICZYCH [Methodological problems of studies on the history of the labor movement and Marxist-Leninist communist and workers' parties]. *Z Pola Walki [Poland] 1978 21(3): 177-202.* Analyzes new methodological approaches to historical studies of communist and other working-class parties: Marxist-Leninist dialectics and gnosiology; historical materialism; and the theory of science in history. 57 notes.   M. A. Zurowski

2643. McNall, Scott G. THE MARXIAN PROJECT. *Sociological Quarterly 1984 25(4): 473-495.* Examines Karl Marx's work and outlines some of the central ideas and concepts with the intention of synthesizing the many different versions of his work.

2644. Meshcheryakova, N. M. FORMIROVANIE PROLETARIATA V OSVESHCHENII K. MARKSA I EGO NOVEISHIKH BURZHUAZNYKH "KRITIKOV" [The formation of the proletariat as explained in the works of Karl Marx and his modern bourgeois critics]. *Vestnik Moskovskogo U. Seriia 9: Istoriia [USSR] 1968 23(3): 13-40.* Divides Marx's works into two periods: 1) 1840-50's when Marx described the essence of the proletariat as a class, its place in bourgeois society and its role in history; and 2) 1850-60's when Marx studied in detail the origins of the proletariat and the objective prerequisites needed for the formation of workers into a class. Also examines bourgeois historical literature on the origins of the proletariat. 170 notes.   L. Kalinowski

2645. Miller, Robert F. WRITING ABOUT COMMUNISM. *Australian J. of Pol. and Hist. [Australia] 1975 21(3): 167-171.* A review of four books: *The Communist Party in Canada: A History* by Ivan Avakumovic (Toronto, 1975); *The Politics of Modernization in Eastern Europe: Testing the Soviet Model* ed. by Charles Gati (New York and London, 1974); *Bureaucracy and Revolution in Eastern Europe* by Chris Harman (London, 1974); and *Organizacija i Funkcije Javne Uprave: Osnovne Uporedne i Istorijske Karakteristike* [The organization and function of public administration: basic comparative and historical characteristics] by Aleksandar Stojanović (Belgrade, 1972). The author compares the books, each of which respectively illustrates four different analytical perspectives—viz., that of the traditional political and historical scholar; that of the current Western (mainly American) scholar striving for scientific objectivity in the comparative analysis of communist systems; that of the Western New Left critiques of existing socialist systems; and finally, the sympathetic but critical analyses of insiders (mainly Yugoslavs) who seek basically nonrevolutionary change to enhance the humanistic and popular elements of their societies. Secondary sources; 4 notes.   R. G. Neville

2646. Mints, I. I. PERVYI SHTURM IMPERIALIZMA (1917-23 GG) [The first assault on imperialism]. *Voprosy Istorii [USSR] 1978 (11): 3-21.* In his polemic with bourgeois historians, who are trying to accuse Lenin of a miscalculation on the question of world revolution which, they maintain, has failed to take place, the author clearly shows by drawing on concrete historical material that the beginning of world revolution—an organized assault on the entire imperialist system—was laid by the Great October Socialist Revolution and from that time on imperialism has been powerless to win back its former stability for a lasting period or to ward off the onslaught of the revolutionary forces.   J

2647. Mokshin, S. I. BOR'BA KOMMUNISTOV ZA INTERNATSIONAL'NUIU SPLOCHENNOST': BURZHUAZNYE VYMYSLY I DEISTVITEL'NOST' [The Communist struggle for international unity: bourgeois fabrications and reality]. *Voprosy Istorii KPSS [USSR] 1980 (4): 90-102.* Examines bourgeois contentions of the postwar disintegration in the Communist movement. Refutes the opposition's claims using as evidence the strength of Communist countries today. 60 notes.   S. J. Talalay

2648. Mokshin, S. I. BURZHOAZNI KONCEPCII ZA DEZINTEGRACIA NA KOMUNISTICHESKOTO DVIZHENIE I TIAHNATA NESUSTOIATELNOST (1945-1977) [Bourgeois notions of the disintegration of the Communist movement and their lack of substance, 1945-77]. *Izvestiia na Inst. po Istoriia na BKP [Bulgaria] 1979 40: 79-114.*

2649. Moravcová, Dagmar. INTERPRETACE FAŠISMU V ZÁPADONĚMECKÉ HISTORIOGRAFII V 60. A 70. LETECH [The interpretation of fascism in West German historiography, 1960's-70's]. *Československý Časopis Hist. [Czechoslovakia] 1978 26(5): 657-675.* Traces changing West German interpretations of fascism since the 1950's. Bourgeois historians in the 1950's used the doctrine of totalitarianism to ally antifascism with anticommunism. In the 1960's Ernst Nolte's phenomenological interpretation of Nazism encouraged perception of Nazism as a heterogeneous movement distinct from monopoly capitalism. Others such as M. Greiffenhagen emphasized Nazi conservatism, D. Schoenbaum and K. D. Bracher noted its revolutionary elements, while H. A. Winkler considered its petit-bourgeois extremism and W. Sauer and I. Fetscher the modernizing aspects of the movement. The 1970's gave rise to a Hitlerian wave with J. C. Fest and W. Maser highlighting the internal conflicts of Nazism. A leftist historical school with R. Kühnl as a representative emphasized the reactionary capitalist basis of fascism. Unlike Marxist historiography these interpretations assign Nazism a large measure of political independence from monopoly capital. 72 notes.   R. E. Weltsch

2650. Mosse, George L.; Ledeen, Michael A., interviewer. ON NAZISM. *Society 1977 14(4): 69-73.* Mosse discusses his historical interpretation of Nazism in Germany and Fascism in Italy, showing why they cannot be understood simply as economic, social, or political phenomena; most importantly they were attempts to actualize irrational myth through state power.

2651. Nemes, Dezső. A FASIZMUS KÉRDÉSÉHEZ [On the question of fascism]. *Párttörténeti Közlemények [Hungary] 1974 20(4): 3-64.* Scolds Marxist historians who have accepted some parts of Western redefinitions of fascism. The East Germans and the Soviets have maintained a leading role in the international ideological struggle while Miklós Lackó, Mihály Vajda, and even Party historians Mária Ormos and Ince Miklós have deviated from Georgi Dimitrov's definition of fascism: An openly terrorist dictatorship of the most reactionary, most chauvinistic, and most imperialistic elements of finance capital. 35 notes. P. I. Hidas

2652. Nezhinski, L. N. AKTUAL'NYE PROBLEMY EDINSTVA STRAN SOTSIALISTICHESKOGO SODRUZHESTVA V OSVESHCHENII SOVREMENNOI SOVETSKOI ISTORIOGRAFII [Topical problems of unity of the countries of socialist cooperation in the light of contemporary Soviet historiography]. *Novaia i Noveishaia Istoriia [USSR] 1980 (3): 3-20.* Examines topical problems of unity and cohesion of the socialist community countries, demonstrates Soviet historiography's contribution to the elaboration of these problems, and stresses the need to highlight some urgent questions. J

2653. Ochocki, Kazimierz. KAROL MARKS I MARKSOLOGIA [Karl Marx and Marxology]. *Studia Filozoficzne [Poland] 1983 (3): 145-158.* Various tendencies in Marxist studies in the West make limited positive contributions to the interpretation of the theory, but they concentrate on providing the theoretical background for an antisocialist campaign. 18 notes. Russian and English summaries.

2654. Orlova, M. I. MARKSISTSKAIA ISTORIOGRAFIIA NOIABR'SKOI REVOLUITSII V GERMANII (K VOPROSU O KHARAKTERE REVOLIUTSII) [Marxist historiography of the November Revolution in Germany: the character of the revolution]. *Voprosy Istorii [USSR] 1980 (5): 59-75.* Analyzes the Soviet and German Marxist historiography of the revolution of 1918-19 in Germany. The author focuses attention on the formation of the Marxist-Leninist conception regarding the character of the German revolution and singles out several stages in its development; in the period of the revolution and of the postwar revolutionary crisis a uniform appraisal of the revolution did not yet crystallize in publicistic literature; from the beginning of the temporary, partial stabilization of capitalism to the latter half of the 1930's the viewpoint was fairly widespread that the proletarian revolution in Germany had suffered a defeat; from the second half of the 1930's to the second half of the 1950's the emphasis was laid on the incompleteness of this revolution, on its bourgeois character; from the second half of the 1950's and particularly in the 1970's it became the generally accepted principle to appraise the revolution of 1918-19 in Germany as a bourgeois-democratic revolution which had a tendency to develop into the socialist revolution. J

2655. Orlova, T. V. VYKRYTTIA RADIANS'KOIU ISTORIOHRAFIIEIU BURZHUAZNOI FAL'SYFIKATSII ROLI KPRS V POLITYCHNII SYSTEMI SYSPIL'STVA ZRILOHO SOTSIALIZMU [Soviet historiography reveals the bourgeois falsification of the role of the CPSU in the political-social system of advanced socialism]. *Ukrains'kyi Istorychnyi Zhurnal [USSR] 1981 (3): 137-144.* Reviews and criticizes capitalist propagandists who in their defense of the capitalist-totalitarian system attack socialism and its advance and progress.

2656. Pancchawa, Ilja D. ROZWINIĘTE SPOŁECZEŃSTWO SOCJALISTYCZNE—WYBRANE PROBLEMY MATERIALIZMU HISTORYCZNEGO [Developed socialist society: select problems of historical materialism]. *Nowe Drogi [Poland] 1975 (1): 56-62.* Examines how the development of Soviet society since 1918 and the emergence of a socialist nation have added new economic, social, and scientific dimensions to the study of dialectical materialism.

2657. Pelinka, Anton. DIE WURZELN DES NATIONALSOZIALISMUS IN VERGANGENHEIT UND GEGENWART [The roots of National Socialism in past and present]. *Frankfurter Hefte [West Germany] 1983 38(8): 32-40.* Both Marxist and liberal theories are too narrow to explain the rise of fascism.

2658. Perz, Bertrand and Safrian, Hans. WEGE UND IRRWEGE DER FASCHISMUSFORSCHUNG [Right and wrong directions in research on fascism]. *Zeitgeschichte [Austria] 1980 7(11-12): 437-459.* Outlines Austrian historical research on fascism in Italy and Germany, and cites historians in the field and their particular interests and publications. Fascism has been defined as totalitarianism, as an agent of monopoly capital, or as an "alliance" of the executive leadership in the state. The relationship of big business and fascism is a permanent subject of dispute. 57 notes. G. E. Pergl

2659. Plener, Ulla. EINIGE PROBLEME DER ARBEITERBEWEGUNG ENTWICKELTER KAPITALISTISCHER LÄNDER IN DER SOWJETISCHEN LITERATUR (1966-1970) [Some problems of the working class movements of developed capitalist countries in Soviet literature, 1966-70]. *Beiträge zur Geschichte der Arbeiterbewegung [East Germany] 1972 14(1): 131-143.* Discusses the 1966-70 research of Soviet historians examining the laws of the world revolutionary process, the economic, social, political, and ideological processes in modern capitalism, the structural changes in the working class after World War II, the development of class consciousness among workers and the role of the Social Democratic parties. Secondary sources; 63 notes. R. Wagnleitner

2660. Pois, Robert A. AN ESSAY ON THE JEWISH PROBLEM IN MARXIST HISTORIOGRAPHY. *East European Q. 1977 11(2): 235-246.* Uses a recent book by John Bunzl, *Klassenkampf in der Diaspora: Zur Geschichte der jüdischen Arbeiterbewegung* (Vienna: Europaverlag, 1975), to illustrate the "Jewish problem" in Marxist historiography. In Bunzl's work "anti-Semitism is attacked but the general legitimacy of Zionism as being any sort of realistic, socially progressive movement [is] severely called into question." The inability of Marxists to accept Zionism as such a movement weakens the intellectual rigor of their historical analyses. 43 notes. C. R. Lovin

2661. Rakhshmir, P. Iu. SOVREMENNAIA BURZHUAZNAIA ISTORIOGRAFIIA O GENEZISE FASHIZMA [Current bourgeois historiography on the genesis of fascism]. *Novaia i Noveishaia Istoriia [USSR] 1982 (3): 33-48.* Criticizes the bourgeois interpretation of the origin of fascism in crisis phenomena of the interwar period, for it ignores the fact that its rise was a symptom of the general crisis of capitalism. Analyzes the relation between worldwide and national factors and examines social, economic, political, and ideological elements. J/S

2662. Rakhshmir, P. Iu. SOVREMENNYE TENDENTSII BURZHUAZNOI ISTORIOGRAFII FASHIZMA [Modern tendencies in the bourgeois historiography of fascism]. *Novaia i Noveishaia Istoriia [USSR] 1971 (6): 26-36.* Western historians have disagreed over what constitutes fascism. Some try to establish a typology of fascism, but others argue that national peculiarities were too great to allow this, or that fascist movements should be distinguished from fascist regimes. Some claim that fascism was basically conservative, but others assert that it was in some ways revolutionary. Others assert that it helped modernization, while some argue that it hindered progress. All ignore the essence of fascism, which the author describes as a "terroristic dictatorship of the most reactionary and aggressive forces of monopoly capitalism." Based on Western books and articles; 79 notes. C. I. P. Ferdinand

2663. Richter, Rolf. ZUR FASCHISMUSINTERPRETATION IN DER BÜRGERLICHEN HISTORIOGRAPHIE DER USA [On the interpretations of fascism in US bourgeois historiography]. *Zeitschrift für Geschichtswissenschaft [East Germany] 1974 22(8):*

789-800. US historians have presented three models of fascism: conservative-reactionary (D. L. Hoggan, H. E. Barnes), bourgeois-liberal (W. L. Shirer, W. Manchester), and anti-imperialist (New Left).

2664. Ruge, Wolfgang. DIE NOVEMBERREVOLUTION UND DER GEGENWÄRTIGE KAMPF ZWISCHEN SOZIALISMUS UND IMPERIALISMUS [The November Revolution and the present struggle between socialism and imperialism]. *Zeitschrift für Geschichtswissenschaft [East Germany] 1969 17(9): 1141-1147.* The German socialist revolution of November 1918 showed German workers that they could be their own masters. The present existence of the German Democratic Republic is the result of the struggle of the German working class to achieve peace, freedom, and democratic government. The duty of German Marxist-Leninist historians is to investigate the socialist struggles of the past and to provide information supporting the current struggle against imperialism. Secondary sources; 17 notes. G. H. Libbey

2665. Saito, Takashi. INTERPRETATIONS OF FASCISM IN THE INTER-WAR PERIOD. *Shakai-Keizai-Shigaku [Japan] 1976 41(6): 6-17.* Of the various interpretations of fascism and its related phenomena, the Marxist proved the most comprehensive and realistic, showing it as a mere tool of declining capitalism under the guise of a revolutionary mass movement and at the same time making clear its international nature. But the subsequent Nazi seizure of power in Germany demonstrated the weakness of the Marxist interpretation. Marxists, since the latter half of the 1920's, have ignored mass psychological factors in the fascist movement. Today's task is to integrate various theories of fascism. In an attempt to pursue such integration the most important tasks are to revise Dimitrov's definition of fascism by analyzing capitalism in the fascist states of Germany, Italy, and Japan; to complement preceding theories with the socioeconomic analyses of contemporary social and behavioral scientists; and to propose a new definition of fascism that takes into account the total process of its origin, maturation, and collapse. J/S

2666. Salov, V. I. OB ANTINAUCHNYKH PRIEMAKH ISPOL'ZOVANIIA ISTOCHNIKOV ZAPADNO-GERMANSKIMI BURZHUAZNYMI ISTORIKAMI [The unscientific use of sources by West German bourgeois historians]. *Voprosy Istorii KPSS [USSR] 1962 (5): 167-176.* Analyzes the use of sources by West German historians, finding that they, sometimes deliberately and sometimes unconsciously, distort sources, especially the works of Lenin, and falsify the history of the Soviet Communist Party.

2667. Salov, V. I. REVOLIUTSIONNYI PROTSESS I SOVREMENNAIA BURZHUAZNAIA ISTORIOGRAFIIA [Revolutionary process and the present-day bourgeois historiography]. *Novaia i Noveishaia Istoriia [USSR] 1981 (1): 77-90.* Analyzes and reveals the theoretical and methodological untenability of bourgeois historiography's interpretation of the world revolutionary process. J

2668. Sapelli, Giulio. LA CLASSE OPERAIA DURANTE IL FASCISMO: PROBLEMI E INDICAZIONI DI RICERCA [The working class during Fascism: problems and research indications]. *Ann. dell'Istituto Giangiacomo Feltrinelli [Italy] 1979-80 20: VII-XCVIII.* Introduction to an issue devoted entirely to the theme of the working class under Fascism. Deals with general methodological questions, such as the classification of Fascism as a power system, its a class nature, authoritarianism, the working class, an interpretative framework, and relations between capitalist development, Fascist domination, and the industrial working class. Extensive review of the relevant literature. 272 notes. J. V. Coutinho

2669. Sarbei, V. H. POCHATOK ZASVOIENNIA MARKSYSTSKYKH IDEI UKRAINSKOI ISTORIOHRAFIIEIU [The beginnings of the assimilation of Marxist ideas in Ukrainian historiography]. *Ukrains'kyi Istorychnyi Zhurnal [USSR] 1971 (11): 12-20.* Assesses the influence of Marxism on the sociopolitical and historical developments in the Ukraine from ca. 1850 to the October Revolution, with details of historical works concerned with this question.

2670. Schmidt, Walter. GESCHICHTSWISSENSCHAFT UND GESCHICHTSBEWUSSTSEIN [Historical science and historical consciousness]. *Zeitschrift für Geschichtswissenschaft [East Germany] 1967 15(2): 205-223.* The revolutionary proletarian class movement is the decisive element of the consciousness for overcoming exploitation and class divisions. 33 notes. R. Wagnleitner

2671. Schmidt, Walter. ÜBER DIE AUFGABEN DER GESCHICHTSWISSENSCHAFT BEI DER SOZIALISTISCHEN BEWUSSTSEINSBILDUNG [The tasks of historiography for the socialist formation of consciousness]. *Zeitschrift für Geschichtswissenschaft [East Germany] 1969 17(1-2): 52-61.* Marxist-Leninist historiography has to strengthen the scientific knowledge of the progressive traditions of the German working class and work out its alliances with other progressive groups of German history to confirm the necessity and justice of the socialist struggle.

2672. Schöllgen, Gregor. DIE BEGRIFFE UND IHRE WIRKLICHKEIT: "ZEITGESCHICHTLICHE KONTROVERSEN" UM FASCHISMUS UND TOTALITARISMUS [Conceptions and reality: "contemporary controversies" about fascism and totalitarianism]. *Hist. Jahrbuch [West Germany] 1983 103(1): 193-198.* Discusses the use of certain conceptions in historical writings without a verification of the applicability of the conceptions to the reality of events. The word fascism is often used indiscriminately to describe events having little to do with the original fascist movement in Italy. Incorrect use of conceptions can distort historic research. In many cases "fascism" should be replaced with "totalitarianism" which characterizes all kind of dictatorships. 9 notes. R. Vilums

2673. Schütz, Rüdiger. PROLETARISCHER KLASSENKAMPF UND BÜRGERLICHE REVOLUTION: ZUR BEURTEILUNG DER NOVEMBERREVOLUTION IN DER MARXISTISCH-LENINISTISCHEN GESCHICHTSWISSENSCHAFT [Proletarian class struggle and bourgeois revolution: the interpretation of the November Revolution in Marxist-Leninist historiography]. *Saeculum [West Germany] 1979 30(1): 22-44.* Before World War II Marxist-Leninist historians usually interpreted the German November Revolution as a socialist or proletarian revolution. Only later works began to use the term bourgeois revolution, the failure of which resulted in the lack of a revolutionary party of the labor movement and the cooperation of revisionist social democrats with bourgeois and reactionary groups. Secondary literature; 115 notes. R. Wagnleitner

2674. Seeber, Eva. DIE DDR-GESCHICHTSSCHREIBUNG ZUR GESCHICHTE DES SOZIALISTISCHEN WELTSYSTEMS [East German historiography of the socialist world system]. *Jahrbuch für Geschichte der Sozialistischen Länder Europas [East Germany] 1971 15(1): 67-80.* Reviews the major works on the history of the socialist world system published in East Germany during the last 10 years. Research and publication must be intensified, expanding on conceptual articles with monographic works of wider scope and discussing longer periods and whole complexes of problems.

2675. Shanin, Teodor. DEFINING PEASANTS: CONCEPTUALIZATIONS AND DE-CONCEPTUALIZATIONS OLD AND NEW IN A MARXIST DEBATE. *Peasant Studies 1979 8(4): 38-60.* Examines the conceptual basis behind the term "peasant," the degree to which it is a product of mystification, and its application in Marxist polemics.

2676. Shanin, Teodor. THE THIRD STAGE: MARXIST SOCIAL THEORY AND THE ORIGINS OF OUR TIME: REMEMBERING MARC BLOCH. *J. of Contemporary Asia [Sweden] 1976 6(3): 289-308* Historiographical essay on the interpretations of the economic and social development of world history in terms of writers of the third stage of Marxist development since the Stalinist era. The first stage was the destruction of the myth of Stalin, the second demonstrated an increase in the number of writers but a decrease in the depth of their Marxist thought. The current third stage exhibits a confrontation of the fundamentals of Marxist thought in a highly critical manner. Pays particular attention to I. Wallerstein's

The Modern World System (New York, 1974), P. Anderson's *Passages from Antiquity to Feudalism* (London, 1974), and *Lineages of the Absolutist State* (London, 1974). These and other writers are recognizing that Marxist historical analysis must itself be studied historically. Based on secondary sources in English; 34 notes.

K. W. Berger

2677. Soldani, Simonetta. GIORGIO GIORGETTI: UNO STORI-CO MARXISTA [Giorgio Giorgetti: a Marxist historian]. *Studi Storici [Italy] 1977 18(4): 111-130.* An analysis of the significance of the historical work of Giorgio Giorgetti occasioned by the publication of a collection of his essays entitled *Capitalism and Agriculture.* The author recounts Giorgetti's study of Marxism after 1945 while teaching in Pisa. In the 1960's Giorgetti undertook the clarification of the theory of surplus value and the historical problem of the accumulation of landed income. The lassitude of capital accumulation and the internal coherence of precapitalistic agriculture, especially in Tuscany, delayed the triumph of capitalistic agriculture, which began in the 18th century, until the 20th century. Based on Giorgetti's writings and secondary sources; 43 notes.

J. R. Banker

2678. Steinbach, Hans-Jurgen. DIE THEORIE DES "ORGANI-SIERTEN KAPITALISMUS" ALS ANTI-MARXISTISCHES KONZEPT ZUR DARSTELLUNG DES STAATSMONOPOLIS-TISCHEN KAPITALISMUS IN DER SOZIALGESCH-ICHTSSCHREIBUNG DER BRD [The theory of "organized capitalism" as an anti-Marxist concept in the presentation of state-monopolistic capitalism in social history in West Germany]. *Jahrbuch für Geschichte [East Germany] 1978 18: 339-372.* Since the early 1970's bourgeois historiography in West Germany has tried to reconstruct its theoretical-methodological approaches to overcome internal crises in bourgeois historical thinking, particularly in social and economic history. Many bourgeois historians have devised the theory of "organized capitalism" to deal with this crisis. Because this theory is devoid of any true Marxist content, it is inadequate in solving the crisis. Reviews the theories and approaches of several contemporary West German historians. 150 notes.

J. B. Street

2679. Šťovíček, Ivan. K NĚKTERÝM PROBLÉMŮM ME-TODIKY VYDÁVÁNÍ NOVODOBÝCH HISTORICKÝCH PRAMENŮ [Problems in publishing modern historical resources]. *Sborník Archivních Prací [Czechoslovakia] 1977 27(1): 192-219.* Analyzes methods of publishing documents for modern history research in Communist countries. The first rules about declassification, editing, and publishing of documents in modern history, were made in Soviet Russia in 1917. Basic rules on publishing exist in all socialist nations. Based on published materials; 91 notes.

G. E. Pergl

2680. Straube, Fritz. DIE LENINSCHE THEORIE DER SOZI-ALISTISCHE REVOLUTION UND IHRE VERFÄLSCHUNG DURCH DIE WESTDEUTSCHE BÜRGERLICHE GESCH-ICHTSSCHREIBUNG [The Leninist theory of the socialist revolution and its falsification by West German bourgeois historians]. *Jahrbuch für Geschichte [East Germany] 1967 2: 193-219.* Certain West German bourgeois historians have sought to cast doubt on the theoretical foundations of V. I. Lenin's theory of revolution, opposing, as it were, Marx with Marx. They have sought to use the writings of Karl Marx and Friedrich Engels to discredit Lenin, forgetting that the former two wrote before the beginning of the age of imperialism, and that therefore their ideas cannot be used to criticize Lenin's new ideas dealing with the new situation of imperialism. 76 notes.

J. C. Billgmeier

2681. Thamer, Hans-Ulrich. ANSICHTEN DES FASCHISMUS. DER ITALIENISCHE FASCHISMUS IN DER POLITISCHEN UND WISSENSCHAFTLICHEN DISKUSSION [Aspects of Fascism: Italian Fascism in the political and scientific discussion]. *Neue Politische Literatur [West Germany] 1977 22(1): 19-35.* The recent discussion of Renzo de Felice's theories of fascism in Italy was characterized by the stressing of the internal political and ideologi-

cal differences of the Fascist Party, its social heterogeneity and loose organizational structure and by a reanalysis of its class origins.

2682. Toman, B. A. SOVESHCHANIE ISTORIKOV PARTII PRIBALTIKI [The meeting of Party historians of the Baltic area]. *Voprosy Istorii KPSS [USSR] 1971 (9): 145-147.* Discusses the papers read at Tallinn on 15-16 June 1971 on the theme of the contemporary state of Communist Party historical studies in the Baltic republics.

2683. Treves, Piero. DITTICO PER UNA STORIA DEL FASCIS-MO [Diptych for a history of fascism]. *Veltro [Italy] 1975 19(3/4): 209-229.* Agrees with Renzo De Felice that it is possible to write a history of fascism; the problem is to define it.

2684. Tupolev, B. M. FASHIZM I NEOFASHIZM. ISTORIIA I SOVREMENNOST [Fascism and neofascism: the history and presence]. *Novaia i Noveishaia Istoriia [USSR] 1979 (1): 210-212.* Reports on the proceedings and papers presented at the conference on fascism and neofascism organized by the Commission of the Historians of East Germany GDR and USSR held in Kiev in 19-21 September 1978.

V. Sobeslavsky

2685. Vaítkiavicius, B. J. ISTORYCHNA NAUKA V LY-TOVS'KYI RSR [Historical studies in the Latvian SSR]. *Ukrains'kyi Istorychnyi Zhurnal [USSR] 1982 (12): 74-78.* Opens with a discussion on the aims of the Communist Party to raise the level of theoretical research, the development of key problems in historical research, and the question of developed socialism, an analysis of the features of Soviet society and the need to strengthen the academic criticism of anticommunism. Discusses the various resolutions passed by the CPSU and the Latvian Communist Party on historical research and the various faculties of history in the Latvian SSR—the main one being the Institute of History of the Latvian SSR, guided by the department of the history of the Latvian SSR. Gives details of various publications, all of which help to build upon the life of Soviet society. 15 notes.

L. Djakowska

2686. Vandalkovskaia, M. G. and Dunaevski, V. A. PERVAIA KONFERENTSIIA ISTORIOGRAFOV SOTSIALISTICHESKIKH STRAN [The first Conference of Historians of the Socialist Countries]. *Istoriia SSSR [USSR] 1980 (2): 222-226.* Describes papers presented at a conference organized by the USSR Academy of Sciences 11-13 December 1978 on "Basic directions in the modern study of the history of historical sciences in Socialist countries." Includes papers presented by Soviet historians I. D. Koval'chenkov and A. O. Chubar'ian.

L. Waters/S

2687. Vargatiuk, P. L. UCHENYE UKRAINY OBSUZHDAIUT NAUCHNYE TRUDY [Ukrainian scholars discuss scientific works]. *Voprosy Istorii KPSS [USSR] 1983 (8): 155-158.* A conference to mark the publication of a series of volumes of essays on the history of the Communist Party of the Ukraine was held in Kiev in 1983. Participants included local Party secretaries, representatives of authors' collectives, scholars from the institute of Party history, and members of public organizations. Summaries of speeches delivered at the conference by I. V. Iurchuk; L. A. Nagornaia, Iu. V. Babko, and others are included.

G. Dombrovski

2688. Veleva, Zhivka. ZA NIAKOI FALSHIFIKATSII NA ISTORIIATA NA KOMUNISTICHESKIIA INTERNATSIONAL [About some falsifications of the history of the Communist International]. *Izvestiia na Instituta po Istoriia na BKP [Bulgaria] 1970 23: 223-240.* A Marxist survey of the errors in Western bourgeois and reformist interpretations of the history of the 3d Communist International, criticizing socialist interpreters such as Isaac Deutscher and J. Rosenthal and attacking the works of Franz Borkenau for setting the example of exaggerating Soviet influence, models, and domination in the Comintern. Soviet foreign policy did not dictate Comintern policies, nor did revolution depend upon the strength of Soviet arms alone. Western historians have invented an imaginary crisis within the 3d International after the stabilization of world capitalism in 1921. Based on secondary sources and research in East Germany; 60 notes. C. S. Masloff

2689. Voigt, Gerd. HISTORIOGRAPHIE UND KOMMUNIS-MUSFORSCHUNG [Historiography and research on communism]. *Zeitschrift für Geschichtswissenschaft [East Germany] 1976 24(5): 501-515.* Imperialist research on communism uses the theory of pluralism, the theory of the Russian renunciation of proletarian internationalism, and the ideological wear and tear of Marxism-Leninism as arguments for the downfall of the socialist system. Based on Western works on Russian history and secondary literature. 54 notes. R. Wagnleitner

2690. Weissbecker, Manfred. DIE "ZEITGESCHICHTLICHEN KONTROVERSEN" KARL DIETRICH BRACHERS: EIN ANTI-KOMMUNISTISCHER ZERRSPIEGEL DER GESCHICHTE UND THEORIE DES FASCHISMUS [The "controversies on contemporary history" of Karl Dietrich Bracher: an anticommunist distorting mirror of the history and theory of fascism]. *Wissenschaftliche Zeitschrift der Friedrich-Schiller-Universität Jena. Gesellschafts- und Sprachwissenschaftliche Reihe [East Germany] 1979 29(2): 291-303.* Karl Dietrich Bracher and most other West German historians try to interpret fascism as being contrary to the capitalist system and liberal-democratic society. These authors even attribute to fascism some characteristic revolutionary theories. 75 notes. R. Wagnleitner

2691. Yasukawa, Etsuko. IGIRISU NI OKERU MARUKUSU SHUGI NO SEIRITSU [The formation of Marxism in Britain]. *Shakai Shiso [Japan] 1972 2(1): 127-162.* Neglect of E. B. Bax's place in English socialist thought shows the gap in the historiography of Marxist thought in Great Britain. Along with W. Morris and H. Hyndman, Bax formed the first generation of Marxist theorists in Britain at the beginning of the 1880's. The author clarifies Bax's thought on philosophy, economics, and socialism. M. Itō

2692. Yatsuyamagi, Ryōjiro. SHIN MEGA TO MARUKUSU KENKY [The new MEGA and Marx Studies]. *Ann. Bull. of the Soc. for the Hist. of Econ. Thought [Japan] 1983 21: 3-10.* Analyzes Japanese and foreign publications concerning Karl Marx's notes on *Das Kapital* included in the *Karl Marx-Friedrich Engels Gesamtausgabe* (MEGA) (1975) divided into three decades: 1840's, 1850's, and 1860's. Table. M. Kawaguchi

2693. Zaharescu, Vladimir. CU PRIVIRE LA DIALECTICA GENERALULUI ŞI PARTICULARULUI ÎN REVOLUŢIA ŞI CONSTRUCŢIA SOCIALISTĂ [On the dialectic of the general and particular in Socialist revolution and construction]. *Anale de Istorie [Rumania] 1973 19(2): 110-137.* Demonstrates methodologically that each revolution manifests a general, universal historic process based on internal socioeconomic contradictions, while at the same time the particular social, economic, political, cultural, ethnic, national, and religious characteristics of each revolutionary situation may differ. Notes important indices of the development of the forces of production and gives the percent of the population engaged in agriculture in various nations, showing that with divergent levels of development at the start of each revolutionary process, the transition to a bourgeois-capitalist or socialist order will display marked differences. Focuses on the powerful impetus provided by World War II in hastening the revolutionary change to democratic and socialist regimes. Compares the Rumanian experience with that of Hungary, Czechoslovakia, and Poland after 1945, focusing on the expropriation of productive facilities and the collectivization of agriculture. Concludes that there is no automatic, rigid formulation applicable universally in building a socialist system; rather, the specific variations are countless and depend on the historic experience and internal necessities of each nation. Secondary sources; 3 tables, 25 notes. G. J. Bobango

2694. Zeisler, Kurt. GENESIS UND FUNKTIONEN DER GEGENWÄRTIGEN IMPERIALISTISCHEN "KOMMUNISMUS-FORSCHUNG" [Origin and functions of present imperialist research on Communism]. *Zeitschrift für Geschichtswissenschaft [East Germany] 1973 21(10): 1157-1181.* Analyzes the economic, political, and ideological background of American and West German research on communist countries. Secondary literature; 62 notes. R. Wagnleitner

2695. Zevelev, A. I. and Pedosov, A. D. REVIEW OF *M. N. POKROVSKII AND SOVIET HISTORICAL SCHOLARSHIP. Soviet Studies in Hist. 1973 12(2): 83-89.* Reviews O. D. Sokolov's *M. N. Pokrovskii and Soviet Scholarship,* covering Pokrovski's views as a Marxist historian and his consolidation of Marxist-Leninist thought, 1905-30.

2696. Zimmermann, Fritz. URSACHEN UND ZIELE DER VERSTÄRKTEN AKTIVITÄT DER BÜRGERLICHEN HISTORIOGRAPHIE DER BDR AUF DEM GEBIET DER GESCHICHTE DER ARBEITERBEWEGUNG [Origins and goals of the increased activity in bourgeois historiography of the Federal Republic of Germany in the field of the history of the workers' movement]. *Beiträge zur Geschichte der Arbeiterbewegung [East Germany] 1974 16(5): 804-808.* West German historians have recently intensified their studies of the international workers' movement. Their approach has been to seek out flaws in socialist histories and supposed differences between the theories of Karl Marx and Friedrich Engels and the theories and applications of V. I. Lenin. Socialist historians should use the present journal to point out and correct these errors. Secondary materials; 9 notes. G. H. Libbey

2697. Zsilák, András. A PÁRTTÖRTÉNETI ÉS MARXIZMUS-LENINIZMUS INTÉZETEK VEZETŐINEK NEMZETKÖZI TANÁCSKOZÁSA [The international consultation of directors of institutes of Party history and Marxism-Leninism]. *Párttörténeti Közlemények [Hungary] 1976 22(4): 211.* An account of the September 1976 conference in Berlin of the directors of institutes of Party history and Marxism-Leninism working in cooperation with the central committees of Communist and Workers' parties. The conference surveyed the results achieved in research since the 1975 Prague meeting and those realized from the long-range research program of the 1974 Budapest conference.

2698. —. HISTORIOGRAFIE K DĚJINÁM MEZINÁRODNÍHO A KOMUNISTICKÉHO HNUTÍ. PUBLIKAČNÍ ČINNOST ÚML A VSP ÚV KSČ [Historiography on the international and communist movement: publications issued by Central Committee of the Communist Party of Czechoslovakia]. *Acta U. Carolinae Phil. et Hist. [Czechoslovakia] 1981 (5): 129-131.* Surveys the publications of original works on history sponsored by the Communist Party of Czechoslovakia. These papers were a result of the Central Committee's decision in 1974 to "enhance the level of political education for the future of socialist society." More than 20 significant publications appeared between 1977-80. Based on official reports; biblio. G. E. Pergl

2699. —. WALKA IDEALOGICZNA PRZECIWKO ANTYKOMUNIZMOWI W DZIEDZINIE HISTORII RUCHU ROBOTNICZEGO I ZADANIA PARTYJNYCH CZASOPISM HISTORYCZNYCH [An ideological struggle against anticommunism in the field of history of the workers' movement and the tasks of Party historical periodicals]. *Z Pola Walki [Poland] 1974 68(4): 3-22.* The peaceful coexistence of countries of different social systems raises the importance of ideological struggle. The field of this struggle is also a science of history, especially the history of the workers' movement. The anticommunist centers publish many books and specialized periodicals aimed at falsifying the ideology of Marxism-Leninism, the history of the international worker and communist movement, the history of particular parties, and of socialist countries. Anticommunist trends are visible in bourgeois and rightist-social democratic historiography as well as in literature originated in extreme leftist and Maoist circles. The article is an analysis of general trends in anticommunist penetration in the field of the history of Polish and international workers' movement. Shortened from a paper presented by the *Z Pola Walki* editorial board to an international conference of Party historical periodicals, Warsaw on 9-11 April 1974. J

Colonialism and Imperialism

2700. Albertini, Rudolf von. ZUR IMPERIALISMUSDEBATTE [The debate on imperialism]. *Schweizerische Zeitschrift für Geschichte [Switzerland] 1978 28(1-2): 104-112.* A discussion of recent works (1976-77) in German, French, and English on imperialism. Historians, non-Marxists and Marxists alike, are divided in their explanations of the causes of European expansion in the 19th century. Causal relationship between capitalism and imperialism is disputed; defensive and social imperialism theories compete with peripheral and integrative ones. H. K. Meier

2701. Anderau, Walter. NEUE ANSÄTZE IN DER IMPERIALISMUSFORSCHUNG [New approaches toward research on imperialism]. *Schweizer Monatshefte [Switzerland] 1972 51(12): 906-910.* Reviews 18 West German, American, and Swiss publications on imperialism since the 18th century and on neoimperialism after World War II.

2702. Bade, Klaus J. IMPERIALISMUSFORSCHUNG UND KOLONIALHISTORIE [Research into imperialism and colonial history]. *Gesch. und Gesellschaft [West Germany] 1983 9(1): 138-150.* Reviews seven recent studies, both in German and English, of late 19th-century European imperialism. In the last few years leading scholars have attempted to avoid Eurocentrism and to study imperialism from the point of view of the natives directly involved. Colonial experiences were very diverse and cannot all be fitted into the established theories of imperialism. C.-H. Geschwind

2703. Chambers, James T. IMPERIALISM: ROMAN AND BRITISH. Parker, Harold T., ed. *Problems in European History,* (Durham, N.C.: Moore Publ., 1979): 138-151. Recent scholarship has brought differences between Roman and British imperialism into higher relief: the inability of the ancient economy, for example, to support a vast bureaucracy made for a simpler and less obtrusive administration. Explanations of Great Britain's expansion have come full circle, stressing again the motive of glory seeking by the man on the spot, after periods of interest in economics, nationalism, and the imperial idea as the sources of imperialism. The continuity between the apparently quiescent imperialism of 1830-80 and the full-blown imperialism of 1880-1900 has become increasingly clear. Discussion of Roman motives for expansion has also described something of a circle, but here the result is a renewed emphasis on economics. Roman tolerance in matters of race and religion helps account for their more enduring success. L. W. Van Wyk

2704. Franklin, Bruce. ON THE REWRITING OF HISTORY. *Monthly Rev. 1982 34(6): 40-47.* Describes factual distortions in the article in the 15th edition of *Encyclopaedia Britannica* (1974) dealing with US and Soviet colonialism after 1914, including the decolonization of Vietnam.

2705. Glubb, John. THE FATE OF EMPIRES. *Blackwood's Mag. [Great Britain] 1976 1934(320): 484-511.* Study of the ascent and decline of empires during the last 3,000 years reveals several characteristics common to each imperial power: a historiography focusing on empires can aid in better understanding contemporary reality.

2706. Green, William A. CREST OF EMPIRE. *Victorian Studies 1975 18(3): 345-354.* A review article of 13 recent books on the general topic of imperialism and the Victorian Empire. Concludes that imperial history is stalemated, with no definitive answers to the origins and motives of European expansion. Asserts the need for scholars to examine the impact of British imperialism on the newly emerging nations of the Third World. T. L. Auffenberg

2707. Guillen, Pierre. MILIEUX D'AFFAIRES ET IMPÉRIALISME COLONIAL [Business circles and colonial imperialism]. *Relations Int. [France] 1974 (1): 57-69.* J. A. Hobson, A. F. Hilferding, and V. I. Lenin maintained that imperialism was the result of an excess of capitalist accumulation, forcing business interests to seek new markets, hence colonies. There are many legitimate objections to this view. Business interests were not unanimous

regarding either their investments or their politics. Many invested at home, or in the United States or Russia, not in the colonies. Colonies were at least as much the creation of military and nationalist as of financial circles. Historians should avoid making generalizations about great movements such as colonialism as did Hobson, Hilferding, and Lenin. 25 notes. J. C. Billigmeier

2708. Gutsche, Willibald. ZUR INTERPRETATION DER ANFÄNGE DES DEUTSCHEN IMPERIALISMUS IN DER HISTORIOGRAPHIE DER BRD [The interpretation of the origins of German imperialism in West German historiography]. *Zeitschrift für Geschichtswissenschaft [East Germany] 1975 23(11): 1274-1286.* Challenged by the increased strength of the socialist states, West German historians have adopted more flexible methods in their struggle against the Marxist-Leninist theory of imperialism. They have attempted to confuse the connection between monopoly and imperialism by presenting the latter as an outcome of temporary disturbances in industrial society. The ruling elites supposedly adopted imperialism to divert the energies of progressive elements or to preserve the remnant of the preindustrial order. In addition, West German historians give economic factors a subordinate role among the many alleged causes of imperialism. Primary works; 82 notes. J. T. Walker

2709. Heath, Ian. TOWARDS A REASSESSMENT OF GORDON IN FIJI. *J. of Pacific Hist. [Australia] 1974 9: 81-92.* Reflects on the shortcomings of biographies on Arthur Charles Hamilton-Gordon, and reassesses his ideas and activities as governor in Fiji as a central protagonist of British colonial government in the late 1870's and early 1880's. 57 notes. D. L. Robinson/S

2710. Khalfin, N. A. and Avetian, A. S. PROBLEMY ISTORII KOLONIALIZMA I NEOKOLONIALIZMA V SOVETSKOI ISTORIOGRAFII 1967-1972G [Problems of the history of colonialism and neocolonialism in Soviet historiography, 1967-72]. *Novaia i Noveishaia Istoriia [USSR] 1973 (4): 146-157.* A bibliography of predominantly monographic materials published in the USSR, 1967-72, on colonialism, neocolonialism, and related subjects. There are works on such broad subjects as racism, colonialism, neocolonialism, and aggression. More numerous, however, are detailed monographs on a variety of more specific topics. The scope of the bibliography is international and has a predominantly late 19th and 20-century chronological bias. 67 notes. D. N. Collins

2711. Khazanov, A. M. ISTORIIA PORTUGAL'SKOGO KOLONIALIZMA V OSVESHCHENII BURZHUAZNOI ISTORIOGRAFII [The history of Portuguese colonialism as presented by bourgeois historiography]. *Novaia i Noveishaia Istoriia [USSR] 1977 (2): 68-82.* The five-century old Portuguese colonial empire about which much has been written collapsed in the early 1970's. The author examines the traditional colonialist trend in bourgeois historiography with its "Luso-tropicalism," the neocolonialist trend which is centered on the search for positive consequences of colonialism, and the bourgeois-liberal trend. J

2712. Klein, Fritz. STAND UND PROBLEME DER ERFORSCHUNG DER GESCHICHTE DES DEUTSCHEN IMPERIALISMUS BIS 1945 [The position and problems of research into the history of German imperialism until 1945]. *Zeitschrift für Geschichtswissenschaft [East Germany] 1975 23(5): 485-493.* East German historians have successfully studied aspects of German imperialism, including the role of imperialists in the causes and conduct of the two world wars, the development of German monopoly capital, and the foreign policy of the Weimar Republic. Topics requiring attention are the influence of economic interest groups on government policies, the relationship between various monopoly capitalist groups and fascism, and imperialism after 1945. 13 notes. J. T. Walker

2713. Koshelev, L. V. OSNOVNYE PROBLEMY KOLONIALIZMA I KOLONIAL'NOI POLITIKI V OSVESHCHENII FRANTSUZSKOI ISTORIOGRAFII I PUBLITSISTIKI V GODY CHETVERTOI RESPUBLIKI (1946-1958 GODY) [Major problems of colonialism and colonial policy as treated in French historiography and the press during the Fourth Republic, 1946-58].

Vestnik Moskovskogo U., Seriia 9: Istoriia [USSR] 1964 19(3): 19-36. Discusses the post-World War II conflict in France between various theoreticians and defending colonialism and the position of the French Communist Party, which opposed colonial rule and considered national liberation movements an expression of anti-imperialist and antifeudal democratic ideas. Evaluates works on colonialism by Jacques Arnault, Georges Bidault, Léon Blum, and Maurice Thorez. 101 notes.   N. Frenkley

2714. Lyytinen, Eino. MUSTAN VAIKO VALKOISEN MIEHEN TAAKKA? 1800-LUVUN LOPUN IMPERIALISMIN SELITYS-MALLEISTA [A burden for the black man or the white man? Explanatory models of imperialism at the end of the 1800's]. *Hist. Arkisto [Finland] 1978 71: 121-136.* Reviews various models of Western imperialism in European and North American historiography from 1870 to 1974. The early concept of a moral, civilizing mission was challenged successively by economic, sociological, and political explanations. Based on international sources; biblio.
R. G. Selleck

2715. Moravcová, Dagmar. IMPERIALISMUS VE VÝKLADU BURŽOAZNÍ HISTORIOGRAFIE NSR V 70. LETECH [Imperialism as interpreted by bourgeois historiography in the 1970's in West Germany]. *Československý Časopis Hist. [Czechoslovakia] 1982 30(4): 580-603.* Since the 1960's, West German historians have worked out theories of imperialism that would invalidate or correct V. I. Lenin's thesis of a crucial interdependence between imperialism and monopoly capital. T. Schieder, J. W. Mommsen, K. D. Bracher, and W. J. Baumgardt continue to emphasize aggressive nationalism and power politics as independent factors. H. U. Wehler, H. Böhme, and J. Kocka attempt a comprehensive socioeconomic approach that allows for the application of Marxist-Leninist insights but tends to oversimplify Lenin's view as one of narrowly economic causation. Even committed antiimperialist historians avoid Lenin's revolutionary conclusions and look to a managed or reformed capitalism as an alternative. 104 notes. Russian and German summaries.   R. E. Weltsch

2716. Mori, Kenzo. "JIYU BOEKI TEIKOKU SHUGI" RONSO NO IGI TO GENKAI [The significance and limitation of the controversy on free trade imperialism]. *Shakai Kagaku Kenkyū [Japan] 1975 26(5): 46-117.* Studies the controversies over John Gallagher and Ronald Robinson's interpretation of free trade imperialism and reexamines their methodological viewpoints. Questions whether the development of British capitalism in the 19th century consistently had an imperialistic character. Viewing British colonial expansion only as the continuity of foreign policy, the author equates imperialism with simple expansionism. Such a viewpoint is the antithesis to the emphasis on the essential difference between the periods of imperialism and free trade which Hobson and Lenin insisted on.
I. Matsui

2717. Parfenov, I. D. NOVYE TENDENTSII V SOVREMENNOI ANGLIISKOI ISTORIOGRAFII KOLONIAL'NOI EKSPANSII XIX VEKA [New tendencies in contemporary English historiography of colonial expansion in the 19th century]. *Voprosy Istorii [USSR] 1978 (3): 183-192.* A considerable increase in the output of literature on colonial expansion in the last third of the 19th century can be seen in contemporary bourgeois historiography. The main topics of discussion are the correlation between capitalism and colonial expansion and motives and stimuli in the creation of empires. The historians of England, the United States, France, West Germany, and Belgium have begun to reevaluate traditional concepts. The author surveys contemporary English historiography and finds that all new theories concerning expansion at the end of the 19th century reject the Marxist-Leninist interpretation but put nothing in its place. Primary sources; 46 notes.   L. Kalinowski

2718. Patrushev, A. I. NESOSTOIATEL'NOST' KONTSEPTSII IMPERIALIZMA V BURZHUAZNOI ISTORIOGRAFII FRG [The untenable concept of imperialism in the bourgeois historiography of West Germany]. *Novaia i Noveishaia Istoriia [USSR] 1978 (5): 50-63.* Discusses the vain attempts by bourgeois ideologists to disprove the Marxist-Leninist theory of socioeconomic formations and regularities in historical development and particularly Lenin's

teaching about imperialism as the highest and final stage of capitalism. He gives a critical analysis of the apologetic concepts of imperialism that are gaining currency in West German bourgeois historiography.   J

2719. Pease, Jane H. THE IMPERIALISM OF STATUS: A SYNTHETIC REVIEW. *R. of Pol. 1970 32(4): 461-475.* Reviews interpretations of imperialism since 1945. A change in the British concept of empire between 1890-1910 occurred at a time of domestic turmoil and uncertainty. Recent studies stress the social and psychological dimensions of imperialism. Primary and secondary sources; 46 notes.   N. A. Kuntz

2720. Rumpler, Helmut. ZUM GEGENWÄRTIGEN STAND DER IMPERIALISMUSDEBATTE [The present state of the debate over imperialism]. *Geschichte in Wissenschaft und Unterricht [West Germany] 1974 25(5): 257-271.* Describes the changing interpretation of imperialism from the 1840's to the present. Originating in party politics, the term imperialism entered into historical discussion through J. A. Hobson who elaborated the major reasons for imperialism, which are still convincing. Hans Ulrich Wehler is the most outspoken German critic of imperialism, and his work bears on the image of Bismarck and has aroused bitter controversies. Wehler defines imperialism as defensive social strategy. Though Wehler's definition is more valid than others, his theory does not quite convince. The controversy surrounding Wehler concerns his use of history to teach politics and his view of historical development. Secondary works; 55 notes.   H. W. Wurster

2721. Schaper, B. W. NIEUWE OPVATTINGEN OVER HET MODERNE IMPERIALISME [New concepts on modern imperialism]. *Bijdragen en Mededelingen betreffende de Geschiedenis der Nederlanden [Netherlands] 1971 86(1): 4-20.* The term imperialism is ambiguous, abused, and perverted. The author reviews conventional and more recent interpretations such as those by Langer, Hobson, and Fieldhouse. Concludes that the balance sheet of imperialism is negative. The costs of expansion were higher than income and imperialism strengthened the forces of totalitarianism. Furthermore, imperialism infested the whole world with the virus of unrestricted strife for power and profit and ideas of materialism and spiritual superiority at the expense of others. Based on published materials; 45 notes.   G. D. Homan

2722. Shtrakhov, A. I. O NESOSTOIATEL'NOSTI KONSERVATORNO-KLERIKAL'NYKH KONTSEPTSII ISPANSKIKH KOLONIAL'NYKH PORIADKOV NA LA-PLATE [The failure of conservative-clerical conceptions of the Spanish colonial system in La Plata]. *Novaia i Noveishaia Istoriia [USSR] 1973 (3): 82-90.* Analyzes Marxist and bourgeois historiography of the Spanish colonization of the Viceroyalty of Río de la Plata. Contemporary Argentinian historiography is divided into two schools: the classical and the revisionist. The conservative -clerical revisionist school stresses the positive aspects of Spanish influence and supports Spain's role as colonizer. Argentinian Marxist historians have given a decided rebuff to this concept. Secondary sources mainly in Spanish; 41 notes.

2723. Simensen, Jarle. COUNTERFACTUAL ARGUMENTS IN HISTORICAL ANALYSIS: FROM THE DEBATE ON THE PARTITION OF AFRICA AND THE EFFECT OF COLONIAL RULE. *Hist. in Africa 1978 5: 169-186.* Considers the value of postulating hypothetical alternatives to actual past events as a method of historical analysis. The views of various historians of the partition and colonialism illustrate the use and misuse of this process. The difficulties posed by employing counterfactual arguments include establishing a plausible starting situation and constructing a reasonable hypothetical process. This process is most successful when its scope is narrowly circumscribed to avoid a complex of variables and to stimulate discussion of new perspectives on specific historical topics. 40 notes.

2724. Trainor, Luke. HISTORIANS AS IMPERIALISTS: SOME ROOTS OF BRITISH IMPERIAL HISTORY, 1880-1900. *New Zealand J. of Hist. [New Zealand] 1981 15(1): 35-48.* The roots of British imperial history are located in the 1880's, much earlier than the establishment of the subject as part of the university curriculum. The early writings, as well as the reactions to them, were essentially political. In time, the Royal Colonial Institute and other organizations gave powerful support to imperial history and the attitudes and policies it fostered. Based on a document in the Public Record Office, London, the writings of imperial historians, and published letters; 34 notes.   P. J. Coleman

2725. Trépanier, Pierre and Trépanier, Lise. RAMEAU DE SAINT-PÈRE ET L'HISTOIRE DE LA COLONIZATION FRANÇAISE EN AMÉRIQUE [Rameau de Saint-Père and the history of French colonization in America]. *Acadiensis [Canada] 1980 9(2): 40-55.* François-Edme Rameau de Saint-Père, author of several histories of French colonization in America, was born in France in 1820. Strongly influenced by France's involvement in Algeria, he was convinced that French failures in America were the fault of the French government, not of French settlers. Between 1877 and 1889, Rameau came to see feudalism rather than liberty as a key element in the development of France's North American colonies. His popularity with French-speaking North Americans is due to their indentification with the social authorities to whom Rameau attributed noble deeds. In Acadia he is the father of traditional historiography. 70 notes.   D. F. Chard

2726. Vahtola, Jouko. AUGUST LUDWIG VON SCHLÖZER JA KOLONISAATION HISTORIA [August Ludwig von Schlözer and the history of colonization]. *Historiallinen Arkisto [Finland] 1984 (82): 291-319.* Examines the historical writings of August Ludwig von Schlözer (1735-1809), a professor at Göttingen University. Though committed to Enlightenment ideals, Schlözer was a founder of modern critical German historiography. His particular research topic was migration and colonial settlement in ancient and medieval Europe. He viewed peaceful colonization as a means of spreading civilization and increasing the wealth of societies. Based on Schlözer's published works and other German history monographs; 132 notes.   R. G. Selleck

2727. Vasudevan, C. P. A. THE NATURE OF THE EUROPEAN EXPANSION. *J. of Indian Hist. [India] 1976 54(2): 441-452.* Continued from a previous article. Examines the reasons and patterns of European expansionism, 15th-20th centuries. Concentrates on British wars, the slave trade, opium smuggling, and other misdeeds in Asia. Reviews the distortions in European and other historical accounts of colonial ventures. Secondary sources; 29 notes.   S. H. Frank

2728. Vinogradov, K. B. LENINSKAIA OTSENKA KOLONIAL'NOI POLITIKI VELIKOBRITANII [Lenin's evaluation of British colonial policy]. *Vestnik Leningradskogo U.: Seriia Istorii, Iazyka i Literatury [USSR] 1980 (3): 11-16.* V. I. Lenin's analysis of imperialism and colonial politics provides a firm base for the study of British expansionism at the end of the 19th century and beginning of the 20th. He wrote on British colonial policy, publishing in 1899 a review of J. A. Hobson's book on the evolution of capitalism. Bourgeois historians have sought to show that Lenin and Hobson employed the same conceptions in their evaluation of imperialism, but a study of their work indicates that this was not the case. They also attempted to justify the colonial past. Soviet historians on the other hand adopted a critical approach and with the aid of Leninist theory have produced a number of important works on the history of British colonialism. Secondary sources; 30 notes.   L. Waters

2729. Vyhovs'kyi, I. I. ROZPAD KOLONIAL'NOI SYSTEMY IMPERIALIZMU U VYSVITLENNI AMERYKANS'KOI BURZHUAZNOI ISTORIOHRAFII [The collapse of imperialism as depicted by American bourgeois historiography]. *Ukrains'kyi Istorychnyi Zhurnal [USSR] 1973 (3): 93-99.* Critically analyzes American historiography of the collapse of colonialism since 1945, with particular reference to US imperialism in Southeast Asia and Africa.

2730. Waller, Bruce. HANS-ULRICH WEHLER ON IMPERIAL GERMANY (1871-1918). *British J. of Int. Studies [Great Britain] 1975 1(1): 60-67.* Discusses Hans-Ulrich Wehler's *Bismarck und der Imperialismus* (1969) in the context of German historiography.

2731. Wesseling, H. L. HET FRANSE IMPERIALISME, 1871-1914: EEN DECENNIUM VAN DISCUSSIE, 1960-1970 [French imperialism, 1871-1914: a decade of discussion, 1960-1970]. *Tijdschrift voor Geschiedenis [Netherlands] 1973 86(4): 544-559.* Discusses French historiography on the causes of imperialism, beginning with Henri Brunschwig's *Mythes et réalités de l'impérialisme colonial français, 1871-1914* (Paris, 1960). The Eurocentric interpretation cites economic, political, and ideological motives. The peripheral interpretation cites the structure of colonies and relations between military and civil authorities. The peripheral explanation, especially regarding France's colonial expansion process, is an important contribution to the history of modern imperialism. 63 notes.   G. Herritt

2732. West, Katharine. THEORISING ABOUT "IMPERIALISM": A METHODOLOGICAL NOTE. *J. of Imperial and Commonwealth Hist. [Great Britain] 1973 1(2): 147-154.* A discussion of the ambiguities surrounding the word imperialism as used by historians and political scientists. Various uses and interpretations of the word are analyzed and its widespread misuse criticized. Based on several recent works on imperialism; 16 notes.

J. A. Casada

2733. —. AMERICAN IMPERIALISM. *Am. Hist. Rev. 1978 83(3): 644-683.*
Field, James A., Jr. AMERICAN IMPERIALISM: THE WORST CHAPTER IN ALMOST ANY BOOK, *pp. 644-668.* The "worst chapter" in works on American foreign relations maintains, through misreading of sources, unverifiable assertion, neglect of technology, repetition, and imprecision, that late 19th century attitudes and export needs led to a Pacific expansionism aimed at the China market. In fact, the coming of steam had shrunk the strategic perimeter. Foreign trade, merchant marine, cable communications, and naval deployment were oriented toward Europe and South America, and the Pacific was a very secondary theater. Incidents conventionally cited as precursors to 1898 were defensive consequences of presumed European threats and of the new technologies of steam propulsion and cable communication. These technologies influenced both the timing and outcome of Dewey's move against the Philippines which, planned as a measure against Spain in Cuba, led to unintended involvement in the Far East.
LaFeber, Walter F. and Beisner, Robert L. COMMENT, *pp. 669-678.*
Field, James A., Jr. REPLY, *pp. 679-683.*   A

Domestic Politics

2734. Baev, V. G. IZUCHENIE ISTORII PARLAMENTARIZMA I POLITICHESKIKH PARTII V FRG [Study of the history of parliamentarism and political parties in West Germany]. *Voprosy Istorii [USSR] 1984 (3): 164-169.* At the end of 1951, a commission on the history of parliamentarism and political parties was formed to study the period from 1848 to the present, and undertook two main activities: monographic research and the publication of documents. Much attention has been paid to the striving of bourgeois and social reformist authors to show the stability of the bourgeois democratic structure in West Germany. 25 notes.

S. J. Talalay

2735. Barker, John. CHANGING FRONTIERS. *Wilson Q. 1983 7(1): 88-99.* Discusses a variety of historical works that have contributed to the development of a national identity and purpose, including John Smith's *A True Relation*, Henry Adams's history of the administrations of John Adams and Jefferson, Frederick Jackson Turner's thesis, and Charles A. Beard's work.

2736. Baum, Dale. "NOISY BUT NOT NUMEROUS": THE REVOLT OF THE MASSACHUSETTS MUGWUMPS. *Historian 1979 41(2): 241-256.* In a pioneering electoral study, Lee Benson challenged the accepted notion that the Mugwumps influenced enough Republican votes toward Cleveland to defeat Blaine; instead he suggested that the decline of Republican votes in Massachusetts from 1880-84 was best explained by support for Benjamin F. Butler. Reexamines this hypothesis through a more detailed analysis of Massachusetts voting returns by ecological regression. Argues that Butler failed to attract Republican votes, and that apathy was more important in the decline of Republican fortunes. Exaggerated importance given to restore political factions plus unsophisticated procedures for estimating voting patterns from aggregate statistics have combined "to give the celebrated bolt of the Mugwumps an importance out of proportion to their raw numerical strength, not only in the 1880's but also later in accounts of the period by many historians." Primary and secondary sources; 9 tables, 29 notes.

R. S. Sliwoski

2737. Belloni, Frank P. and Beller, Dennis C. THE STUDY OF PARTY FACTIONS AS COMPETITIVE POLITICAL ORGANIZATIONS. *Western Pol. Q. 1976 29(4): 531-549.* The study of party factions has been a neglected field in political science, and should be given more attention. The authors survey the extant writings on the subject, and analyze their approaches to political factions. Factions are conceived either as 1) consisting of followers of a prominent leader, or as 2) being a collectivity of like-minded individuals. The two views are not basically inconsistent, but there is a real difference in the basic presumption of the leader-follower quality and the shared-values quality. Political factions can have numerous functions and interests, and their study should contribute to the better understanding of politics in general.

2738. Benczedi, László; Hanák, Péter; Lackó, Miklós; and Várkonyi, Ágnes R.. AZ EGRI "HAZAFIAS TANÁCSKOZÁS" ANYAGÁBÓL [Materials from the conference on "nationalism" in Eger]. *Történelmi Szemle [Hungary] 1972 15(1-2): 235-251.* Summarizes four papers delivered in response to questions of nationalism and internationalism in the study of history. The opinions cited vary on the importance of a nationalistic outlook in historiography, but agree that there is a need to move away from this toward greater objectivity. H. Szamuely

2739. Benson, George C. S. CAUSES AND CURSES OF POLITICAL CORRUPTION. *West Georgia Coll. Studies in the Social Sci. 1975 14: 1-19.* Discusses economic, legal, social class, and ethical aspects of the historiography of political corruption in federal, state, and local government from the 1870's-1970's.

2740. Berkowitz, Edward D. HISTORY, PUBLIC POLICY AND REALITY. *Journal of Social History 1984 18(1): 78-89.* While historians believe their work should be studied to formulate public policy, they often emphasize aspects of their topics that are not useful to policymakers. Historians writing on the development of Social Security have mostly discussed the political process surrounding passage of legislation, though an emphasis on the impact and limitations of programs would be more useful. 16 notes.

2741. Billington, Monroe. RECENT SOUTHERN POLITICAL HISTORY: A REVIEW ESSAY. *Red River Valley Hist. Rev. 1978 3(3): 89-99.* Discusses the political history of the South since the end of World War II.

2742. Blodgett, Geoffrey. THE MUGWUMP REPUTATION, 1870 TO THE PRESENT. *J. of Am. Hist. 1980 66(4): 867-887.* Reviews major interpretations of Republican Party (mugwump) independent reformers by historians from 1910 to 1976 and analyzes evaluations of the mugwumps by their contemporaries of the 1880's. The mugwumps enjoyed a favorable reputation among historians until 1920, when a long period of abuse began at the hands of progressive-liberal historians. Despite Richard Hofstadter's kind treatment of the mugwumps in *The Age of Reform*, their reputation declined further during the 1960's and 1970's. Only recently have American historians been more sympathetic toward the mugwumps. But the rough treatment suffered at the hands of historians has been mild in comparison to the abuse and invective the mugwumps endured from their own contemporaries. 53 notes.

T. P. Linkfield

2743. Boiko, K. DISKUSSIIA O PREZIDENTSKOI VLASTI V SSHA (OBZOR RABOT AMERIKANSKIKH POLITOLOGOV) [The discussion about Presidential power in the USA (a survey of the works of American political commentators)]. *Mirovaia Ekonomika i Mezhdunarodnye Otnosheniia [USSR] 1976 (8): 124-128.* Surveys recent American writing on the presidency in light of the Watergate scandal and its aftermath.

2744. Bolkhovitinov, N. N. "DZHEKSONOVSKAIA DEMOKRATIIA" ISTORIOGRAFICHESKII MIF I REAL'NOST' [The "Jackson Democracy": historiographical myth and reality]. *Voprosy Istorii [USSR] 1978 (12): 83-98.* The article analyzes a number of literary works devoted to the "Jackson democracy." In accordance with the general development of American historiography the author singles out three basic periods: the whig period (19th century), the progressist period (the first half of the 20th century) and the consensus period (after the termination of the Second World War). His analysis enables the author to draw the conclusion that in the 1960's and 1970's the consensus theory began to lose its former influence and to be subjected more and more frequently to well-argumented criticism. On the basis of extensive factual data and published literature the article shows that there was no genuine equality in the U.S.A. either in the 1830's or at any subsequent period, that the "Jackson democracy" was purely bourgeois in its very essence and that its origin was connected with the development of capitalism, notably with the industrial revolution. J

2745. Boyett, Gene W. QUANTITATIVE DIFFERENCES BETWEEN THE ARKANSAS WHIG AND DEMOCRATIC PARTIES, 1836-1850. *Arkansas Hist. Q. 1975 34(3): 214-226.* The progressive historians' view that upper socio-economic classes supported Whigs and lower classes supported Jacksonian Democrats holds more truth in Arkansas than it does in states like New York and Michigan. The revisionists' theories of ethno-cultural differences among voters cannot be profitably applied in Arkansas because of the relative homogeneity of the population. Minor political and religious factors may have influenced voters, but class interests proved most important. Based on newspaper accounts, published documents, and secondary works; 3 tables, 25 notes. T. L. Savitt

2746. Braudel, Fernand; Bertaud, Jean-Paul; Kaplow, Jeffry; and LeRoy Ladurie, Emmanuel. FAUT-IL BRÛLER CLAUDE MANCERON? [Should Claude Manceron be burned?]. *Histoire [France] 1980 (21): 105-116.* An interview with Manceron and review articles based on Manceron's *Les Hommes de la liberté*, vol. 4, *La Révolution qui lève, 1785-1787* [The Revolution in ferment] (Paris: Laffont, 1979).

2747. Brown, Katherine B. THE CONTROVERSY OVER THE FRANCHISE IN PURITAN MASSACHUSETTS, 1954 TO 1974. *William and Mary Q. 1976 33(2): 212-241.* Surveys the controversy among historians during 1954-74 over the extent of the local and provincial franchise in Massachusetts before 1691. Historical interpretations had not previously veered from the view of Massachusetts as oligarchic. Notes challenges of Richard C. Simmons, Larzer Ziff, Richard S. Dunn, and others to the author's 1954 thesis that the true pattern was closer to that of representative democracy. Comments on historians of individual towns. At the root of the disagreement are varying interpretations of the significance of the franchise laws of 1620-91. Examines the problems of assessment. Further evidence confirms that a liberal franchise existed during the period. Based on Samuel Sewall's diary and on town, county, and colony records. Table, 94 notes. H. M. Ward

2748. Butts, R. Freeman. PUBLIC EDUCATION AND POLITICAL COMMUNITY. *Hist. of Educ. Q. 1974 14(2): 165-183.* Discusses conflicting revisionist theories in the historiography of American education. Urges attention to the role of organized public education in building a political community in a society divided along religious, linguistic, racial, ethnic, economic, cultural, and social class lines. Historians should analyze the successes and failures of public education in developing a sense of citizenship appropriate to the goals of a libertarian political community. Based on primary and secondary sources; 45 notes. L. C. Smith

2749. Clavero, Bartolomé. INSTITUCION POLITICA Y DE-RECHO: ACERCA DEL CONCEPTO HISTORIOGRAFICO DE "ESTADO MODERNO" [Political institutions and law: the historiographical concept of "modern state"]. *Rev. de Estudios Pol. [Spain] 1981 (19): 43-57.* The historical concept of "modern state" applied to a political institution predominant in Europe from the 15th to the 18th centuries owes its popularity to its ability to conceal the problem which it is supposed to express. It is not enough to compare a "modern" state with a "medieval" one. It is necessary to analyze earlier "sovereign" political formations from the point of view of their legislative capacity in a constituent sense. 36 notes.   J. V. Coutinho

2750. Collins, Bruce. NON-SECTIONAL ISSUES IN AMERICAN POLITICS, 1830-1875. *Hist. J. [Great Britain] 1978 21(3): 709-719.* Examines a selection of documents edited by Edward Pessen and monographs by Robert W. Johannsen, Richard A. Sewell, William J. Evitts, and James C. Mohr which question the validity of the consensus school of American historiography after World War II. This widely held viewpoint that "American politics was a romance in which the quarrel preceded the kiss" (Louis Hartz) effectively ignored the thoroughly divisive and passionately debated issues, both local and national, which permeated party discourse during 1830-75. These books are said to indicate how far we have moved from a consensus history approach to mid-19th century American politics. 22 notes.   L. J. Reith

2751. Comparato, Vittor Ivo. UN INCONTRO SUL TEMA: IL MITO DI VENEZIA TRA RINASCIMENTO E CONTRORIFORMA [A discussion of the theme: the myth of Venice between the Renaissance and the Counter-Reformation]. *Pensiero Pol. [Italy] 1978 11(2): 249-256.* The myth of republican Venice began during the 16th and 17th centuries when in Europe most of the states were monarchies or principalities. The myth, with its ideals of the universal values of order and liberty, spread throughout Europe and eventually to America. The myth of Venice is nothing else but its ideal image of republicanism utilized in narrow political situations. Today it is the object of study by such historians as Eric Cochrane, Julius Kirshner, Cesare Vasoli, and Renzo Pecchioli. Their object is the discovery of the relationship between the myth and the reality of a state.   S. Ruffo-Fiore

2752. Cunningham, Frank. PLURALISM AND CLASS STRUGGLE. *Sci. & Soc. 1975/76 39(4): 385-416.* Commenting on passages from James Madison's *Federalist* No. 10 and Robert Dahl's *A Preface to Democratic Theory* (Chicago, 1956) and *Pluralist Democracy in the United States* (Chicago, 1967), as well as other early and more recent power politics theorists, examines the position of pluralism as a political ideology since its appearance as an important movement in US universities in the 1950's.

2753. DeMaio, Gerald. THE QUEST FOR THE AMERICAN PUBLIC ORTHODOXY: AN ASSESSMENT. *West Georgia Coll. Studies in the Social Sci. 1975 14: 49-66.* Advocates the concept of public orthodoxy in the historiography of American political traditions, including such topics as: morality, liberalism, federalism, and the Constitution, 1970's.

2754. Droz, Jacques. HISTORIOGRAPHIE D'UN SIÈCLE DE SOCIAL-DÉMOCRATIE ALLEMANDE [Historiography covering a century of German Social Democrats]. *Mouvement Social [France] 1976 (95): 3-23.* Although many works exist on the German labor movement, no overall work on the German Social Democrats is available. Ferdinand Lasselle founded an independent workers' party in 1863 as a political weapon to obtain voting rights for the working class. The Party was first tied to the idea of German unity but the Franco-Prussian War, the creation of the German Empire, and the Paris Commune alienated the German Worker Party from the nation. Antisocialist legislation increased Marxist influence on the Social Democrats. By 1905, having grown into a strong political entity, the Social-Democratic movement nevertheless showed certain internal weaknesses that led to the schism of 1917. After years of waiting for revolution, the party divided—the minority leading toward the coalition of Weimar, and the revolutionary majority without influence outside the labor movement. Since its reconstruction

in 1945, the Social Democratic Party has been a movement for human emancipation rather than a political force that can solve problems. Secondary sources; 130 notes.   M. de Gialluly

2755. Ferling, John E. HISTORY AS JOURNALISM: AN ASSESSMENT OF THEODORE WHITE. *Journalism Q. 1977 54(2): 320-326.* Reviews Theodore White's *Making of the President* books from the 1960 campaign on, including *Breach of Faith* (New York, 1975), and concludes that their author is a liberal Cold War centrist, and that the books—although they have endured surprisingly well for instant histories—are inconsistent and chaotic in applying the writer's philosophy to the events in his narratives.

2756. Folsom, Burton W., II. PARTY FORMATION AND DEVELOPMENT IN JACKSONIAN AMERICA: THE OLD SOUTH. *J. of Am. Studies [Great Britain] 1973 7(3): 217-229.* Analyzes interpretations of Richard P. McCormick, especially those in his *The Second American Party System: Party Formation in the Jacksonian Era* (Chapel Hill: U. of North Carolina Press, 1966). McCormick focuses on institutional factors that engendered the party system, but Folsom challenges the "views of economic and sectional determinists" and emphasizes other key forces in Jacksonian America. Based on secondary sources; 35 notes.   H. T. Lovin

2757. Formisano, Ronald P. TOWARD A REORIENTATION OF JACKSONIAN POLITICS: A REVIEW OF THE LITERATURE, 1959-1975. *J. of Am. Hist. 1976 63(1): 42-65.* Jacksonian era scholars appear slow to integrate into their studies "revisionist social histories of relevance to the period's politics." "Its [the essay's] design . . . will tend to endow Jacksonian writing with a far more interdisciplinary cast than it actually possesses." Compares titles written in the traditional form of emphasizing the political scene and those beginning to bring in the socioeconomic and cultural lifestyle. 55 notes.   V. P. Rilee

2758. Galkin, I. V. PARTIINO-POLITICHESKAIA ISTORIIA SSHA 1920-1930-KH GODOV V OSVESHCHENII AMERIKANSKOI BURZHUAZNOI ISTORIOGRAFII [US political party history of the 1920's-30's in the writings of American bourgeois historians]. *Novaia i Noveishaia Istoriia [USSR] 1983 (5): 166-176.* By the 1970's, American bourgeois historians had established a single, synthesized conception of political party realignment during the New Deal era. They recognize the continuity of development of the main bourgeois political parties in the 1920's-30's, noting that the economic crisis of 1929-33 led to the electorate's disenchantment with the Republican Party and thus guaranteed the victory of the Democrats, who were advocates of the New Deal long before it was actually introduced. This interpretation, however, is a simplification of complex and contradictory political processes. Secondary sources; 47 notes.   G. Dombrovski

2759. George, Juliette L.; Marmor, Michael F.; and George, Alexander L. ISSUES IN WILSON SCHOLARSHIP: REFERENCES TO EARLY "STROKES" IN THE *PAPERS OF WOODROW WILSON. J. of Am. Hist. 1984 70(4): 845-853.* Questions the accuracy and objectivity of Arthur S. Link's *Papers of Woodrow Wilson* (1970-80) on the issue of Wilson's alleged "strokes" of 1896, 1906, and 1907. Link based his editorial position favoring the stroke diagnosis on the findings and opinions of Edwin A. Weinstein in several articles and in *Woodrow Wilson: A Medical and Psychological Biography* (1981). Weinstein's and Link's "stroke" theory is highly questionable and should not be present in a multivolume work intended to serve as a historical record. 21 notes.
T. P. Linkfield

2760. Gerber, Richard Allan. THE LIBERAL REPUBLICANS OF 1872 IN HISTORIOGRAPHICAL PERSPECTIVE. *J. of Am. Hist. 1975 62(1): 40-73.* Reviews major trends in the historiography on the Liberal Republicans of 1872 over the past 100 years. Earlier schools of history described the Liberal Republicans from a "Reunionist" viewpoint (James Ford Rhodes, William A. Dunning, Claude G. Bowers, Paul Buck) or from a "Reformist" viewpoint (Earl D. Ross, Matthew Josephson, Eric F. Goldman). More recent interpretations of Liberal Republicanism center around Revisionist attacks on the "Reunionists" (Robert F. Durden, James M. Mc-

Pherson) and on the "Reformists" (Ari A. Hoogenboom, Matthew Downey, John G. Sproat). The recent work of Patrick Riddleberger and Michael Les Benedict shows the continued research needed to illuminate the relationship between Liberal and Radical Republicanism. Based on secondary works; 72 notes. J. B. Street

2761. Harmond, Richard. TROUBLES OF MASSACHUSETTS REPUBLICANS DURING THE 1880'S. *Mid-America 1974 56(2): 85-99.* The historians Carl Degler and H. Wayne Morgan argue that the Republican Party's appeal to urban dwellers made it better able to deal with new urban and industrial problems than the Democratic Party. Other historians, like Paul Kleppner and Richard Jensen, discern no trend toward urban power in the Republican Party, and suggest that local, ethnic-cultural commitments are a better gauge of party success or failure than national political ideology. A case study of Massachusetts Republicans' mismanagement of local liquor and school issues suggests support for the Kleppner-Jensen hypothesis. Based on primary and secondary sources; 42 notes. T. D. Schoonover

2762. Hopkins, Jerry B. VIOLENCE IN CHICAGO: AN APPRAISAL OF SOURCES ON THE VIOLENCE RELATED TO THE 1968 DEMOCRATIC CONVENTION. *Fides et Hist. 1979 12(1): 7-28.* Examines the diverse opinions about the causes of the violence at the Democratic National Convention in Chicago during August 1968. Among those expressing views were the representatives of the mass media at the convention, who some felt were at least partly responsible for the trouble. This is a clear example of the enormous power wielded by the mass media in their ability to shape and mold public opinion. Christian historians should note such incidents carefully, because they are bound at all times to seek the truth. In so doing, they must use, but must simultaneously treat with skepticism, sources emanating from the mass media, which report often with manipulative intent. Printed primary sources; 43 notes. J. A. Kicklighter

2763. Hoxie, R. Gordon. EISENHOWER AND PRESIDENTIAL LEADERSHIP. *Presidential Studies Q. 1983 13(4): 589-612.* Recent revisionist interpretations of the Eisenhower administration have challenged the initial view that Eisenhower was a passive, sometimes ineffectual president. Eisenhower is now seen as having had great political skill; he was a master of the art of consultation with Congress. He was active in foreign policy, searching for a just world peace. In all areas, using James David Barber's typology, Eisenhower exhibited an active-positive presidential personality, opposite of what had been previously assumed. 108 notes, biblio. D. H. Cline

2764. Hunter, David H. THE EVOLUTION OF LITERATURE ON UNITED STATES INTELLIGENCE. *Armed Forces and Soc. 1978 5(1): 31-52.* The literature of intelligence has been categorized as: 1) "memoirs," 2) "muckraking," and 3) "objective analysis." During 1965-75 a negative attitude toward American intelligence is unquestionably the dominant one. An analysis of the many histories of the intelligence community since 1965 leads to the conclusion that "from a moral perspective, the US intelligence establishment may have benefited from the experience of the past decade. The government and its intelligence components have been forced to examine many professional practices... and to modify or discard those which the American public no longer tolerates." 7 notes, ref. E. P. Stickney

2765. Hutson, James H. COUNTRY, COURT, AND CONSTITUTION: ANTIFEDERALISM AND THE HISTORIANS. *William and Mary Q. 1981 38(3): 337-368.* Surveys treatment of the antifederalists by historians. Emphasis is placed on the Progressive historians, who, following Frederick Jackson Turner's 1893 thesis, portrayed the antifederalists as democrats. Antifederalism was strongest among inland farmers and frontiersmen. The Progressive interpretation of antifederalism as a democratic movement has been challenged since the 1950's, beginning with Merrill Jensen's two works on the Confederation period, stressing radical versus conservative struggle for rule. Cecelia M. Kenyon led the way for the consensus theory. Subsequent historiography on the antifederalists, by both the new revisionists and neo-Progressives, is analyzed. With

the Progressive and consensus schools now finding common ground, the best interpretation is that of "country" versus "court." Based on writings on the adoption of the Constitution; 143 notes. H. M. Ward

2766. Jeffreys-Jones, Rhodri. THE HISTORIOGRAPHY OF THE CIA. *Hist. J. [Great Britain] 1980 23(2): 489-496.* Reviews six new works, suggesting an embryonic historiography of the Central Intelligence Agency, moving away from recriminatory questions to more thoughtful analyses. A. R. Gross

2767. Kelly, Joseph M. SHIFTING INTERPRETATIONS OF THE SAN FRANCISCO VIGILANTES. *Journal of the West 1985 24(1): 39-46.* Discusses the activities and political aims of the San Francisco vigilante committees of 1851 and 1856 and assesses the history of changing perceptions regarding the vigilantes' behavior and success as agents of reform. In 1851 the vigilantes organized to fight abuses within San Francisco's legal system and in 1856 returned to attack political corruption within the city; with only a few notable exceptions, the vigilantes in both instances enjoyed widespread support among their contemporaries. Most modern scholars, by contrast, view the vigilante movements more critically. Historians point out that though the 19th-century vigilantes were generally not racist, antilabor, or anti-immigrant, as were their successors, they were in fact unsuccessful in ushering in legal or long-lasting political reform. Based in part on Hubert Howe Bancroft's *History of California* (1888), and other secondary sources; 3 illus., 71 notes. B. A. Stenslie

2768. Kennedy, Paul M. THE DECLINE OF NATIONALISTIC HISTORY IN THE WEST, 1900-70. *J. of Contemporary Hist. [Great Britain] 1973 8(1): 77-100.* Prominent late 19th- and early 20th-century European and American historians such as Treitschke, Froude, Bancroft, and Mahan emphasized nationalistic, racist, and imperialistic themes in their work. Since the world wars, patriotic history has been countered by an anti-nationalistic, revisionist trend stressing economic realism, neo-Marxism, and internationalism. This has been encouraged and hastened by the changing historical and social world environment occasioned by the world wars, and by the increased professionalization of academic historical writing. 54 notes. B. A. Block

2769. Kleppner, Paul. BEYOND THE "NEW POLITICAL HISTORY": A REVIEW ESSAY. *Hist. Methods Newsletter 1972 6(1): 17-26.* Reviews John M. Allswang's *A House for All People: Ethnic Politics in Chicago, 1890-1936* (Lexington: U. of Kentucky Pr., 1971); Walter Dean Burnham's *Critical Elections and the Mainsprings of American Politics* (New York: Norton, 1970); Richard J. Jensen's *The Winning of the Midwest: Social and Political Conflict, 1888-1896* (Chicago: U. of Chicago Pr., 1971); and Michael P. Rogen and John L. Shover's *Political Change in California: Critical Elections and Social Movements, 1890-1966* (Westport, Conn.: Greenwood, 1970). These books illustrate the growing improvement in statistical techniques over the last 10 years and historians' hesitancy about the function of theory in historical explanation. They go beyond the formulations of Lee Benson whose concept of Jacksonian Democracy is the prime example of the "new political history." 25 notes. D. K. Pickens

2770. Kleppner, Paul. IMMIGRANT GROUPS AND PARTISAN POLITICS. *Immigration Hist. Newsletter 1978 10(1): 1-5.* Examines the historiography (1940's-70's) of the effects of immigrant groups on the political system; calls for further study, specifically of immigrant voting during 1896-1928, attitudinal bases of group partisanship, and party activist and candidate recruitment.

2771. Kozenko, B. D. DZH. VEINSHTEIN I "NASLEDSTVO" AMERIKANSKIKH SOTSIALISTOV [James Weinstein and the legacy of American socialists]. *Voprosy Istorii [USSR] 1971 (3): 182-188.* Discusses the historical concepts and theories of James Weinstein (b. 1925) and particularly the views expressed in his *Decline of Socialism in America 1912-1925* (1967). Describes the background of the American New Left and the radical trend in American historiography, to which Weinstein belongs. He is one of the few American historians to study the socialist movement in the

United States. In his research and published work he has challenged the myth that socialism could not grow on American soil. Secondary sources; 42 notes. E. R. Sicher

2772. Litván, György. JÁSZI OSZKÁR: A NEMZETI ÁLLAMOK KIALAKULÁSA ÉS A NEMZETISÉGI KÉRDÉS C. KÖNYVERÖL [On the book *The Formation of Nation States and the Question of Minorities* by Oszkár Jászi]. *Történelmi Szemle [Hungary] 1981 24(4): 636-649.* Much of the analysis in this work by Oszkár Jászi (1875-1957) is obsolete in several respects, yet his manner of posing the problems is remained relevant for today. 40 notes. R. Hetzron

2773. Loesdau, Alfred. DIE REFLEXION DES NATIONALISMUS IN DER GEGENWÄRTIGEN GESCHICHTSSCHREIBUNG DER USA [The reflection of nationalism in current historiography of the USA]. *Jahrbuch für Geschichte [East Germany] 1976 14: 373-396.* Denounces current historians of and in the United States for allegedly justifying US imperialistic activities around the world. Such bourgeois nationalism is an effort to shore up capitalism on an ideological plane. 81 notes.

J. C. Billigmeier

2774. Malíř, Jiří. K APLIKACI MARXISTICKO-LENINSKÉHO POJETÍ POLITICKÉ STRANY V HISTORII [Applying the Marxist-Leninist concept of a political party in history]. *Časopis Matice Moravské [Czechoslovakia] 1977 96(1-2): 171-184.* Discusses the problem of devising a correct methodological approach to the historiography of political parties, asserting that the best approach is the Marxist-Leninist one of interpreting historical parties in terms of their relationship to the most progressive sections of the population at the time. The basic approach may have to be adapted to specific cases. Based on the writings of Marx, Engels, and Lenin, and on secondary works; 32 notes. M.-M. Petrzilkova

2775. Malov, Iu. K. KRITIKA BURZHUAZNYKH VOZZRENII NA SOTSIAL'NUIU PRIRODU POLITICHESKIKH PARTII [A criticism of bourgeois views on the social nature of political parties]. *Voprosy Istorii KPSS [USSR] 1981 (4): 74-86.* Bourgeois political scientists ignore the social nature of political parties; they deny that parties represent particular classes. In their view, political parties operate autonomously from social and class considerations. Bourgeois studies of the membership, activity, and structure of political parties thereby conceal the real essence of politics. Based on a study of recent Western publications on party politics and on Lenin's *Collected Works;* 40 notes. L. E. Holmes

2776. Malov, Iu. K. LENINSKII PRINTSIP DEMOKRATICHESKOGO TSENTRALIZMA I EGO "KRITIKI" [Lenin's principle of democratic centralism and its critics]. *Voprosy Istorii KPSS [USSR] 1971 (6): 72-83.* Defends V. I. Lenin's ideas on democratic centralism, formulated in the early 20th century, from the arguments of bourgeois historians who attempt to see contradictions in them.

2777. McDonald, Terrence J. PUTTING POLITICS BACK INTO THE HISTORY OF THE AMERICAN CITY. *Am. Q. 1982 34(2): 200-209.* Reviews John M. Allswang's *Bosses, Machines, and Urban Voters: An American Symbiosis* (1977) and *The Age of Urban Reform: New Perspectives on the Progressive Era,* edited by Michael H. Ebner and Eugene M. Tobin (1977). These books were influenced by Samuel P. Hays's 1964 thesis that there are social causes behind political change. However, to write true urban political history, historians must determine who are the beneficiaries of political change. 6 notes. D. K. Lambert

2778. McKay, David H. THE UNITED STATES IN CRISIS: A REVIEW OF THE AMERICAN POLITICAL LITERATURE. *Government and Opposition [Great Britain] 1979 14(3): 373-385.* A review of social science research on the domestic political crisis of the 1960's-70's indicates that despite popular cynicism and distrust the political system remained stable.

2779. Meerse, David E. PRESIDENTIAL LEADERSHIP, SUFFRAGE QUALIFICATIONS, AND KANSAS: 1857. *Civil War Hist. 1978 24(4): 293-313.* Two versions of James Buchanan's Kansas policy have emerged among historians. Allan Nevins's "melodramatic" version has Buchanan submitting a constitution for ratification by bona fide residents. Initially firm, he retreats before a prosouthern Cabinet Directory and southern denunciations. Roy F. Nichols's "legalist" version has Buchanan submitting only "slavery" to voters, becoming distracted by the financial panic of 1857, and accepting the Lecompton Constitution. Both agree on presidential lack of leadership. However, on examination, Buchanan, striving to hold the middleground by accepting de facto slavery settlement, submitted the constitution with the idea of popular amendment. He showed consistency and decisiveness throughout. Published primary and secondary sources; 45 notes.

R. E. Stack

2780. Miller, Sally M. SOCIALIST PARTY DECLINE AND WORLD WAR I: BIBLIOGRAPHY AND INTERPRETATION. *Sci. and Soc. 1970 34(4): 398-411.* Historians writing in the 1960's differed from those of the 1950's in viewing American socialism through a class orientation. All theories of American socialism and its decline after 1913 neglect the reformist wing's willingness to modify traditional socialist ideology. This modification and American socialist opposition to World War I is depicted through the career of Victor Berger. Secondary sources, magazines, and newspapers; 27 notes. W. Marr

2781. Mogensen, Henrik. OVERSIGTER: MCCARTHYISMEN OG MCCARTHY [Surveys: McCarthyism and McCarthy]. *Hist. Tidsskrift [Denmark] 1980 80(2): 500-524.* Analyzes American domestic politics in the 1950's from the position that there is a clear difference between Joseph R. McCarthy and McCarthyism, between the man and the movement. McCarthyism, which began in early 1950, peaked during 1952-53, and ended in December 1954, was an umbrella name for many small reactionary conservative factions, was never a political organization, and was only a sign of the times. McCarthy was McCarthyism's flagbearer but was not identical with it. A historiographical review. 43 notes.

P. D. Walton

2782. Nagel, Paul C. 1831-1981: A SESQUICENTENNIAL ESSAY. *Virginia Mag. of Hist. and Biog. 1981 89(2): 135-142.* Analyzes the changing historiography about the United States since 1831, noting Charles Francis Adams's advocacy of a return to national leadership of wise, principled leaders, rather than reliance on the average man to govern. The force of evil and man's fallen nature are ignored in modern social analysis. The "thoughtful public" has turned to professional writers rather than historians for inspiration as the latter have taken to "indigestible" treatises for themselves. Annual address at the sesquicentennial meeting of the Virginia Historical Society. P. J. Woehrmann

2783. Noël, Jean-François. L'IDEE NATIONALE DANS L'OEUVRE HISTORIQUE DE VICTOR-LUCIEN TAPIÉ [The national idea in the historical work of Victor-Lucien Tapié]. *Histoire, Economie et Société [France] 1983 3(3): 385-398.* A major theme of Tapié's work, particularly his studies of Bohemia and Central Europe in the early modern period, was the idea of the nation, seen as a cultural patrimony, and the organization of peoples and nations into empires. 87 notes. R. Aldrich

2784. Paludan, Phillip S. THE UNION AND THE AMERICAN MIND. *Rev. in Am. Hist. 1975 3(3): 328-333.* Review essay prompted by Major L. Wilson's *Space, Time and Freedom: The Quest for Nationality and the Irrepressible Conflict, 1815-1861* (Westport, Conn.: Greenwood Pr., 1975). Discusses the historiography of pre-Civil War American nationalism, places Wilson's book within the tradition of intellectual histories of pre-Civil War nationalism, and outlines Wilson's analysis of this nationalism particularly as it is manifested by congressional debates.

2785. Pocock, J. G. A. CIVIL WARS, REVOLUTIONS, AND POLITICAL PARTIES. Bonomi, Patricia U., ed. *Party and Political Opposition in Revolutionary America* (Tarrytown, N.Y.: Sleepy

Hollow Pr., 1980): 1-12. Compares the development of political parties as national organizations in Great Britain and the United States and reviews the historiography on party development during the 18th century. Parties in both countries connected the electorate to the government, but the English parliamentary democracy was an extension of the idea of community of the realm, while American republican democracy evolved from the idea of the balance of component parts. Secondary sources; 16 notes.   S

2786. Polsby, Nelson W. DOWN MEMORY LANE WITH JOE MCCARTHY. *Commentary 1983 75(2): 55-59.* The historiography of McCarthyism since the 1950's, may be divided into those who believed McCarthyism to be an elite phenomenon of the Republicans or of the Democrats and those who see it as a mass phenomenon.

2787. Pomaizl, Karel. K PROBLEMATICE NÁRODNÍ NEZÁVISLOSTI [The problem of national independence]. *Slezský Sborník [Czechoslovakia] 1977 75(2): 127-134.* Reviews several historical interpretations of national independence. Explains different stages of national development: the abolition of serfdom, the decline and fall of feudalism, the ascent of bourgeois democracy, and its gradual degeneration into monopoly capitalism which must engage in imperialism to survive. 3 notes.   G. E. Pergl

2788. Prang, Margaret. NATIONAL UNITY AND THE USES OF HISTORY. *Can. Hist. Assoc. Hist. Papers [Canada] 1977: 2-12.* Reassesses the historian's function in relation to the national culture and the sense of community. There has been a tendency to turn away from national themes and to reflect the "contemporary realities" which highlight "fragmentation, dissension, and the growth of regional consciousness," exploring regional and local history. A review of contemporary Canadian studies, however, helps us to realize that even the specialized and limited can in the long run be "compatible with the central traditions of Canadian historiography" and can contribute to a much broader, yet genuine national spirit. 21 notes.   R. V. Ritter

2789. Quester, George H. WAS EISENHOWER A GENIUS? *Int. Security 1979 4(2): 159-179.* Builds on the revisionist view of the 1960's to suggest that Dwight D. Eisenhower was more politically astute than is commonly acknowledged, 1950's.

2790. Radosh, Ronald. THE SUCCESS OF SOCIALIST FAILURE. *Rev. in Am. Hist. 1975 3(3): 371-375.* Review article prompted by Frank Warren's *An Alternative Vision: The Socialist Party in the 1930's* (Bloomington: Indiana U. Pr., 1974); places Warren's book within the historiography of American socialism and suggests the importance of the book to assessing the success of American socialists during the 1930's.

2791. Reeves, Thomas C. MC CARTHYISM: INTERPRETATIONS SINCE HOFSTADTER. *Wisconsin Mag. of Hist. 1976 60(1): 42-54.* Traces the historiography of McCarthyism since the "status politics" interpretation of Richard Hofstadter, published in 1954. Reviews the contributions of sociologists, such as Daniel Bell, David Riesman, Nathan Glazer, Talcott Parsons, and Seymour Martin Lipset; political scientists, such as Nelson Polsby, Earl Latham, and Michael Paul Rogin; a group of "New Left" historians, such as Athan Theoharis, Richard Freeland, and Norman Markowitz; and liberals, such as Alonzo Hamby. Concludes with a plea for more scholarly biographies of McCarthyites and those who opposed them, monographs on the Americans for Democratic Action and the American Civil Liberties Union, and studies of the extent of the Second Red Scare. 4 photos, 45 notes.
N. C. Burckel

2792. Rex, John. NATIONS, NATIONALISM, AND THE SOCIAL SCIENTIST. *Tr. of the Royal Soc. of Can. 1975 13: 51-67.* Discusses "the set of problems which goes under the name of nationalism in comparative and historical perspective" and asks "whether social science can have anything to say about them." Notes that "nations exist prior to the achievement of statehood and states more often than not have been formed so that one nation, class, or other group can coerce another." Remarks on the influence of linguistic communities in nationalism, but notes that a common language has a greater effect in conjunction with historical and cultural forces. Discusses views on nationalism held by Karl Marx, Max Weber, and others, and suggests that modern societies serve the interest of corporate enterprises and do not necessarily seek the greatest happiness for the largest number of people. Criticizes the influence of American sociologists on the social sciences. They try to be value-neutral scientists and become nonintellectual technicians. Says "that social science does not work in a vacuum and insists therefore that instead of claiming to speak pure objective truth unconnected with value, we get our values, the states of affairs which we hold to be desirable, absolutely clear." 15 notes.
J. D. Neville

2793. Roper, Donald M. BEYOND THE JACKSONIAN ERA: A COMMENT ON THE PESSEN THESIS. *New York Hist. 1975 56(2): 226-233.* Edward Pessen's *Riches, Class, and Power before the Civil War* (1973) and other books deny the social egalitarianism of the Jacksonian Era and view the period as one of materialism, opportunism, reckless speculation, and domination by a non-Jacksonian elite. Suggests further investigations to test the validity of the "Pessen thesis." 8 notes.   R. N. Lokken

2794. Shi, David E. *THE POLITICOS: A MODERN LOOK AT A MUCKRAKING CLASSIC. South Atlantic Q. 1981 80(3): 289-304.* In 1938 Matthew Josephson published *The Politicos,* a muckraking popular history responsible for the wide dissemination of a negative view of politics during the Gilded Age. Despite efforts of numerous revisionist scholars, the prophesied demise of the book and its point of view has been greatly exaggerated. With Charles Beard, Josephson, who was not a professional historian, shared the Marxian distrust of politicians and political rhetoric. Thus his work contained numerous factual errors and distortions. He questioned the sincerity of the humanitarian sentiments expressed by Radical Republicans in the post-Civil War era. Yet the value of the work is that it contains a number of penetrating insights and a wealth of information about Gilded Age politics and politicians. Hence it remains popular because many Americans continue to find its essential interpretations persuasive. Based on the Correspondence File of Harcourt, Brace and Jovanovich and the Matthew Josephson Papers, Yale University; 29 notes.   H. M. Parker, Jr.

2795. Sivachev, N. V. DOKLADY SOVETSKIKH ISTORIKOV NA 96-M S'EZDE AMERIKANSKOI ISTORICHESKOI ASSOSTIASTII [The reports of Soviet historians at the 96th annual convention of the American Historical Association]. *Amerikanskii Ezhegodnik [USSR] 1982: 295-298.* Analyzes discussion of the Soviet papers presented at the 96th annual convention of the American Historical Association in 1981 on the principles of the American two-party system and its role during Roosevelt's New Deal. The Americans disagreed with the Soviet methodology and generalization of the subject. The Soviet participants suggested that the use of such concepts as the bourgeois nature of the American parties and the role of the class struggle would give better insight into American party history.   R. Kirillov

2796. Skakkebaek, Mette. OVERSIGTER: AMERIKANSK SOCIALISME OG FAGBEVAEGELSE I BEGYNDELSEN AF DET 20. ARHUNDREDE: AN HISTORIOGRAFISK OVERSIGT [Surveys: American socialism and the labor movement at the beginning of the 20th century: a historiographical survey]. *Hist. Tidsskrift [Denmark] 1980 80(2): 479-499.* Details the development of the socialist parties in the United States, and their relationship with the American labor movement at the beginning of the 20th century, and looks at contemporary historical studies. Marxist socialism of the 1860's led to the dogmatic Socialist Labor Party in 1876, and to the more popular Socialist Party of America in 1901. Farmerlabor parties followed as did the Communist Party from the 1930's. Relations between the socialist parties and the labor movement, particularly the American Federation of Labor (AFL) founded in 1896, were never good, with the latter never wishing to be anything other than a "labor union." 80 notes.   P. D. Walton

2797. Stannard, David E. AMERICAN HISTORIANS AND THE IDEA OF NATIONAL CHARACTER: SOME PROBLEMS AND PROSPECTS. *Am. Q. 1971 23(2): 202-220.* Reviews two works on the subject of national character: David Morris Potter's *People of Plenty: Economic Abundance and the American Character* (Chicago: U. of Chicago Pr., 1954), and Murray G. Murphey's "An Approach to the Historical Study of National Character," in Melford E. Spiro, ed., *Context and Meaning in Cultural Anthropology* (New York: Free Pr., 1965), pp. 144-163. The evidence would indicate that Potter was wrong to connect abundance and national character. Murphey, on the other hand, pioneered techniques to handle the subject—including the statistical—that enabled him to tabulate behavioral responses to reveal the complexities of the concept of national character, and so avoid a "grand scheme" presentation. Historians may in the future be inclined to avoid such a topic, which is more amenable to the empirical methods of social psychologists than traditional historical methods concerned with "deeds and events." 37 notes.   R. V. Ritter

2798. Stockwin, J. A. A. JAPANESE POLITICS: RECENT WRITING AND RESEARCH IN THE WEST. *Japan Interpreter 1972 7(3/4): 409-421.* Discusses American studies of Japanese politics. Two major types of studies exist: a factual coverage of limited institutional or behavioral aspects, and application of general models to Japan, usually theoretical. The main difficulties are the language and the widespread existence of stereotypes and preconceptions about Japan. Research has also been affected by recent trends in American political science, notably the overemphasis on the problem of modernization. "Interaction of industrial power and politics" is suggested as a worthwhile approach.
                                                                F. W. Iklé

2799. Strong, Bryan. HISTORIANS AND AMERICAN SOCIALISM, 1900-1920. *Sci. and Soc. 1970 34(4): 387-397.* Studies the change in American historiography in the 1950's with respect to socialism of the progressive era. A conservative interpretation replaced the progressive interpretation after World War II because the former possessed logical and psychological affinities with cold-war liberalism. The new conservative historiography had a distorted interpretation of American socialism during the progressive era and was equally directed against both communism and McCarthyism. These historians argued that American socialists in the progressive era were basically reformists, and that socialism failed because it was too radical. These arguments are mutually exclusive and incorrect. Based on secondary works; 15 notes.   W. Marr

2800. Sullivan, John. JACKSON CARICATURED: TWO HISTORICAL ERRORS. *Tennessee Hist. Q. 1972 31(1): 39-44.* Discusses problems in political caricature interpretation, citing as examples cartoons of Andrew Jackson in the 1820's.

2801. Teaford, Jon C. FINIS FOR TWEED AND STEFFENS: REWRITING THE HISTORY OF URBAN RULE. *Rev. in Am. Hist. 1982 10(4): 133-149.* Looks at the tendency of urban historians to focus on bossism, corruption, and frustrated reform; urges a broader focus on the larger urban power structure and urban growth.

2802. Thorpe, James A. COLONIAL SUFFRAGE IN MASSACHUSETTS: AN ESSAY REVIEW. *Essex Inst. Hist. Collections 1970 106(3): 169-181.* Traces the historiography of the extent of suffrage in colonial Massachusetts and the relationship of this quantified data to the actual qualifiable degree of democracy prevalent. Estimates analyzed range from John Gorham Palfrey (1876) to Robert E. and B. Katherine Brown (1955). The Palfrey estimate (that one in four to five was eligible to vote in province-wide elections) has been correctly revised upward by the Browns and others. Still, there is no direct correlation between suffrage and democracy, nor is there a consensus on how to define "democracy," let alone how to measure the amount of this unquantifiable variable. 49 notes.   H. M. Rosen

2803. Thuillier, Guy and Tulard, Jean. L'HISTOIRE DE L'ADMINISTRATION DU DIX-NEUVIÈME SIÈCLE DEPUIS DIX ANS: BILAN ET PERSPECTIVES [Administrative history of

the 19th century during the past 10 years: the balance sheet and perspective]. *Rev. Hist. [France] 1977 258(2): 441-455.* An inventory of works printed since 1967 plus problems, observations, and proposals concerning the growing field of administrative history which touches all aspects of life.   G. H. Davis

2804. Vetter, Cesare. COSCIENZA POLITICA E IDEA DI NAZIONE NELL'ITALIA DEL '700. RASSEGNA BIBLIOGRAFICA [Political consciousness and the idea of nation in 18th-century Italy: bibliographic review]. *Pensiero Pol. [Italy] 1983 16(3): 376-401.* Surveys the historiography of the development of modern Italian nationalism and patriotism. 98 notes.   R. Grove

2805. Vivarelli, Roberto. 1870 IN EUROPEAN HISTORY AND HISTORIOGRAPHY. *J. of Modern Hist. 1981 53(2): 167-188.* The year 1870 inaugurated a new phase in European history, characterized by a shift from democratic to authoritarian ideals and from the older notion of patriotism to a new, aggressive nationalism. Both of these changes, although not new in 1870, were given added impetus by the Franco-Prussian War and the unification of non-Austrian Germany. Also occurring at this time were the beginnings of positivism in the cultural sphere and the economic shift from free trade to protectionism. 83 notes.   J. D. Hunley

2806. Walker, Samuel. HISTORIANS ON THE CASE: CONTEMPORARY CRIME POLICY AND THE USES OF HISTORY. *OAH Newsletter 1985 13(1): 13-15.* Historians can and should provide an adequate, accurate, historical perspective for public policy decisions on crime by publishing studies of trends in criminal activity, the politics of criminal justice, and the administration of justice; presently such decisions have been made on the basis of faulty assumptions and untrained research.   R. G. Sherer

2807. Weinstein, Edwin A.; Anderson, James William; and Link, Arthur S. WOODROW WILSON'S POLITICAL PERSONALITY: A REAPPRAISAL. *Pol. Sci. Q. 1978-79 93(4): 585-598.* Reviews the literature on Woodrow Wilson's personality, concentrating on the book *Woodrow Wilson and Colonel House* by Alexander and Juliette George. The authors contend that the Georges' book is based on incorrect assumptions about the relationship between Wilson and his father and offer an alternative view of the dynamics of Wilson's political personality.   J

2808. Whalon, Michael W. THE REPUBLICAN PARTY IN ITS EARLY STAGES: SOME NEW PERSPECTIVES. *Social Sci. Q. 1970 51(1): 148-156.* After examining the historiography and commenting upon historians' relative lack of attention concerning the early Republican Party, Whalon offers a positive explanation of Republican development—that Republicanism acquired strength and attained eventual success because of its widespread and progressive appeal and because of the relative bankruptcy of its opponents.   J

2809. Winitsky, Marvin Laurence. ROGER B. TANEY: A HISTORIOGRAPHICAL INQUIRY. *Maryland Hist. Mag. 1974 69(1): 1-26.* "Whig" historical writing, full of invective against Roger B. Taney's *Dred Scott* decision, and dominated by theories of slaveholder domination of the Supreme Court and Southern conspiracy charges, remained the norm as late as John Bach McMaster's work in 1913. By the 1920's, Progressive historians pointed out Taney's extension of the nationalist construction of the Marshall Court and modified his image as a "pliant instrument of Andrew Jackson" in the Bank War. Taney's own environment, personality, and health problems have dominated more recent scholarship, but "judicial supremacist" remains a recurrent thesis. "Taney as politician, judge, and human being, remains hidden to us." The "reversals, overgeneralizations, and contradictions" in 100 years of Taney scholarship create a confused and distorted picture. Primary and secondary sources; 10 illus., 99 notes.   G. J. Bobango

2810. —. [KENNEDY AND CONGRESS]. *Pol. Studies [Great Britain] 1980 28(4): 567-583.*
Hart, John. ASSESSING PRESIDENTIAL LEADERSHIP: A COMMENT ON WILLIAMS AND KERSHAW, *pp. 567-578.* Comments on R. J. Williams and D. Kershaw's article which

assesses President John F. Kennedy's record of legislative leadership, but adds nothing to the now-familiar revisionist argument, seeing the contrast between promise and performance in terms of undesirable concessions to Southern conservatism. The selection of case studies is unbalanced, and the accounts of minimum wage, aid to education, and civil rights programs are inadequate and distorted. The attempt to establish a causal connection between the circumstances of Kennedy's nomination and his failure is based on very slender evidence. 25 notes.

Williams, Robert J. APOLOGISTS AND REVISIONISTS: A REJOINDER TO HART, pp. 579-583. What Hart calls revisionism is an amalgam of views from different ideological perspectives and does not really exist. He has detected some errors in the essay, but his approach is too quantitive and much of his comment is irrelevant and inaccurate. If he labels his opponents revisionists, then he himself is an apologist. 8 notes.   D. J. Nicholls

2811. —. [MINNESOTA POLITICS]. *Minnesota Hist.* 1980 47(4): 154-161.

Benson, Elmer A. POLITICS IN MY LIFETIME, pp. 154-160. Life-long Farmer-Labor Party stalwart and Minnesota governor during 1937-39, Elmer A. Benson reflects on the politics of the 1920's-30's, concentrating, however, on the give and take between the state's Democratic and Farmer-Labor parties during and after World War II. Moderates' adulation of such Cold War liberals as Hubert Humphrey ignores a fascist strain in US politics.

Youngdale, James M. AFTERNOTE: A CALL FOR NEW AVENUES OF SCHOLARSHIP, pp. 160-161. As Benson indicated, historians have focused too narrowly on communists in US radical movements, neglecting other ideological, occupational, religious, and ethnic elements.   C. M. Hough/S

2812. —. [ROOSEVELT AND THE BRAINS TRUST]. *Pol. Sci. Q.* 1972 87(4): 531-563.

Rosen, Elliot A. ROOSEVELT AND THE BRAINS TRUST: AN HISTORIOGRAPHICAL OVERVIEW, pp. 531-557. The recently opened papers of Raymond Moley and Felix Frankfurter require a reexamination of Schlesinger's hypothesis that the departure of the original Brain Trust signified the abandonment of the partnership. Actually Moley was the most influential single force in shaping the New Deal. In later years he was converted to economic nationalism. The new material shows that "the long-entrenched division into two distinct New Deals is open to question." 41 notes.

Moley, Raymond. COMMENTS, pp. 558-560.

Tugwell, Rexford G. COMMENTS, pp. 560-563.
                                                         E. P. Stickney

Foreign Policy and International Relations
(including Diplomacy and the Cold War)

2813. Aga-Rossi, Elena. RECENTI ORIENTAMENTI DELLA STORIAGRAFIA AMERICANA SULLE ORIGINI DELLA GUERRA FREDDA: L'INTERPRETAZIONE "REVISIONISTA" [Recent attitudes of American historiography concerning the origins of the Cold War: the "revisionist" interpretation]. *Storia contemporanea [Italy]* 1973 4(1): 143-166. Discusses recent "revisionist" interpretations of the origins of the Cold War, characterizing orthodox historians like W. Langer, C. A. Beard, W. H. Chamberlain, then appraising revisionists like W. A. Williams, G. Kolko, D. Fleming, D. Horowitz, G. Alperowitz, and others. Emphasizes the political-ideological position of this literature, its preoccupation with "original blame," its forced theories, and the necessity of using individual contributions to form a more balanced reexamination. Based chiefly on secondary works; 71 notes.   L. R. Atkins

2814. Almaráz, Félix D., Jr. THE STATUS OF BORDERLANDS STUDIES: HISTORY. *Soc. Sci. J.* 1976 12(3): 9-18. Traces the historiography of the US-Mexican border, 1812-1975.

2815. Altherr, Marco. LES ORIGINES DE LA GUERRE FROIDE: UN ESSAI D'HISTORIOGRAPHIE [The origins of the Cold War: a historiographical essay]. *Relations Int. [France]* 1977 (9): 69-81. Notes the extent and passion of the debate among historians about the origins of the Cold War, dividing the opposed opinions into traditional, realist, revisionist, and post-revisionist schools, the revisionists being classified as "hard" and "soft." Reviews leading points of controversy, including eastern Europe, the role of Harry Truman, the atomic bomb, and economic determinism. Generations with different historical experiences helps explain the historiographical disagreements.   R. Stromberg

2816. Altschull, J. Herbert. KHRUSHCHEV AND THE BERLIN "ULTIMATUM": THE JACKAL SYNDROME AND THE COLD WAR. *Journalism Q.* 1977 54(3): 545-551, 565. In 1958, when Soviet Premier Nikita Khrushchev issued a diplomatic note complaining of the presence of West Berlin within USSR-controlled territory, the American press generally and the New York *Times* (the "lion") in particular interpreted the note as an ultimatum, and thereafter the historians (the "jackals") have tended to perpetuate this view, although other interpretations were available.

2817. Ambrosius, Lloyd E. THE ORTHODOXY OF REVISIONISM: WOODROW WILSON AND THE NEW LEFT. *Diplomatic Hist.* 1977 1(3): 199-214. Calls orthodox the New Left interpretation of the Cold War. Woodrow Wilson's (1856-1924) internationalism and view of American leadership in world affairs provided the intellectual framework of the Cold War. In essence, New Left historians did not go beyond Wilson's concepts in their revisionist critiques. In effect, the pluralist critique was more radical, going beyond Wilson's vision of a Pax Americana. 51 notes.   J. Tull

2818. Appatov, S. I. and Koval', I. N. SOVREMENNAIA AMERIKANSKAIA BURZHUAZNAIA ISTORIOGRAFIIA O NEKOTORYKH PROBLEMAKH VOSTOCHNOEVROPEISKOI POLITIKI SSHA (60-70-E GODY) [Contemporary American bourgeois historiography on some problems in the West European policy of the United States (1960's-70's)]. *Amerikanskii Ezhegodnik [USSR]* 1982: 120-135. Considers American historiographic analysis of the relations between the United States and Western socialist countries during the 1960's-70's. The policy was based on the use of detente, negotiations, trade, and cultural exchange, with political pressure to cause disintegration of the Western socialist bloc. A moderate alternate course suggested coexistence and careful studies of the strengths and weaknesses of the socialist countries in order to activate anti-Soviet forces in the future. Secondary sources; 50 notes.   R. Kirillov

2819. Bailey, Thomas A. THE WOODROW WILSON WORSHIPERS. *Soc. for Hist. of Am. Foreign Relations. Newsletter* 1981 12(4): 13-15. Discusses the historical controversies surrounding Woodrow Wilson and his negotiations in the Paris Peace Settlements.

2820. Beck, Kent M. THE KENNEDY IMAGE: POLITICS, CAMELOT, AND VIETNAM. *Wisconsin Mag. of Hist.* 1974 58(1): 45-55. The "*way* that Americans have honored and remembered the thirty-fifth President can tell us much about John F. Kennedy and convey even more about the American experience before and since his passing." He traces the changing attitude of political analysts, historians, and journalists toward the Kennedy administration over the past ten years. Immediate reaction to the slain President's policies was favorable when court histories and first-hand accounts published by his entourage held center stage. As the Vietnam War escalated, revisionists began to see Kennedy's foreign policy as one of the most strikingly negative aspects of his administration. More recently, however, a counter-reaction has set in, emphasizing a more balanced picture of his administration. 5 illus., 52 notes.   N. C. Burckel

2821. Bereznyi, L. A. AMERIKANSKO-KITAISKII DOGOVOR 1844 GODA V OSVESHCHENII AMERIKANSKIKH ISTORIKOV [American historians on the 1844 Sino-American treaty]. *Novaia i Noveishaia Istoriia [USSR]* 1971 (2): 184-193. In the 1840's, China became the object of the expansionist ambitions of the Western Imperialist powers, whose commercial treaties reduced this weak, feudal country to a semicolonial status. American historians take an apologetic stand. The stereotypical treatment of American relations with China to 1949 as friendly and peaceful is also applied to the 1844 Treaty of Wanghia. Now the "institutional" approach has been introduced into this theory and the author discusses its relation to the facts. Secondary sources; 60 notes.

                         E. R. Sicher

2822. Bernstein, Barton J. LES ÉTATS UNIS ET LES ORIGINES DE LA GUERRE FROIDE [The United States and the origins of the Cold War]. *Rev. d'Hist. de la Deuxiéme Guerre Mondiale [France] 1976 26(103): 51-72.* American writers on the origins of the Cold War are divided into realists, revisionists, and antirevisionists. Realists include Walter Lippmann, George Kennan, and others who were impressed by the fierceness of Soviet policy. Revisionists tended to blame American policymakers. Works by Gar Alperovitz, Gabriel Kolko, and especially William Appleman Williams are described here. Anti-revisionists Arthur Schlesinger, Jr. and Adam Ulam are referred to, but about half of this article is a critical examination of John L. Gaddis, *The United States and the Origins of the Cold War* (1972). Although based on extensive archival research, Gaddis's book has astounding shortcomings. 25 notes.

                         G. H. Davis

2823. Bolt, Ernest C., Jr. ISOLATION, EXPANSION, AND PEACE: AMERICAN FOREIGN POLICY BETWEEN THE WARS. Haines, Gerald K. and Walker, J. Samuel, ed. *American Foreign Relations: A Historiographical Review* (Westport, Conn.: Greenwood Pr., 1981): 133-157. American historians have remained fascinated by the roots, ideology, and significance of isolationism during the interwar years. This continued interest stems from the complex and sometimes contradictory nature of the isolationist position, the increasing availability of source materials, and changing American attitudes toward internationalism. Secondary sources; 58 notes.

                         J. Powell

2824. Braeman, John. POWER AND DIPLOMACY: THE 1920'S REAPPRAISED. *Rev. of Pol. 1982 44(3): 342-369.* Post-World War II historiography of diplomacy in the 1920's produced a legalist-moralist indictment that consistently attacked Republican administrations for their failure to support Wilsonian peace and security arrangements, such as the League of Nations. It also has generated a realist indictment blaming the Republicans for their faithful adherence to a diplomacy that favored business interests and persuasion rather than the reality of force and military preparedness, particularly in view of the Japanese military threat. The difficulty with the realist indictments rests with its ignorance of America's overwhelming economic dominance in the 1920's and the unusual security it enjoyed. The 1920's should not be confused with the 1930's, a time when technology and weaponry shifted the balance of power. The diplomacy of the 1920's was realistic and adequate given the circumstances. Secondary sources; 61 notes.

                         G. A. Glovins

2825. Brauch, Hans Günter. ATOMARE DIPLOMATIE UND DER BEGINN DES KALTEN KRIEGES [Atomic diplomacy and the beginning of the Cold War]. *Zeitschrift für Politik [West Germany] 1977 24(3): 303-304.* Both the orthodox apologetic school and the revisionist school of American Cold War historiography are politically preformed and try to initiate an engagement for alternative foreign political strategies.

2826. Brauch, Hans Günter. ENTWICKLUNGEN UND ERGEBNISSE DER FRIEDENSFORSCHUNG [Developments and results of peace research]. *Neue Politische Literatur [West Germany] 1978 23(1): 71-104.* Reviews new publications on the arms race, detente, US and Soviet military strategies, the international arms trade, and the importance of armament for Western and Eastern economies since 1945.

2827. Breccia, Alfredo. LA STORIOGRAFIA ITALIANA SUGLI SLAVI DEL SUD NEL PERIODO 1914-1918 [Italian historiography on South Slavs, 1914-18]. *Storia e Pol. [Italy] 1982 21(4): 738-750.*

2828. Breccia, Alfredo. LA STORIOGRAFIA ITALIANA SUGLI SLAVI DEL SUD NEL 1848-49 [Italian historiography on the South Slavs, 1848-49]. *Storia e Politica [Italy] 1976 15(4): 705-723.* During and after World War I, Italian historiography underlined the ideological aspect of Slavic nationalism, largely ignoring Slavic attempts to collaborate with Italians against the Habsburgs in 1848. After World War II, Angelo Tamborra's works brought to light the relations between Italian and the South Slav national movements. Secondary works; 56 notes.

                         A. Canavero

2829. Brozan, Hugh. AMERICA AND THE COLD WAR. TODAY AND YESTERDAY. *Round Table [Great Britain] 1972 (245): 119-127.* A review article prompted by Lloyd C. Gardner's *Architects of Illusion: Men and Ideas in American Foreign Policy 1941-49* (Chicago: Quadrangle Books, 1971) and Barton J. Bernstein's (ed.) *Politics and Policies of the Truman Administration* (Chicago: Quadrangle Books, 1971). Both take an oversimplified revisionist view of America's role in the Cold War, but "make solid contributions to our knowledge of Cold War origins and of the debate about them." Discusses the Polish question and the Yalta agreements to show how "the revisionists' view of the past has been warped by the facts of the present." However, the revisionists have shown how "American traditions were likely to affect and be affected by the collisions of the mid-1940's" and "how thoroughly the American people had absorbed Cold War manichaeanism" which permitted a false commitment in Vietnam. "Revisionism in general, and these two books in particular, draw our attention to a chain of fatality which ensured that the United States would enjoy some remarkable diplomatic and military successes in the 1940's, only to pay for them in the 1960's with failure."

                         D. H. Murdoch

2830. Campus, Eliza. THE PROBLEMS OF THE 1930'S IN CONTEMPORARY HISTORIOGRAPHY. *Rev. des Études Sud-Est Européennes [Rumania] 1978 16(2): 321-335.* The release of archival material on the 1930's has prompted the appearance of many new and often conflicting monographs about foreign relations between and among the southeastern and Central European states. The author evaluates these works, especially those about the Little Entente and the Balkan Entente. 104 notes.   G. F. Jewsbury

2831. Cantù, Francesca. LA POLITICA ESTERA NEGLI SCRITTI DI CARLO MORANDI: NOTE SU UN ITINERARIO STORIOGRAFICO [Foreign policy in Carlo Morandi's writings: notes on a historiographical itinerary]. *Riv. di Studi Pol. Int. [Italy] 1982 49(4): 555-576.* Traces Carlo Morandi's interest and views on the problems of foreign policy through the four volumes of his recently published *Scritti Storici* (1980) edited by Armando Saitta.

2832. Carroll, F. M. AMERICAN DIPLOMATIC HISTORY: THE STATE OF THE ART. *Can. Rev. of Am. Studies [Canada] 1984 15(2): 221-227.* Reviews Richard Dean Burns's *Guide to American Foreign Relations since 1700* (1983), Gerald K. Haines and J. Samuel Walker's *American Foreign Relations: A Historiographical Review* (1981), and Paul Gordon Lauren's *Diplomacy: New Approaches in History, Theory, and Policy* (1979). Besides noting the richness in monographic material and professionalism that has characterized the writing of diplomatic history since 1945, these volumes point out methodological and theoretical techniques that have also enlivened such writings. 11 notes.

                         H. T. Lovin

2833. Carroll, John M. THE NEW LEFT, THE COLD WAR, AND THE USE OF HISTORICAL EVIDENCE. *Research Studies 1977 45(1): 53-59.* Reviews revisionist historiography on the Cold War 1952-76, emphasizing the rise of the New Left within the field; 23 notes.

2834. Castellan, Georges. LES ÉTATS BALKANIQUES ET SUD-EST EUROPÉENS DANS LES RELATIONS INTERNATIONALES (FIN XVIIIᵉ SIÈCLE—XXeRET SIÈCLE) [The Balkan and southeastern European states in international relations from the end of the 18th to the 20th century]. *Rev. Hist. [France] 1976 255(1): 43-60.* New research techniques may be applied to old problems of historical interpretation. Three groups of problems concerning southeastern Europe include: 1) the knowledge and misconceptions of the Balkans in the policies of the great powers; 2) the economic aspects of the Eastern Question; and 3) the assumptions, models, and sociology of the diplomacy of the Balkan states. In the first case qualitative and quantitative content analyses of the Western press, documentary collections, and libraries may suggest much about the assumptions of great power decision makers. Concerning economic history, the challenge of Fritz Fischer's thesis on the origin of World War I, Pierre Renouvin's technique of relating diplomatic decisions to economic events, the Marxist superstructure-infrastructure investigations and the statistical studies of Jacques Thobie and other quantifications suggest continued research. Finally, the practice of viewing international relations as including entire peoples rather than just diplomats, opens the way for new principles of sociology, psychology, and other social sciences to be applied to historical study of international relations in the Balkans. 16 notes.   G. H. Davis

2835. Chernikov, I. F. ISTORIOHRAFIIA TA DZHERELOZ-NAVSTVO: RADIANS'KA TA ZARUBIZHNA LITERATURA PRO VIDNOSVNY SRSR I TURECHCHYNY U 1935-1972 RR. [Historiography and research: Soviet and foreign literature dealing with the relations of the USSR and Turkey, 1935-72]. *Ukraïns'kyi Istorychnyi Zhurnal [USSR] 1980 (7): 124-130.* Surveys relations between Turkey and the USSR, beginning in the 1920's with Kemal Atatürk and continuing with the period following the Ankara proceedings in 1935.

2836. Chernikov, I. F. OSNOVNI DZHERELA DOSLIDZHEN-NIA RADIANS'KO-TURETS'KYKH VIDNOSYN (1935-1970 RR.) [The main sources for the study of Soviet-Turkish relations, 1935-70]. *Ukrains'kyi Istorychnyi Zhurnal [USSR] 1979 (11): 135-141.* Indicates some of the more important Soviet, Turkish, and foreign sources for research on the development of political, economic, and cultural relations between the USSR and Turkey during the period 1935-70. Criticizes Great Power policy toward Turkey and the Western view of Soviet-Turkish relations. Primary and secondary Soviet, Turkish, and Western sources; 39 notes.
                                                        I. Krushelnyckyj

2837. Cienciała, Anna M. MOCARSTWA WOBEC NOWYCH PAŃSTW W EUROPIE WSCHODNIEJ 1914-1939: PRZEGLĄD PUBLIKACJI [The Great Powers and the new states of Eastern Europe, 1914-39: a survey of publications]. *Zeszyty Hist. [France] 1977 (39): 203-210.* A historiographical survey of the differences in the foreign policies of Great Britain and France concerning Poland, Czechoslovakia, Yugoslavia, Rumania, and the USSR, ca. 1914-39.

2838. Cohen, Michael J. TRUMAN AND PALESTINE, 1945-1948: REVISIONISM, POLITICS AND DIPLOMACY. *Modern Judaism 1982 2(1): 1-22.* Examines the evolution of the Truman administration's attitude toward the Palestine question, focusing on some of the standard works dealing with this subject.

2839. Cohen, Warren I. CONSUL GENERAL O. EDMUND CLUBB ON THE "INEVITABILITY" OF CONFLICT BETWEEN THE UNITED STATES AND THE PEOPLE'S REPUBLIC OF CHINA, 1949-50. *Diplomatic Hist. 1981 5(2): 165-168.* Reprints a letter of Clubb, American consul general in Peking in 1949, about two essays by Michael H. Hunt and Steven M. Goldstein in *Uncertain Years: Chinese American Relations, 1947-1950* (1980). The volume examined newly available material from the archives of the US government and especially the collection of V. K. Wellington Koo, Chinese ambassador to the United States during the period. Clubb finds fault with the thesis that the Sino-American hostility and breach of 1949-50 were inevitable. 3 notes.
                                                        J. V. Coutinho

2840. Combs, Jerald A. COLD WAR HISTORIOGRAPHY: AN ALTERNATIVE TO JOHN GADDIS'S POST-REVISIONISM. *Soc. for Hist. of Am. Foreign Relations. Newsletter 1984 15(2): 9-19.* Takes issue with some of the views of John Gaddis, as expressed in the summer 1983 issue of *Diplomatic History*, regarding differences among orthodox, revisionist, and postrevisionist historians in interpreting the causes and conduct of the Cold War.

2841. Combs, Jerald A. THE ORIGINS OF THE MONROE DOCTRINE: A SURVEY OF INTERPRETATIONS BY UNITED STATES HISTORIANS. *Australian J. of Pol. and Hist. [Australia] 1981 27(2): 186-196.* For 50 years the Monroe Doctrine was virtually ignored, but John Quincy Adams's diary, published in 1874, suggested that Monroe had favored a joint US-British warning against European intervention in Latin America, while Adams favored and secured the unilateral declaration. By the 20th century, writers were arguing that the doctrine also implied intervention in Latin America by the US. The standard work by Dexter Perkins (1927) indicated (using European archives) that the threat from Europe had been nil in 1823, but that the contemporaries could not have been sure and their declaration had been idealistic. Edward Tatum's anti-British interpretation (1936) accorded with isolationist sentiment in the period, which was soon superseded by pro-British interpretations in World War II. Vietnam and Watergate produced Ernest May's view that the motives were concerned with domestic politics (1975). Cold War revisionists see the Monroe Doctrine as the origin of American imperialism. Based on diplomatic monographs and biographies; 58 notes.   W. D. McIntyre

2842. Cushman, Greg and Gilbert, Arthur N. SOME ANALYTICAL APPROACHES TO THE COLD WAR DEBATE. *Hist. Teacher 1977 10(2): 263-280.* Discusses the assumptions and models used by historians of the Cold War. Both traditionalists and revisionist historians have presented interpretations which cross lines. For example, historians in both categories attempt to explain the Cold War from "crossroads" and "roots" perspectives. Similarly, historians in both categories use various political science models. Some deal with the role of individuals, others with the nation-state, and still others with the international political system. The authors therefore see the necessity of uncovering basic assumptions about general approaches to history and political analysis in order to understand the literature about the Cold War. Primary and secondary sources; 41 notes.   P. W. Kennedy

2843. Dashichev, V. ZAKHVATNICHESKAIA VNESHNEPOLI-TICHESKAIA PROGRAMMA GERMANSKOGO FASHIZMA V OSVESHCHENII BURZHUAZNOI ISTORIOGRAFII [The expansionist foreign policy program of German fascism interpreted by bourgeois historiography]. *Voenno-Istoricheskii Zhurnal [USSR] 1969 (5): 40-52.* In spite of the variety of evaluations of Hitler's foreign policy programs by bourgeois historians, the majority of their works have certain common historical conceptions, based either on the interest of certain groups of the imperialist bourgeoisie or on the unscientific interpretation of social occurrences. The most usual approach in these works is subjectively idealistic. This includes the following tendencies: distortion of the moving forces of fascist aggression and the role of German monopolies in the determination of the aggressive foreign policy course; the image of the expansionist program of fascist Germany as something that had arisen strictly from Hitler's own plans; rejection of the existence of previously established plans of conquest; the rejection of the continuity of policies between the expansionist goals of the fascists and of Kaiser's Germany, and the defining of Hitler's expansionist plans in a European framework. Primary sources; 58 notes.
                                                        L. Kalinowski

2844. D'Attorre, Pier Paolo. GUERRA FREDDA E TRASFOR-MAZIONI DELLE SOCIETA OCCIDENTALI NELLA STORIO-GRAFICA AMERICANA [The cold war and transformations of western societies in American historiography]. *Italia Contemporanea [Italy] 1980 32(140): 83-103.* Surveys books and articles dealing with the origin of the cold war between the USSR and the United States during the presidency of Harry S. Truman (1945-53). These studies highlight the relationship between the cold war and the American political system, the international economic policy of the United States, and European-American ties. Many of the studies written since 1972 have taken either a new Left or an anti-New Left perspective. Primary sources; 42 notes.   E. E. Ryan

2845. DeConde, Alexander. THEMES IN THE HISTORY OF AMERICAN FOREIGN POLICY. *Am. Studies Int. 1976 14(3): 3-22.* Surveys the historiography of American foreign policy and presents commentary on major works in foreign policy on chronological and topical subjects. Although most writings emphasize conflict and crisis, there are citations of works stressing peaceful interaction in foreign relations. 　　　　　　　　　　　　　L. L. Athey

2846. Dement'ev, I. P. AMERIKANSKAIA LITERATURA OB ANTIIMPERIALISTICHESKOM DVIZHENII V SSHA NA RUBEZHE XIX-XX VEKA [American literature on the anti-imperialist movement in the United States at the turn of the 19th-20th centuries]. *Voprosy Istorii [USSR] 1973 (8): 177-184.* The aggressive foreign policies of the United States began in the late 19th and early 20th centuries. The Spanish-American War of 1898, the first war of modern American imperialism, inspired the first democratic protest in the United States. The history of that protest movement has been studied only slightly, but is becoming increasingly mentioned in contemporary scholarship. The author discusses the works of M. C. Lanzar, R. L. Beisner, E. B. Tomkins, W. A. Williams, J. W. Rollins, and W. Lafebvre. Secondary sources; 51 notes.

2847. Desiatskov, S. G. REVIZIIA POLITIKI "UMIROTVORENIIA" [Revision of the policy of appeasement]. *Novaia i Noveishaia Istoriia [USSR] 1981 (5): 177-189.* Analyzes and comments on the controversy between the "orthodox" and "revisionist" schools in the study of the appeasement of Hitler in Great Britain. The main proponent and founder of the revisionist school is D. C. Watt and the proponents of the orthodox school are R. W. Seton-Watson, J. W. Wheeler-Bennet, and L. B. Namier. The orthodox school maintains that appeasement was a fundamental error (the Churchillian view), while the revisionists argue that appeasement was an inevitable outcome of British imperial weakness. The revisionist school amounts to a right-wing apologia aimed at the complete rehabilitation of appeasement. Table, 64 notes.

　　　　　　　　　　　　　　　　　　V. Sobell

2848. Doenecke, Justus D. ISOLATIONISTS OF THE 1930'S AND 1940'S: AN HISTORIOGRAPHICAL ESSAY. *West Georgia Coll. Studies in the Social Sci. 1974 13: 5-39.*

2849. Domínguez, Jorge I. CONSENSUS AND DIVERGENCE: THE STATE OF THE LITERATURE ON INTER-AMERICAN RELATIONS IN THE 1970'S. *Latin Am. Res. Rev. 1978 13(1): 87-126.* Examines areas of consensus in recent writings on inter-American relations in addition to eight divergent perspectives. The author proposes a hierarchy of approaches to the study of inter-American relations—at the top, using unorthodox dependency and strategic perspectives; at the middle, organizational ideology and presidential politics perspectives; and at the bottom, the political system perspective. Secondary sources; 2 tables, 103 notes, appendix. 　　　　　　　　　　　　　　J. K. Pfabe

2850. Donnini, Guido. UN MOMENTO DEI RAPPORTI ITALO-RUSSI ALL'INIZIO DEL SECOLO: LA MANCATA RESTITUZIONE DELLA VISITA A VITTORIO EMANUELE III DA PARTE DI NICOLA II NEL 1903 [A moment in Italian-Russian relations at the beginning of the century: Nicholas II's failure in 1903 to reciprocate Victor Emmanuel III's visit]. *Politico [Italy] 1978 43(3): 447-466.* King Victor Emmanuel III visited Russia in 1902; Nicholas II failed to return that visit the next year. Prospects for war in the Far East explain the failure in diplomatic courtesy: Russia instead negotiated the Mürzsteg Program of October 1903 with the Habsburg Empire to block Italy in the Balkans. The author considers Italian scholarship on this issue. 　　　　　J/S

2851. Donway, Roger. THE LIMITS OF CREDULITY. *Freeman 1973 23(9); 537-546.* Analyzes revisionism in histories of the Cold War. 　　　　　　　　　　　　　　　　　　S

2852. Drobysheva, N. G. PROBLEMY ZAVERSHENIIA MIRNOGO UREGULIROVANIIA V EVROPE POSLE VTOROI MIROVOI VOINY V ANGLIISKOI I AMERIKANSKOI BURZHUAZNOI ISTORIOGRAFII [Problems of achieving the regulation of peace in Europe after World War II in English and American bourgeois historiography]. *Vestnik Leningradskogo U.: Seriia Istorii, Iazyka i Literatury [USSR] 1981 (1): 106-108.* A peace settlement after World War II in Europe was really only achieved by the 1970's through Bonn's Ostpolitik. The author

studies Western accounts of the process, showing how they differ from the Soviet view. Bourgeois historians continue to trot out the old cliches about Communist expansionism and the inability to trust treaties with Moscow. Yet overall, the agreements demonstrate how peaceful coexistence can work. Based on secondary sources in English and Russian; 17 notes. 　　　　　　　D. N. Collins

2853. Dukes, Paul. READING HISTORY: THE COLD WAR. *History Today [Great Britain] 1984 34(Dec): 51-52.* Reviews the historiography of the Cold War, noting books published since the 1950's that examine American-Soviet relations.

2854. Dunn, Keith A. CONFLICT OF WORLD VIEWS: ORIGINS OF THE COLD WAR. *Military Rev. 1977 57(2): 14-25.* The difficulties stressed by many revisionist historians did not cause the Cold War, but manifested the larger problem of two opposite views of world organization and of protection from the origins of another World War. 　　　　　　　　　　　　G. E. Snow

2855. Dupeux, Louis. HISTORIOGRAPHIE RÉCENTE DU "TROISIÈME REICH" [Recent historiography of the "Third Reich"]. *Rev. d'Allemagne [France] 1978 10(2): 275-292.* Continued from a previous article. The works of about 100 contemporary historians, mostly German, but also some European and American, are cited with brief critical and descriptive comments. All deal with some aspect of the foreign policy of the Third Reich, including its relation to that of preceding German governments, the relations of Nazi Germany with other European states and the United States, the strategy and tactics of World War II, and the administration of Nazi-occupied countries. Article to be continued. Primary sources; 4 notes. 　　　　　　　　　J. S. Gassner

2856. Egorova, N. VNESHNEPOLITICHESKIE KONTSEPTSII SSHA—MIFY I REAL'NOST' [The external political conceptions of the USA: myths and reality]. *Mirovaia Ekonomika i Mezhdunarodnye Otnosheniia [USSR] 1976 (6): 117-120.* Reviews contributions of revisionist historiography since the 1960's to United State's ideological reassessment of its foreign policy.

2857. Einhorn, Marion and Kölling, Mirjam. URSACHEN, ENTSTEHUNG UND ÜBERWINDUNG DES KALTEN KRIEGES IN DER BÜRGERLICHEN BRITISCHEN GESCHICHTSSCHREIBUNG [The origins, development, and overcoming of the Cold War in bourgeois British historiography]. *Jahrbuch für Geschichte [East Germany] 1978 18: 295-338.* British historians turned much more readily to themes and problems of contemporary issues, 1960's-70's. Bourgeois British historians, however, focused much less on the historiography of the Cold War than their US counterparts. British historiography on the Cold War developed through two phases: 1955-69; and 1970-78 and demonstrated three main directions: militant opposition to detente; flexible accommodation of international changes; and recognition of imperialist responsibility for the Cold War. Demonstrates the crucial interaction of politics, ideology, and history. 177 notes. 　　　　J. B. Street

2858. Eisenberg, Carolyn. REFLECTIONS ON A TOOTHLESS REVISIONISM. *Diplomatic Hist. 1978 2(3): 295-305.* Review article prompted by Daniel Yergin's *Shattered Peace* (Boston: Houghton Mifflin Co., 1977). The traditional view of the Cold War was that it arose as a result of Soviet policy which in turn reflected the intrinsic imperatives of Marxist totalitarianism. A formidable group of revisionist historians challenged that view in the 1960's. These writers claimed that the United States and, at a deeper level, the intrinsic imperatives of liberal capitalism were the ultimate cause of the post-1945 collapse of American-Soviet cooperation. Yergin with an implausible eclecticism presents the problem as arising from a misperception on the part of leading American policymakers, as, for example, George Kennan and James Forrestal, of Soviet aims—a misperception for which he can provide no adequate explanation. 　　　　　　　　　　　　　　　　L. W. Van Wyk

2859. Enssle, Manfred J. STRESEMANN'S DIPLOMACY FIFTY YEARS AFTER LOCARNO: SOME RECENT PERSPECTIVES. *Hist. J. [Great Britain] 1977 20(4): 937-948.* Reexamines the legend of Gustav Stresemann. He contributed both to the international equilibrium of Locarno and to its demise. He was simultaneously cooperative and revisionist on Germany's frontier problem. His foreign policy fluctuated. Based on published primary and secondary sources, and unpublished papers delivered at scholarly meetings; 43 notes.   L. A. McGeoch

2860.   Erdmann, Karl Dietrich. BIOGRAPHISCHES ZU STRESE-MANN: VOM NUTZEN UND NACHTEIL DER JUBILÄUMSLITERATUR [Biographies of Stresemann: virtues and vices of anniversary works]. *Geschichte in Wissenschaft und Unterricht [West Germany] 1979 30(1): 29-32.* Finds fault with Theodor Eschenburg and Ulrich Frank-Planitz's *Gustav Stresemann. Eine Bildbiographie* (1978) and Felix Hirsch's *Stresemann. Ein Lebensbild (1978).* Secondary works; 3 notes.   H. W. Wurster

2861.   Fleury, Antoine. DIPLOMATIE ET RELATIONS ÉCONOMIQUES INTERNATIONALES: CONTRIBUTIONS DE L' ÉCOLE HISTORIQUE FRANÇAISE [Diplomacy and international economic relations: contributions by the French historical school]. *Schweizerische Zeitschrift für Geschichte [Switzerland] 1978 28(4): 531-551.* In the wake of Renouvin's and Duroselle's *Introduction à l'histoire des relations internationales* (1964), French historians approach the history of international relations with a new awareness of the complexities that influence world politics. Jean-Claude Allain's *Agadir 1911*, (1976), Jacques Thobie's *Intérêts et impérialisme français dans l'Empire Ottoman 1895-1914*, (1972), and Jacques Bariéty's *Les relations franco-allemandes après la Première Guerre mondiale,* (1977) illustrate how traditional diplomatic and political history is changed and enriched by the application of social and economic history thus providing a better understanding of the forces at work in the relations between nations.
                                                              H. K. Meier

2862.   Floto, Inga. COLONEL HOUSE IN PARIS: THE FATE OF A PRESIDENTIAL ADVISER. *Am. Studies in Scandinavia [Norway] 1973/74 6(1/2): 21-45.* This historiographical article discusses the break between President Woodrow Wilson and Colonel Edward M. House in 1919 as well as House's competency as an international negotiator. Evaluation is made of numerous historical and psychological works, including Charles Seymour, *The Intimate Papers of Colonel House* (1928); Ray Stannard Baker, *Woodrow Wilson and World Settlement* (1923); Alexander and Juliette L. George, *Woodrow Wilson and Colonel House. A Personality Study* (1956); and the author's own work, *Colonel House in Paris: A Study of American Policy at the Paris Peace Conference 1919* (1973). Based on various private manuscript collections and secondary sources; 64 notes.   J. E. Findling

2863.   Fohlen, Claude. LES HISTORIENS DEVANT LA POLITIQUE AMERICAINE DU SECOND EMPIRE [Historians on the American policy of the Second Empire]. *Rev. d'Hist. Moderne et Contemporaine [France] 1974 21(1): 127-134.* Because Franco-American relations were a relatively minor concern of the Second Empire, traditional historians have given them little attention. The most significant recent works have been by American historians who have shown that economic considerations governed French foreign policy and determined French sympathies during the American Civil War. 11 notes.   S. R. Smith

2864.   Forsyth, Murray. THE CLASSICAL THEORY OF INTERNATIONAL RELATIONS. *Pol. Studies [Great Britain] 1978 26(3): 411-416.* Discusses approaches to the study of international relations with particular reference to the work of Hedley Bull and Martin Wight. Wight's historical approach, which is close to that of a natural scientist approaching physical data, is weak on theory. Bull's work, which was in turn heavily influenced by Wight, exhibits ambiguities and obscurities. Both have failed to define the positive nature of the international world or rather have defined it by what it is not. 21 notes.   R. Howell

2865.   Fretz, Lewis. EISENHOWER AND THE REVISIONISTS. *Political Science [New Zealand] 1984 36(1): 67-76.* Criticizes the conclusions of recent revisionist works about the administration of

President Dwight D. Eisenhower, acknowledging Eisenhower's considerable foreign policy successes but noting that some of his policies created enormous problems for subsequent administrations.

2866.   Frey, Linda and Frey, Marsha. THE FOREIGN POLICY OF FREDERICK I, KING IN PRUSSIA, 1703-1711: A FATAL VACILLATION? *East European Q. 1975 9(3): 259-269.* A reconsideration of the development of the harsh historical judgments on Frederick I's foreign policy. While criticism is warranted, most writers ignore the critical point that it probably would have not been possible for someone to improve on Frederick's actions. His policy was logical within the contexts of Prussia' military might and geographical position. Secondary works; 44 notes.   C. R. Lovin

2867.   Frost, Jess V. A PROBLEM OF BIAS: SOVIET AND U.S. DISTORTION OF HISTORY. *Social Studies 1974 65(2): 58-60.* The problem of bias in history deters better relations between the United States and the USSR. Purposeful distortions seem to be implied on the part of both countries. 3 notes.   L. R. Raife

2868.   Fry, Joseph A. WILLIAM MCKINLEY AND THE COMING OF THE SPANISH-AMERICAN WAR: A STUDY OF THE BESMIRCHING AND REDEMPTION OF AN HISTORICAL IMAGE. *Diplomatic Hist. 1979 3(1): 77-97.* Traces the historiography on President William McKinley (1897-1901) and his role in the coming of the Spanish-American War (1898). McKinley was neither "so weak, pliable, and expedient as his critics suggest" nor "so purposeful or so masterfully in control as portrayed by his supporters." Secondary sources; 64 notes.   T. L. Powers

2869.   Fry, Michael G. and Gilbert, Arthur N. A HISTORIAN AND LINKAGE POLITICS: ARNO MAYER. *Int. Studies Q. [Great Britain] 1982 26(3): 425-444.* Certain historians and political scientists share a common interest in the origins of international conflict and in linkage politics, but still work all too often in traditional modes of intellectual solitude or competition. In particular, political scientists should study the work of Arno Mayer, a historian who has devoted himself to the study of those factors of internal politics that affect the foreign policies of major powers. Mayer has attempted to show that domestic politics determined, in large measure, the incidence and intensity of international conflict in 19th- and 20th-century Great Britain and Germany. 40 notes, fig.
                                                              E. S. Palais

2870.   Gattei, Giorgio. LA STORIOGRAFIA SULLE ORIGINI DELLA GUERRA FREDDA [Historiography on the origins of the Cold War]. *Studi Storici [Italy] 1976 17(4): 185-210.* Revisionism is an ever-reoccurring phenomenon in historiography; now it is being applied to the Cold War. Historians in the United States, and elsewhere, are reexamining the sources of the long confrontation between the Western Allies and the USSR and its satellites. The revisionists maintain that Joseph Stalin took only those countries in Eastern Europe that were his rightful "sphere of influence" and were recognized as such by Winston Churchill. Their opinions of American actions in the last stages of World War II and its immediate aftermath are often critical. The author surveys the revisionists' arguments and critics' replies in detail. 102 notes.
                                                              J. C. Billigmeier

2871.   Gimbel, John. THE AMERICAN REPARATIONS STOP IN GERMANY: AN ESSAY ON THE POLITICAL USE OF HISTORY. *Hist. 1975 37(2): 276-296.* On 3 May 1946 General Lucius D. Clay announced suspension of reparations deliveries from the American zone in Germany. Almost all historians have interpreted this to have been an anti-Soviet act. This study relies principally on papers in the National Archives and US State Department published diplomatic papers, as well as the Department's *Bulletin* for 1946-47 to demonstrate that at the time both Clay and the department attributed the need for the reparations stop not to Soviet provocation but to French refusal to treat Germany as a single economic unit. Speculates about reasons to account for the failure of American historians to view this event in its true light. 91 notes.
                                                              N. W. Moen

2872. Gorshkov, A. I. SOVETSKO-CHEKHOSLOVATSKIE OT-NOSHENIIA 1935-1945 GODOV V ISTORIOGRAFII CHSSR 70-KH GODOV [Soviet-Czechoslovak relations 1935-45 in Czechoslovak historiography of the 1970's]. *Istoriia SSSR [USSR] 1981 (1): 191-205.* Reviews some 170 Czech and Slovak studies, memoirs, popular works, and collections of documents on Soviet-Czechoslovak relations from the signing of the mutual assistance treaty in May 1935 to the liberation of Prague by the Red Army in May 1945. 82 notes.　　　　　　　　N. Frenkley

2873. Graebner, Norman A. et al. ADVISORY COMMITTEE TO THE U.S. DEPARTMENT OF STATE ON HISTORICAL DOCUMENTATION: ANNUAL REPORT, 1979. *PS 1980 13(3): 294-296.* The 23d annual report of the Advisory Committee on Historical Documentation covers such topics as the future of the triennial journal *Foreign Relations,* the budgetary outlook, and publication schedules.

2874. Griffith, Robert. TRUMAN AND THE HISTORIANS: THE RECONSTRUCTION OF POSTWAR AMERICAN HISTORY. *Wisconsin Mag. of Hist. 1975 59(1): 20-50.* Reviews the historical literature on President Harry S. Truman's foreign policy, including changing interpretations and evaluations of the Marshall Plan, Truman Doctrine, Point Four, atomic diplomacy, the Korean War, containment and the origins of the Cold War. Also deals with Truman's domestic policy, highlighting his handling of inflation, domestic security, McCarthyism, housing, civil rights, anti-trust enforcement, and public power programs. Revisionist historians view Truman's administration as a failure because it represented mid-century liberalism which "served only to rationalize an aggressive and militaristic foreign policy, while betraying the cause of social justice at home." Presented at the annual meeting of the Organization of American Historians in 1972. 9 illus., 84 notes, biblio.　N. C. Burckel

2875. Hammett, Hugh B. AMERICA'S NON-POLICY IN EASTERN EUROPE AND THE ORIGINS OF THE COLD WAR. *Survey [Great Britain] 1973 19(4): 144-162.* "The Roosevelt administration did not know what it was doing in Eastern Europe." One result is that historians have been arguing about the origins of the Cold War ever since. Surveys Cold War historiography and discusses the US wartime attitude toward Eastern Europe. Roosevelt had a puzzling, well-intentioned idealism, but never a policy, and this accounts for his behavior at Teheran and Yalta. Truman never reversed Roosevelt's conciliatory policy; he just made the decisions Roosevelt had been putting off. Based on documents and secondary sources; 56 notes.　　　　　　　　R. B. Valliant

2876. Harrington, Michael; Schlesinger, Arthur M., Jr.; Zinn, Howard; and Williams, William Appleman. AMERICA II. *Partisan R. 1970 37(4): 498-527, 1971 38(1): 67-83.* Part I. Three writers comment on the writings of William Appleman Williams. Harrington judges that Williams' *The Roots of the Modern American Empire* (New York: Random House, 1969) gives too much emphasis to agricultural market expansionism in creating historic American foreign policy. Harrington believes that Williams' work is too Leninist in analysis and too pessimistic for any future structural change. Schlesinger criticizes Williams for being too much the economic determinist in ignoring the strategic and political motives in American imperial policy. Schlesinger argues that the essential motives for expansionism were noneconomic. Zinn discounts Williams' account of America's past by stressing its lack of significance or relevance for today's task of a radical reconstruction of American institutions. He rejects Williams as too much the professional historian. Part II. Williams defends his works, and claims that his books were written for differing readers, and hopes to achieve different reactions. He rejects Zinn's models of the radical and professional historians as being pointless and reaffirms his emphasis on agriculture as a source for American market expansionism. Schlesinger reiterates his statement that political and strategic motives have an innate independence from all forms of economic ownership or ideology. The search for power and the search for profits, accordingly, are two different historical processes.　D. K. Pickens

2877. Hillgruber, Andreas. METHODOLOGIE UND THEORIE DER GESCHICHTE DER INTERNATIONALEN BEZIEHUNGEN [Methodology and theory of the history of international relations]. *Geschichte in Wissenschaft und Unterricht [West Germany] 1976 27(4): 193-210.* In Western historiography the field of international relations is to a great extent only covered by the political sciences. Since the Russian revolution the theory of parallel existence of two economic systems is used as the basic model for international relations. Marxist historians interpret international relations as the doctrine of the total system of the action of states. The empirical analysis of individual phenomena must not lose the total perspective of international relations. Based on secondary literature; 58 notes.　　　　　　　　R. Wagnleitner

2878. Hogeboom, Willard L. THE NEW LEFT AND THE REVISION OF AMERICAN HISTORY. *Hist. Teacher 1968 2(1): 51-55.* New Left historians emerged during the 1960's in opposition to the "consensus" school of American historiography, which had challenged the "progressive" writers in the mid-1940's. Mentions individual historians and publications of the movement. Expounds several New Left theories, including a revisionist approach to the origins of the Cold War, and discusses the New Left advocacy of non-elitist history. Based on secondary sources; 10 notes.
　　　　　　　　P. T. Herman

2879. Holsti, Ole R. WILL THE REAL DULLES PLEASE STAND UP. *Int. J. [Canada] 1974-75 30(1): 34-44.* Discusses recent historiography dealing with the diplomacy and foreign policy of US Secretary of State John Foster Dulles 1953-59.

2880. Horn, Rüdiger. DIE "NEW LEFT HISTORY" IN DEN USA ÜBER DEN KALTEN KRIEG ["New Left" history in the USA on the Cold War]. *Zeitschrift für Geschichtswissenschaft [East Germany] 1977 25(7): 803-815.* Influenced by C. Wright Mills and Herbert Marcuse as well as by the protest movement against American involvement in Vietnam, "New Left" historians, led by W. A. Williams, demonstrate that the Cold War was caused by American desire for world hegemony rather than by alleged Soviet expansionism. Nonetheless, these historians, still grounded in bourgeois-democratic ideology, reject Lenin's theory of imperialism as well as other major tenets of the Marxist-Leninist interpretation of history. Based on secondary sources; 85 notes.　　J. T. Walker

2881. Hovi, Kalervo. KANSAINVÄLISTEN SUHTEIDEN HISTORIAN RANSKALAINEN KOULUKUNTA [The French school of the history of international relations]. *Historiallinen Arkisto [Finnish] 1984 (82): 89-99.* Discusses theoretical approaches to the history of international relations developed by European and American historians since 1920. The traditional historicist-positivist school has been challenged by several socioeconomic theories and by the totalist approach represented by Fernand Braudel, Pierre Renouvin, and Jean-Baptiste Duroselle. Based on French, German, and English historiography; 20 notes.　　　　　R. G. Selleck

2882. Iriye, Akira. CONTEMPORARY HISTORY AS HISTORY: AMERICAN EXPANSION INTO THE PACIFIC SINCE 1941. *Pacific Hist. Rev. 1984 53(2): 191-212.* One of the most notable historiographical developments in the last 50 years, the impressive body of monographs on Asian-American relations that has been published since the beginning of World War II is part of the phenomenon of American involvement in the Pacific region. Studying it entails all the usual risks and conceptual problems inherent in the writing of contemporary history. Essay is in six parts: 1941-45, World War II; 1945-49, framework of the Cold War; 1949-53, Korean War era; 1953-61, Eisenhower administration; 1961-69, Vietnam era; and 1969-present.　　　　H. M. Parker, Jr.

2883. Jaffe, Philip J. THE COLD WAR REVISIONISTS AND WHAT THEY OMIT. *Survey [Great Britain] 1973 19(4): 123-143.* Examines the "major historical facts" to prove that the revisionists have a preconceived conclusion and "have omitted or distorted their analysis." Discusses the Duclos affair, the Aleksandrov and Varga disputes, the Hitler-Stalin Pact, the Truman Doctrine and the Marshall Plan, the first Cominform meeting, and Stalin's personality and world view. Revisionists make their points by disregarding, either deliberately or through careless research, important historical facts that are readily accessible to them. Based on documents, memoirs and secondary sources; 3 notes.   R. B. Valliant

2884. Johnston, Whittle. E. H. CARR'S THEORY OF INTERNATIONAL RELATIONS: A CRITIQUE. *J. of Pol. 1967 29(4): 861-884.* Argues that E. H. Carr did not develop a coherent theory of international relations. Instead, he created two theories which run counter to one another. In *The Twenty Years Crisis* (New York: Harper-Row, 1939), Carr held that the major powers by relying on a "harmony of interests" among themselves had neglected morality. So long as they were satisfied, the world was right, and this Carr felt was the source of the "crisis." In *Nationalism and After* (New York: St. Martin, 1945), Carr reversed himself and presented the harmony of interests as helpful. International stability required "successful compromise between international economic and military power on the one hand and political nationalism on the other!" Finally, in *What Is History* (New York: Knopf, 1962), Carr began to move toward utopianism and a theory of history as the story of progress. "Carr thus stands self-incriminated in the light of his own prior analyses." 43 notes.   A. R. Stoesen

2885. Johnston, Whittle. RADICAL REVISIONISM AND THE DISINTEGRATION OF THE AMERICAN FOREIGN POLICY CONSENSUS. *Orbis 1976 20(1): 179-206.* The doctrine guiding US foreign policymakers today is under heavy attack, particularly from the radical revisionists who are "eager to recast the definition of American interest in molds at fundamental variance with those of past doctrines." It is apparent from the presentations they have made regarding the Cold War that the radical revisionists have determined "to flatten the complexities of collective experience into conformity with the strictures of a preconceived ideology, and take as their goal supplanting the intrinsic corruption of society by a new and revolutionary ethic." The radical revisionists "have degraded scholarship for the purpose of ideological argumentation," as is amply demonstrated in the writings of William Appelman Williams, an early revisionist. What is needed is the formulation of adequate alternative perspectives, and a major effort to let the people of this country know that the tendency of the radical revisionists is acceptance of the Russian faith, because for them, "Marxism-Leninism offers rational coherence and universal comprehensiveness, ultimate meaning and daily guidance." A revised version of a paper originally presented at a conference held at the University of Virginia, 14-16 August 1975. 24 notes.
                    A. N. Garland

2886. Jones, R. J. Barry. THE STUDY OF "APPEASEMENT" AND THE STUDY OF INTERNATIONAL RELATIONS. *British J. of Int. Studies [Great Britain] 1975 1(1): 68-76.* Examines 20th-century historiography.

2887. Kanet, Roger E. DIE AUSSENBEZIEHUNGEN DER OSTEUROPÄISCHEN STAATEN [Foreign relations of the Eastern European states]. *Osteuropa [West Germany] 1978 28(1): 79-91.* Reviews new British and US publications on foreign relations between the communist Eastern European states and developing nations.

2888. Kanet, Roger E. WEITERE ENGLISCHSPRACHIGE BÜCHER ÜBER DIE OST-WEST-BEZIEHUNGEN [Further English language books on East-West relations]. *Osteuropa [West Germany] 1978 28(9): 832-844.* Reviews new English and US publications on the arms race, the Cold War, detente, cooperation between Eastern Europe and Western Nations, technological transfer, and Soviet military strategy since 1945.

2889. Kanet, Roger E. WETTRÜSTEN, ENTSPANNUNG UND OST-WEST-HANDEL [Arms race, detente, and East-West trade]. *Osteuropa [West Germany] 1978 28(2): 175-186.* Reviews new British and US publications on foreign relations between Eastern Europe and the Western Nations from the Cold War to detente, and also discusses Soviet world strategy and the influence of detente on Soviet domestic developments.

2890. Kaplan, Lawrence S. THE TREATY OF PARIS, 1783: A HISTORIOGRAPHICAL CHALLENGE. *Int. Hist. Rev. [Canada] 1983 5(3): 431-442.* Reviews historical interpretations of the Treaty of Paris, suggesting the need for more work on the long-term consequences of the treaty, especially with respect to diplomacy, international relations, and the balance of power in Europe. 25 notes.
                    H. M. Parker, Jr.

2891. Kazakevich, L. I. IZUCHENIE ISTORII VNESHNEI I VNUTRENNEI POLITIKI SSHA V TOMSKOM UNIVERSITETE (1976-1982) [The study of the history of US foreign and domestic policy at Tomsk University, 1976-82]. *Amerikanskii Ezhegodnik [USSR] 1983: 299-304.* The study of contemporary US history at Tomsk University is the main focus of American studies in the entire eastern USSR. Under the leadership of Professor S. S. Grigortsevich, studies on US foreign policy have been carried out for the past 20 years. Primary sources; 15 notes.   S. J. Talalay/S

2892. Kazakevich, L. I. OBSUZHDENIE PROBLEM ISTORIOGRAFII VNESHNEI POLITIKI SSHA NA KONFERENTSII V TOMSKOM UNIVERSITETE [Discussion of the problems of the historiography of US foreign policy at the conference at Tomsk University]. *Amerikanskii Ezhegodnik [USSR] 1983: 304-307.* Details speeches presented at the 5th Regional Scientific Conference on Methods of History, Historiography and Historical Knowledge, which took place 18-20 May 1982 at Tomsk University. Organized by western Siberian scholars, the conference was divided into seven sections and focused on US foreign policy and the international youth movement. Further research is needed.   S. J. Talalay

2893. Kedourie, Elie. FROM CLERK TO CLERK: WRITING DIPLOMATIC HISTORY. *Am. Scholar 1979 48(4): 502-512.* The author's *In the Anglo-Arab Labyrinth* (1976) has perhaps made some contribution to the history of Anglo-Arab relations and the history of ideas, but Elie Kedourie intended it to be something more as well. It was an attempt to restore "the meaning of thoughts and actions now dead and gone, which once upon a time were the designs and choices of living men."   F. F. Harling

2894. Kelly, María Patricia Fernández. THE U.S.-MEXICO BORDER: RECENT PUBLICATIONS AND THE STATE OF CURRENT RESEARCH. *Latin Am. Res. Rev. 1981 16(3): 250-267.* Reviews eight books published between 1971 and 1979. They reveal the problematic situation that characterizes the border, an area that could determine the future relationship between the United States and Mexico. 19 notes.   J. K. Pfabe

2895. Kero, Reino and Kostiainen, Auvo. YLEISEN HISTORIAN KIRKKAAT JA HÄMÄRÄT RAJAT [The clear and fuzzy boundaries of general history]. *Hist. Aikakauskirja [Finland] 1982 80(4): 363-366.* Argues that interactions between Finland and other countries, such as international migration, belong to general history, rather than to Finnish domestic history.   R. G. Selleck

2896. Kimball, Warren F. THE COLD WAR WARMED OVER. *Am. Hist. R. 1974 79(4): 1119-1136.* A review article on: John L. Gaddis, *The United States and the Origins of the Cold War, 1941-1947* (Columbia U. Press, 1972), Joyce and Gabriel Kolko, *The Limits of Power: The World and United States Foreign Policy, 1945-1954* (Harper & Row, 1972), and Robert J. Maddox, *The New Left and the Origins of the Cold War* (Princeton U. Press, 1973). Examines the current state of Cold War historiography. Gaddis typifies a new generation of scholars who eclectically combine many of the findings of orthodox and left-revisionist historians. The Kolkos exemplify determinist historians whose arguments often seem to have been forced into a suitable pattern. Maddox's intemperate and sketchy attack on the left-revisionists lacks both civility and validity.   A

2897. Kirichenko, V. P. AMERIKANSKAIA BURZHUAZNAIA ISTORIGRAFIIA O POLITIKE SSHA V LATINSKOI AMERIKE [American bourgeois historiography on US policy in Latin America]. *Voprosy Istorii [USSR] 1981 (7): 148-155.* Latin American studies in the United States has grown at a tremendous rate in the 1970's with a concomitant increase in the number of books and publications dealing with the region. Most US historians tacitly support American policy in the region even when they are claiming to be objective. A number of writers do adopt a critical stance however, such as in the field of economic policy, and argue that economic progress cannot occur where the country is economically dependent on the United States. The works focus on the postwar era. 40 notes.

A. Brown

2898. Koval, M. PRESENT-DAY US HISTORIOGRAPHY ON SINO-US RELATIONS BETWEEN 1928 AND 1937. *Far Eastern Affairs [USSR] 1981 (1): 101-112.* Current Chinese and American historians are actively falsifying Chinese history and the history of Sino-US relations.

2899. Koval', V. S. ZOVNISHNIA POLITYKA SSHA U DRUHII SVITOVII VIINI [US foreign policy during World War II]. *Ukrains'kyi Istorychnyi Zhurnal [USSR] 1968 (10): 140-149.* Discusses the problems involved in studying US foreign policy for Soviet historians such as the difficulty of obtaining sources; reviews and compares treatment of it by American and Soviet historians.

2900. Kramer-Kaske, Liselotte. DIE BÜRGERLICHE HISTORIOGRAPHIE IN DEN USA ZUR ROLLE DES INTERAMERIKANISCHEN SYSTEMS BEI DER HERAUSBILDUNG DER GLOBALEN STRATEGIE DES KALTEN KRIEGES [Bourgeois historiography in the United States on the role of the Inter-American System in the development of the global strategy of the Cold War]. *Jahrbuch für Geschichte [East Germany] 1978 18: 253-294.* Sketches relations between the United States and Latin America from 1945 to 1950, and reviews the major trends in American historiography on the role of Latin America in American Cold War policy in the 1950's and 1960's. In the 1950's American historiography was dominated by an orthodox conventional or semiofficial government view, but important variants included right revisionist and liberal traditional interpretations. Under the changed international conditions of the 1960's the semiofficial government orthodox view split into realistic and strictly orthodox wings. The right revisionists played a minimal role in the 1960's, but a new leftist bourgeois view entered the debates. This article analyzes at length a few representatives of these views. 164 notes.

J. B. Street

2901. Krasnov, I. M. AMERIKANSKAIA BURZHUAZNAIA ISTORIOGRAFIIA O SOVETSKO-AMERIKANSKIKH OTNOSHENIIAKH 1917-1933 GODOV [American bourgeois historiography on Soviet-American relations, 1917-1933]. *Voprosy Istorii [USSR] 1968 (10): 22-40.* American historians have distorted Soviet-American relations and have failed to consider published Soviet versions. They cast doubt on the declared Soviet policy of peaceful coexistence, and they treat too sympathetically the US government's refusal to establish diplomatic relations until 1933. This latter step was forced by the demands of millions of unemployed American workers and by the fear of Japanese militarism. Very few American writers recognize that it was US imperialism that was responsible for strained relations between the two countries. Based on published Soviet and US foreign policy documents, on the *Congressional Record* and newspapers, and on secondary sources; 90 notes.

C. I. P. Ferdinand

2902. Kubyshkin, A. I. AMERIKANSKAIA BURZHUAZNAIA ISTORIOGRAFIIA OB INTERVENTSII SSHA PROTIV REVOLIUTSIONNOI GVATEMALY V 1954 G [American bourgeois historiography concerning US intervention in the Guatemala Revolution of 1954]. *Vestnik Leningradskogo U.: Seriia Istorii, Iazyka i Literatury [USSR] 1978 (3): 48-53.* American interpretations on US intervention in Guatemala range from direct support for the intervention to outright criticism of the imperialistic methods employed, but they all reflect anti-Communism. 25 notes.

G. F. Jewsbury

2903. Kundiuba, D. I. VYSVITLENNIA RADIANS'KO-AMERYKANS'KYKH VIDNOSYN 1933-1939 RR. V BURZHUAZNII ISTORIOGRAFII SSHA [The elucidation in the US bourgeois historiography of Soviet-American relations during 1933-39]. *Ukrains'kyi Istorychnyi Zhurnal [USSR] 1970 (7): 128-134.* Discusses some of the views of US historians on the normal-

ization of Soviet-American relations in 1933 and concludes that "US historiography falsifies the reality and tries to shift the blame for unsatisfactory development of these relations onto the USSR."

2904. Kunina, A. E. NOVYE ISSLEDOVANIIA SOVETSKIKH ISTORIKOV O VNESHNEI POLITIKE SSHA [Soviet historians' new research on US foreign policy]. *Novaia i Noveishaia Istoriia [USSR] 1972 (6): 150-157.* In the late 1940's and early 1950's Soviet historians considered only limited periods of US foreign policy but in the 1960's they adopted a more extensive chronological and theoretical approach. Regional, biographical, and historiographical studies have emerged as well as works considering the struggle of the American nation against the imperialism of the government's foreign policy. Recent important studies have examined US foreign policy, 1945-71, neocolonialism in the 1960's, John F. Kennedy's presidency, US attitudes to European problems, and relations between the USSR and the United States. Soviet secondary sources; 8 notes.

L. Smith/S

2905. Kyrychenko, V. P. FAL'SYFIKATSIA AMERYKANS'KOIU BURZHUAZNOIU ISTORIOGRAFIEIU POLITYKY S SH A V LATYNS'KIY AMERYTSI V 1939-1945 RR. [Falsification of US policy in Latin America in 1939-45 in US bourgeois historiography]. *Ukrains'kyi Istorychnyi Zhurnal [USSR] 1975 (1): 134-138.* US foreign policy in Latin America during 1939-45, formed mutual treaties that appeared to be beneficial for Latin America but were also advantageous to the United States.

2906. Langer, William L. WASHINGTON BUREAUCRAT AND DIPLOMATIC HISTORIAN. *Soc. for Hist. of Am. Foreign Relations. Newsletter 1978 9(2): 2-15, (3): 15-24.* Part I. Based on the author's memoirs, written in 1975; discusses his World War II and postwar diplomatic service in Great Britain, 1941-46. Part II. The author discusses his career as a diplomatic historian, relating his experience with historiography on Vichy France and US foreign policy, 1946-54; mentions European lecture tours and controversy over his published works.

2907. Laqueur, Walter. JEWISH DENIAL AND THE HOLOCAUST. *Commentary 1979 68(6): 44-55.* Describes the dissemination of information about Hitler's Final Solution during the 1940's and Jews' reluctance to believe the extent of Nazi genocide.

2908. Langley, Lester D. AMERICAN FOREIGN POLICY IN AN AGE OF NATIONALISM, 1812-1840. Haines, Gerald K. and Walker, J. Samuel, ed. *American Foreign Relations: A Historiographical Review* (Westport, Conn.: Greenwood Pr., 1981): 33-47. Laments the lack of abroad interpretive studies of the period despite the rich biographical sources available. The three decades after the War of 1812 can be described as an age of nationalis. Secondary sources; 30 notes.

J. Powell

2909. Laptos, Józef. HISTORYCY O ROLI PROPAGANDY POLITYCZNEJ W STOSUNKACH MIĘDZYNARODOWYCH [Historians on the role of political propaganda in international relations]. *Kwartalnik Hist. [Poland] 1976 83(3): 643-648.* Discusses *Propagande et Pressions en Politique Internationale: La Grèce et ses revendications à la Conférence de la Paix* (Paris, 1963) by D. Kitskis and J. Sobczak's *Propaganda zagraniczna Niemiec weimarskich wobec Polski* (Poznan, 1973). Both are pioneering works in interwar historiography, showing the organizational structure, content, methods, and means of propaganda directed at foreign countries as an important arm of diplomacy. Sobczak limits himself only to that part of the Weimar Republic's propaganda which concerns Poland. He neglects its theoretical bases and does not outline the attitude of the West toward Poland. The chief value of his work consists in the data on various organizations and their methods of anti-Polish actions and the interdependence between domestic and external propaganda directed abroad and toward the German nation.

H. Heitzman-Wojcicka

2910. Laroche, Jean. CONTROVERSES SUR L'ORIGINE ET LES CAUSES DE LA GUERRE FROIDE [Controversies on the origin and causes of the Cold War]. *Études Int. [Canada] 1975 6(1): 47-65.* Examines some of the standard interpretations of the

Cold War, classifying them into traditionalist, revisionist, or realist schools. The traditionalist school attributes the Cold War to Soviet expansion. Though the revisionist school has several subdivisions, all revisionist studies point to the United States as the responsible party in bringing on the Cold War. For some, American culpability lies in an inappropriate response to Soviet expansion; for others, in President Harry S. Truman's failure to cooperate with Stalin; and for the extremists, American expansionism was the causative force. The realist school suggests that the Cold War resulted from incomprehensible circumstances which caused a conflict between two modes of thought: American universalism and Soviet zones of influence. 93 notes.   J. F. Harrington, Jr./S

2911.   Latyshev, V. Ia. KOLLOKVIUM ISTORIKOV SSSR I FRG V LENINGRADE [A colloquium of historians of the USSR and West Germany in Leningrad]. *Istoriia SSSR [USSR] 1975 (5): 216-218.* A colloquium of Soviet and West German historians was held on 3 April 1975 in Leningrad. The West German 14-member delegation was headed by professor Werner Konce; the Soviet delegation was headed by A. L. Narochnitski, director of the Institute of History of the USSR of the Academy of Sciences. The colloquium examined two questions: 1) methodology in the history of international relations, and 2) Soviet-German relations, 1918-32.

L. Kalinowski

2912.   Leopold, Richard W. AMERICAN DIPLOMATIC HISTORY: THE VIEWS OF A YOUNGER GENERATION. *Rev. in Am. Hist. 1982 10(3): 320-324.* Reviews *American Foreign Relations: A Historiographical Review* (1981), edited by Gerald K. Haines and J. Samuel Walker, a collection of essays emphasizing changing interpretations and trends in the history of diplomacy since 1783.

2913.   Leopold, Richard W. THE HISTORY OF UNITED STATES FOREIGN POLICY: PAST, PRESENT, AND FUTURE. Delzell, Charles F., ed. *The Future of History: Essays in the Vanderbilt University Centennial Symposium* (Nashville: Vanderbilt U. Pr., 1977): 231-246. Compares the states of diplomatic history today and in 1938, emphasizing the growing availability of sources and shifting areas of interest, specifically the four challenges of 1938, World War II and the origins of the Cold War, a corresponding decline in interest in the period prior to 1865, US policy outside the Western Hemisphere and Europe, and an analysis of internal pressure on foreign policy. Rejects talk of revisionism, the labeling of diplomatic historians, and sweeping generalizations about the history of US foreign policy. Future areas of emphasis will be the internal forces shaping foreign policy, the nature of the decisionmaking process, and the comparative approach, all of which will expand. 22 notes.   P. L. Solodkin

2914.   Levine, Alan J. SOME REVISIONIST THESES ON THE COLD WAR, 1943-1946: A STUDY OF A MODERN MYTHOLOGY. *Continuity 1980 (1): 75-97.* Careful analysis of the strongest arguments on the Cold War presented by revisionist historians who concentrate on Soviet-Western relations in postwar Europe (especially Germany) reveals that their theses are not tenable. Arguments that the United States and Great Britain should take the blame for alienating the USSR because they did not launch a potentially disastrous and certainly bloody second front early enough, that the Allies' postwar united front dissipated because they could not agree on what to do with Germany, and that the USSR "forced Communist regimes on eastern Europe because the West objected to Stalin's forcing Communist governments on eastern Europe" are "uniformly grotesque." The West would be more appropriately criticized for giving in too easily to the USSR between 1943 and 1946.   W. A. Wiegand

2915.   Ligi, H. TSENNYI TRUD PO ISTORII MEZHDUNARODNYKH OTNOSHENII XVI VEKA [A dissertation on international relations in the 16th century]. *Skandinavskii Sbornik [USSR] 1975 20: 214-218.* Reviews Knud Rasmussen's dissertation "Die livländische Krise 1554-1561" [The Livonian crisis, 1554-61] (1973), which discusses the treatment of the period leading to and the beginning of the Livonian War by earlier historical literature.

Not all the theories presented in the book, however, are adequately argued, and there is not enough emphasis on relevant Soviet literature.

2916.   Loesdau, Alfred. ZUR KRISE DER BÜRGERLICHEN HISTORIOGRAPHIE IN DEN USA [On the crisis of bourgeois historiography in the USA]. *Zeitschrift für Geschichtswissenschaft [East Germany] 1976 24(6): 629-641.* American historiography developed from the position of militant anti-Communism via a European-US-centered image of history toward the balance of power model. Based on American works; 55 notes.   R. Wagnleitner

2917.   Lowenthal, Abraham F. UNITED STATES POLICY TOWARD LATIN AMERICA: "LIBERAL," "RADICAL," AND "BUREAUCRATIC" PERSPECTIVES. *Latin Am. Research Rev. 1973 8(3): 3-26.* Reviews and analyzes recent writing on US foreign policy toward Latin America, especially the Alliance for Progress, 1960's.

2918.   Lundestad, Geir. HISTORY AND POLITICS: RESEARCH ON THE UNITED STATES IN NORWAY, 1945-1980. *Am. Studies in Scandinavia [Norway] 1982 14(2): 69-98.* Norwegian historiography about the United States can be grouped into four periods that reflect changes in Norwegian-American relations. During 1945-49, Norwegian historians, such as Sigmund Skard, took a middle-of-the-road approach. Skard praised Franklin D. Roosevelt but feared the materialism of American society and cautioned that Norway must go its own way. At the same time, Norway was cautiously joining the United States in the NATO alliance. During 1949-65, criticism of the United States practically disappeared. Much changed between 1965 and the mid-70's. The Vietnam War, race riots, assassinations, and controversial foreign policies led Norwegian historians to adopt an almost totally critical point of view. Since that time, historical writings have been more favorable but not uncritical. 75 notes.   R. E. Goerler

2919.   Luo Rongqu. SOME QUESTIONS REGARDING THE STUDY OF THE HISTORY OF SINO-AMERICAN RELATIONS AND U.S. HISTORY. *Chinese Studies in Hist. 1982-83 16(1-2): 8-38.* Chinese Marxist historians of the past have dismissed any detailed, analytic study of Sino-American relations as not worthy of attention because of the bourgeois nature of the United States. China's relationship with the United States, however, has been extremely complex. Therefore systematic study of American history by Chinese scholars must be undertaken to understand the underlying bases for Sino-American relations since the 19th century and to facilitate understanding of the American culture and its people. Secondary sources; 21 notes.   A. C. Migliazzo

2920.   Maier, Charles S. MARKING TIME: THE HISTORIOGRAPHY OF INTERNATIONAL RELATIONS. Kammen, Michael, ed. *The Past Before Us: Contemporary Historical Writing in the United States* (Ithaca, N.Y.: Cornell U. Pr., 1980): 355-387. Diplomatic history is not a pioneering field in the 1970's; it has resisted the new methodologies of computers and psychoanalysis. The opening of major archives—the Public Record Office, the Quai d'Orsay, and the records of the German Foreign Ministry—has helped make 20th-century foreign relations the field of overwhelming interest, with emphasis on the interwar period. Interest in wartime diplomacy and the Cold War is beginning, while European diplomacy of the 19th century has languished. There is no *Annales* school equivalent for diplomatic history. American historians tend to continue earlier debates, but there have been moves toward studying the relationship of the social and cultural systems to foreign policy. British and French influence is evident in studies on imperialism, intelligence, and military history. 74 notes.

2921.   Markowitz, Gerald E. PROGRESSIVISM AND IMPERIALISM: A RETURN TO FIRST PRINCIPLES. *Historian 1975 37(2): 257-275.* Almost 25 years ago, William E. Leuchtenburg advanced the thesis that instead of being opposed to-turn-of-the-century US imperialism, the majority of American progressive reformers supported it, arguing that growth, development, and reform at home were possible only in partnership with commercial expansion overseas and the regeneration of the world (particularly Asia and Latin America) along the lines of US capitalism (see Leuchtenburg's "Progressivism and Imperialism: The Progressive Movement and American Foreign Policy, 1898-1916," *Mississippi Valley Historical Review* 1952 39: 483-504). This study examines criticism of the Leuchtenburg essay, corrects two of its limitations, and finds its basic thesis to be sound. 68 notes.   N. W. Moen

2922. Martynenko, B. A. Z ISTORIYI KANADS'KO-AMERYKANS'KYKH VIDNOSYN (1935-1939 RR.) [Extracts from the history of Canadian-American relations, 1935-39]. *Ukrains'kyi Istorychnyi Zhurnal [USSR] 1981 (5): 100-106.* Studies US-Canadian relations and attempts to consider the relatively unexplored field in Soviet historiographical literature. Concentrates on various economic agreements which affected US-Canadian relations.
                                               L. Djakowska

2923. Mazur, Zbigniew. REWIZJONISTYCZNA INTERPRETACJA GENEZY ZIMNEJ WOJNY W HISTORIOGRAFII AMERYKAŃSKIEJ [Revisionist interpretation of the genesis of the Cold War in American historiography]. *Przegląd Zachodni [Poland] 1980 36(5-6): 84-102.* US historians have more to say about the nature and origin of the Cold War, mainly because the files on the subject have been opened. Various schools arose. The orthodox historians saw the US policies as a defense against Soviet expansionism. The realist school held that the war was caused by the closed nature of Soviet society, which bred mistrust and misunderstandings; the villain was the Truman Doctrine with its moralistic undertone and lack of realism. The United States should have recognized the Soviet desire for a sphere of interests. Revisionists arose out of the strife about US aims in Vietnam. Partially on the documents but mainly on ideological grounds, US policies were accused of being imperialistic, insensitive, and immoral.   M. Krzyzaniak

2924. McAliffe, Mary S. EISENHOWER, THE PRESIDENT. *J. of Am. Hist. 1981 68(3): 625-632.* Since the late 1960's revisionist historians have rejected the image of Eisenhower as an unintelligent, bland, and passive president. Instead they have depicted Eisenhower as a strong, decisive leader who led the United States through the Cold War. Revisionists disagree on such issues as Eisenhower's conservatism, his domestic policy, and his use of the Central Intelligence Agency for clandestine operations overseas. 27 notes.   T. P. Linkfield

2925. McCormick, Thomas J. DRIFT OR MASTERY? A CORPORATIST SYNTHESIS FOR AMERICAN DIPLOMATIC HISTORY. *Rev. in Am. Hist. 1982 10(4): 318-330.* Examines traditional, revisionist, and postrevisionist diplomatic historiography, all of which have suffered from a lack of systematic analysis and synthesis.

2926. McMahon, Robert J. UNITED STATES RELATIONS WITH ASIA IN THE TWENTIETH CENTURY: RETROSPECT AND PROSPECT. Haines, Gerald K. and Walker, J. Samuel, ed. *American Foreign Relations: A Historiographical Review* (Westport, Conn.: Greenwood Pr., 1981): 237-270. Surveys the historiography of US relations with Asia in the 20th century, especially the major schools of thought regarding the overall nature of America's encounter with Asia. Focuses on conceptual studies and works which consider American-Asian relations in a broad framework or over a long period of time, writings concerning American relations with East Asia, 1900-19, historical literature for 1919-45, American relations with South and Southeast Asia before 1945, and the turbulent period in United States-Asian relations since World War II. Secondary sources; 125 notes.   J. Powell

2927. Moore, Jamie W. WHY DID THEY LIKE THAT BOOK? COGNITIVE CONSISTENCY, THE SUBLIMINAL ELEMENT OF A. WHITNEY GRISWOLD'S *THE FAR EASTERN POLICY OF THE UNITED STATES. Historian 1975 37(4): 585-597.* Reviews the assumptions and conclusions offered by A. Whitney Griswold in his history of *The Far Eastern Policy of the United States*, covering American foreign policy and diplomacy since 1898. Published in 1938, with the intention of influencing public and official opinion, Moore explains that while the desired effect was not then reached Griswold's judgments "continue to command accep-

tance." This continuing acceptance is explained in terms of the simplistic nature of Griswold's work which fits into cognitive consistency theories. 35 notes.

2928. Moore, John Allphin, Jr. FROM REACTION TO MULTILATERAL AGREEMENT: THE EXPANSION OF AMERICA'S OPEN DOOR POLICY IN CHINA, 1899-1922. *Prologue 1983 15(1): 23-36.* The Open Door policy in the early 20th century was intended to encourage a strong independent China aided by foreign investment that would absorb increased American imports. There are two dominant views on where the policy went wrong. The realist argument, derived from a study by A. Whitney Griswold in 1938, sees the policy alternating between an aggressive/assertive approach and retreating/withdrawing approach whereby the integrity of China, which was to be a means to trade, became an end in itself creating other problems. The revisionist argument, formulated by William Appleman Williams, sees the policy as a calculated, well-planned strategy that would allow the United States all of the benefits of an empire without any of the burdens of colonial administration. Present theory sees shortcomings in both arguments. Based on the Edward Mandell House Papers at Yale University Library, US Department of State Papers, and newspaper accounts; 8 photos, 79 notes.   M. A. Kascus

2929. Nefedova, N. A. SOVREMENNAIA ISTORIOGRAFIIA SSHA O PRINTSIPAKH MIRNOGO SOSUSHCHESTVOVANIIA NA MATERIIAKH ZHURNALA *FOREIGN AFFAIRS* [Contemporary US historiography on the principles of peaceful coexistence: based on the journal *Foreign Affairs*]. *Vestnik Leningradskogo U.: Seriia Istorii, Iazyka i Literatury [USSR] 1980 (3): 99-101.* The articles in *Foreign Affairs* dealing with the Soviet Union illustrate the changes in American attitudes toward peaceful coexistence. In the years 1972-78 Sovietologists and specialists on international relations such as George Kennan moved away from the positions held during the Cold War and insisted that peaceful relations between the United States and the USSR were possible. This shift did not signify a fundamental change in the nature of American imperialism. According to Robert Legvold, war was considered by the Soviet leaders to be a useful method of solving conflict. Under the Carter administration a return to the attitudes of the Cold War took place. Based on secondary sources; 14 notes.

                                               L. Waters

2930. Nezhinski, L. N. SSSR I SOTSIALISTICHESKIE STRANY EVROPY (NEKOTORYE PROBLEMY RAZRABOTKI ISTORII MEZHDUNARODNYKH OTNOSHENI SOTSIALISTICHESKOGO TIPA) [The USSR and the European socialist countries (certain problems of elaborating the history of the socialist-type international relations)]. *Voprosy Istorii [USSR] 1974 (3): 3-26.* Examines problems connected with research in the history of international relations of the new, socialist type on the example of the socialist countries of Europe. Particular attention is devoted to the political and economic relations of these countries. Analyzing in the main the works of Soviet historians, the author briefly describes what has been accomplished in this field and singles out a number of problems which require further elaboration. A conspicuous place is given to the examination of theoretical questions pertaining to the new-type international relations and to the main objectives pursued by a close study of these relations.   J

2931. Novik, F. I. PROBLEMY BOR'BY SSSR ZA MIR I BEZOPASNOST' NARODOV V SOVETSKOI ISTORIOGRAFII 70-X GODOV [The struggle of the USSR for the peace and security of nations in Soviet historiography in the 1970's]. *Sovetskoe Slavianovedenie [USSR] 1981 (1): 9-16.* A review of about a score of Soviet publications 1970-80 dealing with the decade of detente. The tone is set by Lenin, Brezhnev, Kosygin, Gromyko, Suslov, and Ustinov and the Party congresses. The accent is on European security, the arms race, the Warsaw Pact, the constant need for the underlying popular desires to prevail against capitalist opposition to everything socialist. 33 notes.   J. P. H. Myers

2932. Ognev, Y. FACTS OF HISTORY AND THEIR FALSIFI-ERS. *Far Eastern Affairs [USSR] 1983 (1): 143-156.* After the Korean-American treaty of 1882, Americans plundered and robbed Korea, supported the Japanese invasion, and performed other hostile acts; discusses recent historiography on US-Korean relations.

2933. Pachter, Henry. REVISIONIST HISTORIANS & THE COLD WAR. *Dissent 1968 15(6): 505-518.*

2934. Pastorelli, Pietro. MARIO TOSCANO E LA STORIA DEI TRATTATI [Mario Toscano and the history of the treaties]. *Storia e Politica [Italy] 1969 8(4): 581-591.* The methods of historical research in the field of international diplomacy and treaties were argued by Italian historians of the 1930's. Mario Toscano wrote his first book *Patto di Londra* [Treaty of London] in 1931, followed by other works, notably *Storia dei trattati e politica internazionale* (Turin: Giappichelli, 1963). Based on Toscano's works and secondary sources; 10 notes.   C. Bates

2935. Petruf, Pavol. PRÍSPEVOK KU KRITIKE BURŽOÁZNEJ HISTORIOGRAFIE O OTÁZKACH MARSHALLOVHO PLÁNU [Criticism of bourgeois historiography on the question of the Marshall Plan]. *Slovanské Štúdie [Czechoslovakia] 1982 23(1): 67-74.* Reviews the official and liberal historiography (mostly American) on the creation of and results of the Marshall Plan. Bourgeois historiography falsifies the facts by asserting that the United States wanted Soviet cooperation and participation in the plan. Some American authors admitted that behind the US invitation to Moscow was a strong desire to make the USSR responsible for the division of Europe and Germany. Other false interpretations explain the rejection of the plan by nations liberated by Soviet arms as the result of pressure from Moscow, which never existed. 15 notes.
G. E. Pergl

2936. Popov, V. I. FUNDAMENTAL'NYI TRUD PO ISTORII DIPLOMATII [A basic work on diplomatic history]. *Novaia i Noveishaia Istoriia [USSR] 1980 (2): 171-176.* Review article on *Istoriia diplomatii,* vol. 5 (Moscow, 1979). 12 notes.
D. N. Collins

2937. Purnell, Robert. THE RELEVANCE OF ANCIENT HISTORY TO THE CONTEMPORARY STUDY OF INTERNATIONAL POLITICS. *British J. of Int. Studies [Great Britain] 1976 2(1): 27-40.* Discusses parallels between ancient Atheno-Spartan relations and international politics today, suggesting several types of political patterns and processes which can be illuminated by comparative historical approaches.

2938. Reynolds, David. READING HISTORY: AMERICAN ISOLATIONISM. *History Today [Great Britain] 1984 34(Mar): 50-52.* American foreign policy in the 20th century has largely emphasized an independent course free of binding alliances. The historiography on isolationism reflects this perspective.

2939. Rossem, M. van. DRIE RICHTINGEN IN DE HISTORIO-GRAFIE VAN DE AMERIKAANSE BUITENLANDSE POLI-TIEK [Three directions in the historiography of American foreign policy]. *Kleio [Netherlands] 1973 14(8/9): 390-398.* Analyzes three historiographical interpretations of American foreign policy. The orthodox school views Americans as idealists; the realist school regards Americans as "backward bunglers"; and the revisionist school holds that Americans, guided exclusively by economic self-interests, are rogues. All three agree, but for different reasons, that Americans are unique in each regard. Actually, however, "Americans are not unique, neither in their idealism, nor in their stupidity, nor in their perfidy." Biblio.   R. C. Alltmont

2940. Rummel, R. J. A FOREIGN CONFLICT BEHAVIOR CODE SHEET. *World Pol. 1966 18(2): 283-296.* Describes a code sheet drafted to systematize data collection on foreign conflict behavior covering long periods of time, allowing reliability checks, and enabling the punching of data on IBM cards to facilitate taking

different analytical cuts of the data, and to maximize the availability of the data to other researchers. Includes a copy of the code sheet with explanations and reliability tests. 8 notes.
R. V. Ritter

2941. Rykalov, V. S. FRANTSUZSKAIA ISTORIOGRAFIIA SO-VETSKO-FRANTSUZSKIKH OTNOSHENII [French historiography of Soviet-French relations]. *Voprosy Istorii [USSR] 1980 (11): 45-57.* Analyzes French historiography from the establishment of diplomatic relations in 1924 to the present. Describes the consistent struggle of French Marxists for peace and friendship with the USSR, showing that along with anti-Soviet and anti-Communist trends there is a realistic trend motivated by the necessity for cooperation between the two countries.   J/S

2942. Rykalov, V. S. LENINSKII DEKRET O MIRE VO FRANTSUZSKOI LITERATURE [French writings on Lenin's decree on peace]. *Voprosy Istorii [USSR] 1976 (5): 188-195.* Compares French Marxist and non-Marxist historiography, 1917-76, on the significance of Lenin's decree on peace of November 1917. The Marxist writers view it, correctly, as the first step of the new government to pursue its policy of struggle for peace and security and as a turning point in the history of international relations. The non-Marxists attempt to falsify its significance by denying its effect on foreign public opinion, seeing it as a utilitarian measure to provoke European unrest in order to defend Soviet interests. 49 notes.
C. J. Read

2943. Rystad, Göran. IN QUEST OF A USABLE PAST: FOR-EIGN POLICY AND THE POLITICS OF AMERICAN HISTORI-OGRAPHY IN THE 1960S. *Scandia [Sweden] 1982 48(2): 217-230.* During the 1960's American historical writing on foreign policy was characterized by a presentist, instrumentalist, and self-centered view of foreign affairs. Emphasis changed from a multinational, Rankian description of events to an Actonian concern for the failure of American foreign policy. This change was linked with the controversy over American intervention in Vietnam and influenced most by revisionary and New Left historians. 57 notes.
L. B. Sather

2944. Salewski, Michael. MÖGLICHKEITEN UND GRENZEN HISTORISCHER VERGLEICHE IN POLITISCHER ABSICHT ODER: WAS HAT ES MIT DEN JAHRESZAHLEN 1914 UND 1938 AUF SICH? [The possibilities and limits of politically motivated historical comparisons or what has this to do with the years 1914 and 1938?]. *Gesch. in Wiss. und Unterricht [West Germany] 1981 32(10): 585-599.* Responds to political attempts to compare the international crises of 1980 in the Middle East and Afghanistan, to those of 1914 and 1938 in Europe. Discusses the reasons for such comparisons and summarizes the historical situations before each of the two world wars. Though historical analogies can be useful in some cases, comparisons of our contemporary crises to either 1914 or 1938 are not appropriate or defensible. "Whoever has respect for history will not misuse the years 1914 and 1938 for political purposes. These years stand for epochs which are unique and not repeatable." A 1980 lecture delivered at Hermann-Ehlers-Akademie in Kiel.   L. D. Wilcox

2945. Salisbury, Richard V. GOOD NEIGHBORS? THE UNITED STATES AND LATIN AMERICA IN THE TWENTIETH CEN-TURY. Haines, Gerald K. and Walker, J. Samuel, ed. *American Foreign Relations: A Historiographical Review* (Westport, Conn.: Greenwood Pr., 1981): 311-333. An assessment, through a review of recent scholarly publications, of the relationship between the United States and Latin America during the first half of the 20th century. By 1900 the United States had embarked upon an imperial course in Latin America. In the next 50 years inter-American relationships varied from outright military intervention to the overt disavowal of such intervention in both the Good Neighbor policy and to the spirit of hemispheric cooperation during World War II. New interpretations, perspectives, and schools of thought have emerged since 1950, challenging the assumptions and the methodologies of previous generations of diplomatic historians in their analyses of inter-American affairs. Secondary sources; 61 notes.   J. Powell

2946. Sater, William F. LA INTERVENCION NORTEAMERI-
CANA DURANTE LA GUERRA DEL PACIFICO: REFUTAC-
IONES A VLADMIR SMOLENSKI [The North-American
intervention during the War of the Pacific: Refutation of Vladmir
Smolenski]. *Boletin de la Acad. Chilena de la Hist. [Chile] 1970
37(83/84): 185-206.* A detailed criticism of Marxist historian Vladmir Smolenski's article "Los Estados Unidos y la Guerra del Pacifico: historia de una intervención que no llegó a efectuarse" (see
abstract 15: 1234). The author criticizes Smolenski's view that US
capitalism caused the War of the Pacific, the United States inter-
vening to the point of guaranteeing the territorial sovereignty of
Bolivia. This fragile thesis can only be sustained through selective
editing of diplomatic documents, distortion of dates, and outright
falsification. The author has included complete transcripts of the
House and Senate Executive Documents cited by Smolenski to
demonstrate that the US role during the war and the subsequent
Africa Conference of 1880 was neutralist, even after the accession
of the anti-British James G. Blaine as Secretary of State.

L. G. Campbell

2947. Schmid, Georg E. MARGINALE NOTIZEN ZU
NEUEREN ASPEKTEN DES KALTEN KRIEGES [Marginal
notes on new aspects of the Cold War]. *Zeitgeschichte [Austria]
1975 2(11/12): 282-290.* Reviews the New Left revisionist interpretations of the Cold War and the critique of traditional historians.
76 notes.   R. Wagnleitner

2948. Schröder, Hans-Jürgen. ZUR GENESIS DES KALTEN
KRIEGES [On the origin of the Cold War]. *Neue Politische Literatur [West Germany] 1976 21(4): 488-506.* Recent American criticisms of the revisionist school of American Cold War
historiography only brought global attacks without realizing that no
homogeneous revisionist school exists.

2949. Schulzinger, Robert D. MODERATION IN PURSUIT OF
TRUTH IS NO VIRTUE; EXTREMISM IN DEFENSE OF MOD-
ERATION IS A VICE. *Am. Q. 1975 27(2): 222-236.* The books
covered in this review-essay indicate that the debates over the origins of the Cold War have become nearly pointless. Neither the
traditionalists nor the revisionists have emerged victorious, nor has
a new synthesis emerged from the arguments. The "moderate"
books written by John Lewis Gaddis, Robert W. Tucker, George C.
Herring, Jr., Robert James Maddox and Sir John Wheeler-Bennett
are marked by vagueness and lack of rigor in analysis. A multinational analysis of the origins of the Cold War is needed to broaden
the argument of the revisionists who, unlike the "moderates," have
been asking the right questions.   N. Lederer

2950. Schwabe, Klaus. AMERIKANISCHE WELTPOLITIK IN
"REVISIONISTISCHER" SICHT [The "revisionist" view of American world policy]. *Hist. Zeitschrift [West Germany] 1975 221(1):
96-104.* The German edition of William A. Williams's *Tragedy of
American Diplomacy* makes available one of the "neorevisionist"
arguments concerning United States foreign policy. Williams's view
that preservation of the free market distorted the prodemocracy
policy defines one of the consistent American policy trends. Whether it is the chief factor remains questionable. Joyce and Gabriel
Kolko in *The Politics of War* (New York, 1968) try to show aggressive Cold War tendencies in American foreign policy growing
out of domestic policy during the last two years of World War II.
The weakness of this work lies in the lack of attention to secondary
sources and excessive adherence to a leftist viewpoint.

G. H. Davis

2951. Schwabe, Klaus. VERSAILLES, NACH SECHZIG
JAHREN: INTERNATIONALE BEZIEHUNGEN NACH DEM
ERSTEN WELTKRIEG [Versailles, after 60 years: foreign relations
after World War I]. *Neue Politische Literatur [West Germany] 1979
24(4): 446-475.* In contrast to earlier treaties the Versailles peace
treaty has been extensively analyzed and interpreted in international
historiography, including West German and Austrian, since the

1960's. The Treaty of Versailles was not a lost peace from the out-
set, but completely misunderstood, not only in Germany at the
time, but also in the United States. 89 notes.

R. Wagnleitner

2952. Smith, Michael. THE LEAGUE OF NATIONS AND IN-
TERNATIONAL POLITICS. *British J. of Int. Studies [Great
Britain] 1976 2(3): 311-323.* Discusses methodological problems in
the political science and historiography of the League of Nations,
1919-30's; asserts the need for historians to consider the successes
and failures of the League in the context of international social and
political change.

2953. Sogrin, V. V. SOVREMENNAIA AMERIKANSKAIA
"RADIKAL'NAIA" ISTORIOGRAFIIA O VNUTRENNEI I
VNESHNEI POLITIKE SSHA XX V. [Modern American radical
historiography about 20th-century US domestic and foreign
policies]. *Novaia i Noveishaia Istoriia [USSR] 1983 (3): 66-78.*
Analyzes modern American radical historiography on US home and
foreign policy in the 20th century, discloses its continuity in the
American non-Marxist historiography, and the influence other critical trends in present-day Western philosophy and sociology exert
on it. Examines views of radical historians on the working-class
movement, the role of the bourgeoisie and the state in socioeconomic development, and the character and evolution of imperialist
foreign policy.   J/S

2954. Solon, Paul D.; Bailey, Donald A. (commentary). FROM
THE JUSTICE OF WAR TO THE LAW OF CONQUEST: AN
ESSAY ON THE RELATIONSHIP BETWEEN INTERNATION-
AL LAW AND FRENCH HISTORIOGRAPHY IN THE SEVEN-
TEENTH CENTURY. *Pro. of the Ann. Meeting of the Western
Soc. for French Hist. 1980 8: 104-111.* French claims to the Duchy
of Lorraine in the 1630's and 1640's were based more on conceptions of international law than on the right of possession by conquest. Royal historiographers and jurists such as Hugo Grotius had
discovered many legal and historical precedents for the doctrine of
inalienability and for the right of a sovereign power to make war
in order to acquire territories to which it had a just claim. Comments, pp. 125-128. Based on documents in the Bibliothèque Nationale and the Bibliothèque de l'Institut and on secondary works;
21 notes.   T. J. Schaeper

2955. Stepanova, O. L. ISTORIKI-"REVIZIONISTY" O VNESH-
NEI POLITIKE SSHA ["Revisionist" historians on the foreign policy of the USA]. *Voprosy Istorii [USSR] 1973 (3): 93-107.* The
article briefly characterizes the "revisionist" trend in contemporary
American historiography (Williams, Kolko, Alperowitz et al.) which
advanced to the fore of American historical science in the past few
years. The author's attention is focused on the theoretical conceptions linked with the history of the US foreign policy. The "revisionist" historians (who are far removed from Marxism) cite
convincing arguments to prove the invariably expansionist character
of America's foreign policy which was chiefly responsible for the
emergence of the cold war. The article also graphically shows that
the "revisionists" theoretically substantiate the need for the USA to
conduct a "balance of strength" policy in present-day conditions.

J

2956. Sukhorukov, S. R. V. I. LENIN I SOVETSKO-
GERMANSKIE OTNOSHENIIA 1917-1922 GG. V OSVESHC-
HENII   SOVREMENNOI   ZAPADNOGERMANSKOI
BURZHUAZNOI ISTORIOGRAFII [V. I. Lenin and Soviet-
German relations, 1917-22, as described in current West German
bourgeois historiography]. *Istoriia SSSR [USSR] 1970 (1): 194-206.*
West German historians are paying increasing attention to Lenin's
contributions to the theory of foreign policy, even while they con-
tinue to distort his ideas and quote his work out of context. This
survey focuses on the work of W. Grottian, J. O. Grezer, T.
Schieder, and some other West German scholars. Many of the historians whose works are considered recognize the treaties of Brest-
Litovsk and Rapallo as successes of Lenin's foreign policy. 70
notes.   S. P. Dunn

2957. Talpeș, Ioan and Ștefan, Marian. "ADEVĂRURI" LIP-SITE DE ADEVĂR [Truth and the absence of it]. *Magazin Istoric [Romania] 1982 16(3): 39-43.* An account of the Munich negotiations in 1938 taken from René Girault's *Munich: Mythes et Realités* (1979) and of a November 1979 discussion of his conclusions. Article to be continued.

2958. Theoharis, Athan G. MCCARTHYISM: A BROADER PERSPECTIVE. *Maryland Hist. 1981 12(2): 1-7.* A historiographical essay urging scholars to avoid simplistic labeling of Cold War scholars. Material unclassified since 1975 reveals that McCarthyism was rooted in institutions of the Executive Branch. Secondary sources, 15 notes. G. O. Gagnon

2959. Thompson, J. A. LORD CECIL AND THE HISTORIANS. *Hist. J. [Great Britain] 1981 24(3): 709-715.* Considers the treatment by historians of Lord Robert Cecil, pacifist president of the League of Nations Union in Great Britain, and suggests that they have ignored or denied the good political sense of Cecil, that he and his colleagues, "idealists of the age of collective security," are in danger of becoming permanently stereotyped as sentimentalist pacifists or even cranks who obstructed the work of the "keep Britain strong" men like Maurice Hankey. The current image of the leaders of the League of Nations Union is a seriously distorted one; they were far more practical than historians allow, and they deserve more sympathetic historical treatment. 36 notes.

2960. Thompson, J. A. WILLIAM APPLEMAN WILLIAMS AND THE "AMERICAN EMPIRE." *J. of Am. Studies [Great Britain] 1973 7(1): 91-104.* Disputes the interpretations of American foreign policy by William Appleman Williams and his "disciples," most notably Walter LaFeber. The views of Williams and his "school" derive from the theoretical framework outlined by Williams in his pioneering 1959 work, *The Tragedy of American Diplomacy* (New York: Dell, 1972) and several more recent writings, especially his *From Colony to Empire: Essays in the History of American Foreign Relations* (New York: Wiley, 1972) and *The Roots of the Modern American Empire: A Study of the Growth and Shaping of Social Consciousness in a Marketplace Society* (New York: Random House, 1970). Central to the interpretations of Williams and his "disciples" is the thesis that the United States has always practiced expansionism and imperialism. Secondary sources; 76 notes. H. T. Lovin

2961. Trachtenberg, Marc. THE SOCIAL INTERPRETATION OF FOREIGN POLICY. *Rev. of Pol. 1978 40(3): 328-350.* A consideration of the theoretical, methodological, and evidence problems in historical and political science studies of 19th- and 20th-century American and European foreign policymaking as a process and its linkage to social and democratic inputs. Secondary sources; 63 notes.

2962. Trachtenberg, Marc. VERSAILLES AFTER SIXTY YEARS. *J. of Contemporary Hist. [Great Britain] 1982 17(3): 487-506.* All the major works in English on the Paris Peace Conference develop the assumption that an altruistic, moderate Wilson was outfoxed by vindictive, cunning European diplomats who sought to punish Germany. Fresh investigation of the documents of the conference reveals many variations and nuances of opinion. Wilson comes through as a vindicator; the British, for trials of war criminals; the French, as vacillators without plain direction. "This then is the result of the politicization of this field of historiography: historical writing on the peace conference has been used as a vehicle for the projection of political values, and as a result our understanding of the period has been seriously distorted." Based on archival sources; 49 notes. M. P. Trauth

2963. Trask, Roger R. UNITED STATES RELATIONS WITH THE MIDDLE EAST IN THE TWENTIETH CENTURY: A DEVELOPING AREA IN HISTORICAL LITERATURE. Haines, Gerald K. and Walker, J. Samuel, ed. *American Foreign Relations: A Historiographical Review* (Westport, Conn.: Greenwood Pr., 1981): 293-309. Surveys the work of American historians concerning American relations with the Middle East from the 1950's to the 1970's. Only since the end of World War II has the Middle East become a major concern in US foreign policy. The emergence of the Middle East as a major arena of cold war conflict, the critical importance of its oil resources, and the Arab-Israeli dispute have forced the region into the headlines and to a certain degree into the nation's historical consciousness. Secondary sources; 38 notes. J. Powell

2964. Trenard, Louis. HISTOIRE POLITIQUE ET HISTOIRE DIPLOMATIQUE [Political history and diplomatic history]. *Information Hist. [France] 1976 38(1): 48-52.* Continued from previous articles. Reviews the following books concerning political history and international relations, 19th-20th centuries: Alain Dufour's *Histoire Politique et Psychologie Historique* (1966); Jean-Baptiste Duroselle's *Personnalités et Sociétés dans la Naissance des Idéologies* (1968); André-Jean Tudesq's *La Presse et l'Événement* (1973); Pierre Renouvin and Jean-Baptiste Duroselle's *Introduction à l'Histoire des Relations Internationales* (1964); and George Livret's "Gaston Zeller et les Relations Internationales: Une Leçon de Méthode et de Critique Historique" in *Bulletin de la Faculté des Lettres de Strasbourg* 1961 (April): 355-370.

2965. Tulard, Jean. METTERNICH ET SES RÉCENTS HISTORIENS [Metternich and his recent historians]. *Re.v de l'Inst. Napoléon [France] 1973 (127): 53-56.* Discusses Henry Kissinger's interpretation of Metternich in *A World Restored* (Boston, 1957), translated into French under the title, *Le chemin de la Paix* (Paris, 1972).

2966. Utkin, A. I. FRANTSUZSKAIA BURZHUAZNAIA ISTORIOGRAFIIA FRANKO-AMERIKANSKIKH OTNOSHENII [Franco-American relations as reflected in French bourgeois historiography]. *Voprosy Istorii [USSR] 1972 (8): 172-176.* Examines Franco-American relations, particularly in 1962-63, when there was both support for, and opposition to, de Gaulle in America. French bourgeois historiography on this problem of Franco-American relations is characterized by certain weaknesses of method. Often real factors are obscured by excessive attention to differences of opinion between individuals. S. J. Talalay

2967. Vinogradov, K. B. "GAMBURGSKAIA SHKOLA" V OBLASTI IZUCHENIIA ISTORII MEZHDUNARODNYKH OTNOSHENII [The Hamburg School on the study of the history of international law]. *Vestnik Leningradskogo U.: Seriia Istorii, Iazyka i Literatury [USSR] 1982 (2): 16-22.* With the general shift to the left in Germany in the 1960's, the works of the Hamburg School, which accepted the Marxist position that economic and class factors should be taken into consideration when examining foreign policy, contributed to the development of a progressive tendency in the study of the German foreign policy, 1870-1918. Unfortunately, their narrow concentration on *Ostpolitik* and their criticism of dogmatic Marxism has hastened the disintegration of the school from the late 1970's. Secondary sources; 18 notes. G. Dombrovski

2968. Walker, J. Samuel. HISTORIANS AND COLD WAR ORIGINS: THE NEW CONSENSUS. Haines, Gerald K. and Walker, J. Samuel, ed. *American Foreign Relations: A Historiographical Review* (Westport, Conn.: Greenwood Pr., 1981): 207-236. Reviews literature on the cold war period in American history, a topic which has provoked much acrimony. The revisionist challenge to traditional interpretations shattered the consensus that had dominated historiography on the cold war in the 1950's and early 1960's. The ensuing controversy often resembled a political debate more than an academic one as partisans exchanged polemics. In recent years, a vast body of writing, based on extensive research in newly opened sources, has produced a new cold war consensus which draws from both traditional and revisionist interpretations to present a more balanced explanation of the beginning of the cold war. Secondary sources; 53 notes. J. Powell

2970. Watt, D. C. RETHINKING THE COLD WAR: A LETTER TO A BRITISH HISTORIAN. *Pol. Q. [Great Britain] 1978 49(4): 446-456.* On the occasion of the opening to research in January 1978 of the British public records of 1947, argues that the Cold War should now be reassessed and redefined in terms of its chronological and geographical origins, and territorial and ideological issues.

2971. Werking, Richard H. THE BOXER INDEMNITY REMISSION AND THE HUNT THESIS. *Diplomatic Hist. 1978 2(1): 103-106.* The indemnity received by the United States in the wake of the Boxer Rebellion was returned to China, which used it to educate Chinese youth in the United States. In 1972, historian Michael Hunt argued that American pressure forced the reluctant Chinese to spend it in that manner. Further study supports Hunt's thesis. Examination of alternate proposals for use of the indemnity reveals that the remission, and all American policy in this incident, was motivated by self-interest rather than altruism. Based on State Department records; 8 notes. T. L. Powers

2972. Widenor, William C. AMERICAN PLANNING FOR THE UNITED NATIONS: HAVE WE BEEN ASKING THE RIGHT QUESTIONS? *Diplomatic Hist. 1982 6(3): 245-265.* Americans greeted the UN with unwarranted enthusiasm; the organization never lived up to expectations. Regarding those expectations, Franklin D. Roosevelt's defenders emphasize his idealism and/or his realism. His critics fault his naivety regarding Russia and the dynamics of international organizations. These interpretations leave questions unanswered. Perhaps we should not search for rationality in an essentially improvisational US foreign policy, particularly one improvised by Roosevelt, a man difficult to understand. Rather, we should examine the effect of domestic political considerations in that Roosevelt reacted to public enthusiasm over the UN by giving it a priority it did not deserve. Historiographical article; 97 notes. T. J. Heston

2973. Wilensky, Norman M. WAS THE COLD WAR NECESSARY? THE REVISIONIST CHALLENGE TO CONSENSUS HISTORY. *Am. Studies [Lawrence, KS] 1972 13(1): 177-187.* Criticizes the "orthodox" interpretation of the Cold War, and surveys the rise of revisionist historians and their critics. Emphasizes how history is used, not the events themselves. Based on secondary sources; 28 notes. J. Andrew

2974. Zaritski, B. E. KONTSEPTSIIA "SILY" V NEMETSKOI BURZHUAZNOI ISTORIOGRAFII [The concept of power in German bourgeois historiography]. *Voprosy Istorii [USSR] 1976 (9): 81-92.* Traces the continuity and specific nature of the concepts of power elaborated and developed in German bourgeois historiography, and in contemporary West German political science. Shows the narrow, limited character of political thinking typical of the entire realistic school with its intrinsic striving to reduce the whole complexity of the processes taking place in the sphere of foreign policy to an abstract power confrontation of states on the international scene. The changes occurring in international relations have had a definite impact on West German historiography and political science. When interpreting the realistic doctrine today, many West German politicians and historians lay particular accent on the need to make a sober appraisal of the actually existing relation of forces. J

2975. Zawitoski, Jean M. REVISIONIST HISTORIANS' COLD WAR VIEWS. *Towson State J. of Int. Affairs 1977 11(2): 99-109.* Assesses US revisionist interpretations of the origins of the Cold War and their importance for subsequent domestic and foreign policy.

2976. Zingg, Paul J. AMERICA AND NORTH AFRICA: A CASE IN UNITED STATES-THIRD WORLD RELATIONS. *Hist. Teacher 1979 12(2): 253-270.* Until recently this has been a neglected area in American-Third World studies. The author surveys the available material from the Barbary war to the present; the historiography of the field is on the "threshold of sophistication and definition." New work needs to be done on economic, cultural, and ideological factors. Note, biblio. L. C. Smith

2977. —. [ORIGINS OF THE COLD WAR]. *Diplomatic Hist. 1983 7(3): 171-204.*
Gaddis, John Lewis. THE EMERGING POST-REVISIONIST SYNTHESIS ON THE ORIGINS OF THE COLD WAR, *pp. 171-190.* The new interpretation emphasizes America's preoccupation with security rather than economic needs while recognizing the use of economic power to gain political ends. Further, it holds that Stalin, while lacking a blueprint for world revolution, contributed significantly to international tensions; it recognizes the existence of an American empire but indicates that other nations willingly joined it; and it acknowledges that the administration occasionally managed public opinion, but that the public was often already anti-Soviet. Further research is needed in many areas, particularly in the field of comparative empire studies.
Gardner, Lloyd C. RESPONSE, *pp. 191-193.* Agrees that American imperialism does not fit the Leninist model, but an examination of what national security entailed demonstrates the significance of economic factors.
Kaplan, Lawrence S. RESPONSE, *pp. 194-197.* Agrees with Gaddis's thesis. NATO and the absence of isolationism are significant research topics.
Kimball, Warren F. RESPONSE, *pp. 198-200.* While Gaddis's paper opens the door to new concepts, it fails to establish that postrevisionism is anything more than orthodoxy plus archives.
Kuniholm, Bruce R. RESPONSE, *pp. 201-204.* Gaddis provides a common framework for an analysis of postwar US policy. His emphasis on the empire concept and the need for bureaucracy studies is particularly important. Papers presented at the annual meeting of the Organization of American Historians, 8 April 1983; 61 notes. T. J. Heston

2978. —. SYMPOSIUM: RESPONSES TO CHARLES S. MAIER, "MARKING TIME: THE HISTORIOGRAPHY OF INTERNATIONAL RELATIONS." *Diplomatic Hist. 1981 5(4): 354-382.*
Hunt, Michael H., *pp. 354-358.* A legitimate concern with the present makes methodological innovations less applicable to diplomatic history than Maier posits. The field needs a conceptual framework which serves the needs of the present while incorporating a broad outlook. A comparative imperial approach may provide such a framework. Historiographical essay; 6 notes.
Iriye, Akira, *pp. 359-361.* Maier's otherwise valid essay neglects the great strides being made in the study of the interwar years, the collective spirit exemplified by the success of SHAFR, and the studies of cultural relationships as opposed to formal diplomacy. Historiographical essay; 2 notes.
LaFeber, Walter F., *pp. 362-364.* Maier's international systems approach is valid only if one accepts the primacy of the United States in that system. Because of that primacy and the uniqueness of the domestic American liberal system, historians should examine the relationships between American society and global empire as well as between the political system and diplomacy. Historiographical essay; 2 notes.
Leffler, Melvyn P., *pp. 365-371.* Reviews the literature of the last decade to show that diplomatic historians have done more than Maier indicates. Following the publication of several seminal articles in the early 1970's, studies of the influence of socioeconomic, ethnocultural, and administrative factors have significantly contributed to our understanding of the development of American foreign policy. Other works have placed American diplomacy in a comprehensive international context. New techniques and methodologies are valuable, but are not panaceas. Historiographical essay; 12 notes.
Schulzinger, Robert D., *pp. 372-376.* Briefly surveys popular and scholarly works of the last decade to show that the study of diplomatic history is neither better nor worse than it was a decade ago. Our pluralistic, almost incoherent approach means we know more than we did, but we also lack a general theme.

Such diversity is healthy; the government's attempt to cover its errors by restricting access to documents is not. Historiographical essay; 6 notes.

Hoff-Wilson, Joan, *pp. 377-382.* Rebuts Maier's thesis that diplomatic history is "marking time." In the last 10 years, organizational historians of the neocorporatist school have begun to apply the methodologies of political science and economics in foreign policy studies. This methodological innovation has led to a new interpretative emphasis in the form of regional, economic, cultural, and multipolar studies. These developments may lead to a new post-Cold War synthesis. Historiographical essay; 8 notes.   T. J. Heston

Wars and Military History

2979. Aleksandrov, V. A. and Stepanov, A. S. BITVA ZA BERLIN V OTSENKE BURZHUAZNYKH ISTORIKOV [The battle for Berlin in the estimate of bourgeois historians]. *Istoriia SSSR [USSR] 1975 (3): 172-183.* The battle of Berlin is considered by Soviet historians and by historians of other Socialist countries to be one of the largest and most decisive operations of World War II. The authors review Western historiography's errors. Most bourgeois authors ignore the Soviet army's operations to conquer Berlin or describe it as insignificant. H. Maule does not even mention it in his *The Great Battles of World War II.* West German author H. Dahms gives it only one page, while US historian R. Athearn simply says that after Hitler's suicide "the Russian army entered Berlin," and M. Hayle gives only one line. There are even some authors, including E. Kuby, who attempt to prove that "there never was a last battle for Berlin." Primary and secondary sources; 56 notes.   L. Kalinowski

2980. Aleksandrov, V. A. GLAVNY TVORETS POBEDY: SOVETSKII SOIUZ [The chief architect of victory: the USSR]. *Voenno-Istoricheskii Zhurnal [USSR] 1976 (5): 13-20.* Analyzes English-language historiography on the Eastern Front in World War II to refute Western attempts to diminish the role of the USSR in the defeat of Germany and Japan.

2981. Allmayer-Beck, Johann Christoph. DIE GESCHICHTE VON ÖSTERREICHS SEEMACHT ALS HISTORIOGRAPHISCHES PROBLEM [The history of Austria's naval power as a historiographic problem]. *Rev. Int. d'Hist. Militaire [France] 1980 (45): 7-21.* Discusses conventional histories of Austria's Imperial Navy and sketches an approach to the theme, stressing the importance of its presentation in conjunction with the overall history of the country. Any survey of naval activities has to consider the various geographical areas of interest. Other important factors are the interaction between navy and army, the activities of the fleet in peace time, and the multinational character of the navy.
                T. Parker

2982. Andō, Hikotarō. NICHIRŌ SENSŌSHI KENKY NO KADAI: SHUTOSHITE NICCH KANKEISHI NO SHITEN KARA [Historical studies of the Russo-Japanese War: from the viewpoint of Sino-Japanese relations]. *Rekishigaku Kenkyū [Japan] 1960 (238): 29-33.* In the essay *Nichirō Sensōshi no Kenkyū* edited by Seizaburō Shinobu and Jiichi Nakayama, the authors contended that the bourgeoisie did not cause the Russo-Japanese War but that the social unrest inherent to the emperor system inevitably motivated it. This does not take into consideration the conflicting interests of the powers in Asia in 1904-05 and the resulting expansion of armaments in Japan. The subsequent rise of capitalism and military strength led to the alliance with Great Britain and the war with Russia.   B. Evans

2983. Apanovych, O. M. ZBROINI SYLY UKRAINY PERSHOI POLOVYNY XVIII ST. V UKRAINSKII I ROSIISKII ISTORIOHRAFII [The military forces of the Ukraine during the 18th century as noted in Ukrainian and Russian historiography]. *Ukrains'kyi Istorychnyi Zhurnal [USSR] 1971 (11): 21-38.*

2984. Arthur, Anthony. THE CASE OF THE DIMINISHED HERO: FREMONT MEETS DEVOTO. *San José Studies 1977 3(2): 96-106.* Account of the sporadic military career, 1830's-90, of John C. Frémont and the treatment which he receives in Bernard DeVoto's 1943 book, *1846: A Year of Decision.*

2985. Babin, A. I. and Helmert, Heinz. FRIEDRICH ENGELS UND DIE MILITÄRISCHE UND KRIEGSGESCHICHTLICHE LITERATUR SEINER ZEIT [Friedrich Engels, the military, and military historiographical literature of his time]. *Militärgeschichte [East Germany] 1974 13(6): 645-657.* Engels's critical comments on contemporary bourgeois military literature and historiography show his great ability, his realization of the value of the military knowledge and the literature contained, and his attempt to demonstrate how it falsified history in favor of the exploiting class. Proceeding from the class view of the proletariat, he discovered that military systems, armed forces, and military leadership depended on the economic and social relations of society. 25 notes.
                H. D. Andrews

2986. Babin, A. I. SOVĚTSKÁ HISTORIOGRAFIE VELKÉ VLASTENECKÉ VÁLKY [Soviet historiography of World War II]. *Hist. a Vojenství [Czechoslovakia] 1977 26(3): 42-55.* Between 1945 and 1975 over 16,000 publications concerning World War II were published in the USSR. The author mentions some of the major histories, encyclopedias, and memoirs. Soviet historians have demonstrated the decisive role of the Red Army and the Soviet Communist Party in the victory over Germany and Japan. They have also duly stressed the participation of the masses and described the share of the individual Soviet republics in the victory. Many publications have been devoted to the Soviet liberation of various states from the fascist yoke. 18 notes.   L. Short

2987. Barabanov, V. V. KRITIKA BURZHUAZNIKH FAL'SIFIKATSII PRI IZUCHENII TEMY "VTORAIA MIROVAIA VOINA I VELIKAIA OTECHESTVENNAIA VOINA SOVETSKOGO SOIUZA" [A criticism of bourgeois falsifications of the themes of study "World War II and the Great Patriotic War of the Soviet Union"]. *Prepodavanie Istorii v Shkole [USSR] 1984 (3): 34-37.* Discusses the bourgeois falsification of the causes of World War II, its class character and the reasons for the victory of the USSR over Germany.

2988. Barbasov, A. KRATKAIA ISTORIOGRAFIIA RUSSKO-TURETSKOI VOINY 1877-1878 GG [Concise historiography of the Russo-Turkish War of 1877-78]. *Voenno-Istoricheskii Zhurnal [USSR] 1978 (1): 98-103.* Reviews document collections, memoirs, and studies published in Russia, 1880's-1970's on the Russo-Turkish War. The most important sources are the 97-volume collection of documents (St. Petersburg, 1898-1911) and the six-volume *Description of the Russo-Turkish War of 1877-1878* (St. Petersburg, 1901-03), compiled by a commission of the Russian General Staff. Valuable information on domestic and foreign affairs is contained in the diaries of the Minister of War, Dmitri Alekseevich Miliutin (1816-1912). Noteworthy among Soviet studies are V. Belolipetski and A. Kolenkovski's *Russko-turetskaia voina 1877-1878 gg.* [Russo-Turkish War of 1877-78] (Moscow: Voenizdat, 1939) and the joint Soviet-Bulgarian document collection *Osvobozhdenie Bolgarii ot turetskogo iga* [Liberation of Bulgaria from the Turkish yoke] 3 vols, (Moscow: Nauka, 1964). 35 notes.
                N. Frenkley

2989. Barbasov, A. LITERATURA PO VOENNOI ISTORII BOLGARII [Literature on Bulgarian military history]. *Voenno-Istoricheskii Zhurnal [USSR] 1971 (9): 104-109.* Discusses the writing of Bulgaria's military history from the 14th century, especially the fight for freedom from Turkey, 1877-78.

2990. Baumgart, Winfried. PROBLEME DER KRIMKRIEGFORSCHUNG [Problems of Crimean War research]. *Jahrbücher für Geschichte Osteuropas [West Germany] 1971 19(1): 49-109, (2): 243-264, (3): 371-400.* Surveys recent historiography of the Crimean War, focusing on the relations between the belligerents, the attitudes of neutrals, and public opinion.
                G. E. Pergl/S

2991. Beaumont, Roger A. COMMAND METHOD: A GAP IN MILITARY HISTORIOGRAPHY. *Naval War Coll. Rev. 1979 31(3): 61-74.* Military histories tend to avoid analyzing principles of military command and their consequences, 20th century.   J/S

2992. Beeler, John. THE STATE OF THE ART—RECENT SCHOLARSHIP IN LATE MEDIEVAL AND EARLY MODERN MILITARY HISTORY. *Military Affairs 1983 47(4): 193-195.* Survey of recent scholarship on Western European military history, ca. 1300-1600. During this period official records provide a picture of emerging Western European military structures. Increasingly, military historians are turning to the interreaction between warfare and society as a whole.   A. M. Osur

2993. Beeler, John. THE STATE OF THE ART—RECENT SCHOLARSHIP IN LATE MEDIEVAL AND EARLY MODERN MILITARY HISTORY. *Military Affairs 1983 47(3): 141-143.* Review of recent military scholarship on the late medieval and early modern periods. While, "Drum and Trumpet" history continues to be written, military historians are turning to the interaction between warfare and society as a whole.   A. M. Osur

2994. Benjamin, Thomas. RECENT HISTORIOGRAPHY OF THE ORIGINS OF THE MEXICAN WAR. *New Mexico Hist. Rev. 1979 54(3): 169-181.* Surveys the continuing trends and new interpretations since the mid-1960's. Three basic interpretations are discussed, including the Whig thesis, which held that President James K. Polk (1795-1849) was responsible for the war, and the Democratic thesis, which maintained that Mexico was to blame. A third group of studies, which transcends the Whig-Democratic argument, is more evenhanded and significantly improves the quality of Mexican War historiography. A closer look at the origins of the Mexican War is essential to the study of American expansionism and of Mexican and Hispanic-American politics and national character. 48 notes.   P. L. McLaughlin

2995. Bet, G. AKTUAL'NYE PROBLEMY VOENNOI ISTORII NA STRANITSAKH ZHURNALA "MILITERGESHIKHTE" [Topical problems of military history in the journal *Militärgeschichte*]. *Voenno-Istoricheskii Zhurnal [USSR] 1976 (11): 70-75.*

2996. Bidwell, Shelford. WINGATE AND THE OFFICIAL HISTORIANS: AN ALTERNATIVE VIEW. *J. of Contemporary Hist. [Great Britain] 1980 15(2): 245-256.* Acting Major General Orde Wingate took command in Southeast Asia on 25 November 1943. He functioned in that capacity for hardly six months and controlled operations for only twenty days, during which he led two "Chindit" campaigns into Burma, in the second of which he was killed. His main goal was to facilitate Stilwell's Chinese army by operating on the communications of the Japanese facing him. His unorthodox, guerrilla measures were criticized in the official British history, *The War against Japan,* vol. 3. Sir Robert Thompson and Brigadier Peter W. Mead tried to defend him. If Wingate were not the great commander they deem him, he was "certainly one of those bizarre nonconformists who emerge, all too rarely, from the orderly ranks of military establishments and stir them up, much to their benefit." Based on published sources; 11 notes.   M. P. Trauth

2997. Blank, A. S. NIURNBERGSKII PROTSESS I REAKTSIONNAIA ZAPADNOGERMANSKAIA ISTORIOGRAFIIA (K 25-LETIIU OKONCHANIIA NIURNBERGSKOGO PROTSESSA) [The Nuremberg trials and reactionary West German historiography: on the 25th anniversary of the end of the Nuremberg trials]. *Novaia i Noveishaia Istoriia [USSR] 1971 (5): 28-38.* Condemns attempts in West Germany to distort, conceal or reject the verdict of the Nuremberg War Crimes Trial. Such attempts, whether made by professional historians or by ex-Nazis, claim that war was forced on Hitler, that the concentration camps were not as terrible as Allied bombing, and that Nazism was a necessary phase in the development of the German nation. Similar interpretations can occasionally be found in American books. 46 notes.   C. I. P. Ferdinand

2998. Bois, Jean-Pierre. LES ANCIENS SOLDATS DE 1715 À 1815: PROBLEMES ET MÉTHODES [Military veterans, 1715-1815: problems and methods]. *Rev. Hist. [France] 1981 265(1): 81-102.* Research and writing about the history of French war veterans in society is seldom done. It is extremely difficult to devise research strategies, especially for the period 1715-1815, but a new field of research can be developed by combining personal accounts, local history, and government documents. Specific approaches are recommended.   G. H. Davis

2999. Bonadeo, Alfredo. GUERRA, CONQUISTA E RINASCIMENTO NELLA STORIOGRAFIA [War, conquest, and the Renaissance in historiography]. *Pensiero Pol. [Italy] 1983 16(2): 157-188.* The feeble resistance of the Italian states to French invasion in late 15th and early 16th century has been ascribed by historians to inferior technology and organization, poor training, and corruption of the fighting spirit. The author examines these charges and concludes that the reason for the lack of resistance was a moral crisis resulting from generations of violence, which had induced in the Italians a scepticism concerning the results of warfare even in the cause of independence. 102 notes.   J. V. Coutinho

3000. Boog, Horst. GERMANIC AIR FORCES AND THE HISTORIOGRAPHY OF THE AIR WAR. *Aerospace Hist. 1984 31(1): 38-42.* Describes the extent of available archival records of the German air force, the work of the Office of Military History in West Germany, and the principal published studies on the German air arm and identifies topics in need of further examination. The latter include the lives of the major personalities associated with the German air force, the development of air doctrine, the history of civil aviation in Germany, the history of German air armament during World War II, and the story of the Reich air defense. 2 illus.   J. K. Ohl

3001. Borisov, A. NOVEISHAIA ANGLO-AMERIKANSKAIA BURZHUAZNAIA ISTORIOGRAFIIA VELIKOI OTECHESTVENNOI VOINY SOVETSKOGO SOIUZA (1941-1945) [Recent British and American bourgeois historiography of the Soviet Union's Great Patriotic War, 1941-45]. *Istoriia SSSR [USSR] 1975 (3): 154-172.* The main features of British and American works on World War II, just as in the past, are disregard of historical data, subjectivity, the subjugation of historical sciences to political conjuncture, and conscious falsification of the war events. These shortcomings are largely based on the fact that reactionary bourgeois historians were greatly disturbed by the outcome of World War II, i.e., Russia strengthened itself to compete with the United States, Europe was divided, and a Communist government was established in China. 82 notes.   L. Kalinowski

3002. Borisov, A. THE TRUTH AND FALSEHOOD ABOUT THE GREAT PATRIOTIC WAR. *Int. Affairs [USSR] 1975 (5): 89-98.* Discusses alleged inaccuracies in American and British historiography of the USSR's role in the defeat of Germany and fascism in World War II, including aspects of military strategy.

3003. Boros, Zsuzsa. A VICHY KORSZAK ÚJABB FRANCIA TÖRTÉNETE IRODALMÁRÓL [Recent historical studies of the Vichy period]. *Történelmi Szemle [Hungary] 1971 14(3-4): 546-554.* An analysis of French historiography of the Vichy regime, including the collection published by the *Revue de la Deuxième Guerre Mondiale,* which is described as insufficient and one-sided. Only the relationship between Germany and France, and the political submissiveness of the Vichy regime have been well studied. However, the social and political basis of the Vichy regime is still not understood; previous studies have been hampered by the lack of primary sources and by postwar politics. 24 notes.   H. Szamuely

3004. Bracher, Karl Dietrich. ZEITGESCHICHTE IM WANDEL DER INTERPRETATIONEN: ZUR NEUAUSGABE VON K. D. ERDMANN, *DIE ZEIT DER WELTKRIEGE* [Contemporary history in the fluctuation of interpretation: on the new edition of K. D. Erdmann's *The Time of the World Wars*]. *Hist. Zeitschrift [West Germany] 1977 225(3): 635-655.* Combines the author's thoughts on forces affecting interpretation of contemporary history and a review of Karl Dietrich Erdmann's *Die Zeit der Weltkriege,* which is the fourth volume of the ninth edition of the *Handbuch der deutschen Geschichte* (Gebhardt) (Stuttgart: Klett, 1976).

G. H. Davis

3005. Bregman, Alexander. THE SOVIET VERSION OF WORLD WAR II. *Military R. 1963 43(11): 23-34.* Reviews two recent histories of World War II—G. Devorin's *The Second World War* and the collectively authored *The Second World War, 1939-1945*—to illustrate that USSR historians are methodically distorting history to downgrade the West.

3006. Bridge, T. D. READING AFTER 40 YEARS. *Army Q. and Defence J. [Great Britain] 1981 111(4): 448-451.* Surveys 22 books on World War II, with special attention to their worth to the military historian.

3007. Broucek, Peter. MILITÄRHISTORIOGRAPHISCHES NACHBEBEN DES FELDZUGSJAHRES 1859 [The aftershocks of the campaign of 1859 in military historiography]. *Mitteilungen des Österreichischen Staatsarchivs [Austria] 1978 31: 283-297.* Austria's defeat at the hands of the French and Piedmontese in 1859 had not only severe repercussions in the realm of politics, but also in that of military affairs. Pamphlets and other publications soon appeared examining the causes for the Austrian setbacks: poor training of cadets, poor pay, and poor leadership, shown in the lack of aggressiveness and the breaking off of battle at Magenta while victory was still possible. The Austrian military general staff learned little, however, and tasted defeat again in the Seven Weeks War of 1866. Even this did not shake the Habsburg Empire's general staff, which continued to delude itself, though some leading figures were more honest. 69 notes.

J. C. Billigmeier

3008. Bruegel, J. W. et al. REMARKS ON THE ROUNDTABLE "MUNICH FROM THE CZECH PERSPECTIVE." *East Central Europe 1983 10(1-2): 158-164.* A discussion by specialists on the Munich capitulation to Hitler in 1938, which was printed in *East Central Europe* 1983 8(1-2): 62-96. J. W. Bruegel writes that he is in general agreement with the views expressed, but raises numerous objections, especially to Radomír Luža's views. Bruegel states, for example, that Luža cannot be taken seriously when he asserts that the Czech military leaders were ready to defend the country. Luža refutes Bruegel's criticisms in detail, noting his opponent's allegations, which cannot be taken seriously.

R. V. Layton

3009. Brühl, Reinhard. A NÉMET DEMOKRATIKUS KÖZTÁRSASÁG NEMZETI NÉPHADSEREGÉBEN FOLYÓ HADTÖRTÉNELMI KUTATÁSOK IDŐSZERŰ KÉRDÉSEIRŐL [Current problems of military-historical research undertaken by the National People's Army of East Germany]. *Hadtörténelmi Közlemények [Hungary] 1978 25(2): 175-193.* Studies questions raised by the East German army's research into military history, 1945-60. Discusses the historians' ideological and theoretical problems, and asserts that researchers consider the Marxist-Leninist classics to be the model of military-historical science. Secondary sources; 22 notes.

G. and N. H. Foxcroft/S

3010. Brühl, Reinhard. SCHARNHORST UND DIE ERFAHRUNGEN DER GESCHICHTE [Scharnhorst and the experiences of history]. *Militärgeschichte [East Germany] 1983 22(3): 290-298.* Reprinted from *Revue Internationale d'Histoire Militaire.* For 40 years, from age 18 on, Gerhard von Scharnhorst concerned himself with the history of war. He received fundamental impetus from analysis of the wars of the French Revolution. He began to search for the connections among war, armed forces, and society and discovered them. Scharnhorst's perception that the development of military organization depended on progress in social relationships was the driving force for the actions of the great military reformer. Illus., 41 notes.

J/T (H. D. Andrews)

3011. Brühl, Reinhard. SOZIALISTISCHER PATRIOTISMUS UND PROLETARISCHER INTERNATIONALISMUS IN DER MILITÄRGESCHICHTSSCHREIBUNG DER DDR [Socialist patriotism and proletarian internationalism in the military historiography of East Germany]. *Militärgeschichte [East Germany] 1982*

21(3): 276-281. Proceeds from the basic ideological position of a Marxist-Leninist military historian of East Germany to the dialectic of socialist patriotism and internationalism. Explains the essential aspects according to which this problem is considered in research: the concrete historical, Party-based scholarly investigation of patriotic and international modes of behavior in history; the regular inseparable reciprocal connection of both in the military history of East Germany; and the controversy with bourgeois-reactionary views on this issue that aim at a cultivation of nationalist tendencies. 4 notes.

J/T (H. D. Andrews)

3012. Cain, Marvin R. THE MILITARY MEMOIR AS CRITICAL HISTORY: THE CASE OF JAMES M. GAVIN. *Military Affairs 1980 44(4): 177-180. On to Berlin,* the memoir of General James M. Gavin, pioneer airborne commander, is both an account of combat experiences and an analysis of leadership and strategy in World War II. Gavin's memoirs appear to be in the traditional military mode, but also have several characteristics of the new military history. Gavin discusses strategic policymaking, makes uncompromising evaluations, and exhibits a soldier's grasp of war and the perception of men who fight it. These memoirs are unrivalled, raising questions about major events of World War II and suggesting the need for a serious reappraisal of military memoirs as historical sources. Primary sources; bibliographical essay.

A. M. Osur

3013. Cairns, John C. SOME RECENT HISTORIANS AND THE "STRANGE DEFEAT" OF 1940. *J. of Modern Hist. 1974 46(1): 60-85.* A critical examination of all the major studies of France's 1940 defeat and withdrawal from the war, reveals that major inadequacies stemmed from the failure 1) to read the evidence at hand, 2) to correlate the political, social, economic, and military aspects of the problem and to relate them to each other, and 3) to think outside the stereotypes and even caricatures of the time itself. Any real understanding of what happened thus still eludes us. 90 notes.

R. V. Ritter

3014. Caldwell, Frank C. EVERY MARINE AN HISTORIAN. *Marine Corps Gazette 1966 50(3): 33-38.* Reviews the work of the Marine Corps Historical Branch since World War II.

3015. Capriata, Manlio. IL MOSAICO DELLA STORIOGRAFIA MILITARE [The mosaic of military historiography]. *Riv. Militare [Italy] 1969 25(5): 627-632.* A transcript of part of General Manlio Capriata's opening lecture at a conference on military history held in Rome, 17-19 March 1969.

3016. Castellanos, Rafael Ramón. RUFINO BLANCO FOMBONA Y EL SESQUICENTENARIO DE LA BATALLA DE AYACUCHO [Rufino Blanco Fombona and the sesquicentennial of the battle of Ayacucho]. *Bol. de la Acad. Nac. de la Hist. [Venezuela] 1974 57(228): 880-888.* After a brief study of Blanco Fombona's (1874-1944) historiographical work, the author summarizes 63 works related to the battle of Ayacucho which had been studied by Blanco Fombona. Brief notes on contents. Biblio.

M. C. F. (IHE 94088)

3017. Căzănișteanu, Constantin. QUELQUES CONSIDÉRATIONS SUR LA RESPONSABILITÉ DE L'ALLEMAGNE HITLÉRIENNE DANS LE DÉCLENCHEMENT DE LA SECONDE GUERRE MONDIALE [A few considerations on German responsibility for the outbreak of World War II]. *Rev. Roumaine d'Hist. [Romania] 1972 11(1): 125-135.* A revisionist study of the origins of World War II, deemphasizing the responsibility of Adolf Hitler as the principal instigator and pointing to other causes, such as the unequal development of capitalist governments and internal contradictions in capitalist society. Traces the development of Germany's foreign policy, stressing the importance of southeastern Europe in the plan of overall conquest. Romania was among the first countries to feel and react against German pressure. Based on Communist Party archives in Bucharest and secondary sources; 25 notes.

S. Sevilla

3018. Chabert, Henry. A POSSIBLE HISTORICAL MISTAKE: THE CAUSES OF THE ALLIED MILITARY COLLAPSE IN MAY 1940. *Pro. of the Ann. Meeting of the Western Soc. for*

French Hist. 1973 (1): 379-390. The backwardness of the French generals' concepts was not the primary cause of their subsequent defeat. Resistance was not impossible, although the war occurred in the middle of their rearmament program. German and Allied generals employed some of the same tactics the French had been castigated for using. The only logical choice was to enter Belgium. The unexpected suddenness of the German successes meant that "the battle was lost before having been fought because all reinforcements were henceforth bound to arrive too late.... The collapse was really caused by the lack of fighting spirit of a few divisions located side by side at a key point in a crucial moment." Based on primary and secondary material; 48 notes.   L. S. Frey

3019. Chaffee, Wilbur. TWO HYPOTHESES OF SINO-SOVIET RELATIONS AS CONCERNS THE INSTIGATION OF THE KOREAN WAR. J. of Korean Affairs 1976-77 6(3-4): 1-13. Discusses two hypotheses concerning the role of Sino-Soviet relations in the origin of the Korean War. The traditional Cold War hypothesis emphasized Sino-Soviet expansionism and a Communist strategy of world conquest. Another hypothesis emphasized two "conflicting institutional requirements" within the USSR—national security on one hand and friendship with the new Mao regime on the other. Russian security dictated control over buffer zones in the Far East, but friendship with China dictated the abandonment of Russian bases on China's Liaotung Peninsula. Securing a new Russian position in Korea resolved the conflict. The second hypothesis accounts more satisfactorily for the reality of Sino-Soviet tension and the Chinese intervention in the Korean War. Based on English-language secondary sources; 39 notes.   D. M. Bishop

3020. Cherednychenko, V. P. and Troshchyns'kyi, V. P. NESPROMOZHNIST' BURZHUAZNONATSIONALISTYCHNYKH FAL'SYFIKATSII ISTORII DRUHOI SVITOVOI VIINY [The failure of bourgeois nationalists' falsifications of the history of World War II]. Ukrains'kyi Istorychnyi Zhurnal [USSR] 1981 (12): 89-99. The history of World War II has an important place in the present international ideological struggle, and the majority of historians in the United States, Britain, and in other imperialist states scrupulously support false official bourgeois versions of that history. They try to besmirch the peaceful foreign policy of the USSR and thus to justify military preparation in the West. The authors critize materials on the war published by Ukrainian nationalist writers and comment on the activities of Ukrainian bourgeoise nationalists during the war. Based on Communist Party documents and other primary and secondary sources; 23 notes.
I. Krushelnyckyj

3021. Cieślak, Tadeusz. POLSKO-NORWESKIE POWIĄZANIA W WALCE Z HITLERYZMEM [Polish-Norwegian associations in the common front against Nazism]. Przegląd Zachodni [Poland] 1968 24(3): 175-178. Surveys literature on aspects of collaboration between Poles and Norwegians during World War II.

3022. Ciociltan, V. et al. LA SECONDE GUERRE MONDIALE DANS L'HISTORIOGRAPHIE ROUMAINE [World War II in Romanian historiography]. Rev. Roumaine d'Hist. [Romania] 1974 13(4): 647-664. In both general and specific areas of Romanian research on World War II during the past 30 years, there has been an effort to conform historical writing to the scientific Marxist-Leninist thematic and conclusionary structures which older traditional bourgeois historians have ignored. 110 notes.
G. J. Bobango

3023. Cochran, Alexander S., Jr. "MAGIC," "ULTRA," AND THE SECOND WORLD WAR: LITERATURE, SOURCES, AND OUTLOOK. Military Affairs 1982 46(2): 88-92. Bibliographic essay assesses how American and British scholars have risen to the challenge of using the files concerning the successful codebreaking operation against the Germans and Japanese during World War II; examines the literature and criticism, discusses the sources themselves, and offers some tentative remarks about the present situa-

tion and how historians should respond. The revision of World War II historiography to include Magic and Ultra has yet to progress past the initial stage of superficial amazement. 16 notes.
A. M. Osur

3024. Coffman, Edward M. THE UNITED STATES: THE SOCIAL HISTORY OF THE MILITARY TO 1940. Trends in Hist. 1981 2(2): 101-112. Reviews books and articles that discuss the meaning, definition, and interest in military history in America, and focuses on primary and secondary sources for research that reveal the social history of the military before 1940.

3025. Cole, C. Robert. A. J. P. TAYLOR AND THE ORIGINS OF THE SECOND WORLD WAR. Parker, Harold T., ed. Problems in European History, (Durham, N.C.: Moore Publ., 1979): 267-282. A. J. P. Taylor's The Origins of the Second War (1961), represented a rejection of the "Nuremberg Thesis," i.e., of the notion that Hitler was personally responsible for the war and that consequently the governments of Western Europe and the German people were both substantially innocent and could present a morally unassailable front against a Soviet threat much analogous to the former Nazi one. Taylor saw World War II as in the long run inevitable thanks to Versailles and in detail the result of accidents and blunders in which all were more or less equally at fault. F. H. Hinsley accused Taylor of ignoring the role of long-range plans and of conscious choice between available alternatives, and a host of critics found his thesis morally unacceptable. Some of his ideas have been supported by subsequent scholarship. Refs.
L. W. Van Wyk

3026. Collotti, Enzo. L'OCCUPATION ALLEMANDE, LA RÉSISTANCE, LES ALLIÉS: ESSAI D'HISTORIOGRAPHIE [The German occupation, the resistance, the Allies: historiographical essay]. Rev. d'Hist. de la Deuxieme Guerre Mondiale [France] 1973 23(92): 21-36. Since the 1959 colloquium on Italian resistance in World War II, a number of significant works have been published on the German military occupation, the politics and activities of resistance, and the Allied response to the resistance. The establishment of special research institutes and the opening of archival collections have been especially helpful. 42 notes.
G. H. Davis

3027. Constantiniu, Florin. CONSIDERAŢII PRIVIND ISTORIOGRAFIA PARTICIPĂRII ROMÂNIEI LA RĂZBOIUL ANTIHITLERIST [Remarks on the historiography of Romania's participation in the antifascist war]. Rev. de Istorie [Romania] 1975 28(5): 647-655. Notes the importance of the studies devoted to the antifascist armed uprising (August 1944) and the decisive part of the insurrection in destroying the German military dispositions in Southeastern Europe during World War II.   RSA (12:1293)

3028. Cook, Charles O.; Friguglietti, James (commentary). HISTORY, LITERATURE, AND THE FRANCO-PRUSSIAN WAR: AN INTERDISCIPLINARY METHODOLOGY. Pro. of the Ann. Meeting of the Western Soc. for French Hist. 1980 8: 11-19. Compares accounts of the Franco-Prussian War in Emile Zola's The Downfall and Michael Howard's The Franco-Prussian War (1969). Comments pp. 20-21. 24 notes.   T. J. Schaeper

3029. Cookson, J. E. THE SOCIAL IMPACT OF WORLD WAR TWO. Hist. News [New Zealand] 1981 (42): 1-6. Discusses the recent shift from the study of military history to the study of war and society, or the effects of war on social organization, focusing on the social impact of World War II on Great Britain, Germany, and Russia.

3030. Cooper, John Milton, Jr. WOODROW WILSON THROUGH ALIEN EYES. Reviews in Am. Hist. 1975 3(3): 359-364. Review article prompted by Patrick Devlin's Too Proud to Fight: Woodrow Wilson's Neutrality (New York: Oxford U. Pr., 1974); places the book within historiographical context, outlines the book's content, and evaluates the book's character sketch of Wilson and its treatment of the neutrality issue.

3031. Corvisier, André. ASPECTS DIVERS DE L'HISTOIRE MILITAIRE [Various aspects of military history]. *R. d'Hist. Moderne et Contemporaine [France] 1973 20(1): 1-9.* Henri Contamine was the only researcher in the field of military history during the interwar period. The 1940 defeat generated a revival of study in military circles, and Marc Bloch's *L' étrange défaite* (1946) and Émile G. Leonard's *La question sociale dan l'armée française au 18eme siècle* (1958) marked the revival of university interest. Around 1950 the administrative archives of the War Archives were opened to researchers and data processing was adopted by the Ministry of War. Researchers began to submit theses on the army or military affairs, and it was generally realized that the War Archives were a rich source of social information. 13 notes.

K. A. Harvey

3032. Covaci, Maria. LA STORIOGRAFIA ROMENA SULLA SECONDA GUERRA MONDIALE [Romanian historiography on World War II]. *La Seconda Guerra Mondiale nella Prospettiva Storica a Trent'Anni dall'Epilogo* (Como: Casa Editrice Pietro Cairoli, 1977): 327-347. In general, Romanian historiography pinpoints the origins of World War II in the ever-increasing contradictions between the main imperialist powers; contradictions that were rooted in the dichotomies so characteristic of the interwar period: fascism and democracy, socialism and imperialism, conservatism and progressivism. These same contradictions contributed to the growth of the liberation movement within Romania, punctuated by the national antifascist insurrection in August 1944. This event marked not only the beginning of Romanian participation in the war against Hitler but also signaled a turn in the contemporary history of the Romanian people. Biblio.

M. T. Wilson

3033. Cruccu, Rinaldo. LA PRESENZA ITALIANA NEL 2° CONFLITTO MONDIALE: GLI STUDI IN ITALIA [Italy in World War II: Italian studies]. *Riv. Militare [Italy] 1976 99(2): 58-64.* Categorizes and considers the numerous Italian studies on Italy's part in World War II, maintaining that more time must elapse before objective evaluations can be made.

3034. Cunningham, Michael J. REVISIONISM AND THE ORIGINS OF WORLD WAR II: A STUDY OF A. J. P. TAYLOR AND HIS CRITICS. *Midwest Q. 1975 17(1): 8-23.* A. J. P. Taylor's *The Origins of the Second World War* (2d ed.; New York: Fawcett Publications, 1961) remains the most formidable challenge to the traditional view that Germany was responsible for the eruption of World War II. Taylor was attacked in the press and scholarly journals for his thesis and basic assumptions. The article evaluates the book and substantive criticisms of it. Secondary sources; biblio.

H. S. Marks

3035. Czaplinski, Marek. SPÓR O GENEZĘ ZBROJEŃ MORSKICH W CZASACH WILHELMINSKICH [The controversy over the origin of naval armament in William II's Germany]. *Przegląd Zachodni [Poland] 1976 32(3): 67-77.* There are varying interpretations in German historiography of the reasons for the 1898 legislation concerning the building of the naval fleet, in which Admiral Alfred von Tirpitz (1849-1930) played the key role. After World War I, Tirpitz was attacked for squandering money on armored ships. Defenders justify the policy in terms of German *Weltpolitik* and a threatening conflict with Britain. Others see it as the result of an inner political compromise based on common interests and as a solution to inner problems. The policy is also interpreted as a realization of the joint personal interests of the Kaiser, Tirpitz and the naval officer corps. 33 notes.

M. K. Montgomery

3036. Dashichev, V. and Sluch, Sergei. REALITY VERSUS PRECONCEPTIONS. *World Marxist R. [Canada] 1975 18(5): 41-47.* "The controversy between bourgeois and Marxist historians centers on the origins of [World War II], the Soviet contribution to the victory over fascism and the causes of Nazi Germany's defeat."

3037. Davidenko, A. ISTORIOGRAFIIA SOVETSKIKH TANKOVYKH VOISK [The historiography of Soviet tank troops]. *Voenno-Istoricheskii Zhurnal [USSR] 1980 22(10): 81-83.* During the period of the Civil War a number of interesting articles were published on the development and deployment of tank troops. In

1921 a military science society was founded and several specialist journals on military affairs appeared, thus increasing the output of literature. The establishment of the first tank units in the 1930's inspired further discussion of tactics and theory. The volume of work rose rapidly during World War II and the pace of publication has been maintained in the post-1945 period. At the present time one of the main tasks is to counter bourgeois authors such as D. Fuller who falsify the role of the Soviet tank forces in the war. Secondary sources; 92 notes.

L. Waters

3038. Davies, Norman. THE GENESIS OF THE POLISH-SOVIET WAR, 1919-20. *European Studies R. [Great Britain] 1975 5(1): 47-67.* Corrects factual errors and revises conflicting interpretations of Soviet and Western scholars concerning Poland's motives and goals as they relate to the events of the Russo-Polish War which began without premeditation in mid-February 1919. Primary and secondary sources; 41 notes.

C. T. Prukop

3039. Delzell, Charles F. THE ITALIAN ANTI-FASCIST RESISTANCE IN RETROSPECT: THREE DECADES OF HISTORIOGRAPHY. *J. of Modern Hist. 1975 47(1): 66-96.* Utilizes the 30th anniversary of the Anti-Fascist insurrection, 25 April 1945, to review the historiography of the Northern Italian Resistance, 1943-45. Evaluates the roles of the Committees of National Liberation (CLNs) as the symbol of the nation's democratic political unity. Shows how the main currents of Italian historiography have responded to particular political exigencies, thereby limiting the opportunities for research. Suggests new research possibilities. Based on postwar historiographical literature; 68 notes.

P. J. Beck/S

3040. DePaoli, Gianfranco E. CENNI SULLA STORIOGRAFIA MILITARE NAPOLEONICA IN ITALIA DAL 1814 AL 1861 [Notes on Napoleonic military historiography in Italy, 1814-61]. *Rassegna Storica del Risorgimento [Italy] 1980 67(4): 403-416.* Beginnng in the 1840's there appeared in Italy an autobiographical literature which expressed the desire to understand the contribution of Italians to the emperor's campaigns and to reflect on the history still to be made. Napoleon's spirit seems to have communicated to Italians something of his indomitable energy, given them a sense of their national identity, and inspired an unrelenting demand for liberty. 72 notes.

J. V. Coutinho

3041. DiLauro, Ferdinando. DUBBI SU LA VERITÀ DELLA STORIA: NOTE STORIOGRAFICHE IN MARGINE AD UN CONVEGNO DI STORIA MILITARE [Doubts on the truth of history: historiographic marginalia to a miltary history conference]. *Riv. Militare [Italy] 1969 25(10): 1215-1231.* Discusses one of the major themes of the conference on military history held in Rome in March 1969, that of the dimension of truth in history.

3042. Doenecke, Justus D. BEYOND POLEMICS: AN HISTORIOGRAPHICAL RE-APPRAISAL OF AMERICAN ENTRY INTO WORLD WAR II. *Hist. Teacher 1979 12(2): 217-251.* Revisionism is a continual process, particularly in this controversial subject area. The earliest works were by historians and writers such as Beard, Barnes, and Tansil who opposed Roosevelt's interventionism. Internationalist historians who followed defended the basic Roosevelt diplomacy. The key work in this school was by Langer and Gleason. Recently economic factors, particularly in regard to Japan, have received much attention, but the study of religious, ethnic, psychological and emotional factors have continued to be neglected. 156 notes.

L. C. Smith

3043. Doerries, Reinhard R. IMPERIAL BERLIN AND WASHINGTON: NEW LIGHT ON GERMANY'S FOREIGN POLICY AND AMERICA'S ENTRY INTO WORLD WAR I. *Central European Hist. 1978 11(1): 23-49.* Outlines the course of US-German relations during World War I, discusses relevant source materials, and evaluates relevant secondary works on the subject. Concludes that the German government "refused to accept mediation from the American president, even when it appeared highly improbable that the war could be won on the battlefield or on the high seas. Waving aside all possibilities of reconciliation, the German government eventually left the United States with no other alternative but to enter the conflict on the side of the Entente." Based largely on original sources. 76 notes.   C. R. Lovin

3044. Donati, Franco. STORIOGRAFIA NAPOLEONICA: IL TERZO CONGRESSO DI STUDI NAPOLEONICI ALL'ISOLA D'ELBA [Napoleonic historiography: the Third Congress of Napoleonic Studies on the Island of Elba]. *Riv. Militare [Italy] 1969 25(7-8): 1015-1023.* Summarizes the main arguments presented at this 1969 congress, and laments the relative lack of scholarly interest in Napoleonic battles.

3045. Dray, W. H. CONCEPTS OF CAUSATION IN A. J. P. TAYLOR'S ACCOUNT OF THE ORIGINS OF THE SECOND WORLD WAR. *Hist. and Theory 1978 17(2): 149-174.* Examines the causal judgments of A. J. P. Taylor and his critics, particularly Hugh Trevor-Roper and F. H. Hinsley, about World War II as an exercise in the historiography of causation. 44 notes.
                                                        D. A. Yanchisin

3046. Dreetz, Dieter. PROBLEME DER DEUTSCHEN NOVEM-BERREVOLUTION 1918/19 IN NEUEREN MILITÄRHISTORISCHEN PUBLIKATIONEN IN DER BRD [Problems of the November Revolution in Germany, 1918-19, in recent military history publications in West Germany]. *Militärgeschichte [East Germany] 1980 19(3): 315-322.* The numerous recent West German works on the November Revolution in growing measure examine questions of military policy, the role of the soldiers' councils, armed forces, and people's defense units, the alliance between the Army High Command and the Council of People's Commissioners, and especially the solution to the military question. The author determines their basic positions and trends as well as their relation to current politics, compares them with Marxist-Leninist historiography, and argues against interpretations that cannot be defended on scholarly grounds. 42 notes.
                                                        J/T (H. D. Andrews)

3047. Dreisziger, N. F. CONTRADICTORY EVIDENCE CONCERNING HUNGARY'S DECLARATION OF WAR ON THE USSR IN JUNE 1941. *Can. Slavonic Papers [Canada] 1977 19(4): 481-488.* An account of the sequence of the reports and historical interpretations of the bombing raid on Kassa (now Košice) on 26 June 1941, which was followed by Hungary's declaration of war on the USSR. Examines especially the "conspiracy" theory which has usually been based on the reports of Ádám Krudy, an officer of the Royal Hungarian Air Force. He claimed that German aircraft conducted the raid. No final assignment of responsibility for the raid is attempted. Reprints Krudy's new report of February 1946. 23 notes.
                                                        R. V. Ritter

3048. Dülffer, Jost. DAVID IRVING, DER WIDERSTAND UND DIE HISTORIKER [David Irving, the Resistance, and the historians]. *Geschichte in Wissenschaft und Unterricht [West Germany] 1979 30(11): 686-690.* During a lecture tour through West Germany, David Irving revealed the views behind his book on Field Marshal Erwin Rommel. Irving sees Rommel as a victim of the members of the German Resistance, who sacrificed him although he was not one of their number. But Rommel was a member of the Resistance in the sense that he no longer followed Hitler and wanted peace. Irving criticizes and even slanders the Resistance, because he does not believe that they preferred defeat to Nazism. He attacks German historians for presenting a false picture of the Third Reich, but it seems that Irving now shares the views of the extreme right wing and serves neo-Nazi aims.
                                                        H. W. Wurster

3049. Dunaeva, N. LEND-LIZ: FAKTY I VYMSLY [Lend-Lease: facts and fiction]. *Voenno-Istoricheskii Zhurnal [USSR] 1977 (3): 102-106.* Accuses bourgeois historians of exaggerating the importance of Lend-Lease to the Soviet war effort, and presents figures to prove that Allied aid was minimal.

3050. Dunaevski, V. A. OTECHESTVENNAIA VOINA 1812 GO-DA NA SEVERO-ZAPADE ROSSII I V PRIBALTIKE: NEKO-TORYE VOPROSY ISTORIOGRAFII; POSTANOVKA TEMY

[The Patriotic War of 1812 in northwest Russia and the Baltics: some problems of historiography; statement of the subject]. *Latvijas PSR Zinātņu Akadēmijas Vēstis [USSR] 1976 (10): 58-66.* Among historians who have studied the Baltic Area of operations during the Napoleonic Wars were the aristocrats A. I. Mikhailovskii-Danilevskii and M. I. Bogdanovich and later the bourgeois scholars A. N. Popov and N. P. Polikarpov. Early publications and documents concerned with the war in the Baltic theater were I. Tikhonov's *The Defeat of the French in the North* ... (1814), and P. I. Shchukin's *Papers Relating to the Patriotic War of 1812* (Moscow, 1905). Military historian V. E. Zhanov argued that Napoleon lacked a definite plan in his campaign against Riga and St. Petersburg. The Russian fleet was instrumental in preventing Napoleon's Marshal MacDonald from laying seige to Riga. Questions remain concerning the existence of a Moscow attack plan early in Napoleon's campaign. 39 notes.   C. Moody

3051. Dupree, Louis. THE FIRST ANGLO-AFGHAN WAR: FOLKLORE AND HISTORY. *Afghanistan [Afghanistan] 1974 26(4): 1-28.* Investigates the retreat and virtual annihilation of the British army from Kabul to Jalalabad, 6-13 January 1842, in order to test the functional relationships between folklore and the history of a well-known event.

3052. Egan, Clifford L. THE ORIGINS OF THE WAR OF 1812: THREE DECADES OF HISTORICAL WRITING. *Military Affairs 1974 38(2): 72-75.* Discusses the historiography (1941-71) of the origins of the War of 1812. Points out some areas for further research. 25 notes.   K. J. Bauer

3053. Ekman, Stig. SVERIGE UNDER ANDRA VÄRLDSKRIGET PRESENTATION AV ETT FORSKNINGS-PROJEKT [Sweden and WWII: a research project]. *Hist. Tidskrift [Sweden] 1970 (3): 301-326.* Describes a research project on Sweden and World War II which began in 1966 and was to be finished in 1974. Thirty historians worked on the project, most of them recruited from the Historical Institute of Sweden. Gives a detailed analysis of problems and techniques.   B. L. Jeppesen

3054. Engel, Evamaria and Looss, Sigrid. DIE SCHLACHT BEI KÖNIGGRÄTZ IN DER WESTDEUTSCHEN IMPERIALISTIC-HEN GESCHICHTSPUBLIZISTIK [The battle at Königgrätz in the West German imperialist historical publications]. *Zeitschrift für Geschichtswissenschaft [East Germany] 1967 15(2): 301-307.* Review article on recent West German historiography on the battle between Prussia and the Habsburg Empire at Königgrätz, 1866.

3055. Ernst, Volker and Schnitter, Helmut. LITERATUR ZUR MILITÄRGESCHICHTE DES DEUTSCHEN BAUERNKRIEGES [Literature on the military history of the German Peasants' War]. *Militärgeschichte [East Germany] 1975 14(6): 724-729.* Contrasts the socialist treatment of this war of 1524-26 as a real revolution with the Western description of it as peasant disturbances.

3056. Evstigneev, E. and Petrov, V. PODVIG DESANTNIKOV EL'TIGENA [The feat of the landing troops at El'tigen]. *Voenno-Istoricheskii Zhurnal [USSR] 1979 (5): 32-36.* The course of military operations that led to the liberation of the Crimea in World War II and the key operation—the landing at El'tigen in November 1943—have been adequately described in Soviet writings on the history of the war. The author concentrates on several aspects of this story which should receive closer attention. 3 notes.
                                                        V. Sobeslavsky

3057. Fahey, J. C. and Holland, Tim. VICHY: SHIELD OR MIS-CALCULATION? *Melbourne Hist. J. [Australia] 1977 12: 26-34.* Though Marshal Henri Philippe Pétain claimed the Vichy regime of France to be "attentiste"—protecting France while waiting for an Allied victory, eight different historians writing on the period indicate that the Vichy government miscalculated in preparing for an Axis victory, 1943.

3058. Fair, John D. POLITICIANS, HISTORIANS, AND THE WAR: A REASSESSMENT OF THE POLITICAL CRISIS OF 1916. *J. of Modern Hist. 1977 49(3).* Rejects Lord Beaverbrook's account of the political crisis of December 1916, contained in his *Politicians and the War* (1928-32). A fresh examination of the subject reveals that Asquith was dislodged by the "pursuance of a course of cautious opportunism by the entire Conservative leadership." Lloyd George was given an opportunity to form a government first and he offered the Conservatives far more than they could have expected to achieve under Asquith. Abstract only.

E. P. Stickney

3059. Falk, Stanley L. GAPS IN THE PUBLISHED HISTORY OF THE AIR FORCE: CHALLENGE FOR HISTORIANS. *Historian 1982 44(4): 453-465.* Discusses sources and themes in the study of air power. The development of military aviation has had a broad and significant effect on 20th-century society. Additional historical studies of military aviation are needed. 5 notes.

R. S. Sliwoski

3060. Ferretti, Valdo. FRA INGHILTERRA E GERMANIA: UN ASPETTO DELLE ORIGINI DELLA SECONDA GUERRA MONDIALE SECONDO LA RECENTE STORIOGRAFIA GIAPPONESE [Between England and Germany: an aspect of the origins of World War II according to recent Japanese historiography]. *Storia Contemporanea [Italy] 1982 13(6): 1029-1044.* Recent work by Japanese historians throws more light on certain theses defended by Western scholars since the early seventies: that throughout the 1930's the main Japanese conversations were with England, that the decision to go to war with the Western powers was taken by Japan only in 1939-40 after the outbreak of the European war, and that Japanese-American relations must be seen in the context of Anglo-Japanese negotiations. 20 notes.

J. V. Coutinho

3061. Firsov, F. I. KUM VUPROSA ZA MARKSISTO-LENINSKATA METODOLOGIA PRI OTSENKATA NA KHARAKTERA NA VTORATA SVETOVNA VOINA [Marxist-Leninist methodology and the assessment of the character of World War II]. *Izvestiia na Inst. po Istoriia na BKP [Bulgaria] 1981 44: 175-188.* Analyzes the war's transition from a capitalist war into an antifascist war after the attack on the USSR of 22 June 1941. From a December 1979 conference in Sofia, Bulgaria. Secondary sources.

3062. Fischer, Fritz. DER STELLENWERT DES ERSTEN WELTKRIEGS IN DER KONTINUITÄTSPROBLEMATIK DER DEUTSCHEN GESCHICHTE [The place of World War I in the problem of continuity in German history]. *Hist. Zeitschrift [West Germany] 1979 229(1): 25-33.* Whether World War I was a clear break in the historical continuity of structures and tendencies of German history depends on analysis of its relationship to the Prussian-German Empire to 1914, the empire during World War I, and lines connecting the empire to the Third Reich. Lines of continuity are impressive, since the Empire was prepared for World War I and responded to it by developing the Hindenburg-Ludendorff dictatorship. The revolutionary movement and the failed peace were caused more by the weakness of the Weimar republic than by discontinuities caused by World War I. The principles of the Nazi state show clear connections with the pre-World War I empire.

G. H. Davis

3063. Förster, Gerhard. DAS DILEMMA DER IMPERIALISTISCHEN MILITÄRGESCHICHTSSCHREIBUNG DER BRD [The dilemma of imperialist military historiography in West Germany]. *Militärgeschichte [East Germany] 1973 12(4): 389-400.* The continuity of the historical tradition derived from fascist ideology was broken in the 1960's in West Germany; even so, the revisionist school around Ulrich de Maizière continued in a predominantly anti-Communist spirit.

3064. Freeman, Joshua. DELIVERING THE GOODS: INDUSTRIAL UNIONISM DURING WORLD WAR II. *Labor Hist. 1978 19(4): 570-593.* Discusses historiography on industrial unionism during World War II which argues that militancy and conservatism coexisted in a dynamic relationship. Unions became dependent on decisions by government agencies, notably the WLB, but the activity of industrial unionists often had a spontaneous,

even reactionary, quality to it. Widespread support for the war effort helps explain the dichotomy. Based on published works; 46 notes.

L. L. Athey

3065. Gárate Córdoba, José María. LO MILITAR EN LA VIDA Y OBRA DE MENÉNDEZ PELAYO [The military in the life and work of Menéndez Pelayo]. *Rev. de Hist. Militar [Spain] 1978 22(44): 151-177.* Discusses the military and its function in the writings of Marcelino Menéndez Pelayo (1856-1912), Spain's noted historian and polemicist. The author details his views on the militia, Spanish wars, atrocities, the army in Spanish society and his correspondence with military writers. Secondary sources; 13 illus., 53 notes.

K. W. Estes

3066. Genri, E. PRIZNANIIA ANGLIISKOGO ISTORIKA [Acknowledgment by a British historian]. *Mirovaia Ekonomika i Mezhdunarodnye Otnosheniia [USSR] 1978 (2): 110-114.* Reviews A. J. P. Taylor's *The Second World War. An Illustrated History* (London, 1975) and notes that Taylor broke from bourgeois historiography by criticizing the Western powers and correctly evaluating the Soviet role in Germany's defeat.

3067. Gilbert, Felix. FROM CLAUSEWITZ TO DELBRÜCK AND HINTZE: ACHIEVEMENTS AND FAILURES OF MILITARY HISTORY. *J. of Strategic Studies [Great Britain] 1980 3(3): 11-20.* Discussion of how military history has been covered, starting with Niccolò Machiavelli's *Art of War* which stressed triumph in battle. Description of battles continued to be popular in the 19th century, although Karl von Clausewitz placed the battle into a larger context and noted that the battles and campaign are subordinated to the purpose of war. Clausewitz's theories raised the importance of military history, and military history is an integral element of political history, or of history in general. Primary sources; 15 notes.

A. M. Osur

3068. Glasgow, Tom, Jr. COMMENTS ON "LIST OF SHIPS IN THE ROYAL NAVY FROM 1539 TO 1588." *Mariner's Mirror [Great Britain] 1975 61(4): 351-354.* Discusses the shipbuilding, naval battles and historiography of Tudor warships, 1539-88.

3069. Glatz, Ferenc. A MÁSODIK VILÁGHÁBORÚS HISTORIÓGRÁFIAI KONFERENCIA FÖBB VITAKÉRDÉSEI [Vital points of debate at the conference on the historiography of World War II]. *Törtenelmi Szemle [Hungary] 1973 16(3-4): 468-487.* A summary of the issues raised in September 1973 at this conference in Budapest, devoted to World War II, and especially the national and territorial problems connected with the hostilities.

3070. Glazunov, N. ZAPADNOGERMANSKAIA VOENNAIA ISTORIOGRAFIIA O ROLI BUNDESVERA V SISTEME NATO [West German military historiography on the role of the Bundeswehr in NATO]. *Voenno-Istoricheskii Zhurnal [USSR] 1973 (11): 99-105.* Discusses the development of West German military historiographical material on NATO and the role of the Bundeswehr, comparing with Soviet and other evaluations.

3071. Glick, Edward Bernard. INFLUENCE OF A HISTORIAN ON HISTORY. *Military Rev. 1972 52(4): 31-34.* American historian Alfred Thayer Mahan, author of *The Influence of Sea-Power on History, 1660-1783* (1890) has been much feted by the British, and has significantly influenced military historiography.

3072. González Salinas, Edmundo. LA GUERRA DEL PACÍFICO, LA HISTORIA MILITAR Y LOS HISTORIADORES [The War of the Pacific, military history, and the historians]. *Rev. Chilena de Hist. y Geografía [Chile] 1977 (145): 173-185.* Discusses the various authors who have studied the military aspects of the War of the Pacific.

3073. Gooch, John. FIGHTING TALK. *History [Great Britain] 1983 68(223): 258-265.* Reviews seven works that demonstrate the uneven quality of modern Western military historiography. Recent advances have been made in the field, especially through a broadening in the range of interests and skills among military historians; but great pitfalls remain, especially the urge to popularize and to seek out specific lessons for the future. 10 notes.

R. P. Sindermann, Jr.

3074. Gordon, Martin. AMERICAN MILITARY HISTORY. *Am. Studies Int. 1976 15(1): 3-16.* Presents a historiographical survey of American military history citing reference works and new interpretations. Three new directions in military history are multidisciplinary, cooperative endeavors, and efforts to consider military history as a continuous process. Undocumented. L. L. Athey

3075. Gorelik, I. M. DOKUMENTAL'NYE PUBLIKATSII PO ISTORII VELIKOI OTECHESTVENNOI VOINY 1941-1945 GODOV [Documents on the history of the Great Patriotic War, 1941-45]. *Istoriia SSSR [USSR] 1980 (3): 119-127.* Surveys official World War II documents published by the Ministry of Defense, the Communist Party, and the Council of Ministers, mostly works devoted to the local history of the individual republics and dealing mainly with the organizational work of the local branch of the Communist Party. Primary sources; 27 notes. C. Pichelin

3076. Gorelik, I. M. and Salekhov, N. I. FAL'SIFIKATSIIA ISTORII VTOROI MIROVOI VOINY V BURZHUAZNOI ISTORICHESKOI LITERATURE [Falsification of World War II history in bourgeois historical literature]. *Prepodavanie Istorii v Shkole [USSR] 1963 18(1): 46-55.* Distortions of truth with regard to the Soviet Union, rampant in American, British, and West German books on World War II, are seen, for instance, J. F. C. Fuller, *The Second World War, 1939-45, a Strategic and Tactical History* (London, 1948); T. Higgins, *Winston Churchill and the Second Front, 1940-1943* (New York, 1957); H. S. Jacobsen, *1939-1945: der Zweite Weltkrieg in Chronik und Dokumenten* (Darmstadt, 1959); the memoirs of Winston Churchill and Field Marshal Montgomery. This trend in misrepresentation was initiated by the US State Department in *Nazi-Soviet Relations, 1939-1941: Documents from the Archives of the German Foreign Office* (Washington, 1948), which makes no mention of the West's policy of appeasement before and after the Munich Pact. 22 notes. N. Frenkley

3077. Gorn, Michael and Gross, Charles J. PUBLISHED AIR FORCE HISTORY: STILL ON THE RUNWAY. *Aerospace Hist. 1984 31(1): 30-37.* Critically describes the major published works on military aeronautical history. Academic historians have largely ignored military aviation, leaving the field wide open to scholarly exploration by others. 3 illus. J. K. Ohl

3078. Groehler, Olaf. [CAUSES OF GERMAN DEFEAT]. MILITÄRISCHE URSACHEN FÜR DIE NIEDERLAGE DES FASCHISTISCHEN DEUTSCHLANDS IM ZWEITEN WELTKRIEG [Military causes for the defeat of fascist Germany in World War II]. *Militärgeschichte [East Germany] 1977 16(4): 443-455.* In summarizing the results of research on the history of World War II already produced by Soviet and East German historians, the author sketches the most important military causes for the defeat of fascist Germany. The Soviet-German front was the chief front of this war, where German imperialism suffered its decisive defeat. The author examines the role and significance of the anti-Hitler coalition and the problem of the two-front war. DIE POLITISCH-MORALISCHE ÜBERLEGENHEIT DER VÖLKER DER ANTIHITLERKOALITION ALS URSACHE FÜR DIE NIEDERLAGE DES FASCHISTISCHEN DEUTSCHLANDS IM ZWEITEN WELTKRIEG [The political and moral superiority of the nations of the anti-Hitler coalition as cause for the defeat of fascist Germany in World War II]. *Militärgeschichte [East Germany] 1977 16(5): 561-571.* Sketches the political causes of German failure, emphasizing the international anti-fascist resistance struggle and the growing foreign policy isolation of the fascist states. Discusses how with the continuation of the war it became increasingly difficult for German monopoly capital to satisfy the growing demand for weapons and equipment with a rapidly diminishing economic base. J/H. D. Andrews

3079. Groeneveld, Eduard G. DUTCH HISTORIOGRAPHY AND THE SECOND WORLD WAR 1945-75. *La Seconda Guerra Mondiale nella prospettiva storica a trent'anni dall'epilogo* (Como: Casa editrice Pietro Cairoli, 1977): 269-287. In the 30 years since the end of World War II Dutch historians have produced an impressive number of books on war and occupation in the Netherlands and on World War II in general. The author gives an overview under such headings as military operations, German and Dutch Nazi policy, social and economic history, resistance movement, and espionage and secret communications.

J. C. Billigmeier

3080. Groeneveld, Eduard G. LA RÉSISTANCE DANS L'HISTORIOGRAPHIE NÉERLANDAISE [The resistance in Dutch historiography]. *Movimento di Liberazione in Italia [Italy] 1966 (85): 88-92.* Immediately following the liberation in 1945, the Netherlands government set up a National Historiographical Institute to collect material on the Dutch resistance to German forces (1940-45) and to promote scholarly research on the subject. Dutch national television produced a series of programs on the resistance, 1960-65. Biblio. C. Collon

3081. Guboglu, Mihail. BIBLIOGRAFIE TURCĂ REFERITOARE LA RĂZBOIUL DIN 1877-1878 [A bibliography of Turkish publications on the war of 1877-78]. *Rev. Arhivelor [Rumania] 1977 39(2): 279-291.* Lists 263 Turkish books and articles on the Russo-Turkish War of 1877-78.

3082. Haas, Gerhart. MILITÄRISCHE ENTSCHEIDUNGS-FINDUNG UND POLITISCHE FÜHRUNG IM FASCHISTISCHEN DEUTSCHLAND [Military decisionmaking and political leadership in fascist Germany]. *Militärgeschichte [East Germany] 1976 15(5): 584-590.* Reprimands bourgeois German historians for their defense of the German military leadership against responsibility for contributing to aggressive imperialist wars in 1914 and 1939. Cites numerous documented examples of German military influence on war policy decisions. Suggests specific areas of research which would further clarify the war responsibility of the military. Based on published documentary collections and secondary works; 22 notes. J. B. Street

3083. Haikio, Martti and Rusi, Alpo. LA FINLANDE DANS LA SECONDE GUERRE MONDIALE: PRINCIPALES CHARACTÉRISTIQUES DES PUBLICATIONS FINNOISES [Finland in the Second World War: principal characteristics of Finnish publications]. *Rev. d'Hist. de la Deuxième Guerre Mondiale [France] 1974 24(93): 79-88.* Most works on Finnish history during the period 1939-45 treat the three Finnish wars (winter war, 1939-40; continuation war, 1941-44; anti-German war, 1944-45) as strictly military-political phenomena. Forty-six of these works are discussed here. However, about a dozen titles concern the wider experience of society. The large historical research project entitled "Finland in the Second World War" will treat the war as a comprehensive experience of the entire Finnish nation.

G. H. Davis

3084. Haines, Gerald K. ROADS TO WAR: UNITED STATES FOREIGN POLICY, 1931-1941. Haines, Gerald K. and Walker, J. Samuel, ed. *American Foreign Relations: A Historiographical Review* (Westport, Conn.: Greenwood Pr., 1981): 159-185. Reviews the historical interpretations and literature relating to US entry into World War II, especially traditionalist, revisionist, realist, and New Left literature. American participation in World War II ended the great debates over America's international political and economic role. The interpretation of this historical event changes over time with the introduction of new source materials. Secondary sources; 89 notes. J. Powell

3085. Hakobian, A. M. HAYRĒNAKAN MĒTS PATĒRAZMI PATMUTYAN BURZHUAKAN KĒGHTSARARNĒRĒ [The bourgeois falsifiers of the history of World War II]. *Patma-Banasirakan Handes. Istoriko-Filologicheskii Zhurnal [USSR] 1975 (2): 26-35.* In their ideological eagerness to attack socialism, Western historians deliberately minimize the role of the USSR and the Red Army in destroying Nazi Germany.

3086. Hale, Frederick A. FRITZ FISCHER AND THE HISTORIOGRAPHY OF WORLD WAR ONE. *Hist. Teacher 1976 9(2): 258-279.* A discussion of the controversial German historian Fritz Fischer and his work on Germany prior to World War I. The author discusses Fischer's thesis of the continuity of German expansionism and the revival of the war-guilt controversy. Fischer's critics and defenders are surveyed. Primary and secondary sources; 66 notes.   P. W. Kennedy

3087. Hass, Gerhart. DIE SCHLACHT BEI MOSKAU: ZU EINIGEN MILITÄRPOLITISCHEN SCHLUSSFOLGERUNGEN DER BÜRGERLICHEN HISTORIOGRAPHIE [The Battle of Moscow: on some military political conclusions of bourgeois historiography]. *Militärgeschichte [East Germany] 1981 20(5): 517-527.* The Battle of Moscow (1942) even in the 1970's, ranks among the unsurmounted problems of imperialist military historiography. With NATO's renewal of confrontation, the defeat of German troops is increasingly traced to failures and operational errors of the German military leadership, especially Hitler. Its lesson is held to be that the creation of military superiority over the USSR is both necessary and possible. 54 notes.   J/T (H. D. Andrews)

3088. Hass, Gerhart. DIE SOWJETISCHE GESCHICHTSSCHREIBUNG ÜBER DEN GROSSEN VATERLÄNDISCHEN KRIEG [Soviet historiography on the Great Patriotic War]. *Militärgeschichte [East Germany] 1982 21(3): 351-363.* Surveys Soviet historiography on World War II. Organization according to basic political and military topics facilitates rapid location of the most important relevant works. The essay is a valuable resource for utilizing a body of historical literature that is already scarcely possible to survey because of its abundance and variety. 132 notes.   J/T (H. D. Andrews)

3089. Hass, Gerhart. NEUE SOWJETISCHE LITERATUR ZUR GESCHICHTE DES ZWEITEN WELTKRIEGES [New Soviet literature on the history of World War II]. *Zeitschrift für Geschichtswissenschaft [East Germany] 1972 20(11): 1422-1433.* Soviet historians, many working with new archival materials, have contributed to a broader understanding of the war, while correcting the many distortions of bourgeois historians. The following are important themes of recent authors: the causes of the initial collapse of the USSR; the role of the Communist Party and the working class; the battles, especially Stalingrad; the Soviet army; the different regions of the USSR and the war effort; and the origins of the Cold War. 42 notes.   J. T. Walker

3090. Hatton, Peter. THE DEBATE ON THE JULY CRISIS CONTINUES: PROFESSOR FISCHER'S SECOND VOLUME AND ITS AFTERMATH. *European Studies Rev. [Great Britain] 1974 4(2): 165-173.* Surveys the contribution of Fritz Fischer to the debate on the origins of World War I, 1911-14, with particular reference to his *Krieg der Illusionen* (1969).

3091. Heggoy, Alf Andrew. FRONTIER FORCE: THE ROMANCE OF THE FOREIGN LEGION. *Indiana Social Studies Quarterly 1984-85 37(3): 18-30.* The historiography of the French Foreign Legion is replete with romantic myths of intrigue and adventure. Since its founding in 1831, the Foreign Legion has served as an elite military force on the frontline of struggles to protect France and her empire.

3092. Heider, Paul. TRUPPENGESCHICHTE ALS BEREICH MILITÄRGESCHICHTLICHER FORSCHUNG UND MILITÄRISCHER TRADITIONSPFLEGE [History of military units as a field of military history research and cultivation of military tradition]. *Militärgeschichte [East Germany] 1983 22(1): 88-96.* Analyzes East Germany's military unit historiography, considers a series of basic theoretical methodological problems, and examines the experiences of fraternal armies. 14 notes.
                                   J/T (H. D. Andrews)

3093. Heimann, Bernhard and Puschel, Manfred. DIE KONZEPTION DES FRANZÖSISCHEN IMPERIALISMUS FÜR DIE KRIEGFÜHRUNG IN INDOCHINA 1953/54 (NAVARRE-PLAN) [The French imperialist concept of the war effort in Indo-

china, 1953-54 (Navarre plan)]. *Militärgeschichte [East Germany] 1984 23(3): 232-250.* The memorandum of General Henri Navarre of 16 June 1953 confirms Marxist military historiography's view of the origin, motivation, and character of local wars unleashed by imperialists after 1945 as well as the close connection between wars conducted by single imperialist powers and the policy of the US-led imperialist military bloc. The memorandum is published as an appendix. Map, 37 notes.   H. D. Andrews

3094. Herbst, Stanisław. L'HISTORIOGRAPHIE MILITAIRE POLONAISE [Polish military historiography]. *R. Internat. d'Hist. Militaire [Belgium] 1969 (28): 397-402.* Provides a brief survey of the tradition of Polish military historiography originating in the Middle Ages and notes the emphasis on particular aspects of military history at different periods. The foundations of methodical military historiography were laid by three civilian members of paramilitary organizations, the historians Wacław Tokarz (1873-1937), Marian Kukiel (b. 1885), and Bronisław Pawłowski (1883-1962). The Institute of Military History has made great contributions. Since 1956 there has been renewed interest in Polish military historical research. Secondary sources; 10 notes.
                                   P. T. Herman

3095. Higham, Robin. THE HISTORIOGRAPHY OF AMERICAN WRITING ON THE SECOND WORLD WAR IN EUROPE, 1945-1975. *La Seconda Guerra Mondiale nella Prospettiva Storica a Trent'Anni dall'Epilogo* (Como: Casa Editrice Pietro Cairoli, 1977): 419-439. Evaluates US historiography of World War II in Europe, including popular novels, magazines, and government and university publications. 171 notes.   M. T. Wilson

3096. Hillgruber, Andreas. TENDENZEN, ERGEBNISSE UND PERSPEKTIVEN DER GEGENWÄRTIGEN HITLER-FORSCHUNG [Tendencies, interpretations, and perspectives: current Hitler research]. *Hist. Zeitschrift [West Germany] 1978 226(3): 600-621.* Recent historical literature on Adolf Hitler falls into four main categories: detailed collections of previously unknown facts; psychohistorical interpretations; revisionist studies based on social history, which concentrate on Hitler's function within the movement and the system; and a goal-oriented interpretation based on Hitler's architectural ideals. 63 notes.   G. H. Davis

3097. Ho Ying-chin. COMMEMORATING THE JULY 7 ANNIVERSARY OF THE OUTBREAK OF THE WAR OF RESISTANCE AGAINST JAPAN AND REFUTING FOR THE SECOND TIME THE FALSE PROPAGANDA OF THE CHINESE COMMUNISTS. *Issues and Studies [Taiwan] 1972 9(1): 54-61.* Continued from a previous article. Chinese Communist historiography on their role in the defeat of Japan in World War II, 1930's-45, is inaccurate and misleading, especially concerning the role of Chiang Kai-shek.

3098. Hoop, Jean-Marie d'. L'ARMÉE FRANÇAISE DE L'ARMISTICE DE 1940 À LA VICTOIRE DE 1945: ORIENTATION BIBLIOGRAPHIQUE [The French army from the 1940 armistice to victory in 1945: a bibliographical orientation]. *Rev. d'Hist. de la Deuxième Guerre Mondiale [France] 1978 28(110): 103-113.* The history of the French army from the armistice of 1940 to the end of World War II is stormy, complex, and still the subject of much argument and passion. The years 1940-42 Free French fought Vichy forces at Dakar, in Syria, and elsewhere. Things were simplified after the Germans overran unoccupied France in November 1942, though the problems of integrating Gaullists, Giraudists, and former Vichyites were formidable. After 1942, sources are more numerous, and the historiography becomes less tendentious. 44 notes.   J. C. Billigmeier

3099. Horváth, Miklós. A MAGYAR HADTÖRTÉNETÍRÁS FEJLŐDÉSE ÉS FELADATAI [The development of Hungarian military historiography and its tasks]. *Hadtörténelmi Közlemények [Hungary] 1966 13(1): 64-93.* Part II. Continued from a previous article. Investigates the results of several tendencies in the development of Hungarian military historiography between 1914 and 1970 and refers to the recurrent problem of Marxist historical science.

3100. Howard, Michael. THE USE AND ABUSE OF MILITARY HISTORY. *Parameters 1981 11(1): 9-14.* Short of going to war, military professionals can gain an understanding of war only through the study of military history. Yet, military history too often paints an unrealistic picture of war. The very organization of war into military history creates an unrealistic order of what is usually a chaotic situation. To ameliorate the problems of military history, the historian must know what changes with time and what stays the same; the historian must study all facets of a war or campaign and try to gain insight into what it was "really" like. The historian must also place war in its political and social context.

L. R. Maxted

3101. Hürten, Heinz. MILITÄRGESCHICHTE IN DEUTSCH-LAND: ZUR GESCHICHTE EINER DISZIPLIN IN DER SPANNUNG VON AKADEMISCHER FREIHEIT UND GESELLSCHAFTLICHEM ANSPRUCH [Military history in Germany: the history of an academic subject and the controversy between academic freedom and social demands]. *Hist. Jahrbuch [West Germany] 1975 95(2): 374-392.* Describes the development of military historiography in Germany. Since the 18th century the German general staff supervised official military historiography. Its aim was to provide sources for strategic studies. Universities did not include military history in their curriculum. After World War I the general staff was abolished and state archives took charge of compiling historical documents. Universities also began to treat military history as a branch of general history. During the Nazi regime the subject was again restricted and adjusted. After 1945 military history as an academic subject was enlarged by including political, economic, and social aspects of the history of wars. Research concentrated on the causes of wars and on means of preventing future wars. 30 notes.

R. Vilums

3102. Iakovlev, N. N. GOD 1939-I: VZGLIAD 40 LET SPUSTIA [The year 1939: looking 40 years backward]. *Voprosy Istorii [USSR] 1979 (8): 3-18.* Drawing on his careful assessment of the latest American and British historiographical works pertaining to the subject discussed in the article, the author attempts to show how the Western balance of power policy at the close of the 1930's encouraged Hitler's aggression and led to the second world war.

J

3103. Iakushevski, A. BITVA POD MUSKVOI I BURZHUAZNYE FAL'SIFIKATORY ISTORII [The battle of Moscow and bourgeois falsifiers of history]. *Voenno-Istoricheskii Zhurnal [USSR] 1971 (12): 92-100.* The battle of Moscow was one of the greatest and most important battles of World War II. Many Western historians either play down or neglect the importance of the battle or the role of the Soviet Army and falsify the reasons for the German defeat.

3104. Iakushevski, A. KRITIKA BURZHUAZNOI ISTORIO-GRAFII STALINGRADSKOI BITVY [The historic significance of the battle of Stalingrad: a critique of bourgeois historiography]. *Novaia i Noveishaia Istoriia [USSR] 1983 (1): 21-39.* Critically analyzes modern bourgeois historiography of Stalingrad, drawing particular attention to concepts and methods used by bourgeois writers to belittle the battle's world historic significance and disparage the achievements of Soviet armed forces and their military art. He also exposes bourgeois historians' tendentious treatment of the course and importance of the battle, as well as causes of German defeat on the southern flank of the Soviet-German front. J/S

3105. Iakushevski, A. KRITIKA BURZHUAZNYKH FAL'SIFIKATSII KURSKOI BITVY [A critique of bourgeois falsification of the battle of Kursk]. *Voenno-Istoricheskii Zhurnal [USSR] 1983 (8): 29-37.* The presentation of the battle of Kursk, 1943, by bourgeois historians such as R. Payne, A. Conarady, and J. Strawson is increasingly geared to the needs of contemporary imperialist policy. The ideologs of imperialism cannot fail to admit the importance of this battle, but their writings attempt to distort the

real reasons for the defeat of the Wehrmacht, to belittle the achievements of the Soviet troops, and to use the history of these events to glorify German militarism. Secondary sources; 32 notes.

G. Dombrovski

3106. Iakushevski, A. OPERATSII SOVETSKOI ARMII V 1944 GODU V OSVESHCHENII BURZHUAZNOI ISTORIOGRAFII [Operations of the Soviet Army in 1944 as interpreted by bourgeois historiography]. *Voenno-Istoricheskii Zhurnal [USSR] 1974 (6): 74-80.* Surveys a number of books by Western historians, accusing them of a biased evaluation of the strategic and tactical art of the Soviet Army and its victories of 1944.

3107. Iakushevski, A. OSVOBODITEL'NAIA MISSIIA SO-VETSKOGO SOIUZA VO VTOROI MIROVOI VOINE (KRITIKA BURZHUAZNYKH VZGLIADOV) [The Soviet Union's liberating mission during World War II: a critique of bourgeois views]. *Novaia i Noveishaia Istoriia [USSR] 1985 (1): 3-21.* Shows how in order to please the ruling circles of the imperialist powers reactionary bourgeois historiography is trying to deny the Soviet Union's decisive contribution to the defeat of Nazi Germany and her satellites. Documents the role of the Soviet people and their army in World War II noting that they "saved mankind from the threat of fascist enslavement."

J

3108. Iakushevski, A. STALINGRADSKAIA BITVA I FAL'SIFIKATORY ISTORII [The Battle of Stalingrad and the falsifiers of history]. *Voenno-Istoricheskii Zhurnal [USSR] 1982 (12): 41-45.* Bourgeois historians such as R. Seth, J. Jukes, F. Mellenthin, and D. Downing, who have written about the Battle of Stalingrad, have produced analyses full of contradictions. On the one hand they have to admit the importance of the Soviet victory at Stalingrad, but on the other they falsify events so as to play down the achievements of Soviet military art and deny the objective factors leading to the collapse of the Wehrmacht on the Volga. The heroes of Stalingrad were not the soldiers of Hitler's army, as J. Pickalkiewicz and other bourgeois historians argue, but the Soviet soldiers and the Soviet people. 19 notes.

G. Dombrovski

3109. Iatsko, B. O. KRYTYKA FAL'SYFIKATSII ZAKHID-NONIMETS'KOIU BURZHUAZNOIU ISTORIOHRAFIIEIU KERIVNOI ROLI PARTII U PARTYZANS'KOMU RUSI V ROKY VELYKOI VITCHYZNIANOI VIINY [A critique of the falsification by West German bourgeois historiography of the leading role of the Party in the partisan movement during the years of the Great Patriotic War]. *Ukrains'kyi Istorychnyi Zhurnal [USSR] 1979 (10): 143-150.* Treatment of the war period in the Ukraine in the works of West German historians is tendentious, anti-Communist and anti-Soviet. Exposes the limited methodology and distortion of facts in the works of various critics, who slander and cast doubt on the close cooperation between Party and people during the war. Sees their motives as trying to weaken people's vigilance against imperialist aggression and discourage them from "useless" socialist struggle. 36 notes.

V. Packer

3110. Iatsko, B. O. VYKRYTTIA UKRAINSKOIU RADIAN-SKOIU ISTORIOHRAFIIEIU BURZHUAZNYKH FALSYFIKAT-SII PARTYZANSKOHO RUKHU NA UKRAINI [The exposure by Ukrainian Soviet historiography of bourgeois falsifications of the partisan movement in the Ukraine]. *Ukrains'kyi Istorychnyi Zhurnal [USSR] 1980 (6): 136-145.* Numerous American and British authors resort to distortions or outright falsifications of the genesis of the World War II partisan movement in the Ukraine, implying that it was of a compulsory character, ordered from above, and that the guerrillas did not care much about Soviet power. Nothing could be further from the truth than assertions of this kind.

3111. Ibragimbeili, Khadzhi Murat and Sheremet, V. I. SOVREMENNAIA TURETSKAIA ISTORIOGRAFIIA VOSTOCH-NOI (KRYMSKOI) VOINY [Contemporary Turkish historiography of the Crimean War]. *Voprosy Istorii [USSR] 1977 (4): 45-57.* Contemporary Turkish historiography reflected the origin and character of the Crimean War of 1853-56, its economic, military, and political results. The authors examine Russo-Turkish relations, illustrating the relations of the Ottoman Empire with the Western Powers, which led to ruinous economic and political consequences for Turkey. Also discloses the role played by the ruling element of Britain and France in unleashing Russo-Turkish military conflicts in the 18th-19th centuries and shows the interconnection between Turkey's entry into the war of 1853-56 and her receipt of loans from Britain and France.　　　　　　　　　　　　　　　　　　　　　　　J

3112. Ionescu, Vasile G. L'HISTORIOGRAPHIE ROUMAINE DE LA DEUXIÈME GUERRE MONDIALE [Romanian historiography of the Second World War]. *R. d'Hist. de la Deuxième Guerre Mondiale [France] 1968 18(70): 69-81.* Surveys various historical journals and books concluding that Romanian historiography of the Second World War in the postwar years has been oriented toward the major topics surrounding the national antifascist uprising of August 1944. Subjects covered include: opposition of the masses to the 1940 Vienna Dictate; exploitation of the country by the German occupying forces; the people's resistance to the military-fascist regime, manifesting itself in strikes, acts of industrial sabotage, and desertion by soldiers; acts of repression and revenge by Antonescu's forces; preparation and planning of the August 1944 uprising; Romania's part in the forces united against Hitler in Hungary and Czechoslovakia; and the political development of Romania in the year 1944-47. Primary and secondary sources; 22 notes.
　　　　　　　　　　　　　　　　　　　　　　　P. T. Herman

3113. Iur'ev, A. KURSKAIA BITVA I IZMYSHLENIIA BURZHUAZNYKH FAL'SIFIKATOROV [The battle of Kursk and the schemes of bourgeois falsifiers]. *Voenno-Istoricheskii Zhurnal [USSR] 1973 (8): 66-72.* Attacks Western interpretations of the significance of the battle of Kursk in 1943 in which the Soviet forces decisively defeated the Germans.

3114. Iur'ev, A. PROTIV BURZHUAZNYKH FAL'SIFIKATOROV ISTORII [The bourgeois falsifiers of history]. *Voenno-Istoricheskii Zhurnal [USSR] 1972 (11): 73-77.* Discusses the interpretations of a number of US and West German military historians on the role of the Stalingrad victory, 1942-43, in the Allied triumph.

3115. Jacobsen, H. A. ZUR GESCHICHTSSCHREIBUNG DES 2. WELTKRIEGES IN DER BUNDESREPUBLIK DEUTSCHLAND: EIN ÜBERBLICK [The historiography of World War II in West Germany: an overview]. *La Seconda Guerra Mondiale nella prospettiva storica a trent'anni dall'epilogo* (Como: Casa editrice Pietro Cairoli, 1977): 243-258. A detailed bibliographical essay on the treatment by West German historians of World War II.
　　　　　　　　　　　　　　　　　　　　　　　J. C. Billigmeier

3116. Jadjak, Emil. AKTUAL'NIE PROBLEMI ISTORIOGRAFII NARODNOGO VOISKA POL'SKOGO [Essential problems of the historiography of the Polish people's army]. *Voenno-Istoricheskii Zhurnal [USSR] 1976 (1): 61-65.*

3117. Jahn, Wolfgang and Rahne, Hermann. ZU DEN TRUPPEN- UND STANDORTGESCHICHTEN DER BUNDESWEHR UND DES BUNDESGRENZSCHUTZES [On the histories of troop units and garrisons of the Bundeswehr and the Bundesgrenzschutz]. *Militärgeschichte [East Germany] 1982 21(1): 62-72.* The authors show that the Bundeswehr command uses the troop unit historiography aimed at the manipulation of soldiers and the rest of the population in the interest of militarist education. Especially in the last 10 years a growth of the values of reactionary bourgeois historical ideology is observable. So troop unit historiography in West Germany currently contributes to the engendering of ideological readiness for aggression. 5 illus., 36 notes.
　　　　　　　　　　　　　　　　　　　　　J/T (H. D. Andrews)

3118. James, Edith. WILSONIAN WARTIME DIPLOMACY: THE SENSE OF THE SEVENTIES. Haines, Gerald K. and Walker, J. Samuel, ed. *American Foreign Relations: A Historiographical Review* (Westport, Conn.: Greenwood Pr., 1981): 115-131. Reviews World War I historiography of the 1970's, especially Woodrow Wilson's wartime diplomacy, tracing many current concerns—intervention, self-determination, economic expansion, economic regulation, government candor, international cooperation—to

their origins in this era. The 1970's scholarship of the period calls for multiarchival research, multinational perspectives, multicausal analysis, and multidimensional explanations. American involvement in World War I can no longer be seen as stemming strictly from political interests or from purely economic motives, but rather from a complex combination of factors involving national security, moral and legal issues, and diplomatic and economic influences. Secondary sources; 45 notes.
　　　　　　　　　　　　　　　　　　　　　　　J. Powell

3119. Jann, Rosemary. CHANGING STYLES IN VICTORIAN MILITARY HISTORY. *Clio 1982 11(2): 155-164.* Contrasts the historiographical styles of Thomas Arnold (1795-1842) and Thomas Carlyle (1795-1882) with that of Samuel Gardiner (1829-1902). When Arnold and Carlyle wrote military history, they were more concerned with being didactic and imaginative than they were with being militarily accurate or complete. A definite shift from the literary treatment of military history was evident in the work of Samuel R. Gardiner, who was more scientific and dispassionate in his treatment of history. 19 notes.
　　　　　　　　　　　　　　　　　　　　　　　T. P. Linkfield

3120. Jelić, Ivan. NAŠA HISTORIOGRAFIJA O NARODNOOSLOBODILAČKOJ BORBI U HRVATSKOJ 1941. GODINE [Our historiography on the national liberation struggle in Croatia in 1941]. *Vojnoistorijski Glasnik [Yugoslavia] 1971 22(1): 9-41.* Reviews various works on events in 1941 and the beginnings of the armed struggle for the liberation of Croatia, noting that this particular year has rarely been the sole subject of research or analytical studies.

3121. Kaehler, Siegfried A. VIER QUELLENKRITISCHE UNTERSUCHUNGEN ZUM KRIEGSENDE 1918 [A reassessment of critical sources on the end of the war, 1918]. *Nachrichten der Akademie der Wissenschaften in Göttingen: Philologisch-Historische Klasse [West Germany] 1960: 424-481.* A revisionist interpretation of Erich Ludendorff's demand for an armistice in September 1918, the civil and military ramifications of the resignation of Wilhelm II, and the origin of the "stab-in-the-back" theory.

3122. Kahn, David. WORLD WAR II HISTORY: THE BIGGEST HOLE. *Military Affairs 1975 39(2): 74-76.* Certain areas of intelligence operations during World War II merit further historical research; these include codebreaking, aerial reconnaissance, prisoners of war, press coverage, attachés and diplomats, ground reconnaissance, spies, and the evaluation of intelligence. 21 notes.
　　　　　　　　　　　　　　　　　　　　　　　A. M. Osur

3123. Kartashev, N. VELIKAIA OTECHESTVENNAIA VOINA SOVETSKOGO SOIUZA V OTSENKAKH ANGLIISKIKH BURZHUAZNIKH ISTORIKOV [The USSR in World War II in the view of English bourgeois historians]. *Voenno-Istoricheskii Zhurnal [USSR] 1972 (4): 98-104.*

3124. Kathe, Heinz. US-HISTORIKER ÜBER DEN PREUSSISCH-DEUTSCHEN MILITARISMUS [American historians on Prussian-German militarism]. *Wissenschaftliche Zeitschrift. Martin-Luther-Universität Halle-Wittenberg. Gesellschafts- und Sprachwissenschaftliche Reihe [East Germany] 1975 24(5): 29-33.* Recent US historiography on Germany in the 19th and 20th centuries denies the close connection between Prussian-German militarism and imperialism.

3125. Kaulisch, Baldur. BRD-LITERATUR ZUR DEUTSCHEN MARINEGESCHICHTE VON 1898 BIS 1918 [West German literature on the history of the German navy between 1898 and 1918]. *Militärgeschichte [East Germany] 1975 14(1): 97-103.* Although West German historians of the German navy between 1898 and 1918 gave up most of the reactionary positions they had held in the early 1960's and could clear up many questions, they still do not confront German naval policy with a general critique of German imperialism.

3126. Keegan, John. THE HISTORIAN AND BATTLE. *Int. Security 1978-79 3(3): 138-149.* Discusses the historiography of battles which took place during World War I and World War II, 1914-45.

3127. Kennett, Lee. MILITARY HISTORY IN FRANCE. *Military Affairs 1978 42(3): 144-146.* Review of research opportunities in French military history. Examines recent publications, gives some practical research suggestions, and lists guides to published and unpublished sources. Recently, the study of French military history has undergone a renaissance, as seen in dissertations, conferences and colloquia, diverse studies, fruitful exchanges between academics and the military, and an impressive number of books. 2 notes. A. M. Osur

3128. Kimball, Jeffrey. THE CAUSES OF WAR AND THE TEACHING OF PEACE HISTORY: KEITH L. NELSON AND SPENCER C. OLIN, JR., *WHY WAR?: IDEOLOGY, THEORY AND HISTORY,* AND MELVIN SMALL, *WAS WAR NECESSARY?: NATIONAL SECURITY AND U.S. ENTRY INTO WAR. Peace and Change 1984 9(4): 69-73.* Both books address fundamental problems in the field of peace research, including the need for more analysis of historical processes rather than unique cases, and the difficulties of writing nonsubjective historiography.

3129. Klein, Fritz. LITERATURBERICHT: NEUERE VERÖFFENTLICHUNGEN DER BRD ZUR GESCHICHTE UND VORGESCHICHTE DES ERSTEN WELTKRIEGES [Review article: recent publications in West Germany on the history and antecedents of the First World War]. *Zeitschrift für Geschichtswissenschaft [East Germany] 1972 20(2): 203-216.* Reviews the following nine books on the origins and course of the First World War, published by West German bourgeois historians in the years 1968-70: Gerhard Ritter, *Staatskunst und Kriegshandwerk: Das Problem des "Militarismus" in Deutschland,* vol. 4, *Die Herrschaft des deutschen Militarismus und die Katastrophe von 1918* (Munich: Ouldenburg, 1968); Klaus Schwabe, *Wissenschaft und Kriegsmoral: Die deutschen Hochschullehrer und die politischen Grundfragen des ersten Weltkrieges* (Göttingen: Musterschmidt Verlag, 1969); F. Wende, *Die Belgische Frage in der deutschen Politik des Ersten Weltkrieges* (Hamburg, 1969); K. Koszyk, *Deutsche Pressepolitik im ersten Weltkrieg* (Düsseldorf: Droste Verlag, 1968); W. Deist, ed., *Militär und Innenpolitik im Weltkrieg, 1914-1918* (Droste Verlag, 1970); Fritz Fischer, *Krieg der Illusionen: Die deutsche Politik von 1911 bis 1914* (Droste Verlag, 1969); D. Stegmann, *Die Erben Bismarks: Parteien und Verbände in der Spätphase des Wilhelminischen Deutschlands, Sammlungspolitik, 1897-1918* (Berlin: Kiepenheuer & Witsch, 1970); K. Wernecke, *Der Wille zur Weltgeltung: Aussenpolitik und Öffentlichkeit im Kaiserreich am Vorabend des Ersten Weltkrieges,* 2d edition (Droste Verlag, 1970); W. G. Mommsen, *Das Zeitalter des Imperialismus* (Frankfurt and Hamburg, 1969). Lacking a firm theoretical basis, they explain German policy in terms of personalities rather than class interests, while failing to perceive that differences among German leaders were tactical rather than a matter of principle. J. T. Walker

3130. Komolova, N. P. DVIZHENIE SOPROTIVLENIIA V ITALII V OSVESHCHENII ITAL'IANSKOI ISTORIOGRAFII [The resistance as viewed by Italian historiography]. *Novaia i Noveishaia Istoriia [USSR] 1985 (2): 67-84.* Examines the ideological struggle in the Italian historiography over the historico-political issues of the resistance. This struggle became particularly acute in the 1960's and 1970's between the Marxist and Left Radical historiography, on the one hand, and Liberal and Right-wing Catholic historiography, on the other. The author shows the contribution made by Marxist historians to the elaboration of problems of the resistance movement in all its complexity and contradictoriness, and criticizes Liberal, neo-Crocean and Right-wing Catholic historiography. J

3131. Konieczny, Alfred. A MÁSODIK VILÁGHÁBORÚ HISTORIOGRÁFIÁJA KÜLFÖLDI KÉNYSZERMUNKÁSOK ELLENÁLLÁSÁRÓL A HARMADIK BIRODALOM HADIGAZDÁLKODÁSÁBAN [The historiography of resistance movements among foreign forced labor in the German economy during World War II]. *Történelmi Szemle [Hungary] 1973 16(3-4): 440-442.* The available evidence, though scarce, indicates that various forms of resistance were practiced by the forced labor put to work in the German war effort.

3132. Könnemann, Erwin. ZU NEUEREN EINSCHATZUNGEN DES MILITARISMUS IN DER WEIMARER REPUBLIK DURCH HISTORIKER DER BRD [On recent assessments of militarism in the Weimar Republic by historians of the Federal Republic of Germany]. *Militärgeschichte [East Germany] 1980 19(4): 461-466.* Evaluates from a Marxist definition of militarism the papers and commentary of a symposium held in May 1977 by the Hochschule der Bundeswehr in Hamburg as published in K. J. Müller and E. Opitz, ed., *Militär und Militarismus in der Weimarer Republik* (Düsseldorf: Droste Verlag, 1978). 7 notes. H. D. Andrews

3133. Korabljev, J. I. A SZOVJET TÖRTÉNETÍRÁS A SZOVJETUNIÓ RÉSZVÉTELÉRŐL A KELET-ÉS DÉL-KELET-EURÓPAI ORSZÁGOK ÚJTÍPUSÚ FEGYVERES ERŐINEK A KIALAK ÍTÁSÁBAN A MÁSODIK VILÁGHÁBORÚ IDEJÉN [Soviet historiography on the role of the USSR in forming the new armed forces of Eastern and Southeastern Europe during World War II]. *Történelmi Szemle [Hungary] 1973 16(3-4): 376-378.* Soviet historiography has concentrated on the study of the political and theoretical principles that guided the USSR to give military aid to Eastern Europe to support anti-Nazism. Secondary sources; 2 notes. H. Szamuely/S

3134. Korbuly, Dezsö. DISKUSSIONEN UM DIE SCHLACHT BEI MOHÁCS [Discussions about the battle of Mohács]. *Österreichische Osthefte [Austria] 1977 19(4): 305-307.* Hungarian historians believe the Hungarians were defeated by the Turks at the battle of Mohács in 1526 because they were deserted by the Western European states.

3135. Korman, Gerd. WARSAW PLUS THIRTY: SOME PERCEPTIONS IN THE SOURCES AND WRITTEN HISTORY OF THE GHETTO UPRISING. *Yivo Annual of Jewish Social Sci. 1974 (15): 280-296.* Explores the lack of coverage, by American historians, textbooks and newspapers of the uprising in the Warsaw ghetto during World War II. 26 notes. R. J. Wechman

3136. Korotkov, G. and Orlov, A. O POLITIKE I STRATEGII S. SH.A. I ANGLII V ZAPADNOI EVROPE V 1944 G [The policies and strategy of the United States and Great Britain in western Europe in 1944]. *Voenno-Istoricheskii Zhurnal [USSR] 1974 (8): 79-85.* Recent western historiography continues to overemphasize the importance of the second front in the defeat of Germany and to romanticize the imperialistic policies and aims of Great Britain and the United States in World War II.

3137. Korotkov, I. VOPROSY OBSHCHEI TAKTIKI V SOVETSKOI VOENNOI ISTORIOGRAFII (1918-1941 GG) [Questions of general tactics in Soviet military historiography, 1918-41]. *Voenno-Istoricheskii Zhurnal [USSR] 1977 (12): 86-91.* Reviews military-scientific literature, 1918-45, concerning methods and forms of conduct in battle involving land and other forces.

3138. Kostiainen, Auvo. YHDYSVALTAIN LIITTYMINEN ENSIMMÄISEEN MAAILMANSOTAAN HISTORIANTUTKIMUKSEN ONGELMANA [The entry of the United States into World War I: a comparative analysis of American and European historiography]. *Turun Hist. Arkisto [Finland] 1980 34: 196-215.* Before World War II most American historians fell into two categories regarding US entrance into World War I. One group accepted US government explanations that Germany's use of submarine warfare and infringement of the rights of neutral nations could no longer be tolerated. A revisionist group, however, contended that the United States had been partisan from the outbreak of the war. After World War II, US historians began to take a broader view and give importance to such factors as power politics, national interests, public opinion, international economy, and psychology. This trend has brought US historiography on the topic closer to the European viewpoint, but Europeans tend to generalize about US entry into World War I and treat it as a side issue, which is not the case amoung US historians. 40 notes. J/S

3139. Kozlov, L. P. and Orlov, A. S. KAPITAL'NYI TRUD PODGOTOVKE I RAZVIAZYVANII VTOROI MIROVOI VOINY [A major work about the antecedents and beginnings of World

War II]. *Novaia i Noveishaia Istoriia [USSR]* 1976 (3): 161-168. Discusses the period from the eve of World War II to the German attack on the USSR, as it is presented in the second and third volumes of the 12-volume series entitled *History of the Second World War 1939-1945* published by the Soviet Academy of Sciences in 1975. The second volume covers the events from spring 1935 until August 1939; the third volume begins with Germany's attack on Poland (1 September 1939) and ends with the Soviet Union's entry into the war on 22 June 1941. The study is based on a Marxist analysis which investigates the ideological, political, and military aspects of the war, with particular attention to the USSR. 3 notes.

R. Permar

3140. Krupchenko, I. E. BOR'BA ZA KORENNOI PERELOM V GODY VTOROI MIROVOI VOINY [The struggle for the great change in World War II]. *Novaia i Noveishaia Istoriia [USSR]* 1976 (5): 160-168. Analyzes the fourth and fifth volumes of the Soviet *History of the Second World War,* which were published in 1975. The events of the second part of the war are covered: the fourth volume follows the war from June 1941 until April 1942; the fifth volume discusses the events of the summer and fall of 1942. They are written from a Marxist viewpoint and with an emphasis on the USSR. 5 Notes.

R. Permar

3141. Kudriavtsev, I. I. NEKOTORYE VOPROSY ARKHEO-GRAFICHESKOI PODGOTOVKI DOKUMENTAL'NYKH SBORNIKOV PO ISTORII VELIKOI OTECHESTVENNOI VOINY [Certain questions of the archaeographical preparation of collections of documents on the history of World War II]. *Sovetskie Arkhivy [USSR]* 1983 (4): 65-70. Many collections of various types have been published on the labor and military contributions of the workers of republics, regions, and districts to victory in World War II, including collections of military and Party documents, articles from the press, letters, and leaflets. However, there is a great deal more material still to be published. The contributions of the workers of many republics and districts have still to be covered, and many of the collections need to be published in new editions as they suffer from various shortcomings such as errors in the reprinting of leaflets and letters and the inclusion of unverified memoirs and reminiscences. Secondary sources; 17 notes.

G. Dombrovski

3142. Kuehl, Daniel T. MILITARY HISTORY: FOUR APPROACHES. *Air U. Rev.* 1978 29(4): 76-83. Reviews four books that represent different approaches in the writing of military history. Adrian Liddell Hart, editor, *The Sword and the Pen: Selections from the World's Greatest Military Writings* (New York: Thomas Y. Crowell, 1976) is an example of the historiography of military thought and provides a broad but superficial exposure to military thought. Werner Girbig, *Six Months to Oblivion: The Eclipse of the Luftwaffe Fighter Force* (New York: Hippocrene Books, 1975) analyzes Operation Bodenplatte [Baseplate], the Luftwaffe's low-level attack on Allied airfields on 1 January 1945 and provides an excellent example of the operational aspect of military history. Alun Chalfront, *Montgomery of Alamein* (New York: Atheneum, 1976) provides a character study of the British field marshal and an example of the biographical approach. Finally, Anthony Cave Brown, *Bodyguard of Lies* (New York: Harper and Row, 1975), presents an overview of how the Allied knowledge of German plans through *Ultra* was used to aid Operation Overload and is a good example of the grand strategy approach.

J. W. Thacker, Jr.

3143. Kulikov, V. AKTUAL'NYE PROBLEMY VOENNOI ISTORII V SVETE RESHENII XXV S"EZDA KPSS [Topical problems of military history in the light of decisions of the 25th congress of the Communist Party of the USSR]. *Voenno-Istoricheskii Zhurnal [USSR]* 1976 (12): 11-23. Summarizes the achievements of Soviet military historiography, criticizing its many shortcomings, and establishes the mission of contemporary scholars.

3144. Kuskov, V. STROITEL'STVO NATSIONAL'NOI NARODNOI ARMII GDR: (PO STRANITSAM ZHURNALA *VOENNAIA ISTORIIA)* [The development of the national people's army of the GDR: a survey of the journal *Voennaia Istoriia*].

Voenno-Istoricheskii Zhurnal [USSR] 1974 (6): 104-109. Reviews a number of articles on the formation of the army of the German Democratic Republic written by German historians, 1962-72, and stresses the important contribution made by these authors to the strengthening of cooperation between the nations of the Warsaw Pact.

3145. Kuznetsov, I. O NEKOTORYKH NEDOSTATKAKH KNIG O GEROIAKH SOVETSKOGO SOIUZA, VYPUSHCHENNYKH MESTNYMI IZDATEL'STVAMI [Shortcomings of locally published books on the heroes of the Soviet Union]. *Voenno-Istoricheskii Zhurnal [USSR]* 1980 (3): 76-79. The literature on the heroes of World War II brought out by local publishing houses often contain errors, in dates, places and biographical data. A more critical attitude toward sources and greater use of archives and documents could help eliminate errors. Secondary sources; 6 notes.

G. Dombrovski

3146. Labedz, Leopold. THE SPECTRE OF YALTA. *Encounter [Great Britain]* 1981 57(6): 92-96. Criticizes the general Western perception of Soviet aspirations in the 1943-44 period as epitomized by the Yalta conference, citing, and sharply differing with, the opinions of Lord Gladwyn (Gladwyn Jebb) and W. Averell Harriman.

3147. Landaburu, Federico Guillermo C. NUEVOS MÉTODOS EN LA HISTORIOGRAFÍA MILITAR DE LA G. M. II [New methods in the military historiography of World War II]. *Rev. de Hist. Militar [Spain]* 1971 15(30): 145-154. Discusses methods of historiography employed since 1944 to document the events of World War II, citing in particular the attempts of military historians to gather data on military history and to establish its place within the study of history in general.

3148. Lange, Dieter. ÜBER HISTORISCHE FORSCHUNGEN ZUR GESCHICHTE DES ZWEITEN WELTKRIEGES IN DER DEUTSCHEN DEMOKRATISCHEN REPUBLIK [Historical research on World War II in East Germany]. *La Seconda Guerra Mondiale nella prospettiva storica a trent'anni dall'epilogo* (Como: Casa editrice Pietro Cairoli, 1977): 259-267. An account of the historiography of World War II in East Germany, stressing the correctness of its Marxist-Leninist approach and emphasizing the role of the Communist Party in the resistance against the Nazis. 16 notes.

J. C. Billigmeier

3149. Łaniec, Stanisław. OPERACJA WSCHODNIOPRUSKA (1944-1945) W ŚWIETLE RADZIECKIEJ LITERATURY HISTORYCZNEJ [The East Prussian operation, 1944-45, in the light of Soviet historical literature]. *Komunikaty Mazursko-Warmińskie [Poland]* 1974 (3): 339-356. Gives an account of Soviet journalistic articles, memoirs, and serious historical works on the East Prussian campaign of the Soviet army.

3150. Laqueur, Walter. REWRITING HISTORY. *Commentary* 1973 55(3): 53-63. Revisionist historiography is found in the writings pertaining to Nazism, World War II, and the origins of the Cold War.

3151. Larew, Karl G. THE TURKISH STRAITS AS A CAUSE OF THE FIRST WORLD WAR. *Towson State J. of Int. Affairs* 1977 11(2): 81-97. Sketches the historiographical debate about the origins of World War I and discusses international rivalries over the Straits of Turkey as a cause.

3152. Lavi, Theodor. JEWS IN RUMANIAN HISTORIOGRAPHY OF WORLD WAR II. *Soviet Jewish Affairs [Great Britain]* 1974 4(1): 45-52. Describes how the portrayal of the Jews during World War II has changed in Romanian historical literature since 1947, as Stalinism has subsided.

3153. Lesort, Paul-André. LE DÉSASTRE DE 1940 [The disaster of 1940]. *Histoire [France]* 1979 (14): 94-97. The defeat of France by Germany in the spring of 1940 still raises passionate debate among historians and their readers. The author urges former combatants to speak out before more time passes.

3154. Levin, Dov. FACT AND FICTION. *Yad Vashem News [Israel]* 1973 (4): 22-23, 26. Soviet historiography on World War II conceals the identity of Jews killed in battle by classifying them as "Soviet citizens," while the publication of facts on Jewish participation in the regular army or with partisans against the Nazis has been minimal. Examines a recent example concerning the Jewish Lithuanian personality, Genrikas Zimanas (Genia Ziman), an organizer of the Lithuanian partisan movement. Rebuts Zimanas' claim that the blame for the death of thousands of Lithuanian Jews rests with the Zionists.   J. P. Fox

3155. Levine, Herbert M. ARMIES OF DEMOCRACY: A PROBLEM OF HISTORIOGRAPHY. *Studies in Hist. and Soc.* 1975 6(2): 1-30. Surveys the development of national armies in Britain, Switzerland, the United States, France, and Prussia-Germany and evaluates the relationship between military organization and the preservation of democracy. The various types of armies—volunteer, citizen, conscript, mass—present an ambiguous historical legacy. Each has been victorious over, and likewise has lost out to, the other types of armies. Supporters of any form of army can draw examples from military history, but no single form is clearly preferable. Based on standard secondary military histories; 81 notes.
                                                G. H. Libbey

3156. Lévy, Claude. PERSPECTIVE HISTORIQUE DE LA 2ᵉ GUERRE MONDIALE À LA LUMIÈRE DES ÉTUDES FRANÇAISES [A historical perspective on World War II in light of French studies]. *La Seconda Guerra Mondiale nella prospettiva storica a trent'anni dall'epilogo* (Como: Casa editrice Pietro Cairoli, 1977): 137-170. World War II is still extremely painful for France and the French. The collapse of 1940, the collaboration of Vichy with the Nazis, fighting in the colonies between Free French and forces loyal to Vichy, deportations of Jews and others marked by the Nazis for destruction, the fate of French prisoners of war in German hands, and forced labor: all these are still controversial and divisive subjects. Yet an enormous amount of work has been done and is still being done, and the historiography of World War II has never ceased to progress in France. Hope may be placed on the young generation of historians who are free from the taboos and prejudices of the past. 80 notes.   J. C. Billigmeier

3157. Levy, Jack S. THEORIES OF GENERAL WAR. *World Politics* 1985 37(3): 344-374. Examines the theories of general or hegemonic war advanced by Toynbee, Modelski and Thompson, Wallerstein and Chase-Dunn, Gilpin, and Doran, and the related theories of Organski and Kugler, and of Väyrynen. These theories have generated conflicting hypotheses and different lists of general wars. A major impediment to the empirical testing of these divergent hypotheses is the fact that complete operational criteria are rarely provided for the central concept of general war; instead, general war is usually defined broadly in terms of its systemic consequences, so that some key hypotheses on the consequences and causes of general war are reduced to tautologies. An alternative definition, and a compilation of general wars, is offered for the modern great-power system, which is conceived in terms of a Eurocentric focus and the primacy of military security issues.   J

3158. Lewis, B. E. SOVIET TABOO. *Soviet Studies [Great Britain]* 1978 29(4): 603-606. Soviet censorship of Western books usually involves altering the text and footnotes, and the excluded material often reveals taboos about certain subjects. The Russian translation of Liddell Hart's *History of the Second World War* exemplifies this. Material excluded from the book concerns policy mistakes by Joseph Stalin and his generals, Soviet treatment of neighboring states, criticism of the Red Army, and the Red Army's praise of other forces. The worst aspects of Stalin's regime are generally played down. Note.

3159. Lewis, William Gwyn. THE EXACT DATE OF THE BATTLE OF BANBURY, 1469. *Bull. of the Inst. of Hist. Res. [Great Britain]* 1982 55(132): 194-196. There has been disagreement as to whether the battle of Edgecote, near Banbury, was fought on 24 or 26 July 1469. Evidence from contemporary Welsh poetry confirms that of a Latin chronicle that Monday 24 July was the correct date

and also that William Herbert, Earl of Pembroke, was executed on 27 July three days after being taken prisoner in battle. Based on printed primary sources; 20 notes.   D. J. Nicholls

3160. Logunova, T. A. OSVESHCHENIE V ISTORICHESKOI I MEMUARNOI LITERATURE UCHASTIIA SOVETSKIKH GRAZHDAN V EVROPEISKOM DVIZHENII SOPROTIVLENI-IA [The treatment in historical and memoir literature of the participation of Soviet citizens in the European resistance movement]. *Vestnik Moskovskogo U., Seriia 8: Istoriia [USSR]* 1977 32(2): 15-22. Most Soviet prisoners of war took an active role in the resistance to Hitler. They rebelled in the Netherlands when Allied troops were 20 kilometers away. The Buchenwald camp had an organization created by German Communists. V. A. Obolenskaia published an underground Russian newspaper in Paris and she also aided Soviet prisoners. Soviet citizens took an active part in the liberation of Italy. There are many contradictions in the memoirs of members of the Resistance that have to be dealt with by Soviet historians. 27 notes.   D. Balmuth

3161. Luca de Tena, Lucía. LA GUERRA DE LA INDEPENDENCIA ESPAÑOLA EN LA HISTORIOGRAFIA ANGLOSAJONA ACTUAL [The war for Spanish independence in contemporary Anglo-Saxon historiography]. *Hispania [Spain]* 1969 29(111): 181-192. Discusses four English and American books on the Peninsular War published 1963-67, and asserts that they offer viewpoints which, while valuable, reflect English rather than Spanish attitudes.

3162. Lutski, E. A. and Murav'ev, V. A. ISTORIOGRAFIIA ISTORII SSSR V GODY VELIKOI OTECHESTVENNOI VOINY [Historiography of the USSR during World War II]. *Istoriia SSSR [USSR]* 1980 (3): 104-119. Surveys works published between 1941 and 1945 on Soviet history and describes the role of the intelligentsia and Soviet historians during the war. The war had an essential influence on Soviet historical science and proved the superiority of Marxist-Leninist historical science and Communist ideology over the bourgeois interpretation. Primary sources; 88 notes.
                                                C. Pichelin

3163. Maddox, Robert James. ATOMIC DIPLOMACY: A STUDY IN CREATIVE WRITING. *J. of Am. Hist.* 1973 59(4): 925-934. Gar Alperovitz's *Atomic Diplomacy: Hiroshima and Potsdam: The Use of the Atomic Bomb and the American Confrontation with Soviet Power* (New York: Simon and Schuster, 1965) has become a staple of New Left historiography, but Alperovitz' use of his sources distorts and misrepresents the evidence. Arguments cited in support of his thesis in fact refer to other subjects, time sequences are altered, key words are deleted which would invalidate the arguments, certain words are given a sinister weight they do not deserve, and some statements are contradicted by their very sources. The uncritical reception of this lamentable scholarship points to shortcomings in the critical mechanisms of the profession. 43 notes.   K. B. West

3164. Magnusson, Thomas. MOTSTÅNDRÖRELSERNAS MILITÄRA ROLL I SKANDINAVIEN 1940-1945: EN HISTORIOGRAFISK STUDIE [The military role of the resistance movements in Scandinavia, 1940-45: a historiographical study]. *Aktuellt och Hist. [Sweden]* 1977: 5-26. Presents the views of Scandinavian historians Jörgen Haestrup, 1954, Sverre Kjeldstadli, 1959, and Aage Trommer, 1971, and their interpretations of the railroad sabotage in Norway and Denmark in the final stages of World War II. Biblio.

3165. Mahon, John K. BIBLIOGRAPHIC ESSAY ON RESEARCH INTO THE HISTORY OF THE MILITIA AND THE NATIONAL GUARD. *Military Affairs* 1984 48(2): 74-77. A bibliographic essay on the history of the militia and the National Guard, showing how little has been written on the subject, especially on the individual states and overall history. State histories are uneven in historical quality; unit histories are more numerous.
                                                A. M. Osur

3166. Majewski, Wiesław. HISTORIA WOJSKOWA W INSTYTUCIE HISTORYCZNYM UNIWERSYTETU WARSZAWSKIEGO [Military history in the Institute of History of the University of Warsaw]. *Przegląd Hist. [Poland] 1980 71(4): 674-701.* Wacław Tokarz (1873-1937), Janusz Woliński (1894-1970) and Stanisław Herbst (1907-73) are credited with developing the Institute of History of the University of Warsaw into a leading center for the study of Polish military history. Tokarz, a professor at the institute from 1928 to 1937, and Woliński, from 1938 to 1970, concentrated their research on a narrow time-span: the former, on insurrections and conflicts from the 1790's to 1830's; the latter, on battles, campaigns and wars of Jan Sobieski (1629-96), stressing his achievements first as Crown Grand Hetman (from 1668), and then as King of Poland (from 1674). In contrast, Herbst, a professor from 1945 to 1973, chose specific topics from 1410 to 1945. The author examines the most significant publications of these three scholars, as well as those of their students, and evaluates their contributions. At present research in the field of military history continues at the institute in the masters' and doctoral seminars of seven of its professors. Based on publications of Tokarz, Woliński, and Herbst, including those of their students, as well as reviews of their works in scholarly periodicals; 86 notes. Russian and French summaries. A. B. Pernal

3167. Makar, Iu. I. Z ISTORII VARSHAVS'KOHO POVSTANNIA 1944 R. [The Warsaw Uprising, 1944]. *Ukrains'kyi Istorychnyi Zhurnal [USSR] 1970 (6): 91-94.* The Soviets view the 1944 Warsaw Uprising as a military-political adventure of reactionaries and a selfless, heroic struggle of Poles resisting the occupiers.

3168. Mandelbaum, Michael. THE POLITICAL LESSONS OF TWO WORLD WAR II NOVELS: A REVIEW ESSAY. *Pol. Sci. Q. 1979 94(3): 515-522.* Reviews Herman Wouk's *The Winds of War* (Boston: Little, Brown, 1971) and *War and Remembrance* (Boston: Little, Brown, 1978) and points out that although Wouk's works have been disparaged by most literary critics and totally ignored by historians, the fictional approach to the momentous historical events of the last 40 years is an effective means of depicting deeply felt human reactions to the horrors of war and its aftermath. 11 notes.

3169. Marczewski, Jerzy. GERMAN HISTORIOGRAPHY AND THE PROBLEM OF GERMANY'S RESPONSIBILITY FOR WORLD WAR I. *Polish Western Affairs [Poland] 1977 12(2): 289-309.* Nationalism underscored German (and later, West German) historiography on World War I, especially pertaining to responsibility for the war, 1914-60, and furthered German state policy. Historiography since 1960 has drifted away from a nationalistic perspective with a new emphasis on modern Germany.

3170. Marczewski, Jerzy. ORZECZENIE DOTYCZĄCE WYBUCHU I WOJNY ŚWIATOWEJ [Origins of World War I]. *Przegląd Zachodni [Poland] 1970 26(1): 176-190.* Surveys recent German historiography on the origins of and responsibility for World War I initiated by the 1967 publication of *Gedachten zur Kriegsschuldfrage 1914* by Hermann Kantorowicz.

3171. Marushkin, B. AMERIKANSKIE FAL'SIFIKATORY I PODLINNAIA ISTORIIA [American falsifications and real history]. *Mezhdunarodnaia Zhizn' [USSR] 1970 17(5): 26-33.* Using mainly historical writings and political memoirs from 1950-70, shows the links between the postwar military industrial complex and the rewriting of the history of World War II by bourgeois historians seeking to belittle Russian achievements and exaggerate those of the United States; this is a cause of tension and of the futility of current US foreign policy.

3172. Marushkin, B. I. AMERIKANSKIE FAL'SIFIKATORY I PODLINNAIA ISTORIIA [American falsifications and real history]. *Mezhdunarodnaia Zhizn' [USSR] 1970 17(5): 26-33.* Shows the links between the postwar military-industrial complex and western historiography of World War II, in particular the latter's emphasis on the role of the United States.

3173. Mason, T. W. SOME ORIGINS OF THE SECOND WORLD WAR. *Past and Present [Great Britain] 1964 29: 67-87.* Discusses and refutes the following two theses advanced by A. J. P. Taylor in his introductory essay to his *Origins of the Second World War* (1963): 1) that the Third Reich's foreign policies were formulated pragmatically and in response to international situations, not under internal political, ideological, and economic pressures; and 2) that Britain and France dominated the international scene in the 1930's and their policies were decisive. Asserts that Nazism in Germany was the most profound cause of World War II, and that Taylor fails to perceive its distinctive character and role in 20th-century European history. Based on documents of Third Reich Ministries of Labour and Economics; 96 notes.

3174. Massicotte, Guy. LES ÉDITORIALISTES CANADIENS-FRANÇAIS ET LES ORIGINES DE LA SECONDE GUERRE MONDIALE [French Canadian editorialists and the origins of World War II]. *Recherches Sociographiques [Canada] 1976 17(2): 139-165.* Juxtaposes the opinions of eight contemporary historians concerning the origins of World War II with the perceptions of French Canadian editorialists writing in five newspapers during the period 1938-39. The editorialists perceived the movement of international politics in the same light as the contemporary historians. 91 notes. A. E. LeBlanc

3175. Maurach, Bruno. DIE SOWJETISCHE KRIEGSGESCHICHTSSCHREIBUNG [Soviet historiography of World War II]. *Wehrkunde [West Germany] 1960 9(4): 177-185.* In contrast to the great mass of Western publications on World War II, only few and insubstantial Soviet works have been published on that period.

3176. McEwen, J. M LORD BEAVERBROOK: HISTORIAN EXTRAORDINARY. *Dalhousie Rev. [Canada] 1979 59(1): 129-143.* A critical look at Max Aitkin's (Lord Beaverbrook) ability as a historian. Despite certain admirable stylistic qualities the author suggests serious inadequacies of source in Aitkin's *Politicians and the War*. In it he dealt anecdotally with prominent English politicians of the World War I era, primarily Bonar Law, Lloyd George, and Herbert Henry Asquith. While he was often well qualified to describe events cited because "he was there" his comments often extend well beyond his experience with much less basis in fact. Based on Beaverbrook's books, recent secondary sources, and some correspondence; 24 notes. C. Held

3177. Mead, Peter. ORDE WINGATE AND THE OFFICIAL HISTORIANS. *J. of Contemporary Hist. [Great Britain] 1979 14(1): 55-82.* The official history of World War II by General S. Woodburn Kirby et al. (Imperial War Museum—Document 78/2/1) presents Major-General Orde Charles Wingate as both insubordinate and impractical. Wingate's contemporaries, however, eulogized him as a military genius even while they recognized flaws in his character. Wingate organized special night squads in Palestine before the war, commanded the mainly Sudanese and Ethiopian "Gideon Force" which invaded Ethiopia from the west in 1941, and led two Chindit campaigns in Burma in 1943 and 1944, in the second of which he was killed. Primary sources; 66 notes. M. P. Trauth

3178. Mead, Peter and Bidwell, Shelford. ORDE WINGATE—TWO VIEWS. *J. of Contemporary Hist. [Great Britain] 1980 15(3): 401-404.* Peter Mead reiterates his attack on the "infamous malassessment by the British official historians" on Orde Wingate. Shelford Bidwell repeats that Wingate's recommendations "were both indiscreet and a tissue of strategic, political and logistic absurdities." M. P. Trauth

3179. Mertsalov, A. N. STALINGRADSKAIA BITVA V OSVESHCHENII BURZHUAZNOI ISTORIOGRAFII FRG [The battle of Stalingrad in light of West German bourgeois historiography]. *Istoriia SSSR [USSR] 1978 (4): 181-192.* Reviews recent West German historiography on the battle of Stalingrad, 1942-43. On the one hand, West German historiography has devoted much more attention to the nature and significance of the battle than has American and British bourgeois historiography. On the other hand, West German historiography has displayed the same bourgeois emphasis on the role of such factors as leadership, "fatal" mistakes, and missed opportunities by which reactionary historians attempt to conceal the reasons for the Soviet victory which, in fact, are rooted in the superiority of socialist society. 59 notes.   J. W. Long

3180. Mertsalov, A. N. ZAPADNOGERMANSKIE KONSERVATIVNYE ISTORIKI I MEMUARISTY O VTOROI MIROVOI VOINE [World War II in the works of conservative West German historians and memoir writers]. *Voprosy Istorii [USSR] 1969 (11): 78-92.* Review article cites some 100 studies and memoirs on the war and the antecedent Nazi period, published mid-1950's-1968. Unlike Neo-Nazis, West German conservatives condemn Hitler and support the official views of Chancellor Konrad Adenauer's regime. However, their strong anti-Soviet bias makes them distort history and equate Communism with Fascism as two aspects of totalitarianism, while their nationalistic defense of the Wehrmacht causes their evaluation of World War II to differ from that of historians from other imperialist countries. Representative of this Germanic nationalism are the broad studies of Hellmuth Günther Dahms, Walter Görlitz, and Paul Karl Schmidt writing under the pseudonym Paul Carell. More impartial, better researched and less militaristic are topical studies by Hans Mommsen, Hermann Böhme et al. 64 notes.
N. Frenkley

3181. Michel, Henri. LE COMITÉ D'HISTOIRE DE LA DEUXIÈME GUERRE MONDIALE [The Committee for the History of World War II]. *Rev. d'Hist. de la Deuxième Guerre Mondiale [France] 1981 31(124): 1-17.* Recalls 30 years of activity of the Comité d'Histoire de la Deuxième Guerre Mondiale, founded in 1951 by Georges Bidault, Lucien Febvre, Georges Galichon, and the author. The committee collected documents, microfilm, oral history transcripts, and publications and conducted investigations of topics related to French participation in the war. It also published the *Revue d'Histoire de la Deuxième Guerre Mondiale.* Based on documents of the committee and recollections by the author; 30 notes.
G. H. Davis

3182. Milner, Marc. CONVOY ESCORTS: TACTICS, TECHNOLOGY AND INNOVATION IN THE ROYAL CANADIAN NAVY, 1939-1943. *Military Affairs 1984 48(1): 19-25.* Discusses how historians have viewed the convoy escort tactics of the Royal Canadian Navy (RCN) during the battle of the Atlantic. The RCN developed and grew during the campaign, but was affected by the inability of Canadian industry to respond quickly to the needs of operational forces on the nation's very doorstep. Antisubmarine tactics improved rapidly in early 1943, as technological innovations led to greater success. Based on Canadian naval records and other primary sources; 28 notes, 5 fig.   A. M. Osur

3183. Milova, Chr. and Toshkova, Vitka. A BOLGÁR TÖRTÉNETÍRÁS ÉS A DÉLKELET-EURÓPAI NEMZETKÖZI KAPCSOLATOK KÉRDÉSE, VALAMINT BULGARIA KÜLPOLITIKÁJA A MÁSODIK VILÁGHÁBORÚ ALATT [Bulgarian historiography on the problem of Bulgaria's foreign policy and international relations in Southeastern Europe during World War II]. *Történelmi Szemle [Hungary] 1973 16(3-4): 394-401.* Shows how postwar Bulgarian historians have concentrated on the events of 1944, when the country was invaded by Soviet troops and a Communist coup d'etat caused Bulgaria to terminate its Nazi alliance and side instead with the Allies. Secondary sources; 21 notes.
H. Szamuely/S

3184. Minow, Fritz. DIE LANDUNGSOPERATION BEI DIEPPE UND IHRE FUNKTION BEI DER VERZÖGERUNG DER ZWEITEN FRONT IM SPIEGEL DER BÜRGERLICHEN MILITÄRGESCHICHTSSCHREIBUNG [The landing at Dieppe and its function in delaying the second front as reflected in bourgeois military historiography]. *Militärgeschichte [East Germany] 1974 13(6): 689-699.* Bourgeois historiography ignores the fact that British planners designed the Dieppe landing for political ends to demonstrate the futility of launching the second front, which the United States and Great Britain had promised the USSR. Although the landing did demonstrate what was needed for a successful operation, it did not force Germany to maintain troops in France, nor cause the construction of the Atlantic Wall. Rather, it confirmed the

validity of existing German defense plans, including construction of the Wall, and allowed German troop transfers to the eastern front. 40 notes.   H. D. Andrews

3185. Moscardelli, Giuseppe. LA STORIOGRAFIA MILITARE [Military historiography]. *Riv. Militare [Italy] 1974 97(1): 66-70.* Reviews the current state of military historiography in Italy.

3186. Naida, S. F. and Chuzavkov, L. M. ISTORIOGRAFIIA PROBLEMY POSTAVOK S.SH.A. I VELIKOBRITANII SOVETSKOMU SOIUZU V PERIOD VELIKOI OTECHESTVENNOI VOINY [The historiography of US and British military aid to the USSR during World War II]. *Vestnik Moskovskogo U., Seriia 9: Istoriia [USSR] 1975 30(3): 17-31.* Sees a growing literature about alleged Soviet military self-sufficiency during World War II, and denies Western historical claims that the USSR was unprepared for war and dependent on Allied aid. Divides discussion into the periods 1941-47, 1947-60, and 1960-75. Claims that Western scholarship has changed over these periods depending on the political climate, but that Soviet researchers and military memoirists such as G. K. Zhukov have maintained throughout that the Allies deliberately delayed providing supplies to the USSR. 70 notes.
M. R. Colenso

3187. Narochnitski, A. L. VELIKIE DERZHAVY I SERBIIA V 1914 G. [The Great Powers and Serbia in 1914]. *Novaia i Noveishaia Istoriia [USSR] 1976 (4): 22-32.* Analyzes the preconditions for the outbreak of World War I with an emphasis on the role of the contradictions among the Great Powers in the Balkans. Exposes the groundless attempts by some Western authors to prove that Serbia, and not the imperialist governments bear responsibility for the war.   J

3188. Nejedlý, Miloslav. ZÁSADNÍ OBRAT V DRUHÉ SVĚTOVÉ VÁLCE A JEHO BURŽOASNÍ FALZIFIKACE [The decisive breakthrough in World War II and its bourgeois falsification]. *Hist. a Vojenství [Czechoslovakia] 1982 31(6): 23-39.* Soviet victory at Stalingrad 40 years ago was an event of decisive importance. In November 1942 Soviet troops started their counterattack in the Stalingrad area, which ended in German defeat and the loss of a quarter of all enemy forces in Russia. The evaluation of this moment of World War II is often handled by bourgeois historians with attempts at falsification of the facts. Earl F. Ziemke sees Stalingrad not as a result of the success of Soviet strategy but as the final culmination of Hitler's mistakes. Other bourgeois historiographers use a wrong analogy of Stalingrad with Verdun of 1917. Based on published works; 25 notes.   G. E. Pergl

3189. Nem'iatyi, V. M. DOSLIDZHENNIA ISTORII UKRAINS'KOI RSR PERIODU VELYKOI VITCHYZNIANOI VIINY [Studies of the history of the Ukrainian SSR during World War II]. *Ukrains'kyi Istorychnyi Zhurnal [USSR] 1976 (8): 32-44.*

3190. Nesvadba, František. K METODOLOGII VOJENSKÉ HISTORIOGRAFIE: PŘÍSPĚVEK DO DISKUSE [Methodology of military historiography: a contribution to a discussion]. *Hist. a Vojenství [Czechoslovakia] 1983 32(1): 190-200.* Modern historical science stresses the need for constant evaluation of basic methodological problems of military historiography. V. T. Login's *Dialectics of Military Historical Research* (1979) examines problems connected with dialectical understanding and knowledge when applied in military historiography. Based on Login's work; 7 notes.
G. E. Pergl/S

3191. Nesvadba, František. K PROBLEMATICE FALŠOVÁNÍ DĚJIN DRUHÉ SVĚTOVÉ VÁLKY BURŽOAZNÍ HISTORIOGRAFIÍ [Problems of falsification in the history of World War II by bourgeois historiography]. *Československý Časopis Historický [Czechoslovakia] 1985 33(2): 161-189.* Western bourgeois historians ignore imperialism as the crucial underlying cause of World War II and attempt to assign responsibility for it to specific governments and personalities. They usually misrepresent the Soviet position during 1938-41 and indirectly justify Western anti-Soviet policies during and after that period. They exaggerate the Western and belittle the Soviet contributions to the victory over fascism. Their anti-Soviet deductions from World War II include the possibility of a third world war. Based on selected published histories; 3 tables, 84 notes. Russian and German summaries.

R. E. Weltsch

3192. Nesvadba, František. ROK 1944 V SOVĚTSKÝCH DĚJINÁCH DRUHÉ SVĚTOVÉ VÁLKY: POČÁTEK OSVOBOZENÍ ČESKOSLOVENSKA SOVĚTSKOU ARMÁDOU [1944 in the *Soviet History of World War II*: the start of the liberation of Czechoslovakia by the Soviet Army]. *Hist. a Vojenství [Czechoslovakia] 1979 28(2): 34-54.* In its handling of the course of World War II, especially the description and analysis of Soviet military successes and advances in Eastern and Central Europe culminating in the formation of a new front for the Eastern Carpathian operations in July 1944, the coordination of Soviet operations with the progress of the Slovak National Uprising, and the liberation in September 1944 of the first village on Czechoslovak soil, the ninth volume of the *Soviet History of World War II* provides a valuable source of objective Marxist accounts of the period, correcting the falsehoods of bourgeois historiography. Secondary sources; 26 notes.

L. Short

3193. Nesvadba, František. ŠEDESÁT LET SOVĚTSKÉ VOJENSKÉ HISTORIOGRAFIE [Sixty years of Soviet military historiography]. *Hist. a Vojenství [Czechoslovakia] 1977 26(5): 3-27.* Discusses the development of USSR military historiography since 1917. Viewed today as an independent branch of social science associated with military sciences, Soviet historiography enriched the literary scene with many works of importance, 1917-77. The Revolution and World War II are the principal areas of interest. 46 notes.

G. E. Pergl

3194. Nevzorov, B. DLIA CHEGO NUZHNA ETA LOZH' (K VOPROSU O BURZHUAZNOI FAL'SIFIKATSII BITVY POD MOSKVOI) [Why this lie? Bourgeois falsification of the battle for Moscow]. *Voenno-Istoricheskii Zhurnal [USSR] 1982 (4): 48-52.* Bourgeois scholars such as E. Ziemke give a false account of the battle for Moscow, seeking to diminish the significance of the battle by placing it on a level with secondary campaigns of the English and American troops. They denigrate Soviet military art and distort the reasons for the defeat of the German troops. The aim of bourgeois military history is to lower the prestige of the Soviet Union and prepare ground for new wars. Based on secondary sources; 17 notes.

G. Dombrovski

3195. Nikonov, V. A. 40-LETNIAIA GODOVSHCHINA NACHALA VTOROI MIROVOI VOINY. ZASEDANIE UCHENOGO SOVETA ISTORICHESKOGO FAKUL'TETA MGU [The 40th anniversary of the beginning of World War II: session of the Academic Council of the History Department, Moscow State University]. *Vestnik Moskovskogo U., Seriia 8: Istoriia [USSR] 1979 (6): 84-86.* I. S. Galkin holds imperialism responsible for World War II and argues that Great Britain and France conducted a foreign policy that tried to direct Germany against the USSR. N. V. Sivachev deals with Allied diplomatic problems, particularly the second front. V. P. Smirnov surveys French historians of the war and sees bourgeois historians trying to place blame on Germany and Hitler, ignoring the responsibility of imperialism. They are also trying to rehabilitate the Vichy regime and play down the role of the USSR in achieving victory. Based on papers delivered at the session.

D. Balmuth

3196. Noack, Karl-Heinz. ZUM MILITARISMUSBEGRIFF IN DER GESCHICHTSSCHREIBUNG DER BRD [The concept of militarism in the historiography of West Germany]. *Militärgeschichte [East Germany] 1977 16(6): 725-731.* Examines the views of militarism in Germany of various historians. Friedrich Meinecke, Hans Herzfeld, Hans-Joachim Schoeps, and Gerhard Ritter all reject the notion of inherent German militarism; Karl Bucheim saw militarism in Prussia's history, particularly in the use of the army against social democracy; Volker Berghahn, in his histori-

cally based 1975 study of miltarism adopts a comparative approach. The concept of militarism cannot be determined merely by describing its historical manifestations. Secondary works; 44 notes.

A. Alcock

3197. Novoselov, B. N. SSHA, VELIKOBRITANIIA I VTOROI FRONT (KRITIKA NOVYKH TENDENTSII V BURZHUAZNOI ISTORIOGRAFII) [The United States, Great Britain, and the second front: criticism of new trends in bourgeois historiography]. *Novaia i Noveishaia Istoriia [USSR] 1983 (4): 32-48.* Criticizes new trends in Anglo-American historiography of the Second Front. Since the formerly widely entertained versions of the "disinterested" strategy of the United States and Britain in World War II have become unpopular, and the ruling circles of the United States and Britain preach anti-Sovietism, an anti-Soviet conception of priority of national interests has come to the fore in the treatment of the prehistory of the Second Front.

J/S

3198. Novoselov, Boris. THE USA, GREAT BRITAIN AND THE SECOND FRONT. *Social Sciences [USSR] 1984 15(2): 152-168.* Examines new trends in the American and British historiography on the interpretation of the events leading up to the opening of the second front during World War II, noting that the Allies deliberately followed actions detrimental to the alliance and the USSR in order to pursue their own national interests.

3199. Nowak, Tadeusz Marian. STUDIES OF THE HISTORY OF MILITARY TECHNOLOGY IN POLAND. *Kwartalnik Hist. Nauki i Techniki [Poland] 1980 25(4): 721-730.* Discusses the history of Polish military technology from the 10th century until 1918. Methodological knowledge is essential in making use of the vast amount of source material in order to insure that it is correctly categorized. Sources for the history of military technology include both movable objects and standing objects, iconographical materials, and written materials. Primary sources, biblio.

J. Powell

3200. Ogarev, P. V BOIAKH I SRAZHENIIAKH VELIKOI OTECHESTVENNOI VOINY [In the struggles and battles of World War II]. *Voenno-Istoricheskii Zhurnal [USSR] 1977 (1): 112-116.* Examines and evaluates Soviet historiography of World War II.

3201. Orlov, A. S. ISTOKI NASHEI POBEDY I BURZHUAZNAIA ISTORIOGRAFIIA [Sources of our victory and bourgeois historiography]. *Mirovaia Ekonomika i Mezhdunarodnye Otnosheniia [USSR] 1985 (1): 25-36.* Refutes claims of bourgeois historiography which try to misinterpret the roots of the Soviet victory in World War II and depict it not as a logical consequence of the advantages of the socialist system but as a conglomeration of casual circumstances in the belief that victory can be won in a new war against the socialist countries if "past mistakes" are avoided. The USSR gained victory thanks to the heroism of the Soviet army, the modern military equipment produced by the heroic Soviet working class, and superiority in the art of war, the high level of which was acknowledged in the war years by many well-known Western military experts. Refutes the version that the Soviet victory over German fascism was due to the help of the West and stresses the many contemporary leaders of the West who acknowledged that the German defeat on the Eastern front was due to the heroism and blood of the Soviet army. Focuses on the socialist economy, the role of the CPSU and the Soviet government, and the moral and political unity of the Soviet people they forged. The victory of the USSR was prepared by its entire historical development and the possibilities inherent in the socialist system, socialist industrialization, and the collectivization of agriculture.

J/S

3202. Orlov, A. S. ISTORIIA VTOROI MIROVOI VOINY: VAZHNYI FRONT IDEOLOGICHESKOI BOR'BY [The history of World War II: an important front in the ideological struggle]. *Novaia i Noveishaia Istoriia [USSR] 1980 (2): 41-58.* Treats the key problems of World War II, the role in and the contribution to the victory of each of the Great Powers of the anti-Hitler coalition, the historic mission of the Soviet Armed Forces, and the sources of the world-historical victory of the Soviet Union. The article exposes falsifications of the reactionary bourgeois historians trying to minimize the decisive role of the USSR in the defeat of fascist Germany and her allies, to belittle the importance of the Soviet-German front.   J

3203. Orlov, A. S. XXIV S'EZD KPSS I RAZOBLACHENIE BURZHUAZNYKH FAL'SIFIKATOROV ISTORII [The 24th Congress of the Soviet Communist Party and the unmasking of the bourgeois falsifiers of history]. *Voenno-Istoricheskii Zhurnal [USSR] 1972 (10): 3-11.* Criticizes Western historians for their evaluation of the role of the USSR in World War II.

3204. Pacor, Mario. AZ OLASZ TÖRTÉNETÍRÁS A MÁSODIK VILÁGHÁBORÚRÓL A DUNA VÖLGYÉBEN ÉS A BALKÁANON [Italian historiography of World War II in the Danube valley and the Balkans]. *Történelmi Szemle [Hungary] 1973 16(3-4): 411-428.* Italian historians of World War II have shown a continuous interest in those Balkan states that were traditionally in Italy's sphere of influence, as well as in British intrigues in the area.

3205. Park, Hong-Kyu. AMERICAN INVOLVEMENT IN THE KOREAN WAR. *Hist. Teacher 1983 16(2): 249-264.* A review essay on the historiography of the Korean War. Major issues discussed include the origins of the war, the US decision to intervene, the Truman-MacArthur controversy, and the conclusion of the war. 55 notes.   L. K. Blaser

3206. Park, Hong-Kyu. THE KOREAN WAR REVISITED: A SURVEY OF HISTORICAL WRITINGS. *World Affairs 1975 137(4): 336-344.* Surveys books published about the Korean War, 1950's-70's.

3207. Parker, Geoffrey. THE "MILITARY REVOLUTION," 1560-1660—A MYTH? *J. of Modern Hist. 1976 48(2): 195-214.* Michael Roberts of the Queen's University of Belfast is largely responsible for the shift in thinking concerning military history of the early modern period so that it is now regarded "as a time of major change in warfare and military organization." The author examines this "military revolution" in terms of tactics, strategy, the scale of warfare, and its impact on society.

3208. Parrish, Michael. SOVIET HISTORIOGRAPHY OF THE GREAT PATRIOTIC WAR 1970-1985: A REVIEW. *Soviet Studies in History 1984-85 23(3): iii-x.* Over the course of the past 15 years, Soviet studies of World War II have appeared in great numbers. Types of materials published include multi-volume official histories, military memoirs, studies of the army, navy, and airforce, and accounts of individual military districts and units. During this same period, official Soviet policy has insisted that criticism of Stalin and his wartime role is no longer acceptable.

M. R. Yerburgh

3209. Parrish, Noel F. THE INFLUENCE OF AIR POWER UPON HISTORIANS. *Harmon Memorial Lectures in Military Hist. 1979 (21): 1-21.* In the late 19th century Captain Alfred Thayer Mahon in *The Influence of Sea Power Upon History, 1660-1783* did for sea power what now needs to be done for air power. Just as Mahon had witnessed the end of complete dependence on sail, so today we have witnessed the end of complete dependence on wings. But by concentrating on an earlier era of sail power, Mahon discovered important implications for steam and even air technology just as we, by concentrating on earlier decades of air power, can discover implications for our use of the new technology of space. Reviews the work of recent historians of the US Air Force. Primary sources; 54 notes.   E. L. Keyser

3210. Pastorelli, Pietro. LA STORIOGRAFIA ITALIANA DEL DOPOGUERRA SULLA POLITICA ESTERA FASCISTA [Postwar Italian historiography on fascist foreign policy]. *Storia e Politica [Italy] 1971 10(4): 575-614.* After World War II, Italian historians began to seek the reasons for the war and for the Italian failure. Scholars such as Mario Toscano and Gaetano Salvemini studied fascist foreign policy, the key factor in Italy's participation

in the war and defeat. In their writings, they have emphasized Benito Mussolini's guilt, but also the responsibility of the leaders of other European nations for the conflagration. 107 notes.

J. C. Billigmeier

3211. Pate, Clarence W. THE HISTORICAL WRITING OF HANS ROTHFELS AND THE KRIEGSSCHULDFRAGE, 1924-1945. *Montclair J. of Social Sci. and Humanities 1974 3(2): 30-56.* Treats German historiography on the war-guilt question, especially in the work of Hans Rothfels.

3212. Pavlov, B. BURZHUAZNAIA ILLUSTRIROVANNAIA LITERATURA I IDEOLOGICHESKAIA OBRABOTKA MASS [Bourgeois illustrative literature and the ideological cultivation of the masses]. *Voenno-Istoricheskii Zhurnal [USSR] 1976 (1): 66-72.* An examination of the capitalist consensus on the history of World War II.

3213. Pedroncini, Guy. LE HAUT-COMMANDEMENT FRANÇAIS ET LA CONDUITE DE LA GUERRE DE MAI 1917 À NOVEMBRE 1918 [The French High Command and the direction of the war from May 1917 to November 1918]. *Information Historique [France] 1972 34(5): 229-233.* A plea for greater recognition of the original and important contribution of military history to the study of history. The archives of the Service Historique de l'Armée and the 105 volumes of the *Armées Françaises dans la Grande Guerre* should be exploited to demonstrate the role of men, not just battles, toward an understanding of future, even nuclear, conflicts, as well as the past. For example, it was Pétain's decisions and measures that dominated the last year of the war, and influenced the conduct of World War II. Based on primary and secondary sources; 3 notes.   R. K. Adams

3214. Peregontseva, G. PODPOL'NYE I PARTIZANSKIE GAZETY PERIODA VELIKOI OTECHESTVENNOI VOINY KAK ISTORICHESKII ISTOCHNIK [Underground and partisan newspapers from World War II as a historical source]. *Voenno-Istoricheskii Zhurnal [USSR] 1982 (9): 76-78.* By the autumn of 1942 the German invasion forces had occupied Soviet territory in which 45% of the prewar population lived. About 60 million Soviet citizens were under temporary German rule. Besides perpetrating mass terror, the Germans also introduced insidious propaganda. To counter this the Soviet Communist Party and the Red Army printed a number of newspapers, periodicals, and leaflets for those under German occupation. A total of 400 newspapers were published throughout the war years. Some early ones, such as *News of the Soviet Motherland* and *Illustrated Front*, had one prime shortcoming: they failed to provide much news from the occupied regions themselves. This was later rectified, however, and all these publications did much to promote the ideological and political education and agitation of the local population, as well as to suggest methods of resistance. 16 notes.   J. Bamber

3215. Pérez Tenreiro, Tomás. OJEADA AL *CARABOBO* DE DUARTE LEVEL [A look at Duarte Level's *Carabobo*]. *Bol. de la Acad. Nac. de la Hist. [Venezuela] 1982 65(258): 317-324.* General Lino Duarte Level, exiled in New York, wrote a history of Venezuela from its beginnings in pre-Colombian times to the battle of Carabobo in 1821. He wrote it almost from memory and without the benefit of recent documentation, so his judgments on the campaign and battle of Carabobo, one of the decisive engagements of the war of independence, need to be revised, especially regarding the authorship of the plan of operations and the appropriateness of the military decisions taken. Based on secondary material; 3 notes.

J. V. Coutinho

3216. Perona, Gianni. RICERCHE ARCHIVISTICHE E STUDI SULLE RELAZIONI TRA GLI ALLEATI E L'ITALIA [Archival investigations and studies on the relations between the Allies and Italy]. *Italia Contemporanea [Italy] 1981 33(142): 89-101.* Surveys the publications that have resulted from research done on archival material held by the British and American governments since the material became available to scholars in the early 1970's. Among the issues that have been clarified are those dealing with the peace treaty ending World War II and the conduct of the Allied military government in Italy during the period of occupation. More work needs to be done. But it is already clear how international relations have permanently conditioned the internal life of Italy. Primary sources; 45 notes. E. E. Ryan

3217. Petranović, Branko. DNEVNIK JOSIPA SMODLAKE KAO ISTORIJSKI IZVOR [The diary of Josip Smodlaka as a historical source]. *Istorijski Glasnik [Yugoslavia] 1972 (2): 131-148.* The diary of the well-known partisan and publicist Josip Smodlaka has now been published. The diary covers the wartime years 1943-45, when Smodlaka was involved in the negotiations between the exile government in London and the Titoists, and between the Allies and the partisans. As a historical source, the diary throws light on several previously obscure matters in the war's final phase. It is a generally reliable document in its factual aspects, and gives the author's personal impressions of certain events and motivations in an informative and suggestive fashion. P. J. Adler

3218. Polastro, Walter. LA MARINA ITALIANA NELLA SECONDA GUERRA MONDIALE NELL'INTERPRETAZIONE DELLA NOSTRA MEMORIALISTICA [The Italian Navy in World War II as seen by our memoirists]. *Movimento di Liberazione in Italia [Italy] 1972 24(109): 107-113.* While Admiral Angelo Iachino, in *Gaudo e Matapan* (Milan, 1946), attributed Italy's naval debacles to the lack of expertise and initiative on the part of the high command as well as to the almost total absence of air reconnaissance, Antonio Trizzino—*Navi e poltrone* (Milan, 1966)—declares treason to be a decisive factor. Another work by Iachino, *Tramonto di una grande marina* (Milan, 1959), and Admiral Romeo Bernotti's *Storia della guerra in Mediterraneo 1940-43* (Rome, 1960) reveal other basic weaknesses in detail (lack of aircraft carriers, no strategic concept, no real preparations for extended naval operations). H. W. L. Freudenthal

3219. Poltavski, M. A. AVSTRIISKAIA ISTORIOGRAFIIA DVIZHENIIA SOPROTIVLENIIA [Austrian historiography on the resistance movement]. *Voprosy Istorii [USSR] 1972 (1): 183-188.* Discusses the forces involved in the Austrian resistance movement, 1938-45, and recent Austrian publications devoted to this subject. The latter contain much important factual information, but they only represent the first step in the study of the movement, which seriously lacks authentic archive material. 20 notes. R. Permar

3220. Popa, M. and Buşe, C. LUCRĂRI OCCIDENTALE DESPRE PROBLEMA CELUI DE-AL DOILEA FRONT ÎN EUROPA [Western works on aspects of the second front in Europe]. *Analele Universității București: Seria Științe Sociale-Istorie [Romania] 1965 14: 131-46.* World War II continues to be a subject of study and a favorite theme of politicians and military men who took part in it. One of the highlights of the war was the opening of the second front in Europe. Western memoir writers and historiographers have adopted diverse positions on the subject, according to their political and military orientations. For example, K. Tippelskirch, H. Speidel, and J. Thorwald, although in favor of the Anglo-American alliance, criticize Franklin D. Roosevelt for the delay in implementation. The Italian Marxist writer Roberto Battaglia deals with the causes of different Western attitudes from a historical materialist viewpoint. J. Néré considers that in 1941-42 the military necessities of the Anglo-American alliance surpassed realistic possibilities. Secondary sources; 110 notes. P. T. Herman

3221. Porch, Douglas. MILITARY HISTORY. *Hist. J. [Great Britain] 1981 24(4): 981-986.* A review article of André Corvisier's *Armies and Societies in Europe, 1494-1789* (1979), John Gooch's *Armies in Europe* (1980), T. A. Heathcote's *The Afghan Wars, 1839-1919* (1980), Edward M. Spiers's *The Army and Society, 1815-1914* (1980), *The South African War: The Anglo-Boer War 1899-1902* (1980) edited by Peter Warwick and Martin van Creveld's *Supplying War: Logistics from Wallenstein to Patton* (1977). Warfare occupies an important place in European history from the Renaissance to World War II and is worthy of detailed study by historians.

3222. Pospieszalski, K. M. RECHERCHES EN POLOGNE SUR L'HISTOIRE DE LA DEUXIÈME GUERRE MONDIALE [Research in Poland on the history of World War II]. *Rev. d'Hist. de la Deuxième Guerre Mondiale [France] 1960 10(40): 31-46.* A bibliographical report on Polish research on the history of World War II, its scientific organizations, its planning and coordination. Catalogues research organizations by themes or topics dealt with, such as political relations, military relations, German occupation, war crimes, diplomatic relations, national history, judicial proceedings, Polish and Jewish martyrdom, Polish resistance, economic exploitation of Jews, the Warsaw revolt. 61 notes. S. Sevilla

3223. Praun, Albert. VERNACHLÄSSIGTE FAKTOREN IN DER KRIEGSGESCHICHTSSCHREIBUNG [Neglected factors in the writing of military history]. *Wehrwissenschaftliche Rundschau [West Germany] 1970 20(3): 137-145.* Discusses the role of military communications in World War II, a fruitful field of research still largely unexplored. Based largely on printed primary sources (memoirs); 27 notes. J. W. Mishark

3224. Procházka, Zdeněk. DĚJINY DRUHÉ SVĚTOVÉ VÁLKY—ZDROJ TRVALEHO POUCENI [History of World War II: a source of constant instruction]. *Hist. a Vojenství [Czechoslovakia] 1980 29(4): 3-15.* Introductory speech at an ideological conference on the Czech publication of the first six volumes of the Soviet *History of World War II, 1939-1945* and introduction to several papers on the *History* in this issue.

3225. Prokop, Myroslav. ZAIAVA, SHCHO KLYCHE DO DAL'SHYKH ZOBOV'IAZAN' [A declaration which leads to further responsibilities]. *Sučasnist [West Germany] 1975 (12): 93-99.* Discusses the inadequate historical awareness of the Russian dissidents, particularly Andrei Sakharov, who drafted a declaration of guilt in 1975 condemning the USSR's invasion of Poland in 1939 and the subsequent massacre of Polish prisoners at Katyn Forest.

3226. Pugh, Michael. RESISTANCE TO NAZISM: THE CONDITION OF RESISTANCE HISTORY. *Hist. News [New Zealand] 1979 (38): 1-5.* Discusses resistance movements during World War II in Europe, among a varying range of the population and examines historiography of the resistance, 1950's-70's.

3227. Puskás, A. I. A MÁSODIK VILÁGHÁBORÚ TÖRTÉNETÉVEL FOGLALKOZÓ HISTORIOGRÁFIA NÉHÁNY KÉRDÉSÉRŐL [Some problems of the historiography of the Second World War]. *Történelmi Szemle [Hungary] 1975 18(1): 1-9.* In the Soviet works on the international relations and foreign policy of the USSR during World War II significant space is devoted to the problems of the East and Southeast European countries. The author enumerates the most important publications of documents, memoirs and syntheses which have come out recently. In Soviet works, Churchill's plans of a Mediterranean second front and the landing of the troops in the Balkans is interpreted as an anti-Soviet project. This strategy expressed the financial and political interests of the Anglo-American ruling circles, i.e., the maintenance of their positions in this region, the continuation of their colonialist policy in the Near and Middle East. Even the opening of the West European Second Front was determined above all by political motives. On the other hand, the Western Powers wanted to maintain the good relations with the Soviet Union, and at the same time they did not want to let Soviet armed forces liberate Western Europe. The Soviet historians have extensively dealt with the evolution of the works written by their Western colleagues in the last few years. They refute the views which maintain that the steps taken by the Western Powers were primarily motivated by the intention to help the Soviet Union. The author mentions C. P. Macartney's *October Fifteenth* and states that though the book is based on facts, its aim is to defend Horthy's regime. This study is based on his report of research results read out at the conference of the history of the Second World War in Budapest in September 1973. J

3228. Rahne, Hermann. ZUR TRUPPENGESCHICHTSSCHREIBUNG DES DEUTSCHEN MILITARISMUS IN VERGANGENHEIT UND GEGENWART [On German militarist historiography about troops past and present]. *Militärgeschichte [East Germany]* *1980 19(2): 177-189.* Examines the growing flood of military and neofascist literature in West Germany, and investigates the place, role, and significance of German imperialist historiography about troops within the system of political-ideological manipulation of soldiers and civilians. Describes the characteristics and functions of this kind of literature after the First and Second World Wars, and characterizes the authors, initiators, and supporters of reactionary German military historiography from the Weimar Republic through Fascism to West Germany of the seventies. 2 illus., 27 notes.

J/T (H. D. Andrews).

3229. Ranta, Britta. DIE FORSCHUNG ÜBER DIE STELLUNG FINNLANDS IM ZWEITEN WELTKRIEG [Research on Finland's position in World War II]. *La Seconda Guerra Mondiale nella prospettiva storica a trent'anni dall'epilogo* (Como: Casa editrice Pietro Cairoli, 1977). 295-306. Finland's participation in World War II was in two parts: the Winter War of 1939-40 and as an ally of Germany in the operations against the Soviet Union, 1941-44. Questions in Finnish historiography have been over whether Finland should have given in to Soviet demands in 1939 and whether this would have meant the end of Finnish independence, Finland's position between the two phases, and Finland's reasons for joining the Axis in attacking the USSR. 36 notes.

J. C. Billigmeier

3230. Regnery, Henry. HISTORICAL REVISIONISM AND WORLD WAR II. *Modern Age 1976 20(3): 254-265, (4): 402-411.* Part I. Describes revisionist books by George Morgenstern, Charles A. Beard, William Henry Chamberlain, and Charles C. Tansill, the circumstances of their publication, and their reception by reviewers. When World War II ended, the great question of American involvement again became a burning issue. Primary and secondary sources; 13 notes. Part II. Reviews books by Admiral Husband E. Kimmel, George N. Crocker, and Harry Elmer Barnes and asks, "Was the fight for what we thought was historical truth worthwhile?" Finds it difficult to believe that telling the true story, for example of Pearl Harbor, will prevent such occurrences in the future, but argues that if we believe in anything, we must believe that the truth is worthwhile for its own sake. Primary and secondary sources; 22 notes.

M. L. Lifka

3231. Reynolds, Clark G. WRITING ON NAVAL FLYING. *Aerospace Hist. 1984 31(1): 21-29.* Identifies the major works on the history of naval aviation. It has produced a rich lode of historical writing, but much remains to be done, especially in the post-World War II period. 6 illus.

J. K. Ohl

3232. Richter, Karel. BOJ O VÝKLAD DRUHÉ SVĚTOVÉ VÁLKY [The battle over interpretations of World War II]. *Hist. a Vojenství [Czechoslovakia] 1976 25(3): 131-142.* Western historians have falsified the history of World War II, misrepresenting the causes of the war, belittling the decisive role to the USSR, overlooking the role of the masses and the national liberation movements, and depicting the formation of the socialist bloc as a result of Soviet expansionism. West German historians have whitewashed the Wehrmacht and the German general staff. 41 notes.

L. Short

3233. Romer, Jeffrey A. THE GERMAN HIGH SEAS FLEET: A REAPPRAISAL. *US Naval Inst. Pro. 1978 104(1): 56-61.* The German navy was a greater asset to its country than has been generally believed by military and naval historians. Its submarines almost won the war for the Central Powers, while its High Seas fleet contributed to the German war effort by furnishing personnel for the submarine force, by keeping the Baltic Sea under German control, and by keeping the British fleet tied down and unable to support the Allied war effort elsewhere. Secondary sources; 5 photos, 17 notes.

A. N. Garland

3234. Rubenstein, Joshua. WORLD WAR II—SOVIET STYLE. *Commentary 1979 67(5): 65-67.* Examines the distortions and inaccuracies in *The Unknown War,* a series of documentary films on

World War II which portray the conflict between the Soviet Union and Germany on the Eastern front based on footage assembled by Soviet armed forces photographers; appearing on television in 1978.

3235. Rumpler, Helmut. DAS ENDE EINER DISKUSSION. NEUERE LITERATUR ZUR GESCHICHTE DES ERSTEN WELTKRIEGES [The end of a discussion: new literature on the history of World War I]. *Österreichische Osthefte [Austria] 1973 15(4): 392-396.* Reviews new West and East German books on Germany's conservative ruling elite at the outbreak of World War I, Germany's role in the war, Germany's war and peace aims, and German party policies at the beginning of the war. 18 notes.

R. Wagnleitner

3236. Rybkin, E. OSNOVNYE KATEGORII SOTSIOLOGICHESKOGO ANALIZA ISTORII VOIN [Fundamental categories in sociological analyses of the history of war]. *Voenno-Istoricheskii Zhurnal [USSR] 1973 (2): 13-20.* Describes the different categories that can be used in analyzing the history of war, such as: philosophical categories, i.e., objectivity, subjectivity, prejudice; sociological categories, i.e., historical materialism, class struggle, political goals; and military scientific categories including strategy and tactics. The author also examines the sociological analysis of the history of war especially its class origins.

3237. Rzheshevski, O. DAWN OF THE GREAT VICTORY. *Soviet Military Rev. [USSR] 1976 (11): 14-16.* Western accounts of Soviet repulsion of German troops near Moscow, 1941-42, underestimate the dedication and suffering of the Soviet peoples.

3238. Rzheshevski, O. NESOSTOIATEL'NOST' BURZHUAZNOI "TEORII RESHAIUSHCHIKH BITV" [Unsoundness of the bourgeois "theory of decisive battles"]. *Voenno-Istoricheskii Zhurnal [USSR] 1978 (2): 111-118.* Disputes the Western evaluation of World War II battles which applies the term "decisive" primarily to American and British operations. Except for Stalingrad, none were ranked with El Alamein, Tunis, Midway, and Guadalcanal; this conveniently forgets that 70% of the German troops fought against the USSR and that more than 600 German and Axis divisions were defeated or captured in the East. Only recently were bourgeois historians forced to acknowledge the impact of the crucial battles for Moscow and Kursk; e.g., Hanson Baldwin's *The Crucial Years: 1939-1941* (New York: Harper & Row, 1976) and Martin Caidin's *The Tigers Are Burning* (New York: Hawthorn Books, 1974). However, even they falsify data to belittle Soviet military acumen. As for Midway and Guadalcanal, they were hard blows to Japan but did not break its military superiority in the Pacific. 35 notes.

N. Frenkley

3240. Rzheshevski, O. PROTSKHOZHDENIE VTOROI MIROVOI VOINI V OTSENKAKH BURZHUAZNYKH ISTORIKOV SSHA [The origins of World War II according to American bourgeois historians]. *Voenno-Istoricheskii Zhurnal [USSR] 1974 (4): 39-46.* Examines US historiography on the origins of World War II published since the early 1950's.

3241. Saladino, Antonio. LA STORIOGRAFIA SULLA SECONDA GUERRA MONDIALE E LE FONTI DOCUMENTARIE CONSERVATE PRESSO L'ARCHIVIO CENTRALE DELLO STATO IN ROMA [The historiography of World War II and documentary sources in the central state archive in Rome]. *La Seconda Guerra Mondiale nella Prospettiva Storica a Trent'Anni dall'Epilogo* (Como: Casa Editrice Pietro Cairoli, 1977): 57-90. Analyzes the relationship between archival organization and historical methodology. The modern historian must deal with an abundance of sources and must therefore seek means and techniques that allow him to manage the seemingly endless supply of documents. The author provides a detailed description of the organization and contents of the materials housed in the Archivio Centrale dello Stato concerning World War II and discusses the archive's evolution. Note. M. T. Wilson

3242. Samsonov, A. M. VELIKAIA BITVA POD MOSKVOI: K ISTORIOGRAFII PROBLEMY [The great battle near Moscow: the historiography of the problem]. *Istoricheskie Zapiski Akademii Nauk SSSR [USSR] 1977 99: 246-275.* Considers the battle near Moscow between Soviet and German troops, 1941-42, during which the direction of the war began to change.

3243. Savin, A. RAZGROM IAPONII V OSVESHCHENII BURZHUAZNOI ISTORIOGRAFII [The defeat of Japan in bourgeois historiography]. *Voenno-Istoricheskii Zhurnal [USSR] 1975 (9): 55-59.* Criticizes Western historiography for representing the victory against Japan as a US achievement; emphasizes the Soviet contribution to victory.

3244. Schickel, Alfred. ENTSCHIED VERRAT DEN ZWEITEN WELTKRIEG? [Did treachery decide World War II?]. *Geschichte in Wissenschaft und Unterricht [West Germany] 1968 19(10): 608-631.* The voluminous literature on World War II contains an entire subgenre of espionage literature, much of which is devoted to assertions that information provided to the Allies by spies was decisive in bringing about Germany's military defeat. A thorough review of the evidence, however, indicates that it was Hitler's irresponsible policies and military errors that brought defeat of the Third Reich. J. M. McCarthy

3245. Schieder, Wolfgang. ITALIEN UND DEUTSCHLAND 1914/15 [Italy and Germany, 1914-15]. *Quellen und Forschungen aus Italienischen Archiven und Bibliotheken [Italy] 1968 48: 244-259.* Reviews proceedings of a Colloquium on German and Italian war aims in World War I, 13-15 April 1967 at the German Historical Institute in Rome (Deutsches Historische Institut in Rome) and the differing interpretations of this subject in German and Italian studies of the 1960's. The renewed debate on the German war guilt problem was sparked by the declassification of World War I documents and the publication of Fritz Fischer's *Germany's aims in the First World War* (Düsseldorf, 1961 and New York: W. W. Norton, 1967). 27 notes. N. Frenkley

3246. Schmidt, Hans. DIE VERTEIDIGUNG DES OBER-RHEINS UND DIE SICHERUNG SÜDDEUTSCHLANDS IM ZEITALTER DES ABSOLUTISMUS UND DER FRANZÖSISCHEN REVOLUTION: ZUR PROBLEMATIK KRIEGSGESCHICHTLICHER BEURTEILUNG [Defense of the upper Rhine and the protection of southern Germany in the age of absolutism and the French Revolution: problems of military historical evaluation]. *Hist. Jahrbuch [West Germany] 1984 104(1): 46-62.* Discusses military and strategic problems connected with the defense of Germany along the Rhine River against attacks by France during the 17th and 18th centuries. At that time, the defense of the upper Rhine and the passes through the Black Forest were central strategic problems. A successful defense on the banks of the Rhine would protect Germany from devastation, but proved to be impossible with contemporary armies. In the campaign of 1796, Archduke Charles of Austria retreated and permitted the French to temporarily occupy parts of Germany, but later destroyed them in the interior. For that he has been negatively criticized by military historians, although probably unwarrantedly. Primary sources; 47 notes. R. Vilums

3247. Schnitter, Helmut. FEUDALES MILITÄRGEWESEN UND IMPERIALISTISCHE MILITÄRGESCHICHTSSCHREIBUNG [The feudal military system and imperialist military historiography]. *Militärgeschichte [East Germany] 1974 13(2): 174-180.* The West German treatment of military history before 1789 has the political and ideological function of justifying the federal army. Notions of the fascist period such as army and nation support the goal of "integration of the army in the state." Historians ignore the socioeconomic foundations of military developments and idealize the feudal knight. They ignore Eastern Europe and Russia. They misunderstand the nature of the defense system of individual princes and of mercenary armies. The Peasants War is either ignored or misunder-

stood. Imperialist historians celebrate the development of standing armies, claiming that to be the establishment of a real tie among state, people, and army, when in fact it marked the growth of feudal absolutist militarism. Thus, out of a synthesis of military fascist tradition, relics of the Hohenzollern legend, and a social-psychological perception based on bourgeois ethical principles, the picture of the old Prussian army in modern imperialist military history grows. The task of Marxist-Leninist historiography is to prevent imperialists from misusing the progressive military tradition. 22 notes. H. D. Andrews

3248. Schnitter, Helmut; Tomczak, Maria, transl. W KWESTII MIEJSCA PRUSKICH REFORMATORÓW SYSTEMU WOJS-KOWEGO W HISTORIOGRAFII NRD [Placement of Prussian reformers of the military system in East German historiography]. *Przegląd Zachodni [Poland] 1980 36(4): 66-77.* Marxist-Leninist military historians value the reforms instigated in Prussia after the defeat at Jena. The reforms made the Prussian army again a progressive element in the nation. General conscription, abolishment of serfdom, general elementary education, and abolishment of class privileges in the military all played a role in modernizing Prussia and making it a unified state. M. Krzyzaniak

3249. Schraepler, Ernst. DIE FORSCHUNG ÜBER DEN AUS-BRUCH DES ERSTEN WELTKRIEGES IM WANDEL DES GESCHICHTSBILDES 1919-1969 [Research on the outbreak of World War I through changes in historical interpretation, 1919-69]. *Geschichte in Wissenschaft und Unterricht [West Germany] 1972 23(6): 321-338.* Discusses the development of the historical interpretation of the war guilt question from early apologetic works immediately after World War I to the school of Fritz Fischer, who worked out the underlying Social Darwinist tendencies of German imperialistic foreign policy.

3250. Schramm, Tomasz. LA QUESTION POLONAISE ET LA PREMIÈRE GUERRE MONDIALE [The Polish question and World War I]. *Rev. Hist. [France] 1981 265(2): 439-448.* Prevailing opinion among French historians concerning the origins and results of World War I has been shaped by the historical syntheses written by Pierre Renouvin. But Renouvin neglected Poland on several important topics and left the false impression that Poland was a passive element in the origins, conduct, and results of the war. Based on two books by Pierre Renouvin and one book by the Polish historian V. Pajewski; 25 notes. G. H. Davis

3251. Schramm, Tomasz. PROBLEM GENEZY PIERWSZEJ WOJNY ŚWIATOWEJ W HISTORIOGRAFII FRANCUSKIEJ [The origins of World War I in French historiography]. *Roczniki Hist. [Poland] 1979 45: 147-175.* Reviews French historiography and singles out two general stages of research. Works published during and shortly after the war were characterized by their stress on laying the blame on the Central Powers for starting the conflict (Emile Bourgeois and Georges Pagès). During the second half of the 1920's there began to appear more objective works, such as those of Pierre Renouvin and Jules Isaac. Identifies several schools of opinion among French historians for the causes of the war, which were based largely on the same sources; the decisive factor in the changes in the interpretations of French scholars derived from their more complete understanding of the period and more thorough grounding in historical methods. 43 notes. A. B. Pernal

3252. Schumann, Wolfgang. KONZEPTION FÜR DIE AUSAR-BEITUNG EINER VIERBÄNDIGEN "GESCHICHTE DEUTSCHLANDS IM ZWEITEN WELTKRIEG" [Draft for the preparation of a four-volume *History of Germany in World War II*]. *Jahrbuch für Geschichte [East Germany] 1969 3: 9-94.* Outline of a soon to be published four-volume history of Germany from September 1939 to May 1945 by the Authors Collective of the History Institute of the German Academy of Sciences in Berlin. Using the newest work of Marxist historians plus new source materials, the work interprets Hitler's economic, domestic, foreign, and military policies, and emphasizes the contrasts between East and West

German historiography, the underground resistance activities of the German Communist Party, and its extensive preparations for the building of an antifascist, democratic postwar Germany.

M. A. Hoobs

3253. Schumann, Wolfgang and Wappler, Anke. MÁSODIK VILÁGHÁBORÚS TÖRTÉNETI IRODALOM AZ NDK-BAN [Literature on World War II in East Germany]. *Történelmi Szemle [Hungary] 1973 16(3-4): 356-371*. East German military historians dealing with World War II have concentrated on publishing documents concerned with the Southeast European theaters of operation. Some of these publications are discussed here. 78 notes.

H. Szamuely/S

3254. Scurtu, I. N. IORGA DESPRE CAUZELE IZBUCNIRII ŞI CARACTERUL PRIMULUI RĂZBOI MONDIAL [N. Iorga on the origins and character of World War I]. *Analele Universităţii Bucureşti: Istorie [Rumania] 1967 16: 97-108*. As an active participant in the political life of the country and as a historian, Nicolae Iorga analyzed the various aspects of World War I in newspaper articles, scientific communications, conferences, and university courses. Although Iorga's general conception of history was idealistic, he discerned the fact that the war had economic causes and spoke against occupation of countries for the development of new markets and the acquisition of natural resources. He credited the "materialism" which characterized the second half of the 19th century for the war and the spreading of warlike theories among the masses. Iorga showed that German imperialism relied on the philosophy of Nietzsche and social Darwinism. Iorga's humanism rejected the use of science to destroy people and he sympathized with the nations fighting for liberty, independence, and national unity. Primary and secondary sources; 76 notes.   T. Z. Herman

3255. Sekistov, V. A. K VOPROSU O FAL'SIFIKATSII ISTORII VTOROI MIROVOI VOINY I VELIKOI OTECHESTVENNOI VOINY SOVETSKOGO SOIUZA [On the problem of the falsification of the history of World War II and the Great Patriotic War of the Soviet Union]. *Voprosy Istorii KPSS [USSR] 1974 (4): 34-45*. Western writers on World War II such as B. H. Liddel Hart and A. Seaton continue to participate in an ideological struggle against socialism. They ignore the role the Communist Party played in mobilizing the Soviet people; grossly underestimate the Soviet contribution to the war against Japan and especially Germany; attribute Germany's defeat not to the heroism of the party and Red Army but to Germany's weak leadership and Russia's size; and ignore or distort the USSR's liberation of Eastern Europe. Based on Western historical studies on World War II; 58 notes.

L. E. Holmes

3256. Sekistov, V. A. KRITIKA BURZHUAZNYKH FAL'SIFIKATSII ITOGOV I UROKOV VTOROI MIROVOI VOINY [Criticism of bourgeois falsifications of the conclusions and lessons of the Second World war]. *Voprosy Istorii KPSS [USSR] 1975 (4): 81-92*. Despite detente the ideological struggle continues as bourgeois historians distort the history of World War II with four main falsehoods. 1) They blame only Nazi Germany or so-called Soviet imperialism, not Western imperialism including the Munich Pact, for the war's origin. 2) They claim the USSR's victory stemmed only from Hitler's mistakes and such Western assistance as lend-lease. 3) Only the USSR, not European and Asian socialism in general, is regarded as victorious. 4) The USSR rather than Western anti-Sovietism is blamed for the Cold War. Based on an analysis of British and American publications; 59 notes.

L. E. Holmes

3257. Sekistov, V. A. RAZOBLACHENIE HOVEISHIKH BURZHUAZNYKH FAL'SIFIKATSII ISTORII VTOROI MIROVOI VOINY [Exposure of the latest bourgeois falsifications of the history of World War II]. *Voprosy Istorii KPSS [USSR] 1981 (3): 113-122*. Western imperialist circles have recently tried to revise the history of World War II and to suggest that the USSR is a threat to world peace. They accuse the USSR of expansionism, but in reality it is NATO which is aggressively imperialist. During World War II the USSR played an honorable role while America and Great Britain tried to weaken both Germany and the USSR

for their own economic advantage. Bourgeois myth sees the United States as the principal adversary of fascism, but it was the USSR which was the real hero. However antisocialist and anti-Soviet western propaganda may be, people will recognize and value the USSR's role in the thwarting of fascism and in the construction of peace. Based on Soviet and Western press reports, and on political speeches; 62 notes.   A. J. Evans

3258. Seleznev, K. L. VOENNO-TEORETICHESKIE PROBLEMY V BURZHUAZNOI I MELKOBURZHUAZNOI "MARKSOLOGII" 70-KH GODOV XX V [Military-theoretical problems in bourgeois and petit bourgeois Marxology of the 1970's]. *Voprosy Istorii KPSS [USSR] 1979 (7): 81-92*. Analyzes studies published during the 1970's by such Western writers as Robert Tucker, Bertram Wolfe, Schlomo Avineri, W. O. Henderson, and M. Berger which examine the views of Karl Marx (1818-83) and Friedrich Engels (1820-95) on the use of military force and the role of armed forces in history. Isolating the statements of Marx and Engels on armed force from the overall Marxist conception of society and history, many Western analysts have distorted the meaning and applicability of Marxism by ignoring Marx's primary emphasis on the working class and a political party representing its interests. Secondary sources; 83 notes.   L. E. Holmes

3259. Semin, V. VOENNO-POLITICHESKII SOIUZ STRAN SOTSIALIZMA I BOEVOE SODRUZHESTVO IKH VOORUZHENNYKH SIL KAK OB"EKT ISSLEDOVANIIA [The military and political defensive union of the socialist countries and the military cooperation of their armed forces as an object of research]. *Voenno-Istoricheskii Zhurnal [USSR] 1982 (7): 67-74*. The writings of Soviet military scholars faithfully reflect the history of the Warsaw Pact. However the attempts to establish the periods of its development have not produced a consensus. Furthermore several theoretical questions on the collective defense of the socialist countries have as yet been insufficiently researched. 17 notes.

G. Dombrovski

3260. Shankovsky, Lev. NARYS UKRAINS'KOI VOIENNOI ISTORIOGRAFII: UKRAINS'KA VOENNO-ISTORYCHNA NAUKA V PERIODI MIZH VIINAMY (1921-1939) [An outline of Ukrainian war historiography: Ukrainian military history between the wars, 1921-39]. *Ukrains'kyi Istoryk 1974 11(1-3): 48-64*. A critical review of literature available on the operations of the Ukrainian Galician Army and fighting in the Ukraine, 1921-39.

3261. Shankovsky, Lev. NARYS UKRAÏNSKOÏ VOIENNOÏ ISTORIOGRAFI [A sketch of Ukrainian military historiography]. *Ukraïns'ki Istorik [USSR] 1972 9(3/4): 55-71*. Describes the military-historical, cultural, and patriotic activities of Ukrainian military units in emigration throughout Central and Western European countries, especially in Czechoslovakia, where the most numerous army units of Ukrainians were admitted by the Czechoslovakian government after the Russian Revolution and civil war.

A. Mina

3262. Shapiro, Edward S. THE MILITARY OPTIONS TO HIROSHIMA: A CRITICAL EXAMINATION OF GAR ALPEROVITZ'S *ATOMIC DIPLOMACY*. *Amerikastudien/Am. Studies [West Germany] 1978 23(1): 60-72*. Gar Alperovitz's *Atomic Diplomacy* (1965) is a polemical revisionist tract. At no time was President S. Truman advised by his military chiefs that Japan was on the verge of surrender or that Japanese capitulation would occur without use of the atomic bomb. Of little value in understanding the circumstances surrounding the dropping of the atomic bomb in 1945, *Atomic Diplomacy* reveals much about the outlook and methodology of one representative revisionist diplomatic historian.   J

3263. Shekhovtsov, N. SOVETSKOE STRATEGICHSKOE RUKOVODSTVO I IZMYSHLENIIA FAL'SIFIKATOROV [Soviet strategic leadership and the falsifiers' fabrications]. *Voenno-Istoricheskii Zhurnal [USSR] 1974 (3): 45-52*. Analyzes and refutes Western criticism of the leadership and activities of the Soviet High Command during World War II.

3264. Shilin, Pawel. DIE KLASSIKER DES MARXISMUS-LENINISMUS ÜBER KRIEG UND MILITÄRGESCHICHTE [The classics of Marxism-Leninism on war and military history]. *Militärgeschichte [East Germany] 1984 23(2): 99-106.* A characteristic trait of the military history works of Marx and Engels consisted of the broad political, economic, and even military strategy analysis of war as well as the investigation of its origins, course, conclusion, and social consequences. Because they studied military history from a dialectical materialist position, they worked out the scientific foundation and methodological principles for research and can justly be called the founders of the discipline of military history. V. I. Lenin worked in a different historical situation—the transition of capitalism to its imperialist stage. His outstanding contributions were to preserve the inheritance of Marx and Engels from bourgeois revisionist and leftist tendencies and to systematize Marxist military theory and military history knowledge, developing it creatively in the conditions of a new epoch and placing it in the service of the working class. 21 notes. H. D. Andrews

3265. Showalter, Dennis E. MILITARY HISTORY IN GERMANY, 1979-80: AN OVERVIEW OF PERIODICAL LITERATURE. *Military Affairs 1981 45(2): 85-86.* Survey of the periodical literature about German military history published in East and West Germany during 1979-80. A significant trend in German military history is the growing convergence of interpretation and lines of argument in the two Germanies. A. M. Osur

3266. Sikorski, Janusz. REVUE DES RECHERCHES EN MATIÈRE D'HISTOIRE MILITAIRE JUSQUE 1914 EN RÉPUBLIQUE POPULAIRE DE POLOGNE [Review of research on military history topics up to 1914 in Poland]. *R. Internat. d'Hist. Militaire [Belgium] 1969 (28): 621-640.* Describes topics of recent Polish military historiography from the origins of the Polish state to World War I. Also discusses Polish centers of scholarship and journals devoted to military history. Primary and secondary sources; 94 notes. P. T. Herman

3267. Smallwood, James. A HISTORICAL DEBATE OF THE 1960S: WORLD WAR II HISTORIOGRAPHY—THE ORIGINS OF THE WAR, A. J. P. TAYLOR, AND HIS CRITICS. *Australian J. of Pol. and Hist. [Australia] 1980 26(3): 403-410.* A summary of the controversy concerning A. J. P. Taylor's *Origins of the Second World War* (1961). Taylor argued that Adolf Hitler was only an ordinary German who wanted to free Germany from the trammels of Versailles and let it be Europe's greatest power. He followed no preconceived plans and was helped to his gains by the British policy of appeasement. Taylor got some support from E. H. Carr, David L. Hoggan, Sebastian Haffner, David Marquand, John Vincent, and E. M. Robertson, but the orthodox school, who stress Hitler's long-term goal and demonic personality, have held sway. A major difference in interpretation concerns *Mein Kampf* and the Hossbach memorandum. Taylor regarded these as mere ramblings, while the orthodox school accept them as evidence of long-term aims. Based on works on World War II; 27 notes. W. D. McIntyre

3268. Smirnov, V. P. NOVYE FRANTSUZSKIE RABOTY PO ISTORII DVIZHENIIA SOPROTIVLENIIA [New French works on the history of the Resistance movement]. *Novaia i Noveishaia Istoriia [USSR] 1971 (1): 158-166.* Surveys ideological trends in the historiography of the French World War II Resistance movement, especially the role of the Communist Party of France. E. R. Sicher

3269. Smith, Ralph B. READING HISTORY: VIETNAM WAR. *History Today [Great Britain] 1984 34(Oct): 45-48.* Evaluates the historiography of the Vietnam War, describing books written during 1966-84.

3270. Solov'ev, B. PROVAL TRET'EGO NASTUPLENIIA VERMAKHTA NA VOSTOKE [The failure of the Wehrmacht's third eastern offensive]. *Voenno-Istoricheskii Zhurnal [USSR] 1970 12(7): 33-42.* Accuses Western historians of falsifying the history of the Soviet-German Battle of Kursk, July 1943.

3271. Stafford, D. A. T. UPSTAIRS-DOWNSTAIRS: BRITISH FOREIGN POLICY AND SPECIAL OPERATIONS IN EUROPE 1940-45. *J. of European Studies [Great Britain] 1975 5(1): 55-61.* Reviews several official and semi-official histories and reminiscences about British special operations, including M. R. D. Foot's *SOE in France* (1966); L. Woodward's *British Foreign Policy in the Second World War* (1970); and Winston Churchill's *History of the Second World War* and asserts that they concentrate unduly on the upper ranks.

3272. Strieter, Terry W. THE STATE OF MILITARY HISTORY: SOME UPDATINGS AND NEW FINDINGS FOR EUROPEAN ARMIES, 1494-1815. *Armed Forces and Soc. 1982 8(3): 499-504.* Reviews André Corvisier's *Armies and Societies in Europe, 1494-1789* (1979), translated by Abigail T. Siddall, and Samuel F. Scott's *The Response of the Royal Army to the French Revolution: The Role And Development of the Line Army, 1787-1793* (1978), with major emphasis on Corvisier's book. Both authors avoid viewing military history as a series of battles and focus on the human aspects of European military society: the life and times of the officers and enlisted personnel who comprised the garrisons and fought the battles. D. Powell

3273. Stromberg, Roland. ON CHERCHEZ LE FINANCIER: COMMENTS ON THE ECONOMIC INTERPRETATION OF WORLD WAR I. *Hist. Teacher 1977 10(3): 435-443.* Discusses the validity of the economic interpretation of the origins of World War I. Holds that the war was not primarily economic in origin; rather its roots were deeper, more complex, and more varied. Basically, politics determined economics. Economic interests merged into sentimental and ideological ones. Support for this view is found in neo-Marxian interpretations of the origin of the war. The economic interpretation is antiquated and simplistic. Primary and secondary sources; 26 notes. P. W. Kennedy

3274. Syrett, David. THE SECRET WAR AND THE HISTORIANS. *Armed Forces and Soc. 1983 9(2): 293-328.* Reviews the historiography of military intelligence and counterintelligence during World War II. Much vital information is still unavailable to historians. 91 notes. R. Grove

3275. Szabo, Agnes. BEITRÄGE ZUR HISTORIOGRAPHIE DER GESCHICHTE DES II. WELTKRIEGES [The historiography of World War II]. *La Seconda Guerra Mondiale nella prospettiva storica a trent'anni dall'epilogo (Como: Casa editrice Pietro Cairoli, 1977): 317-326.* Hungary was the last of Hitler's European allies to capitulate. Italy left in 1943, and Finland, Romania, and Bulgaria in 1944. But Hungary under the Fascist Szálasi regime which seized power on 15 October 1944, continued to fight alongside its Nazi cobelligerent until the bitter end. After the war, Hungarian historians ignored the great conflict, preferring older, safer themes. Not until the late 1950's did they begin to consider World War II. Since then a flood of histories have appeared, which the author discusses in some detail. J. C. Billigmeier

3276. Thiel, Werner. DIE ENTWICKLUNG DER SOWJETISCHEN TRUPPENGESCHICHTSSCHREIBUNG IM ÜBERBLICK [The development of Soviet historiography of military units]. *Militärgeschichte [East Germany] 1980 19(1): 25-32.* Histories of military units have formed an essential part of Soviet military historiography since 1918. They have covered both the Soviet army and navy and have been used to teach patriotism in the armed services and to spur the defense training of youth. The historiography of military units entered new phases in 1941, 1945, and the mid-1950's. 16 notes, 2 biblio. J/T (H. D. Andrews)

3277. Thompson, Robert and Mead, Peter. WINGATE—THE PURSUIT OF TRUTH. *Army Q. and Defense J. [Great Britain] 1978 108(3): 335-340.* Focuses on the inaccuracies of the official Cabinet Office histories of World War I and World War II, specifically the record of the reputation of Major-General Orde Wingate established in four successful military campaigns between 1936 and 1944 in the British Army.

3278. Tiushkevich, S. O PRINTSIPE PARTIINOSTI V VOENNOI ISTORII [Party spirit in military history]. *Voenno-Istoricheskii Zhurnal [USSR] 1972 (1): 3-10.* The correct Communist Party attitude is an essential attribute of the Soviet military historian, and the cause of socialism benefits in various ways from history written in this spirit.

3279. Tønnesson, Stein. TRETTIÅRSKRIGEN I INDOKINA 1945-1975 SOM EMNE FOR HISTORISK FORSKNING [The Thirty Years War in Indochina, 1945-75, as a topic for historical research]. *Int. Pol. [Norway] 1984 (1): 105-119.* After an assessment of problems related to periodization of the war and a presentation of some main perspectives regarding the nature of this war, argues that the most important issues now for a political and historical Indochina war research effort ought to be the outbreak of the war in 1945, the internationalization of the war in 1950, and the Geneva negotiations and agreement in 1954. J

3280. Torrey, Glenn. ROMANIAN HISTORIOGRAPHY ON THE FIRST WORLD WAR. *Military Affairs 1982 46(1): 25-28.* Discusses the most important of the recent Romanian books on the experience of World War I when, at a heavy cost, the historic Romanian lands were united for the first time since 1600. 12 notes. A. M. Osur

3281. Toškova, Vitka. INTERNATIONALE WISSENSCHAFTLICHE KONFERENZ ZUM THEMA "DIE HISTORIOGRAPHIE ÜBER DEN ZWEITEN WELTKRIEG IN MITTEL- UND OSTEUROPA" [International scientific conference on the historiography of World War II in central and eastern Europe]. *Bulgarian Hist. Rev. [Bulgaria] 1974 2(1): 103-109.* Reviews the conference held at Budapest, 27-29 September 1973, in which 19 countries took part at Hungary's invitation. Its main aim was to summarize the results of research into the history of World War II over the last five years, and to discuss future research. The main Hungarian reports are considered in detail and the findings of the three conference discussion groups are examined. Although some gaps do exist the wealth of literature already produced has heralded a new era in the study of World War II: the stage of systematic compilation. 10 notes. A. Armstrong

3282. Tóth, Sándor. MAGYARORSZÁG KATONAI SZEREPE A MÁSODIK VILÁGHÁBORÚBAN [Hungary's military role in World War II]. *Történelmi Szemle [Hungary] 1973 16(3-4): 339-355.* Considers the historiography of Hungary's military involvement, 1939-45. Historians concerned with this subject have produced numerous specialized monographs, but no general or synthetic works as yet. Secondary sources; 99 notes. H. Szamuely/S

3283. Trainor, Luke. THE EUROPEAN STATES SYSTEM AND THE ORIGIN OF THE FIRST WORLD WAR, 1903-1915: THE FISCHER SCHOOL AND THE GERMAN ROLE IN WAR ORIGINS. *New Zealand J. of Hist. [New Zealand] 1975 9(2): 171-178.* The Fischer controversy is only gradually being absorbed into the body of historical scholarship, though Fritz Fischer has established that the German government took actions which it knew were likely to lead to war. His work invites comparative studies of France, Britain, Russia, and Austria. Secondary sources; 17 notes. P. J. Coleman

3284. Trenard, Louis. LA BATAILLE DE CASSEL, 1677 [The Battle of Cassel, 1677]. *Rev. du Nord [France] 1979 61(242): 581-592.* Compares three centuries of historiography of the battle of Cassel between William of Orange and the Duc d'Orléans, brother of Louis XIV of France. Following the eyewitness accounts of the battle came 18th-century opinions which expressed political overtones. The Duc d'Orléans was rehabilitated while Louis XIV was criticized. Nineteenth-century historians were more demanding. The Flemish scholar De Smyttère brought precision to the phases of the battle while sympathizing with the conqueror. Contemporary historiography attaches much less importance to the battle although it insured the taking of St. Omer and the annexation of maritime Flanders. 2 illus., map, 31 notes. J/S

3285. Trgo, Fabijan. IZVORI I LITERATURA ZA HISTORIJU NARODNOOSLOBODILAČKOG RATA [Sources and literature for the history of the National Liberation War]. *Vojnoistorijski Glasnik [Yugoslavia] 1967 18(2): 7-93.*

3286. Turnbaugh, Roy. HARRY ELMER BARNES AND WORLD WAR I REVISIONISM: AN ABSENCE OF DIALOGUE. *Peace and Change 1978 5(2-3): 63-69.* Schooled in the liberalism and revisionism popular in intellectual circles during the 1920's and influenced by his employment as a propagandist for the Allied cause during World War I, Harry Elmer Barnes in *The Genesis of the World War* (1926) typified the extreme of revisionist thought, but was severely criticized for unhistorical attitude, pro-Germanism, and tendency to reduce the conflict to personal terms.

3287. Turner, L. C. F. AUSTRALIAN HISTORICAL AND BIOGRAPHICAL WRITING RELATING TO THE SECOND WORLD WAR. *La Seconda Guerra Mondiale nella Prospettiva Storica a Trent'Anni dall'Epilogo* (Como: Casa Editrice Pietro Cairoli, 1977): 397-409. After a brief consideration of the apparent lack of academic attention by Australian scholars to war history, the author lists and reviews the existing Australian historiography and documents on World War II. M. T. Wilson

3288. Usikov, A. and Shevchenko, V. NORMANDSKAIA DESANTNAIA OPERATSIIA [The Normandy landing]. *Voenno-Istoricheskii Zhurnal [USSR] 1984 (6): 61-69.* Rejects the view of the crucial importance of the D-Day landing in 1944 held by the Western historians, who see the opening of the second front in Europe as the decisive factor in victory over Germany. The overwhelming Soviet military victories since 1942 had finally spurred the Allies, worried about the fast pace of the Red Army, into opening the second front. Fig., 23 notes. M. Hernas

3289. Valabrega, Guido. ECHI DEL PROCESSO EICHMANN NELLA PUBBLICISTICA ITALIANA [Echoes of the Eichmann trial in Italian publications]. *Movimento di Liberazione in Italia [Italy] 1961 63(2): 63-67.* Reviews five books published in Italy in 1960-61, providing background information on Adolf Eichmann's Jerusalem trial for Nazi war crimes; more than an individual, the Nazi regime and weak Western democracies were on trial.

3290. Vargin, N. F. KRASNYI FLOT (1918-1920 GG) V SOVETSKOI ISTORICHESKOI LITERATURE [The Red Fleet (1918-20) in Soviet historical literature]. *Istoriia SSSR [USSR] 1972 (4): 89-101.* Since the historiography of the Soviet Red Fleet is part of general historiography on the civil war in the USSR, the author does not examine the literature on the Red Fleet by periods, but rather attempts to determine to what extent its most important themes have been studied, i.e.: the formation of the Red Fleet; its fundamental organization; the preparation and the acceptance of the decree on the creation of the fleet and the practical transfer of the big and complex naval agency and the fleet to its new basis; the struggle to save the Baltic fleet from German conquest; the fate of the Black Sea fleet; the Red Fleet in combat; the Red Fleet on Soviet rivers; the naval forces in the Far East; the political life of the Red Fleet; and its leadership. Primary and secondary sources; 59 notes. L. Kalinowski

3291. Vargyai, Gyula. A MÁSODIK VILÁGHÁBORÚ KÉRDÉSEIVEL FOGLALKOZÓ NÉHÁNY ÚJABB NYUGATNÉMET HADTÖRTÉNELMI MUNKÁRÓL [On some recent West German military historical works dealing with the questions of World War II]. *Hadtörténelmi Közlemények [Hungary] 1983 30(4): 686-692.* Reviews Dieter Ose's *Entscheidung im Westen 1944* [Decision in the West 1944] (1982), Helmut Krausnick and Hans Heinrich-Wilhelms's *Die Truppe des Weltanschauungskrieges* [The troops of the war of ideology] (1981), Romedio Galeazzo Graf von Thun-Hohenstein's *Der Verschwörer. General Oster und die Militäropposition* [The conspirator: General Oster and the military opposition] (1982), Hans von Herwath's *Erlebte Zeitgeschichte 1931-1945* [Witness to contemporary history]

(1982), and Albert Speer's *Der Sklavenstaat* [The slave state] (1981). These works differ in quality, the first two being the most scholarly and containing the most new information.

G. Jeszenszky

3292. Vasilevsky, Alexander. SERVING THE PEOPLE. *Soviet Military Rev.* [USSR] 1975 (9): 40-42. Interview with Marshal Aleksandr Vasilevski, in which he discusses Soviet military science, attempts made by Western historiography to belittle its use in World War II, and his participation in World War II, 1941-45.

3293. Vehviläinen, Olli. NEUE FINNISCHE LITERATUR ZUR GESCHICHTE DES ZWEITEN WELTKRIEGES [New Finnish literature on the history of World War II]. *Jahrbücher für Geschichte Osteuropas* [West Germany] 1981 29(2): 246-257. A new phase in Finnish historiography began in 1974 with the establishment of Research Project Finland in the Second World War, directed by Olli Vehviläinen and under the auspices of the Ministry of Education and the Finnish Academy. Numerous colleges and scientific institutes began collaborating in a 10-year effort to develop a multifaceted picture of Finland and its society during the war. With the major military histories already completed, the Research Project turned its attention to such diplomatic, economic, and domestic questions as Finland's war aims, the devastation and reconstruction of Lapland, internal political issues, and plans for unification with Sweden. 16 notes.

S. A. Welisch

3294. Veryha, Wasyl. THE GALICIA UKRAINIAN DIVISION IN POLISH AND SOVIET LITERATURE. *Ukrainian Q.* 1980 36(3): 253-270. In 1943 a Ukrainian military unit known as the Galicia Division was formed under German auspices to fight against the Soviet army on the eastern front. After engaging in action in several areas, most of the Galicia unit surrendered to the British in 1945. Several Polish sources have claimed that this unit was deeply and brutally involved in the 1944 Warsaw uprising and in other Polish atrocities, but such claims have repeatedly been proven false. Soviet sources, while also ascribing crimes to the Galicia Division, minimized its role, preferring to emphasize the obvious anti-Soviet cast of the unit. Ukrainian partisans have also denigrated the role of the Galicia Division, claiming it acted only as a guerrilla unit. 47 notes.

K. N. T. Crowther

3295. Vigezzi, Brunello. LUGLIO 1914: UNA STORIA DI BREVE O DI LUNGO PERIODO? [July 1914: a short- or long-period history?]. *Ann. della Facoltà di Sci. Pol.: Materiali di Storia* [Italy] 1980-81 17(5 part 2): 135-150. In the light of recent studies on World War I examines the methodological implications of research on the crisis of July 1914 and the origins of the war, in terms of long- and short-term theories.

3296. Vinogradov, A. PRAVDA O TOM, KAK ITALIIA VYSHLA IZ VTOROI MIROVOI VOINY [The truth about how Italy left World War II]. *Voprosy Istorii* [USSR] 1979 (5): 121-130. Discusses the circumstances of Italy's abandonment of alliance with Nazi Germany in 1943. The royalist bourgeois regime which ruled after the removal of Mussolini in July 1943 was willing to sign a capitulation to the Allies and to follow the path of containment of communism, but some elements of the regime continued to assure the Germans about Italy's adherence to the Berlin-Rome axis. On 8 September Italy abandoned the axis, and the following day the king and key government figures fled the country, leaving it defenseless. The motive for their defection was sheer cowardice, not concern for the people or an effort to avoid armed conflict with the Germans, as the bourgeois historiography claims. Secondary sources, 44 notes.

V. Sobeslavsky

3297. Vinogradov, K. B. OSNOVNYE NAPRAVLENIIA BURZHUAZNOI ISTORIOGRAFII AVSTRO-SERBSKOGO KONFLIKTA I VOZNIKONOVENIIA PERVOI MIROVOI VOINY [Basic trends in the bourgeois historiography of the Austro-Serbian conflict and the origins of the first world war]. *Uchenye Zapiski Inst. Slavianovedeniia Akademii Nauk SSSR* [USSR] 1962 (24): 169-196. Available European and US publications are too preoccupied with secondary politics and superficial diplomacy.

3298. Wegner, Bernd. DIE GARDE DES "FÜHRERS" UND DIE "FEUERWEHR" DER OSTFRONT: ZUR NEUERER LITERATUR ÜBER DIE WAFFEN-SS [The Führer's guard and the "fire brigade" of the Eastern Front: recent literature on the Waffen SS]. *Militärgeschichtliche Mitteilungen* [West Germany] 1978 (1): 210-236. Discusses historiography, written 1965-77, on the role of the German Waffen SS.

3299. Weinland, Robert G.; Herrick, Robert W.; MccGwire, Michael; and McConnell, James M. ADMIRAL GORSHKOV'S "NAVIES IN WAR AND PEACE." *Survival* [Great Britain] 1975 17(2): 54-63. Discuss USSR Admiral S. G. Gorshkov's historical analysis of the role of navies in war and peace and in military strategy, and its relevance to the USSR's current military and foreign policy.

3300. Wiggershaus, Norbert. DIE AMTLICHE MILITÄRGESCHICHTSFORSCHUNG IN DER DIENSTSTELLE BLANK UND IM BUNDESMINISTERIUM FÜR VERTEIDIGUNG 1952 BIS 1956: VORSTELLUNGEN UND PLANUNGEN [The official military history research in the so-called Dienststelle Blank and in the defense ministry of West Germany: conceptions and planning]. *Militärgeschichtliche Mitteilungen* [West Germany] 1976 (2): 115-121. Surveys the founding, organization, and scientific results of the official systematic military history research of West Germany and the meaning of its activities for German historiography. 45 notes.

3301. Wiltz, John Edward. TRUMAN AND MACARTHUR: THE WAKE ISLAND MEETING. *Military Affairs* 1978 42(4): 169-176. Summarizes historical evaluations of the October 1950 meeting between President Harry S. Truman and General of the Army Douglas MacArthur at Wake Island, giving the background to and a detailed account of the meeting. Many accounts contain inaccuracies and mistaken assumptions. Truman's purpose in calling the meeting was "public relations" for the upcoming election, and historians should be careful not to assume exalted motives for exalted personages. Based on the *Log of President Truman's Trip*, interviews, and secondary sources; 34 notes.

A. M. Osur

3302. Windisch, Aladarne. MILITÄRHISTORISCHE PUBLIKATIONEN IN UNGARN IN DEN 70ER JAHREN [Publications on military history in Hungary in the 1970's]. *Militärgeschichte* [East Germany] 1977 16(3): 354-359. Describes relevant institutions and journals and provides a topical overview of publications of Hungarian Marxist-Leninist military historiography, 1970-75.

H. D. Andrews

3303. Young, Kenneth Ray. THE STILWELL CONTROVERSY: A BIBLIOGRAPHICAL REVIEW. *Military Affairs* 1975 39(2): 66-68. Reviews General Joseph W. Stilwell's career in Asia and examines the controversy over Stilwell's effectiveness as the China-India-Burma Theater commander (1942-44). Summarizes the different viewpoints and concludes that Stilwell's mission to China was doomed from the start. 23 notes.

A. M. Osur

3304. Young, Marilyn B. REVISIONISTS REVISED: THE CASE OF VIETNAM. *Soc. for Hist. of Am. Foreign Relations. Newsletter* 1979 10(2): 1-10. None of the recent revisionist histories of the Vietnam War reveals the actual imperialistic and anti-self-deterministic nature of US intervention.

3305. Zaitsev, I. ARDENSKAIA OPERATSIIA [The Ardennes Operation]. *Voenno-Istoricheskii Zhurnal* [USSR] 1969 11(12): 40-46. Denies claims by Western historians that the German attack during the Battle of the Bulge, 1944, was mounted at the cost of weakening their forces on the Eastern Front.

3306. Zakharov, M. V. ISTORICHESKAIA POBEDA SOVETSKOGO NARODA I EGO VOORUZHENNYKH SIL [The historic victory of the Soviet people and her armed forces]. *Voprosy Istorii KPSS* [USSR] 1970 (5): 3-15. Assesses key factors in the USSR's victory over Germany in World War II, and laments attempts by bourgeois historians to underestimate its importance.

3307. Zaniewicki, Witold. UN MOYEN DE RECHERCHES EN HISTOIRE MILITAIRE: L'ÉTUDE DES MOUVEMENTS DE TROUPES (LE RETOUR DE L'ARMÉE À PARIS, MARS-JUIN 1848) [A method of research in military history: the study of troop movements (the return of the army to Paris, March-June 1848)]. *Rev. d'Hist. Moderne et Contemporaine [France] 1975 22(4): 583-600.* Immediately after the Revolution of 1848 and the proclamation of the Second French Republic, the army was sent to the frontiers. In May it was necessary to recall the troops to Paris to keep order. An analysis of the troop movements shows that the Minister of War, Louis Eugène Cavaignac (1802-57) executed this mission ably, transferring enough troops to maintain order without making an excessive military display. The army assumed police duties in Paris during May and June and was well prepared to crush the insurrection that broke out on June 23. Based on documents in military archives, and secondary works; 40 notes. J. D. Dawson

3308. Zhilin, P. A. O PROBLEMAKH ISTORII VTOROI MIROVOI VOINY [Some problems on the history of World War II]. *Novaia i Noveishaia Istoriia [USSR] 1973 (2): 3-19.* The study of World War II highlights the vigilance necessary to maintain peace. Bourgeois historians have questioned the role of the USSR in World War II to smear it, and to detract from the Soviet Communist Party's reputation as the inspirer of anti-fascist resistance. Led by the Communist Party, the Soviet people, fulfilling their internationalist duty, defeated the Nazis. The experience gained in World War II increases our understanding of the modern world, where the conflict between capitalism and socialism is being waged. Based on the works of Lenin and Leonid Brezhnev; 16 notes. A. J. Evans

3309. Zhilin, P. A. PROTIV IZVRASHCHENIIA ROLI SOVETSKOGO SOIUZA VO VTOROI MIROVOI VOINE [Against the distortion of the USSR's role in World War II]. *Voprosy Istorii KPSS [USSR] 1965 (5): 52-64.* Analyzes English, American, West German and French studies of the war, which tend to distort the USSR's role because of their intent to falsify history.

3310. Zhilin, P. A. VOENNAIA ISTORIIA I SOVREMENNOST' [Military history and the contemporary world]. *Voenno-Istoricheskii Zhurnal [USSR] 1975 (5): 70-80.* Stresses the importance of military history, presents a survey of sources, particularly those relating to World War II, and criticizes bourgeois historians for the their distortion of the facts.

3311. Zhilin, P. A. VSEMIRNO-ISTORICHESKAIA POBEDA SOVETSKOGO NARODA V VELIKOI OTECHESTVENNOI VOINE [The historic victory of the Soviet people in the Great Patriotic War]. *Novaia i Noveishaia Istoriia [USSR] 1975 (2): 3-20.* Discusses the causes, character, course, and results of World War II. Particular attention is devoted to its main component part—the Great Patriotic War of the Soviet Union. The author considers the tasks of Soviet historians and the results of their work in the field of research of the history of World War II. J

3312. Zhukov, Georgi. THE WAR AGAINST HITLER AND THE FALSIFIERS OF HISTORY. *New World Rev. 1970 38(3): 71-84.* Continued from a previous article. A study of the battles of Moscow, Stalingrad, the Kursk Bulge, and Berlin as illustrations of the differences between historians with a Marxist-Leninist and those with an idealist understanding of the historical process. Rebuts the Western theory that the success of the Soviet army was due to other causes than "the heroism of the Soviet soldiers and the skill and courage of their officers." Reprinted from *Kommunist* 1970 (1). 4 notes. R. V. Ritter

3313. Zinchenko, Iu. I. PYTANNIA VZAIEMODII PARTYZANIV Z CHASTYNAMY CHERVONOI ARMII PID CHAS VYZVOLENNIA PRAVOBEREZHNOI UKRAINY V RADIANS'KII ISTORIOHRAFII [The matter of interaction between partisans and units of the Red Army during the liberation of right-bank Ukraine in Soviet historiography]. *Ukrains'kyi Istorychnyi Zhurnal [USSR] 1978 (7): 137-141.* Many articles and works have been written by Soviet historians about the cooperation between partisans and Red Army units in the liberation of right-bank

Ukraine 1943-44, but the subject is far from exhausted. The author suggests that more attention should be paid to highlighting the organization and effectiveness of this interaction, which was praised even by the Germans. Primary sources; 34 notes. V. Packer

3314. Zolotarev, V. AZ 1877-78: ÉVI HÁBORÚ AZ OROSZ KATONAI IRODALOMBAN [The war of 1877-78 in the Russian military literature]. *Hadtörténelmi Közlemények [Hungary] 1981 28(3): 428-449.* The Russo-Turkish War led to the liberation of the Balkan nations and constituted an important stage in the development of Russian military art. This is a survey of studies and evaluations of this war by S. P. Zikov, 1881-82, P. A. Geisman in 1880, N. A. Jepančin in 1891, E. I. Martinov in 1900, M. A. Domontovič in 1900, A. K. Puzirevskij in 1881, and a collective study by several authors published between 1901 and 1920. The conservative tendencies, reflecting the policies of imperialism of the tsarist regime, left their mark to some extent on the character and contents of research on the Russo-Turkish War. 135 notes. R. Hetzron

3315. Zvenzlovski, A. O NEKOTORYKH CHERTAKH FRANTSUZSKOI ISTORIOGRAFII VTOROI MIROVOI VOINY [Certain aspects of the French historiography of World War II]. *Voenno-Istoricheskii Zhurnal [USSR] 1972 (10): 100-107.* Surveys the writings of French historians on World War II and accuses authors who work from a non-Marxist perspective of distorting the facts.

3316. Zvenzlovski, A. TREKHTOMNOE ISSLEDOVANIE FRANTSUSKOGO ISTORIKA O VELIKOI OTECHESTVENNOI VOINE [A French historian's three-volume study of World War II]. *Voenno-Istoricheskii Zhurnal [USSR] 1971 (11): 109-115.*

3317. —. [HISTORIOGRAPHY OF WORLD WAR II IN EAST CENTRAL EUROPE]. *Történelmi Szemle [Hungary] 1973 16(3-4): 289-329, 437-439.*

Ránki, György. KELET-KÖZÉP-EURÓPA MÁSODIK VILÁGHÁBORÚS TÖRTÉNETI IRODALMÁNAK KÉRDÉSEI [Issues of historical literature on World War II in East Central Europe], *pp. 289-311.* Argues for a regional, rather than general approach to the history of World War II. Relying on new sources, the author reexamines the relationship of the Danubian lands with Germany, and the effect of changing Allied policy on them. 71 notes.

Juhász, Gyula. POLITIKAI ÉS DIPLOMACIA-TÖRTÉNETI IRODALOM MAGYARORSZÁG MÁSODIK VILÁGHÁBORÚS TÖRTÉNETÉRŐL [Political and historical literature about Hungary's role in World War II], *pp. 312-329.* Examines the relation between Hungary's foreign and domestic policies during World War II, and its effect on Miklós Horthy's leadership. 14 notes.

Macartney, C. A. HOZZÁSZÓLÁS A RÁNKI GYÖRGY ÉS JUHÁSZ GYULA ELŐADÁSÁRÓL POLYTATOTT VITÁHOZ [Notes on the debate over Ranki's and Juhasz's papers], *pp. 437-439.* Outlines the British view of the problem of the Danubian lands during World War II, denying that the British government was intent on buttressing the Horthy regime. H. Szamuely/S

3318. —. K 20-LETIIU SLAVNOI POBEDY SOVETSKOGO NARODA [The 20th anniversary of the glorious victory of the Soviet people]. *Voprosy Istorii KPSS [USSR] 1962 (1): 230-233.* Describes and expresses certain reservations about the proceedings of a historical conference on Germany's military defeat outside Moscow in 1941, held in Moscow in December 1961. A number of speakers attacked distortions caused by Stalin's personality cult.

3319. —. LOS CENTROS HISTORICO-MILITARES ESPAÑOLES [Spanish centers of military history]. *Rev. Int. d'Hist. Militaire [France] 1984 (56): 263-305.* Describes the organization and activities of the various centers of historical documentation and services of the Spanish armed forces. Included are the central archive and library of the Military Historical Service, the Museum of the Army, the Institute of Naval History and Culture, and the Historical and Cultural Service of the Army of the Air. 10 color plates.

J. V. Coutinho

3320. —. [WORLD WAR I: THE FISCHER THESIS IN GERMAN TEXTBOOKS]. (German text).

Bruckmann, Klaus. ERSTER WELTKRIEG—URSACHEN, KRIEGSZIELE, KRIEGSSCHULD: FRITZ FISCHERS THESEN IN DEUTSCHEN SCHULGESCHICHTSBÜCHERN [World War I—origins, war aims, war guilt: Fritz Fischer's theses in German school history textbooks], *Gesch. in Wiss. und Unterricht [West Germany] 1981 32(10): 600-617.* Evaluates the influence of Fritz Fischer's views of World War I on the school history textbooks of six major publishers or groups of publishers in West Germany. Fischer's emphasis on German responsibility for World War I, an interpretation spread by Fischer and his students over the past 20 years, has unduly influenced history texts. Most of the textbooks discussed present a one-sided, even deterministic, interpretation of the origins of the Great War and the responsibility for it. The textual treatments are slanted in favor of the Fischer school in a fashion which seems contrary to the spirit of objective historical analysis which such materials should encourage among students. A few exceptions are noted. Based in part on primary sources; 121 notes.

Plass, Jens. KRITIK [Critique], *Gesch. in Wiss. und Unterricht [West Germany] 1982 33(4): 227-231.* Challenges Bruckmann's accuracy, especially the biased presentation of Fritz Fischer's interpretation of the origins of World War I.

Hug, Wolfgang. KRITIK [Critique], *Gesch. in Wiss. und Unterricht [West Germany] 1982 33(4): 232-237.* Responds to the criticism of his school text, *Geschichtlichen Weltkunde,* and presents evidence from his text to counter Bruckmann's charge of a one-sided interpretation.

Bruckmann, Klaus. ANTIKRITIK [Reply], *Gesch. in Wiss. und Unterricht [West Germany] 1982 33(4): 238-246.* Defends his article as a response to those who have argued that Fischer's thesis on the origins of World War I has not been integrated into West German school texts. Also responds to the specific criticisms of his previous article by Plass and Hug. 54 notes.

L. D. Wilcox

3321. —. WORLD WAR II IN FIGURES. *World Marxist R. [Canada] 1975 18(5): 49-58.* Presents a Marxist interpretation of the war, based on Soviet data.

3322. —. ZIELSETZUNG UND METHODE DER MILITÄRGESCHICHTSSCHREIBUNG [Objective and methodology in military historiography]. *Militärgeschichtliche Mitteilungen [West Germany] 1976 (2): 9-20.*

Revolutions and Rebellions

3323. Antoljak, Stjepan. DOSADAŠNJI ISTRAŽIVAČKI RADOVI O POKRETU MATIJA IVANIĆA I NEKA NOVONASTALA PITANJA I PROBLEMI O NJEMU [Research on Matij Ivanić's movement and new questions and problems relating to it]. *Radovi: Inst. za Hrvastku Povijest [Yugoslavia] 1977 10: 7-26.* Lists historiography on the commoners' revolt on the Adriatic island of Hvar, 1510-14, and clarifies questions regarding the activities of its leader, Matij Ivanić.

3324. Antoljak, Stjepan. NEKOLIKO MARGINALNIH OPASKI O SELJAČKOJ BUNI 1573. GODINE [Marginalia about the peasant rebellion of 1573]. *Radovi: Inst. za Hrvatsku Povijest [Yugoslavia] 1973 5: 93-111.* Refutes purported facts about the 1573 peasants' revolt in Croatia and Slovenia: the leader Mathias Gubec never called himself a king, nor was he executed on 15 February 1573. Questions estimates of those killed.

3325. Barg, M. A. SRAVNITEL'NO-ISTORICHESKOE IZUCHENIE BURZHUAZNYKH REVOLIUTSII XVI-XVIII VV. [The comparative historical study of bourgeois revolutions in the 16th-18th centuries]. *Voprosy Istorii [USSR] 1975 (9): 69-88.* The problem of applying the comparative historical method in studying the bourgeois revolutions of the 16th-18th centuries has now advanced to the foreground of historiography. The method that has become firmly rooted in Western historiography in recent years is based on the synchronous approach to the investigation of the above-mentioned problem, which leads to a comparison of the crises that do not lend themselves to comparison by their very nature, such as inter-formation revolutions, the riots and disturbances flaring up within the framework of one or another formation, etc. The author proposes the method of examining each of the three bourgeois revolutions of that period embracing the whole of Europe, the Reformation and the Peasants' War in Germany in the 16th century, the English Revolution of the mid-17th century, and the French Revolution of the end of the 18th century, stage by stage. This will make it possible to bring out the distinctive features of each of these revolutions and at the same time to disclose the general laws intrinsic to all of them.   J

3326. Berindei, Dan. DESPRE CONVENŢIA DINTRE VLADIMIRESCU ŞI ETERIE ŞI ALTE PROBLEME ALE REVOLUŢIEI DIN 1821 [The agreement between Vladimirescu and Eterie and other problems of the revolution of 1821]. *Revista de Istorie [Romania] 1981 34(8): 1555-1559.* Mircea T. Radu declared in a book published in 1978 that the documents pertaining to the revolution of 1821 include "contradictory affirmations" and that Andrei Oţetea, historian and specialist on the complex problems of the revolution of 1821, is inaccurate in his observations. Describes M. T. Radu's own inaccuracies and declares that the agreement reached by Tudor Vladimirescu and Eterie was "an inauthentic act" and characterizes Radu's entire conception of the revolution of 1821 as unjustified polemic. Secondary sources; note.

T. Z. Herman

3327. Boneschi, Mario. NINO BIXIO A BRONTE: UN COLPO ALLA NUCA [Nino Bixio in Bronte: a blow at the nape of the neck]. *Risorgimento [Italy] 1975 27(1-2): 41-46.* A recent film by Nino Bixio depicting the tragic 1860 uprising in Bronte, Sicily, mistakenly draws revolutionary implications from what was essentially a peasant monarchist revolt. In depicting Garibaldi as a political hero in the South, Bixio ignores the fact that it was the conservative Catholic clergy which really guided peasant political action. In fact, Garibaldi, and the late 19th-century liberal historiography recognized the historical improbability of agrarian revolution in 1860. Therefore it is necessary to rectify such apparently reputable distortions of Risorgimento history as that created by Bixio.

L. R. Atkins/S

3328. Brownstein, Lewis. THE CONCEPT OF COUNTERREVOLUTION IN MARXIAN THEORY. *Studies in Soviet Thought [Netherlands] 1981 22(3): 175-192.* Summarizes the historiography of counterrevolution. Discusses counterrevolution as historical movement, as Thermidor, as empire (or world system), as tactic, as Fascism, and as revolution. Concentrates on the specific contributions of Marx, Engels, and Lenin on the topics of counterrevolution and the class war and dictatorship of the proletariat as tactics to gain and maintain power. Primary sources; 57 notes.

R. B. Mendel

3329. Cesa, Claudio. KARL GRIEWANK (E OLTRE) SUL CONCETTO DI RIVOLUZIONE [Karl Griewank and others on the concept of revolution]. *Ponte [Italy] 1979 35(7-8): 816-832.* Discusses Griewank's work, 1942-52, on modern revolutionary theory, particularly his studies of the Revolution of 1848. Describes his academic career which was retarded by his refusal to join the Nazi Party, and examines his legacy in the development of subsequent historiography on revolutionary theory in East and West Germany.

3330. Church, C. H. FORGOTTEN REVOLUTION: RECENT WORK ON THE REVOLUTIONS OF 1830 IN EUROPE. *European Studies Rev. [Great Britain] 1977 7(1): 95-106.* There has been a considerable neglect of the revolution of 1830 in favor of that of 1848. The author studies the recent revival of interest in the former. 20 notes.   S. P. Carr

3331. Cobb, R. C. MODERN FRENCH HISTORY IN BRITAIN. *Pro. of the British Acad. [Great Britain] 1974 60: 271-294.* Renewed interest in the French Revolution commenced with its centennial and continued through World War I, but it "is now almost extinct as a research subject in France." The quest has been assumed by English scholars. 25 notes.   E. L. Furdell

3332. Constantiniu, Florin and Densuşianu, Nicolae. IN SECOLUL LUI HOREA: HOREA, CLOŞCA ŞI CRIŞAN [The century of Horea: Horea, Cloşca, and Crişan]. *Magazin Istoric [Romania] 1980 14(10): 2-7, 50.* The background and course of the revolt in Transylvania in 1784, here described, led by Nicolae Horea, Cloşca, and Crişan, has been dealt with by N. Iorga in *Le Place des Roumains dans l'Historie Universelle,* as seen against the 18th-century outbreak of peasant unrest in Europe, and in detail by N. Densuşianu in his *Răscoala Lui Horea.*

3333. De Mattei, Roberto. AUGUSTIN COCHIN E LA STORIOGRAFIA CONTRORIVOLUZIONARIA [Augustin Cochin and counterrevolutionary historiography]. *Storia e Pol. [Italy] 1973 12(4): 570-585.* Augustin Cochin (1876-1916) was a representative of counterrevolutionary historiography on the French Revolution, who followed in the wake of Augustin Barruel (1741-1820), Edmund Burke (1728-97), and Hippolyte Taine (1828-93). According to Barruel, an anti-Christian conspiracy of atheists and Freemasons caused the French Revolution. In the same way Cochin thought that a minority of agitators, who would become victims of their own conspiracy, organized it. Cochin censured bitterly the democratic system. 51 notes.   A. Canavero

3334. Drabkin, Ia. S. PROBLEMATIK DER NOVEMBER-REVOLUTION IM IDEENKAMPF—60 JAHRE HISTORIOGRAPHIE: LEGENDEN UND ERKENNTNISSE [Problematics of the November revolution in the battle of ideas—60 years of historiography: legends and knowledge]. *Wiss. Zeits. der Humboldt-Universität zu Berlin. Gesellschafts- und Sprachwissenschaftliche Reihe [East Germany] 1980 29(3-4): 299-308.* Explores how historical change led to changed interpretations of the justifications for the occurrences after the November 1919 revolution in Germany.

3335. Dupaquier, Jacques and Berg-Hamon, Christine. VOIES NOUVELLES POUR L'HISTOIRE DÉMOGRAPHIQUE DE LA RÉVOLUTION FRANÇAISE: LE MOUVEMENT DE LA POPULATION DE 1785 À 1800 [New channels for the demographic history of the French Revolution: the change of population, 1785-1800]. *Ann. Hist. de la Révolution Française [France] 1975 47(219): 3-29.* Examines the problems and sources of demographic research 1785-1800, during which there was a decisive mutation in the population of France. Up to 1799 the French Revolution increased the number of births to a new record, largely because of the increase of marriages. Based on documents in the Archives Nationales, the Bibliothèque Nationale, departmental archives, and secondary works; map, 2 tables, 5 graphs, 25 notes.
                                                        L. S. Frey

3336. Dychenko, O. A. PROBLEMY VYVCHENNIA HRUD-NEVOHO ZBROINOHO POVSTANNIA 1905 R. NA UKRAINI V NOVITNII RADIANS'KII ISTORIOHRAFII [Problems in the study of the Revolution of 1905 in the Ukraine in modern Soviet historiography]. *Ukrains'kyi Istorychnyi Zhurnal [USSR] 1980 (3): 138-143.* Notes and discusses some of the existing written material dealing with the history of the December 1905 armed uprising in the Ukraine. Soviet historians have shed sufficient light on the course of revolutionary events, the Bolsheviks' role in preparing and organizing armed activities, the Mensheviks' disruptive role, and the positive role of the councils of workers' deputies. 38 notes.
                                                   I. Krushelnyckyj

3337. Einstein, Elizabeth et al. SYMPOSIUM: CASTE, CLASS, ELITES, AND REVOLUTION. *Consortium on Revolutionary Europe 1750-1850: Pro. 1979: 25-73.* Provides a transcript of a panel

discussion, which treats the following themes: the continuity of elites under the French Revolution and the Napoleonic periods; the Marxist interpretation of the Revolution; revolutionary rhetoric; and the federalist revolt of 1793. Most of the discussion concerns various social aspects of the Revolution. The classic Marxist view has been revised in several important ways.   T. J. Schaeper

3338. Furet, François. AU CENTRE DE NOS REPRESENTA-TIONS POLITIQUES [The center of our political representations]. *Esprit [France] 1976 44(9): 172-178.* Historians of revolutions have either identified with the values of revolutionaries or developed critical conceptualizations of revolutionary experience, 1790's-1917.

3339. Fursenko, A. A. and McArthur, Gilbert H., transl. THE AMERICAN AND FRENCH REVOLUTIONS COMPARED: THE VIEW FROM THE U.S.S.R. *William and Mary Q. 1976 33(3): 481-500.* Compares historiography of the American Revolution with that of the French Revolution from a Marxist perspective, observing the different conditions under which the two revolutions took place. The American Revolution was chiefly an agrarian uprising, as there was no demographic pressure. The two revolutions had a similarity in that both signalized the rise of progressive capitalism, although the American Revolution belongs in the world revolutionary tradition. 73 notes.   H. M. Ward

3340. Grab, Walter. DIE FRANZÖSISCHE REVOLUTION IM SPIEGEL DER HISTORISCHEN FORSCHUNG [The French Revolution mirrored in historical research]. Grab, Walter and Koplenig, Hilde, ed. *Die Debatte um die Französische Revolution* (Munich: Nymphenburger, 1975): 9-28. Legends, especially about the dictatorship of the Jacobins, lingered on throughout the 19th century because a critique of sources on the French Revolution was lacking. Idealistic historical philosophy, contempt for the masses, and moralizing disdain of Jacobin theories explain the conservative historians' negative evaluation of the revolution. Liberal-bourgeois historiography stressed the change to a legal and constitutional state, while left-wing historiography pointed to the radical-democratic phase of 1793-94 as most important for combining the antifeudal classes in France. Based on secondary literature on the French Revolution; 10 notes.   R. Wagnleitner

3341. Hampson, Norman. 1789 & ALL THAT: FRENCH MARXISTS VS. THE "ANGLO-SAXONS." *Encounter [Great Britain] 1980 54(5): 78-81.* Reports on a conference on the French Revolution in Bamberg, particularly the debate there between Marxists and non-Marxists on the class character and general significance of the revolution.

3342. Hobsbawm, Eric J. A FORRADALOM [The revolution]. *Világtörténet [Hungary] 1981 (2): 88-120.* Research on revolutions cannot be separated from the background of the historical era or from the author's political opinions. The definition of revolution demands that it should include: sudden and upsetting actions, open resistance to existing society, and an ideology with positive goals for the advancement of humanity. Most revolutions never manage to accomplish their utopian unrealistic goals. Revolutionary energy will never follow the pattern designated by its creators. The best the creators can do according to Lenin is to gain as much benefit as possible for themselves from the new and unpredictable situations as they develop. Based on a lecture at the 1975 International Congress of Historical Sciences in San Francisco.   T. Kuner

3343. Holzapfel, Kurt. DIE JULIREVOLUTION 1830 IN FRANKREICH: MEINUNGEN, KONTROVERSEN, FOR-SCHUNGSDESIDERATA [The July 1830 revolution in France: opinions, controversies, and lacunae in research]. *Zeits. für Geschichtswissenschaft [East Germany] 1981 29(8): 710-725.* The French revolution of 1830 has recently been rediscovered by researchers, and the ongoing debate concerns a multitude of controversial aspects of this revolution. This study touches on some problems of a theoretical, methodological, and political character, with focus on the conflicting points of view of bourgeois and Marxist historiography. The traditional view of the revolution, its origins, and effects are discussed. The opinions of Metternich, Ranke, Tocqueville and others are quoted and set in historical perspective. This contribution

is a revised version of the main lecture given at the meeting in Leipzig in 1980 of the International Colloquy of the Research Group of Comparative Revolutionary History of Modern Times.
T. Parker

3344. Holzapfel, Kurt. ROBESPIERRE UND PREUSSEN [Robespierre and Prussia]. *Zeitschrift für Geschichtswissenschaft [East Germany] 1978 26(10): 878-886.* Bourgeois historiography argues that it was Maximilien Robespierre's Reign of Terror which was the only cause of the failure of the peace negotiations between revolutionary France and the first coalition of European countries led by England. Asserts that this argument is inaccurate and that after Robespierre had successfully suppressed internal-Jacobin opposition, his peacekeeping policy had a greater chance of success. Indeed the stabilization of radical-bourgeois forces in France ironically enabled the negotiation of a separate peace between France and Prussia on 5 April 1795.
S. Boehnke/S

3345. Hürten, Heinz. DIE NOVEMBERREVOLUTION: FRAGEN AN DIE FORSCHUNG [The November Revolution: open questions]. *Geschichte in Wissenschaft und Unterricht [West Germany] 1979 30(3): 158-174.* Proposes a new interpretation of the German revolution of 1918. Present interpretations see 1918 not as mere breakdown, but as a revolution, in which the Social Democratic Party missed its chance and followed the path of a parliamentary instead of a socialist democracy. According to the recognized criteria of revolutions there was no revolutionary situation in 1918, and because of the vulnerability of a developed industrial society, even the revolutionaries hesitated making fundamental changes in politics and society. The workers' and soldiers' councils were no means for a socialist transformation; they lacked the strength and social basis to oust the forces represented in parliament. Thus the Weimar Republic had to be built on the Social Democratic Party and the parties of the center. 59 notes.
H. W. Wurster

3346. Kinner, Klaus. DIE INTERNATIONALISTISCHE SICHT DER REVOLUTION VON 1848/49 IM GESCHICHTSBILD DER KPD IN DEN JAHREN DER WEIMARER REPUBLIK [The internationalist view of the Revolution of 1848 from the historical viewpoint of the Communist Party of Germany during the Weimar Republic]. *Beiträge zur Geschichte der Arbeiterbewegung [East Germany] 1973 15(2): 252-261.* Analytic tools for the revolutionary fight of the 1920's were found as early as November 1918 in the doctrines of the Revolution of 1848-49. In contrast to the right-wing Social Democrats who limited their studies of the 1848 revolution to Germany, the German Communists were mainly interested in its international implications, stressing the continuity of the Revolution of 1848, the Paris Commune of 1871, and the revolution of the sailors in Petrograd. The Social Democrats, in separating the German Revolution of 1848 from the European context, created a bourgeois-liberal-idealistic historiography. Secondary sources; 34 notes.
R. Wagnleitner

3347. Kolejka, J. NÁRODNOSTNÍ OTÁZKA V REVOLUCI 1848-1849 [The question of nationality, 1848-49]. *Slovanský Přehled [Czechoslovakia] 1980 66(3): 224-231.* Although the historiography of the Revolution of 1848 is vast, even as late as the 1960's, many historians, including Marxist ones, persisted in interpreting the events in nationalist terms and tended to be sympathetic to their own nationality's struggle of that time. The time has come for the use of an objective criteria in assessing those events and in judging the reactions of the founders of scientific socialism, Karl Marx and Friedrich Engels. 42 notes.
B. Reinfeld

3348. Kudrna, Jaroslav. ZUR TYPOLOGIE DER BÜRGERLICHEN HISTORIOGRAHIE IN DER ERSTEN HÄLFTE DES XIX. JAHRHUNDERTS [Towards a typology of bourgeois historiography in the first half of the 19th century]. *Sborník Prací Filosofické Fakulty Brněnské U.: Řada Hist. [Czechoslovakia] 1982 31(29): 57-69.* Early 19th-century historiography can be classified according to the writers' attitudes to the French Revolution or to their own bourgeois society: pro-reform historians attempted to explain some aspects of social life; counter-

revolutionary historians regarded history as irrational or partial. Based on secondary sources in French, German, and Russian; 27 notes.

3349. Küttler, Wolfgang. FORMATIONSANALYSE, TYPOLOGIE UND REVOLUTIONSGESCHICHTSFORSCHUNG IM WERK LENINS [The analysis of social formation, typology, and research into the history of revolutions in Lenin's works]. *Zeitschrift für Geschichtswissenschaft [East Germany] 1977 25(7): 765-786.* V. I. Lenin analyzed the relationship between the stages of capitalism in a number of countries and the varying character of their bourgeois revolutions, in order to determine the correct revolutionary course for the proletariat in Russia. He posited the theory of bourgeois revolutions, showing how they are consolidated in stages in varying countries, thereby explaining why the bourgeois revolution was yet to be completed in Russia. 112 notes.
J. T. Walker

3350. Lefebvre, Henri. WHAT IS THE HISTORICAL PAST? *New Left R. [Great Britain] 1975 (90): 27-34.* Albert Soboul's *The Paris Sans-Culottes and the French Revolution 1793-4* (Oxford, 1964) suggests new solutions to the methodological problems of historiography.

3351. Lipsky, William E. COMPARATIVE APPROACHES TO THE STUDY OF REVOLUTION: A HISTORIOGRAPHY ESSAY. *Rev. of Pol. 1976 38(4): 494-509.* Although revolutions have been discussed since the time of Plato and Aristotle, interpretations of revolutions since the French Revolution of 1789 fall into two general categories: 1) historical narrative focusing on a specific revolution, or aspects of it, or 2) a theoretical approach which examines revolutions in general and seeks, by analyzing several examples, to "develop a general statement capable of explaining its what and why." Despite numerous studies and a movement from monocausationist to multicausationist treatments, there remains much that is unknown about revolutions because the data has not been gathered to evaluate revolution theories in a variety of historical settings. 58 notes.
L. E. Ziewacz

3352. Lönne, Karl-Egon. ZUR BEDEUTUNG DER UNTERSCHICHTEN FÜR DIE REVOLUTION VON 1848 IN DEUTSCHLAND [The significance of the lower classes in the Revolution of 1848 in Germany]. *Zeitgeschichte [Austria] 1978 5(8): 311-321.* The 1848 German revolutions have long been viewed as bourgeois-led events; even historians of East Germany accepted this interpretation. Although not leaders of the revolutions, the lower classes were clearly involved; contemporary estimates of the numbers involved range upward from one-half of the population, far more than the middle-class segment of the whole population. Emphasis on middle-class leadership has marked past historical study of the revolutions; objective study of the role of the lower classes is now essential to balance the earlier bias. 32 notes.
G. H. Libbey

3353. Mattheisen, Donald J. HISTORY AS CURRENT EVENTS: RECENT WORKS ON THE GERMAN REVOLUTION OF 1848. *Am. Hist. Rev. 1983 88(5): 1219-1237.* A review of recent literature on the German Revolution of 1848, which concludes that no consensus has yet materialized. "For the present generation, the ultimate consequences of the revolution are still matters of dispute." 50 notes.
R. Schlesinger

3354. Narulin, K. K. MARKS I F. ENGEL'S OB OSOBENNOSTIAKH REVOLIUTSIONNYKH I OSVOBODITEL'NYKH VOIN XIX VEKA [K. Marx and F. Engels on the peculiarities of the 19th-century revolutionary wars and the wars of independence]. *Voenno-Istoricheskii Zhurnal [USSR] 1973 (7): 91-96.* Reviews Karl Marx and Friedrich Engels's analyses of revolutionary wars and wars of independence which occurred in their lifetimes including the American Civil War and various European conflicts.

3355. Nelson, Douglas T. THE LEGEND OF THE DEMOCRATIC REVOLUTION: CREATING AN ORTHODOXY. *Consortium on Revolutionary Europe 1750-1850: Pro. 1976: 121-132.* Both Jules Michelet and Edgar Quinet appraised the past in the light of its significance for their own day. Their aims as historians often became confused with their aims as social reformers. To alert the French to their new historical identity they resorted to the myth of a democratic revolution in the 1790's. 32 notes.

R. Howell, Jr.

3356. Nisbet, Robert. HANNAH ARENDT E LA RIVOLUZIONE AMERICANA [Hannah Arendt and the American Revolution]. *Comunità [Italy] 1981 35(183): 81-95.* In *On Revolution,* Hannah Arendt saw that revolutions aim at power not liberty: unlike the French and the Russian revolutions, the American revolution did not extend the bureaucratic power structure; Arendt did not see other aspects of that revolution.

3357. Oliinyk, L. V. REVOLIUTSIIA 1905-1907 RR. NA UKRAINI V RADIANS'KII ISTORIOHRAFII [The Soviet historiography about the 1905-07 revolution in the Ukraine]. *Ukrains'kyi Istorychnyi Zhurnal [USSR] 1980 (12): 134-139.*

3358. Oliinyk, L. V. VIDOBRAZHENNIA V RADIANS'KII ISTORIOHRAFII REVOLIUTSIINYKH PODII 1848 NA UKRAINI [The Revolution of 1848 in the Ukraine in Soviet historiography]. *Ukrains'kyi Istorychnyi Zhurnal [USSR] 1973 (2): 52-58.*

3359. Perrot, Jean-Claude. VOIES NOUVELLES POUR L'HISTOIRE ÉCONOMIQUE DE LA RÉVOLUTION [New channels for the economic history of the Revolution]. *Ann. Hist. de la Révolution Française [France] 1975 47(219): 30-65.* Reviews the literature on basic economic problems of the French Revolution and raises additional questions on the transfer of property, fiscal reforms, price structure, agricultural and industrial production. Primary and secondary sources; table, 86 notes.

L. S. Frey

3360. Petrić, Nikša. RADOVI O PUČKOM USTANKU MATIJA IVANIĆA [The study of Matij Ivanić's commoners' revolt]. *Radovi: Inst. za Hrvatsku Povijest [Yugoslavia] 1977 10: 541-549.* Lists historiography, published 1769-1976, on the commoners' revolt on the Adriatic island of Hvar, 1510-14.

3361. Plongeron, Bernard. LE FAIT RELIGIEUX DANS L'HISTOIRE DE LA RÉVOLUTION FRANÇAISE: OBJET, METHODES, VOIES NOUVELLES [Religious fact in the history of the French Revolution: object, methods, new channels]. *Ann. Hist. de la Révolution Française [France] 1975 47(219): 95-133.* Reviews the research of the last decades, principally in France and Italy, on religious fact. The actual lack of religious concern in the general interpretation of the revolution underlines the slowness of its assimilation. Religious fact encompasses "men and events, doctrines and beliefs, cults and religious practices." Secondary sources; 50 notes.

L. S. Frey

3362. Popkin, Jeremy D. THE FRENCH REVOLUTIONARY PRESS: NEW FINDINGS AND NEW PERSPECTIVES. *Eighteenth-Century Life 1979 5(4): 90-104.* Summarizes recent historiography on the newspapers published during the era of the French Revolution, noting the role of the government in publishing, and the profitability and readership of the papers.

3363. Prince, Hugh. RICHARD COBB: A SPY IN REVOLUTIONARY FRANCE. *J. of Hist. Geography 1977 3(4): 363-372.* Richard Cobb has been a student of the French Revolution since 1935. His books have a social perspective and a strong sense of regional geography. He has written mostly about the lower classes, including drifters and criminals. Based on these books by Cobb: *The Police and the People: French Popular Protest, 1789-1820* (Oxford U. Pr., 1970), *Reactions to the French Revolution* (Oxford U. Pr., 1972), *Paris and Its Provinces, 1792-1802* (Oxford U. Pr., 1975), *A Sense of Place* (Duckworth, 1975), and *Tour de France* (Duckworth, 1976); 53 notes.

F. N. Egerton

3364. Robek, Antonín. DER BÖHMISCHE BAUERNAUFSTAND VON 1775 IM SPIEGEL VOLKSTÜMLICHER CHRONIKAUFZEICHNUNGEN [The Bohemian peasant revolt of 1775 in the mirror of popular chronicles]. *Jahrbuch für Volkskunde und Kulturgeschichte [East Germany] 1977 20: 137-145.* While Bohemian peasant chronicles interpret the peasant revolt of 1775 in social and economic terms, chronicles written by priests and teachers saw the rebellion as a result of Hussite and Prussian propaganda against the Habsburgs.

3365. Rudé, George. THE STUDY OF REVOLUTIONS. *Can. Hist. Assoc. Hist. Papers [Canada] 1976: 13-19.* Most models of revolution since Crane Brinton's *Anatomy of Revolution* (1938) are "natural history" models dealing with the developments stage by stage. Charles Tilly and James Rule have recently propounded a political process model that concentrates on the activities of rival contenders in the revolutionary process. V. I. Lenin, in 1915, stressed the need for leaders who were willing and able to take power. In addition, there is a need to study the change in consciousness of the mass of population caused by the spread of revolutionary ideas. Secondary sources; 12 notes.

G. E. Panting

3366. Rumpler, Helmut. REVOLUTIONSGESCHICHTSFORSCHUNG IN DER DDR [Research into revolutions in East Germany]. *Geschichte in Wissenschaft und Unterricht [West Germany] 1980 31(3): 178-187.* Revolutions play an important role in the Marxist world view and research into revolutions is of great importance at the research center at the University of Leipzig. During the period 1500-1917 historians were concerned less with general theories than with the vastness of historical realities. Orthodox Marxist historians criticize their results, which imply new interpretations of Marxist concepts of history. 27 notes.

H. W. Wurster

3367. Rürup, Reinhard. DEMOKRATISCHE REVOLUTION UND "DRITTER WEG": DIE DEUTSCHE REVOLUTION VON 1918/19 IN DER NEUEREN WISSENSCHAFTLICHEN DISKUSSION [Democratic revolution and the "third way": the German revolution of 1918-19 in recent scholarly discussion]. *Gesch. und Gesellschaft [West Germany] 1983 9(2): 278-301.* A revisionist school of thought, accepted by most researchers, has overcome the traditional interpretations of the German revolution of 1918-19, but has not yet appeared in textbooks because of its political content. The revisionists hold that the revolutionary movement was a mass movement seeking to democratize the army and the bureaucracy and thereby attempting to restructure German society to make democracy viable. Based on secondary sources; 58 notes.

C.-H. Geschwind

3368. Schaper, B. W. REVOLUTIE EN CONTRAREVOLUTIE [Revolution and counterrevolution]. *Spiegel Historiael [Netherlands] 1973 8(1): 9-15.* Surveys the current literature on revolutionary movements in Central Europe, 1917-19, focusing especially on the German Revolution of 1918 and communist uprisings. The Spartacists failed because they were dilettantish, utopian, and uncertain of themselves; they actually strengthened the counterrevolution. The German revolution was a victory of moderate elements supported by the generals. The same development did not occur in Austria where the Socialists did not need the support of the military. Biblio.

G. D. Homan

3369. Schilfert, Gerhard. ÜBER VERGLEICHENDE GESCHICHTE DER NEUZEITLICHEN REVOLUTIONEN [The comparative history of modern revolutions]. *Zeitschrift für Geschichtswissenschaft [East Germany] 1982 30(5): 435-439.* Examines the work of historians in East Germany on modern revolutions, particularly the comparative history of 18th- and 19th-century revolutions and their economic causes. Discusses similarities and differences between the developments from feudalism that led to economic, social, and industrial progress, the agricultural and industrial revolutions in England, developments in Germany leading to the Revolution of 1848, and developments in Japan, 1850-89. Secondary sources; 2 notes.

G. N. Neville

3370. Schilfert, Gerhard. ZEITGENÖSSISCHE DEUTSCHE HISTORIKER ÜBER DIE AMERIKANISCHE BÜRGERLICHE REVOLUTION [Contemporary German historians on the American bourgeois revolution]. *Zeitschrift für Geschichtswissenschaft [East Germany] 1979 27(8): 736-750.* During the 18th century, professional historians in Germany based their positive or negative evaluations of the American Revolution on Enlightenment philosophy. Matthias Christian Sprengel (1746-1803) recognized the world historical importance of the revolution. Daniel Ebeling (1741-1817) lectured and published on constitutional and economic developments in North America. Julius August Remer (1738-1803) and Johann Christian Schmohl (b. 1736) were also pro-American. In contrast, the prominent historian August Ludwig von Schlözer was critical of the rebellious Americans. 73 notes.   J. T. Walker

3371. Schleier, Hans. ZUR REVOLUTIONSINTERPRETATION IN DER DEUTSCHEN GESCHICHTSSCHREIBUNG ZWISCHEN 1848 UND 1933 [The interpretation of revolution in German historiography, 1848-1933]. Zeitschrift für Geschichtswissenschaft [East Germany] 1984 32(6): 515-525. Traces the influence of the French Revolution on the philosophy of history in Germany relating to revolutionary movements. Bourgeois dominance of German historiography led to constant concern to relate revolution to mere reform. The most accurate theory of revolution occurred among historians active in the labor movement, rather than among those in colleges and universities. Presented to the 7th Colloquium of Historians of the Republic of France and the German Democratic Republic, Paris, October 1983. 63 notes.   R. Grove

3372. Scott, Tom. THE PEASANTS' WAR: A HISTORIOGRAPHICAL REVIEW, PART I. Hist. J. [Great Britain] 1979 22(3): 693-720. A bibliographic and historiographic study of 14 titles produced by East German historians, 1968-75, in which the Peasants War of 1524-26 is interpreted in a Marxist ideological framework. They see the Peasants War as an initial expression of the revolutionary tradition of "the first worker and peasant state on German soil." These titles discussed relate only to specific aspects of the Peasant War itself. 143 notes.   R. V. Ritter

3373. Scott, Tom. THE PEASANTS' WAR: A HISTORIOGRAPHICAL REVIEW: PART II. Hist. J. [Great Britain] 1979 22(4): 953-974. Continued from a previous article. A historiographical and bibliographical review of the literature on the Peasants' War in Germany, 1524-26, considering rural-urban relationships, the role of the Imperial Free Cities, the spread of the rebellion to other parts of Germany, the disarray of Charles V's Habsburg Empire in the face of the revolt, and its social, economic, and demographic consequences. The events need to be placed in a broader context not just within Germany but all over Europe. Unfortunately, very little has been published in English. 258 notes.

3374. Sekistov, V. A. PRAVDA I VYMYSEL OB OTKRYTII VTOROGO FRONTA V EVROPE [Truth and fabrications about the opening of the second front in Europe]. Voenno-Istoricheskii Zhurnal [USSR] 1984 (5): 74-82. Rejects the view of such Western historians as R. Weigley and A. Seaton of the crucial importance of the second front created by the Allies in 1944 in the defeat of Germany. Despite Western propaganda concerning D-Day, the turning point of World War II came about in 1943, as a result of the successful Soviet offensive. 43 notes.   M. Hernas

3375. Shashko, Philip. A SELECTIVE BIBLIOGRAPHY ON THE APRIL UPRISING OF 1876. Southeastern Europe 1977 4(2): 322-346. Selects about 300 of the most significant titles, including guides and bibliographies, published documents, memoirs and contemporary accounts, books, articles, and works of fiction. A few of the fictional accounts are, at times, more effective than some of the scholarly works in conveying the spirit and flavor of the rebellion in Bulgaria.   W. R. Hively

3376. Shulim, Joseph I. THE MARXIST INTERPRETATION OF THE FRENCH REVOLUTION: SOME OBSERVATIONS. Consortium on Revolutionary Europe 1750-1850: Pro. 1974: 34-44. Analysis of the tradition of Marxist historiography of the French Revolution. While Marxist historians have, through massive archival research, made the Revolution a more and more complex event, they have continued to present it within the Marxist a priori context. But glaring contradictions now exist between the Marxist interpretation of the Revolution and the facts as revealed by the latest

research. This is examined with respect to the connection between capitalism and the Revolution and the question of social relations in 18th-century France. 37 notes.   R. Howell

3377. Soboul, Albert. JAURÈS, MATHIEZ ET L'HISTOIRE DE LA RÉVOLUTION FRANÇAISE [Jaurès, Mathiez and the history of the French Revolution]. Ann. Hist. de la Révolution Française [France] 1979 51(3): 443-454. Albert Mathiez was greatly influenced by the historical writings of Jean Jaurès on the French Revolution, especially his economic and social interpretation, even though Mathiez disagreed with him on various problems. Jaurès's influence was limited by Mathiez's Robespierrism and view of the revolution from above rather than from below. The work of Mathiez serves as a bridge between the political history of Alphonse Aulard and the social history of Georges Lefebvre. Reprinted from Bulletin de la Société d'Études Jaurésiennes, 1978 (69-70). Based on Mathiez's writings; 13 notes.   J. Friguglietti

3378. Sogrin, V. V. SOVREMENNAIA AMERIKANSKAIA ISTORIOGRAFIIA O BURZHUANYKH REVOLIUTSIIAKH V SSHA [Current American historiography on bourgeois revolutions in the United States]. Novaia i Noveishaia Istoriia [USSR] 1982 (1): 20-38. Reviews books on the American Revolution and the Civil War.

3379. Ștefănescu, Ștefan. 1784: RĂSCOALĂ SAU REVOLUȚIE? [1784: insurrection or revolution?]. Revista de Istorie [Romania] 1981 34(7): 1359-1361. Defines the peasants' antifeudal activities of 1784 in Transylvania as an insurrection confirming D. Prodan's definition based on historiographic research. Some historians, including N. Densușianu, Al. Odobescu, and I. Lupaș, had previously defined these activities as revolution.   T. Z. Herman

3380. Streisand, Joachim. DIE NOVEMBERREVOLUTION IM GESCHICHTSBILD [The November revolution in the historical picture]. Wiss. Zeits. der Humboldt-Universität zu Berlin. Gesellschafts- und Sprachwissenschaftliche Reihe [East Germany] 1980 29(3-4): 309-311. Gathers evidence for a new look at Germany's 1919 revolution, trying to counter evaluations that see it as a revolution from above rather than a working-class revolution.

3381. Suratteau, Jean-René. LE DIRECTOIRE: POINTS DE VUE ET INTERPRETATIONS D'APRES DES TRAVAUX RECENTS [The Directory: points of view and interpretations based upon recent works]. Ann. Hist. de la Révolution Française [France] 1976 48(2): 181-214.

3382. Tateishi, Hirotaka. KASUTERIYA NO KOMUNIDADESU NI KANSURU SHYOKENKYU [Studies on the revolt of the Comunidades of Castile]. Shigaku Zasshi [Japan] 1979 88(7): 58-78. The name Comunidades has been given to the rebellion of Castilian cities in Toledo in April 1520 over the abuse of the king's rights and in April 1521 when the king's aristocratic army was defeated. What was called a mass riot in the 17th and 18th centuries is today called an uprising for freedom against absolutism. In 1963 J. A. Maravall described the rebellion as the first step in replacing medieval social group democracy with modern democracy. Recent studies cover the social, economic, and political influences of the rebellion. Analyzes the viewpoints of J. Perez and Gutierrez Nieto. 116 notes.   M. Kawaguchi

3383. Terni, Massimo. RICONSIDERAZIONI SU JAURÈS E L'INTERPRETAZIONE ECONOMICA DELLA RIVOLUZIONE FRANCESE [Reappraisals of Jaurès and the economic interpretation of the French Revolution]. Studi Storici [Italy] 1979 20(2): 373-397. Surveys the historiography of the French Revolution, seen as the victory of the capitalist bourgeoisie over feudalism, from Karl Marx to Alfred Cobban. Reconsiders Jean Jaurès's concept of the French Revolution as the bourgeois revolution based on the third edition of Histoire socialiste de la révolution française (Paris, 1969-73). Jaurès's initial concept is modified in such a way that he loses sight of the revolution as a class movement and concentrates instead on the heroic individuals who shaped events, spurred on by an almost personified idea of revolution itself. 91 notes.

R. D. Black

3384. Villari, Rosario. STORICI AMERICANI E RIBELLI EUROPEI [American historians and European rebellions]. *Studi Storici [Italy] 1980 21(3): 487-502.* Investigates US historiography since 1958 on social conflict in Europe from the early 16th century to the French Revolution. Some historians see events such as the 1584 revolt in Naples as isolated incidents, while others view them as a general move toward revolution. The dispute has brought new interest to a study of the relationship between the French Revolution and the social conflicts of the two preceding centuries. 34 notes.

E. E. Ryan

3385. Zagorin, Perez. THEORIES OF REVOLUTION IN CONTEMPORARY HISTORIOGRAPHY. *Pol. Sci. Q. 1973 88(1): 23-52.* Examines various definitions of revolution and reviews modern theories of revolution, mainly from the 1960's-70's including: the study of revolutionary populations (elites, masses) and their relation to economic and social oppression; the comparative history of different revolutions; theoretical approaches concerned with societies, governments, and revolutions; the study of millenarianism and its relation to revolution; studies of social psychology dealing with frustration, aggression, and the personal experience of discontent; revolution as part of a process of modernization; and the incompatibility of institutions with the processes of society. Secondary sources; 55 notes.

B. C. Tharaud

3386. Zajewski, Władysław. WPŁYW REWOLUCJI LIPCOWEJ 1830 R. NA NOC 29 LISTOPADA 1830 R. W POLSCE [The influence of the Revolution of 1830 on the night of 29 November 1830 in Poland]. *Kwartalnik Hist. [Poland] 1980 87(3-4): 621-634.* The Polish historians of the interwar years did not pay attention to the influence of the French 1830 Revolution on the November insurrection in Poland until Marceli Handelsman in 1932 pointed to the interdependence of the revolutions in France, Belgium, and Poland. The notion that the French carbonari brought the revolutionary ideas to Poland has not been proven and it seems to have been conceived by Klemens von Metternich. France has simply been a model showing the Poles how to act against a tyrant who violated the constitution. 47 notes, French summary.

H. Heitzman-Wojcicka

3387. —. ["MYTH OF THE ARTISAN"]. *International Labor and Working Class History 1984 (25): 37-46.*

Newman, Edgar. RESPONSE TO J. RANCIERE, "THE MYTH OF THE ARTISAN," *pp. 37-38.* Disputes Rancière's thesis challenging the view that revolutions are carried out by well-organized artisans proud of their class and status.

Papayanis, Nicholas. RESPONSE TO J. RANCIERE "THE MYTH OF THE ARTISAN," *pp 39-41.* Takes exception to Rancière's view of the role of Alphonse Merrheim in French labor history.

Rancière, Jacques. A REPLY, *pp. 42-46.* Redefines the democratic meaning of "worker militancy" in his analysis of the importance of democratic feeling in the working class movement.

9. TOPICS IN HISTORIOGRAPHY

Women

3388. Adams, Carol. OFF THE RECORD: WOMEN'S OMIS-SION FROM CLASSROOM HISTORICAL EVIDENCE. *Teaching Hist. [Great Britain] 1983 (36): 3-6.* The new focus on women's history shows female workers, during the Industrial Revolution in England, as strong, competent laborers with pride in their new freedom and financial independence.

3389. Apodaca, Maria Linda. THE CHICANA WOMAN: AN HISTORICAL MATERIALIST PERSPECTIVE. *Latin Am. Perspectives 1977 4(1-2): 70-89.* Critiques the treatment of the Chicana by most Chicano historiography and points out the need for a class analysis. Also, traces the important historic roots of the Chicana's subjugation from Aztec society, through Spanish and Mexican feudalism, to the division of labor in the capitalist mode of production. Thesis is complemented by a biographical essay on an immigrant woman. J. L. Dietz

3390. Armstrong, Patricia. MARXISM AND FEMINISM. *Atlantis [Canada] 1979 4(2): 125-132.* Discusses books and essays on Marxism and feminism in this examination of the women's movement in Canada since the 1960's, based on Marxist thought, in order to understand women's position in society, the inequality between men and women, and to analyze cross-cultural differences over time among women

3391. Barr, Marleen. DEBORAH NORRIS LOGAN, FEMINIST CRITICISM, AND IDENTITY THEORY: INTERPRETING A WOMAN'S DIARY WITHOUT THE DANGER OF SEPARAT-ISM. *Biography 1985 8(1): 12-24.* Feminist scholars are devoting much attention to unearthing women's diaries and letters. As they develop new theories to interpret these noncanonical works, feminists should not dismiss other theories generated by the male critical establishment. Examines the diary of Deborah Norris Logan in terms of Norman N. Holland's notions about identity theory in order to provide one link between new feminist scholarship and existing male-generated theory. J/S

3392. Beddoe, Deirdre. TOWARDS A WELSH WOMEN'S HIS-TORY. *Llafur: J. of the Soc. for the Study of Welsh Labour Hist. [Great Britain] 1981 3(2): 32-38.* Describes the need for a history of women in Wales, examines the reasons it has not been written, and provides a brief historiographical study of Welsh women's history. Originally given as a lecture to the Llafur Annual General Meeting at the Polytechnic of Wales, Pontypridd, 22 November 1980. G. L. Neville

3393. Beecher, Maureen Ursenbach. UNDER THE SUNBON-NETS: MORMON WOMEN WITH FACES. *Brigham Young U. Studies 1976 16(4): 471-484.* Mormon women of the 19th century have a stereotyped image compounded of romanticized generalizations and overt sentimentality. Historians should include the impact of women in their writings on the history of the Mormon Church and Mormon culture. Mentions successful Mormon women in education, telegraphy, business, law, and medicine. M. S. Legan

3394. Berch, Bettina. "THE SPHINX IN THE HOUSEHOLD": A NEW LOOK AT THE HISTORY OF HOUSEHOLD WORKERS. *Rev. of Radical Pol. Econ. 1984 16(1): 105-120.* Reexamines the writings of Lucy Maynard Salmon, a 19th-century investigator of household work. Women whose options were limited by race as well as sex became household technicians rather than factory industrial workers. Based on the Lucy Maynard Salmon Papers at Vassar College and secondary sources; table, 2 notes, ref. D. R. Stevenson/S

3395. Berkin, Carol Ruth. REMEMBERING THE LADIES: HIS-TORIANS AND THE WOMEN OF THE AMERICAN REVOLU-TION. Fowler, William M., Jr. and Coyle, Wallace, ed. *The American Revolution: Changing Perspectives* (Boston: Northeastern U. Pr., 1979): 47-67. Reviews books and articles written during the 1970's on the relationship of women to the American Revolution. Some studies merely discussed the extent to which women participated in the Revolution. More sophisticated studies have sought to determine the effect of the Revolution on the self-identity of women and how women's participation in the war helps to describe the nature of the Revolution. 24 notes. S

3396. Branca, Patricia. REVIEW ESSAY: WOMEN'S HISTORY: COMMENTS ON YESTERDAY, TODAY AND TOMORROW. *J. of Social Hist. 1978 11(4): 575-579.* Review article prompted by William H. Charf's *Women and Equality: Changing Patterns in American Culture* (New York: Oxford U. Pr., 1977), Nancy F. Cott's *The Bonds of Womanhood: "Woman's Sphere" in New England, 1780-1835* (New Haven, Conn.: Yale U. Pr., 1977) and Ann Douglas's *The Feminization of American Culture* (New York: Knopf, 1977). Finds Cott's study of 18th and 19th century development of the cult of domesticity superior to Douglas' chiefly because the latter is too narrowly Marxist. Chafe's study of the politics of the struggle for equality also serves her critical reservations about Douglas's concentration of oppression. M. Hough

3397. Bravo, Anna; Passerini, Luisa; and Piccone Stella, Simonetta. MODI DI RACCONTARSI E FORME DI IDENTITA NELLE STORIE DI VITA [Modes of telling and forms of identity in life stories]. *Memoria: Riv. di Storia delle Donne [Italy] 1983 (8): 101-113.* A dialogue between three women researchers into women's life histories discussing the self-image of their interviewees, recurring themes in their accounts, and the implications for research of the differing points of view and reference frames of researcher and subject. Biblio. J. V. Coutinho

3398. Bridenthal, Renate and Koonz, Claudia. INTRODUCTION. Bridenthal, Renate and Koonz, Claudia, ed. *Becoming Visible: Women in European History* (Boston: Houghton Mifflin, 1977): 1-10. In the introduction to their compilation of essays on European women's history, the authors propose a feminist historiography to challenge traditional periodization of history. Research and methodology in women's history must include consideration of the changes within the family and the social change brought about by industrialization. Note. J. Brown

3399. Buhle, Mari Jo; Gordon, Ann G.; and Schrom, Nancy. WOMEN IN AMERICAN SOCIETY: AN HISTORICAL CON-TRIBUTION. *Radical Am. 1971 5(4): 3-66.* Discusses the historical role of women in the 19th and 20th centuries and how in spite of economic, technological, and social changes, the ideological assumptions regarding women have remained the same.

3400. Chianese, Gloria. DONNA, FAMIGLIA, AMORE: QUES-TIONI DI METODO NELLA RECENTE STORIOGRAFIA [Woman, family, love: questions of method in recent historiography]. *Italia Contemporanea [Italy] 1981 33(143): 69-82.* Reviews eight recent books displaying three common lines of approach: an analysis of the socioeconomic changes in the family, a study of the history of behavior, and a study of the history of feelings and emotions. Primary sources; 28 notes. E. E. Ryan

3401. Crunden, Robert M. THE IMPACT OF FEMINISM ON AMERICAN HISTORIOGRAPHY. *Indian J. of Am. Studies [India] 1983 13(2): 3-8.* The historiography on Progressivism has been a totally masculine one in which feminism was an issue of little importance. However, the activities of women such as Jane Addams were integral to the Progressive era. The activities of women led to new institutions, new political platforms, and new ideas.

L. V. Eid

3403. Degler, Carl. WHAT THE WOMEN'S MOVEMENT HAS DONE TO AMERICAN HISTORY. *Soundings 1981 64(4): 403-421.* Surveys attempts to rewrite American history from the perspective of women, concluding that the influence of women must be integrated into the picture in a balanced rather than in a reactionary, one-sided manner.

3404. Degler, Carl. *WOMAN AS FORCE IN HISTORY* BY MARY BEARD. *Daedalus 1974 103(1): 67-73. Woman as Force in History* (New York, 1946) never caught on, even during the current period of interest in women's history. Not a traditional feminist, Mary R. Beard did not accept conventional feminist interpretations of history. Rejecting the notion that women were subjected in the past, Beard preferred to emphasize the achievements of women. Primary and secondary sources; 6 notes.

E. McCarthy

3405. Doughty, Frances. LESBIAN BIOGRAPHY, BIOGRAPHY OF LESBIANS. *Frontiers 1979 4(3): 76-79.* Discusses lesbian historiography in terms of biography of lesbians and biography by lesbians, particularly the difficulty in establishing whether or not women were lesbians, using as examples American author Janet Flanner who lived in Paris from the 1920's to the 1970's and kept her private and public lives separate, and her contemporary Margaret Anderson whose private and public lives were the same.

3406. DuBois, Ellen et al. POLITICS AND CULTURE IN WOMEN'S HISTORY: A SYMPOSIUM. *Feminist Studies 1980 6(1): 26-64.* Discusses the political and theoretical significance of the current interest in describing the women's culture of 19th-century America. This interest has at times threatened to overshadow pressing political issues in the feminist movement. At best such studies can provide the framework for reexamining women's social status and life in that era. Includes a discussion of women's culture and politics from European and Third World perspectives, focusing upon class as a factor in how women experience the world. 47 notes.

G. V. Wasson

3407. Eichler, Margrit and Nelson, Carol Ann. HISTORY AND HISTORIOGRAPHY: THE TREATMENT IN AMERICAN HISTORIES OF SIGNIFICANT EVENTS CONCERNING THE STATUS OF WOMEN. *Historian 1977 40(1): 1-15.* Examines the extent to which historians have dealt with woman suffrage in America. Two complementary approaches are taken: 1) an index search concerning suffragism as compared to other contemporaneous issues in works of general history; and 2) an examination of major reform histories and their treatment of the question. The historians examined either totally ignored woman's suffrage or dealt with it in a summary fashion. Because a lack of available information cannot be used to explain the historiographic deficiencies found, evidently sexual bias existed.

M. S. Legan

3408. Engman, Max. DEN OGIFTA KVINNANS ARBETE, MYNDIGHET OCH SAMLEVNADSPROBLEM [The work, legal status, and cohabitation problems of the unmarried woman]. *Historisk Tidskrift för Finland [Finland] 1984 69(3): 201-206.* Comments on research in women's history in general and as currently carried out in Finland.

R. G. Selleck

3409. Fauré, Christine; Robinson, Lillian, transl. ABSENT FROM HISTORY. *Signs 1981 7(1): 71-80.* French feminist theory remains generally unknown to American scholars, although theory should be an underlying concern of feminist historiography. The author recognizes the subjectivity of history and its anachronistic nature. Michelet and Comte also recognized it, but silence on women's questions remained. Women's roles were ignored in 1848 as anecdotal, and Emmanuel Le Roy Ladurie, who uncovered a wealth of materials tied women to sex roles. Likewise, studies of witchcraft focus on the judges rather than on the accused, who were frequently female. Based primarily on the writings of the *Annales* school; 26 notes. Introduction by translator, pp. 68-70.

S. P. Conner

3410. Fox-Genovese, Elizabeth. GENDER, CLASS AND POWER: SOME THEORETICAL CONSIDERATIONS. *Hist. Teacher 1982 15(2): 255-276.* Few writers have examined carefully the close interactions between Marx's concept of class and the recent feminist analysis of sexism or gender related inequalities in society. Michel Foucault's recent revisionist work represents one of the best attempts, but even his work suffers from too little attention to the notion of gender and its relation to power. Presents a brief description of gender, class, and power relationships in precapitalist, early capitalist, and modern Western cultures. Calls for more detailed studies. Based on published sources; 19 notes.

L. K. Blaser

3411. Franchini, Silvia. IL NEOFEMMINISMO E LA "NEW WOMEN'S HISTORY" IN GRAN BRETAGNA [Neofeminism and the new women's history in Great Britain]. *Movimento Operaio e Socialista [Italy] 1981 4(3): 299-317.* In Great Britain the historiography resulting from the development of neofeminism has not yet found an institutional environment comparable to that which it enjoys in US universities. The article brings together some of the themes, methods, categories, and approaches found in the new women's history and concludes that, although it is somewhat limited in scope and fragmented, recent work is rich in theoretical revisions and new interpretative hypotheses. 64 notes.

J. V. Coutinho

3412. Freedman, Estelle B. THE NEW WOMAN: CHANGING VIEWS OF WOMEN IN THE 1920'S. *J. of Am. Hist. 1974 61(2): 372-393.* Historians have not been consistent in their evaluation of the women's movement in the 1920's. They have differed in their evaluation of the uses to which women put the newly acquired economic parity with men, and in their attitudes toward the reality of the sexual revolution of the 20's. Most recent works by William O'Neill and William Chafe see women as having made little progress in either the political or non-political realms in the period, though they differ in whether this failure should be attributed to splits within the feminist movement or to social barriers to full emancipation. Common to nearly all studies is a tendency toward broad and unsubstantiated generalizations about women without fully recognizing class, race, region, and ethnicity. 63 notes.

K. B. West

3413. Goldin, Claudia. HISTORIANS' CONSENSUS ON THE ECONOMIC ROLE OF WOMEN IN AMERICAN HISTORY. *Hist. Methods 1983 16(2): 74-81.* In this summary of nine books a consensus emerges; women in sex segregated jobs received lower wages than men and suffered from an ideology of domesticity. Agrees with these conclusions, but sees the need for a better methodology to strengthen them. 11 notes.

D. K. Pickens

3414. Gordon, Ann D.; Buhle, Mari Jo; and Dye, Nancy Schrom. THE PROBLEM OF WOMEN'S HISTORY. Carroll, Berenice A., ed. *Liberating Women's Hist.* (Chicago: U. of Illinois Pr., 1976): 75-92. Historians have traditionally looked upon women's spheres as monolithic, passive, and isolated from social change, with current historiography reflecting these beliefs. In the study of women's history present categories of historical methodology are bound by the traditional notion that only public and political spheres are of historical significance, areas in which women are not highly visible.

Feminists, opposed to this line of inquiry, seek to develop categories to fit women into history and to redefine significant events to encompass personal and subjective experiences. 31 notes.

B. Sussman

3415. Gordon, Linda; Hunt, Persis; Peck, Elizabeth; Ruthchild, Rochelle Goldberg; and Scott, Marcia. HISTORICAL PHALLACIES: SEXISM IN AMERICAN HISTORICAL WRITING. Carroll, Berenice A., ed. *Liberating Women's Hist.* (Chicago: U. of Illinois Pr., 1976): 55-74. Identifies and analyzes sexism in contemporary historical books and articles on American women. Explores why sexism, the belief in men's superiority over women, must lead to distorted historical interpretations of women's oppression. An examination of works by Robert Riegel, William O'Neill, Christopher Lasch, James R. McGovern, Carl Degler, David Potter, and Page Smith reveals that their historical writings on women are badly skewed because of sexist bias. 51 notes.   B. Sussman

3416. Gordon, Linda. WHAT SHOULD WOMEN'S HISTORIANS DO: POLITICS, SOCIAL THEORY, AND WOMEN'S HISTORY. *Marxist Perspectives 1978 1(3): 128-137.* Sees a need for total coverage of women's psychological, social, political, and economic position in historiography, rather than for strict concentration on feminism.

3417. Green, Rayna. NATIVE AMERICAN WOMEN. *Signs 1980 6(2): 248-267.* Reviews literature on Native American women written in the United States and Canada since the 17th century. The first trend was "an almost pathological attachment" to wars and the John Smith mythology. By 1900, two new topics emerged: a discussion of the American Southwest and biographies of individual Indians, which eventually were written from a Freudian perspective. After World War I, marriage customs entered the discussion, and the first major work was published—Ruth Landes's *The Ojibwa Woman.* After World War II, interest turned to matriarchy. Other notable works have appeared since 1960, highlighting anthropological and medical problems. Further studies are needed, but feminist theory is probably inapplicable and unwelcome. 33 notes.

S. P. Conner

3418. Groppi, Angela and Pelaja, Margherita. L'IO DIVISO DELLE STORICHE [The divided I of historians]. *Memoria: Rivista di Storia delle Donne [Italy] 1983 (9): 7-19.* Discusses the relationship of woman's history to social history, and notes the connection between socialist and leftist theory and feminism, and the mediation of militant feminists with professional historians. New demands have expanded the field of historical research and led to a reexamination of ideological presuppositions. There is, at present, a split between the practice of historians and the history lived by members of social liberation movements.   J. W. Houlihan

3419. Hackett, Amy and Pomeroy, Sarah. MAKING HISTORY: THE FIRST SEX. *Feminist Studies 1972 1(2): 97-108.* Review of Elizabeth Gould Davis' *The First Sex* (New York: Penguin Books, 1971). Challenges her use of history as an ally for feminists. Davis demonstrates through myth, archaeology, anthropology, biology, and history that females once ruled males and credits woman with all culture and invention. She uncritically accepts J. J. Bachofen's assumption of the universality of matriarchy in prehistory (*Myth, Religion and Mother Right,* 1861) and depicts Christianity as almost the sole historical agent of women's degradation. Neither historiography nor feminism are well served by Davis' speculations and polemics. 18 notes.

3420. Hageman, Elizabeth H. RECENT STUDIES IN WOMEN WRITERS OF TUDOR ENGLAND. *English Literary Renaissance 1984 14(3): 409-439.* Part 1. WOMEN WRITERS, 1485-1603, EXCLUDING MARY SIDNEY, COUNTESS OF PEMBROKE. After presenting a list of 33 books and articles that might serve as background studies to work on women writers of 16th-century England, surveys recent studies of 15 English women who wrote between 1485 and 1603. Except for occasional ground-breaking work by scholars such as Myra Reynolds, Ruth Hughey, and Charlotte Kohler, most of the articles and books treated here were published in the 1970's and the early 1980's—the years of the burgeoning new

scholarship on women. Although as yet none of the "standard" textbooks of the period include substantial excerpts by women writers, and although no general literary history of Tudor England allots appropriate space to them, enough of their works have been edited and examined to make it clear that women writers of Tudor England deserve careful study. Part 2. MARY SIDNEY, COUNTESS OF PEMBROKE. Only in the past 20 years have critics begun to explore the subtle verbal play and artistry of the Countess of Pembroke's literary works. J. C. A. Rathmell's edition (1963) of the *Psalms* of Sidney and Pembroke, the first to appear in nearly 150 years, has led to a reassessment of the countess's key role in revising her brother's first 43 psalms and in completing the collection. Recent studies by Barbara Lewalski, Coburn Freer, G. F. Waller, and others have recognized the rich diversity of tone and meaning in the countess's psalms and have shown their importance in the development of the 17th-century religious lyric. The countess's play *Antonie* continues to provoke controversy over its intrinsic merit and its possibility as a source for Shakespeare's *Antony and Cleopatra.* Although the countess's translations and occasional poems have been edited, there is still an urgent need for a complete critical edition of the *Psalms,* which exist in 17 manuscripts with extensive variants.   J

3421. Hammerton, A. J. NEW TRENDS IN THE HISTORY OF WORKING WOMEN IN BRITAIN. *Labor Hist. [Australia] 1976 (31): 53-60.* Examines changing attitudes toward the history of working women and discusses recent relevant works in British historiography.

3422. Harris, Barbara J. RECENT WORK ON THE HISTORY OF THE FAMILY: A REVIEW ARTICLE. *Feminist Studies 1976 3(3/4): 159-172.* Gerda Lerner has recently warned against equating family history with women's history. However, family history is certainly an important element in the history of women. Only when changes in the modern family are understood will we have an accurate picture of women's role in the transition to modern society. Christopher Lasch attacked the "modernization theory" supporting much current work on family history in a series of articles in the *New York Times Review of Books,* 1975. The theory assumes that the change from an extended to a nuclear family marks the transition from traditional to industrial society. Lasch is mistaken in questioning the importance of current research on family structure, since that structure in itself is vital because of its connection with demography. The question of the relation of family history to women's history remains. The changing role of women in modern family structures is a study vitally needed to complete our understanding of the total history of modern women. 51 notes.

S. R. Herstein

3423. Harrison, Brian and McMillan, James. SOME FEMINIST BETRAYALS OF WOMEN'S HISTORY. *Hist. J. [Great Britain] 1983 26(2): 375-389.* There are many faults in Patricia Hilden's recent article on women's history (see entry 35A:8124). Her historiographical perspective is inspirational but inaccurate; her assessment of the relationship between feminism and historical scholarship is misleading; and her treatment of past and present antifeminist ideas is confused. To be done in a fair, accurate, and truthful way, women's history must eventually be absorbed into a richer, invigorated history of society. Primary sources; 46 notes.

A. C. Drysdale

3424. Havice, Christine. FEMINIST ART HISTORY: A REVIEW ESSAY. *Southern Q. 1979 17(2): 87-94.* Reviews *Women and Art: A History of Women Painters and Sculptors from the Renaissance to the 20th Century* (Allanheld & Schram, 1978) by comparing it to the other works on art history that stress the importance of women's contributions to the arts in the past and present. The work is inspirational and an important contribution to the historiography of the subject.   B. D. Ledbetter

3425. Hilden, Patricia. WOMEN'S HISTORY: THE SECOND WAVE. *Hist. J. [Great Britain] 1982 25(2): 501-512.* Distinguishes three principal subdivisions in the "first wave" of women's history, from the mid-1960's to about 1975: combatant history, separate sphere history, and compensary or empirical retrieval history.

Critically evaluates a recent work on various aspects of women's history in 19th- and 20th-century Britain, America, and Germany insofar as it reproduces or transcends the characteristic strengths and weaknesses of each of these types of women's history. Based on nine works on political, economic, and social aspects of women's history published between 1978 and 1981. 19 notes.

M. J. Clark

3426. Hufton, Olwen. WOMEN IN HISTORY: EARLY MODERN EUROPE. *Past & Present [Great Britain] 1983 (101): 125-141.* The study of women in the past is part of a venerable tradition going back to the 19th century. There is no single history of women, and different historiographical approaches have been used. Sex differential demography has been of vital concern to historians of women since R. Kennedy's *The Irish: Emigration, Marriage and Fertility.* Demographic work recently has been linked with the history of the family. More work in class specific demography and the area of sex differentials in mortality rates is also needed. Other topics on women that require attention include labor, religion, charitable work and early professional activities.   J. G. Packer/S

3427. Hutson, James H. WOMEN IN THE ERA OF THE AMERICAN REVOLUTION: THE HISTORIAN AS SUFFRAGIST. *Q. J. of the Lib. of Congress 1975 32(4): 290-303.* More than 50 years after the passage of the 19th amendment, the women's suffrage movement is still shaping the character of present-day writing about women during the era of the American Revolution. The first comprehensive work was *The Women of the American Revolution,* by Elizabeth F. Ellet, 1848-1850. This work was second in importance only to the *History of Woman Suffrage,* by Elizabeth Cady Stanton, Susan B. Anthony and others. The new field of women's history is largely controlled by the propagandistic work written nearly a century ago. More attention should be given to traditional information. Illus., 44 notes.   E. P. Stickney

3428. Jameson, Elizabeth. WOMEN AS WORKERS, WOMEN AS CIVILIZERS: TRUE WOMANHOOD IN THE AMERICAN WEST. *Frontiers 1984 7(3): 1-8.* Historians have often based their treatment of Western women on prescriptive literature that reflects either male or Victorian female views; oral histories, however, indicate that these traditional literature sources do not accurately reflect the role of women in Western society.

3429. Jensen, Joan M. and Miller, Darlis A. THE GENTLE TAMERS REVISITED: NEW APPROACHES TO THE HISTORY OF WOMEN IN THE AMERICAN WEST. *Pacific Hist. Rev. 1980 49(2): 173-213.* Examines the ways in which historians have viewed women in the West and explores new possibilities for historical analysis. Women have been largely ignored in traditional histories of the West. A multicultural approach to the history of women of different ethnic groups, a study of cross-cultural relations of women, studies of the role of women in the urban process, and the effect of woman suffrage on western politics will result in a more representative history of men and women in the Trans-Mississippi West. Secondary sources; 120 notes.   R. N. Lokken

3430. Johannson, Sheila Ryan. "HERSTORY" AS HISTORY: A NEW FIELD OR ANOTHER FAD? Carroll, Berenice A., ed. Liberating Women's Hist. (Chicago: U. of Illinois Pr., 1976): pp. 400-430. Discusses methodological changes necessary if women's historical experience is to become more than a series of interesting facts unrelated to the mainstream of historical concerns. Suggests this can be accomplished by developing the relationship between the lives and social roles of women, and the nature of social change. To this end various aspects of women's history must be explored: the complex problem of status, attitudes and values of men toward females, the importance of production, reproduction, sexuality, and socialization, and, most important, how women have been instrumental in changing the structure and function of their societies. 55 notes.   B. Sussman

3431. Kealey, Linda. WOMEN'S WORK IN THE UNITED STATES: RECENT TRENDS IN HISTORICAL RESEARCH. *Atlantis [Canada] 1979 4(2): 133-142.* Discusses trends in the study of women's history, particularly of the 19th-century woman's role,

and the interest in Marxism as an analytical tool for research on the history of working women; reviews books, essays, and articles on working women in US history published in the 1970's.

3432. Kirk, Neville; Salveson, Paul; and Walker, Ann. REFLECTIONS ON HISTORY WORKSHOP 17. *International Labor and Working Class History 1984 (25): 92-95.* Activities of History Workshop 17 at Manchester Polytechnic in November 1983 emphasizes the need to involve the working class in historical discussions relevant to labor and women's history.

3433. Ku Yen. CHIANG CH'ING'S WOLFISH AMBITION IN PUBLICIZING "MATRIARCHAL SOCIETY." *Chinese Studies in Hist. 1979 12(3): 75-79.* Jiang Qing (Chiang Ch'ing) and the Gang of Four stepped up their plot to usurp Party leadership and seize state power at the death of Chairman Mao. One of her tricks was to build a case for a long-standing historical precedent for a matriarchal society and the exercise of power by women. An examination of history reveals no basis for such programs. Rather, everywhere and always the significant factor has been class struggle. "History is made by the people," and reactionaries can only hold back the course of history, but never ultimately dominate it. From the *Guangming Ribao* [Guangming Daily], 23 November 1976.   R. V. Ritter

3434. Ladner, Joyce A. RACISM AND TRADITION: BLACK WOMANHOOD IN HISTORICAL PERSPECTIVE. Carroll, Berenice A., ed. Liberating Women's Hist. (Chicago: U. of Illinois Pr., 1976): pp. 179-193. Past historiography has generally compared the black family to middle-class whites, a method which emphasizes the weaknesses of the blacks and overlooks their positive features. To begin to comprehend the position of black women in today's society, an analysis must be undertaken of family life in precolonial African cultures and the structural effects of slavery and modern oppression of blacks. In this way a true assessment of the strengths of the black personality can be made. 39 notes.

B. Sussman

3435. Lavrin, Asunción. SOME FINAL CONSIDERATIONS ON TRENDS AND ISSUES IN LATIN AMERICAN WOMEN'S HISTORY. Lavrin, Asunción, ed. *Latin American Women* (London: Greenwood Pr., 1978): 302-332. The history of Latin American women has been approached in two ways: women have been defined according to sources which reflect cultural norms, such as legislative and educational material, or in terms of individual biographies of exceptional women. Historians must amplify this limited picture by seeking a definition of the ideals that served as guidelines for behavior and by studying behavior in its historical reality. Important areas for consideration are prescriptive and educational literature written for women, the impact of the law on women's lives, and women's roles in politics, the work force, feminism, and women's associations. Questions about the differences between rural, urban, white, Indian, and black families and the changes in them resulting from the formation of a new society also merit attention. 70 notes.   S. Tomlinson-Brown

3436. Lerner, Gerda. THE MAJORITY FINDS ITS PAST. *Current Hist. 1976 70(416): 193-196, 231.* Discusses shortcomings in the historiography of women, sexual mores, and the role of women in society, 1970's.

3437. Lerner, Gerda. NEW APPROACHES TO THE STUDY OF WOMEN IN AMERICAN HISTORY. *J. of Social Hist. 1969 3(1): 53-62.* Rejects the traditional framework for studying women in American history, and suggests a new conceptual model incorporating psychology, role playing, status differentiation, and societal expectations counterpointed against reality. The feminist writers of the Progressive years, with few exceptions, saw American women as an oppressed group struggling for equality of rights; however, they ignored women's accomplishments outside of the suffrage movement. In retrospect their framework was too middle-class, nativist, and moralistic to be of use to scholars any longer. Suggests a new approach which provides a wider framework, yet permits a narrower focus on specific groups of women or individuals in America's past. Based on secondary sources, feminist literature, and biographies, 13 notes.   J. P. Harahan

3438.   Lerner, Gerda. PLACING WOMEN IN HISTORY: A 1975 PERSPECTIVE. Carroll, Berenice A., ed. Liberating Women's Hist. (Chicago: U. of Illinois Pr., 1976): pp. 357-367. No single methodology and conceptual framework can organize the historical experience of all types of women. Methods are only tools for analysis, to be used when needed and then replaced by new tools when necessary. A new history is essential, a universal history that is equally concerned with men, women, and the establishment and passing of patriarchy. To achieve this goal historians must become aware of the sexist bias that pervades the culture and recognize that women have always been an essential part of history. 14 notes.
                                                            B. Sussman

3439.   Lerner, Gerda. PLACING WOMEN IN HISTORY: DEFINITIONS AND CHALLENGES. Feminist Studies 1975 3(1/2): 5-14. Women's history has been considered an independent field by American historians for the last five years. Writing in traditional ways, historians have begun by studying exceptional women and their societal contributions, the struggle for women's rights, the economic problems of women, and questions relating to marriage, divorce, and female sexuality. New methods are developing to deal with the reality of females' experience in the past, including the use of letters, diaries, autobiographies, and oral history projects. Women's history is currently in transition and later stages may include the study of the tensions between male and female culture and the effect of patriarchal assumptions on women in society. Primary and secondary sources; 12 notes.   S. R. Herstein

3440.   Maack, Mary Niles. TOWARD A HISTORY OF WOMEN IN LIBRARIANSHIP: A CRITICAL ANALYSIS WITH SUGGESTIONS FOR FURTHER RESEARCH. J. of Lib. Hist. 1982 17(2): 164-185. Historians need to further refine their conceptual frameworks concerning women's history and librarianship, especially 19th-century developments, to avoid inaccurate generalizations. Attention should be focused on women who attempted to enhance the library profession, as well as their own careers. There are significant problems in obtaining the personal papers of many women who deserve study, but two works, American Library History: A Bibliography and The Role of Women in Librarianship, are among the many available materials that offer some help in this field. Secondary sources; 67 notes.   J. S. Coleman

3441.   Macintyre, Martha Bruton. RECENT AUSTRALIAN FEMINIST HISTORIOGRAPHY. Hist. Workshop J. [Great Britain] 1978 (5): 98-110. Surveys recent Australian feminist literature on the evolution of woman's social role in the country. Most of the works are psychological or sociological writings; their authors mostly ask why women have such low social status in one of the world's most advanced countries. 23 notes.   N. Dejevsky

3442.   May, Elaine Tyler. EXPANDING THE PAST: RECENT SCHOLARSHIP ON WOMEN IN POLITICS AND WORK. Rev. in Am. Hist. 1982 10(4): 216-233. Recent scholarship in women's history challenges basic historical approaches and assumptions; an examination of the role of women in politics and work necessitates an expanded definition of those concepts.

3443.   McClave, Heather. SCHOLARSHIP AND THE HUMANITIES. Women's Ann. 1982-83: 205-229. Surveys the progress of women's studies and its contributions to literary criticism, historiography, religious studies, black studies, lesbian studies, music history, and art history.

3444.   McGinnis, Janice P. Dickin. SEXISM IN THE NEW ENCYCLOPEDIA BRITANNICA. Dalhousie Rev. [Canada] 1979 59(2): 250-264. Criticizes the 1974 edition of the Encyclopedia Britannica for its historical and biographical treatment of women. Examines articles on Babe Didrikson, Emma Hamilton, Maximilian of Austria and his wife Elizabeth, Mary Wollstonecraft, Carrie Nation, Isabella I of Castile, Anne Boleyn, Catherine Howard, Catherine Parr, Madame de Staël, Elizabeth of Russia, Queen Mary (of

Teck), Christina of Sweden, Marie Antoinette, Anne of Brittany, Eleanor of Aquitaine, and a large number of lesser figures including missing entries for important women.   C. H. Held

3445.   Morantz, Regina Markell. THE PERILS OF FEMINIST HISTORY. J. of Interdisciplinary Hist. 1974 4(4): 649-660. Many current feminist histories locate the source of 20th-century problems in the apparent injustices of the 19th century, playing on the theme of woman as victim. Often this is not history but polemics. The point is examined with respect to recent writing on 19th-century medical therapeutics in the treatment of women's diseases and on the attitudes and self-images of pioneering women doctors. 20 notes.   R. Howell

3446.   Moreau, Thérèse. REVOLTING WOMEN: HISTORY AND MODERNITY IN JULES MICHELET. Clio 1977 6(2): 167-179. Although Jules Michelet's (1798-1874) style and approach are outdated, his "ideology of the Third Republic," where he projected woman upon the entire historical system is not. Constructing an Oedipal family relationship in which the woman was sexually repressed, Michelet projected that relationship onto French society to explain the early stages of the French Revolution of 1789. He described the qualities of the woman and the masses as identical. Speech given at an interdisciplinary colloquium on Jules Michelet. 6 notes.   T. P. Linkfield

3447.   Moseley, Eva S. SOURCES FOR THE "NEW WOMEN'S HISTORY." Am. Archivist 1980 43(2): 180-190. The writing of women's history, particularly the history of poor women, requires use of nontraditional sources such as personnel, reform school, prison, court, and hospital records. Also useful are reports of people such as teachers and employers about poor women and papers of women's organizations and oral history interviews. Archivists must change collecting policies where necessary to acquire these records, seek them in existing holdings, and provide better indexing to lead researchers to them. Based on the author's personal experience and secondary sources; 32 notes.   G.-A. Patzwald

3448.   Norton, Mary Beth and Berkin, Carol Ruth. WOMEN AND AMERICAN HISTORY. Berkin, Carol Ruth and Norton, Mary Beth, ed. Women of America: A History (Boston: Houghton Mifflin Co., 1979): 3-15. The historiography of American women can be said to have begun with Elizabeth Fries Lummis Ellet's The Women of the American Revolution (1848). It was followed by the History of Woman Suffrage by Elisabeth Cady Stanton, Susan B. Anthony, et al. (completed in 1922), and Elizabeth Dexter's Colonial Women of Affairs (1924), written to exhibit that American women had been involved in business enterprises in the past. The authors include a summary of the common view of women's history and recent scholarly trends, including fields of study in women's history.   K. Talley

3449.   O'Brien, Jo. WRITING WOMEN BACK INTO ENGLISH HISTORY. Internat. Socialist Rev. 1971 32(1): 18-22. Discusses the lack of information concerning the role of women in working-class political associations in the 1840's in the historiography of Great Britain. Also examines the political activities of the women's liberation movement, 1968-70.

3450.   Perrot, Michelle. SUR L'HISTOIRE DES FEMMES EN FRANCE [On the history of women in France]. Rev. du Nord [France] 1981 63(250): 569-579. Points out major directions of research into women's history and the groups, centers, publications connected with it, especially at the university level. Indicates the contemporary specifications of this history, its aims and limits, and its relations with the place of women in French society.   J/S

3451.   Pierson, Ruth. WOMEN'S HISTORY: THE STATE OF THE ART IN ATLANTIC CANADA. Acadiensis [Canada] 1977 7(1): 121-131. Since the history of women in the Atlantic Provinces is just beginning to emerge, a coherent historiography has yet to be developed, but there is a current scattering of essays, papers, and books, as demonstrated in this bibliographic essay.

3452. Pirzio, Paola. DONNE NELLA POLITICA E NELLA STORIA [Women in politics and in history]. *Italia Contemporanea* [Italy] 1982 (148): 81-96. Surveys recent Italian books and articles on the feminist movement in the 20th century. The interpretation of the movement and its relationship to politics is controversial due to conflicting assumptions about the role of women. Primary sources; 56 notes.   E. E. Ryan

3453. Porter, Marilyn. "SHE WAS SKIPPER OF THE SHORE-CREW": NOTES ON THE HISTORY OF THE SEXUAL DIVISION OF LABOUR IN NEWFOUNDLAND. *Labour* [Canada] 1985 (15): 105-123. Most feminist studies of maritime societies have assumed that the rigors of the seafaring life and the consequent development of a "tough" male ethic led almost necessarily to the subordination of women. In Newfoundland the history of women reveals a strong woman's culture and a very low level of domestic violence. Women were few in the early stages of colonial life and were extremely important in the growth of the colony. Although women almost never engaged in fishing, their other contributions, such as drying and packing, were a major part of the industry's work. Secondary sources; 49 notes.
                                                J. W. Houlihan

3454. Rausa-Gomez, Lourdes and Tubangui, Helen R. REFLECTIONS ON THE FILIPINO WOMAN'S PAST. *Philippine Studies* [Philippines] 1978 26(1-2): 125-141. Examines foreign written observations on the occupations, role in the family and business, beauty, and morals of Filipino women. Most quotes are by 19th-century Spaniards and 20th-century Americans. The Filipina was unusual in Asia. She was visibly subordinate in the household, but wielded much subtle social and economic power.
                                                D. Chaput

3455. Riegelhaupt, Joyce F. WOMEN, WAR, AND FAMILY: SOME RECENT WORKS IN WOMEN'S HISTORY. *A REVIEW ARTICLE. Comparative Studies in Soc. and Hist.* [Great Britain] 1982 24(4): 660-672. Reviews five recent works in women's history. Thomas Dublin's *Women at Work: The Transformation of Work and Community in Lowell, Massachusetts, 1826-1860* (1979) demonstrates that the perception and structuring of work and the form of labor organization and agitation are historically related to the roles of women. Carl Degler's *At Odds: Women and the Family in America from the Revolution to the Present* (1980) suggests that equality for women and the maintenance of the family are incompatible. Darlene Levy, Harriet Applewhite, and Mary Johnson's *Women in Revolutionary Paris 1789-1795* (1979) and *Women, War and Revolution* (1980) maintain that opportunities for changing gender roles have emerged during periods of social unrest, such as the French Revolution. Susan Kennedy's *All We Did Was to Weep at Home: A History of White Working-Class Women in America* (1979) provides a 25 page bibliography on her topic.
                                                S. A. Farmerie/S

3456. Riemer, Eleanor S. and Fout, John C. WOMEN'S HISTORY: RECENT JOURNAL ARTICLES. *Trends in Hist.* 1979 1(1): 3-22. Discusses articles which appeared in US and European periodical literature in 1978 on major trends in the study of women's history: sexuality, the family, women and war, attitudes toward women, education, and immigrants.

3457. Robertson, Darrel M. THE FEMINIZATION OF AMERICAN RELIGION: AN EXAMINATION OF RECENT INTERPRETATIONS OF WOMEN AND RELIGION IN VICTORIAN AMERICA. *Christian Scholar's Rev.* 1978 8(3): 238-246. Traces the feminization of American religion during 1820's-30's, identified as a romanticization or sentimentalization of religion by traditional historians, discussed as feminization in Barbara Welter's essay, "The Feminization of American Religion," published in 1973.

3458. Roe, Jill. MODERNISATION AND SEXISM: RECENT WRITINGS ON VICTORIAN WOMEN. *Victorian Studies* 1977 20(2): 179-192. Recent scholarship has directed attention to women as wives, mothers, and workers. Yet books focusing on the atypical Victorian woman—one struggling for legal or educational reform—still receive the bulk of attention. Five of the nine books

reviewed deal with the suffrage question. Considers the current status of historiography in the field and proposes profitable new avenues of approaching the topic. 47 notes.   T. L. Auffenberg

3459. Rouse, Parke, Jr. BELLE HUNTINGTON, HER MEN AND HER MUSE. *Virginia Mag. of Hist. and Biog.* 1980 88(4): 387-400. Surveys the life of Mrs. Collis P. Huntington, later Mrs. Henry E. Huntington, treating it as a historiographical problem. Important both as the wife of these railroad magnates and as an art collector in her own right, Mrs. Huntington effectively kept her affairs, especially her early life and premarital relations with Collis Huntington, from contemporaries and, subsequently, historians. Her privacy was assured when her son destroyed her papers upon her death. Covers ca. 1860-1924. Photo, 22 notes.
                                                P. J. Woehrmann

3460. Rupp, Leila J. REFLECTIONS ON TWENTIETH-CENTURY AMERICAN WOMEN'S HISTORY. *Rev. in Am. Hist.* 1981 9(2): 275-284. "Attempts to apply some of the approaches and concepts that have emerged in research and writing on nineteenth-century American women's history to the twentieth century," focusing on work, women's culture, and feminism based on numerous books and articles published 1970-80.

3461. Sangster, Joan. WOMEN AND UNIONS IN CANADA: A REVIEW OF HISTORICAL RESEARCH. *Resources for Feminist Res.* [Canada] 1981 10(2): 2-6. A review of Canadian historical studies on women workers since 1891 shows a paucity of research in spite of evidence of women's organizability and militancy.

3462. Scarpaci, J. Vincenza. *LA CONTADINA*: THE PLAYTHING OF THE MIDDLE CLASS WOMAN HISTORIAN. *J. of Ethnic Studies* 1981 9(2): 21-38. Interest in Italian-American women among researchers, predominantly women, reflects "the tendency of scholars to apply their own preconceptions to the people they study, and the dangers of this are examined in four current forums of analysis: the monad theory, the generational sequence pattern, the creator of a women's culture, and history through empathy. Studies representative of each approach are analyzed, and each is found lacking in "acknowledgment of women's many roles." Instead "women are dumped into a category where their commonality becomes more important than their individual behavior." Primary and secondary written sources and oral sources; 28 notes.
                                                G. J. Bobango

3463. Schultz, Constance B. DAUGHTERS OF LIBERTY: THE HISTORY OF WOMEN IN THE REVOLUTIONARY WAR PENSION RECORDS. *Prologue* 1984 16(3): 139-153. Discusses the Revolutionary War pension records and bounty-land warrant application files, part of the records of the Veterans Administration, as a rich source of 19th-century social history. The files are an especially rich resource for women's history. The women's material falls into two categories: anecdotal information, providing insight into a wide variety of women's lives; and economic and demographic information, providing data for the analysis of change in the lives of groups of women. Based on Revolutionary War pension and bounty-land warrant application files; 15 illus., 30 notes.
                                                M. A. Kascus

3464. Schwarz, Judith. QUESTIONNAIRE ON ISSUES IN LESBIAN HISTORY. *Frontiers* 1979 4(3): 1-12. Reprints the responses of 24 women doing research in women's studies, to a 1979 questionnaire on lesbian history, including brief descriptions of their work, their definition of lesbians, the relationship of lesbian history to women's history, and difficulties in research; sees a need for studying lesbian history.

3465. Scott, Joan Wallach. WOMEN IN HISTORY: THE MODERN PERIOD. *Past & Present* [Great Britain] 1983 (101): 141-157. Examines the assumptions and methods of the various approaches to women's history drawing upon recent scholarship. The first approach narrates women's experience either alongside or outside conventional historical frameworks, describing historical topics that have been ignored. The second approach is closely associated with social history, emphasizing the relationship of women to larger historical themes. The third approach emphasizes gender as a fundamental part of the analysis, examining women and men in relationship to each other. 38 notes. J. G. Packer/S

3466. Sicherman, Barbara. THE NEW SCHOLARSHIP: REVIEW ESSAYS IN THE HUMANITIES: AMERICAN HISTORY. *Signs: J. of Women in Culture and Soc. 1975 1(2): 461-485.* Rapidly accumulating scholarly work on women's historical experiences has not yet developed a consensus on an appropriate conceptual framework for women's history. Rather, historians are mainly impressed with the complexities of women's experiences. The most important current issue is the impact of industrialization on women's status, with individual studies touching on demography, sexual differentiation, economic and familial roles, psychology, and social structures. Secondary sources; 79 notes. S. E. Kennedy

3467. Silverman, Eliane Leslau. WRITING CANADIAN WOMEN'S HISTORY, 1970-82: AN HISTORIOGRAPHICAL ANALYSIS. *Can. Hist. Rev. [Canada] 1982 63(4): 513-533.* Based on articles and books on Canadian women's lives, thoughts, and activities by professional historians. The article analyzes themes that the literature suggests and points to new directions for the scholarship. It concluded that while women have created spheres both within and alongside of male culture, their history must be integrated to create a new Canadian history. A

3468. Skidmore, P. G. REFORMING WOMEN. *Can. Rev. of Am. Studies [Canada] 1983 14(4): 437-446.* Reviews Claudia L. Bushman's *"A Good Poor Man's Wife": Being a Chronicle of Harriet Hanson Robinson and Her Family in Nineteenth-Century New England* (1981), Mark Thomas Connelly's *The Response to Prostitution in the Progressive Era* (1980), Barbara Leslie Epstein's *The Politics of Domesticity: Women, Evangelism, and Temperance in Nineteenth Century America* (1981), and Estelle B. Freedmen's *Their Sisters' Keepers: Women's Prison Reform in America, 1830-1930* (1981), which profile feminist reformers and reflect the new professionalism in women's history. H. T. Lovin

3469. Smith, Bonnie. THE CONTRIBUTION OF WOMEN TO MODERN HISTORIOGRAPHY IN GREAT BRITAIN, FRANCE, AND THE UNITED STATES, 1750-1940. *American Historical Review 1984 89(3): 709-732.* Evaluates the contributions of British, French, and American women scholars to women's history. These historians faced a variety of prejudices and problems in undertaking their research and writing. In part, they were challenged by their male counterparts, who often regarded books on women as frivolous, trivial, and "outside the boundaries of history." Despite political and social changes, women's history remains professionally suspect by some traditional historians. Secondary sources; 88 notes. S

3470. Smith, Bonnie G. SEEING MARY BEARD. *Feminist Studies 1984 10(3): 399-416.* Reviews Mary Beard's historiography, using the viewpoint she herself applied to history. Just as she noted that women are invisible to historians, her work has been largely ignored or misunderstood by others. She rejected the accumulation of facts as a tool for understanding history. Crucial to understanding Mary Beard's "weirdness and asymmetry" is a recognition of her belief in history as viewpoint, and that the absence or presence of women in history depends entirely on the perspective of the historian. The fact that she did not receive full recognition for her work, whereas her husband Charles Beard was given both blame and credit for it, reinforces her own observations about history and historians. 27 notes. K. Phenix

3471. Smith, Hilda. FEMINISM AND THE METHODOLOGY OF WOMEN'S HISTORY. Carroll, Berenice A., ed. Liberating Women's Hist. (Chicago: U. of Illinois Pr., 1976): pp. 369-384. Women's history must be viewed from the feminist perspective of women as a distinct sociological group. Sexual division has created a separate past for men and women, and regardless of individual differences among women, they are distinguished from all other groups because of this division. In reassessing women's role, women must not be isolated from historical experiences because women were always a part of society, absorbed its values, and in turn affected life through their own peculiar experiences. A comparison between male and female lifestyles and value systems is essential if we are to uncover the realities of women's past. 14 notes. B. Sussman

3472. Smith-Rosenberg, Carroll. THE FEMINIST RECONSTRUCTION OF HISTORY. *Acad.: Bull. of the AAUP 1983 69(5): 26-37.* The beginning of the modern women's movement in the 1960's drew scholars and students to the field of history, and feminist issues formed the questions that women's historians first addressed; their goal was to integrate their studies of women's history with traditional history.

3473. Smith-Rosenberg, Carroll. THE NEW WOMAN AND THE NEW HISTORY. *Feminist Studies 1976 3(1/2): 185-198.* Contrary to Elizabeth Janeway's view that there is no such thing as "women's history," there is indeed a women's history. In fact, in the mid-1970's there are actually two women's histories. One is a traditional and politically oriented study of women. The second "New Women's History" results from the interplay of forces between the women's movement and the "New Social History." Utilizing new methodologies including family reconstruction, demographic studies, and other statistical constructs, historians seek answers to new questions regarding the tensions and influence of hitherto private places—the household, the nursery, the bed, etc. Male-female interaction, as well as female-female interaction, is being studied. Middle-class and working-class women's history are evolving and can in the future contribute to a synthesis of the female experience. Primary and secondary sources; 27 notes. S. R. Herstein

3474. Stearns, Peter N. OLD WOMEN: SOME HISTORICAL OBSERVATIONS. *J. of Family Hist. 1980 5(1): 44-57.* Old women are the latest in that long line on neglected historical topics. Lacking few prime movers ("great men") that traditionally attracted historians and even the romance or scandal that occasionally got young women into the history books, old women were relegated to old wives tales. This group deserves more attention by family historians and demographers because of their unique vital patterns and social roles. 8 notes, biblio. T. W. Smith

3475. Stoddart, Jennifer. LE PAYSAGE DE L'HISTOIRE CHANGE: LA PRODUCTION FRANÇAISE RÉCENTE EN HISTOIRE DES FEMMES [The picture of history is changing: recent French works on the history of women]. *Resources for Feminist Res. [Canada] 1981 10(3): 4-11.* Reviews several recent French books on the history of women. They are innovative in French historical writing through their explanations of history according to feminine criteria.

3476. Struna, Nancy L. BEYOND MAPPING EXPERIENCE: THE NEED FOR UNDERSTANDING IN THE HISTORY OF AMERICAN SPORTING WOMEN. *J. of Sport Hist. 1984 11(1): 120-133.* The historiography of women in American sports is limited both in quality and interpretation. Historians have focused only on educated, middle-class women, and they have failed to examine women's motives for participating in sports. 31 notes. M. Kaufman/S

3477. Stuard, Susan Mosher. THE ANNALES SCHOOL AND FEMINIST HISTORY: OPENING DIALOGUE WITH THE AMERICAN STEPCHILD. *Signs 1981 7(1): 135-143.* In Lucien Febvre's interests in marriage patterns, social revolt, sexual frustrations, and other parts of total history were the beginnings of feminist concerns and theory. In works such as these, women's history was legitimized; but in spite of the interest, women's history still remains glaringly underrepresented because of the nonideological structuralist theory. In fact, no member of the Centre de Recherches Historiques is primarily a historian of women. Only Christiane Klapishe-Zuber and David Herlihy's *Les Toscans et Leurs Familles* addresses women's issues directly. 11 notes. S. P. Conner

3478. Treckel, Paula A. AN HISTORIOGRAPHICAL ESSAY: WOMEN ON THE AMERICAN FRONTIER. *Old Northwest 1975 1(4): 391-403.* In 150 years only four major works have been published about women on the frontier. These women have been inadequately considered; for the writings, all by men, have male chauvinist standard biases. The works are deficient in source, neglecting a wealth of material written by pioneer women. Since many of these women did not fit the stereotype of loving, virtuous peacemakers, they were ignored by male historians. Secondary works; 25 notes.   J. N. Dickinson

3479. Ulrich, Laurel Thatcher. VIRTUOUS WOMEN FOUND: NEW ENGLAND MINISTERIAL LITERATURE, 1668-1735. *Am. Q. 1976 28(1): 20-40.* Examines 17th- and 18th-century New England ministerial elegies, memorials, funeral sermons, and works of practical piety concerning women indicating a tension existing in male minds between a view of the private worth and the public position of women. Ministers' genuine concern for sex equality eventually generated discrete and ultimately confining notions of femininity. The common historiographical view of Puritan women being regarded as inferior by their male counterparts must be reexamined in the light of the evidence presented.   N. Lederer

3480. Vallance, Elizabeth. WRITING WOMEN BACK IN. *Pol. Studies [Great Britain] 1982 30(4): 582-590.* Reviews feminist books, which have attempted to make women realize their own historical exclusion, except as appendages, from the male world and which have tried to write women back into history and into social and political theory and practice. The books are divided into the categories of women at work, women in politics, the politics of sex and reproduction, and theoretical studies of women's position in social and political life. Particular attention is focused on C. Aldred's *Women at Work* (1981), A. Pollert's *Girls, Wives, Factory Lives* (1981), J. Lovenduski's *Women in British Political Studies* (1981), S. J. Pharr's *Political Women in Japan* (1981), J. Week's *Sex, Politics and Society: The Regulation of Sexuality since 1800* (1981), *Building Feminist Theory: Essays from Quest* (1981), edited by A. Rogin, and M. O'Brien's *The Politics of Reproduction* (1981). 55 notes.   G. L. Neville

3481. Volk, S. S. and Tishkin, G. A. ZARUBEZHNYE AVTORY O ZHENSKOM DVIZHENII I SEM'E V ROSSII XIX NACHALA XX V. [Foreign authors on women's movements and the family in Russia in the 19th and beginning of the 20th centuries]. *Voprosy Istorii [USSR] 1981 (11): 164-166.* The problem of women's emancipation and their increasing role in society played an important part in the prerevolutionary liberation movement in Russia. After the October Revolution the Soviet authorities carried out a series of reforms for the liberation of women. This prompted many foreign authors to study the struggle for women's rights and to shed light on the connection between the family and the economic and cultural development of Russia.   S. M. Levy/S

3482. Zinich, M. S. IZUCHENIE TRUDOVOI DEIATEL'NOSTI ZHENSHCHIN V GODY VELIKOI OTECHESTVENNOI VOINY (1941-1945) [Female employment during the Great Patriotic War, 1941-45]. *Istoricheskie Zapiski Akademii Nauk SSSR [USSR] 1976 97: 237-262.* Discusses the existing historiography of women's activities in the USSR during World War II, in particular 1941-45, indicating a number of related topics still to be studied.

Religion

3483. Aguirre, Emilio. APUNTES PARA UNA BIOGRAFIA DEL P. GUILLERMO VAZQUEZ NUÑEZ, DESDE SU EPISTO-LARIO COMO PROVINCIAL [Notes for a biography of Father Guillermo Vázquez Núñez from his correspondence as provincial]. *Estudios [Spain] 1984 40(146-147): 117-126.* The letters from Guillermo Vázquez Núñez, provincial of Castile for the Order of Our Lady of Mercy, to Alberto Barros Fernández in Rome indicate his concern for the religious education and formation of novices, personal and economic difficulties, and the historiography of the order.

3484. Ajayi, J. F. Ade and Ayandele, E. A. EMERGING THEMES IN NIGERIAN AND WEST AFRICAN RELIGIOUS HISTORY. *J. of African Studies 1974 1(1): 1-39.* Discusses the 19th- and 20th-century writings on religious history in West Africa

where the dominant religions have been native animism, Islam, and Christianity. The latter has been in the vanguard of sociopolitical change and modernism, but has failed to replace the traditional value system. Islam has more adherents and has proved to be very adaptable. Native animism remains the most satisfying religion to the majority. 56 notes.   V. L. Human

3485. Allen, James B. and Cowan, Richard O. THE TWENTIETH CENTURY: CHALLENGE FOR MORMON HISTORIANS. *Dialogue 1972 7(1): 26-36.* Much of recent Mormon history is unstudied and unrecorded.

3486. Arnal, Oscar L. LUTHER AND THE PEASANTS: A LUTHERAN REASSESSMENT. *Sci. & Soc. 1980-81 44(4): 443-465.* Marxist and Christian scholars of the German Democratic Republic have been trying to integrate their particular insights into the old debate of how Martin Luther (1483-1546) could have advocated the bloody suppression of the German peasants in 1525. Luther's radical religious ideas on Christian liberty were rooted in his troubled psyche, while his entire family background and education easily led him to defend the political status quo. That Luther could not appreciate the quite different environment of the peasants is the great tragedy of the Reformation. Based on *Luther's Works* with some references to relevant secondary accounts.   L. V. Eid

3487. Arrington, Leonard J. HISTORIAN AS ENTREPRENEUR: A PERSONAL ESSAY. *Brigham Young U. Studies 1977 17(2): 193-209.* Author traces his own academic development and career. He provides candid insights into the Historical Department of the Mormon Church; the developing historiography of Mormonism, and the Church's attitude toward its vast primary source holdings on western Americana.   M. S. Legan

3488. Arrington, Leonard J. THE WRITING OF LATTER-DAY SAINT HISTORY: PROBLEMS, ACCOMPLISHMENTS AND ADMONITIONS. *Dialogue 1981 14(3): 119-129.* An overview of the writing of Mormon history from the denomination's founding until 1980. Most of the study focuses on the work of the past decade, highlighting the contributions of the History Division of the Church of Jesus Christ of Latter-day Saints and the growing professionalization of such historical studies. Reconciling faith and history constitutes one of the major problems facing Mormon historians. 22 notes.   M. G. Bishop

3489. Ayandele, E. A. and Ade Ajayi, J. F. WRITING AFRICAN CHURCH HISTORY. *African Historical Studies* (Totowa, N.J.: Frank Cass, 1979): 230-252. Scholars of African church history have long denied the authenticity of churches that broke away from mission churches, thus contributing to their ambiguous position in African society; yet the imprinting of national characteristics on Christianity is valid.

3490. Balevics, Z. V. ISTORICHESKOE ZNANIE V FORMIROVANII NAUCHNO-MATERIALISTICHESKOGO MIROVOZZRENIIA [The role of the knowledge of history in the formation of the scientific and materialistic world outlook]. *Latvijas PSR Zinatnu Akademijas Vestis [USSR] 1976 (6): 67-79.* It is easy to fall back on a religious explanation of life and man's role in it without a thorough knowledge of history and a grounding in Marxist-Leninist materialism. Emigré falsifiers exploit this weakness when they distort the history and present status of religion in Latvia and other parts of the Soviet Union. The historical spirituality of Latvians and other peoples of what is now the USSR is grossly exaggerated by rightist emigré clerics in the West, especially with regard to the mid-19th century. As religious concepts are increasingly discredited, religions attempt to maintain their power by claiming involvement in popular social movements, but historically they have supported the establishment. Soviet works on cultural history are generally weak and schematic, allowing religious interpretations in this field to retain their influence.   C. Moody

3491. Balmer, Randall H. THE PRINCETONIANS, SCRIPTURE, AND RECENT SCHOLARSHIP. *J. of Presbyterian Hist. 1982 60(3): 267-270.* In 1881 Archibald Alexander Hodge and Benjamin Breckinridge Warfield of Princeton coauthored an article on inspiration, which held that biblical inspiration extends to the very words of Scripture, that the Bible itself teaches its own inerrancy, and that inerrancy extends only to the original autographs and not to later translations. In recent years Ernest Sandeen, Jack Rogers, and Donald McKim have urged that the article formulated a new theory of inspiration in response to the attacks of biblical criticism. The 1881 article, however, not only was quite consistent with earlier Princeton theories, but it was also in harmony with a much wider contingent of 19th-century American theologians. Warfield and the young Hodge did not pioneer a new theory of inspiration nor did they hold peculiar views about Scripture. 15 notes.

H. M. Parker, Jr.

3492. Bammel, Ernst. ALBERT SCHWEGLER ÜBER JESUS UND DAS URCHRISTENTUM [Albert Schwengler on Christ and early Christianity]. *Zeit. für Kirchengeschichte* [West Germany] 1980 91(1): 1-10. Discusses the work of German philosopher and historian A. Schwengler about the early Christians in a paper commended by the Protestant Theological Faculty in Tübingen in 1839. When in 1841 the author published his *Montanism and the Church of Christ,* he was acclaimed a "young man of many hopes for the future of German philosophy." Manuscript sources; 44 notes.

G. E. Pergl/S

3493. Ban, Joseph D. WAS JOHN BUNYAN A BAPTIST? A CASE-STUDY IN HISTORIOGRAPHY. *Baptist Quarterly* [Great Britain] 1984 30(8): 367-376. Surveys views of British author John Bunyan's (1628-88) religious identity. Calling him a Baptist or a Congregationalist may imply distinctions not applicable in his day. 24 notes.

3494. Bannon, John Francis. THE MISSION AS A FRONTIER INSTITUTION: SIXTY YEARS OF INTEREST AND RESEARCH. *Western Hist. Q. 1979 10(3): 303-322.* Herbert Eugene Bolton's 1917 faculty research lecture at the University of California at Berkeley, subsequently printed and reprinted several times, became "a veritable seed piece." Entitled "The Mission as a Frontier Institution in the Spanish American Colonies," it continues to affect the study of the Spanish Borderlands history. Reviews a selection of the historiography of the subject under several headings: geographic areas, missions, missions and protection, missions and civilization/Hispanicization, and scholars other than historians who study missions. Selected biblio.

D. L. Smith

3495. Bartel, Horst and ˙Schmidt, Walter. DAS HISTORISCHMATERIALISTISCHE LUTHERBILD IN GESCHICHTE UND GEGENWART [Historical materialism and the portrayal of Luther in past and present]. *Zeitschrift für Geschichtswissenschaft* [East Germany] 1984 32(4): 291-301. Neither Marx nor Engels concerned themselves unduly with Martin Luther, yet by their collective attitudes they implied a new qualitative comprehension of Luther. He was rejected due to his opposition to the Peasants War in 1524, which was obviously inexcusable. However, during the past eight years modern Marxist historians, with deeper insight into the many different aspects of Luther's character, are greatly impressed by his socialist and work ethics and consider him in a much more favorable light. 37 notes.

T. Kuner

3496. Bartel, Horst. DAS LUTHERBILD DER REVOLUTIONÄREN DEUTSCHEN ARBEITERBEWEGUNG [The image of Luther in the revolutionary German working-class movement]. *Beiträge zur Gesch. der Arbeiterbewegung* [East Germany] 1983 25(6): 786-796. Analyzes the evolution of the image of Martin Luther in Marxist-Leninist historiography of the 19th- and 20th-century German working-class movement through an examination of the works of eight East German writers whose works have been published between 1970 and 1982. The author discusses the historiographical foundations of the image of Luther in the revolutionary working-class movement and the historical and political context in which this image originated and evolved. He also discusses how Marx and Engels viewed Luther within the universal political context of the Reformation and the peasants' wars and

demonstrates how the views of Engels in particular were supported by the German revolutionary working-class movement, particularly during the 1880's and 1890's. Secondary sources; 47 notes.

G. L. Neville

3497. Baubérot, Jean. LE PROTESTANTISME FRANÇAIS ET SON HISTORIOGRAPHIE [French Protestantism and its historiography]. *Archives des Sciences Sociales des Religions* [France] 1984 58(2): 175-186. This bibliographical essay presents 12 recent works on the history of French Protestantism. In this last half century a subtle change has taken place in the Protestants' attitude to their own history, from a theological and pastoral approach to a certain indifference to spiritual meanings.

J. V. Coutinho

3498. Becker, Gerhard. MARTIN LUTHER—GESCHICHTLICHE STELLUNG UND HISTORISCHES ERBE INTERNATIONALE WISSENSCHAFTLICHE KONFERENZ ZUM 500. GEBURTSTAG DES REFORMATORS IN HALLE [Martin Luther—historical place and heritage: international scientific conference in Halle on the 500th anniversary of the birth of the reformer]. *Zeitschrift für Geschichtswissenschaft* [East Germany] 1984 32(3): 236-242. The conference in Halle-Wittenberg in 1983 discussed the Marxist-Leninist approach to Luther and to the German Democratic Republic. The 500 historians and other East German representatives and 67 visitors from six socialist and 14 capitalist countries produced useful and stimulating discussions between theologians and Marxist historians on several subjects, including the new insights gained by Marxist research on Luther.

T. Kuner

3499. Belardinelli, Mario. DÖLLINGER E L'ITALIA: PER UNA STORIA DEL DIBATTITO SULLA "LIBERTA NELLA CHIESA" NELL'OTTOCENTO [Döllinger and Italy: toward a history of the debate on the "freedom of the Church" in the 19th century]. *Riv. di Storia della Chiesa in Italia* [Italy] 1982 36(2): 381-407. Presents the first part of a study on Ignaz von Döllinger (1799-1890) in the context of the ecclesiastical political debate in Italy concerning the "freedom of the Church." The author deals primarily with the period before the opening of Vatican Council I (1869-70) and includes a historiographical survey of recent literature on Döllinger's role in the debate. Based on documents in the Vatican archives and Biblioteca Ambrosiana, Milan and secondary sources; 86 notes. Article to be continued.

A. A. Strnad

3500. Berens, John F. RELIGION AND REVOLUTION RECONSIDERED: RECENT LITERATURE ON RELIGION AND NATIONALISM IN EIGHTEENTH-CENTURY AMERICA. *Can. Rev. of Studies in Nationalism* [Canada] 1979 6(2): 233-245. Surveys the historiography of religion and the American Revolution, then reviews recent monographs by Carl Bridenbaugh, Catherine L. Albanese, Henry F. May, James West Davidson, Nathan O. Hatch, and Mark A. Noll. These books lay to rest the notion that providential rhetoric in the Revolutionary era was only rhetoric; refute the contention that millenarianism was always a stimulus to patriotism; and argue that religion and politics were not competing for control of the American mind, but were both central. 7 notes.

R. Aldrich

3501. Bergsten, Torsten. DIE TÄUFERBEWEGUNG DES 16. JAHRHUNDERTS ALS PROTEST UND KORREKTIV [The Anabaptist movement of the 16th century as protest and as a corrective]. *Kyrkohistorisk Årsskrift* [Sweden] 1977: 100-106. Discusses recent changes in historiographical opinion on the Anabaptist movement, now considered to have originated independently in three branches of which Swiss Anabaptism represents a presectarian phenomenon and the late stage of a radical reform movement. A typical representative of this movement is Balthasar Hubmaier (d. 1528) whose protest was also meant as a corrective of Luther's and Zwingli's Reformation. In his *Von der christlichen Taufe der Gläubigen* [The Christian baptism of the faithful] Hubmaier defends the Anabaptist movement against accusations of rebellion, sectarianism, and spiritual arrogance raised by his opponents in the Reformation. Based on recent historiographical works and on Hubmaier's writings.   G. Herritt

3502. Blackburn, Gilmer W. THE PORTRAYAL OF CHRISTIANITY IN THE HISTORY OF TEXTBOOKS OF NAZI GERMANY. *Church Hist. 1980 49(4): 433-445.* Early histories written by National Socialists said little or nothing at all about Christianity, while works published after 1943 unmasked the regime's full enmity for the Christian faith. However, the government's attitude toward religion was characterized by the duplicity of trying to preserve the religious influence of traditional German heroes like Charlemagne and Martin Luther, while working to dismantle the Christian church structure. 72 notes.   M. D. Dibert

3503. Boles, John B. RELIGION IN THE SOUTH: A TRADITION RECOVERED. *Maryland Hist. Mag. 1982 77(4): 388-401.* Three recent books on Southern religious history point to the current interest in a topic sadly neglected in scholarship until recently. After a historiographic review of reasons for this lag and milestone works of the period 1941-78, analyzes Anne C. Loveland's *Southern Evangelicals and the Social Order, 1800-1860* (1980), Charles Reagan Wilson's *Baptized in Blood: The Religion of the Lost Cause, 1865-1920* (1980), and Samuel S. Hill, Jr.'s, *The South and the North in American Religion* (1980). These, combined with forthcoming books, suggest that southern religion has become a tradition recovered. Primary and secondary sources; 26 notes.
                                    G. J. Bobango

3504. Bolle, Kees W. REFLECTIONS ON THE HISTORY OF RELIGIONS AND HISTORY. *Hist. of Religions 1980 20(1-2): 62-80.* Although there has been intellectual chaos in the study of the religious history for some time, the proper use of the discipline is essential to the understanding of history in general. Recognition of the fact that religions in all times and places are institutions may help preserve the proper use of the intellect in the study of history. Such recognition will allay unnecessary fear of religious subjectivity in historical investigation. 30 notes.   M. E. Quinlivan

3505. Bosco Naitza, Giovanni and Pisu, Gianpaolo. IL MOVIMENTO CATTOLICO TRA FASCISMO E REPUBBLICA: ELEMENTI PER UNA BIBLIOGRAFIA ORIENTATIVA [The Catholic movement between Fascism and Republic: elements for an orienting bibliography]. *Italia Contemporanea [Italy] 1977 29(126): 73-94.* The Catholic political movement has undergone many changes in fortune since World War I: resurgence, eclipse under Fascism, revival during World War II as part of the resistance, and, finally, political power under Alcide De Gasperi, Dossetti, and the banner of the Christian Democratic Party. The authors discuss works presenting various interpretations of and attitudes toward political Catholicism and the Christian Democrats, most of them recent, but including others from the immediate postwar period. 12 notes.   J. C. Billigmeier

3506. Bowden, Henry Warner. LANDMARKS IN AMERICAN RELIGIOUS HISTORIOGRAPHY. *J. of the Am. Acad. of Religion 1974 42(1): 128.* Sidney Ahlstrom's *A Religious History of the American People* (New Haven, Conn.: Yale U. Press, 1972) is "a landmark in modern historiography" which combines a study of organized religious groups with a study of those movements not included in the structured patterns, and which shows how religion has been connected with the social and political life of America.
                                    E. R. Lester

3507. Bowden, Henry Warner. MODERN DEVELOPMENTS IN THE INTERPRETATION OF CHURCH HISTORY. *Hist. Mag. of the Protestant Episcopal Church 1974 43(2): 105-124.* Examines the views of church historians regarding the relation of one's faith to the interpretation of historical events, focusing on Kenneth Scott Latourette (1884-1968) and William Warren Sweet (1881-1959). "Each pursued his craft within the context of modern epistemological and methodological structures, and both of them brought their

Christian faith to bear creatively on those standards." They achieved workable hypotheses while reconciling temporal knowledge and transcendental convictions. 44 notes.   R. V. Ritter

3508. Boyle, Marjorie O'Rourke. ERASMUS AND THE "MODERN" QUESTION: WAS HE A SEMI-PELAGIAN? *Archiv für Reformationsgeschichte [West Germany] 1984 75: 59-77.* Analyzes the literary genre of the *diatriba*, which theologians have ignored as essential to an understanding of Desiderius Erasmus's *De Libero Arbitrio* Diatribē *sive Collatio [Diatribē* or comparison about free will] (1524), which discusses the question of whether human beings have free will or not. Emphasizes the error in methodology of theologians who impose their speculative discipline on historical materials. 81 notes. German summary.   R. Grove

3509. Bradshaw, Brendan. THE REFORMATION AND THE COUNTER-REFORMATION. *Hist. Today [Great Britain] 1983 33(Nov): 42-45.* Recent scholarship has sought to balance the "confessional" images of Luther and Calvin by restoring their links with the Catholic tradition, and to balance the confessional image of Protestantism as a radical religious revolution by directing attention to its continuity with the medieval past.

3510. Brady, Thomas A., Jr. THE POLITICAL MASKS OF MARTIN LUTHER. *Hist. Today [Great Britain] 1983 33(Nov): 27-30.* Reviews the political purposes of changing evaluations of the contribution of Martin Luther, particularly his admission to the ranks of those who fought for progressive social values during the Luther jubilee in East Germany in 1983.

3511. Britsch, R. Lanier. ANOTHER VISIT WITH WALTER MURRAY GIBSON. *Utah Hist. Q. 1978 46(1): 65-78.* An evaluation of Gwynn Barrett's "Walter Murray Gibson: The Shepherd Saint of Lanai Revisited" reveals that Barrett failed to produce evidence discrediting the works of Thomas G. Thrum and Andrew Jenson. Historical sources relating to Gibson and the Mormons are too abundant and unified to support a new, more sympathetic appraisal of Gibson. They also prove the "tradition" that Gibson stole the Hawaiian island of Lanai from the Mormon Church immediately after his excommunication in 1864, not years later as Barrett asserts. Primary and secondary sources; illus., 37 notes.
                                    J. L. Hazelton

3512. Brodeur, Raymond. L'HISTOIRE DE L'ÉGLISE DU QUEBEC: ÉTAT ET ORIENTATION DES TRAVAUX QUEBECOIS [The history of the Church of Quebec: state and orientation of works by Quebecois]. *Rev. d'Hist. de l'Église de France [France] 1981 67(178): 91-110.* Outlines works on the history of the Catholic Church in Quebec. It outlines the principal phases of the Church's history since the first settlement, describes the evolution of the historiography of the Church, noting various works produced before 1970 and describing in greater detail those published subsequently, and analyzes the teaching of the history of the Catholic Church in Quebec in the various French-Canadian universities. 120 notes.
                                    W. S. Reid

3513. Brox, Norbert. FRAGEN ZUR "DENKFORM" DER KIRCHENGESCHICHTSWISSENSCHAFT [Questions on the "intellectual structures" of science of church history]. *Zeitschrift für Kirchengeschichte [West Germany] 1979 90(1): 1-21.* Analyzes the theoretical deficit of German studies on church history, especially in the context of objectivity and perspective, theology and theory of science, and demands the inclusion of church history into the general discussion of scientific theories.

3514. Brunkow, Robert deV. AN ANALYSIS OF COTTON MATHER'S UNDERSTANDING OF THE RELATIONSHIP OF THE SUPERNATURAL TO MAN AS SEEN IN HISTORY. *Hist. Mag. of the Protestant Episcopal Church 1973 42(3): 319-332.*

3515. Burhoe, Ralph Wendell. THE HUMAN PROSPECT AND THE "LORD OF HISTORY." *Zygon 1975 10(3): 299-375.* Discusses the humanist philosophy of Robert L. Heilbroner, speculating on the possibility of a new wave of religious vision shaped by a scientifically informed theology, in the 20th century.

3516. Burr, Nelson R. THE AMERICAN CHURCH HISTORIAN AND THE BIBLICAL VIEW OF HISTORY. *Hist. Mag. of the Protestant Episcopal Church 1970 39(4): 347-359.* After defining the Biblical view of history as a philosophy of history that regards events as "meaningful, related to one supreme God, who has a purpose for mankind," the author traces its influence in American historiography from colonial times to the 20th century. Particular attention is given to church historians. Primary sources and unpublished dissertations; 16 notes.   A. J. Stifflear

3517. Bushman, Richard L. THE HISTORIANS AND MORMON NAUVOO. *Dialogue 1970 5(1): 51-61.*

3518. Butler, Jon. MAGIC, ASTROLOGY, AND THE EARLY AMERICAN RELIGIOUS HERITAGE, 1600-1760. *Am. Hist. Rev. 1979 84(2): 317-346.* This article criticizes the church-orientation of American religious history and the narrow conceptualizations of religion used by American historians by describing the development and decline of occult religious practices in the colonies before the Revolution. It uses library lists, court records, almanacs, diaries, and other literary evidence to outline a widespread resort to occult practices by colonists from South Carolina to Puritan New England and suggests that these practices supplemented Christianity for some colonists and replaced it for others. The article traces their eighteenth-century decline to a combination of dissension among occult practitioners and supporters, withdrawal of elite support for occult beliefs, continued opposition from mainstream Christian groups, and government use of the law and courts to suppress occult crafts in ways that labeled them socially deviant.   A

3519. Cannon, Donald Quayle. ANGUS M. CANNON AND DAVID WHITMER: A COMMENT ON HISTORY AND HISTORICAL METHOD. *Brigham Young U. Studies 1980 20(3): 297-299.* Angus M. Cannon was apparently the last Mormon to see David Whitmer (1805-88), the last survivor of the three witnesses to the Book of Mormon, while he was alive. Repeats a story purporting to be Angus M. Cannon's recollection of Whitmer's testimony to him. The author states that he was skeptical of its authenticity, so while researching he discovered the item in Angus M. Cannon's diary, indicating that apparently the reminiscence was embellished. Here is a good example of the difference between a reminiscence and a journal entry; both containing the core issues, but with the former adding detail and color. Both are important to the historian in helping him understand the past. Based on the George Cannon family newsletter and Angus M. Cannon journal; 2 notes.
                          E. R. Campbell

3520. Cantimori, Delio. CHABOD STORICO DELLA VITA RELIGIOSA ITALIANA DEL '500 [Chabod, historian of Italy's 16th-century religious life]. *Riv. Storica Italiana [Italy] 1960 72(4): 687-711.* Reviews Federico Chabod's historical writings on the Renaissance and Counter-Reformation in Italy with special reference to his views on the religious aspects of 16th-century Italian history. Notes a development in presentation as Chabod became conscious of the importance of changing popular attitudes to religion. Based on Chabod's writings and other secondary sources; 28 notes.
                          F. Pollaczek/S

3521. Carter, John Ross. *DHAMMA* AS A RELIGIOUS CONCEPT: A BRIEF INVESTIGATION OF ITS HISTORY IN THE WESTERN ACADEMIC TRADITION AND ITS CENTRALITY WITHIN THE SINHALESE THERAVADA TRADITION. *J. of the Am. Acad. of Religion 1976 44(4): 661-674.* Traces the significant interpretations of the concept of *dhamma* as expressed by scholars of the Western world in the past century and a half. Primarily, however, the author explores what *dhamma* has meant to Theravada Buddhists. *Dhamma* is the central religious concept in the tradition of Theravada Buddhism, an interpretation which has not yet been fully developed by Western scholars. Primary and secondary sources; 65 notes.   E. R. Lester

3522. Case, Thomas. SAN DIEGO AND HIS BIOGRAPHERS. *J. of San Diego Hist. 1983 29(4): 235-246.* Reviews the historiography of the Spanish missionary and saint, San Diego de Alcalá (d. 1463), for whom San Diego, California, was named.

3523. Clayton, John Powell. PERSPECTIVES ON PROTESTANT AND CATHOLIC THOUGHT IN THE NINETEENTH CENTURY. *European Studies Rev. [Great Britain] 1980 10(2): 247-262.* Reviews recent research on 19th-century theology as reflected in an interconfessional series of 31 academic monographs issued between 1972 and 1977 by the Gottingen publishing house of Vandenhoeck and Ruprecht. Includes an extensive interpretation of these works as they relate to other theological studies. 42 notes.
                          J. G. Smoot

3524. Clebsch, William A. TOWARD A HISTORY OF CHRISTIANITY. *Church Hist. 1974 43(1): 5-16.* None of the numerous books written about the history of Christianity try to explain Christianity in its various cultural contexts. Previous histories have either concerned themselves with the history of doctrine or tried to interpret Christianity through general history categories "mostly borrowed from interpretations of primitive and Oriental religions." A history should be written which tries to understand Christianity in terms of the life styles that have been generated by the Christian faith, particularly in the West. "Christianity has been *relevant*—to times and places, to events and people," and its relationship to major cultural crises in past centuries should be explored.
                          D. C. Richardson

3525. Cochrane, Eric. WHAT IS CATHOLIC HISTORIOGRAPHY? *Catholic Hist. Rev. 1975 61(2): 169-190.* Occasionally Catholic historians have written uncritical accounts out of respect for Church authority. This separated them from non-Catholic historians. Consequently, they failed to achieve the interconfessional dialogue called for by Vatican Council II. Internal contradictions are now being examined more openly to win respect for Catholic historiography from both historians and theologians. Religious conviction need not be compromised, however: theology and historiography are not incompatible. 98 notes.   R. V. Ritter

3526. Daniel, David P. THE HISTORIOGRAPHY OF THE REFORMATION IN SLOVAKIA. *Sixteenth Cent. Biblio. 1977 (10): 1-50.* A bibliography on the Reformation and Lutheranism in Slovakia, 16th century.

3527. Davidson, Alan. NEWSLETTER 1984. *Recusant History [Great Britain] 1984 17(1): 96-102.* A bibliography of articles, books, manuscripts, and graduate theses related to the history of the Catholic Church in Great Britain between the accession of Queen Elizabeth I and the first Vatican Council. Biblio.

3528. Decavele, Johan. HISTORIOGRAFIE VAN HET ZESTIENDE-EEUWS PROTESTANTISME IN BELGIE [Historiography of 16th-century Belgian Protestantism]. *Nederlands Archief voor Kerkgeschiedenis [Netherlands] 1982 62(1): 1-27.* The work of historians of the last 100 years has been surveyed regarding 16th century Flemish Protestantism. Dozens of entries are listed among the following categories: the Spanish Inquisition, Alva and the Council of Blood, Martyrologies, Biographical Studies, and Radical Reformation, and Iconoclasm in 1566-67. Additional studies and publications are noted in the origins of the Flemish Reformation, the Reformation and the revolution, churches in exile, diaries, and memoirs. Future studies are being carried out on the economic impact of the Reformation. Based on secondary sources; 72 notes.   F. Frankfort

3529. Delumeau, Jean. LES CHRÉTIENS AU TEMPS DE LA REFORME [Christians at the time of the Reformation]. *Social Hist. [Canada] 1977 10(20): 235-248.* Traditional explanations of the Reformation focus on church abuses and Marxist arguments about economic evolution. The former does not explain why Erasmus remained faithful to Rome and the latter does not explain why Italy, the most advanced European state, remained faithful to Catholicism. In fact, Europe was influenced by its incomplete Christianity and two centuries of religious ferment before the Reformation. Conscious Christians were a minority for whom reform permitted expansion. 16 notes.   D. F. Chard

3530. Devesa, Juan. LOS MERCEDARIOS FAUSTINO DE-
COROSO GAZULLA GALVE Y GUILLERMO VAZQUEZ
NUÑEZ, DOS GRANDES HISTORIOGRAFOS COETANEOS
QUE TRABAJARON EN SOLITARIO [Mercedarians Faustino De-
coroso Gazulla Galve and Guillermo Vázquez Núñez, two great
contemporary historians who worked alone]. *Estudios [Spain] 1984
40(146-147): 163-169.* Considers the personalities and historiography of the Order of Our Lady of Mercy of two historians of the
Spanish order.

3531. Droulers, Paul. A PROPOS DU *PAPE FORMOSE* DU P.
ARTHUR LAPOTRE [A propos of the *Pape Formose* of Arthur
Lapôtre]. *Arch. Hist. Pontificiae [Italy] 1981 19: 327-332.* The doctoral thesis of the Jesuit historian Arthur Lapôtre, *Le Pape Formose, Rome et Photius,* which he partly destroyed and was
reprinted in 1978, is the occasion of this note on the vicissitudes of
this work on the 9th-century popes.

3532. Dümmerth, Dezső. LES COMBATS ET LA TRAGEDIE
DU PERE MELCHIOR INCHOFER S.J. A ROME (1641-1648):
(LA NAISSANCE DE L'HISTORIOGRAPHIE HONGROISE BA-
SEE SUR LA CRITIQUE DES SOURCES, RELATION DU
THEOLOGIEN JANSENISTE JEAN BOURGEOIS, ET LA RE-
FORME AVORTEE DE LA SOCIETE DE JESUS) [The battles
and the tragedy of Father Melchior Inchofer, S.J., in Rome, 1641-
48: the birth of Hungarian historiography based on source criticism,
connection with the Jansenist theologian Jean Bourgeois, and the
abortive reform of the Society of Jesus]. *Ann. U. Sci. Budapestinen-
sis de Rolando Eötvös Nominatae: Sectio Hist. [Hungary] 1976 17:
81-112.* Chronicles the censorship of the Austrian-Italian historian
Melchior Inchofer's *Annales Ecclesiastici Regni Hungariae* [Church
annals of the Kingdom of Hungary] for its historical method, its
sympathetic view of Hungary, and its nonconformity with dogmatic
positions of the Catholic Church.

3533. Dyck, Cornelius J. THE LIFE OF THE SPIRIT IN ANA-
BAPTISM. *Mennonite Q. R. 1973 47(4): 309-326.* Discusses the
historiography of Anabaptism with particular emphasis on Robert
Friedmann's *Mennonite Piety Through the Centuries* (Goshen, Ind.:
Mennonite Historical Society, 1949).

3534. Eccleshall, Robert. RICHARD HOOKER'S SYNTHESIS
AND THE PROBLEM OF ALLEGIANCE. *J. of the Hist. of Ideas
1976 37(1): 111-124.* Richard Hooker's (1554?-1600) reputation
has suffered from the misinterpretations of historians more anxious
to impose their own preconceptions on his work than to understand
him in his own terms. *Of the Laws of Ecclesiastical Polity* "has
been taken as a precursor of contractualism, rationalism, and positivism" rather than as the powerful synthesis of medieval and 16th
century ideas. Hooker's sources, purposes, and achievement are examined and appraised to that end. Primary and secondary sources;
19 notes.   D. B. Marti

3535. Edwards, M. U., Jr. THE LUTHER QUINCENTENNIAL.
*Journal of Ecclesiastical History [Great Britain] 1984 35(4): 597-
613.* Surveys recent writings on Martin Luther under three headings: recent biographies, the younger Luther, and the older Luther.
66 notes, biblio.   P. H. Hardacre

3536. Edwards, Paul M. THE IRONY OF MORMON HISTORY.
Utah Hist. Q. 1973 41(4): 393-409. Deals with the problems of
faith and history as they concern Mormon historiography. The integrity of questions is as important as are questions of integrity.
Many Mormon would-be historians waste their energies in "scholastic antiquarianism." There is not, and there never should be, an official Mormon philosophy of history. The historian's first tool is
interest in and love of the past with a "willingness to become half
lost in the imagination of previous days." Illus., 29 notes.
                                                       D. L. Smith

3537. Ellacuría, Ignacio. IGLESIA Y REALIDAD HISTÓRICA
[Church and historical reality]. *Estudios Centroamericanos [El
Salvador] 1976 31(331): 213-220.* In examining the role of the

Catholic Church in Latin American history, theological considerations aid in understanding the Church's use and abuse of its social
and political influence.

3538. Ellis, William E. EVOLUTION, FUNDAMENTALISM,
AND THE HISTORIANS: AN HISTORIOGRAPHICAL REVIEW.
Historian 1981 44(1): 15-35. The historiography of fundamentalism
and evangelicalism is divided into three time periods: the participants and observers in the 1920's; scholars trained in the liberal
tradition and irritated by the restraints of the McCarthy era; and
revisionists of the 1960's. Examines those studies of the most prominent secular and church historians that illustrate interpretive viewpoints or develop new trends. Contrary to the hopes of moderates
and liberals in the church and sciences, anti-evolutionism has not
completely died, consequently evangelicalism and its fundamentalist
wing demonstrate no sign of weakening and will continue to play
a major role in US religion and culture. 46 notes.
                                                       R. S. Sliwoski

3539. Ernst, Eldon G. WINTHROP S. HUDSON AND THE
GREAT TRADITION OF AMERICAN RELIGIOUS HISTORI-
OGRAPHY. *Foundations 1980 23(2): 104-126.* Winthrop S. Hudson is discussed in the tradition of American church history laid
down by Robert Baird, Philip Schaff, Daniel Dorchester, Leonard
Woolsey Bacon, and William Warren Sweet. Hudson's strong points
are presented in terms of this background along with his weaknesses, some of which were found in predecessors. Hudson's book
Religion in America is well balanced on showing the place of not
only Protestantism, but of other groups such as Jews and American
Indians. 66 notes.   E. E. Eminhizer

3540. Esplin, Robert K. FROM THE RUMORS TO THE RE-
CORDS: HISTORIANS AND THE SOURCES FOR BRIGHAM
YOUNG. *Brigham Young U. Studies 1978 18(3): 453-465.*
Brigham Young and Mormons have been maligned unjustly in both
19th- and 20th-century sources. Challenges historians to investigate
the available primary materials and correct the "systematic distortions." The present arrangement of the extensive Young manuscript
collections in the Mormon Church Archives should enable scholars
to gain new insights and correct the twisted views of critics.
                                                       M. S. Legan

3541. Field, Clive D. BIBLIOGRAPHY OF METHODIST HIS-
TORICAL LITERATURE, 1977. *Pro. of the Wesley Hist. Soc.
[Great Britain] 1979 42(2): 55-63.* A bibliography of Methodist historical literature published in Great Britain and the United States,
1970-77.

3542. Field, Clive D. BIBLIOGRAPHY OF METHODIST HIS-
TORICAL LITERATURE, 1981. *Pro. of the Wesley Hist. Soc.
[Great Britain] 1983 44(1): 16-21.* The 1981 bibliography on historical activities involving Methodists and Methodism, comprised of 94
entries organized under 14 topics.

3543. Finnestad, Ragnhild Bjerre. DEN HELLIGE NATUR OG
RELIGIONSHISTORIKERENS ONTOLOGISKE PARADIGMER:
ET ANLIGGENDE FOR DET SAMMENLIKNENDE RELI-
GIONSSTUDIUM [Sacred nature and the ontological paradigms of
the historian of religion: a requirement for the comparative study
of religion]. *Norsk Teologisk Tidsskrift [Norway] 1984 85(1): 17-
37.* Discusses problems that arise in comparative historical studies
of religion when scholars presuppose a dualistic separation of man
from nature. In many religions human beings are viewed as part of
nature and nature itself as ultimate reality. Such views must be tak-
en into account in analyzing these traditions. Based on published
monographs, mainly in English; 27 notes.   R. G. Selleck

3544. Fitzsimons, M. A. THE ROLE OF PROVIDENCE IN HIS-
TORY. *R. of Pol. 1973 35(3): 386-397.* Examines the concept of
providence in the study of history and surveys the philosophy of
Christianity, Augustine, and Georg W. Hegel.

3545. Foster, Claude R., Jr. THE RADICAL REFORMATION
AND REVOLUTIONARY TRADITION. *Worldview 1976 19(5):
43-46.* As the Protestant-Catholic polemic is eased, modern Chris-

tian historians are more receptive to Marxist interpretations of German history, which link Martin Luther and Thomas Münzer to Karl Marx.

3546. Freehof, Solomon B. SOME LESSONS OF HISTORY. *Western Pennsylvania Hist. Mag. 1966 49(4): 279-288.* Uses Biblical history to assess the meaning of historiography. Though material entities die away, lose essence, and are forgotten, the spirit of humanity continues.

3547. Friesen, Abraham. WILHELM ZIMMERMANN AND FRIEDRICH ENGELS: TWO SOURCES OF THE MARXIST INTERPRETATION OF ANABAPTISM. *Mennonite Q. Rev. 1981 55(3): 240-254.* Examines the influence of Wilhelm Zimmermann's *Bauernkrieg* (first edition) on Friedrich Engels's thought on the Anabaptists, particularly Thomas Münzer, who Engels considered a prototype Marxist. The first edition was full of errors which were corrected in the second edition (Stuttgart, 1856) but which Engels would not use. Because of Engels's insistence on using Zimmermann's interpretation in the first edition, Marxist historians have had to revise the Marxist view on the Reformation. Based on the first and second editions of Wilhelm Zimmermann's *Geschichte des Grossen Bauernkriegs;* 51 notes.   E. E. Eminhizer

3548. Frijhoff, Willem. VAN "HISTOIRE DE L'EGLISE" NAAR "HISTOIRE RELIGIEUSE." DE INVLOED VAN DE *ANNALES*-GROEP OP DE ONTWIKKELING VAN DE KERKGESCHIEDENIS IN FRANKRIJK EN DE PERSPECTIEVEN DAARVAN VOOR NEDERLAND [From history of the church to religious history: the influence of the *Annales* school on the development of church history in France and the perspective for the Netherlands]. *Nederlands Archief voor Kerkgeschiedenis [Netherlands] 1981 61(2): 113-153.* Until quite recently French historiography on the history of Christianity has been written along strict sectarian lines. The influence of the *Annales* school has been to shift the emphasis of historical interest from institutional (church history) to religious life and motivation (religious history). The interdisciplinary nature of the *Annales* school brought about this shift through its emphasis on sociology of religion, text analysis, and the study of folklore. 95 notes.   F. Frankfort

3549. Gadille, Jacques. GEORGES GOYAU, HISTORIEN DES MISSIONS [Georges Goyau, historian of missions]. *Rev. Française d'Hist. d'Outre-Mer [France] 1978 65(4): 585-601.* To fill a gap in French historiography, Georges Goyau established a foundation for the study of Catholic missions, 1918-39. His work was rather circumspect in its treatment of political, colonial, and mercantile affairs. It focused on the spiritual motivation of laymen, clergy, monks, and, especially, nuns. 41 notes.   D. G. Law

3550. Gleason, Philip. COMING TO TERMS WITH AMERICAN CATHOLIC HISTORY. *Societas 1973 3(4): 283-312.* Discusses the ambiguity in the use of the crucial terms Americanism and Americanization in the history of American Catholicism. Catholic discussion shows a shift that is "evidence that a profound change has taken place in the way scholars in the historical discipline view the relation of religion to life and the Church to the world." 76 notes.
E. P. Stickney

3551. Goeckel, Robert F. THE LUTHER ANNIVERSARY IN EAST GERMANY. *World Politics 1984 37(1): 112-133.* Analysis of the celebration of the 500th anniversary of Martin Luther's birth indicates the dynamics of ideological and political change in the Communist regime in East Germany. The long-term shift toward a more positive view of Luther in official Marxist historiography and the extensive state celebration of Luther challenged the churches, resulting in their arm's length cooperation with the state. The regime's new stance toward Luther suggests that it seeks to adapt to, rather that transform, its political culture. The study reveals however, that short-range factors—the improved church-state relationship and the more relaxed inter-German relationship in the Honecker era, as well as the limitations on these relationships, also had con-

siderable impact on the Luther celebration. Comparison with other Soviet-bloc regimes confirms the uniqueness of the church-state relationship in East Germany.   J

3552. Goichot, Emile. DEUX HISTORIENS A L'ACADEMIE (SUITE ET FIN) [Two historians at the academy. Part 2]. *Revue d'Histoire Ecclésiastique [Belgium] 1983 78(2): 373-396.* Continued from a previous article. Concludes the history of Henri Bremond's discourse, tracing the text's five stages during the year before his May 1924 reception as he mitigated his views on historiography about the Church but still defended Louis Duchesne's new history against the reactions of friends and foes. Based on the Bremond Papers at the Bibliothèque Nationale, Paris.   R. Burns

3553. Gómez, Elías. ESPIRITUALIDAD EN EL P. GUILLERMO VAZQUEZ NUÑEZ, "MISIONERO" DOCTO E ILUMINADO [Spirituality in Father Guillermo Vázquez Núñez, learned and enlightened "missionary"]. *Estudios [Spain] 1984 40(146-147): 135-148.* Guillermo Vázquez Núñez found the dynamic motivation for his histories of the Order of Our Lady of Mercy in his deep internalization of the spirituality of the Mercedarians of Spain.

3554. Gonnet, Giovanni. LE INTERPRETAZIONI TIPICHE DEL VALDISMO [Typical interpretations of Waldensianism]. *Protestantesimo [Italy] 1974 29(2): 65-91.* Studies the origins of the Waldensians from a philosophical standpoint. Analyzes "heresy" etymologically (from the Greek *hairein*, to choose) in Medieval church history as compared to the terms "orthodoxy" and "heterodoxy." Modern Marxist historians equate heresy with class struggle. Secondary sources; 74 notes.   C. Bates

3555. Gonnet, Giovanni. REMARQUES SUR L'HISTORIOGRAPHIE VAUDOISE DES XVIe ET XVIIeRET SIÈCLES [Remarks about Waldensian historiography of the 16th and 17th centuries]. *Bull. de la Soc. de l'Hist. du Protestantisme Française [France] 1974 120(3): 323-365.* Beginning in 1603 several Waldensian Protestant synods authorized official histories of the movement. They were based partly on 16th-century manuscripts, which in turn were based on earlier manuscripts, documents, and oral traditions going back to the 12th century. Much of this material was placed in the Cambridge University Library in 1655, where it was rediscovered in 1899. Major portions have been published recently, and this article critically analyzes the material. Based on manuscripts and monographs; map, 137 notes.   O. T. Driggs

3556. González Castro, Ernesto. LA *HISTORIA GENERAL* DE GABRIEL TELLEZ EN EL CONJUNTO DE LA HISTORIOGRAFIA MERCEDARIA DEL SIGLO XVI [Gabriel Téllez's *General History* in the context of 16th-century historiography of the Order of Mercy]. *Estudios [Spain] 1981 37(132-135): 537-574.* A comparison of Tirso de Molina's history of his order, written and published in 1639, with the work of other historians before and after him, brings out the originality and modernity of his book, which combines historical and autobiographical material.

3557. Grass, Nikolaus. ZUR JÜNGSTEN KANONISTISCHEN WISSENSCHAFTSGESCHICHTE IN ÖSTERREICH [Recent canon law history in Austria]. *Österreichisches Archiv für Kirchenrecht [Austria] 1971 22(3): 177-183.* Reviews new approaches towards the historical research of canon law in Austria. Secondary works; 2 notes.   R. Wagnleitner

3558. Green, Lowell C. THE FORMULA OF CONCORD: AN HISTORIOGRAPHICAL AND BIBLIOGRAPHICAL GUIDE. *Sixteenth Cent. Biblio. 1977 (11): 1-58.* Provides background material and bibliographies relating to the Formula of Concord, the theological document written in 1577 seeking to reunite the Lutheran Church.

3559. Greiner, Albert. LUTHER VU PAR LES FRANÇAIS DU XIXe ET DU XXeRET SIÈCLES [Luther viewed by Frenchmen of the 19th and 20th centuries]. *Francia [France] 1977 5: 708-713.* A review article which examines Gerhard Philipp Wolf's *Das Neuere Französische Lutherbild* (Wiesbaden: Franz Steiner, 1974), which describes French evaluations of Martin Luther. Unlike German writers, French Germanists have always written mediocre works on Luther probably because they have viewed him as peripheral to the history of religion in Germany. Note.   G. E. Pergl

3560. Griffin, John. NEWMAN'S *DIFFICULTIES FELT BY ANGLICANS:* HISTORY OR PROPAGANDA? *Catholic Hist. Rev. 1983 69(3): 371-383.* John Henry Newman's lectures of 1850, *Difficulties Felt by Anglicans,* claim to be a history of the origins and logical development of the religious revival of 1833, better known as the Oxford Movement. But the lectures are usually dismissed as one of Newman's satiric or polemic works, for the Newman version of the Oxford Movement does contradict the now established version of the Catholic revival in the Church of England. Yet Newman had been one of the most active members of the original revival, and the lectures are filled with quotations from the writings of those who had participated in the first Oxford Movement.   A

3561. Griffiths, Gordon. SAINT BARTHOLOMEW REAPPRAISED. *J. of Modern Hist. 1976 48(3): 494-505.* Reviews *Actes du colloque "L'Amiral de Coligny et son temps"* (Paris: Soc. de l'Hist. du Protestantisme Francais, 1974) and Alfred Soman's *The Massacre of St. Bartholomew: Reappraisals and Documents* (The Hague: Martinus Nijhoff, 1974) consisting (between the two editions) of 44 essays by current historians reappraising the meaning of the 1572 massacre of Huguenots in France.

3562. Hagen, Kenneth. AV OG OM LUTHER PÅ NORSK [By and about Luther in Norwegian]. *Norsk Teologisk Tidsskrift [Norway] 1981 82(2): 79-101.* A critical survey and extensive bibliography of Norwegian studies of Martin Luther and translations of his works. Around 1900, writing on Luther began to reflect on attitudes to the Norwegian nationalist movement. For the most part, contemporary Norwegian writing about Luther is informative and concerned with independence. Biblio.   K. S. Williams

3563. Hanley, Thomas O'Brien. BERDYAEV AND CHRISTIAN HISTORY. *Hist. Bull. [Philippines] 1956 34(2): 82-95.* Examines the writings and influence of Nicholai Berdyaev on Christian interpretations of the impact of communism, 1920's-40's.

3564. Hartweg, Frédéric. VOM "FÜRSTENKNECHT" ZUM "WEGBEREITER" UND "MITBEWEGER UNSERER GESCHICHTE": DAS MARXISTISCHE LUTHERBILD UND DAS LUTHERJUBILÄUM IN DER D. D. R. [From the "princes' servant" to the "pioneer" and "prime mover of our history": the Marxist image of Luther and the 500th anniversary of Luther in East Germany]. *Rev. d'Allemagne [France] 1983 15(4): 348-386.* Although earlier Marxists had a generally negative attitude toward Martin Luther (1483-1546), after 1960 East German historians began to revise this view and to credit him with initiating the dialectic of the class conflict without which the social progress and democracy of the present could not have been attained. In the 1970's they saw in the Reformation the ingredients of a revolutionary ideology. In preparation for the 500th anniversary of Luther's birth, he was described as a leader of the first bourgeois revolution in world history and one of the most important humanists. The rehabilitation of Luther culminated in 1983 when politicians and academicians agreed that Luther's heritage is preserved in the socialist culture of East Germany and his theology was recognized as socially relevant. Luther may have become a national hero of the German Democratic Republic. 141 notes.   J. S. Gassner

3565. Hatch, Roger D. INTEGRATING THE ISSUE OF RACE INTO THE HISTORY OF CHRISTIANITY IN AMERICA: AN ESSAY-REVIEW. *J. of the Am. Acad. of Religion 1978 46(4): 545-569.* Sidney Ahlstrom, Robert T. Handy, and Martin E. Marty in (respectively) *A Religious History of the American People; Righteous Empire: The Protestant Experience in America;* and *A Christian America: Protestant Hopes and Historical Realities* agree that past attempts to write a history of Christianity in America have not adequately covered the issue of race, but the author contends that each of these historians has failed to make up this lack. Explains the two approaches of these writers: including race as a new topic, thus adding additional chapters; and integrating race into the com-

monly discussed topics of religious history. Both are insufficient because race is still regarded as somewhat external to the history. Chart, 4 notes, biblio.   E. R. Lester

3566. Hench, John B. OBITUARY: FREDERICK BARNES TOLLES. *Pro. of the Am. Antiquarian Soc. 1975 85(2): 367-369.* A remembrance of Frederick Barnes Tolles (1915-75). Tolles was born in New Hampshire. He was educated at Harvard University, where he converted from Unitarianism to Quakerism, a decision that was to alter his entire life. He began teaching at Swarthmore College, a Quaker institution, and refused induction in World War II as a conscientious objector, doing alternative work instead. His primary academic thrust was in the direction of the history of Quakerism in the American society and he published a number of books on the subject. Tolles was elected to membership in the American Antiquarian Society in 1967. He was proud of the honor, but distance and poor health prevented him from taking an active part in the Society's activities.   V. L. Human

3567. Hendrix, Scott H. LUTHER'S IMPACT ON THE SIXTEENTH CENTURY. *Sixteenth Century Journal 1985 16(1): 3-14.* Martin Luther did not expect to have much impact on his own century but he abolished old religious practices which he deemed harmful and created a theological base for new ones: clerical marriage, increased lay self-confidence, and secularization. 36 notes.

D. R. Stevenson

3568. Hersche, Peter. UNGLAUBE IM 16. JAHRHUNDERT. EIN LEICHT KETZERISCHER BEITRAG ZUM LUTHERJUBILÄUM IN FORM EINER LITERATURBESPRECHUNG [Unbelief in the 16th century: a slightly heretical contribution to the Luther jubilee in the form of a historiographical review]. *Schweizerische Zeitschrift für Geschichte [Switzerland] 1984 34(2): 233-250.* Irreligiosity and atheism in the 16th century are, in contrast to the overabundant Luther scholarship, still a wide open field for historical investigation. There are direct connections between the Reformation and the growth of unbelief in Epicurian and libertarian circles, about which we are informed from the letters of the reformers, through the rising debate on toleration, and through the antitrinitarian Socinians. In addition, one has to consider literary atheism and the works of certain painters. Italy and France played a major role in the formation of modern unbelief. Research on witchcraft indicates that there may have been a widespread, autonomous non-Christian folk culture in many parts of Europe. 81 notes.   H. K. Meier

3569. Hibbard, Caroline. EARLY STUART CATHOLICISM: REVISIONS AND RE-REVISIONS. *J. of Modern Hist. 1980 52(1): 1-34.* Examines the historiography on English Catholics with full discussion of two works of synthesis: J. C. H. Aveling's *The Handle and the Axe: The Catholic Recusants in England from Reformation to Emancipation* (London, 1976) and John Bossy's *The English Catholic Community, 1570-1850* (London, 1975). The county histories fail to "provide a grass-roots background for the national politics of no-popery." The high point of the English Catholic Counter-Reformation was from 1600 to 1640, a period dominated by the Jesuits, where the strength was not in the counties but in a national network of clergy, schools, and book distribution. Anti-Catholic legislation was aimed at the upper classes to get them to conform; those who refused were removed from positions of authority. The real threat was the "potential collaboration" between English Catholics and foreign governments. 91 notes.

3570. Hill, Marvin S. JOSEPH SMITH THE MAN: SOME RECOLLECTIONS ON A SUBJECT OF CONTROVERSY. *Brigham Young U. Studies 1981 21(2): 175-186.* Discusses some controversial and contradictory reports by eyewitnesses and friends of Joseph Smith, which the author, as a historian, tries to reconcile. Quotes examples of contradictory opinions and descriptions of Smith. The historian discovers the truth by examining the evidence for accuracy in light of the age and condition of the witness and by weighing the amount and substance of contradictory evidence. Based on diaries, personal journals, letters, autobiographies, reminiscences, newspapers, Wayne County, New York history, and sermons; 58 notes.

E. R. Campbell

3571. Hölvényi, György. A MAGYAR JEZSUITA TÖRTÉNETÍRÓK ÉS A JEZSUITA REND [The Hungarian Jesuit historiographer and the Order of Jesuits]. *Magyar Könyvszemle [Hungary] 1974 90(3-4): 232-248.* Hungarian historiography was founded by Jesuit historians. As a result of their debates with Protestants, they developed an interest in history, although this was never more than tolerated in the Order. In Hungary the major Jesuit historians were Gábor Hevenesi (1656-1715), Sámuel Timon (b. 1675), István Kuprinai (1714-86), György Pray (1723-1801), Károly Wágner (1732-1790). The author describes their lives and major contributions. 92 notes. R. Hetzron

3572. Honée, Eugène. ACCENTVERSCHUIVINGEN IN DE HISTORIOGRAPHIE VAN DE AUGSBURGSE RIJKSDAG 1530 [Changes in emphasis in the historiography of the Diet of Augsburg, 1530]. *Nederlands Archief voor Kerkgeschiedenis [Netherlands] 1976 56(2): 396-412.* Review of Herbert Immerkötter's *Um die Einheit im Glauben: Die Unionsverhandlungen der Augusburger Reichstages in August und September 1530* [For the unity of the faith: the negotiations to establish unity at the Diet of Augsburg in August and September 1530] (Münster, 1973). This work is an important contribution to the history of the meeting in Augsburg in 1530 because it includes many of the new interpretations of the last few decades. 31 notes.

3573. Hornsby, Samuel G., Jr. RECENT STUDIES IN THE 1611 "AUTHORIZED VERSION" OF THE BIBLE. *English Literary Renaissance 1983 13(3): 345-353.* Recent scholars have extended the study of the Bible from purely theological considerations to modes of literary and historical analysis. A number of scarce studies on the English Bible have recently been reprinted and provide an important supplement to new publications. These works are listed and summarized under several headings which identify specific topics: available texts of English versions; historical background; principles and problems of translation; and matters of style, grammar, and literary analysis. J

3574. Hovey, Kenneth Alan. THE THEOLOGY OF HISTORY IN *OF PLYMOUTH PLANTATION* AND ITS PREDECESSORS. *Early Am. Literature 1975 10(1): 47-66.* The historiography of William Bradford's *Of Plymouth Plantation* combines the dominant theological emphasis of each of three previous Plymouth histories—"A Brief Relation of the Discovery and Plantation of New England," "Mourt's Relation," and "Good News from New England"—into a single impression of the complex relationship of God and man. Based on primary and secondary sources; 15 notes.

D. P. Wharton

3575. Hultkrantz, Åke. THE CONCEPT OF THE SUPERNATURAL IN PRIMAL RELIGION. *Hist. of Religions 1983 22(3): 231-253.* The dichotomy between the natural and supernatural is the basic and universal principal in religion. During the 19th century, historians of religion were influenced by cultural evolutionary theory, differentiating between primitive and "higher" conceptions of religion. Later psychological interpretations focused on the human need to explain the mysterious. Contrary to ideas current among anthropologists, North American Indians do make a distinction between the natural and supernatural. Though the particulars may differ from culture to culture, a basic division between the two realms is constant. Based on a lecture delivered at the Department of Religion, Northwestern University; 96 notes.

3576. Jansen, Reiner. KEIN PLATZ FÜR DIE JUDEN? LUTHER, DIE REFORMATION UND DIE JUDEN: IN BÜCHERN ÜBER DIE GESCHICHTE DER KIRCHE [No room for the Jews? Luther, the Reformation, and the Jews: books on the history of the church]. *Judaica [Switzerland] 1983 39(3): 179-192.* Explores the way in which recent books deal with Luther's relationship to the Jews.

3577. Jemolo, Arturo Carlo. IL NODO DEL CONCORDATO [The bond of the Concordat]. *Nuova Antologia [Italy] 1974 521(2084): 469-473.* In response to Piero Agostino d'Avack's radical revision of the significance of the Lateran Treaties, the author offers a more pessimistic view of the Catholic Church's position in Italian society, as evidenced by the approval of the referendum for divorce and the general decline in Papal authority.

3578. Jemolo, Arturo Carlo. SULLA SOGLIA DEL VATICANO [The threshold of the Vatican]. *Nuova Antologia [Italy] 1971 513(2051): 312-325.* A preface to the new edition of Giuseppe Manfroni's *Sulla Soglia del Vaticano* in which the author offers a brief biography of Manfroni and describes the history of the Vatican in the last half of the 19th century.

3579. Johnson, Kathryn L. THE MUSTARD SEED AND THE LEAVEN: PHILIP SCHAFF'S CONFIDENT VIEW OF CHRISTIAN HISTORY. *Hist. Mag. of the Protestant Episcopal Church 1981 50(2): 117-170.* Philip Schaff (1819-93), born in Germany, came to the United States in 1843 and became one of the leading figures in American religion and theological education. Compares Schaff's historiographical philosophy with those of Hegel, Bauer, Neander, and Newman. While he is closest to Neander, it was his opinion that an adequate philosophy of church history had yet to be produced. Failing to find such, he sought to follow truth wherever he found it. His approach was that of a practicing historian and an expositor of ideas rather than a participant in philosophical debates. He believed that some especially knotty questions could be resolved not philosophically or theologically but only historically. But above all, he remained an optimist. Based on Schaff's writings and studies in historiography; 290 notes. H. M. Parker, Jr.

3580. Jurden, D. A. A HISTORIOGRAPHY OF AMERICAN DEISM. *Am. Benedictine R. 1974 25(1): 108-122.* Reviews several seminal studies of the history of American Deism and concludes that most studies obscure the varieties, and thus the nature, of Deism that existed in America in the 18th and 19th centuries. This conclusion is demonstrated by a review of the beliefs espoused by significant Deists such as Benjamin Franklin, Thomas Jefferson, Elihu Palmer, and Ethan Allen. 45 notes. J. H. Pragman

3581. Juszczyk, Jan. O BADANIACH NAD JUDAIZANTYZMEM [Research into Judaizerism]. *Kwartalnik Hist. [Poland] 1969 76(1): 141-151.* The controversy concerning Judaizerism is a difficult problem because of the scarcity of historical sources. Soviet historians dealing with the Novgorod-Moscow heresy rejected the name itself, suggesting either of the following: "religious free-thinking," "anti-Trinitarianism" and "anti-feudal heretical movement." The author criticizes the Soviet suggestions, pointing out that it was a religious movement motivated by the Old Testament concepts and therefore stepping outside Christianity and he calls it a "dogmatic radicalism." 66 notes. J. Wilczek

3582. Kantzenbach, Friedrich Wilhelm. KRITISCHE KIRCHENGESCHICHTSSCHREIBUNG. ZUR BEGRÜNDUNG VON KIRCHENKRITIK IM PROTESTANTISCHEN GESCHICHTSBEWUSSTSEIN DER NEUZEIT [Critical church historiography: the origin of church criticism in Protestant historiography of the modern age]. *Zeitschrift für Religions- und Geistesgeschichte [West Germany] 1978 30(1): 19-35.* Discusses the roots of some central motifs of a critical approach to church history. Reformers such as Joachim of Floris (1145?-1202?) and Martin Luther detected corruption in the Church, but believed God has always provided it with witnesses of the truth. Those dissatisfied with eschatological church historiography, including Franz Overbeck, view church history as part of general history and point out the distance to modernity of earlier periods of Christianity. The Anabaptists have viewed the history of the Church as that of a great apostasy by those who want to restitute the original, apostolical Church. Restitution seems futile to the spiritualized view of church history, held by Sebastian Franck and Gottfried Arnold, which believes in an invisible church constituted by heretics, while every visible church has fallen under the influence of the anti-Christ. Arnold's *History of Heresy* (1699), written by a theologian deeply concerned about the state of his church, was utilized by Arthur Schopenhauer and Friedrich Nietzsche to repudiate Christianity altogether. 30 notes.

G. Hollenberg

3583. Kaplanoff, M. D. CHOSEN PEOPLE. *J. of Ecclesiastical Hist. [Great Britain] 1984 35(1): 124-140.* Reviews seven works on American religious history. 13 notes. P. H. Hardacre

3584. Karp, Hans-Jürgen. AUFSÄTZE UND FORSCHUNGS-BERICHTE ZUR KIRCHENGESCHICHTSFORSCHUNG IN VOLKSPOLEN [Research on ecclesiastical history in People's Poland]. *Zeitschrift für Ostforschung [West Germany] 1976 25(1): 1-36.* Surveys postwar Polish research on church history. Surveys denominational research centers, where work has unfolded to a considerable degree since 1956, when the Church regained its right to exist. The nondenominational Marxist-oriented research approaches ecclesiastical history in a more narrow sense—without history of philosophy and science of religion, and without research on the Reformation and Counter-Reformation in cultural history. The author discusses recent works in Polish ecclesiastical history. A Marxist synthesis of the role of the Church in Polish history has yet to be composed. J/S

3585. Kent, J. PROBLEMS IN CHURCH HISTORY: TWENTY YEARS ON. *Southern History [Great Britain] 1983 5: 13-26.* Analyzes the historiography (ca. 1962-82) of church history concerning Great Britain and the British Empire. The author notes the principal changes and cites many published works.

3586. Koch, H. G. DAS LUTHERBILD DER KOMMUNISMUS [Luther as viewed by the Communists]. *Zeitwende [West Germany] 1965 36(4): 263-270.* The interpretations of Martin Luther as given by both earlier Marxists and modern Communist writers follow the same line; Luther is viewed and judged solely from a political and sociological standpoint, and his religious and theological motives are entirely ignored. T. Gunther

3587. Köhler, Joachim. WAR JOHANN ADAM MÖHLER (1796-1838) EIN PLAGIATOR? BEOBACHTUNGEN ZUR AR-BEITSTECHNIK UND ZU DER LITERARISCHEN ABHÄNGIGKEIT IN DER KATHOLISCHEN "TÜBINGER HI-STORISCH-KRITISCHEN SCHULE" DES 19. JAHRHUNDERTS [Was Johann Adam Möhler (1796-1838) a plagiarist? The working technique and literary dependency of the Catholic "historical-critical school of Tübingen" in the 19th century]. *Zeitschrift für Kirchengeschichte [West Germany] 1975 86(2): 186-207.* The German Catholic theologian Johann Adam Möhler in his first lecture at Tübingen in 1829 misquoted, did not cite his sources, or omitted passages of quotes which did not fit his argument.

3588. Kornev, V. I. K IZUCHENIIU BUDDIZMA [On the study of Buddhism]. *Voprosy Istorii [USSR] 1981 (6): 76-90.* Demonstrates a new approach to the study of Buddhism through the Buddhist symbolism of numbers which allows the creation of a model leading to the correct interpretation of main Buddhist terms. Thus obtained the conditional system of Buddhist philosophy serves as the key to an analysis of the contemporary Buddhist dogmas translated into religious practice and to the creation of a new pattern of the development of Buddhism from ancient times to the present. J

3589. Kovács, Elisabeth. DIE PERSÖNLICHKEIT DES WIENER FÜRSTERZBISCHOFS VINZENZ EDUARD MILDE IM SPIE-GEL DER HISTORIOGRAPHIE [The personality of the Viennese Prince Archbishop Vinzenz Eduard Milde in the mirror of historiography]. *Jahrbuch des Vereins für Geschichte der Stadt Wien [Austria] 1978 34: 218-238.* As a typical representative of the Franciscan period the Viennese Prince Archbishop Vinzenz Eduard Milde (1777-1852) promoted the Austrian state-church system, reformed the training of priests, and stressed the charitable works of the Viennese Catholic Church. R. Wagnleitner

3590. Krejci, Jaroslav. THE MEANING OF HUSSITISM. *J. of Religious Hist. [Australia] 1974 8(1): 3-20.* Reevaluates the traditional approaches to Hussitism by utilizing new sociological and historical perspectives, comparing the present Czech and Western developments in Hussite research with English developments. Hussitism was the most significant force to emerge from Bohemia and Moravia with implications throughout Europe. Secondary sources; 47 notes. W. T. Walker

3591. Kucherenko, G. S. O SOTSIAL'NO-KATOLICHESKIKH INTERPRETATSIIAKH IDEINOGO NASLEDIIA SEN-SIMONA [Social-Catholic interpretations of the ideological heritage of Saint-Simon]. *Novaia i Noveishaia Istoriia [USSR] 1973 (6): 167-175.* Shows that the increasing study of utopian socialism has changed previous attitudes to Saint-Simon (1760-1825). Criticizes and analyzes social and Catholic works on Saint-Simon's philosophy, 1953-73, and relates Philippe Buchez's attitude to Saint-Simon. Represents the latter as the founder of a new Christianity. 60 notes. C. R. Pike

3592. Kucherenko, G. S. SEN-SIMON I A. BAZAR [Saint-Simon and A. Bazard]. *Novaia i Noveishaia Istoriia [USSR] 1975 (1): 105-118.* Describes the thinking of Saint-Amand Bazard, who became one of the disciples of Comte de Saint-Simon in 1825. After Saint-Simon's death, Bazard founded the periodical *Le Protecteur* to disseminate Saint-Simon's ideas. The author repudiates Western historians' view of Saint-Simonianism in favor of the Marxist-Leninist analysis. Discusses the extent to which Bazard continued the ideas of Saint-Simon. In some respects, such as his pantheism, Bazard was among the epigones of Saint-Simon. Primary sources; 78 notes. E. R. Sicher

3593. Kuykendall, John W. *PRESBYTERIANS IN THE SOUTH* REVISITED—A CRITIQUE. *J. of Presbyterian Hist. 1983 61(4): 445-459.* Examines Ernest Trice Thompson's *Presbyterians in the South* (1963-73), the most complete study of any American Presbyterian Church. Focuses on Thompson's methodology, the central purpose of the study, and the influence and permanent value of the book. Based on book reviews; illus., 26 notes.

H. M. Parker, Jr.

3594. Lanaro, Silvio. MOVIMENTO CATTOLICO E SVILUPPO CAPITALISTICO NEL VENETO FRA '800 E '900 [The Catholic movement and capitalistic development in Venetia, 1800-1900]. *Studi Storici [Italy] 1974 15(1): 57-105.* Outlines the historiographical orientation of recent studies by Catholics of the post-unification Catholic movement. Disagrees with their view of a Catholic opposition and shows how Catholic cooperatist models in Venetia in the 1870's-80's were linked to the general interest of the emerging aristocratic-capitalist class. Unpublished archival and secondary sources; 77 notes. E. J. Craver

3595. Langlois, Claude. DES *ÉTUDES D'HISTOIRE ECCLE-SIASTIQUE LOCALE* À LA SOCIOLOGIE RELIGIEUSE HI-STORIQUE. RÉFLEXIONS SUR UN SIÈCLE DE PRODUCTION HISTORIOGRAPHIQUE [From *Studies of local ecclesiastical history* to the historical sociology of religion: reflections on a century of historiographic production]. *Rev. d'Hist. de l'Église de France [France] 1976 72(169): 329-347.* Discusses the development of French ecclesiastical historiography from the French Revolution to the present. While much attention was paid to the medieval and early modern periods, little was written about the history of the 19th century itself, except in the form of biographies. Most of the histories were concentrated on localities and regions, while the biographies concentrated on important local ecclesiastical figures. Since World War I, under the influence of writers such as Lucien Fevre, a laicized type of church history has become common. Even more important was the impact of sociologists such as G. Le Bras by which a new approach has been developed to explain such phenomena as the gradual loss of the church's influence over the working class. Such histories have attempted to use the techniques of both sociology and political science. This has opened new opportunities to apply other scientific methods to contemporary history of the church. 86 notes. W. S. Reid

3596. Langlois, Claude and Mayeur, Jean-Marie. SUR L'HISTOIRE RELIGIEUSE DE L'ÉPOQUE CONTEMPORAINE [On religious history in the contemporary epoch]. *Rev. Hist. [France] 1974 252(2): 433-444.* A definite revival of interest in religious aspects of history is taking place despite the secular tenor of the age and the dangers of subjectivity in contemporary history. Dozens of works mentioned herein deal with religious aspects of 20th century life or with religions themselves. Demographical and geographical studies, history of mentalities, and other topics deal with religions from the "outside," What is needed is more study from the "inside," accepting the faith of religions as real in their own terms. Based on modern and contemporary histories of religion; 66 notes. G. H. Davis

3597. Lannie, Vincent P. CHURCH AND SCHOOL TRIUMPHANT: THE SOURCES OF AMERICAN CATHOLIC EDUCATIONAL HISTORIOGRAPHY. *Hist. of Educ. Q. 1976 16(2): 131-146.* Examines sources from the 19th century.

3598. Lapteva, L. P. OSVESHCHENIE GUSISTSKOGO DVIZHENIIA V NOVEISHEI ISTORICHESKOI LITERATURE SSHA [Interpretation of the Hussite movement in recent American historical literature]. *Vestnik Moskovskogo U., Seriia 9: Istoriia [USSR] 1961 16(1): 58-72.* Reviews studies published in the mid-1950's by Frederick G. Heymann, especially his *John Žižka and the Hussite Revolution* (Princeton: Princeton U. Pr., 1955), Howard Kaminsky, and Paul P. Bernard on this 15th-century Bohemian religious reform movement. Their typically bourgeois idealistic emphasis on religion underrates or denies the significance of economic factors and class struggle. In contrast, contemporary Communist, mainly Czech, literature is unbiased and factual. 65 notes. N. Frenkley

3599. Lapteva, Ludmilla P. JAN HUS UND DIE DEUTSCHE REFORMATION IN DER BÜRGERLICHEN RUSSISCHEN HISTORIOGRAPHIE [John Hus and the German Reformation in bourgeois Russian historiography]. *Wissenschaftliche Zeitschrift der Ernst-Moritz-Arndt-U. Greifswald [East Germany] 1977 26(2): 113-119.* Mid-19th-century Russian historiography presented Martin Luther only as a follower of the Slav reformer, John Hus, but by 1912-17 this Slavophile view gave way to an interpretation which, while noting the connection between the Reformation in Bohemia and Germany, took into account the developments initiated by Luther.

3600. Launay, Michel. POLITIQUE SOCIAL ET CHRISTIANISME [Social policy and Christianity]. *Rev. d'Hist. Moderne et Contemporaine [France] 1974 21(4): 623-630.* The history of French Catholic social action in the early 20th century is described in Paul Droulers' *Politique sociale et Christianisme: le Père Desbuquois et l'Action populaire, débuts, syndicalisme et intégristes (1903-1918)* (Paris, 1969), based in part on the Jesuit archives in France and Rome and the publications of *Action populaire*. Émile Poulat attacked Droulers' methodology in *Archives de sociologie des religions* (1969, 28: 131-147) on the ground that it lacked scientific objectivity. The article evaluates Poulat's criticism. 3 notes.
J. S. Gassner

3601. Lazarus-Yafeh, Hava. CONTEMPORARY RELIGIOUS ATTITUDES OF MUSLIM ARABS TOWARD THE KA'AB AND THE HAJJ. *Asian and African Studies [Israel] 1978 12(2): 173-201.* Surveys contemporary Egyptian writing on Islamic institutions which sees increasing fundamentalist orthodoxy at all levels encouraged by both the intellectual community and the secular goverment.

3602. LeBrun, Jacques. SENS ET PORTÉE DU RETOUR AUX ORIGINES DANS L'OUEVRE DE RICHARD SIMON [Meaning and import of the return to origins in the work of Richard Simon]. *Dix-Septième Siècle [France] 1981 33(2): 185-198.* Richard Simon, author of *Histoire Critique du Vieux Testament*, was devoted to the search for religious truth, especially in the Vulgate. 98 notes.
W. J. Roosen

3603. Levin, David. WHEN DID COTTON MATHER SEE THE ANGEL? *Early Am. Lit. 1980-81 15(3): 271-275.* Defends 1685 as the year of Cotton Mather's alleged angelic vision, not 1693 as proposed by Professor Kenneth Silverman in a paper delivered at the Essex Institute on 29 September 1979. 12 notes.
T. P. Linkfield

3604. Lienhard, Marc. CONFLITS THEOLOGIQUES ET HISTORIOGRAPHIE: LES JUGEMENTS PORTES AU XIXᵉ SIECLE SUR LA REFORME STRASBOURGEOISE DU XVIeRET SIECLE [Theological conflicts and historiography: 19th-century judgments on the 16th-century Reformation in Strasbourg]. *Rev. d'Hist. et de Phil. Religieuses [France] 1981 61(4): 379-387.* Through a selection of 19th-century works by religious historians of different currents of opinion on Alsatian Protestantism, analyzes the great divergences and biases of their judgments toward the various aspects of the 16th-century Reformation in Strasbourg.

3605. Lienhard, Marc. LA PLACE DE LUTHER EN RFA EN 1983 [Martin Luther's place in West Germany in 1983]. *Rev. d'Allemagne [France] 1983 15(4): 387-401.* The 500th anniversary of the birth of Martin Luther (1483-1546) was celebrated in the Federal Republic of Germany by at least 30 exhibitions in museums and libraries, by numerous conferences and colloquiums of Protestant and Catholic theological faculties and scholarly societies, and by solemn statements of church leaders. In addition to many pamphlets and articles, over 60 books were published; these included new editions of Luther's works and nearly 15 biographies. Political leaders took the opportunity to declare how Luther supported their policies. Fortunately Luther's nationalism was not heavily emphasized. 48 notes. J. S. Gassner

3606. Littell, Franklin H. ETHICS AFTER AUSCHWITZ. *Worldview 1975 18(9): 22-26.* Outlines the problems of ethics and historiography posed for Christian churches by the Holocaust.

3607. Llera, Luis de. LA STORIOGRAFIA DEL DOPOGUERRA SUL CATTOLICESIMO SOCIALE CONTEMPORANEO IN SPAGNA (1868-1936) [Postwar historiography on contemporary social Catholicism in Spain, 1868-1936]. *Bol. dell'Arch. per la Storia del Movimento Sociale Cattolico in Italia [Italy] 1982 17(3): 289-314.* Surveys postwar writing on the history of the Catholic Church's involvement in social matters from the arrival in Spain of the 1st International to the outbreak of the 1936 civil war.

3608. Locher, Gottfried W. ZUR ZWINGLI-BIOGRAPHIE VON GEORGE POTTER [The Zwingli biography by George Potter]. *Zwingliana [Switzerland] 1978 14(10): 597-603.* Reviews George R. Potter's *Zwingli* (Cambridge: Cambridge U. Pr., 1976). Although the author's English vantage point makes it objective, the work labors the obvious. The author follows the interpretation of Walther Köhler and Oskar Farner in assessing Zwingli's place in the Protestant Reformation. The work is a major study, but Zwingli's theology is not handled profoundly, and Zwingli looms too large because Oekolampadius, Vadian, Haller Manuel, and other figures are not described adequately. D. R. Stevenson

3609. Loewenberg, Robert J. NEW EVIDENCE, OLD CATEGORIES: JASON LEE AS ZEALOT. *Pacific Hist. Rev. 1978 47(3): 343-368.* Traditional interpretation of Jason Lee as a devoted yet worldly missionary, a colonizer who cared little about Indians and a great deal about Americanizing Oregon, requires revision. Hitherto unused letters from Lee and letters and diaries of other Oregon Methodists reveal Lee was primarily an Indian missionary who believed in Christianizing before civilizing. The misinterpretation stems from historians' adherence to a naturalistic philosophy which assumes religious life is a shadow play of more "basic" economic and social realities. Primary and secondary sources; 60 notes.
W. K. Hobson

3610. Lucas, Glenn. CANADIAN PROTESTANT CHURCH HISTORY TO 1973. *Bull. of the United Church of Can. [Canada] 1974 (23): 5-50.* Outlines the history of the Methodist, Presbyterian, Anglican, Baptist, Congregational, and Lutheran churches in Canada and the United Church of Canada since 1825; includes bibliographies and historiography.

3611. Lukacs, John. THE HISTORIOGRAPHICAL PROBLEM OF BELIEF AND OF BELIEVERS: RELIGIOUS HISTORY IN THE DEMOCRATIC AGE. *Catholic Hist. Rev. 1978 64(2): 153-167.* The difficulties in reconstructing certain historical developments in the age of democracy have not yet been generally recognized, despite the concise warnings of Alexis de Tocqueville, among others. These difficulties are particularly evident when it comes to religious history: to what people believe or profess to believe. This was true of modern Germany and of the United States in the 20th century. On the one hand, "intentions must be gathered from acts"; on the other hand, we must attempt a kind of sociography, considering elements such as that of successive generations, or the desire for respectability among large masses of people. Religious ideas are no longer confined to ecclesiastical history. It must be "inside" history, requiring the historian's sympathetic participation. It must be microcosmic and sociographic, not sociological and generalizing.

A

3612. Luker, Ralph E. REVIVALISM AND REVISIONISM REVISITED. *Fides et Hist. 1982 14(2): 70-74.* Timothy L. Smith's *Revivalism and Social Reform* (1957) was not only a pioneering study of American urban religious history, it refuted both the notion that revivals were frontier phenomena and that they were cyclical events tied to economic factors. Contrary to Professor Guelzo's claims, Smith's *Revivalism* is not a rejection of intellectual history, nor did Smith fail in shifting the religious focus to the preachers who were nearer the laity. Smith's focus was narrow, concentrating on Northern evangelicals and virtually ignoring the existence of religious feeling in the South. Finally, perfectionism must also be viewed as a divisive force in antebellum Protestantism particularly in reference to the slavery issue. Secondary sources; 10 notes.   G. A. Glovins

3613. Lyon, T. Edgar. CHURCH HISTORIANS I HAVE KNOWN. *Dialogue 1978 11(4): 14-22.* The author reminisces about the lives and work of four Mormon historians who influenced his own development as a Mormon historian. B. H. Roberts, author of *The History of the Church* and president of the Church of the Latter Day Saints, attempted to break away from writing church history as propaganda. Andrew Jenson represents an earlier type of Mormon historian who collected historical information and documents, a chronicler striving for complete and accurate coverage. Similarly, A. William Lund, assistant historian in the Church Historian's Office, saw his responsibility as preserving documents and books, rather than making them accessible for use. Church historian Howard W. Hunter visited the author in Nauvoo, Illinois, and praised him for the concept of a church history that was people-oriented, not concerned only with abstractions. Based on an address to the Mormon History Association, Salt Lake City, Utah, 12 April 1973.   C. B. Schulz

3614. Mader, Hubert. LO SVILUPPO DEL MOVIMENTO SOCIALE CATTOLICO IN AUSTRIA (XVIII-XX SECOLO) SECONDO LA RECENTE STORIOGRAFIA [The development of the Catholic social movement in Austria, 18th-20th centuries, according to recent historiography]. *Bol. dell'Arch. per la Storia del Movimento Sociale Cattolico in Italia [Italy] 1982 17(3): 315-354.* Catholic involvement in social and political matters in Austria developed into an independent movement, which unlike similar movements elsewhere, was not controlled by the Church hierarchy.

3615. Madsen, Truman G. B. H. ROBERTS AND THE BOOK OF MORMON. *Brigham Young U. Studies 1979 19(4): 427-445.* A review of the perspectives of Elder Benson Howard Roberts, Mormon clergyman, historian and missionary, on the Book of Mormon. Considered are his views as circumstantial analyst, historian, translation analyst, advocate and defender, wisdom seeker, creative writer, doctrinal teacher, devil's advocate, avid spiritualist, and ideological prophet. Though never purely scientific, Roberts pos-

sessed a keen understanding of human nature, which, with patient and rigorous labor, caused him to break new ground in the understanding of the book of faith.   V. L. Human

3616. Mahan, Harold E. "MOST PLEASANT SCHOOL OF WISDOM": MARTIN J. KERNEY AND A CATHOLIC VISION OF HISTORY. *Maryland Hist. 1984 15(1): 19-26.* Reviews the historical works of Martin J. Kerney, a Marylander whose writings were an antidote to the strongly Protestant histories of the era and were used in Catholic schools. Based on Kerney's works and secondary sources; illus., 17 notes.   G. O. Gagnon

3617. Manselli, Raoul. LA STORIOGRAFIA RELIGIOSA ITALIANA DEL SECONDO DOPOGUERRA [Italian religious historiography since World War II]. *Italian Q. 1982 23(89): 55-61.* Several Italian historical studies about Christianity have appeared since 1945, especially in relation to the Franciscans and Benedictines; the most significant contributions have been made by Ernesto Buonaiuti.

3618. Manselli, Raoul. LUDWIG VON PASTOR—DER HISTORIKER DER PÄPSTE: KATHOLISCHE TRADITION UND POSITIVISTISCHE METHODOLOGIE IN DER GESCHICHTSSCHREIBUNG [Ludwig von Pastor, the historian of the popes: Catholic tradition and positivist methodology in historiography]. *Römische Hist. Mitteilungen [Austria] 1979 21: 111-126.* Considers the Catholic historiography and the methodology of Austrian academic Ludwig von Pastor (b. 1854) in his work on the popes. The author pays particular attention to the influence which German writers such as Caesar Baronius and Leopold von Ranke had on the development of historiography in Germany during the 19th century. This gave rise to great debates which took place in Germany, 1850-1900, when sharp ideological divisions emerged in both political and religious circles. Pastor's work was based partly on the methodological approach to history adopted by writers such as Ranke, Burkhardt, and Janssen, and partly on the traditional approach through the results of his own research. Based on Pastor's letters and diary and secondary sources; 45 notes.

G. L. Neville

3619. Mansfield, B. E. ERASMUS, LUTHER AND THE PROBLEM OF CHURCH HISTORY. *Australian J. of Pol. and Hist. [Australia] 1962 8(1): 41-56.* Discusses how traditional theological controversy in the Catholic Church, has affected Catholic historians' views, with particular reference to their assessments of the personalities, work, and influence of Desiderius Erasmus and Martin Luther. Emphasizes the need for cooperation between theologians and historians for a full understanding of 16th-century issues. 72 notes.   C. A. McNeill

3620. Marchadier, Bernard. SUR LE LIVRE VLADIMIR RJABUŠINSKIJ: *LA VIEILLE FOI ET LE SENTIMENT RELIGIEUX RUSSE* [Vladimir Riabushinski's The Old Faith and Russian Religious Feeling]. *Cahiers du Monde Russe et Soviétique [France] 1980 21(1): 83-107.* Places the Riabushinski family in the social background to which it belonged: that of Muscovite merchants of the 19th century, in which attachment to traditional values and to the priority of the spiritual domain was not deemed inconsistent with the good management of worldly interests. The author then considers Riabushinski's work as a study of Russian history and religious sensibility. The well-known questions, such as the quarrel between Joseph of Volokolamsk and Nil of Sora, the Slavophile philosophy, Tolstoy's populism and the works of writers such as Leont'ev, Solov'ev, and Rozanov, acquire a new meaning when dealt with by the Old-Believer Riabushinski. Stress is laid on the contribution of Old Believers to Russian literature and thought.

J/S

3621. Markova, Z. BULGARSKIIAT TSURKOVEN VUPROS V RUSKATA ISTORICHESKA LITERATURA [The Bulgarian religious question in Russian historical literature]. *Istoricheski Pregled [Bulgaria] 1975 31(3): 111-124.* The struggle in Bulgaria for an independent Orthodox Eastern Church began in the 1840's, and was a chief item in the program for national liberation. Russia's interest in the controversy was substantial because of its political ambitions in the region. In the 1870's T. I. Filipov argued that the Bulgarians should have limited autonomy in religious matters, but no independent church. This view was challenged toward the end of the century by Evgenii Galubinski who thought that the Bulgarians should indeed have their own church. This belief was echoed by most Russian historians. Based on the works of G. Trubetskoi, V. Teplov, and E. Golubinski; 72 notes. A. J. Evans

3622. Marmion, John P. CARDINAL POLE IN RECENT STUDIES. *Recusant Hist. [Great Britain] 1975 13(1): 56-61.* During the last 25 years many facets of the life and thoughts of Cardinal Reginald Pole have been examined. Walker and Trimpe have examined Pole's theology; Macaluso his humanism and politics. Fisher has contrasted his theology with that of Pope Paul IV; Fenelon has examined the Viterbo set. His role in the Counter Reformation has been analyzed as has his relationship with Ignatius Loyola and the Marian restoration. But there is still a need to publish the legatine registers, Pole's *De Reformatione*, and investigate his contacts with Cromwell and Contarini. Based on archives, published letters, secondary works; 13 notes. D. F. Schafer

3623. Maron, Gottfried. LUTHER UND DIE "GERMANISIERUNG DES CHRISTENTUMS": NOTIZEN ZU EINER FAST VERGESSENEN THESE [Luther and the "Germanization of Christianity": notes on an almost forgotten thesis]. *Zeits. für Kirchengeschichte [West Germany] 1983 94(3): 313-337.* Arthur Bonus (1864-1941) first coined the phrase "Germanization of Christianity" in 1896, defining it as the "modernization of Christianity." The resulting confused mixture of enthusiasm and decisiveness aimed at a "new" Germanic world-view and was based upon the organic philosophy of Social Darwinism. The opinion of Reinhold Seeberg (1859-1935) and other contemporary historians that Martin Luther (1483-1546) had proposed such a program was denounced by Karl Barth (1886-1968) and Heinrich Boehmer (1869-1927), as well as by other scholars. But Luther as "German prophet" was very critical of the Germans; his message was: "Do penance, Germany, while the time of grace is there; the time is ripe." The falsely understood "Germanization" was nothing more than a product of nationalistic cant. L. J. Reith

3624. Marshall, Norma. LORD ACTON AND THE WRITING OF RELIGIOUS HISTORY. *J. of Religious Hist. [Australia] 1979 10(4): 400-415.* J. E. E. D. Acton's approach to the writing of religious history was altered several times during the last four decades of the 19th century. From his work with Richard Simpson and the staff of *The Rambler* in the early 1860's to his years as Regius Professor of Modern History at Cambridge, Acton's approach to religious history was transformed. Acton's Catholicism, his German education, and his early commitment to scientific history distinguished him from his English contemporaries and affected his views on religious history. Primary sources; 70 notes.
W. T. Walker, III

3625. Massaut, Jean Pierre. HISTOIRE, HUMANISME, ET THÉOLOGIE, UN ÉRASME DES PROFONDEURS [History, humanism, and theology: an Erasmus of depth]. *R. d'Hist. Ecclésiastique [Belgium] 1974 69(2): 453-469.* Most Humanists were religious, a factor giving to Renaissance studies today a new coloration. Erasmus particularly is acquiring impressive stature as a theologian. R. I. Burns

3626. May, Dean L. THE MAKING OF SAINTS: THE MORMON TOWN AS A SETTING FOR THE STUDY OF CULTURAL CHANGE. *Utah Hist. Q. 1977 45(1): 75-92.* Mormon communities are historical specimens of a central theme of American experience: the tension between preservation of order and libertarian ideologies. Past studies of Mormon towns failed to examine the process of change over time. Techniques used for New England towns by such historians as Philip Greven, John Demos, Kenneth Lockridge, and Michael Zuckerman suggest questions to ask about Mormon communities. These scholars identified forces of disintegration. Mormon studies may show forces of reintegration. Primary and secondary sources; illus., 38 notes. J. L. Hazelton

3627. McBride, Paul. THE ITALIAN-AMERICANS AND THE CATHOLIC CHURCH: OLD AND NEW PERSPECTIVES. *Italian Americana 1975 1(2): 265-279.* Reviews Enrico C. Sartorio's *Social and Religious Life of Italians in America* (Clifton, New Jersey: Augustus M. Kelley, 1974) and Silvano Tomasi's *Piety and Power: The Role of the Italian Parishes in the New York Metropolitan Area* (New York: Center for Michigan Studies, 1975), and discusses problems of historical objectivity. S

3628. McLeod, Hugh. RELIGION IN THE CITY. *Urban Hist. Y. [Great Britain] 1978: 7-22.* Surveys the study of religion in the cities of Europe and America over the past 150 years. Considers various schools which have developed in this field, especially *sociologie religieuse.* 50 notes. N. Dejevsky

3629. McMillan, James. SCOTTISH CATHOLICS AND THE JANSENIST CONTROVERSY: THE CASE REOPENED. *Innes Rev. [Great Britain] 1981 32(1): 22-33.* Reviews the limited existing historiography of Jansenist penetration of the Scottish Catholic mission in the 18th century. Based on manuscripts in the Scottish Catholic Archives, Vatican Secret Archives, and Bibliothèque de l'Arsenal; 65 notes.

3630. Michaelsen, Robert S. RED MAN'S RELIGION/WHITE MAN'S RELIGIOUS HISTORY. *J. of the Am. Acad. of Religion 1983 51(4): 667-684.* Native Americans, viewed by Europeans as having either no religion or a false one, became objects of Christian missionary endeavor. This sentiment is reflected in histories of religion in America. 8 notes. E. R. Lester

3631. Michiels, R. HET VERANDERENDE BEELD VAN MAARTEN LUTHER [The changing image of Martin Luther]. *Spiegel Historiael [Netherlands] 1983 18(10): 512-518.* A review of the changing historical perspective on Martin Luther on the 500th anniversary of his birth. The Protestant image of Luther before 1914 was shaped by nationalism as well as Protestant piety. The Catholic view was largely based on the polemics of Johannes Cochlaeus, 1549, and the early 20th-century work of Heinrich Denifle, 1904, and Hartmann Grisar, 1911-12. 20th-century scholarship has been dominated by H. Borkamm, K. A. Meissinger, Joseph Lortz, R. Weijenborg, Remigius Bäumer, and Erwin Iserloh.
C. W. Wood, Jr.

3632. Mills, Frederick V., Sr. THE PROTESTANT EPISCOPAL CHURCHES IN THE UNITED STATES 1783-1789: SUSPENDED ANIMATION OR REMARKABLE RECOVERY? *Hist. Mag. of the Protestant Episcopal Church 1977 46(2): 151-170.* Church historians have interpreted the post-Revolutionary War period as one of stagnation at best, decline at worst, for the Protestant Episcopal Church. However, the records of the plans, hopes, and accomplishments of the churchmen, despite extensive disorganization and a prolonged series of reserves, show that this period was one of remarkable recovery. The achievements of the Episcopalians raise the distinct possibility that religion was not passé between 1775 and 1800, as it has been described. Based on diocesan histories; 2 tables, 82 notes. H. M. Parker, Jr.

3633. Miscamble, Wilson D. CATHOLICS AND AMERICAN FOREIGN POLICY FROM MCKINLEY TO MCCARTHY: A HISTORIOGRAPHICAL SURVEY. *Diplomatic Hist. 1980 4(3): 223-240.* Catholics exerted no identifiable significant influence on the formulation and conduct of US foreign policy from the Spanish-American War to the Cold War. Even on those rare occasions when the Church made the attempt, the establishment was unable to unify all believers in bringing pressure on the government. Only in its opposition to the lifting of the embargo on the Loyalist government during Spain's Civil War (1936-39) did the Church succeed in influencing policy, and even then other factors contributed heavily to President Franklin D. Roosevelt's decision. The Church "itself was influenced more by the course of American foreign relations than American foreign policy was influenced by Catholics." Mostly secondary sources; 60 notes. T. L. Powers

3634. Moir, John S. COMING OF AGE, BUT SLOWLY: AS-
PECTS OF CANADIAN RELIGIOUS HISTORIOGRAPHY
SINCE CONFEDERATION. *Sessions d'Etude: Soc. Can. d'Hist. de
l'Eglise Catholique [Canada] 1983 50(1): 89-98.* Surveys problems
in the development of a formal discipline of church history in Canada.

3635. Montgomery, Ingun. 1500-TALETS KONFESSIONELLA
HISTORIESKRIVNING [Confessional historical writings of the
16th century]. *Norsk Teologisk Tidsskrift [Norway] 1974 75(2):
121-140.* Traces the development of church history from Eusebius
of Caesarea, Saint Augustine, Erasmus, and Luther to Gerhard
Ebeling and Kurt Dietrich Schmidt, with particular reference to the
works of Matthias Flacius Illyricus (1520-72) and Caesar Baronius
(1538-1607). The former's *Magdeburg Centuries* (1559-74) is a polemic, regarding sources criticizing the pope as unconditionally true.
The latter's *Annales Ecclesiastici* (1588-1607) puts forward the pro-
papal viewpoint. Biblio.   U. G. Jeyes

3636. Mork, Gordon R. MARTIN LUTHER'S LEFT TURN:
THE CHANGING PICTURE OF LUTHER IN EAST GERMAN
HISTORIOGRAPHY. *Hist. Teacher 1983 16(4): 585-596.* East
German historiography has traditionally taken a negative view of
Martin Luther, emphasizing instead the more radical Thomas Mun-
tzer and the Peasants War. Beginning around 1980 a more positive
and revolutionary picture of Luther began to emerge. Reasons for
the new more favorable view of Luther include the importance of
his 500th birthday anniversary as a tourist event and internal and
external political needs of the East German government. Based on
published sources; 27 notes.   L. K. Blaser

3637. Moses, H. Vincent. NATIONALISM AND THE KING-
DOM OF GOD ACCORDING TO HANS KOHN AND CARL-
TON J. H. HAYES. *J. of Church and State 1975 17(2): 259-274.*
Discusses the nationalism and religious attitudes of historians Hans
Kohn and Carlton J. H. Hayes in the 1950's and 60's.

3638. Mounger, Dwyn M. HISTORY AS INTERPRETED BY
STEPHEN ELLIOTT. *Hist. Mag. of the Protestant Episcopal
Church 1975 44(3): 285-317.* Stephen Elliott (1806-66) was the
first Episcopal bishop of Georgia. Through his sermons and voluminous writings he conceived of history from the traditional Christian
point of view: the fulfillment of the divine will. He was one of the
major apologists for the southern way of life. He viewed slavery as
intricately woven into the fabric of southern life, decried abolitionism, led the way in evangelizing slaves, and favored the southern
cause during the Civil War. Never wavering in his belief that God
was on the side of the Stars and Bars, he anticipated Confederate
victory down to the last battle. Even the defeat he accepted as the
work of God, not of man. His greatest delusion in historical interpretation lay in his claim to be able to read the approval and con-
demnation of God in the events of history, despite the fact that on
occasion he would admit that discernment was difficult. Only the
Confederate defeat changed him from a strict Deuteronomist in history. Based largely on Elliott's writings; 117 notes.
                                                    H. M. Parker, Jr.

3639. Murphy, Francis X. THE FIRST HISTORIANS OF THE
SECOND VATICAN COUNCIL. *Catholic Hist. Rev. 1963 49(4):
540-547.* Reviews 10 books written in the period 1962-63 reporting
on and interpreting the events of Vatican Council II.

3640. Niemeyer, Gerhart. HISTORY AND CIVILIZATION.
Anglican Theological Rev. 1976 59(Supplement 7): 81-98. Assesses
Augustinian historiography in terms of centrality of theme and uni-
ty and compares it methodologically to the writing of Voltaire.

3641. Nohl, Frederick. WHAT I WOULD LIKE TO SEE HAP-
PEN IN TOMORROW'S CONCORDIA HISTORICAL INSTI-
TUTE. *Concordia Hist. Inst. Q. 1972 45(3): 178-180.* Calls upon
the Concordia Historical Institute to be more honest, daring, and
ecumenical in its approach to historical writings on the Lutheran
Church.

3642. Noll, Mark A. THE CHURCH AND THE AMERICAN
REVOLUTION: HISTORIOGRAPHICAL PITFALLS, PROB-
LEMS, AND PROGRESS. *Fides et Hist. 1975 8(1): 2-19.*
Historiographical examination of the relationships between the various Protestant Churches and the American Revolution. Calls for
fuller investigation of the easy merger of Protestantism and support
for the revolution; of the religious sources of Loyalist thought; and
of the more complex thought of those patriots who, while supporting the revolution, continued to also press a distinctly Christian ethic. Based on primary and secondary sources; 58 notes.
                                                    R. E. Butchart

3643. Noll, Mark A. THE CONFERENCE ON FAITH AND
HISTORY AND THE STUDY OF EARLY AMERICAN HISTO-
RY. *Fides et Hist. 1978 11(1): 8-18.* Calls on Christian historians
to broaden their audience, their research, and their methodologies
while affirming their faith in God's influence on history. Includes
an evaluation of the research into early American history (1607-
1865) by members of the Conference on Faith and History. Secondary sources; 12 notes.   R. E. Butchart

3644. Norwood, Frederick A. SOME FACETS OF THE HISTO-
RY OF BISHOPS IN AMERICAN METHODISM. *Methodist Hist.
1984 22(3): 174-188.* Stresses the need for a history of the episco-
pacy of the Methodist Church and discusses such features as existing studies of the office of bishop, different periods of episcopal
history, elections to the office, and some of the able ministers who
almost became bishops. 10 notes.   H. L. Calkin

3645. Pace, Enzo. THE DEBATE ON POPULAR RELIGION IN
ITALY. *Sociological Analysis 1979 40(1): 71-75.* A look at the recent upsurge of interest in popular religion in southern Italy. Current Catholic ritual is being increasingly forsaken in favor of feast
celebrations which fall somewhere between primitive pagan and
modern Christian rites. Sociologists and folklorists differ on the reasons for this development. Marxists argue that the phenomenon is
class connected, but that seems not to be the case. The most convincing explanation is that the rapidly modernizing trends current
in southern Italy have dislodged people from their traditional moor-
ings and thus in these half-pagan feasts they temporarily touch
again a past that has gone. 5 notes, ref.   V. L. Human

3646. Packull, Werner O. LUTHER AND MEDIEVAL MYSTI-
CISM IN THE CONTEXT OF RECENT HISTORIOGRAPHY.
Renaissance and Reformation [Canada] 1982 6(2): 79-93. No consensus exists regarding Luther's relationship, let alone his indebtedness to medieval mysticism. Heiko Oberman's approach is best
because it allows the relationship to be examined on a variety of
different levels. While Steven Ozment stresses Luther's indebtedness
to medieval nominalism and Bengt Hoffman emphasizes Luther's
closeness to mysticism, neither scholar is totally convincing. Luther's
works and secondary sources; 59 notes.   D. R. Stevenson

3647. Parente, Fausto. ERNESTO BUONAIUTI STORICO
[Ernesto Buonaiuti historian]. *Riv. Storica Italiana [Italy] 1972
84(3): 756-776.* Ernesto Buonaiuti was a historian who felt a need
to renew the essence of Christianity and to free it from its institutionalization by the Catholic Church. Buonaiuti's contribution to the
interpretation of ancient Christianity and its historic development
centered around the controversy between Adolf von Harnack and
Alfred Loisy. Discusses the "synthesis of his work as a historian
and religious thinker" and his three volume *Storia del
Cristianesimo* (1942-43). 71 notes.   M. T. Wilson

3648. Parente, Fausto. LA FIGURA STORICA DI GESÚ NEL-
LA STORIOGRAFIA TEDESCA DA H. S. REIMARUS A D. F.
STRAUSS (1775-1865) [The historical figure of Jesus in German
historiography from H. S. Reimarus to D. F. Strauss, 1775-1865].
Problemi di Ulisse [Italy] 1976 13(81): 96-112. Traces changes in
the view of theologians toward the historical Jesus Christ from the
16th century until the work of Hermann Reimarus and David Friedrich Strauss in the 18th and 19th centuries, stressing the humanizing trend.

3649. Payne, Harry. REVIEW ESSAY: REMAKING ONE'S MAKER—THE CAREER OF RELIGION IN THE EIGHTEENTH CENTURY. *Eighteenth-Century Life 1984 9(1): 107-115.* Summarizes and critiques historical scholarship in the 1980's that explores religion during the Enlightenment.

3650. Peace, Nancy E. ROGER WILLIAMS: A HISTORIOGRAPHICAL ESSAY. *Rhode Island Hist. 1976 35(4): 103-113.* Analyzes writings about Roger Williams, from accounts by his contemporaries to recent works by theologians. 58 notes.
P. J. Coleman

3651. Pender-Cudlip, Patrick. RELIGION AND CHANGE IN AFRICAN HISTORY. *Int. J. of African Hist. Studies 1974 7(2): 304-311.* A discussion and critique of Jan Vansina's review [*IJAS* 1973 6(1)] of T. O. Ranger and Isaria Kimambo's *The Historical Study of African Religion* (Berkeley: U. of California Pr., 1972). The questions which Vansina raises (the definition of religion, the difficulty of documenting change in African religions, and the attack upon the assumption that religion must have undergone continual change in precolonial Africa) are important but not urgent. They can only be answered through the collection and analysis of historical evidence. Secondary sources; 16 notes.
M. M. McCarthy

3652. Penedo Rey, Manuel. MI CONVIVENCIA CON EL P. GUILLERMO, EMINENTE RESTAURADOR [My cohabitation with Father Guillermo, eminent restorer]. *Estudios [Spain] 1984 40(146-147): 127-134.* Transcribes a recording made for *Jornadas Mercedarias,* which reminisces about Mercedarian Guillermo Vázquez Núñez, who worked to restore the Order of Our Lady of Mercy in Castile, and with whom the speaker lived and studied the history of the Mercedarians.

3653. Perko, F. Michael. OF CROSS AND CLASSROOM: PROSPECTS FOR CATHOLIC EDUCATIONAL BIOGRAPHY IN THE POST-CONCILIAR ERA. *Vitae Scholasticae 1983 2(1): 73-92.* Describes the biases in most American Catholic historiography: a monolithic view of the Catholic Church with little awareness of the various groups that compose it; ignoring the relationship between Catholics and other Americans; lack of intellectual biography; and domination by male and hierarchical interests. Proposes a new focus on neglected historical figures, on women, on the internal life of parochial schools, and on Hispanic educators. Discusses new methodologies to suit the field's needs. 42 notes. Spanish summary.
R. Grove

3654. Pikaza, Xabier. EL P. GUILLERMO VAZQUEZ Y SU VISION DE LA BIBLIA [Father Guillermo Vázquez Núñez and his vision of the Bible]. *Estudios [Spain] 1984 40(146-147): 149-161.* Guillermo Vázquez Núñez's *Temas Bíblicos* (1984), vol. 3 of his posthumous *Obras Completas* reveals his historian's and theologian's methodology of studying the Bible as well as the effects on his spirituality of his pilgrimage to the holy places in Palestine.

3655. Plongeron, Bernard and Godel, Jean. 1945-1970: UN QUART DE SIÈCLE D'HISTOIRE RELIGIEUSE À PROPOS DE LA GÉNÉRATION DES "SECONDES LUMIÈRES" (1770-1820) [A quarter century of religious history, 1945-70: the generation of the Enlightenment, 1770-1820]. *Ann. Hist. de la Révolution Française [France] 1972 44(2): 181-203.* The generation of the late Enlightenment lived from 1770 to 1820; it was preceded by the Baroque and succeeded by Romanticism. These classicists were the second lights, the First being those of the generation of Voltaire and Rousseau. Since 1945, historians have paid increasing attention to the religious life of the classical generation. This is perhaps because today Europe is enjoying a period of peace uncontaminated by nationalism, such as it has not been since the 18th century. Like the philosophes, Western thinkers today feel themselves part of an Atlantic community. 80 notes.
J. C. Billigmeier

3656. Pope, Robert G. NEW ENGLAND VERSUS THE NEW ENGLAND MIND: THE MYTH OF DECLENSION. *J. of Social Hist. 1969/70 3(2): 95-108.* Declension, a concept depicting spiritual deadness, loss of piety, and religious apathy among 17th century

New Englanders, has characterized historical scholarship from Perry Miller to Jack P. Greene. This traditional portrait is rejected and a different chronological model is substituted for interpreting the process of settlement, religious organization, community order, and growth. Tensions existed within early Puritan society between the church governing the community and the "gathered sects" of visible saints, identified by their spiritual conversions. During 1640-75 the saints triumphed, but the price they paid was a heavy one: the separation of the church from the community. After 1675, a series of crises forced the two to coalesce again. Based on the author's *The Half-Way Covenant* (Princeton, 1969), primary sources, religious literature, church membership rolls, and secondary works; 27 notes.
J. P. Harahan

3657. Rasmussen, Tarald. KAN TEOLOGIEN TRENGE EN HISTORISMEDEBATT? [Might theology need a historicism debate?]. *Norsk Teologisk Tidsskrift [Norway] 1982 83(4): 255-276.* Traces 20th-century developments in theology and ecclesiastical history against the background of the German tradition of historicism, which dominated the period 1870-1920, re-established its ascendancy by the 1930's, and came under fire again in the 1960's. Historicism has had special relevance to theology, its atheoretical nature being reflected in modern systematic theology, which developed in the 1920's and is responsible for the failure of ecclesiastical history to respond to the new "profane" interest in historical theory. Based on a lecture given in Theological Convent, Oslo, 27 September 1982. Primary and secondary sources; 62 notes.
D. F. Spade

3658. Reid, W. Stanford. THE FOUR MONARCHIES OF DANIEL IN REFORMATION HISTORIOGRAPHY. *Hist. Reflections [Canada] 1981 8(1): 115-123.* Protestant historians of the 16th century such as Luther, Philip Melanchthon, and Johannes Sleidan (1505-56), used the four monarchies prophecy of the book of Daniel (chapters 2 and 7) to interpret contemporary history. Feeling threatened by the Turks, the ecclesiastical establishment, led by the Pope, and the civil governments of Europe, these writers found in Daniel a source of continuity of God's plan. They could look forward with optimism. 22 notes.
M. Schumacher

3659. Reid, W. Stanford. IS THERE A CHRISTIAN APPROACH TO THE WRITING OF HISTORY? *Fides et Hist. 1980 12(2): 104-113.* A review essay on Earle E. Cairns's, *God and Man in Time: A Christian Approach to Historiography* (Grand Rapids: Baker Book House, 1979). Although since the late 1930's Christian and other historians have sought to describe the ultimate meaning of human history, their efforts have hitherto been largely theoretical with little concern for speciic events. Christian historians have also never come to terms with the best ways to express their beliefs in teaching and writing. Cairns's book is designed for the undergraduate. 12 notes.
J. A. Kicklighter

3660. Reinalter, Helmut. REFORMKATHOLIZISMUS ODER STAATSKIRCHENTUM? ZUR BEWERTUNG DES JOSEPHINISMUS IN DER NEUEREN LITERATUR [Reform Catholicism or a state Church? The evaluation of Josephinism in recent literature]. *Römische Hist. Mitteilungen [Austria] 1976 18: 283-307.* Until recently, historians of the Church reforms carried through by Habsburg Emperor Joseph II have either presented them as wise attempts to reform and modernize the Catholic Church or as an effort to have the state control the Church. The new generation of historians, led by Eduard Winter, Fritz Valjavec, and Ferdinand Maass, are avoiding apologetics for either Joseph or for the Church hierarchy, and are attempting to make objective analyses of Joseph's Church policy and of the resistance to it. 79 notes.
J. C. Billigmeier

3661. Reinerman, Alan J. PAPACY AND PAPAL STATE IN THE RESTORATION (1814-1846): STUDIES SINCE 1939. *Catholic Hist. Rev. 1978 64(1): 36-46.* Surveys the books and articles written since 1939 on the papacy and the Papal States during the restoration, 1814-46. Although much has been accomplished, much remains to be done before our understanding of this period can be considered satisfactory. Indicates several areas where further work would be desirable.
A

3662. Reingrabner, Gustav. ZUR KONZEPTION DER ÖSTER-REICHISCHEN PROTESTANTENGESCHICHTSSCHREIBUNG [The conception of Austrian Protestant historiography]. *Jahrbuch der Gesellschaft für die Gesch. des Protestantismus in Österreich [Austria] 1980 96(1-3): 189-207.* The establishment of the Society for the History of Protestantism in Austria in 1879 marked the beginning of systematic research and publications concerning the history of Austrian Protestantism and Protestant church matters in the Habsburg and Austrian lands. The author traces the development of Protestant theological historiography in Austria, 1879-1979, with reference to Protestant education, the position of Protestants prior to the Charter of Tolerance of 1849, Reformation and Counterreformation in Austria, and the problems of emigration. Secondary sources; 33 notes.   G. L. Neville

3663. Rempel, David G. C. B. SCHMIDT, HISTORIAN: FACT OR FICTION? *Mennonite Life 1974 29(1/2): 33-37.* Corrects misconceptions brought out in the historical writings of C. B. Schmidt, who wrote a history of the Mennonites from their beginnings in Germany and Russia through their immigration to the New World; attempts to clear up misstatement of fact and outright fallacies perpetrated by Schmidt.

3664. Reynolds, Noel B. THE DOCTRINE OF AN INSPIRED CONSTITUTION. *Brigham Young U. Studies 1976 16(3): 315-340.* Examines the views of the founding fathers and the general political theories of government in the 18th century to determine to what degree the American Constitution was inspired by God. Discusses the attitudes of modern-day historians on the question and criticizes secular revisionist historians for breaking the traditional inspirational view held by the Latter-Day Saints. The ultimate constitutional document may have come as a result of the evolution of God's inspirations rather than by direct revelations to the founding fathers.   M. S. Legan

3665. Rischin, Moses. THE NEW AMERICAN CATHOLIC HISTORY. *Church Hist. 1972 41(2): 225-229.* Catholicism experienced a resurgent spirit in the United States after 1960. The election of the first Catholic president, John Kennedy, and the dynamic, progressive papacy of John XXIII accentuated a renewed Catholic consciousness in this nation. Studies in 20th-century US Catholic history went beyond the traditional denominational approach to a wider view of American history as seen from the Catholic perspective. Current Catholic history, written primarily by Catholics, takes an introspective and often self-critical view of the Catholic experience in America. That Catholic experience is being increasingly recognized as complex and difficult to quantify. Many different nationalities, all trying to establish themselves in a non-Catholic nation, comprise American Catholicism. The Catholic contribution to American history needs to be given its proper importance by general historians. Based on recently published material; 11 notes.   S. C. Pearson, Jr.

3666. Roberts, Frank. GOTTFRIED ARNOLD ON HISTORICAL UNDERSTANDING: AN EARLY PIETIST APPROACH. *Fides et Hist. 1982 14(2): 50-59.* Though largely ignored in English and American scholarship, the German Pietist Church historian Gottfried Arnold (1606-1714) was an integral figure in modern church historiography. Frustrated by what he viewed as the blatant biases and apologetics of the traditional church historians, Arnold endeavored to correct their errors and reinterpret church history in a more objective light. Emphasizing a return to original sources which characterized Renaissance scholarship, Arnold proposed a methodology of impartiality. The historian should not only be cognizant of the origin of the documents but should strive to maintain a mild disposition, control passion, and maintain a healthy skepticism. 55 notes.   G. A. Glovins

3667. Roth, Guenther. RELIGION AND REVOLUTIONARY BELIEFS: SOCIOLOGICAL AND HISTORICAL DIMENSIONS IN MAX WEBER'S WORK—IN MEMORY OF IVAN VALLIER. *Social Forces 1976 55(2): 257-272.* How adequate is Max Weber's world historical sociology of religion in relation to ongoing secularization, especially the rise of quasi-religious political movements and ideologies? His work retains a considerable degree of conceptual adequacy in the face of new historical developments for both analytical and historical reasons. The author distinguishes between Weber's developmental theory of modern revolutionary beliefs and his sociology of ideological virtuosi and of social marginality. The model of revolutionary religious virtuosity is applied to the Catholic opposition against church and state in the United States. The essay concludes with some observations on the counterculture in the light of Weber's developmental theory and sociohistorical model.   J

3668. Russo, Carla. STUDI RECENTI DI STORIA SOCIALE E RELIGIOSA IN FRANCIA: PROBLEMI E METODI [Recent studies in social and religious history in France: problems and methods]. *R. Storica Italiana [Italy] 1972 84(3): 625-682.* Examines recent French studies of the church history of France in the 17th and 18th centuries. While there has always been ample material on major questions in church history, recent works have dealt with the daily life and work of the clergy. Summarizes the main historical lines taken in recent studies. Secondary sources; 64 notes.   C. Bates

3669. Sakakibara, Gan. MY PILGRIMAGE TO ANABAPTISM. *Mennonite Life 1973 28(1): 12-15.* Traces the author's life in the context of his contacts with and ultimate promotion of Anabaptism as a religion and a way of life. Particular attention is devoted to his efforts in publishing works of Anabaptist history in Japan and the development of his religious and philosophical outlook. Illus.   J. A. Casada

3670. Sandon, Leo, Jr. H. RICHARD NIEBUHR'S PRINCIPLES OF HISTORIOGRAPHY. *Foundations 1975 18(1): 61-74.* The principles of H. Richard Niebuhr's historiography were Troeltschian, but modified by Henri Bergson. One cannot show the influence of Troeltsch on Niebuhr by explicit statement only. Ernest Troeltsch thought that even though historical investigation was subjective to some degree, it was not a matter of personal judgement. Troeltsch did not think history could be interpreted psychologically only, but that natural cause had to be considered. Niebuhr held in *The Kingdom of God in America* (1937), that historical thought was conceptual thought, and attempted to see American Christianity as an "historic totality" in Troeltschian terms. Henri Bergson held to two kinds of religion and morality: closed morality supported by state religion, and open morality supported by dynamic religion. Niebuhr equates static religion with institutional religion, and sees the true church as a "movement." 55 notes.   E. E. Eminhizer

3671. Schäfer, Gerhard. "DAS GUTE BEWAHREN, ABWEGE ABER VERHÜTEN": ZUR GESCHICHTE DES WÜRTTEMBERGISCHEN PIETISMUS [To preserve the good but avoid error: the history of Pietism in Württemberg]. *Blätter für Württembergische Kirchengeschichte [West Germany] 1982 82: 218-236.* Examines both the history and historiography of Swabian Pietism.

3672. Schieder, Wolfgang. RELIGION IN THE SOCIAL HISTORY OF THE MODERN WORLD: A GERMAN PERSPECTIVE. *European Studies Rev. [Great Britain] 1982 12(3): 289-299.* German historical scholarship has ignored religion as a force in history leaving this task to special disciplines to explore the role of religion as a legitimate historical concern. The weakness in this approach has permitted ecclesiastical historians to concentrate almost exclusively on Christianity while comparative religion scholars have treated religion phenomenologically and those specializing in the sociology of religion have largely ignored the historical dimension of their field. Research in religion as social history should be approached from the broadest perspective, religious phenomena should be seen from the wider context of the society and not from the focal point of the state, and the history of religion should not be isolated from other forces that shaped the past. 31 notes.   J. G. Smoot

3673. Schorsch, Ismar. GERMAN ANTISEMITISM IN THE LIGHT OF POST-WAR HISTORIOGRAPHY. *Leo Baeck Inst. Y. [Great Britain] 1974 19: 257-272.* An ever growing literature endeavors to explore the roots of German anti-Semitism and its nexus to the traditional Christian perception of the Jew. Christian anti-Semitism deserves to be considered only as one component of a complex matrix. Eva Reichmann and Hannah Arendt point out that the decline of Christianity during the early modern period and the rise of the nation state produced the roots of the modern totalitarian state in which extermination of the Jewish minority became a reality. Other major contributions were made by Paul Massing and Eleonore Sterling in their examination of 19th-century political and social anti-Semitic attitudes.   F. Rosenthal

3674. Schulin, Ernst; Watson, U., transl. LUTHER'S POSITION IN GERMAN HISTORY AND HISTORICAL WRITING. *Australian Journal of Politics and History [Australia] 1984 30(1): 85-98.* Summarizes Martin Luther's place in German historiography by reflecting on the jubilees of 1817, 1883, 1917, and 1983. Discusses the views of Gotthold Ephraim Lessing, Johann Wolfgang von Goethe, Michael Schmidt, Leopold von Ranke, Heinrich von Treitschke, Johannes Janssen, Heinrich Denifle, Hartman Grisar, Ernst Troeltsch, and Gerhard Ritter. Based on German histories, biographies, and monographs; 37 notes.   W. D. McIntyre

3675. Segal, Lester A. JACQUES BASNAGE DE BEAUVAL'S *L'HISTOIRE DES JUIFS:* CHRISTIAN HISTORIOGRAPHICAL PERCEPTION OF JEWRY AND JUDAISM ON THE EVE OF THE ENLIGHTENMENT. *Hebrew Union College Annual 1983 54: 303-324.* Reviews *L'Histoire des Juifs* (1706-07) by Jacques Basnage de Beauval (1653-1723), which was the first comprehensive history of the Jewish people to appear since the first century. As such, it is a significant historiographical document—one that has to be read, however, with the knowledge that the author was a Protestant theologian who often allowed religious doctrine to distort his historical objectivity. Nevertheless, *L'Histoire* served as the authoritative source on the Jewish past during the Enlightenment. 87 notes.   B. Reiner

3676. Shea, Daniel B. JONATHAN EDWARDS: THE FIRST TWO HUNDRED YEARS. *J. of Am. Studies [Great Britain] 1980 14(2): 181-197.* Before 1903, the thinking and literary achievements of American colonial theologian Jonathan Edwards (1703-58) were subjects for lively controversy among historians, theologians and literary analysts, and for 19th-century American eulogists, his work represented the "rising glory in America." These numerous revisionist writings provided essential insights to 20th-century scholars who subsequently have interpreted Edwards's influence on American literature and thought. 40 notes.   H. T. Lovin

3677. Sheils, Richard D. THE SECOND GREAT AWAKENING IN CONNECTICUT: CRITIQUE OF THE TRADITIONAL INTERPRETATION. *Church Hist. 1980 49(4): 401-415.* Lyman Beecher credited Yale president Timothy Dwight with bringing about the Second Great Awakening. Beecher also maintained that the Second Awakening was contrived for political purposes and caused a change in preaching techniques. These three themes expressed by an elderly Beecher have traditionally formed the basis for historians' interpretation of revivalism during the period, but records of the Connecticut Missionary Society indicate that many of Beecher's conclusions may be too narrow. They suggest that the Second Great Awakening might be viewed as a folk movement. 38 notes.   M. D. Dibert

3678. Šidak, Jaroslav. PROBLEM HERETIČKE "CRKVE BOSANSKE" U NAJNOVIJOJ HISTORIOGRAFIJI (1962-75) [The problem of the heretical Bosnian Church in recent historiography, 1962-75]. *Hist. Zbornik [Yugoslavia] 1974-75 27-28: 139-182.* An account based on the most recent literature dealing with the heretical Bosnian Church. The author presents a critical analysis of this scholarship from the examination of the documents. A number of approaches to the problems pertaining to the study of the *Crkva bosanska* and the sect of the Bogomils are suggested. 147 notes.   A. C. Niven

3679. Sil, Narasingha Prosad. LUTHER, ERIKSON, AND HISTORY: A STRANGE ENCOUNTER. *Q. Rev. of Hist. Studies [India] 1982 22(3): 21-35.* Since its appearance in 1958, Erik H. Erikson's *Young Man Luther: A Study in Psychoanalysis and*

History has commanded continuing attention. However, further analysis and recognition of Martin Luther as a fundamentally religious man argues the case against the psychoanalytical emphasis in interpretation. Luther's concept of God's *potentia* and the essence of the *evangelium* render the Erikson approach futile. A more legitimate psychological approach to the study of Luther would be based on the concepts of Søren Kierkegaard. Based on primary and secondary sources; 48 notes.   W. T. Walker

3680. Silke, John J. THE ROMAN CATHOLIC CHURCH IN IRELAND 1800-1922: A SURVEY OF RECENT HISTORIOGRAPHY. *Studia Hibernica [Ireland] 1975 15: 61-104.* Sufficient scholarship appeared between 1960 and 1975 to allow meaningful historiographical assessment. During the union, contemporary Irish Catholicism emerged. Despite work on the prefamine Catholic Church, more is needed to determine the extent to which religious traditions of the penal era affected the era of Cardinal Paul Cullen (1803-78). Daniel O'Connell's success in wielding mass opinion aroused Protestant reaction which bore fruit in Ulster nationalism. In the post-Parnell era the Church managed relations with the state and nation so as to protect and augment its interests. Though concentration on insular history has impoverished Irish historiography, recent scholarship has broadened that perspective and has illuminated the external relationships of the Church under the union. Under Sources and Guides, the author discusses periodicals and bibliographical, archival, printed and calendared sources. Survey of books and articles is classified by period and topics. Secondary sources; 141 notes.   T. F. Moriarty

3681. Smith, Melvin T. FAITHFUL HISTORY/SECULAR FAITH. *Dialogue 1983 16(4): 65-71.* Explores the relationship of religious faith to historical methodology. Examines the problems of historical study of the Prophet Joseph Smith, of Mormon revelations, and of the church history of the Church of Jesus Christ of Latter-day Saints. Presented at the Mormon History Association annual meeting, May 1982, Omaha.   R. Grove

3682. Soto Pérez, José Luís. PROYECTO ESPAÑOL DE UNA *HISTORIA GENERAL DE LA TERCERA ORDEN REGULAR DE SAN FRANCISCO* (SIGLO XVIII) [Spanish plan for a general history of the third order of St. Francis, 18th century]. *Arch. Ibero-Americano [Spain] 1980 40(157): 37-72.* Outlines the history of the third order of Franciscans in Spain and Portugal from the 14th century, including administrative structure and organization, jurisdiction, and leadership. Three letters dated 1793-95 from Fr. Pedro Joaquín de Salas concerning his plans for a general history of the order, a description of the establishment of the province of the third order in Andalucia by Padre Laín Rojas in 1819, a Latin catalogue of 50 provincial ministers of the 17th and 18th centuries, and official nominations of the provincial chapter of Andalucia in 1783 are examined. Based on documents in the Évora Public Library; 16 notes, 3 appendixes.   P. J. Durell

3683. Spadolini, Giovanni. CHIESA E RELIGIOSITÀ IN ITALIA [Church and religiosity in Italy]. *Nuova Antologia [Italy] 1973 518(2070): 151-158.* In the form of a letter to Michele Maccarone, author of *Chiesa e religiosità in Italia dopo l'unità (1861-1876)* (Vita e Pensiero, 1973), the author critiques the new work, calling for a more complete historiography of the cooperation between the Catholic Church and the anticlerical opposition during the early post-Unification period.

3684. Speck, William A. WHAT SHOULD BE THE ROLE OF CHRISTIAN HISTORIANS? *Fides et Hist. 1975 8(1): 76-81.* Review essay of C. T. McIntire's *The Ongoing Task of Christian Historiography* (Toronto: Inst. for Christian Studies, 1974). McIntire calls on Christian historians to return to a historiographic tradition in which biblical truths figure largely in interpretive stances. Based on McIntire and secondary sources; 11 notes.   R. E. Butchart

3685. Stalnaker, John C. ANABAPTISM, MARTIN BUCER, AND THE SHAPING OF THE HESSIAN PROTESTANT CHURCH. *J. of Modern Hist. 1976 48(4): 601-643.* Examines the historiography concerning Martin Bucer (1491-1551), Landgrave Philip the Magnanimous of Hesse (1504-67), religious liberty, Anabaptism, and the infant Hessian Protestant Church, 1520's-40's. Examines as well Bucer's experiences in Strasbourg as they relate to Hesse. The Ziegenhain ordinance, designed to introduce discipline into the established church as a means of social control, broke the power of Anabaptism but did not solve popular anticlericalism or indiscipline.   S

3686. Staper, James M. REFLECTIONS AND RETRACTIONS ON *ANABAPTIST AND THE SWORD. Mennonite Q. Rev. 1977 51(3): 196-212.* The author reviews his *Anabaptists and the Sword,* 2d ed. (Lawrence: Coronado Pr., 1976), pointing out the areas where he still holds to his thesis and those where he has changed his views. The scholarship concerning the "evangelical Anabaptists" needs more consideration. Discusses current problems of Anabaptist historiography. 45 notes.   E. E. Eminhizer

3687. Stayer, James M.; Packull, Werner O.; and Depperman, Klaus. FROM MONOGENESIS TO POLYGENESIS: THE HISTORICAL DISCUSSION OF ANABAPTIST ORIGINS. *Mennonite Q. Rev. 1975 49(2): 83-121.* The controversy between Ernest Troeltsch and Karl Holl over the 16th-century origins of Anabaptism in Zurich has "in some respects obstructed the study of its history." A review of the Swiss Brethern, early South German Anabaptism, and Anabaptism in the Netherlands offers a different, polygenesis perspective on the origins of Anabaptism. 137 notes.

E. E. Eminhizer

3688. Steinmetz, Max. THOMAS MÜNZER IN DER FORSCHUNG DER GEGENWART [Thomas Münzer in present day research]. *Zeitschrift für Geschichtswissenschaft [East Germany] 1975 23(6): 666-685.* The triumph of socialism in this century has caused both Marxist and bourgeois historians to focus on Thomas Münzer (d. 1525), who previously received little attention. In capitalist countries theologians and church historians have done most of the research on Münzer, while Marxist historians have concentrated upon the impact of his doctrines on the early bourgeois revolution. The author discusses how Münzer's activist theology differed from Martin Luther's doctrines, which fostered passivity in both religious and secular matters. 73 notes.   J. T. Walker

3689. Stineback, David C. THE STATUS OF PURITAN-INDIAN SCHOLARSHIP. *New England Q. 1978 51(1): 80-90.* Analyzes recent Puritan-Indian scholarship. Alden Vaughan has overemphasized Puritan missionary work. Both he and Francis Jennings have underestimated the importance of Puritan theology in determining the Puritans' Indian policy. Believing themselves to be God's chosen people, the Puritans expected Indians to readily accept the superiority of an English way of life and to adopt it. When Indians failed to convert to Christianity and to adopt English ways, the Puritans believed that they must be allied with Satan and they were being used by God to chastise his people for their sins. Indian-Puritan conflict "is best described as a religious confrontation with economic, political, and military ramifications." Primary and secondary sources; 33 notes.   J. C. Bradford

3690. Strauss, Gerald. SUCCESS AND FAILURE IN THE GERMAN REFORMATION. *Past and Present [Great Britain] 1975 (67): 30-63.* Briefly describes the historiographical controversy relating to whether the Reformation in Germany resulted in a change for the "better or worse in the hearts and minds of men." Asks such questions as, "Were men and society improved in some way?" and "Had the adult population in Lutheran territories acquired some basic religious knowledge by the end of the sixteenth century?" The author concludes that, contrary to early hopes, Lutheranism failed to accomplish a general elevation of morality; it did not succeed in making an impact on the population at large; experiments in mass indoctrination were unsuccessful; the "Gospel had not been implanted in the hearts and minds of men," and an attitude of indifference prevailed toward the established religion. However, there were German Lutherans of "serious, sincere and informal piety." Primary and secondary sources; 146 notes.

R. G. Neville

3691. Stump, Wolfgang. ZUR GESCHICHTE DES REICHSKONKORDATS VOM 20. JULI 1933 [Concerning the history of the Concordat of 20 July 1933]. *Hist. Jahrbuch [West Germany] 1974 94: 333-342.* A review of recent German publications, interpretations, and arguments commemorating the 40th anniversary of the Concordat. The Concordat was a defensive measure of the Catholic Church in an exceptional situation. It offered new possibilities for the protection of the Church even though Hitler violated the agreement from the beginning. 44 notes.   G. Bassler

3692. Sytenko, L. T. MODERNIZM I KONSERVATYZM RELIHIINOHO ROZUMINNIA ISTORII [Modernism and conservatism in a religious interpretation of history]. *Ukrains'kyi Istorychnyi Zhurnal [USSR] 1971 (5): 62-70.* Suggests that the modernization of religious history is undertaken by those historians who wish to introduce the scientific spirit of the 20th century into their work. Compares these works and their Biblical source material to the approach of 19th-century and Marxist-Leninist historians.

3693. Thadden, Rudolf von. KIRCHENGESCHICHTE ALS GESELLSCHAFTSGESCHICHTE [Church history as social history]. *Gesch. und Gesellschaft [West Germany] 1983 9(4): 598-614.* Until recently, church history in Germany has been undertaken in isolation from other areas of history. However, since churches are a part of society and reflect society in their structure, church and religious history should become more a part of social history. Recently, several works on church history have appeared that show the value and necessity of tools, concepts, and methods of social history in this field. Secondary sources; 62 notes.   C.-H. Geschwind

3694. Toews, John B. THE RUSSIAN MENNONITES. SOME INTRODUCTORY COMMENTS. *Mennonite Q. R. 1974 48(4): 403-408.* Describes development of Mennonite ethnocentrism in 19th-century Russia and its influence on Russian Mennonite historiography.   S

3695. Tökés, István. WEITERLEBEN UND AKTUALITÄT ZWINGLIS IN DER UNGARISCHSPRACHIGEN REFORMIERTEN KIRCHE [Range and reality of Zwingli in the Hungarian-speaking Reformed Church]. *Zwingliana [Switzerland] 1984 16(3): 217-238.* Reviews 19th- and 20th-century Hungarian Protestant historiography of Zwingli and his influence in Hungary. 70 notes.

D. R. Stevenson

3696. Trénard, Louis. LA VIE RELIGIEUSE AU XVIIᵉ SIECLE [Religious life in the 17th century]. *Information Hist. [France] 1969 31(1): 23-29, (2): 66-72.* Part I. Examines the studies carried out 1963-68 on religious life in 17th-century France. Considers in particular the links between religion and political life, the role of the Church in 17th-century French society, the evolution of the Jansenist movement, and the renaissance of Catholicism. Part II. Examines works concerning the role of missionaries, the activities of the parish priest, pastoral work in the diocese, and the position of the reformed churches.

3697. Vahle, Hermann. CALVINISMUS UND DEMOKRATIE IM SPIEGEL DER FORSCHUNG [Calvinism and democracy in the light of scholarly research]. *Archiv für Reformationsgeschichte [West Germany] 1975 66: 182-212.* Investigates the historical substance of theories about the democratic content of Calvinism and its significance for the development of democratic ideas. The literature on the subject reveals no direct equation in intellectual history between the Calvinism of Geneva and the theoreticians of modern democratic theory. Far from advocating a modern concept of popular sovereignty, John Calvin (1509-64) promoted individual religious and political freedom under the aegis of a mixed aristocratic-democratic constitution, thus contributing to the ideas of democratic freedom. The Calvinist "Monarchomachs" went beyond Calvin in the direction of a democratization of the right of resistance. Mercier Morelli and Petrus Ramus (1515-72) represented a democratic wing of 16th-century Calvinism. Marxist historians have tended to interpret Calvinism as an ideology of the rising middle classes with a profoundly liberalizing, if not revolutionary, impact. 190 notes.

L. J. Reith

3698. Van Kley, Dale. DOOYEWEERD AS HISTORIAN. *Christian Scholar's Rev. 1975 5(2): 129-145.* Continued from a previous article. Analyzes the Christian view of history developed by Herman Dooyeweerd (1932-75).

3699. Vaussard, Maurice. ÉCLAIRCISSEMENTS SUR LA CONSTITUTION CIVILE DU CLERGÉ [Elucidations on the Civil Constitution of the Clergy]. *Ann. Hist. de la Révolution Française [France] 1970 42(2): 287-293.* Attempts to correct the imbalance in previous discussions of the Civil Constitution of the Clergy. Discusses the errors on both the Catholic and pro-Revolutionary sides in the historiography of the French Revolution. Among the latter group was Albert Mathiez who failed to appreciate the importance of contemporary Italian religious history in explaining the conduct of Pope Pius VI and who underestimated the Jansenist current in the Constituent Assembly. 9 notes. J. C. Billigmeier

3700. Vázquez, Luis. LA HISTORIA DE LA MERCED, DE TIRSO (1639), Y LA DE LOS MERCEDARIOS DE LA CONGREGACION DE PARIS (1685) [The history of the Mercedarians written by Tirso de Molina (pseud. of Gabriel Téllez) 1639, and by members of the Paris congregation of the order, 1685]. *Estudios [Spain] 1981 37(132-135): 575-604.* Compares the two histories and the differences in the choice and interpretation of material between their respective authors.

3701. Vázquez de Parga, Luis. LOS BENEDICTINOS Y LA ERUDICION HISTORICA [The Benedictines and historical scholarship]. *Rev. de Arch., Bibliotecas y Mus. [Spain] 1979 82(3): 395-406.* Briefly surveys the contributions to historical science made by the monks of Saint Benedict, especially by Jean Mabillon (1632-1707) and the Congregation of St. Maur, often against strong opposition in the name of the Rule. Describes an unsuccessful Spanish attempt to emulate Mabillon's achievement. J. V. Coutinho

3702. Vecchi, Alberto. SULLA NOZIONE DI STORIA DEL CRISTIANESIMO [On the notion of the history of Christianity]. *Convivium [Italy] 1959 27(2): 207-212.* The history of Christianity is not simply the history of its origins, its dogmas, or its institutions but the discernment of a certain ferment of grace which raises the events of normal history to a new dimension.

3703. Villers, David H. CONNECTICUT ANGLICANISM AND SOCIETY TO 1783: A REVIEW OF HISTORIANS. *Hist. Mag. of the Protestant Episcopal Church 1984 53(1): 45-59.* Examines the historiography of Connecticut Anglicans, focusing on interpretations of their role in the American Revolution. 44 notes.

3704. Vocke, Harald. ROSE UNTER DEN DORNEN: MARONITENGESCHICHTE IN DER SICHT WESTLICHER HISTORISCHER FORSCHUNG [A rose beneath thorns: Maronite history in the view of Western historical research]. *Ostkirchliche Studien [West Germany] 1982 31(4): 334-337.* Surveys Western historiography of Lebanon's Maronite Catholic community.

3705. Vogler, Günter. L'HISTORIOGRAPHIE MARXISTE ET MARTIN LUTHER [Marxist historiography and Martin Luther]. *Rev. d'Hist. et de Phil. Religieuses [France] 1983 63(1-2): 155-166.* Considers Martin Luther's place in German history and the revolutionary influence of his work and of the Reformation in the context of Marxist historiography.

3706. Vorländer, Herwart. ZUM SELBSTVERSTÄNDNIS DER BEKENNENDEN KIRCHE IM DRITTEN REICH [On the self-understanding of the Confessing Church in the Third Reich]. *Geschichte in Wissenschaft und Unterricht [West Germany] 1968 19(7): 393-407.* The question of the self-understanding of the German Confessing Church is not identical with the question of its structure. It is rather a question posed by the moral dilemma of the church with regard to its attitude toward the Nazi government's actions during World War II. Whether opposition to that war was a function of groups or movements within the church or a stance of the church itself posed an ecclesiological question of enormous significance for this church, and its historiography does not end in 1945. 31 notes. J. M. McCarthy

3707. Wellenreuther, Hermann. THE POLITICAL DILEMMA OF THE QUAKERS IN PENNSYLVANIA, 1681-1748. *Pennsylvania Mag. of Hist. and Biog. 1970 94(2): 135-172.* A documentary and historical analysis of the accuracy of "the historians' understanding of the peace testimony, as the Quakers themselves called their pacifistic principles," and whether it is identical with the one held by Pennsylvania Quakers between 1681 and 1748, and the further question of "whether the acts and deeds of the Quaker politicians have been interpreted by their historians in terms congenial to conceptions held by these politicians in the first half of the eighteenth century." A study of the Assembly's actions in this period should affect our understanding of the events of the Seven Years' War, and should emphasize the importance of the peace testimony as the most contested and most important political doctrine of the Quakers. Though the doctrine was not given up there was agitation for a broader understanding of it. 84 notes. R. V. Ritter

3708. White, Joseph M. HISTORIOGRAPHY OF CATHOLIC IMMIGRANTS AND RELIGION. *Immigration Hist. Newsletter 1982 14(2): 5-11.* Until the 1970's, church historians had little to say about Catholic immigrants' religious adaptations.

3709. White, Peter. REASON AND INTUITION IN THE THEOLOGY OF THEODORE PARKER. *J. of Religious Hist. [Australia] 1980 11(1): 111-120.* Since the 1920's, historians such as Vernon Parrington, Henry Steele Commager, Herbert W. Schneider, John E. Dirks, and H. Shelton Smith have investigated the complex nature of Unitarian Theodore Parker's theology. The basic problem in their assessment of Parker has been their failure to recognize that transcendentalism, and its essential issue of reason versus intuition, did not emerge in 1800, but rather had a very extensive historical tradition. When this factor is considered, one can detect Parker's debt to the New England rationalist tradition and his concerns of Antinominian dangers which were evident within transcendentalism. Primary sources; 33 notes. W. T. Walker III

3710. White, Robert. FIFTEEN YEARS OF CALVIN STUDIES IN FRENCH (1965-1980) *J. of Religious Hist. [Australia] 1982 12(2): 140-161.* A historiographical analysis of Calvin studies in French, 1965-80, indicates that works in French were fewer than those in German and English. However, major contributions have been advanced by Francois Wendel, Henri Meylan, Rodolphe Peter, Richard Stauffer, and Alexandre Ganoczy. Institutional support for Calvinist research has been provided by the Ecole Pratique des Hautes Etudes and the Societe de l'Histoire du Protestantisme Francais (Paris), the Institut d'Histoire de la Renaissance et de la Reforme (Liège), the Centre d'Histoire de la Reforme et du Protestatisne (Montpellier), and the Faculte de Theologie Protestante (Strasbourg). A historiographical essay based on secondary sources; 27 notes. W. T. Walker III

3711. Whittaker, David J. [LEONARD J. ARRINGTON: HIS LIFE AND WORK AND A BIBLIOGRAPHY]. *Dialogue 1978 11(4): 23-47.*
LEONARD JAMES ARRINGTON: HIS LIFE AND WORK, *pp. 23-32.* Uses the 20-year anniversary of the 1958 publication of Arrington's *Great Basin Kingdom* as opportunity to celebrate the personal and professional accomplishments of the church historian of the Church of the Latter Day Saints (Mormons). A Mormon by faith, and a historian trained at the University of North Carolina, Arrington personifies the new generation of Mormon historians who have integrated into Mormon studies a larger understanding of institutional, social, and economic developments in western history. Illus., list of six sources.
BIBLIOGRAPHY OF LEONARD JAMES ARRINGTON, *pp. 33-47.* Lists chronologically all work published by Arrington between the beginning of his career in 1935 and the present. For each year, writings are divided into the following categories:

articles in professional publications, articles in nonprofessional publications, reviews, books, addresses and duplicated papers, and monographs. C. B. Schulz

3712. Woolley, Paul. FAITH AND SCHOLARSHIP IN A CHRISTIAN STUDY OF HISTORY. *Fides et Hist. 1978 10(2): 70-75.* Review article on George Marsden and Frank Roberts, eds., *A Christian View of History?* (Grand Rapids: Eerdmans, 1975), noting the effort of Christian historians to balance the demands of faith and scholarship. 16 notes. R. E. Butchart

3713. Yardeni, Miriam. NEW CONCEPTS OF POST-COMMONWEALTH JEWISH HISTORY IN THE EARLY ENLIGHTENMENT: BAYLE AND BASNAGE. *European Studies Rev. [Great Britain] 1977 7(3): 245-258.* The new, secular concept of history in the early Enlightenment influenced Jewish historiography. This new approach is expressed in the works of two Frenchmen, Jacques Basnage (1653-1723) and Pierre Bayle (1647-1706). Both were French Protestants living in Holland who saw parallels to their religion in the historic persecution of the Jews. Basnage believed in God's choosing of the Jews, but focused his *Histoire des Juifs* on the secondary and rational causes of Jewish history. Bayle applied a rationalist and critical approach to the problem of hatred of the Jews. Bayle and Basnage shared Enlightenment rationalism with the Jews and showed Jewish history to be understandable in universal terms. 63 notes. J. L. White

3714. Yoder, John H. "ANABAPTISTS AND THE SWORD" REVISITED: SYSTEMATIC HISTORIOGRAPHY AND UNDOGMATIC NONRESISTANTS. *Zeitschrift für Kirchengeschichte [West Germany] 1974 85(2): 126-139.* Historians have too rigidly characterized the Anabaptists as apolitical.

3715. Zeman, Jarold Knox. ANABAPTISM: A REPLAY OF MEDIEVAL THEMES OR A PRELUDE TO THE MODERN AGE? *Mennonite Q. Rev. 1976 50(4): 259-271.* Discusses differing interpretations of Anabaptism. Some historians have approached it as a product of Erasmian humanism, a continuation of asceticism in the spirit of the Franciscan spiritualists, a product of mysticism, an expression of the scholastic tradition or of a popular deity. Others have seen it as an expression of apocalypticism, and yet others as a revolution and as an expression of sectarian dissent. These latter interpretations are discussed under the headings of personalism, pluralism, and egalitarianism, perceptions which more accurately assess Anabaptism's place in church history. 47 notes.
E. E. Eminhizer

3716. Zhukovskaia, N. L. IZUCHENIE LAMAIZMA V SSSR (1917-1976) [The study of lamaism in the USSR, 1917-76]. *Narody Azii i Afriki [USSR] 1977 (2): 187-196.* Traces Russian research on lamaism, the religion of three Siberian peoples, the Buryats, Kalmyks, and Tuvinians, from its beginnings in the 17th century. The most active periods of Soviet lamaist research were the 1920's and since the late 1950's. The 1920's was a period of reconstruction of the people's outlook following the revolution, and efforts were devoted to antireligious propaganda. The author mentions several scholarly works on lamaism published in that period. Since the 1950's, in addition to the continuing flow of antireligious materials, the Buryat branch of the Soviet Academy of Sciences' Siberian department has sponsored extensive research on the history and ideology of lamaism and the economic position of the monasteries and the lamas. 45 notes. L. Kalinowski

3717. Ziegler, P. Albert. ZWINGLI—EINE KATHOLISCHE AUFGABE, EIN ÖKUMENISCHES ANLIEGEN [Zwingli—a Catholic problem, an ecumenical request]. *Zwingliana [Switzerland] 1984 16(3): 201-216.* Surveying the research of Gottfried Locher, Oskar Vasella, Ulrich Gäbler, to name just the recent scholars of Zwingli, from the Catholic point of view, the reviewer concludes that Zwingli represents a historical problem because he was a pastor whose concern was nationalistic—as opposed to Luther who was an individualist monk—and a theological problem because of

his opposition to the papal-headed "universal" church. Zwingli still envisioned Christianity as universal, and here is his ecumenical request. 62 notes. D. R. Stevenson

3718. Zybkovets, V. F. PROBLEMA PROISKHOZHDENIIA RELIGII V SOVREMENNOI BURZHUAZNOI ISTORIOGRAFII [The origin of religion as reflected in contemporary bourgeois historiography]. *Voprosy Istorii [USSR] 1970 (10): 56-69.* Analyzes the crisis of the bourgeois science of religion caused by the progress of modern historical knowledge. The latest discoveries in paleoanthropology, paleoarchaeology, historical psychology, and other branches of scientific knowledge have completely demolished creationistic conceptions. That explains the attempts of bourgeois sociologists to construct new religious conceptions (entelechic, praetheistic, etc.) which are allegedly distinguished for more "elasticity" and do not come into direct conflict with science. All such attempts are futile, however, for the religious-mystical and the scientific world outlooks are incompatible. Shows that every new achievement of historical knowledge, which deepens and renders more precise scientific conceptions of the genesis of ideological phenomena, confirms the Marxist conception of religion as an historically transient phenomenon.

3719. —. [A CHRISTIAN FOCUS FOR HISTORICAL STUDY]. *Fides et Hist. 1981 14(1): 6-20.*
McIntire, C. T. THE FOCUS OF HISTORICAL STUDY: A CHRISTIAN VIEW, *pp. 6-17.* The fragmentation in contemporary historiography can be remedied by understanding all historical reality as the "ongoing response by all God's creatures to God's will in creation" and recognizing that the focus of human historical study is "temporal culturation, or culture-making as time process."
Miller, David. C. T. MCINTIRE'S *THE FOCUS OF HISTORICAL STUDY:* ANOTHER ANGLE OF VISION, *pp. 18-20.* McIntire's focus on history as enculturation views history as nothing more than human activity. 40 notes.
M. E. Quinlivan

3720. —. [EVANGELICALS AND THE AGE OF REFORM, 1870-1930]. *Fides et Historia 1984 16(2): 74-89.*
Mathisen, Robert. EVANGELICALS AND THE AGE OF REFORM, 1870-1930: AN ASSESSMENT, *pp.74-85.* Historians often neglect or understate the role of American evangelicals in promoting social reform between the Civil War and the Depression, and though they are largely in agreement upon the causes of the decline of evangelical social concern (prosperity, post-World War I malaise, disillusionment) they have been unable to agree upon a specific time referent for the decline.
Barlow, Jack. RESPONSE, *pp.86-89.* Takes issue with Mathisen's working definitions of "evangelical" and of "social gospel," and questions the propriety of speaking of the social postures of such disparate figures as Woodrow Wilson and William Jennings Bryan in similar terms. 54 notes. L. J. Howell

3721. —. [THE HISTORY DIVISION OF THE MORMON CHURCH]. *Dialogue 1983 16(3): 9-33.*
Bitton, Davis. TEN YEARS IN CAMELOT: A PERSONAL MEMOIR, *pp. 9-20.* Prints a personal history of the History Division of the Church of Jesus Christ of Latter-Day Saints, recollections of Mormon historians and historiography, and an overview of the reorganization of institutions related to Mormon church history.
Beecher, Maureen Ursenbach; Anderson, Kathleen H.; and Lilenquist, Debbie. HISTORY DIVISION PUBLICATIONS, *pp. 20-33.* Prints a bibliography of recent publications of members of the Mormon Church's History Division and of the Joseph Fielding Smith Institute of Church History. R. Grove

3722. —. ["MAMLEKHET KOHANIM" KESISMAH PERUSHIT] ["A Kingdom of Priests" as pharisaic slogan].
Schwartz, Daniel R. HISTORIA VEHISTORIOGRAFIA—"MAMLEKHET KOHANIM" KESISMAH PERUSHIT [History and historiography—"A kingdom of priests" as Pharisaic slogan]. *Zion [Israel] 1980 45(2): 96-117.* Reviews ancient sources for allusions to the verse from

Exodus, "You shall be unto Me a kingdom of priests" and finds that the text is rarely mentioned and virtually never given the democratic and universalist meaning often ascribed to it. In fact, leaders of 19th-century German and American Reform Judaism, centered in the Lehranstalt für die Wissenschaft des Judentums and Hebrew Union College, popularized the slogan and attributed it to the Pharisees in order to supply themselves with historical precedent and legitimization.

Meyer, Michael A. LEMAAMARO SHEL D. SCHWARTZ: "HISTORIA VEHISTORIOGRAFIA—'MAMLEKHET KOHANIM' KESISMAH PERUSHIT" [Concerning D. R. Schwartz's "History and Historiography—'A Kingdom of Priests' as Pharisaic Slogan"]. *Zion [Israel] 1981 46(1): 57-58.* The Exodus text was employed as a slogan more broadly than Schwartz allows, being found, for instance, in the works of Samson R. Hirsch and Nahman Krochmal.

Schwartz, Daniel R. TESHUVAH LEHEARAH [Rejoinder]. *Zion [Israel] 1981 46(1): 59-60.*   J. D. Sarna/S

3723. —. [PROBLEMS OF ANABAPTIST HISTORY: A SYMPOSIUM]. *Mennonite Q. Rev. 1979 53(3): 175-218.*
—. INTRODUCTION, p. 175.
Goertz, Hans-Jurgen. HISTORY AND THEOLOGY: A MAJOR PROBLEM OF ANABAPTIST RESEARCH TODAY, *pp. 177-188.* Discusses theology's influence on interpretations of Anabaptism's 16th-century origins, and the need to avoid coupling questions of contemporary relevance with historical fact, and recommends a thorough critique of Marxist-Leninist interpretations, particularly those of Gerhärd Zschäbitz and Claus-Peter Clasen. James M. Stayer's intellectual history, rather than social history offers the most competent challenge to traditional views of the Anabaptists. Theology must not be granted primacy in studying church history; instead, theology must "recognize the legitimate sphere of historical investigation." 30 notes.
Lindbergh, Carter. *FIDES ET INTELLECTUS EX AUDITU:* A RESPONSE TO HANS-JURGEN GOERTZ ON "HISTORY AND THEOLOGY," *pp. 189-192.* Disagrees with Goertz on present values affecting historical conclusions. Historians have commitments as do theologians, and are as involved in hermeneutics. Historical understanding must relate to the present. 6 notes.
Oyer, John S. GOERTZ'S "HISTORY AND THEOLOGY": A RESPONSE, *pp. 192-197.* Criticizes Goertz's methodological problems and encourages a variety of viewpoints based on canons of historical integrity. 19 notes.
Klassen, William. HISTORY AND THEOLOGY: SOME REFLECTIONS ON THE PRESENT STATUS OF ANABAPTIST STUDIES, *pp. 197-200.* Discusses historians of Anabaptism and welcomes questions on historians' involvements in their subjects' relevance to present issues.
Davis, Kenneth R. VISION AND REVISION IN ANABAPTIST HISTORIOGRAPHY: PERCEPTIONAL TENSIONS IN A BROADENING SYNTHESIS OR ALIEN IDEALIZATION?, *pp. 200-208.* Opposes separation of history and theology and advocates a larger synthesis recognizing each perception of historical reality.
Packull, Werner O. A RESPONSE TO "HISTORY AND THEOLOGY: A MAJOR PROBLEM OF ANABAPTIST RESEARCH TODAY," *pp. 208-211.* Points out that the many new perspectives result from the professionalization of Anabaptist history. 5 notes.
Stayer, James M. LET A HUNDRED FLOWERS BLOOM AND LET A HUNDRED SCHOOLS OF THOUGHT CONTEND, *pp. 211-218.* Outlines five schools of thought and hopes to avoid a consensus on "methodological atheism." 25 notes.
D. L. Schermerhorn

Science and Technology

3724. Abir-Am. Pnina. THEMES, GENRES, AND ORDERS OF LEGITIMATION IN THE CONSOLIDATION OF NEW SCIENTIFIC DISCIPLINES: DECONSTRUCTING THE HISTORIOGRAPHY OF MOLECULAR BIOLOGY. *History of Science [Great Britain] 1985 23(1): 73-117.* Contrary to reconstructionist scientific analysis, the development of the ultra-discipline of molecular biology was a conceptual innovation—a result of sociopolitical restructuring and dislocation of the traditional scientific order. Each of the four authors cited (Robert Olby; Edward Yoxen; Horace Judson, and H. Sajet) has interpreted past events in terms of later discoveries thus perpetuating "second-order legitimations" whereby the power of the scientific elite to shape the writing of scientific history is demonstrated. Secondary sources; 55 notes.
L. M. Newman

3725. Babkov, V. V. PERECHITYVAIA CHETVERIKOVA (POLVEKA EVOLIUTSIONNOI GENETIKI) [Rereading Chetverikov (a half century of evolutionary genetics)]. *Voprosy Filosofii [USSR] 1977 (1): 126-137.* Analyzes the methodological principles of S. S. Chetverikov, the outstanding Soviet geneticist, who initiated the synthesis of Darwin's theory of evolution and Mendel's genetics. Western geneticists relied mainly on methodological principles, making assumptions which greatly simplified the real pattern of the interaction of genes in a genome. Soviet geneticists, including Chetverikov, strove for the generalization of the data obtained by experimental genetics, as a result of biometric and mathematical studies of evolution and of naturalists' studies into the variability in natural populations. A considerable part of the article deals with problems of the history of science. The author describes S. S. Chetverikov's methods of organizing joint studies.   J

3726. Barone, Francesco. LA CONTEMPORANEA DISCUSSIONE METODOLOGICA E LA STORIOGRAFIA DELLA SCIENZA [Contemporary discussion of methodology and the historiography of science]. *Physis [Italy] 1980 22(2): 191-209.* In this century the problem of the relations between the history of science and the methodology of science has had two extreme solutions: the first, which was maintained by logical empiricists, conceives methodology as a normative discipline without any reference to the history of science; the second maintains, on the contrary, that the actual history of science destroys the very possibility of a methodology of science. Both solutions are unacceptable. In particular the contradiction within the second or "anarchist" solution is examined as well as the overstatements of its historical reconstructions. The kernel of the solution proposed here concerns a re-evaluation of some empiricists' tenets against the convulsive apriorism of the anarchists.   J

3727. Bates, George E., Jr. SEVENTEENTH-AND-EIGHTEENTH-CENTURY AMERICAN SCIENCE: A DIFFERENT PERSPECTIVE. *Eighteenth-Century Studies 1975 9(12): 178-192.* The Whig interpretation of the history of early American science errs in stressing the importance of the Copernican revolution. In spite of Newton's remarkable success with theories of matter in motion, Newton himself continued to consider science as an adjunct to theology. This dualistic conception of nature was more at home with the study of natural science and the divining of God's will than with theories of matter in motion in an autonomous universe. Those historians who stress an abrupt change to an essentially modern view in the 18th century are guilty of anachronism. 41 notes.
W. W. Elison

3728. Benvenuti, Giovanni. QUANDO LA DURATA DIVENTA STORIA [When the duration becomes history]. *Ponte [Italy] 1979 35(11-12): 1448-1454.* Traces the development of the study of natural history since the Enlightenment and reviews Giuliu Barsanti's *Dalla storia naturale alla storia della natura* (Milan: Feltrinelli, 1979) which focuses on the thought of Lamarck, the birth of biology as a legitimate science, and the growth of the historiography of science, 1790's-1820's.

3729. Boia, Lucian. CLIMATOLOGIA ISTORICĂ [Historical climatology]. *Rev. de Istorie [Romania] 1979 32(6): 1119-1130.* Traces the development of the historical study of climate from the speculations of Greek philosophers and historians to the more scientific researches of the last 20 years in Western Europe and the United States, particularly the important and influential works of Emmanuel LeRoy Ladurie. Methods used in various recent research include the gathering of general meteorological observations from chronicles, the examination of the more precise meteorological data gathered over the last two to three centuries, information gathering from the growth patterns of plants by examining historical agricultural procedures or the growth rings of trees, the study of glaciers and the study of pollen traces. The various conclusions of such studies are enumerated and the difficulty of correlating historical events with historical climate is stressed. 17 notes. French summary.

R. O. Khan

3730. Brožek, Josef. CONTEMPORARY EAST EUROPEAN HISTORIOGRAPHY OF PSYCHOLOGY. *Hist. of Sci. [Great Britain] 1977 15(4): 233-251.* Examines and evaluates recent work done in Czechoslovakia, Poland, Yugoslavia, and Romania on the history of psychology. Primarily covers work done in the 1960's and 1970's. Biblio. L. R. Maxted

3731. Brožek, Josef and Dazzi, Nino. CONTEMPORARY HISTORIOGRAPHY OF PSYCHOLOGY: ITALY. *J. of the Hist. of the Behavioral Sci. 1977 13(1): 33-40.* Discusses works in the historiography of psychology during the 1970's from Italy, dividing the works into five categories: original works, new editions, editions of classic science, readings, and translations.

3732. Brožek, Josef. CONTEMPORARY WEST EUROPEAN HISTORIOGRAPHY OF PSYCHOLOGY. *Hist. of Sci. [Great Britain] 1975 13(1): 29-60.* This bibliographical essay surveys contemporary (mostly 1960-) West European sources for the history of psychology using the following categories: French-speaking areas, German-speaking areas, Great Britain, Holland, Italy, and Scandinavia. Biblio. T. L. Underwood

3733. Brožek, Josef. THE PSYCHOLOGY AND PHYSIOLOGY OF BEHAVIOR: SOME RECENT SOVIET WRITINGS ON THEIR HISTORY. *Hist. of Sci. [Great Britain] 1971 10: 56-87.* A review of Soviet writings, 1960-71, on the history of the psychology and physiology of behavior. Soviet psychology is directed toward the study of consciousness while Soviet physiology is oriented toward the study of behavior and its mechanisms. Presents short reviews and descriptions of selected articles and books, and tries to tie each in with general trends in the USSR on this subject during the 11-year period considered. Primary sources; biblio.

L. R. Maxted

3734. Brožek, Josef. SOVIET HISTORIOGRAPHY OF PSYCHOLOGY. *J. of the Hist. of the Behavioral Sciences 1973 9(2): 152-161, (3): 213-216; 1974 10(2): 195-201, (3): 348-351.* Part I. SOURCES OF BIOGRAPHIC AND BIBLIOGRAPHIC INFORMATION. Discusses Soviet writings on the history of psychology and the Pavlovian behavior theory, 1917-71. Part II. CONTRIBUTIONS OF NON-RUSSIAN AUTHORS. Discusses the development of psychology in non-Slavic areas of the Soviet Union, 1917-57, emphasizing the contributions of P. M. Pelekh, G. S. Kostyuk, and V. M. Bekhterev. Part III. BETWEEN PHILOSOPHY AND HISTORY. Discusses the contributions to psychology since 1818 of theorists S. L. Rubinshtein, E. A. Budilova, A. V. Brushlinskii, and A. I. Karamyan. Part IV. HISTORY OF PSYCHOLOGY ABROAD. Discusses the writings of noted Soviet historiographers on foreign developments since 1881 in psychology and the history of psychology. S

3735. Bystritski, E. K. KONTSEPTSIIA PONIMANIIA V ISTORICHESKOI SHKOL'E FILOSOFII NAUKI [The notion of understanding in the historical school of the philosophy of science]. *Voprosy Filosofii [USSR] 1982 (11): 142-149.* Surveys the developments in the philosophic concept of understanding contemporary Western scientific thought, focusing on M. Polanyi, St. Toulmin, and K. Popper, whose post-positivist approach aligns them with the historical school of thought.

3736. Cantor, G. N. THE EIGHTEENTH CENTURY PROBLEM. *Hist. of Sci. [Great Britain] 1982 20(1): 44-63.* Reviews *The Ferment of Knowledge: Studies in the Historiography of Eighteenth Century Science,* edited by G. S. Rousseau and Roy Porter (1980).

This collection of 12 essays delineates the present state of scholarship and highlights some of the conflicting interpretations of 18th-century science. 13 notes. J. G. Packer

3737. Cantor, G. N. THE HISTORIOGRAPHY OF "GEORGIAN" OPTICS. *Hist. of Sci. [Great Britain] 1978 16(31): 1-21.* A review of recent and important elder writings on the development of physical optics in Great Britain from 1727 to 1830. Examines some of the prevalent historiographical assumptions, suggests various ways of approaching the subject, and presents questions about the conceptual development of optics in need of study. 32 notes, biblio. L. R. Maxted

3738. Cappelletti, Vicenzo. ATTUALITÀ DELLA STORIOGRAFIA SCIENTIFICA [Reality in scientific historiography]. *Physis [Italy] 1972 14(4): 395-406.* Examines the problems of scientific historiography, including the origins and evolution of science and the application of scientific principles and methods to the study of nature. Note. C. King

3739. Cardwell, Donald S. L. THE ACADEMIC STUDY OF THE HISTORY OF TECHNOLOGY. *Hist. of Sci. [Great Britain] 1968 7: 112-124.* Traces the links between the development of technology and the history of ideas, and shows the importance of the scientific revolution in the 17th century for technological developments in Europe.

3740. Caron, François. HISTOIRE TECHNIQUE ET HISTOIRE ÉCONOMIQUE [Technical history and economic history]. *Hist., Econ. et Soc. [France] 1983 2(1): 7-17.* Reviews historical questions posed by history of technology, particularly the relations between science, the state, and capitalism. The technical and research revolution of the post-World War II period makes an appreciation of these questions of renewed importance. Biblio. R. Aldrich

3741. Certeau, Michel de. L'HISTOIRE DANS UNE POLITIQUE DE LA SCIENCE [The place of history in science]. *Esprit [France] 1981 (10-11): 120-129.* Expresses thoughts on the relationship between science and fiction and the need for a politicization of the sciences and "historicization" of historiography.

3742. Cherniak, Vladimir Senenovich. OPYT STRUKTURNOGO ANALIZA ISTORII NAUKI; PO POVODU ISTORIOGRAFICHESKOI KONTSEPTSII DZH. KHOLTONA [An attempt at structural analysis of the history of science; the historiographical concept of G. Holton]. *Voprosy Filosofii [USSR] 1983 (2): 42-51.* The prerequisites for Gerald J. Holton's theory of science, e.g., the relationship between structural analysis and the dialectic method, belong to the framework of universal thought structures. 34 notes.

3743. Christie, J. R. R. and Golinski, J. V. THE SPREADING OF THE WORD: NEW DIRECTIONS IN THE HISTORIOGRAPHY OF CHEMISTRY 1600-1800. *Hist. of Sci. [Great Britain] 1982 20(4): 235-266.* An intrinsic historiography of the science of chemistry, emphasizing it as a didactic practice, involves analysis of the functions of chemical texts in their historical contexts. Owen Hannaway proposes the existence of a formal tradition underlying the development of chemistry as an academic discipline at the beginning of the 17th century. Examination of the works of Lémery shows the introduction of mechanistic rationalizations; John Freind relied on a geometric reductionist method, and Boerhaave in the mid-18th century conceived of chemistry as an "art." Joseph Priestly's study of air was an expression of his philosophical interests. Lavoisier's use of a new nomenclature was critical in its effect. Chemistry emerged as a process whose "interactive oppositions" included factors perpetuating its discipline and practice with a sense of its own identity, and other factors from outside the science which influenced its nature. Primary sources; 2 diagrams, 126 notes.

J. G. Packer

3744. Churchill, Frederick B. IN SEARCH OF THE NEW BIOLOGY: AN EPILOGUE. *J. of the Hist. of Biology [Netherlands] 1981 14(1): 177-191.* Places the scholarly dispute in a larger historiographic context, and urges that greater attention be directed to biology as inquiry: as a spectrum of biological institutions contributing to, facilitating, and together constituting the discipline.

D. K. Pickens/S

3745. Cohen, I. Bernard. [ESSAY REVIEW: THE HISTORY OF ELECTRICITY]. *Isis 1981 72(263): 480-489.* Reviews *Aepinus's Essay on the Theory of Electricity and Magnetism,* translated by P. J. Connor (1979); Willem D. Hackmann's *Electricity from Glass: The History of the Frictional Electrical Machine 1600-1850* (1978); and J. L. Heilbron's *Electricity in the 17th & 18th Centuries: A Study of Early Modern Physics* (1979). M. M. Vance

3746. Cohen, I. Bernard. THE MANY FACES OF THE HISTORY OF SCIENCE. Delzell, Charles F., ed. *The Future of History: Essays in the Vanderbilt University Centennial Symposium* (Nashville: Vanderbilt U. Pr., 1977): 65-110. Although the history of science has no apparent value to the pursuit of scientific investigation, its place is assured by the need to deal with the exotic scientific language of the past, as in Newton's *Principia.* Extensive review of the historiography points up the dearth of studies on the social history of science shown by two important examples: the development of the synthetic dyestuff industry, which had far-reaching effects on human society, and the tensions involved in the development of English medicine in conjunction with the Puritan revolution. Today there is a need for well-edited texts of original manuscripts and a further investigation of the relationship between science and government policy, a field initiated by Derek de Solla Price. The history of science is necessary to provide a complete view of man as well as an important tool of the scientific community. 112 notes.

P. L. Solodkin

3747. Coleman, William. [ESSAYS IN THE HISTORY OF ECOLOGY]. *Isis 1980 71(256): 150-152.* Frank N. Egerton's *History of American Ecology* (New York: Arno Pr., 1977), an anthology of nine essays, demonstrates the chaos of thought and terminology in the field of ecology and illuminates the problem of writing the history of such a diverse subject. M. M. Vance

3748. Crombie, Alistair C. HISTORIANS AND THE SCIENTIFIC REVOLUTION. *Physis [Italy] 1969 11(1-4): 167-180.* Voltaire was the first historian to treat the history of science as part of the history of civilization, in contrast to 19th-century historians who concentrated on political events. Predecessors who had attempted to include science in their histories were Tommaso Campanella (1568-1639), Francis Bacon (1561-1626), René Descartes (1596-1650), and their students. The present interest in social, intellectual, and scientific history is a return to the ideas of Voltaire. 34 notes.

S. Košak

3749. Crosland, Maurice. HISTORY OF SCIENCE IN A NATIONAL CONTEXT. *British J. for the Hist. of Sci. [Great Britain] 1977 10(35): 95-113.* Surveys the advantages and disadvantages of writing the history of science in a single country. Discusses the ability to focus upon the institutional context of science to understand its rate of progress, and the danger that scholars will glorify contributions from their nation. Scholars should study the history of science in a foreign country and compare it with their own. 34 notes.

F. N. Egerton

3750. Degler, Carl. CAN A HISTORIAN OR SOCIAL SCIENTIST LEARN ANYTHING FROM SOCIOBIOLOGY? AN ATTEMPT AT AN ANSWER. *Hist. Methods 1981 14(4): 173-179.* In reviewing the issues of sociobiology, the genetic basis of behavior, the author sees the human family as the structural or sociological equivalent to Edward O. Wilson's concept. It is, however, a very tentative suggestion. The answer might be contained in the differential sexuality of males and females. While not convinced of sociobiology's answers, the author notes that historians ask different questions about the human condition from the sociobiologists' inquiries, although both scholarly groups are concerned about the same human behavior. 10 notes. D. K. Pickens

3751. Demandt, Alexander. NATUR- UND GESCHICHTSWISSENSCHAFT IM 19. JAHRHUNDERT [Natural and historical science in the 19th century]. *Hist. Zeits. [West Germany] 1983 237(1): 37-66.* The ideas of history and nature were originally very close together. As historical sciences developed in the 19th century, historicism tended to isolate the study of history from the natural sciences. The influence of economics, biology, and positivistic social research challenged historicist attitudes. Various scientific approaches to the study of history focused on ideas of determinism, cycles, and progress. The separation of the natural sciences from humanistic influences created ethical problems. There are some trends in historical scholarship which seem to bring natural and historical sciences closer together. Based on original works of scientists and historians; 70 notes. G. H. Davis

3752. Dhombres, J. G. FRENCH TEXTBOOKS IN THE SCIENCES, 1750-1850. *History of Education [Great Britain] 1984 13(2): 153-162.* Historians of education tend to focus on institutional changes or on pedagogical ideas; historians of science generally prefer either to attack one scientific theme or to follow scientists' careers. Sociologists try to delineate scientific communities and their structure. The educational interplay between science as it is practiced and its popularization through teaching is often neglected. Studies this interplay by scrutinizing published scientific books, comparing the number and the quality of editions according to different scientific subjects, and drawing conclusions concerning the practical as well as the ideological role played by the sciences, 1750-1850. 4 tables. J. F. Harrington, Jr.

3753. Dupree, A. Hunter. DOES THE HISTORY OF TECHNOLOGY EXIST? *J. of Interdisciplinary Hist. 1981 11(4): 685-694.* Reviews volumes 6-7 of the *History of Technology* series, published together as *A History of Technology: The Twentieth Century, c. 1900 to c. 1950* (1979), edited by Trevor I. Williams. These volumes are a collection of histories of technological components as told by British participants in their development.

C. R. Gunter, Jr.

3754. Elkhadem, Hosam. L'HISTORIOGRAPHIE DES SCIENCES DU MOYEN AGE ISLAMIQUE CHEZ GEORGE SARTON [The historiography of science of the Islamic Middle Ages in the writings of George Sarton]. *Technologia [Belgium] 1984 7(3): 73-87.* Critically examines the outlines of the historiography of Muslim science in the Middle Ages in the writings of George Sarton. Sarton concluded that a history of science that ignores the oriental contribution is not only incomplete but also bound to be false. Evaluates this view and its relationship to previous and contemporary histories of medieval science in general, and Muslim science in particular. J/S

3755. Finocchiaro, M. A. A CROCEAN PHILOSOPHY OF THE HISTORIOGRAPHY OF SCIENCE. *Physis [Italy] 1976 18(3-4): 274-286.* J. Agassi's *Towards an Historiography of Science* (The Hague, 1963) was followed by M. A. Finocchiaro's *History of Science as Explanation* (Detroit, 1973). The author points out similarities and differences between the two, and concludes that his own approach is both positivist and idealist, and accords with the ideas of Benedetto Croce and Michael Scriven. 3 notes. S. Košak

3756. Finocchiaro, M. A. LOGIC AND SCHOLARSHIP IN KOYRÉ'S HISTORIOGRAPHY. *Physis [Italy] 1977 19(1-4): 5-27.* Analyzes the investigation by Alexandre Koyré of the arguments used by Galileo Galilei in his *Two Chief World Systems.* Koyré, in *Études galiléennes* [Galileo studies] (1966), wrongly estimated the value of Galileo's writing. Koyré used superficial logical analysis, and was guilty of exaggerations and questionable manipulation of texts. Correctly understood, Galileo's work exhibits a number of insights. Primary sources; 23 notes. E. E. Ryan

3757. Fores, Michael. TECHNICAL CHANGE AND THE "TECHNOLOGY" MYTH. *Scandinavian Econ. Hist. Rev. [Finland] 1982 30(3): 167-188.* Identifies the problem of classifying technical change. General historians, historians of technology, and economists, have all tended to make false distinctions between technological change deriving from empirical experiment with hardware and that deriving from pure science. All science is potentially applicable and the purest science is the most often applied. The main determinant of technical change is not science but skill. Hence the commonly argued view of the Industrial Revolution as characterized by the discontinuity between artisanal tinkering and specialized scientific imperatives is wrong. Based on secondary sources and the published works of Francis Bacon; 76 notes. M. C. Pugh

3758. Fox, Frank W. THE GENESIS OF AMERICAN TECHNOLOGY, 1790-1860: AN ESSAY IN LONG-RANGE PERSPECTIVE. *Am. Studies 1976 17(2): 29-48.* Surveys the historiography of early American technology, and examines the American inventive genius concept. The rapid collapse of a deferential order unleashed the spirit of innovation, particularly the rise of such ideas as individualism, egalitarianism, ambition, and open-endedness. Primary and secondary sources; 51 notes. J. Andrew

3759. Frandsen, K. E. HISTORISK GEOGRAFI [Historical geography]. *Hist. Tidsskrift [Denmark] 1978 78: 460-473.* Summarizes recent developments in historical geography in Great Britain, Germany, France, and Scandinavia, commenting on the most recent works on the subject, in particular: Alan R. H. Baker, ed., *Progress in historical Geography* (Newton Abbot: David and Charles, 1972); Alan Mayhew's *Rural Settlement and Farming in Germany* (London: Batsford, 1972); Martin Born's *Die Entwicklung der deutschen Agrarlandscaff;* Hans-Jürgen Nitz, ed., *Historisch-genetische Siedlungsforschung;* and Henry Clifford Darby, ed., *A new Historical Geography of England* (Cambridge: Cambridge U. Pr., 1973). M. A. Bott

3760. Gorokhov, V. G. METODOLOGICHESKIE PROBLEMY ISTORII I FILOSOFII NAUKI [Methodological problems of history and the philosophy of science]. *Voprosy Filosofii [USSR] 1982 (4): 129-135.* Examines the necessary link between history of science and philosophical-methodological approaches, warning it may lead to uncritically accepting certain "obvious" and therefore believable facts. Based on the works of J. Hacking, J. Sneed, and others; 14 notes.

3761. Greenaway, Frank. THE HISTORY OF SCIENCE AND THE SCIENCE OF HISTORY. *Pro. of the Royal Inst. of Great Britain [Great Britain] 1973 46: 99-115.* Examines various problems and perspectives in the study of the historical development of science and the relationship between the methodology of historians and scientists. Particular attention is devoted to the history of the philosophy of science. J. A. Casada

3762. Grigorian, A. T. and Kirsanov, V. S. ISSLEDOVANIIA PO ISTORII MEKHANIKI [Research into the history of mechanics]. *Voprosy Istorii Estestvoznaniia i Tekhniki [USSR] 1981 (2): 22-25.* The historian of mechanics must also be a social historian, sociologist, methodologist, and philosopher. This is made clear in the collection of monographs *Mekhanika i Tsivilizatsiia* [Mechanics and civilization] (1978), edited by A. T. Grigorian and B. G. Kuznetsov, which traces the historical cultural evolution of mechanics in the 17th-19th centuries. Another useful study of recent research into the history of mechanics is *Mekhanika i Fizika Vtoroy Poloviny XVIII V.* [Mechanics and physics of the late 18th century], edited by A. N. Bogoliubov, and *Mekhanika v SSSR* [Mechanics in the USSR] (1977), by A. T. Grigorian and B. N. Fradlinii. J. Bamber

3763. Grigorian, A. T. and Filatowa, L. A. SOWJETISCHE BEITRÄGE ZUR GESCHICHTE DER KLASSISCHEN MECHANIK [Soviet contributions to the history of classical mechanics]. *Archives Internationales d'Histoire des Sciences [Italy] 1983 33 (110): 118-125.* Surveys Soviet historiography dealing with the history of science in the area of mechanics from the 16th to the 18th centuries. Deals with editions of the works of scientists such as Copernicus, Galileo, von Huygens, and Newton, as well as with studies, including some on the philosophy of science. 28 ref.; biblio. R. Grove

3764. Hall, Diana Long and Glick, Thomas F. ENDOCRINOLOGY: A BRIEF INTRODUCTION. *J. of the Hist. of Biology [Netherlands] 1976 9(2): 229-233.* An introduction to

the issue's special section on endocrinology. Outlines the major controversies in the historiography of endocrinology. The major confusion turns on the fact that endocrinology is a field, not a discipline. It lacks common techniques and concepts. Social factors have also contributed to the varied scientific arguments. 2 tables, 4 notes. D. K. Pickens

3765. Hankins, Thomas L. SEEING THROUGH THE ENLIGHTENMENT. *Isis 1982 73(267): 274-279.* Reviews *The Ferment of Knowledge: Studies in the Historiography of Eighteenth Century Science* (1980), edited by G. S. Rousseau and Roy Porter, which demonstrates that historians of science are now in a position to play a leading role in the ongoing reinterpretation of the Enlightenment. M. M. Vance

3766. Heilbron, J. L. QUANTUM HISTORIOGRAPHY AND THE ARCHIVE FOR HISTORY OF QUANTUM PHYSICS. *Hist. of Sci. [Great Britain] 1968 7: 90-111.* Describes the historiography of the Quantum Theory in physics in Western Europe and the United States and lists such secondary sources as general treatises, biographies, autobiographies, and monographs.

3767. Hindle, Brooke. A RETROSPECTIVE VIEW OF SCIENCE, TECHNOLOGY, AND MATERIAL CULTURE IN EARLY AMERICAN HISTORY. *William and Mary Q. 1984 41(3): 422-435.* Reflections on the author's work as a fellow of the Institute of Early American History and Culture. Analyzes the development of the history of science, the history of technology, and early American material culture. Contribution to "Early American Emeriti: A Symposium of Experience and Evaluation." H. M. Ward/S

3768. Hofmann, Gustav. VÝVOJ, STAV A ÚKOLY NAŠÍ METROLOGIE [The development, condition, and tasks of Czechoslovak metrology]. *Archivní Časopis [Czechoslovakia] 1974 (4): 215-222.* In spite of the importance of research in economic history, Czechoslovak historians have nonetheless neglected the study of metrology as an auxiliary science. The author outlines the history of this science beginning in 1541, comments on the complicated system of measurements in the Habsburg Empire until the introduction of the metric system in 1871-75, and cites works on metrology. Primary sources; 44 notes. G. E. Pergl

3769. Hollinger, David A. [THE HISTORY OF SCIENCE AND JOSEPH NEEDHAM]. *Hist. & Theory 1976 15(1): 85-94.* Reviews *Changing Perspectives in the History of Science: Essays in Honour of Joseph Needham* (Dordrecht and Boston: D. Reidel, 1973), edited by Mikuláš Teich and Robert Young. These essays by students and admirers of Joseph Needham feature 11 essays on the historiography of science, eight essays on pseudoscientific developments and comparative studies in the history of science, and an interesting autobiographical sketch of Needham signed by his alterego, Henry Holorenshaw. 10 notes. D. A. Yanchisin

3770. Holmes, Frederic L. LAVOISIER AND KREBS: THE INDIVIDUAL SCIENTIST IN THE NEAR AND DEEPER PAST. *Isis 1984 75(276): 131-142.* In comparing the problems of writing the history of contemporary science to those of doing older science, the author discusses similarities and differences between the thought and methods of Antoine Lavoisier and those of Hans A. Krebs, whose work he has studied, partly through interviews. The opportunity to discuss his ideas with a contemporary subject has made him more critical of his inferences concerning subjects of the past who are unable to respond to them. Based primarily on personal experience; diagram, 11 notes. M. M. Vance

3771. Hounshell, David A. ON THE DISCIPLINE OF THE HISTORY OF AMERICAN TECHNOLOGY. *J. of Am. Hist. 1981 67(4): 854-865.* Although the history of technology, flourishing since 1958, is a new and healthy historical discipline it faces two serious challenges. The more immediate challenge is the technology historians' tendency toward introspection. The major challenge for these historians, however, is to produce a synthetic study of their scholarly work. An adequate synthesis of technology in American history would provide much-needed guidance for the field. 32 notes.   T. P. Linkfield

3772. Hughes, Thomas P. EMERGING THEMES IN THE HISTORY OF TECHNOLOGY. *Technology and Culture 1979 20(4): 697-711.* Since 1972 American historians of technology have tended away from the science-technology relationship as a major theme and toward invention, development, and innovation as the key to understanding technological change. At the same time general historians have begun to devote more attention to "the pervasive influence of technology in recent history." 32 notes.   C. O. Smith

3773. Jacob, Margaret. EARLY MODERN EUROPE: SCIENCE AND SOCIETY. *Trends in Hist. 1979 1(2): 30-39.* Surveys literature of the 1970's that pertains to science and its relation to 17th- and 18th-century Europe.

3774. James, Frank A. J. L. THE CREATION OF A VICTORIAN MYTH: THE HISTORIOGRAPHY OF SPECTROSCOPY. *History of Science [Great Britain] 1985 23(1): 1-24.* The view that Robert Bunsen and Gustav Kirchhoff's use of line spectra for chemical analysis (1859) was merely the culmination of many years of earlier investigations by others is not accurate since this interpretation is largely based on the writings of Victorian chemists who ignored the physical concerns which had originally driven spectroscopic studies. Based on primary sources; 107 notes.
L. M. Newman

3775. Jennings, Edward M. THE FERMENT OF KNOWLEDGE: THE HISTORIOGRAPHY OF EIGHTEENTH-CENTURY SCIENCE. *Eighteenth Cent.: Theory and Interpretation 1983 24(3): 244-256.* Reviews G. S. Rousseau and Roy Porter's *The Ferment of Knowledge: Studies in the Historiography of Eighteenth-Century Science* (1980). The first section deals with philosophy and principles of investigation, the second with revisionist-contextualist conceptualizations, and the third with case studies.
H. T. Blethen

3776. Jílek, František. ROZWÓJ BADAŃ NAD HISTORIĄ TECHNIKI W CZECHOSŁOWACJI [The development of the studies of the history of technology in Czechoslovakia]. *Kwartalnik Hist. Nauki i Techniki [Poland] 1982 27(1): 51-75.* Interest existed in the late 19th century, but writing the history of Czechoslovak technology had a later start than the collecting of technological artifacts. After long efforts by Josef Šusta, the Archive of the History of Industry, Trade, and Technical Works was founded as an autonomous part of the older Museum of Technology in Prague in 1932. Starting in the early 1950's, the Commission of the History of Technology, later the Association of the History of Sciences and Technology, a part of the Czechoslovak Academy of Sciences, came to the forefront of the study of technology. Translated from Czech. German and Russian summaries.   L. A. Krzyzak

3777. Judson, Horace Freeland. REFLECTIONS ON THE HISTORIOGRAPHY OF MOLECULAR BIOLOGY. *Minerva [Great Britain] 1980 18(3): 369-421.* With the view that the history of biology offers an overdue corrective to certain long-fashionable ideas based almost entirely on classic examples from the history of physics, the author discusses Rene J. Dubos's biography of the molecular biologist Oswald Avery, Erwin Chargaff's *Heraclitean Fire: Sketches from a Life before Nature,* and other histories dealing with molecular biology and biochemistry, and establishes the fundamental character of the change in thinking that marked the rise of molecular biology.

3778. Kevles, Daniel J. GENETICS IN THE UNITED STATES AND GREAT BRITAIN, 1890-1930: A REVIEW WITH SPECULATIONS. *Isis 1980 71(258): 441-455.* Historical studies published during the last 15 years have greatly expanded our understanding of the early development of genetics, but several important questions remain unanswered. This survey discusses both the contributions and the unanswered questions. Historical publications and manuscript sources; 43 notes.   M. M. Vance

3779. Kimura, Yojiro. KAEMPFER, THUNBERG AND SIEBOLD. *Japanese Studies in the Hist. of Sci. [Japan] 1976 15: 1-13.* Discusses the work of visiting naturalists Carl Peter Thunberg (1743-1828), E. Kaempfer, and Philipp Franz van Siebold (1796-1866), in Japanese botany, and lists Japanese studies on these men.

3780. Kohler, Robert E. THE HISTORY OF BIOCHEMISTRY: A SURVEY. *J. of the Hist. of Biology [Netherlands] 1975 8(2): 275-318.* In this historiographic review of current writings, the author maintains that the ideal historian of the discipline must combine the internal history of scientific discoveries with the external history of social systems and institutions. He supports the historical model of periods and generations, constructing the article around these concepts. 136 notes.   D. K. Pickens

3781. Kozlov, B. I. K ISTORII TEKHNIKI PODVODNYKH RABOT (OB ISSLEDOVANIIAKH R. A. ORBELI) [The history of underwater engineering: the research of R. A. Orbeli]. *Voprosy Istorii Estestvoznaniia i Tekhniki [USSR] 1982 (1): 28-35.* Describes the completion of the first Soviet scientific work on the world history of underwater engineering by R. A. Orbeli in 1942.   J

3782. Kragh, Helge. HISTORIOGRAPHY OF ELECTRONIC VALENCE THEORY. *Ann. of Sci. [Great Britain] 1983 40(3): 289-295.* Reviews A. N. Stranges's *Electrons and Valence. Development of the Theory, 1900-1925* (1982), which describes the role of the electron in valence theory from the experiments by J. J. Thompson to the birth of quantum physics. The book, although informative, fails to include explanatory and analytical aspects in recounting the development of this theory. It is too narrowly descriptive and does not include the views held by contemporary chemists.
D. Powell

3783. Kröber, Günter. NAUCHNO-TEKHNICHESKAIA REVOLIUTSIIA, NAUKA I OBSHCHESTVO [The scientific and technological revolution, science and society]. *Voprosy Filosofii [USSR] 1974 (3): 41-48.* From the standpoint of Marxist-Leninist theory, science is a social phenomenon, and its development can be explained only in connection with social development. In bourgeois philosophy, sociology, and the theory of science there prevail concepts which examine the development of science irrespective of the development of society or at best admit the influence of scientific progress on the progress of society. That is why in stating such empirical natural concomitants of the development of science (such as the growth of the number of scientific journals, the number of people employed in research, and the rise in the expenditure of science and research), bourgeois scholars are unable to separate the essential from the nonessential and to formulate the main factors of the development of science and their corollary. The question of the increasing role of science is a corollary of fundamental qualitative change in the relationship of science and society and science and production. The specific laws governing the development of science are mainly laws of the interaction of science with other spheres of social life, above all with material production.   J/S

3784. Laver, A. Bryan. THE HISTORIOGRAPHY OF PSYCHOLOGY IN CANADA. *J. of the Hist. of the Behavioral Sci. 1977 13(3): 243-251.* Brief but comprehensive in scope, the author covers everything from history programs, undergraduate and graduate, to recent surveys and publishing outlets. 36 notes.
D. K. Pickens

3785. Lavers, Annette. FOR A "COMMITTED" HISTORY OF SCIENCE. *Hist. of Sci. [Great Britain] 1970 9: 101-105.* Examines the scientists, research questions and methods with which the historiography is concerned; considers its relations with history, science and philosophy. Concludes that "the history of science cannot but be philosophical; and it cannot be philosophical without being conscious of contemporary human realities, or, as it used to be called, 'committed.'"   L. R. Maxted

3786. Littman, Richard A. PSYCHOLOGY'S HISTORIES: SOME NEW ONES AND A BIT ABOUT THEIR PREDECESSORS—AN ESSAY REVIEW. *J. of the Hist. of the*

Behavioral Sci. 1981 17(4): 516-532. Reviews six books on the history of psychology written by psychologists, and provides a brief history of histories of psychology since Aristotle. J. Powell

3787. López Sánchez, José. PANORAMA DE LA CIENCIA EN CUBA AL COMIENZO DE LA GUERRA DE LOS DIEZ AÑOS [A panorama of science in Cuba at the beginning of the Ten Years War]. *R. de la Biblioteca Nacional José Martí [Cuba] 1968 10(3): 105-138.* A historiographical review of the writings of 19th-century Cuban scientists encompassing all branches of science. Primary sources; biblio. M. W. Szewczyk

3788. Lumpkin, Beatrice. HISTORY OF MATHEMATICS IN THE AGE OF IMPERIALISM. *Sci. and Soc. 1978 42(2): 178-184.* Historians of mathematics influenced by European-centered imperialist ideas of the late 19th and early 20th centuries negated the important contributions of Africans and Asians to the evolution of mathematical thought. Recent historiographical research has uncovered significant contributions to theoretical mathematical development made by the ancient Egyptians and Mesopotamians as well as by the Moslems during the medieval period. A new historiography of mathematics must be constructed embodying within it the contributions of non-Europeans and of women in their proper important relationship to the evolution of the discipline. Secondary sources. N. Lederer

3789. Marx, Otto M. HISTORY OF PSYCHOLOGY: A REVIEW OF THE LAST DECADE. *J. of the Hist. of the Behavioral Sci. 1977 13(1): 41-47.* Examines the range of opinion and critical analysis displayed in articles published in the *Journal of the History of the Behavioral Sciences,* 1967-77, as it relates to historiography in psychology.

3790. May, Kenneth O. MATHEMATICS IN RUSSIA. *Hist. of Sci. [Great Britain] 1971 10: 122-127.* Justifies national histories of mathematics such as A. P. Yushkevich's *Istoriya Matematiki v Rossii do 1917 goda* [History of mathematics in Russia to 1917] (1968). Cultural influences and the nationalistic support given to mathematics make such historiography necessary, their current disrepute notwithstanding. Mainly secondary sources; 6 notes. L. R. Maxted

3791. Mayr, Otto. THE SCIENCE-TECHNOLOGY RELATIONSHIP AS A HISTORIOGRAPHIC PROBLEM. *Technology and Culture 1976 17(4): 663-673.* "Attempts to construct permanent and universal definitions" of science and technology are futile. The historian should seek "not to discover what the science-technology relationship actually has been in history but what previous eras and cultures have thought it to be." 9 notes. C. O. Smith

3792. McCartney, Paul J. CHARLES LYELL AND G. B. BROCCHI: A STUDY IN COMPARATIVE HISTORIOGRAPHY. *British J. for the Hist. of Sci. [Great Britain] 1976 9(32): 175-189.* Both Giovanni Battista Brocchi's (1772-1826) *Conchiologia Fossile Subappennina* (2 vols., 1814) and Charles Lyell's (1797-1875) *Principles of Geology* (3 vols., 1830-33) have extensive historical introductions which bolstered the theoretical positions of their works. Although Brocchi's adherence to Abraham Gottlob Werner's (1750-1817) theory of the earth was incompatible with Lyell's uniformitarianism, Lyell nevertheless relied heavily upon Brocchi's historical discussion when discussing early Italian contributions to paleontology. The author discusses Lyell's distortion of Brocchi's information. Primary and secondary sources; 51 notes. F. N. Egerton

3793. Mikulinski, S. R. MNIMYE KONTRAVERZY I REAL'NYE PROBLEMY TEORII RAZVITIIA NAUKI [Imaginary controversies and real problems of the theory of development of science]. *Voprosy Filosofii [USSR] 1977(11): 88-104.* Shows the essence of major methodological trends in the analysis of the development of science, and proves the untenability of internalism and externalism. Neither internalism, nor externalism can provide a theoretical basis for studies of the history of science. There cannot be any choice between them like there is no alternative between vitalism and mechanism. An attempt to synthesize them cannot be fruit-

ful either. Therefore, the author classes internalism-externalism controversy, which has been regarded for about half a century as the main methodology of the historiography of science, as an imaginary problem. The author sees the way out of this situation in the rejection of these theoretical structures and in the elaboration of a theory of the development of science on the basis of the Marxist teaching of science. The author formulates the basic principles of such a theory and analyzing the history of the creation of Charles Darwin's theory of evolution, suggests a concrete way of reconstructing the genesis of a scientific theory. J

3794. Minchinton, W. E. EARLY TIDE MILLS: SOME PROBLEMS. *Technology and Culture 1979 20(4): 777-786.* A survey of the literature on when, where, and for what purposes tide mills were employed in the Middle Ages reveals wide differences of opinion among scholars. But it does show that this innovation was a significant aspect of the medieval drive to harness available sources of power. 2 illus., 40 notes. C. O. Smith

3795. Molodshi, V. N. "MATEMATICHESKIE RUKOPISI" K. MARKSA I RAZVITIE ISTORII MATEMATIKI V SSSR ["Mathematical manuscripts" of Karl Marx and the development of the history of mathematics in the USSR]. *Voprosy Istorii Estestvoznaniia i Tekhniki [USSR] 1983 (2): 29-34.* Considers the main trends in the studies of Soviet historians of mathematics in relation to the ideas expressed in the "mathematical manuscripts" of Marx. J

3796. Murata, Tamotsu. L'ÉTAT ACTUEL DES RECHERCHES EN HISTOIRE DES MATHÉMATIQUES AU JAPON [The present state of research into the history of mathematics in Japan]. *Japanese Studies in the Hist. of Sci. [Japan] 1976 15: 21-36.* Examines the development of mathematics in Japan, 1872-1976, and provides a bibliography and a review of works on the history of mathematics which have been published in Japanese, 1937-76. Also examines the current state of research into the history of mathematics in Japan.

3797. Murata, Tamotsu. SOME PHILOSOPHICAL ASPECTS OF THE HISTORIOGRAPHY OF MATHEMATICS. *XIVth International Congress of the History of Science, Proceedings No. 4* (Tokyo and Kyoto: Science Council of Japan, 1975): 187-199. Due to the radically changed nature of mathematics in the 20th century, a history of modern mathematics needs to be written.

3798. Myllyntaus, Timo. TEKNOLOGIAN HISTORIA TIETEENALANA [The history of technology as a field of scholarship]. *Hist. Aikakauskirja [Finland] 1984 82(1): 56-62.* Describes the development of the study of the history of technology in Europe and North America during the 1900's. The three major approaches are traditional engineering, economic history, and industrial archaeology. All of these have been criticized, and the field as a whole lacks a distinct methodology and body of theory. It will nevertheless become an increasingly important area of research. Based on European and American monographs; 29 notes. R. G. Selleck

3799. Nakayama, Shigeru. EXTERNALIST APPROACH OF JAPANESE HISTORIANS OF SCIENCE. *Japanese Studies in the Hist. of Sci. [Japan] 1972 (11): 1-10.* Reviews the development of the Marxist approach to the history of science in Japan from the 1920's, when Ogura Kinnosuke, the first president of Minshu-shugi Kagakusha Kyokai [Society of Democratic Scientists] and the second president of the History of Science Society of Japan, described Japanese science as being an imported product, imitative and superficial, and lacking a social conscience. Based on a Festschrift for Professor D. Struik to be published in the Boston Studies in the Philosophy of Science; 11 notes. M. Elmslie

3800. Nowak, Tadeusz Marian. STAN BADAŃ NAD HISTORIĄ TECHNIKI W POLSCE [The state of the studies of the history of technology in Poland]. *Kwartalnik Hist. Nauki i Techniki [Poland] 1982 27(1): 91-106.* 97 notes. Russian and German summaries.

3801. Nye, Mary Jo. SCIENTIFIC DECLINE: IS QUANTITATIVE EVALUATION ENOUGH? *Isis 1984 75(279): 697-708.* Examines the frequently expressed contention that French science "declined" after the early 19th century, and concludes that it is impossible to determine whether science declined in France or simply advanced in other countries. Reasons for the complexity of this question and some studies that might contribute to its resolution are discussed. 44 notes. M. M. Vance

3802. Oldroyd, David R. BY GRID AND GROUP DIVIDED: BUCKLAND AND THE ENGLISH GEOLOGICAL COMMUNITY IN THE EARLY NINETEENTH CENTURY. *Annals of Science [Great Britain] 1984 41(4): 383-393.* Reviews Nicholaas A. Rupke's *The Great Chain of History: William Buckland and the English School of Geology (1814-1849)* (1983) and Martin Rudwick's "Cognitive Styles in Geology" in *Essays in the Sociology of Perception* (1982) edited by M. Douglas. Checks the results of Rudwick's use of "grid/group" analysis on the early 19th-century British geological community, including William Buckland, against Rupke's portrayal of the latter as an intelligent, open-minded, and not necessarily catastrophist exponent of the English school of geology. 2 fig., 48 notes. B. Rivers

3803. Onuma, Masanori and Doke, Tatsumasa. RECENT STUDIES IN JAPAN ON THE HISTORY OF CHEMISTRY. *Japanese Studies in the Hist. of Sci. [Japan] 1973 12: 5-14.* Reviews Japanese studies on the history of chemistry, 1965-72, and discusses scholars' views on chemistry teaching in Japan, government policy on science and technology, and environmental pollution by chemicals and the chemical industry.

3804. Pahaut, Serge and Stengers, Isabelle. LA DECOUVERTE DES HORIZONS TEMPORELS PAR LA PHYSIQUE POSE-T-ELLE UNE QUESTION A L'HISTOIRE? [Can the discovery of temporal horizons through physics investigate history?]. *Cahiers de Clio [Belgium] 1981 (67): 48-52.* A study of the temporality of physics on the basis of the discoveries in chemistry of 1977 Belgian Nobel laureate Ilya Prigogine.

3805. Pelet, Paul-Louis. L'HISTOIRE DES TECHNIQUES AVANT LA REVOLUTION INDUSTRIELLE [The history of technology before the industrial revolution]. *Schweizerische Zeits. für Gesch. [Switzerland] 1982 32(2): 324-337.* The history of technology has become so scientifically exacting since the industrial revolution as to demand scientists or engineers for its writing. For earlier times professional historians are better suited, since the research is centered on old documents. Yet written sources are scarce, and remnants of old tools and machines are at best a partial remedy. Scientific and technological treatises are the most important guides. Difficulties arise over the meaning of terms, which change from province to province, dates of inventions that cannot be fixed, and the fact that old and new lived side by side. A humanistic history of technology realizes that a simple hierarchy of efficiency that does not take into account the adaptation of means to the needs of the society under study gives a misleading measurement of civilization. 23 notes; biblio. H. K. Meier

3806. Pomian, Krzysztof. L'HISTOIRE DE LA SCIENCE ET L'HISTOIRE DE L'HISTOIRE [The history of science and the history of history]. *Ann.: Écon., Soc., Civilisations [France] 1975 30(5): 935-952.* Study of parallels between the history of science and the history of history. The change in the nature of history in the 16th and 17th centuries is seen as parallel to the changes occurring in science. In science, direct knowledge was replaced by mediate knowledge; the growing critique of sources and the methods for employing them was the corresponding historical development. Bibliographical note. R. Howell

3807. Porter, Glenn. TECHNOLOGY AND BUSINESS IN THE AMERICAN ECONOMY. Frese, Joseph R. and Judd, Jacob, ed. *An Emerging Independent American Economy 1815-1875* (Tarrytown, N.Y.: Sleepy Hollow Pr., 1980): 1-28. A history of the role of business and technology in the rise of American capitalism. Covers the impotence of government in affecting business trends and decisions and the importance of European ideas and money in tech

nological innovation. The majority of inventions and advancements of the early years came from outside the firm. Entrepreneurs tended to be generalists. Covers the writing of histories of technology and business, the gulfs between the two and between the activities they studied, and remarks that only in recent years have effective steps been taken to bridge these gaps. 26 notes. V. L. Human

3808. Price, Michael H. MATHEMATICS IN ENGLISH EDUCATION 1860-1914: SOME QUESTIONS AND EXPLANATIONS IN CURRICULUM HISTORY. *Hist. of Educ. [Great Britain] 1983 12(4): 271-284.* Discusses mathematics curriculum historiography in two major areas: who should benefit from the study of mathematics and the causes of changes in curricula and the forces of resistance. Discusses liberal secondary education preceding any form of specialization in mathematics, such as for preparation for university. Fig., 72 notes. J. F. Harrington

3809. Prillinger, Ferdinand. GESCHICHTE DER GEOGRAPHIE [History of geography]. *Österreich in Geschichte und Literatur [Austria] 1969 13(1): 38-46.* The history of geography must include the study of geographic discoveries and research, the discipline itself, the teaching of geography, and the history of territories.

3810. Pursell, Carroll W., Jr. THE HISTORY OF TECHNOLOGY AND THE STUDY OF MATERIAL CULTURE. *Am. Q. 1983 35(3): 304-315.* A bibliographic survey of the historiography of US technology and its relation to material culture. This data can also be used to explore nonmaterial aspects of the culture. 38 notes. R. Grove

3811. Rabb, Theodore K. THE HISTORIAN AND THE CLIMATOLOGIST. *J. of Interdisciplinary Hist. 1980 10(4): 831-837.* Discusses the implications for interdisciplinary work between historians and climatologists suggested by the papers in this volume. Physical scientists are able to contribute climatic data to historians, though the latter may have problems relating this data to historical concerns. The time scale of much climatological data is irrelevant to the historian. Nevertheless, significant advances can be made if both historians and climatologists genuinely collaborate rather than simply supply information to one another. This presupposes agreement about the context, aims, and methods of research. Note. J. Powell

3812. Rapp, Friedrich. STRUCTURAL MODELS IN HISTORICAL WRITING: THE DETERMINATION OF TECHNOLOGICAL DEVELOPMENT DURING THE INDUSTRIAL REVOLUTION. *Hist. and Theory 1982 21(3): 327-346.* Investigates the largely implicit theoretical parameters of historical writing by using study of proposed determinants of the technological developments in the 18th- and 19th-century West. Different disciplines imply that the topic will be approached from different angles and with focuses on different aspects and causal explanations. The literature in the area reveals nine conceptual models and the "internalist" historiography of technology tends to concentrate on five factors. Becoming aware of these theoretical priorities does not vitiate the primacy of the factual data relating to the subject but makes the variety of accounts less incommensurable and more evident and complementary. 31 notes. W. J. Reedy

3813. Ravindra, R. EXPERIMENT AND EXPERIENCE: A CRITIQUE OF MODERN SCIENTIFIC KNOWING. *Dalhousie Rev. [Canada] 1975/76 55(4): 655-674.* Examines scientific inquiry and its techniques as applied to history and the study of man. Presented at the World Philosophy Conference in New Delhi, December 1975. 23 notes. C. Held

3814. Redondi, Pietro. NOTE CRITIQUE: LES TENSIONS ACTUELLES DE L'HISTOIRE DES SCIENCES [A critical note: current tensions in the history of science]. *Ann.: Écon., Soc., Civilisations [France] 1981 36(4): 572-590.* Reviews Thomas S. Kuhn's *Essential Tension: Selected Studies in Scientific Tradition and Change* (1977), a sequel to and reformulation of ideas contained in his *Structure of Scientific Revolutions,* and comments on the development in Kuhn's mind of his concepts of a scientific community, paradigms, and the incommensurability of different scientific theories. 3 notes, biblio.   J. V. Coutinho

3815. Reingold, Nathan. CLIO AS PHYSICIST AND MACHINIST. *Rev. in Am. Hist.* 1982 10(4): 264-280. Discusses the growth of studies in American science, technology, and medicine in the larger context of general American history and the history of science.

3816. Richards, Robert J. WHY DARWIN DELAYED, OR INTERESTING PROBLEMS AND MODELS IN THE HISTORY OF SCIENCE. *J. of the Hist. of the Behavioral Sci.* 1983 19(1): 45-53. Though Darwin had formulated his theory of evolution by natural selection by early fall of 1837, he did not publish it until 1859 in the *Origin of Species*. Darwin thus delayed publicly revealing his theory for some twenty years. Why did he wait so long? Initially this may not seem an important or interesting question, but many historians have so regarded it. They have developed a variety of historiographically different explanations. This essay considers these several explanations, though with a larger purpose in mind: to suggest what makes for interesting problems in history of science and what kinds of historiographic models will best handle them.
                                                                      J

3817. Rousseau, Philip. STRUCTURE AND EVENT IN ANTHROPOLOGY AND HISTORY. *New Zealand J. of Hist.* [New Zealand] 1975 9(1): 22-40. Historians can learn about their discipline by examining the methods and discoveries of anthropology. The author illustrates the argument by drawing on examples from the works of Malinowski, Radcliffe-Brown, Evans-Pritchard, and Lévi-Strauss. Based on anthropological and historical studies, especially by the authors named.   P. J. Coleman

3818. Rudwick, M. J. S. THE GLACIAL THEORY. *Hist. of Sci.* [Great Britain] 1969 8: 136-157. Reviews a new edition of Louis Agassiz's (1807-73) *Studies on Glaciers* and Albert V. Carozzi's edition of Agassiz's *Discourse of Neuchâtel* (New York: Hafner, 1967), and summarizes the controversy in mid-19th century historiography about glacial and diluvial theories. Describes the key personalities and writings in the debate.

3819. Sandler, Iris. SOME REFLECTIONS ON THE PROTEAN NATURE OF THE SCIENTIFIC PRECURSOR. *Hist. of Sci.* [Great Britain] 1979 17(3): 170-190. Historians of science who have attempted to identify scientific precursors—individuals whose scientific activities were used by later scientists such as Charles Darwin in constructing major theories—have often been guilty of studying the precursor's achievement with reference to the present.

3820. Schaffer, Simon. PRIESTLEY'S QUESTIONS: AN HISTORIOGRAPHIC SURVEY. *Hist. of Sci.* [Great Britain] 1984 22(2): 151-183. Historians need to break out of a somewhat restricted model of Joseph Priestley's questions, a historiography legitimated by sources in his texts. Historiography that stays at the level of matter theory and metaphysics can be enriched by attention to the social practices of Priestley and his colleagues, and the varying interests at play with such groups. Historians have concentrated on his dispute with Lavoisier as the self-evident goal of their interpretation of Priestley's chemistry, and defined that chemistry and its community using the French group as a standard of comparison. However, it is important to reject an account that adopts a teleology directed exclusively toward his failure to see the significance of developments in French chemistry. Priestley connected assent to political and religious authority with assent to matters of fact, and his concern for divisive allegiance characterizes most of the historiography devoted to his thought style, and, in fact, is its most instructive aspect. Primary sources; 101 notes.   J. G. Packer

3821. Schiller, Brent. TECHNOLOGY—HISTORY—SOCIAL CHANGE: A METHODOLOGICAL COMMENT AND AN OUTLINE OF A NORDIC ACCOUNT. *Scandinavian J. of Hist.* [Sweden] 1983 8(2): 71-82. Interprets the history of technology as a broad topic requiring a methodology that accounts for the relationship of technology to all aspects of society. In the past, most studies in the history of technology, in both international and Nordic contexts, have failed to include aspects of social change. Such disciplines as economic history, history, and sociology have their own preoccupations which discourage an understanding of the history of technology as an independent discipline. This field of study will improve only with a more interdisciplinary focus on theory and synthesis. Based on secondary sources; 31 notes.   B. Stenslie

3822. Shtokalo, I. Z. and Anisimov, Iu. A. ISTORIKO-NAUCHNYE ISSLEDOVANIIA V UKRAINSKOI SSR [Research on the history of science in the Ukrainian SSR]. *Voprosy Istorii Estestvoznaniia i Tekhniki* [USSR] 1982 (4): 10-15. The study of the history of the natural sciences and technology began to develop in the Ukraine on a wide scale at the end of the 1940's and beginning of the 1950's when relevant departments were set up under the leadership of V. V. Danilevski and I. Z. Shtokalo. The establishment of the Ukrainian section of the Soviet Association of the History and Philosophy of Natural Sciences and Technology in 1958 gave a further impetus to research. The regularly published collection of essays on the history of science also plays an important role in stimulating scholarly work. Secondary sources.   G. Dombrovski

3823. Sörbom, Per. OM SPRIDNING AV SPRIDNINGSTEORIER: EXEMPLET KOMPASSEN [The diffusion of diffusion theories: e.g. the compass]. *Lychnos* [Sweden] 1984: 27-65. Although the mariner's compass was known for over a century in China before it appeared in the Western nations, there is in fact no evidence that it spread from China to the West via India and the Islamic world. Traces the history of diffusion theories about the compass and reflects on the fact that diffusionism remained respectable among historians long after others, e.g. anthropologists, discredited it. 169 notes. English summary.   R. Grove

3824. Staudenmaier, John M. WHAT SHOT HATH WROUGHT AND WHAT SHOT HATH NOT: REFLECTIONS ON TWENTY-FIVE YEARS OF THE HISTORY OF TECHNOLOGY. *Technology and Culture* 1984 25(4): 707-730. In three thematic areas, the articles published in *Technology and Culture* since 1958 show that the Society for the History of Technology has "developed a new language about technological change which is . . . liberated from the excesses so often found in progress talk." Yet signs of Whiggery still abound, while too little attention has been given to technical failures, the workers' perspective, cultural conflict in technology transfer, non-Western technologies, critical interpretation of Western capitalism, and the perspectives of women.
                                                                      C. O. Smith

3825. Stout, Harry S. and Taylor, Robert. SOCIOLOGY, RELIGION, AND HISTORIANS REVISITED: TOWARDS AN HISTORICAL SOCIOLOGY OF RELIGION. *Historical Methods Newsletter* 1974 8(1): 29-38. Discusses Robert W. Doherty's "Sociology, Religion and Historians". Stout and Taylor urge that, unlike Doherty's model, historians use both substantive and functional analysis. This mode of scholarship can be furthered by creating intellectual and social typologies which can be correlated and empirically validated with one another.
                                                                      D. K. Pickens

3826. Suzuki, Zenji. RECENT STUDIES IN THE HISTORY OF BIOLOGY BY JAPANESE HISTORIANS. *Japanese Studies in the Hist. of Sci.* [Japan] 1972 (11): 11-21. Reviews the 89 Japanese journal articles, 1965-72, on the history of biology, mainly from the *Seibutsugakushi Kenkyu* [Japanese Journal of the History of Biology], *Kagakushi Kenkyu* [Journal of the History of Science], and *Japanese Studies in the History of Science*.   M. Elmslie

3827. Swinton, W. E. HISTORICAL INTERRELATIONS OF GEOLOGY AND OTHER SCIENCES. *J. of the Hist. of Ideas* 1975 36(4): 729-738. Surveys and criticizes historical literature bearing upon geology. The standard general works are now old and, in the view of current researchers, unsophisticated. "The periods of assimilation and gestation are nearing their end," and new works are beginning to appear.   D. B. Marti

3828. Thackray, Arnold. HISTORY OF SCIENCE IN THE 1980S: SCIENCE, TECHNOLOGY, AND MEDICINE. *J. of Interdisciplinary Hist. 1981 21(2): 299-314.* The history of science has been affected by the changes in the demography of the historical profession, the employment situation, and the transformation of tools. The redefinition of science in the last decade has carried with it also a different historical awareness. The interdisciplinary nature of the field and a new emphasis on science in its social and cultural setting is going to have an enduring impact on the history of science. Historians of science are turning toward questions like the social dimensions of scientific thought, the politics of knowledge, or the institutions of science. Secondary sources; 21 notes.

H. J. Kaiser

3829. Urusov, V. S. OSNOVNYE ETAPY RAZVITIIA I VZAIMODEISTVIIA IDEI GEOKHIMII I KRISTALLOKHIMII [Stages of development and interaction of geochemistry and crystallography]. *Voprosy Istorii Estestvoznaniia i Tekhniki [USSR] 1984 (1): 63-70.* Considers the historiographical problem of the interaction of geochemistry and crystallography in connection with the works of A. E. Fersman. Two main stages in the development of these sciences are outlined. The first stage is the period of accumulation of empirical facts and the establishment of empirical rules; the second stage is the formulation of theories and laws. Analyzes the transition from the first stage to the second.

J/S

3830. Uselding, Paul. STUDIES OF TECHNOLOGY IN ECONOMIC HISTORY. *Res. in Econ. Hist. 1977 (supplement 1): 159-219.* Reviews the significant literary sources in the field of technology and its role in American economic history. Covers the original work of H. J. Habakkuk on why Americans developed a mechanical technology and the British did not, leading to the American system of mechanical frontierism; the transfer and diffusion of technological ideas and innovations; issues of techniques choice, productivity standards, and the role of learning effects in technological development. The literature is more than quantitatively adequate, but certain areas have perhaps been overstudied, and others not studied at all. Covers ca. 1600-1970's. 120 notes, ref.

V. L. Human

3831. Vecchio, Bruno. GEOGRAFIA E STORIA [Geography and history]. *Studi Storici [Italy] 1982 23(4): 919-923.* The traditional geographic monograph is in crisis. Despite attempts to update it, geographers tend to abandon it, realizing the multiplicity of processes that affect a given territory; it is impossible for a single scholar to master all of them. Attention is more focused on single processes in an interdisciplinary approach, which treats a place as a privileged observation ground for a number of significant dynamisms, refusing all deterministic or tautological explanations. 6 notes.

J. V. Coutinho

3832. Wächtler, Eberhard. METHODISCHE PROBLEME DER DARSTELLUNG DER ENTWICKLUNG DER TECHNIK IN DER HISTORIOGRAPHIE DER NEUESTEN ZEIT [Methodological problems in the representation of the development of technology in the historiography of recent times]. *XIVth International Congress of the History of Science, Proceedings No. 3* (Tokyo and Kyoto: Science Council of Japan, 1975): 197-200. Discusses methodological problems in the representation of technological development in the historiography of recent years from a Marxist perspective, with the mining industry as an example.

3833. Wettersten, John R. THE HISTORIOGRAPHY OF SCIENTIFIC PSYCHOLOGY: A CRITICAL STUDY. *J. of the Hist. of the Behavioral Sci. 1975 11(2): 157-171.* Surveys the important historiographical contributions to scientific psychology, 1820-1974.

3834. Weyant, Robert G. [EIGHTEENTH-CENTURY SCIENCE]. *J. of the Hist. of the Behavioral Sci. 1983 19(3): 226-233.* Reviews *The Ferment of Knowledge: Studies in the Historiography of Eighteenth-Century Science* (1980), a collection of papers edited by G. S. Rousseau and Roy Porter.

3835. Weyer, Jost. CHEMIEGESCHICHTSSCHREIBUNG IM 19. UND 20. JAHRHUNDERT [Historiography of chemistry in the 19th and 20th centuries]. *Südhoffs Archiv [West Germany] 1973 57(2): 171-194.* Examines the historiographical principles and methods of the most important of the approximately 70 "Histories of Chemistry" published since the end of the 18th century. 56 notes.

C. F. Latour

3836. Weyer, Jost. THE IMAGE OF ALCHEMY IN 19TH AND 20TH CENTURY HISTORIES OF CHEMISTRY. *Ambix [Great Britain] 1976 23(2): 65-79.* Historians of chemistry tend to reflect contemporary stereotypes of alchemy rather than the actual facts of the subject. The author attempts to analyze the attitudes found in major histories published since the late 18th century, with the greatest emphasis on works originally published in German. Current stereotypes emphasize religio-philosophic aspects of alchemy, rather than the technical aspects that had been central to other periods. Chiefly primary sources; 65 notes.

W. B. Whitham

3837. Witthöft, Harald. LITERATUR ZUR HISTORISCHEN METROLOGIE 1945-1981 [A bibliographical essay on historical metrology, 1945-82]. *Vierteljahrschrift für Sozial- und Wirtschaftsgeschichte [West Germany] 1982 69(4): 515-541.* A review of developments in the field of historical metrology, its evolving methodologies, general theories, and areas of research, primarily since World War II. Over a hundred works are discussed, including handbooks, dictionaries, documentary collections, contributions of other fields, and a more detailed review of important recent research. 95 notes.

D. Prowe

3838. Worster, Donald. HISTORY AS NATURAL HISTORY: AN ESSAY ON THEORY AND METHOD. *Pacific Hist. Rev. 1984 53(1): 1-19.* Develops an ecological perspective on history by tracing the history and theoretical models of the impact of ecology on history, beginning with Walter Prescott Webb and James Malin, and working through other ecological historians such as Samuel Hays, Roderick Nash, and Donald Swain. Some historians are beginning to grasp the relationship between ecology, or natural history, and political history and social development. Two such "premodern" historians are LeRoy Ladurie and Fernand Braudel. If the ecological perspective will not make us more scientific, it may at least open our imaginations and permit us to look deeper into the past around us. Secondary sources; 32 notes.

H. M. Parker, Jr.

3839. Xi Zezong. CHINESE STUDIES IN THE HISTORY OF ASTRONOMY, 1949-1979. *Isis 1981 72(263): 456-470.* A report on the work of contemporary Chinese scholars in the history of astronomy in China. 68 notes.

M. M. Vance

3840. Yoxen, Edward. THE HISTORY OF MOLECULAR BIOLOGY. *British J. for the Hist. of Sci. [Great Britain] 1978 11(39): 273-278.* Review essay on Robert C. Olby's *The Path to the Double Helix* (London: Macmillan, 1974) and Franklin H. Portugal and Jack S. Cohen's *A Century of DNA: a History of the Discovery of the Structure and Function of the Genetic Substance* (Cambridge, Mass. and London: MIT Press, 1977). The history of modern science is an expanding area of scholarship, but even the best works thus far tend to ignore or downplay the insights of the social sciences and philosophy.

J. H. Sweetland

3841. —. [A CHRISTIAN VIEW OF AMERICAN SCIENTIFIC HISTORY]. *Fides et Hist. 1981 14(1): 21-41.*

Noll, Mark. SCIENTIFIC HISTORY IN AMERICA: A CENTENNIAL OBSERVATION FROM A CHRISTIAN POINT OF VIEW, pp. 21-37. Analysis of the scientific history of the first half-century of American professional history (1880's-1930's) from a Christian point of view. The Christian perspective "allows scope for the strengths of scientific history while excluding some of its weaknesses."

Schlossberg, Herbert. SCIENTIFIC HISTORY IN CHRISTIAN PERSPECTIVE: A COMMENT ON MARK NOLL'S ARTICLE, *pp. 38-41.* Noll errs in accepting the battleground staked out by empiricists and relativists. The Christian historian need not choose between "brute factuality and scepticism." 86 notes.
M. E. Quinlivan

3842. —. [CRITICAL PROBLEMS IN THE HISTORY OF MODERN PHYSICS]. *XIVth International Congress of the History of Science, Proceedings No. 4* (Tokyo and Kyoto: Science Council of Japan, 1975): 207-238.

Kuhn, Thomas S. ADDENDUM TO THE "QUANTUM THEORY OF SPECIFIC HEATS," *p. 207.* Acknowledges the contribution made by Martin J. Klein in the preparation of the author's paper on Nernst's interest in Einstein's quantum theory.

Takabayasi, Takehiko. QUANTUM TRANSITION, MATTER WAVE, AND THE FORMATION OF QUANTUM MECHANICS, *pp. 208-222.* Traces the development in thought and data collection in the development of the quantum theory and quantum mechanics, 1900-27.

McCormmach, Russell. COMMENTARY FOR THE SYMPOSIUM ON CRITICAL PROBLEMS IN THE HISTORY OF MODERN PHYSICS, *pp. 223-231.* Examines principles of world situation, professionalism, and teaching activities of physicists in relation to their impact on modern physics historiography, 20th century.

Nisio, Sigeko. COMMENT: SOMMERFELD'S QUANTUM THEORY OF 1911, *pp. 232-235.* Chronicles the origin and development of Sommerfeld's quantum theory, 1909-11, which applied action in aperiodic processes.

3843. —. ISSLEDOVANIIA PO ISTORII ESTESTVOZNANIIA I TEKHNIKI V DESIATOI PIATILETKE [Research on the history of natural science and technology during the 10th Five-Year Plan]. *Voprosy Istorii Estestvoznaniia i Tekhniki [USSR] 1981 (1): 3-12.* Traces the most important achievements in the area of the historiography of science and technology during the years of the 10th Five-Year Plan (1976-80). The main directions of research in this area were determined by the Presidium of the USSR Academy of Sciences proceeding from the objectives defined by the resolutions of the XXVth Congress of the CPSU. Among the aims pursued were the elaboration of Marxist-Leninist doctrine on science and technology and criticism of bourgeois conceptions; the working out of the subdivisions of the history of science; and the study of the sociological, organizational, and psychological problems of scientific activity. Cites the major works in the history of Soviet and world science.
J/S

3844. —. KANTTEKENINGEN BIJ EEN THEMANUMMER [Marginal notes on a theme issue]. *Tijdschrift voor de Geschiedenis der Geneeskunde, Natuurwetenschappen, Wiskunde en Techniek [Netherlands] 1982 5(3): 118-130.*

Berkel, K. van. WAT IS ER MIS MET HET ISME? [What is wrong with the "ism"?], *pp. 118-125.* Notes with disapproval the critical tenor of the contributions to an earlier thematic issue of this journal (1982 5(1)) and their basic assumption that "isms" as terms for trends in science history are neutral descriptive labels.

Hakfoort, C. ER IS IETS MIS MET DE ISME-GEBRUIKER: ANTWOORD AAN VAN BERKEL [There is something wrong with the "ism" user: in answer to van Berkel], *pp. 125-130.* Acknowledges van Berkel's emphasis on the logical status of historical narration, but objects to his polar analysis of the texts. 17 notes.
G. Herritt

3845. —. [THE NEED FOR ACCURACY AND THEORY IN HISTORIOGRAPHY]. *J. of the Hist. of the Behavioral Sci. 1976 12(2): 178-182.*

Littman, Richard A. THE NEED FOR ACCURACY IN HISTORIOGRAPHY, *pp. 178-181.* John R. Wettersten's article contains too many errors. The author corrects the footnotes, indicates some inaccuracies, and challenges the reference to Ivan Pavlov as the first major theorist in the history of scientific psychology.

Kurt Lewin was not the last systematic Gestalt psychologist. Wettersten's description of Hermann von Helmholtz's research is incorrect. Note.

Wettersten, John R. RESPONSE TO LITTMAN: THE NEED FOR RECOGNITION OF THEORY IN HISTORIOGRAPHY, *pp. 181-182.* Maintains that the charge of "substantive" errors involves misrepresentation of the original article. Littman failed to note that Pavlov was proposing an alternative to traditional explanations of learning. In discussing Lewin, the author was indicating the death of the last Gestalt psychologist rather than of a school. Wettersten insists that the understanding of the history of psychology requires study and criticism of various viewpoints. He cites the reactions and proposals of such psychologists as Carl Jung, Reich, and Gordon Allport, indicating that personal and subjective influences are involved with research of the human personality. 25 notes.
R. I. Vexler

3846. —. PROTOCOLE FINAL DE LA REUNION DE TRAVAIL—SOFIA, 10-12 MAI 1983 [Final communiqué of the working meeting, Sofia, 10-12 May 1983]. *Etudes Balkaniques [Bulgaria] 1984 20(3): 136-140.* Summarizes the proceedings of a meeting preparing UNESCO's history of science and culture. Representatives from the USSR, France, East Germany, Bulgaria, Romania, Hungary, Czechoslovakia, and Poland discussed the need to relate the science of various regions to social conditions and economic conditions.
R. Grove

3847. —. THE ROANOKE CONFERENCE—CRITICAL ISSUES IN THE HISTORY OF TECHNOLOGY: ROANOKE, VIRGINIA, AUGUST 14-18, 1978. *Technology and Culture 1980 21(4): 617-632.*

Pursell, Carroll W., Jr. I. SUMMARY, *pp. 617-620.*

Sivin, Nathan. II. CONCLUDING REMARKS ON CONFERENCE, *pp. 621-632.*

A summary of the proceedings and an analysis of the issues raised at the Roanoke Conference of the Society for the History of Technology: Is the history of technology a discipline? How is it related to the history of science and to economic analysis? How can it be made more accessible to the public and better integrated into history textbooks?
C. O. Smith, Jr.

Medicine

3848. Achenbaum, W. Andrew. FURTHER PERSPECTIVES ON MODERNIZATION AND AGING: A (P)REVIEW OF THE HISTORICAL LITERATURE. *Social Sci. Hist. 1982 6(3): 347-368.* A review essay on historical gerontology, with an emphasis on the relationship of modernization and aging. Recent work has dispelled traditional myths of a "golden age" for the aged in earlier Western history and emphasizes variety and complexity in the elderly experience. A summary of major issues and findings of US historians of the aged provides a more detailed case study of their work and their effect on modernization theory. Review essay based on secondary sources; note, biblio.
L. K. Blaser

3849. Appleby, Andrew B. DISEASE, DIET AND HISTORY. *J. of Interdisciplinary Hist. 1978 8(4): 725-735.* Reviews selected recent historiography on the biological aspects of history. While there are pitfalls in this type of interdisciplinary history, some of the recent work shows the considerable promise available in the uncovering of the role of diseases and diet in the past. 10 notes.
R. Howell

3850. Atwater, Edward C. MEDICAL SCHOOLS: HOW SHOULD WE WRITE THEIR HISTORIES? *Bull. of the Hist. of Medicine 1980 54(3): 455-460.* During 1905-43, no medical college history was published. A trickle then began in the 1940's, turning into a flood in the 1970's. Most authors have been senior or retired faculty. Of the 34 persons who could be identified, 24 were professors or professors emeritus at the college under study, three were medical practitioners on a full-time basis, and only six were historians. One motive for the recent increase in medical school histories is fund raising. The four most recent works reviewed here are among the best and most readable that have yet appeared. W. David Baird and Martin Kaufman provide the broadest perspective and the most historical analysis.   M. Kaufman

3851. Bell, Whitfield J., Jr. JOSEPH M. TONER (1825-1896) AS A MEDICAL HISTORIAN. *Bull. of the Hist. of Medicine 1973 47(1): 1-24.* Discusses the contribution to medical historiography of Joseph Meredith Toner, practicing physician and leader of the profession.   S

3852. Bell, Whitfield J., Jr. RICHARD HARRISON SHRYOCK, 1893-1972. *Bull. of the Hist. of Medicine 1972 46(5): 499-503.* Shryock made important contributions to the modernization of medical historiography in the 20th century.   S

3853. Benison, Saul. GEORGE ROSEN: AN APPRECIATION. *J. of the Hist. of Medicine and Allied Sci. 1978 33(3): 245-253.* Tribute to George Rosen (1910-77), specialist in public health, and the history of medicine and public health. Aside from his massive research and publication record, Rosen instructed a generation of medical historians and sociologists, as editor of the *Journal of the History of Medicine and Allied Sciences.* Moreover, as editor and member of the board of the *American Journal of Public Health,* he taught medical history to thousands of public health workers and physicians. He wrote more than 200 papers, and published many books, including a *History of Public Health,* a *History of Preventive Medicine,* and later work on urban history. His living legacy will grow and develop, as young minds use his analyses and findings and address themselves to the problems facing medical thought, practice, and care. 26 notes.   M. Kaufman

3854. Bujosa i Homar, Francesc. LA AFASIA Y SU HISTORIO-GRAFIA [Aphasia and its historiography]. *Dynamis [Spain] 1981 1: 131-163.* Reviews the historiography of aphasia, dividing it in two periods separated by the publication of the work of Henry Head (1861-1940) in 1920. Underlines the profusion of the literature on the subject, which precludes an exhaustive treatment, and comments on the more significant works. 108 notes, biblio.
                J. V. Coutinho

3855. Camp, Charles. FOODWAYS IN EVERYDAY LIFE. *Am. Q. 1982 34(3): 278-289.* Divides the literature on dietary patterns into 15 categories based on five areas of activity (production or gathering of foodstuffs, distribution of foodstuffs, cookery, distribution of foods, and consumption) and three types of analysis (descriptive, patterning, and interpretive). Discusses prominent works in each category. Table, 41 notes.   D. K. Lambert

3856. Debus, Allen G. HISTORY WITH A PURPOSE: THE FATE OF PARACELSUS. *Pharmacy in History 1984 26(2): 83-96.* Assesses the neglect of historiographical studies of the histories of science, medicine, and pharmacy by examining the interpretations of the works of Renaissance scholar Paracelsus (1493-1541). In the late 16th-early 17th centuries, many established medical authorities, notably Guinter of Anderbach (ca. 1505-74) and Daniel Sennert (1572-1637), suggested a compromise of accepting the chemically prepared medicines advocated by Paracelsus while retaining the predominant Galenic medicine and pharmacy; but they rejected "the religious mysticism of Paracelsian cosmology." This compromise was accepted by the late 17th and 18th-century academicians, mostly the mechanists. Physician-scholars John Freind (1675-1728) and Hermann Boerhaave (1668-1738) and their contemporaries, continued to ignore and criticize the influence of Paracelsus. Recognition of Paracelsus's contributions appeared in the works of Abbé Nicholas Lenglet du Fresnoy (1674-ca. 1752), Antoine-Joseph Pernety (1716-ca. 1800), and other medical scholars who were outside the new scientific establishment of the academics. Most 19th-century historians of science, medicine, and pharmacy summarily dismissed Paracelsus while concentrating on the Newtonian impact on the Scientific Revolution. Based on original texts and secondary sources; 2 fig., photo, 58 notes.   S. C. Morrison

3857. Ell, Stephen R. INTERHUMAN TRANSMISSION OF MEDIEVAL PLAGUE. *Bull. of the Hist. of Medicine 1980 54(4): 497-510.* Medieval records ascribe plague patterns to transmission by the human flea. Seasonality, low rat mortality, and multiple cases per household argue against rat-borne plague; bubonic presentation rules against pneumonic plague. There is no adequate explanation for the disappearance of the disease in the early medieval period. Based on recent medical studies as well as medieval sources in various languages; 91 notes.   M. Kaufman

3858. Faccini, Luigi. STORIA SOCIALE E STORIA DELLA MEDICINA [Social history and the history of medicine]. *Studi Storici [Italy] 1976 17(2): 257-264.* Until recently, Italian historians showed little interest in social history. This is now changing with considerable focus on medical history, in particular diseases such as smallpox, cholera, and malaria in Italy well into the 19th century and their demographic and social effects. New works on epidemics and Italian efforts to combat them examine both the state of medical science and the structure of medical and public health services. 18 notes.   J. C. Billigmeier

3859. Federn, Ernst. ON THE DIFFICULTY OF WRITING HISTORY OF IDEAS: A REPLY. *J. of the Hist. of the Behavioral Sci. 1980 16(1): 45-49.* [Response to Nathan G. Hale, Jr.'s "From Bergasse XIX to Central Park West: The Americanization of Psychoanalysis, 1919-1940".] Its author described an important work in psychoanalysis with disregard to the facts and with an apparent lack of knowledge of the book. American historians may have unusual difficulties when writing about European ideas which may lead to a false presentation of historical facts.   J

3860. Folch Jou, G. and Muñoz Calvo, S. APORTACIÓN DE OLMEDILLA Y PUIG AL DESARROLLO DE LA HISTORIOGRAFÍA FARMACÉUTICA EN ESPAÑA [Contributions of Joaquin Olmedilla y Puig to the development of pharmaceutical historiography in Spain]. *Bol. de la Soc. Española de Hist. de la Farmacia [Spain] 1980 31(123): 205-234.* Joaquin Olmedilla y Puig's unfinished manuscript, *Historia Crítico-Literaria de la Farmacia,* includes biographies of pharmacists and notes on their writings, related persons, and monographs on a variety of subjects.

3861. Gorham, Deborah. BIRTH AND HISTORY. *Social History [Canada] 1984 17(34): 383-394.* Until the 1970's, the physician's point of view dominated the history of birth, equated technological and male intervention in birth with progress, and linked traditional midwifery with backwardness. In 1973, an essay by Barbara Ehrenreich and Deirdre English, feminist academics, challenged the traditional point of view, emphasizing the importance of feminine participation in a feminine event. Since then, feminists have devoted much attention to demonstrating, though simplistically, that history supports Ehrenreich and English's view. Social historians of medicine have also challenged the traditional interpretation, and have taken a more balanced position. 26 notes.   D. F. Chard

3862. Hebert, Raymond G. HISTORY OF NURSING: HISTORY AND HISTORICAL METHOD FOR PRE-PROFESSIONALS. *Pro. and Papers of the Georgia Assoc. of Hist. 1980: 34-39.* Describes a course in the history of nursing at Thomas More College, Fort Mitchell, Kentucky. The course sets the profession in historical context, enabling students to see the changes that occurred in the past in order to encourage them to become agents of change in the future. 10 notes.   R. Grove

3863. Hornblower, Henry, II. HENRY FURBUSH HOWE. *Massachusetts Hist. Soc. Pro. 1977 89: 184-186.* A memoir of Henry Furbush Howe (1905-77), physician and historian of New England. A graduate of Phillips Academy, Yale, and the Harvard Medical School, Henry Howe achieved prominence in occupational health, rising to the position of director of the Department of Occupational Health of the American Medical Association in 1962. A member of the Massachusetts Historical Society for 30 years, Henry Howe also published several anecdotal, popular histories, primarily based on secondary sources. Based on the author's friendship with Howe.   G. W. R. Ward

3864. Jacyna, L. S. IMAGES OF JOHN HUNTER IN THE NINETEENTH CENTURY. *Hist. of Sci. [Great Britain] 1983 21(1): 85-108.* The history of science has generally been a study of the lives and careers of great men. Like Newton and Cuvier, John Hunter (1728-93) was seen as a "catastrophic" figure whose career marked a turning point. The conventional view is that he brought science and medicine firmly into alliance, demonstrated the relevance of physiology to pathology and therapeutics, and showed that the world could be ordered into a "natural system" based on the correlation of structure with function. The architects of this image were the early Hunterian orators at the Royal College of Surgeons. Contemporary surgeons wished to burnish Hunter's image so that they could aspire to the rank of gentlemen. They wished to stress the intellectual significance of surgery and assert that they were a learned profession. Examination of Hunter's own writings is needed to determine his true contribution as opposed to a reputation based on a conscription of his name for polemical purposes. Based on primary sources; 76 notes. J. G. Packer

3865. James, Janet Wilson. WRITING AND REWRITING NURSING HISTORY: A REVIEW ESSAY. *Bull. of the Hist. of Medicine 1984 58(4): 568-584.* Reviews eight recent books on the history of nursing, and provides information on sources for understanding nursing history. 9 notes. M. Kaufman

3866. King, Lester S. OF WHAT USE IS MEDICAL HISTORY? *Bull. of the Hist. of Medicine 1977 51(1): 107-116.* A philosophical analysis of the use of history in general, and medical history in particular. M. Kaufman

3867. Lippard, Vernon W. THE JOSIAH MACY, JR. FOUNDATION PROGRAM IN THE HISTORY OF MEDICINE AND THE BIOLOGICAL SCIENCES. *Bull. of the Hist. of Medicine 1969 43(3): 262-269.* The foundation was established in 1965 to educate physicians on historical events in medical history and to advance understanding of the relationship between medicine and social, economic, and cultural advances. S

3868. Livi-Bacci, Massimo. THE NUTRITION-MORTALITY LINK IN PAST TIMES: A COMMENT. *Journal of Interdisciplinary History 1983 14(2): 293-298.* The complexities of the histories of Europe and the Americas belie the theory that nutrition has played the key role in mortality trends. Childrearing practices and environmental conditions, among other factors, were also significant in determining mortality rates. Secondary sources; 35 notes. R. deV. Brunkow

3869. Midelfort, H. C. Erik. MADNESS AND CIVILIZATION IN EARLY MODERN EUROPE: A REAPPRAISAL OF MICHEL FOUCAULT. Malament, Barbara C., ed. *After the Reformation: Essays in Honor of J. H. Hexter* (Philadelphia: U. of Pennsylvania Pr., 1980): 247-265. Examines the challenges and difficulties posed by studies of the poor, the working class, criminals, and especially mental illness as described in Michel Foucault's *Madness and Civilization* (New York, 1965). Historiography on these subjects, including the history of medicine, has often displayed a "myopic bias toward modern problems," especially by psychiatrists who lack training in history. The 16th century marked the beginning of real cruelty in Europe toward the mentally ill, a situation not changed until the late 18th and early 19th centuries. Empirical evidence refutes many of Foucault's arguments and many of his "broadest generalizations are oversimplifications." 91 notes.

3870. Miller, Genevieve. THE FIELDING H. GARRISON LECTURE. IN PRAISE OF AMATEURS: MEDICAL HISTORY IN AMERICA BEFORE GARRISON. *Bull. of the Hist. of Medicine 1973 47(6): 586-615.* Examines medical historiography from 1856 to 1913, when Fielding H. Garrison's *Introduction to the History of Medicine* was published. Read at the 46th annual meeting of the American Association for the History of Medicine at Cincinnati, Ohio, 3 May 1973. S

3871. Numbers, Ronald L. THE HISTORY OF AMERICAN MEDICINE: A FIELD IN FERMENT. *Rev. in Am. Hist. 1982 10(4): 245-263.* The increasing number of nonphysicians writing

medical history has led to internecine squabbles with physician-historians, but has also encouraged a redefinition of the field to include topics once regarded as peripheral.

3872. Öberg, Lars. MEDICINHISTORIA [The history of medicine]. *Historielärarnas Förenings Årsskrift [Sweden] 1982-83: 31-33.* Describes general outlines of the history of medicine as treated by contemporary European historians. Scandinavian secondary sources. R. G. Selleck

3873. Olagüe de Ros, Guillermo. LA EPIDEMIA EUROPEA DE GRIPE DE 1708-1709; DIFUSION TEMPORO-ESPACIAL E INTERPRETACIONES CONTEMPORANEAS: G. M. LANCISI, B. RAMAZZINI Y K. F. HOFFMANN [The European influenza epidemic of 1708-09: its diffusion in space and time and contemporary interpretations: G. M. Mancisi, B. Ramazzini and K. F. Hoffmann]. *Dynamis [Spain] 1981 1: 51-86.* The influenza epidemic of 1708-09 had important social and scientific consequences that have been little studied by historians. Three contemporary accounts of the epidemic, its causes, extent, and duration are analyzed. 147 notes. J. V. Coutinho

3874. Quinn, Kevin F. BANTING AND HIS BIOGRAPHERS: MAKER OF MIRACLES, MAKERS OF MYTH. *Queen's Q. [Canada] 1982 89(2): 243-259.* Frederick Grant Banting's winning of the Nobel Prize (1923) for his discovery of insulin, followed by his untimely death while on active duty in World War II, caused him to become for Canadians a cultural hero of mythic proportions. The biographies of Banting that attempt to explain why he was great by focusing on what he did are doomed to failure, for it was not what he did but what he meant to Canadian nationalism that was important. Secondary sources; 15 notes. L. V. Eid

3875. Riera, Juan. HISTORIOGRAFÍA MÉDICA CATALANA: LUIS COMENGE Y FERRER (NOTA PREVIA) [Catalonian medical historiography: Luis Comenge y Ferrer; a preliminary note]. *Cuadernos de Hist. de la Medicina Española [Spain] 1971 10: 87-108.* A biographical sketch of Luis Comenge y Ferrer, a medical historian (1854-1916). His work goes beyond the bibliographical method represented by Antonio Hernández Morejón (1773-1836). He was an innovator in the use of archival documents and legal sources, and in promoting the use of the social history of medicine. J. S. (IHE 91097)

3876. Roeder, Beatrice A. HEALTH CARE BELIEFS AND PRACTICES AMONG MEXICAN AMERICANS: A REVIEW OF THE LITERATURE. *Aztlán 1982 13(1-2): 223-256.* Surveys the historical development of research on the medical care beliefs and practices of Mexican Americans. Published studies fall into four categories: works on the historical development and sources of Mexican folk medicine, pioneering studies (1894-1954), the research of Lyle Saunders and his followers in placing Mexican American health practices in a cultural context, and research in the 1970's examining socioeconomic factors and criticizing Saunders's approach. Scholars in the field differ regarding the frequency of use of health care facilities by Mexican Americans and how such facilities can better serve Mexican-American needs. Note, ref. A. Hoffman

3877. Rosen, George. THE PEDIATRICIAN AS HISTORIAN: JOHN RUHRÄH AND ERNEST CAULFIELD. *Bull. of the Hist. of Medicine 1977 51(2): 188-201.* John Ruhräh (1872-1935) and Ernest Caulfield (1893-1972) contributed significantly to the history of pediatrics. Ruhräh collected and read old books on children's diseases, occasionally contributing a historical paper. In 1925 he published his major contribution, a history of pediatrics entitled *Pediatrics of the Past.* It was traditional in terms of focusing on the pediatricians of the past. Caulfield, however, made a greater contribution. He was an early advocate of the social history of medicine, publishing in 1931 *The Infant Welfare Movement in the Eighteenth Century,* and in 1939 *A True History of the Terrible Epidemic vulgarly called the Throat Distemper which occurred in His Majesty's New England Colonies between the Years 1735 and 1740.* In 1949

Carl Bridgenbaugh reviewed the book and called it "the ablest study of colonial medical history" he had ever encountered. 2 illus., 27 notes.   M. Kaufman

3878. Rousseau, G. S. EPHEBI, EPIGONI, AND FORNICALIA: SOME MEDITATIONS ON THE CONTEMPORARY HISTORIOGRAPHY OF THE EIGHTEENTH CENTURY. *Eighteenth Cent.: Theory and Interpretation* 1979 20(3): 203-226. During the last two decades two different types of histories of medicine have been written: the general survey which tries to fill in gaps, to synthesize and to build on the works of others; and thesis oriented history prompted by the discovery of material, which leads to a thesis purporting to reconstruct the field of knowledge. Secondary sources; 45 notes.   H. T. Blethen

3879. Scrimshaw, Nevin S. THE VALUE OF CONTEMPORARY FOOD AND NUTRITION STUDIES FOR HISTORIANS. *Journal of Interdisciplinary History* 1983 14(2): 529-534. Conclusion of a special issue on "Hunger and History" identifying areas for further research: the role of nutrition on disease, population, and cognitive behavior; the effects of chronic energy, vitamin, and mineral deficiencies; and adverse nonnutritional effects of food. Secondary sources; 7 notes.   R. deV. Brunkow

3880. Scull, Andrew. HUMANITARIANISM OR CONTROL? SOME OBSERVATIONS ON THE HISTORIOGRAPHY OF ANGLO-AMERICAN PSYCHIATRY. *Rice U. Studies* 1981 67(1): 21-41. Describes various attempts by historians to assess the 19th-century asylums in the United States and Great Britain, their origins, functions, and failings, and emphasizes the need to understand the fundamental shift in consciousness that, guided by notions of progress, regarded the insane no longer as brutes but as socially redeemable human beings; discusison, pp. 75-78.

3881. Shortt, S. E. D. BANTING, INSULIN AND THE QUESTION OF SIMULTANEOUS DISCOVERY. *Queen's Q. [Canada]* 1982 89(2): 260-273. The host of US and Canadian contenders, especially Frederick Grant Banting for the title of discoverer of insulin, is an example of that relentless urge to assign priority for biomedical discoveries, which is one of the least endearing features of medical historiography. Historians are better advised to follow Thomas Kuhn's heuristic lead and study the factors leading to multiple discovery. The multiple claims for insulin's discovery become intelligible and indeed, with hindsight, inevitable against the early 20th-century background of the demands for a scientific medicine, the growth of biochemistry as a new discipline, and the study of "internal secretions." Secondary sources; 30 notes.   L. V. Eid

3882. Shortt, S. E. D. THE CANADIAN HOSPITAL IN THE NINETEENTH CENTURY: AN HISTORIOGRAPHIC LAMENT. *J. of Can. Studies [Canada]* 1983-84 18(4): 3-14. The historiography of 19th-century Canadian hospitals is marked by institutional rather than social studies. Themes in British and US hospital history also hold true for Canada: hospitals were not death houses but were moral-reclamation centers serving the poor, and they acted as a medium for the professionalization of medicine. Based on studies of 19th-century Canadian, British, and US hospitals; 49 notes.
                                                  H. M. Narducci, Jr.

3883. Shortt, S. E. D. CLINICAL PRACTICE AND THE SOCIAL HISTORY OF MEDICINE: A THEORETICAL ACCORD. *Bull. of the Hist. of Medicine* 1981 55(4): 533-542. Medical historians include practicing physicians as well as professional historians, and in each group there are those who deride the contributions of the other group. They argue whether a lack of personal medical experience and understanding precludes the writing of accurate medical history. The debate over internal versus external, analytical versus antiquarian, personal experience versus comprehensive research, obscures a major point of congruence. The new social history of medicine is based on philosophical assumptions that are closely related to attitudes underlying recent developments in clinical practice. Awareness of this relationship may provide the basis

for a detente within the history of medicine. Based on analysis of recent work in the history of medicine and clinical developments in medicine; 52 notes.   M. Kaufman

3884. Siraisi, Nancy G. SOME CURRENT TRENDS IN THE STUDY OF RENAISSANCE MEDICINE. *Renaissance Quarterly* 1984 37(4): 585-600. Reviews two areas of scholarly interest during the past five years in the study of Renaissance medicine (ca. 1300-1600). Those areas are the social history of medicine and the range of intellectual and scientific activity within the academically trained Renaissance medical community. Based on secondary sources; 53 notes.   J. H. Pragman

3885. Sonnedecker, Glenn. WRITING THE HISTORY OF PHARMACY IN THE U.S.A. *Pharmacy in Hist.* 1978 20(1): 3-16. A 1977 address to the International Academy of the History of Pharmacy summarizes the main phases in the writing of pharmacy history in the United States. Prior to the 1920's, humanistically-oriented pharmacists of Germanic background produced most of the American pharmaco-historical literature. Dr. Edward Kremers (1865-1941), Director of the School of Pharmacy at the University of Wisconsin, epitomized this first phase. Kremers' work emphasized thorough multi-source research and a comprehensive presentation of material and the collection and preservation of American pharmaco-historical documents and artifacts. From 1904 American pharmacy historians profited from a forum in the Section on Historical Pharmacy of the American Pharmaceutical Association and the Association's *Journal*. Kremers' successor, Dr. George Urdang (1882-1960), advocated the creation of the American Institute of the History of Pharmacy (f. 1941) to advance the study, research, teaching, publishing, and recognition of pharmacy history in the United States. Currently, American pharmaco-historical research and writing by the small number of trained scholar-teachers remains "strongly internalist in its orientation," "traditionalist" in its historiographic methods, and noninterdisciplinary in practice. Primary and secondary sources; 6 fig., 14 notes.   S. C. Morrison

3886. Sournia, Jean-Charles. HISTOIRE ET MEDECINE [History and medicine]. *Rev. des Travaux de l'Acad. des Sci. Morales et Comptes Rendus de ses Séances [France]* 1981 134(4): 655-672. Despite the differences between them, history and medicine are both "arts" rather than "sciences." Historians and physicians share much in the way of approach and methodology and should engage in more cooperative ventures to cast new light on the past. Comments by Maurice Le Lannou, Jean-Baptiste Duroselle, Fernand Gambiez, Pierre George, François Lhermitte, André Piettre, and Henri Guitton.   J. R. Vignery

3887. Stroppiana, Luigi. I RAPPORTI CULTURALI E MEDICO-STORICI TRA ITALIA E ROMANIA [Cultural and medical-historical relations between Italy and Romania]. *Balcanica [Italy]* 1983 2(1): 77-82. Surveys historiography on the influence of Italian physicians and medical science in Romania.

3888. Viney, Wayne and Bartsch, Karen. DOROTHEA LYNDE DIX: POSITIVE OR NEGATIVE INFLUENCE ON THE DEVELOPMENT OF TREATMENT FOR THE MENTALLY ILL. *Social Sci. J.* 1984 21(2): 71-82. Challenges recent criticisms of social reformer Dorothea Dix's efforts to improve institutions for the mentally handicapped.

3889. Zainaldin, James S. and Tyor, Peter L. ASYLUM AND SOCIETY: AN APPROACH TO INSTITUTIONAL CHANGE. *J. of Social Hist.* 1979 13(1): 23-48. Studies two 19th-century asylums in Boston, one for the poor and the other for the feeble-minded. Covers the history of the institutions, discussing the sources of institutional policy and its reformulation, institutional operation, external perception and internal fact, and the social functions which the institution provides. Closes with an examination of the conclusions of other authors and a possibly fruitful path for additional studies. 7 tables, 57 notes.   V. L. Human

Other Topics in Historiography

3890. Abbott, Carl. BUILDING WESTERN CITIES: A REVIEW ESSAY. *Colorado Heritage 1984 (1): 39-46.* Traces the historiography of the growth of cities in the western United States. Urban planning was first based on a visionary idealism that sought to transform the wilderness into civilization. Urban history must tie the growth of cities to social conditions, economic conditions, and politics. 3 photos, biblio.   R. Grove

3891. Adelman, Melvin. ACADEMICIANS AND ATHLETICS: HISTORIANS' VIEWS OF AMERICAN SPORT. *Maryland Historian 1973 4(2): 123-137.* A historiographical essay chastizing historians for their superficial examination of the phenomenon of American Sports, summarizing the scanty studies which have been made. Secondary sources, 39 notes.   G. O. Gagnon

3892. Adelman, Melvin. ACADEMICIANS AND AMERICAN ATHLETICS: A DECADE OF PROGRESS. *J. of Sport Hist. 1983 10(1): 80-106.* Several surveys of American athletics appeared in the past decade, including John R. Betts's *America's Sporting Heritage* and John Lucas and Ronald Smith's *Saga of American Sport.* A collection of essays has been published and edited by William J. Baker and John M. Carroll *Sports in Modern America,* and in 1983 Benjamin Rader's *American Sports* appeared. There is need for less emphasis on details and more on a conceptual framework. Authors have been influenced by recent developments in historiography generally, including the questions of sport and social control, sport and the city, and sport and demographic groups. Although there have been many studies on American sport, there has been too little attempt to develop a synthesis. Based on books and articles on sport history; 73 notes.   M. Kaufman

3893. Allen, Robert C. HISTORIOGRAPHY AND THE TEACHING OF FILM HISTORY. *Film and Hist. 1980 10(2): 25-31.* Most film history survey courses are inadequate; discusses ways of "integrating historiography into the teaching of film history," including specific classroom curricula on film historiography dating to 1908 and the movies of D. W. Griffith.

3894. Almeida Camargo, Ana Maria de. ESTUDOS SÔBRE CIDADES: UMA "COLEÇÃO DE EXEMPLOS" [Studies of cities: a collection of examples]. *Rev. de Hist. [Brazil] 1970 41(83): 213-235.* Gives an overview of the topics covered in Oscar Handlin and John Burchard, ed., *The Historian and the City* (1966).
                                                    P. J. Taylorson/S

3895. Altamira, Rafael. POSIBILIDADES DE ESCRIBIR LA HISTORIA CONTEMPORANEA [Possibilities of writing contemporary history]. *Bol. del Archivio General de la Nación [Venezuela] 1969 59(216): 99-104.* Considers the problems in writing contemporary history, the impossibility of being impartial, the lack of documents, and the danger of involving those still alive.

3896. Amsden, Jon. HISTORIANS AND THE SPATIAL IMAGINATION. *Radical Hist. Rev. 1979 (21): 11-30.* Deliberate human creations, Spanish plazas, French bistros, and inner city lots reveal information about individuals and class relations; historians wrongfully neglect the evidence of social and political values to be found in urban and regional space.

3897. Aradi, Nóra. A SZOCIALISTA KÉPZŐMŰVÉSZEK CSOPORTJA ÉS A MŰVÉSZETTÖRTÉNET-ÍRÁS [The Group of Socialist Artists and the historiography of art]. *Párttörténeti Közlemények [Hungary] 1978 24(4): 198-210.* This group was first formed in 1934, then again in 1939, and ceased to exist in 1942 for political reasons. The study of their history was neglected for a long time. The author provides a chronicle of exhibitions of graphic art by the Hungarian painter, Gyula Derkovits, the forerunner of the group, and examines scholarly publications about his work. Argues that research on the group could contribute to the history of the labor movement. 18 notes.   R. Hetzron/S

3898. Baker, William J. THE STATE OF BRITISH SPORT HISTORY. *J. of Sport Hist. 1983 10(1): 53-66.* Until recent times, sport history was done exclusively by amateurs and ignored by most serious historians, except Peter McIntosh and Dennis Brailsford. Over the past decade various scholars have researched aspects of British sport history, but the full story cannot be told since research on the medieval and recent periods is deficient. The period from the Renaissance to the Industrial Revolution has been covered much better. Secondary sources; 80 notes.   M. Kaufman

3899. Bale, John. INTERNATIONAL SPORTS HISTORY AS INNOVATION DIFFUSION. *Canadian Journal of History of Sport [Canada] 1984 15(1): 38-63.* Describes the development and spread of various sports offering a model incorporating predictability rather than a model of chance structuring and parallel development.

3900. Baranowski, B. STAN I POTRZEBY BADAŃ NAD NOWOŻYTNA, HISTORIA, KULTURY MATERIALNEJ [State and need for studies on modern history of material culture]. *Kwartalnik Hist. Kultury Materialnej [Poland] 1972 2(4): 687-691.* Discusses the current state of studies on the history of material culture, which began in Poland in the 1930's, with extensive work after the 1953 establishment of the Institute for History of Material Culture within the Polish Academy of Science.

3901. Bardach, Juliusz. SCIENCES HISTORICO-JURIDIQUES: 1945-1977 [History of the legal sciences: 1945-77]. *Czasopismo Prawno-Historyczne [Poland] 1979 31(1): 11-29.* Gives an account of Poland's activity in legal history, centering on research, pedagogy, and publications, from the end of World War II, when it reconstructed its bases, until 1977. Examines its methodological orientation, teamwork, syntheses, monograph research, law historiography, studies in Slavic history and Roman law, political, legal, and administration histories, and international participation and exchanges. Stresses the necessity of maintaining a historical approach that demonstrates the mutual bonds between sociopolitical institutions and the system of law. Based on an expanded version of a lecture given during the 25th anniversary of the University of Warsaw Law History Institute, 25 April 1977; 15 notes.
                                                    G. P. Cleyet

3902. Barolsky, Paul. WALTER PATER'S RENAISSANCE. *Virginia Q. Rev. 1982 58(2): 208-220.* Analyzes *The Renaissance* of the elusive Victorian scholar, Walter Pater. Historians of art and literature often comment upon Pater's "unhistorical approach to his subject." The author disagrees, although he argues that in Pater's work "its historical value has to be excavated." He points out that *The Renaissance* describes the influence of Neoplatonism, relates the era to other great historical periods, is somewhat autobiographical, and is conspicuously about philosophy. There is, however, an "omnipresent sense of history." Based on Pater's *Renaissance.*
                                                    O. H. Zabel

3903. Bauman, John F. DOWNTOWN VERSUS NEIGHBORHOOD: FOCUSING ON PHILADELPHIA IN THE METROPOLITAN ERA, 1920-1980. *Pennsylvania Hist. 1981 48(1): 3-20.* This historiographical essay sees a need for studies of the postindustrial period and suggests additional works dealing with the post-World War II diaspora of the white middle class to suburbia. 36 notes.
                                                    D. C. Swift

3904. Bentley, Jerry H. RENAISSANCE CULTURE IN RECENT SOVIET HISTORICAL STUDIES. *Soviet Studies in Hist. 1980 19(2): 6-11.* Critiques three Russian articles on Renaissance figures, Petrarch, Giannozzo Manetti, and Leonardo da Vinci, translated in this issue of *Soviet Studies in History.* All three articles seek to interpret the Renaissance in terms of its utter worldliness and these figures in terms of their disdain of the transcendental and the beliefs of the Roman Catholic Church. 4 notes.

3905. Bergeron, Louis and Roncayolo, Marcel. DE LA VILLE PRÉINDUSTRIELLE À LA VILLE INDUSTRIELLE. ESSAI SUR L'HISTORIOGRAPHIE FRANÇAISE [From the preindustrial to the industrial town: an essay on French historiography]. *Quaderni Storici [Italy] 1974 9(3): 827-876.* Examines French urban historiography which defines models, and analyzes and interprets the processes of social change. The new urban history precisely identifies the areas that the city organizes. The authors examine four main areas of research: urban structure and its evolution in the 18th and 19th centuries, the principal contribution of geographers; urban demography, an analysis of preindustrial and industrial models of city growth; city and society, from the definition of social groups to urban dynamics in which urban growth and change are linked with fundamental behavior patterns of the urban social classes; and the construction of urban areas including works dedicated to the physical forms of cities (Haussmannization and social divisions within cities, with particular reference to the 19th century). J/S

3906. Bewell, Alan J. PORTRAITS AT GREYFRIARS: PHOTOGRAPHY, HISTORY, AND MEMORY IN WALTER BENJAMIN. *Clio* 1982 12(1): 17-29. For Walter Benjamin (1892-1940) photography, historical reflection, and memory shared the same "image-space" provided by 19th-century cities like Paris, London, and Berlin. In *A Short History of Photography* (1931), Benjamin argued that these cities provided images that allowed the historian to reconstruct the past. 31 notes. T. P. Linkfield

3907. Bogucka, Maria. LES RECHERCHES POLONAISES DES ANNÉES 1969-1978 SUR L'HISTOIRE DES VILLES ET DE LA BOURGEOISIE JUSQU'AU DÉCLIN DU XVIIIᵉ SIÈCLE [Polish studies, 1969-78, on the history of towns and of the bourgeoisie up to the end of the 18th century]. *Acta Poloniae Hist.* [Poland] 1980 (41): 239-257. A review article of Polish studies on the history of cities. 63 notes. H. Heitzman-Wojcicka

3908. Brockstedt, Jürgen. REGIONALGESCHICHTLICHE FORSCHUNGSANSÄTZE ZUR GEOGRAPHISCHEN MOBILITÄT IN SCHLESWIG-HOLSTEIN [Regional history research principles on geographical mobility in Schleswig Holstein]. *Hist. Social Res.* [West Germany] 1980 (14): 34-47. Briefly examines the historiography on geographical mobility.

3909. Brown, Marshall. THE CLASSIC IS THE BAROQUE: ON THE PRINCIPLE OF WÖLFFLIN'S ART HISTORY. *Critical Inquiry* 1982 9(2): 379-404. Assesses the continuing influence of Heinrich Wölfflin's approach to the history of art since the Renaissance, principally his insights into the complexity and difficulty of style formation.

3910. Brownell, Morris R. "BURSTING PROSPECT": BRITISH GARDEN HISTORY NOW. *Eighteenth-Century Life* 1983 8(2): 5-18. Due to the research of English historians, garden history has grown from a secondary interdisciplinary study to a separate discipline in its own right.

3911. Buck, August. ÜBERLEGUNGEN ZUM GEGENWÄRTIGEN STAND DER RENAISSANCEFORSCHUNG [Considerations on the place of contemporary Renaissance research]. *Bibliothèque d'Humanisme et Renaissance* [Switzerland] 1981 43(1): 7-38. Interdisciplinary historiographical essay on the following topics: the concept of the Renaissance, the Renaissance and Antiquity, the Renaissance and natural science, the seamy side of the Renaissance, the Italian Renaissance and Europe, Erasmus, and the Renaissance and religion. Diversity characterizes the historiography since World War II. 156 notes.

3912. Burke, Peter. "THE EARLY MODERN TOWN"—ITS HISTORY AND HISTORIANS: A REVIEW ARTICLE. *Urban Hist. Y.* [Great Britain] 1981: 55-58. Prompted by the publication of C. Phythian-Adams's *Desolation of a City* (1979), J. T. Evans's *17th-Century Norwich* (1979), and D. Palliser's *Tudor York* (1979), one by an American (J. T. Evans), considers whether there are distinctive schools of preindustrial urban history in Britain and America, and if so whether this is because the towns studied are different or because the historical traditions of the students are different. Compares and contrasts English studies on English towns with the French histories of French towns published ca. 1941-81,

and discusses the traditions of the French school of urban history, in particular the fundamental influences of Lucien Febvre, Fernand Braudel, Ernest Labrousse, and the *Annales* school. 5 notes.

3913. Burt, E. S. ROUSSEAU THE SCRIBE. *Studies in Romanticism* 1979 18(4): 629-667. Examines the problems facing historians in the writing of history and autobiography as expressed in Jean Jacques Rousseau's *Dialogues* and *Rousseau juge de Jean Jacques.*

3914. Caracciolo, Alberto. CITTÀ COME MODERNITÀ, CITTÀ COME "MALE": SPUNTI E LINEE DI LETTURA IN DUE SECOLI DI STORIA INGLESE [The town as modernity, the town as evil: suggestions and possible readings in two centuries of British history]. *Quaderni Storici* [Italy] 1981 16(2): 556-573. Taking as a starting point the "ambiguous" aspect presented by all modern urban phenomena, discusses this contradiction in relation to the English town, from Manchester to the New Towns. Apart from its concrete historical reality, the town (and especially the big city) incarnates infinite plans, efforts, even utopias, aiming at achieving the utmost degree of organization and rationality. At the same time, however, in the same period and country, it once again appears as a place of alienation, degradation and "evil." Historical analyses have seldom found a way out of this dilemma by way of more articulated research going beyond a prejudicial choice of values. J

3915. Cardini, Franco. MEDIOEVO "PROSSIMO VENTURO," "PRESENTE INATTUALE" O "PASSATO PROSSIMO?" SIGNIFICATI, EQUIVOCI E PROSPETTIVE DI UN REVIVAL [Middle Ages: "near future," "noncurrent present," or "present perfect?" Meanings, ambiguities, and prospects of a revival]. *Storia della Storiografia* [Italy] 1983 (4): 99-112. Discusses the Middle Ages in the awareness of 20th-century persons. The repulsion of the Enlightenment and the Romanticism of the 18th century survived. The Middle Ages themselves survived or were revived not only in historiography but also in popular culture and the arts. Popular representations of the Middle Ages, as projections of 20th-century social conditions, offer opportunities to study 20th-century society. 20 notes. R. Grove

3916. Ciliberto, Michele. INTERPRETAZIONI DEL RINASCIMENTO [Interpretations of the Renaissance]. *Studi Storici* [Italy] 1979 20(4): 759-777. Analyzes the essays in the volume, *Il Rinascimento: Interpretazioni e problemi* [The Renaissance: interpretations and problems], published to mark the 70th birthday of Eugenio Garin. The essays, all written by other than Italian scholars, reflect contrasting views about the ideological character of the concept of the Renaissance, and about the relationship between the Renaissance and humanism. Primary sources. E. E. Ryan

3917. Coing, Helmut. HISTORIA DEL DERECHO Y DOGMATICA JURIDICA [History of law and legal dogmatics]. *Rev. de Estudios Histórico-Jurídicos* [Chile] 1981 6: 105-118. Compares the discipline of legal history with the study of current juridical dogma, the latter emerging as the "systematic comprehension of the content of a specific ordinance" in 19th-century Germany.

3918. Colburn, David R. and Pozzetta, George E. BOSSES AND MACHINES: CHANGING INTERPRETATIONS IN AMERICAN HISTORY. *Hist. Teacher* 1976 9(3): 445-463. Discusses the literature dealing with the urban boss and the growth of American cities during the past century. The authors evaluate changing interpretations from the critical viewpoints at the turn of the century to the more favorable accounts of recent years. Urban bosses were not always inimical to reform; a number of them utilized reform movements to enhance the strengths of their own organizations. Based on primary and secondary sources; 4 illus., 18 notes. P. W. Kennedy

3919. Craig, Gordon A. THE CITY AND THE HISTORIAN. *Can. J. of Hist.* [Canada] 1970 5(1): 47-55. General observations on writing urban history designed to save the discipline from being frozen "into a kind of descriptive exercise" based on techniques learned from the social sciences. 17 notes. R. V. Ritter

3920. Curran, Donald J. HISTORICAL APPROACH TO A STUDY OF A METROPOLITAN AREA. *Land Econ. 1966 42(2): 209-215.*

3921. Czeczot-Gawrak, Zbigniew. NOTES ON THE GENERAL THEORY OF THE FILM DOCUMENT. *Cultures [France] 1974 2(1): 241-248.* Discusses film as historical document addressing the problems of historical consciousness, the impact of sociological or technological revolutions, and the methods of transmitting historical memory.

3922. Dahl, Hans Frederik. THE ART OF WRITING BROAD-CASTING HISTORY. *Gazette [Netherlands] 1978 24(2): 130-137.* With 50 years of experience behind it, broadcasting is ripe for historical study. The administration of broadcasting institutions has produced large collections of data which most historians have not consulted. Only in the area of the news broadcasts will the broadcasting historian find a dearth of primary source materials. Current secondary sources on broadcasting history reveal that programs have a folklore-like quality and have become increasingly uniform; and that broadcasting institutions have become monopolies which obtain income from mass membership. W. A. Wiegand

3923. Darnton, Robert. WHAT IS THE HISTORY OF BOOKS? *Daedalus 1982 111(3): 65-84.* Discusses the history of books as a discipline, and the various elements and perspectives which have comprised the subject area over time.

3924. Dew, Lee A. NARROW-GAUGE RAILROADS IN THE MID-MISSISSIPPI VALLEY: FRUSTRATIONS AND OPPORTU-NITIES FOR HISTORIANS. *Midwest Q. 1972 14(1): 65-78.* Enumerates four classes of transportation historians: 1) the "high iron" men; 2) the "house historians"; 3) the economists; and 4) the "hobby historians." The hobby historians "have shown the professionals how remiss they have been in their neglect of transportation generally and railroads in particular. The history of railroading in the mid-Mississippi valley has hardly been touched. The narrow-gauge era, for instance, has had hardly a word written about it, although it is a subject of great worth in itself, and essential to an understanding of the overall economic development of the region...." D. D. Cameron

3925. Dirnberger, Franz. THEATERGESCHICHTE UND THE-ATERLEGENDE. BEMERKUNGEN ZUM SCHRIFTGUT DER THEATERVERWALTUNG [Theater history and theater legend: remarks on the documentary sources of theater administration]. *Mitteilungen des Österreichischen Staatsarchivs [Austria] 1975 28: 210-225.* The supervision and administration of Vienna's court theaters have frequently changed; consequently many administrative records and other written sources have been lost and destroyed. Yet current theater problems require a knowledge of the precedents which can only be acquired through the documents. A knowledge of the pertinent sources is further required to preclude legends passing for theater history. The author describes some theater legends which he thinks developed because of insufficient use of sources, e.g., the legend that Joseph II was the founder of a truly national (German) theater when in reality he only revitalized the court theater. Theater history will have to be based on solid sources, no matter how hard they are to find. 33 notes. E. Sicher

3926. Dobkowski, Michael N. AMERICAN ANTISEMITISM AND AMERICAN HISTORIANS: A CRITIQUE. *Patterns of Prejudice [Great Britain] 1980 14(2): 33-43.* Examines the differing approaches of some American historians toward anti-Semitism in America and surveys the general character of that phenomenon since the late 19th century.

3927. Dyos, H. J. A CASTLE FOR EVERYMAN. *London J. [Great Britain] 1975 1(1): 118-134.* Examines the concept of suburbia as it has been presented in a range of books published, 1898-1963.

3928. Ebner, Michael H. URBAN HISTORY: RETROSPECT AND PROSPECT. *J. of Am. Hist. 1981 68(1): 69-84.* Analyzes the development of American urban history as a subfield of social his-

tory and assesses its current circumstances. Urban history should avoid becoming too preoccupied with technical scholarship. Urban historians should have three priorities for the future: adaptation of methods from other disciplines, further study of urban public policy, and the application of Marxist analysis. 38 notes.
T. P. Linkfield

3929. Eichberg, Henning. REKONSTRUKTION EINES CHAO-TEN: DIE VERÄNDERUNG DES JAHNBILDES UND DIE VERÄNDERUNG DER GESELLSCHAFT [Reconstruction of a chaotic person: changes in Jahn's image and changes in society]. *Stadion [West Germany] 1978 4(1): 262-291.* Friedrich Ludwig Jahn's (1778-1852) image has radically changed through the ages. Today, the criticisms of established political and social culture by a younger generation enables us to recognize the "chaotic figures" around Jahn as radicals. Gymnastics as an alternative physical culture appears as a bygone part of an antibourgeois subculture, as an attempt at "another life." 63 notes. M. Geyer

3930. Elsner, Jürgen. MUSIKETHNOLOGIE—MUSIKGESCHICHTE —MUSIKWISSENSCHAFT [Music ethnology, music history, music science]. *Wissenschaft Zeitschrift der Humboldt-U. zu Berlin. Gesellschafts- und Sprach-wissenschaftliche Reihe [East Germany] 1980 29(1): 35-37.* Contemporary research into music history combines ethnological and sociological concepts with historical, philosophical, stylistic, and biographical approaches.

3931. Ernst, Wolfgang. *DISTORY: CINEMA AND HISTORICAL DISCOURSE. J. of Contemporary Hist. [Great Britain] 1983 18(3): 397-409.* "Film is like history, absent in the representation...; history is like film, another genre but the same narrative pattern..." Even documentary film is fictional, if only in the point of view involved. Similarly, the historical-political film presents atmospheres which may or may not have been there at the time depicted. Numerous examples of recent films illustrate the point that "the paradigmatic validity of historiography can be applied to 'history through pictures.'" Based on secondary sources; 40 notes.
M. P. Trauth

3932. Feibach, Hans-Joachim and Münz, Rudolf. THESEN ZU THEORETISCH-METHODISCHEN FRAGEN DER THEATER-GESCHICHTS-SCHREIBUNG [Theses on the theoretic-methodical problems of theater historiography]. *Wissenschaftliche Zeitschrift der Humboldt-Universität zu Berlin: Gesellschafts- und Sprach-wissenschaftliche Reihe [East Germany] 1974 23(3/4): 359-367.* A wide-ranging methodological consideration of factors to be taken into account in any historiography of the theater. The authors discuss theater as it is, as it should be, and sometimes as it has developed, dwelling especially on the essence of theater, relations between dramatic literature and its stage production, between production and the audience, and between theater and society in any given era, especially as regards economic factors and class structure. Any historiographical consideration of theater must approach it as a unity of artistic conception and practice. M. Faissler

3933. Fenger, Ole. MELLEM JUSTITIA OG CLIO ELLER RE-TSHISTORIKERENS DILEMMA [Between Justitia and Clio, or, the dilemma of a legal historian]. *Tidsskrift for Rettsvitenskap [Norway] 1973 (5): 580-589.* Shows how legal historians are open to criticism from both jurists and historians.

3934. Fidler, Douglas K.; Goroneos, George; and Tamburro, Michael. FREDERICK JACKSON TURNER, THE REVISIONISTS, AND SPORT HISTORIOGRAPHY. *J. of Sport Hist. 1975 2(1): 41-49.* Applies the Turner thesis to sports, asserting that sports by 1917 had become the new safety valve, a cure-all for industrial pressure. Since sports were present before the development of the city, the safety valve theory has been challenged. Concludes that technological advance helped reduce urban tension, while sports are described as part of the American way of life. 22 notes.
M. Kaufman

3935. Figlio, Karl. THE HISTORIOGRAPHY OF SCIENTIFIC MEDICINE: AN INVITATION TO THE HUMAN SCIENCES. *Comparative Studies in Soc. and Hist. [Great Britain] 1977 19(3): 262-286.* Survey of the historiography of the interconnection of the history of science and the history of medicine, 1800-1977.

3936. Friedman, Lawrence M. THE STATE OF AMERICAN LEGAL HISTORY. *Hist. Teacher 1983 17(1): 103-120.* Prior to 1950, legal history could mostly be classified as "doctrinal," concentrating on legal doctrines and their origins. After 1950, the Wisconsin school, associated with J. Willard Hurst, emerged. The Wisconsin school focused on how external social factors, especially the economic system, shape and determine law. Recently a Critical school has begun to challenge the Wisconsin School's domination. Critical-school legal historians emphasize the ways in which law legitimizes the status quo. A major challenge is to combine the best features of the Wisconsin and Critical schools of legal history. Secondary works; ref. L. K. Blaser

3937. Friesel, Evyatar. CRITERIA AND CONCEPTION IN THE HISTORIOGRAPHY OF GERMAN AND AMERICAN ZIONISM. *Zionism [Israel] 1980 1(2): 285-302.* Discusses the history of Zionism as the movement developed in both Germany and the United States. American Zionist historians claim that Zionism in America fulfilled many important functions in American Jewish life. German Zionists perceived their work toward a Zionist entity as a rationalization to continue their lives in Germany without consideration of Aliya themselves. Statistics of Aliya are not germane to the success or failure of the Zionist movement. Historical and philosophical questions face the historian examining Zionism because of the ambiguous nature of the Zionist movement. Based partially on Central Zionist Archives materials; 43 notes. T. Koppel

3938. Frisch, Michael. AMERICAN URBAN HISTORY AS AN EXAMPLE OF RECENT HISTORIOGRAPHY. *Hist. and Theory 1979 18(3): 350-377.* Describes and criticizes the evolution of urban history in the United States since the mid-1960's. Before the early (1964) work of Stephan P. Thernstrom, research on the urban past was divided between those who clung to a more traditional idiographic orientation and those who were beginning to make use of methodologies borrowed from the social sciences. The so-called New Urban History won preeminence in the profession with the social-geographical mobility studies of the late 1960's. But these publications were flawed, because they let contemporary middle-class criteria and quantitative techniques limit their results. The infusion of a Marxist perspective and the influence of the European *Annales* school promise a more productive future for American social history as a whole. W. J. Reedy

3939. Furet, François. HISTOIRE DU LIVRE DANS LA SOCIETE MODERNE. RECHERCHES, METHODES, PROBLEMATIQUE [The history of the book in modern society: research, methods, issues]. *Rev. Roumaine d'Hist. [Rumania] 1970 9(3): 507-516.* Contends that quantitative methods can provide important insights into the social conditions prevailing when books were produced. The books of 18th-century France reveal a cultural diversity contrary to traditional interpretations, attesting not only to progressive and reactionary movements, but also to the varied purposes served by books. The ideas in books must, by various historical means, be integrated into contemporary society. One such idea was that of history as a factual documentation of the past, an idea flourishing during the 18th century despite attempts to romanticize historiography. A sociological history of the book in France would clarify contradictions inherent in society. A. W. Howell

3940. García-Gallo, Alfonso. CUESTIONES DE HISTORIOGRAFÍA JURÍDICA [Questions in legal historiography]. *Anuario de Hist. del Derecho Español [Spain] 1974 44: 741-764.* Considers a justification of the history of law and the possibility of a history of European law, on the occasion of the appearance of the collected methodological studies of Bruno Paradisi and the first volume of a work on European legal literature, directed by Helmut Coing. The author defends his well-known position on the institutional history of law, studied strictly from a legal angle. He also singles out the strong limitations to be met by any legal history attempting to go beyond the national framework presently encompassing it. J. L. A. (IHE 93052)

3941. Gieysztor, Aleksander. REMARQUES SUR L'HISTOIRE DU DROIT ET LES SCIENCES HISTORIQUES [Remarks on legal history and the historical sciences]. *Czasopismo Prawno-Historyczne [Poland] 1979 31(1): 31-37.* Discusses the close bonds between legal history and history in a broad sense in Poland. Historians specializing in legal history have often written works on national history, philology, or literature; they also have combined their research or comparative studies with history and other historical sciences. Deplores the separation of legal history from history *sensu largo* and expresses the wish for historians' cooperation with legal historians in comparative research. G. P. Cleyet

3942. Gilson, Estelle. ON THE TRAIL OF ANTI-SEMITISM. *Present Tense 1978 6(1): 51-54.* Discusses Léon Poliakov, a self-taught historian born in Leningrad, and his work, *The History of Anti-Semitism,* covering more than 2,000 years of Jewish life.

3943. Goldman, Martin S. TEACHING THE HOLOCAUST: SOME SUGGESTIONS FOR COMPARATIVE ANALYSIS. *J. of Intergroup Relations 1977 6(2): 23-30.* Comparative historiography of the Nazi treatment of Jews and the discrimination against Negroes and Indians in the United States would increase cultural understanding and cure prejudice.

3944. Gordon, Amy Glassner. CONFRONTING CULTURES: THE EFFECT OF THE DISCOVERIES ON SIXTEENTH-CENTURY FRENCH THOUGHT. *Terrae Incognitae 1976 8: 45-57.* Henri de LaPopelinière (1541-1608), the French historian, realized the significance of newly-discovered primitive cultures on historiography; he attempted to write the history of civilization, not just to chronicle events. Studying non-European societies encouraged understanding of contemporary life. 34 notes. C. B. Fitzgerald

3945. Gordon, Robert W. INTRODUCTION: J. WILLARD HURST AND THE COMMON LAW TRADITION IN AMERICAN LEGAL HISTORIOGRAPHY. *Law and Soc. Rev. 1975 10(1): 9-55.* Discusses the contribution of J. Willard Hurst and other scholars to the common law tradition and to analyses of the social and governmental functions of law, 1880's-1970.

3946. Goy, Joseph. L'HISTOIRE DE LA CULTURE MATÉRIELLE EN FRANCE: PROGRÈS RÉCENTS ET RECHERCHES FUTURES [Material history in France: recent progress and future research]. *Material Hist. Bull. [Canada] 1979 (8): 83-88.* Examines the current state of material history in France, a young and as yet not precisely defined field of study, discussing the prehistorian's, the Marxist's, and Fernand Braudel's definitions of material history, and research in the fields of technological history, economic history, medieval archaeology, and industrial archaeology.

3947. Grant, H. Roger. THE WRITING OF RAILROAD HISTORY. *Railroad Hist. 1983 (148): 9-12.* Discusses the state of railroad historiography in 1983, focusing on recent trends in company-sponsored histories, problems of interpreting large and often disorganized collections of railroad records, and the continuing dearth of studies on railroad labor, trade associations, and other topics.

3948. Guerci, Luciano. NOTE SULLA STORIOGRAFIA ILLUMINISTICA [Notes on historiography in the Enlightenment]. *Pensiero Pol. [Italy] 1979 12(2): 236-262.* Assesses recent critical works on historiography in the 18th century. An important characteristic of the Enlightenment is the value attached to time, a development naturally influenced by the growth of a secular state based on constitutional principles. Another characteristic is morality as it was portrayed in popular works often of a moralizing and didactic nature. Based on papers delivered at a conference on "The Study of Man and the Study of Society in the 18th Century." A. Alcock/S

3949. Gumilev, L. N. MESTO ISTORICHESKOI GEOGRAFII V VOSTOKOVENDNYKH ISSLEDOVANIIAKH [The place of historical geography in Oriental research]. *Narody Azii i Afriki [USSR] 1970 (1): 85-94.* Stresses the importance of examining the geographical aspects of human history. Geographical factors offer useful insights into the influence of the geographical environment on man as well as his on it. The author gives several examples of the use of geographical data in ancient and modern Oriental studies. Secoday works; 21 notes.   A. P. Oxley

3950. Guttman, Allen. WHO'S ON FIRST? OR, BOOKS ON THE HISTORY OF AMERICAN SPORTS. *J. of Am. Hist. 1979 66(2): 348-354.* Summarizes the important American and European histories of American sports from 1838 to 1978. The current interest in sports by historians is an inevitable result of the broader interest in popular culture. Although many of the recent American histories are professional, all but a few suffer from scholarly isolation; most American writers ignore recent works by social theorists and even histories of American sports by European writers. 31 notes.
                                                        T. P. Linkfield

3951. Halkin, Léon-E. LE JOURNALISTE, HISTORIEN DU PRÉSENT? [The journalist, a historian of the present?]. *Cahiers de Clio [Belgium] 1980 (63): 5-15.* Analyzes the work, role, and duties of the journalist who, applying the same rules as the historian, may be considered the real historian of the present. Lecture at the University of Liège, Belgium, 6 March 1980.

3952. Hammack, David C. ANOTHER SNARK? PURSUING URBAN HISTORY. *Reviews in American History 1984 12(3): 343-346.* Reviews *The Pursuit of Urban History* (1983), edited by Derek Fraser and Anthony Sutcliffe, an eclectic collection of current work on the elusive subject of urban history in the United States and Europe.

3953. Handlin, Oscar. A TWENTY YEAR RETROSPECT OF AMERICAN JEWISH HISTORIOGRAPHY. *Am. Jewish Hist. Q. 1976 65(4): 295-309.* Compares his 1948 evaluation of writing of the American Jewish past with the progress made since then. Greater abundance of material and its availability coupled with professionalization of authors and the elimination of an apologetic approach has contributed to greater scholarship. Setting the Jewish experience in America in a comparative, often sociological relationship to the contemporary trends in other immigrant religions and community organizations leads to a better understanding of the story, even though the extent of leakage through intermarriage, conversion, and apathy has not yet been assessed. The history of American anti-Semitism, 1900-40, also still remains to be written. Delivered at the 73rd annual meeting of the American Jewish Historical Society, 4 May 1975. 43 notes.   F. Rosenthal

3954. Hardt, Hanno. THE RISE AND PROBLEMS OF MEDIA RESEARCH IN GERMANY. *J. of Communication 1976 26(3): 90-95.* Discusses research problems in the historiography and sociology of the role of the press in Germany, 1885-1970's.

3955. Harris, Michael H. TWO YEARS' WORK IN AMERICAN LIBRARY HISTORY, 1969-1970. *J. of Lib. Hist. 1972 7(1): 33-49.* Examines library history research (1969-70) on theory and method, sources, biography, libraries in early America, public libraries, academics and research Libraries, state, national and international libraries, and library education and library association. A significant amount of the work is published in fulfillment of graduate degree requirements. 73 notes.   L. G. Will

3956. Havig, Alan R. BEYOND NOSTALGIA: AMERICAN RADIO AS A FIELD OF STUDY. *J. of Popular Culture 1978 12(2): 218-227.* Reviews research and historiography of the broadcasting industry, assesses business, historical, political, popular, and literary reasons for studying the area, and suggests areas to investigate, 1930's-60's.

3957. Heilman, Robert B. PASTS, PRESENT, AND FUTURE IN THE RENAISSANCE. *Southern Q. 1975 14(1): 1-16.* Examines contemporary reasons for making the European Renaissance a focal

point of study and discusses humanism, religion, and the visual arts in relation to it. Applies Renaissance ideas, concepts, and attitudes to modern society. Based on various literary works and their authors.   R. W. Dubay

3958. Hill, Christopher. DRAMA AS HISTORY. *Lit. and Hist. [Great Britain] 1983 9(2): 250-254.* Reviews the following books on drama and the theater: Phillip Edward et al.'s *The Revels History of Drama in English, Vol. IV, 1613-1660* (1981), Alexander Leggatt's *Ben Jonson: His Vision and His Art* (1981), A. Coleman and A. Hammond's *Poetry and Drama, 1570-1700: Essays in Honour of Harold F. Brooks* (1981), Ann J. Cook's *The Privileged Playgoers of Shakespeare's London, 1576-1642* (1981), and Simon Shepherd's *Amazons and Warrior Women: Varieties of Feminism in Seventeenth-Century Drama* (1981). These books illustrate how such varied social themes as censorship, feminism, and class differences affected the theater and how the drama of that time reflected these concerns.   M. M. A. Lynch

3959. Hillier, Bevis. GOING ON EXPLORATION: SURVEYS OF ART. *Encounter [Great Britain] 1982 59(6): 62-69.* Discusses and evaluates various histories and surveys of art.

3960. Hoffecker, Carol E. THE EMERGENCE OF A GENRE: THE URBAN PICTORIAL HISTORY. *Public Hist. 1983 5(4): 37-48.* Discusses pictorial urban histories published by Continental Heritage Press, in Tulsa, Oklahoma; Donning Company Publishers, in Norfolk, Virginia; and Windsor Publications, Inc., in Woodland Hills, California.

3961. Hofmann, Etienne. NOUVELLES ÉTUDES SUR LE "GROUPE DE COPPET" [New studies on the Coppet Group]. *Schweizerische Zeitschrift für Geschichte [Switzerland] 1978 28(4): 522-530.* Members of the Coppet Group included Benjamin Constant, Jean-Charles Sismondi, the Schlegel brothers, and Charles Victor de Bonstetten and they were centered around Madame de Staël (1766-1817). This circle resembled no other; it was neither an academy nor purely a salon, not a club nor a party. It had its self-imposed task of safeguarding and adopting for the future those aspects of the Enlightenment which its members considered to be most worthy. Reviews a number of publications concerning the group that originated in international colloquia held in Coppet and Geneva in 1973 and 1974.   H. K. Meier

3962. Holly, Edward G. THE PAST AS PROLOGUE: THE WORK OF THE LIBRARY HISTORIAN. *J. of Lib. Hist. 1977 12(2): 110-127.* Critiques many works of library history from 1877 to 1945, and discusses the difficulties inherent in researching and reporting what really happened. Primary and secondary sources; 41 notes.   A. C. Dewees

3963. Hošek, Emil. ZPRACOVÁNÍ A VÝZNAM HISTORIE LESŮ [The processing and significance of the history of forests]. *Archivní Časopis [Czechoslovakia] 1983 33(4): 193-206.* Because of the long-term nature of forest economy and the basically unchanging prevailing conditions in any given forest, forest history is just as important as standard research in contributing to knowledge of and progress in forestry. Systematic records have been kept since the late 19th century on large estates, but major historical research on all Czech forests has only been conducted since 1950. This has been carried out in three cycles in progressively more detailed frameworks. All available archival records, some going back to the 16th century, have been used to detail the physical history of forests, the state of soils, species introduction, seed sources, wild animal populations, damage and losses due to weather and animals, and economic questions. Work in some areas has yet to be completed. 4 notes.   D. Short

3964. Huovinen, Lauri. RENAISSANCE RESEARCH TODAY. *U. of Turku. Inst. of General Hist. Publ. [Finland] 1967 1: 7-15.* Discusses the historiography of the Italian Renaissance, from Torsten and Werner Söderhjelm's *Italiensk Renässans* (1908), and reviews the work of the most famous historians of the Renaissance.

3965. Hurst, James Willard. THE STATE OF LEGAL HISTORY. *Rev. in Am. Hist. 1982 10(4): 292-305.* Describes the expansion of legal historiography from its earlier narrow focus on New England, the colonial era, and the courts to include regional and contextual studies.

3966. Hyman, Paula E. THE HISTORY OF EUROPEAN JEWRY: RECENT TRENDS IN THE LITERATURE. *J. of Modern Hist. 1982 54(2): 303-319.* Review article on some 16 recent works on European Jews. Mentions older literature, points to fruitful areas for research, and presents the thesis that "if histories of European Jewry rightly continue to be preoccupied by emancipation and its diverse consequences, they are probing more deeply the connections, and tensions, between ideology and behavior, between elites and masses, between acculturation and the assertion of minority-group identity." J. D. Hunley

3967. Ilsøe, Grethe. ADMINISTRATIONSHISTORIE—UNDER FLERE SYNSVINKLER [Administration history—from several points of view]. *Arkiv [Denmark] 1980 8(1): 54-58.* Administration history cannot be sharply divided into auxiliary science and independent research. The archivist is best qualified for evaluating the archive material in its historical context. Analyses based on governmental output are not possible for the period before 1848. The historian here particularly needs the source material. Administrative history can learn from administrative science's formulation of questions and contact between the two disciplines might prove highly beneficial. K. S. Williams

3968. Izdebski, Hubert. HISTORIA ADMINISTRACJI A HISTORIA BIUROKRACJI [The history of administration and the history of bureaucracy]. *Panstwo i Prawo [Poland] 1975 30(5): 60-72.* Examines the close links between the history of administration, and the history and theory of bureaucracy, as seen in world history, 1500-1975.

3969. Kedourie, Elie. REFLECTIONS ON JEWISH HISTORY. *Am. Scholar 1981 50(2): 231-235.* Explores the perennial conflict in Jewish historiography that views history as ceaseless change and immense variety on the one hand and rabbinical revelation of truth on the other. These two competing notions, with their mutual tensions and ambiguities, constitute the ever-shifting framework and distinguishing landmarks of Jewish history. F. F. Harling

3970. Kedward, Roderick. FILM AND HISTORY. *History [Great Britain] 1980 65(215): 405-413.* Discusses the study of films—primarily newsreels, documentaries, political, and feature films—in modern historiography. Based on seven histories of modern filmmaking in Great Britain, the USSR, and Nazi Germany. R. P. Sindermann, Jr.

3971. Kirkinen, Heikki. HYTTYNEN VALTAMERESSÄ ELI MAAN IHMISLAJIN VIUHAHDUS UNIVERSUMISSA: ALKUA IHMISKUNNAN HISTORIAN EKOLOGISEKSI KEHITYSMALLIKSI [A mosquito in the ocean, or the buzz of earth's humanity in the universe: sketch for an ecological development model of human history]. *Hist. Arkisto [Finland] 1978 71: 302-319.* Presents an ecological model of human history, placed in a cosmic and global time frame, and constructed in a pattern of interrelated human and natural systems. Energy and information are major resources for growth, while the content of human development is shaped by such factors as changes in population levels, in technology and in modes of human interaction. Table, 4 charts. R. G. Selleck

3972. Klaw, Barbara. IMAGES OF A LIFETIME. *Am. Heritage 1983 34(6): 16-25.* In 1951, Marshall Davidson authored *Life in America,* a history in pictures and words that opened the way to wider acceptance of pictorial history. Presents 14 of the pictures, ranging from a map published in 1651 to a bridge painting done in 1922, that have special meaning for Davidson. 14 photos, illus. J. F. Paul

3973. Kochan, Lionel. A MODEL FOR JEWISH HISTORIOGRAPHY. *Modern Judaism 1981 1(3): 263-278.* Creates a model of Jewish historiography that removes Jewish history from the nation-

alistic framework and locates it in the category of utopian thought and action, focusing on the concept of community as it has evolved over the years in Jewish society. 67 notes.

3974. Köhler, Oskar et al. VERSUCH EINER "HISTORISCHEN ANTHROPOLOGIE" [An attempt at "historical anthropology"]. *Saeculum [West Germany] 1974 25(2-3): 129-246.* Tries to establish a useful kind of historiography for the present generation with the help of the comparative study of three topics: 1) aggressive and imperial expansion in ancient, medieval, and modern human history on all continents; 2) the social and individual phenomenon of the monk in different societies; and 3) the foundation of various legal systems.

3975. Kooij, P. STADSGESCHIEDENIS EN DE VERHOUDING STAD-PLATTELAND [Urban history and rural-urban relations]. *Econ.-en Sociaal-Hist. Jaarboek [Netherlands] 1975 38: 124-140.* Surveys recent studies on urban histories in the United States, Great Britain, and Germany, with special attention given to problems of rural-urban relations. G. D. Homan

3976. Kornieieva, M. H. TENDENTSIIA DO INTEHRATSII NAUKOVOHO ZNANNIA—ZAKONOMIRNIST' ROZVYTKU SUCHASNOI NAUKY [Trends toward the integration of scientific knowledge: the regularity of development in current historical science]. *Ukrains'kyi Istorychnyi Zhurnal [USSR] 1971 (10): 21-25.* Review of the increasing specialization found in all branches of the natural and social sciences and the parallel development, in particular in history, of disciplines embracing the achievements of multidisciplinary approaches.

3977. Kovács, Sándor V. AZ ELSŐ MAGYAR NYOMDATÖRTÉNET ISMERETLEN KÉZIRATA [The unknown manuscript of the first Hungarian history of printing]. *Magyar Könyvszemle [Hungary] 1973 89(3-4): 332-348.* The first synthesis of Hungarian printing history is a set of lecture notes from 1788 entitled *Prima Lineamenta Artis Typographicae apud Hungaros* by Jakab Ferdinánd Miller, professor of history. 2 photos, 6 notes. R. Hetzron

3978. Kozlov, V. I. O BIOLOGO-GEOGRAFICHESKOI KONTSEPTSII ETNICHESKOI ISTORII [The biological-geographical conception of ethnic history]. *Voprosy Istorii [USSR] 1974 (12): 72-85.* A critical analysis of the concept put forward by L. N. Gumilev in a number of his works. The author shows that it represents a peculiar combination of long-evolved conceptions of geographical determinism with biological and psychological conceptions of social development. Exaggerating the role of geographical factors in the origin and historical development of nations, attaching decisive significance in the historical process to local and genetically emerging "spontaneous" forces which manifest themselves most clearly in the activity of one or another outstanding historical personality (Alexander the Great, Mohammed, Napoleon, etc.), and unjustifiably identifying historico-social processes with natural-biological and physical phenomena, Gumilev arrives at a number of patently erroneous and even reactionary conclusions which, moreover, can well create an absolutely wrong impression about the actual views held by Soviet historians and ethnographers. J

3979. Krenzlin, Ulrike. DIE ROMANTIK ALS EUROPÄISCHE ERSCHEINUNG: HISTORISCHE UND METHODOLOGISCHE PROBLEME EINER VERGLEICHENDEN ANALYSE [Romanticism as a European phenomenon: historical and methodological problems of a comparative analysis]. *Wiss. Zeits. der Greifswalder Ernst-Moritz-Arndt-Universität. Gesellschafts- und Sprachwissenschaftliche Reihe [East Germany] 1979 28(1-2): 72-75.*

3980. Kroeber, A. L. AN ANTHROPOLOGIST LOOKS AT HISTORY. *Pacific Hist. Rev. 1957 26(3): 281-288.* Expounds on the place which history's sister social sciences (anthropology, archaeology, and ethnology) and hard sciences (geology, biology, and astronomy) play in historiography.

3981. Kuehl, Jerry. T. V. HISTORY. *Hist. Workshop J.* *[Great Britain]* 1976 1: 127-135. Considers the nonpolitical constraints on television documentary producers. A documentary program has two basic components: the footage of film available and the sound recordings to match it. When new films or recordings are made the producer often finds that his subjects are deliberately selective in what they offer for the record. At times financial limitations will prevent the producer from interviewing the people who are most important for the subject of his program. Some interesting people prove unable to communicate their views when being interviewed. The single basic constraint on producers who want to become historians stems from the very nature of program production, which is a collective task, whereas the writing of history is a solitary one. The author repeatedly illustrates his points with reference to two documentary films, *Destination America* and *The World at War*.

A. J. Evans

3982. Kurlat de Korin, Itta R. LA NUMISMATICA COMO CIENCIA AUXILIAR DE LA HISTORIA [Numismatics as an auxiliary science to history]. *Historia* *[Argentina]* 1963 9(32): 136-146. Comments on the types of coinage known to history, particularly in Europe, and on the significance of numismatics for historians.

3983. Laird, J. T. T. E. LAWRENCE: THE PROBLEM OF INTERPRETATION. *Australian Q.* *[Australia]* 1960 32(1): 93-99. Discusses the development of the Lawrence of Arabia legend through various interpretations written since the 1920's, concluding that T. E. Lawrence's own account, *Seven Pillars of Wisdom,* is still the best source for his experiences in World War I.

3984. Le Riverend, Julio. PROBLEMAS HISTÓRICOS DE LA CONQUISTA DE AMÉRICA. LAS CASAS Y SU TIEMPO [Historical problems of the conquest of America: Las Casas and his times]. *Casa de las Américas* *[Cuba]* 1974 15(85): 4-15. Discusses the 16th-century explorer Fra. Bartolomé de Las Casas (1474-1566), discussing his *Historia de las Indias* and its effects on later conquests of America.

3985. Lees, Andrew. HISTORICAL PERSPECTIVES ON CITIES IN MODERN GERMANY: RECENT LITERATURE. *J. of Urban Hist.* 1979 5(4): 411-446. Despite a recent interest in German urban history in the modern period the field is still underdeveloped. No scholarly survey or synthetic treatment of German urban development and structure exists. Most studies are particularistic in coverage, narrative in organization, and routine in subject. Important themes such as social response to or causes of urbanization are rarely discussed. 35 notes.

T. W. Smith

3986. Leham, Emil. THE GIST OF IT ALL. *Midstream* 1979 25(2): 34-42. Discusses the need for a unifying field theory of Jewish history and the need to assemble the points of departure for the examination of the forces driving the Jews through time.

3987. Lehotská, D. SCIENCES AUXILIAIRES HISTORIQUES EN 1960-1977, LEUR ÉVOLUTION ET LEUR APPORT [Historical auxiliary sciences, 1960-77: their evolution and contribution]. *Studia Hist. Slovaca* *[Czechoslovakia]* 1980 (11): 229-273. Slovak auxiliary sciences include history of diplomacy and administration, paleography, chronology, heraldry, metrology, numismatics, historical geography, topography, demography and statistics. Notes the satisfactory methodology used, but gives suggestions on how to develop research in these sciences, in particular, about the production of works of syntheses. Primary sources; note.

G. P. Cleyet

3988. Lemaire, Jacques. L'IMAGE DE VOLTAIRE DANS L'HISTORIOGRAPHIE MAÇONNIQUE DE LANGUE FRANÇAISE [Voltaire's image in the French historiography of freemasonry]. *Rev. de l'U. de Bruxelles* *[Belgium]* 1977 (3-4): 310-344. Examines the reasons for and extent of Voltaire's involvement in freemasonry and analyzes the historiography of this involvement, 18th century-1970's.

3990. Liess, Andreas. MUSIKGESCHICHTE UND MUSIKGESCHICHTEN [Music history and music histories]. *Wissenschaft und Weltbild* *[Austria]* 1969 22(2): 133-138. Reviews a number of works in the field of music history.

3991. Ling, Jan. BÜRGERLICHE KONZEPTIONEN DER MUSIKGESCHICHTSSCHREIBUNG: VERSUCH EINER ALTERNATIVE [Bourgeois conceptions of music historiography: attempt at an alternative]. *Wissenschaftliche Zeitschrift der Humboldt-U. zu Berlin. Gesellschafts- und Sprachwissenschaftliche Reihe* *[East Germany]* 1980 29(1): 31-34. Briefly examines sources and approaches used in the study of music history in Scandinavian countries and notes the trend toward incorporating the use of music in different social milieus into music history research.

3992. MacDonald, William W. THE ENLIGHTENMENT AND THE HISTORIANS. *Res. Studies* 1970 38(1): 1-12. Discusses the historiographical study of the Enlightenment, by examining the works of numerous historians both before and after World War II.

3993. Marquez Castro, Diego. EL HOMBRE Y EL DESEQUILIBRIO ECOLOGICO A TRAVÉS DE LA HISTORIA [Man and the ecological imbalance through history]. *Bol. Hist.* *[Venezuela]* 1975 (38): 141-151. Traces the history of mankind in the light of the modern ecological reform movement. Based on secondary works; 24 notes.

F. Pollaczek

3994. Martinet, Chantal. LES HISTORIENS ET LA STATUE [French historians and 19th-century statues]. *Mouvement Social* *[France]* 1985 (131): 121-130. The public sculpture of the last century is now the object of a great interest; many historians and art historians have been working on the topic in order to explain the significance of public sculpture for the spirit of the 19th century.

J

3995. McCreary, Eugene C. FILM CRITICISM AND THE HISTORIAN. *Film & History* 1981 11(1): 1-8. Analyzes the role of film critic as chronicler of the milieu which produced a particular film, using as an example the career of French critic and film maker Louis Delluc who, from 1910 to his death in 1924, drew from the then-current developments in music, art, and psychology to describe film as a cinematic representation of the burgeoning 20th-century experience, whose stress ought to be on the modern technology that produced it.

3996. McRoberts, Meg. THE FRENCH PHILOSOPHES AND THE JEWS: AN HISTORIOGRAPHICAL INQUIRY. *Pro. of the Ann. Meeting of the Western Soc. for French Hist.* 1974 2: 208-216. Analyzes Arthur Hertzberg's thesis in his *The French Enlightenment and the Jews* (New York: Columbia U. Pr., 1968), an outstanding work in the historiography of the Enlightenment. Until Hertzberg there was little deviation from Heinrich Graetz's 1876 view of anti-Semitism as religious and medieval, its continued existence due to a time-lag. Hertzberg claims that the philosophes, especially Voltaire, echoed Christian anti-Semitism but also "transformed it into the secular anti-Semitism" of today. Biblio.

J. D. Falk

3997. Mergen, Bernard. WORK AND PLAY. *Am. Q.* 1980 32(4): 453-463. Reviews six books published in 1977 or 1978 on the subjects of work and play in history. These two subjects have been treated separately: the history of work has been handled by economic, social, and labor historians, while the history of play has been studied by a small, but different group of scholars. All the books reviewed add to our understanding of work and play, but only one tries to treat both at once. What is needed is an end to the false dichotomy of work and play, and a synthesis of research already done.   D. K. Lambert

3998. Michael, Reuven. THE CONTRIBUTION OF "SULAMITH" TO MODERN JEWISH HISTORIOGRAPHY. *Zion [Israel] 1976 39(1/2): 86-113.* The appearance of the journal *Sulamith* in 1806 as the successor to *Ha-Meassel* is further evidence of the dissemination of the German language among Central European Jews. In this Enlightenment journal designed to continue the spirit of the German Haskalah, several historical essays appeared which were to constitute important contributions to the development of modern Jewish historiography. Most of the authors of these essays belonged to the Prague circle of the Haskalah. Their contribution to Jewish historiography lies in their departure from the chroniclers and in their opening horizons to a more profound and comprehensive historical view.   J

3999. Mignot, Claude. HENRI SAUVAL ENTRE L'ERUDITION ET LA CRITIQUE D'ART [Henri Sauval between erudition and art criticism]. *Dix-Septième Siècle [France] 1983 35(1): 51-66.* Analyzes the works of Henri Sauval (1623-76), his appraisals of Paris monuments, churches, and other works of art and his appreciation of artists. Sauval contributed to the birth of art criticism in France, but after 1660 he lost much of his interest in criticism in favor of historical scholarship. Based on Bibliothèque Nationale archival documents; 19 notes.   G. P. Cleyet

4000. Mironov, B. N. AMERIKANSKAIA BURZHUAZNAIA ISTORIOGRAFIIA RUSSKOGO FEODAL'NOGO GORODA [American bourgeois historiography of the Russian feudal town]. *Voprosy Istorii [USSR] 1984 (7): 29-42.* American historians concentrate mainly on the difference and similarities between the Russian and the Western European town and associate them with the broader question of the Russian and Western development patterns and the causes behind the Russian revolutions. The current American concept counterpoising the Russian and Western European town is merely a variant of the opinion held by Russian prerevolutionary historians. Both the Russian and the Western European town served basically the same purpose and settled the same problems, though in a different sequence and by different means. The urbanization processes in both parts of Europe followed the same patterns, were similar in essence, but often differed in form.   J

4001. Molchanov, Iu. V. TRUDY 'MEZHDUNARODNOGO OBSHCHESTVA PO IZUCHENIIU VREMENI' [Works of the International Society for the Study of Time]. *Voprosy Filosofii [USSR] 1977 (5): 159-166.* Describes the development of the International Society for the Study of Time, set up in New York in 1967, and traces the progress of Western research in this field by summarizing the papers presented at the three conferences of the Society in 1969, 1973, and 1976.

4002. Morgan, H. Wayne. THE GILDED AGE. *Am. Heritage 1984 35(5): 42-48.* Presents a number of revisions that have been made to the stereotypical views of the Gilded Age. Closer examination of politics, economics, labor, literature, and art all suggest variances from earlier generalizations. This period ought correctly to be viewed as a transition and a new interpretation of the period is needed. 4 illus.   J. F. Paul

4003. Morrow, Don. CANADIAN SPORT HISTORY: A CRITICAL ESSAY. *J. of Sport Hist. 1983 10(1): 67-79.* Canadian sport history received its impetus from the graduate program of Dr. Maxwell Howell at the University of Alberta. The impact of that program combined with the publication of the *Canadian Journal of History of Sport and Physical Education* (May 1970) must be considered in any evaluation of the state of Canadian sport history over the past decade. Much work has been published in that journal and in the *Journal of Sport History.* In the latter journal 8.5% of the articles relate to Canada, and 23.1% in the *Canadian Journal* are on Canadian sport history. In terms of methodology, most historians have used the narrative-descriptive approach, and only two

authors have used theory to interpret the facts. Most authors are trained in physical education and not in history. Based on recent books and articles; 60 notes.   M. Kaufman

4004. Mott, Morris. PERSPECTIVES ON SPORTS AND URBAN STUDIES: CANADIAN SPORTS HISTORY: SOME COMMENTS TO URBAN HISTORIANS. *Urban Hist. Rev. [Canada] 1983 12(2): 25-29.* In the last 10 or 15 years a considerable number of publications on the history of Canadian sport have appeared. Most of these are of little consequence to serious scholars, but a few are useful and informative to urban historians. The existence of several exemplary studies on the history of sport and leisure in Great Britain and the United States, together with the current acceptance of the idea that good sports history can be good social or cultural history, should encourage more and better studies of Canadian sporting developments.   J/S

4005. Motte, Olivier. LA ESCUELA DE LOS ANALES Y LA HISTORIA DEL DERECHO [The *Annales* school and the history of law]. *Rev. de Estudios Histórico-Jurídicos [Chile] 1981 6: 317-330.*

4006. Münz, Rudolf. ZWISCHEN "THEATERKRIEG" UND "NATIONALTHEATERIDEE"—ZU DEN ANFÄNGEN DER BÜRGERLICHEN DEUTSCHEN THEATERHISTORIOGRAPHIE [Between "theater war" and "national theater idea": on the beginnings of bourgeois German theater historiography]. *Wissenschaftliche Zeitschrift der Humboldt-Universität zu Berlin. Gesellschafts- und Sprachwissenschaftliche Reihe [East Germany] 1969 18(1): 15-36.* Opposition to the theater by German Protestant groups (Puritans, Calvinists, Pietists) in the 18th century was slowly overcome by the growing importance of the bourgeoisie which used the theater for political and ideological ends, such as national unification in the 19th century.

4007. Nahon, Gérard. LES MARRANES ESPAGNOLS ET PORTUGAIS ET LES COMMUNAUTÉS JUIVES ISSUES DU MARRANISME DANS L'HISTORIOGRAPHIE RÉCENTE (1960-75) [Spanish and Portuguese Marranos and the Jewish communites descended from Marranism in recent historiography, 1960-75]. *Rev. des Études Juives [France] 1977 136(3-4): 297-367.* Reviews the development of Marranism, from the 15th to the 20th centuries with particular reference to work carried out on the subject, 1960-75. Shows the evolution of Marranism in Spain and Portugal and their territories, the dispersal of the Marranos, and major trends in Marrano historiography. Also considers other Jewish communities, for example, in Italy, the Ottoman Empire, Morocco, Europe, and the United States which have descended from the Marranos in France, Holland, England, Ireland, and Germany. Studies the sources, archaeology, groupings, biographies, economy, religious practices, community institutions, decisions by the rabbis, intercommunity relations, mentality, culture, and persecutions. Based on English, French, Spanish, Italian, and other secondary sources; appendix, 30 notes.   G. L. Neville

4008. Nauert, Charles G., Jr. RENAISSANCE HUMANISM: AN EMERGENT CONSENSUS AND ITS CRITICS. *Indiana Social Studies Q. 1980 33(1): 5-20.* Discusses the role of humanism, especially as advanced by Paul Oskar Kristeller, in the evolving views of the nature of the Renaissance.

4009. Nord, David Paul. WHAT WE CAN DO FOR THEM: JOURNALISM HISTORY AND THE HISTORY PROFESSION. *Journalism Hist. 1982 9(2): 56-60.* Assesses trends in journalism historiography, including agenda-setting research, information diffusion studies, organization studies, economic-restraints research, and socialization studies.

4010. Parker, John. ORIGINAL SOURCES AND WEIGHTY AUTHORITIES: SOME THOUGHTS ON REVISIONISM AND THE HISTORIOGRAPHY OF DISCOVERY. *Terrae Incognitae 1981 13: 31-34.* There is a need to reevaluate the interpretations of earlier historians who wrote on discovery and exploration. Later information and scientific advances may add new dimensions to older, but still valid research. In addition, some topics, such as the impact of religion on the age of discovery and naval logistics need more work.   C. B. Fitzgerald

4011. Pastore, Nicholas and Rosen, Edward. ALBERTI AND THE CAMERA OBSCURA. *Physis [Italy] 1984 26(2): 259-269.* Examines two different interpretations of a passage in an anonymous biography (through the year 1437) of Italian painter Leon Battista Alberti (1404-72) that describes Alberti's *demonstrationes* [optical displays]. In the late 18th century, G. Tiraboschi used this description to ascribe to Alberti, rather than to the 16th-century natural philosopher Giambattista Porta, the invention of the *camera obscura* [dark box]. James Waterhouse's "Camera Obscura, History" in the 11th edition of the *Encyclopaedia Britannica* (1910) interprets the passage as referring to a show box for paintings. Concludes that Waterhouse's interpretation better fits the passage itself. Fig., 40 notes. Italian summary.   R. Grove

4012. Pérez-Prendes y Muñoz de Arracó, José Manuel. SOBRE EL CONOCIMIENTO HISTORICO DEL DERECHO [On historical knowledge of law]. *Estudios de Deusto [Spain] 1969 17: 337-403.* Discusses the relations between law and history, between the dogmatic and historical understanding of law, and the historical influences which helped create Spanish law.

4013. Perini, Giovanna. LA STORIOGRAFIA ARTISTICA A BOLOGNA E IL COLLEZIONISMO PRIVATO [Art history in Bologna and private collections]. *Ann. della Scuola Normale Superiore di Pisa: Classe di Lettere e Filosofia [Italy] 1981 11(1): 181-243.* A comparison of Bologna with Venice, Florence, and Milan with respect to art history literary production since the 15th century reveals that Bologna began late; while Florence produced biographies and Milan produced treatises, Bologna, like Venice, emphasized the city guide.

4014. Petrovich, Michael B. CROATIAN HUMANISTS AND THE WRITING OF HISTORY IN THE FIFTEENTH AND SIXTEENTH CENTURIES. *Slavic Rev. 1978 37(4): 624-639.* Examines briefly the roots of humanism and traces humanistic development throughout Europe. Lists and discusses 11 15th- and 16th-century Croatian humanist writers and their works: Koriolan Cipiko, Marko Marulić, Ludovik Crijević, Feliks Petancić, Vinko Pribojević, Stjepan Brodarić, Antum Vrancić, Bartol Djurdjević, Matija Vlacić, Franjo Petris, and Dinko Zavorović. 68 notes.
                                                    R. B. Mendel

4015. Phillipson, N. T. HENRY THOMAS BUCKLE ON SCOTTISH HISTORY AND THE SCOTTISH MIND. *Hist. of Educ. Q. 1974 14(3): 407-417.* Discusses the work of Henry Thomas Buckle, who attempted in the 19th century to write the history of liberty and to discover the laws determining society's progress, with reference to Scotland.

4016. Pollak, Michael. PRINTING IN VENICE—BEFORE GUTENBERG? *Lib. Q. 1975 45(3): 287-308.* A brief and completely erroneous statement by the sixteenth-century Hebrew chronicler Joseph ha-Kohen [1496-1578?] to the effect that an unnamed book had been printed in Venice in 1428 set off a bitter debate which was to engage the energies of several generations of printing historians. The chronicler's remark was manipulated in such a way as to cause it to become a key factor in the centuries-long dispute over whether printing had been invented in Germany by Johannes Gutenberg or in Holland by Laurens Coster. The deeply partisan and often emotional arguments regarding the validity of the ha-Kohen claim demonstrate quite plainly that when the facts did not support their own convictions, certain printing historians were not above twisting them about or sweeping them under the rug. Although some scholars attempted to judge ha-Kohen's statement solely on its merits, too many others did not. Generally speaking, the treatment of ha-Kohen's allegation regarding the existence of printing in 1428 represents a low point in the writing of printing history and serves as a reminder that the works of the early printing historians must be read wtih considerable caution.   J

4017. Pucheu, René. LA PRESSE ET SON HISTOIRE [History of the press]. *Histoire [France] 1978 (5): 87-90.* Reviews the historiography of the press in France with particular reference to Claude Bellanger, Jacques Godechot, Pierre Guiral, and Fernand Terrou, eds., *Histoire cénérale de la presse française* (Paris: P.U.F., 1969-76).

4018. Quaintance, Richard E. WALPOLE'S WHIG INTERPRETATION OF LANDSCAPING HISTORY. *Studies in Eighteenth-Century Culture 1979 9: 285-300.* Horace Walpole felt that the English "respect for local vitality and circumstance" was expressed in landscape gardening as well as in politics. Landscaping was laissez-faire, and was Whig just as much as parliamentary politics were. This is expressed in his "On Modern Gardening" (1771). 28 notes.
                                                            S

4019. Radojčić, Svetozar. O SRPSKOJ ISTORIJI UMETNOSTI [Serbian art history]. *Jugoslovenski Istorijski Časopis [Yugoslavia] 1977 16(1-2): 3-8.* Summarizes the historiography of Serbian art, especially painting. Urges the adoption of the critical methods of Ilarion Ruvarac and the comparison and synthesis of Serbian art history with other modern European schools of art history.

4020. Rakestraw, Lawrence. CONSERVATION HISTORIOGRAPHY: AN ASSESSMENT. *Pacific Hist. R. 1972 41(3): 271-288.* A recent boom in the field of conservation history is due to increased interest in the environment, availability of new sources, improved service of federal and state archives, and the increase in oral history. Describes some of the existing conflicts among the non-academic and academic conservation historians and writers, and suggests that the writing is sometimes superficial, with faulty hypotheses, overemphasized conflict, and stereotypes. There is need for more careful and responsible writing, if the historian is to contribute to the conservation field and aid in decisionmaking for the future. 37 notes.
                                                    E. C. Hyslop

4021. Rebérioux, Madeleine. CINEMA ET HISTOIRE, HISTOIRE ET CINEMA: QUELQUES TEXTES RECENTS [Cinema and history, history and cinema: some recent studies]. *Mouvement Social [France] 1982 (121): 117-121.* Discusses the relationship between history and films in the light of recent articles and books. Film does not precisely reflect society; it is a representation as intended by the producer in a perspective introducing history in sociology. The cinema can also be viewed as a source that breaks with institutional or bureaucratic systems. 25 notes.   G. P. Cleyet

4022. Redmond, Gerald. SPORT HISTORY IN ACADEME: REFLECTIONS ON A HALF-CENTURY OF PECULIAR PROGRESS. *British Journal of Sports History [Great Britain] 1984 1(1): 24-40.* Outlines the recent academic study of sports, which has increased significantly and gained respect in academe. Notes prominent educators in the United States, Canada, and Europe who have promoted sports history as an integral part of cultural and social history, and cites recent valuable additions to the historiography of this subdiscipline. Secondary sources; 75 notes.   S

4023. Reulecke, Jürgen and Huck, Gerhard; Sutcliffe, Anthony, transl. URBAN HISTORY RESEARCH IN GERMANY: ITS DEVELOPMENT AND PRESENT CONDITION. *Urban Hist. Y. [Great Britain] 1981: 39-54.* Though there is a long, honorable tradition of urban studies in Germany, modern urban history is only now beginning to function as an independent specialism in both East and West Germany. Progress has been gradual, and compared to Great Britain and the United States, Germany is underdeveloped as far as sustained and varied urban historical research is concerned. This slow development is explained in terms of the general orientation of German historiography, traced from the 19th century. Discusses a number of problems involved with methodology and the interdisciplinary nature of urban studies. 105 notes.   S

4024. Riess, Steven A. SPORT AND THE AMERICAN DREAM. *J. of Social Hist. 1980 14(2): 295-303.* Examines literature on the backgrounds of boxers, baseball players, soccer and cricket players in English-speaking countries, soccer players in Latin America, and blacks in several sports. In some cases work on amateur sport, at least of the collegiate variety, has been done to give a broader perspective. The studies raise questions about the role of sports in upward social mobility. 21 notes.   C. M. Hough

4025. Roman, Louis. SCIENCES DE L'HISTOIRE, DEMOGRAPHIE ET DEMOGRAPHIE HISTORIQUE [Historical sciences, demography, and historical demography]. *Analele U. Bucureşti: Istorie [Romania] 1980 29: 99-109.* Although a descriptive history of events is admirable, the historian who desires to know the deeper currents in a society must pay attention chiefly to historical demography, socioeconomic history, and philosophy. No important factor of social evolution can be adequately studied without looking at its historical demographic aspects. However, historical demography must be seen in its limits and must be correlated with other disciplines. These conclusions are supported by the results of scholarly efforts in recent decades.   J. V. Coutinho

4026. Romano, Giovanni. DOCUMENTI FIGURATIVI PER LA STORIA DELLE CAMPAGNE NEI SECOLI XI-XVI [Figurative documents and the history of farmlands from the 11th to the 16th centuries]. *Quaderni Storici [Italy] 1976 11(1): 130-201.* Warns against the risk of possible misunderstandings when historians use figurative works as conclusive evidence. Artistic masterpieces in Italian art should be treated as explicit historical documents only with great circumspection. The direct representation of nature and history was undertaken only by a few great innovators who dared to fly in the face of the tradition of masters, classical models, and academic rules. The author mainly refers to the Po area, covering in particular the development of scientific culture and the illustration of works on botany, medicine, and hygiene which show agricultural occupations month by month; the decoration of secular buildings; landscape painting; peasant satire; the empirical culture of artisans and craftsmen; and astrological documents.   J

4027. Roodenburg, Marie-Cornélie. KOSTUUMHISTORISCH ONDERZOEK IN NEDERLAND [Historical research on costumes in the Netherlands]. *Spiegel Hist. [Netherlands] 1975 10(11): 602-605.* Discusses the development of costume history in the Netherlands in the 20th century, with special reference to the work of Professor Willem Vogelsang (1875-1954). Illus., biblio.

G. D. Homan

4028. Rozman, Gilbert. URBAN NETWORKS AND HISTORICAL STAGES. *J. of Interdisciplinary Hist. 1978 9(1): 65-91.* Proposal for a general strategy for comparative research on the premodern city. The proposed "urban networks approach" derives from the insights of central place theory and charts an evolutionary course through the changing urban distributions before the 19th century. The author illustrates the urban networks approach with respect to variables relating to settlement size and suggests that it indicates a common sequence of distinct stages. Other indicators of societal evolution such as human resources, patterns of settlement, organizational contexts, redistributive processes, and aspects of personal relationships might vary as a function of changing stages of urban networks. 3 tables, 2 graphs, 19 notes.   R. Howell

4029. Rubio de Hernández, Rosa Luisa. RELACIONES INTERDISCIPLINARIAS: HISTORIA—FILOLOGIA—LINGUISTICA [Interdisciplinary relations: history, philology, linguistics]. *Histórica [Peru] 1979 3(1): 121-131.* Argues that the disciplines of philology and linguistics are valuable to historians. Employs examples from recent French, Soviet, and Peruvian historiography and especially from the author's own research on Hugo de Paganis, the 13th-century founder of the Knights Templar. Based on published works; 10 notes, biblio.

D. P. Werlich

4030. Rushing, Stan. A CASE FOR ART IN BAPTIST HISTORIOGRAPHY. *Baptist Hist. and Heritage 1977 12(3): 170-174.* Most Baptists are not enthusiastic about history, but the past can come alive for people when historians give new life to their historiogra-

phy. A lively style is not a panacea, but it is essential for curing the aversion to the past that afflicts so many people. Urges excitement and fascination in historiography. 13 notes.

H. M. Parker, Jr.

4031. Rusu, Adrian Andrei. L'ÉTUDE DES CHÂTEAUX EN TRANSYLVANIE: LA CASTELLOLOGIE ROUMAINE À L'ÉPOQUE DU ROMANTISME [The study of castles in Transylvania: Romanian castle studies during the romantic era]. *Rev. Roumaine d'Hist. [Romania] 1979 18(1): 155-164.* Romanian romantic historiography of the mid-19th century made two important contributions to the study of fortresses: 1) an expansion of information based on direct observation of monuments and 2) on medieval documents. This made possible the formation of an autonomous branch of research. Romanticism also suggested most of the directions of future research. 52 notes.   J. V. Coutinho

4032. Sarlós, Robert K. A. M. NAGLER AND THEATRE HISTORY IN AMERICA. *Theatre Res. Int. [Great Britain] 1984 9(1): 1-6.* Assesses Alois M. Nagler's contribution to theater history.

4033. Schafer, William J. BREAKING INTO "HIGH SOCIETY": MUSICAL METAMORPHOSES IN EARLY JAZZ. *J. of Jazz Studies 1975 2(2): 53-60.* Uses the jazz number "High Society" as an example of how turn-of-the-century jazzmen used popular music of the day as the basis for their compositions and discusses how musicologists traced it.   S

4034. Schafer, William J. THOUGHTS ON JAZZ HISTORIOGRAPHY: "BUDDY BOLDEN'S BLUES" VS. "BUDDY BOTTLEY'S BALLOON." *J. of Jazz Studies 1975 2(1): 3-14.* Describes the difficulty in finding accurate sources of information concerning early jazzmen, using the controversy over Buddy Bolden's New Orleans jazz band, circa 1895, and Buddy Bartley, a black balloonist living in New Orleans at approximately the same time, as an example.

4035. Schillinger, Philippe. CINEMA ET HISTOIRE [Motion pictures and history]. *Rev. Hist. des Armées [France] 1977 4(1): 117-126.* Because motion pictures are of historical value as propaganda, a mode of international communication, the expression of social problems, and the reflection of the manners and morals of a society, they have become one of the tools of historians and must be preserved as archives. During World War I, the French army established a military film library at Fort d'Ivry, where thousands of news films, documentaries, and fiction films are being catalogued for the use of future historians. 6 photos, 7 notes.

J. S. Gassner

4036. Schlesinger, Roger. THE RENAISSANCE DEBATE. Parker, Harold T., ed. *Problems in European History,* (Durham, N.C.: Moore Publ., 1979): 19-35. The concept of the "Renaissance," which dates from the period itself, was given definitive form by Jacob Burckhardt (1860), and further developed by such writers as John Addington Symonds. Its present status has been profoundly influenced by the decline of classical learning and by growing attention to the period's relative paucity of scientific and technological innovations. Jerrold Seigal has noted that perceived Medieval-Renaissance differences may in part reflect the abiding contrast between Italy and Northern Europe. More recently the concept has found a new generation of defenders. Elizabeth Eisenstein, for example, has emphasized the crucial impact of printing, and art historians have pointed to such undeniable innovations as mathematical perspective. Secularization may be the key concept for understanding the period. 16 notes, ref.   L. W. Van Wyk

4037. Schneider, John C. URBANIZATION AND THE MAINTENANCE OF ORDER: DETROIT, 1824-1847. *Michigan Hist. 1976 60(3): 260-281.* Detroit, as a transitional urban community during the second quarter of the 19th century, offers instructive comparison with the existing historical studies of law and order in that era's villages and cities. Paralleling experiences elsewhere, citizens of Detroit were devoted to the American ideal of individualism and to public order and had allowed crime to become an acute problem by the early 1830's. Refusing to admit the need for a permanent police force, residents preferred temporary expedients, and countenanced them until the late 1840's, when a second period of rapid growth forced the idea of a professional approach to come into its own. Primary sources; 7 illus., map, 56 notes.

                                                                    D. W. Johnson

4038. Schwarzlose, Richard A. FIRST THINGS FIRST: A PROPOSAL. *Journalism Hist.* 1975 2(2): 38-39, 63. A response to James W. Carey's "The Problem of Journalism History" *(Journalism History* 1(1): 3-5, 27), questioning his inattention to fundamental research as the basis of improved journalism history.

4039. Sheedy, Arthur. POUR UNE HISTORIOGRAPHIE PROPRE AUX PHÉNOMÈNES DE L'ÉDUCATION PHYSIQUE ET DU SPORT: LA SOCIOLOGIE DE LA CONNAISSANCE [For a proper historiography of physical education and sports phenomena: the sociology of knowledge]. *Can. J. of Hist. of Sport and Physical Educ.* [Canada] 1978 9(1): 19-30.

4040. Solie, Ruth. MELODY AND THE HISTORIOGRAPHY OF MUSIC. *J. of the Hist. of Ideas* 1982 43(2): 297-308. There is a general lack of a widely accepted method for analyzing melody, especially in music of the 18th and 19th centuries. Indeed, texts since the 19th century have normally relegated melody to a "primitive" or "instinctive" category within a developmental outlook on music that, taking Western musical history as its paradigm, sees harmony as the inevitable and more advanced successor of melody. This trend, spurred on by the vogue of evolutionary thinking, is exemplified in many musical compendiums from around 1850 to the present. Many of these imply that melody is unworthy of serious analysis and that cultures musically centered around it will eventually follow the lead of the West in its harmonic innovations. 37 notes.

                                                                    W. J. Reedy

4041. Sonnichsen, C. L. THE POETRY OF HISTORY. *Am. West* 1975 12(5): 26-27, 59-60. Poetry and history have much in common. While "poetry may get along without history...history without poetry is dead, or in a state of suspended animation." While "the poet is impelled to communicate his feelings,...the scholar is usually content to convey information." A professional historian should remember and teach that "bricks alone do not make a building. An architect is needed to make something out of the bricks."

                                                                    D. L. Smith

4042. Spisarevska, Ioanna. KONFERENTSIIA NA MEZHDUNARODNITE KOMISII PO ISTORIIA NA GRADOVETE I PO MORSKA ISTORIIA [The conference of the international commissions of the history of cities and naval history]. *Istoricheski Pregled* [Bulgaria] 1977 33(5-6): 312-314. Describes the conference organized by the International Committee of Historians, the Institute of Balkan Studies of the Bulgarian Academy of Sciences, and the regional council of Varna and held at Varna on 7-10 May 1977. Fifty-five scholars from Europe and the United States read papers concerning port cities at various periods of history.

                                                                    F. B. Chary

4043. Spufford, Margaret. THE TOTAL HISTORY OF VILLAGE AND COMMUNITIES. *Local Hist.* [Great Britain] 1973 10(8): 398-401. Argues for the need to relate the economic, demographic, political, and spiritual aspects of the culture of preindustrial British villages.

4044. Stead, Peter. BRITISH SOCIETY AND BRITISH FILMS. *Bulletin of the Society for the Study of Labour History* [Great Britain] 1985 (48): 72-75. Examines the historiography of British cinema, noting the place that films occupy in popular culture, the role of censorship, the system of production, and distribution, the obstacles that constrain filmmakers, and the social impact of film. Includes a selected bibliography.

4045. Sullivan, Donald. THE END OF THE MIDDLE AGES: DECLINE, CRISIS, OR TRANSFORMATION? *Hist. Teacher* 1981 14(4): 551-566. Describes the major recent interpretations of the late Middle Ages. Before 1945 the period was often seen as one of decay or decline, but after 1945, a crisis approach emphasized

agricultural and demographic crisis, but not universal retrogression or value-oriented decline. More recently a transformation theory emphasized the emergence of a new culture and civilization during these years. Historians whose work is considered include Johan Huizinga, Michael Postan, Perry Anderson, and Wallace Ferguson. 47 notes.

                                                                    L. K. Blaser

4046. Summers, David. CONVENTIONS IN THE HISTORY OF ART. *New Literary Hist.* 1981 13(1): 103-125. By defining artistic style, iconography, and metaphors of convention as exemplified from Egyptian to modern art, shows how convention clarifies certain general stylistic phenomena and how the conception of historical change in art is a continuous sequence of formal innovations, with some variations or refinements, and some inventions that begin new sequences that correspond to a notion of creativity that is, in itself, a convention, a specific historical assumption about a relationship with many possible historical forms.

4047. Szymański, József. BÁDÁNÍ O POLSKÉ EPIGRAFICE [Research on Polish epigraphy]. *Archivni Časopis* [Czechoslovakia] 1975 25(4): 203-219. Evaluates the system of historical research in which inscriptions and records on various materials such as stone, steel, and brick are scrutinized and decoded. Describes results achieved in Polish historical research when epigraphy was used, including the case of a royal coronation sword, inscriptions on famous bells, and inscriptions on knightly armor. Epigraphy has become an important source of information about the past. 73 notes.

                                                                    G. E. Pergl

4048. Tarling, Nicholas. HISTORY AND HISTRIONICS. *New Zealand J. of Hist.* [New Zealand] 1977 11(2): 105-111. Historians, dramatists, producers, and actors share common goals, the recreation of a world. Though the task is impossible, craftsmanship can be used to come closer to the goal. Based on secondary works dealing with the philosophy of history and theater craft; 21 notes.

                                                                    P. J. Coleman

4049. Trinkaus, Charles. HUMANISM, RELIGION, SOCIETY: CONCEPTS AND MOTIVATIONS OF SOME RECENT STUDIES. *Renaissance Q.* 1976 29(4): 676-713. Reviews the content and motivation of English-language Renaissance historiography during the last decade. Arranges the discussion under the following heads: trends in recent Renaissance historiography; recent trends and studies on humanism; religious movements and their social contexts in the Renaissance; and society, community, and social utopias. This essay was prepared for the 1975 session of the International Federation of Societies and Institutes for the Study of the Renaissance at the 14th International Congress of Historical Science.

                                                                    J. H. Pragman

4050. Trunk, Isaih. YIVO UN DI YIDISHE HISTORISHE VISNSHAFT [YIVO and Jewish historiography]. *Yivo Bleter* 1980 46: 242-254. Discusses the historical research conducted at YIVO Institute of Jewish Research, particularly the work done and inspired by Elias Tcherikover, founder and secretary of YIVO'S History Department. This division opened up new areas of research such as the history of the Jewish labor movement, Yiddish in its cultural dimensions, the study of youth, and regional research—all of which called for innovative methodology and the training of fresh young scholars.

                                                                    J

4051. Turnau, Irena. STAN I POTRZEBY BADAŃ NAD HISTORIĄ TECHNIKI SKÓRNICZYCH NA ZIEMIACH POLSKICH [The state and requirements of research on the history of leather techniques in Poland]. *Kwartalnik Hist. Nauki i Techniki* [Poland] 1980 25(3): 523-536. Discusses the present state and possible directions that historians of the leather industry in Poland ought to undertake. There has been a considerable amount of archaeological work done on medieval leather fabrics, and studies have been written about tanners and other leather craftsmen from the 13th century to the present, but work still needs to be done on the transition from traditional methods of leather manufacture to modern industrial methods. 64 notes.

                                                                    M. A. Zurowski

4052. Uscatescu, George. TEORIA DEL RINASCIMENTO [Theory of the Renaissance]. *Nuova Antologia [Italy] 1973 518(2069): 47-57.* Examines the humanistic content of the cultural revolution that was the Renaissance and the differing interpretations of it through time.

4053. Vann, Richard T. THE NEW DEMOGRAPHIC HISTORY. Iggers, Georg G. and Parker, Harold T., ed. *International Handbook of Historical Studies: Contemporary Research and Theory* (Westport, Conn.: Greenwood Pr., 1979): 29-42. Because of the great strides made in historical demography since World War II, and especially since 1955 when *Population Index* was first published, no social history can be written without some knowledge of demographic concepts. The production of a vast array of statistics based on parish registers and local censuses does not necessarily tell much about institutions, social conndtions, or political attitudes. Even more controversial is the relation between demography and psychology; does the great rise in prenuptial pregnancies in the late 18th century, for example, represent rebellion by working-class women against parental authority? There is a great difference between historical demography and demographic history. The latter is not just a subspecialty of history, but it is clear that it has yet to make much impression upon popular historical consciousness. 38 notes, biblio.   S

4054. Vecoli, Rudolph J. THE RESURGENCE OF AMERICAN IMMIGRATION HISTORY. *Am. Studies Int. 1979 17(2): 46-66.* The current emphasis on ethnicity brought immigration history to the fore. Governmental and private agencies created an infrastructure of facilities and resources—research centers and collections, microform and reprint editions, reference tools, historical societies, and publications. Recent immigration scholarship examines the causes of mass migrations, the experiences of particular groups including some hitherto neglected, and the ethnic diversity of particular states and regions; it employs theories of modernization, cliometrics, and oral history, and emphasizes the persistence of ethnic cultures. It presages a rewriting of US history which will be multiethnic, multiracial, and multilingual. 3 photos, 31 notes.   R. E. Noble

4055. Villa, Renzo. LA PROSTITUZIONE COME PROBLEMA STORIOGRAFICO [Prostitution as a historiographic problem]. *Studi Storici [Italy] 1981 22(2): 305-314.* The 19th century is exemplary for the study of prostitution as a form of marginalization and deviance. Among the sources for the study are police archives, debates carried on by legislatures and other governing bodies, and government or private investigations. Such a study reveals the prostitute as a member of a stigmatized and segregated group, without protection or autonomy, in a society that was often brutal. Primary sources; 21 notes.   E. E. Ryan

4056. Vital, David. THE HISTORY OF THE ZIONISTS AND THE HISTORY OF THE JEWS. *Studies in Zionism [Israel] 1982 (6): 159-170.* Historical works on Zionism are generally poorly researched and therefore fail to make any significant contribution toward understanding the Zionist movement. There are some intrinsic problems to studying Zionism, including the need to know five or six languages, huge numbers of uncatalogued and unorganized documents, and the need for expertise in several distinct areas of current world history. The significance of the Zionist movement is far greater than the numbers of useful articles on Zionism would imply. 2 notes.   T. Koppel

4057. Vovelle, Michel. L'HISTORIEN ET LA DECOUVERTE DE LA FETE AUJOURD'HUI [The historian and the current rediscovery of festivity]. *Etudes Rurales [France] 1982 (86): 9-17.* Examines the reasons underlying the recent rediscovery of festive celebration as both a collective social need and an object of historical study. Can the historian be of any use to today's social worker or community leader in their search for models and references? While perhaps not, such dialogue is useful, serving to clarify the issue at hand.   J

4058. Walling, William. THE POLITICS OF JAZZ: SOME PRELIMINARY NOTES. *J. of Jazz Studies 1975 2(1): 46-60.* Describes a methodology for jazz historiography and criticism during 1920-45 and notes that articles on jazz often reflect "certain basic assumptions about the nature of power and influence in this country."

4059. White, Dana F. "THE UNDERDEVELOPED DISCIPLINE": DIRECTIONS/MISDIRECTIONS IN AMERICAN URBAN HISTORY. *Am. Studies Int. 1984 22(2): 122-140.* Assesses the state of urban history and reviews recent literature on the subject. Urban history is still searching for a coherent and governing conceptual focus. It is to applied rather than academic urban history that we must look for the promise of the future.   R. E. Noble

4060. Whitfield, Stephen J. THE PRESENCE OF THE PAST: RECENT TRENDS IN AMERICAN JEWISH HISTORY. *Am. Jewish Hist. 1980 70(2): 149-167.* The question of survival, of how Jews have managed to endure, is central to American Jewish historiography. In the past much of this writing oversimplified Jewish history, either by glorifying achievements or by deploring persecution. In the 1960's and 1970's, however, writers, often untrained as historians, have produced valuable local and oral histories. Important topics for further study include the role of Jewish women, the Jewish leftist tradition, and especially the representation of Jews in popular culture.   E. L. Keyser

4061. Wojtowicz, Jerzy. STAN BADAŃ NAD WOLNOMULARSTWEM EUROPEJSKIM W LATACH 1970-1981 [The state of research, 1970-81, on European Freemasonry]. *Kwartalnik Hist. [Poland] 1982 89(4): 659-663.* Discusses the principal publications in French, German, Italian, English, Polish, and Russian during the years 1970-81 dealing with the history of European Freemasonry during the Enlightenment. Interest on this topic has increased with new research and recent publications based on methodological improvements. 18 notes.   J. J. Kulczycki

4062. Worster, Donald. WORLD WITHOUT BORDERS: THE INTERNATIONALIZING OF ENVIRONMENTAL HISTORY. *Environmental Rev. 1982 6(2): 8-13.* Recent environmental history has focused largely on issues within nations or national cultures; greater success will be achieved if the scope of research is expanded to an international perspective.

4063. Zeitlin, Solomon. THE NEED FOR SYSTEMATIC JEWISH HISTORY. *Jewish Q. Rev. 1967 58(4): 261-273.* Reviews the works of several Jewish scholars which indicate the need for a history which shows the development and integration of Jewish history to the 20th century.

4064. Zlatkin, I. I. A. TOYNBEE ON THE HISTORICAL PAST AND PRESENT SITUATION OF NOMADIC PEOPLES. *Soviet Studies in Hist. 1973 11(4): 371-397.* Arnold Toynbee, in Volume III of his *A Study of History* (London, 1934), bases his ideas on the conclusions of the 1903-04 Pumpelly expedition and the climatic theories of Huntington, and is therefore almost totally wrong in his analysis of how and why nomadism arose, flourished, and declined from its origins, ca. 4000-5000 B.C., to the present.

4065. —. [CARLO GINZBURG'S METHODOLOGY OF ART HISTORY]. *Quaderni Storici [Italy] 1982 17(2): 692-727.*
Pinelli, Antonio. IN MARGINE A *INDAGINI SU PIERO* DI CARLO GINZBURG [In the margins of Carlo Ginzburg's *Indagini su Piero*], *pp. 692-701.* Discusses Carlo Ginzburg's *Indagini su Piero*, acknowledging the validity of Ginzburg's procedure of combining iconographic analysis with inquiries on the commissioning of works of art (for more exact dating or interpretation), but criticizes his use of sets of clues that are too faint to provide real evidence rather than mere conjecture.
Ginzburg, Carlo. MOSTRARE E DIMOSTRARE: RISPOSTA A PINELLI E ALTRI CRITICI [To show and demonstrate: a reply to the criticism of Pinelli and others], *pp. 702-727.* Analyzes the meaning of demonstration in art history, referring to Roberto Longhi and his example, based primarily on stylistic analysis and the intuition of the historian, but also on com-

pletely external elements (such as the size of a painting, iconographic information, or details of its commissioning) that provide concrete and immediately communicable factual evidence. As to his "reading" of Piero della Francesca's *Flagellation*—the major object of contention on the part of both Pinelli and of other critics—Ginzburg affirms his opinion as to the commissioning and dating of the painting and clarifies some of the contradictions present in his original interpretation.   J

4066. —. A REEXAMINATION OF A CLASSIC WORK IN AMERICAN JEWISH HISTORY: MOSES RISCHIN'S *THE PROMISED CITY*, TWENTY YEARS LATER. *Am. Jewish Hist.* 1983 73(2): 133-204.
Gurock, Jeffrey S. INTRODUCTION, *p. 133.*
Moore, Deborah Dash. THE IDEAL SLUM, *pp. 134-141.* Rischin's depiction of New York's Lower East Side as an "ideal slum" has stood up well amid the spate of social and urban studies it spawned.
Berrol, Selma. GERMANS VERSUS RUSSIANS: AN UPDATE, *pp. 142-156.* Rischin minimized the hostility between German and Russian Jews and therefore failed to explain its origins.
Dubofsky, Melvyn. "THE POLITICAL WILDERNESS," *pp. 157-162.* Though traditional, Rischin's description of politics was suggestive of modern approaches, too.
Joselit, Jenna Weissman. WHAT HAPPENED TO NEW YORK'S "JEWISH JEWS"? *pp. 163-172.* Concerned to show how immigrant Jews fit into American culture, Rischin gave inadequate attention to Jewish attempts to preserve religious traditions.

Goren, Arthur A. THE PROMISES OF *THE PROMISED CITY*: MOSES RISCHIN, AMERICAN HISTORY, AND THE JEWS, *pp. 173-184.* Fits Rischin and his book into the maturing of American Jewish historical scholarship after World War II.
Rischin, Moses. RESPONSE, *pp. 185-204.* Responds appreciatively to, though sometimes in sharp disagreement with, his critics.
         R. A. Keller

4067. —. [THE STATE OF THE ART OF WRITING LIBRARY HISTORY]. *J. of Lib. Hist.* 1978 13(4): 432-450.
McMullen, Haynes. THE STATE OF THE ART OF WRITING LIBRARY HISTORY, *pp. 432-440.* Reviews published English-language historiography of libraries and librarians. Gives directions for writing readable history while avoiding slanted interpretation. Revision of a talk to the Research Interest Group, Association of American Library Schools, January 1978. 17 notes.
Milum, Betty. COMMENT, *pp. 441-444.* Criticizes McMullen's article for failing to cite some of his sources and for inconsistent use of statistics. Note.
Kraus, Joe W. COMMENT, *pp. 445-447.* Eulogizes the *Journal of Library History* and urges library historians to fill in certain gaps, to analyze collections, to study worthy librarians more deeply, and to write more about the influence of libraries. Note.
Dickinson, Donald C. COMMENT, *pp. 448-450.* Urges continued study of American libraries since 1876 before placing more emphasis on earlier or foreign library history.

SUBJECT INDEX

Subject Profile Index (ABC-SPIndex) carries both generic and specific index terms. Begin a search at the general term but also look under more specific or related terms. This index includes selective cross-references.

Each string of index descriptors is intended to present a profile of a given article; however, no particular relationship between any two terms in the profile is implied. Terms within the profile are listed alphabetically after the leading term. The variety of punctuation and capitalization reflects production methods and has no intrinsic meaning; e.g., there is no difference in meaning between "History, study of" and "History (study of)."

Cities, towns, and counties are listed following their respective states or provinces; e.g., "Ohio (Columbus)." Terms beginning with an arabic numeral are listed after the letter Z. The chronology of the bibliographic entry follows the subject index descriptors. In the chronology, "c" stands for "century"; e.g., "19c" means "19th century."

Note that "United States" is not used as a leading index term; if no country is mentioned, the index entry refers to the United States alone. When an entry refers to both Canada and the United States, both "Canada" and "USA" appear in the string of index descriptors, but "USA" is not a leading term. When an entry refers to any other country and the United States, only the other country is indexed.

The last number in the index string, in italics, refers to the bibliographic entry number.

A

Abipon. Argentina (La Plata). Colonialism. Jesuits. Social Customs. 1527-19c. *661*
Abolition Movement. 1831-65. 1980. *2122*
—. Anti-institutionalism (concept). Elkins, Stanley M. 1829-60. 1954-76. *2161*
Abolitionism. Elkins, Stanley M. (review article). Slavery. 1450-1865. *2137*
Abolitionists (image). Attitudes. 1830's-60. 19c-20c. *705*
Abraham, David (*Collapse of the Weimar Republic*). Fraud. Historians. Scandals. 1982-85. *787*
Absolute. Social organization. Theory. 1920-61. *1360*
Absolutism. Aretin, Karl Otmar von. Hubatsch, Walther. ca 17c. *2535*
—. Hobbes, Thomas (*Behemoth*). Political science. 1679-82. *2545*
Absolutism (colloquium). Germany. 1500-1800. 1970. *2595*
Academic Degrees. *See* Degrees, Academic.
Academic freedom. Germany. Military history. 1779-1975. *3101*
Academicians. Education. Social problems. Teacher training. 20c. *2318*
Academy of Sciences. Bibliographies. Lithuania. 1979. *1*
Academy of Sciences (Historiographic Wednesdays). USSR. 1977. *1128*
Academy of Sciences Institute of History. International cooperation. USSR. 15c-1980. *19*
Acadia. Clergy. Elites. 17c-20c. *475*
Acculturation. *See also* Assimilation.
—. Immigration. Jews. New York City. Rischin, Moses (*Promised City*). 1870-1914. *4066*
Achehnese. Epic literature. Language. Muslims. Netherlands East Indies. Sumatra. 19c-20c. *488*
Achievement (review article). McClelland, David C. Psychology. 1961. *1492*
Acosta Rodríquez, Antonio. Census. Colonial Government. Louisiana. Spain. 1763-1803. 1976-80. *1720*
Action Française. Bainville, Jacques. France. Monarchy. ca 1914-36. *374*
Acton, J. E. E. D. Great Britain. Stubbs, William. 1724-1978. *1323*
—. Religious history. 1860-1900. *3624*
Adams family. Conservatism. 17c-1910's. *650*
Adams, Henry Brooks. 1838-1918. *239*
—. 1880-1910. *297*
—. 1893-1918. 1981. *1546*
—. Becker, Carl. 20c. *569*
Adams, Henry Brooks (*History of the United States*). Democracy. Diplomacy. Jefferson, Thomas. National Characteristics. 1800-17. 1889-91. *563*
—. Impressionism. National Characteristics. Pragmatism. 1800-17. 1880's. *556*
Adams, Herbert Baxter. New History. Presentism. 1850-1901. *1184*
—. Scholarship. 1874-76. *774*
Administration. Archives. Research. 18c-20c. *76*
—. Archivists. Denmark. 19c-20c. *3967*
—. Archivists. Research. 20c. *160*
Adorno, Theodor W. Frankfurt School (review article). Horkheimer, Max. Tar, Zoltán. 1920-50. *2224*
Advertising. *See also* Propaganda; Public Relations.
—. Fugitive Slaves. Jackson, Andrew (papers). Newspapers. *Tennessee Gazette.* 1804. 1977. *2125*

Advisory Committee on Historical Documentation (report). Foreign Relations. Publishers and Publishing. State Department. 1979. *2873*
Aepinus, Franz. Electricity (review article). Hackmann, Willem D. Heilbron, J. L. 17c-20c. *3745*
Aeronautics, Military. *See also* Air Warfare.
—. 1914-82. *3077*
—. Navies. 1914-1983. *3231*
Aesthetics. Auerbach, Erich (*Mimesis*). 1940's. *1273*
—. Historians. Philosophy. Poland. Tatarkiewicz, Władysław (obituary). 1910-80. *890*
Afghan War, 1st. Folklore. Great Britain. 1842. *3051*
Africa. 20c. *516*
—. Asia. Mathematics. -20c. *3788*
—. Asia, Southeast. Imperialism. 1945-60's. *2729*
—. Blacks. Racism. Women. 17c-20c. *3434*
—. Christianity. Church history. Missions and Missionaries. 19c-20c. *3489*
—. Colonial government. Delavignette, Robert (obituary). France. 1897-1976. *771*
—. Colonization. Methodology. 1870's-20c. *2723*
—. Economic history. 19c-20c. *2021*
—. Europe. Family. Methodology. 1730-1870. *2480*
—. Historians. Hodgkin, Thomas (obituary). 1930's-82. *1056*
—. Methodology. Oral Tradition. 15c-20c. *421*
—. Religion. Prehistory-1970's. *3651*
—. Slave trade. 16c-19c. 1950's-70's. *2108*
—. Slavery. 11c-20c. *2165*
—. Slavery. Prehistory-20c. *2104*
—. Slavery (review article). 18c-19c. *2133*
—. Westermann, Diedrich (tribute). 19c-20c. *1005*
Africa, North. Foreign Relations. 1785-1975. *2976*
Africa, Sub-Saharan. Culture. Linguistics. 15c-19c. *359*
Africa, West. Animism. Christianity. Islam. Religious history. 19c-20c. *3484*
—. Colonies. France. Historical sources. Slave trade. 1713-93. *2140*
Agaja, King. Dahomey. Lambe, Bulfinch. Slave trade. 18c. *2129*
Agassi, J. Croce, Benedetto. Finocchiaro, M. A. Philosophy of science (review article). 20c. *3755*
Agassiz, Louis. Books (editions). Glaciers. 1820-40. *3818*
Aged. *See also* Death and Dying; Public Welfare.
—. Women. 1980. *3474*
Aging (review article). Modernization. 1600-1980. *3848*
Agrarian history. Quantitative methods. Russia. ca 1800-50's. 1966-. *1722*
Agrarian problems. Marxist interpretations. Slovakia. 1848-1918. *2055*
Agricultural History. Kocka, J. Puhle, H.-J. 1970-78. *1887*
Agricultural Labor. *See also* Peasants.
—. Germany (Thuringia). 1400-1550. *1943*
Agricultural Labor (contract). Agricultural Technology and Research. Labor movement. Social Change. Sugar. 19c. *1909*
Agricultural Production. Capitalism. Industrialization. Social History. 19c-20c. *1942*
Agricultural Revolution. Enclosures. Great Britain. 16c-18c. *2070*
Agricultural Technology and Research. Agricultural Labor (contract). Labor movement. Social Change. Sugar. 19c. *1909*
—. Crops (rotation). France. 1450-19c. *1917*
Agriculture. *See also* Agricultural Labor; Conservation of Natural Resources; Crops; Farms; Forests and Forestry; Land; Plantations.

—. 17c-18c. *1865*
—. *Annales* school. 1929-78. *2076*
—. Barrows, Henry D. California (Los Angeles). Education. Law Enforcement. Republican Party. 1854-77. *884*
—. Capitalism. Giorgetti, Giorgio. Italy. Marxism. 18c-20c. *2677*
—. Capitalism. Research. ca 1800-1914. *1977*
—. Climate. Economic conditions. Methodology. Netherlands. 17c-18c. *1190*
—. Collective farms. Peasants. Ukraine. 1917-75. *1965*
—. Collectivization. Communist Countries. 1918-77. *1901*
—. Eastern Illinois University. Fite, Gilbert C. Georgia, University of. Great Plains. Oklahoma, University of. 1930's-79. *840*
—. Great Britain. Industrial Revolution (review article). 1650-1815. *2014*
—. Great Plains. Illinois, University of. Shannon, Fred A. 1920's-63. *871*
—. Hungary. 9c-16c. *2060*
—. Hungary. Szeremlei, Sámuel. Towns. 1850-1908. *1080*
—. Marxism. -19c. *1941*
—. Objects. Research. 1600-1976. *1473*
—. Thaer, Albrecht Daniel. 1807-28. *1971*
Ahlstrom, Sidney. Christianity (review article). Handy, Robert T. Marty, Martin E. Race (issue). 16c-1978. *3565*
—. Religion. 17c-1974. *3506*
Ahnlund, Nils. Lönnroth, Erik. Sweden. 20c. *567*
Air Forces. *See also* Air Warfare.
—. Air Warfare. Bibliographies. Germany. Germany, West. 1920's-84. *3000*
—. Research. 1920's-81. *3059*
—. Space Flight. 1660-1978. *3209*
Air Warfare. *See also* names of wars with the subdivision aerial operations, e.g. World War II (aerial operations), etc.
—. Air forces. Bibliographies. Germany. Germany, West. 1920's-84. *3000*
Alabama, University of, Library. Economic Conditions. Reconstruction. Shelby Iron Company. 1862-1923. *1997*
Alberti, Leon Battista. Camera Obscura. Inventions. Italy. Painters. Photography. 15c-1910. *4011*
Alchemy. 1775-1970. *3836*
—. Austria (Villach). Historians. Moro, Gotbert. Paracelsus. Physicians. 1493-1531. 1950-79. *957*
—. Psychohistory (review article). 1978-80. *1814*
Aleksandrov, Vadim A. (tribute). Russia. 1982. *1124*
Alienation. Psychoanalysis. 1975. *1797*
Allen, Ethan. Deism. Franklin, Benjamin. Jefferson, Thomas. Palmer, Elihu. 1750-1820. *3580*
Allen, Frederick Lewis (*Only Yesterday*). Journalism. Liberalism. Puritanism. 1931. *912*
Alliance for Progress. Foreign policy. Latin America. USA. 1960's. *2917*
Allies. Archives. Foreign Relations. Italy. Military government. World War II. 1939-46. *3216*
—. Italy. Military occupation, German. Resistance. World War II. 1939-45. *3026*
Allswang, John M. City Politics (review article). Ebner, Michael H. Tobin, Eugene M. 1867-1920. *2777*
Almanacs. France. Great Britain. Italy. Popular Culture. Public opinion. 18c. *2432*
Alperovitz, Gar. Atomic bomb (review article). Decisionmaking. Japan (Hiroshima). World War II. 1945-65. *3262*

C

—. Clubb, O. Edmund. Foreign Relations. Goldstein, Steven M. Hunt, Michael H. Letters. 1949-50. *2839*

—. Compass. Diffusion Theory. Western nations. 1088-1220. 17c-20c. *3823*

—. Economic Conditions. Social Conditions. 11c-18c. *309*

—. Ethnocentrism. 1950's-70's. *275*

—. Fairbank, John King. Latourette, Kenneth Scott. 19c-20c. *652*

—. Foreign Policy. Imperialism. Wanghia, Treaty of. 1844. *2821*

—. Foreign Relations. 1928-37. 1970's. *2898*

—. Foreign Relations. Japan. Russo-Japanese War. 1904-05. *2982*

—. Foreign Relations. Korean War (origin). USSR. 1943-50. *3019*

—. Foreign Relations. USA. 19c-20c. *2919*

—. Geography. Martini, Martino. 17c. *746*

—. Government. Jiang Qing. Political Factions. Women. 1975-76. *3433*

—. Hay, John. International Trade. Open Door policy. Revisionism. 1899-1901. *1861*

—. Islam. Western Civilization. 600 BC-20c. *1464*

—. Li Zhi. Philosophy. 1527-1602. 20c. *1117*

—. Open Door policy. 1899-1922. *2928*

—. Stilwell, Joseph W. World War II (China-India-Burma Theater). 1942-44. *3303*

—. Zhao Yi. Zhexi' Historians. 18c. *581*

China, Republic of (1949-). *See* Taiwan.

Ch'ing Dynasty. China. Zhao Yi. 1740's-1814. *662*

Christian churches. Ethics. Genocide. Holocaust. Jews. 1933-70's. *3606*

Christian Democrats. Italy. Politics. 1918-76. *3505*

Christian history. Schaff, Philip. 1843-93. *3579*

Christianity. *See also* Catholic Church; Deism; Missions and Missionaries; Protestantism; Theology.

—. 20c. *3702*

—. Africa. Church history. Missions and Missionaries. 19c-20c. *3489*

—. Africa, West. Animism. Islam. Religious history. 19c-20c. *3484*

—. American history. Conference on Faith and History. 17c-1865. 1977. *3643*

—. Anti-Semitism. Germany. 19c-20c. *3673*

—. Augustine, Saint. Hegel, Georg. Philosophy. Providence (concept). 410-1970. *3544*

—. Berdiaev, Nikolai. Communism. 1920's-40's. *3563*

—. British North America. Deviant Behavior. Government. Magic. Occult Sciences. 1600-1760. *3518*

—. Buonaiuti, Ernesto. 1908-26. *3647*

—. Buonaiuti, Ernesto. Italy. 1945-82. *3617*

—. Cairns, Earle E. 1938-79. *3659*

—. Germanization. Luther, Martin. Nationalism. 1500-1984. *3623*

—. Germany. Nazism. Textbooks. 1933-45. *3502*

—. Germany. Schwengler, Albert. Theology. 1839-41. *3492*

—. Marsden, George. Roberts, Frank. 1975. *3712*

—. McIntire, C. T. 20c. *3684*

—. McIntire, C. T. Philosophy of History (review article). 1930-81. *3719*

—. Methodology. 1880-1981. *3841*

—. Philosophy of History. 1c-20c. *234*

—. Secularization. Troeltsch, Ernst. 16c-20c. *692*

Christianity (cultural contexts). 1974. *3524*

Christianity (review article). Ahlstrom, Sidney. Handy, Robert T. Marty, Martin E. Race (issue). 16c-1978. *3565*

Chronicles. Israelites. Methodology. Old Testament. 1830's-70's. *614*

—. Marxism-Leninism. Methodology. 1917-77. *1608*

—. Mustafa Efendi, Selânikî. Ottoman Empire. 1566-1600. *657*

—. Nikon. Russia. 16c-17c. *379*

Chronology. Renaissance. Scaliger, Joseph Justus. 1500-1700. *1244*

Church administration. Barros Fernández, Alberto. Letters. Mercedarians. Spain (Castile). Vázquez Núñez, Guillermo. 1914-18. *3483*

Church and Social Problems. Catholic Church. D'Avack, Piero Agostino. Italy. Lateran Treaty. 1929-74. *3577*

Church and State. *See also* Religious Liberty.

—. Anniversaries. Germany, East. Luther, Martin. 1483-1546. 1945-84. *3551*

—. Civil Religion. Political Theory. 395-20c. *678*

—. Declension, myth of. New England. Puritan society. 17c. 20c. *3656*

—. England. Jesuits. Missions and Missionaries. More, Henry (*Historia Missionis Anglicanae Societatis Jesu*). 1580-1635. *422*

—. Habsburg Empire. Joseph II. Religious reform. 18c. *3660*

Church and State (review article). Catholic Church. Italy. Maccarone, Michele. 1861-76. *3683*

Church Councils. *See* Councils and Synods.

Church historians. Bible (historical viewpoint). 17c-20c. *3516*

Church history. Africa. Christianity. Missions and Missionaries. 19c-20c. *3489*

—. Baronius, Caesar. Flacius Illyricus, Matthias. 1520-1607. *3635*

—. British Empire. Great Britain. 16c-20c. 1962-82. *3585*

—. Canada. 20c. *3634*

—. Catholic Church. 1875-1975. *697*

—. Clergy. Daily Life. France. 17c-18c. 1972. *3668*

—. Etymology (heresy). Waldensians. 13c-20c. *3554*

—. Europe. Reformation. Zwingli, Ulrich. ca 1520. *401*

—. France. Sociology. 1789-20c. *3595*

—. Germany. 1979. *3513*

—. Germany. Philosophy of History. Pietism. 1670-1700. *3666*

—. Latourette, Kenneth Scott. Sweet, William Warren. ca 1910-65. *3507*

—. Poland. Protestantism. 1950's-70's. *3584*

—. Protestantism. 15c-19c. *3582*

—. Religious history. Social history. 1890-1945. *3693*

Church of England. *See also* Puritans.

—. American Revolution. Connecticut. 18c-20c. *3703*

—. Great Britain. Newman, John Henry. Oxford Movement. 1833-50. *3560*

—. Religion. 1775-1800. *3632*

Church of Jesus Christ of Latter-Day Saints (History Division). Bibliographies. Joseph Fielding Smith Institute of Church History. Mormons. Personal narratives. 19c-20c. *3721*

Church Schools. *See also* Religious Education.

—. Catholic Church. Kerney, Martin J. Maryland. 1845-50. *3616*

Churchill, Winston. 15c-20c. *904*

Cioranescu, Alexandre. Bibliographies (review article). France. Literature. 16c-18c. *178*

Cities. *See also* headings beginning with the word city and the word urban; names of cities and towns by state; Metropolitan Areas; Sociology; Suburbs; Urbanization.

—. Prehistory-20c. *3894*

—. Benjamin, Walter. Photography. 19c. 1920-40. *3906*

—. Bibliographies. Research. Prehistory-20c. *37*

—. Bossism. Reform. 1850-1976. *3918*

—. Continental Heritage Press. Donning Company Publishers. Photographs. Publishers and Publishing. Windsor Publications. 1970's-83. *3960*

—. Cultural change. Mormons. Utah. 1849-1970's. *3626*

—. Demography. France. Social change. 18c-19c. *3905*

—. Europe. Religion. ca 1820's-1970's. *3628*

—. Germany. 1800-1970's. *3985*

—. Germany. Great Britain. Rural-urban relations. USA. 1975. *3975*

—. Germany. Reformation (conference). 1520's. 1978. *2173*

—. Great Britain. 19c-20c. *3914*

—. Naval history. ca 14c-20c. 1977. *4042*

—. Political power. 19c-20c. *2801*

—. Slavery. Southwest. Wade, Richard C. ca 1860-65. *630*

—. Urban history. 1970. *3919*

Cities (review article). Middle Classes. 15c-1800. 1969-78. *3907*

Cities (size). Business leaders. Iron Industry. Social Classes. 1874-1900. *1955*

City Politics (review article). Allswang, John M. Ebner, Michael H. Tobin, Eugene M. 1867-1920. *2777*

Civil Constitution of the Clergy. Catholic Church. French Revolution. Mathiez, Albert. 1790-91. *3699*

Civil Religion. Church and State. Political Theory. 395-20c. *678*

Civil War. *See also* battles and campaigns by name; Reconstruction; Slavery.

—. American Revolution. 18c-19c. 1960's-81. *3378*

—. Catton, Bruce. Literature. 1952-66. *654*

—. Catton, Bruce (interview). Methodology. 20c. *779*

—. Chile. 1891. *323*

—. England. 17c. *441*

—. England. Literary criticism. Marvell, Andrew (*Horatian Ode upon Cromwell's Return from Ireland*). Poetry. 1649-50. *2372*

—. Ideology. Labor. Politics. Slavery. 1860-76. 1970-79. *315*

—. Interpretive changes. Politics (essays). Quantitative Methods. Reconstruction. 1850's-76. 1960's-75. *512*

—. Louisiana State University. Military. Political history. South. Williams, T. Harry (obituary). 1941-79. *1115*

—. Moore, Glover (festschrift). Race Relations. South. 19c-20c. *288*

—. Navies. USSR. 1918-20. *3290*

—. Russian Revolution (October). Siberia. 1917-20. *461*

Civil War (antecedents). Intellectual History. Nationalism. Wilson, Major L. (review article). 1815-61. 1946-75. *2784*

Civilization. Boundaries. 20c. *2287*

—. Culture. Prehistory-19c. *2322*

—. History. Science. -20c. *1482*

Civilization (concept). Guizot, François. 18c. *2426*

Civil-Military Relations. Gorshkov, S. G. Navies. USSR. 1956-80. *998*

Clarendon, 1st Earl of. Bibliographies. England. Historians. Political Leadership. 1630's-74. *468*

Clark, G. Kitson. Attitudes. Callcott, George H. Postan, M. M. Richter, Melvin. Small-group theory. 1970-71. *1462*

Clark, Manning. Australia. 1915-63. *354*

Class analysis. Marxism-Leninism. Skazkin, S. D. USSR. ca 500-1700. 20c. *777*

Class consciousness. Ethnic Groups. Labor movement. 1963-82. *1902*

—. Middle Classes. Subjectivity. 1969. *2194*

Class struggle. Economic theory. Enfantin, Barthélemy Prosper. Saint-Simon, Comte de. 1825-40. *1976*

—. Feudalism. Peasants. 16c-18c. *2209*

—. Germany, East. 1949-69. *2593*

—. Labor. 19c-20c. *1994*

—. Methodology. Social sciences. 20c. *1345*

—. Public Schools. 1950's-70's. *2347*

—. Socialism. 1967. *1618*

—. USSR. World War II. 1940-45. *2987*

Classes. *See* Social Classes.

Classical history. Critical history. 19c-20c. *1198*

Classification. Archives. Yugoslavia. 1965. *119*

—. Technical change. Technology. 17c-18c. *3757*

Classification systems. Information sciences. -1975. *16*

Clausewitz, Karl von. Military history. 1450-1980. *3067*

Claval, Paul. Geography. Kuhn, Thomas S. Science, history of. Wright, John K. 1978. *555*

Clay, Lucius D. Germany. Reparations. USA. 1946-47. *2871*

Clemens, Samuel Langhorne. *See* Twain, Mark.

Clergy. *See also* specific denominations by name.

—. Acadia. Elites. 17c-20c. *475*

—. Catholic Church. Fordham University. Sievers, Harry J. (obituary). 1921-77. *973*

—. Catholic Church. Polish Americans. Swastek, Joseph Vincent (obituary). 1913-77. *915*

—. Church history. Daily Life. France. 17c-18c. 1972. *3668*

Climate. Agriculture. Economic conditions. Methodology. Netherlands. 17c-18c. *1190*

—. Methodology. Prehistory-20c. *473*

Climatology. LeRoy Ladurie, Emmanuel. 5c BC-20c. *3729*

—. Research (interdisciplinary). 1980. *3811*

Cliometrics. Econometrics. Economic history (review article). North, Douglass C. 1950's-81. *1973*

Clive, John. Maldelbaum, Maurice. Rearich, Charles. White, Hayden. 19c. 1974. *1146*

Clubb, Jerome M. Quantitative Methods. Scheuch, Erwin K. 1980. *1698*

Clubb, O. Edmund. China. Foreign Relations. Goldstein, Steven M. Hunt, Michael H. Letters. 1949-50. *2839*

Cobb, Richard. French Revolution (review article). 1789-1820. *3363*

Cochin, Augustin. Counterrevolution. French Revolution. 19c-20c. *3333*

Cochrane, Eric. Burrow, J. W. Butterfield, Herbert. Kenyon, John. Wormell, Deborah. 5c BC-20c. *1547*

Coin Collecting. *See* Numismatics.

Cold War. *See also* Detente.

—. 1945-68. *2933*

—. 1945-70. *2923*

—. 1945-77. *2842*

—. 1945-84. *2853*

—. 1947-78. *2970*

—. Cuban Missile Crisis. USA. USSR. 1962. *647*

—. Domestic Policy. Foreign policy. Revisionism. 1962-70's. *2895*

—. Economic policy. Foreign Relations. Political Systems. 1945-52. *2844*

—. Europe. Great Britain. Revisionism. USSR. World War II. 1943-46. *2914*

D

Druzhinin, Nikolai M. Bensing, Manfred. Germany, East. Letters. Methodology. USSR. 1969. *1567*

Duarte Level, Lino. Carabobo (battle). Independence, war of. Venezuela. 1821. *3215*

Dubnow, Simon. Diaspora. Jews. Russia. 1880-1941. *903*

—. Jews. Poland. 1860-1941. *1059*

Dubois, Jean. France. Lexicology (review article). Vocabulary. 1869-72. *1680*

DuBois, W. E. B. Empiricism. Fiction. Morality. 1909-40. *579*

—. Phillips, Ulrich B. Slavery. South. ca 1620-1865. 1896-1940. *2155*

DuBois, W. E. B. (works). ca 1920-55. *689*

DuChaillu, Paul. Discovery and Exploration. 1831-1903. *754*

Duchesne, Louis. Bremond, Henri. Catholic Church. France. Historians. 1900-24. *3552*

Duichev, Ivan. Bulgaria. 20c. *823*

Dulles, John Foster. Diplomacy. Foreign policy. 1953-59. 1970's. *2879*

Dunning, William A. Race Relations. Reconstruction. 1865-77. 1900-25. *622*

Durkheim, Emile. *Annales* school. Mauss, Marcel. Structuralism. 20c. *1636*

—. Berr, Henri. France. Lamprecht, Karl. Methodology. Sociology. 1900-11. *1328*

—. Merton, Robert K. Sociology. Spencer, Herbert. -1974. *2226*

Duroselle, Jean Baptiste. France. Strategy. 1969. *1367*

Dutch-Romanian Colloquium of Historians, 1st. Romania. 1848-1918. 1977. *330*

Dwight, Timothy. Beecher, Lyman. Connecticut. Documents. Great Awakening, 2d. Popular movements. 1770-1840. 1970. *3677*

Dyrvik, Ståle. Daily Life. Norway. Popular Culture. 1720-84. *2489*

E

East Prussia. Leo, Jan. Poles. 1572-1635. *864*

—. USSR. World War II. 1944-45. *3149*

Eastern Front. Armies. USSR. World War I. Zaionchkovski, A. M. 1862-1926. *902*

—. USSR. World War II. 1941-45. *2980*

Eastern Illinois University. Agriculture. Fite, Gilbert C. Georgia, University of. Great Plains. Oklahoma, University of. 1930's-79. *840*

Eastern Question. Bibliographies. 1875-78. 1978-80. *133*

Ebner, Michael H. Allswang, John M. City Politics (review article). Tobin, Eugene M. 1867-1920. *2777*

Ecology. *See also* Conservation of Natural Resources; Environment.

—. 1920's-83. *3838*

—. Prehistory-1975. *3993*

—. DeVoto, Bernard (letters). Fictionwriting. 1920's-55. *289*

—. Egerton, Frank N. 20c. *3747*

—. Models. 1978. *3971*

Econometric history. Economic theory. 1971. *2078*

Econometrics. Cliometrics. Economic history (review article). North, Douglass C. 1950's-81. *1973*

Economic change. Family history. Social Theory. 19c-20c. 1950's-70's. *2503*

Economic Conditions. *See also* terms beginning with Economic; Business Cycles; Natural Resources; Statistics.

—. Agriculture. Climate. Methodology. Netherlands. 17c-18c. *1190*

—. Alabama, University of, Library. Reconstruction. Shelby Iron Company. 1862-1923. *1997*

—. Beard, Charles. Constitutions. Political Theory. 18c. 20c. *2527*

—. Canada. Foreign Relations. USA. 1935-39. *2922*

—. China. Social Conditions. 11c-18c. *309*

—. Culture. Science, history of. Social conditions. UNESCO. Prehistory-20c. *3846*

—. Depression. Social Organization. 1900-33. *1851*

—. Domesticity. Income. Women. 1780-1980. *3413*

—. Frontier and Pioneer Life. Social Conditions. Western States. 19c. *537*

—. Jews. Poland. Schipper, Yitzhak. 12c-18c. *399*

—. New Deal. Political Parties. 1920's-30's. *2758*

—. New South. Political Leadership. ca 1865-1979. *1855*

—. Populism. Social Change. 1880's-1980. *2236*

—. Slavery. South. 17c-1865. 1974. *2119*

Economic cooperation. Comecon. Foreign policy. USA. Western nations. ca 1948-71. *2015*

Economic decline. McCloskey, Donald. Rapp, Richard T. Workshop papers. 17c-20c. 1977. *1896*

Economic Development. *See also* National Development.

—. 18c-20c. *392*

—. Blacks. South. 1850's-20c. *2079*

—. Business. Technology. 1815-75. *3807*

—. Canals. 1810-50. *2044*

—. Economic History. Marxism. 19c-20c. *559*

—. England. Protoindustrialization (concept). 14c-18c. *1883*

—. Germany. Industrialization. 19c. 1960's. *2068*

—. Industrial Revolution. Political Change. Social Change. 1640-1880's. *1913*

—. Khalatbari, Parviz. Migration (conference). 16c-20c. *1946*

—. Mississippi Valley. Railroads, narrow-gauge. Transportation history. 1870-1900. 1970. *3924*

—. Philosophy of History. 17c. *1853*

—. Sociology. Prehistory-1977. *2087*

Economic Development (documents). Industrialization. USSR. 1917-72. 1950-70. *96*

Economic Development (review article). Gould, J. D. 19c-20c. *1866*

Economic Growth. *See also* Business History; Economic History; Economic Policy; Industrialization; Modernization.

—. Franklin, Benjamin. Manufactures. Puritanism. Trade. 18c. *1848*

—. Great Britain. Quantitative Methods. 1880's-90's. *659*

—. Income. Population. Regions. South. ca 1840-60. *675*

—. Italy. Melis, Federigo. Renaissance. 14c-15c. *1894*

—. North, Douglass C. (*The Economic Growth of the United States, 1790-1860*). 1790-1860. *1910*

—. Rostow, W. W. 20c. *2057*

Economic growth debate. Australia. Veblen, Thorstein. ca 1899-1923. *1888*

Economic History. 1930-80. *1875*

—. 1950-80. *2058*

—. 1969-70's. *1911*

—. ca 1900-45. *1918*

—. ca 1950-75. *1920*

—. Africa. 19c-20c. *2021*

—. *Annales* School. France. Social History. 1949-68. *609*

—. Archives, local. Phillips, Ulrich B. Slave prices. Texas (Harrison County). 1849-60. *2101*

—. Balkan states. Diplomacy. Great powers. International relations. 18c-20c. *2834*

—. Balkans. Bibliographies. 1975. *1979*

—. Bujak, Franciszek. Madurowicz-Urbańska, H. Methodology. Poland. ca 1840's-1920's. *834*

—. Business. Canada. Laurentian thesis. 1960-73. *2025*

—. Capitalism. Germany, West. 1970-77. *2678*

—. Denmark. 1933-74. *1949*

—. Economic Development. Marxism. 19c-20c. *559*

—. Economic theory. Yugoslavia. 19c-20c. *1923*

—. Einaudi, Luigi. 1910-61. *2031*

—. Europe. 9c-18c. *1881*

—. Finance. Genoa. Occupations. 1000-1815. *2085*

—. France. Marxism. Meuvret, Jean. 1971. *821*

—. French Revolution. 1789-1815. *3359*

—. Germany. Nazism. 1945-70. *1905*

—. Great Britain. ca 1875-1920. *1936*

—. Great Britain. Habakkuk, H. J. Technology. ca 1600-1976. *3830*

—. Great Britain. Social History. 1750-1850. *2571*

—. Industrial Revolution. "Robber Barons". 1880's-1900. *1970*

—. International Congress of Economic History, 7th. 15c-20c. 1978. *1878*

—. Japan. 1603-1940. *420*

—. Japan. 1603-1940. *510*

—. Kondratieff cycle. 15c-17c. 20c. *1864*

—. Models, theoretical. 1955-72. *1992*

—. Money. 1956-76. *1862*

—. Museum of History. Museums. Yugoslavia (Belgrade). ca 1850-1979. *2074*

—. Periodicals. 1976-82. *1922*

—. Quantitative history. 1930-. *1876*

—. Quantitative methods. 1940's-70's. *2069*

—. Quantitative Methods. 1965. *1856*

—. Quantitative Methods. 19c-20c. *1991*

—. Science and Government. Technology. 1850-1980. *3740*

Economic history, New. 20c. *2005*

Economic History (review article). 18c-20c. *1846*

—. Cliometrics. Econometrics. North, Douglass C. 1950's-81. *1973*

—. Government activity. 1970. *2013*

Economic influence. France. Ideology. Saint-Simonians. 1830's-1960's. *2030*

Economic interest. Conservatism. Hofstadter, Richard. Liberalism. 1955-68. *1048*

Economic order. Constitutional law. Federalism. Supreme Court. 1789-1910. *2039*

Economic Policy. *See also* Free Trade; Industrialization; International Trade; Modernization.

—. Business. Government. Liberalism, corporate. 20c. *1940*

—. Cold war. Foreign Relations. Political Systems. 1945-52. *2844*

—. Depressions. Hoover, Herbert C. 1930's-70's. *1974*

—. Fascism. Italy. Monetary policy. 1920-39. *1916*

—. Hamilton, Alexander. 1789-1967. *2006*

Economic Regulations. *See also* Federal Regulation.

—. Property rights. 19c. *2095*

Economic Structure. Business Cycles. 19c-20c. 1930-84. *2007*

—. Family. Vital Statistics. 1607-1790. *1742*

—. Federal Policy. Labor Unions and Organizations. New Deal. Politics. Revisionism. 1921-38. *704*

—. Methodology. Social Status. 1925-77. *1181*

Economic theory. Ayres, Clarence E. Institutionalism. Veblen, Thorstein. 20c. *1947*

—. Business. Great Britain. 17c-1880. *1882*

—. Capitalism. Imperialism. 1891-1980. *1914*

—. Class struggle. Enfantin, Barthélemy Prosper. Saint-Simon, Comte de. 1825-40. *1976*

—. Dobb, Maurice. Heckscher, Eli F. Mercantilism. 17c-19c. *1931*

—. Econometric history. 1971. *2078*

—. Economic history. Yugoslavia. 19c-20c. *1923*

—. Europe. Protoindustrialization. 16c-19c. 1970's. *2040*

—. Germany, West. Imperialism. Lenin, V. I. 1960's-70's. *2715*

—. Gray, Simon. 1890's-1960's. *1989*

—. Hicks, John. 1974. *1852*

—. Imperialism. 1870-1965. *2052*

—. Japan. 1760's-20c. 1940's-80. *2045*

—. Luxemburg, Rosa. Political Theory. 1900's-19. 1950's-70's. *1904*

—. Marxism. Slavery. 1840-1977. *2138*

—. Methodology. Snooks, Graeme. 1957-74. *1995*

—. Smith, Adam (*Wealth of Nations*). 1776. 20c. *2063*

—. USSR. 1920-80. *2019*

Economic Theory (classical). Social Darwinism. 18c-1978. *1962*

Economic Theory (review article). Denis, H. Fusfeld, D. R. Gill, R. 1970. *2003*

Economics. *See also* Business; Credit; Depressions; Finance; Income; Industry; Labor; Land; Money; Political Economy; Population; Prices; Socialism; Trade.

—. 15c-20c. *1985*

—. Education, compulsory. Political systems. Social classes. 1840-20c. *2388*

—. Europe. Japan. Revolution. 18c-19c. *3369*

—. Foreign Relations. Ideology. USA. USSR. 1918-33. *545*

—. Psychology. Sociology. 1930's-80's. *1456*

—. Social sciences. Prehistory-1969. *1863*

Economics, cyclical. France. Labrousse, Ernest (review article). Quantitative Methods. Social Organization. ca 1960-70. 1974. *1723*

Economics (research). Engerman, Stanley L. Fogel, Robert William. Slavery (review article). South or Southern States. ca 1820-1974. *2162*

Economism. Dobb, Maurice. Humanism. Johnson, Richard. Socialism. 20c. *1880*

Economists. Methodology. 1929-70. *1172*

Edgecote (battle; date). Battles. England. Pembroke, Earl of (William Herbert). 1469. *3159*

Editors and Editing. *See also* Press.

—. *American Historical Review*. Jameson, John Franklin. Periodicals. 1880's-1928. *1002*

—. Blegen, Theodore C. (tribute). Immigrant studies. Local history. Minnesota, University of. Norwegian-American Society. 1925-60. *990*

—. Butterfield, Lyman Henry. 1944-82. *737*

—. Croatia. Kukuljević, Ivan. 1850-75. *1037*

—. Czechoslovakia. Historians. History Teaching. Král, Václav (obituary). Sociology. 1926-83. *1122*

—. Factories. Gorky, Maxim. *History of Factories and Plants*. Ukraine. 1931-35. *1953*

—. Faulk, Odie B. Southwest. 1960's-79. *868*

—. Greenslet, Ferris. Massachusetts Historical Society. 1916-59. *896*

—. *Historisk Tidskrift*. Periodicals. Swedish Historical Society. 1900-61. *151*

—. Massachusetts Historical Society. Mitchell, Stewart (obituary). 20c. *802*

—. Massachusetts Historical Society. Sedgwick, Ellery. 1914-59. *1031*

—. Papers. 1950's-80. *1510*

—. Periodicals. Self-Managed Interest Society for Scientific Endeavors. Yugoslavia (Croatia). 1981. *85*

—. *Radical History Review*. 1981. *9*

—. Scholarship. 17-18c. *15*

Education. *See also* names of classes of people with the subdivision education, e.g. Women (education); subjects with the subdivision study and teaching, e.g. Art History (study and teaching); headings beginning with education and educational; Audiovisual Materials; Colleges and Universities; Curricula; Higher Education; Military Education; Religious Education; Scholarship; Secondary Education; Teaching; Textbooks.
—. 17c-18c. 1959-78. *2344*
—. 17c-20c. *2316*
—. 1873-1979. *561*
—. 18c-20c. *582*
—. 1900-75. *278*
—. 1950's-81. *2392*
—. 1960's-70's. *2310*
—. 1978. *2309*
—. Academicians. Social problems. Teacher training. 20c. *2318*
—. Agriculture. Barrows, Henry D. California (Los Angeles). Law Enforcement. Republican Party. 1854-77. *884*
—. American history. FitzGerald, Frances (review article). Textbooks. Values. 1492-1980. *2401*
—. Attitudes. Human Relations. Methodology. 18c-20c. *1174*
—. Bailyn, Bernard (review article). Family. 1915-74. *2431*
—. Bibliographies. 17c-20c. 1973-74. *58*
—. Boxer Rebellion. China. Foreign Policy. Hunt, Michael (thesis). Reparations. 1900-06. 1972. *2971*
—. Carbone, Peter, Jr. Rugg, Harold Ordway. Social Theory. 20c. *2172*
—. Catholic Church. 19c. *3597*
—. Center for Study and Research in Education and Culture. Culture. France (Ardennes, Champagne). Rheims, University of. 1975. *2183*
—. Committee on the Role of Education in American History. Cremin, Lawrence. Revisionism. 20c. *663*
—. Corporate state. Revisionism. Spring, Joel (review article). 1974. *2356*
—. Culture. Czechoslovakia. Hungary. 18c-20c. *2511*
—. Dewey, John. Liberalism. Revisionism. 1920-79. *565*
—. Dewey, John. Liberalism. Social Change. 1970-78. *2229*
—. Europe. Teachers. 19c. *2342*
—. Ford Foundation (Fund for the Advancement of Education). National characteristics. 1954-70's. *2378*
—. France. 1679-1979. *230*
—. France. National Institute for Pedagogical Research. 1977. *2312*
—. France. National Institute for Pedagogical Research. 1978. *2313*
—. France. Science. Textbooks. 1750-1850. *3752*
—. History teaching. Italy. Research. 1968-82. *1450*
—. Humanism. 1981. *1281*
—. Radicals and Radicalism. Ravitch, Diane (review article). Revisionism. 1965-78. *2350*
—. Ravitch, Diane (review article). 1960's-78. *2387*
—. Revisionism. 1960's-70's. *2348*
—. Revisionism. Spring, Joel. 1750-1978. *2358*
—. Teachers. 1960-65. *2390*
Education, compulsory. Economics. Political systems. Social classes. 1840-20c. *2388*
Education, history of. Social sciences. 1960-70. *2319*
Education, public. Political community. 1930-74. *2748*
Education (review article). France. 19c-20c. *2321*
Education (symposium). Institutionalization. 1800-1975. *2299*
Edwards, Jonathan. Fiering, Norman. Miller, Perry. New England. Philosophy (review article). Puritans. 1640-1760. *2379*
—. Literature. Revisionism. 1758-1903. *3676*
—. New England. Scripture. 17c-1750's. *658*
Edwards, Jonathan (works). Scripture. Theology. 18c. *447*
Egerton, Frank N. Ecology. 20c. *3747*
Eichmann, Adolf (review article). Trials. War crimes. World War II. 1940-45. 1960-61. *3289*
Einaudi, Luigi. Economic History. 1910-61. *2031*
Eisenhower, Dwight D. Foreign policy. 1952-60. *2865*
—. Politics. Revisionism. 1950's. *2789*
—. Presidency. 1953-61. *2763*
Eisenhower, Dwight D. (administration). 1953-61. 1965-80. *2924*
Electricity (review article). Aepinus, Franz. Hackmann, Willem D. Heilbron, J. L. 17c-20c. *3745*
Electrification. Siberia (Buryatia). USSR. 1926-80. *2035*

Electrons. Chemistry. Scientific Experiments and Research. Stranges, A. N. Valence theory. 1900-25. *3782*
Eliade, Mircea. Anthropology, cultural. 1944-79. *2510*
—. Freud, Sigmund. Toynbee, Arnold J. Prehistory-20c. 1912-60. *790*
Elias, Norbert. Social theory. 1935-77. *841*
Eliot, George. 19c. 1945-75. *2338*
Elites. *See also* Decisionmaking; Social Classes; Social Status.
—. Acadia. Clergy. 17c-20c. *475*
—. Community studies. Pluralism. 1957-77. *1255*
—. French Revolution. Rhetoric. Social Conditions. 1789-99. *3337*
—. Intellectual history. 1930-70. *2375*
Elkins, Stanley M. Abolition Movement. Anti-institutionalism (concept). 1829-60. 1954-76. *2161*
—. Bibliographies. 1957-77. *929*
—. Blassingame, John W. Slavery (review article). South. 1619-1865. *2128*
—. Hofstadter, Richard (review article). McKitrick, Eric. 1940's-70's. *747*
Elkins, Stanley M. (review article). Abolitionism. Slavery. 1450-1865. *2137*
Eller, Paul. Bolvig, Axel. Iconography (review article). 1500-1945. *1488*
Elliott, Stephen. Episcopal Church, Protestant. South. 1840-66. *3638*
Ellsworth, S. George (account). Periodicals. *Western Historical Quarterly*. 1969-79. *45*
El'tigen (landing). Kerch (battle). USSR (Crimea). World War II. 1943. *3056*
Elton, G. R. Fogel, Robert William. 1983. *1279*
Emigrants. Bakalov, Georgi. Bulgaria. Plekhanov, G. V. Revolutionary Movements. Russia. 1860's-1917. *836*
Emigration. *See also* Demography; Immigration; Population; Race Relations.
—. Czechoslovakia. Europe, Central and Western. Military units. Russian Revolution. Ukrainians. 1917-39. *3261*
Eminescu, Mihai. Poems. Romania. Romanticism. 1870-79. *857*
Emotional history. 1983. *1811*
Emotions. Methodology. 1941-81. *1247*
—. Methodology. Personality. 1970's-80's. *1819*
Empiricism. DuBois, W. E. B. Fiction. Morality. 1909-40. *579*
Employment. *See also* Occupations.
—. USSR. Women. World War II. 1941-45. *3482*
Enclosures. Agricultural Revolution. Great Britain. 16c-18c. *2070*
Encyclopedia Britannica. Colonialism. USA. USSR. 1914-75. *2704*
—. Europe. USA. Women. 12c-19c. 1974. *3444*
Encyclopedias, General. Biography. Bombing. World War II. 1939-45. *688*
Encyclopédie. Diderot, Denis. Philosophy. 1751-1800. *633*
Endocrinology. 1890-1956. *3764*
Enfantin, Barthélemy Prosper. Class struggle. Economic theory. Saint-Simon, Comte de. 1825-40. *1976*
Engagement. Objectivity. 20c. *1228*
Engels, Friedrich. 1884-95. *2634*
—. Anabaptism. Books (editions). Marxism. Zimmermann, Wilhelm (*Bauernkrieg*). 1840-1980. *3547*
—. Berlin, University of. Hegel, Georg. Pamphlets. Philosophy. Schelling, Friedrich von. 1841-45. *1077*
—. Germany. *Junker* (definition). Marx, Karl. 1845-90. *1695*
—. Independence, War of. Marx, Karl. Revolution. 1850-70. *3354*
—. Marx, Karl. Philosophy of History. Social Classes. 1850's-90's. *1603*
—. Military. 19c. *2985*
—. Political Theory. 1844-91. *2618*
Engels, Friedrich (*Peasant War in Germany*). Germany. Peasants war. 1850. *1556*
Engels, Friedrich (*The Origin of the Family, Private Property, and the State*). 19c. *2418*
Engerman, Stanley L. Economics (research). Fogel, Robert William. Slavery (review article). South or Southern States. ca 1820-1974. *2162*
—. Fogel, Robert William. Genovese, Eugene D. Leadership qualities. Slave drivers. 1800's-60. 1930's-70's. *2163*
—. Fogel, Robert William. Methodology. Slavery (review article). South or Southern States. 17c-1860. 1975. *2120*
—. Fogel, Robert William. Quantitative methods. Slavery. Social Mobility. 1800's-50's. 1930's-70's. *2151*
—. Fogel, Robert William. Slavery (review article). 19c. 1974. *2121*

—. Fogel, Robert William. Slavery (review article). South. 1830-60. 1974. *2097*
Engineering industry. Great Britain. Lockouts. 1852. *2009*
Engineering, underwater. Orbeli, R. A. 8c BC-1942. *3781*
England. 1307-16c. *333*
—. Aubrey, John. Folklore. L'Estrange, Nicholas. Oral history. 17c. *1757*
—. Authors. Pembroke, Countess of (Mary Herbert). Women. 1485-1621. *3420*
—. Authors. Wollstonecraft, Mary. 1759-97. *994*
—. Aveling, J. C. H. Bossy, John. Catholics (review article). Counter-Reformation. Legislation. 1600-40. *3569*
—. Battles. Edgecote (battle; date). Pembroke, Earl of (William Herbert). 1469. *3159*
—. Bible. Scholarship. Translating and Interpreting. 1611. 17c-20c. *3573*
—. Bibliographies. Clarendon, 1st Earl of. Historians. Political Leadership. 1630's-74. *468*
—. Bibliographies. Hurstfield, Joel. Tudors. 16c. 1944-78. *1112*
—. Chase, Myrna. Halévy, Elie (review article). 1870-1937. *1047*
—. Chaytor, Miranda. Family. Methodology. 1580's-1640's. *2452*
—. Church and State. Jesuits. Missions and Missionaries. More, Henry (*Historia Missionis Anglicanae Societatis Jesu*). 1580-1635. *422*
—. Civil War. 17c. *441*
—. Civil War. Literary criticism. Marvell, Andrew (*Horatian Ode upon Cromwell's Return from Ireland*). Poetry. 1649-50. *2372*
—. Dickens, A. G. Reformation. 15c-16c. *290*
—. Economic Development. Protoindustrialization (concept). 14c-18c. *1883*
—. Enlightenment. 1700-50's. *656*
—. Family (review article). 1500-1800. 1977-78. *2270*
—. France. Netherlands. Political Theory. Sidney, Philip (*New Arcadia*). ca 1560-1600. *2557*
—. Hallam, Henry. 1812-59. *270*
—. Harrison, William. Historians. Holinshed, Raphael. 1573-87. *972*
—. Hexter, J. H. Hill, Christopher. Methodology. 17c. 1930's-70's. *1629*
—. Historians. Law. Maitland, Frederic William. 10c-19c. 1884-1906. *300*
—. Ireland. Scotland. 10c-20c. 1966-84. *479*
—. Landscaping. Walpole, Horace. 1771. *4018*
—. Literature. 1475-1642. 1981-83. *2359*
—. Literature. 1534-1979. *576*
—. Manuscripts. Oxford University (Bodleian Library). Walsingham, Thomas. 15c. *164*
—. Methodology. Namier, Lewis. Politics. 18c. *2555*
—. Methodology. Population (review article). 1541-1871. *1718*
—. Milton, John (*Paradise Lost*). 17c. *591*
—. Poetry. 1600-60. *641*
—. Politics. Progressivism. Religion. 19c. *562*
—. Renaissance. 16c-1630. *308*
—. Social Reform. 19c-20c. *544*
—. Victorian History. 11c-19c. *253*
England (London). Urbanization. 19c. *298*
England (Worcestershire). Population. Statistics. 1646. *1737*
English Canadians. Canada. Nation (term). Race (term). 1873-1980. *1684*
Enlightenment. *See also* Rationalism.
—. 18c. *3948*
—. 20c. *3992*
—. American Revolution. Germany. 1775-87. *3370*
—. Basnage, Jacques. Bayle, Pierre. Jews. ca 1650-1725. *3713*
—. Becker, Carl. Structuralism. 20c. *1439*
—. Bertelli, Sergio. 16c-18c. 1973. *2304*
—. Coppet Group. Staël, Madame de. 1800-20. *3961*
—. Dialectical materialism. France. Marxism. Philosophy of History. 18c. *1597*
—. England. 1700-50's. *656*
—. Europe. ca 1750-72. *1693*
—. Europe. Religious life. 1770-1820. 1945-70. *3655*
—. Europe, Central. Jews. Periodicals. *Sulamith*. 1800-25. *3998*
—. Fiction. France. Literary Criticism. 18c-19c. *324*
—. France. Hazard, Paul. 18c-20c. *996*
—. Germany. 1690-1780. 1945-79. *2314*
—. Germany. Lessing, Gotthold Ephraim. Middle Ages. 18c. *707*
—. Germany. Wolf, Friedrich August. 1795-1824. *860*
—. Habermas, Jürgen. 18c. 1950's-82. *1018*
—. Habermas, Jürgen. Koselleck, Reinhart. *Öffentlichkeit* (concept). Political Participation. Public opinion. 18c-20c. *2516*

—. Industrialization. Methodology. Research. 19c. 255

—. Irving, David. Nazism. Resistance. Rommel, Erwin. 1941-45. 3048

—. Jesus Christ. Theology. 16c-19c. 3648

—. Judaism, Reform. Lehranstalt für die Wissenschaft des Judentums. Pharisees. 19c. 3722

—. Labor, forced. Resistance. World War II. 1940-45. 3131

—. Labor history. Labor movement. Methodology. Social Classes. Social history. 1866-1933. 2255

—. Lamprecht, Karl. 1890's-1900's. 835

—. Lamprecht, Karl. Royal Saxonian Institute for Cultural and Universal History. 1890's-1915. 1017

—. Luther, Martin. 16c. 19c-20c. 3495

—. Luther, Martin. Reformation. 1517-1983. 3674

—. Luther, Martin. Reformation. 16c. 19c-20c. 3705

—. Luther, Martin (review article). Reformation. Wolf, Gerhard Philipp. 16c. 19c-20c. 3559

—. Lutheranism. Morality. Reformation. 16c. 3690

—. Madajczyk, Czesław (tribute). Military Occupation. Poland. 20c. 918

—. Marxism. Reformation. 16c. 3545

—. Marxism-Leninism (conference). 1969. 2636

—. Meinecke, Friedrich. 1890-1954. 1021

—. Methodology. Political Factions. 1859-1979. 1447

—. Militarism. 1860's-1945. 3196

—. Militarism (symposium). 1918-33. 3132

—. Military history. 1380-1980. 3265

—. Military history. 500-1789. 3247

—. Myths and Symbols. Revolution of 1848. 1848-1930's. 1945-70's. 240

—. Näf, Werner. 15c-20c. 1019

—. Nationalism. Treitschke, Heinrich von (political career). ca 1850-1900. 783

—. Navies. World War I. 1914-18. 3233

—. Nazism. 1920's-67. 2588

—. Nazism. 1930's-45. 351

—. Nazism. 1933-45. 350

—. Nazism. Psychohistory. ca 1940-78. 1804

—. November Revolution. Parliamentary government. Social Democratic Party. 1918-19. 3345

—. November Revolution. 1918-19. 1930's-70's. 2654

—. November Revolution. 1918-79. 2673

—. Parliamentarism. Political parties. 1848-20c. 1951-83. 2734

—. Peasants. Rebellions. 1525. 19c-20c. 709

—. Peasants War. 1524-26. 20c. 3055

—. Peasants War. 1525. 1968-75. 3372

—. Political Factions. Social Democratic Party. 1863-1963. 2754

—. Political Participation. Revolution of 1848. Working class. 1848. 3352

—. Press. Research. 1885-1970's. 3954

—. Ranke, Leopold von. World and Universal History. ca 1877-1900. 1343

—. Research sources. Thirty Years War. 1618-48. 463

—. Revolution. 1919-80. 3334

—. Revolution. Working Class. 1919. 3380

—. Revolution of 1848. 1848. 1970's-83. 3353

—. Rheinfelder, Hans (tribute). Spanish studies. 1972. 961

—. Rothfels, Hans. War-guilt question. World War I. 1924-45. 3211

—. Schiller, Friedrich von. 1791-93. 1390

—. Schultz, G. Social History (review article). 19c-20c. 2193

—. Social history. 1870-1933. 1960's-70's. 2182

—. Social movements. USA. 1919-60's. 1387

—. Social sciences. 1949-79. 540

—. Taylor, A. J. P. (tribute). 1938-45. 847

—. Tirpitz, Alfred von. Warships. 1898-1914. 1914-73. 3035

—. USA. Zionism. 1900-35. 3937

—. USSR. World War II. 1941-69. 3306

—. Waffen SS. World War II. 1933-45. 1965-77. 3298

—. Working class. 1920's-40's. 1899

—. World War I. 1914-18. 1960's. 3170

—. World War I. 1968-70. 3129

—. World War I (antecedents). 1914-70. 3169

—. World War II. 1939-45. 3252

—. Ziekursch, Johannes. 17c-20c. ca 1925-30. 1016

Germany, East. ca 19c-20c. 1955-62. 2581

—. Anniversaries. Church and State. Luther, Martin. 1483-1546. 1945-84. 3551

—. Armies. Periodicals. Voennaia Istoriia. 1962-72. 3144

—. Attitudes. Luther, Martin. 1500's-46. 1950-83. 3636

—. Beiträge zur Geschichte der Arbeiterbewegung. Communist parties and movements. Periodicals. Working class. 19c-20c. 1958-83. 192

—. Bensing, Manfred. Druzhinin, Nikolai M. Letters. Methodology. USSR. 1969. 1567

—. Bibliographies. Communist Parties and Movements. Socialist Unity Party. 1848-1961. 68

—. Business history. 1970's. 1891

—. Class struggle. 1949-69. 2593

—. Communism. Methodology. USSR. 1917-82. 1569

—. Germany, West. Methodology. Urban studies. 19c-1981. 4023

—. Historical consciousness. Marxism-Leninism. 20c. 1579

—. Industrial history. Labor movement (review article). Socialist Unity Party (10th Congress). 1945-80. 1898

—. International System. Socialism. 1917-70. 1960-70. 2674

—. Leipzig, University of. Marxism. Revolution (theory). 1500-1917. 1971-78. 3366

—. Luther, Martin. Politics. 1517-1983. 3510

—. Marx, Karl (Karl Marx Year). Marxism-Leninism. 1953. 2609

—. Marxism. Methodology. Research. 1970's. 1600

—. Methodology. 1967-78. 1271

—. Military. Patriotism. Proletarian internationalism. Socialism. 1952-82. 3011

—. Military history. Prehistory-20c. 3009

—. Military History (unit histories). 1949-79. 3092

—. November Revolution. Socialism. 1918-69. 2664

—. Periodicals. Socialism. 1978. 92

—. Periodicals. Zeitschrift für Geschichtswissenschaft. 1953. 65

—. Research. Socialism. 1960-70. 2627

—. Social consciousness. 1969. 2671

—. Socialism. 1969. 1617

—. USSR. World War II (Soviet-German Theater). 1943-45. 3078

—. World War II. 1939-75. 3148

Germany, East (Halle). Luther, Martin (conference). 16c. 1983. 3498

Germany (Hesse). Anabaptism. Bucer, Martin. Philip the Magnanimous, Landgrave. Religious liberty. Ziegenhain ordinance. 1520's-40's. 3685

Germany (Jena). Curricula. Friedrich-Schiller University. Marxism. Prehistory-20c. 1945-65. 1354

Germany (Prussia). Foreign Relations. France. 1918-47. 380

Germany (Thuringia). Agricultural labor. 1400-1550. 1943

Germany, West. 1945-61. 2666

—. 1945-70's. 1539

—. 1945-75. 1335

—. 1949-75. 2548

—. 20c. 1254

—. ca 1958-66. 1967. 6

—. Air forces. Air Warfare. Bibliographies. Germany. 1920's-84. 3000

—. Annales school. France. Social history. 1950-79. 303

—. Annales school. France. Sozialgeschichte. 1946-81. 1420

—. Anti-Communist Movements. Maizière, Ulrich de. Military History. 1950's-70's. 3063

—. Begriffsgeschichte. Words. 1960's-80's. 1694

—. Bibliographies. World War II. 1939-75. 3115

—. Capitalism. Economic History. 1970-77. 2678

—. Defense ministry. Dienststelle Blank. 1952-76. 3300

—. Economic Theory. Imperialism. Lenin, V. I. 1960's-70's. 2715

—. Family History (review article). 1200-1950. 2428

—. Fischer, Fritz. Textbooks. World War I (antecedents). 1905-14. 3320

—. Foreign policy. Lenin, V. I. USSR. 1917-22. 2956

—. Foreign Policy. Politics. 1945-79. 456

—. Foreign policy. Power concept. 19c-20c. 2974

—. Foreign Relations. Methodology. USSR. 1918-75. 2911

—. France. Social sciences. 1945-80. 1525

—. Germany. Navies. 1898-1970's. 3125

—. Germany. November Revolution. 1918. 1966-78. 3046

—. Germany, East. Methodology. Urban studies. 19c-1981. 4023

—. Herzfeld, Hans (tribute). Historians. 1892-1982. 738

—. Historians. Matthias, Erich (obituary). Political science. 1921-83. 1089

—. Historicism. Methodology. 20c. 1417

—. Imperialism. 20c. 2718

—. Imperialism. Lenin, V. I. Revolution (theory). 20c. 2680

—. Labor movement. 1945-75. 1939

—. Leninism. 1950-69. 2611

—. Luther, Martin. 1483-1546. 1983. 3605

—. Methodology. Social history. 1970's. 2240

—. Military. 1919-80. 3228

—. Military History (unit histories). 1978-80. 3117

—. Nuremberg trials. World War II. 1933-71. 2997

—. Political history. Social sciences. 19c-20c. 2561

—. Social history. 1960-79. 2222

—. Structuralists. 1951-74. 1376

—. Theory. ca 1960-81. 1318

Germany, West (Berlin; Dahlem). Archives. 1874-1974. 74

Gerschenkron, Alexander. Marxism. Methodology. 20c. 1405

—. Methodology. 1976. 1404

Geschichte und Gesellschaft. Germany. Periodicals. Social History. 20c. 44

—. Periodicals. Social history. 20c. 2221

Giannone, Pietro. Europe. Philosophy. 18c. 217

Gibbon, Edward. 1776-91. 839

—. Ferguson, Adam. Great Britain. Hume, David. Italy. 1736-65. 1062

—. Gossman, Lionel. Methodology (review article). 18c. 1138

—. Historians. 1780's. 329

Gibbon, Edward (Autobiography). Great Britain. 1737-94. 982

Gibbon, Edward (review article). Braudy, Leo. Jordan, David. Parkinson, R. N. 18c. 1084

Gibson, Walter M. Barrett, Gwynn. Hawaii (Lanai). Mormons. 1859-64. 1972-78. 3511

Giddens, Paul H. (Standard Oil Company). Oil Industry and Trade. Personal narratives. Standard Oil Company (Indiana). 1946-56. 1926

Gilbert, Felix. Hintze, Otto (review article). Sociology. 1890-1978. 965

Gilded Age. ca 1868-1900. 4002

—. Industrialization. Urbanization. 1865-1900. 1895

—. Josephson, Matthew (Politicos). Politics. 1865-1900. 1938-80. 2794

—. Modernization. Trachtenberg, Alan. Wiebe, Robert. ca 1865-90. 2065

—. Political Culture. 1870-1900. 2526

Gill, R. Denis, H. Economic Theory (review article). Fusfeld, D. R. 1970. 2003

Ginzburg, Carlo. Art history. Methodology. 15c-19c. 4065

Giorgetti, Giorgio. Agriculture. Capitalism. Italy. Marxism. 18c-20c. 2677

Girault, René. Munich Agreement. 1938. 2957

Giurescu, Constantin C. National Development. Romania. 18c-20c. 1103

—. Romania. 15c-20c. 311

—. Romania. 1901-77. 1104

Gjurmime Albanologjike. Periodicals. Yugoslavia (Kosovo). 16c-20c. 100

Glaciers. Agassiz, Louis. Books (editions). 1820-40. 3818

Glasgow, Ellen. Novels. South. Women. 1855-1941. 595

Godwin, William. Japan. Owen, Robert. ca 1770-1836. 1036

Goethe, Johann Wolfgang von (Faust II). Poetry. 19c. 628

Goetz, Leopold Karl. Germany. Pan-Slavism. Slavs. USSR. 8c-20c. 1100

Gold rushes. California. May, Philip Ross (obituary). New Zealand. 1960's-77. 932

Goldstein, Steven M. China. Clubb, O. Edmund. Foreign Relations. Hunt, Michael H. Letters. 1949-50. 2839

Goodfield, June. Kammen, Michael. Reinitz, Richard. Strout, Cushing. Wilson, Daniel J. 1940-82. 1400

Gookin, Daniel (writings). Indians. Massachusetts Bay Colony. Puritan attitudes. 1656-86. 637

Gordlevsky, Vladimir. Philology. Turkey. 1976. 874

Gorky, Maxim. Editors and Editing. Factories. History of Factories and Plants. Ukraine. 1931-35. 1953

Gorshkov, S. G. Civil-Military Relations. Navies. USSR. 1956-80. 998

Gorshkov, S. G. (Navies in War and Peace). Foreign policy. Military strategy. Navies. USSR. ca 1970's. 3299

Gossman, Lionel. Gibbon, Edward. Methodology (review article). 18c. 1138

Göttingen University. Germany. 18c-19c. 1164

—. Germany. Historians. 1760-1800. 1289

—. Germany. Scholarship. 18c. 1165

Gottschalk, Louis. Generalization (concept). ca 1960-65. 1227

Gould, J. D. Economic Development (review article). 19c-20c. 1866

Goulemot, Jean-Marie. France. 20c. 1635

—. Architecture. Parthenon. 1750-1850. *664*
—. Odessa, University of. Papadimitriou, Synodis D. Russia. 1880-1921. *969*
Greeks. Balkans. Cantemir, Dimitrie. 18c. *1085*
Greene, A. C. (interview). Local history. Texas (western). 1977. *1789*
Greenslet, Ferris. Editors and Editing. Massachusetts Historical Society. 1916-59. *896*
Greer, Colin. Historical context. Matz, Michael B. Public schools. Revisionism. 19c. 1970's. *2330*
Grekov, Boris D. (tribute). Russia. 1912-52. *831*
Griewank, Karl. Germany. Revolution (theory). 18c-19c. 1942-52. *3329*
Grigorovich, Viktor. Bulgaria. 1815-92. *922*
Griswold, A. Whitney (influence). Diplomacy. Far East. Foreign policy. USA. 1898-1938. *2927*
Gross, Mirjana. Marxism. 1970-80. *1424*
Gross National Product. *See* GNP.
Groulx, Lionel. Canada. French Canadians. 1900's-67. 1978. *808*
—. Catholic Church. French Canadians. Quebec. 20c. *1088*
—. French Canadians. Quebec. 1920-67. *819*
—. Quebec. 1878-1967. *310*
Groulx, Lionel (tribute). Catholic Church. French Canadians. Quebec. 1878-1967. *894*
Grünebaum, Gustave von. Islamic studies. Methodology. ca 11c. ca 20c. *1333*
Grushin, B. A. Methodology (review article). Social sciences. 1961. *1437*
Guarracino, Scipione. History Teaching. Methodology. 15c-20c. *1166*
Guatemala. Anti-Communism. Intervention. Revolution. 1954-78. *2902*
Gubec, Mathias. Croatia. Peasants. Rebellions. Slovenia. 1573. *3324*
Guicciardini, Francesco. Political Theory. Prudence. Reason of state. 1561-17c. *644*
Guizot, François. Civilization (concept). 18c. *2426*
Gullah (language). Hancock, Ian. Language. Pidgin English. Slave trade. South Carolina. West Indies. 1651-70. *2102*
Gura, Philip. Bridgman, Richard. Rose, Anne C. Thoreau, Henry David. Transcendentalists (review article). 1820-50. *2343*
Gymnastics. Jahn, Friedrich Ludwig. Social Change. 1820-1978. *3929*

H

Habakkuk, H. J. Economic history. Great Britain. Technology. ca 1600-1976. *3830*
Habermas, Jürgen. Enlightenment. 18c. 1950's-82. *1018*
—. Enlightenment. Koselleck, Reinhart. *Öffentlichkeit* (concept). Political Participation. Public opinion. 18c-20c. *2516*
Habsburg Empire. *See also* constituent parts, e.g. Hungary, Bohemia, etc.; Austria; Czechoslovakia; Hungary.
—. Bibliographies. 1975-76. *194*
—. Bibliographies. Germany. Peasants War. 1524-26. *3373*
—. Church and State. Joseph II. Religious reform. 18c. *3660*
—. Diplomacy. Serbia. World War I (antecedents). 1912-14. *3297*
—. Hungary. Nationalities. Research. Szekfü, Gyula. 1907-25. *824*
—. Italy. Military Campaigns. 1859-80. *3007*
—. Königgrätz (battle). Prussia. 1866. *3054*
—. Navies. 1600-1918. *2981*
—. Periodization of History. 1815-48. *1207*
—. Seton-Watson, R. W. (centennial). Slovakia. 1879-1914. *940*
Habsburg Empire (Vienna). Theater administration (sources). 1750-1975. *3925*
Hackmann, Willem D. Aepinus, Franz. Electricity (review article). Heilbron, J. L. 17c-20c. *3745*
Hagen, Karl. Germany. Reformation. Wirth, Johann. 1840-49. *949*
Hahn, Philipp Matthäus. Bibliographies. Germany. 1770-1980. *985*
Haines, Gerald K. Burns, Richard Dean. Foreign Relations (review article). Lauren, Paul Gordon. Walker, J. Samuel. 1945-83. *2832*
—. Diplomacy (review article). Walker, J. Samuel. 1783-1980. *2912*
Hakluyt, Richard. Discovery and Exploration. 1552?-1616. *457*
Ha-Kohen, Joseph. Printing. Venetia. 1428. 16c. *4016*
Hale, Nathan G., Jr. Europe. Ideas, history of. Psychoanalysis. 1919-40. 1978. *3859*
Halévy, Elie (review article). Chase, Myrna. England. 1870-1937. *1047*
Haley, J. Evetts. Southwest. 20c. *851*
—. Texas. 20c. *465*

Hallam, Henry. England. 1812-59. *270*
Halsted, Caroline Amelia. Richard III. 1460's-85. *340*
Hamburg School. Germany. International law. Marxism. 1870-1918. 1925-79. *2967*
Hamelin, Jean. *Annales* school. Ouellet, Fernand. Quebec. 1952-72. *1645*
Hamilton, Alexander. Economic Policy. 1789-1967. *2006*
Hamilton-Gordon, Arthur Charles. Colonial government. Fiji. 1875-85. *2709*
Hammer-Purgstall, Josef von. Austria. Diplomats. Methodology. Ottoman Empire. Topography. Travel accounts. 1798-1852. *793*
Hancock, Ian. Gullah (language). Language. Pidgin English. Slave trade. South Carolina. West Indies. 1651-70. *2102*
Handbook. Family history. ca 1900-74. *539*
Handicrafts. *See* Arts and Crafts.
Handlin, Oscar. 1979. *341*
—. Truth (review article). 1950-80. *1180*
Handlin, Oscar (review article). 1970's. *1187*
Handlin, Oscar *(Uprooted)*. Immigrants. 1951. *2264*
Handy, Robert T. Ahlstrom, Sidney. Christianity (review article). Marty, Martin E. Race (issue). 16c-1978. *3565*
Hardin-Simmons University. Regional history. Richardson, Rupert Norval. Texas. 1917-79. *726*
Harrison, William. England. Historians. Holinshed, Raphael. 1573-87. *972*
Harvard University. Asia, East. China. Foreign Relations. 19c-20c. *413*
—. Hudson, Winthrop. Massachusetts Bay Colony. Morison, Samuel Eliot. Religious Education. 1636-50. 20c. *665*
Haupt, Georges. Labor movement. Social history. 20c. *2260*
—. Socialism. 1949-72. *893*
Hawaii (Lanai). Barrett, Gwynn. Gibson, Walter M. Mormons. 1859-64. 1972-78. *3511*
Hay, John. China. International Trade. Open Door policy. Revisionism. 1899-1901. *1861*
Hayes, Carlton J. H. Kohn, Hans. Nationalism. Religious attitudes. 1950's-60's. *3637*
Hazard, Paul. Enlightenment. France. 18c-20c. *996*
Head, Henry. Aphasia. 1875-1981. *3854*
Heckscher, Eli F. Dobb, Maurice. Economic Theory. Mercantilism. 17c-19c. *1931*
Hegel, Georg. Augustine, Saint. Christianity. Philosophy. Providence (concept). 410-1970. *3544*
—. Berlin, University of. Engels, Friedrich. Pamphlets. Philosophy. Schelling, Friedrich von. 1841-45. *1077*
—. Burckhardt, Jacob. Comte, August. Dilthey, Wilhelm. Fustel de Coulanges, Numa Denis. 13c-19c. *1342*
—. Documents. Rosenkranz, Karl. 19c. *1262*
Hegel, Georg (review article). Lukács, George. Marxism. Philosophy. 1790's. *832*
Heilbron, J. L. Aepinus, Franz. Electricity (review article). Hackmann, Willem D. 17c-20c. *3745*
Heilbroner, Robert L. (review essay). Humanism. Religion and Science. ca 20c. *3515*
Heine, Heinrich. France. Germany. Larra, Mariano José de. Literature. Spain. 1831-37. *712*
Hempel, Carl G. Murphey, Murray. Philosophy, analytic. 1973. *1832*
Henry, Howell M. Black seamen acts. Slave codes. South Carolina. 1793-1865. *2167*
Herbert Hoover Presidential Library. Iowa, University of. Libraries. State Historical Society of Iowa. 20c. *514*
Herder, Johann Gottfried. Germany. Idealism. Luther, Martin. Ranke, Leopold von. Reformation. 16c-19c. *585*
Heresy. Bibliographies. Bogomils. Bosnia. 12c-16c. *3678*
Hermeneutics. Germany. Philosophy. Sociology of knowledge. 19c-20c. *1406*
Hermerén, Göran *(Värdering och Objektivitet)*. Objectivity. 1970's-83. *1336*
Heroes. Myths and Symbols. Nationalism. Romanticism. Totalitarianism. 19c-20c. *1764*
—. Publishers and Publishing (local). USSR. World War II. 1953-77. *3145*
Heroes (review article). USSR. Working Class. 1917-83. *2034*
Hertzberg, Arthur. Enlightenment. Jews. Philosophes. Voltaire. 18c. 1876-1968. *3996*
Herzfeld, Hans (tribute). Germany. Germany, West. Historians. 1892-1982. *738*
Hexter, J. H. 1961-80. *1379*
—. Bibliographies. Ideas, History of. 16c-17c. 1936-80. *1123*
—. England. Hill, Christopher. Methodology. 17c. 1930's-70's. *1629*
—. Great Britain. Hill, Christopher. 17c. *1231*

—. Italy. 1935-80. *880*
Hexter, J. H. (essays). 1951-77. *349*
Hexter, J. H. (review essay). Fischer, David Hackett (review essay). Logic. 1900-70. *1278*
Heymann, Frederick G. Bernard, Paul P. Bohemia. Hussite movement (review aricle). Kaminsky, Howard. 15c. 1950's. *3598*
Hicks, John. Economic theory. 1974. *1852*
Higginbotham, A. Leon (review article). Blacks. Slavery. 18c. 1960's-78. *2145*
High Schools. *See also* Secondary Education.
—. Japan, Treatments of. Textbooks. 1951-72. *626*
—. Slavery. Textbooks. 20c. *620*
"High Society" (composition). Music (jazz). Popular Culture. ca 1900. 1950's. *4033*
Higher Education. *See also* Colleges and Universities.
—. 1965. *1361*
—. Europe. 16c-18c. *2308*
—. Political science. 20c. *2559*
—. Racism. Reconstruction. Textbooks. 1865-76. 1960-73. *596*
Hildebrand, Emil. *Historisk Tidskrift*. Periodicals. Sweden. 1881-1900. *75*
Hilden, Patricia. Feminism. Women. 19c-20c. *3423*
Hill, Christopher. England. Hexter, J. H. Methodology. 17c. 1930's-70's. *1629*
—. Great Britain. Hexter, J. H. 17c. *1231*
Hill, Samuel S., Jr. Loveland, Anne C. Religion (review article). South. Wilson, Charles Reagan. 1941-81. *3503*
Hillgruber, Andreas. Germany. 1871-1945. *849*
Hinsley, F. H. Causation. Taylor, A. J. P. Trevor-Roper, Hugh. World War II. 1961-78. *3045*
Hinton, James. Great Britain. Labor history. Montgomery, David. USA. Workers' control. ca 1870's-1918. *2092*
Hintze, Otto (review article). Gilbert, Felix. Sociology. 1890-1978. *965*
Hispanic American Historical Review. Bibliographies. 1956-75. *472*
Hiss, Alger. Communism. Liberalism. McCarthy, Joseph R. Textbooks. 1950-80. *2523*
Histoire de la Littérature Allemande. Germany. Literature (review article). 1835-1959. *172*
Histoire Generale de Languedoc. Benedictines. France (Languedoc). Maurists. 1715-45. *680*
Histoire raisonnée. Enlightenment. 1660-1720. *1334*
—. Mézeray, François Éudes de. 1610-83. *2237*
Historians. 18c-20c. *258*
—. 20c. *1432*
—. Abraham, David *(Collapse of the Weimar Republic)*. Fraud. Scandals. 1982-85. *787*
—. Aesthetics. Philosophy. Poland. Tatarkiewicz, Władysław (obituary). 1910-80. *890*
—. Africa. Hodgkin, Thomas (obituary). 1930's-82. *1056*
—. Alchemy. Austria (Villach). Moro, Gotbert. Paracelsus. Physicians. 1493-1531. 1950-79. *957*
—. Ariès, Philippe. Autobiography. Family (review article). 1930-70. *2490*
—. Attitudes. Death. Thullier, Guy. 1980. *1513*
—. Attitudes. French Revolution. 19c. *3348*
—. Balaban, Meyer (tribute). Jews. Poland. ca 13c-20c. *854*
—. Beard, Mary. Women. 1930-80. *3470*
—. Bibliographies. Clarendon, 1st Earl of. England. Political Leadership. 1630's-74. *468*
—. Biography. Dictionaries. Latin America. 16c-20c. *517*
—. Biography. Moorman, Mary. Trevelyan, George Macauley (review article). 1876-1965. *750*
—. Books (editions). Droysen, Johann Gustav *(Historik)*. Germany. 1850's-84. *820*
—. Bremond, Henri. Catholic Church. Duchesne, Louis. France. 1900-24. *3552*
—. Bulgaria. Zhivkova, Liudmila (obituary). 1942-81. *1118*
—. Butterfield, Herbert. Liberalism. 1930-83. *1297*
—. Cambridge University. Colleges and Universities. Great Britain. Oxford University. ca 1870-1900. *1292*
—. Capitalism. Nejedly, Z. (tribute). 1878-1962. *1083*
—. Cherepnin, Lev (tribute). Russia. 14c-18c. 1930's-77. *956*
—. Communist Party. Lenin, V. I. Popov, N. N. USSR. 1906-30's. *938*
—. Czechoslovakia. Editors and Editing. History Teaching. Král, Václav (obituary). Sociology. 1926-83. *1122*
—. Delpech, François (obituary). France. Jews. Lyons, University of. Religion. 1935-82. *768*
—. Democracy. Germany. Human rights. Schlözer, August Ludwig von. 1717-1809. *2553*
—. DiManzano, Francesco. Italy (Friuli). 11c-19c. *1010*

I

Inchofer, Melchior (*Annales Ecclesiastici Regni Hungariae*). Catholic Church. Censorship. Hungary. Jansenism. 1641-48. *3532*
Income. Domesticity. Economic Conditions. Women. 1780-1980. *3413*
—. Economic Growth. Population. Regions. South. ca 1840-60. *675*
—. Real estate. Webb, Walter Prescott. Western States. 1930's-63. *1007*
Independence. National development. -1976. *2787*
Independence Movements. *See also* Anti-Imperialism; Nationalism.
—. Anticolonialism. Kenya. Kikuyu. Mau Mau. 1951-60. *251*
—. Bulgarians. Macedonia. Ottoman Empire. 1878-1912. 1945-79. *181*
—. Mijares, Augusto. Venezuela. 18c-20c. 1931-72. *910*
Independence, War of. Bibliographies. Germany. Marxism. Napoleonic Wars. 1813-14. *150*
—. Carabobo (battle). Duarte Level, Lino. Venezuela. 1821. *3215*
—. Engels, Friedrich. Marx, Karl. Revolution. 1850-70. *3354*
India. Art. 19c-20c. *265*
—. Sepoy Mutiny. 1857-59. *266*
Indiana (Indianapolis). Police. Social Control. 1820-83. *708*
Indiana, University of. Transportation. Western States. Winther, Oscar Osburn. 1920's-70. *1079*
Indians. *See also* terms beginning with the word Indian; names of Indian tribe, e.g. Delaware Indians; Acculturation.
—. Anglos. Ethnocentrism. Mexican Americans. New Mexico Territory. Racism. 17c-20c. *672*
—. Authors. French Canadians. New France. Stereotypes. 1534-1663. 19c-20c. *495*
—. Bibliographies. 16c-20c. *511*
—. Blacks. Folklore. Utah. ca 1850-1973. *1791*
—. Boas, Franz. British Columbia. Ethnology. Myths and Symbols. 1890-20c. *412*
—. Books (editions). Franciscans. Mexico. Torquemada, Juan de (*Monarquía Indiana*). 16c-1624. *394*
—. Canada. USA. Women. 17c-20c. *3417*
—. Gookin, Daniel (writings). Massachusetts Bay Colony. Puritan attitudes. 1656-86. *637*
—. Great Plains. Sioux Indians. Winter Counts. 1796-1926. *267*
—. Lee, Jason. Methodism. Missions and Missionaries. Oregon. 1838-43. *3609*
—. Massachusetts (Boston). Overland Journeys to the Pacific. Parkman, Francis. Psychology. 1840's-90's. *1794*
—. Religion. 19c-20c. *3630*
—. Religion. Supernatural. 19c-20c. *3575*
Indian-White Relations. Colonialism. New England. Puritans. 17c. *365*
—. New England. Puritans. Theology. 17c-20c. *3689*
Indochina. *See also* Asia, Southeast.
—. Bibliographies. Mkhitarian, S. A. (tribute). Vietnam. 1945-81. *941*
—. War. 1945-75. *3279*
Industrial archaeology. 1960-79. *2056*
—. Bibliographies. Great Britain. Technological change. 19c-20c. *78*
Industrial development. Estonia. Working class. 1960-80. *1958*
Industrial history. Germany, East. Labor movement (review article). Socialist Unity Party (10th Congress). 1945-80. *1898*
Industrial Revolution. Crime. Great Britain. USA. ca 1775-19c. *2235*
—. Economic Development. Political Change. Social Change. 1640-1880's. *1913*
—. Economic History. "Robber Barons". 1880's-1900. *1970*
—. Europe, Western. Standard of Living. Textile industry. Working conditions. 19c. *1944*
—. Great Britain. Labor. Women. 18c-19c. *3388*
—. Great Britain. Social Change. 18c-19c. 1950's-70's. *1912*
Industrial Revolution (review article). Agriculture. Great Britain. 1650-1815. *2014*
Industrial Society (theory). 1940's-60's. *2032*
Industrial Workers of the World. American Federation of Labor. Labor. 1905-69. *1886*
—. Brissenden, Paul F. 20c. *1885*
Industrialization. *See also* Economic Growth; Modernization.
—. Agricultural Production. Capitalism. Social History. 19c-20c. *1942*
—. Atkinson, Edward. New England. Walker, Francis A. Wells, David A. Wright, Carroll D. 17c-19c. 1890's. *1950*
—. Banking. Italy. 18c-20c. 1960's-80's. *2036*
—. Capitalism. Laue, Theodor von. Russia. 1900-17. *822*

—. Economic development. Germany. 19c. 1960's. *2068*
—. Economic Development (documents). USSR. 1917-72. 1950-70. *96*
—. France. 19c. *1927*
—. Germany. Methodology. Research. 19c. *255*
—. Gilded Age. Urbanization. 1865-1900. *1895*
—. Italy. Labor Unions and Organizations. ca 1870-1914. *2020*
—. Models, theoretical. Political Culture. Social Organization. 1950-71. *2217*
—. Saint-Simon, Comte de. Socialism. 19c. *2024*
—. USSR. 1920's-30's. 1960's-70's. *2062*
Industrialized Countries. *See also* Developing Nations; Western Nations.
—. Natural Resources. Social Conditions. 1980. *2051*
Industry. *See also* individual industries, e.g. Iron Industry, etc.; Industrialization; Management; Manufactures.
—. Communist Party. Technological progress. Ukraine. 1959-75. *1964*
—. Conferences. Lowell Conference on Industrial History. 1815-1920. *2075*
—. Factory histories. Hungary. Labor movement. 1960's. *2046*
—. Labor Unions and Organizations. Netherlands. 1890's-1940. *2066*
—. Labor Unions and Organizations. World War II. 1941-45. *3064*
—. Personnel Managers. Reform. 1897-1920. *629*
—. Ukraine. 20c. *1870*
Inerrancy. Bible. Hodge, Archibald Alexander. Theology. Warfield, Benjamin Breckinridge. 1800-1962. *3491*
Inflation. Hungary. Wages. 1867-1945. *1871*
Influenza. Epidemics. Europe. Hoffmann, K. F. Mancisi, G. M. Ramazzini, B. 1708-09. *3873*
Information. Research Sources. 20c. *14*
Information access. Documents. Government. Research. 1970's-83. *135*
Information Sciences. *See also* Information Storage and Retrieval Systems.
—. Classification systems. -1975. *16*
—. Europe, Eastern. USSR. 1960's-70's. *11*
Information Storage and Retrieval Systems. *See also* Computers.
—. Austria. Graz, University of (Institut für Maschinelle Dokumentation). 1945-81. *1706*
—. Bibliographic References. Graduate Study and Research. Physical Education. 1973. *646*
—. Methodology. 1969. *1705*
Information Storage and Retrieval Systems (input). Methodology. 1977. *1702*
Information Theory. Research (sources). 1861-1901. *1325*
Innis, Harold Adams. Communications. McLuhan, Marshall. 1930-79. *770*
Innovation. Diffusion. Sports. 19c-20c. *3899*
Insanity. *See* Mental Illness.
Institut Français de l'Histoire Sociale. *Mouvement Social*. Periodicals. Working class. 1960-82. *2180*
Institute for History of Material Culture. Material culture. Poland. 1930's-70. *3900*
Institute of Croatian History. Yugoslavia (Croatia). 1971-81. *214*
Institutional history. Social history. 1865-1900. *2207*
Institutionalism. Ayres, Clarence E. Economic theory. Veblen, Thorstein. 20c. *1947*
Institutionalization. Education (symposium). 1800-1975. *2299*
Institutions. Modernization. 1950-80. *2450*
Insulin. Banting, Frederick Grant. Biochemistry. Canada. Medical Research. USA. 1890's-1962. *3881*
—. Banting, Frederick Grant. Canada. Medicine. Nobel Prizes. 1902-72. *3874*
Insurrections. *See* Rebellions.
Intellectual history. 1870's-1975. *2323*
—. 1960-80. *2305*
—. 19c-20c. *385*
—. American studies. Culture concept. 1972. *2300*
—. Civil War (antecedents). Nationalism. Wilson, Major L. (review article). 1815-61. 1946-75. *2784*
—. Cultural history. 1940-80. *2186*
—. Elites. 1930-70. *2375*
—. Foucault, Michel. France. 1970-72. *2353*
—. Foucault, Michel. Methodology. 17c-20c. *2402*
—. Methodology. Miller, Perry. New England. ca 1630-1740. 1930's-70's. *2385*
Intellectuals. *Arguments*. France. Periodicals. 1956-62. *34*
—. Bossuet, Jacques. France. 17c. 20c. *1024*
—. Buckle, Henry Thomas. Europe, Eastern. Great Britain. Jews. Russia. 1860-1905. *1032*

—. Buckle, Henry Thomas (*History of Civilization in England*). Culture. Great Britain. Romania. 1860's. *1102*
—. Cold War. Ideas, History of. *Partisan Review*. Periodicals. Totalitarianism. 1934-48. *627*
—. Feminism. Ideology. 19c-1981. *470*
—. Iqbal Ashtiyani, 'Abbas. Iran. 1905-56. *560*
Intelligence Service. *See also* Espionage; Military Intelligence.
—. Reform. 1965-75. *2764*
Intelligentsia. Ivanov, Razumnik. Russia. USSR. 1903-33. *816*
Interdisciplinary approach. 1967-77. *1655*
Interdisciplinary research. Sociology. 1810-1970. *2231*
Interdisciplinary studies. 1965. *1291*
—. 20c. *3976*
—. Jacksonian era. Politics. 1820's-30's. 1959-75. *2757*
—. Marxism. Public policy. Urban history. 1940-80. *3928*
Internal Migration. *See* Migration, Internal.
International Commission on Historiography. *History of Historiography*. International Congress of Historical Sciences, 15th. Periodicals. 18c-20c. 1980-84. *156*
International Congress of Economic History, 7th. Economic History. 15c-20c. 1978. *1878*
International Congress of Historical Sciences. California (San Francisco). USSR. 1975. *1703*
—. Methodology. 1955-65. *1428*
International Congress of Historical Sciences (General). Methodology. 1977. *169*
International Congress of Historical Sciences, 12th. Austria (Vienna). Methodology. 1965. *64*
International Congress of Historical Sciences, 14th. 1975. *134*
—. Brezzi, P. Sestan, E. ca 1800-1975. *38*
—. Ideology. Methodology. 1975. *148*
International Congress of Historical Sciences, 15th. 1975-79. *99*
—. 1980. *98*
—. 1980. *156*
—. Contemporary History. Modern History. 16c-20c. *61*
—. *History of Historiography*. International Commission on Historiography. Periodicals. 18c-20c. 1980-84. *156*
International cooperation. Academy of Sciences Institute of History. USSR. 15c-1980. *19*
International Law. *See also* Boundaries; International Relations (discipline); Slave Trade; Treaties; War.
—. France. Lorraine. War. 1630-48. *2954*
—. Germany. Hamburg School. Marxism. 1870-1918. 1925-79. *2967*
—. Multinational corporations. ca 1945-70. *2089*
International Longshoreman's and Warehouseman's Union. Bridges, Harry. California. Communist Party. 1934-79. *2042*
International relations. 19c-20c. *2920*
—. Appeasement. 1919-74. *2886*
—. Balkan states. Diplomacy. Economic history. Great powers. 18c-20c. *2834*
—. Carr, E. H. (review article). Political nationalism. 1939-62. *2884*
—. France. 1920-83. *2881*
—. Marxism. Western Nations. 20c. *2877*
International Relations (discipline). *See also* Foreign Relations.
—. France. 19c-20c. 1960-78. *2861*
—. Methodology. Philosophy of History. 1600-1970. 20c. *551*
—. Political history (review article). 1800-1973. *2964*
International Relations Theory. Bull, Hedley. Wight, Martin. 20c. *2864*
International research. Quantitative Methods (review). 1950-74. *1709*
International Society for the Study of Time. Time (conferences). Prehistory-1977. *4001*
International System. Diplomacy. Maier, Charles S. Methodology. 1970-80. *2978*
—. Germany, East. Socialism. 1917-70. 1960-70. *2674*
International Trade. China. Hay, John. Open Door policy. Revisionism. 1899-1901. *1861*
International, 1st. 1864-77. ca 1960-66. *2616*
—. Socialism. 1864-76. 1954-64. *2625*
International, 2d. 1889-1914. *2626*
Internationalism. Labor movement. Methodology. Marxist. Poland. 19c-20c. *1972*
Interpretation. 1971. *1372*
—. Generalization. Methodology. 1979. *1415*
—. Historians. Research. 5c BC-20c. *1455*
Interpretive changes. Civil War. Politics (essays). Quantitative Methods. Reconstruction. 1850's-76. 1960's-75. *512*

Intervention. Anti-Communism. Guatemala. Revolution. 1954-78. *2902*

Interviews. Methodology. Oral History. 1975. *334*

Interviews, tape-recorded. Film. 1972. *1763*

Intuition. New England. Parker, Theodore. Reason. Theology. Transcendentalism. Unitarianism. 18c-1860. 1920-79. *3709*

Inventions. Alberti, Leon Battista. Camera Obscura. Italy. Painters. Photography. 15c-1910. *4011*

Inventive genius concept. National Characteristics. Technology. 1790-1860. *3758*

Investments. Business. Imperialism. 19c-20c. *2707*

Iorga, Nicolae. *Annales: Économies, Sociétés, Civilisations.* Europe, Southeastern. Periodicals. *Revue Historique du Sud-Est Européen.* 1924-46. *168*

—. Enlightenment. Modernization. Romania. 17c-19c. *921*

—. Kogălniceanu, Mihail. Philosophy. Politics. Romania. ca 1840-90. *1106*

—. Methodology. 1890-1940. *1550*

—. Methodology. Romania. 1890-1940. *991*

—. World War I (causes). 1850-1945. *3254*

Iowa, University of. Herbert Hoover Presidential Library. Libraries. State Historical Society of Iowa. 20c. *514*

Iqbal Ashtiyani, 'Abbas. Intellectuals. Iran. 1905-56. *560*

Iran. Intellectuals. Iqbal Ashtiyani, 'Abbas. 1905-56. *560*

Ireland. *See also* Great Britain.

—. Bennet, Arthur (*Wars of Ireland*). 1844. *966*

—. Catholic Church. 1800-1922. 1960-75. *3680*

—. England. Scotland. 10c-20c. 1966-84. *479*

Irish Americans. Immigration. ca 1830's-1970's. *2419*

Iron Industry. *See also* Steel Industry.

—. Business leaders. Cities (size). Social Classes. 1874-1900. *1955*

—. James, Thomas. Maramec Iron Works. Massey, Samuel. Missouri. Slavery. 1828-50. 1950's-70's. *2124*

Irony. Methodology. 20c. *1443*

—. Niebuhr, Reinhold. 20c. *462*

Irregular Warfare. *See* Guerrilla Warfare.

Irving, David. Germany. Nazism. Resistance. Rommel, Erwin. 1941-45. *3048*

Irving, Washington. Biography. Literature. 1807-59. *2307*

Irving, Washington (*Conquest of Granada, History of New York*). 19c. *699*

Iskra. Lenin, V. I. Newspapers. 1885-1971. *130*

Islam. 20c. *338*

—. 20c. *3601*

—. Africa, West. Animism. Christianity. Religious history. 19c-20c. *3484*

—. Ameer 'Alī, Syed. Great Britain. Imperialism. Shiblī Nu 'Mani, Mohammed. 19c. *557*

—. Arabs. Culture. Western Civilization. 1980. *2412*

—. China. Western Civilization. 600 BC-20c. *1464*

—. Middle East. Orientalism. 19c-20c. *358*

Islamic studies. Grünebaum, Gustave von. Methodology. ca 11c. ca 20c. *1333*

Isolationism. Foreign policy. 1919-39. *2823*

—. Foreign policy. 20c. *2938*

—. Foreign Policy. History Teaching. 1920's. 1970's. *589*

—. World War II. 1930's-40's. *2848*

Israelites. Chronicles. Methodology. Old Testament. 1830's-70's. *614*

Istoricheski Pregled. Bulgaria. Communist Party. Periodicals. 1945-60. *125*

—. Bulgaria. Periodicals. 1944-64. *90*

—. Bulgaria. Periodicals. 1944-69. *91*

—. Bulgaria. Periodicals. 1960. *207*

Istoriia Diplomatii (series, review article). Diplomacy. 1960-79. *2936*

Istorijski Zapisi. Cultural History. Periodicals. Yugoslavia (Montenegro). 1927-77. *33*

—. Periodicals. Yugoslavia (Montenegro). 1927-77. *12*

Istprofs (labor history commissions). Labor movement. USSR. 1920-39. *1954*

Italian Americans. Catholic Church. Objectivity. Sartorio, Enrico C. (review article). Tomasi, Silvano (review article). 1918. 1975. *3627*

—. Middle Classes. Women. 1939-78. *3462*

—. Schiavo, Giovanni. 1924-62. *736*

Italy. *See also* Tuscany, Venetian Republic, etc.

—. Agriculture. Capitalism. Giorgetti, Giorgio. Marxism. 18c-20c. *2677*

—. Alberti, Leon Battista. Camera Obscura. Inventions. Painters. Photography. 15c-1910. *4011*

—. Allies. Archives. Foreign Relations. Military government. World War II. 1939-46. *3216*

—. Allies. Military occupation, German. Resistance. World War II. 1939-45. *3026*

—. Almanacs. France. Great Britain. Popular Culture. Public opinion. 18c. *2432*

—. *Annales: Économies, Sociétés, Civilisations.* France. Periodicals. 1940's-70's. *1634*

—. *Annales: Économies, Sociétés, Civilisations.* Labor Movement. Periodicals. 1940's-70's. *1644*

—. *Annales* School. 20c. *1661*

—. *Annales* school. France. 20c. *1663*

—. *Archivio Storico Italiano. Nuova Rivista Storica.* Periodicals. 1860-1945. *13*

—. *Archivio Storico Italiano.* Periodicals. Political Change. Poriani, Ilaria. Risorgimento. 19c. *154*

—. *Archivio Storico Italiano.* Periodicals. Risorgimento. 1842-61. *452*

—. Aristotle. Patrizi da Cherso, Francesco (*Discussiones Peripateticae*). Renaissance. 1571-81. *2363*

—. Banking. Industrialization. 18c-20c. 1960's-80's. *2036*

—. Baroque. 16c-1750. *1177*

—. Bibliographies. Feminism. Politics. Women. 1900-81. *3452*

—. Bibliographies. Mazzini, Giuseppe. Risorgimento. 19c. 1981-83. *1108*

—. Bibliographies. Ragionieri, Ernesto. 1946-75. *1109*

—. Buonaiuti, Ernesto. Christianity. 1945-82. *3617*

—. Cantimori, Delio. Culture. Periodicals. Popular culture. *Società.* 1947-53. *114*

—. Capitalism, industrial. Merli, Stefano. Working Class (review article). 1880-1900. *1925*

—. Catholic Church. Church and Social Problems. D'Avack, Piero Agostino. Lateran Treaty. 1929-74. *3577*

—. Catholic Church. Church and State (review article). Maccarone, Michele. 1861-76. *3683*

—. Catholic Church. Döllinger, Ignaz von. Religious Liberty. 1850-70. *3499*

—. Center for the History of the University of Padua. Padua, University of. 13c-20c. 1922-82. *202*

—. Chabod, Federico. Religion. 16c. *3520*

—. Chabod, Federico. Renaissance. 13c-16c. *1028*

—. Christian Democrats. Politics. 1918-76. *3505*

—. Conference. Germany. War aims. World War I. 1914-15. *3245*

—. Conquest. War. 15c-16c. *2999*

—. Croce, Benedetto (works; editions). Text structure. 1890-1950. *909*

—. Cultural relations. Medicine. Physicians. Romania. 15c-19c. 20c. *3887*

—. DeFelice, Renzo. Fascism. ca 1920-45. *2683*

—. DeFelice, Renzo. Fascism. Political Theory. 1920's-30's. 1970's. *2681*

—. DeFelice, Renzo (review essay). Fascism. Revolution. 1922-45. 1975. *2632*

—. Dejung, Christoph. Fascism. Totalitarianism (term). 20c. *2600*

—. Diplomacy. Toscano, Mario. Treaties. 1930's-60's. *2934*

—. Economic growth. Melis, Federigo. Renaissance. 14c-15c. *1894*

—. Economic Policy. Fascism. Monetary policy. 1920-39. *1916*

—. Education. History teaching. Research. 1968-82. *1450*

—. Epidemics. Medicine. Social history. 14c-19c. *3858*

—. Europe. Ferrero, Guglielmo. Social Change. 1900-42. *600*

—. Fascism. Foreign policy. 1947-71. *3210*

—. Fascism. Labor Unions and Organizations. 1926-43. *2029*

—. Fascism. Mussolini, Benito. 1922-45. *262*

—. Fascism. Resistance. 1922-45. *2598*

—. Fascism. Working class. 1922-43. *2668*

—. Ferguson, Adam. Gibbon, Edward. Great Britain. Hume, David. 1736-65. *1062*

—. Financial aid. National Research Council. Research. 1967-82. *3*

—. Foreign policy. Morandi, Carlo (*Scritti Storici*). 1926-50. *2831*

—. Foreign Relations. Mürzsteg Program. Nicholas II (visit). Russia. 1903. *2850*

—. France. Oriani, Alfredo. Political culture. 5c-19c. 1920's. *917*

—. France. Positivism. ca 1854-1912. *1508*

—. Habsburg Empire. Military Campaigns. 1859-80. *3007*

—. Hexter, J. H. 1935-80. *880*

—. Historians. Renaissance. 15c-16c. *272*

—. Humanism. Ideology. Renaissance. 1200-1500. *3916*

—. Industrialization. Labor Unions and Organizations. ca 1870-1914. *2020*

—. Landscape. Social history. 15c-20c. 1960's-70's. *2259*

—. Local history. Methodology. 1946-79. *1209*

—. Lombards. Sclopis, Federico. 700-1900. *948*

—. Lunacharski, Anatoli. 1905-17. *959*

—. Machiavelli, Niccolò. 16c. *872*

—. Machiavelli, Niccolò. Martelli, Mario. 16c. *758*

—. Machiavelli, Niccolò. Political Theory. 1494-1527. *360*

—. Memoirs. Navies. World War II. 1940-43. *3218*

—. Methodology. National Institute for the Study of the History of the Liberation Movement. 1979. *1219*

—. Military History. 1974. *3185*

—. Military History. Napoleon. 1814-61. *3040*

—. Mosca, Gaetano. Political Theory. Social Classes. 1880's-20c. *937*

—. Namier, Lewis. 18c. *741*

—. Nationalism. Patriotism. 18c. 19c-20c. *2804*

—. Neo-Kantianism. Positivism (review article). 19c. *2332*

—. *Nuova Rivista Storica.* Periodicals. 1917-45. *40*

—. Periodicals. 1982. *102*

—. Philosophy. Pico della Mirandola, Giovanni. 15c. *282*

—. Photography. 1975-82. *132*

—. Political Culture. Religion. 1970's. *3645*

—. Psychology. 1970's. *3731*

—. Renaissance. 16c. 20c. *3964*

—. Surrender. World War II. 1943. *3296*

—. Venice. 15c-16c. *444*

—. World War II. 1941-76. *3033*

—. World War II (Balkan Theater). 1939-45. *3204*

Italy (Bologna). Art history. Literature. 15c-20c. *4013*

Italy (Friuli). DiManzano, Francesco. Historians. 11c-19c. *1010*

Italy (Liguria). Labor movement. Perillo, Gaetano. 1897-1975. *1924*

Italy (northern). Resistance. 1943-45. *3039*

Italy (Po River). Art. Documents, Figurative. Farms. 11c-16c. *4026*

Italy (Rome). Archivio Centrale dello Stato. Methodology. World War II. 1939-45. 1922-75. *3241*

—. French Academy. Geffroy, Auguste. *Mélanges d'Archéologie et d'Histoire.* Periodicals. 1877-82. *124*

Italy, southern. Family. Marriage. Social change. 16c-20c. *2443*

Ivanić, Matij. Dalmatia (Hvar). Rebellions. 1510-14. *3323*

—. Dalmatia (Hvar). Rebellions. 1510-14. 1769-1976. *3360*

Ivanov, Razumnik. Intelligentsia. Russia. USSR. 1903-33. *816*

J

Jackson, Age of. Quantitative Methods. Working Class. 1828-48. 1972. *2022*

Jackson, Andrew. Cartoons. Political caricatures. 1827-34. *2800*

—. Democracy. 19c-20c. *2744*

Jackson, Andrew (papers). Advertising. Fugitive Slaves. Newspapers. *Tennessee Gazette.* 1804. 1977. *2125*

Jackson, Andrew (presidency). Pessen, Edward (thesis). Social History. 1828-36. *2793*

Jacksonian Democracy. 1828-41. 19c-1974. *603*

—. 19c-20c. *2572*

Jacksonian era. Interdisciplinary studies. Politics. 1820's-30's. 1959-75. *2757*

Jacksonianism. Politics. Social Classes. 1828-30's. *2289*

Jahn, Friedrich Ludwig. Gymnastics. Social Change. 1820-1978. *3929*

—. Nationalism. Prussia. 19c. *814*

Jahrbuch für die Geschichte Mittel- und Ostdeutschlands. Bibliographies. Germany. Historic Commission of Berlin. Periodicals. Poland. 15c-20c. 1952-84. *129*

Jails. *See* Prisons.

Jamaica. Blacks. Ethnic groups. Myalism. Religion. 18c-19c. *2164*

James, Thomas. Iron Industry. Maramec Iron Works. Massey, Samuel. Missouri. Slavery. 1828-50. 1950's-70's. *2124*

Jameson, John Franklin. *American Historical Review.* Editors and Editing. Periodicals. 1880's-1928. *1002*

—. Colleges and Universities. 1879-1937. *668*

Janik, Allan. Ideas, History of (review article). Marcus, Stephen. Toulmin, Stephen. 19c. 1973-74. *2354*

Jansenism. Catholic Church. Censorship. Hungary. Inchofer, Melchior (*Annales Ecclesiastici Regni Hungariae*). 1641-48. *3532*

—. Catholic Church. Scotland. ca 1713-80. *3629*

Japan. Americanology. National self-image. Social conditions. 19c-20c. 1969-73. *2219*

—. Arai Hakuseki (*Tokushi Yoron*). 9c-16c. *226*

—. Arai Hakuseki *(Tokushi yoron)*. Confucianism. 1700's-25. *213*

—. *Baishōron (work)*. Ideology. *1868-1912.* 703

—. Bibliographies. Mathematics. Research. 1872-1976. 1937-76. *3796*

—. Biology (review article). 1965-72. *3826*

—. Botany. Kaempfer, E. Siebold, Philipp Franz van. Thunberg, Carl Peter. 17c-20c. *3779*

—. Business history. Methodology. 1965. *2093*

—. Chemistry. 19c-1970. 1962-72. *3803*

—. China. Foreign Relations. Russo-Japanese War. 1904-05. *2982*

—. Culture. 15c-20c. *225*

—. Economic History. 1603-1940. *420*

—. Economic History. 1603-1940. *510*

—. Economic Theory. 1760's-20c. 1940's-80. *2045*

—. Economics. Europe. Revolution. 18c-19c. *3369*

—. Feudalism. Norman, E. H. 17c-19c. 1940-75. *844*

—. Films. Popular Culture. *Shōgun.* 1600. 1980. *496*

—. Foreign Relations. Great Britain. USA. World War II (antecedents). 1934-41. *3060*

—. Foreign Relations. Imperialism. Korea. 1882-1980's. *2932*

—. Godwin, William. Owen, Robert. ca 1770-1836. *1036*

—. Government. Nationalism. 14c-20c. *248*

—. Marxism. Ogura Kinnosuke. Science. 1920's-60's. *3799*

—. Military defeat. USA. USSR. World War II. 1942-45. *3243*

—. Politics. USA. 1972. *2798*

Japan (Hiroshima). Alperovitz, Gar. Atomic bomb (review article). Decisionmaking. World War II. 1945-65. *3262*

Japan, Treatments of. High Schools. Textbooks. 1951-72. *626*

Jaspers, Karl. Philosophy of history. Politics. 20c. *1836*

Jászi, Oszkár. Minorities. State Formation (review article). 1908-49. *2772*

Jászi, Oszkár (reputation). Hungary. Politics. 1919-61. *769*

Jaurès, Jean. French Revolution. Lefebvre, Georges. 1789-99. *1057*

—. French Revolution. Mathiez, Albert. 1789-99. 1874-1932. *3377*

—. French Revolution. Social Classes. 1789-99. *3383*

Jaurès, Jean *(Armée nouvelle)*. Middle Classes. 1859-1914. *2223*

Jeanneret, Charles Edouard. *See* Corbusier, Le.

Jedin, Hubert. Catholic Church. Reformation. 16c. *552*

Jefferson, Thomas. Adams, Henry Brooks *(History of the United States)*. Democracy. Diplomacy. National Characteristics. 1800-17. 1889-91. *563*

—. Allen, Ethan. Deism. Franklin, Benjamin. Palmer, Elihu. 1750-1820. *3580*

—. Brodie, Fawn M. Children. Slaves. ca 1771-89. 1974-76. *2135*

Jefferson, Thomas *(Notes on the State of Virginia)*. Geography, historical. Research (sources). 18c-20c. *1208*

Jensen, Merrill. Antifederalists. Kenyon, Cecelia M. Turner, Frederick Jackson. 1776-1800. 1893-1974. *2765*

—. Ideology. Main, Jackson T. 20c. *1520*

Jensen, Richard (interview). Illinois (Chicago). Newberry Library (Family and Community History Center). Quantitative Methods. 1971-82. *1721*

Jenson, Andrew. Hunter, Howard W. Lund, A. William. Lyon, T. Edgar (reminiscences). Mormons. Roberts, B. H. 1913-70. *3613*

Jesuits. Abipon. Argentina (La Plata). Colonialism. Social Customs. 1527-19c. *661*

—. Church and State. England. Missions and Missionaries. More, Henry *(Historia Missionis Anglicanae Societatis Jesu)*. 1580-1635. *422*

—. Hungary. 1591-1801. *3571*

—. New France. Parkman, Francis. 17c. 1840's-60's. *833*

Jesus Christ. Germany. Theology. 16c-19c. *3648*

Jewish Historical Institute. Korczak, Janusz. Poland. 1967-79. *77*

Jews. See also Anti-Semitism; Judaism; Zionism.

—. -20c. *3986*

—. 19c-20c. *3969*

—. 20c BC-20c. *549*

—. Prehistory-20c. *4063*

—. ca 1290 BC-20c. *3973*

—. ca 1780-1980. *4060*

—. Acculturation. Immigration. New York City. Rischin, Moses *(Promised City)*. 1870-1914. *4066*

—. Assimilation. Europe. Katz, Jacob (review article). Social Change. 18c. *1039*

—. Balaban, Meyer (tribute). Historians. Poland. ca 13c-20c. *854*

—. Basnage, Jacques. Bayle, Pierre. Enlightenment. ca 1650-1725. *3713*

—. Basnage, Jacques *(L'Histoire des Juifs)*. Europe. 18c. *3675*

—. Bibliographies. Germany. 15c-20c. 1945-79. *51*

—. Bibliographies. Poland. -1870. *80*

—. Buckle, Henry Thomas. Europe, Eastern. Great Britain. Intellectuals. Russia. 1860-1905. *1032*

—. Christian churches. Ethics. Genocide. Holocaust. 1933-70's. *3606*

—. Crime and criminals. Social history. 19c-20c. *2265*

—. Delpech, François (obituary). France. Historians. Lyons, University of. Religion. 1935-82. *768*

—. Diaspora. Dubnow, Simon. Russia. 1880-1941. *903*

—. Dubnow, Simon. Poland. 1860-1941. *1059*

—. Economic Conditions. Poland. Schipper, Yitzhak. 12c-18c. *399*

—. Enlightenment. Europe, Central. Periodicals. *Sulamith.* 1800-25. *3998*

—. Enlightenment. Hertzberg, Arthur. Philosophes. Voltaire. 18c. 1876-1968. *3996*

—. Genocide. Germany. Psychology. World War II. 1941-54. 1940's. *2907*

—. Genocide. Holocaust. Nazism. World War II. 1939-45. *285*

—. Jost, Isaak Markus. Zunz, Leopold. 1800-60. *1020*

—. Labor. 20c. *2080*

—. Luther, Martin. 16c. 1945-82. *3576*

—. Marranos. Portugal. Spain. 15c-20c. *4007*

—. Methodology. Tcherikover, Elias. YIVO Institute of Jewish Research. 1920's-60's. *4050*

—. Poland. Press. USA. Warsaw ghetto uprising. World War II. 1942-43. *3135*

—. Romania. World War II. 1939-73. *3152*

—. Scholarship. 1948-76. *3953*

—. Zionism. 19c-1982. *4056*

—. Zunz, Leopold. 1810's-20's. *1093*

Jews, Lithuanian. USSR. World War II. Zimanas, Genrikas. 1960-70's. *3154*

Jews (review article). Europe. 18c-20c. *3966*

Jiang Qing. China. Government. Political Factions. Women. 1975-76. *3433*

Johannsen, Robert W. Evitts, William J. Mohr, James C. Pessen, Edward. Politics (review article). Sewell, Richard A. 1830-75. 1945-78. *2750*

Johnson, Richard. Dobb, Maurice. Economism. Humanism. Socialism. 20c. *1880*

—. Marxism. 20c. *1602*

Johnson, Samuel. Humanism. 1454-1582. 1755-84. *2380*

Jonge, Johannes Cornelius de. Great Britain. Letters. Macaulay, Thomas Babington *(History of England)*. Netherlands (The Hague). 1847-49. *1094*

Jordan, David. Braudy, Leo. Gibbon, Edward (review article). Parkinson, R. N. 18c. *1084*

Joseph Fielding Smith Institute of Church History. Bibliographies. Church of Jesus Christ of Latter-Day Saints (History Division). Mormons. Personal narratives. 19c-20c. *3721*

Joseph II. Church and State. Habsburg Empire. Religious reform. 18c. *3660*

Josephson, Matthew. 1934-40. *677*

Josephson, Matthew *(Politicos)*. Gilded Age. Politics. 1865-1900. 1938-80. *2794*

Josiah Macy, Jr. Foundation. Medicine. Science and Society. 1965-69. *3867*

Jost, Isaak Markus. Jews. Zunz, Leopold. 1800-60. *1020*

Journal of Broadcasting. Bibliographies. Broadcasting. Periodicals. 20c. *93*

Journal of the History of the Behavioral Sciences. Bibliographies. Psychology. 1967-77. *3789*

Journalism. *See also* Editors and Editing; Films; Newspapers; Periodicals; Press.

—. 1980. *3951*

—. Allen, Frederick Lewis *(Only Yesterday)*. Liberalism. Puritanism. 1931. *912*

—. Culture. Methodology. 19c-20c. *2421*

—. Political Commentary. White, Theodore. 1960-75. *2755*

—. Research. 1960's-82. *4009*

—. Research. 19c-1975. *4038*

—. Sciranka, John Coleman. Slovak Americans. Social Organizations. 1924-78. *1061*

Journals. *See* Diaries; Periodicals.

Judaism. *See also* Anti-Semitism; Jews; Zionism.

—. Baer, Isaac. Bibliographies. 1913-79. *8*

—. Cabala. Mysticism. Scholem, Gershom. 20c. *237*

Judaism, Reform. Germany. Lehranstalt für die Wissenschaft des Judentums. Pharisees. 19c. *3722*

Judaizerism. Russia. 1440-1555. *3581*

Judson, Edward Zane Carroll. *See* Buntline, Ned.

Junker (definition). Engels, Friedrich. Germany. Marx, Karl. 1845-90. *1695*

K

Kaempfer, E. Botany. Japan. Siebold, Philipp Franz van. Thunberg, Carl Peter. 17c-20c. *3779*

Kalabiński, S. Methodology (review article). Poland. Quantitative methods. 20c. *1711*

Kaminsky, Howard. Bernard, Paul P. Bohemia. Heymann, Frederick G. Hussite movement (review aricle). 15c. 1950's. *3598*

Kammen, Michael. Goodfield, June. Reinitz, Richard. Strout, Cushing. Wilson, Daniel J. 1940-82. *1400*

—. Social history. 1979-80. *1206*

Kammen, Michael (review article). 1940's-80. *1314*

—. 1979-80. *1302*

Kansas. Buchanan, James. Lecompton Constitution. Political Leadership. Slavery. Suffrage. 1857. 20c. *2779*

—. Great Plains, northern. Kansas, University of. Malin, James C. 1920's-64. *766*

Kansas, University of. Great Plains, northern. Kansas. Malin, James C. 1920's-64. *766*

Karamzin, Nikolai. Partitions. Pogodin, Mikhail. Poland. Russia. Soloviëv, Sergei. 1772-93. *742*

Kardelj, Edvard (obituary). Slavs, South. 1945-79. *721*

Katyn Forest. Dissent. Poland. Sakharov, Andrei. USSR. World War II. 1939-40. 1975. *3225*

Katz, Jacob (review article). Assimilation. Europe. Jews. Social Change. 18c. *1039*

Kedourie, Elie. Anglo-Arab Relations. Diplomatic history. 1976. *2893*

Keller, Fred. Colleges and Universities. Personalized System of Instruction. 1977. *2360*

Kellner-Hostinský, Peter. Hungary. Slovaks. 9c-19c. *916*

Kennan, George F. Russian Studies. USA. 1865-1905. *700*

Kennedy, John F. 1960-63. *403*

—. Congress. Political Leadership. Revisionism. 1961-63. *2810*

Kennedy, John F. (changing image). Foreign policy. Vietnam War. 1963-73. *2820*

Kentucky. *See also* South or Southern States.

—. Baptists. Missions and Missionaries. 19c. *685*

Kentucky (Fort Mitchell). Curricula. Medicine, history of. Nurses and Nursing. Thomas More College. 19c-20c. 1975-78. *3862*

Kenya. Anticolonialism. Independence Movements. Kikuyu. Mau Mau. 1951-60. *251*

—. Methodology. 15c-20c. *500*

Kenyon, Cecelia M. Antifederalists. Jensen, Merrill. Turner, Frederick Jackson. 1776-1800. 1893-1974. *2765*

Kenyon, John. Burrow, J. W. Butterfield, Herbert. Cochrane, Eric. Wormell, Deborah. 5c BC-20c. *1547*

Kerch (battle). El'tigen (landing). USSR (Crimea). World War II. 1943. *3056*

Kerney, Martin J. Catholic Church. Church Schools. Maryland. 1845-50. *3616*

Keylor, William R. Carbonell, Charles-Olivier. France. 1866-1914. *1479*

Keynesianism. Capitalism. Periodization of History. 1913-83. *1845*

Khalatbari, Parviz. Economic Development. Migration (conference). 16c-20c. *1946*

Khmelnitsky, Bogdan. Cossacks. Documents. Ukraine. 1620-54. *1033*

Khrushchev, Nikita. Berlin "ultimatum.". Germany. USA. USSR. 1958. *2816*

Kidrič, Boris. Slovenia. 1934-51. *989*

Kikuyu. Anticolonialism. Independence Movements. Kenya. Mau Mau. 1951-60. *251*

Kirby, S. Woodburn. Great Britain. Wingate, Orde. World War II. 1939-44. *3177*

Kissinger, Henry *(A World Restored)*. Diplomacy. Metternich. 1790's-1859. 1957. *2965*

Klein, Magnus. Austria. Middle Ages. Paleography. 1717-83. *1074*

Kliuchevski, V. O. Russia. 10c-19c. *378*

Kliuchevski, Vasili Osipovich. Russia. 1870's-1911. *1060*

Kluge, Alexander. Literature. 20c. *1157*

Knunyants, Bogdan. Centennial Celebrations. Revolution of 1905. Russia. Soviets. 1897-1911. *859*

Kocka, J. Agricultural History. Puhle, H.-J. 1970-78. *1887*

Kogălniceanu, Mihail. Iorga, Nicolae. Philosophy. Politics. Romania. ca 1840-90. *1106*

—. Kogălniceanu, Vasile M. Romania. 1893-1942. *882*

—. Romania. 19c. *1107*

Kogălniceanu, Vasile M. Kogălniceanu, Mihail. Romania. 1893-1942. *882*

Kogan-Bernshtein, Faina Abramovna. Bibliographies. 1927-79. *1078*

Kohli-Kunz, Alice. Psychology. Radkau, Joachim. Radkau, Orlinde. 1972. *1131*

Kohn, Hans. Hayes, Carlton J. H. Nationalism. Religious attitudes. 1950's-60's. *3637*

Kolko, Gabriel. Business-government relations. Government regulation. Railroads. 1877-1916. 1965-72. *1873*

—. Foreign policy. Kolko, Joyce. Neorevisionism. Williams, William Appleman. 1975. *2950*

Kolko, Gabriel *(Triumph of Conservatism)*. Federal regulation. Progressivism. 1901-16. *1847*

Kolko, Joyce. Foreign policy. Kolko, Gabriel. Neorevisionism. Williams, William Appleman. 1975. *2950*

Kommunistul Moldovei. Communist Party. Moldavia. Periodicals. USSR. 20c. *62*

Kondratieff cycle. Economic History. 15c-17c. 20c. *1864*

Koneski, Blazhe. Literature. Macedonia. Nationalism. 19c-20c. *720*

Königgrätz (battle). Habsburg Empire. Prussia. 1866. *3054*

Korczak, Janusz. Jewish Historical Institute. Poland. 1967-79. *77*

Korea. Foreign Relations. Imperialism. Japan. 1882-1980's. *2932*

Korean War. Bibliographies. 1950's-70's. *3206*

—. Bibliographies. USA. 1950-55. *3205*

—. MacArthur, Douglas. Politics. Public relations. Truman, Harry S. Wake Island. 1950. *3301*

Korean War (origin). China. Foreign Relations. USSR. 1943-50. *3019*

Korhonen, Arvi. Finland. Operation Barbarossa. Philosophy of History. World War II. 1961. *1838*

Kormanowa, Żanna (tribute). Bibliographies. Working class. 1925-80. *877*

Kornilov, Aleksandr A. Historians. Russia. 19c. *397*

Koselleck, Reinhart. Enlightenment. Habermas, Jürgen. *Öffentlichkeit* (concept). Political Participation. Public opinion. 18c-20c. *2516*

Košice (air raid). Hungary. USSR. War, declaration of. World War II. 1941-46. *3047*

Kousser, J. Morgan. Social Sciences. 1977-80. *2171*

Koyré, Alexandre. Epistemology. Science. 17c. 1917-64. *368*

Koyré, Alexandre *(Études galiléennes)*. Galileo (Two Chief World Systems). 1632. *3756*

Kraditor, Aileen. Radicals and Radicalism (review article). 1880-1917. *1538*

Král, Václav (obituary). Czechoslovakia. Editors and Editing. Historians. History Teaching. Sociology. 1926-83. *1122*

Krandžalov, Dimitr (obituary). Bulgaria. Europe, Eastern. 1907-71. *1071*

Krasnaia Letopis'. Periodicals. *Proletarskaia Revoliutsiia.* USSR. 1922-41. *71*

Krause, Karl. Baron, André. Krausism. Menéndez Pelayo, Marcelino. Sanz del Río, Julián. Spain. 19c. 1936-72. *2351*

Krausism. Baron, André. Krause, Karl. Menéndez Pelayo, Marcelino. Sanz del Río, Julián. Spain. 19c. 1936-72. *2351*

Krebs, Hans A. Lavoisier, Antoine. Science. Scientists. 18c. 20c. *3770*

Kremers, Edward. Pharmacy. Urdang, George. 19c-20c. *3885*

Kristeller, Paul. Humanism. Renaissance. 1300's-1980. *4008*

—. Humanism. Renaissance. 1350-1650. *1344*

—. Ideology. Objectivism. Renaissance. Truth in history. 15c-16c. *1561*

Križanić, Juraj. 1638-83. *828*

Kronstadt mutiny. Lenin, V. I. Trotsky, Leon. 1921. *393*

Krzywicki, Ludwik. Memoirs. Poland. Political Parties. Proletariat. Working Class. 1875-84. *1857*

Kuczynski, Jürgen. Marxism. Working Class (definition). 20c. *1984*

—. Social Sciences (review article). 1970-79. *2238*

Kuhn, Thomas S.. Burke, Kenneth. Wise, Gene. 1975. *799*

—. Claval, Paul. Geography. Science, history of. Wright, John K. 1978. *555*

—. Iggers, Georg G. 1962-75. *1451*

—. Paradigms. 1962-79. *1161*

—. Science. Structuralism. 1957-79. *1477*

Kuhn, Thomas S. (review article). Science. 15c-20c. *3814*

Kuhn, Thomas *(Structure of Scientific Revolutions)*. Palmer, Robert R. *(Age of Democratic Revolution)*. Rostow, W. W. *(Stages of Economic Growth)*. Social Change. 1960-70. *1272*

Kukuljević, Ivan. Croatia. Editors and Editing. 1850-75. *1037*

Kursk (battle). USSR. World War II. 1943. *3105*

—. USSR. World War II (Soviet-German Theater). 1943. *3270*

—. World War II. 1943. *3113*

Kurz, Anton. German. Periodicals. Research. Transylvania. 1840's. *128*

Kutsch, Thomas. Social change. Social Theory. Wiswede, Günter. 20c. *2206*

Kwartalnik Historii Nauki i Techniki. Periodicals. Poland. Science, history of. 1956-80. *144*

Kwartalnik Historyczny. Methodology. Periodicals. Poland. 1970-76. *167*

L

Labastida, Jaime. Humboldt, Alexander von. ca 1790-1845. *967*

Labor. *See also* Agricultural Labor; Capitalism; Communism; Employment; Lockouts; Socialism; Strikes; Wages; Working Class; Working Conditions.

—. American Federation of Labor. Industrial Workers of the World. 1905-69. *1886*

—. Americas (North and South). Plantations. Slavery. Social Organization. 17c-19c. 1959-79. *2111*

—. Anarchism and Anarchists. Communism. Ethnic Groups. 1880's-1920's. *1869*

—. Bibliographies. Hobsbawm, Eric. Thompson, E. P. 1960's-70's. *2091*

—. Capitalism. Mining. Mozambique. South Africa. 1890-1945. *613*

—. Civil War. Ideology. Politics. Slavery. 1860-76. 1970-79. *315*

—. Class Struggle. 19c-20c. *1994*

—. Commons, John R. Foner, Philip S. 19c-20c. 1918-82. *1903*

—. Depression. New Left. 1930-45. *1867*

—. Depressions. Ethnicity. 1930's. 1970-82. *2053*

—. Great Britain. 19c-20c. *2027*

—. Great Britain. Ideology. -1974. *1948*

—. Great Britain. Industrial Revolution. Women. 18c-19c. *3388*

—. Immigration. 1877-1920's. *353*

—. Jews. 20c. *2080*

—. Marxism. Research. Sex roles. Women. 19c. 1970's. *3431*

—. Methodology. 19c-1940's. 1950-78. *1868*

—. Mexican Americans. Oral history. 1920's-30's. *1788*

—. New Left. 1950's-70's. *2050*

—. Politics. Women. 19c-20c. *3442*

—. South. 19c-20c. *1919*

—. USA. USSR. 1976. *2047*

Labor Disputes. *See also* Lockouts; Strikes.

—. 1917-79. *1932*

Labor, division of. Finland (Tampere). Working Class (concept). 1830-1920. *1935*

Labor, forced. Germany. Resistance. World War II. 1940-45. *3131*

Labor history. 1920-70. *2088*

—. Associations. Denmark (Ringkøbing). 1983. *1956*

—. Copenhagen, University of. Denmark. 1982. *1849*

—. Germany. Labor movement. Methodology. Social Classes. Social history. 1866-1933. *2255*

—. Great Britain. Hinton, James. Montgomery, David. USA. Workers' control. ca 1870's-1918. *2092*

—. Research. Sociology. Working class. 18c-20c. *1930*

Labor History Institute. Communist Party. Hungary. 1946-73. *2094*

Labor movement. 1960-75. *2696*

—. 19c-20c. *2096*

—. 19c. *1938*

—. 19c. *2083*

—. Agricultural Labor (contract). Agricultural Technology and Research. Social Change. Sugar. 19c. *1909*

—. *Annales: Economies, Sociétés, Civilisations.* Italy. Periodicals. 1940's-70's. *1644*

—. Belgium. 1860-1979. *2028*

—. Bibliographies. China. 1895-1949. *264*

—. Bibliographies. Slovenia. Socialism. 19c-20c. *86*

—. Capitalism. Western nations. 2049

—. Chartism. Doherty, John. Europe. Great Britain. Radicals and Radicalism (review article). 19c. *2064*

—. Class consciousness. Ethnic Groups. 1963-82. *1902*

—. Comintern. Foreign Relations. Labor Unions and Organizations. Socialism. 1979. *2607*

—. Communism. Germany. Socialism. 1914-45. *2023*

—. Czechoslovakia. Marxism. 1789-1977. 1948-78. *2090*

—. Depressions. Social Change. 1929-39. *2257*

—. Europe. 1870-1970. *1937*

—. Factory histories. Hungary. Industry. 1960's. *2046*

—. Germany. Labor history. Methodology. Social Classes. Social history. 1866-1933. *2255*

—. Germany, West. 1945-75. *1939*

—. Great Britain. 1919-39. 1950's. *1983*

—. Great Britain. Methodism. Wearmouth, Robert Featherstone. 19c. *1076*

—. Haupt, Georges. Social history. 20c. *2260*

—. Historical consciousness. Revolutionary movements. 20c. *2670*

—. Internationalism. Methodology, Marxist. Poland. 19c-20c. *1972*

—. *Istprofs* (labor history commissions). USSR. 1920-39. *1954*

—. Italy (Liguria). Perillo, Gaetano. 1897-1975. *1924*

—. Lenin, V. I. USSR. ca 1917-70's. *1975*

—. Luxemburg, Rosa. Nettl, Peter. ca 1900-14. *2576*

—. Manitoba (Winnipeg). Strikes. 1890's-1919. *415*

—. Methodology. Political Parties. 19c-20c. *2642*

—. Methodology. Working class. 19c-20c. *1276*

—. Rasputnis, B. I. 1950-80. *1900*

—. Research. 18c-20c. *2081*

—. Russia. 19c-20c. *1981*

Labor movement (conference). 1977. *1966*

Labor movement, international. 1850-1970. 1971-76. *1969*

Labor movement (review article). 20c. *1929*

—. Germany, East. Industrial history. Socialist Unity Party (10th Congress). 1945-80. *1898*

Labor Unions and Organizations. *See also* names of labor unions and organizations, e.g. American Federation of Labor, United Automobile Workers, etc.; Lockouts; Strikes.

—. Canada. Leftism. Logan, Harold. Thompson, E. P. 20c. *1998*

—. Canada. Research. Women. 1891-1980. *3461*

—. Catholic Church. Quebec. Social Classes. 1864-1979. *343*

—. Comintern. Foreign Relations. Labor movement. Socialism. 1979. *2607*

—. Denmark. 1950-80. *2054*

—. Economic Structure. Federal Policy. New Deal. Politics. Revisionism. 1921-38. *704*

—. Fascism. Italy. 1926-43. *2029*

—. France. 1945-75. *2033*

—. Industrialization. Italy. ca 1870-1914. *2020*

—. Industry. Netherlands. 1890's-1940. *2066*

—. Industry. World War II. 1941-45. *3064*

—. Socialism. 1890-1930. *2796*

Labrousse, Ernest. Braudel, Fernand. Mentalities. 18c-20c. *2395*

—. Rebellions. Social Conditions. 18c-20c. *2285*

Labrousse, Ernest (review article). Economics, cyclical. France. Quantitative Methods. Social Organization. ca 1960-70. 1974. *1733*

Lamaism. Religion. Siberia. USSR. 1919-76. *3716*

Lambarde, William. Literature. Manuscripts (collection). Nowell, Laurence. Travel. 1568-72. *743*

Lambe, Bulfinch. Agaja, King. Dahomey. Slave trade. 18c. *2129*

Lamprecht, Karl. Berr, Henri. Durkheim, Emile. France. Methodology. Sociology. 1900-11. *1328*

—. Finland. Ranke, Leopold von. 1900-50. *1295*

—. Germany. 1890's-1900's. *835*

—. Germany. Royal Saxonian Institute for Cultural and Universal History. 1890's-1915. *1017*

—. Ranke, Leopold von. Treitschke, Heinrich von. 19c. *419*

Land. *See also* Agriculture; Real Estate.

—. Gates, Paul W. Western States. 1920's-79. *733*

—. Millenarianism. Nationalization. Radicals and Radicalism. Spence, Thomas. 1780-1814. *2550*

—. Speculators (role). 18c-20c. *2059*

Land reform. Livonia. Peasants. Schoultz-Ascheraden, Baron von. 1760's. *2011*

—. Peasants. Stolypin, Pëtr. Yanly, George L. 1907-15. *2017*

Land use. Biography. Documents. War. ca 1800-1950. *1252*

Land warrants. American Revolution. Bounties. Pension records. Social history. Women's history. 19c. *3463*

Landscape. Italy. Social history. 15c-20c. 1960's-70's. *2259*

O

P

—. *Annales* school. Russia (Moscow). 16c-17c. 1949-81. *1672*
—. Antifeudalism. Rebellions. Terminology. Transylvania. 1784. *3379*
—. Bohemia. Rebellions. 1775. *3364*
—. Capitalism. 19c-20c. *2067*
—. Class struggle. Feudalism. 16c-18c. *2209*
—. Colloquium of American and Soviet Historians. Slavery. USSR. 1975. *2100*
—. Croatia. Gubec, Mathias. Rebellions. Slovenia. 1573. *3324*
—. Germany. Rebellions. 1525. 19c-20c. *709*
—. Land reform. Livonia. Schoultz-Ascheraden, Baron von. 1760's. *2011*
—. Land reform. Stolypin, Pëtr. Yanly, George L. 1907-15. *2017*
—. Luther, Martin. Political repression. 1520-33. *3486*
—. Marxism. 1905-78. *2675*
—. Marxism. Public Policy. 1919-50. *2592*
—. Social Organization. 1545-1700. *2253*
—. Sociology (rural). 1971. *2269*
Peasants (typologies). Socioloqy, rural. 1973. *2002*
Peasants War. Bibliographies. Germany. Habsburg Empire. 1524-26. *3373*
—. Engels, Friedrich *(Peasant War in Germany)*. Germany. 1850. *1556*
—. Germany. 1524-26. 20c. *3055*
—. Germany. 1525. 1968-75. *3372*
Peckham, Howard H. *American Heritage.* American history. Periodicals. Personal narratives. 1930-84. *2366*
Pedagogy. See Education; Teaching.
Pediatrics. Caulfield, Ernest. Physicians. Ruhräh, John. 18c. 1899-1972. *187*
Pembroke, Countess of (Mary Herbert). Authors. England. Women. 1485-1621. *3420*
Pembroke, Earl of (William Herbert). Battles. Edgecote (battle; date). England. 1469. *3159*
Penal system. Sociology. 18c-19c. *2239*
Penedo Rey, Manuel. Mercedarians. Personal narratives. Spain (Castile). Vázquez Núñez, Guillermo. 1922-36. *3652*
Peninsular War (review article). Great Britain. USA. 1808-15. *3161*
Pennsylvania. Fertility. Marriage. Methodology. Occupations. 1850-80. *2446*
—. Friends, Society of. Pacifism. Politicians. 1681-1748. *3707*
Pennsylvania (Philadelphia). Metropolitan Areas. Migration, Internal. 1920-80. *3903*
Pension records. American Revolution. Bounties. Land warrants. Social history. Women's history. 19c. *3463*
Pépin III. Attitudes. Germany. Methodology. 19c. 751-68. *1129*
Pereiaslav Agreement. Russia. Ukraine. 1654. *233*
Perillo, Gaetano. Italy (Liguria). Labor movement. 1897-1975. *1924*
Periodicals. *See also* Editors and Editing; Newspapers; Press.
—. 1970. *110*
—. *American Heritage.* American history. Peckham, Howard H. Personal narratives. 1930-84. *2366*
—. *American Historical Review.* Editors and Editing. Jameson, John Franklin. 1880's-1928. *1002*
—. *Annales: Économies, Sociétés, Civilisations. Bloch, Marc. Febvre, Lucien. 1929-79.* 1675
—. *Annales: Économies, Sociétés, Civilisations. Bloch, Marc. Febvre, Lucien.* France. Social sciences. *1929-79.* 1665
—. *Annales: Économies, Sociétés, Civilisations.* Europe, Southeastern. Iorga, Nicolae. Revue Historique du Sud-Est Européen. 1924-46. 168
—. *Annales: Économies, Sociétés, Civilisations.* France. Italy. 1940's-70's. *1634*
—. *Annales: Économies, Sociétés, Civilisations.* Italy. Labor Movement. 1940's-70's. *1644*
—. *Annales* school. France. *Nouvelle Histoire.* 1920's-83. *1633*
—. *Archives. Sovetskie Arkhivy.* USSR. 1922-82. *177*
—. *Archives of the Ukraine.* Ukraine. USSR. 1925-80. *79*
—. *Archivio Storico Italiano.* Italy. *Nuova Rivista Storica.* 1860-1945. *13*
—. *Archivio Storico Italiano.* Italy. Political Change. Poriani, Ilaria. Risorgimento. 19c. *154*
—. *Archivio Storico Italiano.* Italy. Risorgimento. 1842-61. *452*
—. *Arguments.* France. Intellectuals. 1956-62. *34*
—. Armies. Germany, East. *Voennaia Istoriia.* 1962-72. *3144*
—. Austria. ca 1800-48. *558*
—. Austria. Bibliographies. 15c-20c. *32*
—. Austria (Lower Austria). Bibliography. Daily life. Newspapers. Social customs. 1918-82. *113*

—. Bazard, Saint-Amand. *Protecteur.* Saint-Simonianism. 1825-32. *3592*
—. *Beiträge zur Geschichte der Arbeiterbewegung.* Communist parties and movements. Germany, East. Working class. 19c-20c. 1958-83. *192*
—. Berr, Henri. France. Methodology. *Revue de Synthèse Historique.* 1900-07. *1327*
—. Bibliographies. Broadcasting. *Journal of Broadcasting.* 20c. *93*
—. Bibliographies. Germany. Historic Commission of Berlin. *Jahrbuch für die Geschichte Mittel-und Ostdeutschlands.* Poland. 15c-20c. 1952-84. *129*
—. Bibliographies. Poland. Pomerania. 10c-19c. 19c-1908. *153*
—. Bibliographies. Romania. 15c-20c. *157*
—. Bulgaria. 1878-1944. *193*
—. Bulgaria. Communist Party. *Istoricheski Pregled.* 1945-60. *125*
—. Bulgaria. *Istoricheski Pregled.* 1944-64. *90*
—. Bulgaria. *Istoricheski Pregled.* 1944-69. *91*
—. Bulgaria. *Istoricheski Pregled.* 1960. *207*
—. Cantimori, Delio. Culture. Italy. Popular culture. *Società.* 1947-53. *114*
—. Cold War. Ideas, History of. Intellectuals. *Partisan Review.* Totalitarianism. 1934-48. *627*
—. Communist Party. Great Britain. Morris, John. *Past and Present.* 1952-58. *2613*
—. Communist Party. *Kommunistul Moldovei.* Moldavia. USSR. 20c. *62*
—. *Cuadernos Americanos.* Mexico. Political Commentary. Silva Herzog, Jesús. 1940's-70's. *489*
—. *Cuadernos de Historia Moderna y Contemporanea.* Spain. 1980. *116*
—. Cultural History. *Istorijski Zapisi.* Yugoslavia (Montenegro). 1927-77. *33*
—. *Daedalus.* Social sciences. 1969-70. *1224*
—. Decorations. Red Banner of Labor. USSR. *Voprosy Istorii.* 1978. *70*
—. *Diogène.* Toynbee, Arnold J. *(Study of History).* 1956. *723*
—. Economic history. 1976-82. *1922*
—. Editors and Editing. *Historisk Tidskrift.* Swedish Historical Society. 1900-61. *151*
—. Ellsworth, S. George (account). *Western Historical Quarterly.* 1969-79. *45*
—. Enlightenment. Europe, Central. Jews. *Sulamith.* 1800-25. *3998*
—. Europe, Western. Middle Ages (review article). *Srednie Veka.* 11c-17c. 1968-82. *10*
—. Family. Leftism. *Radical History Review.* Slavery. 17c-20c. 1970's. *2123*
—. *Foreign Affairs.* Foreign Relations. USA. USSR. 1972-78. *2929*
—. France. Literature. Melodrama. Vaudeville. 1789-1800. *2365*
—. France. Propaganda. *Revue Historique.* World War I. 1914-18. *115*
—. French Academy. Geffroy, Auguste. Italy (Rome). *Mélanges d'Archéologie et d'Histoire.* 1877-82. *124*
—. German. Kurz, Anton. Research. Transylvania. 1840's. *128*
—. Germany. *Geschichte und Gesellschaft.* Social History. 20c. *44*
—. Germany, East. Socialism. 1978. *92*
—. Germany, East. *Zeitschrift für Geschichtswissenschaft.* 1953. *65*
—. *Geschichte und Gesellschaft.* Social history. 20c. *2221*
—. *Gjurmime Albanologjike.* Yugoslavia (Kosovo). 16c-20c. *100*
—. Great Britain. *Past and Present.* 1959-82. *103*
—. Hildebrand, Emil. *Historisk Tidskrift.* Sweden. 1881-1900. *75*
—. *History of Historiography.* International Commission on Historiography. International Congress of Historical Sciences, 15th. 18c-20c. 1980-84. *156*
—. Hungary. *Levéltári Közlemények. Történelmi Szemle.* 1970-74. *158*
—. Hungary. *Voenno-Istoricheskii Vestnika.* World War II. 1944-45. 1969-72. *52*
—. Institut Français de l'Histoire Sociale. *Mouvement Social.* Working class. 1960-82. *2180*
—. *Istorijski Zapisi.* Yugoslavia (Montenegro). 1927-77. *12*
—. Italy. 1982. *102*
—. Italy. *Nuova Rivista Storica.* 1917-45. *40*
—. *Krasnaia Letopis'. Proletarskaia Revoliutsiia.* USSR. 1922-41. *71*
—. *Kwartalnik Historii Nauki i Techniki.* Poland. Science, history of. 1956-80. *144*
—. *Kwartalnik Historyczny.* Methodology. Poland. 1970-76. *167*
—. Lenin, V. I. *Ukrains'kyi Istorychnyi Zhurnal.* USSR. 1968-70. *155*

—. *Magazin Istoric.* Mass Media. National Self-image. Romania. 1967-82. *139*
—. *New Literary History.* Theater. 20c. *690*
—. *Novaia i Noveishaia Istoriia.* USSR. 20c. 1971-72. *145*
—. *Pacific Historical Review.* 19c. 1974-81. *170*
—. Poland. Resistance. *Wojskowy Przegląd Historyczny.* World War II. 1941-45. 123
—. Poland. *Śląski Kwartalnik Historyczny Sobótka.* 1946-80. 55
—. Poland. *Zapiski Historyczne.* 1908-79. *82*
—. *Problemy Slavianoznavstva.* Slavic studies. Ukraine. USSR. 1970's. *175*
—. *Revue des Etudes Sud-Est Européennes.* Romania. 1963-67. *43*
—. Social sciences. Yugoslavia (Montenegro). *Zapisi.* 1927-33. *180*
—. Sociology. *Thought and Word.* 1970-80. *2177*
—. Ukraine. *Ukrains'kyi Istorychnyi Zhurnal.* 1957-61. *176*
—. Ukraine. *Ukrains'kyi Istoryk.* 1963-83. *182*
—. USSR. *Voprosy Istorii.* 14c-20c. *69*
—. USSR. *Voprosy Istorii KPSS.* 1970-72. *95*
Periodicals, historical. Editors and Editing. Self-Managed Interest Society for Scientific Endeavors. Yugoslavia (Croatia). 1981. *85*
—. *Literature and History.* 1982. *2377*
—. Romania. 1944-74. *36*
Periodization of history. 1979. *1548*
—. Biography (seminar). 1981. *1524*
—. Capitalism. Keynesianism. 1913-83. *1845*
—. Europe. Women. 1976. *3398*
—. Habsburg Empire. 1815-48. *1207*
—. Music. ca 5c BC-20c. *605*
Persecution. See also Anti-Semitism; Religious Liberty.
—. Bibliographies. Witchcraft. 16c-17c. 1945-. *1779*
—. Europe. USA. Witchcraft. 16c-17c. 1966-80. *1766*
—. Europe. Witchcraft. 16c-17c. 1762
Personal narratives. 1930-84. *1388*
—. *American Heritage.* American history. Peckham, Howard H. Periodicals. 1930-84. *2366*
—. American history. Material culture. Science, history of. Technology. 1930-84. *3767*
—. Bibliographies. Church of Jesus Christ of Latter-Day Saints (History Division). Joseph Fielding Smith Institute of Church History. Mormons. 19c-20c. *3721*
—. Folklore. 1970-80. *1787*
—. Giddens, Paul H. *(Standard Oil Company).* Oil Industry and Trade. Standard Oil Company (Indiana). 1946-56. *1926*
—. Mercedarians. Penedo Rey, Manuel. Spain (Castile). Vázquez Núñez, Guillermo. 1922-36. *3652*
—. Methodology. Smith, Joseph. ca 1820-44. *3570*
—. Social history. 1930-84. *2278*
Personality. Emotions. Methodology. 1970's-80's. *1819*
—. Political Leadership. Weiner, M. 1801-48. *2573*
Personality, cult of (conferences). Bulgaria. 1946-63. *1527*
Personality, modern. Models. Modernization, concept of. Underpopulation. ca 1600-1865. 20c. *1795*
Personalized System of Instruction. Colleges and Universities. Keller, Fred. 1977. *2360*
Personnel Managers. Industry. Reform. 1897-1920. *629*
Peru. Garcilaso de la Vega. Linguistics. Spanish Conquest. Translating and Interpreting. 1605-16. *624*
—. Garcilaso de la Vega *(Comentarios Reales).* Incas. Linguistics. 15c-16c. *711*
Pessen, Edward. Evitts, William J. Johannsen, Robert W. Mohr, James C. Politics (review article). Sewell, Richard A. 1830-75. 1945-78. *2750*
Pessen, Edward (observations). 1975. *1421*
Pessen, Edward (thesis). Jackson, Andrew (presidency). Social History. 1828-36. *2793*
Pétain, Henri Philippe. France. Military history. World War I. 1917-18. *3213*
Peter I. Russia. 1680's-1725. 18c-20c. *464*
Petrarch. Culture. Leonardo da Vinci. Manetti, Giannozzo. Renaissance (review article). 14c-15c. *3904*
Petroleum. See Oil and Petroleum Products.
Petronio, Giuseppe. Literary History (review article). 15c-20c. *2369*
Peucer, Kaspar. Melanchthon. 1525-1602. *800*
Pharisees. Germany. Judaism, Reform. Lehranstalt für die Wissenschaft des Judentums. 19c. *3722*
Pharmacy. See also Botany; Chemistry.
—. Kremers, Edward. Urdang, George. 19c-20c. *3885*
—. Medicine. Paracelsus. Science. 15c-19c. *3856*

—. Olmedilla y Puig, Joaquin. Spain. ca 1902. *3860*
Phenomenology. Husserl, Edmund. 1890's-1930's. *1004*
—. Time. 1970-80. *1251*
Philip the Magnanimous, Landgrave. Anabaptism. Bucer, Martin. Germany (Hesse). Religious liberty. Ziegenhain ordinance. 1520's-40's. *3685*
Philippines. Discovery and Exploration. Magellan, Ferdinand. Pigaffeta, Antonio. 1520-21. *450*
—. Women. 19c-20c. *3454*
Phillips, Ulrich B. Archives, local. Economic History. Slave prices. Texas (Harrison County). 1849-60. *2101*
—. DuBois, W. E. B. Slavery. South. ca 1620-1865. 1896-1940. *2155*
—. Race Relations. Slavery. South or Southern States. 1900-34. *667*
—. Slavery. 1800-65. ca 1904-80. *2156*
—. Slavery, treatment of. South. 1908-34. 1976. *2107*
Philology. *See also* Language; Lexicology; Linguistics; Literature.
—. Gordlevsky, Vladimir. Turkey. 1976. *874*
—. Linguistics. Research (interdisciplinary). 1979. *4029*
Philosophers. Historians. Scotland. 18c. *2326*
Philosophes. Enlightenment. Hertzberg, Arthur. Jews. Voltaire. 18c. 1876-1968. *3996*
Philosophy. *See also* Ethics; Existentialism; Free Will and Determinism; Mysticism; Pragmatism; Rationalism; Transcendentalism.
—. 1976. *2317*
—. 5c BC-20c. *2405*
—. Prehistory-20c. *280*
—. Aesthetics. Historians. Poland. Tatarkiewicz, Władysław (obituary). 1910-80. *890*
—. Atheism. Germany. Spinoza, Baruch. 17c-19c. *2333*
—. Augustine, Saint. Christianity. Hegel, Georg. Providence (concept). 410-1970. *3544*
—. Bayle, Pierre. Magic. 1686-1706. *2301*
—. Berlin, University of. Engels, Friedrich. Hegel, Georg. Pamphlets. Schelling, Friedrich von. 1841-45. *1077*
—. Chernyshevski, Nikolai. Russia. 19c-20c. *936*
—. China. Li Zhi. 1527-1602. 20c. *1117*
—. Collingwood, R. G. (*Autobiography*). Vico, Giambattista. 1939. *1835*
—. Diderot, Denis. *Encyclopédie*. 1751-1800. *633*
—. Europe. Giannone, Pietro. 18c. *217*
—. France. Montesquieu, Charles de. Political Theory. Tacitus. 1700's-55. *2519*
—. Geijer, Erik Gustav. 19c. *952*
—. Germany. Hermeneutics. Sociology of knowledge. 19c-20c. *1406*
—. Hegel, Georg (review article). Lukács, George. Marxism. 1790's. *832*
—. Ideas, history of. 1975. *1842*
—. Ideas, history of. Social history. 1920-83. *2349*
—. Ideas, history of. Vico, Giovanni Battista. 18c. *2337*
—. Iorga, Nicolae. Kogălniceanu, Mihail. Politics. Romania. ca 1840-90. *1106*
—. Italy. Pico della Mirandola, Giovanni. 15c. *282*
—. Marxism. Methodology. 198t. *414*
—. Marxism-Leninism. 19c. *2335*
—. Methodology. Science. 1982. *3760*
—. Militarism. Russia. Tolstoy, Leo (*War and Peace*). 1866. *785*
—. Pawlicki, Stefan. Poland. 1839-1916. *825*
—. Political change. Romania. 1848-66. *1843*
—. Quebec. 1853-1970. *386*
—. Renaissance. 15c-16c. *2389*
—. Rousseau, Jean Jacques. 1740-78. *2303*
—. Simmel, Georg. 1905-18. *974*
—. Skovoroda, Grigori. Ukraine. 1721-1970. *2364*
—. Slavery. 4c BC-20c. *2142*
—. Spinoza, Baruch. 17c. 1960-77. *2391*
—. Strauss, Leo. Tradition. 1933-79. *1063*
—. Technology. -20c. *250*
—. Wolff, Christian. 18c. *2357*
—. World Congress of Philosophy, 15th. 1973. *2383*
Philosophy, analytic. Hempel, Carl G. Murphey, Murray. 1973. *1832*
Philosophy (natural). Franklin, Benjamin. Science. Theology. 17c-19c. *352*
Philosophy of history. 19c-20c. *1823*
—. 20c. *1154*
—. 20c. *1468*
—. 20c. *1615*
—. 5c BC-20c. *1303*
—. Analogy. 400 BC-1980's. *1824*
—. Archivo General de la Nación. Latin America. Mexico. 1980. *445*
—. Boorstin, Daniel. Naturalism. 17c-19c. 1955-71. *1830*
—. Bossuet, Jacques. France. Voltaire. 18c. *1841*

—. Butterfield, Herbert. Religion. 20c. *789*
—. Chastellain, Charles (review article). Delclos, J. -C. 1419-74. *1837*
—. Christianity. 1c-20c. *234*
—. Church history. Germany. Pietism. 1670-1700. *3666*
—. Communist Party. France. Resistance. World War II. 1945-70. *3268*
—. Communist Party. Marx, Karl. Methodology. 1850-90. *1613*
—. Concept history. 15c-20c. *1833*
—. Conference. Methodology. Rossi, Paolo (*Teoria della Storiografia Oggi;* review article). 20c. *1339*
—. Culture. 19c-1965. *2494*
—. Dialectical materialism. Enlightenment. France. Marxism. 18c. *1597*
—. Dialectical materialism. USSR. Vipper, Robert I. 1880's-1954. *911*
—. Drama. Hochhuth, Rolf. World War II. 1939-45. *1827*
—. Droysen, Johann Gustav (*Historik*). Germany. 1750-1900. *1150*
—. Economic Development. 17c. *1853*
—. Engels, Friedrich. Marx, Karl. Social Classes. 1850's-90's. *1603*
—. Finland. Korhonen, Arvi. Operation Barbarossa. World War II. 1961. *1838*
—. France. Literature. 16c. *590*
—. Germany. Ideology. Political Theory. Social Classes. 19c. *1494*
—. Historians. Steen, Sverre. 20c. *1113*
—. Hume, David. 1711-76. *826*
—. Ideas, History of. 12c-17c. *435*
—. International Relations (discipline). Methodology. 1600-1970. 20c. *551*
—. Jaspers, Karl. Politics. 20c. *1836*
—. Language. 15c-20c. *224*
—. Marx, Karl. 1840's-20c. *1592*
—. Marxism. 15c-20c. *535*
—. Mentalities. 1930's-80's. *2346*
—. Metaphysics. Poetics. 1970's. *1839*
—. Methodology. 1980's. *1829*
—. Methodology. 19c. *1509*
—. Methodology. 20c. *522*
—. Methodology. 20c. *1199*
—. Methodology. 20c. *1572*
—. Methodology. Norway. Seip, Jens Arup. 1940-83. *1222*
—. Methodology. Science, history of. Values. 1880-1984. *1140*
—. Methodology (review article). Narrative. Ricoeur, Paul. 1983. *1825*
—. Mexico. Nationalism. Veytia, Mariano. Prehistory-16c. 18c. *423*
—. Mexico. Ó'Gorman, Edmundo. 1945-70's. *580*
—. Myths. Research. 15c-20c. *1752*
—. Pokrovski, M. N. Political Theory. USSR. 1890-1930's. *953*
—. Pokrovski, M. N. USSR. 1896-1960's. *954*
—. Porter, Dale H. 20c. *453*
—. Ranke, Leopold von. World and Universal History. 20c. *458*
—. Romania. Xenopol, Alexander D. 1866-1913. *1844*
—. Savigny, Friedrich Karl von. 1883. *920*
—. Skovoroda, H. S. Ukraine. 18c. 19c-1917. *1014*
—. Subjectivity. 5c BC-20c. *765*
—. Voegelin, Eric. 1957. *2394*
—. Western Nations. 5c BC-20c. *242*
—. World and Universal History. 1982. *1374*
Philosophy of History (organic connections). Dilthey, Wilhelm ("Allgemeine Landrecht"). 1875-1911. *1826*
Philosophy of History (review article). 1970-72. *1828*
—. Christianity. McIntire, C. T. 1930-81. *3719*
—. Estonia. Loone, Eeero N. 20c. *1471*
Philosophy of science (review article). Agassi, J. Croce, Benedetto. Finocchiaro, M. A. 20c. *3755*
Philosophy (review article). 600 BC-1980. *2382*
—. DelTorre, Maria Assunta. 17c-20c. *2367*
—. Edwards, Jonathan. Fiering, Norman. Miller, Perry. New England. Puritans. 1640-1760. *2379*
Photographs. Archives. Documents. Theft. 1950's-78. *185*
—. Archives. Documents. Theft. 1950's-78. *186*
—. Cities. Continental Heritage Press. Donning Company Publishers. Publishers and Publishing. Windsor Publications. 1970's-83. *3960*
—. Daily life. Great Britain. Material culture. Research sources. Social customs. 19c. *118*
—. Methodology. 1975-77. *1460*
Photography. *See also* Films.
—. 20c. *363*
—. Alberti, Leon Battista. Camera Obscura. Inventions. Italy. Painters. 15c-1910. *4011*
—. Benjamin, Walter. Cities. 19c. 1920-40. *3906*

—. Italy. 1975-82. *132*
Physical Education. Bibliographic References. Graduate Study and Research. Information Storage and Retrieval Systems. 1973. *646*
Physicians. Alchemy. Austria (Villach). Historians. Moro, Gotbert. Paracelsus. 1493-1531. 1950-79. *957*
—. Caulfield, Ernest. Pediatrics. Ruhräh, John. 18c. 1899-1972. *3877*
—. Cultural relations. Italy. Medicine. Romania. 15c-19c. 20c. *3887*
—. Diseases. Feminist history. Medical therapeutics. Women. 19c. *3445*
Physics. *See also* Chemistry.
—. Chemical analysis. Spectroscopy. 1820-59. *3774*
—. Chemistry. Methodology. Prigogine, Ilya. 1981. *3804*
—. Europe, Western. Quantum Theory. USA. 1900-30. *3766*
—. Quantum theory. 1900-27. *3842*
Physiology. Behavior. Bibliographies. Psychology. USSR. 1960-71. *3733*
Pico della Mirandola, Giovanni. Italy. Philosophy. 15c. *282*
Pidgin English. Gullah (language). Hancock, Ian. Language. Slave trade. South Carolina. West Indies. 1651-70. *2102*
Pierson, George W. Berthoff, Rowland T. Demography. Population. Turner, Frederick Jackson. 1920-79. *1741*
Pietism. Church history. Germany. Philosophy of History. 1670-1700. *3666*
—. Württemberg. 17c-18c. *3671*
Pigaffeta, Antonio. Discovery and Exploration. Magellan, Ferdinand. Philippines. 1520-21. *450*
Pirenne, Henri (*History of Europe*). Rhetoric. 4c-16c. *1188*
Pirenne, Henri (review essay). Lyon, Bryce. 1863-1976. *751*
Pistone, Sergio. Germany. Imperialism. Meinecke, Friedrich (review article). Political Theory. 20c. *2517*
Place Names. *See* Toponymy.
Plagiarism. Möhler, Johann Adam (lecture). Theology. 1829. *3587*
Plague. 1348-1915. *3857*
Plantation societies. British West Indies. Slavery. 18c-19c. 1970's. *2106*
Plantations. Americas (North and South). Labor. Slavery. Social Organization. 17c-19c. 1959-79. *2111*
—. Bibliographies. Slavery. South or Southern States. 18c-20c. *2110*
Platt, Anthony. Rothman, David. Social control theory. 19c. *2249*
Platt, Gerald M. Psychosocial history (review article). Weinstein, Fred. 1969-75. *1816*
Play. Work. 1825-1978. *3997*
Playwrights. *See* Dramatists.
Plekhanov, G. V. Bakalov, Georgi. Bulgaria. Emigrants. Revolutionary Movements. Russia. 1860's-1917. *836*
Plumb, J. H. 1969. *1549*
Pluralism. Community studies. Elites. 1957-77. *1255*
—. Dahl, Robert. *Federalist* No. 10. Madison, James. Political ideology. 1950's-70's. *2752*
—. Lipset, Seymour Martin. Politics. Social Organization. 1950-79. *2546*
Plymouth Plantation. Bradford, William. Theology. 1630. *3774*
Poems. Eminescu, Mihai. Romania. Romanticism. 1870-79. *857*
Poetics. Metaphysics. Philosophy of history. 1970's. *1839*
Poetry. *See also* Poetics.
—. 1975. *4041*
—. Biography. Howe, Mark. 1880's-1960. *976*
—. Civil War. England. Literary criticism. Marvell, Andrew (*Horatian Ode upon Cromwell's Return from Ireland*). 1649-50. *2372*
—. Doolittle, Hilda. Fiction. 1920's-61. *570*
—. England. 1660-1978. *641*
—. Franco Mendes, David. 18c. *806*
—. Goethe, Johann Wolfgang von (*Faust II*). 19c. *628*
—. Literary criticism. Marvell, Andrew. ca 1640-78. 1945-70's. *2381*
Pogodin, Mikhail. Karamzin, Nikolai. Partitions. Poland. Russia. Soloviëv, Sergei. 1772-93. *742*
Pokrovski, Alexei (tribute). Russia. USSR. 1875-1954. *924*
Pokrovski, M. N. Marxism. Research. USSR. 1920's. *1045*
—. Philosophy of History. Political Theory. USSR. 1890-1930's. *953*
—. Philosophy of History. USSR. 1896-1960's. *954*
—. Research. USSR. 1917-31. *1046*
—. USSR. 1868-1932. *782*

—. Communist Party (Central Committee). Czechoslovakia. Political education. 1977-80. *2698*

—. Europe. Ideas, History of. Marxism. Working class. 19c-20c. *2386*

—. France. Lapôtre, Arthur (*Pape Formose, Rome et Photius*). Papal States. Rome. 1882-88. *3531*

—. National Academy of History (Publications Department). Venezuela. 16c-20c. 1958-83. *50*

—. Poland. Research sources. 1980-83. *112*

—. Regnery, Henry (account). Revisionism. Truth. World War II (causes). 20c. *3230*

Publishers and Publishing (local). Heroes. USSR. World War II. 1953-77. *3145*

Puhle, H.-J. Agricultural History. Kocka, J. 1970-78. *1887*

Punishment. Crime. Foucault, Michel. 1750-1950. *2252*

Puritan attitudes. Gookin, Daniel (writings). Indians. Massachusetts Bay Colony. 1656-86. *637*

Puritan society. Church and State. Declension, myth of. New England. 17c. 20c. *3656*

Puritan Studies. Miller, Perry. ca 1940-73. *640*

Puritanism. Allen, Frederick Lewis (*Only Yesterday*). Journalism. Liberalism. 1931. *912*

—. Economic growth. Franklin, Benjamin. Manufactures. Trade. 18c. *1848*

—. Great Britain. Massachusetts (Salem). Witchcraft (review article). 16c-1692. *1786*

Puritans. *See also* Calvinism; Church of England; Congregationalism.

—. Colonialism. Indian-White Relations. New England. 17c. *365*

—. Edwards, Jonathan. Fiering, Norman. Miller, Perry. New England. Philosophy (review article). 1640-1760. *2379*

—. Indian-White Relations. New England. Theology. 17c-20c. *3689*

—. Miller, Perry. 17c-18c. 1960's-81. *756*

—. Ministers. New England. Sexes (equality). Women, position of. 1668-1735. *3479*

—. New England. Nonconservatism. Social Organization. 17c. 1930's-60's. *2200*

Pushkin, Alexander (*Captain's Daughter*). Political Attitudes. Russia. 1834-36. *660*

Q

Quakers. *See* Friends, Society of.

Quality. Standards. 1945-80. *1438*

Quantification. Literature (narrative). 20c. *1519*

Quantitative analysis. Computers. 18c. *1719*

—. Computers. 20c. *1734*

—. Great Britain. Political History. 1971. *228*

Quantitative analysis (case studies). Social research. 1970. *513*

Quantitative history. Economic history. 1930-. *1876*

Quantitative Methods. *See also* Methodology.

—. 1950's-70's. *1738*

—. 1960-75. *1714*

—. 1967-76. *1743*

—. 1970's. *1739*

—. 1973. *313*

—. 1975. *1745*

—. 20c. *1968*

—. Agrarian history. Russia. ca 1800-50's. 1966-. *1722*

—. *Annales* school. France. Marxism. 1930's-70's. *1235*

—. Belgium. 1830-1913. *1728*

—. Biography, collective. Political Leadership. Progressivism. 1950's-77. *1708*

—. Books. France. 1700-1970. *3939*

—. Central University of Venezuela. Colonial Government. Treasury. Venezuela (Caracas). 1930's-70's. *1699*

—. Civil War. Interpretive changes. Politics (essays). Reconstruction. 1850's-76. 1960's-75. *512*

—. Clubb, Jerome M. Scheuch, Erwin K. 1980. *1698*

—. Computer analysis. Scotland. Social conditions. ca 18c. 1970's. *1707*

—. Computers. 1969. *1730*

—. Computers. Reynolds, Ben. Reynolds, Siân. 1978. *396*

—. Economic Growth. Great Britain. 1880's-90's. *659*

—. Economic history. 1940's-70's. *2069*

—. Economic history. 1965. *1856*

—. Economic history. 19c-20c. *1991*

—. Economics, cyclical. France. Labrousse, Ernest (review article). Social Organization. ca 1960-70. 1974. *1733*

—. Engerman, Stanley L. Fogel, Robert William. Slavery. Social Mobility. 1800's-50's. 1930's-70's. *2151*

—. Estonia. 1960-84. *1723*

—. Fertility. Norway. Sorcery. Statistics. 16c-1910. *1713*

—. France. 1900-75. *1236*

—. Illinois (Chicago). Jensen, Richard (interview). Newberry Library (Family and Community History Center). 1971-82. *1721*

—. Jackson, Age of. Working Class. 1828-48. 1972. *2022*

—. Kalabiński, S. Methodology (review article). Poland. 20c. *1711*

—. Marxism. Research. 1960's-82. *1147*

—. Massachusetts (Cambridge, Dedham, Ipswich). Suffrage. 1640-1700. *1749*

—. Methodology. Statistics. 20c. *1748*

—. Methodology (review article). 1970's. *1704*

—. Political Theory. 17c-18c. *481*

—. Research. 1540-1964. *1736*

—. Research. Southwest. Prehistory-20c. *1717*

—. Romania. 1973. *1729*

—. Sex. Slavery. Women. 19c. 1970's. *2117*

—. Slave trade. 18c-19c. *2115*

—. Social Sciences. 1957-79. *1726*

—. Social sciences. 1957-80. *1725*

—. Social Theory. 1960's-70's. *1740*

—. USA. USSR. 1980. *1744*

—. USSR. 1100-1970. *1727*

—. USSR. ca 1970-79. *1746*

Quantitative Methods (code sheet). Foreign conflict behavior. 1966. *2940*

Quantitative Methods (conference). USA. USSR. 1981. *1700*

Quantitative Methods (review). International research. 1950-74. *1709*

Quantitative Methods (review article). 1970's. *1732*

Quantum Theory. Europe, Western. Physics. USA. 1900-30. *3766*

—. Physics. 1900-27. *3842*

Quebec. 1840-1920. *321*

—. *Annales* school. Hamelin, Jean. Ouellet, Fernand. 1952-72. *1645*

—. Bibliographies. Catholic Church. 1608-1980. *3512*

—. Catholic Church. French Canadians. Garneau, François-Xavier. Nationalism, Theories of. 1831-1945. *642*

—. Catholic Church. French Canadians. Groulx, Lionel. 20c. *1088*

—. Catholic Church. French Canadians. Groulx, Lionel (tribute). 1878-1967. *894*

—. Catholic Church. Labor Unions and Organizations. Social Classes. 1864-1979. *343*

—. Creighton, Donald. Trudel, Marcel. 19c-1980. *1072*

—. Febvre, Lucien. Social Sciences. 1979. *320*

—. French Canadians. Groulx, Lionel. 1920-67. *819*

—. Groulx, Lionel. 1878-1967. *310*

—. Philosophy. 1853-1970. *386*

—. Working class. 1897-1974. *1884*

Quebec Act (1774). Canada. Colonial Government. Great Britain. 1774. *432*

Quebec (Lower Canada). Rebellion of 1837. 1837-38. *236*

Quebec (St. Maurice). Steel Industry. ca 1890-20c. *525*

Quinet, Edgar. Democracy. French Revolution. Michelet, Jules. Social reform. 1789-19c. *3355*

R

Raabe, Wilhelm. Fiction, historical. Germany. 19c. *577*

Race. Attitudes. Ethnicity. Social Classes. 1865-1919. *220*

—. Domestic service. Salmon, Lucy Maynard. Women. 19c. *3394*

Race (issue). Ahlstrom, Sidney. Christianity (review article). Handy, Robert T. Marty, Martin E. 16c-1978. *3565*

Race Relations. *See also* Acculturation; Emigration; Ethnology; Human Relations; Immigration; Indian-White Relations.

—. Civil War. Moore, Glover (festschrift). South. 19c-20c. *288*

—. Dunning, William A. Reconstruction. 1865-77. 1900-25. *622*

—. Phillips, Ulrich B. Slavery. South or Southern States. 1900-34. *667*

Race (term). Canada. English Canadians. Nation (term). 1873-1980. *1684*

Racism. Africa. Blacks. Women. 17c-20c. *3434*

—. Anglos. Ethnocentrism. Indians. Mexican Americans. New Mexico Territory. 17c-20c. *672*

—. Higher Education. Reconstruction. Textbooks. 1865-76. 1960-73. *596*

—. Holocaust. Methodology (comparative analysis). Teaching. USA. 20c. *3943*

Rački, Franjo. Croatia. Ruvarac, Ilarion. Serbia. 1875-99. *942*

Radical History Review. Editors and Editing. 1981. *9*

—. Family. Leftism. Periodicals. Slavery. 17c-20c. 1970's. *2123*

Radicals and Radicalism. *See also* Leftism; Political Reform; Revolution; Social Reform.

—. Denmark. 19c-20c. *410*

—. Domestic Policy. Foreign policy. 20c. *2953*

—. Education. Ravitch, Diane (review article). Revisionism. 1965-78. *2350*

—. Land. Millenarianism. Nationalization. Spence, Thomas. 1780-1814. *2550*

Radicals and Radicalism (review article). Chartism. Doherty, John. Europe. Great Britain. Labor movement. 19c. *2064*

—. Kraditor, Aileen. 1880-1917. *1538*

Radio. *See also* Audiovisual Materials.

—. Research. 1930's-60's. *3956*

—. Television. 1925-75. *3922*

Radkau, Joachim. Kohli-Kunz, Alice. Psychology. Radkau, Orlinde. 1972. *1131*

Radkau, Orlinde. Kohli-Kunz, Alice. Psychology. Radkau, Joachim. 1972. *1131*

Radu, Mircea T. Oţetea, Andrei. Revolution of 1821. Vladimirescu, Tudor. Wallachia. 1821. *3326*

Raemond, Florimond de. Counter-Reformation. Europe. 1560's-1601. *698*

Ragionieri, Ernesto. Bibliographies. Italy. 1946-75. *1109*

Ragionieri, Ernesto (obituary; review article). Historians. 1940's-75. *810*

Railroads. 1983. *3947*

—. Business-government relations. Government regulation. Kolko, Gabriel. 1877-1916. 1965-72. *1873*

—. Collectors and Collecting. Huntington, Arabella Yarrington. Huntington, Collis P. Huntington, Henry E. ca 1860-1924. *3459*

—. Resistance. Sabotage. Scandinavia. World War II. 1940-45. *3164*

Railroads, narrow-gauge. Economic development. Mississippi Valley. Transportation history. 1870-1900. 1970. *3924*

Ramazzini, B. Epidemics. Europe. Hoffmann, K. F. Influenza. Mancisi, G. M. 1708-09. *3873*

Rameau de Saint-Père, François-Edme. Colonization. France. North America. 16c-1889. *2725*

Ramsay, David. Nationalism. 1763-1825. *804*

Ranke, Leopold von. Finland. Lamprecht, Karl. 1900-50. *1295*

—. Fischer, Fritz. Germany. 1960's-70's. *1286*

—. Germany. Herder, Johann Gottfried. Idealism. Luther, Martin. Reformation. 16c-19c. *585*

—. Germany. Imperialism. Lenz, Max. Seeley, John Robert. 1880's-1932. *848*

—. Germany. World and Universal History. ca 1877-1900. *1343*

—. Lamprecht, Karl. Treitschke, Heinrich von. 19c. *419*

—. Methodology. 1825-1980. *1526*

—. Philosophy of History. World and Universal History. 20c. *458*

Ranum, Orest. *Annales* school (review article). Forster, Robert. Stoianovich, Traian. 1929-78. *1657*

Raombana. Historians. Madagascar. 16c-19c. *425*

Rapp, Richard T. Economic decline. McCloskey, Donald. Workshop papers. 17c-20c. 1977. *1896*

Rasmussen, Knud. Foreign Relations. Livonian War (review article). Russia. Sweden. 1554-61. *2915*

Rasputnis, B. I. Labor movement. 1950-80. *1900*

Rationalism. *See also* Atheism; Deism; Enlightenment.

—. Belknap, Jeremy. Romanticism. Social happiness (concept). 1760-1979. *2181*

Rationality. Weber, Max. 19c-20c. *1298*

Ravitch, Diane (review article). Education. 1960's-78. *2387*

—. Education. Radicals and Radicalism. Revisionism. 1965-78. *2350*

Raynal, Guillaume. American Revolution. 1770-80. *2245*

Read, Conyers. Beard, Charles. Becker, Carl. Croce, Benedetto. Presentism. 1945-76. *1605*

Real estate. Income. Webb, Walter Prescott. Western States. 1930's-63. *1007*

Realism. Idealism. 1824-1975. *1233*

Reality. Cattle Raising. Western States. 1978. *2399*

—. Truth in history. 1967. *1265*

Reapportionment. *See* Apportionment.

Rearich, Charles. Clive, John. Maldelbaum, Maurice. White, Hayden. 19c. 1974. *1146*

Reason. Intuition. New England. Parker, Theodore. Theology. Transcendentalism. Unitarianism. 18c-1860. 1920-79. *3709*

S

—. Caribbean Region. 1600-1875. 1959-83. *2105*
—. Children. Mortality. Nutrition. South. 1840's-60's. *2132*
—. Cities. Southwest. Wade, Richard C. ca 1860-65. *630*
—. Civil War. Ideology. Labor. Politics. 1860-76. 1970-79. *315*
—. Colloquium of American and Soviet Historians. Peasants. USSR. 1975. *2100*
—. Cuba. 1500-1980. *2136*
—. Developing nations. Political attitudes. Rural problems. ca 17c-20c. *2098*
—. DuBois, W. E. B. Phillips, Ulrich B. South. ca 1620-1865. 1896-1940. *2155*
—. Economic Conditions. South. 17c-1865. 1974. *2119*
—. Economic Theory. Marxism. 1840-1977. *2138*
—. Engerman, Stanley L. Fogel, Robert William. Quantitative methods. Social Mobility. 1800's-50's. 1930's-70's. *2151*
—. Family. 18c-20c. *2166*
—. Family. Leftism. Periodicals. *Radical History Review.* 17c-20c. 1970's. *2123*
—. Genovese, Eugene D. 1800-65. 1963-79. *2152*
—. Genovese, Eugene D. 1850's. *2130*
—. Genovese, Eugene D. Marxism. South. 18c-19c. 1970's. *2149*
—. Genovese, Eugene D. (review article). 18c-19c. 1974-75. *2113*
—. Genovese, Eugene D. (review article). Marxism. South. 17c-1860. 1970's. *2131*
—. High Schools. Textbooks. 20c. *620*
—. Iron Industry. James, Thomas. Maramec Iron Works. Massey, Samuel. Missouri. 1828-50. 1950's-70's. *2124*
—. Methodology. *Time on the Cross* (critique). ca 1800-60. *337*
—. Models. 19c-20c. *649*
—. Phillips, Ulrich B. 1800-65. ca 1904-80. *2156*
—. Phillips, Ulrich B. Race Relations. South or Southern States. 1900-34. *667*
—. Philosophy. 4c BC-20c. *2142*
—. Protestant ethic. 18c-19c. *2168*
—. Quantitative Methods. Sex. Women. 19c. 1970's. *2117*
—. Rhodes, James Ford (*History of the United States from the Compromise of 1850*). Wilson, Woodrow. ca 1890-1920. *2157*
—. Russia. ca 1300-17c. 1970-75. *2126*
—. South. 1800-60. 1956-79. *2160*
—. South or Southern States. 17c-19c. 1918-77. *2118*
—. Stone, Alfred Holt. 17c-1865. 1901-40's. *2154*
—. Williams, Eric. 15c-19c. *2139*
Slavery (review article). Africa. 18c-19c. *2133*
—. Blassingame, John W. Elkins, Stanley M. South. 1619-1865. *2128*
—. Economics (research). Engerman, Stanley L. Fogel, Robert William. South or Southern States. ca 1820-1974. *2162*
—. Engerman, Stanley L. Fogel, Robert William. 19c. 1974. *2121*
—. Engerman, Stanley L. Fogel, Robert William. Methodology. South or Southern States. 17c-1860. 1975. *2120*
—. Engerman, Stanley L. Fogel, Robert William. South. 1830-60. 1974. *2097*
—. South or Southern States. 19c. 1970. *2099*
Slavery, treatment of. Phillips, Ulrich B. South. 1908-34. 1976. *2107*
Slaves. Brodie, Fawn M. Children. Jefferson, Thomas. ca 1771-89. 1974-76. *2135*
Slaves (testimony). Douglass, Frederick. South. 1830's-60. 1930's-70's. *2143*
Slavic Studies. Bibliographies. ca 19c-20c. 1977. *203*
—. Bibliographies. ca 19c-20c. 1977. *211*
—. Dissertations. 1973-77. *41*
—. Periodicals. *Problemy Slavianoznavstva.* Ukraine. USSR. 1970's. *175*
Slavík, J. Czechoslovakia. Russian Revolution. 1920-69. *729*
Slavs. Germany. Goetz, Leopold Karl. Pan-Slavism. USSR. 8c-20c. *1100*
—. Hungary. Slovakia. Timon, Samuel. 1690's-1735. *925*
Slavs, South. Kardelj, Edvard (obituary). 1945-79. *721*
—. Nationalism. Revolution of 1848. 19c-20c. *2828*
—. Nikitin, Sergei (obituary). 1926-79. *786*
—. World War I. 1914-82. *2827*
Slovak Americans. Journalism. Sciranka, John Coleman. Social Organizations. 1924-78. *1061*
Slovakia. Agrarian problems. Marxist interpretations. 1848-1918. *2055*
—. Archives. 1960-77. *104*
—. Auxiliary sciences. 1960-77. *3987*
—. Bibliographies. Reformation. 16c. *3526*

—. Daxner, Š. M. National Self-image. 19c. *978*
—. Feudalism. 1500-1800. 1960-77. *179*
—. Habsburg Empire. Seton-Watson, R. W. (centennial). 1879-1914. *940*
—. Hungary. Slavs. Timon, Samuel. 1690's-1735. *925*
—. Matunák, Michal. Methodology. Ottoman Empire. 16c-17c. 1889-1932. *885*
—. Sasinek, F. V. 19c. *889*
—. Timon, Samuel. 11c-17c. 1702-37. *926*
—. Vlček, Jaroslav. 1836-1900. *1044*
Slovaks. Hungary. Kellner-Hostinský, Peter. 9c-19c. *916*
Slovene. Bibliographies. Yugoslavia. 1979. *146*
Slovenia. Bibliographies. 15c-20c. 1978. *147*
—. Bibliographies. Labor movement. Socialism. 19c-20c. *86*
—. Bleiweis, Janez. 1840's-81. 1982. *1054*
—. Croatia. Gubec, Mathias. Peasants. Rebellions. 1573. *3324*
—. Kidrič, Boris. 1934-51. *989*
—. Rutar, Simon. 1870-99. *837*
Small, Melvin. Nelson, Keith L. Olin, Spencer C., Jr. Peace Research (review article). 19c-20c. *3128*
Small-group theory. Attitudes. Callcott, George H. Clark, G. Kitson. Postan, M. M. Richter, Melvin. 1970-71. *1462*
Smelser, Neil. American Revolution (antecedents). Collective Behavior. Government. Resistance to. *Liberty* Riot. Social Theory. 1765-75. 1970-78. *2189*
Smets, Georges. Behavior. Ethnology. Veyne, Paul. Waxweiler, Emile. 19c-20c. *2281*
Smith, Adam (*Wealth of Nations*). 1755-1975. *1850*
—. Economic Theory. 1776. 20c. *2063*
Smith, David. Appalachia. Campbell, Alan. Francis, Hywel. Gaventa, John. Miners (review article). Scotland (Lanarkshire). Wales (South). 18c-20c. *1963*
Smith, Henry Nash. Literary history. 1950-. *2328*
Smith, Henry Nash (influence). American Studies. Behavior. Collective images. 1950-75. *2233*
Smith, John. Autobiography. Discovery and Exploration. Romanticism. 1608-30. *830*
Smith, Joseph. Methodology. Personal narratives. ca 1820-44. *3570*
Smith, Timothy L. (*Revivalism and Social Reform*). Revivals. Social reform. 1830-60. *2205*
—. Revivals. Social Reform. 1830-60. *3612*
Smodlaka, Josip (diary). Partisans. World War II. Yugoslavia. 1943-45. *3217*
Smolenski, Vladimir. Bolivia. Foreign Relations. USA. War of the Pacific. 1879-80. 1970. *2946*
Snooks, Graeme. Economic theory. Methodology. 1957-74. *1995*
Soboul, Albert. Belgium. 1960's-82. *780*
—. French Revolution. 1789-90's. *901*
—. French Revolution. 1789-90's. *923*
—. French Revolution. 1789-90's. *960*
—. French Revolution. Historians (Japanese). Takahashi, H. Kohachiro. 1789-90's. *1035*
—. French Revolution (Paris). Social Classes (sans-culottes; review article). 1793-94. 1975. *3350*
Soboul, Albert (obituary). French Revolution. USSR. 1914-82. *1120*
Soboul, Albert (tribute). French Revolution. Historians. 1914-82. *753*
Social action. Catholic Church. Droulers, Paul. France. Poulat, Émile. 1903-18. *3600*
Social analysis. Poland. 1963. *1152*
Social Change. *See also* Economic Growth; Industrialization; Modernization.
—. 18c-20c. *1544*
—. Agricultural Labor (contract). Agricultural Technology and Research. Labor movement. Sugar. 19c. *1909*
—. Americas (North and South). 19c-20c. *2188*
—. Assimilation. Europe. Jews. Katz, Jacob (review article). 18c. *1039*
—. Cities. Demography. France. 18c-19c. *3905*
—. Culture. Working Class. 20c. *2000*
—. Daily Life. Popular culture. 16c-20c. *2187*
—. Democracy. Germany. Revolution. 1918-19. *3367*
—. Depressions. Labor movement. 1929-39. *2257*
—. Dewey, John. Education. Liberalism. 1970-78. *2229*
—. Economic Conditions. Populism. 1880's-1980. *2236*
—. Economic Development. Industrial Revolution. Political Change. 1640-1880's. *1913*
—. Europe. Ferrero, Guglielmo. Italy. 1900-42. *600*
—. Family. Italy, southern. Marriage. 16c-20c. *2443*
—. Family. Modernization. ca 19c-20c. *2449*
—. Great Britain. Hunter, John. Medicine. Science. Surgeons. 18c-19c. *3864*
—. Great Britain. Industrial Revolution. 18c-19c. 1950's-70's. *1912*

—. Great Britain. Progress (concept). 1730-80. *687*
—. Gymnastics. Jahn, Friedrich Ludwig. 1820-1978. *3929*
—. Kuhn, Thomas (*Structure of Scientific Revolutions*). Palmer, Robert R. (*Age of Democratic Revolution*). Rostow, W. W. (*Stages of Economic Growth*). 1960-70. *1272*
—. Kutsch, Thomas. Social Theory. Wiswede, Günter. 20c. *2206*
—. Luther, Martin. Reformation. Secularization. Theology. 16c. *3567*
—. Medicine. Rosen, George. 19c-20c. *469*
—. Methodology. Technology. 1958-80. *3821*
—. Revolution. 16c-1960's. *1874*
—. Sensibility (concept). Sex (concept). 1680-1790. *2478*
—. Socialism. 1960-76. *1321*
—. Tocqueville, Alexis de. 1835-59. *2267*
—. Women, role of. 19c-20c. *3399*
Social Change (essays). Behavioral science. 1900-72. *271*
Social Classes. *See also* Aristocracy; Class Struggle; Elites; Middle Classes; Social Mobility; Social Status; Working Class.
—. 17c-1950. *2190*
—. 1970's-80's. *2408*
—. Arkansas. Democrats. Revisionism. Whigs. 1836-50. *2745*
—. Attitudes. Ethnicity. Race. 1865-1919. *220*
—. Business leaders. Cities (size). Iron Industry. 1874-1900. *1955*
—. Canada. 20c. *2466*
—. Catholic Church. Labor Unions and Organizations. Quebec. 1864-1979. *343*
—. Economics. Education, compulsory. Political systems. 1840-20c. *2388*
—. Engels, Friedrich. Marx, Karl. Philosophy of History. 1850's-90's. *1603*
—. Ethnicity. 1970-82. *2213*
—. French Revolution. Jaurès, Jean. 1789-99. *3383*
—. French Revolution (conference). 1790's. *3341*
—. Germany. Ideology. Philosophy of History. Political Theory. 19c. *1494*
—. Germany. Labor history. Labor movement. Methodology. Social history. 1866-1933. *2255*
—. Ideology. Williams, William Appleman. 18c-20c. 1950's-70's. *895*
—. Italy. Mosca, Gaetano. Political Theory. 1880's-20c. *937*
—. Jacksonianism. Politics. 1828-30's. *2289*
—. Mexican Americans. Women. 17c-20c. *3389*
—. New France. St. Lawrence Valley. 16c-18c. *2254*
—. Political parties. 1956-76. *2775*
—. Political Power. Sex. 18c-19c. *3410*
Social Classes (essays). British North America. Literary sources. Public Records. 17c-1775. *431*
Social Classes (sans-culottes; review article). French Revolution (Paris). Soboul, Albert. 1793-94. 1975. *3350*
Social Classes (stratification). Models, theoretical. Political systems, community. 17c-19c. 1973. *2191*
Social Conditions. *See also* Cities; Daily Life; Economic Conditions; Family; Labor; Marriage; Migration, Internal; Popular Culture; Social Classes; Social Mobility; Social Problems; Social Reform; Standard of Living.
—. 1969. *2244*
—. 1980's. *1504*
—. American Revolution (causes). Massachusetts (Boston). Methodology. 18c. *1532*
—. Americanology. Japan. National self-image. 19c-20c. 1969-73. *2219*
—. *Annales* school. Ideas, History of. 1920's-70's. *1652*
—. China. Economic Conditions. 11c-18c. *309*
—. Computer analysis. Quantitative Methods. Scotland. ca 18c. 1970's. *1707*
—. Culture. Economic conditions. Science, history of. UNESCO. Prehistory-20c. *3846*
—. Economic Conditions. Frontier and Pioneer Life. Western States. 19c. *537*
—. Elites. French Revolution. Rhetoric. 1789-99. *3337*
—. Films. 1925-76. *437*
—. Films. Great Britain. Popular culture. 20c. *4044*
—. Food. Nutrition. 1982. *3879*
—. Industrialized countries. Natural Resources. 1980. *2051*
—. Labrousse, Ernest. Rebellions. 18c-20c. *2285*
—. Middle Ages. 15c-20c. *3915*
—. Middle Classes. South. 19c. *408*
—. Military History. War. 1300-1600. *2993*
—. Military organization. Reform. Scharnhorst, Gerhard von. War. 1755-1813. *3010*
—. Mortality. Nutrition. 16c-19c. *3868*
—. Sexual mores. Women. 1970's. *3436*
—. Wiebe, Robert (review article). 1950-75. *2184*

Tirpitz, Alfred von. Germany. Warships. 1898-1914. 1914-73. *3035*

Tirso de Molina. Mercedarians. 1639-85. *3700*

Tirso de Molina (*Historia General de la Orden de la Merced*). Historians. Mercedarians. Spain. 1639. *3556*

Titulescu, Nicolae. Political Leadership. Romania. 1917-80. *778*

Tobin, Eugene M. Allswang, John M. City Politics (review article). Ebner, Michael H. 1867-1920. *2777*

Tocqueville, Alexis de. Social change. 1835-59. *2267*

Tolles, Frederick Barnes (obituary). Friends, Society of. 1915-75. *3566*

Tolstoy, Leo (*War and Peace*). Militarism. Philosophy. Russia. 1866. *785*

Tomasi, Silvano (review article). Catholic Church. Italian Americans. Objectivity. Sartorio, Enrico C. (review article). 1918. 1975. *3627*

Tomsk University. American history. Domestic policy. Foreign Policy. USSR. 1962-82. *2891*
—. Research. USSR. 1963-69. *47*

Toner, Joseph Meredith. Medicine (history of). ca 1850-96. *3851*

Topography. Austria. Diplomats. Hammer-Purgstall, Josef von. Methodology. Ottoman Empire. Travel accounts. 1798-1852. *793*

Topolski, Jerzy. Marxism. Methodology (review article). 1976. *1505*

Toponomy. Research. Romania. 1931-80. *1678*

Torquemada, Juan de (*Monarquía Indiana*). Books (editions). Franciscans. Indians. Mexico. 16c-1624. *394*

Torrente Ballester, J. B. de (*Saga/Fuga*). Literature. Regionalism. Spain (Galicia). 19c. *702*

Torres Agredo, Mauro (tribute). Colombia. Social Psychology. 20c. *1820*

Történelmi Szemle. Hungary. *Levéltári Közlemények*. Periodicals. 1970-74. *158*

Total history. Michelet, Jules. 1820-55. *1189*

Total history (concept). Carlotti, Anna Lisa. Prehistory-1979. *1414*

Totalitarianism. *See also* Communism; Fascism; Nazism.
—. Cold War. Ideas, History of. Intellectuals. *Partisan Review*. Periodicals. 1934-48. *627*
—. Communism. 1920-75. *2577*
—. Heroes. Myths and Symbols. Nationalism. Romanticism. 19c-20c. *1764*
—. Political Theory. Rousseau, Jean Jacques. 1778-1980. *730*

Totalitarianism (term). 20c. *2524*
—. Dejung, Christoph. Fascism. Italy. 20c. *2600*

Totality. Genovese, Eugene D. Marxism. Wallerstein, Immanuel. 15c-19c. *1967*

Toulmin, Stephen. Ideas, History of (review article). Janik, Allan. Marcus, Stephen. 19c. 1973-74. *2354*

Towns. Agriculture. Hungary. Szeremlei, Sámuel. 1850-1908. *1080*
—. Feudalism. Russia. USA. 15c-19c. *4000*

Towns (review article). France. Great Britain. Urban studies. USA. ca 15c-20c. 1941-81. *3912*

Toynbee, Arnold J. 20c. *801*
—. Eliade, Mircea. Freud, Sigmund. Prehistory-20c. 1912-60. *790*
—. Nomads and Nomadism. ca 4000 BC-20c. *4064*

Toynbee, Arnold J. (*Study of History*). Diogène. Periodicals. 1956. *723*

Trachtenberg, Alan. Gilded Age. Modernization. Wiebe, Robert. ca 1865-90. *2065*

Trade. *See also* International Trade.
—. Economic growth. Franklin, Benjamin. Manufactures. Puritanism. 18c. *1848*
—. New England. Triangular trade myth. 1795-1950. *2016*

Trade, balance of. British North America. Shipbuilding. 1763-75. 1913-72. *2026*

Trade Union Movements. *See* Labor Movement.

Trade Unions. *See* Labor Unions and Organizations.

Tradition. 15c-20c. *1183*
—. Cultural change. Methodology. Prehistory-20c. *2475*
—. Czechoslovakia. Military education. 1982. *1449*
—. Denmark. 1880-1979. *1216*
—. Philosophy. Strauss, Leo. 1933-79. *1063*

Transcendentalism. Intuition. New England. Parker, Theodore. Reason. Theology. Unitarianism. 18c-1860. 1920-79. *3709*

Transcendentalists (review article). Bridgman, Richard. Gura, Philip. Rose, Anne C. Thoreau, Henry David. 1820-50. *2343*

Transfer Tax. *See* Inheritance and Transfer Tax.

Transition period. Mill, John Stuart. 19c-20c. *1682*

Translating and Interpreting. Bible. England. Scholarship. 1611. 17c-20c. *3573*

—. Garcilaso de la Vega. Linguistics. Peru. Spanish Conquest. 1605-16. *624*
—. Marx, Karl. Methodology. 19c-20c. *1588*

Translation. Fiction. Literary criticism. 1976. *1268*

Transportation. *See also* names of transportation vehicles, e.g. Automobiles, Ships, Buses, Trucks, Railroads, etc.; Canals.
—. Indiana, University of. Western States. Winther, Oscar Osburn. 1920's-70. *1079*

Transportation history. Economic development. Mississippi Valley. Railroads, narrow-gauge. 1870-1900. 1970. *3924*

Transylvania. *See also* Rumania.
—. Antifeudalism. Peasants. Rebellions. Terminology. 1784. *3379*
—. Barițiu, Gheorghe. Culture. Romanians. 1840-93. *411*
—. Castles. Romanticism. 19c. *4031*
—. German. Kurz, Anton. Periodicals. Research. 1840's. *128*
—. Horea, Nicolae. Rebellions. 1784-85. *3332*
—. Romania. Seton-Watson, R. W. 1879-1951. *980*

Travel. Lambarde, William. Literature. Manuscripts (collection). Nowell, Laurence. 1568-72. *743*

Travel accounts. Austria. Diplomats. Hammer-Purgstall, Josef von. Methodology. Ottoman Empire. Topography. 1798-1852. *793*

Treasury. Central University of Venezuela. Colonial Government. Quantitative Methods. Venezuela (Caracas). 1930's-70's. *1699*

Treaties. *See also* names of treaties, e.g. Utrecht, Treaty of (1713), Nazi-Soviet Pact; names beginning with Convention, Agreement, Protocol, etc.
—. Diplomacy. Italy. Toscano, Mario. 1930's-60's. *2934*

Treitschke, Heinrich von. Droysen, Gustav. Germany. Nationalism. Sybel, Heinrich von. ca 1830-1900. *1212*
—. Lamprecht, Karl. Ranke, Leopold von. 19c. *419*

Treitschke, Heinrich von (political career). Germany. Nationalism. ca 1850-1900. *783*

Trent, Council of. Catholic Church. Sarpi, Paolo. Sforza, Cardinal. Vatican II. Venice. 17c. 20c. *621*

Trevelyan, George Macaulay. 19c. *725*

Trevelyan, George Macauley (review article). Biography. Historians. Moorman, Mary. 1876-1965. *750*

Trevor-Roper, Hugh. 8c BC-1914. *400*
—. Causation. Hinsley, F. H. Taylor, A. J. P. World War II. 1961-78. *3045*

Trials. *See also* Crime and Criminals.
—. Eichmann, Adolf (review article). War crimes. World War II. 1940-45. 1960-61. *3289*

Triangular trade myth. New England. Trade. 1795-1950. *2016*

Trivia. Research. 1900-79. *1507*

Troeltsch, Ernest. Bergson, Henri. Morality. Niebuhr, H. Richard. Religion. 1925-37. *3670*

Troeltsch, Ernst. Christianity. Secularization. 16c-20c. *692*

Troitski, S. M. Bibliographies. Russia. 1600-1800. *988*

Tropes. Narrative. Rhetoric. Social sciences. Struever, Nancy S. White, Hayden (*Metahistory*; review article). 1970-80. *1397*

Tropfke, Johannes. Mathematics, elementary. Prehistory-19c. ca 1902-39. *524*

Trotsky, Leon. Kronstadt mutiny. Lenin, V. I. 1921. *393*

Trotsky, Leon (*History of the Russian Revolution*). Russian Revolution. 20c. *881*

Trotsky, Leon (*1905*). Political culture. 1901-17. *2537*

Trudel, Marcel. Creighton, Donald. Quebec. 19c-1980. *1072*

Truman, Harry S. Domestic policy. Foreign policy. Liberalism. 1945-52. *2874*
—. Korean War. MacArthur, Douglas. Politics. Public relations. Wake Island. 1950. *3301*

Truman, Harry S. (administration). Diplomacy. Palestine. Politics. 1945-48. *2838*

Truman, Harry S. (research). 1945-53. 1960's-72. *377*

Truth. Military History (conference). 1969. *3041*
—. Publishers and Publishing. Regnery, Henry (account). Revisionism. World War II (causes). 20c. *3230*

Truth in history. -1960's. *1598*
—. 1960's. *1330*
—. Historians. 1450-1984. *1359*
—. Ideology. Kristeller, Paul. Objectivism. Renaissance. 15c-16c. *1561*
—. Imagination. ca 1000-1966. *1370*
—. Myths. -20c. *1205*
—. Objective. 19c-20c. *1472*
—. Objectivity. -1974. *1240*
—. Reality. 1967. *1265*

Truth (review article). Handlin, Oscar. 1950-80. *1180*

Tuchman, Barbara. History. 1936-79. *526*

Tudors. Bibliographies. England. Hurstfield, Joel. 16c. 1944-78. *1112*

Tuhanuku, Daniel. Oceania (Bellona). Oral tradition. Wawn, William T. 1893-1970's. *1768*

Turkey. *See also* Ottoman Empire.
—. 1979. *1408*
—. Atatürk, Kemal. Foreign Relations. USSR. 1935-72. *2835*
—. Foreign Relations. USSR. 1935-70. *2836*
—. Gordlevsky, Vladimir. Philology. 1976. *874*
—. Straits Question. World War I (antecedents). 19c-1914. *3151*

Turks. Hungary. Mohács (battle). 1526. *3134*

Turnbull, Andrew. Fitzgerald, F. Scott. Fitzgerald, Zelda. Mayfield, Sara. Milford, Nancy. Mizener, Arthur. 1910's-40's. *2315*

Turner, Frederick Jackson. Antifederalists. Jensen, Merrill. Kenyon, Cecelia M. 1776-1800. 1893-1974. *2765*
—. Berthoff, Rowland T. Demography. Pierson, George W. Population. 1920-79. *1741*
—. Billington, Ray Allen (review article). 1890's-1932. 1973-75. *875*
—. Folklore. Myths and Symbols. 20c. *1774*
—. Frontier thesis. 1861-1932. *238*
—. Presentism. 19c. *796*
—. Rhetoric. 1880's-1932. *259*

Turner, Frederick Jackson (career). Billington, Ray Allen (review article). Frontier thesis. Sectional interaction. ca 1890-1924. *744*

Turner, Frederick Jackson (papers). Frontier thesis. 1890's-1932. *528*

Turner, Frederick Jackson (thesis). Sports. 20c. *3934*

Twentieth Century. American History. 1900-75. *269*

U

Ukraine. Agriculture. Collective farms. Peasants. 1917-75. *1965*
—. *Archives of the Ukraine*. Periodicals. USSR. 1925-80. *79*
—. Armies. Partisans. World War II. 1943-44. *3313*
—. Bibliographies. Doroshenko, Dmytro. 1904-51. *1099*
—. Bulgaria. 15c-20c. 1945-80. *83*
—. Communist Party. Industry. Technological progress. 1959-75. *1964*
—. Cossacks. Documents. Khmelnitsky, Bogdan. 1620-54. *1033*
—. Editors and Editing. Factories. Gorky, Maxim. *History of Factories and Plants*. 1931-35. *1953*
—. Industry. 20c. *1870*
—. Marxism. 1840-80. 1921-28. *2623*
—. Marxism. 1850's-1917. *2669*
—. Military. 18c. *2983*
—. Military history. 1921-39. *3260*
—. Partisans. World War II. 1941-45. *3110*
—. Pereiaslav Agreement. Russia. 1654. *233*
—. Periodicals. *Problemy Slavianoznavstva*. Slavic studies. USSR. 1970's. *175*
—. Periodicals. *Ukrains'kyi Istorychnyi Zhurnal*. 1957-61. *176*
—. Periodicals. *Ukrains'kyi Istoryk*. 1963-83. *182*
—. Philosophy. Skovoroda, Grigori. 1721-1970. *2364*
—. Philosophy of history. Skovoroda, H. S. 18c. 19c-1917. *1014*
—. Revolution of 1848. 1848. *3358*
—. Revolution of 1905. 1905-07. *3357*
—. Revolution of 1905. 1905. *3336*
—. Science. Technology. USSR. 1928-81. *3822*
—. Workers' control. 1917-18. *1879*
—. World War II. 1945-76. *3189*

Ukraine (Kiev). Communist Party. Communist Party (congress). 1890's-1983. *2687*

Ukraine (Poltava Oblast). Folklore. Research. 1960-74. *1750*

Ukrainian Historian. USSR (Ukraine). 1963-73. *183*

Ukrainians. Atrocities. Galicia Division. Poland. USSR. World War II. 1943-45. *3294*
—. Czechoslovakia. Emigration. Europe, Central and Western. Military units. Russian Revolution. 1917-39. *3261*

Ukrains'kyi Istorychnyi Zhurnal. Lenin, V. I. Periodicals. USSR. 1968-70. *155*
—. Periodicals. Ukraine. 1957-61. *176*

Ukrains'kyi Istoryk. Periodicals. Ukraine. 1963-83. *182*

Ultra. Bibliographies. Cryptography. Magic. Military Intelligence (review article). World War II. 1939-45. *3023*

UN. Foreign Policy. Roosevelt, Franklin D. 1943-47. *2972*

X

Y

Z

AUTHOR INDEX

Emanuel, Gary Lynn 596
Emerson, Roger L. 2326
Emmer, P. C. 301 1458
Ende, Aurel 1821
Endo, Teruaki 1908
Engel, Evamaria 3054
Engelberg, Ernst 1204 1556 1583 2194
Engel-Janosi, Friedrich 790 1205
Engerman, Stanley L. 1909 1910 1911 2166 2195
Engman, Max 3408
Enriquez del Arbol, Eduardo 46
Enssle, Manfred J. 2859
Enteen, George M. 302 1206
Entenmann, Robert 9
Epshtein, A. D. 47
Erbe, Michael 303
Erdélyi, Ilona T. 1207
Erdmann, Karl Dietrich 48 2529 2860
Erényi, Tibor 2530
Erickson, Ann K. 791
Ermakov, V. T. 2436
Ernst, Eldon G. 3539
Ernst, Joseph E. 1208
Ernst, Volker 3055
Ernst, Wolfgang 3931
Erofeev, N. A. 792 1912 1913 2531
Esler, Anthony 2437
Esplin, Robert K. 3540
Estes, Leland L. 1762
Esteva, Juan 1647
Etherington, Norman 1914
Etulain, Richard W. 2327 2328
Evans, Michael Jay 597
Evans, Richard William 598
Evselevs'kyi, L. I. 1870
Evstigneev, E. 3056
Eyice, Semavi 793
Ezergailis, Andrew 2532

F

Faber, Karl-Georg 1584 1648
Faccini, Luigi 3858
Fahey, J. C. 3057
Fair, John D. 3058
Fairchild, Sharon Louise 599
Falcionelli, Alberto 2597
Falk, Stanley L. 3059
Falk, Waltraud 1915
Falla, P. S. 351
Faragasso, Frank Thomas 600
Farina, Francesco 1916
Farquharson, John 350
Farr, James Fulton 601
Farsobin, V. V. 1679
Faucher, Daniel 1917
Faulenbach, Bernd 304
Faulk, Odie B. 305 794
Fauré, Christine 3409
Fay, Victor 2533
Fearnley-Sander, Mary 795
Feather, John 2329
Federn, Ernst 3859
Feenstra, R. 49
Feibach, Hans-Joachim 3932
Feinberg, Walter 2330
Felice Cardot, Carlos 50
Feliu, Gaspar 1918
Fell, John L. 306
Felt, Thomas E. 307
Femia, Joseph 2534
Fenger, Ole 3933
Ferguson, Arthur B. 308 2438
Ferling, John E. 2755
Fernández Vargas, Valentina 2196
Ferrante, Lucia 2439
Ferrari, Liliana 1209
Ferretti, Valdo 3060
Ferriss, William H. 796
Feuerwerker, Albert 309
Fidler, Douglas K. 3934
Field, Clive D. 3541 3542
Field, Frank 2331
Field, James A., Jr. 2733
Field, Martha Heineman 2197
Figlio, Karl 3935

Filatowa, L. A. 3763
Filene, Peter G. 2198
Filion, Maurice 310
Fine, John V. A., Jr. 797
Fink, Gary M. 1919
Finkelstein, Barbara 2440
Finley, M. I. 1210 2116
Finn, Peter Elliott 855
Finnestad, Ragnhild Bjerre 3543
Finocchiaro, M. A. 3755 3756
Firsov, F. I. 3061
Fischer, Fritz 3062
Fischer, Wolfram 1920
Fischer-Galati, Stephen 311
Fishbone, Jonathan D. 798
Fitch, Nancy E. 1712
Fitzsimons, M. A. 312 3544
Flaherty, David H. 1211
Flaig, Herbert 1212
Flanary, Barbara Jean Dawson 602
Flandrin, Jean-Louis 2441
Flatt, Donald Franklin 603
Fleischer, Cornell Hugh 604
Fleischer, Dirk 1150
Fleury, Antoine 2861
Flint, John T. 1213
Florea, Ion 1214
Flores, Marcello 2442
Floto, Inga 799 1215 1216 2862
Floud, Roderick 313
Flynn, Dennis O. 1921
Foa, Anna 1217
Foerg, Irmgard 51
Fogel, Robert William 314 2117
Fohlen, Claude 2118 2119 2863
Folch Jou, G. 3860
Folsom, Burton W., II 2756
Fomin, V. 52
Foner, Eric 315 2120
Fontaine, P. F. M. 800
Fontana i Làzaro, Josep 1649
Fores, Michael 3757
Formisano, Ronald P. 2757
Förster, Gerhard 3063
Forster, Robert 1673
Forsyth, Murray 2864
Foster, Claude R., Jr. 3545
Fourquin, Guy 2199
Fout, John C. 3456
Fowler, William M., Jr. 3395
Fox, Edward Whiting 801
Fox, Frank W. 3758
Fox-Genovese, Elizabeth 2121 3410
França, José Agosto 1218
Franchini, Silvia 3411
Francovitch, Carlo 2598
Frandsen, K. E. 3759
Franklin, Bruce 2704
Frantz, Joe B. 316
Franzina, Emilio 1219
Frazer, Derek 317
Frederickson, George M. 1220
Freedman, Estelle B. 3412
Freehof, Solomon B. 3546
Freeman, Joshua 3064
Freiberg, Malcolm 802
Freidel, Frank 803
Freitag, W. D. 605
Fremdling, Rainer 1922
French, Valerie 398
Frese, Joseph R. 3807
Fretz, Lewis 2865
Frey, Linda 2866
Frey, Marsha 2866
Fricke, Dieter 1585
Friedman, Edward 1556
Friedman, Lawrence 804 2122 3936
Friesel, Evyatar 3937
Friesen, Abraham 3547
Frigo, Gian Franco 2332 2333
Friguglietti, James 805 960 3028
Frijhoff, Willem 3548
Frisch, Michael 3938
Frolova, I. I. 53
Frost, Elsa Cecilia 394
Frost, Jess V. 2867
Fry, Joseph A. 2868

Fry, Michael G. 2869
Fuchs, Peter 2535
Fuks-Mansfeld, R. G. 806
Fulton, Richard M. 318
Fumaroli, Max 1221
Fure, Eli 1713
Fure, Odd-Bjørn 1222
Furet, François 1223 1650 3338 3939
Furman, Necah Stewart 319
Fursenko, A. A. 3339
Furtek, Joanne 606
Fuzitsu, Seiji 2093

G

Gabel, Christopher R. 54
Gaddis, John Lewis 2977
Gadille, Jacques 3549
Gadzhiev, K. S. 807 1224 2200
Gagné, Suzanne 808
Gagnon, Nicole 320
Gagnon, Serge 321 1225
Galante Garrone, Alessandro 809
Galasso, Giuseppe 2443
Galkin, I. S. 1586 2758
Gallerano, Nicola 1226 2123
Galos, Adam 55
Galvão de Andrada Coelho, Ruy 2201
Gamson, Ian Calder 607
Ganz, Peter 322
Gárate Córdoba, José María 3065
Garcia, Hazel Dicken 505 506
Garcia de la Huerta I., Marcos 323
García-Gallo, Alfonso 3940
Gardiner, Patrick 1227
Gardner, Lloyd C. 2977
Garin, Eugenio 810
Garlato, Francesco 811
Garrard, John 2536
Garrett, Wendell D. 812
Gattei, Giorgio 2870
Gaus, Helmut 1228
Gaustad, Edwin S. 1696
Gavigan, Johannes 813
Gavrila, Irina 1714
Gawrecki, Dan 1587 2599
Gay, Peter 1229
Gearhart, Suzanne 324
Gégot, Jean-Claude 2202
Geldbach, Erich 814
Gemkow, Heinrich 2581
Génicot, Léopold 1230
Genri, E. 3066
George, Alexander L. 2759
George, C. H. 1231
George, Juliette L. 2759
Georgescu, Valentin Al 815
Georgian, Lucia 56
Gephart, Ronald Michael 608
Gerardi, Donald F. 57
Geras, Norman 2537
Gerber, Richard Allan 2760
Gericke, Helmuth 524
Gersman, Elinor Mondale 58
Gerstein, Linda 816
Gerster, Patrick 325
Gestrin, Ferdo 1923
Giard, Luce 1232
Gibbs, William E. 817
Gibelli, Antonio 1924 1925
Giddens, Paul H. 1926
Gieysztor, Aleksander 818 3941
Giguère, Georges-Émile 819
Gilbert, Arthur N. 2842 2869
Gilbert, Felix 820 3067
Gillet, Marcel 1927
Gilliam, Harriet 1233
Gilmore, Al-Tony 326
Gilson, Estelle 3942
Gimbel, John 2871
Gindin, Claude 821
Gindin, I. F. 822
Ginsberg, Arlin J. 1749
Ginsburg, Jerry 1832
Ginter, Donald E. 1702
Ginzburg, Carlo 4065
Girard, Louis 1680
Girardet, Raoul 2444

Giuzelev, Vasil 823
Givsan, Hassan 1928
Glasberg, Ronald Peter 609
Glasgow, Tom, Jr. 3068
Glatz, Ferenc 824 1234 1588 3069
Glaubauf, K. 610
Glazunov, N. 3070
Gleason, Philip 3550
Glénisson, Jean 1235 1236
Glick, Edward Bernard 3071
Glick, Thomas F. 3764
Głombik, Czesław 825
Glubb, John 2705
Godechot, Jacques 327
Godel, Jean 3655
Goeckel, Robert F. 3551
Goertz, Hans-Jurgen 3723
Goetz, Hans-Werner 1833
Goetz, Helmut 59 2600
Goetzmann, William H. 1237
Gogarten, Hermann 826
Goggin, Jacqueline Anne 611
Gogoneață, Nicolae 827
Goichot, Émile 3552
Goldberg, A. L. 828
Goldberg, Barry 1929
Goldie, Mark 1238
Goldin, Claudia 3413
Goldman, Lawrence 1715
Goldman, Martin S. 3943
Goldmann, Sonja 1899
Goldstein, Warren 9
Gołębiowski, Bronisław 2096
Gołębiowski, Janusz W. 1930 2096
Golinski, J. V. 3743
Golob, Eugene O. 1239
Golub, Arno 1898
Gómez, Elías 3553
Gómez Martínez, José L. 829
Gonçalves Melo, Jayro 1931
Gonen, Jay Y. 1821
Gonnet, Giovanni 3554 3555
González Castro, Ernesto 3556
González Salinas, Edmundo 3072
Gooch, John 3073
Goodale, Jesse Robinson 612
Goodman, Jennifer Robin 830
Goodman, R. S. 1763
Goodway, David 2538
Goodwyn, Lawrence 328
Gool, S. Y. 613
Goranov, Stefan 2601
Gordon, Amy Glassner 3944
Gordon, Ann D. 3414
Gordon, Ann G. 3399
Gordon, Linda 3415 3416
Gordon, Martin 3074
Gordon, Robert W. 3945
Gorelik, I. M. 3075 3076
Goren, Arthur A. 4066
Gorham, Deborah 3861
Gorman, J. L. 1240
Gorn, Michael 3077
Gorn, Tatiana 302
Gorodetski, E. N. 1241 1242 1243 2602
Gorokhov, V. G. 3760
Goroneos, George 3934
Gorshkov, A. I. 2872
Gorskaia, N. A. 831
Gossman, Lionel 329
Gottfried, Paul 832 1834
Gottlieb, Roger S. 2603
Gottschling, Ernst 1589
Goubert, Pierre 2445
Goudoever, A. P. van 330
Goulding, Stuart D. 833
Goveia, Elsa V. 331
Goy, Joseph 3946
Gràb, Walter 3340
Grabmüller, Hans-Jürgen 60
Grabski, Andrzej F. 834 835
Gracheva, L. E. 836
Graebner, Norman A. 2873
Gräfe, Karl-Heinz 2604
Grafenauer, Bogo 837
Grafton, Anthony T. 1244
Graham, Matt Patrick 614
Granasztói, György 1716
Gransden, Antonia 333
Granstein, J. L. 332
Grant, H. Roger 838 3947
Grass, Nikolaus 3557

Graubard, Stephen R. 839
Graus, František 1245
Green, Barbara L. 2124
Green, Donald E. 840
Green, Lowell C. 3558
Green, Rayna 3417
Green, William A. 2706
Greenaway, Frank 3761
Gregor, A. James 2605
Greiner, Albert 3559
Grele, Ronald J. 334
Grendi, Edoardo 841 1553
Greussing, Kurt 1556
Grew, Raymond 1246
Gribaudi, Maurizio 2334
Griffin, John 3560
Griffith, Robert 2874
Griffiths, Gordon 3561
Grigoraş, Nicolae 842
Grigorian, A. T. 3762 3763
Grigulevich, I. R. 61
Grishin, V. M. 62
Griswold del Castillo, Richard 1717
Grob, Gerald N. 2203
Groehler, Olaf 3078
Groenendijk, L. F. 2491
Groeneveld, Eduard G. 3079 3080
Grogono, Peter 1702
Grönroos, Gun 63
Groppi, Angela 1247 3418
Gross, Charles J. 3077
Gross, David L. 1248
Gross, Mirjana 214
Groth, Margit 1932
Gruzdeva, V. P. 2606
Guadarrama González, Pablo 2335
Guboglu, Mihail 3081
Gudavicius, E. 2204
Guelzo, Allen C. 2205
Guerci, Luciano 3948
Guggisberg, Hans Rudolf 335
Guillen, Pierre 2707
Gumilev, L. N. 3949
Gunnarson, Gisli 1933
Gunnell, John G. 2539
Guntau, Martin 336
Gurock, Jeffrey S. 4066
Gurría Lacroix, Jorge 394
Gustavson, Carl G. 2336
Gutman, Herbert G. 337 2166
Gutman, Myron P. 1718
Gutnova, E. V. 1934
Gutsche, Willibald 2708
Guttman, Allen 3950

H

Haapala, Pertti 1935
Haas, Gerhart 3082
Haberl, Othmar Nikola 2607
Hackett, Amy 3419
Haddad, Yvonne Yazbeck 338
Haddock, B. A. 2337
Haecker, Dorothy A. 615
Haenens, Albert d' 1249
Hageman, Elizabeth H. 3420
Hagen, Kenneth 3562
Häikiö, Martti 843 3083
Hail, Francina Kercheville 616
Haines, Gerald K. 339 2823 2908 2926 2945 2963 2968 3084 3118
Haines, Michael A. 2446
Hakfoort, C. 3844
Hakobian, A. M. 3085
Hale, Frederick A. 3086
Halkin, Léon-E. 3951
Hall, A. Rupert 1250
Hall, Diana Long 3764
Hall, John R. 1251
Hall, John Whitney 844
Hall, Peter Dobkin 2299
Hall, Stuart 1590
Halperin, John 845 2338
Halpern, Jeanne W. 2339
Halsted, Caroline Amelia 340
Hamelin, Jean 320
Hamlin, Cyrus 2340
Hammack, David C. 3952
Hammerstein, Notker 2341

McArthur, Gilbert H. 3339
McAuley, James J. 1370
McAvoy, William C. 2359
McBride, Paul 3627
McCaa, Robert 1731
McCaffrey, Larry 929
McCaffrey, Raymond
Aloysius 643
McCartney, Paul J. 3792
McClave, Heather 3443
McClelland, Peter D. 1992
McCloskey, Donald 1993
McComb, David 2360
McConnell, James M. 3299
McCormach, Russell 3842
McCormick, Richard P. 1371
McCormick, Thomas J. 2925
McCreary, Eugene C. 3995
McCullagh, C. Behan 1372
1373
McDonald, Roderick A.
2139
McDonald, Terrence J. 2777
McDonnell, Lawrence T.
1994
McEwen, J. M 3176
McFarlane, Bruce 1995
McGill, William J. 930
McGinnis, A. C. 931
McGinnis, Janice P. Dickin
3444
McGuire, Barbara 1996
McGwire, Michael 3299
McIntire, C. T. 3719
McIntyre, W. D. 932
McKay, David H. 2778
McKenzie, Lionel Andrew
644
McKenzie, Robert H. 1997
McKinley, Blaine 2551
McKinney, Gordon B. 933
McLennan, Gregor 414 1602
McLeod, Hugh 3628
McMahon, Robert J. 2926
McMillan, James 3423 3629
McMullen, Haynes 4067
McNall, Scott G. 2643
McNaught, Kenneth 415
1998
McNeill, John T. 934
McNeill, William H. 1374
McPartland, Thomas Joseph
645
McQuaid, Kim 1999
McRoberts, Meg 3996
McShane, Clay 2243
Mead, Peter 3177 3178 3277
Mealy, Charles Richard 646
Medland, William James 647
Medvedev, Roy A. 416
Meerse, David E. 2779
Megill, Allan 935
Meier, Helmut 1580
Meier, M. S. 216
Meikle, Jeffrey L. 117
Meilink-Roelofsz, M. A. P.
417
Melanson, Richard A. 418
Melent'ev, Iu. S. 936
Mellon, Stanley 2552
Meloni, Vittorio 937
Mende, Georg 2244
Mercier, Roger 2245
Mérei, Gyula 1375 1376
Mergen, Bernard 3997
Merrens, H. Roy 1208
Mertsalov, A. N. 3179 3180
Meshcheryakova, N. M.
2644
Meshkov, O. V. 938
Mettas, Jean 2140
Metz, Karl Heinz 419
Meyer, Klaus 939
Meyer, Michael A. 3722
Michael, Reuven 3998
Michaelsen, Robert S. 3630
Michalski, Stanisław 2000
Michel, Henri 3181
Michiels, R. 3631
Midelfort, H. C. Erik 3869
Miehls, Don George 648
Mignot, Claude 3999
Mikell, Charles 979
Mikio Sumiya 420
Mikkeli, Heikki 2465
Mikkelsen, Flemming 2001
Mikulinski, S. R. 3793
Mikus, Joseph A. 940
Milani, Piero A. 2142

Miliband, S. D. 941
Milis, L. 1685
Millar, David 2466
Miller, Darlis A. 3429
Miller, David 3719
Miller, David Harry 1377
Miller, Genevieve 3870
Miller, Joseph C. 421
Miller, Randall M. 2143
Miller, Robert F. 2645
Miller, Sally M. 2780
Miller, Stuart T. 118
Mills, Frederick V., Sr. 3632
Milner, Marc 3182
Milošević, Miloš 119
Milova, Chr 3183
Milum, Betty 4067
Milutinović, Kosta 942 943
Minchinton, W. E. 3794
Minei, Nicolae 1378
Mink, Louis O. 1379
Minoski, Mikhailo 120
Minow, Fritz 3184
Mints, I. I. 2646
Mintz, Lawrence E. 2467
Mintz, Sidney 2002
Mironets, N. I. 1380 1381
Mironov, B. N. 4000
Miscamble, Wilson D. 3633
Miskimin, Harry 1732
Mitchell, Allan 2361 2362
Mitrofanova, A. V. 2073
Mogensen, Gunnar Viby
1949
Mogensen, Henrik 2781
Mogil'nitski, B. G. 1603
1604
Mohrmann, Ute 1771
Moir, John S. 3634
Mokshin, S. I. 2647 2648
Molchanov, Iu. V. 4001
Molesti, Romano 2003
Moley, Raymond 2812
Molnar, Miklos 2246
Molodshi, V. N. 3795
Momigliano, Arnaldo 1382
1383
Mommsen, Wolfgang J. 944
1384 1686
Monberg, Torben 1768
Monds, Jean 2092
Monguillot, Manuel Salvat
945
Monkkonen, Eric H. 2247
Monod, Gabriel 121
Monter, E. William 2248
Montgomery, David 1385
2004
Montgomery, Ingun 3635
Monticone, Alberto 122
Montpensier, Roy Stone de
946
Moore, Deborah Dash 4066
Moore, Jamie W. 2927
Moore, John Allphin, Jr.
2928
Moore, R. Lawrence 1696
1696
Moore-Rinvolucri, Mina 533
Moote, A. Lloyd 1657
Morales Lezcano, Víctor
2005
Moramarco, Fred 2006
Morantz, Regina Markell
3445
Morato, Josefina 947
Moravcová, Dagmar 2649
2715
More, Henry 422
Moreau, Thérèse 3446
Morel, Bernard 1386
Moreno, Diego 2468
Moreno Bonett, Margarita
423
Morgan, H. Wayne 4002
Morgan, James Calvin 649
Morgenthau, Hans 1387
Mori, Kenzo 2716
Morineau, Michel 2007
Morison, Samuel Eliot 424
Moritz, Erhard 123
Mork, Gordon R. 3636
Mörner, Magnus 2144
Moroz, V. K. 175
Morris, Richard B. 1388
Morrison, Katherine Long
650
Morrow, Don 4003
Morton, Desmond 2008

Mosca, Liliana 425
Moscardelli, Giuseppe 3185
Moscati, Laura 948
Moscow Institute of the
International Working
Class Movement 426
Moseley, Eva S. 3447
Moses, H. Vincent 3637
Moses, Wilson J. 2145
Mosolov, V. G. 2625
Mosse, George L. 2650
Motoike, Ritsu 1658
Mott, Morris 4004
Motte, Olivier 124 4005
Mounger, Dwyn M. 3638
Moutsopoulos, E. 1389
Mozzarelli, Cesare 427 2469
Muccillo, Maria 2363
Mudroch, Vaclav 428
Mühlpfordt, Günter 949
2553
Muise, D. A. 429
Muller, C. F. J. 430
Müller, Joachim 1390
Mulryan, John 950
Muñoz Calvo, S. 3860
Munz, Peter 1391
Münz, Rudolf 3932 4006
Muraskin, William A. 2249
Murata, Tamotsu 3796 3797
Murav'ev, V. A. 1392 3162
Muret, Philippe 1837
Murphy, Francis X. 3639
Murphy, George G. S. 1393
Murphy, James J. 1394
Murphy, Lawrence R. 1772
Murphy, P. J. 2009
Murrah, David J. 951
Murru, Furio 1687
Mutnick, Barbara 393
Myllyntaus, Timo 3798
Myslivchenko, A. G. 952
Mytrovych, Kyrylo 2364

N

Naganuma, Muneaki 2250
Nagel, Paul C. 2782
Nagl-Docekal, Herta 1395
Nahon, Gérard 4007
Naida, S. F. 3186
Naidenov, M. E. 953
Nakagawa, Keiichiro 2093
2093
Nakamura, Hiroji 2010
Nakayama, Shigeru 3799
Namias, Jerome 1190
Naphtali, Zvia Segal 651
Nardin, A. V. V. 954
Narochnitski, A. L. 3187
Narulin, K. 3354
Nash, Gary B. 431
Nasko, Siegfried 955
Natan, Zhak 125
Nauert, Charles G., Jr. 4008
Naumov, V. P. 126
Navasardian, R. G. 1626
Nazarov, V. D. 956
Neatby, Hilda 432
Nedoncelle, Maurice 1396
Nefedova, N. A. 2929
Negoiu, I. 127
Neils, Patricia C. 652
Nejedlý, Miloslav 3188
Nelson, Carol Ann 3407
Nelson, Douglas T. 3355
Nelson, John S. 1397
Nemes, Dezső 2651
Nem'iatyi, V. M. 3189
Nesvadba, František 3190
3191 3192 3193
Netchkina, M. V. 1557
Neuman, R. P. 1810
Neumann, Victor A. 128
Neumann, Wilhelm 957
Neuschäffer, Hubertus 2011
Neveux, Hugues 1733
Nevler, V. E. 958 959
Nevzorov, B. 3194
Newell, William Dixon 653
Newman, Edgar 960 3387
Newman, Peter 1989
Newmyer, Kent 433
Nezhinski, L. N. 2554 2652
2930
Nichiţelea, Pamfil 1605
Nicholls, David 2251
Nichols, William W. 2146

Niederhauser, Emil 2511
Niedermayer, Franz 961
Nielsen, Sabine 129
Niemeyer, Gerhart 3640
Nies, Fritz 2365
Nikiforov, E. A. 1398
Nikonov, V. A. 3195
Nilsson, Carl-Axel 2012
Ninomiya, Hiroyuke 1035
Nisbet, Robert 3356
Nisio, Sigeko 3842
Nissen, Henrik S. 1399
Noack, Karl-Heinz 3196
Noble, David W. 1400
Noël, Jean-François 2783
Nohl, Frederick 3641
Noll, Mark A. 344 3642
3643 3841
Nolte, Ernst 1606
Nord, David Paul 4009
Nore, Ellen 1401
Norman, Birger 962
Norris, Colin J. 2412
Norris, James D. 2013
Norris, Roy William 654
North, Douglass C. 1673
Norton, Mary Beth 3448
Norwood, Frederick A. 3644
Nostrand, Richard L. 507
508
Novack, George 434
Novik, F. I. 2931
Novoselov, B. 3197 3198
Nowak, Tadeusz Marian
3199 3800
Numbers, Ronald L. 3871
Nunis, Doyce B., Jr. 963 964
Nusbaum, Mary Antoine 655
Nybom, Thorsten 1402
Nye, Mary Jo 3801

O

Oakley, Francis 435
Öberg, Lars 3872
O'Brien, Jo 3449
O'Brien, Michael 436
O'Brien, P. K. 2014
O'Brien, Patricia 2252
Ochocki, Kazimierz 2653
O'Connor, John E. 437
Oestreich, Gerhard 965
Ogarev, P. 3200
Ognev, Y. 2932
O'Gorman, Frank 2555
Okie, Packard Laird, Jr. 656
Okinshevich, Leo 438
Olagüe de Ros, Guillermo
3873
Oldfield, Adrian 1403
Oldroyd, David R. 3802
Olegina, I. N. 1404 1405
Oliver, Ivan 1406
Oliver, Peter 1773
Olmi, Giuseppe 427
Olsen, Ib 2470
Olson, Gordon L. 1996
Olson, James S. 439 2147
O'Muiri, Reamonn 966
Oñate, Modesta 947
O'Neill, James E. 440
Onuma, Masanori 3803
Opie, John 1774
Opitz, Peter J. 2394
Orban, Peter 1821
Orekhov, V. A. 130
Orlik, I. I. 2015
Orlov, A. S. 3136 3139 3201
3202 3203
Orlova, M. I. 2654
Orlova, T. V. 2655
Ortega y Medina, Juan A.
967
Ory, Pascal 2471
Osinovskii, I. N. 1407
Østberg, Berit 2472
Österberg, Eva 2253
Ostrander, Gilman M. 2016
Otruba, Gustav 131
Otsuka, Hisao 2093
Ouellet, Fernand 2254
Owens, W. R. 441
Oyer, John S. 3723
Özbaran, Salih 1408

P

Pace, Enzo 3645
Pach, Zsigmond Pál 968
Pachter, Henry 2933
Packull, Werner O. 3646
3687 3723
Pacor, Mario 3204
Pahaut, Serge 3804
Painter, Borden W. 262
Pallot, Judith 2017
Palm, Erwin Walter 1111
Palmer, Bryan D. 442 2018
2473
Palmer, William G. 1629
Palmieri, Stefano 1688
Palonen, Kari 1838
Paludan, Phillip S. 2784
Pamlényi, Ervin 1409
Pancchàwa, Ilja D. 2656
Papa, Antonio 132
Papadrianos, Ioannês A. 133
Papayanis, Nicholas 3387
Papoulidis, Constantin 969
Paquette, Jean-Marcel 970
Parente, Fausto 3647 3648
Parente, Luigi 971
Parfenov, I. D. 2717
Park, Hong-Kyu 3205 3206
Parker, Christopher J. W.
1410
Parker, Geoffrey 3207
Parker, Harold T. 1235 1286
1287 1411 1412 1412
1692 2069 2552 2703
3025 4036 4053
Parker, John 4010
Parkerson, Donald 1413
Parlato, Giuseppe 1414
Parrish, Michael 3208
Parrish, Noel F. 3209
Parry, G. J. R. 972
Partington, Gordon Geoffrey
1415
Pascoe, Louis B. 973
Pascoe, Rob 443
Pashkov, Anatolii Ignat'evich
2019
Paskaleva, Virginia 134
Passell, Peter 392
Passerini, Luisa 3397
Passos, Maria Lúcia Perrone
de Faro 1416
Pasternak, Jakob 1559
Pastore, Nicholas 4011
Pastorelli, Pietro 2934 3210
Patch, William L., Jr. 2255
Pate, Clarence W. 3211
Paterson, Thomas G. 135
Patrushev, A. I. 1417 2718
Pavlenko, O. H. 892
Pavlenko, V. V. 83
Pavličević, Dragutin 214
Pavlov, B. 3212
Payne, Harry 3649
Payne, Walter 1110
Pazdur, Jan 136
Peace, Nancy E. 3650
Peachy, William Samuel 657
Pearl, Valerie 400
Pease, Jane H. 2719
Pecchioli, Renzo 444
Peck, Elizabeth 3415
Peckham, Howard H. 2366
Pedosov, A. D. 2695
Pedroncini, Guy 3213
Peeters, H. F. M. 2474
Pelaja, Margherita 3418
Pelinka, Anton 2657
Peltier, Michel 1418
Pender-Cudlip, Patrick 3651
Penedo Rey, Manuel 3652
Pentti, Raili 137
Pepe, Adolfo 2020
Perceval-Maxwell, Michael
1419
Peregontseva, G. 3214
Pereyra, Carlos 445
Pérez, Louis A. 446
Pérez Tenreiro, Tomás 3215
Pérez-Prendes y Muñoz de
Arracó, José Manuel
4012
Perinbaum, B. Marie 2021
Perini, Giovanna 4013
Perko, F. Michael 3653
Perlak, Bernard 1420
Perona, Gianni 3216

LIST OF PERIODICALS

A

Abside (ceased pub?) |Mexico|
Academe: Bulletin of the AAUP
Acadiensis: Journal of the History of the Atlantic Region |Canada|
Acta Historiae Neerlandica (ceased pub) |Netherlands|
Acta Historica |Hungary|
Acta Poloniae Historica |Poland|
Acta Sociologica |Norway|
Acta Universitatis Carolinae Philosophica et Historica |Czechoslovakia|
Acta Universitatis Palackianae Olomoucensis: Historica |Czechoslovakia|
Action Nationale |Canada|
Actualité de l'Histoire (see Mouvement Social) |France|
Actualité Economique |Canada|
Aerospace Historian
Affari Esteri |Italy|
Afghanistan |Afghanistan|
Afro-Americans in New York Life and History
Agrártörténeti Szemle |Hungary|
Agricultural History
AHA Newsletter (see AHA Perspectives)
AHA Perspectives
Air University Review
Aktuellt och Historiskt (see Militärhistorisk Tidskrift) |Sweden|
Ambix |Great Britain|
American Archivist
American Behavioral Scientist
American Benedictine Review
American Heritage
American Historical Review
American History Illustrated
American Jewish History
American Journal of Economics and Sociology
American Journal of Legal History
American Journal of Sociology
American Political Science Review
American Presbyterians: Journal of Presbyterian History
American Quarterly
American Scholar
American Slavic and East European Review (see Slavic Review)
American Speech
American Studies in Scandinavia |Norway|
American Studies International
American Studies (Lawrence, KS)
American West
Amerikanskii Ezhegodnik |Union of Soviet Socialist Republic|
Amerikastudien/American Studies |German Federal Republic|
Anais da Academia Portuguesa da História |Portugal|
Anais de História (ceased pub 1977) (IHE) |Brazil|
Anale de Istorie |Romania|
Analele Universităţii Bucureşti: Filosofie |Romania|
Analele Universităţii Bucureşti: Istorie |Romania|
Anales de Economía (IHE) |Spain|
Anglican Theological Review
Annales: Economies, Sociétés, Civilisations |France|
Annales Historiques de la Révolution Française |France|
Annales Universitatis Scientiarum Budapestinensis de Rolando Eötvös Nominatae: Sectio Historica |Hungary|
Annali della Facoltà di Scienze Politiche: Materiali di Storia |Italy|
Annali della Fondazione Luigi Einaudi |Italy|
Annali della Scuola Normale Superiore di Pisa: Classe di Lettere e Filosofia |Italy|
Annali dell'Istituto Giangiacomo Feltrinelli |Italy|
Annals of Science |Great Britain|
Annals of the American Academy of Political and Social Science
Année Politique et Economique (ceased pub 1975) |France|
Annual Bulletin of the Society for the History of Economic Thought |Japan|
Anuario de Historia |Mexico|
Anuario de Historia Contemporánea |Spain|
Anuario de Historia del Derecho Español (IHE) |Spain|
Anuarul Institutului de Istorie şi Arheologie "A. D. Xenopol" |Romania|
Anzeiger der Österreichischen Akademie der Wissenschaften: Philosophisch-Historische Klasse |Austria|
Appalachian Journal
Arbejderhistorie |Denmark|

Årbog for Arbejderbevaegelsens Historie |Denmark|
Arbor (IHE) |Spain|
Archiv für Kulturgeschichte |German Federal Republic|
Archiv für Reformationsgeschichte |German Federal Republic|
Archiv für Sozialgeschichte |German Federal Republic|
Archivar |German Federal Republic|
Archives de Sciences Sociales des Religions |France|
Archives Européennes de Sociologie (see European Journal of Sociology = Archives Européennes de Sociologie = Europäisches Archiv für Soziologie) |Great Britain|
Archives Internationales d'Histoire des Sciences |Italy|
Archivio Storico Italiano |Italy|
Archivmitteilungen |German Democratic Republic|
Archivní Casopis |Czechoslovakia|
Archivo Hispalense (IHE) |Spain|
Archivo Ibero-Americano |Spain|
Archivum Historiae Pontificiae |Italy|
Arhivist |Yugoslavia|
Arizona and the West
Arkansas Historical Quarterly
Arkiv |Denmark|
Armed Forces & Society
Armenian Review
Armidale and District Historical Society Journal and Proceedings |Australia|
Army Quarterly and Defence Journal |Great Britain|
Asian and African Studies |Israel|
Atlantis: A Women's Studies Journal |Canada|
Australian and New Zealand Journal of Sociology |Australia|
Australian Economic History Review |Australia|
Australian Journal of Politics and History |Australia|
Australian Quarterly |Australia|
Austrian History Yearbook
Aztlán

B

Balcanica: Storia, Cultura, Politica |Italy|
Baptist History and Heritage
Baptist Quarterly |Great Britain|
Beiträge zur Geschichte der Arbeiterbewegung |German Democratic Republic|
Belfagor: Rassegna di Varia Umanità |Italy|
Belleten |Turkey|
Biblioteconomía (IHE) |Spain|
Bibliothèque d'Humanisme et Renaissance |Switzerland|
Bijdragen en Mededelingen betreffende de Geschiedenis der Nederlanden |Netherlands|
Biography
Biuletyn Żydowskiego Instytutu Historycznego (see Biuletyn Żydowskiego Instytutu Historycznego w Polsce) |Poland|
Biuletyn Żydowskiego Instytutu Historycznego w Polsce |Poland|
Blackwood's Magazine (ceased pub 1980) |Great Britain|
Blätter für Württembergische Kirchengeschichte |German Federal Republic|
Bleter far Geszichte (pub suspended 1971-79) |Poland|
Boletín de Historia y Antigüedades |Colombia|
Boletín de la Academia Chilena de la Historia (IHE) |Chile|
Boletín de la Academia Nacional de la Historia |Venezuela|
Boletín de la Biblioteca Menéndez Pelayo |Spain|
Boletín de la Sociedad Española de Historia de la Farmacia |Spain|
Boletín del Archivo General de la Nación |Venezuela|
Boletín Histórico (ceased pub 1978) |Venezuela|
Bollettino della Domus Mazziniana |Italy|
Bollettino dell'Archivio per la Storia del Movimento Sociale Cattolico in Italia |Italy|
Brigham Young University Studies
British Journal for the History of Science |Great Britain|
British Journal of Educational Studies |Great Britain|
British Journal of International Studies (see Review of International Studies) |Great Britain|
British Journal of Political Science |Great Britain|
British Journal of Sociology |Great Britain|
British Journal of Sports History |Great Britain|
British Studies Monitor
Bulgarian Historical Review = Revue Bulgare d'Histoire |Bulgaria|

Bulletin de la Société de l'Histoire du Protestantisme Français |France|
Bulletin de la Société d'Histoire Moderne |France|
Bulletin des Séances de l'Académie Royale des Sciences d'Outre-mer |Belgium|
Bulletin d'Histoire Moderne et Contemporaine |France|
Bulletin of Bibliography
Bulletin of Bibliography and Magazine Notes (see Bulletin of Bibliography)
Bulletin of the Committee on Archives and History of the United Church of Canada |Canada|
Bulletin of the History of Medicine
Bulletin of the Institute of Historical Research |Great Britain|
Bulletin of the Society for the Study of Labour History |Great Britain|
Bulletin of the United Church of Canada (see Bulletin of the Committee on Archives and History of the United Church of Canada) |Canada|
Business History Review

C

Cahiers de Clio |Belgium|
Cahiers d'Histoire |France|
Cahiers du Monde Russe et Soviétique |France|
Cahiers Pédagogiques |France|
California Historian
California History
Canadian Historical Association Historical Papers (see Historical Papers = Communications Historiques) |Canada|
Canadian Historical Review |Canada|
Canadian Journal of History = Annales Canadiennes d'Histoire |Canada|
Canadian Journal of History of Sport = Revue Canadienne de l'Histoire des Sports |Canada|
Canadian Journal of History of Sport and Physical Education (see Canadian Journal of History of Sport = Revue Canadienne de l'Histoire des Sports) |Canada|
Canadian Library Journal |Canada|
Canadian Oral History Association Journal = Journal de la Société Canadienne d'Histoire Orale |Canada|
Canadian Review of American Studies |Canada|
Canadian Review of Studies in Nationalism = Revue Canadienne des Etudes sur le Nationalisme |Canada|
Canadian Slavonic Papers = Revue Canadienne des Slavistes |Canada|
Canadian-American Slavic Studies
Caribbean Quarterly |Jamaica|
Carinthia I |Austria|
Casa de las Américas |Cuba|
Časopis Matice Moravské |Czechoslovakia|
Časopis za Zgodovino in Narodopisje |Yugoslavia|
Catholic Historical Review
Centennial Review
Center Magazine
Central European History
Československý Časopis Historický |Czechoslovakia|
Chinese Studies in History
Christian Scholar's Review
Church History
Cithara
Civil War History
Colorado Heritage
Commentary
Communication Monographs
Communications Historiques (see Historical Papers = Communications Historiques) |Canada|
Comparative Political Studies
Comparative Studies in Society and History |Great Britain|
Computer Studies in the Humanities and Verbal Behavior (ceased pub 1974)
Computers and the Humanities
Comunità |Italy|
Concordia Historical Institute Quarterly
Consortium on Revolutionary Europe 1750-1850: Proceedings
Contemporary Review |Great Britain|
Continuity
Convivium (ceased pub 1969) |Italy|
Criminal Justice History
Critica Storica |Italy|
Critical Inquiry
Critique |Great Britain|
Cuadernos de Historia de la Medicina Española |Spain|
Cuadernos de Historia Económica de Cataluña = Quaderns d'Història Econòmica de Catalunya (ceased pub 1980) |Spain|

Cuadernos Hispanoamericanos |Spain|
Cultures: Dialogue between the Peoples of the
 World (ceased pub 1985) |France|
Current Anthropology
Current History
Czasopismo Prawno-Historyczne |Poland|

D

Daedalus
Dalhousie Review |Canada|
Défense Nationale |France|
Dialogue: A Journal of Mormon Thought
Diogenes |Italy|
Diplomatic History
Dissent
Dix-Septième Siècle |France|
Durham University Journal |Great Britain|
Dynamis |Spain|

E

Early American Literature
East Central Europe
East European Quarterly
Economia e Storia |Italy|
Economic History Review |Great Britain|
Economic Journal |Great Britain|
Economisch- en Sociaal-Historisch Jaarboek
 |Netherlands|
Economy and History (merged with Scandinavian
 Economic History Review 1981) |Sweden|
Ecrits de Paris |France|
Education and Urban Society
Eesti NSV Teaduste Akadeemia Toimetised.
 Ühiskonnateadused |Union of Soviet Socialist
 Republic|
Eighteenth Century: Theory and Interpretation
Eighteenth-Century Life
Eighteenth-Century Studies
Einheit |German Democratic Republic|
Ekonomista |Poland|
Encounter
English Historical Review |Great Britain|
English Literary Renaissance
Environmental Review
Esprit |France|
Essex Institute Historical Collections
Estudios |Spain|
Estudios Centroamericanos |El Salvador|
Estudios de Asia y Africa |Mexico|
Estudios de Cultura Náhuatl |Mexico|
Estudios de Deusto (IHE) |Spain|
Estudios Sociales |Dominican Republic|
Etudes Balkaniques |Bulgaria|
Etudes Historiques Hongroises |Hungary|
Etudes Internationales |Canada|
Etudes Rurales |France|
Europa (ceased pub 1982) |Canada|
Europäisches Archiv für Soziologie (see European
 Journal of Sociology = Archives Européennes
 de Sociologie = Europäisches Archiv für
 Soziologie) |Great Britain|
European History Quarterly |Great Britain|
European Journal of Sociology = Archives
 Européennes de Sociologie = Europäisches
 Archiv für Soziologie |Great Britain|
European Studies Review (see European History
 Quarterly) |Great Britain|
Explorations in Economic History
Explorations in Entrepreneurial History (see
 Explorations in Economic History)

F

Far Eastern Affairs |Union of Soviet Socialist
 Republic|
Feminist Studies
Fides et Historia
Film & History
Flinders Journal of History and Politics |Australia|
Fortid og Nutid |Denmark|
Forum der Letteren |Netherlands|
Foundations: A Baptist Journal of History and
 Theology (superseded by American Baptist
 Quarterly)
Francia |France|
Frankfurter Hefte |German Federal Republic|
Freeman
French Historical Studies
Frontiers

G

Gazette: International Journal for Mass
 Communication Studies |Netherlands|
Georgia Historical Quarterly
Georgia Review

German Studies Review
Geschichte in Wissenschaft und Unterricht |German
 Federal Republic|
Geschichte und Gesellschaft: Zeitschrift für
 Historische Sozialwissenschaft |German Federal
 Republic|
Geschichtsdidaktik |German Federal Republic|
Godišnjak Društva Istoričara Bosne i Hercegovine
 |Yugoslavia|
Goriški Letnik |Yugoslavia|
Government and Opposition |Great Britain|
Great Plains Journal

H

Hadtörténelmi Közlemények |Hungary|
Harmon Memorial Lectures in Military History
Harvard Educational Review
Harvard Library Bulletin
Hebrew Union College Annual
Heimen |Norway|
Helikon Világirodalmi Figyelő |Hungary|
Hispania |Spain|
Histoire |France|
Histoire de l'Education |France|
Histoire, Economie et Société |France|
Historia (IHE) |Argentina|
Historia |South Africa|
Historia Mexicana |Mexico|
Historia Scientiarum |Japan|
Historiallinen Aikakauskirja |Finland|
Historiallinen Arkisto |Finland|
Historian
Histórica |Peru|
Historical Bulletin |Philippines|
Historical Journal |Great Britain|
Historical Journal of Film, Radio and Television
 |Great Britain|
Historical Magazine of the Protestant Episcopal
 Church
Historical Methods
Historical Methods Newsletter (see Historical
 Methods)
Historical New Hampshire
Historical News |New Zealand|
Historical Papers = Communications Historiques
 |Canada|
Historical Reflections = Réflexions Historiques
 |Canada|
Historical Social Research = Historische
 Sozialforschung |German Federal Republic|
Historical Studies |Australia|
Historické Štúdie |Czechoslovakia|
Historický Časopis |Czechoslovakia|
Historie |Denmark|
Historie a Vojenství |Czechoslovakia|
Historielärarnas Förenings Årsskrift |Sweden|
Historijski Zbornik |Yugoslavia|
Historische Zeitschrift |German Federal Republic|
Historisches Jahrbuch |German Federal Republic|
Historisk Tidskrift |Sweden|
Historisk Tidskrift för Finland |Finland|
Historisk Tidsskrift |Denmark|
Historisk Tidsskrift |Norway|
History |Great Britain|
History and Theory
History in Africa
History of Education |Great Britain|
History of Education Quarterly
History of European Ideas |Great Britain|
History of Political Economy
History of Religions
History of Science |Great Britain|
History Teacher
History Today |Great Britain|
History Workshop Journal |Great Britain|
Humánitas |Mexico|

I

Illinois Historical Journal
Immigrants & Minorities |Great Britain|
Immigration History Newsletter
Indian Historical Review |India|
Indian Journal of American Studies |India|
Indiana Magazine of History
Indiana Social Studies Quarterly (superseded by
 International Journal of Social Education)
Information Historique |France|
Innes Review |Great Britain|
Inquiry |Norway|
Inter-American Review of Bibliography = Revista
 Interamericana de Bibliografía
Internasjonal Politikk |Norway|
International Affairs |Union of Soviet Socialist
 Republic|
International History Review |Canada|
International Journal |Canada|

International Journal of African Historical Studies
International Journal of Politics
International Labor and Working Class History
International Review of Social History
 |Netherlands|
International Security
International Social Science Journal |France|
International Social Science Review
International Socialist Review
International Studies Quarterly |Great Britain|
Internationale Wissenschaftliche Korrespondenz zur
 Geschichte der Deutschen Arbeiterbewegung
 |German Federal Republic|
Isis
Islas |Cuba|
Issues & Studies |Taiwan|
Istoricheski Pregled |Bulgaria|
Istoricheskie Zapiski |Union of Soviet Socialist
 Republic|
Istoriia SSSR |Union of Soviet Socialist Republic|
Istorija: Spisanie na Sojuzot na Drushtvata na
 Istoricharite na SR Makedonija |Yugoslavia|
Istorijski Glasnik |Yugoslavia|
Istorijski Zapisi |Yugoslavia|
Italia Contemporanea |Italy|
Italian Americana
Italian Quarterly (pub suspended 1977-79)
Izvestiia na Instituta po Istoriia na BKP |Bulgaria|
Izvestiia na Instituta za Istoriia (pub suspended
 1975-78) |Bulgaria|
Izvestiia Sibirskogo Otdeleniia Akademii Nauk
 SSSR. Seriia Istorii, Filologii i Filosofii |Union
 of Soviet Socialist Republic|

J

Jahrbuch der Gesellschaft für die Geschichte des
 Protestantismus in Österreich |Austria|
Jahrbuch des Instituts für Deutsche Geschichte
 |Israel|
Jahrbuch des Oberösterreichischen Musealvereines
 |Austria|
Jahrbuch des Vereins für Geschichte der Stadt Wien
 |Austria|
Jahrbuch für die Geschichte Mittel- und
 Ostdeutschlands |German Federal Republic|
Jahrbuch für Geschichte |German Democratic
 Republic|
Jahrbuch für Geschichte der Sozialistischen Länder
 Europas |German Democratic Republic|
Jahrbuch für Geschichte von Staat, Wirtschaft und
 Gesellschaft Lateinamerikas |German Federal
 Republic|
Jahrbuch für Volkskunde und Kulturgeschichte
 |German Democratic Republic|
Jahrbuch für Wirtschaftsgeschichte |German
 Democratic Republic|
Jahrbücher für Geschichte Osteuropas |German
 Federal Republic|
Japan Interpreter (pub suspended 1980) |Japan|
Japanese Studies in the History of Science (see
 Historia Scientiarum) |Japan|
Jednota Annual Furdek
Jewish Quarterly Review
Journal of African History |Great Britain|
Journal of African Studies
Journal of American Culture
Journal of American Ethnic History
Journal of American Folklore
Journal of American History
Journal of American Studies |Great Britain|
Journal of Area Studies |Great Britain|
Journal of Baltic Studies
Journal of California and Great Basin Anthropology
Journal of Canadian Studies = Revue d'Etudes
 Canadiennes |Canada|
Journal of Church and State
Journal of Communication
Journal of Contemporary Asia |Sweden|
Journal of Contemporary History |Great Britain|
Journal of Ecclesiastical History |Great Britain|
Journal of Economic Literature
Journal of Ethnic Studies
Journal of European Economic History |Italy|
Journal of European Studies |Great Britain|
Journal of Family History: Studies in Family,
 Kinship, and Demography
Journal of Historical Geography
Journal of Imperial and Commonwealth History
 |Great Britain|
Journal of Indian History |India|
Journal of Interdisciplinary History
Journal of Intergroup Relations
Journal of Japanese Studies
Journal of Jazz Studies (superseded by Annual
 Review of Jazz Studies)
Journal of Korean Affairs (ceased pub 1977)
Journal of Libertarian Studies

Journal of Library History, Philosophy, &
    Comparative Librarianship
Journal of Medieval and Renaissance Studies
Journal of Mississippi History
Journal of Modern History
Journal of Negro History
Journal of Pacific History [Australia]
Journal of Peasant Studies [Great Britain]
Journal of Political and Military Sociology
Journal of Politics
Journal of Popular Culture
Journal of Presbyterian History (see American
    Presbyterians: Journal of Presbyterian History)
Journal of Psychohistory
Journal of Religious History [Australia]
Journal of San Diego History
Journal of Social History
Journal of Social Issues
Journal of Southern History
Journal of Sport History
Journal of Strategic Studies [Great Britain]
Journal of the American Academy of Religion
Journal of the Early Republic
Journal of the History of Biology [Netherlands]
Journal of the History of Ideas
Journal of the History of Medicine and Allied
    Sciences
Journal of the History of Philosophy
Journal of the History of the Behavioral Sciences
Journal of the Illinois State Historical Society (see
    Illinois Historical Journal)
Journal of the Polynesian Society [New Zealand]
Journal of the Society of Archivists [Great Britain]
Journal of the West
Journal of the West Virginia Historical Association
Journal of Urban History
Journalism History
Journalism Quarterly
Judaica [Switzerland]
Jugoslovenski Istorijski Časopis [Yugoslavia]

K

Keieishigaku [Japan]
Kentucky Folklore Record: A Regional Journal of
    Folklore and Folklife
Kleio [Netherlands]
Kleio [South Africa]
Komunikaty Mazursko-Warmińskie [Poland]
Kronika [Yugoslavia]
Kwartalnik Historii Kultury Materialnej [Poland]
Kwartalnik Historii Nauki i Techniki [Poland]
Kwartalnik Historyczny [Poland]
Kyrkohistorisk Årsskrift [Sweden]

L

Labor History
Labour = Travail [Canada]
Labour History [Australia]
Land Economics
Landfall [New Zealand]
Latin American Perspectives
Latin American Research Review
Latvijas PSR Zinatnu Akademijas Vestis [Union of
    Soviet Socialist Republic]
Law & Society Review
Leo Baeck Institute. Year Book [Great Britain]
Liberal Education
Library Quarterly
Library Review [Great Britain]
Lietuvos Istorijos Metrastis [Union of Soviet
    Socialist Republic]
Lietuvos TSR Mokslų Akademijos. Darbai. Serija
    A: Visuomenes Mokslai [Union of Soviet
    Socialist Republic]
Literature and History [Great Britain]
Llafur: Journal of the Society for the Study of
    Welsh Labour History [Great Britain]
Local Historian [Great Britain]
Local Population Studies [Great Britain]
Lock Haven Review (ceased pub 1974)
London Journal [Great Britain]
Louisiana History
Louisiana Studies (see Southern Studies: An
    Interdisciplinary Journal of the South)
Lychnos [Sweden]

M

Macedonian Review [Yugoslavia]
Magazin Istoric [Romania]
Magyar Könyvszemle [Hungary]
Magyar Tudomány [Hungary]
Magyar Tudományos Akadémia Filozófiai és
    Történettudományok Osztályának Közleményei
    (ceased pub 1981) [Hungary]

Majallat al-Buhūth al-Tarīkhīya (Journal of
    Historical Researches) [Libya]
Makedonika [Greece]
Manuscripta
Manuscripts
Marine Corps Gazette
Mariner's Mirror [Great Britain]
Marxist Perspectives (ceased pub 1980)
Maryland Historian
Massachusetts Historical Society Proceedings
Massachusetts Review
Material History Bulletin = Bulletin d'Histoire de
    la Culture Matérielle [Canada]
Medina, Mimshal ve-Yahasim Benleumiyim [Israel]
Mélanges de la Casa de Velázquez (IHE) [France]
Mélanges de l'Ecole Française de Rome. Moyen
    Age-Temps Modernes [Italy]
Melbourne Historical Journal [Australia]
Memoria: Rivista di Storia delle Donne [Italy]
Mennonite Life
Mennonite Quarterly Review
Methodist History
Mezhdunarodnaia Zhizn' (see International Affairs)
    [Union of Soviet Socialist Republic]
Michigan History
Mid-America
MidContinent American Studies Journal (see
    American Studies (Lawrence, KS))
Midstream
Midwest Quarterly
Militärgeschichte [German Democratic Republic]
Militärgeschichtliche Mitteilungen [German Federal
    Republic]
Militärhistorisk Tidskrift [Sweden]
Military Affairs
Military Review
Minerva: A Review of Science, Learning and Policy
    [Great Britain]
Minnesota History
Mirovaia Ekonomika i Mezhdunarodnye
    Otnosheniia [Union of Soviet Socialist Republic]
Missouri Historical Review
Mita Gakkai Zasshi [Japan]
Mitteilungen des Instituts für Österreichische
    Geschichtsforschung [Austria]
Mitteilungen des Kremser Stadtarchivs [Austria]
Modern Age
Modern Asian Studies [Great Britain]
Modern Judaism
Mondo Cinese [Italy]
Montclair Journal of Social Sciences and
    Humanities (ceased pub 1974)
Monthly Review
Mouvement Social [France]
Movimento di Liberazione in Italia (see Italia
    Contemporanea) [Italy]
Movimento Operaio e Socialista [Italy]
Musées de Genève [Switzerland]

N

Nachrichten der Akademie der Wissenschaften in
    Göttingen: Philologisch-Historische Klasse
    [German Federal Republic]
Narody Azii i Afriki [Union of Soviet Socialist
    Republic]
Nationalities Papers
Nationaløkonomisk Tidskrift [Denmark]
Nauka Polska [Poland]
Naval War College Review
Nederlands Archief voor Kerkgeschiedenis
    [Netherlands]
Negro History Bulletin
Neue Politische Literatur [German Federal
    Republic]
New England Quarterly
New Left Review [Great Britain]
New Literary History
New Mexico Historical Review
New Scholar
New World Review
New York History
New Zealand Journal of History [New Zealand]
Nghien Cuu Lich Su [Vietnam]
Nineteenth-Century Fiction
Nordeuropa [German Democratic Republic]
Norsk Teologisk Tidsskrift [Norway]
North Dakota Quarterly
Norwegian-American Studies
Notes and Queries [Great Britain]
Nouvelle Revue des Deux Mondes (see Revue des
    Deux Mondes) [France]
Novaia i Noveishaia Istoriia [Union of Soviet
    Socialist Republic]
Nowe Drogi [Poland]
Nuova Antologia [Italy]
Nuova Rivista Storica [Italy]

O

OAH Newsletter
Økonomi og Politik [Denmark]
Old Northwest
Oral History Review
Orbis
Organon (ceased pub 1972)
Österreich in Geschichte und Literatur [Austria]
Österreichische Osthefte [Austria]
Österreichisches Archiv für Kirchenrecht [Austria]
Osteuropa [German Federal Republic]
Ostkirchliche Studien [German Federal Republic]
Oxford Slavonic Papers [Great Britain]

P

Pacific Historian
Pacific Historical Review
Pacific Northwest Quarterly
Paedagogica Historica [Belgium]
Państwo i Prawo [Poland]
Papers of the Bibliographical Society of America
Partisan Review
Párttörténeti Közlemények [Hungary]
Passato e Presente: Rivista di Storia
    Contemporanea
Past and Present [Great Britain]
Patma-Banasirakan Handes. Istoriko-Filologicheskii
    Zhurnal [Union of Soviet Socialist Republic]
Patterns of Prejudice [Great Britain]
Peace and Change
Peasant Studies
Peasant Studies Newsletter (see Peasant Studies)
Pennsylvania History
Pennsylvania Magazine of History and Biography
Pensée [France]
Pensiero Politico [Italy]
Perspectives in American History (suspended pub
    1980-83)
Pharmacy in History
Philippine Studies [Philippines]
Phylon
Physis [Italy]
Plantation Society in the Americas
Polish Perspectives [Poland]
Polish Review
Polish Western Affairs = Pologne et les Affaires
    Occidentales [Poland]
Political Quarterly [Great Britain]
Political Science [New Zealand]
Political Science Quarterly
Political Studies [Great Britain]
Political Theory: An International Journal of
    Political Philosophy
Politico [Italy]
Politics [Australia]
Politics & Society
Politiikka [Finland]
Polity
Ponte [Italy]
Prepodavanie Istorii v Shkole [Union of Soviet
    Socialist Republic]
Present Tense
Presidential Studies Quarterly
Prispevki za Zgodovino Delavskega Gibanja
    [Yugoslavia]
Problemi di Ulisse [Italy]
Proceedings and Papers of the Georgia Association
    of Historians
Proceedings of the American Antiquarian Society
Proceedings of the Annual Meeting of the Western
    Society for French History
Proceedings of the British Academy [Great Britain]
Proceedings of the Royal Institution of Great
    Britain [Great Britain]
Proceedings of the South Carolina Historical
    Association
Proceedings of the Wesley Historical Society [Great
    Britain]
Prologue: the Journal of the National Archives
Protestantesimo [Italy]
Przegląd Historyczny [Poland]
Przegląd Zachodni [Poland]
PS
Psychohistory Review
Public Historian

Q

Quaderni per la Storia dell'Università di Padova
    [Italy]
Quaderni Storici [Italy]
Quarterly Journal of Speech
Quarterly Journal of the Library of Congress
    (ceased pub 1983)
Quarterly Review of Historical Studies [India]
Queen's Quarterly [Canada]

Quellen und Forschungen aus Italienischen Archiven und Bibliotheken [German Federal Republic]

R

Radical America
Radical History Review
Radovi: Institut za Hrvatsku Povijest [Yugoslavia]
Railroad History
Rassegna degli Archivi di Stato [Italy]
Rassegna Storica del Risorgimento [Italy]
Recherches Sociographiques [Canada]
Recherches Sociologiques [Belgium]
Recusant History [Great Britain]
Red River Valley Historian (ceased pub 1980)
Rekishi Hyōron [Japan]
Rekishigaku Kenkyū [Japan]
Relations Internationales [France]
Renaissance and Reformation = Renaissance et Réforme [Canada]
Renaissance Quarterly
Rendezvous
Research in Economic History
Research Studies (suspended pub 1983)
Resources for Feminist Research = Documentation sur la Recherche Féministe [Canada]
Review (Fernand Braudel Center)
Review of International Studies [Great Britain]
Review of Politics
Review of Radical Political Economics
Reviews in American History
Revista Arhivelor [Romania]
Revista Chilena de Historia y Geografía [Chile]
Revista de Archivos, Bibliotecas y Museos [Spain]
Revista de Ciencias Sociales [Puerto Rico]
Revista de Estudios Histórico-Jurídicos [Chile]
Revista de Estudios Internacionales (supersedes Revista de Política Internacional) [Spain]
Revista de Estudios Políticos [Spain]
Revista de Filosofía de la Universidad de Costa Rica [Costa Rica]
Revista de História (suspended pub 1977-82) [Brazil]
Revista de Historia Americana y Argentina [Argentina]
Revista de Historia Económica [Spain]
Revista de Historia Militar [Spain]
Revista de Istorie [Romania]
Revista de la Biblioteca Nacional "José Martí" [Cuba]
Revista de la Universidad Complutense de Madrid [Spain]
Revista de Occidente (IHE) [Spain]
Revista do Instituto Histórico e Geográfico Brasileiro [Brazil]
Revista Española de Investigaciones Sociológicas [Spain]
Revista Española de la Opinión Pública (superseded by Revista Española de Investigaciones Sociológicas) [Spain]
Revista Internacional de Sociología (IHE) [Spain]
Revue Belge de Philologie et d'Histoire [Belgium]
Revue Bulgare d'Histoire (see Bulgarian Historical Review = Revue Bulgare d'Histoire) [Bulgaria]
Revue d'Allemagne [France]
Revue de l'Institut de Sociologie [Belgium]
Revue de l'Institut Napoléon [France]
Revue de l'Université de Bruxelles [Belgium]
Revue des Deux Mondes [France]
Revue des Etudes Italiennes [France]
Revue des Etudes Juives [France]
Revue des Etudes Sud-Est Européennes [Romania]
Revue des Sciences Morales & Politiques [France]
Revue des Travaux de l'Académie des Sciences Morales et Politiques & Comptes Rendus de ses Séances (see Revue des Sciences Morales & Politiques) [France]
Revue d'Histoire de la Deuxième Guerre Mondiale et des Conflits Contemporains [France]
Revue d'Histoire de l'Amérique Française [Canada]
Revue d'Histoire de l'Eglise de France [France]
Revue d'Histoire Diplomatique [France]
Revue d'Histoire Ecclésiastique [Belgium]
Revue d'Histoire Economique et Sociale (ceased pub 1977) [France]
Revue d'Histoire et de Philosophie Religieuses [France]
Revue d'Histoire Moderne et Contemporaine [France]
Revue du Nord [France]
Revue Economique [France]
Revue Française de Science Politique [France]
Revue Française d'Histoire d'Outre-Mer (ceased pub 1980) [France]
Revue Historique [France]
Revue Historique des Armées [France]

Revue Internationale d'Histoire de la Banque [Switzerland]
Revue Internationale d'Histoire Militaire [France]
Revue Roumaine d'Histoire [Romania]
Rhetorica: A Journal of the History of Rhetoric
Rhode Island History
Rice University Studies (ceased pub 1981)
Rinascimento [Italy]
Risorgimento [Italy]
Rivista Critica di Storia della Filosofia [Italy]
Rivista di Storia della Chiesa in Italia [Italy]
Rivista di Studi Politici Internazionali [Italy]
Rivista Italiana di Scienza Politica [Italy]
Rivista Militare [Italy]
Rivista Storica Italiana [Italy]
Rocky Mountain Social Science Journal (see Social Science Journal)
Roczniki Historyczne [Poland]
Römische Historische Mitteilungen [Austria]
Round Table (suspended pub 1982) [Great Britain]
Russian History
Russian Review

S

Saeculum [German Federal Republic]
Samtiden [Norway]
San José Studies
Sborník Archivních Prací [Czechoslovakia]
Sborník Národního Muzea v Praze. Řada A: Historie [Czechoslovakia]
Sborník Prací Filosofické Fakulty Brněnské University: Řada Historická [Czechoslovakia]
Scandia [Sweden]
Scandinavian Economic History Review [Norway]
Schweizer Beiträge zur Allgemeinen Geschichte (ceased pub 1963) [Switzerland]
Schweizer Monatshefte [Switzerland]
Schweizerische Zeitschrift für Geschichte = Revue Suisse d'Histoire = Rivista Storica Svizzera [Switzerland]
Science & Society
Scottish Historical Review [Great Britain]
Seanchas Ard Mhacha: Journal of the Armagh Diocesan Historical Society [Great Britain]
Secolas Annals
Sessions d'Etude: Société Canadienne d'Histoire de l'Eglise Catholique (published simultaneously in one volume with Study Sessions: Canadian Catholic Historical Association) [Canada]
Shakai Kagaku Kenkyū [Japan]
Shakaikeizaishigaku (Socio-Economic History) [Japan]
Shigaku Zasshi [Japan]
Shisō (Iwanami Shoten) [Japan]
Signs: Journal of Women in Culture and Society
Sixteenth Century Bibliography
Sixteenth Century Journal
Skandinavskii Sbornik [Union of Soviet Socialist Republic]
Śląski Kwartalnik Historyczny Sobótka [Poland]
Slavic Review: American Quarterly of Soviet and East European Studies
Slezský Sborník [Czechoslovakia]
Slovanské Štúdie [Czechoslovakia]
Slovanský Přehled [Czechoslovakia]
Social Forces
Social History [Great Britain]
Social History = Histoire Sociale [Canada]
Social Policy
Social Research
Social Science (see International Social Science Review)
Social Science History
Social Science Journal
Social Science Quarterly
Social Sciences [Union of Soviet Socialist Republic]
Social Service Review
Social Studies
Societas (ceased pub 1978)
Society
Society for Historians of American Foreign Relations. Newsletter
Sociological Analysis
Sociological Inquiry
Sociological Quarterly
Soundings (Nashville, TN)
South Atlantic Quarterly
Southeastern Europe
Southern Economic Journal
Southern Folklore Quarterly
Southern History [Great Britain]
Southern Quarterly
Southern Speech Communication Journal
Southern Studies: An Interdisciplinary Journal of the South
Sovetskaia Etnografiia [Union of Soviet Socialist Republic]

Sovetskie Arkhivy [Union of Soviet Socialist Republic]
Sovetskoe Gosudarstvo i Pravo [Union of Soviet Socialist Republic]
Sovetskoe Slavianovedenie [Union of Soviet Socialist Republic]
Soviet Jewish Affairs [Great Britain]
Soviet Military Review [Union of Soviet Socialist Republic]
Soviet Studies [Great Britain]
Soviet Studies in History
Speech Monographs (see Communication Monographs)
Spiegel Historiael [Netherlands]
Srednie Veka [Union of Soviet Socialist Republic]
Ssu yü Yen = Thought and Word [Taiwan]
Stadion [German Federal Republic]
State, Government and International Relations (see Medina, Mimshal ve-Yahasim Beneumiyim) [Israel]
Storia Contemporánea [Italy]
Storia della Storiografia = Histoire de l'Historiographie = History of Historiography = Geschichte der Geschichtsschreibung [Italy]
Storia e Politica (suspended pub 1984) [Italy]
Strahovská Knihovna [Czechoslovakia]
Studi Storici [Italy]
Studia Filozoficzne [Poland]
Studia Hibernica [Republic of Ireland]
Studia Historiae Oeconomicae [Poland]
Studia Historica Slovaca [Czechoslovakia]
Studia Nauk Politycznych [Poland]
Studia Rosenthaliana [Netherlands]
Studies in Comparative Communism [Great Britain]
Studies in Comparative International Development
Studies in Eighteenth-Century Culture
Studies in History and Society (suspended pub 1977)
Studies in Romanticism
Studies in Soviet Thought [Netherlands]
Studies in Zionism [Israel]
Studii și Articole de Istorie [Romania]
Studime Historike [Albania]
Studium [Italy]
Sučasnist [German Federal Republic]
Sudhoffs Archiv für Geschichte der Medizin und der Naturwissenschaften (see Sudhoffs Archiv: Zeitschrift für Wissenschaftsgeschichte) [German Federal Republic]
Sudhoffs Archiv: Zeitschrift für Wissenschaftsgeschichte [German Federal Republic]
Südost-Forschungen [German Federal Republic]
Survey [Great Britain]
Survival [Great Britain]
Svensk Tidskrift [Sweden]
Swedish Pioneer Historical Quarterly (see Swedish-American Historical Quarterly)
Swedish-American Historical Quarterly
Synthesis [Romania]
Századok [Hungary]

T

Tarih Dergisi [Turkey]
Tarih Enstitüsü Dergisi [Turkey]
Tarikh [Nigeria]
Társadalmi Szemle [Hungary]
Teachers College Record
Teaching History [Great Britain]
Teaching History: A Journal of Methods
Technologia [Belgium]
Technology and Culture
Tennessee Historical Quarterly
Terrae Incognitae
Theatre Research International [Great Britain]
Thought
Thought and Word (see Ssu yü Yen = Thought and Word) [Taiwan]
Tidsskrift for Rettsvitenskap [Norway]
Tijdschrift voor de Geschiedenis der Geneeskunde, Natuurwetenschappen, Wiskunde en Techniek [Netherlands]
Tijdschrift voor Geschiedenis [Netherlands]
Tijdschrift voor Rechtsgeschiedenis = Revue d'Histoire du Droit = Legal History Review [Netherlands]
Történelmi Szemle [Hungary]
Towson State Journal of International Affairs
Tradition (see Zeitschrift für Unternehmensgeschichte) [German Federal Republic]
Transactions of the Royal Historical Society [Great Britain]
Transactions of the Royal Society of Canada = Mémoires de la Société Royale du Canada [Canada]
Trends in History

Turun Historiallinen Arkisto |Finland|

U

Uchenye Zapiski Instituta Slavianovedeniia Akademii Nauk SSSR |Union of Soviet Socialist Republic|
Ukrainian Quarterly
Ukrains'kyi Istorychnyi Zhurnal |Union of Soviet Socialist Republic|
Ukrains'kyi Istoryk
Umoja: A Scholarly Journal of Black Studies
University of Toronto Quarterly |Canada|
University of Turku. Institute of General History. Publications |Finland|
Unsere Heimat |Austria|
Urban History Review = Revue d'Histoire Urbaine |Canada|
Urban History Yearbook |Great Britain|
U.S. Naval Institute Proceedings
Utah Historical Quarterly

V

Valkanika Symmeikta |Greece|
Veltro |Italy|
Verifiche |Italy|
Veröffentlichungen des Verbandes Österreichischer Geschichtsvereine (ceased pub 1971) |Austria|
Vestnik Leningradskogo Universiteta: Seriia Istorii, Iazyka i Literatury |Union of Soviet Socialist Republic|
Vestnik Moskovskogo Universiteta: Istoriko-Filologicheskaia Seriia (superseded by Vestnik Moskovskogo Universiteta, Seriia 9: Istoriia) |Union of Soviet Socialist Republic|
Vestnik Moskovskogo Universiteta, Seriia 8: Istoriia |Union of Soviet Socialist Republic|
Vestnik Moskovskogo Universiteta, Seriia 9: Istoriia (see Vestnik Moskovskogo Universiteta, Seriia 8: Istoriia) |Union of Soviet Socialist Republic|
Victorian Studies
Vierteljahrschrift für Sozial- und Wirtschaftsgeschichte |German Federal Republic|
Vierteljahrshefte für Zeitgeschichte |German Federal Republic|
Viewpoints: Georgia Baptist History
Világtörténet |Hungary|
Virginia Magazine of History and Biography
Virginia Quarterly Review
Vitae Scholasticae: The Bulletin of Educational Biography
Voenno-Istoricheskii Zhurnal |Union of Soviet Socialist Republic|
Vojnoistorijski Glasnik |Yugoslavia|
Voprosy Ekonomiki |Union of Soviet Socialist Republic|
Voprosy Filosofii |Union of Soviet Socialist Republic|
Voprosy Istorii |Union of Soviet Socialist Republic|
Voprosy Istorii Estestvoznaniia i Tekhniki |Union of Soviet Socialist Republic|
Voprosy Istorii KPSS |Union of Soviet Socialist Republic|

W

Wehrkunde |German Federal Republic|
Wehrwissenschaftliche Rundschau (ceased pub 1970) |German Federal Republic|
West Georgia College Studies in the Social Sciences
West Tennessee Historical Society Papers
West Texas Historical Association Year Book
Western Historical Quarterly
Western Humanities Review
Western Pennsylvania Historical Magazine
Western Political Quarterly
Wiener Beiträge zur Geschichte der Neuzeit |Austria|
Wiener Geschichtsblätter |Austria|
William and Mary Quarterly
Wilson Library Bulletin
Wilson Quarterly
Wisconsin Magazine of History
Wissenschaft und Weltbild |Austria|
Wissenschaftliche Zeitschrift der Friedrich-Schiller-Universität Jena. Gesellschafts- und Sprachwissenschaftliche Reihe |German Democratic Republic|
Wissenschaftliche Zeitschrift der Ernst-Moritz-Arndt- Universität Greifswald. Gesellschaftswissenschaftliche Reihe |German Democratic Republic|

Wissenschaftliche Zeitschrift der Humboldt-Universität zu Berlin. Gesellschafts- und Sprachwissenschaftliche Reihe (see Wissenschaftliche Zeitschrift der Humboldt-Universität zu Berlin. Gesellschaftswissenschaftliche Reihe) |German Democratic Republic|
Wissenschaftliche Zeitschrift der Karl-Marx-Universität Leipzig. Gesellschafts- und Sprachwissenschaftliche Reihe |German Democratic Republic|
Wissenschaftliche Zeitschrift der Martin-Luther-Universität Halle-Wittenberg. Gesellschafts- und Sprachwissenschaftliche Reihe |German Democratic Republic|
Wissenschaftliche Zeitschrift der Universität Rostock. Gesellschafts- und Sprachwissenschaftliche Reihe (see Wissenschaftliche Zeitschrift der Wilhelm-Pieck-Universität Rostock. Gesellschaftswissenschaftliche Reihe) |German Democratic Republic|
Wissenschaftliche Zeitschrift der Wilhelm-Pieck-Universität Rostock. Gesellschaftswissenschaftliche Reihe |German Democratic Republic|
Women's Annual
Women's Studies International Forum
World Affairs
World Marxist Review |Canada|
World Politics
Worldview
Wort und Wahrheit (ceased pub 1973) |German Federal Republic|

Y

Yad Vashem News |Israel|
Yivo Annual of Jewish Social Science
Yivo Bleter

Z

Z Pola Walki |Poland|
Zbornik Istorijskog Muzeja Srbije |Yugoslavia|
Zbornik Matice Srpske za Društvene Nauke |Yugoslavia|
Zbornik Matice Srpske za Istoriju |Yugoslavia|
Zbornik za Društvene Nauke (see Zbornik Matice Srpske za Društvene Nauke) |Yugoslavia|
Zbornik za Istoriju (see Zbornik Matice Srpske na Istoriju) |Yugoslavia|
Zbornik za Zgodovino Naravoslovja in Tehnike |Yugoslavia|
Zeitgeschichte |Austria|
Zeitschrift für Geschichtswissenschaft |German Democratic Republic|
Zeitschrift für Kirchengeschichte |German Federal Republic|
Zeitschrift für Ostforschung |German Federal Republic|
Zeitschrift für Politik |German Federal Republic|
Zeitschrift für Religions- und Geistesgeschichte |German Federal Republic|
Zeitschrift für Unternehmensgeschichte |German Federal Republic|
Zeitschrift für Württembergische Landesgeschichte |German Federal Republic|
Zeitwende |German Federal Republic|
Zeszyty Historyczne |France|
Zgodovinski Časopis |Yugoslavia|
Zion |Israel|
Zionism (see Studies in Zionism) |Israel|
Zwingliana |Switzerland|
Zygon: Journal of Religion and Science

LIST OF ABSTRACTERS

A

Adams, R. K.
Adler, P. J.
Alcock, A.
Aldrich, R.
Alexander, G. M.
Alltmont, R. C.
Andersen, H. C.
Andrew, J.
Andrew, J. A., III
Andrews, H. D.
Ardia, D.
Athey, L. L.
Atkins, L. R.
Auffenberg, T. L.
Auten, A. H.

B

Bailey, C. B.
Bailey, E.
Balmuth, D.
Bamber, J.
Banker, J. R.
Barnard, J. D.
Bassler, G.
Bates, C.
Bauer, K. J.
Baylen, J. O.
Bazillion, R. J.
Beck, P. J.
Beer, S.
Belles, A. G.
Bender, V.
Berger, K. W.
Billigmeier, J. C.
Bishop, D. M.
Bishop, M. G.
Black, R. D.
Blaser, L. K.
Bleaney, C. H.
Blethen, H. T.
Block, B. A.
Blum, G. P.
Blumberg, A.
Bobango, G. J.
Boehnke, S.
Bohm, F. C.
Bott, M. A.
Bowers, D. E.
Bradford, J. C.
Brown, A.
Brown, C. C.
Brown, J.
Brunkow, R. deV.
Burckel, N. C.
Burns, R.
Buschen, J.
Bushnell, D.
Butchart, R.
Butler, M. A.

C

Calkin, H. L.
Cameron, D. D.
Campbell, E. R.
Campbell, L. G.
Canavero, A.
Carr, S. P.
Casada, J. A.
Chan, L. B.
Chaput, D.
Chard, D. F.
Chary, F. B.
Christianson, J. R.
Clark, M. J.
Cleyet, G. P.
Cline, D. H.
Coleman, J. S.
Coleman, P. J.
Colenso, M. R.
Collins, D. N.
Collon, C.
Conner, S. P.
Coutinho, J. V.
Crapster, B. L.
Craver, E. J.
Cregier, D. M.
Crowther, K. N. T.
Cushnie, J.

D

Dalby, A. K.
Darshana-Reed, B.
David, G. H.
Davies, T. B.
Davis, G. H.
Dawson, J. D.
Dejevsky, N.
Dewees, A. C.
Dibert, M. D.
Dickinson, J. N.
Dietz, J. L.
Diuk, N. M.
Djakowska, L.
Dodd, D.
Dombrovski, G.
Driggs, O. T.
Drysdale, A. C.
Dubay, R. W.
Dunn, S. P.
Durell, P. J.

E

Egerton, F. N.
Eid, L. V.
Eidlin, F. H.
Eilan, N.
Elison, W. W.
Elmslie, M.
Eminhizer, E. E.
Engler, D. J.
English, J. C.
Erlandsson, A.
Erlebacher, A.
Estes, K. W.
Evans, A. J.
Evans, B.

F

Faissler, M.
Falk, J. D.
Farmerie, S. A.
Fenn, A.
Ferdinand, C. I. P.
Fetter, B. S.
Findling, J. E.
Fitzgerald, C. B.
Forgus, S. P.
Fox, J. P.
Foxcroft, G. and N. H.
Frank, S. H.
Frankfort, F.
Frenkley, N.
Freudenthal, H. W. L.
Frey, L. S.
Friguglietti, J.
Fulton, R. T.
Furdell, E. L.

G

Gagnon, G. O.
Garfield, R.
Garland, A. N.
Gassner, J. S.
Geschwind, C.-H.
Geyer, M.
Gialluly, M. de
Gilbert, J. M.
Gillam, M. R.
Gillespie, C. G. P.
Glasrud, B. A.
Glovins, G. A.
Goerler, R. E.
Goldman, J. R.
Gromen, R. J.
Gross, A. R.
Grove, R.
Grusin, J. R.
Gunter, C. R.
Gunther, T.

H

Harahan, J. P.
Hardacre, P. H.
Harling, F. F.
Harrington, J. F.
Harvey, K. A.
Hayashida, S.
Hazelton, J. L.
Hegstad, P. A.

Heitzman-Wojcicka, H.
Held, C.
Herman, P.
Herman, T. Z.
Hernas, M.
Herrick, J. M.
Herritt, G.
Herstein, S. R.
Heston, T. J.
Hetzron, G.
Hetzron, R.
Hewlett, G. A.
Hidas, P. I.
Hildenbrand, S.
Hively, W. R.
Hobson, W. K.
Hočevar, T.
Hoffman, A.
Hoidal, O.
Hollenberg, G.
Holmes, L. E.
Homan, G. D.
Hont, I.
Hoobs, M. A.
Horn, D. E.
Hough, C. M.
Hough, M.
Houlihan, J. W.
Howell, A. W.
Howell, L. J.
Howell, R.
Howlett, C. F.
Human, V. L.
Hunjic, M.
Hunley, J. D.
Hyslop, E. C.

I

Iklé, F. W.
Ingram, J. L.
Itô, M.

J

Jennison, E. W.
Jeppesen, B. L.
Jeszenszky, G.
Jewsbury, G. F.
Jeyes, U. G.
Johnson, B. D.
Johnson, D. W.
Johnson, L.
Jones, S. F.

K

Kaiser, H. J.
Kalinowski, L.
Kascus, M. A.
Kaufman, M.
Kaufman, S. L.
Kawaguchi, M.
Keller, R. A.
Kellogg, F.
Kennedy, P. W.
Kennedy, S. E.
Keyser, E. L.
Khan, R. O.
Kicklighter, J. A.
Kimmel, B.
King, C.
Kirillov, R.
Kittell, A. H.
Klass, L. J.
Knafla, L. A.
Koppel, T.
Košak, S.
Krogstad, E. E.
Krompart, J. A.
Krushelnyckyj, I.
Krzyzak, L. A.
Krzyzaniak, M.
Kulczycki, J. J.
Kuner, T.
Kuntz, N. A.

L

Lambert, D. K.
Larson, A. J.
Latour, C. F.
Law, D. G.
Layton, R. V.
LeBlanc, A. E.

Ledbetter, B. D.
Lederer, N.
Legan, M. S.
Leonardis, M. de
Lester, E. R.
Levy, S. M.
Lewis, J. A.
Libbey, G. H.
Lifka, M. L.
Lindgren, R. E.
Linkfield, T. P.
Lokken, R. N.
Long, J. W.
Lovin, C. R.
Lovin, H. T.
Lubelski, B.
Lucas, M. B.
Lukes, I.
Lynch, M. M. A.

M

MacCarthy, E.
Malwitz, I.
Marks, H. S.
Marr, W.
Marti, D. B.
Masloff, C. S.
Massey, T. P.
Matsui, I.
Maxted, L. R.
Mayer, T. F.
McCarthy, E.
McCarthy, J. M.
McCarthy, M. M.
McDonald, D. R.
McGeoch, L. A.
McGinnis, D.
McIntyre, W. D.
McLaughlin, P. L.
McNeil, D. O.
McNeill, C. A.
Meier, H. K.
Mendel, R. B.
Michelson, P. E.
Migliazzo, A. C.
Miller, H. J.
Mills, J. C.
Mina, A.
Mishark, J. W.
Moen, N. W.
Montgomery, M. K.
Moody, C.
Moore, J.
Moriarty, T. F.
Morrison, S. C.
Mtewa, M.
Mulligan, W. H.
Munro, G. E.
Murdoch, D. H.
Murdock, E. C.
Myers, J. P. H.

N

Naçi, G.-D. L.
Narducci, H. M.
Nassibian, A.
Nelson, L. H.
Neville, G. L.
Neville, J. D.
Neville, R. G.
Newhouse, N. A.
Newman, L. M.
Nicholls, D. J.
Nielson, D. G.
Niven, A. C.
Noble, R. E.
Novitsky, A. W.

O

Ohl, J. K.
Ohrvall, C. W.
Olbrich, W. L.
Olson, C. W.
Orr, R. B.
Orton, L. D.
Osur, A. M.
Oxley, A. P.

P

Pach, B. R.
Packer, J. G.

Packer, V.
Palais, E. S.
Panting, G. E.
Papalas, A. J.
Parker, H. M.
Parker, T.
Pasadas-Ureña, C.
Patzwald, G.-A.
Paul, J. F.
Pearson, S. C.
Pergl, G. E.
Perkins, J. A.
Permar, R.
Pernal, A. B.
Petrzilkova, M.-M.
Pfabe, J. K.
Phenix, K.
Pichelin, C.
Pickens, D. K.
Piehl, C. K.
Piersen, W. D.
Pike, C. R.
Pizzimenti, G.
Pogany, A. M.
Pollaczek, F.
Powell, D.
Powell, J.
Powers, T. L.
Pragman, J. H.
Preda, M. A.
Preece, C. A.
Prowe, D.
Prukop, C. T.
Pugh, M. C.
Pusateri, C. J.

Q

Quinlan, S. J.
Quinlivan, M. E.

R

Raife, L. R.
Read, C. J.
Reedy, W. J.
Reid, W. S.
Reiner, B.
Reinfeld, B.
Reith, L. J.
Renaldo, J. J.
Richardson, D. C.
Richardson, T. P.
Rilee, V. P.
Ritter, R. V.
Rivers, B.
Robbins, R. C.
Robinson, D. L.
Rocchitta, S.
Rockwood, D. S.
Rodger, R. G.
Roosen, W. J.
Rosen, H. M.
Rosenthal, F.
Roth, D.
Ruffo-Fiore, S.
Ryan, E. E.

S

Samaraweera, V.
Sarna, J. D.
Sather, L. B.
Savitt, T. L.
Sbacchi, A.
Schaeper, T. J.
Schafer, D. F.
Schermerhorn, D. L.
Schlesinger, R.
Schmidt, L. H.
Schoonover, T.
Schroeder, G. R.
Schuetz, A.
Schulz, C. B.
Schumacher, M.
Schweitzer, D. R.
Seitz, R.
Selleck, R. G.
Senn, A. E.
Sevilla, S.
Seymour, L. J.
Shepherd, L. J.
Sherer, R. G.
Short, D.
Short, L.

Sicher, E.
Sicher, E. R.
Simmerman, T.
Sindermann, R. P.
Sirriyeh, E. M.
Sliwoski, R. S.
Smith, C. O.
Smith, D. L.
Smith, G.
Smith, L.
Smith, L. C.
Smith, S. R.
Smith, T. W.
Smoot, J. G.
Snow, G. E.
Sobell, V.
Sobeslavsky, V.
Solodkin, P. L.
Soos, E. E.
Spade, D. F.
Sprague, S. S.
Stack, R. E.
Stanley, T. C.
Stenslie, B.
Stevenson, D. R.
Stickney, E. P.
Stifflear, A. J.
Stoesen, A. R.
Street, J. B.
Strnad, A. A.
Stromberg, R.
Sussman, B.
Sweetland, J. H.
Swift, D. C.
Szamuely, H.
Szewczyk, M. W.

T

Talalay, S. J.
Talley, K.
Tate, M. L.
Taylorson, P. J.
Thacker, J. W.
Tharaud, B. C.
Tomlinson-Brown, S.
Touchstone, D. B.
Trauth, M. P.
Troebst, S.
Tull, J.
Turk, E. L.
Twisdale, R. M.
Twyman, L. G. G.

U

Underwood, T. L.

V

Valliant, R. B.
Vance, M. M.
Velicer, L. F.
Vexler, R. I.
Vignery, J. R.
Vilums, R.

W

Wagner, F. S.
Wagnleitner, R.
Walker, J. T.
Walker, W. T.
Walton, P. D.
Ward, G. W. R.
Ward, H. M.
Wasson, G. V.
Waters, L.
Wechman, R. J.
Welisch, S. A.
Weltsch, R. E.
Werlich, D. P.
West, K. B.
Wharton, D. P.
White, J. L.
Whitham, W. B.
Wiegand, W. A.
Wilcox, L. D.
Wilczek, J.
Wilkinson, J.
Will, L. G.
Williams, K. S.
Wilson, M. T.
Woehrmann, P. J.
Wojcicka, H. Heitzman
Wood, C. W.
Woodward, R. L.
Wrigley, W. D.

Wurster, H. W.
Wyk, L. W. Van

Y

Yanchisin, D. A.
Yasamee, F. A. K.
Yerburgh, M. R.
Young, R. G.

Z

Zabel, O. H.
Ziewacz, L. E.
Zornow, W. F.

DATE DUE

GAYLORD			PRINTED IN U.S.A.